# DATE DUE

| | | | |
|---|---|---|---|
| | | | |
| | | | |
| | | | |
| | | | |
| | | | |
| | | | |
| | | | |
| | | | |
| | | | |
| | | | |
| | | | |
| | | | |
| | | | |
| | | | |
| | | | |
| | | | |
| | | | |
| | | | |
| | | | PRINTED IN U.S.A. |

OCT 1 1 2013

# Japan at War

# Japan at War

## AN ENCYCLOPEDIA

Louis G. Perez, Editor

ABC-CLIO

Santa Barbara, California • Denver, Colorado • Oxford, England

**Library of Congress Cataloging-in-Publication Data**

Japan at war : an encyclopedia / Louis G. Perez, editor.
    p. cm.
  Includes bibliographical references and index.
  ISBN 978–1–59884–741–3 (hard copy : alk. paper) — ISBN 978–1–59884–742–0 (e-book)
1.  Japan—History, Military—Encyclopedias.  I. Perez, Louis G.
DS838.J368   2013
355.00952′03—dc23          2012030062

ISBN: 978–1–59884–741–3
EISBN: 978–1–59884–742–0

17  16  15  14  13      1  2  3  4  5

This book is also available on the World Wide Web as an eBook.
Visit www.abc-clio.com for details.

ABC-CLIO, LLC
130 Cremona Drive, P.O. Box 1911
Santa Barbara, California 93116-1911

This book is printed on acid-free paper (∞)

Manufactured in the United States of America

In memory of three who dedicated their lives to teaching Japanese history to undergraduate students: Sidney DeVere Brown, Mikiso Hane, and Sharon Sievers.

# Contents

# Guide to Related Topics by Era

Topics preceded by an asterisk (*) are located in the Primary Documents chapter.

## Prehistoric Period

Ainu, Military Resistance to

Early Mytho-histories: *Kojiki* and *Nihon shōki*

Himiko-Iyo Succession Crisis

Isshi Incident

Jimmu Tennō

Jingū Kōgō

*Kusanagi-no-Tsurugi*

Language: Change in the Sixth to Eighth Centuries

Nara (Heijō-kyō) to Heian-kyō

*Seventeen-article Constitution

## Heian Period

Cloister Government (*Insei*)

Fujiwara Family

*Ritsu-ryō*

*Shōen* and Rise of *Bushi*

Shōtoku Taishi

Taika Reforms

## Kamakura Period

Ashikaga Takauji

*Azuma kagami*

Buke Shohatto

Go-Daigo

*Hara-kiri (Seppuku)*

*Heike monogatari*

Hogen-Heiji-Gempei Wars

Hôjô Masako

Hōjō Tokimune

Jôkyû War of 1221

Kamakura *Bakufu*

Kitabatake Chikafusa

Minamoto Yoritomo

Minamoto Yoshitsune

Mongol Invasions of Japan

Nichiren

Nitta Yoshisada

*Taiheiki*

Taira-no-Masakado

Warrior Tales

## Muromachi Period

Ashikaga Takauji

Kakitsu Disturbance

Muromachi *Bakufu*

Southern Court (Yoshino)

## Sengoku Period

Civil Wars, Sengoku Era

Hansan, Battle of

Ikkō *Ikki*

Imjin War

*Ninja*

Oda Nobunaga

Ōnin War

*Sōhei* ("Monk Warriors")

Takeda Shingen

Toyotomi Hideyoshi

## Edo Period

Aizawa Seishisai

Aizu Samurai Spirit

Bakumatsu Fencing Schools and
    Nationalism

Boshin Civil War

Colonization of Hokkaidō

Colonization of Taiwan

Dutch on Deshima

Harris, Townsend

Heusken, Henry

Hitotsubasi Keiki (Tokugawa Yoshinobu)

Ii Naosuke

Kagoshima, Bombardment of

*Kakure*

Loyalist Verse (*Shishi-gin*)

Matsudaira Sadanobu

Mito School

Namamugi Incident

Ōshio Yoshio and the 47 Rōnin

Osaka Castle, Battle of

Ōshio Heihachirō

Perry, Matthew

Sakamoto Ryōma

*Sakoku*

Sakuradamon Incident

*Sankin kōtai* (Alternate Attendance)

Sekigahara, Battle of

Shimabara Rebellion

Shimoda Treaty

Shimonoseki, Bombardment of

Tanuma Okitsugu

Tokugawa *Bakufu* Political System

Tokugawa Bakumatsu Military Reforms

Tokugawa Ieyasu

Tokugawa Loyalism: Boshin War

Tokugawa Nariaki

Yoshida Shōin

## Meiji Period

Anglo-Japanese Alliances

Boissonade de Fontarabie, Gustave Émile

Boxer Rebellion

Emigrants from Japan

Fukuzawa Yukichi

Golovnin Incident

Gōtō Shinpei

Great Kanto Earthquake

Hara Takashi

High Treason Incident

Hiratsuka *Raichō*

Ichikawa Fusae

*Imperial Rescript for Soldiers and Sailors

*Imperial Rescript on Education

## Taishō Period

Saigō Takamori

Saigō Tsugumichi

Satchō Oligarchy

Triple Intervention

Tsushima, Battle of

Twenty-One Demands

Versailles Treaty

Washington Naval Conference

World War I

Yamagata Aritomo

## Shōwa Period

AMPO: United States–Japan Security Treaty

Anti-Comintern Pact

Anti-Narita Airport Movement

Anti-Vietnam War Movement

Araki Sadao

Atomic Bombs: Surrender of Japan

Bataan Death March

Bikini Island Atomic Tests

Buddhism Copes with Imperialism

Burma Air Campaign

*The Constitution of Japan, 1947

Continental Adventurers

Comfort Women

Corregidor Battle

Dōmei News Agency (Dōmei Tsūshinsha)

February 26 Incident

Gen'yōsha Nationalism

Gordon, Beate Sirota

Greater East Asia Co-prosperity Sphere

Guadalcanal, Land Battle for

Guam, Battle for

Hakkō Ichiu

Hashimoto Kingoro

History Textbooks Controversy

Ienaga Saburō

Ikeda Hayato

International Military Tribunal for the Far

Ishiwara Kanji

Iwo Jima, Battle for

Jiang Jieshi (Ch'iang K'ai-shek)

Kamikaze (Tokkōtai)

Kawakami Soroku

Kita Ikki

Kokutai and Ultra-nationalism

Konoe Fumimaro

Korean War

Kwantung Army Adventurism

Leyte Gulf, Battle of

London Naval Conference

MacArthur, Douglas

Malaya Campaign

Manchukuo

Maruyama Masao

Matsuoka Yōsuke

Midway, Battle of

Minobe Tatsukichi

Mishima Yukio

Mukden Incident: Lytton Report

Nanjing Massacre

Nativism, Rise of

New Religions in Imperial and Postwar Japan

Newsreels

Nomonhan/Khalhin-Gol, Battle

Occupation of Japan

Okinawa, Invasion of (Operation Iceberg)

## Heisei Period

# Guide to Related Topics by Subject

## Atrocities

Atomic Bombs: Surrender of Japan

Bataan Death March

Comfort Women

History Textbooks Controversy

International Military Tribunal for the Far

Manila, Battle for

Nanjing Massacre

Pal, Radhabinod

Shanghai, Battle of

Unit 731

World War II, Japanese Atrocities

Yasukuni Shrine Controversy

## China

Anti-Japanism in China

Colonization of Taiwan

Continental Adventurers (*Tairiku Rōnin*)

Jiang Jieshi (Ch'iang K'ai-shek)

Language: Change in the Sixth to Eighth
  Centuries

Manchukuo

May Fourth Movement

Mongol Invasions of Japan

Nanjing Massacre

Port Arthur Siege

Pu-yi (Henry)

Qingdao, Siege of

Russian Invasion of Manchuria

Shanghai, Battle of

Siberian Intervention

South Manchurian Railway

Sun Yat-sen and the Japanese

Taiwan Expedition

Tanaka Memorial

Twenty-One Demands

Xi'an Incident

Zhang Zuolin

## Constitution and Law

Boissonade de Fontarabie, Gustave Émile

*Charter Oath (1868)

Gordon, Beate Sirota

Itō Hirobumi

Jiyu Minken Undo

Law on Assembly and Political Association
  (1890)

*1947 Constitution

Meiji Constitution

Peace Preservation Law
Potsdam Proclamation (1945)
Meiji Press Laws
San Francisco Peace Treaty
Seventeen-article Constitution
Shimoda Treaty

Shimonoseki, Treaty of
Taika Reforms
Tripartite Pact
Unequal Treaties
Versailles Treaty

## Diplomats

Hara Takashi
Iwakura Mission
Iwakura Tomomi
Komura Jutarō
Matsuoka Yōsuke

Mutsu Munemitsu
Saionji Kinmochi
Shidehara Kijuro
Takahashi Korekiyo
Uchida Yasuya

## Economics

Matsukata Masayoshi
Meiji economic Reforms (1880s)
Meiji Land Tax
Rice Riots

*Shōen* and Rise of *Bushi*
Tanuma Okitsugu
*Zaibatsu*

## Emperors

Akihito (Heisei), Emperor
Go-Daigo
*Hakkō Ichiu*
Himiko-Iyo Succession Crisis
Jimmu Tennō
Loyalist Verse (*Shishi-gin*)
Meiji Emperor
Minobe Tatsukichi

Nitta Yoshisada
Organ Theory of the State
Shōwa Emperor (Hirohito)
Shōwa Restoration
*Sonno-jōi*
Southern Court (Yoshino)
Taishō Emperor

## Foreigners in Japan

Boissonade de Fontarabie, Gustave Émile
Dutch on Deshima
Golovnin Affair
Gordon, Beate Sirota
Harris, Townsend
Heusken, Henry
Namamugi Incident

Occupation of Japan
Otsu Incident
*Oyatoi Gaikokujin*
Pal, Radhabinod
Perry, Matthew
*Sonno-jōi*

## Internationalism

Dōmei News Agency (Dōmei Tsūshinsha)

Emigrants from Japan

Iwakura Mission

League of Nations, Mandates

London Naval Conference

*Maria Luz* Incident

Portsmouth Treaty

*Potsdam Declaration (1945)

Saionji Kinmochi

Siberian Intervention

Washington Naval Conference

## Island Hopping

Corregidor, Battle of

Guadalcanal, Land Battle for

Guam, Battle for

Iwo Jima, Battle for

Kamikaze (*Tokkōtai*)

Leyte Gulf, Battle of

Malaya Campaign

Manila, Battle for

Midway, Battle of

Okinawa, Invasion of (Operation Iceberg)

Pearl Harbor, Attack on

Tarawa, Battle of

World War II, Pacific Theater

## Japanese-ness

Aizawa Seishisai

Amau Doctrine

Loyalist Verse (*Shishi-gin*)

*Sonno-jōi*

## Korea

Hansan, Battle of

Imjin War

Jingū Kōgō

Kim Ok-kyun

Korea Added to the Empire

Korean War

Mongol Invasions of Japan

## Literature

Early Mytho-histories: *Kojiki* and *Nihon shōki*

*Heike monogatari*

History Textbooks Controversy

*Imperial Rescript for Soldiers and Sailors

*Imperial Rescript on Education

Loyalist Verse (*Shishi-gin*)

*Taiheiki*

Warrior Tales

## Martyrs

Christian Era, Suppression (*Fumi-e*)

Heusken, Henry

Ii Naosuke

*Kakure Kirishitan*

Kim Ok-kyun

Minamoto Yoshitsune

Minobe Tatsukichi

Mito School

Muromachi *Bakufu*

Nara (Heijō-kyō) to Heian-kyō

Occupation of Japan

Organ Theory of the State

*Ritsu-ryō*

Taika Reforms

Tokugawa *Bakufu* Political System

## Rebellions

Boxer Rebellion

High Treason Incident

Ikkō *Ikki*

Isshi Incident

kakitsu Disturbance

Kotōku Shūsui

Meiji-Era Peasant Uprisings

Ōshio Yoshio and the 47 Rōnin

Ōnin War

Osaka Castle, Battle of

Red Army (Sekigun)

Rice Riots

Saga Rebellion

Seinan (Satsuma) Rebellion

Shimabara Rebellion

Taira-no-Masakado

Zengakuren

## Religion

Buddhism Copes with Imperialism

Ikkō *Ikki*

*Kakure Kirishitan*

New Religions in Imperial and Postwar Japan

Nichiren

*Sōhei* ("Monk Warriors")

State Shintō

State Shintō, Exporting to the Colonies

Zen Buddhism and Militarism

Zen Buddhism in Japanese Sports

## Warrior Cult

Aizu Samurai Spirit

Bakumatsu Fencing Schools and
Nationalism

Buke Shohatto

*Bushidō*

*Hara-kiri* (*Seppuku*)

Kamikaze (*Tokkōtai*)

*Kokutai* and Ultra-nationalism

Meiji Ishin Shishi

Minamoto Yoshitsune

Mishima Yukio

Nativism, Rise of

*Ninja*

Nitobe Inazō

Ōshio Yoshio and the 47 Rōnin

Sakamoto Ryōma

Sasakawa Ryōichi

Shiba Ryōtarō and *Bushidō*

*Sōhei* ("Monk Warriors")

Tanaka Chigaku

Tôyama Mitsuru

Yoshida Shōin

Zen Buddhism and Militarism

## Women

Himiko-Iyo Succession Crisis

Hiratsuka *Raichō*

Hôjô Masako

Ichikawa Fusae

Itō Noe

*Seito* (*Bluestockings*)

Senninbari and "Comfort Bags"

Women during World War II: Kokubo Fujinkai and Aikoku Fujinkai

Yosano Akiko

## World War II (see also Island Hopping)

Burma Air Campaign

Hong Kong, Battle of

Jiang Jieshi (Ch'iang K'ai-shek)

Manchukuo

Mukden Incident: Lytton Report

Nanjing Massacre

Nomonhan/Khalhin-Gol, Battle of

Russian Invasion of Manchuria

Shanghai, Battle of

World War II, Continental Theater

# Preface

There are very few serious scholars living outside of countries ruled by authoritarian regimes (China, Iran, Cuba, Myanmar, Vietnam, North Korea) who still slavishly follow a single interpretative historical system. There are simply too many human exceptions to the hard-and-fast rules required by those systems. Yet all of those discredited systems can provide insights into history. The Marxists remind us that economic pressures do have power in determining historical outcomes. We do well to remember that the Post-Modernists have given us a valuable tool in understanding human power relationships. Feminism reminds us that the male ego is a powerful, yet fragile biological urge. The Freudians, Maoists, Trotskyites, and the various religious fundamentalists all give us an insight into the human condition that we would do well to remember—namely, that irrational ideas can often affect historical outcomes.

With that caveat in mind, we can safely say that there is no one overriding "secret system" to understanding Japanese history. There are, however, a few valuable interpretative hints.

First and foremost is that there was a continuing tension between central imperial power on the one hand, and the overweening ambition of local warrior–land owners on the other hand. The so-called feudal period (1190–1868) of its history is filled with attempts by emperors to restore themselves to actual political power. Their champions were often merely opportunists, hoping to carve out more power for themselves by posing as "loyalists." Nevertheless, a few of those warriors can properly be called royalists. A few probably truly believed that Japan would be better served by a centralized imperial regime than by the often ragtag coalition of self-interested military adventurers who only occasionally thought of the collective society.

Whether any loyalists actually believed that the emperor was semi-divine is a moot question, perhaps. The men who helped "restore" the Meiji Emperor to power in 1867 acted as if they really did. And they certainly instituted a philosophical educational system that convinced several generations that true patriotism required blind faith and loyalty, and that they become crusading evangelists, spreading State Shintō throughout the world—whether those Asians actually wanted to be "liberated" or not. The so-called *shishi* ("men of spirit") at the end of the Tokugawa era (1860s) and the *shishi* of the Shōwa Restoration (1920s and 1930s) were prepared to kill anyone who stood in their way; both sets of terrorists were willing to die for their irrational beliefs.

Second, one can argue that Japanese history is electric with the tension between the sacred versus the profane—though it is probably more a case of philosophical orthodoxy versus heterodoxy, because neither Shintō nor Buddhism had the complete religious dominance over Japan that Roman Catholicism enjoyed over Medieval Europe. The Confucian and Neo-Confucian sociopolitical philosophies were simply too strongly entrenched to allow for such homogeneity. Secular leaders used religious men to achieve their political ends. Oda Nobunaga used Christianity to eradicate his Buddhist enemies. Various warlords pitted one Buddhist sect against another. The men of the Meiji Restoration chose to use Shintō to conquer the Tokugawa regime. They attacked Buddhism not so much on religious doctrinal issues, as because the myriad sects had been so closely allied with the Tokugawa regime. Later, the same men re-embraced Buddhism to counter the power of Western Christianity. For their part, the Buddhists "rediscovered" the imperial house and allied themselves to it to rejoin the sacred.

Third, the struggle between nativism and the power of foreign sense and sensibility was a recurring dynamic. The two antagonists often cooperated in such ideas as Ryobu-Shintō (the idea that the native Shintō kami were actually local incarnations of Indo-Chinese Buddhas) and Zen Buddhism. Nevertheless, more often than not, the adherents of "Japanese-ness" were constantly at odds with those who were educated in foreign philosophies. This held true in the struggle between the Shintō nativists and the Chinese Buddhists in the eighth century and again in the 18th century, as well as between nativists and Christians in the 16th century and again in the 19th century.

Finally, the samurai warriors constantly sought to legitimize the violence that kept them in power. Whether it was though the creation of the eclectic *bushidō* (literally "the way of the warrior") or the 13th-century Chinese Neo-Confucianism (Zhu Xi) employed by Toyotomi Hideyoshi and Tokugawa Ieyasu at the turn of the 17th century, the rustic warriors firmly ensconced themselves at the top of Japanese culture by virtue of their service to the society. They flocked to the scholars who could help them reconcile the *Bun* and *Bu* (learning and martial arts, respectively). They came to power by the sword, but wanted to rule with the writing brush.

With these ideas in mind, we attempt to examine Japan at war in this encyclopedia. This topic encompasses not just the warriors, their weapons, and their strategies and tactics, but also how the warrior ethic became predominate in Japan. Reams and megabytes have been devoted to the *katana* (long sword), the samurai, and the rōnin-*sohei-ninja* killer cults with decidedly more heat than light. We seek here to briefly examine also the philosophical "roads not taken," the ignored diplomats, and the battles and wars left unfought. The reader is reminded that while the military adventurers too often wielded power in Japanese history, many other voices preached the virtues of peace, rationality, and international cooperation. Japan was ravaged by periods of horrible civil and international war, but enjoyed long stretches of peace as well. Compare the two centuries of relative peace during the Tokugawa era (roughly 1640–1850) with the wars of conquest that tore the rest of the world apart at the same time. Contrast Japan's seven decades of peace since World War II with the seemingly endless civil and international strife that has plagued the rest of the world.

The roughly 300 encyclopedic entries herein often glimpses into Japan at war. They are alphabetically arranged for quick, convenient reference, but also include "see also" cross-references to other entries that will help the reader to understand the wider context. Of course, one cannot list every trace and link in each entry, so the Guides to Related Topics preceding this Preface suggest links by general topic that are not immediately transparent and obvious. For instance, if one reads the entry on the Russo-Japanese War of 1904–1905, the Rebellions, Warrior Cult, World War II and Island Hopping sections of the Guide to Related Topics by Subject refers one to some of the generals (Tōgō and Nogi), and battles (Port Arthur and Tsushima), but also to the Treaty of Portsmouth, the Triple Intervention, and the Rise of the Modern Army. The Guide to Related Topics by Era points the reader to such entries such as the *Oyatoi*, the Otsu Incident, and the Unequal Treaties—all entries that one might not otherwise read. The "Martyrs" section of the Guide to Related Topics by Subject illuminates commonalities between the *Kakure Kirishitan*, Kim Ok-kyun, Ōshio Heihachirō, and Yoshida Shōin, and the "Constitution and Law: section makes the connection between Shōtoku Taishi's 17-article Constitution with the Meiji Constitution that came 1,300 years later.

Each encyclopedic entry also contains a brief list of scholarly sources that are suggested as Further Reading. These lists are by no means exhaustive; they are intended to indicate the best scholarship (in the mind of the writer and editor) on the topic. The reader can, if interested, access that monograph and then use the bibliography of that article or book to suggest other related works.

The five dozen or so authors who have contributed entries to the encyclopedia were selected because they are generally considered to be premier specialists in the field. One should not be surprised that the authors have listed one of their own articles or books in the list of Further Reading. This is not immodesty, but rather an indication that the contributing author is preeminent in the field. In at least four cases, the author has not listed his or her own work, but the editor chose to do so.

The reader is encouraged to read more widely in the field than to merely consult one specific entry. The entries are designed as interpretive and evocative essays. One can find the muzzle velocity of the Nambu machine gun or the land-air speed of the Zero fighter plane elsewhere. The entries in this encyclopedia are designed to inform but also to cause the reader to think.

A glossary is provided to help the reader identify an event or idea that is not otherwise completely defined or explained in each entry. Often an item is cross-referenced in both Japanese and English languages. The intent is to provide a quick reference. One should also employ the index for further clarification. Finally, a bibliography includes all of the sources cited in the Further Reading sections of each entry.

I wish to thank a number of people whose names do not appear among the contributors, but contributed to this project. First of all is Pat Carlin, who is Manager of Editorial Development for Military History for the publisher ABC-CLIO. Pat initially approached me with ideas about the project and then helped guide me through the editorial process. He has been most helpful and patient. Editors Cathleen Casey and Andy McCormick were very helpful at various stages of production as well.

I also wish to thank several friends and colleagues who made suggestions along the way. They include (alphabetically) Scott

O'Bryan, Tom Burkman, Scott Clark, Sally Hastings, Laura Hein, Marvin Marcus, Noriko Reider, Jennifer Robertson, and Sara Thal. All of these individuals made valuable topic suggestions as well as recommended possible contributors.

I especially wish to thank Larissa Kennedy, Philip Streich, Yu Chang, and Gerry Iguchi. They helped immeasurably by stepping in when other contributors had to withdraw. They took on unfamiliar topics that required some considerable additional research. Friends who are willing to "stretch" beyond their comfort zones to help you are good friends indeed.

Finally, I am indebted to my late good friend Sidney DeVere Brown, who was always willing to offer suggestions and encouragement when they were most needed. I'll miss you, Sid.

# Introduction

Early archeological evidence indicates that a hunting and gathering civilization emerged in the southern reaches of the Japanese archipelago more than 250,000 years ago. Pottery shards, shell mounds, and other relics suggest that the humans who migrated to the islands came from what is now the Russian Maritime Provinces and probably island-hopped down from Sakhalin through the Kurile Islands. Other relics also trace these peoples' ancestry from the South Pacific islands, probably transported on the strong Black Current that sweeps up through the Taiwan Straits.

Approximately 1200 B.C.E. the peoples in Japan coalesced into what has become known as the Jōmon people, who populated the area around what is now the Kyoto-Osaka region. They subsisted on fish, small game, and various gathered fruits, nuts, berries, seeds, and roots. Skeletal remains show evidence of violence even then. Obviously those people defended their hunting and gathering grounds against interlopers with stone and bone weapons.

About the third century B.C.E. a new wave of migrants brought metal tools, wheel-thrown pottery, and, most importantly, wet-rice cultivation to the region. This group, called Yayoi, probably came from the Asian mainland down through the Korean Peninsula. These people also brought the first metal swords, spear tips, and arrowheads. Whether these were Japan's first warriors is open to debate, but some evidence indicates that warfare was not unknown among these sedentary people. They dug defensive moats and built stone walls to protect their homelands.

By the so-called Yamato Era (third century C.E.), the Japanese people had evolved to include a warrior caste. The distinctive keyhole-shaped tombs (*kofun*) of this era contain military artifacts and the terracotta figurines (*haniwa*) depicting armored horse riders and foot soldiers. A female shaman named Himiko sent an emissary to China early in that era; the Chinese historical records indicate that the Chinese recognized Himiko as the legitimate Queen of Japan. She sent 10 slaves as a tributary gift to the Chinese and indicated that she had pacified most of Japan after a generation of warfare. We do not have very much information about the nature of that warfare, but it appears that Japanese became involved in political disputes in Korea, sending troops to aid their allies there.

In the first quasi-historical writings (the *Kojiki* and *Nihon-shōki*) that appeared in the eighth century, we are told that warfare was endemic throughout much of the early history of Japan. The fighting described was mostly between clans over land disputes, but the writings also recount the first defensive battles against the northern *Ainu* (also called *emishi*), who formed a distinct culture and raided Japanese settlements from time to time.

During this time Japan began to emulate Chinese culture, importing and adapting the predominating Confucian political philosophies to its own use. The resulting Chinese-influenced society in the so-called Nara Era (named after the first permanent capital modeled on the Chinese capital Chang-an) tried to establish civil control over the military clan *(uji)* leaders. The society that emerged was called Heian after the new capital established in 794. The next three centuries were heavily influenced by the secular humanist Confucianism of Tang China, but also by the predominance of Buddhism, which formed a curious syncretic amalgam with the native animism (*Shintō*). Both Confucianism and Buddhism eschewed warfare and violence, so we may say that this is the most peaceful era of Japanese history; even the death penalty was abolished in the Nara Era.

Personal vendettas and interfamily rivalries continued, but the warfare was still very personal. Charismatic warlords led small bands of mounted warriors; great store was placed on honor, valor, and personal loyalties. The mounted warrior wielded a sword and shield, and often the battles began with a flurry of arrows before the hand-to-hand combat ensued.

The next period of history was decidedly more violent. In the 11th century, a series of attempted military coups led Japan into the first of the so-called feudal periods. The rise of the warrior-dominated Kamakura *bakufu* (*bakufu* means "tent government") was the result of two decades of almost constant warfare. Minamoto Yoritomo, who led the feudal coalition that ultimately triumphed at the end of the 12th century, was a brutal warrior who massacred his enemies and even killed his half-brother and nephews to eliminate any rivals to his position of military deputy (*shōgun*) to a powerless emperor. When he died, his two sons briefly succeeded him, but before long his widow Hōjō Masako (called the "Nun-Shōgun" because she had taken the Buddhist tonsure after Yoritomo's death) had to engineer a coalition with the imperial house to preserve power. The era was replete with sporadic warfare, punctuated by two attempted invasions of the country by the Mongols of Kublai Kahn.

In many ways, Japanese warfare was changed forever as a result of the superior military tactics and weaponry of the Mongols. The invaders came armed with catapults, explosives, and horse war tactics that had already conquered almost half of the known world at the time. Japan was saved by two opportune typhoons that the Japanese called *kamikaze* ("divine winds"). Because the Mongols never gained full purchase on Japanese soil, they were unable to fully mount the fearsome phalanxes and cavalry charges that had laid waste to the steppes and grasslands of Asia.

The Japanese warriors began to mimic the Mongol use of foot soldiers (*ashigaru*) armed with iron-tipped pikes (*naginata*). The more aristocratic samurai armed themselves with razor-sharp long swords (*katana*) and shorter dirks (*wakizashi*) that were used for in-close warfare, for ritually taking of trophy heads, and, ultimately, for committing suicide (*hara kiri*—literally "stomach cut" or *seppuku*) if necessary to avoid capture or disgrace. By the end of the period, Japanese iron mongers were turning out tensile steel weapons.

The Kamakura *bakufu* met its end after an attempt by Emperor Go-Daigo to recover actual power from the *bakufu*. A turncoat, Ashikaga Takauji, who was sent to suppress the imperial restoration established a new *bakufu* in Kyoto. He captured Go-Daigo and instituted a new feudal government called Muromachi after the neighborhood of Kyoto where the new *bakufu* was ensconced. Ashikaga's descendants ruled for about 150 years, but by the 1450s the country dissolved into a century of civil war (called the *Sengoku* or "warring states").

The semi-independent warlords (*daimyō*) carved out little fiefdoms surrounding the construction of increasingly more elaborate castles. The *daimyō* occasionally turned on one another, allying themselves with other warlords in the hopes of replacing the shōgun. The 15th century was perhaps the nadir of Japanese history as sons turned against fathers, brothers (and sometimes sisters) turned against cousins, and vassals killed their feudal lords. Indeed, this period has also been called *Gekoku-jo*, which means "superiors overcome by subordinates." It was during this period that ritualized torture and suicide became endemic. A bloody quasi-religious warrior philosophy called *bushidō* ("The Way of the Warrior") advocated loyalty and self-sacrifice (which was rarely practiced) between comrades in arms. The *samurai* ("warrior") were discouraged from trusting women, who were deemed to be evil and enervating.

The endemic treachery and bloodshed continued for decades until a series of military chieftains finally reunited the country under a new *bakufu*. Oda Nobunaga (called the "Destroyer") triumphed over his peers by military genius and strategic terror. He managed to incorporate the guns (*teppo*) brought by the Portuguese into his war machine. He had conquered almost two-thirds of the country when his life ended with an ignominious suicide in 1582 after he was surrounded by forces led by a former subordinate. Nobunaga's chief military ally Toyotomi Hideyoshi used subterfuge to inherit Nobunaga's budding kingdom. By 1587, he had crafted a complex coalition and was able to bring a very short period of peace to the country before he died in 1598. Part of that subterfuge was a concerted effort to conquer Korea, forcing his enemies to commit their troops to the quixotic *Imjin* War on the peninsula instead of fighting in Japan.

Hideyoshi's longtime rival Tokugawa Ieyasu managed to conquer the coalition led by Hideyoshi's young son. Ieyasu defeated his rivals at the Battle of Sekigahara in 1600 and shortly thereafter established a new *bakufu* in the eastern fishing village of Edo. Assuming (and then quickly passing on to his son) the title of shōgun, he crafted a complex political system that managed to check every possible source of power. Hideyoshi surrounded his rivals with family and allies, placed the emperor under close confinement, forbade intermarriage between *daimyō*, and "froze" the society into four classes, each enjoined from social mobility. The other major control mechanism was the virtual seclusion of the country and the eradication of Roman Catholicism. Only the Dutch (who were Protestants), a few Chinese, and Koreans were allowed to enter the country to trade, and all Japanese were forbidden to leave the country on pain of death.

The Tokugawa regime managed to enforce the peace through a series of complex and draconian controls. Some of them, begun by Hideyoshi in the previous century, included forcing virtually all *ashigaru* to give up their careers as soldiers. These warriors were disarmed, except for the dirk (*wakizashi*) that was worn as a ceremonial badge of authority, and ensconced as peasant village leaders. Everyone was enjoined from changing careers, and the country was flooded with Neo-Confucian tutors who taught that people were born into immutable classes. Peasants were not allowed to leave their farms, merchants and artisans were relegated to their burgeoning castletowns (*jokamachi*), and samurai were bottled up in their cramped castle quarters.

Ieyasu confiscated all guns and cannon, and forced the samurai warrior class into a peacetime bureaucracy. Except for two extended battles, the era was remarkably free of real warfare. A castle siege at Osaka in 1614–1615 finally disposed of Hideyoshi's heir Hideyori as well as many of his supporters. In 1637, a rebellion arose in Shimabara close to Nagasaki. Although the uprising was basically a rebellion against a corrupt tax collector, it took on the color of a religious war because many of the warriors who joined the doomed uprising were dispossessed Christians. In both cases, the sieges that slowly starved the inhabitants of the surrounded castle were matters of attrition, not war. The end was more butchery than warfare.

For the next two centuries, Japan was a police state ruled by the most dangerous and despicable form of human life: the armed bureaucrat. Samurai were required to remain ready for war, but they did so perfunctorily, with all the skill and precision of an American Legion close-order drill before a Labor Day parade. Those samurai who drew a sword in anger during those two centuries were punished with remarkable vigor. In one such incident, the so-called Ako Incident of 1703, all 47 samurai who drew swords to avenge their *daimyō* were required to commit suicide for having disturbed the peace.

These two centuries of peaceful isolation spared Japan from the warfare that ravaged the rest of the world. While the rest of the world was writhing in the agonies of religious, colonial, and civil wars of every description, Japan blossomed culturally and artistically. This fact alone should belie any claims that Japan was somehow more violent and its culture more conducive to warfare than other societies.

To be sure, the samurai were encouraged to balance their lives between the personal cultivation of the artistic and literary arts (*bun*) and the martial arts (*bu*), but most only dabbled in the latter because social and political rewards came only for the former. Some honed their skills in the unarmed gymnastics of *karate, judo, jujutsu*, and even *sumo*, and even fewer practiced fencing with wooden swords (*kendo*), fencing with real swords (*kenjutsu*), mounted archery (*yabusame*), sword handling (*battōjutsu*), drawing of swords (*Iaijutsu*), and many other forms of "playing at war." Very few continued to practice with guns (*teppo jutsu*), partially because such warfare had mostly been the purview of the lowly *ashigaru*. Indeed, Japanese society was one of the few in the world that consciously stepped *backward* in terms of military technology after about the middle of the 17th century. Of course, when Japan "reentered" the world in the 1850s, it would suffer briefly because the rest of the world had continued to use and perfect guns and cannons. It rapidly closed that gap, as we shall see.

Despite its enforced isolation, Japan was cognizant of world affairs. The Dutch who were relegated to Deshima, a tiny artificial island in Nagasaki harbor, were required to make scheduled reports of world affairs to the *bakufu*. As a consequence, Japan knew about the European colonial acquisitions in the Americas and Africa, as well as the various and sundry wars that sprang up from time to time. Japan was obviously very interested in the extension of European (and American) interests into Asia.

The Dutch were only too happy to try to gain financial advantage through Japan's growing paranoia about the Opium Wars in China in the 1840s and beyond. Also, there were sporadic "close encounters" with Westerners in Japanese waters. British and Russian ships appeared in the home archipelago seeking water, food, and supplies in the late 18th century. Americans' extension of their naval activity into the far Pacific due to whaling and trade with China and other parts of Asia also brought them into Japanese waters.

Despite the anti-Christian policies (aimed chiefly against Roman Catholic Spain and Portugal) in Japan, the study of Western science and technologies (called *Rangaku* or "Dutch studies" in Japan) was allowed to a few Japanese scholars. Increasingly in the early 19th century, a number of these scholars began to shift from Western medicine to the other sciences and technologies.

Therefore, the Japanese were not totally unprepared for Commodore Matthew Perry's momentous visit to Edo bay in 1853. The American demands that Japan open a few ports for purposes of trade were not to be rebuffed as easily as Japan had chased away single Western ships in search of supplies. The letter from American president Millard Fillmore was roundly discussed in *bakufu* circles. The *bakufu* realized that Japan was in no military position to keep the West at arm's length. After all, if the Chinese giant could not defeat the British, how could tiny Japan hope to win?

The Japanese began to try to catch-up with Western military power. The *bakufu* accepted an offer from France to train Japanese samurai and the Tokugawa hurriedly began to buy guns, cannons, and a few gunships to defend Japan. Unfortunately for the *bakufu*, however, some of its ancient feudal enemies began to do the same. The *tozama* (literally "far people") domains (*han*) of Chōshū, Satsuma, and Tosa began to acquire arms from Western smugglers around Nagasaki. The *bakufu* fared poorly in this arms race because their more conservative elders preferred the status quo. The *tozama han*, however, had more to gain than to lose by building up their military power.

Ultimately, the *tozama* overcame their fear of Tokugawa retribution and began to harass the intrepid foreigners who braved a visit to a very dangerous Japan. Young swashbuckling xenophobes who called themselves *shihi* ("men of spirit") slipped their feudal traces and declared themselves to be independent (*rōnin*) loyalists to a newly rediscovered emperor. When the *bakufu* could not control these vicious swordsmen, the Western nations began to take matters into their own hands.

As a partial response to the murder of one of their citizens by Satsuma samurai, the British bombarded the castletown capital of Kagoshima in 1863. Similarly, a joint flotilla of British, Dutch, and French (with an American observer) gunships bombarded the Chōshū-controlled Shimonoseki Straits after the Chōshū forces had strafed passing Western ships. In both cases, the overwhelming Western firepower destroyed the Japanese emplacements and forced those *han* governments to recognize the need to stifle their xenophobic elements. Both *han* governments promoted more moderate "modernizers" within their governments who began to approach the British for military assistance.

So it was that when the inevitable clash between the *bakufu* and the *tozama* came in 1867–1868, the *bakufu* forces showed themselves to be remarkably inept against a more "modern" combined Satsuma-Chōshū army.

The *tozama* won almost every battle of the short-lived Boshin War, and the Tokugawa sued for peace. This development ushered out the *bakufu*, and with it, nearly seven centuries of feudal government and warfare.

The new government, which was named after the newly crowned 13-year-old Emperor Meiji, chose to continue the French military tutelage begun under the Tokugawa. After the Germans defeated the French in 1871, however, the Japanese hired Germans to train their army. Indeed, Japan hired hundreds of foreigners called *oyatoi* ("honorable employees") to come to train young Japanese in the science and technologies of the West after an exploratory mission led by the imperial courtier Iwakura Tomomi identified which nations specialized in particular fields. British naval tutors trained the new Japanese navy, Americans taught the Japanese how to establish a public education system, the French explained the intricacies of criminal law, and the Germans helped establish medical schools.

While Japan "modernized," it began to consider whether it would be advisable to extend its territorial borders given that imperialism seemed to be the path to wealth and power in the 19th century. The Iwakura Mission scurried back to Japan from Europe when the delegates discovered that their governmental peers were considering a punitive military mission to Korea. Among those who advocated a mission to punish the Koreans for a diplomatic slight against the Japanese was one of the heroes of the Boshin War, Saigō Takamori. Not only did Saigō wish to use the "Korean Question" to expand Japan's influence into East Asia, but he also thought that the mission should be staffed by samurai instead of the newly trained military. Disgruntled samurai who were being eased out of their ancient warrior

caste by universal conscription in the military could die honorably in Korea, he argued, rather than waste away as discharged bureaucrats.

Those who had seen the Western nations up close as part of the Iwakura Mission counseled against such a quixotic venture until Japan was stronger. Saigō and many others resigned from the Meiji government in protest. A hastily considered alternative mission was mounted to punish the Taiwanese who had slaughtered some Okinawan sailors. Saigō's young half-brother Tsugumichi was made head of that mission. The venture—Japan's first foray into international warfare—was nearly a disaster. Although the Japanese managed to force China to formally apologize and pay an indemnity for the behavior of the Taiwanese, the Japanese forces stumbled about, nearly losing battles to the aborigines, and suffering more casualties to the island diseases than to the actual battles.

The next two incidences of warfare, however, were domestic. Another former Boshin hero, Etō Shimpei, led a brief rebellion in Saga *han* in 1874, an uprising that was put down rather easily by the new conscription army against Etō's samurai. The samurai showed themselves to be sadly unsuited to the new type of warfare that involved large coordinated military units firing and maneuvering in strategic battle plans. Three years later, another rebellion arose among the dissatisfied samurai in Satsuma. After the rebellion had started, Saigō Takamori was lured out of retirement to lead the ragtag band of rebels. The new army crushed this rebellion as well, and Saigō and many of his men committed suicide rather than be tried as rebels.

Many historians point to this failed rebellion as the last gasp of the old samurai class and of feudalism itself. The rest of Japan's warfare would take place in foreign lands and be led by the new military. Two decades later, Japan's slide into the Valley of Darkness began. For the next five decades, Japan would be caught up in continental military expansionism. The siren song of imperialism lured the Japanese into horrific warfare.

Foreign warfare, once it had begun in 1894, escalated quickly. Japan fought three wars in less than a decade. The first was against China and began over the issue of Korean independence. Korea had long been a dependency of China and when a local uprising cropped up in 1893, the Koreans asked for Chinese help. Japan seized on the opportunity to force its way into continental affairs, and before long China and Japan were at war. Japan was incredibly lucky to win virtually every battle and the war—its victories came not because of any Japanese military superiority, but mainly because of Chinese corruption and inefficiency. The Treaty of Shimonoseki, which ended the First Sino-Japanese War (as it was later called), granted Japan the cession of Taiwan, the declared independence of Korean (soon to be annexed), a large indemnity, and China's Liaoning Peninsula, gateway to Manchuria. Before the ink had dried on the treaty, however, France, Germany, and Russia declared themselves jointly in opposition to Japan's acquisition of Liaoning. The Triple Intervention, as it came to be known, merely postponed Japan's entry into Continental Asia, as we shall see.

A few years later in 1900, Japan sent troops to help squash a xenophobic war in China called the Boxer Rebellion. Japanese troops acquitted themselves very well, refusing to execute prisoners or to fire on suspected Chinese supporters of the Boxers. Indeed, the Western military leaders praised the Japanese and granted them the lead position in the victory parade into Beijing. The Russians, however, seemed to be spoiling for a fight after the war. Despite promises to vacate their position in China and Korea as a result of the rebellion, the Russians seemed intent on using the pretext to expand their empire into East Asia.

This Russian incursion, along with the expansion of the Trans-Siberian Railway into Manchuria, frightened the British as well—enough so to convince them that an Anglo-Japanese alliance would serve both interests against Russia. Two years after the alliance agreement was signed in 1902, Japan broke off diplomatic negotiations with Russia and attacked the new Russian naval port at the tip of the Liaoning Peninsula. The resulting Russo-Japanese War was one of horrific battle attrition. Japanese frontal assaults against Russian emplacements led to horrendous battle casualties on both sides. Apart from the carnage, the results caused the Japanese to come to believe in the efficacy of such spirited charges. Thousands of Japanese would die because of this belief within the next three decades. Also, the "miracle" of Japan's naval victory at the Battle of Tsushima in 1905 convinced Japan's naval leaders that a "fell swoop" deciding victory would lead to Japan's ultimate triumph.

Now that Japan was fully committed to continental expansion, its military and political leaders thirsted for more. It all seemed so easy, after all. Perhaps Japan was truly divinely destined to establish hegemony in Asia, as some of its more radical nationalists argued.

Japan honored its commitments to Britain in 1914 and attacked the German positions at Qingdao in China's Shandong Peninsula at the beginning of World War I. After a bloody siege involving more Japanese frontal assaults, the beleaguered Germans surrendered and once again Japan's military machine triumphed. Two decades of Japanese meddling into Chinese affairs ensued until Japan was drawn into the ultimate morass. After Japanese troops overran Manchuria in 1931, Japan was sucked increasingly down toward a seemingly inevitable war with China.

Full-fledged warfare came in 1937. After achieving some initial easy victories, the Japanese army became bogged in a vicious war. Japanese atrocities at Shanghai (bombing civilians) were followed by the very nadir of Japan's descent into madness. Japan attacked the undefended capital of Nanjing in December 1937 and began to rape, pillage, and slaughter civilians by the thousands. If this horror had been an anomaly, a one-time paroxysm in the "fog of war," perhaps one could understand. But it was not, for the next eight years Japanese troops spread such atrocities across Asia. Horrors abounded, including the "Three-All" ("Kill-all, loot-all, and burn-all") campaigns and the Massacres at Manila, Sook Ching, Wake Island, Banka Island, and many more. Mistreatment of prisoners of war, biological experiments on humans, sexual slavery (the so-called Comfort Women), and scores of other war crimes make this period of Japanese history a disgusting and reprehensible one at best.

American and British aid to China during the war resulted in Japanese expansion into Southeast Asia in search of oil and rubber, and, eventually, into the infamous attacks on Pearl Harbor, Hong Kong, Guam, and the rest of the South Pacific. The following four years brought the horror home. By 1944, Japan was being fire-bombed by the allies almost at will. Bloody battles in the South Pacific killed perhaps 500,000 Japanese, a least 100,000 of them Japanese civilians. The use of nuclear weapons at Hiroshima and Nagasaki, coupled with Russia's seizure of Manchuria, finally brought Japan to its knees and surrender.

The next 70 years were as peaceful as the previous 70 had been filled with war. The constitution of 1947 renounced war and militarism; Japan became the center of pacifism and of the anti-nuclear war movement. Every attempt to amend the constitution to allow re-militarism has been sounded defeated by the Japanese electorate.

This postwar peace, coupled with other long periods of peace (the Nara and Heian eras as well as the two centuries of Tokugawa peace), might suggest that war is an anomaly in Japan. Japan certainly sank into horrific war several times in its history, but perhaps less so than in the last three centuries of American, European and world history. Japan's seven centuries of feudalism is a long history to be sure, but shorter than most of Europe's history and less bloody than China's. Japan's horrific history of war crimes,[*] when compared to the history of war crimes in the world prior to their commission (Wounded Knee, Trail of Tears, Philippine Insurrection, Algeria, Amritsar, the Holocaust, Armenia, and Katyn Woods) and since (Rwanda, Croatia, Biafra, and Cambodia), gives us neither hope nor solace. It does, however, argue against the notion that war is either endemic or natural in Japan.

# A

## Ainu, Military Resistance to

Archeologists have reached a consensus that around 400 B.C.E., the Japanese population arose from an influx of Yayoi peoples carrying wet-rice farming technology from the Korean peninsula. Starting from northern Kyushu, the Yayoi migrated across the Japanese archipelago, bringing trade, conquering territory, and intermarrying with previously settled Jōmon peoples. With the establishment of the Yamato State in the late seventh century C.E., this expansion was institutionalized through the development of a feudal military system. By the 11th century, the feudal military organization extended to the Tohoku region of northern Honshu, where it was in contact with peoples called *Emishi* by the Japanese.

Some sources have argued that the *Emishi* and the Ainu are largely the same people and that Ainu culture developed in the 13th century due to an influx of Japanized *Emishi* fleeing military rule and the appropriation of hunting land for agriculture. The Chinese characters for the word *Emishi* are the same as those used in *Ezo*, the premodern Japanese term for both Hokkaidō and the Ainu.

Archeologists have dated the emergence of Ainu culture to the 13th century C.E. based on a shift from the use of pit-houses to wood and thatch houses (*chise* in the Ainu language) and from ceramic pottery to lacquerware obtained through trade with Japanese. The ancestors of the Ainu were a mixture of two distinct peoples: Jōmon hunter-gatherers who occupied the entire Japanese archipelago from Okinawa to

Hokkaidō from about 10,000 years ago, and Oktohosk marine-based hunter-gatherers originating in Northeast Asia.

The Japanese warlords of northern Honshu recognized the benefits of controlling trade with the Ainu. In addition to abundant wildlife and rich seas within Ainu territory that yielded food as well as status goods such as hawks and bearskins, the Ainu were connected to Chinese merchants through a northern trade network. The Ainu traded furs and other products of the forests and the seas, sometimes directly, but usually through intermediaries, for Chinese silks and other manufactured goods from Chinese outposts on the Amur River. In the 13th century, the Japanese Ando clan established a military trading post on the southern peninsula of Hokkaidō and participated actively in trade between Honshu and Hokkaidō through the port of Tosaminato, near present-day Aomori City. In the Japanese civil wars of the 16th century, the Kakizaki clan, originally retainers of the Ando, rose to hegemony over the southern portion of Hokkaidō; in 1590, Toyotomi Hideyoshi recognized Yoshihiro Kakizaki as the *daimyō* of this territory. With the establishment of the Tokugawa *bakufu* in 1603, the Kakizaki clan changed its name to Matsumae, and clan members were invested as *daimyō* based on a monopoly of trade with the Ainu rather than on the production of rice.

Ainu society was organized into independent villages (*kotan*), each with a well-defined territory (*iwor*), in which village members had resource-gathering rights. Each *kotan* had a chief chosen for his ability to defend the *iwor* and bring wealth to the *kotan* through trade. Ainu leaders sometimes formed alliances and fought other groups to defend or expand territory or gain access to trading partners. The Kakizaki/Matsumae's desire to establish and maintain a trade monopoly on Hokkaidō inevitably drew them into these conflicts, in most cases complicating and escalating them.

In 1456, a major conflict arose when a Japanese blacksmith killed an Ainu in a dispute over a poorly sharpened knife. The following year, a large Ainu force overwhelmed nearly all the Japanese strongholds in Hokkaidō, but was finally defeated by the Kakizaki. However, intermittent warfare continued until the Kakizaki were able to broker an uneasy peace in 1551. In 1669, the Ainu leader Shakushain led a large group of Ainu on a march toward the main stronghold of the Matsumae, killing Japanese traders and officials in Shiraoi and Yoichi along the way. Shakushain was finally defeated by a large Matsumae force at Kunnui, and was murdered the following year by Matsumae samurai who had invited him to a feast under the pretense of peace. This conflict, known as Shakushain's War, marks a shift in Ainu-Matsumae relations, as it finally established Matsumae military and economic dominance in Hokkaidō. Finally, in 1789, a group of 37 Ainu were executed by Matsumae samurai after a failed uprising by indebted Ainu fishery workers on Kunashiri Island and in eastern Hokkaidō— the last instance of armed resistance by Ainu people against the Japanese in Hokkaidō.

While the immediate causes of each of these conflicts were unique, and Ainu groups fought on both sides of all of the major conflicts, they reflect Ainu efforts to counter their increasing economic dependence on the Matsumae, and the Japanese merchants who exercised the monopoly. This dependence had several causes, including steady rises in the prices of rice and sake due to gouging by Japanese merchants, and the depletion of natural resources in Hokkaidō to meet the increasing consumption demands of early-modern Japanese society. In the mid-18th century, many Ainu became dependent on seasonal wage labor in the commercial herring fishery. Meanwhile, on Sakhalin, Ainu traders could not procure enough furs to purchase Chinese goods for trade with Japanese merchants, and many became indebted and enslaved to North Sakhalin middlemen. Between 1809 and 1812, the *bakufu* took control of the Sakhalin trade, absolving Ainu debts, but also closing the last independent market for Ainu trade. The failure of Ainu military resistance allowed the Matsumae to tighten their trade monopoly and fix the terms of trade to their advantage. Perhaps even more importantly, it prevented the formation of a united Ainu political structure that might have threatened Matsumae, or even *bakufu* military power.

In 1871, the new Meiji government transferred all Ainu to Japanese family registers, officially making them nationals within the modern Japanese nation-state, though discrimination against Ainu people continues to the present day. Still, despite their historical experience of economic exploitation, the Ainu have proudly preserved their language and culture, and many among them have achieved considerable success in Japanese society while maintaining a distinct Ainu identity. In 2008, the Ainu people were recognized as the indigenous people of Hokkaidō by the Japanese government.

*Joel Legassie*

**See also:** Civil Wars (1467–1570), Consequences; Civil Wars, Sengoku Era; Colonization of

Hokkaidō; Fujiwara Family; Tokugawa *Bakufu* Political System; Toyotomi Hideyoshi.

## Further Reading

Dubreuil, Chisato O., and William W. Fitzhugh, eds. *Ainu: Spirit of a Northern People*. Washington, DC: Arctic Studies Center National Museum of Natural History Smithsonian Institution in association with University of Washington Press, 1999.

Irish, Ann B. *Hokkaidō: A History of Ethnic Transition and Development on Japan's Northern Island*. Jefferson, NC: McFarland & Co., 2009.

Siddle, Richard. *Race, Resistance, and the Ainu of Japan*. New York: Routledge, 1996.

Sjöberg, Katarina. *The Return of the Ainu: Cultural Mobilization and the Practice of Ethnicity in Japan*. Langhorne, PA: Harwood Academic Publishers, 1993.

Walker, Brett L. *The Conquest of Ainu Lands: Ecology and Culture in Japanese Expansion, 1590–1800*. Berkeley: University of California Press, 2001.

## Aizawa Seishisai (1782–1863)

Aizawa Seishisai is considered one of the intellectual founders of modern Japanese national ideology. As a Confucian scholar in the service of the Mito Domain Lord Tokugawa Nariakai, Aizawa originated the idea of *kokutai* as a basis for Japanese nationalism, and was the most famous propagator of the doctrine of *sonnō jōi* (Revere the Sovereign, Expel the Barbarians). Aizawa's views were most notably put forward in his 1825 work *Shinron* ("New Theses"). Here Aizawa concentrated on the threat posed to Japan by Western imperialism. He argued that to preserve the shōgunal realm, radical reform of the country was necessary. Aizawa proposed that the shōgunate should exploit the charismatic power of the emperor to gain mass loyalty from the Japanese population. *Sonno-jōi* became the rallying cry for the anti-shōgunate rebels who enacted the Meiji Revolution, while the idea of *kokutai* served as the key plank of Japanese nationalist ideology until defeat in World War II.

A low-level samurai retainer of the Mito branch of the Tokugawa house, Aizawa studied under the famous Mito School scholar Fujita Yūkoku from the age of 10. At 18, Aizawa was appointed to the Mito Academy to work on its famous *Dai nihon shi* ("History of Great Japan") project. He was also responsible for lecturing senior Mito nobles, including the future domain lord Tokugawa Nariaki. Together with Fujita Yūkoku's son Fujita Tokō, Aizawa represented the core of a faction of intellectually elite but hereditarily low-class samurai within the Mito domain who lobbied for the appointment of Nariaki as domain lord. After Nariaki's appointment, this faction, with Aizawa playing a central role, led major reforms of Mito domain governance carried out during the 1830s and early 1840s. Aizawa provided not only intellectual inspiration and planning for these reforms, but through appointment by Nariaki to senior government positions such as county magistrate (in 1830), was also directly involved in governance of the domain. In 1841, Aizawa was appointed the first head of the Kōdōkan, a revamped Mito Academy that Nariaki and Aizawa constructed to spread the Mito reform agenda to the rest of Japan. The Kōdōkan proved very effective in carrying out this task, with the ideas of Aizawa and Fujita Tokō spreading quickly throughout Japan, and a range of important figures in later Japanese history—for instance, Yoshida Shōin—coming to Mito to study at the academy.

The ideas of Aizawa—particularly his anti-Westernism and promotion of the doctrine of sonnō jōi—were ultimately radicalized to an extent that unsettled Aizawa. After Tokugawa Nariaki's defeat in the internal shōgunal political struggles of 1858, many young Mito samurai turned to direct action, carrying out insurgent attacks on shōgunal figures and installations in Tokyo. As a senior Mito domain elder, Aizawa was involved in the domain government's suppression of these radical samurai followers of the sonnō jōi ideology he had himself originated. Ironically, sonnō jōi ultimately became an anti-shōgunate rallying cry, employed to bring down the very same Tokugawa regime that Aizawa and Nariaki had been trying to preserve.

*Kiri Paramore*

**See also:** *Sonno-jōi;* Tokugawa Nariaki; Yoshida Shōin.

### Further Reading

Paramore, Kiri. *Ideology and Christianity in Japan*. New York: Routledge, 2009.

Wakabayashi, Bob Tadashi. *Anti-foreignism and Western Learning in Early-Modern Japan: The New Theses of 1825*. Cambridge, MA: Harvard University Press, 1986.

## Aizu Samurai Spirit

The origin of Aizu samurai spirit can be traced back to Hoshina Masayuki (1611–1673), the founder of Aizu domain. Masayuki was the illegitimate son of Hidetada, the second Tokugawa shōgun. In 1643, after Hidetada's death, Masayuki received 230,000 *koku* of fertile land in northeast Japan from Iemitsu, the third shōgun, and became the founding *daimyō* of Aizu. Not only was Masayuki wise in domain building, but he also served Iemitsu conscientiously. Iemitsu, in turn, valued the loyalty of his half-brother so much that he entrusted his heir, the next shōgun, to the care of Masayuki. Grateful of such trust,

Masayuki promulgated in 1668 the Aizu Creed, the first clause of which reads: "Always serve the shōgun with single-minded loyalty and never conduct yourselves by the examples of other domains." This notion of single-minded loyalty to the shōgun became the founding principle of Aizu domain.

That principle, however, brought tragic disaster to Aizu during the tumultuous Bakumatsu period. In 1862, Matsudaira Katamori, the ninth Aizu *daimyō*, was appointed Kyoto Protector. This position thrust Aizu into the center of Japan's political turmoil. The position was newly created to protect the emperor and restore order to the capital, which had been thrown into chaos by widespread terrorism. The perpetrators were radicals from Chōshū and other domains bent on revenge for the Ansei Purge, a crackdown in 1858 on opposition to the opening of the country and *kōbugattai*, a movement to unite the court and the shōgunate. Fully recognizing the political risk the position entailed, Katamori initially declined the appointment. His chief retainer even warned that taking the position is "to put out fire by carrying wood to the site." But representatives of the Shōgunate council—one of them being Tokugawa Yoshinobu—pressed the case by citing Hoshina Masayuki and the Aizu Creed. This left Katamori without choice. He took office in December 1862. A proponent of *kōbugattai*, he identified serving the shōgun with serving the emperor and Japan.

Meanwhile, the situation in Kyoto deteriorated. What had been revenge for the Ansei Purge and opposition to the opening of the country had now become a political plot to overthrow the Tokugawa shōgunate. The shift was graphically demonstrated in a "heavenly curse" incident in February 1863 in which the "beheaded" wooden statues of three Muromachi shōguns were put on public display with a signboard enumerating the crimes of the "usurpatory traitors" since the end of the Heian Period when the warrior class took power away from the emperor. Katamori took swift action. He rounded up those guilty of the incident and followed up with a series of crackdowns. Then on August 18, 1863, he assisted Emperor Kōmei, a xenophobic ruler but a strong believer of *kōbugattai*, in launching a coup that successfully expelled from Kyoto courtiers guilty of forgery of imperial rescripts to assist the radicals, along with their Chōshū colluders. Pleased with Katamori's loyalty, Emperor Kōmei bestowed on him a letter of commendation in October 1863.

Katamori was gratified that Aizu loyalty was recognized, but his crackdown made Aizu the enemy of the radicals, particularly Chōshū. In July 1864, Chōshū became the enemy of the emperor for attempting to recapture the Imperial Palace, which led to an expedition against Chōshū by the *bakufu* army led by Aizu and Satsuma. However, Satsuma betrayed Aizu soon after by joining Chōshū in a secret anti-shōgunate alliance to restore imperial rule by force. The year 1866 witnessed precipitous changes in Japanese politics. The 14th shōgun died in July, and Yoshinobu became the 15th shōgun in November; Emperor Kōmei died in December. By the time Emperor Meiji was enthroned in January 1867, it was obvious that the shōgunate could no longer hold out against the better-equipped Satchō forces. Yoshinobu voluntarily surrendered power to the emperor on October 14, 1867, but Satchō leaders, obtaining a forged imperial ordinance dated one day earlier, resolved to subjugate Bukufu and the pro-shōgunate Aizu by force. On January 3, 1868, Satchō forces seized the Imperial Palace and proclaimed an "imperial restoration," stripping Yoshinobu of his lands and abolishing all *bakufu* offices. These moves outraged Yoshinobu, who sent Aizu and other pro-shōgunate troops to recapture the court, leading to the Battle of Toba-Fushimi in which Aizu suffered more than 270 casualties. Yoshinobu, pledging submission to the Meiji government, then began to distance himself from Katamori, leaving Aizu the main target of the Satchō hatred. Thus, despite its loyal service to, and the enormous sacrifice for, the shōgunate and the court, Aizu was rejected by both the shōgunate and the Meiji government, the self-claimed representatives of the young emperor.

By the time Aizu surrendered in September 1868, it lost 2,500 more men. Many books have been written to tell the story of Aizu samurai spirit, the best known of which is perhaps Saotome Mitsugu (1926–2008)'s prize-winning 21-volume novel *The Soul of Aizu Samurai* (Aizu shikon, 1985–2001). While a touching tale of the Meiji Restoration from the loser's perspective, it fails to note that some former Aizu samurai, such as Shiba Shirō, in their eagerness to prove their loyalty to Japan, were instrumental in Japan's aggression against Asian countries during Japan's rise to modernization.

*Guohe Zheng*

**See also:** Hitotsubasi Keiki (Tokugawa Yoshinobu); Shiba Ryōtarō and *Bushidō*.

## Further Reading

Ishimitsu, Mahito, ed. *Remembering Aizu: The Testament of Shiba Gorō*. Translated by Teruko Craig. Honolulu: University of Hawai'i Press, 1999.

Shiba, Ryotarō. *Drunk as a Lord: Samurai Stories*. Translated by Eileen Kato. Tokyo: Kodansha International, 2001.

Shiba, Ryōtarō. *The Last Shōgun*. Translated by Juliet Carpenter. Tokyo, Japan: Kodansha, 1998.

Zheng, Guohe. *From Patriotism to Imperialism.* Ph.D. dissertation, The Ohio State University, 1997.

## Akihito (Heisei), Emperor (b. 1933)

Akihito was born December 23, 1933, in Tokyo as the first son and fifth child of Hirohito, Emperor Shōwa, and Nagako, Empress Kojun. He is considered to be the 125th direct descendant of Emperor Jimmu, Japan's first emperor. He has one younger brother, Prince Masahito, four elder sisters, and one younger sister. His first cousin is Prince Tomohito.

In 1940, Akihito began his elementary education at Gakushuin, the Peers' School, which was then called the Imperial Household Ministry School; it became a private school in 1949. In the last years of World War II, Akihito and his brother moved out of Tokyo to escape the American bombing of Tokyo and remained in Nikko until 1945. Because of his youth, Akihito was not commissioned as an Army officer or connected to the war.

After the war, Akihito returned to Gakushuin to receive his secondary education. He was also privately tutored by Mrs. Elizabeth Gray Vining, an American Quaker, and was introduced to English and Western manners and values. In 1952, he entered the Faculty of Politics and Economics at Gakushuin University. Akihito received a wide range of training, including Japanese history, constitutional law, Western culture, and English, and later developed an academic interest in ichthyology, the study of fish. Akihito completed his university education in 1956.

In November 1952, his Coming-of-Age Ceremony was held at the Tokyo Imperial Palace and Akihito was invested as heir to the Japanese throne. He then began to carry out official duties as Crown Prince. In June 1953, he made his first overseas journey to London to attend the coronation of Queen Elizabeth II of the United Kingdom. Between March and October of that year, he made a round of visits to the United States, Canada, and 12 European countries.

In August 1957, at the age of 23, Akihito met Shoda Michiko, the first daughter of Shoda Hidesaburo, the president and later honorary chairman of the Nisshin Flour Milling Company. Michiko was a commoner and not related by either blood or marriage to the Imperial House, but was a valedictorian at the University of the Sacred Heart in Tokyo. On April 10, 1959, Crown Prince Akihito married Michiko. The Imperial Household Council, headed by the Prime Minister, gave its unanimous consent to the marriage. In the history of the Imperial House of Japan, Michiko was the first commoner to marry into the imperial family. Akihito and Michiko have three children: Prince Naruhito (born February 23, 1960), Prince Fumihito (November 30, 1965), and Princess Sayako (April 18, 1969).

After the death of Emperor Hirohito on January 7, 1989, Akihito acceded to the throne as the 125th emperor of Japan. On November 12, 1990, he was formally enthroned. The era of Akihito's reign was designated Heisei. In accordance with the Constitution of Japan, he became the first Japanese monarch to ascend to the Chrysanthemum Throne as "the symbol of the state and the unity of the people."

Akihito has visited all 47 prefectures, including a visit to Okinawa in 1993, and has so far made official visits to 49 countries. In cases of major natural disaster, Akihito and Michiko have paid sympathy visits, consoling the survivors and encouraging those in relief operations. In 2009, the Commemoration Ceremony of the Twentieth Anniversary of

His Majesty the Emperor's Accession to the Throne was held at the National Theatre of Japan in Tokyo.

*Hiroyuki Yamamoto*

**See also:** Shōwa Emperor (Hirohito).

**Further Reading**

Shillony, Ben-Ami. *The Emperors of Modern Japan*. Leiden: Brill, 2008.

Vining, Elizabeth Gray. *Windows for the Crown Prince: An American Woman's Four Years as Private Tutor to the Crown Prince of Japan*. New York: Harper Collins, 1952.

**Alternative Attendance.** *See* Sankin Kōtai.

## Amau Doctrine

Following the Manchurian Incident (1931), the creation of Manchukuo (1932), and Japan's leaving of the League of Nations (1933), Japanese policy in East Asia was marked by an increasing emphasis on the creation of an institutionalized regional bloc of some kind under Japanese leadership. While ideas of Pan-Asianism had a long pedigree in Japan, they remained largely foreign to mainstream politics, but rather were a policy option advocated by the opposition. For decades, the government's preferred course had been a policy of joining the "club" of Western powers and following imperialist practices, while keeping aloof from the affairs of other Asian nations—or, at least, not officially siding with them or showing sympathy for the various Asian independence movements. Unofficially, however, leaders of Asian national independence movements had received support from civilian Japanese pan-Asian organizations since the late 19th century.

In the 1930s, Japan felt sufficiently self-confident to attempt a change in its foreign policy course and to openly pursue the idea of a pan-Asian bloc with a strong anti-Western orientation. Japanese Pan-Asianists now argued that Japan should lead Asia and free it from Western domination. On April 17, 1934, against the background of intensifying Japanese expansion in Northern China, a Foreign Ministry spokesman, Amau Eiji (1887–1968), made a statement that, to Western ears, suggested an abrupt change of course in Japanese diplomacy. The statement claimed "special responsibilities for Japan in East Asia" and was frequently interpreted as a declaration by Japan of an "Asian Monroe Doctrine"—that is, a call for noninterference by the Western powers in China. The statement emphasized that Japan "opposes any joint action on the part of foreign Powers that tends to militate against the maintenance of peace and order in Eastern Asia. . . . Owing to the special position of Japan in her relations with China, . . . it must be realized that Japan is called upon to exert the utmost effort in carrying out her mission and in fulfilling her special responsibilities in East Asia."

This statement was never published in written form. Instead, the news agency Renmei issued an explicitly "unofficial communiqué" summarizing Amau's statement. Notwithstanding its ambiguous legal character, the Amau statement was widely quoted in the contemporary Western media, as it seemed to signify a change of direction in Japan's foreign policy and was considered proof that Japan was becoming increasingly aggressive. The British, French, American, and Italian governments demanded that the Japanese government clarify the meaning of the statement. The Japanese Foreign Ministry explained that it had no intention of questioning the rights of other powers in China or the principles underlying the open door policy in China. To appease the Western powers, the Amau statement was several times revised and even revoked in part in the course of these diplomatic exchanges.

In the years that followed, the results of Japanese foreign policy—continuing to expand its influence in Northern China; in 1937, waging a full-scale war against the Republic of China under Chiang Kai-shek; and, in 1938, declaring a "New Order" in East Asia—seemed to confirm that Japan was, indeed, following the intent of the 1934 statement. Thus the Amau statement was frequently invoked whenever Japan's expansion in Asia was discussed in the Western media in the late 1930s and early 1940s. The increasing use of Pan-Asian propaganda in Japanese attempts to legitimize the Pacific war seemed to confirm, ex post facto, that the Amau Declaration had meant exactly what it said (or appeared to say)—notwithstanding Japanese efforts to respond to Western criticism immediately after the announcement was made in 1934.

After World War II, the statement was soon forgotten and resurfaced only in the course of research on Pan-Asianism in recent years. Amau himself pursued a successful diplomatic career after 1934. In 1937, he was appointed ambassador to Switzerland and later ambassador to Italy, and in 1941, he became Vice Minister for Foreign Affairs. In December 1945, Amau was arrested by the occupation authorities, but was released in 1948 without facing trial as a war criminal. He was rehabilitated in 1951 and later became chairman of the Japanese United Nations Association (Nihon Kokusai Rengô Kyôgikai). He died in 1968.

*Sven Saaler*

**See also:** Pan-Asianism; Tōyama Mitsuru.

## Further Reading

FRUS, United States Department of State. *Papers Relating to the Foreign Relations of the United States, Japan: 1931–1941*, vol. I, pp. 224–229. Washington, DC: U.S. Government Printing Office, 1931–1941. Available at: http://digital.library.wisc.edu/1711.dl/FRUS.FRUS193141v01

Saaler, Sven, and Christopher W. A. Szpilman. "Introduction: The Emergence of Pan-Asianism as an Ideal of Asian Identity and Solidarity, 1850–2008," in Sven Saaler and Christopher W. A. Szpilman (eds), *Pan-Asianism: A Documentary History. Volume 1: 1859–1920*. Lanham, MD: Rowman & Littlefield, 2010:1–41.

## American Anti-alien Movement

Opposition to Asian immigration has been a consistent force in U.S. history that has, at critical moments, congealed into significant actions in regional and national politics and the history of U.S.-East Asian relations. From the earliest days of Asian immigration, Asians within the United States have faced claims that they are "aliens" who cannot be assimilated into the cultural or ethnic fabric of the nation. Asian exclusion—a policy of blocking Asian immigrant participation in American society—began as restrictions on the right to citizenship. As Asian American communities and the number of U.S. citizens of Asian heritage expanded, so did the complexity of anti-alien politics. The most striking example of anti-alien exclusion, the removal and confinement of Japanese Americans from the West Coast during World War II, reflected decades of political maneuvering and popular debate about the place of Asian immigrants in American society.

Following the first wave of Chinese immigration to the United States in the 1860s, agitation on behalf of exclusionary laws

Dr. Soyeda Juichi, of the Associated Chambers of Commerce of Japan and the Japanese American Society of Tokyo, and Kamiya Tadao, chief secretary of the Tokyo Chamber of Commerce, on a visit to the United States, where they were lobbying against proposed anti-Japanese legislation in California, 1913. (Library of Congress)

against Chinese labor gained political traction throughout the 1870s and 1880s. Exclusion usually came in the form of state or local laws passed to restrict places of work or residence for Chinese laborers or to impose unique and burdensome requirements to carry documentation proving right of residence. Politicians also pursued outright limits or bans on immigration. Agitation for such laws turned violent with tragic results. In an emblematic episode, known as the Rock Springs Massacre of 1885, Wyoming miners rampaged through a settlement of Chinese workers as part of a labor dispute with the Union Pacific Railway. Dozens were left brutally murdered.

Exclusion fever arose through a combination of forces. An undercurrent of blinding racial prejudice served as either an implicit or explicit justification for legal exclusion. Specific historical circumstances transformed these racial fears into exclusionary politics. The concentration of Asian immigrants along the U.S. West Coast made that population particularly susceptible to exclusionary politics. Moreover, cyclical economic depressions afflicted the United States throughout the last decades of the 19th century, raising anxieties about the uneven nature of economic growth in the region. These anxieties expressed themselves in nativist claims that industrious Asian laborers and the low wages they would accept constituted a threat to the cohesion of American culture. The close balance between Democrats and Republicans in national politics in those decades also encouraged crude political maneuvering in an effort to swing narrow voting constituencies. These disparate forces coalesced to produce legislation that made anti-alien exclusion a national policy: the Chinese Exclusion Act of 1882.

China was a weak international power with limited diplomatic capacity to protest exclusion. As Japan's modernization lurched forwarded, however, the United States experienced an upsurge of Japanese immigration in late 1880s. Many of these immigrants came as so-called *dekasegi* émigrés—migrating workers seeking to improve their fortunes abroad before returning to Japan. Many workers, however, stayed. Japan's rise to global prominence after its victory in the Russo-Japanese War inspired American journalists to fan the flames of war hysteria in the United States and to look upon Japanese immigrants as a new threat. American and Japanese diplomats entered into a gentleman's agreement in 1907 to diffuse these war scares by restricting Japanese emigration to the United States. The agreement still allowed wives and family members to flow into Japanese communities, and Japanese residents in Hawaii could also still enter the United States. Politicians in California responded to this wave of immigration with the 1913 Alien Land Law, which barred

Japanese immigrants—but not their citizen offspring—from owning land. The law, while viciously exclusionary in intent, did not stem the growing importance of the Japanese community to the economic life of the region.

In the aftermath of World War I, issues of race and international politics collided ever more forcefully. Japanese negotiators at the Paris Peace Conference of 1919 proposed to end discrimination against its nationals by including a statement of racial nondiscrimination in the final treaty. In an atmosphere of nationalist protest against imperial domination, many colonized peoples were quick to view the proposal as a call for the leading states of the Western world to abide by their high-minded principles of equality and self-determination. When the proposal failed, critics in Japan and elsewhere noted the hypocrisy of a status quo that exclusively benefited "white" states. Nativists and racial theorists were just as quick to warn of an impending global racial conflict. In this heated atmosphere, the United States adopted a new immigration law in 1924 that effectively banned further Japanese immigration. The ban undercut the position of Japanese proponents of cooperative diplomacy with the West and hardened Japanese elite attitudes regarding the duplicity of American behavior. The U.S.-educated internationalist Nitobe Inazō vowed not to send foot in the United States until the ban was lifted.

Throughout the 1930s, Japanese and American policymakers alike viewed faltering U.S.-Japanese diplomatic relations through the lens of this racial history. Japan's attack on Pearl Harbor in 1941 and particularly the string of Japanese military successes afterward ignited hysteria over supposed Japanese spies and saboteurs throughout the Japanese American population. Although government agencies found little basis for such claims, President Franklin Roosevelt signed Executive Order 9066 in February 1942, leaving the disposition of the Japanese community to the regional military command. The military response was to exclude all people of Japanese ancestry, regardless of citizenship, from the West Coast. Approximately 120,000 ethnic Japanese, most U.S. citizens, were relocated forcibly to desolate, isolated camps throughout the western interior. Driven by necessity to sell off their land and possessions quickly, many in the Japanese American community suffered grievous economic losses.

Although the relocation faced legal challenges during the war, the U.S. Supreme Court refused to overturn exclusionary policies enacted in the name of military necessity. The exclusion order was rescinded in early 1945 as any threat of a Japanese invasion of the West Coast faded, and the camps closed by 1946. Throughout the postwar era, efforts were made to revisit and undo this ugly history. In 1988 and 1992, acts of Congress, signed by Presidents Ronald Reagan and George H. W. Bush, respectively, aimed to bring the era of anti-alien exclusion to a close. The laws paid compensation to victims of the wartime policies and issued formal apologies from the U.S. government.

*Michael A. Schneider*

**See also:** Nitobe Inazō ; Pearl Harbor Attack; Russo-Japanese War, Consequences; World War II, Pacific Theater.

### Further Reading

Azuma, Eiichiro. *Between Two Empires: Race History and Transnationalism in Japanese America*. New York: Oxford University Press, 2005.

Daniels, Roger. *The Politics of Prejudice: The Anti-Japanese Movement in California and the Struggle for Japanese Exclusion*. Berkeley: University of California Press, 1962.

Hunt, Michael H. *The Making of a Special Relationship: The United States and China to 1914*. New York: Columbia University Press, 1983.

Robinson, Greg. *A Tragedy of Democracy: Japanese Confinement in North America*. New York: Columbia University Press, 2009.

## AMPO: United States–Japan Security Treaty (1951)

The United States–Japan Security Treaty was signed simultaneously with the Treaty of Peace with the Allied powers, which together restored full sovereignty to Japan in 1951. The Security Treaty granted the United States the right "to dispose of United States land, air, and sea forces in and about Japan" so as "to contribute to the maintenance of international peace and security in the Far East and the security of Japan against armed attack." It also stipulated that U.S. forces "may be utilized to put down large-scale internal riots and disturbances in Japan."

The United States–Japan Security Treaty differed from other defensive arrangements entered into by the American government, such as the U.S.–South Korea and the U.S.-Philippines treaties, in that Japan did not have an obligation to defend U.S. territory. This fundamental difference is explained by limitations placed on postwar Japan's military structure, which was allowed only to exercise the right of self-defense under the war renunciation clause established in the Japanese constitution of May 3, 1947. Japan's limited military capabilities turned the Security Treaty into a rather asymmetrical agreement, in that the United States would provide military protection in return for basing rights in Japan.

This asymmetry engendered Japanese criticism of the treaty, which was considered one-sided and unfair. The Japanese government was concerned about the risk of becoming involved in an American military confrontation in the Far East, despite the fact that the treaty did not obligate the Japanese to mutual defense. In addition, the "internal disturbance" clause raised Japanese suspicions that the agreement essentially retained vestigial remnants of the postwar U.S. occupation period.

After a review process in the late 1950s, Japan and the United States concluded a Treaty of Mutual Cooperation and Security on January 19, 1960. The asymmetrical nature of the original Security Treaty remained relatively unchanged in the 1960 revision, as it granted U.S. forces the use of "facilities and areas in Japan" for "the security of Japan and the maintenance of international peace and security in the Far East." However, the revision improved on the reciprocity of the Security Treaty in several ways.

First, it acknowledged Japan's obligation to maintain and develop its own capabilities to resist armed attack in conjunction with the U.S. obligation to defend Japan, recognizing that Japan now had an obligation to assist American forces in a future conflict involving Japanese territories. Second, the revised treaty introduced a consultative mechanism regarding the implementation of the agreement. Now, "the use of facilities and areas in Japan as bases for military combat operations" would be "subject to prior consultation with the Government of Japan." Third, it encouraged political and economic cooperation between the two signatories. Finally, and perhaps most important to the Japanese, the 1960 treaty eliminated the so-called internal disturbance clause and established a 10-year term for the treaty, subject to renegotiation upon notice of each party.

*Takeda Yasuhiro*

**See also:** American Occupation; Self-Defense Forces.

### Further Reading

Buckley, Roger. *US-Japan Alliance Diplomacy, 1945–1990*. New York: Cambridge University Press, 1992.

Olsen, Edward A. *U.S.-Japan Strategic Reciprocity: A Neo-Internationalist View*. Stanford, CA: Hoover Institution Press, 1985.

Weinstein, Martin E. *Japan's Postwar Defense Policy, 1947–1968*. New York: Columbia University Press, 1971.

## Anglo-Japanese Alliances (1902–1921)

The idea of an alliance between Britain and Japan had its origins in the late 1890s. Following Japan's victory in the Sino-Japanese War (1894–1895), China ceded the Liaodong Peninsula to Japan. Three continental European powers (Germany, France, and Russia) advised the Japanese to return the peninsula to China in the famous Triple Intervention. The sting of the intervention intensified the isolated Japan's desire to find an ally. At the time, the most likely partner was Britain, which had refused to participate in the intervention. The British were increasingly wary of defending their far-flung colonies at a time when the powers were expanding their empires, especially in East Asia. Impressed with Japanese efforts to put down the Boxer Rebellion in China in 1900, the British signaled that they were open to ending their "splendid isolation" with an alliance with Japan.

Movement for an alliance quickened in 1901, when Russia made clear its intentions to dominate Manchuria and move into Korea. A British alliance, along with an agreement with Russia over spheres of influence on the mainland, offered a possible solution to the new Russian threat. A change in government in Japan, whereby the pro-alliance Katsura Tarō replaced the Russia-leaning Itō Hirobumi as prime minister, put negotiations with Britain on the fast track. Japanese ambassador Hayashi Tadasu began hashing out the alliance terms in London. Itō, however, was still determined to reach an accord with Russia, and he traveled to St. Petersburg for direct talks. In the end, the Russia's position proved unsatisfactory, and Ito consented to the alliance, which already had the approval of the cabinet and emperor. Signed in January 1902, the five-year agreement stipulated that each ally would come to the aid of the other if it were engaged in a war with two powers. The parties were to remain neutral if warring with only one power.

The effect of the alliance was immediate. Japan continued negotiations with Russia concerning Manchuria and Korea, but it also prepared for war, buoyed by the fact that the treaty would most likely keep Russia's ally, France, on the sidelines. Even before achieving its formal victory in the Russo-Japanese War, Japan renewed its alliance with Britain in August 1905. The renewed pact was expanded to include Japanese support for British rule in India and British recognition of Japanese control over Korea.

The alliance was renewed a second time in 1911. At that time there was debate in Japan over the future utility of the alliance in protecting Japanese interests on the mainland. Since 1905, Japan had grown increasingly closer to its erstwhile enemy Russia in an effort by the two to protect their respective rights in northeastern China from meddling powers, especially the United States. As a result, some Japanese leaders believed that reorienting Japanese diplomacy toward a pact with Russia made more sense than continuing the alliance with Britain. Proponents of the alliance in Japan, such as Komura Jutarō (foreign minister) and Katō Takaaki (ambassador to London), were able to overcome this resistance and renewed the alliance for a 10-year period. In fact, Katō, as foreign minister in 1914, invoked the alliance in declaring war on Germany in World War I.

Because it violated the League of Nations Covenant, the alliance required modification or abrogation after World War I. While the Japanese were open to altering the alliance to make it consistent with the League's provisions, the British, noting Canadian and American objections to the pact, suggested to the Japanese a triple alliance that would include the United States. The Hara Takashi cabinet was open to the possibility if it would continue the alliance. Ultimately, talks of convening a Pacific Conference that would include the United States came to supplant renewal discussions. The Four-Power Treaty that resulted from the Washington Conference in 1921 served to replace the Anglo-Japanese Alliance. In the treaty, Britain, Japan, the United States, and France agreed to consult with the other signatories if a disagreement arose between them regarding their possessions in the Pacific.

*Rustin Gates*

**See also:** Boxer Rebellion; Itō Hirobumi; Komura Jutarō; Russo-Japanese War, Causes; Triple Intervention; Washington Naval Conference; World War I.

## Further Reading

Nish, Ian. *Alliance in Decline: A Study in Anglo-Japanese Relation, 1908–1923*. London: Athlone Press, 1972.

Nish, Ian. *The Anglo-Japanese alliance: The Diplomacy of Two Island Empires, 1894–1907*. London: Athlone Press, 1966.

O'Brien, Phillips Payson, ed. *The Anglo-Japanese Alliance, 1902–1922*. London: RoutledgeCurzon, 2004.

## Anti-Comintern Pact (1936)

German Special Ambassador Plenipotentiary Joachim von Ribbentrop first proposed an anti-Comintern agreement between Germany and Japan in 1935, but the German Foreign Office and the army opposed it. Since World War I, the Germans had worked to develop a close relationship with China. This pact would nullify these efforts, as Japan and China were at loggerheads over the Japanese takeover of Manchuria. Nevertheless, Adolf Hitler's approval ended discussion of the matter. Hitler hoped that the pact would pressure Great Britain not to interfere with Germany's military buildup and his plans for eastward expansion. In any case, British leaders were concerned about the escalating Japanese threat to their own interests in the Far East.

Developed from conversations between Ribbentrop and Japanese military attaché Major General Oshima Hiroshi, the Anti-Comintern Pact was Hitler's effort to tie Japan to Germany. Japanese leaders saw it as an important step toward finding an ally in an increasingly hostile world. Alienated from the West by its takeover of Manchuria, Japan was also involved in armed clashes with Soviet forces in the Far East. The Japanese hoped that a pact with Germany would strengthen their country's position vis-à-vis the Soviet Union. Thus the wording of the pact was more important to the Japanese than to the Germans.

On the same day that the Anti-Comintern Pact was signed, Germany and Japan signed another agreement providing that in case of an unprovoked attack by the Soviet Union against Germany or Japan, the two nations would consult on which measures to take "to safeguard [their] common interests," and in any case they would do nothing to assist the Soviet Union. They also agreed that neither nation would make any political treaties with the Soviet Union. Germany also recognized Manchukuo, the Japanese puppet regime in Manchuria.

Germany later employed the Anti-Comintern Pact as a litmus test to determine the loyalty of minor allies. Italy adhered to the pact on November 6, 1937. The pact was renewed in 1941, with 11 other countries as signatories.

To many observers, the pact symbolized Germany's resurgence as the most powerful country in Europe. The threat of global cooperation between Germany and Japan directly imperiled the overextended empires of France and Great Britain. However, the pact, much like Germany's actual capabilities, was more illusion than reality. Both signatories failed to cooperate, and only rarely did one even inform the other of its intentions. An even greater indication of the pact's worthlessness was Hitler's breaking of its terms when he signed the German-Soviet Non-aggression Pact in August 1939.

*Captain C. J. Horn*

**See also:** Manchukuo; World War I.

## Further Reading

Boyd, Carl. *The Extraordinary Envoy: General Hiroshi Æshima and Diplomacy in the Third Reich, 1934–1939*. Washington, DC: University Press of America, 1980.

Schroeder, Paul W. *The Axis Alliance and Japanese-American Relations, 1941.* Ithaca, NY: Cornell University Press, 1958.

## Anti-Japanism in China

Anti-Japanism became a significant phenomenon in China after Japan seized concessions in China following its victory in the Sino-Japanese War of 1894–1895. In 1915, Japan forced Chinese leaders to sign the Twenty-One Demands, which would allow it to gain further political and economic control of China. This measure ignited popular protests against Japanese imperialism. During the signing of the Treaty of Versailles in 1919, Chinese students took to the street against Japanese imperialism when previously held German concessions in Shandong were transferred to Japan. Similar protests erupted in China in the ensuing decades in response to Japan's continued colonial expansion in China, especially after Japan established a puppet state in Manchuria in 1931 and committed wartime atrocities in Nanjing (1937) and elsewhere.

Negative feelings toward Japan remained strong in China after Japan's defeat in 1945, although they were partially ameliorated after some Japanese war criminals and Chinese collaborators were put on trial and punished. After the normalization of relations between Japan and the People's Republic of China (PRC) in 1972, anti-Japanese expressions were discouraged by the PRC authorities. However, in recent decades, incidents involving anti-Japanism have reemerged in China over issues such as the Japanese history textbook controversies, territorial disputes over the Diaoyu/Senkaku islands, visits by the prime minister to the Yasukuni shrine, and other unresolved historical conflicts associated with Japan's wartime atrocities.

In the spring of 2005, Japan's effort to seek a permanent seat on the UN Security Council sparked anti-Japanese protests all over Asia. The demonstrations in China led to the vandalism of businesses with Japanese connections and some Japanese nationals being injured.

The disputes over the sovereignty of the Diaoyu/Senkaku islands, located between Taiwan and Okinawa in the East China Sea, have provoked a number of anti-Japanese demonstrations by patriotic and nationalistic Chinese since the early 1970s. The islands, known as Diaoyu and Senkaku by Chinese and Japanese, respectively, were annexed by Japan during the Sino-Japanese War of 1894–1895 and were administered by the U.S. occupation government between 1945 and 1972. After Japan resumed control of the islands in 1972, a number of overseas Chinese groups have organized anti-Japanese protests, and several patriotic groups from Hong Kong and Taiwan have attempted to land on these islands to demonstrate Chinese sovereignty over them. Some mainland Chinese activists have also participated in *Bao-Diao* (protecting Diaoyu Islands) activities and demonstrations. The disputes over these islands reached a new height in September 2010, when a Chinese fishing boat collided with two Japanese Coast Guard vessels in the water near the islands. The captain of the fishing boat was arrested and detained by the Japanese Coast Guard. Thousands of Chinese demanding the immediate release of the captain participated in anti-Japanese protests in Beijing, Shanghai, and other Chinese cities. The incident ended with the release of the captain. In August 2012, another wave of anti-Japanese protests swept through China after a ship of activists from Hong Kong had successfully landed on one of the islands in protest of Japan's plan to purchase or nationalize three of the islands.

Anti-Japanism in China can be traced back to the anti-imperialistic efforts by Chinese during Japan's colonial expansion in Asia in the first half of the 20th century. It continues to shape the contour of Sino-Japanese relations, as Japan struggles to come to terms with its wartime responsibilities. In recent years, anti-Japanism has also been associated with the rise of nationalism in China, whose citizens have become more vocal in demanding more political participation.

*Yu Chang*

**See also:** History Textbooks Controversy; Sino-Japanese War; Twenty-One Demands; Versailles Treaty; War World II, Japanese Atrocities; Yasukuni Shrine Controversy.

## Further Reading

Gong, Gerrit, and Teo, Victor, eds. *Reconceptualising the Divide: Identity, Memory, and Nationalism in Sino-Japanese Relations*. Newcastle: Cambridge Scholars, 2010.

Heazle, Michael, and Knight, Nick, eds. *China-Japan Relations in the Twenty-First Century: Creating a Future Past?* Cheltenham, UK/Northampton, MA: Edward Elgar, 2007.

Rose, Caroline. *Sino-Japanese Relations: Facing the Past, Looking to the Future?* London/New York: RoutledgeCurzon, 2005.

Zheng, Yongnian. *Discovering Chinese Nationalism in China: Modernization and International Relations*. Cambridge, UK/New York: Cambridge University Press, 1999.

## Anti-Narita Airport Movement

In 1962, the Japanese national government announced intentions to build an alternative to the very crowded Haneda airport in Tokyo. Because it was impossible to expand the old airport due to the high cost of adjacent land near the center of Tokyo, it was decided to build near the city of Narita, some 35 miles outside Tokyo. The government reasoned that land would be much cheaper around Narita, in part because a large agricultural tract was owned by the Imperial Household Ministry.

Farmers in the designated area around the villages of Sanrizuka and Shibayama protested that the government agents designated to acquire the land were acting "arrogantly and disrespectfully" by demanding that land owners settle for low prices without the usual Japanese way of consensus building and compromise (*nemawashi*). Perhaps the issue would have died quietly had not a coalition of leftist student and labor unions rushed to support the farmers.

In the vanguard was the so-called *Chūkaku-ha* ("Middle Core Faction") of the Japan Revolutionary Communist League. Founded only a few years before, after the Japan Communist Party had splintered, *Chūkaku-ha* was looking for a national issue that would serve as a basis to recruit new members. The party announced that it had "discovered" that the real reasons for a new airport were to reward a number of construction companies friendly to the ruling Liberal Democratic Party, and to provide a new facility that the United States could use for planned military actions against Communist China and the Soviet Union. *Chūkaku-ha* began to send members to help the farmers protest the heavy-handed methods of the government.

When the government ignored these protests, a number of leftist parties and remnants of Zengakuren joined the fray. The latter student group had led the movement against the renewal of the U.S.-Japan

Mutual Security Pact (AMPO) in 1960. Later that year, an umbrella organization of rural farmers and leftist unions joined to form the Sanrizuka-Shibayama Union to Oppose the Airport (*Sanrizuka-Shibayama Rengo Kūkō Hantai Dōmei*). The union began to throw up roadblocks around the area to stop work crews. Soon the prefectural police began to use heavy-handed methods to disperse the crowds of chanting students, union toughs, and farmers. Before long, the protests turned violent. The nation was treated to almost weekly scenes of bloodied protesters and police fighting under the klieg lights of the national television news crews. Many of the same protesters who were involved in the anti-Vietnam War movement participated in both movements. A few of the student leaders vied with one another to see how many times they could be arrested for demonstrating.

The protests escalated in 1971 when the government began to forcibly expropriate land. Nearly 300 farmers were arrested when they chained themselves to their homes. The grand spectacle came to a head on September 16, 1971, when thousands of protesters and police clashed. Hundreds on both sides were injured in the riot, and three policemen were killed in an explosion. Both sides seemed to be shocked by the violence, and efforts were made at negotiation and compromise.

The protests took a comedic turn as protestors erected a series of fences and ditches to impede construction. When those impediments were torn down or repaired, the protestors built bamboo (and eventually steel) towers and concrete blockhouses and dug underground tunnels. Violence flared again a few years later, however, when on March 26, 1978, protestors drove a stolen car onto one of the new runways, throwing flaming Molotov cocktails at the police.

Others broke into the new control tower and smashed equipment, doing more than $500,000 worth of damage.

The airport was finally opened in May 1978, but for more than a decade the facility was guarded like a military installation by thousands of police. Passengers were subject to intense searches—a practice unheard of until airport antiterrorism systems were instituted worldwide after the September 11, 2001, terrorist attacks in New York.

Scholars have focused on the anti-Narita Airport contretemps in a number of studies on postwar citizens movements. Some see the movement as an expression of popular discontent with the ruling Liberal Democratic Party. Others claim that it was merely an opportunist event by the so-called New Left (after the split of the Japan Communist Party). In any case, it was a case of political irony when very conservative rural landowners became "strange bedfellows" with urban leftists.

*Louis G. Perez*

**See also:** AMPO: United States–Japan Security Treaty; Zengakuren.

**Further Reading**

Apter, David, and Nagayo Sawa. *Against the State: Politics and Social Protest in Japan.* Cambridge, MA: Harvard University Press, 1984.

Dower, John. *Peace and Democracy in Two Systems: External Policy and Internal Conflict.* Berkeley: University of California Press. 1993.

# Araki Sadao (1877–1966)

A general and statesman who promoted spiritual mobilization in the army and society during the 1930s, the Tokyo-born Araki graduated from the Army Academy and, later, the Army War College. After serving as captain and unit commander in the Russo-Japanese War, Araki was posted to Russia as military attaché during the First World War. While in Russia, he witnessed the Russian Revolution—an experience that, combined with his subsequent deployment to the Russian Far East in the Siberian Expedition, made him strongly anticommunist.

Following his return to Japan, Araki occupied several important posts within the army, including head of the military police, principal of the War College, division chief in the General Staff, Inspector-General of Military Education, and Minister of War (1931–1934; the Inukai Tsuyoshi and Saitō Makoto cabinets).

As war minister, Araki, in an attempt to remake the army according to his own beliefs, purged officers within army central headquarters who were supporters of the concept of "total war." Araki replaced them with officers who, like Araki, believed that the Japanese spirit was more important in war than material strength. He and his like-minded colleagues rewrote army manuals to highlight élan and morale as the key to maintaining an offensive spirit that could defeat any enemy. Araki was a strong proponent of Japan's recognition of Manchukuo and, along with Uchida Yasuya, advocated leaving the League of Nations. While minister, Araki began adding the expression "imperial" to specific words, rendering, for example, the army the "imperial army" (*kōgun*), thereby linking the army to the imperial institution. He also introduced the wearing of samurai-style swords by Japanese officers. Because of his constant use of this expression, Araki and his supporters became known as the Imperial Way faction (*Kōdōha*).

After resigning as war minister in 1934, Araki became a member of the Supreme War Council, a post he occupied during the February 26 Incident in 1936. Araki met with the rebel leaders during the incident and agreed to help them achieve their aims, one of which was the appointment of Araki as Kwantung Army commander. The emperor did not consent to the rebels' demands and branded them mutineers. Again sympathetic to the rebels, Araki requested that the rebellion be put down without the use of force. He was subsequently retired into the reserves because of his seemingly tacit approval of the rebellion.

Araki returned to the government from 1938 to 1939 as education minister in the Konoe Fumimaro and Hiranuma Kiichiro cabinets. In 1939, he attempted to revitalize the Movement for Spiritual Mobilization by holding rallies, enlisting the aid of celebrities, and stressing the campaign at meetings of the neighborhood associations. After World War II, Araki was arrested and put on trial as a Class A war criminal before the International Tribunal for the Far East, partially due to his involvement with the 1936 mutineers. Found guilty, he was sentenced to life in prison but was paroled due to ill health in 1954 and later pardoned. He died in November 1966.

*Rustin Gates*

**See also:** February 26 Incident; International Tribunal for the Far East; Konoe Fumimaro; Manchukuo; Siberian Expedition; Uchida Yasuya.

**Further Reading**

Blair, Alexander. "Justice Undone: The Trial of General Araki Sadao." *International Journal of Interdisciplinary Social Sciences.* 5, no. 4 (2010): 107–120.

Crowley, James. *Japan's Quest for Autonomy: National Security and Foreign Policy, 1930–1938.* Princeton, NJ: Princeton University Press, 1966.

# Ashikaga Takauji (1305–1358)

Ashikaga Takauji was born in A.D. 1305 and descended from the imperial Seiwa branch of the same clan as Minamoto Yoritomo, the founder of the Kamakura shōgunate. The Ashikaga family was an important house controlled through marriage by the Hōjō regency. The Hōjō connection was actively maintained throughout the Kamakura period until Takauji's father, Ashikaga Yoriuji, married outside of the Hōjō clan. Significantly, although Takauji's wife was Hōjō, his mother was from the powerful Uesugi house, which created a weakness in Hōjō supremacy.

In 1333, Takauji betrayed the Kamakura shōgunate and defected to Emperor Go-Daigo's movement against the *bakufu* government. As reported in the *Taiheiki*, in an event known as the Kemmu Restoration, Takauji made public his resolve to defect with the claim that the Hōjō were commoners while his line was regal. At the time of his defection, Takauji had been dispatched by the *bakufu* to defend the city of Kyoto, which had just avoided capture by the princes who were against the *bakufu*. He received a written commission from Go-Daigo and raised an army in his mother's home province of Tamba; he then attacked Kyoto and forced the city's defenders and the puppet emperor Kogon to flee for Kamakura. Unbeknownst to Kogon, the city of Kamakura had fallen to another rebellious Hōjō vassal, Nitta Yoshisada, the day before. After those two victories, Emperor Go-Daigo rejected Kogon's claim by edict and restored Japan's imperial control. The Kamakura *bakufu* was over.

Takauji and Emperor Go-Daigo spent 1333 and most of 1334 in precarious coexistence. When the emperor publicly announced the Kemmu Restoration, Takauji did not take office in any of Go-Daigo's various governmental posts. Although Takauji was the new shōgun in all but name, the emperor had created an imperial government that would displace him. Takauji had his brother, Tadayoshi, appointed guardian to the heir, Prince Morinaga, but in a failed Hōjō bid for power in 1335, Tadayoshi murdered the young prince.

Subsequently, Takauji led his own army to Kamakura and assumed the mantle of shōgun. Go-Daigo retaliated and declared Takauji an enemy of the throne. In full rebellion now, Takauji attempted to retake Kyoto but was forced to retreat. By mid-1336, he had enough allies to return to Kyoto. Takauji and the Ashikaga house won a decisive battle and entered Kyoto with the retired emperor Kogon's brother, Prince Yutahito, whom they installed as Emperor Komyo. He then sought to legitimize himself further by beginning construction in Kyoto, taking high court rank, and adopting the role of the chief of the warrior estate. He was officially appointed shōgun in 1338.

Although the Ashikaga controlled Kyoto, Go-Daigo set up a southern court in the mountainous region of Yoshino. Takauji's military rivals followed Go-Daigo to the southern court, but they died in battles by 1338. Without any real military support, the exiled southern court unofficially accepted Ashikaga rule. After Go-Daigo's death in 1339, the southern court continued to exist until 1392.

Between 1339 and 1358, Takauji organized the new *bakufu*. By 1350, a rift over policy and responsibilities had developed between Takauji and his brother Tadayoshi, and Ashikaga loyalties split between the two brothers. With a divided court, Takauji was ever more reliant on military power to enforce his edicts. In his first open battle, he was forced to take the field against his own son, Tadafuyu, who had been adopted by Tadayoshi. In the beginning of 1352, Takauji had his brother poisoned, but it was not until 1355 that he put down all resistance to his control.

Takauji died on June 7, 1358, in Kyoto and was succeeded as head of the Ashikaga shōgunate by Yoshiakira, his second son.

*Tim Barnard*

**See also:** Go-Daigo; Kamakura *Bafuku*; Minamoto Yoritomo; Muromachi *Bakufu*; Nitta Yoshisada; Southern Court (Yoshino).

### Further Reading

Hall, John Whitney, and Jeffrey P. Mass, eds., *Medieval Japan: Essays in Institutional History*. New Haven: Yale University Press, 1974.

Yamamura, Kozo, ed. *The Cambridge History of Japan. Volume 3: Medieval Japan*. Cambridge, UK: Cambridge University Press, 1990.

## Atomic Bombs: Surrender of Japan (August 15, 1945)

By early 1945, it was clear to most observers that Japan could not hope to win World War II. The United States captured Iwo Jima in February 1945. Okinawa, secured in June of that year, could be used as a staging area for a U.S. invasion of the Japanese home islands. Germany, Japan's only remaining ally, had been defeated in May. Meanwhile, B-29 Superfortresses flying from the Marianas

The ruins of Hiroshima after the atomic bomb. (Getty Images)

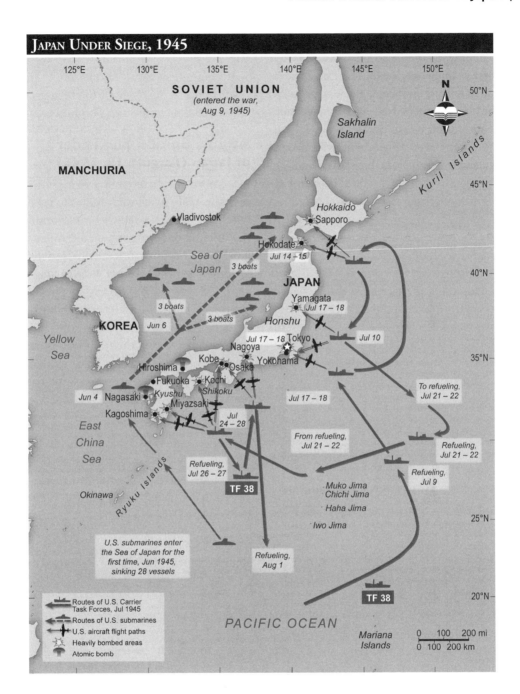

JAPAN UNDER SIEGE, 1945

Routes of U.S. Carrier Task Forces, Jul 1945
Routes of U.S. submarines
U.S. aircraft flight paths
Heavily bombed areas
Atomic bomb

were destroying Japan's cities, while submarines cut off Japanese seaborne trade and B-29 aerial mining eliminated much of the important coastal trade, raising the specter of starvation for the Japanese people. Still, Japan fought on.

Revisionist historians have held that because the Japanese government was by this time seeking desperately to leave the war, employing the atomic bomb against Japan was unnecessary. Intercepted diplomatic messages, however, indicate that

Japan had still not reached the decision to surrender when the first bomb was dropped. Although Emperor Hirohito and his principal advisers had concluded that Japan could not win the war, they hoped for a negotiated settlement after a last "decisive battle" that would force the Allies to grant more favorable peace terms. On July 28, the Japanese government formally rejected acceptance of the Potsdam Declaration, as demanded by U.S. President Harry S Truman two days before—a refusal that led Truman to decide to employ the atomic bomb.

On August 6, 1945, the United States dropped an atomic bomb on the Japanese city of Hiroshima. Approximately 100,000 people perished outright or died later from radiation effects; another 40,000 were injured, and most of the remaining population suffered some long-term radiation damage. Even so, this carnage was less than that inflicted in the firebombing of Tokyo in March 1945. Meeting with the emperor, the army leadership still strongly opposed accepting the Potsdam Declaration.

On August 8, the Soviet Union declared war on Japan, with Josef Stalin honoring his pledge at Yalta to enter the war against Japan "two or three months after the defeat of Germany." One day later, Soviet troops invaded Manchuria in force. That same day, a B-19 bomber dropped a second atomic bomb, this time on Nagasaki. The blast there claimed approximately 70,000 lives, either killed outright or dying later from radiation, and injured as many more.

After prolonged meetings with his top advisers, Emperor Hirohito made the decision for peace on August 14. He stated that as onerous as it would be to order the surrender, have the Japanese homeland occupied, and see loyal servants face possible trial as war criminals, these considerations had to be weighed against the devastation facing the Japanese people in a continuation of the war.

Braving possible assassination by high-level fanatics determined to stage a coup d'état and fight to the end, Hirohito communicated this decision over the radio on August 15 at noon Tokyo time, the first occasion on which the Japanese people had heard his voice. In the course of his remarks, Hirohito said, "We have resolved to pave the way for a general peace for all generations to come by enduring the unendurable and suffering what is unsufferable." He referred specifically to the atomic bombs when he said, "Moreover, the enemy has begun to employ a new and more cruel bomb, the power of which to do damage is indeed incalculable, taking the toll of many innocent lives." On September 2, the final terms of surrender were signed aboard the battleship *Missouri* in Tokyo Bay, and the Japanese islands came under the rule of a U.S. army of occupation.

*Spencer C. Tucker*

**See also:** Potsdam Declaration; Russian Invasion of Manchuria; Shōwa Emperor (Hirohito).

**Further Reading**

Butow, Robert J. C. *Japan's Decision to Surrender*. Stanford, CA: Stanford University Press, 1954.

Craig, William. *The Fall of Japan*. New York: Dial Press, 1967.

Frank, Richard B. *Downfall: The End of the Imperial Japanese Empire*. New York: Random House, 1999.

## *Azuma kagami*

*Azuma kagami* ("The Mirror of the East") is an official record of the activities of the Kamakura shōgunate from the time of the

Genpei War (1180–1185) through 1266. Its date of composition is unknown, but it was probably compiled by functionaries working for the Kamakura shōgunate between 1266 and 1301. The work was sponsored by the Hōjō family, who served as shōgunal regents. The text is written in *kanbun*, a hybrid form of Chinese popular in the warrior class during the medieval period.

The *kagami* (mirror) of the work's title identifies it as a history; in the Chinese tradition, history was thought to be a mirror of past events. In Japan, starting with the late 11th century, *Ōkagami* ("Great Mirror"), a tradition of *kagamimono* ("Mirror Works"), emerged and flourished. In the main, *kagamimono* are narratives that follow the structure of Sima Qian's *Shi ji* ("Records of the Historian"), including biographies of important figures and exemplary episodes involving emperors or extraordinary figures. *Azuma kagami*, by contrast, is organized as a chronicle in imitation of the *Rikkokushi* ("Six National Histories"), but several years are missing from extant manuscripts, including one significant year (1183) during the Genpei War.

*Azuma kagami* comprises a series of dated entries for a period lasting almost 100 years, and each entry records events as viewed from Kamakura, the new warrior capital. *Azuma kagami* thus is at once a replica of other sorts of histories produced in the aristocratic capital of Kyoto (or Heian-kyō) and a challenge to them, because it centers its world in what had represented the distant provinces (*Azuma*, the east country) for earlier generations of writers and readers. It is an important document describing the development of warrior society and the various conflicts in the early years of warrior rule that helped shape the role of the warrior

government and the cultural place of the samurai. It unfortunately ends before the two Mongol Invasions (1274 and 1281), so its role is primarily in documenting domestic affairs of the early warrior age.

Many of the entries for later years in *Azuma kagami* record the everyday activities of the shōgunate as it adjudicated disputes, promulgated regulations, and responded to the actions—both supportive and challenging—of members of the newly powerful warrior elite. Numerous decrees and judgments are replicated in the pages of *Azuma kagami*, giving it an air of authenticity and historicity. In fact, the later years seem to have been recorded in real time, and the entries, while not necessarily unbiased, record actual events as they were interpreted when they happened. For the early days of the shōgunate, including the Genpei War years, however, *Azuma kagami* seems to derive from a number of less reliable historical sources, chief among them the variants of the *Tales of the Heike* and other narrative accounts. The effect of presenting pieces from retrospective narrative accounts of the war in an otherwise more journalistic account of the workings of the shōgunate serves to fix sometimes fictional events as part of the historical record.

*Elizabeth A. Oyler*

**See also:** *Heike monogatari*; Hogen-Heiji-Gempei Wars; Kamakura *Bakufu*.

## Further Reading

Mass, Jeffrey. *Yoritomo and the Founding of the First Bakufu*. Stanford, CA: Stanford University Press, 1999.

Shinoda, Minoru. *The Founding of the Kamakura Shōgunate 1180–1185, with Selected Translations from the* Azuma Kagami. New York: Columbia University Press, 1960.

# B

## Bakumatsu Fencing Schools and Nationalism

During the final decades of the Tokugawa period, the number of fencing academies (*dōjō*) and swordsmanship styles (*ryūha*) increased. The first styles of fencing and other martial arts developed in the background of the Sengoku Era, but were not used to train common troops. Instead, they developed as one cultural art among many. In one famous example, the writings of the Noh theater master Zeami, who professionalized Noh and systematized how it should be taught, influenced the swordsman Yagyū Munenori. Yagyū copied many of Zeami's pedagogical tools—for example, maintaining secret teachings given only to trusted students who could pay the required fee. He and his ancestors monopolized their family style, Yagyū Shinkage ryū, and were instructors to the successive Tokugawa shōgun.

With war and concern for martial valor disappearing by the late 17th century, swordsmanship entered a period of stagnation. Much of the same criticism directed against the samurai during the Genroku Period (1688–1704)—namely, that they had become too extravagant and lazy—was also leveled at swordsmanship, then seen as a simple flowery dance.

Later, swordsmanship again became popular as a path for self-perfection. Moreover, changes in the equipment allowed swordsmanship to be practiced as fencing. Certain schools adopted the use of bamboo swords and armor, the predecessors of modern kendō. Practitioners could engage in full-power striking and sparring, which were previously considered too dangerous with wooden swords. During the 19th century, two interrelated trends dominated the spread of fencing: the increasing number of commoner practitioners and the spread of armored fencing.

Martial art schools catered to different sectors of samurai society. Fencing styles for low-ranking samurai, for example, received little support from domain authorities. Instructors received only a pittance of a stipend, and they rarely enjoyed demonstration audiences with the *daimyō* or shōgun, unlike styles practiced by high-ranking samurai. However, this also meant that styles practiced by low-ranking samurai were not as strictly managed by officials. Consequently, they tended to engage in practices considered unorthodox, such as holding matches with swordsmen from other schools, or cross-training. This was especially so among commoner-dominated styles in the countryside. In theory, martial arts, as a possible tool for violence, were supposed to be monopolized by samurai. The shōgunate and domains repeatedly issued edicts throughout the 19th century forbidding the practice among commoners. But for disaffected rōnin wandering the countryside, and even within Edo itself, teaching fencing to commoners was one of the few sources of income. Commoners who claimed descent from a former warrior family, sometimes called "rural samurai," could reinforce their identity by practicing swordsmanship. Growing numbers of rural entrepreneurs also translated their financial capital into social and cultural capital, investing in rural Noh theater, and forming poetry and nativist (*kokugaku*) study groups. Rural swordsmanship became yet another art that gave local elites a chance to imitate their social betters, the samurai. As disorder spread in the form of peasant protests, gangs, and wandering disaffected samurai throughout the Kanto region surrounding Edo during the *bakumatsu* period, local elites used swordsmanship for self-protection. Some became rank-and-file members of newly created peasant militias. Others even found employment within domains that wanted to reform samurai martial spirit by forcing their men to train in competitive fencing, which was deemed more realistic.

For much of the Tokugawa period, fencing focused on self-cultivation, a mix of Buddhist and Confucian teachings, and lessons from the Chinese military classics. Thus, during the 19th century, sport fencing meshed with a broad range of philosophical teachings that reflected the politics of the day—in particular, anti-foreign and pro-emperor teachings. Edo *dōjō* became meeting sites for like-minded samurai from various domains, and the biographies of many Meiji Restoration figures on both sides of the conflict, such as Kido Kōin, Katsu Kaishū, and Sakamoto Ryōma, were practitioners of popular styles of the day. After the Meiji Restoration, many former fencing instructors continued to teach in private *dōjō*, becoming the forerunners of modern kendō.

*Michael Wert*

**See also:** *Bushidō* in Sports; Katsu Kaishū; Sakamoto Ryōma; *Sonno-jōi*; Tokugawa *Bakumatsu* Military Reforms; Tokugawa-Era Peasant Uprisings.

## Further Reading

Hurst, G. Cameron. *Armed Martial Arts of Japan: Swordsmanship and Archery.* New Haven: Yale University Press, 1998.

Morinaga, Maki I. *Secrecy in Japanese Arts: "Secret Transmission" as a Mode of Knowledge.* New York: Palgrave Macmillan, 2005.

Rogers, John M. "Arts of War in Times of Peace: Archery in *Honchō Bugei Shōden.*" *Monumenta Nipponica* 45, no. 3 (Fall 1990): 253–284.

Rogers, John M. "Arts of War in Times of Peace: Swordsmanship in *Honchō Bugei Shōden*, Chapter 5." *Monumenta Nipponica* 45, no. 4 (Winter 1990): 413–447.

Rogers, John M. "Arts of War in Times of Peace: Swordsmanship in *Honchō Bugei Shōden*, Chapter 6." *Monumenta Nipponica* 46, no. 2 (Summer 1991): 174–202.

Rogers, John M. 1998. *The Development of the Military Profession in Tokugawa Japan.* Ph.D. thesis, Harvard University, Cambridge, MA.

## Bataan, Battle of (1941–1942)

Bataan is a peninsula on the big island of Luzon in the Philippines; it is some 25 miles long and roughly 20 miles wide and extends south into Manila Bay. The peninsula figured prominently in General Douglas MacArthur's plans for defending the Philippines against a Japanese invasion in World War II. The original plan called for U.S. and Philippine forces to withdraw into the Bataan Peninsula, and there fight an extended defensive battle until reinforcements arrived from the United States.

MacArthur changed this plan prior to the U.S. entry into the war following the December 7, 1941, attack on Pearl Harbor. He believed that, even with mobilization of the Filipino army and promised reinforcements from the United States, he could defend the entire Philippine Islands against a Japanese invasion. When elements of Lieutenant General Homma Masaharu's 14th Army landed at Lingayen Gulf on December 22, however, it became apparent that MacArthur's new plan would not work. Japanese forces quickly broke through MacArthur's lines north and south of Manila, forcing him to fall back on the original plan but not in an orderly fashion. Vast quantities of supplies were lost in the process. By the end of December, more than 67,500 Filipino and 12,500 U.S. troops, as well as 26,000 civilians, were in the Bataan Peninsula. The shortage of supplies put everyone on half rations. Malnutrition, dysentery, and malaria were soon commonplace, with many soldiers unable to fight.

Even so, U.S. and Filipino troops put up a stout defense. They lost their main line of defense in late January 1942, but at their secondary line, they stopped Homma's forces by mid-February. The defenders bravely fought on, halting two battalion-sized Japanese landings in late January and early February.

Meanwhile, most of Homma's best troops were diverted to the Netherlands East Indies; with more than 2,700 dead, 4,000 wounded, and 13,000 sick, Homma was temporarily unable to mount additional attacks. MacArthur used this pause in the siege to shore up his defensive positions, but the realization that no relief force was coming from the United States caused bitter disappointment. The Americans and Filipinos called themselves the "Battling Bastards of Bataan." And in the wake of U.S. defeats at Pearl Harbor, Guam, and Wake Island, as well as the British defeat at Singapore, the resistance that was mounted in Bataan boosted morale on the U.S. home front.

President Franklin D. Roosevelt ordered MacArthur to leave the Philippines on March 11, 1942, and command of U.S.-Filipino forces fell to Major General Jonathan Wainwright. He inherited a hopeless cause. Homma received reinforcements, and his troops finally broke through the U.S.-Filipino lines on April 3. MacArthur ordered Wainwright not to surrender, but the U.S. ground forces commander, Major General Edward P. King, Jr., realizing that the cause was hopeless, decided to end the fight and capitulated on April 9.

More than 20,000 Americans and Filipinos perished in the campaign, but roughly 2,000 escaped to the nearby island of Corregidor and fought on there until they in turn were forced to surrender on May 5. The 76,000 prisoners of war of the battle for Bataan—some 64,000 Filipino soldiers and 12,000 Americans—then were forced to endure what came to be known as the Bataan Death March as they were moved into captivity. They had succeeded, however, in delaying the Japanese conquest of the Philippines for 148 days and briefly inspiring the Allied cause during the dark early days of U.S. participation in World War II.

*Lance Janda*

**See also:** Bataan Death March; MacArthur, Douglas; War in the Pacific, World War II; World War II, Japanese Atrocities.

## Further Reading

Mallonée, Richard. *Battle for Bataan: An Eyewitness Account.* New York: I Books, 2003.

Morton, Louis. *United States Army in World War II: The War in the Pacific—Fall of the Philippines.* Washington, DC: Office of the Chief of Military History, Department of the Army, 1953.

Whitman, John W. *Bataan: Our Last Ditch—The Bataan Campaign, 1942.* New York: Hippocrene Books, 1990.

## Bataan Death March (April 1942)

On April 3, 1942, Japanese General Homma Masaharu launched a new offensive against the defenders of the Bataan Peninsula in the Philippines during World War II. Before leaving, the U.S. Far Eastern commander, General Douglas MacArthur, had ordered the troops to continue to fight, but six days later, with his men worn down by the strain of constant combat, disease, and starvation, Major General Edward P. King, commander of the forces on Bataan, ordered them to surrender. The troops had been on half rations since January.

Homma had decided that he would hold the prisoners at Camp O'Donnell, 100 miles away. The Japanese forced the 12,000 American and 64,000 Filipino prisoners to march 52 miles from Mariveles to San Fernando, Pampanga, to be transported by rail to Capas, Tarlac. They would then walk another 8 miles to Camp O'Donnell. King expressed concern about his men being able to make this trip and asked that trucks transport them to their final location. Homma rejected the request.

The trek began on April 10, 1942, and lasted for more than a week. The march is remembered for its sheer brutality, but before it even began, each prisoner was searched, and anyone found to possess a Japanese souvenir was executed on the spot. Allied soldiers were, for the most part, denied food and water by their guards until the completion of their journey. The only food that

Captured Filipino and American soldiers move north on a forced march along the 100-kilometer route from Bataan to Camp O'Donnell. (Library of Congress)

some received was a bit of rancid rice. The prisoners of war were given only a few hours of rest each night in crowded conditions. One of the worst forms of punishment inflicted on the captives was known as the sun treatment, in which the prisoner, denied any water, was forced to sit in the scalding Philippine sun without the protection of a helmet. Prisoners were beaten, kicked, and killed for falling behind or violating the smallest rule.

Between 7,000 and 10,000 of the prisoners died before reaching Camp O'Donnell. The Japanese had failed to take into consideration both the poor health of their captives and their numbers. Although a few of the prisoners escaped into the jungle, most were physically unable even to make the attempt. A number were murdered at random by their guards.

Many who survived the march died in the overcrowded, suffocating boxcars on the rail trip to Capas. In the two months after reaching the camp, 1,600 Americans and 16,000 Filipinos died of starvation, disease, and maltreatment. The cruelty of the march became well known, and U.S. commanders used the story of the Bataan Death March to motivate their troops in subsequent fighting against the Japanese. After a trial in 1946, General Homma was executed for his actions.

*T. Jason Soderstrum*

**See also:** Bataan, Battle of; MacArthur, Douglas; War in the Pacific; World War II, Japanese Atrocities.

**Further Reading**

Falk, Stanley Lawrence. *Bataan: The March of Death.* New York: Norton, 1962.

Young, Donald J. *The Battle of Bataan: A History of the 90-Day Siege and Eventual Surrender of 75,000 Filipino and United States Troops to the Japanese in World War II.* Jefferson, NC: McFarland, 1992.

## *Beheiren:* Anti-Vietnam War Movement

The Japanese movement against American involvement in the Vietnam War burgeoned in the mid-1960s when Oda Makoto, one of the founders of the movement, criticized Prime Minister Satō Eisaku for giving the United States Japan's unilateral support for the war. Oda, a noted novelist and essayist (*Hiroshima* and *Gyokusai*), joined with philosopher Tsurumi Shunsuke and writer Kaiko-Takeshi in 1965 to form *Betonamu ni Heiwa o Shimin Rengo* ("Citizen's League for Peace in Vietnam"), commonly shortened to *Beheiren.* Oda blasted the Satō government in 1967 when he suggested that failure to criticize America for its racist war made Japanese "all guilty of complicity in the Vietnam War."

Despite many attempts to link *Beheiren* with other leftist political movements, it remained focused on the unpopular war. Some members became embroiled with the Return Okinawa movement, but the leadership tried to keep the anti-Vietnam War movement independent. Oda and the other ad hoc leaders (they refused to organize like a political party) steered clear of the traditional student, communist, and socialist parties, refusing both political and economic support. They encouraged local anti-war activists to plan their own demonstrations but did not construct normal political party committees (e.g., finance, printing, communication).

Oda stated that it was better for Japan to become something like a "conscientious objector nation." *Beheiren* staged public demonstrations and handed out anti-war leaflets to American service members outside of the military bases. In the late 1960s, *Beheiren* even assisted at least a dozen American military men to defect to Sweden (through the Soviet Union).

Because the movement chose to focus on the single issue of the Vietnam War and preferred a "grass-roots," local method of loose organization, many members drifted into the more tightly organized leftist movements, particularly the indigenous Okinawan groups. Oda and other leaders occasionally appeared on television to popularize their anti-war views, but only rarely personally appeared at the public demonstrations.

*Louis G. Perez*

**See also:** Zengakuren.

**Further Reading**

Havens, Thomas. *Fire across the Sea: The Vietnam War and Japan 1965–1975*. Princeton: Princeton University Press, 2006.

Tanaka Yuki. "Oda Makoto, Beheiren and 14 August 1945: Humanitarian Wrath Against Indiscriminate Bombing." *Japan Focus: The Asia-Pacific Journal* 25, no. 2 (September 28, 2007): 25–31.

## Bikini Island Atomic Tests (1946–1958)

Bikini Atoll is located in the westernmost Marshall Islands in the Central Pacific. The Marshalls are approximately 4 degrees north of the equator and 2,000 miles southwest of Pearl Harbor, Hawaii. Japan had acquired the islands from Germany following World War I, and the United States conquered them in 1944. The Marshalls became a U.S. trust territory in 1947.

In 1946, Bikini was the site for Operation Crossroads, a U.S. experiment to gauge the effects of atomic weapons on ships. Vice Admiral William Blandy commanded the joint army-navy nuclear tests. On July 1, 1946, following extensive publicity, the United States exploded the first atomic bomb in peacetime. It was an air burst, dropped over 73 unmanned naval vessels at Bikini Atoll with the explosive power of about 20,000 tons of TNT, roughly equivalent to the size of the bomb dropped on Nagasaki in August 1945. Five of the ships were sunk outright, and 45 were damaged. Ninety percent of the test animals aboard the ships survived the initial blast but died later from radiation exposure.

On July 25, a second bomb was detonated, this one underwater. The blast sent into the air a column of 1 million tons of water half a mile in diameter and sank 10 of 75 unmanned ships. Following the initial tests, Bikini and nearby Enewetak Atoll became the Pacific Proving Grounds of the U.S. Atomic Energy Commission.

The United States conducted additional tests at Bikini in 1954, 1956, and 1958, including a hydrogen bomb explosion on March 1, 1954. Unexpected widespread radiation fallout from this test inflicted radiation burns on Japanese fishermen 70–90 miles from the blast site and also affected residents of Kwajalein Island, 176 miles distant. This test triggered widespread alarm, especially in Japan, that helped to bring about the 1958 moratorium on atmospheric nuclear weapons tests.

*Spencer C. Tucker*

**See also:** Atomic Bombs: Surrender of Japan; Versailles Treaty.

**Further Reading**

Ball, Howard. *Justice Downwind: America's Atomic Testing Program in the 1950s*. New York: Oxford University Press, 1986.

Weisgall, Jonathan M. *Operation Crossroads: The Atomic Tests at Bikini Atoll*. Annapolis, MD: Naval Institute Press, 1994.

**Bluestockings.** *See* Seito.

## Boissonade de Fontarabie, Gustave Émile (1825–1910)

Born in Vincennes, France on June 7, 1825, Gustave Boissonade received a doctorate of law from the University of Paris-Sorbonne and began his career in 1864 as an adjunct professor of law at Grenoble University. He also taught at his alma mater, where in 1873 he lectured Inoue Kowashi and other Japanese exchange students. This work led to an invitation to serve as an adviser to Japan's Ministry of Justice, where Boissonade worked for more than 20 years.

At the time of Boissonade's arrival in 1873, the Meiji government was pursuing comprehensive legal reform. Collapse of the Tokugawa shōgunate meant the dissolution of the old legal order. Meanwhile, foreign powers had since the 1850s claimed that Japan's barbaric legal system justified extraterritoriality. The Napoleonic Code, then the world standard, offered Meiji justice officials an expedient blueprint for renovating the legal order and centralizing the judiciary. Boissonade gained distinction as the consulting architect for this project, leading a team of Japanese interpreters of French law and other foreign advisers, including Georges Hilaire Bousquet. Replacing the temporary Chinese code topped his agenda. Even as Boissonade objected to torture and stressed the presumption of innocence, his approach to the civilizing mission reflected attention to local practice. For example, contrary to European norms, the draft Criminal Code tolerated male-male sexuality. As a result of combined efforts, the Ministry of Justice completed a draft Criminal Code in 1878. The Genrōin passed the Code into law in 1880; it took effect in 1882.

In the meantime, Boissonade drew on his deep knowledge of French law to begin compiling a draft Civil Code. Building on earlier translation efforts, the draft Code of 1880 served as the basis for court rulings through 1896. It did not become official, however. Over the course of the 1880s, enthusiasm for French legal models waned and the juridical field became fractured. Republican France became less an object of emulation for emperor-focused Meiji oligarchs, and interest in other European—particularly Germanic—models soared. As a sign of changing times, Boissonade had little influence on the drafting of the Meiji Constitution and his draft Civil Code foundered. Partisans of divergent legal traditions at the universities, on the boards of legal journals, and in the Ministry of Justice blocked adoption of the draft Code because it was too foreign and too French. Even so, Boissonade's influence on Japan's Civil Code remained in the sections on property, securities, and evidence.

In addition to advising the Ministry of Justice and the Genrōin, Boissonade served the Ministry of Foreign affairs. From the start of his tenure, diplomats queried Boissonade on international law, including how to advance Japan's position vis-à-vis the great powers in the wake of its 1874 expedition to Taiwan. The treaty revision debates of 1887 elicited Boissonade's crowning contribution to Japan's external affairs. Boissonade argued that inclusion of foreign judges in Japanese courts would infringe on Japanese sovereignty, drain the purse, and lead to popular rebellion. His powerful opposition, joined with that of senior statesmen including Inoue Kowashi, prevailed.

While providing policy advice to the Meiji government, Boissonade also worked as a legal educator. From 1874, he lectured on French law at the Ministry of Justice legal training program; he later taught at private institutions, including the Tokyo Law School, forerunner of Hōsei University, and Meiji Law School, forerunner of Meiji University. Boissonade authored extensive works on Japanese law, and his work on French law included titles such as the *History of the Rights of the Surviving Spouse*.

In 1909, Boissonade received the Order of the Rising Sun, First Class, for his contributions to Japan's modern legal foundation.

*Darryl Flaherty*

**See also:** Oyatoi Gaikokujin; Unequal Treaties.

### Further Reading

Ikeda, Masako Kobayashi. *French Legal Advisor in Meiji Japan (1873–1895): Gustave Émile Boissonade de Fontarabie*. Ph.D. thesis, University of Hawaii, 1997.

Ōkubo Yasuo. *Nihon kindaihō no chichi—Bowasonaado*. Tokyo: Iwanami, 1977.

## Boshin Civil War (1867–1868)

The Boshin Civil War was a relatively short-lived conflict and not very significant considering that very few battles were fought and few casualties suffered. In terms of historical importance, however, it was a major watershed in Japanese history. The war brought down the Tokugawa *bakufu* after more than 260 years of rule, and the so-called medieval feudal period was ended after seven centuries.

The war had been brewing for over a decade. The Tokugawa regime was caught between the expansionist forces of the Western powers and the xenophobic Japanese, who welcomed domestic political change, but not at the expense of more Western influence. After the intrusion of the American Commodore Matthew Perry in 1853–1854, the *bakufu* had tried to keep the foreigners at bay. When they signed the Treaty of Kanagawa in 1854,

however, they opened a Pandora's box of troubles. By allowing the Americans entry, the Tokugawa had ignored the Emperor Kōmei's wishes and had also thumbed their noses at their feudal vassals who had also counseled continued international seclusion.

Most of the anti-foreign sentiments centered on the western hans of Satsuma, Chōshū, Tosa, and Hizen, but also had significant support of Mito, one of the three Tokugawa collateral han. The *bakufu* had tried to stifle this dissent in 1860 when Ii Naosuke, the head of the coalition government, had arrested the chief dissenters and even executed a few (among them, the firebrand Yoshida Shōin) in the so-called Ansei Purge. The anti-*bakufu* coalition who styled themselves as pro-emperor, loyalist "men of action" (*shishi*) and proclaimed a *sonno-jōi* ("Revere the Emperor—Expel the Barbarian") movement. The "modernist" courtiers around the emperor (including Iwakura Tomomi) had fed an increasingly rebellious upsurge by secretly issuing edicts calling for more "direct actions" against the Tokugawa.

The *sonno-jōi* rebels had exacerbated an already tenuous position for the *bakufu* by unilaterally attacking foreigners. The *bakufu* had been unable to ferret out and punish the culprits, which of course led the foreigners to act. The British and French had led punitive bombardment raids against first the Satsuma bastion of Kagoshima in 1863 and against the Chōshū port of Shimonoseki later that year. Otherwise-neutral han then began to criticize the *bakufu* for being unable or unwilling to protect Japanese citizens. After all, the full Tokugawa title (*sei-itai-shōgun*) meant "barbarian-subduing generalissimo." The title was originally aimed at the ninth-century northern Ainu, but here were new barbarians to subdue.

The *bakufu* had been preparing for the inevitable struggle with the rebellious western han (and also against the Western treaty powers, if necessary). They had sought French help, had obtained eight Western gunboats, and had trained a contingent of Tokugawa loyalists with the new Western weapons. Yet their last shōgun, Yoshinobu, had no stomach for civil war. Yoshinobu was the son of the Mito patriot (arrested during the Ansel Purge of 1860) Tokugawa Nariaki and had been tutored by strident xenophobes, yet he knew that the British had long specialized in backing Asian regimes in civil wars against their domestic rivals so as to wield power and influence. Yoshinobu had heeded the advice of cooler heads, including that of Yamanouchi Yodo, the *daimyō* of Tosa. Upon the death of the Emperor Komei in 1867, Yoshinobu announced that he wished to resign his office and turn over actual political control to the new teenage emperor Meiji.

The young rebels led by Saigō Takamori and Ōkubo Toshimichi of Satsuma and Kido Takayoshi of Chōshū would not allow Yoshinobu to go quietly into the night. They knew that if the popular idea of a national assembly came to fruition, the Tokugawa would wield considerable influence on the strength of their control of approximately 30 percent of the country. Thus they engineered a series of provocative actions to force the Tokugawa to fight. They hired some ruffians to attack various Tokugawa government emplacements, including their Edo castle bastion. Before Yoshinobu could pacify his troops, they responded in kind, attacking the Satsuma mansion in Edo the next day.

A brief full-scale battle ensued at Toba-Fushimi just outside Kyoto on January 27, 1868. The *bakufu* forces had more than 15,000 troops in the field, many armed and trained by the French. Although the imperial forces under the titular command of an imperial prince Ninnajinomiya Yoshiaki (who never saw action, remaining in Kyoto) claimed victory, the battle was actually somewhat of a standoff. Of course, the Tokugawa could now be branded as rebels, which is exactly what Saigō, Ōkubo, and Kido wanted.

When Tokugawa allies began to wither away, Yoshinobu decamped from Osaka on February 7. The Tokugawa castle at Osaka was surrounded and capitulated a few days later. The *bakufu* did, however, win the first naval battle of the war at Awa on January 28. The gunboats purchased from the French acquitted themselves well against the few Satsuma ships. Saigō led the imperial army against the Tokugawa and won two decisive battles. The first, at Kōshū-Katsunuma, routed the *bakufu* forces (who lost almost 180 men) on March 29. Saigō then surrounded Edo and won another victory at Ueno on July 4. Yoshinobu had repaired to the Kan'ei-ji Temple, where his defenders repulsed a frontal charge by the impetuous Saigō. Much to his chagrin, Saigō's forces were rescued by the Chōshū and Tosa forces and Yoshinobu was forced to retreat. The Tokugawa lost nearly 300 troops.

For all intents and purposes, the war ended when the Tokugawa forces surrendered Edo castle. Katsu Kaishū, a *bakufu* stalwart, negotiated the peaceful surrender of the remaining Tokugawa forces. A few thousand troops, however, boarded the remaining *bakufu* ships and escaped north to Hokkaidō. There they continued to offer resistance, even establishing the short-lived Republic of Ezo with Enomoto Takeaki elected as its first president. The Republic was probably the first democratically elected government in Asia.

The Ezo Republic established an army in part led by Jules Brunet, the former French military attaché to the *bakufu*. The government held out until April 1869, when it was defeated by the future Meiji *genrō* Kuroda

Kiyotaka at the battle of Hakodate. Enomoto himself surrendered the Republic to Kuroda without substantial loss of life, an act for which he was given an imperial pardon. Enomoto later served as foreign minister of Japan in the early 1890s. Katsu also was later rehabilitated and served the Meiji government in a number of positions. A third Ezo officer, Ōtori Keisuke, served as Army Minister and later entered the Meiji government. He was minister to Korea at the beginning of the Sino-Japanese War. The last shōgun, Tokugawa Yoshinobu, was later rewarded for his service to Japan by being named a prince in the new Meiji nobility.

*Louis G. Perez*

**See also:** Hitotsubasi Keiki (Tokugawa Yoshinobu); Ii Naosuke; Iwakura Tomomi; Katsu Kaishū; Meiji Emperor; Ōkubo Toshimichi; Perry, Matthew; Saigō Takamori; *Sonno-jōi;* Tokugawa Nariaki; Treaty of Kanagawa; Yoshida Shōin.

**Further Reading**

Kitaoka, Shin'ichi. "The Army as a Bureaucracy: Japanese Militarism Revisited." *Journal of Military History* 57, no. 5 (Special Issue, October 1993): 67–86.

Totman, Conrad. *The Collapse of the Tokugawa Bakufu, 1862–1868.* Honolulu: University Press of Hawai'i, 1980.

## Boshin Civil War, Causes

After a series of struggles with the rebellious Western han, the Tokugawa *bakufu* seemed poised for war. The Tokugawa *bakufu* were caught between the proverbial immovable object and the irresistible force in the 1860s. On the one hand, the foreign powers (primarily Great Britain and the United States) demanded more concessions from the *bakufu* to facilitate international trade. On the other hand, most Japanese were solidly against allowing any further concessions. In fact, most of this latter group were already angry with the *bakufu* because they had signed treaties with the foreigners without imperial consent.

The *bakufu* had tried to silence their critics in the so-called Ansei Purge. In 1860, many of the critics had been arrested and some even executed. Now, many took out their frustrations through "direct action" against the few and vulnerable foreigners in the country. The *bakufu*, being merely the head of a feudal coalition of semi-independent warlords, could not control the anti-foreign terrorists of the *sonno-jōi* ("Revere the Emperor—Expel the Barbarians") movement. The attacks on foreigners by these firebrands elicited demands by the foreign powers that the *bakufu* punish the perpetrators. The *bakufu* often had absolutely no idea who the attackers were, much less how to punish them.

Because the Tokugawa were in no position to meet foreign demands, the foreigners took matters into their own hands. The *bakufu* had been beset by the Western powers because of the Tokugawa failure to punish samurai who had attacked Western citizens. Chōshū had taken the Emperor Komei's March 1863 "Order to Expel Barbarians" seriously and had attacked the British legation and fired on Western ships as they sailed through the Shimonoseki Straits. A small flotilla of mixed foreign ships banded together to bombard the Chōshū batteries there, just as they had bombarded the Satsuma capital of Kagoshima a year earlier in response to the assassination of the British civilian Charles Richardson. Of course, the *bakufu* were now criticized by the *sonno-jōi* for not protecting Japan from these foreign vigilante actions.

The *bakufu* mounted two successive punitive campaigns against Chōshū; the first ended inconclusively, and the second was saved from a complete Tokugawa fiasco by the death of the shōgun Iemochi. A succession dispute turned the Tokugawa attention from the fractious western han for a while.

Satsuma and Chōshū had been purchasing Western arms with the help of the Scottish merchant Thomas Blake Glover in Nagasaki. Both domains had begun to train their samurai with the new weapons. Chōshū had gone so far as to include non-samurai in that training, an effort that came to fruition during the second *bakufu* campaign. The samurai-led peasant soldiers proved to be both effective and trustworthy. At this time the junior samurai leaders of both Satsuma and Chōshū managed to forge a peaceful coalition with the help of the Tosa rōnin Sakamoto Ryōma. Both han had made preliminary negotiation attempts with the British diplomat Ernest Satow.

The *bakufu* had also been preparing for battle for a number of years. With the technical assistance of the French, they had trained a regiment of samurai with modern weapons and had acquired eight Western-style warships. Despite such preparations, the new shōgun Yoshinobu (also known as Hitosubashi Keiki) had no taste for war. The son of the Mito firebrand Tokugawa Nariak (who had been arrested in the Ansei Purge), Yoshinobu feared that a Japanese civil war would allow the French and British to gain advantage against whichever side ultimately won. The British, for example, had previously used such crises to gain power in India and Africa. The Tokugawa had long been warned of such tactics by the Dutch as well as by the martyr Yoshida Shōin, who had been executed in the Ansei Purge.

In 1867, Emperor Komei died, which brought the new emperor Meiji to the throne at age 13. Within his entourage, a number of "modernist" nobles sought to use this crisis to restore power to the imperial house. Led by Iwakura Tomomi, the "modernists" managed to elicit a secret order on November 9, 1867, in the name of the new emperor calling upon "loyal subjects" to "slaughter the traitorous subject Yoshinobu." Four han (Satsuma, Tosa, Hizen, and Chōshū) responded to the call and began to march on Edo. In the meantime, Yoshinobu had tried to avoid the war by resigning his position and "restoring" power to the emperor.

Saigō Takamori, the young leader of the Satsuma forces, reasoned that if the Tokugawa were allowed to quietly resign, they might retain considerable influence in the new government by virtue of their extensive land holdings (approximately 30 percent) throughout the country. There had been considerable talk about replacing the *bakufu* with a national parliament consisting of proportional representation according to population. If that happened, the Tokugawa would still predominate. Saigō sought to avoid that possibility at virtually any cost. He engineered a series of provocations that forced the Tokugawa to fight. He hired some adherents of the *sonno-jōi* movement to attack Edo castle and other Tokugawa sites. Naturally, the Tokugawa samurai responded. Saigō managed to have the entire Tokugawa regime branded as rebels and enemies of the emperor. Once Saigō had his *casus belli*, he was free to mount a full-fledged attack on the *bakufu* from all sides.

The Tokugawa soon realized that very few of its old allies could be counted on to risk all for their defense.

*Louis G. Perez*

**See also:** Boshin Civil War; Boshin Civil War, Consequences; Hitotsubasi Keiki (Tokugawa Yoshinobu)Iwakura Tomomi; Kagoshima, Bombardment of; Meiji Emperor; Saigō

Takamori; Sakamoto Ryōma; Shimonoseki, Bombardment of; Tokugawa Nariaki.

### Further Reading

Kitaoka, Shin'ichi. "The Army as a Bureaucracy: Japanese Militarism Revisited." *Journal of Military History* 57, no. 5 (Special Issue, October 1993): 67–86.

Totman, Conrad. *The Collapse of the Tokugawa Bakufu, 1862–1868.* Honolulu: University Press of Hawai'i, 1980.

## Boshin Civil War, Consequences

Despite the fact that desultory warfare continued in Hokkaidō for more than a year, for the most part the Boshin Civil War was over as soon as the final shōgun Yoshinobu surrendered his forces in Edo only weeks after the battle had started. Yoshinobu was not a decisive leader, but he was a patriot. He knew that if the war continued for much longer, it would escalate, as his supporters throughout the country would be forced to defend their homelands. An escalation of the war would, in turn, allow the French and British to make political inroads. Thus Yoshinobu quickly sued for peace.

Because the Tokugawa had been lured into warfare even after Yoshinobu had surrendered his office to the emperor in 1867, they were declared to be rebels. Not surprisingly, Saigō Takamori, who had engineered the provocations that caused the Tokugawa to fight, now announced that all rebel lands would be confiscated. Yoshinobu complied and counseled his family and allies not to resist. The "confiscation" was actually something of a sham because the "loyalist" han (chiefly Satsuma, Tosa, Hizen, and Chōshū) also surrendered their tax registers to the emperor in a symbolic act of establishing the new government.

The war served to clear away the debris from the Tokugawa regime, but it was left to the peace to fundamentally change the country. The changes that were about to occur would have been unthinkable scarcely a year before the war. The establishment of the new government was a very messy affair, indeed. The fundamental problem was the availability of too many alternatives. Most of the victors would probably have preferred to substitute themselves for the Tokugawa, but there were so many conflicting ideas of who would rule, and how that would be accomplished, to make it an easy transition. Although the samurai were divided in their views about who should rule and as to the nature of the new government, they were absolutely united in their fear of Western incursions. They knew only too well of British domination in India, parts of Africa, and the Americas. They had been warned by the Dutch (who they knew dominated the East Indies) of French, German, Russian, and even American intrigues all over the world.

Not surprisingly, then, the primary efforts of these young samurai was to strengthen their rag-tag collection of armies. They had been sufficient for the task of defeating the *bakufu*, but they needed considerable reforms to compete with any Western nation. Among the first reforms undertaken by the Meiji men was to continue the military instructions begun by the French. Of course, after the Franco-Prussian War of 1870–1871, they switched to German instructors for their army. Without question, their choice for naval modernization was Great Britain.

Absolutely no one among the victors had the slightest idea how a centralized bureaucratic state could be ruled by a teenage emperor who had no experience at governing at all. Even the loyal courtiers around Meiji had no ready models at hand. When the emperor and his extensive entourage left the cramped imperial palace in Kyoto and headed for the Tokugawa castle in Edo, which had been selected as the new center of imperial power, the leaders struggled to cobble together a new government.

The new Meiji government leaders initially acted as a collegial confederation. Soon, however, huge assembly proved to be too unwieldy, and a smaller group of men began to act as an unofficial political council. The official *Daijō-kan* (Grand Council of State) of three imperial ministers (Right, Center, and Left) was a copy of the imperial government that had existed some 700 years before the first *bakufu* had been established in the end of the 12th century. The imperial prince Sanjo Sanetomi was joined by the courtier Iwakura Tomomi in that government, but both men were only in their early thirties and had no real previous experience in government. They were joined by a small group of men, chiefly from Satsuma and Chōshū, who rose to leadership chiefly due to their charisma. Saigō Takamori and Ōkubo Toshimichi represented Satsuma, and Kido Takayoshi represented Chōshū.

Fortunately, the new leaders listened to the British minister Sir Harry Parkes, who advised them not to treat the Tokugawa loyalists harshly. A few of the Tokugawa leaders were briefly imprisoned, but within a few years any man who swore loyalty to the emperor was allowed to join the new society. Katsu Kaishū, the officer who surrendered Edo castle, later served as Navy Minister in the 1870s; Enomoto Takeaki, the erstwhile president of the quixotic Ezo Republic in Hokkaidō, later served as foreign minister; Ōtori Keisuke, the Army Minister of that republic who had convinced Enomoto to surrender peacefully, was later rehabilitated and was the Japanese minister to Korea at the beginning of the Sino-

Japanese War. Tokugawa Yoshinobu, the last shōgun, was later rewarded for his service to the nation by being named an imperial prince.

Ironically, many of the men who had been on the victors' side of the Boshin Civil War ended up on the wrong side of history. Thousands of the Satsuma samurai died as rebels in the Seinan War of 1877, as did their reluctant leader Saigō Takamori. Etō Shimpei was executed as a rebel after the Saga Rebellion of 1874. Mutsu Munemitsu served four years in prison for his treason as part of the Seinan War, but was rehabilitated in time to be the foreign minister who managed to revise the hated Unequal Treaties.

Obviously, the Boshin War served as a watershed in Japanese history, ushering out the old feudal regime and helping to establish the new Meiji government. It also signaled the end of the samurai, who were stripped of their social and political power in a series of reforms in the 1870s. The Buddhist establishment was briefly attacked, chiefly for its support of the old feudal regime; it survived when the Meiji modernizers needed philosophical support against those who wished for a Christian conversion of the country. Shintō had long lain dormant during the Tokugawa Era, but it was revitalized by the *sonno-jōi* imperial loyalists. The resulting State Shintō created by the new regime bore little resemblance to the quiet, rural, animist faith that nurtured the peasants in their agricultural pursuits.

Curiously, those samurai who died on the "wrong side" of the Boshin War were for many years treated as rebels against Imperial Japan. After World War II, the managers of the Yasukuni Shrine proposed to enshrine them together with all of the other 3 million honored war dead. A brief controversy ensued that was not settled until after the Shrine secretly enshrined the seven men who were convicted of war crimes by the Tokyo War Crimes Tribunal. The Boshin War dead were also quietly added to the list of warriors who died in service to the nation.

*Louis G. Perez*

**See also:** Boshin Civil War; Boshin Civil War, Causes; Enomoto Takeaki; Iwakura Tomomi; Kido Takayoshi; Meiji Early Political Reforms; Mutsu Munemitsu; Ōkubo Toshimichi; Ōtori Keisuke; Saga Rebellion; Saigō Takamori; Seinan War; State Shintō; Tokugawa Yoshinobu; Unequal Treaties; Yasukuni Shrine Controversy.

### Further Reading

Jansen, Marius B., and Gilbert Rozman, eds. *Japan in Transition: From Tokugawa to Meiji.* Princeton: Princeton University Press, 1986.

Totman, Conrad. *The Collapse of the Tokugawa Bakufu, 1862–1868.* Honolulu: University Press of Hawai'i, 1980.

## Boxer Rebellion (1898–1900)

The Boxer Rebellion was initiated by the secret organization known as the Righteous and Harmonious Society Movement or Righteous and Harmonious Fists (known in the West as the Boxers). The Boxers were so named because most of the adherents of the movement practiced martial arts, including Eastern-style boxing.

In November 1897, the German government retaliated against China for the murder of two missionaries in Shandong Province by occupying the port of Qingdao. In December 1897, the Russians seized Lushun, located in southern Liaoning. The British joined in by occupying Weihai, while the French seized Zhanjiang. The U.S. open door policy, initiated in 1899, was also seen by Chinese Nationalists as a further incursion on Chinese sovereignty.

The Boxers at first were hostile toward the ruling Manchu Qing dynasty. After suffering a stinging defeat during an engagement with imperial troops in October 1898, however, they suspended their antigovernment campaign to focus their assaults on Christian missionaries and converts, whom they saw as agents of Western imperialism.

The growing strength of the Boxers encouraged the Dowager Empress Cixi to deploy them as a force to expel the Western powers from China. She issued edicts in January 1900 defending the Boxers. This move drew vociferous complaints from foreign diplomats. By November 1899, the Boxers had begun to launch widespread attacks against Western interests throughout northern China.

In response to spreading Boxer depredations, Western nations began to build up their forces on the Chinese coast in April 1900. A mixed force of 4,500 troops was landed to safeguard Western interests in Tianjin, and on May 31, 430 marines and sailors from eight nations were dispatched to Beijing to reinforce the forces guarding the legations there. On June 10, 1900, British vice admiral Sir Edward Seymour led a multinational force of some 2,100 troops (mostly marines and sailors) to go to the aid of troops already in place defending foreign embassies at Beijing.

The Western troops met with stiff resistance from imperial troops and had to retreat to Tianjin, arriving there on June 25 after losing 350 men. The imperial government ordered all foreigners to leave Beijing. The following day, the Boxers, joined by elements of the imperial army, attacked the foreign compounds inside Beijing. The American, British, Dutch, French, and Russian legations—all of which were located in close proximity to the imperial compound known as the Forbidden City—joined together to form a fortified compound into which the staff of the Belgian and Spanish legations and other foreign citizens fled. The German legation, however, was on the other side of the city and was stormed before the staff could escape.

Imperial Chinese troops, in the meantime, had reinforced the Dagukou forts at the mouth of the Haihe River, cutting off the allied fleet from the forces it had landed. At 1:00 a.m. on June 17, a fierce artillery interchange between the forts and shoal-draft elements of the allied fleet commenced, after which allied landing forces assaulted the forts. By 6:30 a.m., the forts had been captured, along with four destroyers that had been seized by naval boarding parties.

Dagukou became a beachhead for the buildup of strong forces to relieve the troops at Tianjin and advance on Beijing. By early July, 51 warships from eight nations were deployed in the mouth of the Haihe River. They brought with them 4,750 marines and naval landing forces, along with almost 50,000 other troops—the great majority from Japan (20,840), Russia (13,150), and Britain (12,020), with smaller contingents from France (3,520), the United States (3,420), Germany (900), Italy (80), and Austria-Hungary (75). This allied force successfully assaulted Tianjin on July 13 and commenced its advance to Beijing on August 4.

The march to Beijing was opposed by approximately 70,000 imperial troops and between 50,000 and 100,000 Boxers. On August 5, 1900, Beicheng fell, and the following day American and British troops prevailed in a fierce engagement at Yangcun.

Following the capture of Beijing, allied troops spread out over northern China, breaking up Boxer concentrations. On February 1, 1901, the imperial government officially abolished the Boxers. On September 7,

1901, imperial officials had no choice but to sign the so-called Boxer Protocol. The Qing government was obliged to permit fortifications of foreign legations and the installation of foreign garrisons along the Beijing-Tianjin railroad. It was also compelled to execute 10 officials linked to the outbreak of the rebellion and to pay war reparations of $333 million. Britain, Japan, and the United States subsequently allocated much of their portions of the indemnity for the education of Chinese students at overseas institutions.

Japan's extensive involvement in the suppression of the Boxers contributed to the respect of its army by Westerners. The fact that by and large the Japanese did not commit atrocities against captured Boxers and did not participate in the raping and looting by Western troops against civilian Chinese won high praise by many foreign journalists. Even some Western military commanders recognized Japan's "professional and civil behavior," a supreme irony considering Japanese atrocities in World War II.

*Paul E. Fontenoy*

**See also:** World War II, Japanese Atrocities.

### Further Reading

Harrington, Peter. *China, 1900: The Eyewitnesses Speak; The Boxer Rebellion as Described by Participants in Letters, Diaries and Photographs*. London: Greenhill Books, 2000.

Preston, Diana. *The Boxer Rebellion: The Dramatic Story of China's War on Foreigners That Shook the World in the Summer of 1900*. New York: Walker, 2000.

## Buddhism Copes with Imperialism (1900–1945)

Modern Japanese Buddhism, from 1900 to1945, became an important instrument for the nation-state's policies of modernization and imperialism. After the threat of total eradication of *Haibutsu-Kishaku* ("Abolishing the Buddha and Destroying the Shakyamuni") after the Meiji Restoration in 1868, the Meiji Buddhists argued that Buddhism was an important ideological foundation in establishing a unified nation-state centered on the emperor because the expansion of Christianity and Western liberal democracy threatened it. Japanese Buddhist opposition to Christian colonialism led the Japanese to favor Buddhist Pan-Asianism. To counter Western Christianity and colonialism, it was thought, all Asians who suffered under Western imperialism must unite around their common cultural treasures led by Japanese Buddhism.

After Japanese Buddhists attended the World's Parliament of Religions in Chicago in 1893, they became convinced that Japanese Buddhism was the synthesis of the best of Asian culture and the West. They believed that Japan had a mission to enlighten the materialistic West and educate all other Asian Buddhists.

*Shinshū Ōtani-ha*, one of two largest denominations of True Pure Land Buddhism (*Honganji-ha*), first sent a missionary Ogurusu *Kōchō* (1831–1905) to China in 1873. Ogurusu was determined to revive Asia by uniting Buddhist movements in India, China, and Japan and thereby counter Christian missionary activities in Asia. In China, Buddhism was in decline. Thus Ogurusu tried to educate Chinese Buddhists through the modernity of Japanese Buddhism. The Pure Land Buddhist missionaries went to the areas where Japanese residents lived but gradually made contact with local Chinese by building schools and hospitals. Both Pure Land Buddhist denominations requested that the Japanese government pressure the Chinese government to grant an equal right to their missionary work with that of the Western Christian missionaries. After Japan's victory in the Russo-Japanese War in 1905, more Japanese Buddhist missionaries went to Manchuria, Korea, Taiwan, and other areas of China. In turn, Chinese, Taiwanese, and Korean Buddhist leaders came to Japan to study Japanese Buddhism, which had been successful in modernization and integration in the society and the state.

However, after Japan's annexation of Korea in 1910, the Mukden Incident in 1931, and the China-Japan War in 1937, young Chinese and Korean Buddhist leaders questioned Japanese Buddhism and its missionary activities. Some Japanese Buddhist missionaries working with the Japanese military abroad as chaplains were uncritical of the military aggression, and even became agents provocateurs or spies to give information about local pro/anti-Japanese Chinese Buddhists to the military.

Nichiren Buddhism became more nationalistic after the Meiji Restoration. Tanaka Chigaku and Honda Nisshō preached a new interpretation of Nichiren doctrines: 2,500 years after Gautama Buddha's death, *mappō* must come for the Right Dharma to prevail and return to India from Japan. Nichiren predicted that *mappō* would come when the Right King comes to restore the Right Dharma. The Right King must be the Japanese emperor.

Ishiwara Kanji, a student of Tanaka Chigaku, was the leader of the Kwantung Army in Manchuria. Ishiwara experienced a spiritual revelation when he visited the Ise Shintō Shrine in 1927; when he recited the *Lotus Sutra*, he saw a bright light rising from the west (Manchuria). This experience confirmed Ishiwara's faith in Nichiren's prophecy: after *mappō*, the Right Dharma is returned to India from Japan. Ishiwara was convinced that he would do decisively the right things to expand Japan's mission in Manchuria. Ishiwara became the key architect for the Manchuria Incident in 1931, which sought to establish Japan's puppet nation of Manchukuo.

Japanese Buddhist Pan-Asianism became instrumental in the Japanese military aggression to justify the ideology of the "Greater East Asia Co-prosperity Sphere." Japanese Buddhists initiated three large Pan-Asian Buddhist Youth Conferences in 1930 in Hawaii, and in 1934 and 1943 in Tokyo. Chinese Buddhists refused to attend in 1934 because Manchurian Buddhists attended with equal status with Chinese Buddhists; the latter group did not recognize Manchukuo. Japanese Buddhists accused Chinese Buddhists of confusing politics with religion: this logic was self-contradictory because Japanese Buddhist political neutrality was used in demanding that Chinese Buddhists not fight Japanese military aggression. At the Conference in 1943, Japanese Buddhists persuaded South Asian Buddhists in Thailand, Burma, and Vietnam, among others, that they should cooperate with the Japanese military operation in the Pacific War to protect Buddhism from Western Christian colonialism, as Christians and Communists controlled the Chinese government and Allied nations.

In Korea, Buddhists were persecuted by advocates of the Chosŏn Dynasty's Neo-Confucian ideology; in fact, Buddhists were not even allowed to enter the capital of Seoul. After Japan's annexation of Korea in 1910, Korean Buddhists welcomed the modernity of Japanese Buddhism as an instrument for reforming Korean Buddhism. The Korean Buddhist denominations were controlled by the head of Japanese denominations according to "The Temple Act" of 1911. For example, according to Zen Buddhism, Takeda Hanshi, a Sōtō Zen priest, came to control Korean Zen Buddhism *Wonjong* by merging

it with Sōtō Zen in 1911. It has been debated whether he was involved in the assassination of Queen Min, who cooperated with Russia in 1895.

After the Korean independence movement exploded on March 1, 1919, the Japanese Governor of Korea realized the importance of controlling the population's minds by cultural rather than military means. The Governor of Korea requested that Japanese Buddhists cooperate with Korean Buddhists to disseminate the *Naisen-Ittai* policy ("unity of Japanese and Koreans as one people under the emperor") by the so-called *Shinden* movement ("cultivating mind" movement).

The Japanese Buddhists considered that because of their modernity, they were in a good position to educate Asian Buddhists by means of Buddhist Pan-Asianism. Eventually, however, they found themselves used by Japanese imperialism during the 1900–1945 period.

*Kunihiko Terasawa*

**See also:** Ishiwara Kanji; Nichiren; Pan-Asianism; Tanaka Chigaku.

**Further Reading**

Sueki Fumihiko. "Religion and the Japanese Empire," in Jaffe, Richard ed., *Japanese Journal of Religious Studies* 37, no. 1 (2010): 1–7; Nanzan Institute for Religion and Culture.

Victoria, Brian. *Zen at War*, 2nd ed. Lanham, MD: Rowman & Littlefield, 2006.

Victoria, Brian. *Zen War Stories*. London/New York: RoutledgeCurzon, Taylor & Francis Group, 2003.

# Buke Shohatto

The Buke shohatto was one of the foundational laws of the Tokugawa shōgunate (1603–1868). It regulated aspects of the relationship between the domain lords and the shōgunate, and also provided general guidelines for samurai conduct. The first Buke shohatto was drafted by Isshin Sūden on the orders of Tokugawa Ieyasu in 1615, directly after the eradication of the Toyotomi house in the second siege of Osaka Castle. Tokugawa Ieyasu had already handed the shōgunal title on to his son Tokugawa Hidetada by this time, and it was therefore the second shōgun Tokugawa Hidetada who proclaimed the law before the assembled *daimyō* at Fushimi Castle in Kyoto on July 7, 1615.

This first version of the Buke shohatto, known as the "Genwa Proclamation" (*Genwa rei*), was addressed primarily to the *daimyō*. It emphasized good conduct, along with the importance of reporting criminal acts and unauthorized fortification works in bordering domains to the central authorities. It also mentioned the duty of domain lords to pursue criminals and rebels, and to supply service to the shōgunate. Each of the 19 articles of the law in this first version was followed by a "commentary," which explicated the article through citations of classical Japanese and Chinese literature and philosophy. The significance of the Buke shohatto in 1615 was that it changed the way the shōgunate exercised power over the domains. Previously, the Tokugawa shōgun had influenced *daimyō* on an individual basis through their capacity to change the allocation of domains. The Buke shohatto, in contrast, represented direct central rule over the *daimyō* through a standard law.

In 1629, Hidetada revised the law slightly, removing the clause that prohibited *daimyō* from "harboring" people from other provinces. The third shōgun Iemitsu revised the law more substantially in 1635. He removed the commentaries from all articles but the first, thereby giving the law a more legal and less literary character. He also added

articles that has the following effects: (1) regulated the conduct of the new system of alternate attendance (*sankin kōtai*) for *daimyō* at Edo; (2) further clarified the ban on the building of new castles, and required *daimyō* to apply for shōgunal approval for castle repairs; (3) required *daimyō* to militarily assist one another in the case of local outbreaks of rebellion; (4) banned private alliances or conflicts; (5) ensured the maintenance of highways and banned private tolls; (6) stopped the construction of larger shipping vessels; and (7) acknowledged temple and shrine ownership of certain lands. This revision of the law was known as the Kan'ei proclamation (*kan'ei rei*).

In 1663, Shōgun Tokugawa Ietsuna further revised the law (the Kanbun proclamation), removing the commentary to the first article, extending the law requiring shōgunal permission for *daimyō* marriages to the imperial aristocracy, and emphasizing the duty of *daimyō* to suppress Christianity and punish unfilial behavior. The law was further revised in 1683 by Shōgun Tokugawa Tsunayoshi (the Tenwa proclamation), in 1710 by Shōgun Tokugawa Ienobu (the Shōtoku proclamation), and in 1717 by Shōgun Tokugawa Yoshimune (the Kyōho proclamation).

*Kiri Paramore*

**See also:** Tokugawa *Bakufu* Political System; Tokugawa Ieyasu.

**Further Reading**

de Bary, William Theodore, et al., eds. *Sources of Japanese Tradition*, 2nd ed., vol. 2. New York: Columbia University Press, 2005.

## Bunmei kaika

The phrase *bunmei kaika* means "Civilization and Enlightenment," and was one of the many Meiji-era four-kanji character slogans that appear in the classic Confucian model of "rectification of names." Others include *sonnoi-jōi* ("Honor the Emperor—Expel the Barbarian"), *shokusan kōgyō* ("Encourage Industry"), and *fukoku kyōhei* ("Rich Country—Strong Military").

The Meiji leaders of the time wished to encourage "modernization" of Japan, but what they really implied was the Westernization of the country. The idea was to learn from the West so as to ensure Japan's independence in the face of European and American imperialism.

The phrase *bunmei kaika* had been coined and popularized by Fukuzawa Yukichi, whose series of books *Seiyō Jijō* ("Conditions in the West") and *Bunmeiron no gairyaku* ("Outline and Theory of Civilization") had been best-sellers and manuals on Westernization. Fukuzawa had been at the forefront of the Meiji-era movement. He wrote that "civilization can be defined as that which advances man's knowledge and virtue." Fukuzawa advocated sloughing off the ancient cultural ideas that had doomed China to a century of stagnation. His phrase *datsua nyūo* ("Abandon Asia—Join Europe") argued that Japan must move into the European sphere of reason and science and leave behind Confucian and Buddhist superstitions.

The ideas of *bunmei kaika* were embodied into the Charter Oath of 1868, which had set out the intentions of the new Meiji state. Two of the five "oaths" included "Evil customs of the past shall be broken off and everything based upon the just laws of Nature" and "Knowledge shall be sought throughout the world so as to strengthen the foundations of imperial rule."

The brunt of Westernization had been borne in the political and economic spheres, but some of its influence had spilled over into the social realm as well. The wholesale political changes had been accompanied by wrenching and revolutionary social changes such as the abolition of the samurai class; an institutionalized universal conscription of all classes into the military; mandatory education; abolition of the outcaste *eta* (now euphemistically called *burakumin* ["hamlet people"]); a new land tax system; and the first faltering steps into representative government.

Concomitantly, however, thousands of silly social trappings had swept the nation. Ballroom dancing, Western clothes (in wildly inappropriate combinations: top hats worn with *zori* sandals, petticoats worn outside dresses, and waxed moustaches worn with traditional samurai *chonmage* topknots), beef-eating, beer drinking, turnip-sized vest pocket watches (with no vests to house them), elaborate walking canes, pet animals, cigar smoking, and taking of snuff all proliferated in the burgeoning cities.

Thousands of young men (and a few women) flocked to foreign-language schools, dancing academies, Western musical schools, millinery and haberdashery shops, and Western-style restaurants, all in the headlong stampede to be au courant. By the 1880s, Fukuzawa himself despaired that his countrymen had missed the point of Westernization. He groused, "Must we emulate every silly European habit?"

Indeed, something of a backlash occurred against the wide-scale abandonment of Japanese traditions. Traditional cultural mores made something of a comeback after a frightening anti-Asian campaign including *Haibutsu kishaku* ("abolish Buddhism and destroy Shakyamuni"), which had destroyed many temples in the larger cities. The traditional cultural arts (e.g., flower arranging, tea ceremonies, Noh theater) staged a revival, and many people reverted to the wearing of more comfortable Japanese clothes. After a brief effort to eradicate Sino-Japanese written *kanji* in favor of a Western alphabet (Romaji), the nation chose to regularize and unify the somewhat chaotic Japanese oral and written language. Native literature and the fine arts experienced a renaissance as well.

Some historians argue that this conservative cultural backlash was highly influential in the swing back to Neo-Confucianism evidenced in the Imperial Rescript on Education and the Meiji Constitution, both issued in 1890. It has also been argued that the institutionalization of State Shintō as a sociopolitical ethos had much to do with the backlash as well.

*Louis G. Perez*

**See also:** Charter Oath; Fukuzawa Yukichi; Imperial Rescript on Education; Meiji Constitution; *Sonno-jōi*.

**Further Reading**

Black, John R. *Young Japan: Yokohama and Yedo 1858–79*. Oxford, UK: Oxford University Press, 1969.

Craig, Albert M. *Civilization and Enlightenment: The Early Thought of Fukuzawa Yukichi*. Cambridge, MA: Harvard University Press, 2009.

# Burma Air Campaign (1941–1942)

By the time the United States entered World War II, China had been at war for four years. Virtually the only American force fighting the Axis powers anywhere in the world in December 1941 was the American Volunteer Group (AVG), popularly known as the Flying Tigers. Since August 1941, members of the AVG had been training at the British fighter base in Toungoo, Burma.

The Nationalist Chinese government headed by Jiang Jieshi was not only at war with the Japanese but also locked in an uneasy truce with Chinese Communist forces led by Mao Zedong. By late 1941, Jiang's troops had failed to block the Japanese move toward Burma, threatening the only land supply route into China that ran over the Himalayas, along the hairpin mountain curves of the Burma Road.

As the Japanese advance threatened Burma, the British requested one of the AVG's three squadrons to help defend Rangoon. On December 12, 1941, the AVG 3rd Squadron moved south to Rangoon to join units of the Royal Air Force (RAF), while the other two squadrons flew to Kunming in China to cover the terminus of the Burma Road.

The AVG's first combat occurred over Yunnan Province in China on December 20. The group shot down 9 of 10 Japanese bombers, losing only 1 of their own P-40Bs. On December 23, together with RAF aircraft, they shot down 6 Japanese bombers and 4 fighters over Rangoon. The RAF lost 5 aircraft in the battle, and the AVG lost 4. On Christmas Day, the Japanese sent 80 bombers over Rangoon in two waves, escorted by 48 fighters. The AVG knocked down 23 of the planes without suffering a single loss. The Japanese attacks continued through New Year's Eve. After 11 days of fighting, the AVG had shot down 75 Japanese aircraft, losing only 4 fighters and 2 pilots in the process.

In early January 1942, 8 aircraft from the AVG's 1st Squadron reinforced the 3rd Squadron in Rangoon. The rest of the 1st Squadron followed by midmonth. The AVG went on the offensive, attacking Japanese air bases in Thailand. During one raid alone, AVG pilots destroyed more than 60 Japanese aircraft on the ground. On January 23, the Japanese again hit Rangoon with 72 aircraft. The AVG shot down 21, suffering only a single loss.

The air battles over the Burmese capital continued until March 9, 1942, when the city finally fell to Japanese ground attack. The Japanese captured the remainder of Burma in May, effectively cutting China off from ground access. For most of the rest of the war, the United States supplied China by air from India in the massive airlift that became known as flying "the Hump."

During the 10 weeks the AVG fought in the skies over Rangoon and the Burma Road, it had only 5 to 20 operational fighters in Burma at any given time. Yet in 31 separate air battles, its pilots destroyed a confirmed total of 217 Japanese aircraft and probably shot down 43 more. In the process, the AVG lost 6 pilots and 16 P-40s. Fighting alongside the AVG, the RAF had 74 confirmed kills and 33 probables, losing 22 Buffaloes and Hurricanes.

*David T. Zabecki*

See also: Jiang Jieshi.

**Further Reading**

Byrd, Martha. *Chennault: Giving Wings to the Tiger.* Tuscaloosa: University of Alabama Press, 1987.

Ford, Daniel. *Flying Tigers: Claire Chennault and the American Volunteer Group.* Washington, DC: Smithsonian Institution Press, 1995.

Greenlaw, Olga. *The Lady and the Tigers: Remembering the Flying Tigers of World War II.* Ed. Daniel Ford. San Jose, CA: Writers Club Press, 2002.

## Bushidō

The "invention of tradition" is generally considered a modern venture, but in the case of *bushidō*—"the Way of the Warrior"—the initial fabrication occurred centuries earlier, in the Edo period (1600–1868). During the first half of the Pax Tokugawa, when warring among warriors was explicitly forbidden, a handful of samurai scholars set brush and ink to paper, musing openly about their *raison d'être* and social value. The texts they produced were expressions of an existential crisis among the more contemplative members of Japan's warrior elite. While those treatises constitute a canon for modern articulations of *bushidō* (and have been applied to everything from business and martial arts to modern battle strategy and nation building), they are also a discrete reflection of their own times, distinct from both what preceded them and what came afterward.

Indeed, the inventors of the *bushidō* "tradition" were quite deliberately critiquing their times and their contemporaries through their formulations of ideal samurai conduct. Yet they did so without over-reliance on nostalgic references to exemplary heroes of a bygone golden age. Rather, the ideal they envisioned was an unprecedented combination of the martial and intellectual, the rugged and the refined, the quick-to-act and the thoughtfully deliberative, that was more in keeping with the new roles peacetime required of warriors. This ideal was embodied in a novel combination of Chinese ideographs that Chinese and Koreans would have read as oxymoronic: *bu* (Ch: *wu*) for martial, and *shi* (Ch: *shì*) for gentleman or scholar. *Bushidō* was, therefore, "the way of the gentleman warrior."

There are few fundamental incongruities between the core *bushidō* treatises, but different authors did emphasize specific virtues: Yamaga Sokō (1622–1685) propounded on the samurai's responsibility to exhibit moral conduct to commoners; Yamamoto Tsunetomo (1659–1720) advocated mental preparation for meeting death without hesitation; the prolific Neo-Confucian Kaibara Ekken (1630–1714) instructed his readers in the proper observance of ritual hierarchy and the importance of study. However, for these men, arguably the most basic of all warrior virtues was selflessness, an attribute their medieval forebears neither exalted nor displayed with any consistence.

In earlier times, when warfare was endemic, samurai expected to be well rewarded for their services. Victorious warriors could anticipate a portion of the spoils from vanquished estates; when they did not receive those in the desired quantities, they either deserted or revolted. Abstract concepts such as unquestioning loyalty to one's lord or service to the nation had little effect on their personal manners or battlefield conduct. The soldiers who fought off the Mongol invasions of 1274 and 1281 were so aggrieved by the lack of compensation that they openly defied the Hōjō regency in Kamakura, permanently undermining its viability. The much-touted samurai virtue of personal honor was manifested mostly in violent efforts at self-redress (*jiriki kyūsai*)—that is, responding to any perceived insult with lethal vengeance. *Jiriki kyūsai* was so pervasive that most medieval legal documents—from the Jōei Code (1232) to the house laws of individual warlords—explicitly and repeatedly forbade any efforts by warriors to settle disputes among themselves without adjudication.

If the 16th century was the samurai's heyday—with bloodletting aplenty—it was certainly not because of widespread observance of an intangible code among men of arms. If anything, that era's phenomenon of *gekokujō* ("those below topple those above") was a *negative* example against which the later codifiers of *bushidō* held up the virtue of loyalty to one's lord. Most samurai of the Warring States period (ca. 1467–1590) would have regarded the "way of the gentleman warrior" to be foolhardy, even suicidal; conversely, the warrior-philosophers of the 17th and 18th centuries scorned the self-aggrandizing, opportunistic treachery of that discredited, chaotic epoch.

Only in the relative calm imposed by the Tokugawa shōguns did introspective warriors feel moved to pontificate about what made their calling so distinctively noble and socially beneficial. Those who did so were informed by philosophical strains from Zen Buddhism and Neo-Confucianism, which they melded with the martial proficiency valorized in the earlier, nebulous phrase *yumiya no narai* ("learning the bow and arrow") to fashion a more comprehensive ethos. The earliest of the canonical texts— *Book of the Five Rings* (*Gorin no sho*) by Miyamoto Musashi (1584–1645)—might be considered a transitional piece, in that it teaches military strategy and combat techniques, yet anticipates the philosophical tendencies of later treatises with closing remarks on the Void, "that which cannot be seen."

Subsequent texts were somewhat less esoteric, going into considerable detail about proper samurai comportment and attitude, and reflecting the intense interest in Neo-Confucianism in the early Edo period, but devoting relatively little attention to specific martial arts techniques. "The samurai code requires that samurai rise at dawn," Yamaga Sokō instructed, "wash their face and hands, groom themselves, dress properly, and prepare their weapons." "It is bad taste to yawn in front of people," Yamamoto Tsunetomo admonished. Daidōji Yūzan's (1639–1730) *Primer on the Martial Way* (*Budō shoshinshū*) included chapters on frugality, courtesy, laziness, modesty, and cultural refinement, in addition to horsemanship and vassalage. In *The Great Learning for Women* (*Onna daigaku*, 1672), a didactic text for women of the warrior caste, Kaibara Ekken wrote that "A woman must always be on the alert and keep a strict watch over her own conduct" to avoid the "five infirmities" to which her gender was prone: "indocility, discontent, slander, jealousy, and silliness." *Bushidō* should thus be embodied in every mannerism and social interaction, rather than just in combat.

In his *Way of the Samurai (Shidō)*, Yamaga admitted that "the samurai eats food without growing it, uses utensils without manufacturing them, and profits without buying or selling. What is the justification for this?" The samurai's role, he answered himself, was to "uphold the proper moral principles in the land. . . . The three classes of the common people make him their teacher and respect him. By following his teachings, they are able to understand what is fundamental and what is secondary." In an age in which their martial skills were rarely required, samurai were to be the living exemplars of Confucian virtues such as filial piety, trustworthiness, selflessness, and wisdom.

Yamamoto's *Hagakure* (1716) proposed an elegantly simple, straightforward definition of *bushidō*: "The Way of the Samurai is found in death. When it comes to either/or, there is only the quick choice of death. It is not particularly difficult. Be determined and advance. . . . If by setting one's heart right every morning and evening, one is able to live as though his body were already dead, he gains freedom in the Way." Daidōji likewise contended that "The foremost concern of a warrior, no matter what his rank, is how he will behave at the moment of his death." For these thinkers, controlling the circumstances of one's death was the reward for a lifetime of physical and mental training. This fixation on "dying pretty" intensified in the wake of the infamous Akō vendetta of 1703, in which the retainers of Asano Naganori plotted and carried out the assassination of his tormenter, Kira Yoshinaka, and were sentenced to ritual suicide (*seppuku*) after extensive debate among government magistrates. The Akō vendetta laid bare the inconsonance between the unwritten warrior code's emphasis on loyalty to one's lord unto death and beyond, and the rule of law designed to preclude a return to the chaotic violence of the Warring States era. The government's efforts to criminalize the "47 loyal retainers" were countered by a widespread popular reverence for their heroics.

The codifiers of *bushidō* were, indeed, disgusted with what they considered to be the wretched state of warrior virtues in their own times ("Today," Yamamoto lamented, "there are no models of good retainers."). Nevertheless, their influence on the "men of purpose" (*shishi*) who challenged the Tokugawa regime in the mid-19th century was profound. Their words echo in the writings of Yoshida Shōin (1830–1859), mentor to several architects of the Meiji Restoration: "From the beginning of the year to the end, day and night, morning and evening, in action and repose, in speech and in silence, the warrior must keep death constantly before him and always have in mind that the one death [that he has to give] should not be suffered in vain." The very fact that Yoshida felt compelled to restate this is proof enough that *bushidō* has always been an evolving set of *ideal* principles and behaviors that responds to particular historical circumstances, rather than a timeless, universally observed "Japanese tradition." In the Edo period, these principles and behaviors were expected only of hereditary warriors; in modern times they were reimagined as a defining element of Japanese nationhood, which all people (*kokumin*) were required to exemplify.

*E. Taylor Atkins*

**See also:** Civil Wars, Sengoku Era; Mongol Invasions of Japan; Tokugawa *Bakufu* Political System; Yoshida Shōin.

## Further Reading

Ames, Roger. "*Bushidō*: Mode or Ethic?" In *Japanese Aesthetics and Culture*, edited byNancy Hume. Albany: SUNY Press, 2002: 279–294.

Cleary, Thomas, trans. *The Code of the Samurai: A Modern Translation of the* Bushidō Shoshinshū *of Taira Shigesuke* [Daidōji Yūzan]. Rutland, VT: Tuttle, 1999.

Friday, Karl F. *Samurai, Warfare and the State in Early Medieval Japan*. London: Routledge, 2003.

Yamamoto Tsunetomo. *Hagakure: Book of the Samurai*. Trans. William Scott Wilson. Tokyo: Kōdansha International, 2002.

## *Bushidō* in Japanese Sports

Like the American cowboy, the samurai has served as a symbol of Japanese masculinity for hundreds of years. Although the samurai and their "warrior code of ethics," called *bushidō*, are often seen as the wellspring of the values of Japanese athletes, their current place in Japanese sports is actually the product of various claims by a few influential men in Japanese baseball history. These men were seeking to justify their own participation in the sport by appealing to this powerful symbol. *Bushidō*'s legend grew the more they appealed to its symbolism.

*Bushidō* has taken hold in Japanese sports for a variety of reasons. First, many point to the powerful links between competitive sport and the spiritualism of and mental preparation demanded by Zen Buddhism, which *bushidō* draws upon. Second, *bushidō*'s lasting influence owes much to the fact that Japanese sports competitions are perceived to be "battles," "contests," or "wars." Third, the practical wisdom offered by these ancient warriors, especially in terms of battle strategy, patience and poise in competition, and honor in defeat, have all appealed to modern-day "samurai-athletes." But above all, *bushidō* persists because it remains the dominant form of masculinity into which young Japanese athletes, especially baseball players, are socialized.

Sports were introduced to Japan after it opened itself to the West in the late 19th century. *Bushidō* was thereafter appropriated to defend the playing of baseball, a Western sport not initially well received by all Japanese people at the time. Some thought the sport was immoral because it lauded "stealing" bases. Infusing *bushidō* into baseball solved this problem because it showed how Japanese could play this Western import in a Japanese—and thus a moral—way. *Bushidō* was called upon to "Japanize" baseball. Because Japan was a relatively new member of the global community and was seeking to establish a national identity, many saw *bushidō* as the "essence" of Japan, that which made the country "unique." It did not hurt that foreigners who visited Japan around this time often said the same thing.

One baseball coach who played a particularly significant role in equating baseball with *bushidō* was Tobita Suishū (1886–1965), of Waseda University. Tobita asserted a link between education and sports and believed that baseball coaches had the power to inculcate samurai values. He argued that coaches should teach "athletic *bushidō*," in part because his father was against his own participation in the sport and wanted him to instead follow a traditional Japanese martial art. Borrowing spiritual practices from Buddhism, Tobita was a proponent of "ascetic training," professed the importance of instilling "guts" in his players, and has been referred to as the "god of [Japanese] baseball."

The idea that baseball should be used to inculcate *bushidō* values has since come to hold significant sway over coaches in many

Japanese sports. The masculine stoicism asserted by *bushidō* appeals to many modern Japanese athletes, even in lesser-known sports. For example, Kai Shūji insists that the "samurai spirit" helped him become the *futsal* champion. The terms "samurai" and "*bushidō*" are also used in titles of golf books and by sprinters such as Tamesue Dai, who calls himself a "samurai hurdler."

Baseball, however, has been most prone to samurai and *bushidō* invocations, none more influential than the work of the bestselling author and journalist Robert Whiting. The Japanese have embraced Whiting's prose, translating much of it back into their native tongue. The mass media today refer to the national baseball team as "Samurai Japan."

Some argue that the idea of *bushidō* is strongest in baseball because baseball bats symbolize samurai swords, and because the battle between pitcher and batter is like a battle between dueling samurai. Japanese professional baseball teams are arms of large corporations, meaning baseball players serve their employers in the same way that samurai used to serve their feudal masters. Playing baseball is, therefore, said to foster the *bushidō* values of loyalty, honor, and courage. *Bushidō*'s place in Japanese sports is secure thanks to this perception.

*Aaron L. Miller*

**See also:** *Bushidō*; Nitobe Inazō; Orientalism; Zen Buddhism in Japanese Sports.

**Further Reading**

Blackwood, Thomas. "Bushidō Baseball? Three 'Fathers' and the Invention of a Tradition." *Social Science Japan Journal* 11, no. 2 (2008): 223–240.

Kelly, William. "The Spirit and Spectacle of School Baseball: Mass Media, Statemaking and 'Edu-tainment' in Japan, 1905–1935." *Senri Ethnological Studies* 52. Osaka: National Museum of Ethnology, 2000.

Whiting, Robert. *You've Gotta Have Wa*. New York: Vintage, 1990.

# C

## Christian Era, Suppression (*Fumi-e*)

Portuguese traders first arrived in Japan in 1543, followed by Roman Catholic missionaries in 1549. Hence, the Japan Christian century extends from 1549 to approximately 1650. Roman Catholicism was first brought to Japan by members of the Society of Jesus, which was newly founded in 1540. More commonly known as Jesuits, the first of these missionaries to arrive in Japan were a Basque, Francis Xavier (one of the original seven members of order), along with Cosme de Torres and Juan Fernandez. The trio landed in Kagoshima on Japan's southernmost island of Kyushu on August 15, 1549. A samurai named Yajiro, whom the Jesuits had met in Malacca, accompanied the Jesuits as their interpreter.

Language became a problem immediately for the missionaries, as Yajiro was using Buddhist terms to refer to the Christian God, so that some thought the religion was a form of Buddhism. To clarify, the Jesuits starting using Portuguese and Latin terms to designate words not found in the Japanese language. The Jesuits began by trying to make inroads among the elite of society. They first attempted to meet with the emperor. However, they quickly came to realize that the emperor, while the symbolic head of the country, held no actual power during this period of Japan's history—it was the shōgun they needed to approach. The samurai were the highest-ranking class in Japan at this time, under the shōgun and *daimyō*.

Several decisions needed to be made at the outset. First, the young Jesuits decided that they would reach as many people as possible with some of the most important elements of the faith, and then later return and provide more in-depth teaching. They trained young Japanese to act as lay teachers, called *dojuku* (fellow lodgers), and they established confraternities of believers called *companhia* in Portuguese. These would remain after the Jesuits had given a brief introduction and converted willing Japanese to Catholicism.

The Jesuits also tried to understand the Japanese culture and did not forbid Japanese from participating in local festivals and practices that might have had Shintō or Buddhist overtones. Newly brought to light for readers of English is the work of prominent Japanese women whom the Jesuits trained and who had a profound influence on their mission activity. Women were drawn to Christianity because of its inclusion of salvation for women, the agency it provided them to preach the Christian message, and the fact that they could choose to be Christian. These powerful women carried the Christian message with no thought to their own safety.

The early years of the conversions were aided by the missionaries accompanying the traders to the various han. One historian of Japan says that the Jesuits used trade for the kingdom of God, while the traders used the kingdom of God for trade. As conversions multiplied, Japanese officials worried that their country might not be safe from these foreigners whose religion had a God who was above the emperor. The first ban on Christianity was announced by Toyotomi Hideyoshi in 1587, but not enforced. Meanwhile, Franciscan friars arrived as missionaries in Japan to proselytize, and took a different stance from the Jesuits. The friction that arose among the Jesuits and the new arrivals disturbed Hideyoshi, culminating in Japan's first persecution of Christians. In 1596, 24 Christians were paraded through the streets from Kyoto all the way to Nagasaki. In the original group were 6 Franciscans and 18 Japanese; 3 of the latter were Jesuits. Two more persons were picked up on the road, and 26 were crucified in Nagasaki on February 4, 1597.

Persecutions ceased for a time. Then, on January 27, 1614, an order regarding the new religion was issued by the Tokugawa shōgun, banning all Christian priests. Moreover, *daimyō* were ordered to destroy any vestiges of Christianity in their domains. Japanese earned rewards from authorities for turning in Christians, with the amounts varying during the years 1614 to 1640: 200 to 500 pieces of silver for a priest; 100 to 300 pieces of silver for a brother; and 50 to 100 pieces of silver for a Japanese catechist.

Another method of surfacing Christians was the *goningumi*. Villages were arranged by *kumi*, five or more households grouped to keep order in the village. Authorities demanded that these groupings report any Christian in the group. If failure to do so came to light, the entire *kumi* was liable to suffer the same punishment as the Christian.

*Fumi-e* were Christian pictures or religious medals that Japanese officials used to test the sincerity of Japanese who claimed they were not Christian. The images were placed on the ground, and the person in question was ordered to step on a sacred Christian image, such as that of Christ, the cross, or the Virgin Mary. Paper images were eventually replaced by more durable large copper medals. In addition, each family was required to register at a Buddhist temple, become a member of a Buddhist sect, and obtain a temple certificate.

The final blow for Japanese Christianity came in a series of edicts issued between 1633 and 1639, resulting in the closing of Japan to the outside world, with the exception of the Dutch, who were required to live on Deshima, a man-made island in Nagasaki harbor. The Japanese allowed some Koreans and Chinese to continue limited trade. In 1640, a Christian Suppression Office was established (*Kirishitan Shumon aratame-yaku*) by order of the shōgun. The Japanese feared not only Christianity, but the takeover of Japan by Western powers as well.

In 1614, scholars believe, there were approximately 300,000 Christians in Japan. By the time of the final *sakoku* (closed country) edict, only 150,000 Christians remained. These persons were the original *kakure kirishitan* (hidden Christians), who attempted to keep the faith alive underground. The majority of these Japanese were peasants, merchants, and artisans.

One of the most dramatic events that led to the closed country edict was the Shimabara Rebellion, which raged from 1637 to 1639. The *bakufu* government called this conflict a Christian rebellion because many of the participants were Christian. In fact, scholars have shown that the conditions in the area for the inhabitants of Shimabara and Amakusa were actually terribly difficult due to the inhumane treatment by the leaders of the area and a severe series of crop failures.

No matter the cause, the result of the ban was severe repression of Christianity, and the closure of Japan to the outside world, until the mid-19th century. What Christianity survived was carried out underground with practices that were camouflaged with a veneer of Shintō, Buddhist, or folk ceremony.

*Ann M. Harrington*

**See also:** Dutch on Deshima; Shimabara Rebellion; Tokugawa *Bakufu* Political System; Toyotomi Hideyoshi.

### Further Reading

Fujita, Neil S. *Japan's Encounter with Christianity: The Catholic Mission in Pre-modern Japan*. New York: Paulist Press, 1991.

Harrington, Ann M. *Japan's Hidden Christians*. Chicago: Loyola University Press, 1993.

Jennes, Joseph. *A History of the Catholic Church in Japan from Its Beginnings to the Early Meiji Era, 1549–1871*. Revised ed. Tokyo: Oriens Institute for Religious Research, 1973.

Ward, Haruko Nawata. *Women Religious Leaders in Japan's Christian Century, 1549–1650*. Burlington, VT: Ashgate, 2009.

## Civilization and Enlightenment
*See Bunmei kaika.*

## Civil Wars (1467–1570), Causes

The era 1467–1570 is given the name *Sengoku* ("Warring States") to mimic those periods of civil war between dynasties in Chinese history. The period began with the Ōnin War (1467–1477) when two rival military houses, the Hosokawa and the Yamana, battled for a decade for the right to name and control the heir to the Ashikaga *bakufu*. Although the period was characterized by almost constant civil war between the semi-independent warlords (*daimyō*, which means something like "famous name"), there was technically a "national" government still in Muromachi, a section of Kyoto. The *bakufu* founded by Ashikaga Takauji in the 1330s had fallen upon hard times. In fact, it was only marginally better off than the emperor's court, for which the *bakufu* nominally served as military deputy. As the *bakufu* weakened, it could no longer hold together the coalition of vassal-led armies that had once kept the peace.

New military leaders rose up to wrest power from their ancestral warlords. New coalitions were formed and dissolved virtually overnight. Old feudal bonds and obligations broke down rapidly as the new *daimyō* began to carve out their own spheres of power. The period is also called the *Gekokujo* ("rule of superiors by inferiors") era, in recognition of the upheaval that occurred as old leaders were conquered by their former vassals.

To better defend their agricultural lands, the *daimyō* lured their own vassal samurai into castles built to concentrate their defenses. To feed this burgeoning army in the castles, *daimyō* lured merchants and artisans to settle around the castles. The sprawling cities (*jokamachi*) that grew around the castles spawned new markets and neighborhoods where craftsmen produced all the materials needed by feudal warriors. The *jokamachi* merchants formed supply networks that cut across old military alliances. In turn, these long-distance commercial lines forced a change in the methods of trade and exchange. The old barter systems became cumbersome and costly, so some of the larger merchant alliances began to issue their own paper money when the available Chinese coins could no longer service the trade.

Among those who benefited most from this new trade within and between these burgeoning castle towns were the various Buddhist temples around the country. Several became feudal powers unto themselves.

They had acquired large tracts of land—some from pious legacies, others through usurious money lending and pawn brokering methods. Several temples became such financial powerhouses that they maintained large militias of "warrior monks" (*sōhei*) to protect their holdings. A loose coalition of Buddhist Pure Land lay organizations in the center of the country also fielded large self-governing armies (*ikkō*) that defended their territories ferociously. This proved to be their undoing during the period, however, as several *daimyō* coveted their accumulated wealth.

Almost continual civil war ravaged the country for nearly a century until a trio of powerful and cunning men managed to bring all of the warring parties together into another *bakufu*.

*Louis G. Perez*

**See also:** Ashikaga Takauji; Civil Wars (1467–1570), Consequences; Civil Wars, Sengoku Era (1467–1570); Muromachi *Bakufu*; Ōnin War; Warrior Monks.

**Further Reading**

Hall, John Whitney. "Foundations of the Modern Japanese Daimyō." *Journal of Asian Studies* 20, no. 3 (May 1961): 317–329.

Lorimer, Michael James. *Sengokujidai: Autonomy, Division and Unity in Later Medieval Japan*. London: Olympia Publishers, 2008.

## Civil Wars (1467–1570), Consequences

The era 1467–1570 is given the name *Sengoku* ("Warring States") to mimic those periods of civil war between dynasties in Chinese history. Almost continual civil war ravaged the country for nearly a century until a trio of powerful and cunning men

managed to bring all of the warring parties together into another *bakufu*. This consolidation took nearly 30 years to achieve and involved many short-lived coalitions and treacheries. The three men hailed from the same area around present-day Nagoya. The first, Oda Nobunaga, had been feudal overlord to Toyotomi Hideyoshi, and the last, Tokugawa Ieyasu began his career as hostage to Nobunaga.

The period ended (at least for historians) with the capture and murder of the last Ashikaga shōgun by Nobunaga in 1570, but the endemic civil war continued until Ieyasu won a conclusive battle of coalitions at Sekigahara in 1600. Once in titular control of the coalition of *daimyō*, Ieyasu established the *bakufu* that was to last almost three centuries. When he took the title *Sei-itai-shōgun* ("barbarian-subduing generalissimo") in 1603, Ieyasu crafted a complex political system called *bakuhan* by many historians. The name implies a combination of the traditional *bakufu* and the *daimyō* landholdings called *han*.

Ieyasu and his heirs divided the country into a checkerboard of han, each balanced and checked by others. His extensive family (*shimpan*) controlled roughly 30 percent of the arable land, and their holdings were placed strategically next to those of his erstwhile enemies (*tozama*), who controlled almost 40 percent of the land. His long-time lieutenants (*fudai*) received tracts of land totaling the remaining 30 percent and were placed astride the three main roads leading to Ieyasu's capital of Edo (present-day Tokyo). The *fudai* also served as rotating officers within the *bakufu* administration.

All *daimyō* served at the pleasure of the shōgun, but in reality Ieyasu and his heirs rarely interfered with the local *daimyō* administration as long as they remained peaceful. In the first few decades of the *bakufu*, a few *daimyō* were forced to resign in favor of their heirs, and a few were forced to relocate their holdings, exchanging han with another *daimyō*. These two actions were taken to make examples of troublesome *daimyō*, but did not reoccur very often.

The shōgun also controlled these 270-some *daimyō* by forcing them to spend half of their careers in attendance in Edo, and the other half back at their home castles. Their immediate families were required to stay in Edo as hostages. This system called "alternate attendance" (*sankin kōtai*) forced huge expenditures on the *daimyō* because they had to maintain a suitable residence in Edo as well as their own castle towns. They were also compelled to undertake large-scale public improvements such as seawalls, roads, drainage canals, and the transportation of hardwoods and construction materials to repair Tokugawa castles. They were allowed one castle of their own, but had to obtain permission to repair it from the shōgun himself.

The *bakufu* controlled the major port cities of Osaka, Nagasaki, and Sendai. They also seized all silver, copper, gold, iron, and coal mines as well as the major hardwood forests and stone quarries. The *bakufu* kept the imperial house under close surveillance and denied all requests by *daimyō* to visit the ancient capital unless escorted by *bakufu* guards. The one-time large Buddhist temple complexes were stripped of their *sohei* warrior monks and their landholdings reduced severely to what could barely maintain the few priests that were allowed.

Because the Portuguese and Spaniards had caused Ieyasu many sleepless nights, he got rid of them and began two centuries of persecution of Christian converts in the country. He hedged Toyotomi Hideyoshi's heir Hideyori about with spies until the young man was forced to commit suicide, ending a brief rebellion of Ieyasu's allies at Osaka in 1614–1615.

Historians claim that most of these seemingly paranoid feudal controls were foisted upon Ieyasu by his long experience in the Sengoku civil wars. He was powerful enough to require these checks and balances, but not powerful enough to rid himself of his enemies. He sought to balance and nullify the powers ranged against him; his heirs continued these controls. In fact, they went beyond his system when they secluded the country (*sakoku*) in 1640, allowing only a few Dutch, Chinese, and Korean traders to come to Nagasaki and no Japanese to leave the country upon pain of death.

*Louis G. Perez*

**See also:** Civil Wars (467–1570), Causes; Civil Wars, Sengoku Era (1467–1570); Oda Nobunaga; *Sakoku*; *Sankin kōtai*; *Sōhei*; Tokugawa Ieyasu; Toyotomi Hideyoshi.

**Further Reading**

Bolitho, Harold. *Treasures Among Men: The Fudai Daimyō in Tokugawa Japan*. New Haven: Yale University Press, 1974.

Totman, Conrad. *Politics in the Tokugawa Bakufu, 1600–1843*. Cambridge, MA: Harvard University Press, 1967.

# Civil Wars, Sengoku Era (1467–1570)

Japan's Sengoku era, also known as the Warring States period, generally designates the period between the start of the Ōnin War in 1467 and the Battle of Sekigahara in 1600. This era encompasses the last century of the Muromachi period (1336–1573) and the Azuchi-Momoyama period (1573–1600). This anarchic period in Japanese history is notable for the collapse of the Ashikaga shōgunate; the resulting breakup of Japan into independent, warlord-run domains; and near-continuous warfare among the feudal lords.

The origins of the Sengoku era can be traced back to the conditions under which the Ashikaga shōgunate was established. This shōgunate was established during the War Between the Northern and Southern Courts (1336–1392), a civil war between supporters of Emperor Go-Daigo and his line (the Southern Court) and the Ashikaga shōgunate and its hand-chosen emperor (the Northern Court). To maintain authority during the war, the shōgunate relied on provincial governors (shugo), who were granted autonomy and wide-ranging powers in their jurisdictions, such as the ability to confiscate land. This relatively dependent position of the shōgunate vis-à-vis the provincial governors laid the foundation for the breakup of Japan into the independent domains of the Sengoku era.

After the death of the third Ashikaga shōgun, Yoshimitsu (1358–1408), a series of ineffective shōguns weakened the personal power of the shōgun. Infighting between governors serving in positions in the shōgunal administration spread, while those governors outside of central Japan began paying less heed to the shōgunal authority in Kyoto. The infighting erupted into the Ōnin War in 1467, whereupon the shōgun retreated from his duties in Kyoto and the warring parties ravaged the city.

Many of the governors who served in the shōgunate eventually began making their way back to their home provinces, only to find their authority usurped by their deputy governors (shugo-dai), vassals, or independent samurai (jizamurai). Other vassals split off from their lords to become independent rulers. As the locus of power diffused to the provinces, the number of independent warlords increased to well over 200.

The new provincial rulers were known as the Sengoku daimyō. They were new in the sense that their authority derived from neither the emperor nor the shōgunate, but rather from their own personal military power and the ruling structures they created to establish legitimacy. Each daimyō naturally needed military power, but many also saw the need for legal structures. Many warlords thus created law codes for their vassals and their domain's inhabitants. These law codes provided for a nominal monopoly on the use of coercion within their domains while also recognizing the existence of other domains, making Sengoku Japan similar to a small multistate system.

Daimyō houses in central Japan, primarily the Hosokawa and Miyoshi clans, continued to fight for control over Kyoto and the remnants of the powerless shōgunate. They exiled and appointed their own puppet shōguns at will, but they held no authority over other daimyō.

The frequent vacuums of power and constant warfare sometimes led to peasant uprisings known as ikki. In certain instances, these ikki, in concert with Buddhist militants or independent samurai, were able to accomplish self-rule in their areas. The most impressive example of such an arrangement occurred in Kaga Province on the Japan Sea coast, in which an ikki led by the True Pure Land Buddhist sect (Ikkō ikki) conquered and ruled the entire province.

In the mid-16th century, there emerged a group of "great power" warlords, who created superior military organizations and were able to substantially expand their territories at the expense of their weaker neighbors. Examples of such powerful daimyō houses include the Uesugi, Takeda, and Go-Hōjō clans in the east, and the Mōri, Shimazu, and Ōtomo clans in the west.

These warlords all had important roles in the unification campaigns of the last three decades of the 16th century.

The unification campaigns were driven by three warlords: Oda Nobunaga (1534–1582), Toyotomi Hideyoshi (1536–1598), and Tokugawa Ieyasu (1542–1616). From 1568 until 1582, Nobunaga fought relentlessly against the Takeda, Uesugi, and Mōri clans, the Ikkō *ikki*, and several smaller clans. He came to control most of central Japan at the time of his death. His general and successor Hideyoshi pacified the remaining warlords and brought all of Japan under his rule in 1590. Then, two years after Hideyoshi's death in 1598, Nobunaga's old ally Ieyasu fought the final campaign of the Sengoku era, defeating his rivals at the Battle of Sekigahara. He established the long-lasting Tokugawa shōgunate in 1603.

*Philip Streich*

**See also:** Oda Nobunaga; Ōnin War; Sekigahara, Battle of; Takeda Shingen; Tokugawa Ieyasu; Toyotomi Hideyoshi.

## Further Reading

Asao Naohiro, "The Sixteenth-Century Unification," in *The Cambridge History of Japan. Vol. 4: Early Modern Japan*, edited by J. W. Hall. New York: Cambridge University Press, 1991:40–95.

Berry, Mary Elizabeth. *The Culture of Civil War in Kyoto*. Berkeley: University of California Press, 1994.

Berry, Mary Elizabeth. *Hideyoshi*. Cambridge, MA: Harvard University Press, 1982.

Lamers, Jeroen. *Japonius Tyrannus: The Japanese Warlord Oda Nobunaga Reconsidered*. Leiden, Netherlands: Hotei Publishing, 2000.

Sansom, George. *A History of Japan, 1334–1615*. Stanford: Stanford University Press, 1961.

## Cloister Government (*Insei*)

A cloister government (*insei* is a system of government (*sei*) in which a retired emperor, rather than the reigning emperor, exercised power from his monastery or cloister (*in*). The practice of retired emperors making political decisions for the reigning emperor, especially when he was a minor, already existed in the Nara period (710–794). Nevertheless, it was Emperor Shirakawa (1053–1129, reign 1073–1087) who was the first retired emperor to wield actual power upon his abdication by creating a separate political center in the Cloister Office (*In no Chō*). The *insei* system was politically dominant from 1087 until the establishment of the warrior government in 1192, and was resurrected intermittently until 1840.

Shirakawa's father, Emperor Go-Sanjō (1034–1073, reign 1068–1073), is credited for paving the way for the *insei*, although he did not live to see its establishment. Go-Sanjō chose to retire early so that he could free himself from the political influences of the Fujiwara regent (*sesshō* or *kampaku*). During the Heian period (794–1185), the northern branch of the Fujiwara family exerted much political influence in the imperial court by marrying their daughters into the imperial family and assuming the office of the regent to the emperor. In other words, the Fujiwara patriarch was often the maternal grandfather, uncle, or father-in-law of the emperor. Emperor Go-Sanjō, however, was an exception—his mother was not a Fujiwara. With his weak Fujiwara connection, he was less affected by the domineering forces of the Fujiwara regency. As long as he was the reigning emperor, however, he could not entirely avoid such influence. Eventually, he decided to abdicate the throne early, hoping to reassert imperial rule in his retirement without Fujiwara influence, but he died too soon to realize his plan.

It was Shirakawa who established the *insei* after he passed his throne to his son Horikawa (1079–1107, reign 1087–1107) in 1087. Taking Buddhist vows, Shirakawa ruled the country from his Cloister Office for more than 40 years, expanding its authority and functions. The prestige of the Cloister Office, which was staffed with capable non-Fujiwara administrators and clerks, came from two sources. First, the retired emperor exerted patriarchal authority on his son or grandson, who was the reigning emperor. In this way, the retired emperor bypassed the traditional court and bureaucracy in ruling the country. His edicts were regarded as more authoritative than imperial edicts. Second, the prestige of the Cloister Office came from its growing economic and military influence. In theory, the reigning emperor owned all the land in Japan, but in reality he did not have personal access to the resources from the land, nor did he keep a standing army. In contrast, through the Cloister Office, whose activities were not constrained by the rules applied to the imperial court, the retired emperor continued to amass private landholdings in various provinces and hired samurai to manage and protect his lands. As a result, the retired emperor had direct access to considerable military and economic resources.

Because an emperor could gain financial and political independence by abdicating his throne, a number of emperors followed in Shirakawa's footsteps by retiring early during their prime. Therefore, at any one point in time, it was possible for two retired emperors to coexist. For example, in 1123, while Shirakawa was the retired emperor, the reigning emperor Toba (1103–1156, reign 1107–1123) decided to pass his throne to his young son Sutoku (1119–1164, reign 1123–1142), becoming a retired emperor himself. From 1123 until the death of Shirakawa in 1129, both Shirakawa and Toba were the retired emperors. The senior retired emperor (*hon'in*)—in this case, Shirakawa—was the one who exercised real power, although the junior retired emperor also had considerable influence. A similar scenario took place again in 1142, when Sutoku passed his throne to his son Konoe (1139–1155, reign 1142–1155). Between 1142 and 1155, both Toba and Sutoku were the retired emperors, with Toba being the senior.

Multiple abdications soon created tensions between retired emperors when they all sought to exert influence on the reigning emperor. This was the case between retired emperors Toba and Sutoku, for example. Both wanted to control the young Emperor Konoe. When Konoe died in 1155 at the age of 16, their tension escalated as they argued over who should succeed Konoe. Finally, despite Sutoku's objection, his younger brother Go-Shirakawa (1127–1194, reign 1155–1158) succeeded to the throne. Sutoku had wanted his own son to be the next emperor, so that he could control the imperial court much more easily. Now that Go-Shirakawa was the emperor, Sutoku's authority was seriously challenged.

In 1156, when Toba died, his sons, Sutoku and Go-Shirakawa, continued their family feud, which led to the Hōgen Civil War. The rivals sought support from both the aristocracy and provincial warrior leaders. The major warrior families, Taira and Minamoto, became involved in the armed conflicts in the capital city of Kyoto. The war resulted in the exile of Emperor Sutoku to Shikoku Island. Go-Shirakawa emerged victorious, but he, too, chose to abdicate early in 1158. From then until 1192, Go-Shirakawa continued to wield actual power throughout the reigns of five successive emperors.

The *insei* system had a number of repercussions. First, it significantly eroded the power of Fujiwara regents. Second, it led to the further privatization of public land by retired emperors and other court aristocracies. Third, because retired emperors relied on samurai for protecting their interests, the *insei* system encouraged the rise of local warrior families such as the Taira and Minamoto. A number of armed conflicts similar to the Hōgen War would eventually allow the samurai to gain further power. In 1193, the Kamakura *bakufu* (or shōgunate) was established by the Minamoto clan, thereby ushering in the age of warrior rule.

*Yu Chang*

**See also:** Fujiwara Family; Hogen-Heiji-Gempei Wars; Kamakura *Bakufu*.

### Further Reading

Hall, John W. *Government and Local Power in Japan, 500–1700: A Study Based on Hizen Province*. Princeton: Princeton University Press, 1966; Ann Arbor, MI: University of Michigan Press, 1999.

Hurst, G. Cameron III. *Insei: Abdicated Sovereigns in the Politics of Late Heian Japan*. New York: Columbia University Press, 1976.

## Colonization of Hokkaidō

Hokkaidō did not become part of Japan until the late 19th century. Hokkaidō was first mentioned, as Watarishima, in the account of an expedition against the Emishi in 658 in *Nihon shōki*, Japan's oldest official history, completed in 720. It was not until the Kamakura period, however, that Japanese frontier reached the northern tip of Honshū. Even before then, though, the Japanese had been trading with the Emishi aborigines, known as Ezo, from the 12th century. They provided timber, fur, and sea products for the Japanese; in return, the Ezo received products of more advanced civilizations, such as iron, lacquerware, and silk. From the 1310s, the port of Tosaminato in the northwest tip of Honshū began to serve trade with the Ezo in Hokkaidō. By the middle of the Muromachi period, a settlement in southern Oshima Peninsula was created by the Japanese, among whom were retainers of powerful clans in Northern Honshū who were appointed the middlemen of Ezo trade. Twelve trading posts (*dōnan jūni tate*) were built along the southern coast of Oshima Peninsula as administrative centers of these retainers, who were known as *wataritō*, or "those who crossed the Tsugaru Strait." The large influx of Japanese into Hokkaidō and their unfair business threatened the livelihood of the Ezo, triggering numerous revolts against the Japanese.

Things changed with Kakizaki Yoshihiro (1548–1616), who was given the grant of a special fief—the exclusive right to Ezo trade—from Toyotomi Hideyoshi (1593) and Tokugawa Ieyasu (1604). Yoshihiro changed his family name to Matsumae in 1599 and founded the Matsumae domain in southwest Oshima Peninsula.

Unlike in any other domain in the Edo period, the salary of Matsumae retainers was not paid with land with a yield of rice—Hokkaidō climate does not allow rice growing and Matsumae domain did not own the rest of Ezo land—but rather by grant of the right to certain Ezo trade markets from which to gain profits (*akinaiba chigyō sei*). To the Ezo, also known as Ainu now, this system meant that their free trade with any Japanese became restricted first to Matsumae domain and then to designated markets, at rates out of their control. To make things worse, Matsumae retainers were poor managers: being samurai, they eventually rented their markets to shrewd and greedy merchants from Honshū (*basho ukeoi sei*). This practice gradually turned the Ainu from trade partners to laborers bound to the markets, leading to Ainu bitterness and uprisings against the Japanese.

In the mid-18th century, the Russian Empire began to expand eastward, reaching the Kuril Islands in 1750s. Perceiving the Russian ambition, the Tokugawa *bakufu* took Hokkaidō under its direct control in 1799–1821 and again from 1855 until the end of the Tokugawa regime.

During the Meiji Restoration, some pro-shōgunate forces led by Enomoto Takeaki (1836–1908) escaped to Hokkaidō and proclaimed its independence as the Republic of Ezo. Their resistance was crushed in May 1869 by Meiji government troops. In the same year, the Japanese name Hokkaidō was adopted, for the first time, to replace Ezochi ("land of the Ezo"), the premodern name of the island. The Colonization Commission (*kaitakushi*) was also created that year, beginning a period of rapid modernization of the island. Massive numbers of Japanese immigrants rushed in, roads were built, ports were constructed, and forests were burned down to create farmland. The Ainu, uprooted from their land, became farmers or laborers living on their wages. Moreover, in 1899, a law of national assimilation, in the name of protecting the Ainu (*Hokkaidō kyūdojin hogo hō*), was imposed upon them, officially taking Ainu land from them, banning hunting and fishing as a way of their life, banning Ainu customs, and forcing them to adopt Japanese language and Japanese names. In 1947, Hokkaidō acquired equal status as other prefectures in Japan, but the fight of the Ainu for their rights never stopped—as seen, for example, in the abolition of the 1899 law and the adoption of the Ainu Culture Revitalization Law (*Ainu bunka shinkō hō*), both in 1997.

*Guohe Zheng*

**See also:** Ainu, Military Resistance to; Tokugawa Ieyasu; Toyotomi Hideyoshi.

**Further Reading**

Howell, David L. *Geographies of Identity in Nineteenth-Century Japan*. Berkeley, CA: University of California Press, 2005.

Irish, Ann B. *Hokkaidō: A History of Ethnic Transition and Development on Japan's Northern Island*. Jefferson, NC: McFarland & Company, 2009.

Miyajima, Toshimitsu. *Land of Elms: The History, Culture, and Present Day Situation of the Ainu People*. Etobicoke, ON: United Church Publishing House, 1998.

Walker, Brett L. *The Conquest of Ainu Lands: Ecology and Culture in Japanese Expansion, 1590–1800*. Berkeley, CA: University of California Press, 2001.

## Colonization of Taiwan (1895–1945)

After the First Sino-Japanese War, Taiwan was officially ceded to Japan as part of the Treaty of Shimonoseki (1895). Initially, the native people did not readily surrender to the imposition of colonial rule, but instead continued to snipe at their new masters through guerrilla warfare. The Governor-General position was a political sinecure, so a succession of former bureaucrats and military men shuffled through the position, some of whom never actually resided on the island.

In 1898, Gōtō Shimpei was appointed Chief of Home Affairs. Gōtō was a politician who fancied himself a British-style enlightened colonial administrator. During his eight-year tenure, he instituted public institutions to foster education, transportation, communication, railways, sanitation, drainage, modern agriculture, public health, and other social reforms. His greatest accomplishment was to establish a sugar production system that nearly paid for the colonial administration.

Although some Japanese civilians came to the island, chiefly as bureaucrats and merchants, immigration was not really encouraged until after 1919, when prime minister Hara Takashi instituted a new colonial system. Hara believed that the native Taiwanese could be assimilated into the empire, so Japanese were encouraged to come to Taiwan to "civilize" the natives.

After 1937, the administration of Taiwan became increasingly harsher, as natives were required to speak Japanese in public and take Japanese names. Thereafter, the study of Chinese literature and history were forbidden. In 1943, Buddhism was discouraged and State Shintō became the official religion of the island. Many Taiwanese women were lured into prostitution to serve Japan's military. Many Taiwanese were drafted into the Japanese military, primarily as laborers, but some were formed into segregated combat units. From 1937 to 1945, some 126,750 Taiwanese joined and served in the military of the Japanese Empire, while a further 80,433 were conscripted between 1942 to 1945. Of the sum total, 30,304 (15 percent) died in Japan's war in Asia. Because Japan had established military bases on the island and built war materials factories there, Taiwan suffered from significant bombing by American forces during the later part of World War II.

With the surrender of Japan in August 1945, the island was occupied by Chinese Nationalist (Guomintang) forces. The island became the "temporary restaging area" for Jiang Jieshi's regime as it fled the mainland during the Chinese Civil War of 1947–1949. In 1949, Taiwan became part of Jiang's "government in exile" and has been established as the capital of the Republic of China.

*Louis G. Perez*

**See also:** Gōtō Shinpei; Hara Takashi; Jiang Jieshi (Ch'iang K'ai-shek); Shimonoseki Treaty; Sino-Japanese War; State Shintō.

### Further Reading

Ka, Chih-ming. *Japanese Colonialism in Taiwan: Land Tenure, Development and Dependency, 1895–1945.* Boulder, CO: Westview Press, 1995.

Takekoshi Yosaburo. *Japanese Rule in Formosa.* Taipei: Longman's Green and Company, 1997.

**Comfort bags.** *See* Senninbari

## Comfort Women

In the last decade of the 20th century, the world began to learn the tragic stories of some of the forgotten victims of World War II—the "comfort women." These women were forced into sexual servitude by the Japanese imperial army during the war. Although Japanese, Chinese, Taiwanese, Filipino, Indonesian, and Dutch women worked as comfort women, the majority—at least 80 percent—were Korean.

During World War II, more than 200,000 girls and women, ages 14 to 30, were conscripted from Japan's prewar colonies and occupied territories. They were sent to the front for the duration of the war, housed in brothels, and forced by the Japanese military into institutionalized sexual slavery on a massive scale. The women were originally called "voluntary corps." Later, the Japanese government coined the term "military comfort women." Historical documents found both in Washington, D.C., and Japan indicate that the procurement of comfort women was

Former South Korean comfort women, who were forced to serve for the Japanese Army as sexual slaves during World War II, shout slogans during a rally to demand an official apology and compensation from the Japanese government in front of the Japanese Embassy in Seoul, South Korea, October 19, 2011. (AP Photo/Ahn Young-joon)

institutionalized to prevent soldiers from raping local women, which would have encouraged local opposition; to protect soldiers from the spread of venereal disease; and to safeguard military secrets.

At the beginning of World War II, the Japanese army brought Japanese prostitutes to the front for the soldiers. (The institution of prostitution was not prohibited legally by Japan until 1957.) However, many of the women were already infected with venereal diseases and, in turn, infected the soldiers, which rendered them unfit for combat. Therefore, Japanese brokers recruited Korean village girls by offering money to their impoverished families.

Toward the end of the war, the supply of women was enlarged by more indiscriminate kidnapping of women, including married women. The Military Compulsory Draft Act (1943) allowed the Japanese

imperial army to take more women, and as many as 70,000 to 80,000 were sent as comfort women to work in "comfort stations" on the front lines in Asia. When the war was over, many of the comfort women were deserted by the Japanese army, while others were massacred. Some women committed suicide because they were unable to overcome the shame, and others lived in silence.

On December 6, 1991, three Korean comfort women filed suit demanding justice for the crimes against humanity committed against them. They demanded an official apology, compensatory payment, a thorough investigation of their cases, the revision of Japanese school textbooks identifying that issue as part of the colonial oppression of the Korean people, and the building of a memorial museum.

Eighteen former comfort women from the Philippines filed a class action suit in

April 1992. Subsequently, four more groups did the same. In December 1992, a public hearing was held in Tokyo at which former comfort women from six countries testified. One of the plaintiffs explained that her decision to finally disclose what had happened to her was prompted by the fact that because all her close family members had died, there was no one left who would be shamed because of her past.

On April 26, 2000, the Yamaguchi district court in southwestern Japan ruled that "the Japanese government which inherited Imperial Japan has the duty to make restitution for damage done in the war, in particular for the pain and suffering of the comfort women. Its failure to do this has resulted in increased pain suffered by victims. The comfort women system was sexual and racial discrimination, violating fundamental rights of women." The court ordered the Japanese government to pay 360,000 yen ($3,540) to each of the South Korean comfort women but said it could not direct government policy regarding the apology.

For 47 years, the Japanese government denied any role in the comfort women scheme. However, in January 1992, documents from Japan's defense agency's archives surfaced that directly linked the Japanese military with the brothels. In August 1993, the Japanese government admitted that Japanese military authorities were in constant control of women who were forced to provide sex for soldiers before and during World War II.

Since then, Japanese prime ministers have made personal apologies to the women, but they have not issued an official apology or set up an official compensation plan. They maintain that the violations against the rights of the comfort women were not in violation of the Japanese legal system existing at the time they were committed and that all claims for compensation for citizens of various countries have already been settled by virtue of the various treaties of peace with Japan negotiated after the war.

On March 26, 2007, Prime Minister Abe Shinzo, after first denying that women were forced into wartime prostitution, issued a public apology in which he acknowledged that he had been mistaken. Within a month the world responded. A number of parliamentary resolutions on behalf of the women were passed in the United States (April 26, 2007), Dutch Lower House (November 20, 2007), Canadian Lower House (November 28, 2007), and the European Parliament (December 13, 2007). The government of Japan has not responded to those resolutions.

*ABC-CLIO and Louis G. Perez*

### Further Reading

Tanaka, Yuki. *Japan's Comfort Women: Sexual Slavery and Prostitution During World War II and the US Occupation*. London: Routledge, 2002.

Wakabayashi, Bob Tadashii. "Comfort Women: Beyond Litigious Feminism." *Monumenta Nipponica* 58 (Spring 2003): 2.

## Continental Adventurers (*Tairiku Rōnin*)

It is difficult to understand the concept of *tairiku rōnin* (usually translated as "continental adventurers") without understanding the Pan-Asianism they espoused as a Japanese version of Western imperialist ideology demonstrated by concepts such as Rudyard Kipling's "white man's burden" and France's *mission civilisatrice*. Without such a comparison in mind, it may be difficult to make sense of the mixture of concern with the plight of colonized Asians and the Japanese nationalism that motivated them. For these people, as with many Japanese before 1945, defeat of the West and desire to liberate others became inextricably linked with an ideology of Japanese imperialism that conceptually disguised itself as an exploitation of overseas markets, resources, and people that rivaled that of the West.

*Tairiku rōnin* depended upon infrastructural support provided by political societies, the most important of which was the Gen'yō-kai (Dark Ocean Society), founded in 1881 by disgruntled former samurai led by Tōyama Mitsuru (1895–1944). The "Gen'yō" in the group's name referred to the Genkai Nada ("Dark Open Sea") that separated Tōyama's native northwestern Kyushu from Korea and the rest of Asia. By 1882, Tōyama was sending young men to China to facilitate what he regarded positive change. Gen'yōsha activists were involved in the prelude to the Sino-Japanese War, trying to provide a pretext for Japanese intervention that would challenge Chinese influence in Korea by inciting violence on the peninsula. Once the war began, Gen'yōsha members and other *tairiku rōnin* assassinated the Korean Queen Min, using extralegal means to help secure the beginnings of Japanese hegemony on the continent.

Originally affiliated with a movement seeking to expand the rights of "the people" in Japan during the 1880s, the Gen'yōsha, the groups it spawned, and the *tairiku rōnin* network it supported came to serve the national interests of Japan, a country they imagined as an organic totality untroubled internally by conflicting interests. They furthermore sought solutions for modernity's endemic problems such as the unequal distribution of wealth and power and racial discrimination across the planet in the panacea of Japanese-led development in Asia, where they challenged the dominance of the West and worked at toppling traditional regimes such as that of Qing China and the Joseon dynasty in Korea.

Prior to the 1904–1905 Russo-Japanese War, Geny'ōsha member Uchida Ryōhei made his home on the continent in Vladivostok, where he opened a martial arts academy. He also ran a *tairiku rōnin* network serving Japanese military forces in the context of the looming war with Russia. Like T. E. Laurence and British agents operating in India's hinterlands, *tairiku rōnin* "went native" to a remarkable degree. Uchida, for example, studied Russian and visited St. Petersburg before settling in Vladivostok. Uchida also founded the Kokuryūkai (Black Dragon or Amur River Society) in 1901. "Kokuryū," meaning "black dragon," is also the Chinese name for the river that forms much of the border between Russia and Manchuria. Chinese- and Korean-speaking *tairiku rōnin* organized by Uchida spied and scouted for the Japanese military in that border zone, posing as commercial photographers, Buddhist priests, barbers, tailors, martial arts instructors, and launderers.

In addition to the two organizations discussed previously, which supported and trained *tairiku rōnin*, state elements provided institutional backing for the continental adventurers' activities. For example, Konoe Atsumarō—an imperial prince and member of the House of Peers, who became that body's president in 1896—founded the Dōbunkai (Common Culture Association) in 1898, which evolved into the Tōa (East Asia) Dōbunkai later that year. The organization developed cultural policies and language skills meant to unify Japan with China. Konoe wanted Japanese who would work in Asia as *tairiku rōnin* to collaborate with Chinese in defeating what he called the "White Peril" of Western imperialism. Toward these ends, Konoe's society opened the Tōa Dōbunkai Shin in 1901, a school in Shanghai for Japanese persons studying Chinese language and culture.

In 1909, the Tōa Dōbunkai, the Kokuryū-kai, and the Gen'yōsha were also involved in founding the Ajia Gi Kai (Association for the Defense of Asia), which intended to improve relationships between anti-Western Muslims and the Japanese empire. Ajia Gi Kai founders included Tōyama and Uchida, as well as Russian Muslim activist Abdurre-şid İbrahim. While traveling to Istanbul soon after the founding of the Ajia Gi Kai, Ibrahim met Kokuryūkai member and Muslim convert Yamaoka "Omar" Kōtarō, and the two visited Mecca and Medina together, making Yamaoka the first known Japanese to do so. Later, Yamaoka lectured in Istanbul, made contacts with Chinese Muslims, and helped train Muslim Japanese agents such as Hadji Nur Tanaka Ippei. Yamaoka apparently saw no contradiction between serving Japan and sincerely embracing Islam.

Another semi-official support for *tairiku rōnin* was Ōkawa Shūmei's Shōwa Gogaku Kenkyūjo. Ōkawa was trained at Tokyo Imperial University in the Indian Studies. After his 1909 graduation, an encounter with Sir Henry Cotton's *New India or India in Transition* (1905)—an account of the British effect on contemporary India—caused him to repudiate his earlier cosmopolitanism in favor of pan-Asianism. In 1919, while working as a university lecturer and for the Tokyo Research Bureau of the South Manchurian Railway, Ōkawa went to Shanghai to recruit Kita Ikki, a *tairiku rōnin* who, as a Kokuryūkai affiliate, participated in China's 1911 Revolution. Together they formed the Yūzonsha (Survivors Society). Both went on to influence rebellious young military officers in the 1930s, until Kita's execution in 1937. Ōkawa's role in a 1932 coup attempt led a five-year prison sentence in 1935. He served only two years, however. By 1938, he had obtained

funding from the Manchurian Railway Company, the army, and the Foreign Ministry to run the Far East Asian Economic Research Bureau, which was simply known as the Ōkawa Juku (Ōkawa School). In a two-year program there, future *tairiku rōnin* studied either English or French, and an Asian language, including Hindi, Urdu, Thai, Malay, Arabic, Persian, or Turkish.

*Gerald Iguchi*

**See also:** Gen'yōsha Nationalism; Kita Ikki; Kwantung Army Adventurism (1926–1936); Pan-Asianism; Russo-Japanese War; Sino-Japanese War; Tōyama Mitsuru.

**Further Reading**

Aydin, Cemil. *The Politics of Anti-Westernism in Asia.* New York: Columbia University Press, 2007.

Esenbel, Selçuk. "Japan's Global Claim to Asia and the World of Islam: Transnational Nationalism and World Power, 1900–1945." *American Historical Review* 109, no. 4 (October 2004): 1140–1170.

Norman, E. Herbert. "The Genyōsha: A Study in the Origins of Japanese Imperialism." *Pacific Affairs* 17, no. 3 (September 1944): 261–284.

Siniawer, Eiko Maruko. *Ruffians, Yakuza, Nationalists: The Violent Politics of Modern Japan, 1860–1960.* Ithaca: Cornell University Press, 2008.

# Coral Sea, Battle of (May 7–8, 1942)

Following their successful attack on Pearl Harbor and early military triumphs in World War II, Japanese leaders were reluctant to continue with their original strategy of shifting to a defensive posture. They feared the adverse impact that such a change in strategy might have on their forces' fighting spirit and believed that it would work to

The aircraft carrier *USS Lexington* explodes at the Battle of the Coral Sea, one of several major naval battles of the Pacific Theater preceding the Battle of Midway. (Library of Congress)

Japan's disadvantage by allowing the Western powers time to regain their strength.

Japanese naval leaders, in particular, were anxious to occupy the Hawaiian Islands and Australia—the two chief points from which U.S. forces might mount offensive operations. U.S. carriers were operating out of Pearl Harbor, still the headquarters of the U.S. Pacific Fleet. If Japanese forces could take the Hawaiian Islands, it would be virtually impossible for the U.S. Navy to conduct long-range Pacific naval operations. Also, securing the islands to the north and east of Australia—the Solomons, New Caledonia, and Samoa—would enable the Japanese to establish bases to cut the Allied lifeline from the United States to Australia. Japanese long-range

bombers would then be able to strike targets in Australia itself, preparatory to an invasion and occupation of that continent.

The Japanese army was not enthusiastic about either proposal. Most of its assets were tied down in China, and the army continued to garrison Manchukuo. Invading Australia and occupying even the populated areas would require significant military resources that the army could not spare. Thus the Army Ministry and General Staff in Tokyo advocated holding the gains already achieved in the southern advance and shifting resources to China. The army formally vetoed the navy plan in early April 1942, but in effect, it was dead by the end of January of that year. Japanese navy leaders hoped, however, that a success either eastward toward Pearl Harbor or southwest toward Australia might overcome army opposition.

Admiral Yamamoto Isoroku and the Combined Fleet Staff favored taking Midway Island, 1,100 miles west of Pearl Harbor, as a preliminary step to invading Hawaii. Yamamoto expected this move would provoke a strong U.S. naval reaction, enabling him to set a trap for and destroy the U.S. aircraft carriers. The Japanese Naval Staff, however, preferred the southeasterly drive to isolate Australia. By the end of March, the Japanese had already advanced from Rabaul into the Solomon Islands and along the northern coast of New Guinea. The Japanese Imperial General Staff searched for a strategy to follow up their successes. Initially, the Naval General Staff favored assaulting Australia, fearing an Allied buildup there might lead to a counteroffensive against the Japanese defensive perimeter. The army rejected an Australian operation because of the long distances involved, insufficient troops, and inadequate transportation. In January 1942, both army and navy agreed on a less demanding joint invasion of Lae and Salamaua in New Guinea; the seizure of Tulagi in the Solomons; and the capture of the Australian base of Port Moresby in Papua, New Guinea.

On March 8, 1942, American carriers, sent to beleaguer the Japanese base at Rabaul northeast of New Guinea, interdicted Japanese landing operations at Lae and Salamaua on the Papuan peninsula of eastern New Guinea. Two carrier task forces sailed into the Gulf of Papua on the opposite side of the peninsula. Together, on the morning of March 10, they sent 104 aircraft across the high Owen Stanley Mountains to emerge undetected and find Japanese ships discharging troops and supplies at the two villages. The attacking American aircraft sank three Japanese ships, including the converted light cruiser *Kongo Maru*, at a cost of only one plane and one aviator lost.

The action caught the Japanese by surprise and convinced them that conquest of New Guinea would have to be postponed until they could secure fleet carriers for protection. That opportunity came only after the return of the carriers from the Japanese raids into the Indian Ocean.

In early April 1942, the attention of the Imperial Naval General Staff was on southeast operations (seizure of strategic points in New Guinea, New Caledonia, the Fiji Islands, and Samoa) to isolate Australia. However, the April 1942 (Doolittle) raid on Tokyo refocused their attention on the destruction of the U.S. carriers and forced an earlier date for the Tulagi and Port Moresby operations, with the New Caledonia, Fiji, and Samoa operations to follow after Midway.

The Japanese broke their forces into five groups: two invasion groups to land army and naval forces at Tulagi and Port Moresby; a support group to establish a seaplane base in the Louisiade Archipelago off New Guinea; a small covering group with the light carrier *Shoho*; and the main striking force of two fleet carriers, *Shokaku* and *Zuikaku*, plus escorts. This striking force was to support both landings and protect the entire force from American carriers.

At Pearl Harbor, the Americans determined from intercepts that the Japanese would probably attack Port Moresby on May 3. On April 29, the *Yorktown* group was ordered to operate in the vicinity of the Coral Sea beginning on May 1. The *Lexington* group and the American-British-Dutch-Australian Command (ABDACOM) combined naval force of two Australian cruisers, the American heavy cruiser *Chicago*, and two U.S. destroyers were also placed under that tactical command. The two carrier groups formed Task Force 17 (TF 17) when they rendezvoused on May 1 some 250 miles off the New Hebrides. While the *Lexington*'s group refueled, the *Yorktown*'s group sailed north on May 2 to reconnoiter, having received reports of approaching Japanese naval forces.

On May 3, the Japanese Tulagi invasion group began landing forces without opposition. Learning of the landings, the Americans decided to strike Tulagi the next morning without waiting for the *Lexington* to join them. The commander sent his fleet oiler and its escorts to order them to join him 300 miles south of Guadalcanal on May 5. The *Yorktown* then closed on Tulagi undetected on May 4 and launched three air strikes that met little resistance. The Japanese carrier striking force had been delayed and was nowhere near Tulagi. Inexperienced as they were, the American attackers were ineffective, only damaging a destroyer to the point that it had to be beached and sinking three small minesweepers and four landing barges. They also shot up some grounded aircraft. Nevertheless, even this small success was enough to send the rest of the Tulagi force steaming back to Rabaul.

Withdrawing southward, on May 5, TF 17 then moved northwest, expecting to catch Japanese forces as they emerged from the Jomard Passage into the Coral Sea. Although sightings were made by both sides on May 6, essentially ineffective reconnaissance led to little significant action by either party.

Before dawn on May 7, the opposing fleet carriers passed within 70 miles of each other. At dawn, both sides sent out search planes over the Coral Sea. The Japanese sighting of an American "carrier and cruiser" led to the sinking of the destroyer *Sims* and the severe mauling of the oiler *Neosho*. At about the same time, an American scout reported two Japanese carriers north of the Louisiades. After the *Lexington* and *Yorktown* launched their aircraft, they discovered that their forces had been sighted by a Japanese scout plane. The action prompted by the American sighting turned out to be a wild goose chase, but the *Lexington* and *Yorktown* pilots stumbled on the light carrier *Shoho* and sank her.

Early the next morning, the two carrier forces found each other. The American planes concentrated their attack on the fleet carrier *Shokaku* but hit the ship with just three bombs, causing only modest damage. The fleet carrier *Zuikaku* escaped attack by hiding in a rainsquall. The *Shokaku*'s damage was sufficient to prevent launch-and-recovery operations, and when the Americans withdrew, it turned north toward Japan.

Meanwhile, planes from the *Shokaku* and *Zuikaku* found the *Lexington* and *Yorktown*. Diving out of the sun, torpedo planes hit the *Lexington* twice on the port side, and dive-bombers scored two minor hits. The *Yorktown* was hit by only one bomb, which did no major damage. Confident they had sunk the *Saratoga*, the *Lexington*'s sister ship, and the *Yorktown*, the Japanese pilots withdrew. Neither ship sank, however, until gasoline vapors aboard the *Lexington* reignited fires that eventually became uncontrollable; as a result, the ship was abandoned and scuttled by torpedoes from a nearby destroyer.

Both sides hailed their achievements in the Coral Sea and scored themselves a win. Tactically, the Japanese came out ahead. The Americans were hurt most by the loss of the *Lexington*, one of its largest carriers, whereas the Japanese lost only the light carrier *Shoho* and suffered severe damage to the large carrier *Shokaku*. However, although the Japanese scored a tactical win, the Americans had finally blunted a Japanese offensive thrust, preventing the occupation of Port Moresby and thereby winning the strategic victory. In addition, significant losses in aircraft, aircrew, and repairs to the *Shokaku* prevented both Japanese carriers from taking part in the critical Battle of Midway a month later.

*Arthur T. Frame*

**See also:** Doolittle Raid; Tokyo Bombing; Yamamoto Isoroku.

### Further Reading

Hoyt, Edwin P. *Blue Skies and Blood: The Battle of the Coral Sea.* New York: S. Eriksson, 1975.

Millet, Bernard. *The Battle of the Coral Sea.* Annapolis, MD: Naval Institute Press, 1974.

Spector, Ronald H. *Eagle Against the Sun: The American War with Japan.* New York: Vintage Books, 1985.

## Corregidor, Battle of (April–May 1942)

Known officially as Fort Mills, Corregidor was the final bastion of U.S. and Filipino forces in the Philippines and the largest of the islands off the entrance to Manila. The island's chief installations included the post headquarters, a huge barracks, and coastal batteries. Contained within the tail of the island was a vast underground network known as Malinta Tunnel, which measured 1,400 feet in length and 30 feet in width, with twenty-five 400-foot laterals branching from it. The tunnel was the administrative and operational heart of the island fortress. Kindley Airfield was situated on the extremity of the tail on the second-highest point of the island. The island also had batteries with an array of eighteen 12-inch and 10-inch coastal guns and twenty-four 12-inch mortars, plus antiaircraft guns and machine-gun positions. Almost all of the armament on the island was obsolete in 1942, but as long as the troops on Corregidor held the island, they could effectively keep the Japanese fleet from using Manila Bay. This was the basic mission of the troops on Corregidor.

On the departure of General Douglas MacArthur and his staff to Australia, Major General Jonathan M. Wainwright assumed command of these forces beginning on March 12, 1942. The Japanese had bombed and shelled the island constantly since February. For 27 days, from April 9 to May 6, the Japanese forces daily increased the shelling. By May 5, the beach defenses had been destroyed, the huge seacoast guns had been silenced, and the antiaircraft batteries had been reduced to scrap. All wire communication had been destroyed, and every attempt to restore it failed. Even the geography of Corregidor had changed; the island lay scorched, leafless, and covered in the dust of thousands of explosions.

By the beginning of May, the 9,400 men on Corregidor knew a Japanese attack was imminent. The island's defenders had sustained 600 casualties since April 9, and those men who had not been injured were beginning to succumb to malnutrition and malaria. General Wainwright wrote on May 4 that there was only enough water to last for four days and that the fortress' power supply would only hold out for one week at most.

Late in the night of May 5, the long-awaited Japanese attack began, following a particularly intense artillery bombardment. Shortly before 10:00 p.m., as Japanese landing craft steamed toward the eastern end of the island, an order went out for all able-bodied troops to resist the landing.

The fight for Corregidor lasted only 10 hours. Japanese troops cut across the island, then turned west toward Malinta Tunnel. Most of the fighting during the night and the early morning of May 6 took place at Battery Denver, on a ridge near the east entrance of the tunnel. U.S. troops, including coast artillerymen and a battalion of 500 sailors, fought bravely. At 8:00 a.m., after the Japanese had taken tanks and artillery ashore for a frontal assault, General Wainwright committed the last of his reserves on the island. The final blow to the defenders came when the Japanese sent three tanks into the action. The first sight of armor panicked the defenders and caused some to flee from the lines.

By 10:00 a.m., the situation was critical, with the defenders having no means of stopping the Japanese tanks. Already, 600 to 800 U.S. troops had been killed, and another 1,000 were wounded. Every reserve had been thrown into the battle, and the Japanese had destroyed all defensive artillery. The Japanese were planning to mount an attack on the other side of the island and would reach Malinta Tunnel, which sheltered 1,000 wounded, in a few hours. Fearing a

slaughter, Wainwright decided to surrender. By 12:00 noon on May 6, all weaponry larger then .45 caliber had been destroyed; all codes, radio equipment, and classified materials had been burned; and the surrender message had been broadcast to the Japanese. The U.S. flag was lowered and burned, and a white flag was hoisted. Wainwright then communicated to President Franklin D. Roosevelt that he had made the decision to surrender. It had taken the Japanese five months to seize the island, instead of the two months they had originally estimated.

*Frank Slavin III*

**See also:** MacArthur, Douglas.

### Further Reading

James, D. Clayton. *The Years of MacArthur. Vol. 2: 1941–1945*. Boston: Houghton Mifflin, 1970.

Morton, Louis. *United States Army in World War II: The War in the Pacific—The Fall of the Philippines*. Washington, DC: Department of the Army, 1952.

# D

## Dōmei News Agency (Dōmei Tsūshinsha)

The Dōmei News Agency (*Dōmei Tsūshinsha*) was wartime Japan's national representative news agency from 1936 to 1945. It was formed through the merger of two major news agencies, *Nihon Denpō Tsūshinsha* (Japan telegraph news agency), popularly known as Denstū, and *Nihon Shinbun Rengō-sha* (associated press of Japan). It was to be the "ears and voice" of Japan as the nation's chief purveyor of international news. At its height, it maintained a news network throughout the Japanese empire and East Asia, as well as correspondents and bureaus in Europe, South America, and, prior to 1942, the United States. Its news reached the public through newspapers and other publications, radio, photographs, and newsreels. Originally Dōmei was intended to counter the British-dominated flow of international news in and out of Asia, but after the outbreak of war it became part of Japan's wartime media control.

Dōmei's origins begin in 1913 with the creation of the Kokusai (international) News Agency (*Kokusai Tsūshinsha*), Japan's first attempt to establish a national news agency. Its Japanese backers soon found their efforts hindered by the treaties made by the three major European news agencies: Reuters (Britain), Havas (France), and Wolff (Germany). In 1923, in an effort to strengthen Kokusai, the original director, former AP Tokyo correspondent John Russell Kennedy, was replaced by Iwanaga

Yūkichi, who made the creation of a "national representative news agency" his objective. In 1926, he oversaw the reorganization of Kokusai as *Nihon Shinbun Rengō-sha*, modeled along the lines of the United States' Associated Press (AP). Iwanaga also joined forces with AP general manager Kent Cooper to successfully overcome the strict control Reuters held on the flow of news within its news empire. These restrictions seriously limited Rengō's ability to distribute news outside Japan at a time when Japan was anxious to achieve a stronger international voice, especially in China and the United States.

To Iwanaga and his supporters, information was a vital weapon in a nation's arsenal; consequently, they urged the creation of a single news agency for Japan. From their point of view, this was how the major countries of the world operated, with Reuters, Havas, Wolff, and even AP representing their respective nations. In 1931, following the Manchurian Incident, the advocates for a Japanese national news agency urged the merger of Dentsū's news operations with Rengō. The merger was opposed by Dentsū's founder and president Mitsunaga Hoshirō and Dentsū's client newspapers, which had favorable news and advertisement contracts. Their resistance delayed the merger until 1936. While the two sides negotiated, Iwanaga, concerned about a news vacuum in Manchuria, successfully lobbied for the establishment of a national news agency in Manchuria. *Manshukoku Tsūshinsha* (Manchurian News Agency), known by its byline

*Kokutsu*, was organized in 1932 and became East Asia's first national representative news agency.

On January 1, 1936, Rengō was reorganized as Dōmei; in July, it was finally merged with Dentsū. The new agency was organized as a corporation of news companies, with Iwanaga as president to oversee day-to-day affairs. In July 1936, Dōmei had 187 member newspapers in Japan, Taiwan, and Korea, and two broadcast companies, making it the first news agency to include radio among its members. Besides providing the Japanese press with international news, Dōmei also collected and distributed domestic news among its member newspapers within the Japanese empire. As war spread from China into Southeast Asia, Dōmei established news bureaus throughout East Asia for the collection and dissemination of news, and the military gave it responsibility for developing Singapore and Malaysia's news media.

Iwanaga died unexpectedly in 1939 and was succeeded by Dōmei's vice president, Furuno Inosuke. By this time the original vision of a national news agency had become blurred with the growing authoritarianism of Japan's wartime regime. Any change in Dōmei's mission, however, should be traced to changes in circumstances and not necessarily leadership. Furuno was a career journalist who began as a copy-boy for Reuters and AP and later was a correspondent in China and London for Kokusai and Rengō. He also shared Iwanaga's commitment to a national news agency and lobbied vigorously for the creation of Kokusai, Rengō, Kokutsu, and Dōmei.

When the Pacific War ended in 1945, the Supreme Commander of the Allied Powers' (SCAP's) press restrictions, censorship of the Japanese press, and attitude toward Dōmei led Furuno to conclude that Dōmei's termination at the hands of SCAP was imminent. In October, Furuno authorized the self-liquidation of Dōmei to preserve the agency's surviving assets, which were divided between the new Jiji and Kyōdō news agencies.

*R. W. Purdy*

See also: Manchukuo; Occupation of Japan; World War II, Pacific Theater.

## Further Reading

Cooper, Kent. *Barriers Down*. New York: Farrar and Rinehart, 1942.

Purdy, R. W. "Fanning the Flames or Holding the Blaze at Bay? Furuno Inosuke and Japan's Wartime Press," in *Mutsu Munemitsu and Identity Formation of the Individual and the State in Japan*, edited by Louis G. Perez. Lewiston, NY: Edwin Mellen Press, 2001:266–286.

Purdy, R. W. "Nationalism and News: 'Information Imperialism' and Japan, 1910–1936." *Journal of American-East Asian Relations* (Fall 1992): 295–323.

## Doolittle Raid (April 18, 1942)

On April 18, 1942, 16 U.S. Army Air Forces (AAF) B-25 Mitchell bombers, launched from the aircraft carrier *Hornet*, bombed Tokyo and other Japanese cities. The aircraft were led by Lieutenant Colonel James ("Jimmy") Doolittle. Although the physical damage caused by the Doolittle raid was slight, the psychological and military impacts were considerable.

The original idea to launch twin-engine army bombers against Japan from a navy ship came from Captain Francis Low, a submariner on Chief of Naval Operations Admiral Ernest J. King's staff. The mission was planned at the highest levels and had the full support of President Franklin D. Roosevelt. Doolittle, the army liaison officer, secured command of the mission. He and his handpicked crews trained on short landing fields, but none had made a takeoff with a fully loaded aircraft from a carrier until the actual mission. The plan required each B-25 to drop 1 ton of bombs on its specified target; fly to Zhuzhou, China, to refuel; and then proceed 800 miles farther to Chungking. Unfortunately, the U.S. ships were spotted early by a Japanese picket boat.

Task force commander Vice Admiral William "Bull" Halsey decided to launch the aircraft about 200 miles early, 650 miles from the coast. Most of the planes dropped their loads, each consisting of two 500-pound high-explosive bombs and two 500-pound incendiary bombs, on Tokyo, although others hit Kobe, Yokohama, and Nagoya. The Americans were lucky in attacking soon after a practice air-raid drill, when defenses were relaxed.

The combination of the early launch, inaccurate maps, and the lack of a radio at Chuchow meant that the B-25s had no place to land. Most of the crews headed for friendly Chinese territory and bailed out or ditched, although one plane landed at Vladivostok (the crew was interned in the USSR). All of the planes were lost. Of the 80 crewmen, 3 were killed, 4 were seriously injured, 5 were interned, and 8 were captured by the Japanese. Of the latter group, 3 were executed after a show trial and 1 died in captivity. Their experience inspired the classic 1944 propaganda movie *The Purple Heart*. The Japanese also killed many thousands of Chinese in retaliation for the assistance given the crewmen who escaped.

Although bomb damage from the mission was insignificant, its results were important. President Roosevelt's announcement of the raid launched from "Shangri-La" (his mountain retreat in the Catoctin Hills of Maryland) boosted American morale, and the attack shocked the Japanese nation and embarrassed the government in Tokyo. The Japanese Supreme Command overreacted by assigning extra fighter groups to protect Japan and ordering the Chinese Expeditionary Army to root out enemy air bases there. Most important, the impact of the Doolittle raid allowed Admiral Yamamoto Isoroku to gain final approval for his operation to take the island of Midway and destroy the American carriers, setting the stage for the decisive Battle of Midway in June 1942.

*Conrad C. Crane*

**See also:** Midway, Battle of; Yamamoto Isoroku.

**Further Reading**

Doolittle, James H. *I Could Never Be So Lucky Again*. New York: Bantam Books, 1991.

Glines, Carroll V. *The Doolittle Raid: America's Daring First Strike against Japan*. New York: Orion, 1988.

Schultz, Duane. *The Doolittle Raid*. New York: St. Martin's Press, 1988.

# Dutch on Deshima (1641–1859)

The first Dutch factory was established in Japan in 1609 on Hirado, an island north of Nagasaki. Hirado was known for ceramics founded by Korean potters, whale oil, cattle, and a flourishing Jesuit mission. Increasing suspicion toward the motives of foreigners in Japan prompted the shōgunate to force the Dutch to move to the island of Deshima in 1641, the final phase of the *sakoku* ("closed country") edicts.

Deshima was a small, fan-shaped artificial island in the harbor of Nagasaki. In 1636, all Portuguese in Japan were forced to move behind its walls because Japanese anti-Christian policy conflicted with Portuguese practice that combined missionary activity with trade. When the Portuguese were banished in 1639 after the outbreak of the Christian-led Shimabara Rebellion, the buildings stood empty until the Dutch were ordered to move there in 1641.

The move came as a shock to the Dutch, who after a profitable year had built an expensive stone warehouse. The engraving of "anno Domini 1639" over the door was the thin excuse used to demolish the warehouse and isolate the Dutch traders. Deshima had only two entrances: a guarded bridge that connected to the port city of Nagasaki, and a water port where the long boats, gigs, and dinghies from the large ships would dock. The 1,850-square-foot island contained warehouses; offices for interpreters, inspectors, and officials; residences for the Dutchmen who stayed on the island year-round and their servants; housing for the captain of the trade vessels; a cook house; a bath house; and a garden.

The number of Dutchmen on Deshima varied, declining over time, from as many as 20 to as few as 8, reflecting the profitability of trade in Japan. These numbers swelled for the two or three months in which the ship was in port, but after the mid-17th century did not exceed 40 because the Japanese found it too difficult to control the rowdy sailors. Only upper-ranked officers were allowed ashore. In addition to the factory members, the Dutch usually brought perhaps half-dozen personal slaves, usually from Bengal or Java. Many Japanese also lived and worked on the island. Some were officials of the shōgunate, some local officials, and some day workers. A small population of Japanese prostitutes also worked on the island. (To ensure that the Dutchmen left regularly, they were forbidden from bringing women with them.) Initially these women had to leave daily, but over time they often stayed for extended periods, and close relationships were formed.

Although Deshima was walled, it was not actually a prison. The residents were allowed to take trips into town. They rarely availed themselves of this pleasure because these forays were quite expensive. The Dutchmen had to pay not only for themselves but also for an entourage of interpreters and bodyguards required to accompany them. Moreover, the factory head, the doctor, and a varying number of other officials had to take a trip each year until 1790 (thereafter reduced to once every four years because of declining profits) to pay their respects to the shōgun. The trip took about three months, and included official visits to the magistrates of Osaka and Kyoto. The factory members often took this opportunity to sightsee and enjoy local attractions such as the theater. Scholars of Western sciences (*rangaku*) visited the Dutchmen to ask questions.

For most of the 17th century, trade was profitable for both sides despite aggressive competition from Chinese traders after 1644, when the Qing removed trade restrictions. This trade was heavily based on export of precious and base metals. As the mines became depleted, the shōgunate initiated measures to further restrict trade. The Nagasaki *kaisho* (Dutch, *Geldkamer*) was established in 1698 to allow the shōgunate to control prices. Traders were required to sell their goods to the *kaisho* at set prices. Two years later, ships were limited to five a year, and then in 1715, to only two, although this quota was not strictly maintained.

Restricting bullion exports and ships slowly choked off trade because nothing else was as profitable for the East India Company. Some historians think the decline in Japanese copper sales caused the Dutch East India Company to go bankrupt in 1795. The Dutch government maintained the trading post on Deshima until 1859 in part out of national pride, but also because individuals profited from trade even when the government did not.

*Martha Chaiklin*

**See also:** *Sakoku*; Shimabara Rebellion.

## Further Reading

Blusse, Leonard, Willem Remmelink, and Ivo Smits, ed. *Bridging the Divide: 400 Years of the Netherlands and Japan.* Leiden: Hotei Publishing, 2000.

Chaiklin, Martha. *Cultural Commerce and Dutch Commercial Culture: The Influence of European Material Culture on Japan, 1700–1850.* Leiden: CNWS, 2003.

# E

## Early Meiji (1868–1890) Political Reforms

Although historians have tended to praise the vision, selflessness, and forward-looking policies of Meiji statesmen, their early reforms demonstrated profound fears. Their anxiety was not for the distant future, but about the recent past and the events that had culminated in their Tokugawa rival's destruction. Simply put, the samurai who took control of Japan in January 1868 had a tiger by the tail. The military toppling of the shōgunate happened perhaps faster than even the victors expected. It had merely required three bold steps: capturing the Kyoto Imperial Palace and compelling the 15-year-old Emperor to endorse the rebels' actions; mounting a lightning-fast coup d'état to stop the heart of Tokugawa rule in central Edo; and waging a slower but equally effective military campaign to pacify the Shōgun's few and generally isolated regional allies.

Within months of these acts, the imperial government stood "restored" and its young-ish leaders for the moment militarily unrivaled. The tottering old regime had been weakened internally by inflation, samurai radicals who used terror to degrade Tokugawa rule, and increasingly sharp intellectual attacks on its legitimacy. It had also been destabilized from without. In less than two decades, Western powers had saddled it with disadvantageous tariffs, aggressively forced open Japanese ports, and successfully secured residency and extraterritorial rights for foreigners, including widely despised Christian missionaries. Paradoxically, soon after the Meiji Restoration's onset, its leaders—men whose success resulted from the Tokugawa's internal collapse accelerated by external pressure—now found themselves faced with the same stubborn problems that had destroyed the regime from which they had snatched power. This dangerous context, one fraught with instability within Japan and the threat of external aggression, shaped the political reforms undertaken by the new Meiji leaders between 1868 and 1890. In the early 1870s, the inherited problems of economic instability and weak defenses soon led Tokyo's new leaders to announce an overarching national policy of "Rich Country, Strong Military" (fukoku-kyōhei). The slogan signaled a concerted drive to do whatever necessary to secure the fiscal resources required to run a state that simply had to be more centralized and united if it were to survive.

To assuage the Western powers and secure time to implement reforms, the Meiji Emperor's Five-Point Charter Oath (Gokajō no seimon) promulgated in March 1868 declared that "Knowledge would be drawn from throughout the world" to remedy the ills of the past. But the fundamental reforms to achieve "Rich Country" objectives first began at home. In 1869, the imperial government compelled daimyō lords to return their domains to the emperor's control. This single step channeled tax resources that had once been dispersed throughout the county into central coffers. This measure, together with the 1871 revision of the land tax that mandated a 3 percent assessment on the value of agricultural land to be paid by individually designated landowners, provided more than 70 percent of the national budget over the next several decades. Also in 1871, 72 new prefectures administered by a centrally appointed governor replaced the domains. This arrangement provided an enduring administrative structure that would continue to enable the Meiji state to tap regional resources and reallocate funds from the national funds as Tokyo's oligarchic leaders deemed appropriate.

Many *daimyō* lords, happy to be free of debt-ridden domains and well compensated with money and peerage honors for giving them up, did not resist these first centralizing administrative and fiscal reforms. The samurai and farming classes, however, suffered real declines in economic and social standing. Although national defense against Westerners was ever on the Meiji leaders' minds, the gradual elimination of warrior social privileges and rise in the number of impoverished landless farmers gave added domestic impetus for Meiji "Strong Army" policies. Ōmura Masujirō, a Chōshū samurai and the early Restoration's leading military reformer, first proposed universal conscription to create a truly national army as early as 1869. His recommendation earned him not praise but assassination at the hands of a fellow samurai. A version of his measure— hated by both peasants, who called it a "blood tax," and former warriors, who condemned it as another step in social leveling that usurped their role—nevertheless became law in 1873. The defeat of samurai forces at the hands of commoners in the Seinan War, a rebellion in 1877 led by Restoration's most famous military hero, Saigō Takamori, validated the "Strong Army" policy based on service by all classes.

The ability of the Meiji center to hold in 1877 deterred future military attempts to overthrow the nascent Tokyo government, but it also gave rise to new political challenges that shaped the direction of reforms during the 1880s. The rise of political parties, initially organized by and for disaffected samurai but soon joined by tens of thousands of farmers angered by new tax burdens and a lack of political representation, prompted the Meiji oligarchy to respond with "candy and whip" policies to resist a wider sharing of power. The candy came in the form of the 1881 central government announcement that it would promulgate a national constitution within a decade; the whip took the form of several new laws that limited freedom of speech, publication, and political party activities. Together these steps weakened the political parties. In strategic terms, they took away one of the new parties' most attractive features by usurping their promise of representative institutions. At the same time, the measures tactically frustrated the parties' ability to organize, publicize, and fund their organizations.

The nature of the Constitution of 1889, arguably the greatest political reform of the early Meiji decades, continues to be debated. As the first modern written constitution in Asia, it provided rule by law, a national assembly, voting rights, and other representative institutions and practices simply unprecedented outside the West. It also provided for rule by a legally transcendent emperor open to direct manipulation by a powerful military establishment that before 1945 contributed to social control and jingoism at home and aggressive expansionism abroad.

*Michael Lewis*

**See also:** Charter Oath; Meiji Constitution; Meiji Land Tax; Saigo Takamori; Seinan (Satsuma) Rebellion.

**Further Reading**

Jansen, Marius B. "The Meiji Restoration," in *The Cambridge History of Japan. Vol. 5: The Nineteenth Century*, edited by Marius B. Jansen. Cambridge, UK: Cambridge University Press, 1989.

Lewis, Michael. *Becoming Apart: Local Politics and National Power in Tōyama, 1868–1945*. Cambridge, MA: Harvard University Press, 2000.

## Early Mytho-histories: *Kojiki* and *Nihon shōki*

Japan's earliest "literary texts" are two mytho-histories composed in the early eighth century. *Kojiki* ("Record of Ancient Matters," 712) was commissioned by the Tenmu emperor (reign 672–686) and completed during the reign of Genmei (reign 707–715) by the scribe Ō no Yasumaro. *Nihon shōki* ("Record of Japan," 720) was probably commissioned and begun at the same time, but it was not completed until the reign of Genshō (reign 715–725). A later history credits Prince Toneri, a son of Tenmu, as the compiler of that work.

Both *Kojiki* and *Nihon shōki* include descriptions of the mythical origins of the islands of Japan, the natural world, and the early Japanese people. Its final focus is the genealogy of the royal family who served as consolidating power in the Yamato region at the time these works were written, which both works trace to the Sun Goddess, Amaterasu. Not many traces of writing can be found in Japan predating this period, and these two works are considered to be foundational texts in the development of written language in Japan as well as to represent its first histories.

*Kojiki* consists of three books, describing the creation of the land and the early generations of gods, the descent to earth of the first

sovereign, and the mostly legendary early generations of sovereigns. *Nihon shōki* comprises 30 volumes, and is far longer than *Kojiki*. Like *Kojiki*, it traces the ancestry of the legendary first ruler, Jimmu, directly back to Amaterasu. Where *Kojiki* ends its narrative with the Sovereign Suiko (reign 592–618), however, *Nihon shōki* traces the lineage up to the period of Tenmu and his wife and successor, Jitō (reign 687–696).

Although the works share a focus on origins and include many of the same myths, they embrace significantly different forms. *Kojiki*, whose preface claims that it is a faithful recording of ancient matters as narrated by a reciter known as Hieda no Are, is written in a style intended to evoke the reciter's voice. This hybrid style, as *manyōgana* (a term derived from the *Manyō'shū*, a near-contemporary poetry collection also using this style), utilizes Chinese characters sometimes for their sounds and sometimes for their meanings within any given text. This early attempt to render the sounds of spoken Japanese in writing was very cumbersome and became more or less incomprehensible to later generations. By contrast, *Nihon shōki* is written in Chinese. The use of Chinese and the adaptation of Chinese modes of historiography in *Nihon shōki* represented a form that would be adopted by five later histories; together, the *Nihon shōki* and its followers make up the *Rikkokushi* ("Six National Histories"). In contrast to *Kojiki*, whose use of *manyōgana* resulted in it being largely ignored until relatively modern times, the *Nihon shōki* was read, referred to, and interpreted throughout the classical and medieval ages.

*Kojiki* and *Nihon shōki* were both products of a nascent polity asserting its right to rule, but the different characteristics of the texts imply that the best method for doing so was very much a matter for debate. *Kojiki* recounts that the earliest motivator of creation was a spontaneous generative force, whereas *Nihon shōki* frames creation as the product of yin and yang working together—a distinctly continental interpretation of the origins of the world. While attributing the *Kojiki*'s account to native belief and *Nihon shōki*'s to Chinese influence is an oversimplification, the heavy reliance in *Nihon shōki* on Chinese forms is one of its defining characteristics. Another indication of Chinese influence is the multiple alternative versions of myths included in *Nihon shōki*, which suggests that it was in part an ethnographic project aimed at recording variant beliefs, even as it organized them under a master narrative centered on the ancestry of the royal family.

During the medieval period, the myths contained in *Nihon shōki* served as an important cultural reference point for historians and the writers of *gunki monogatari* ("war tales"). It was therefore vitally important for the warrior class as they thought and wrote about their origins and roles. *Kojiki*, in contrast, was not recovered until nativist scholar Motoori Norinaga (1730–1801) published his *Kojiki-den* ("*Kojiki* commentary"), in which he rendered the difficult writing system of the text into contemporary Japanese.

Norinaga's treatment of *Kojiki* as a pure, native expression of Japanese belief became increasingly popular as Japan was opened to the West. The implied identification of the Japanese spirit as pure and unsullied by external influence was then mobilized during Japan's imperial period, when cultural artifacts with foreign associations, including Buddhist institutions and Chinese language, were subordinated to what were considered to be the indigenous beliefs embodied by Shintō.

*Elizabeth A. Oyler*

**See also:** Language: Change in the Sixth to Eighth Centuries; Warrior Tales.

## Further Reading

Aston, W. G. *Nihongi: Chronicles of Japan from the Earliest Times A.D. to 697 C.E.* Rutland, VT: Tuttle, 1972.

Bialock, David T. *Eccentric Spaces, Hidden Histories: Narrative, Ritual, and Royal Authority from* The Chronicles of Japan *to* The Tale of the Heike. Stanford, CA: Stanford University Press, 2007.

Brownlee, John S. *Political Thought in Japanese Historical Writing, from* Kojiki *(712)* *to* Tokushi yoron *(1712).* Waterloo, ON: Wilfrid Laurier University Press, 1991.

Sakaki, Atsuko. *Obsessions with the Sino-Japanese Polarity in Japanese Literature.* Honolulu, HI: University of Hawaii Press, 2006.

Tsunoda Ryusaku et al., eds. *Sources of Japanese Tradition*, vols. 1 and 2. New York: Columbia University Press, 1958.

## Emigrants from Japan

Japan's emigration can be divided into three periods: (1) before 1641; (2) 1868–1945, after the Meiji Restoration through World War II; (3) the post-World War II period.

### Before 1641: The Sengoku Era

In the 13th century, Japanese pirates, known as *wakō*, started appearing in the Pacific along the Korean peninsula and China. During the Sengoku era (1467–1570), Japan was in chaos. As a result, by the 15th century commoners and merchants started going overseas for businesses, and *wakō* pirates and smugglers became prevalent as far away as Southeast Asian waters, where they formed residential areas known as Nihon-machi (Japantowns). These Japantowns thrived in major ports and some major cities across Southeast Asia, such as Hoi An in central Vietnam, Ayutthaya in Thailand, Manila in the Philippines, and Jakarta in Indonesia.

In the 16th century, samurai and Christian refugees also began heading to these Nihon-machi. Many samurai who had fought on losing sides lost their masters and land and became *rōnin* (masterless samurai). Many rōnin could not see a future in Japan and, therefore, left for these overseas Nihon-machi. In the late 16th and early 17th centuries, a new type of rōnin began coming to the Nihon-machis. In 1584, Toyotomi Hideyoshi took central political power. Attempting to solidify the nation's political structure and economy under a single regime, Hideyoshi sent a 242,700- man army to the Korean peninsula during a first invasion (1592–1593), and 122,100 soldiers in the second invasion (1597–1598). While losing local battles in Korea, and confronting political complications in Japan, Hideyoshi still needed to face warlords such as Tokugawa Ieyasu and Date Masamune. During these struggles for political power, some Japanese veterans of the Korean conflict fled to the Nihon-machis instead of returning to Japan.

In spite of initially following the policy established by Oda Nobunaga of protecting Japanese Christians, Hideyoshi prohibited the practice of Christianity in 1587. Although he banned the religion as part of his attempt to consolidate power, he kept foreign trade open to enrich the national economy. In turn, many Christians either were deported or emigrated from Japan to the Nihon-machis. The Tokugawa regime established in 1600 continued the practice of banning Christianity; in fact, the largest religious deportations in the history of Japan occurred during this period. For example, after being arrested, the devout Christian warlord Takayama Ukon and more than 100 of his

Christian samurai followers were deported to Manila in 1611.

The majority of emigrants in the Sengoku era were men. It is not known how many emigrants left at this time. However, just in Ayuttaya in Siam (current-day Thailand) alone, it is estimated that as many as 1,500 Japanese resided in the local Japantown. These Japanese men usually married local women. After the Tokugawa government imposed isolation in 1639 and closed the doors to Japan (both in and out), many of these men returned to Japan by themselves, leaving their wives and mixed children left behind.

### The Japón Lineage in Spain

The last emigrants of this period were sent abroad by a powerful local warlord, Date Masamune. He ordered his family servant, Hasekura Tsunenaga, to lead a delegation of 180 people to visit the Pope in Rome. The official reason for this delegation was to solidify social, political, and economic ties between Japan and the West. However, it is also said that Masamune wished to gain power to oppose the Tokugawa shōgunate, and economic and military ties to the West were one way of obtaining his goal. A year after this party left Japan in 1613, the Tokugawa government banned all Christians in Japan; while the delegation was still in the West, Japan's policy moved toward self-imposed isolation. The official law prohibiting foreigners entering Japan was ordered in 1639 and completed in 1641. After this point in time, Dutch and Chinese merchants were limited to the tiny artificial island of Deshima in Nagasaki harbor.

Because the delegation was a diplomatic mission under the auspices of the Tokugawa government, its members were able to return to their homeland if they renounced

Christianity. This was a very difficult choice for some of the people, especially those who had been baptized in Rome. As a result, while some returned to Japan in 1620, others did not. Recently, the historical records of six members of the delegation were discovered, and it is clear now that they moved to southern Spain. They settled in and around the village of Coria del Río and married into the community, where many of their descendants remain today, carrying their surname, Japón.

## 1868–1945: After the Meiji Restoration through World War II

After Commodore Matthew Perry and his fleet of American steamships came to Japan and demanded that the nation be opened to the outside world in 1853, Japan entered a civil war that lasted for the next 15 years.

### The First Economic Emigrants

The Tokugawa government sent a delegation to Washington, D.C., in 1860 to ratify the U.S.-Japan Treaty of Amity and Commerce of 1858. It was the first Japanese official voyage abroad in the modern times. The delegation also stopped by Hawaii. Soon after this visit, the king of Hawaii sent an official request to the Tokugawa government though Eugene M. Van Reed (an American businessman and Consul General of Hawaii) asking for migratory farmhands. At that time, discrimination against Chinese was strong in Hawaii, and not many Chinese were coming to the islands. However, because of the American Civil War (1861–1865), the demand of sugar had grown rapidly and Hawaiian plantation owners were desperately looking for plantation laborers.

Van Reed got permission from the Tokugawa government to recruit some 300 people. Before preparations for their emigration were made, however, Japan's civil war ended. The new Meiji government denied permission to emigrate, revoking the permission that the Tokugawa government had issued. As a result, Van Reed could take only 149 Japanese (141 men, 6 women, and 2 children)—without government permission—to Hawaii. Because these people left in the first year of the new Meiji Era, they were called *gan'nen-mono* ("first-year persons"). Later that year, another 42 Japanese left for Guam to work in the sugar plantations. In both locations, the migrants were treated little better than slaves, so many ran away before their contracts ended.

Regardless of the treatment of their fellow countrymen, many Japanese still wished to work outside Japan. This desire arose because of the steps the new government was taking in its efforts to modernize the country. For example, so that it would have a stable fixed income for each fiscal year, the new government established a draconian tax system that led to an increase in land tenancy, as many farmers had to sell their land to pay their taxes, especially in years of bad harvests. Furthermore, the new military conscription and compulsory education programs took people from the land. By 1908, almost the half of the nation's farmers were tenant farmers. Wishing to make money to buy back their ancestors' farmlands, many went abroad to earn hard cash.

In addition, the new Meiji government eliminated the samurai and other classes as it modernized the country. Some samurai continued to fight against these new government policies, including Matsudaira Katamori of the Aizu-Wakamatsu domain and many of the samurai of Satsuma. After losing the last fight against the Meiji government, some ex-samurai chose to immigrate overseas. Natural catastrophes such as the Great Kanto Earthquake of 1923, along with several nationwide famines, merely worsened the plight of the economically strapped Japanese farmers.

Some also left because they feared the newly instituted draft.

Because the demand for emigration was high—and as an attempt to decrease economic and population pressure—the Meiji government allowed its citizens to emigrate in 1885. At that time, several individual *toriasukainin* (private immigration agents) in Yokohama and Kobe helped potential emigrants complete their legal paperwork and obtain passports. As a result, by 1930, Japanese residents accounted for 46.3 percent of the Hawaiian population, which totaled some 140,000.

Financial hardships in Japan also caused some women to be sold into prostitution. Known as *Karayuki-san* ("someone who goes to China"), their number in 1935 was reported as at least 13,000. Including these women, between 1868 and the beginning of World War II in the Pacific in 1941, more than 1 million people left Japan. The majority of emigrants in this period planned to come back to Japan as soon as they made money, so that most emigrants left their family back home. In reality, few who left actually came back, as the first-generation immigrants generally could not make enough money to return.

### The Political Emigrants

A number of political refugees also left Japan during this period. For example, after being forced to give up his castle and turn himself over to the government in 1868, Matsudaira Katamori of the Aizu-Wakamatsu domain sent his wife and some 20 others—including samurai, servants, carpenters, and farmers—from his domain to America. With the help of a German (or possibly Dutch or Prussian) merchant, Edward (or John Henry) Schnell, they arrived in Gold Hill, in El Dorado County, California, in 1869.

Very little is known about the Wakamatsu Tea and Silk Colony. The people of the Colony brought with them mulberry bushes, silk cocoons, tea plants, bamboo roots, Zelkova trees, and other agricultural products to use in their new home. They also brought cooking utensils, swords, and a large banner bearing the crest of the Aizu-Wakamatsu domain. The Wakamatsu area is known as one of the best tea-producing areas in Japan. Thus the settlers probably wished to produce tea and silk, products for which Japan was world-famous at this time. Today, at the site of the Wakamatsu colony, one can find a huge Zelkova tree that was brought over with the Wakamatsu refugees. Given that the Aizu clan was known for their *keyaki* Zelkova tree artifacts, it is possible that the settlers were also planning on doing woodworking at the colony.

### Immigration to Hawaii and the United States

After Hawaii was annexed by the United States in 1898, many Japanese remigrated to the mainland. In 1900 alone, more than 12,000 Japanese remigrated to California from Hawaii, where approximately 61,000 Japanese were already living. This rapid growth of the Japanese population accelerated anti-Asian discrimination on the West Coast, where feelings against Chinese immigrants already ran deep. Both the governments of the United States and Canada requested the Japanese government not to send new immigrants in 1908. However, the definition of "new immigrants" did not include family members of the migrants who were already in North America.

Hearing about the new restrictions on immigration, those Japanese who were already in North America thought that soon no one would be allowed to come from Japan. Those people who had wives back in Japan called their wives over. The people who were not married decided to acquire wives though arranged marriages. Not being able to afford to return themselves, they sent their pictures instead. Their wives-to-be often had marriage ceremonies with only their new husbands' pictures in Japan. They submitted marriage licenses to the Japanese government, and acquired all the documents they needed to immigrate to North American. Once they arrived, they had real marriage ceremonies with their new husbands.

### Seasonal Migrants to British Columbia

The history of the Japanese in Canada started in 1877, when Nagano Manzo first landed and became a permanent resident. In 1897, a year before Hawaii became a territory of the United States and massive Japanese immigration started, the Japanese Fishermen's Association was established in Steveston, British Columbia. Japanese had been seasonal migrants in Canada for salmon fishing before that time, but now that Japanese had settled down permanently in the area, they became a dominant social force. Japanese held 1,958 of the total number of 4,722 fishing licenses. Moreover, the 1,999 licenses issued to the canneries were used mainly to employ Japanese fishermen. By 1941, there were 23,149 Japanese and their children were living in Canada.

### Immigration to Latin America

Immigration to Latin America occurred much earlier than immigration to Canada. In 1893, 132 Japanese plantation workers who finished their contracts in Hawaii remigrated to Guatemala in search of better working conditions. These remigrants suffered from poor working conditions as well as serious tropical diseases such as malaria, typhoid, and yellow fever. They then left Guatemala for Mexico.

Three years prior to their departure, the first Japanese consulate in Latin America

had opened in Chiapas, Mexico, in 1891 and Enomoto Takeaki became a Minister of Foreign Affairs. He was ordered by the government to investigate the possibility of having Japanese settlement areas in Mexico in 1893. The Japanese government bought 600 square kilometers of farmland in Chiapas on a 15-year installment plan in 1897, and sent 35 Japanese there. Because the area was chosen by Enomoto, it was called the Enomoto colony. However, as in Guatemala, people suffered from tropical diseases and many fled from the area. By the following year, the colony had closed down.

Although the first two Latin American immigration plans failed, 790 Japanese arrived at Callao, Peru, in 1877. These Japanese immigrants also suffered from poor working conditions, tropical diseases, and racial, language, and cultural barriers. Within a year, 143 had died and 93 fled to Bolivia (the first Japanese immigrants to come to that country). Because of these difficulties, a second wave of emigration from Japan did not happen. However, in 1903, the Japanese government reopened the immigration path to Peru. That year Japanese immigration to Chile also started with 126 coal miners. Despite the notable discrimination against Asians in Peru, since 1903 Japanese had been regularly arriving, and they continued to do so until the Pacific War broke out in 1941. Today, there are approximately 85,000 Japanese Peruvians (about 0.3 percent of Peruvian population) covering four generations. In contrast, only 519 Japanese legally had immigrated to Chile by 1941.

The Japanese Brazilian community began in 1908 with 781 coffee plantation workers. The Japanese Argentinean community began with 150 remigrants from Brazil in 1909. The Japanese government started aggressively sending families to Brazil in the 1920s and 1930s, especially to four

Japanese government-sponsored villages in São Paulo and Paraná. Before Brazil closed its door to Japanese immigrants in 1941, more than 188,000 Japanese entered the country.

The growth and development of Japanese communities in Latin America were directly connected to racial discrimination in North America. After immigration to Canada and the United States was outlawed in 1924, Japanese emigrants turned to South America as well as to Japan's colonies in Asia to settle. Although most Japanese originally came to the plantations as agricultural laborers, many in Peru and Chile eventually moved to the cities and developed urban Japanese communities: in Lima, many Japanese opened barbershops, and in Buenos Aires, many were engaged in the laundry businesses. Japanese also suffered great racial discrimination in Peru. Nevertheless, they produced the first president of a Latin American country of Japanese descent, Alberto Fujimori. Japanese residents in Brazil stayed in the farm areas until after World War II, when the young generation sought higher education in major cities.

### Immigration to the Colonies: Korea, Manchuria, and Sakhalin

After the Russo-Japanese War (1904–1905), Russia acknowledged Japan's "paramount political, military, and economic interest" in Korea under the Treaty of Portsmouth in 1905. Around the time of the First Sino-Japanese War (1894–1895), Japanese merchants began settling in Korea. After 1905, Japan invaded Korea. Prior to the annexation treaty of 1910, Japanese land ownership was legalized in 1906. Because the Korean traditional land ownership system did not require legal documents, Japanese denied the legality of Koreans' ownership of their own land, and the Japanese government sold the properties at subsidized cost to Japanese who were

willing to settle in Korea. Because many Japanese farmers had their farms confiscated for failure to pay taxes, more than 170,000 Japanese immigrated to Korea until 1945.

Following the Manchurian Incident in 1931 and the establishment of Manchukuo, the last Manchu emperor, Pu-yi, was then placed on the throne to lead a Japanese puppet government. Manchukuo was established in 1932 under the auspices of Japan's Kwantung Army. By 1945, some 270,000 Japanese settlers migrated there. Approximately 700,000 Koreans were living in Manchuria at the time of the Manchuria Incident in 1931, and the Japanese made more Koreans immigrate to Manchukuo, so the numbers of Koreans grew rapidly to more than 2 million by 1945.

Although the majority of emigrants left from Yokohama or Kobe, there was one other important seaport: Wakkanai in Hokkaidō. Although it is a small local port, some 400,000 Japanese left for new homes from there. After the Russo-Japanese War ended in 1905, Sakhalin Island was divided in half, with land south of the 50th parallel becoming Japanese territory. After World War II, although the majority of Japanese residents in Sakhalin returned to Japan, some 300 Japanese who had obtained Russian citizenship remained. The majority of these Japanese were women who had married Koreans. Although no records exist (the Japanese army destroyed them after the war), it is estimated that some 43,000 Koreans came to Sakhalin via Japan to work in the coal mines.

### The Post-World War II Period
#### War Brides

Although Japanese were not allowed to immigrate to the United States because of the Immigration Act of 1924, which remained in effect until the Immigration and Nationality Act of 1965 was passed,

48,912 Japanese women left Japan with their American husbands between 1947 and 1965, according to the *Yearbook of Immigration Statistics*. The actual number of war brides could be larger than this official number, as some followed their future husbands and were married in the United States. They faced strong discrimination in their new homes, both because of the effects of World War II and because Japanese Americans had been placed in internment camps from 1942 to 1946. Many in-laws and neighbors of Japanese war brides held deep prejudices. War brides in the American Midwest and the East Coast felt less racial discrimination than on the West Coast, but there was more isolation in the former areas because of the smaller Japanese American communities.

### *Emigration of Mixed Children after World War II*

According to some estimates, between 5,000 and 10,000 mixed-blood babies were born in Japan by 1952. Facing financial difficulties and social discrimination, many women abandoned their interracial children. Sawada Miki, granddaughter of Iwasaki Yataro, the founder of the Mitubishi *zaibatsu*, decided to found an orphanage for these interracial children in Oiso, Kanagawa, in 1948 (named the Elizabeth Saunders Home in honor of the first donor). There she took care of some 2,000 children, and sent about 600 to families in the United States.

*Nobuko Adachi*

**See also:** Colonization of Hokkaidō; Colonization of Taiwan; Comfort Women; Korea Added to Empire (1910); Manchukuo; Meiji Economic Reforms; Meiji-Era Peasant Uprisings; Meiji Land Tax; Rice Riots.

### Further Reading

Adachi, Ken. *The Enemy That Never Was.* Toronto, ON: McClelland and Stewart, 1991.

Adachi, Nobuko, ed. *Japanese Diasporas: Unsung Past, Conflicting Presents, and Uncertain Futures.* London/New York: Routledge, 2006.

Adachi, Nobuko, ed. *Japanese and Nikkei at Home and Abroad: Negotiating Identities in a Global World.* New York: Cambria Press, 2010.

Adachi, Nobuko. "Racial Journeys: The Japanese-Peruvians in Peru, the United States, and Japan." *Japan Focus* (2007). Available at: http://www.japanfocus.org/products/topdf/2517.

Azuma, Eiichiro. "Wakamatsu Colony," in *Encyclopedia of Japanese American History: An A to Z Reference from 1868 to the Present*, edited by Niiya, Brian. New York: Checkmark Books. 2000:406.

Crawford, Miki Ward, Katie Kaori Hayashi, and Shizuko Suenaga. *Japanese War Brides in America: An Oral History.* Santa Barbara: ABC-Clio, 2010.

Masterson, Daniel M., with Sayaka Funada-Classen. *The Japanese in Latin America.* Urbana/Chicago: Universtiy of Illinois Press, 2004.

Okihiro, Gary Y. *Cane Fires: The Anti-Japanese Movement in Hawaii 1865–1945.* Philadelphia: Temple University Press, 1991.

Uchida, Yoshiko. *Samurai of Gold Hill.* Berkeley: Creative Arts Book Company, 1985.

Yamazaki, Tomoko. *Sandakan Brothel No. 8: An Episode in the History of Lower-Class Japanese Women.* Translated by Kren Colligan-Taylor. London/New York: M. E. Sharpe, 1999.

## Enomoto Takeaki (1836–1908)

Born in 1836 to a Tokugawa samurai family in Edo, Enomoto was early recognized as a brilliant child and at a young age was admitted as a student of Dutch at the *bakufu* Naval

Training Center in Nagasaki. From 1862 to 1867, he studied in the Netherlands, returning with a newly purchased gunboat just in time for the Boshin War of 1867–1868. Enomoto commanded a gunboat during the short war. When Edo castle fell to the Meiji imperial troops, he refused to surrender, taking his ship and a few others north to the island of Hokkaidō.

Despite the Tokugawa surrender, a few thousand samurai continued to resist. On Christmas Day 1868, Enomoto was elected at age 32 as the president of the newly formed Ezo Republic. In later years he would humorously boast that he was the "youngest president of the first democratically-elected government in Asia." The Republic lasted only a few months. When surrounded by the Meiji imperial navy led by Kuroda Kiyotaka, Enomoto was persuaded by his Army Minister Ōtori Keisuke to surrender peacefully. Initially, Enomoto intended either to die fighting or to commit suicide. His friend Ōtori convinced him to abandon those plans by saying, "Dying is easy; you can do that anytime."

Enomoto was convicted of treason and sentenced to prison. He was pardoned in 1872 and two years later accepted a vice-admiral's commission in the new navy. Recognized for his brilliance, he was appointed ambassador to Russia to negotiate the Treaty of St. Petersburg. Upon his return to Japan, he was rewarded for his service, being named viscount in the new Meiji nobility in 1887—an ironic honor considering that he had spent four years in prison for treason. Later Enomoto was named Education Minister and eventually in 1891 reached his highest office, serving as Foreign Minister.

In his later years, Enomoto pursued a quixotic scheme to encourage immigration to the Americas. Because he was criticized for the negative implications of emigration, he ultimately resigned his membership in the Privy Council where he had served for many years.

*Larissa Castriotta Kennedy*

**See also:** Boshin Civil War; Boshin Civil War, Consequences; Ōtori Keisuke.

### Further Reading

Hillsborough, Romulus. *Shinsengumi: The Shōgun's Last Samurai Corps.* New York: Tuttle Publishing, 2005.

Ravina, Mark. *The Last Samurai: The Life and Battles of Saigō Takamori.* Hoboken, NJ: Wiley, 2004.

# F

## February 26 Incident (1936)

In the wee hours of February 26, 1936, more than 1,400 troops simultaneously attacked multiple targets in Tokyo, including the high-ranking government officials, the Army Ministry, and the Metropolitan Police Headquarters. Of the six officials targeted, Lord Keeper of the Privy Seal Saitō Makoto, Finance Minister Takahashi Korekiyo, and Army Inspector General of Military Training Watanabe Jōtarō were killed, and Grand Chamberlain Suzuki Kantarō was seriously wounded. Prime Minister Okada Keisuke, though on top of the target list, survived the assassination but only because his secretary was mistaken for him and killed instead.

The rebel troops were led by officers in the army's Imperial Way Faction (*kōdōha*), so called because they were fanatic advocates of direct rule of the country by the emperor. Influenced by Kita Ikki, a right-wing political philosopher, they believed that high-ranking government officials, financiers, and advisers to the emperor were to blame for all of Japan's woes. The solution to the problems, in their view, was to remove these people and return power to the emperor. Evoking the slogan "Revere the Emperor—Expel the Barbarians" (*sonno-jōi*) during the Meiji Restoration, they acted under the slogan "Revere the Emperor—Eliminate the Evils (*sonno-tōkan*)" in an attempt to launch a "Shōwa Restoration."

Rivaling against the *kōdōha* was the Control Faction (*tōseiha*), so called because it pushed for a reform of the country by legal means under the control of the Army Ministry. The rivalry had been going on for several years and led to the Army Academy Incident (*rikugun shikan gakkō jiken*) in 1934, in which several *kōdōha* officers were arrested for plotting a coup, and the Aizawa Incident in August 1935, in which *tōseiha* leader Nagada Tetsuzan was assassinated in retaliation for the removal of *kōdōha* leader Mazaki Jinzaburo from his office the month before. Then, at the height of the rivalry, an order came on February 22, 1936, that the 1st Division, home of most of the *kōdōha* officers, was to be dispatched to Manchuria. The rebel leaders advanced the action to February 26 to accomplish their "restoration" before the dispatch.

Now occupying the country's political and military center, rebel leaders delivered a manifesto of their grievances, along with the demand that *kōdōha* generals be appointed to important posts to carry out their reforms. Sympathetic to the rebels, army authorities responded by issuing a bulletin, in the name of Army Minister Kawashima Yoshiyuki, that recognized the patriotism of the rebels and promised to relay their manifesto to the emperor. But the emperor, shocked and furious that his closest advisers were killed in the coup, ordered immediate suppression. Because three of the targeted officials (Okada, Suzuki, and Takahashi) were former admirals, the navy was also determined to suppress the uprising. Sympathy toward the rebels, however, remained strong in the army. Repeated appeals for the rebels were made to the emperor by the Army Minister and Honjō Shigeru, aide-de-camp to the emperor, until the emperor shouted that he would personally lead the suppression forces if no one obeyed his order. Because of this, martial law in Tokyo was not declared until 5:00 a.m, on February 27, and no suppression was ordered until 11:00 p.m, on February 28, when the rebels were identified as "insurgents" for the first time.

The subjugation began on the morning of February 29 with a radio broadcast of an "Advice to the Soldiers," telling them that it was not too late to return to their units but that anyone who chose to resist would be considered a traitor to the emperor and be treated accordingly. Bills to the same effect were dropped from an airplane. Most of the common soldiers—recruits in their first year—quickly abandoned their posts. All rebel leaders were arrested by 5:00 p.m, of the day, with the exception of two who committed suicide. Of the arrested, 16 were executed, as were their civilian mentors, Kita Ikki and his disciple Nishida Mitsugi.

Alarmed by the way the military interfered with politics in the incident, public opinion strongly supported a reform of the army, proposed by Diet member Saitō Takao in May 1936. However, the military took advantage of the reform and worked aggressively to seize control of the cabinet.

The February 26 Incident was the last and worst of a series of attempted armed coups d'etat in Japan in the early to mid-1930s that, though suppressed in 4 days, became a landmark in Japan's road to militarism.

*Guohe Zheng*

**See also:** Kita Ikki; Kwantung Army Adventurism; Shōwa Emperor (Hirohito); *Sonno-jōi*; Young Officer Movement.

**Further Reading**

Harries, Meirion. *Soldiers of the Sun: The Rise and Fall of the Imperial Japanese Army.* New York: Random House, 1994.

Shillony, Ben-Ami. *Revolt in Japan: the Young Officers and the February 26, 1936 Incident.* Princeton, NJ: Princeton University Press, 1973.

## Firearms in Premodern Japan

Popular impressions regarding firearms in premodern Japan tend to follow one of two lines. One view suggests that they were present but not necessarily a major force on Japanese battlefields during the 16th century. That view is based on popular images of the samurai from the Edo period that emphasize the wearing of a long sword and a short sword as a mark of class distinction. A second view is that firearms were important but that the Japanese "gave up the gun" at the beginning of the Edo period in a kind of backing-off process from an unnecessarily deadly weapon.

A more accurate explanation of firearms in the premodern period is that they were quickly adopted onto the battlefield and grew in number to the point they decided many conflicts during the 16th century. During the Edo period it was not a matter of giving up guns so much as letting firearms technologies stagnate at their early 17th-century level, for lack of use.

Another widely held impression is that firearms first appeared in Japan in 1543, brought to Tanegashima by Portuguese sailors whose ship had blown off course. However, there is evidence that earlier firearms, possibly of Chinese or Korean design, had previously appeared in Japan. Some textual evidence indicates that firearms had been used in Japan by the early 16th century. These early firearms seem to have had little military importance in Japan, although they might have been central to conflicts in other parts of Asia at the time. Just how and when European-style firearms reached

Japan also is subject to debate. Some scholars have asserted that they arrived before 1543, while others suggest that they spread following successive waves of introduction.

The weapons first brought by the Portuguese to Tanegashima arguably transformed the Japanese battlefield. Almost immediately upon their arrival, the lord of the island, Tanegashima Shigetoki and his son, Tokitaka, recognized their military potential. The pair had iron smiths start to reproduce the muskets, and before long they learned the necessary techniques. Musket manufacture soon spread from Tanegashima to other locations.

Militarily, these weapons were used primarily for sniper missions, small-scale attacks, and similar harassment deployments. During the succeeding decades, another major change in tactics took place that would provide the basis for widespread use of muskets in large formations. Similar to what happened in Switzerland during the 14th century, Japanese tacticians realized that formations of foot soldiers (*ashigaru*) holding pikes and backed with archers could stop the charges of horse-mounted warriors. High-ranking warriors at this time depended primarily on the use of bows or lances in battle, but this gave the lower-ranking foot soldiers a tactical advantage.

In 1575, Oda Nobunaga combined *ashigaru* at the battle of Nagashino. There, he had ranks of musketeers fire in formation against the mounted horsemen of the Takeda clan with devastating effect. The textual account of the battle itself is not completely trustworthy in its assertion that Nobunaga's 3,000 musketeers fired in well-organized volleys. Yet there is no question that this battle was the first in which musketeers showed that they could decimate an oncoming charge of mounted warriors. From this time, the major battles that followed up to

and including the decisive battle of Sekigahara in 1600 made use of musket formations, which often proved key to battlefield outcomes. The three major figures—Oda Nobunaga, Toyotomi Hideyoshi, and Tokugawa Ieyasu—all used the musket to great effect in battles that often fielded tens of thousands of warriors and were key to the unification of the country. Contemporary Western descriptions of Japanese warriors described the musket as central to battlefield outcomes, which also helped persuade Europeans that any forceful attempt to create a foothold in Japan would be futile. Artillery pieces also were key to siege warfare at this time, and because of their great weight often were created *en situ*.

Despite the role that firearms played on the battlefield during the 16th century, once peace was established following the rise of the Edo *bakufu* in 1603, firearms fell into disuse. Samurai needed little more than their swords to claim their monopoly on the use of coercive violence in society. Yet when Japanese warriors faced new Western firearms technologies in the mid-19th century, the experience of history made it clear that they had to adopt the newer technology to survive militarily. In no small part, this realization led to the changes that resulted in the fall of the *bakufu* itself in 1868 and the establishment of a conscription army in the years that followed.

*William Johnston*

See also: Oda Nobunaga; Tokugawa *Bakufu*; Tokugawa Ieyasu; Toyotomi Hideyoshi.

## Further Reading

Perrin, Noel. *Giving Up the Gun: Japan's Reversion to the Sword, 1543–1879.* Boulder, CO: Shambhala, 1979.

Sun, Laichen. "Military Technology Transfers from Ming China and the Emergence of Northern Mainland Southeast Asia

(c. 1360–1527)." *Journal of Southeast Asian Studies* 34 no. 3 (2003): 495–517.

Udagawa Takehisa. *Teppō denrai: heiki ga kataru kinsei no tanjō* [The Arrival of the Musket: The Birth of the Early Modern as Told by Military Weapons]. Tokyo: Chuo Koronsha, 1990.

## Fujiwara Family

The Fujiwara family ascended to power by monopolizing the position of regents to the emperors of Japan. Until the Kamakura shōgunate, the Fujiwara dominated Japanese society, both by serving as the conduits to aristocratic ancestry that bound provincials to the imperial court and by simply awing the same provincials with their power. The Fujiwara family bypassed state institutions and controlled Japan through private rule until their position was challenged by Emperor Go-Sanjo in 1068.

The family's founder, Fujiwara Kamatari, dominated events surrounding the Taika reforms of 645. The fortunes of the Fujiwara grew in the mid-Nara period through marriage until 806, when the family's monopoly over the role of chief court minister began. In 858, Fujiwara Yoshifusa established a hereditary claim to the position of *sessho* (regent) by placing his nine-year-old grandson on the throne, making him Emperor Seiwa. The Fujiwara family became the most powerful family at court and the first regents in Japanese history outside of the imperial line. However, the assent of the Fujiwara family was solidified through their control of court ministries. The Fujiwara reached their highest point of power and prestige under Fujiwara Michinaga circa 1000. At the time, they kept the throne impotent by making sure that it was usually occupied by little boys or Fujiwara women.

The Fujiwara regency ushered in a powerful aristocratic culture that affected every facet of public and private life. Fujiwara dominance over the imperial court played an important role in establishing architecture, religion, and fashion during the Heian period (794–1185). Beginning in 793, Emperor Kammu sent Fujiwara no Oguromaro to plan the building of the new imperial capital at Kyoto. Architecturally, Fujiwara Japan developed a preoccupation with harmonizing buildings with settings so that each building imitated the natural landscape. Japanese fascination with harmony derived from the culture's aesthetic ideas of beauty. Another aspect of Fujiwara influence on Japanese culture was their encouragement of Buddhism as a naturalized Japanese religion. By the end of the Fujiwara regency, their power rested not only on their ability to control the throne and court ministries, but also on their capability to protect Buddhist temples and shrines.

In many ways, the Fujiwara regency institutionalized a cyclical shifting balance of power between the imperial line and noble clans that had been characteristic of Japanese government. After Emperor Go-Sanjo challenged Fujiwara power in 1068, the growing influence of the Minamoto and Taira families further eroded the family's power, ushering in the Kamakura shōgunate after the Gempei War.

*Tim Barnard*

**See also:** Hogen-Heiji-Gempei Wars; Kamakura *Bakufu*; Taika Reforms.

### Further Reading

Hall, John Whitney, and Jeffrey P. Mass, eds. *Medieval Japan: Essays in Institutional History*. New Haven: Yale University Press, 1974.

Inoue, Mitsusada. *Introduction to Japanese History before Meiji*. Tokyo: Kokusai

Bunka Shinkokai (Japan Cultural. Society), 1962.

Jansen, Marius B. *Warrior Rule in Japan.* Cambridge, UK: Cambridge University Press, 1995.

## Fukuzawa Yukichi

Fukuzawa was born on January 10, 1835, into the family of an impoverished, low-ranking samurai in Kyushu. His father, Fukuzawa Hyakusukc, died when Fukuzawa was only one year old. In 1854, Fukuzawa moved to Nagasaki to study Western gunnery techniques. The following year, he went to Osaka, where he entered a school for Dutch studies. By 1857, Fukuzawa was the leading student at the Dutch school. On orders from the officials of his domain, he opened a school for Dutch studies at Teppozu in Edo, which later grew to be Keio University.

Fukuzawa Yukichi was the most influential thinker of the Meiji era in Japan after 1868. (Fukazawa Memorial Center for Modern Japanese Studies, Keio University)

Fukuzawa quickly learned that Dutch was not generally spoken by the Westerners who visited Japan, so he began to teach himself English. In 1860, he traveled to the United States aboard the *Kanrin Maru* as a part of the embassy delegation sent by the shōgun to ratify the treaty between the United States and Japan that had been forced by the naval activities of Matthew C. Perry. After his return to Japan, Fukuzawa was named the official in charge of translations pertaining to foreign affairs. In 1861, he was again sent abroad, to visit England, France, Germany, and Russia.

The impressions from Fukuzawa's European tour formed the basis of his first major work, *Seiyo Jijo* ("Conditions in the West"). This three-volume tome was published in 1866, 1868, and 1870. It gave a simple, very readable account of everyday Western customs and institutions and became enormously popular in Japan. The first volume sold more than 150,000 copies in 1866 alone. Fukuzawa became known as an authority on the West.

During the internal military conflicts that resulted in the Meiji Restoration in 1868, Fukuzawa remained strictly neutral. He willingly took the status of commoner and renounced any government position to remain a private citizen. Fukuzawa believed in the importance of education to the transformation of Japan; much of his time was spent teaching at Keio University. He began a publishing house in 1869, eventually founding a newspaper, *Jiji Shimpo*, in 1882 to more effectively spread his ideas. In 1870, he prepared a survey of police systems of Western countries at the request of the Tokyo government. In 1873, Fukuzawa joined with other intellectuals to form a society to encourage Western studies. Known as the Meirokusha, the society published a journal entitled *Meiroku Zasshi* to popularize its ideas. Fukuzawa defined a new concept of *jitsugaku*, or practical knowledge, based on Western positivism and liberalism.

Fukuzawa wrote his own works on many different topics. These included *Gakumon No Susume* ("An Encouragement of Learning"), which criticized old ways of thinking and encouraged new ones. In 1875, he published *Bummeiron No Gairyaku* ("An Outline of a Theory of Civilization"), which reviewed his interpretations of Western civilization. In all of his works, Fukuzawa challenged many of the traditional beliefs accepted by Japanese. Some of his most radical ideas had to do with the rights of individuals. Fukuzawa believed in a compromise between popular rights and government powers. Imperialist expansion on the Asian mainland, through such projects as Korean independence and modernization, were considered as desirable goals by Fukuzawa. He also believed that women should have equivalent rights to men. Not only should women receive higher education, but they should also have their own jobs outside the home and property rights independent of the males in their family. Despite Fukuzawa's controversial ideas, however, his writings were so readable and popular that sales reached 3.4 million copies before his death.

Fukuzawa suffered a stroke in 1898. He continued his work, however, until another stroke took his life on February 3, 1901. His funeral procession consisted of 1,500 students and 10,000 mourners, all on foot. The *Japan Weekly Mail* offered the opinion that no other style of funeral would have better fit the simple lifestyle that marked Fukuzawa's life.

*Tim Watts*

**See also:** Dutch on Deshima; Jiyu Minken Undo; Meiji Emperor; Perry, Matthew; Tokugawa Shōgunate.

## Further Reading

Blacker, Carmen. *The Japanese Enlightenment: A Study of the Writings of Fukuzawa Yukichi*. Cambridge, UK: Cambridge University Press, 1964.

Fujita, Shozo. "The Spirit of the Meiji Revolution." *Japan Interpreter* 6, no. 1 (Spring 1970): 78–88.

Fukuzawa, Yukichi. *The Autobiography of Yukichi Fukuzawa*. New York: Columbia University Press, 1966.

Kinmonth, Earl H. "Fukuzawa Reconsidered: Gakumon No Susume and Its Audience." *Journal of Asian Studies* 37, no. 4 (August 1978): 677–696.

# G

**Gempei Wars.** *See* Hogen-Heiji-Gempei Wars.

**Genrō.** *See* Satchō Oligarchy.

## Gen'yōsha Nationalism

Gen'yōsha means "Dark Ocean Society," a reference to the Genkai Nada, the narrow sea passage separating Kyushu from Korea. Hiraoka Kotarō, Tōyama Mitsuru (1885–1940), and others founded the organization in 1881. Hiraoka—the group's first official leader—was significant for his financial contributions, but the group's true leader was always Tōyama, the son of a poor samurai family from Fukuoka. The group's initial members were disaffected former samurai.

The Gen'yōsha also had roots in the Freedom and Popular Rights movement led by former Tōsa samurai such as Itagaki Taisuke and Etō Shimpei. Both Saigō Takamori's rebellion and the activism of Tōsa men who called for a constitution, expanded civil liberties, and more representative government originated in the anger of elite contemporaries of the Meiji oligarchy. They differed from the oligarchs, however, in that they had been relatively excluded from power in the aftermath of the 1868 Meiji Restoration.

Before the Gen'yōsha, Fukuoka was home to disgruntled former warriors who gathered and discussed politics. The Kōyōsha (Sun-Facing Society) was one of many groups that formed there. The Kōyōsha morphed into the Gen'yōsha, which claimed three founding principles: reverence for the emperor, respect for the nation, and defense of people's rights. By 1882, Tōyama was sending young men to China to gather information and make contacts with Japanese military intelligence. For the Gen'yōsha, furtherance of its principles always involved Japanese-led advancement via anticolonialism and the toppling of traditional policies in Asia.

In 1882, a mutiny among Korean troops whose commanders worked with Japanese advisers caused Gen'yōsha frustration over Japan's lackluster response, and the group mustered an army. An advance team hijacked a steamship, forcing it to Busan. However, the crisis was over by the time that the ship arrived. In 1884, the society attempted to raise another army to stage a Japan-friendly Korean coup, but this also failed. In 1889, a Gen'yōsha member named Kurushima Tsuneki attempted to assassinate Foreign Minister Ōkuma Shigenobu, whom the group disliked due to his alleged kowtowing to the West. Tōyama involved himself in providing explosives that Kurushima threw under Ōkuma's carriage. Incorrectly believing that he had killed Ōkuma, Kurishima slit his own throat and died. Afterward, police investigated 40 Gen'yōsha members, but only one was ultimately imprisoned.

In 1894, Gen'yōsha members joined with other Japanese in Korea to form the Ten'yūkyō (Heavenly Grace and Chivalry). They engaged in violence intended to cause a reaction that would provide a pretext for Japanese intervention. During the 1894–1895 Sino-Japanese War, Tun'yūkyō members assassinated Korea Queen Min at the behest of the Japanese minister to Korea. Forty-eight group members were charged, but all were released.

In elections held in 1892, the Gen'yōsha sided with the government, acting at the behest of the Home, War, and Navy Ministers, and worked alongside organized criminals to intimidate voters, facilitating returns favoring illiberal candidates. The quid pro quo was government support for military spending increases and aggressive foreign policy. Gen'yōsha activities in the context of these elections solidified Gen'yōsha's alliance with the Japanese state. Group members continued to work outside the law but increasingly clearly in the interests of the state, performing duties that the state itself could not openly do. During the Russo-Japanese War, Gen'yōsha members formed a *Tokubetsu Inmutai* (special duties corps), which worked with Manchurian outlaws in guerrilla warfare and reconnaissance operations.

The influence of the Gen'yōsha extended into other groups and across the globe. Gen'yōsha member Uchida Ryōhei formed the Kokuryūkai in 1901. Because "kokuryū" in the group's name—taken from the Japanese reading of the Chinese name for the Amur River that separates China from Russia—literally means "black dragon," the group became a horrific caricature of evil Japanese in Western representation. The Kokuryūkai continued Gen'yōsha activities during and after the Russo-Japanese War. It also sponsored pro-Japanese activities in the United States. Tōyama had a hand in Kokuryūkai affairs. Well into the 20th century, Tōyama perpetuated what he considered Japanese interests by hosting anti-colonial Asian nationals at his Tokyo home. These individuals included Sun Yat-sen and Jiang Jieshi of China, the Philippines' Emilio Aguinaldo, Rabindranath Tagore of India, and even Abdurreşid İbrahim, a Russian Muslim nationalist opposed to Moscow.

*Gerald Iguchi*

**See also:** Continental Adventurers (*Tairiku Rōnin*); Itagaki Taisuke; Jiang Jieshi (Ch'iang K'ai-shek); Kita Ikki; Kwantung Army Adventurism; Pan-Asianism; Saigō Takamori; Russo-Japanese War; Seikanron; Seinan (Satsuma) Rebellion; Sino-Japanese War; Sun Yat-sen and the Japanese; Tôyama Mitsuru.

**Further Reading**

Aydin, Cemil. *The Politics of Anti-Westernism in Asia*. New York: Columbia University Press, 2007.

Esenbel, Selçuk. "Japan's Global Claim to Asia and the World of Islam: Transnational Nationalism and World Power, 1900–1945." *American Historical Review* 109, no. 4 (October 2004): 1140–1170.

Norman, E. Herbert. "The Gen'yōsha: A Study in the Origins of Japanese Imperialism." *Pacific Affairs* 17, no. 3 (September 1944): 261–284.

Siniawer, Eiko Maruko. *Ruffians, Yakuza, Nationalists: The Violent Politics of Modern Japan, 1860–1960*. Ithaca: Cornell University Press, 2008.

# Gilbert Islands Campaign (November 1943)

The 16 atolls that constitute the Gilbert Islands lie astride the equator. The Americans invaded the Gilbert Islands in late November 1943; approximately 200 ships and more than 30,000 troops seized the atolls of Makin, Tarawa, and Abemama in Operation Galvanic.

Following preparatory air strikes against Rabaul, the 11 fleet carriers in Task Force 50, which were divided into 4 different carrier groups, neutralized Japanese bases in the Marshall Islands and pounded Makin and Tarawa in preparation for landings there. At the latter two atolls, 7 battleships and accompanying cruisers bombarded the shore for more than an hour on the morning of the invasion. On November 20, Task Force 54 landed elements of the army's 27th Division on Butaritari Island; 2nd Marine Division troops landed on on Betio Island.

At Butaritari, 4 battalions from the 27th Division assaulted Beach Yellow in the lagoon and Beach Red on the western face of the island. Although the reef line forced the men in the lagoon to wade the last 300 yards to shore, initial resistance was light because only 300 Japanese combat troops defended the island. The attack became bogged down by enemy snipers and small counterattacks, however, and it took three days to secure the island. The army suffered 64 killed and 150 wounded.

Resistance was heavier on Betio, a small but well-fortified island defended by 4,000 Japanese troops. Initially, three Marine battalions landed on Beach Red along the wide lagoon side of the island. These troops ran into heavy fire, and, as low tide prevented heavy equipment from crossing the reef line, the attack stalled in the face of determined Japanese resistance. Two additional battalions landed as reinforcements later that day, and a sixth battalion landed the following morning. All suffered heavy casualties in the process. The situation improved late on the second day when destroyers and aircraft supported the landing of a seventh battalion at the narrow western end of Betio.

Using tanks, grenades, TNT blocks, and flamethrowers, the Marines secured most of the island by November 22. Two Japanese counterattacks were repulsed that evening, and the entire atoll was cleared six days later. The United States lost 980 Marines and 29 sailors killed; 2,106 troops were wounded. Only 17 Japanese survived the battle; they were taken prisoner along with 129 Korean laborers.

Although the Japanese surface navy did not intervene, Japan's air and submarine units did strike the American invasion force. At dusk on November 20, 16 twin-engine "Betty" bombers attacked a carrier group off Tarawa and torpedoed the light carrier *Independence*. The explosion killed 17 sailors and wounded 43, and it forced the carrier to retire for repairs. At least three similar raids followed over the next week, although none scored hits because American air cover—including the first use of night-combat air patrols—broke up the attacks.

More deadly were Japanese submarines, one of which torpedoed and sank the escort carrier *Liscombe Bay* on November 24, killing 642 sailors. Overall, the Gilbert landings cost the lives of roughly 1,800 Americans and 5,000 Japanese, including the crews of 4 lost Japanese navy submarines. The Gilbert Islands Campaign provided important lessons in amphibious operations, and it paved the way for the next U.S. amphibious operation, which was conducted against the Marshall Islands in January and February 1944.

*Timothy L. Francis*

**See also:** Tarawa Battle; World War II, Pacific Theater.

### Further Reading

Crawford, Danny J. *The 2nd Marine Division and Its Regiments*. Washington, DC: History and Museums Division, Headquarters, U.S. Marine Corps, 2001.

Morison, Samuel E. *History of United States Naval Operations in World War II. Vol. 7: Aleutians, Gilberts and Marshalls, June 1942–April 1944*. Boston: Little, Brown, 1951.

## Go-Daigo

Go-Daigo was born Kameyama Takaharu on November 26, 1288, of Daikaku-ji heritage; his father was the 91st imperial ruler, Go-Uda. The Daikaku-ji line patronized the new Chinese culture: Song dynasty Confucianism, Zen Buddhism, and calligraphy.

Beginning with the 89th emperor, Go-Fukakusa, the Jimyo-in line had an equal claim to the throne. Unlike the Daikaku-ji line, the Jimyo-in line patronized the traditional Japanese culture in literature, calligraphy, and Buddhism. Balancing the succession between the two lines was often a peaceful process left to the Kamakura shōguns and the retired emperors; however, those cultural differences, coupled with the economics of landholdings, deepened tensions between the two lines. With tensions high, the Kamakura shōgunate stringently adhered to the practice of alternate succession between the lines and held that each emperor would rule no more than 10 years.

Go-Daigo initially received support as the 94th emperor, but his younger brother, Go-Nijo, was favored when he produced an heir. After his brother's enthronement and then sudden death in 1308, the Jimyo-in line nominated Hanazono as the 95th emperor. Court intrigue and charges of treason brought the youthful Hanazono shame, which ended with his abdication. By 1318, Prince Takaharu was enthroned as Go-Daigo, the 96th imperial ruler of Japan.

With Go-Daigo's ascension, the Daikaku-ji line came to dominate the highest levels of imperial hierarchy. Such dominance was not in the Kamakura shōgunate's best interest, so it attempted to set aside Go-Daigo's nephew Prince Kuniyoshi, as the practice of alternate succession warranted. Soon after he began his reign, however, Go-Daigo set out to rule Japan as more than a mere puppet.

Go-Daigo began with staffing his court with men of ability, especially men whose interests were in Song Confucianism. Moreover, recognizing that controlling commerce was an immense source of power and revenue, he ordered the first-ever collection of taxes from sake brewers in Kyoto. During a period of famine, he issued edicts that stabilized prices and ordered hoarding merchants to sell their goods at special markets. Go-Daigo also contemplated bringing down the Kamakura shōgunate because it could not protect the countryside from increased banditry.

Initially, Go-Daigo sought political allies against the Kamakura government through the powerful Enryaku-ji monks. Accordingly, he placed his two sons, Morinaga and Munenaga, at the top of the clerical hierarchy. Furthermore, Go-Daigo sought the support of dissatisfied warrior houses, as well as from the bandits. Meanwhile, Prince Kuniyoshi died, and the Kamakura shōgunate chose Kazuhito (Kogon) as heir, which infuriated Go-Daigo.

In 1331, Go-Daigo's covert conspiracy against the shōgunate was exposed and resulted in his forced abdication. He was exiled to Oki, and many of his followers were punished with death or banishment. With Go-Daigo's exile began the "northern emperors" period in Japanese history. Although they were often considered illegitimate, all subsequent emperors descended from them. The first of the northern emperors was Kogon, who replaced Go-Daigo when he was forced into retirement.

The problem was that Go-Daigo did not want to retire, so he escaped from exile and raised a rebellion against the Hōjō family regency and the Kamakura *bakufu* instead. That "restoration" of the emperor actually briefly succeeded in 1333 with Kogon's forced retirement and the destruction of the Kamakura.

Go-Daigo's Kemmu Restoration was short-lived, however, due to a falling-out between Go-Daigo and his samurai supporters, especially Ashikaga Takauji. In 1336, Go-Daigo fled the capital, and a rival emperor, Komyo, was installed by Takauji. Go-Daigo established himself at Yoshino, and the schism created the period of northern and southern courts in Japanese history. Go-Daigo died on December 19, 1339, at his southern court at Yoshino.

*Tim Barnard*

**See also:** Ashikaga Takauji; Kamakura *Bakufu*; Southern Court (Yoshino).

**Further Reading**

Hall, John Whitney, and Jeffrey P. Mass, eds. *Medieval Japan: Essays in Institutional History*. New Haven: Yale University Press, 1974.

Inoue, Mitsusada. *Introduction to Japanese History before Meiji*. Tokyo: Kokusai Bunka Shinkokai (Japan Cultural. Society), 1962.

Yamamura, Kozo, ed. *The Cambridge History of Japan. Vol. 3: Medieval Japan*. Cambridge, UK: Cambridge University Press, 1990.

## Golovnin Affair (1811–1813)

In 1811, the Russian sloop *Diana* was on a surveying trip in the Kurile Islands, as part of the Russian push eastward that had begun in the 17th century. Some of the crew were captured when they went ashore in Etorofu in search of desperately needed supplies. They were imprisoned by the Japanese for two years before being repatriated. The details of their captivity were widely known throughout the world because Lieutenant Commander Vasily Mikhailovitch Golovnin (1778–1831) wrote a book about his experiences that was translated into several languages. The English version, *Narrative of My Captivity in Japan during the Years 1811, 1812 & 1813*, was issued in London in 1818. It also contained an account by Lieutenant Commander Petr Ivanovich Rikord (1776–1855), who had remained on board the *Diana* and negotiated the release of the captured crew members. Well written, entertaining, and accurate to the degree that Golovnin's captivity allowed him access to information, the book gave some of the first new information on Japan to appear in the West in decades, and served to heighten interest about Japan in the United States and Europe.

Until the late 18th century, relations between the Russians and Japanese were uneasy but there was no real friction, even when the 1739 expedition led by Martin Spanburg landed not only in Hokkaidô, but also in Sendai, which was much closer to major population centers. One reason the relationship between Russia and Japan changed for the worse was the arrival of Count Moritz Aladar von Benyowsky, a Hungarian adventurer, in 1771. In an echo of the *San Filipe* affair, he presented a letter containing news of a pending attack on Matsumae, the single Japanese outpost on the island of Ezo (now called Hokkaidô). Although Benyowsky had manufactured the information, it created an interest in Ezo among scholars such as Kudô Heisuke and Hayashi Shihei, who advocated increasing defenses in the north.

An expedition was sent to explore the region in 1785–1786 but little else was done. In 1792, Eric Laxman, a Finn in the employ of the Russian government, arrived in Nemuro to return the castaway merchant Kôdayû and negotiate for trade. Although Kôdayû was extensively debriefed, Laxman was sent on his way with the message that all foreign negotiations were conducted in Nagasaki. Internal affairs prevented an immediate response from Russia, but in 1804 an official diplomatic mission was sent under Nikolai Rezanov. The Japanese had no interest in negotiating and Rezanov was not a particularly skilled negotiator—his imperious manner alienated the Japanese. After keeping the Russian mission virtually imprisoned for almost six months, the Japanese officials refused all gifts brought for the shōgun and sent the Russian mission on their way in April 1805. An angry Rezanov colluded with Gavriil Davydof and Nikolay Khvostov, who were in the employ of the Russian American Company. The latter two staged several attacks over the next two years, burning towns and seizing ships in the Kuriles and in Hokkaidô. The Japanese responded by increasing soldiers in the region.

This was the state of affairs when the *Diana* entered Japanese waters. Golovnin, however, was a very different man from Resanov. He was much more interested in creating a good impression, teaching the Japanese and learning as much as he could about Japan. He suffered through the interrogations meant to establish whether Russia intended to attack Japan with good grace. He demanded equally good behavior from his crew. Even though he had refused to teach Russian language in fear of being kept captive, when Rikord secured his freedom, he and his Japanese captors companionably feasted together in farewell.

Rikord accomplished the Russians' release by setting up a blockade of the port of Hakodate, capturing a large merchant vessel, and trading this crew for that of the *Diana*. When Golovnin was released, he was given a letter to the Russian government that pronounced Japan's continued seclusion policy. The time spent by Golovnin and his crew in Hokkaidô served to alleviate Russo-Japanese tensions. It was the last real effort to establish relations with Japan through the Kuriles, and Russian activity in the area temporarily halted. Thereafter, shipwrecked Japanese were brought only as far as the Kurile Islands. Golovnin's reassurance that Davydof and Khvostov had not acted with imperial sanction calmed Japanese fears enough that they paid little attention to Hokkaidô in the decades that immediately followed. Golovnin's reports on the Japanese also caused the Russian government to view the Japanese with more respect. Ultimately, the Russian push eastward was only slowed, not stopped.

*Martha Chaiklin*

**See also:** *Sakoku.*

### Further Reading

Golovnin, Vasili, M. *Narrative of My Captivity in Japan during the Years 1811, 1812 & 1813.* 2 vols. Richmond, UK: Japan Library, 2000.

Kimura, Hiroshi. *Kurillian Knot: A History of Japanese-Russian Border Negotiation.* Stanford, CA: University of Stanford Press, 2008.

Lensen, George. *The Russian Push toward Japan.* Princeton, NJ: Princeton University Press, 1958.

## Gordon, Beate Sirota (b. 1923)

Born October 25, 1923, in Vienna, Beate Sirota was the only child of Ukranian Jews who had fled persecution in Russia. Her father, pianist Leo Sirota, later moved the family to Japan, where he taught at the Imperial Academy of Music in Tokyo.

Sirota lived in Tokyo for 10 years. She first attended the German school in Japan, but her parents decided that there was too much Nazi influence there. At the age of 12, she transferred to the American School in Japan. In 1939, she moved to Oakland, California, to attend Mills College; her parents remained in Japan.

During World War II, Sirota worked for the Foreign Broadcast Information Service of the Federal Communications Commission, the Office of War Information, and as a researcher for *Time* magazine. She returned to Japan after the war to search for

Beate Gordon, age 74, adjusts her glasses during a press luncheon in Tokyo, September 21, 1998. Gordon, who helped write the section on women's rights in Japan's constitution after World War II, praised the advances women have made in Japan in the last half-century. (AP Photo/Chiaki Tsukumo)

her parents. Fluent in Japanese and English, she was employed as a translator and researcher for the Supreme Commander of the Allied Powers (SCAP).

SCAP interpreted sections of the Potsdam Declaration to mean that the Japanese had to revise the Meiji Constitution of 1889. However, the Japanese resisted changing it, and in February 1946, when Japanese attempts at a constitutional revision were deemed too conservative and too close to the Meiji Constitution, General Douglas MacArthur ordered his American staff to draft a constitution that reflected the intentions of the Potsdam Declaration. Sirota was one of two women enlisted to help with that effort; she was one of only a few members of the constitutional committee who had any experience in, or knowledge of, Japan. She worked on the subcommittee for civil rights. Scholars credit her with drafting the articles that guaranteed women equal rights under the law, as well as marriage and property rights.

In 1947, Major General Charles A. Willoughby targeted Sirota in his investigation of leftist infiltration in the Japanese government. He failed to prove any allegations against her.

Sirota returned to the United States in 1947 and began promoting cross-cultural exchanges first between Japan and the United States. She sought to teach Americans about the rich East Asian cultural traditions by bringing Japanese artists, dancers, and musicians to the United States. She worked for the Japan Society as director of student activities, and later as the first director of the Performing Arts Program of the Japan Society, a position she held until 1991.

She resides in New York City, and goes by her married name, Gordon.

*Larissa Castriotta Kennedy*

See also: MacArthur, Douglas; Meiji Constitution; Potsdam Declaration.

**Further Reading**

Bendersky, J. W. *The Jewish Threat: Anti-Semitic Politics of the U.S. Army*. New York: Basic Books, 2000.

Dower, John W. *Embracing Defeat*. New York: W. W. Norton and Company, 1999.

Gordon, Beate Sirota. *The Only Woman in the Room*. Tokyo: Kodansha International, 1997.

## Gōtō Shinpei

Gōtō Shinpei was born in the Mizusawa domain as the son of a samurai of the Sendai domain on June 4, 1857. As a child, he idolized Takano Choei, a scholar-physician. Gōtō determined that he, too, wanted to become a doctor. Gōtō took up medicine at the Sukagawa Igakko in the Fukushima Prefecture. He graduated in 1876 and continued his studies at the Nagoya Medical School. Gōtō also worked at the Aichi Prefectural Hospital.

In 1877, Gōtō served as a physician for government forces during the Satsuma Rebellion. In 1881, at the age of 25, he became president of the Nagoya Medical School. He gained fame for his outspoken views on hospital management, social welfare, and health education. In 1882, when Itagaki Taisuke was attacked and stabbed, Gōtō took charge of his successful treatment. In that same year, Gōtō entered government service, serving in the Health Bureau, which was attached to the Home Ministry.

Gōtō was sent to Germany in 1890 to study medical administrative methods. When he returned to Japan in 1892, he was appointed chief of the Health Bureau, becoming Japan's highest-ranking medical officer. When the Sino-Japanese War of 1894–1895 broke out, Gōtō urged the establishment of a quarantine system patterned on European and American models. In 1895, he was appointed director of the Army Quarantine Office to prevent the spread of disease.

In 1898, Gōtō was sent to Taiwan, which had become a Japanese possession as a result of the Sino-Japanese War. Under the military administrator, Gōtō was the civilian governor in charge of administering Taiwan. He sought to establish a constructive and even-handed civil rule, despite opposition from the local population. He used the civil police to put down the Taiwanese who refused to submit to Japanese rule. A combination of force, amnesty, and cash rewards led to pacification. Gōtō created monopolies in camphor and salt, built railroads, encouraged industries,

and founded educational and health facilities. He created the infrastructure that led to an influx of investment from Japan and laid the basis for a thriving colonial economy in Taiwan. His efficiency was rewarded when he was appointed in 1903 to the House of Peers of the Diet with the title of count.

Gōtō was appointed head of the government-owned South Manchuria Railway Company in 1906. His success in dealing with the difficulties in that position resulted in an appointment in 1908 as Minister of Communications in the second Katsura Taro cabinet. At the same time, he served as president of the Railway Bureau and vice president of the Colonization Bureau. Gōtō played a very active role in Japanese affairs in Manchuria, including the immigration of Japanese settlers to Japanese-controlled areas and the exploitation of Manchurian resources. In 1912, Gōtō again served as Minister of Communications in the third Katsura cabinet. Following the Taishō Political Crisis of 1912–1913, Gōtō assisted Katsura in organizing a new political party, the Rikken Doshikai, which brought together groups opposing Hara Takashi.

In 1916, Gōtō was appointed Home Minister in the Terauchi Masatake cabinet. In 1918, he became Foreign Minister. Gōtō advocated an aggressive and expansionist foreign policy. As an avid Pan-Asianist, he promoted the establishment (with government funds) of an East Asian Economic League that would rely on Japanese capital and Chinese labor. Funds intended for this project were used to finance corrupt activities abroad, however, leading to scandal and criticism of Gōtō in Japan. Gōtō also advocated the dispatch of Japanese troops to Siberia following the Bolshevik Revolution; the eventual expulsion of the Japanese troops prompted further criticism of Gōtō.

In 1920, Gōtō was appointed mayor of Tokyo. In 1923, he was named Home Minister in the second Yamamoto Gombei cabinet. In September 1923, the Great Kanto Earthquake devastated Tokyo; Gōtō headed the agency that planned and oversaw the reconstruction of the city.

Gōtō retired from government after the rebuilding of Tokyo but continued to be active. He devoted himself to broadcasting enterprises. He was also an organizer and president of the Boy Scouts of Japan, head of the Japan-Russia Society, president of Takushoku University, an active member of the Association of East Asian Societies, and a vigorous promoter of ethical government. He wrote on a number of topics, including the effective use of ocean water, problems of public health, political ethics, and the Swiss system of worker's compensation. Gōtō died on April 4, 1929, on a trip to Okayama.

*Tim Watts*

**See also:** Boshin Civil War; Great Kanto Earthquake; Hara Takashi; Itagaki Taisuke; Japan-Soviet Neutrality Pact; Pan-Asianism; Seinan (Satsuma) Rebellion; Siberian Intervention; Sino-Japanese War; South Manchurian Railway.

**Further Reading**

Chen, Edward I. "Gōtō Shimpei, Japan's Colonial Administrator in Taiwan: A Critical Reexamination." *American Asian Review* 13, no. 1 (1995): 29–59.

Iwao, Seiichi, ed. *Biographical Dictionary of Japanese History*. Trans. Burton Watson. Tokyo: International Society for Educational Information, 1978.

# Greater East Asia Co-prosperity Sphere

The origins of the Greater East Asia Co-prosperity Sphere date to long before the phrase was coined in 1940. In the late 19th century, Japan began aggressively modernizing, aspiring to become accepted as a world power. The Japanese were particularly interested in acquiring colonies, which added to a nation's prestige. More importantly, colonies could supply Japan's growing industrial economy with the raw materials the home islands lacked and absorb some of Japan's excess population. The Japanese were also motivated by a sense of racial superiority over both Europeans and other Asians. They wanted to extend their political and economic domination over the entire western Pacific Rim.

Japan's desire to become a world power began and ended in just five decades. In 1895, after a brief war with China, Japan acquired Taiwan and the Ryukyu and Pescadores island chains. The Japanese victory in the Russo-Japanese War of 1904–1905, fought over competing interests in Manchuria, increased Japanese influence in northeastern Asia. Japan annexed Korea in 1910, and at the end of World War I, was granted the former German possessions of the Caroline, Marshall, and Mariana island groups. In 1932, the Japanese established a puppet government in Manchuria, calling the new state of Manchukuo. Five years later, Japan went to war with China. Although initially successful, the campaign soon lost momentum.

To support their operations in China, the Japanese had to import resources from overseas. Before hostilities began, Japan secured the cooperation of Thailand, arranging for its troops to operate from that country, and forced France, which had been conquered by Germany in May 1940, to make similar concessions regarding Indochina. Shortly afterward, Japanese Foreign Minister Matsuoka Yōsuke gave a speech calling for the "establishment of a sphere of cooperative economies" in Asia that would provide "the foundation of [a] national defense economy" for Japan. This was the first time the expression "Greater East Asia Co-prosperity Sphere" (*dai-tōa-kyoeiken*) was used.

The United States, however, soon placed an embargo on scrap metal and oil, in addition to freezing Japanese assets in 1941, in an attempt to compel the Japanese to withdraw from China. The Netherlands similarly refused to sell oil to Japan. The Japanese ignored the demands and began making plans to acquire the raw materials they needed by force.

The Pacific War began in early December 1941 with near-simultaneous Japanese attacks on the U.S. Pacific Fleet at Pearl Harbor; the British colony of Malaya, a source of rubber; and the Philippines, an American possession that lacked resources but was strategically placed. The Japanese then moved on to take the Netherlands East Indies, with its oil, tin, and rubber resources. The Dutch, too, had been weakened by the fighting in Europe and by May 1942 the Japanese had achieved all of their territorial objectives in Asia and the Pacific.

At first, many Asians welcomed the Japanese as liberators, believing Japan's promises of "Asia for Asians." Soon, however, the conquerors proved to be as oppressive and exploitive as the Europeans they had displaced. The Japanese lacked an adequate civil administration, so local army commanders governed the conquered territories. Japanese troops brutally repressed subject civilians. Local culture was suppressed under a policy of "Japanization." By the end of the Pacific War, most areas under Japanese control had thriving resistance movements.

The Japanese never realized fully the benefits of empire, not having time to exploit the resources, and lacking the shipping to transport these resources to Japan, which in any case came under relentless U.S.

submarine attack. The economic infrastructures of the occupied areas, which were damaged during the initial fighting (and later by Allied strategic bombing), never fully recovered. Japanese mismanagement also impaired productivity. Allied aircraft and submarines crippled the Japanese merchant fleet, reducing even further the amount of food, fuel, and resources reaching Japan. The blockade of the Japanese home islands was so effective that some have argued that neither an invasion of Japan nor the dropping of the atomic bombs were necessary to compel the Japanese to surrender.

After the war, Japan was stripped of most of its territorial possessions outside the home islands.

*Roger Horky*

**See also:** Korea Added to the Empire; Manchukuo; Matsuoka Yōsuke; Pan-Asianism; Pearl Harbor, Attack on; Russo-Japanese War; Versailles Treaty; World War I; World War II, Pacific Theater.

### Further Reading

Morley, James William. *The Fateful Choice: Japan's Advance into Southeast Asia, 1939–1941*. New York: Columbia University Press, 1980.

Myers, Ramon Hawley, Mark R. Peattie, and Ching-chih Chen. *The Japanese Colonial Empire, 1895–1945*. Princeton, NJ: Princeton University Press, 1984.

Nish, Ian. *Japanese Foreign Policy in the Interwar Period*. Praeger Studies of Foreign Policies of the Great Powers Series. Westport, CT: Praeger, 2002.

## Great Kanto Earthquake (1923)

On September 1, 1923, one of the deadliest and most destructive earthquakes of the 20th century devastated Japan's populous Kanto plain. The Great Kanto Earthquake destroyed much of Japan's industrial heartland, killed more than 100,000 people, slowed the Japanese economy for years, and revealed tensions among sectors of Japan's population as well as between Japan and its Korean colonial subjects.

The Great Kanto Earthquake, an estimated magnitude 8.3 quake, lasted for at least 4 minutes and perhaps as long as 10 minutes. The initial quake struck at lunchtime, and more than 800 aftershocks occurred in the hours and days that followed. The fires that resulted spread from wood and charcoal cooking stoves in Japanese houses and proved to be as destructive as the powerful quake itself. High winds fanned the flames, which often trapped groups of refugees even after they had managed to escape from their shattered homes and businesses. Ultimately, as many as 143,000 people lost their lives, and another 50,000 were injured. Some 71 percent of the population of Tokyo and 85 percent of Yokohama's residents lost their homes.

The Kanto region was Japan's industrial core. The damage caused by the quake and its aftermath seriously disrupted Japan's industrial and commercial infrastructure by placing huge burdens on an already strained economy. A short-lived reconstruction boom did little to lift the general economic gloom, and recovery was slow to come to the region.

The earthquake was taken by many rural Japanese as a judgment on the nature of modern civilization; that the fruits of modernity could so easily be reduced to rubble prompted many farmers to redouble their efforts to eschew modern urban values in favor of local rural ones.

In addition, rumors that Korean residents of the Kanto area planned to use the chaos that followed the earthquake to loot, riot, or otherwise threaten the Japanese led to the widespread abuse of Koreans by groups of Japanese vigilantes. Government pleas to recognize the official imperial policy of assimilation and declarations that "Japanese and Koreans are one people" fell largely on deaf ears, as an estimated 6,000 to 10,000 Koreans were killed in the aftermath of the quake. In the disorder that followed, anarchists Itō Noe and Osugi Sakae were arrested and were strangled in their cell by a captain of the Tokyo military police.

*Kirk Larsen*

**See also:** Itō Noe.

### Further Reading

Allen, J. Michael, "The Price of Identity: The 1923 Kanto Earthquake and Its Aftermath," *Korean Studies* 129 (1996): 64–93.

Hammer, Joshua. *Yokohama Burning: The Deadly 1923 Earthquake and Fire That Helped Forge the Path to World War II.* New York: Simon & Schuster 2006.

## Guadalcanal, Land Battle for (August 1942–February 1943)

The battle for Guadalcanal was actually a series of naval and land battles fought in and around the island of Guadalcanal in the Solomon Island archipelago.

In January 1942, Japanese amphibious forces had landed in the Bismarck Archipelago between New Guinea and the Solomon Islands. They quickly wrested Kavieng on New Ireland Island and Rabaul on New Britain from the Australians. The Japanese consolidated their hold and turned Rabaul into their principal southwest Pacific base. By early March, the Japanese had landed at Salamaua and Lae in Papua and on Bougainville. Their advance having gone so well, they decided to expand their defensive ring to the southeast to cut off the supply route

Bodies of dead Japanese soldiers lie on a beach on Guadalcanal, Solomon Islands, while U.S. Marines consolidate their position. (Library of Congress)

from the United States to New Zealand and Australia. On May 3, the Japanese landed on Tulagi and began building a seaplane base there. Between May and July, they expanded their ring farther in the central and lower Solomons. The first Japanese landed on Guadalcanal on June 8. On July 6, their engineers began construction of an airfield near the mouth of the Lunga River.

The discovery of the Japanese effort on Guadalcanal led to the implementation of Operation Watchtower. Conceived by U.S. Chief of Naval Operations Admiral Ernest J. King, it called for securing Tulagi as a base to protect the United States–Australia lifeline and as a starting point for a drive up the Solomons to Rabaul.

The Japanese airfield on Guadalcanal would allow its aircraft to bomb the advanced Allied base at Espiritu Santo. In recognition of

that fact, U.S. plans to take the offensive were stepped up, and a task force was hurriedly assembled. From Nouméa, Vice Admiral Robert Ghormley dispatched an amphibious force under Rear Admiral Richmond K. Turner, lifting Major General Alexander A. Vandegrift's 19,000-man reinforced 1st Marine Division. A three-carrier task force under Vice Admiral Frank J. Fletcher provided air support. This operation involved some 70 ships.

Although hamstrung by a lack of adequate resources because of the sealift required for Operation Torch (the British and American invasion of North Africa), Ghormley pieced together forces from the United States, Australia, and New Zealand for the invasion. Resources were so meager that some of his officers nicknamed the plan Operation Shoestring.

The U.S. Navy's tasks were to sustain forces ashore and provide naval and air protection for the Marines defending the airfield, which was captured shortly after the landing and renamed Henderson Field for a Marine aviator killed in the Battle of Midway. The lack of a harbor compounded supply problems. The Japanese operated aircraft from Rabaul and later from other closer island airfields, but Allied "coast watchers" on islands provided early warning of many Japanese naval movements.

On August 7, 1942, the Marines went ashore at Tulagi, Florida, Tanambogo, Gavutu, and Guadalcanal, surprising the small Japanese garrisons (2,200 on Guadalcanal and 1,500 on Tulagi). On the same day, the Marines seized the harbor at Tulagi, and by the next afternoon they had also secured the airfield under construction on Guadalcanal, along with stocks of Japanese weapons, food, and equipment. Supplies for the Marines were soon coming ashore from transports in the sound between Guadalcanal and Florida Islands, but this activity came under attack by Japanese aircraft based at Rabaul.

The stakes were high for both sides. The fiercest fighting occurred for Henderson Field. Vandegrift recognized its importance and immediately established a perimeter defense around it. Eating captured rations and using Japanese heavy-construction equipment, the U.S. 1st Engineer Battalion completed the airfield on August 17. As early as August 21, the day the Japanese mounted a major attack on the field, the first U.S. aircraft landed there. The Japanese now found it impossible to keep their ships in waters covered by the land-based American aircraft during the day, and they found it difficult to conduct an air campaign over the lower Solomons from as far away as Rabaul.

The surrounding coral reef and lack of a harbor compounded U.S. supply problems, as did Japanese aircraft attacks. The battle on Guadalcanal became a complex campaign of attrition.

On August 8 in the Battle of Savo Island, a Japanese cruiser squadron overwhelmed an Allied force of equal size, sinking one Australian and three U.S. cruisers and damaging several destroyers, while losing none of Japan's own ships. The battle clearly showed the superiority of Japanese night-fighting techniques. The battle was the worst defeat ever suffered by the U.S. Navy, but it was only a tactical success, because the Japanese failed to go after the vulnerable American troop transports off Guadalcanal and Tulagi.

Nonetheless, the Battle of Savo Island and Japanese air attacks led to the withdrawal of supporting naval forces from Guadalcanal, leaving the Marines ashore isolated, bereft of naval support, and short of critical supplies. Long-range aircraft and destroyers did bring in some resources. The Japanese made a critical mistake in not capitalizing on the U.S. vulnerability to commit their main fleet to this area. For the most part, they sent only smaller units in driblets, chiefly in the form of fast destroyers. The so-called Slot was controlled by the United States during the day but the Japanese owned it at night.

Concern over the vulnerability of the U.S. transports led to their early removal on the afternoon of August 9, along with most of the heavy guns, vehicles, construction equipment, and food intended for the Marines ashore. The Japanese sent aircraft from Rabaul, while initially U.S. land-based aircraft flying at long range from the New Hebrides provided air cover for the Marines as fast destroyer transports finally brought in some supplies. American possession of Henderson Field tipped the balance. U.S. air strength there gradually increased to about 100 planes.

At night the so-called Tokyo Express—Japanese destroyers and light cruisers—steamed down the Slot and into the sound to shell Marine positions and to deliver supplies. The latter effort was haphazard and never sufficient; often, drums filled with supplies were pushed off the ships to drift to shore. One of the great what-ifs of the Pacific War was the failure of the Japanese to exploit the temporary departure of the U.S. carrier task force on August 8 by rushing in substantial reinforcements.

Actions ashore were marked by clashes between patrols on both sides. Colonel Kiyonao Ichiki, who had arrived with his battalion on Guadalacanal in early August, planned a large-scale attack that took little account of U.S. Marine dispositions. His unit was effectively wiped out in the August 21, 1942, Battle of the Tenaru River. Ichiki's men refused to surrender, and they and their commander were killed in the fighting. Marine losses were 44 dead and 71 wounded; the Japanese lost at least 777 men.

The next major confrontation at sea off Guadalcanal came on the night of August 24–25 in the Battle of the Eastern Solomons. American carrier-based aircraft intercepted and attacked the covering group for a Japanese convoy of destroyers and transports carrying 1,500 troops to Guadalcanal. The Americans sank the Japanese light carrier *Ryujo* and damaged another ship, but the U.S. fleet carrier *Enterprise* was located and attacked by Japanese aircraft and badly damaged. The Japanese destroyers and transports delivered the reinforcements and the destroyers and then shelled Henderson Field, although a U.S. Army B-17 sank one of the Japanese ships.

On August 31, the U.S. carrier *Saratoga* was torpedoed by a Japanese submarine and put out of action for three months. That left only the carrier *Wasp* available for operations in the South Pacific. From September 12 to 14, strong Japanese land forces attempted to seize U.S. Marine positions on Lunga Ridge overlooking Henderson Field from the south. The Japanese left 600 dead; American casualties were 143 dead and wounded. Both sides continued building up their strength ashore as naval and air battles raged over and off Guadalcanal.

On September 15, the *Wasp* was torpedoed and sunk while it was accompanying transports lifting the 7th Marine Regiment to Guadalcanal from Espiritu Santo. A Japanese torpedo also damaged the battleship *North Carolina*, which, however, held its place in the formation. The Americans continued to Guadalcanal, delivering the 7th Marine Regiment safely three days later.

Then came the naval Battle of Cape Esperance during the night of October 11–12. The Japanese sent in their supply ships at night. U.S. ships equipped with radar detected a Japanese convoy. In the ensuing fight, the Japanese lost a cruiser and a destroyer, and another cruiser was heavily damaged. The Americans lost only a destroyer and had two cruisers damaged. The first Allied success against the Japanese in a night engagement, the Battle of Cape Esperance provided a great boost to U.S. morale.

From October 23 to 25, the Japanese launched strong land attacks against Henderson Field. Fortunately for the Marine defenders, the attacks were widely dispersed and uncoordinated. In these engagements, the Japanese suffered 2,000 dead, while U.S. casualties were fewer than 300. Immediately after halting this Japanese offensive, Vandegrift began a six-week effort to expand the defensive perimeter to a point beyond which the Japanese could not subject Henderson to artillery fire.

A major naval engagement occurred on October 26–27 in the Battle of the Santa Cruz Islands. Task Force 16, centered on the carrier *Enterprise*, engaged Japanese forces. Each side conducted carrier strikes against the other. U.S. aircraft inflicted severe damage on the heavy carrier *Shokaku*, putting the ship out of action for nine months, and damaged the light carrier *Zuiho*. On the U.S. side, the heavy carrier *Hornet* was badly damaged and had to be abandoned while under tow; it was soon sunk by Japanese destroyers. Japan had won a major victory over the Americans, but had lost 100 aircraft and experienced pilots, half again as many as the Americans.

During November 12–15, a series of intense sea fights occurred in what became known as the Naval Battle of Guadalcanal. It took place near the entrance to Ironbottom Sound (so named because it was the resting place of many Allied and Japanese ships) off Savo Island. U.S. ships and aircraft fought to block reinforcement of the island by 13,000 Japanese troops in 11 transports, escorted by destroyers. At the same time, a powerful squadron arrived to shell Henderson Field. In a confused engagement, both sides suffered heavily. The Japanese lost the battleship *Hiei* and two cruisers sunk; all other Japanese vessels were damaged. The Americans lost two cruisers and four destroyers. A cruiser and a destroyer were close to sinking, and all other ships, save one, were damaged. The Japanese were obliged to retire, and the planned Japanese bombardment of Henderson Field did not occur.

On November 13–14, the Japanese returned, and their heavy cruisers shelled Henderson Field. The Americans, however, sank seven Japanese transports and two cruisers. During the third phase of the engagement on November 14–15, U.S. warships met and defeated yet another Japanese forces near Savo Island. The Americans lost two destroyers, but Japan lost the battleship *Kirishima*

and a destroyer. The net effect of the three-day battle was that Japan landed only some 4,000 troops, whereas the Americans regained control of the waters around the island.

The last major naval battle for Guadalcanal occurred on November 30 at Tassafaronga Point. The Japanese again attempted to land reinforcements on the island and were surprised by a larger U.S. Navy task force. However, the Japanese once more demonstrated their superior night-fighting ability. In the exchange, the Japanese lost a destroyer and the Americans lost a cruiser.

Fighting on land continued. On December 8, the 2nd Marine Division replaced the veteran 1st Marine Division and the 25th Infantry Division. At the beginning of January 1943, there were 58,000 Americans present in the Guadalcanal area, whereas Japanese strength was then less than 20,000.

Meanwhile, on January 10, the U.S. military began an offensive to clear the island of Japanese forces, mixing Army and Marine units as the situation dictated. In a two-week battle, the Americans drove the Japanese from a heavily fortified line west of Henderson Field. At the end of January, the Japanese were forced from Tassafaronga toward Cape Esperance, where a small American force landed to prevent them from escaping by sea. Dogged Japanese perseverance and naval support, however, enabled some defenders to escape. The Japanese invested in the struggle 24,600 men (20,800 troops and 3,800 naval personnel).

Japanese leaders now came to the conclusion that they could no longer absorb such losses in trying to hold on in Guadalcanal. The final battle of the campaign was a skirmish off Rennell's Island on January 30, 1943. In daring night operations during February 1–7, 1943, Japanese destroyers evacuated 10,630 troops (9,800 army and 830 navy).

The United States committed 60,000 men to the fight for the island; of these forces, the Marines lost 1,207 dead and the army 562. U.S. casualties were far greater in the naval contests for Guadalcanal; the U.S. Navy and Marines lost 4,911 men and the Japanese at least 3,200. Counting land, sea, and air casualties, the struggle for Guadalcanal claimed 7,100 U.S. lives.

Ultimately, the Americans won the land struggle for Guadalcanal thanks to superior supply capabilities. The Americans were now well fed and well supplied, but the Japanese were desperate, losing many men to sickness and simple starvation.

The Americans won the naval campaign thanks largely to their superior supply capability and the failure of the Japanese to throw enough resources into the battle. The Tokyo Express down the Slot was haphazard and inadequate. The campaign for Guadalcanal proved to be as much a turning point for the United States as the Battle of Midway. The Japanese advance had been halted, opening the way for the long island-hopping advance toward Japan. In addition to the loss of lives, the Japanese lost 1 light carrier, 2 battleships, 3 heavy cruisers, 1 light cruiser, 14 destroyers, and 8 submarines. Particularly serious from the Japanese point of view was the loss of 2,076 aircraft (1,094 to combat) and many trained pilots. U.S. Navy losses included 2 heavy carriers, 6 heavy cruisers (including the Royal Australian Navy *Canberra*), 2 light cruisers, and 15 destroyers, but new U.S. naval construction more than offset the U.S. losses. The campaign also destroyed the myth of Japanese naval superiority.

U.S. control of the air had rendered the Japanese ships vulnerable to attack. It also allowed Allied forces to determine the timing and location of offensive operations without Japanese foreknowledge. The Japanese advance was halted, and the U.S. could begin the long and bloody return to the Philippine Islands.

*William P. McEvoy, Troy D. Morgan and Spencer C. Tucker*

**See also:** Midway, Battle of; World War II, Pacific Theater.

**Further Reading**

Frank, Richard B. *Guadalcanal: The Definitive Account of the Landmark Battle*. New York: Random House, 1990.

Hamel, Eric M. *Guadalcanal: Decision at Sea: The Naval Battle of Guadalcanal, November 13–15, 1942*. New York: Crown, 1988.

Lundstrom, John B. *The First Team and the Guadalcanal Campaign*. Annapolis, MD: Naval Institute Press, 1994.

Morison, Samuel Eliot. *History of United States Naval Operations in World War II. Vol. 5: The Struggle for Guadalcanal, August 1942–February 1943*. Boston: Little, Brown, 1948.

Mueller, Joseph N. *Guadalcanal 1942: The Marines Strike Back*. London: Osprey, 1992.

Tregaskis, Richard. *Guadalcanal Diary*. New York: Random House, 1943.

## Guam, Battle for (July 21–August 10, 1944)

Guam was the only one of the Mariana Islands controlled by the United States before World War II, it having been acquired in 1898 as a consequence of the Spanish-American War. Little had been done to prepare the island against attack, and its 200-man Marine garrison, supported by Guamanian police and volunteers, was overwhelmed on December 10, 1941, following three days of fighting, by a 5,500-man Japanese brigade.

U.S. Admiral Ernest King, chief of naval operations, argued as early as January 1943 for an invasion of the Mariana Islands. The invasion of Guam was delayed by more than a month because operations against Saipan took longer than anticipated and the task force reserve of the 27th Division had to be ordered there.

Its limestone terrain veiled in labyrinthine vegetation, Guam was well suited for defense. The island's numerous ridges, hills, valleys, and caves allowed Lieutenant General Takashina Takeshi's 18,500 defenders to magnify their limited artillery resources. In close proximity to one another on the western shore were the two most important military installations: the fortified air base on Chote Peninsula and the navy yard at Apra Harbor.

The invasion was preceded for two days by the longest sustained naval bombardment of the Pacific islands campaigns to that point. The invasion force came ashore on the morning of July 21 in a two-pronged assault five miles apart. The 3rd Marine Division landed on the beach north of Apra Harbor to capture the nearby navy yard; the 1st Provisional Marine Brigade joined with the foremost elements of the 77th Infantry Division below the harbor to take the large airfield on the Orote Peninsula. Poor maps and stiff Japanese resistance prevented an advance of more than a few miles beyond the two designated American beachheads for four days. Enough Japanese guns survived the preliminary naval bombardment to inflict numerous casualties on the exposed American troops.

Late in the afternoon of July 25, the 1st Provisional Marine Brigade finally seized the road bisecting the neck of the Orote Peninsula, severing Japanese access to the island's interior. That night, the trapped Japanese troops attempted to escape in General Takashina's ill-conceived banzai attack, only to be shattered by concentrated Marine artillery fire. Surviving Japanese were gradually eliminated over the next few days.

In an attempt to splinter the American beachhead north of Apra Harbor, at about 3:00 a.m. on July 26 Takashina mounted a well-planned, 3,900-man counterstrike against the unsuspecting 3rd Marine Division. Exploiting an unintended gap between two Marine regiments, the attackers swiftly penetrated the American position. Wild fighting ensued, involving support personnel as well as frontline defenders.

Despite its initial gains and the infliction of 800 Marine casualties, after three hours the Japanese attack ground to a complete halt. It had left an astounding 3,500 (95 percent) of the attacking force dead. Takashina's expensive counterattack proved catastrophic to his already inadequate force. Intermittent fighting continued for several weeks across much of the island's thickly forested interior as organized Japanese resistance slowly dissolved in the face of the Americans' steady northward advance.

The loss of Guam and the remainder of the Marianas deprived the Japanese navy of airfields and anchorages and cut Japan's major supply artery with the South Pacific and its large air and naval base at Truk in the Caroline Islands. The United States launched devastating B-29 bombing raids against Japan itself after it gained control of Guam, Saipan, and Tinian.

*William B. Rogers*
*and Phillip M. Sozansky*

**See also:** World War II, Pacific Theater.

## Further Reading

Gailey, Harry. *The Liberation of Guam: 21 July–10 August, 1944.* Novato, CA: Presidio Press, 1988.

Morison, Samuel Eliot. *History of United States Naval Operations in World War II. Vol. 8: New Guinea and the Marianas, March 1944–August 1944.* Boston: Little, Brown, 1953.

## Hakkō Ichiu

The phrase *hakkō ichiu* literally means "eight cords, one roof" but may be freely translated as "the whole world under one roof." The phrase became incorporated into Japan's ultranationalist vision of the future in the early part of the 20th century to indicate that Japan's destiny was to rule the world.

The saying was popularized by the Nichiren Buddhist ultranationalist Tanaka Chigaku. He claimed that Jimmu, the human descendant of Japan's chief deity the Sun Goddess Amaterasu-no-mi-kami, had uttered the phrase as he ascended to become Japan's first emperor. Tanaka said that Jimmu had prophesized that Japan's pure Shintō morality would expand to encompass the entire world.

Strangely, the fusion of this brand of Buddhism and Shintō was seized upon by those who wished to "restore" the Shōwa emperor to real power. Like "nativists" the world over, the adherents chose to ignore rationality in favor of anything that proved that what was native was superior to anything foreign. Like the Aryanism nonsense of German Nazis and the Geomancy (*feng shui*) of the Chinese Boxers, this Japanese world-view conflated Tanaka's interpretation of Nichiren with Kokugaku atavism with no sense of irony.

Kita Ikki, the ideological leader of national socialism in Japan, adopted the phrase *hakkō ichiu* in his writings in the 1920s. Ishiwara Kanji, an army officer and member of Tanaka's Kokuchukai (National Pillar Society), used Tanaka's teachings in his plans for the 1931 Manchurian Incident. Eventually, Konoe Fumimaro, the prime minister in 1940, used the phrase to explain why Japan had invaded China: to save it from itself. Perhaps this circular logic was no more irrational than the ravings of the American "Know Nothing Party," whose advocates eschewed Native Americans as part of their attempt to preserve American Native purity, or the madness of the Ku Klux Klan, whose members wished to preserve American Christianity at the expense of native Roman Catholics.

In April 1940, a huge obelisk was raised to commemorate the 2,500th anniversary of the founding of Japan's Imperial Dynasty, dating from the alleged ascension of Jimmu to the throne in 660 B.C.E. The phrase *Hakkō Ichiu* was carved on one side of the monument. Perversely, when World War II was clearly going against Japan after 1944, the government urged the people onward, even to mass suicide, to accomplish the goals of *hakkō ichiu*. Curiously, the inscription was removed from the monument in the immediate postwar era when the obelisk was rechristened the "Peace Tower." The inscription was restored in the 1990s, but the monument continues to be called a "prayer for peace."

*Louis G. Perez*

**See also:** Ishiwara Kanji; Kita Ikki; Konoe Fumimaro; Mukden Incident: Lytton Report; Tanaka Chigaku.

### Further Reading

Brownlee, John. *Japanese Historians and the National Myths, 1600–1945: The Age of the Gods.* Vancouver: University of British Columbia Press, 1997.

Edwards, Walter. "Forging Tradition for a Holy War: The *Hakkō Ichiu* Tower in Miyazaki and Japanese Wartime Ideology." *Journal of Japanese Studies* 29, no. 2 (2003): 289–324.

Lee, Edwin. "Nichiren and Nationalism: The Religious Patriotism of Tanaka Chigaku." *Monumenta Nipponica* 30, no. 1 (1975): 19–35.

# Hansan, Battle of (1592)

In 1592, Toyotomi Hideyoshi had decided to conquer Korea on the road to conquering China. Hideyoshi had recently defeated his rivals to unify Japan, and he needed an outlet for the energies of many unemployed soldiers. In April 1592, the Japanese made a surprise landing at Pusan and quickly captured the nearby fortifications. Within 20 days, the Japanese occupied Seoul. Every Korean army sent to stop them was soundly defeated. The Japanese forces were veteran troops, and they were well armed with firearms, a weapon in short supply in the Korean Army.

Korean Admiral Yi Sun Sin mounted a naval squadron to attack the Japanese ships. Although Yi was born into a scholar-official family in Korea, he entered the military, instead. By 1592, Yi had advanced to command the Korean fleet in the Cholla Province. One important innovation was his creation of "turtle ships." Known in Korean as *kobukson*, these ships were normal warships whose decks were covered with a curved iron roof, like a turtle's back. The roof was covered with spikes to prevent enemy soldiers from boarding. The turtle ships were armed with cannons and other firearms that could fire in all directions. They were also armed with an iron ram so they could smash other ships

and sink them. Like all Korean ships, the turtle ships were flat-bottomed so they could sail close to Korea's rocky shores and operate in harbors and rivers. They were powered mainly by oars, although two sails were also used. For psychological reasons, Yi added a dragon head to each ship, which could breathe out smoke and fire. The turtle ships were very maneuverable and held a technological edge over the Japanese ships available at that time.

Yi first attacked Japanese ships at the Battle of Okpo, where he quickly destroyed 26 of his opponent's ships without losing any himself. That success was soon followed by other victories. On July 7, 1592, Yi defeated a Japanese fleet carrying reinforcements in the Korean Strait. He used a familiar tactic of pretending to flee to make the Japanese ships follow him and lose their formation. Off the island of Hansan, Yi joined the rest of his fleet, and the Koreans turned on their pursuers. Yi used a formation he called the "Crane" formation—two lines of ships that enveloped the Japanese fleet and used cannon fire to disrupt and destroy it. The same line-ahead formation was first being used at that time in European fleets. The Japanese were overwhelmed. More than 120 of their warships were burned or sunk, while most of a convoy carrying 100,000 soldiers was destroyed.

After the Battle of Hansan, the Japanese refused to fight Yi at sea. The Korean Navy patrolled the waters around Korea and intercepted most of the supplies and communications between Korea and Japan. Yi followed up his victory with an attack on Japanese shipping in Pusan harbor, the main Japanese naval base. By some accounts, 470 Japanese ships were there. Yi attacked with only 166 ships, using cannon fire and fireships to destroy 133 Japanese vessels without losing any of his own.

Yi's victories led the Korean king to promote him to commander-in-chief of the navy. He briefly fell into disfavor in 1597 after being accused of not pursuing the enemy. Following a defeat by the Japanese, Yi was recalled. He soon regained naval superiority, however. At the Battle of Noryang, the final battle of the war, Yi was killed by a stray shot.

*Tim Watts*

See also: Toyotomi Hideyoshi.

**Further Reading**

Park, Yune-hee, *Admiral Yi Sun-Sin and His Turtleboat Armada: A Comprehensive Account of the Resistance of Korea to the 16th Century Japanese Invasion*, Seoul: Hanjin, 1973.

Sadler, A. L. "The Naval Campaign in the Korean War of Hideyoshi (1592–1598)." *Transactions of the Asiatic Society of Japan*, Second Series, 14 (June 1937): 179–208.

**Hara Kei.** *See* Hara Takashi.

## *Hara-kiri (Seppuku)*

*Hara-kiri* or *seppuku* is a form of ritual suicide performed by cutting open the abdomen; it was viewed as a way to provide samurai with an honorable death other than in battle. *Hara-kiri* is the Japanese reading of the Chinese characters for "stomach" and "to cut" and may be translated as "belly slitting." *Seppuku* is the Chinese reading of the same characters in reverse order and may be translated as "disembowelment." The abdomen is focus of the ritual because it is the central core of the physical body and, according to Asian thought, is where the soul is located. In the past, the ethics and values of Japan allowed for suicide. While neither Shintō nor Buddhism openly approve of suicide, neither do they outright condemn it. Buddhism, especially, with its teachings of rebirth and discipline and the infinite forgiveness of Amida, was amenable to the act.

The ritual evolved over time. Self-immolation through disembowelment seems to have its origin among the Minamoto clan, especially during the Gempei War. While suicide to avoid capture and disgrace can be found in *Nihongi* and *Kojiki*, early Japanese histories, the first recorded act of *hara-kiri* was by Minamoto Tametomo in 1177. The legendary bowman, who reportedly stood nearly seven feet tall, had been banished to the island of Oshima following the 1156 Hōgen War. His enemies had cut the tendons in his arms to render him harmless as an archer, but when he attempted to seize power on the island the Taira sent a force to stop him. Rather than face defeat and ignominious death, Minamoto cut open his stomach. A formal model for the ritual was established at the beginning of the Gempei War when Minamoto Yorimasa performed the act in relatively peaceful isolation after writing a poem. With the end of the Warring States era (mid-15th century to 1600), there was no longer the need for a warrior-chosen suicide as a way to escape defeat and capture but the Tokugawa *bakufu* allowed *hara-kiri* as an option for samurai to avoid execution like common criminals.

Throughout history, *hara-kiri* was performed for a variety of reasons, including avoiding capture and defeat, as an option to being executed as a common criminal, and *junshi* (following one's lord in death). *Junshi* was outlawed in the 17th century by the Tokugawa *bakufu*, which feared that the suicides of a deceased lord's retainers could lead to political instability. The last historically significant act of ritual suicide occurred in 1970, when author Mishima Yukio committed *hara-kiri* as an act of political the-ater after staging a coup in the headquarters of the Self-Defense Forces.

Under the regulations established by the Tokugawa *bakufu*, a feudal lord would be charged with the custody of the condemned. He would see that the site and resources for the act were prepared. The most important official functionary at the suicide was the *ken-shi* (inspector), who was appointed by the *bakufu*. It was his responsibility to pronounce the sentence and ensure the ritual was prop-erly carried out. Preparation for the formal suicide ceremony included providing a site, about 20 feet square, special meals, and gar-ments, including a white kimono for the act of disembowelment. White symbolized purity and the condemned's commitment to accept death. Before the condemned was presented with the knife, a priest would offer a prayer. The condemned would then slit his abdomen from left to right with a short knife. As a final act of bravado, the warrior might end with an upward cut. At the same time the con-demned warrior reached for the knife and began the incision, the *kaishaku* (an attendant or second) would behead the victim. Prior to the Tokugawa era, the use of the *kaishaku* was dependent on circumstances and war-rior's preference, but it was instituted by the *bakufu* to spare the condemned warrior the pain of disembowelment.

Traditional depictions of *hara-kiri* in liter-ature and art, such as the classic story of the 47 loyal retainers (*Chūshingura*), often por-tray the act as heroic and even romantic. Kobayashi Masaki's 1962 film *Harakiri* (*Sep-puku*), in contrast, exposes a dark side of the tradition as cruel and brutal. Mishima's *hara-kiri* also raised doubts about the act's nobility when his *kaishaku* was reportedly unable to efficiently carry out his responsibil-ity with a single cut.

*R. W. Purdy*

**See also:** *Bushidō*; Civil Wars, Sengoku Era; Hogen-Heiji-Gempei Wars; Mishima Yukio; Tokugawa *Bakufu* Political System.

## Further Reading

Ikegami Eiko. *The Taming of the Samurai.* Cambridge, MA: Harvard University Press, 1995.

Pinguet, Maurice. *Voluntary Death in Japan.* Cambridge, UK: Polity Press, 1993.

Seward, Jack. *Hara-kiri: Japanese Ritual Sui-cide.* Tokyo: Charles E. Tuttle Company, 1968.

## Hara Takashi (1856–1921)

Born in Morioka in northern Japan on Febru-ary 9, 1856, Hara Takashi joined the Japanese Foreign Ministry in November 1882. His acquaintance with Mutsu Munemitsu, who was appointed foreign minister in the second cabinet of Itō Hirobumi in August 1892, helped Hara obtain a series of key posts in Japan's Foreign Service. Hara left the For-eign Ministry upon Mutsu's death in Septem-ber 1897 and became a senior editor for the *Osaka Mainichi Shinbun*. He assumed the daily newspaper's presidency the following year. When the Rikken Seiyūkai Party was organized in September 1900, Hara was recruited into its ranks by the party's first presidents, Itō and Inoue Kaoru. In December of that year, Hara became the party secretary-general. He was elected to his first term in the House of Representatives in 1902 and became the Seiyūkai Party's third president in June 1914. In the interim, Hara served in a series of cabinet posts.

When Terauchi Masatake, a member of the early Meiji oligarchy, formed a cabinet in October 1916, Hara remained neutral and was appointed to the Emergency For-eign Affairs Research Council. Concerned about U.S. reaction, Hara was reluctant to

Hara Takashi played a pivotal role in the founding and development of the Seiyūkai political party. In 1918, he became the first party politician and member of the lower house of the Diet (Japan's legislature) to hold the office of prime minister. (Corbis)

send troops to the Allied military expedition to Siberia following the Bolshevik Revolution of November 1917. His appointment as premier in September 1918 was the first for an elected lower house member in Japanese history. As Hara was not a member of the nobility, he was nicknamed the "commoner" prime minister.

Hara played a central role in shifting post-World War I Japanese foreign policy toward international cooperation and in the withdrawal of Japanese troops from Siberia. Domestically, he implemented substantial reform programs, including expansion of higher education and improvements in infrastructure such as the expansion of railroads and port facilities. Although his government did expand the franchise, it rejected universal male suffrage. Hara's government also adopted suppressive policies toward internal unrest (the Rice Riots) and the Korean independence movement. Accusations of corruption and scandal led to Hara's assassination at the Tokyo Railway Station on November 4, 1921. The assassin, Nakaoka Konichi, charged that the Hara cabinet had pursued partisan rather than national interests.

*Kurosawa Fumitaka*

**See also:** Inoue Kaoru; Itō Hirobumi; Mutsu Munemitsu; Rice Riots; Siberian Intervention.

## Further Reading

Oka, Yoshitake. *Five Political Leaders of Modern Japan: Itô Hirobumi, Ōkuma Shigenobu, Hara Takashi, Inukai Tsuyoshi, and Saionji Kinmochi.* Trans. Andrew

Fraser and Patricia Murray. Tokyo: University of Tokyo Press, 1986.

Olson, L. A. *Hara Kei: A Political Biography.* Unpublished doctoral dissertation, Harvard University, Cambridge, MA, 1954.

Tesuo Najita. *Hara Kei in the Politics of Compromise, 1905–1915.* Cambridge, MA: Harvard University Press, 1967.

## Harris, Townsend (1804–1878)

Townsend Harris was born in Sandy Hill, New York. Primarily a merchant and importer of Chinese goods, he was also involved in politics. Harris served as the president of the New York City Board of Education from 1846 to 1848. Recognizing the importance of education for all, he founded the Free Academy of the City of New York, which later became City College of New York. Townsend Harris High School emerged out of the secondary-level curriculum. The Free Academy provided a free education to the city's working class.

Harris's connection to Japan came as a part of American expansion in the Pacific. In 1853, Commodore Matthew Perry arrived at Edo and requested that the Japanese open ports for trade and provisioning. The Treaty of Kanagawa, signed in March 1854, was the result of this request. The treaty allowed American ships to trade at two specifically designated ports, guaranteed the safety of shipwrecked sailors, and allowed a representative of the American government to reside in Shimoda. President Franklin Pierce appointed Harris as the first Consul General to Japan. He set up the first American Consulate on the grounds of Gyokusen-ji Temple in Shimoda in 1856. The Japanese government did not warmly welcome Harris, but instead attempted to isolate him, throwing up obstacles to further diplomatic and trade relations with the United States.

In spite of Japanese attempts to stall diplomatic relations, in 1858 Harris negotiated the Treaty of Amity (Peace) and Commerce, also known as the Harris Treaty. Harris relied on diplomacy rather than threat of force to secure the terms of this treaty. He persuaded Japanese officials to accept the terms he proposed, out of friendship and goodwill, adding that any terms demanded by the British and French would be less favorable. The Japanese government ultimately agreed and this treaty secured a trade relationship between the United States and Japan. It opened more ports to trade— Edo, Kobe, Nagasaki, Niigata, and Yokohama—and fixed a low tariff on trade goods. The Harris treaty also granted the right of extraterritoriality to Americans in Japan, based on the belief that it would be unfair to expect Americans to follow Japanese laws and custom. The treaty was ratified in 1860 when the first Japanese embassy traveled to the United States. In addition, it served as the model for treaties that Japan later signed with other nations. As a group, these treaties came to be known as the Unequal Treaties.

In January 1861, a group of samurai from Satsuma assassinated Harris's translator and friend, Henry Heusken, as he returned home after assisting the Prussian delegation in their treaty negotiations. Tensions were high as Western nations attempted to negotiate their own treaties with the Japanese government. After the assassination, the French, British, and Prussian delegations withdrew from Edo, but Harris refused to retreat. Instead, he stayed on and negotiated an indemnity for Heusken's mother.

Harris returned to the United States in 1861. He retired to New York City, where he remained active in politics until his death in 1878.

*Larissa Castriotta Kennedy*

See also: Perry, Matthew; Shimoda Treaty; Unequal Treaties.

### Further Reading

Cosenza, Mario Emilio, ed. *The Complete Journal of Townsend Harris, First American Consul General and Minister to Japan*. New York: Doubleday, 1930. Reprint Rutland: Charles E. Tuttle, 1968.

Dulles, Foster Rhea. *Yankees and Samurai: America's Role in the Emergence of Modern Japan, 1791–1900*. New York: Harper and Row, 1965.

Griffis, William Elliot. *Townsend Harris, First American Envoy in Japan*. New York: Houghton, Mifflin, 1895. Reprint Freeport: Books for Libraries Press, 1971.

Perrin, Noel. *Giving Up the Gun*. Boulder, CO: Shambhala, 1979.

## Hashimoto Kingoro (1890–1957)

Born in Okayama City on February 19, 1890, Hashimoto Kingoro joined the army in 1911 and graduated from the Army Staff College in 1920. He then served in Manchuria with the Guandong (Kwantung) Army from 1922 to 1925. Hashimoto believed that Japan's future demanded territorial expansion, and he was attracted to nationalist organizations that promoted this cause. While in Manchuria, Hashimoto helped to plan the Mukden Incident, in which elements of the Japanese military staged an attack on their own interests and used it as an excuse to seize most of Manchuria. This led to the establishment by Japan of the puppet state of Manchukuo.

In 1930, Hashimoto and Captain Isamu Cho founded the Sakurakai (Cherry Blossom Society) to promote Japanese imperialism. Hashimoto also published widely; his most famous essay is "The Need for Immigration and Expansion." His writings became the philosophical basis for most Japanese extreme nationalists. Hashimoto attracted many followers, especially among mid-level army officers. He held various regimental assignments in Japan between 1931 and 1935. During this time, he continued his extremist nationalist activities He was cashiered from the Japanese army for his involvement in the attempted coup on February 26, 1936, against the Japanese government.

When war with China began in July 1937, Hashimoto was recalled to active duty. Promoted to colonel, he received command of the 13th Heavy Field Artillery Regiment. Hashimoto was implicated in atrocities committed in Nanjing (Nanking) in December 1937. He also ordered his troops to fire on the British gunboat *Ladybird* and on the U.S. Navy gunboat *Panay*. Despite Western protests, Hashimoto retained his command until 1939.

On his retirement from the army, Hashimoto dedicated himself to political activities. He organized and led the Dai Nippon Seinen-to (Great Japan Youth Party), later known as the Dai Nippon Sekisei-kai (Great Japan Sincerity Association). Hashimoto also became executive director of the Imperial Rule Assistance Association in 1940. He was elected to the Diet in 1944.

After World War II, Hashimoto was tried as a war criminal for his part in atrocities in China and in promoting aggressive war. Sentenced to life imprisonment, he was paroled in 1954. Hashimoto died in Tokyo on June 29, 1957.

*Tim J. Watts*

See also: February 26 Incident; International Military Tribunal for Far East; Kwantung Army Adventurism; Manchukuo; Mukden Incident; World War II, Japanese Atrocities.

## Further Reading

Hayashi, Saburo. *Kogun: The Japanese Army in the Pacific War.* Westport, CT: Greenwood Press, 1959.

Koginos, Manny T. *The Panay Incident: Prelude to War.* Lafayette, IN: Purdue University Studies, 1967.

Toland, John. *Rising Sun: The Decline and Fall of the Japanese Empire, 1936–1945.* New York: Random House, 1970.

## Heike monogatari

The *Heike monogatari* ("Tales of the Heike") is a long, narrative account the Genpei War (1180–1185), its causes, and its immediate aftermath. It describes the conflict in terms of a clash between two great warrior clans, the Taira (or Heike) and the Minamoto (or Genji). The first large-scale civil conflict in Japan's history, the Genpei War led to the establishment of the first shōgunate in Kamakura (south of Yokohama), thus attenuating the power of the aristocratic government in Kyoto.

As an account of the foundational event in the rise of the samurai class, *Heike monogatari* is unequaled among the *gunki monogatari* (war tales) as the most beloved and influential. Its important characters appear in the Noh and Kabuki drama and narratives from the late medieval and early modern period, and they have also been the subject of modern drama and film. The most memorable of these characters include Minamoto Yoshitsune, his cousin Kiso Yoshinaka, and the generals of the Taira clan, such as Tadanori, Shigehira, and Koremori, as well as less clearly historical figures such as Taira Atsumori and the female dancer Giō. Both *Heike monogatari* and works influenced by it have played an important role in shaping the cultural memory of the war for later generations.

There are approximately 80 variant texts of *Heike monogatari*, which are generally divided into two lineages: the recited-text lineage, or *kataribonkei*, and the read-text lineage, or *yomihonkei*. The "recited" texts are associated with the recitational practice of *Heike biwa* (alt. *heikyoku*), in which blind, male performers called *biwa hōshi* ("biwa priests"), who accompanied their singing of the tale with the *biwa*, or Japanese lute. That *Heike monogatari* takes its title from the name of the losing side suggests a general sympathy for the fallen as well as a placatory dimension associated with this lineage—one role of the work appears to have been to assuage the spirits of those killed in battle. The "read" variants, by contrast, were originally intended to be read as records of the war and were not part of the performance tradition. The recited-text lineage is the better known of the two, and its finest representative, the *Kakuichi-bon*, is usually chosen for translations into English and other languages of *Heike monogatari*.

As with most *gunki monogatari*, *Heike monogatari* cannot be ascribed to a particular author, and scholars tend to think of it as an accretion of numerous shorter narratives coalesced under the direction of a compiler or compilers. Moreover, specific dates are hard to ascribe to the variants, although the colophon of the *Engyō-bon*, a read-text lineage variant dates it to 1309 (the earliest date for any *Heike* variant) and a colophon on the *Kakuichi-bon* dates it to 1371. Later variants were being created well into the 15th century. Scholars believe the *Kakuichi-bon* was probably compiled at Enryaku-ji, the Tendai Buddhist complex on Mt. Hiei, just northeast of Kyoto, an assertion supported by a comment in Yoshida Kenkō's *Tsurezuregusa* ("Essays in Idleness") that the Tendai Abbot Jien had a hand in editing the work.

*Elizabeth A. Oyler*

See also: *Early Mytho-histories: Kojiki* and *Nihon shōki*; Hogen-Heiji-Gempei Wars; Kamakura *Bakufu*; Minamoto Yoshitsune.

## Further Reading

Bialock, David T. *Eccentric Spaces, Hidden Histories: Narrative, Ritual, and Royal Authority from* The Chronicles of Japan *to* The Tale of the Heike. Stanford, CA: Stanford University Press, 2007.

McCullough, Helen C. *The Tale of the Heike.* Stanford, CA: Stanford University Press, 1988.

Oyler, Elizabeth A. *Swords, Oaths, and Prophetic Visions: Authoring Warrior Rule in Medieval Japan.* Honolulu: University of Hawaii Pres, 2006.

Varley, Paul. *Warriors of Japan as Portrayed in the War Tales.* Honolulu: University of Hawaii Press, 1994.

**Heisei Emperor.** *See* Akihito, Emperor.

## Heusken, Henry (1832–1861)

Born Henricus Conradus Joannes Heusken January 20, 1832, in Amsterdam. At age 15, Heusken returned from school in Brabant to join the family business in Amsterdam. His father's death soon afterward left him in charge but Henry was unable to maintain the business. Facing bankruptcy, Heusken immigrated to the United States in 1853, at age 21. He drifted from job to job in increasingly impoverished circumstances.

Heusken's fortunes changed for the better, at least temporarily, when he was hired as secretary and interpreter to Townsend Harris, the recently appointed the Consul-General to Japan. The new legation needed a Dutch speaker because after the expulsion of all other Western nationalities by 1639, Dutch was the language of diplomacy with Western powers. Heusken departed with Harris from New York on October 25, 1855, arriving in Shimoda on August 21, 1856. Harris was charged with negotiating diplomatic and commercial treaties. A commercial treaty was signed in 1856. The pair transferred to Edo, the shōgunal capital, in November 1857. Before the 1856 treaty took effect, a new one was signed in 1858 that was more favorable to the United States.

Heusken was an important factor in the success of the American mission. He was well liked by the Japanese officials with whom they negotiated, and he liked and respected them in return. Fluent in Dutch, English, French, and German, Heusken was commended as able and efficient. Not only was he an effective translator, but he was also a popular member of the foreign community. Harris claimed to have loved him like a son. In addition to his duties for the American legation, Heusken sometimes assisted other foreign dignitaries, as when he was loaned to the British for two weeks in 1858.

Notwithstanding his efforts on the behalf of Western diplomacy, Heusken is best remembered for his death. He was attacked in the waning hours of January 15, 1861, the first foreigner in the diplomatic corps to be assassinated. Heusken was assisting Friedrich Albrecht Graf zu Eulenburg, the Prussian Plentipotentiary, in treaty negotiations with the Japanese. Harris had advised Heusken not to go out after dark because the tense political situation had already resulted in several assassinations over the past year and a half. Moreover, Heusken had been threatened and assaulted several times in the streets already. Heusken did not heed this warning and regularly returned late. He was cut down in the street despite being accompanied by four grooms and an armed escort of six Japanese. Left at the scene while help was sought, he bled to death from wounds sustained to the chest and abdomen because he did not receive medical help for 90 minutes. The attackers are believed to have been Ibuta Shohei, Masumitsu Shinpachirō, Kandabashi Naosuke, Hiwatari Hachibei, and one more member known only as Owaki, all from Satsuma, led by Koyokawa Hachirō, a rōnin from Shonai. There were rumors that another attack would be made on the foreign ministers at Heusken's funeral on January 18. Shōgunal officials advised the foreigners to avoid the funeral and stay at home. Instead, Dutch and Prussian armed soldiers accompanied the procession. The five *bugyō* (ministers) of Edo also attended.

Harris negotiated an indemnity of $10,000 for Heusken's mother. Heusken's assassination caused the French, British, and Prussian envoys to withdraw from Edo to Yokohama. Townsend Harris refused to follow, standing his ground in Edo. This stance caused ongoing friction between Harris and Rutherford Alcock, the British Consul. Heusken's death also put pressure on the Japanese government to negotiate because they feared retaliation. Heusken was portrayed by Sam Jaffe in the 1958 John Wayne film, *The Barbarian and the Geisha*.

*Martha Chaiklin*

See also: Harris, Townsend.

**Further Reading**

Harris, Townsend. *The Complete Journal of Townsend Harris*, 2nd ed. Edited by Mario E. Cosenza. Tokyo/Rutland, VT: Charles E. Tuttle, 1958.

Hesselink, Reinier H. "The Assassination of Henry Heusken." *Monumenta Nipponica* 49, no. 3 (Autumn 1994): 331–351.

Heusken, Henry. *Japan Journal, 1855–1861*. Translated by Jeannette C. van der Corput and Robert A. Wilson. New Brunswick, NJ: Rutgers University Press, 1964.

**Hidden Christians.** *See Kakure Kirishitan.*

## High Treason Incident (1910–1911)

The 1911 execution of 12 left-wing radicals for a plot against the Meiji Emperor's life, known as the Kōtoku Incident and the Great Treason Incident, marked a turning point between the relatively unihibited, lively speech of the Meiji years and a time of increasing government control over public discourse—a time when socialists, in particular, found it ever more difficult to operate. The episode foreshadowed the Japanese authoritarianism of the 1930s.

Serving as a backdrop to the incident was the government's attempt in the preceding years to control a small but outspoken left-wing movement, which had emerged after the Sino-Japanese War (1894–1895) when a brilliant group of young intellectuals used the country's major thought journals, as well as their own newspaper, the *Heimin Shimbun* ("Commoners Newspaper"), to advocate everything from socialism to anarchism. With images of the French Revolution and Europe's radical Marxism in mind, officials had shut down the *Heimin Shimbun* and had sent numerous left-wingers to jail, particularly in the 1908 Red Flag Incident, when activists used banners to agitate on behalf of extreme socialist views such as anarchism and anarcho-communism.

The High Treason Incident began with the police's discovery in May 1910 of potential bomb-making materials in the apartment of Miyashita Takichi, a factory worker in mountainous Nagano Prefecture. Convinced by their investigation that Miyashita was part of a broader group, the authorities arrested 26 leftists, charging them with plans to harm the emperor, an offense for which Japan's Criminal Code prescribed death. The trial was conducted in secret before the nation's highest court, with material about the proceedings so tightly controlled that most details about the episode emerged only decades later, after World War II.

Chief prosecutor Hiranuma Kiichirō focused on Kōtoku Shūsui, Japan's best-known socialist, even though it was clear that Kōtoku had withdrawn from the group's discussions months before the raid on Miyashita's residence. A clearer case could be made for Miyashita and two colleagues, Niimura Tadao and Furukawa Rikisaku, as well as for the only woman in the group, Kanno Suga, one of the era's most outspoken socialist activists and, for a time, Kōtoku's partner. All 26 were labeled by the prosecution as dangerous terrorists. In contrast, the head of the defense team, Hiraide Shū, argued—in a view generally supported by historians—that none except the central group had been involved in anything but the most peripheral way and that even the core five had made no efforts to actually commit the deed.

The verdict, handed down on January 18, 1911, found all 26 defendants guilty. Two were given lengthy prison terms, the other 24 death by hanging. A day later, the emperor commuted half of the death sentences to life in prison. Eleven of the others were hanged January 24, with Kanno suffering the same fate a day later.

The most significant feature of the incident may have been the public response, which generally supported the government's use of the imperial symbol to prohibit "radical" speech. With only the rarest exception, writers across the ideological spectrum proclaimed horror that any Japanese could even imagine an attack on the throne. Even the secrecy of the trials (some 250 security officials guarded the court) and the heavy censorship of information drew almost no press comment. When the novelist Tokutomi Rōka made a speech on February 1 before the Debate Club of the First National Higher School, condemning the plotters' act but lauding their dream of "liberty and equality" and deploring their execution, the press castigated him, and the Education Ministry censured the school's principal, Nitobe Inazō, for allowing the talk. When the mainstream opinion journal *The Sun* (*Taiyō*) ran a short story in 1913 raising questions about the executions, officials banned the issue.

The 1910s have been called the "winter years" for Japanese socialists, a period when government harassment and public indifference drove Marxists into silence. They would reemerge temporarily in the 1920s, before being destroyed in the militarist 1930s. There is little question about the importance in this chain of the High Treason Incident, when conservatives and progressives alike expressed outrage over the activists' plot and writers of all stripes felt constrained to keep silent about censorship and secret trials.

*James L. Huffman*

**See also:** Kōtoku Shūsui; Meiji Emperor; Nitobe Inazō.

### Further Reading

Cronin, Joseph. *The Life of Seinosuke: Dr. Oishi and the High Treason Incident.* Kyoto: White Tiger Press, 2007.

Notehelfer, F. G. *Kōtoku Shūsui: Portrait of a Japanese Radical.* Cambridge, UK: University Press, 1971.

Rubin, Jay. *Injurious to Public Morals: Writers and the Meiji State.* Seattle: University of Washington Press, 1984.

## Himiko-Iyo Succession Crisis (Third Century C.E.)

Himiko is mentioned in a number of third-century Chinese dynastic histories. The Chinese report that after several decades of civil war in Japan, the people decided to install an aged virgin woman as queen. She ruled for several years during which she "occupied herself with magic and sorcery, bewitching the people." Himiko was seldom seen, preferring to communicate her wishes through her brother. She kept a large entourage of "one thousand women as attendants."

The Chinese recognized Himiko as Queen of Japan (the Kingdom of the Wa) after she sent an embassy to the court of Wei emperor Cao Rui in 238 C.E. They sent her a number of gifts including a gold imperial seal and charged her, "O Queen, to rule your people in peace." Later, another entry reported that Himiko died and was buried together with "over a hundred male and female attendants" in a large tumulus (*kofun*). A male tried to take over as king but civil war ensued until Iyo, a 13-year-old girl was named queen.

The Himiko-Iyo story continues to be a source of controversy in Japanese studies. Neither queen is mentioned by name in the two Japanese eighth-century quasi histories (*Kojiki* and *Nihon shōki*), although some scholars claim that the two are conflated into Yamato-totohi-momoso-hime-no-mikoto, the aunt of Emperor Sujin; Yamatohime-no-mikoto, the daughter of Emperor Suinin; and Empress Jingū.

Some scholars point to the queen succession as evidence of matriarchy. They suggest that evidence of uxorial marriage, matrilineal inheritance, female shamanism, polyandry, and the fact that the chief Shintō deity is a woman (the Sun Goddess Amaterasu) all suggest that Japan was ruled by women.

In any case, the story of the succession crisis was the first mention of Japan in any written history.

*Louis G. Perez*

**See also:** Early Mytho-histories: *Kojiki* and *Nihon shōki*.

### Further Reading

Akima Toshio. "The Myth of the Goddess of the Undersea World and the Tale of Empress Jingū's Subjugation of Silla." *Japanese Journal of Religious Studies* 20, no. 2 (1993): 95–185.

Farris, William Wayne. "Sacred Texts and Buried Treasures: Issues in the Historical Archaeology of Ancient Japan." *Monumenta Nipponica* 54, no. 1 (1998): 123–126.

Kidder, Jonathan Edward. *Himiko and Japan's Elusive Chiefdom of Yamatai*. Honolulu: University of Hawai'i Press, 2007.

## Hiratsuka *Raichō*

Hiratsuka was born in 1886 with the name Hiratsuka Haruko. She was the daughter of the vice president of the Board of Audit, an important government position. Hiratsuka's father had studied constitutional law in Europe during the early days of the Meiji Restoration, and she was exposed to Western ideas and learning from a very early age. Zen Buddhism was also a part of her early life, and she practiced Zen meditation throughout her life. Hiratsuka attended Ochanomizu Girls' High School and graduated from the home economics course of Nihon Women's College in 1906. She first aroused public criticism in 1908, when she planned to commit double suicide with the writer Morita Sohel. This episode became known as the Baien Incident, after Morita later wrote about it in the novel *Baien* ("Smoke").

Hiratsuka *Raichō* (fifth from right), one of the foremost feminists of early 20th-century Japan, meets with fellow suffragists. (Underwood & Underwood/Corbis)

In 1911, Hiratsuka joined with other young, unmarried women from upper-middle-class backgrounds who had an interest in literature. They formed the Seitosha (Bluestockings Society) with the avowed aim to work for the emancipation of Japanese women. In 1912, they began publishing the magazine *Seito* ("Bluestockings") by women and for women only, "promoting the self-awakening of women, bringing forth the inborn talent of each woman and giving birth to the female genius." Hiratsuka was editor and introduced the first issue with her manifesto entitled *"Genshi josei wa taiyo de atta"* ("In the Beginning Woman Was the Sun"). This slogan was repeated on the cover of each subsequent issue and became a rallying cry for Japanese feminists of the time. Finances for the magazine came from savings intended for Hiratsuka's wedding.

The magazine served as an inspiration and forum for liberal young women during the Taishō period of 1912–1926. Circulation increased rapidly, especially among young women. *Seito* became less of a literary magazine and more a source of criticism directed against Japanese society. One issue was banned by the government because of its content. Eventually, Hiratsuka turned her controlling interests and editorial duties over to Itō Noe, a far more radical feminist. *Seito* eventually ceased publication in February 1916.

In 1914, as *Seito* was prospering, Hiratsuka left her parents' home and moved in with Okumura Hiroshi, a man five years her junior who dreamed of being a painter. Hiratsuka disagreed with the marriage laws and refused to formally register her marriage to Okumura. She gave birth to a son and a daughter, but the family faced severe financial difficulties.

Okumura rarely sold his paintings and squandered the money he received when one did sell. Hiratsuka responded to critics of her lifestyle by responding that they did not understand the "new woman" that she had become. Ichikawa Fusae, in particular, came in for criticism by Hiratsuka, who accused Fusae of lacking individuality and creativity and being merely a practical administrator, a career woman who was the model of the "professional female."

Hiratsuka was especially interested in the concepts of Ellen Key, a Swedish feminist, whose *Love and Marriage* was widely read in Japan. Key advocated freedom to marry and divorce as love dictated, the improvement of the status of marriage, children's rights, and the social reforms necessary to achieve these goals. Inspired by these ideas, Hiratsuka stressed the protection of motherhood and engaged woman poet Yosano Akiko in a published debate in 1918. She also formally married Okumura in the same year.

In 1920, Hiratsuka founded the Shin Fujin Kyokai (New Woman's Association) with feminists Fusae and Oku Mumeo. The organization's goal was to reform the social and legal position of women, especially regarding Section 5 of the Peace Preservation Law, which forbade any political activity by women. Despite great difficulties in lobbying members of the Diet, Hiratsuka and her colleagues were successful. In 1922, the Diet passed a revision to the law, and women, although still under great handicaps, were able to begin to participate in politics.

During the remainder of the 1920s, Hiratsuka largely withdrew from feminist politics. Not until 1929 did she again step onto the national stage. In that year, Hiratsuka formed an all-women consumers' union called Warera no Ie, with herself as director. In 1930, she joined the Proletarian Women's Art Alliance formed by Takamura Itsue, a historian of Japanese women. She contributed articles to the alliance's radical magazine, *Fujin Sensen* ("Women's Battlefront").

After World War II, Hiratsuka again spoke out about the need for broad social reform, emphasizing pacifism and democracy and rejecting war. She became president of the Nihon Fujin Dantai Rengokai (Federation of Japanese Women's Societies); she would remain the organization's honorary president until her death. In 1954, Hiratsuka's "Japanese Women's Appeal" was a call to all the women of the world to help ban the hydrogen bomb, and it led to the holding of the World Mothers' Convention.

While her calls for equality for women and her unconventional lifestyle both contributed to her notoriety, Hiratsuka remained known primarily as a strong champion for social reform until her death in 1971.

*Tim Watts*

**See also:** Ichikawa Fusae; Itō Noe; Peace Preservation Law; *Seito* (*Bluestockings*); Yosano Akiko; Zen Buddhism and Militarism.

**Further Reading**

Iwao, Seiichi, ed. *Biographical Dictionary of Japanese History*. Trans. Burton Watson. Tokyo: International Society for Educational Information, 1978.

Kiyoko, Takeda. "Ichikawa Fusae: Pioneer for Women's Rights in Japan." *Japan Quarterly* 31, no. 4 (1984): 410–415.

Miyamoto, Ken. "Itō Noe and the Bluestockings." *Japan Interpreter* 10, no. 2 (Autumn 1975): 190–204.

**Hirohito.** *See* Shōwa Emperor.

# History Textbooks Controversy

School textbooks for teaching history in Japan, until the country's defeat at Allied hands in 1945, were anchored in myths and legends rather than in verifiable fact. Official standardized textbooks written by the imperial government—the only ones permitted in compulsory education—stressed Japan's unique *kokutai* ("national essence") and its subjects' ultimate virtue of dying in loyal service to their imperial dynasty reputed to be of divine descent. This national essence was the presumed basis of Japan's moral eminence and justified its self-proclaimed holy war to build a "New Order" in East Asia by liberating local peoples from Western colonial oppression. Thus the imperial government instilled extremist nationalism (also known as "ultra-nationalism") plus values of militaristic aggression in children through history education. The victorious Allies identified this issue in their occupation (1945–1952) as one key area to remake Japan into a peace-loving democratic nation under the "MacArthur peace constitution" that guaranteed basic human rights for citizens and renounced war as a sovereign right of the state. Old textbooks were scrapped and new ones written along liberal, pacifistic lines.

After the occupation ended in 1952, the textbook accreditation process became far more open than ever—although not totally transparent and accountable to the public—under a system whereby multiple publishers submitted draft copies of proposed texts for screening and accreditation by the Ministry of Education (MoE). Thus diversity and a broad range of choice emerged in textbooks used in public schools. Also, as democratic and pacifistic values took root in postwar Japan, bitter disputes erupted over textbooks, which continue today. Leftists in or allied with the Japan Teachers' Union (JTU) challenged conservative MoE textbook screeners, Asian governments and nongovernmental organizations (NGOs)

later denounced the MoE for whitewashing Japan's war crimes, and the MoE in turn came under fire from nationalist critics at home who berated it for capitulating to foreign demands in education, which should be an internal Japanese affair.

## Early Struggles

Shrewdly attuned to their occupation masters, numerous education bureaucrats, school principals, and classroom teachers nimbly discarded their now-discredited militarism in favor of democracy after 1945. Their questionable integrity produced fierce clashes with more sensitive cohorts, alarmed by the danger of an equally deft backslide into militarism and ultra-nationalism should political conditions change. The JTU issued a clarion call, "Never send our students to war again," which has fueled leftist opposition on textbook issues ever since. Its platform of total pacifism and unremitting hostility to patriotic symbols—seen in its denunciation of the national flag and anthem—won broad support in mainstream postwar society and created an intense ideological opposition to rearmament unseen even in West Germany, which began military conscription in 1956.

In 1955 the ruling party attacked one JTU-backed textbook for being ideologically slanted because it mentioned wartime atrocities, and in 1956 the MoE responded by creating a system of full-time screeners charged with tightening government control over textbooks. As a result, authors were banned from describing Japan's war crimes and from calling its actions in Asia "aggression." Such restrictions prompted one university history professor, Ienaga Saburô (1913–2002), and his supporters to file lawsuits against the MoE over the content of textbooks as well as their process of state accreditation in 1965, 1967, and 1984. Under the new Fundamental Law of Education and Constitution, he contended, textbook authors had the right to describe and students had the right to study atrocities committed by imperial Japan, such as its brutal crushing of independence movements in colonial Korea, its systematic mass murders and numerous rapes at Nanjing, Unit 731's chemical and biological warfare in China, and military orders for Okinawan civilians to kill themselves en masse rather than surrender. Ienaga conceded the legality of textbook screening to correct minor factual errors, typos, and grammatical mistakes. But, he insisted, it was illegal for the MoE to order major changes in content based on arbitrary and inconsistent procedures or on empirically flawed criteria. Ienaga won a partial victory in the Supreme Court that, coupled with the foreign pressure discussed later in this article, compelled MoE screeners to include limited mention of Japanese atrocities in history textbooks.

During the Cold War, most Asian countries that had earlier been victimized by Japan were in no position to lodge effective protests against the MoE. Thus, apart from the JTU and other civic groups inside Japan that backed dissidents such as Ienaga, the MoE faced scant pressure to make substantive textbook changes. Later, owing to foreign protests starting in the late 1970s, the government added a new criterion for accrediting textbooks in 1982. It stipulated that MoE screeners "take the history of neighboring countries into due consideration from the perspective of international understanding and cooperation." In practice, this forced screeners to approve brief and guarded accounts of Japanese atrocities such as the Unit 731 activities and the Nanjing Massacre, along with the army's wartime policy of enslaving women of Korean and other nationalities—euphemistically termed "comfort women"—which later came to light in the 1990s.

Foreign and domestic left-wing criticism amounted to this: by whitewashing, if not glorifying, Japan's past wars, the MoE was exploiting textbooks to instill patriotism in Japanese youths so that they would not oppose waging future wars, after the "MacArthur peace constitution" had undergone revision and Yasukuni Shrine—dedicated to Japan's war dead, including war criminals—had molted itself of all ultra-nationalist, militaristic associations.

## Later Developments

Nationalistically minded educators, some at Japan's finest universities, reacted harshly to textbook accounts of shameful wartime issues, especially the Nanjing Massacre, "comfort women," and forced mass suicides of Okinawan civilians. These educators derided such accounts as "masochistic" and the MoE as weak-kneed for bowing to foreign pressure. They also berated undue leftist influence over education and in society overall, which, they claimed, harmed the nation's well-being. In 1997, they formed the Society for History Textbook Reform. Since then, this group has published three successive editions of *A New History Textbook* (*NHT*), which vies for MoE accreditation and for a share of Japan's textbook market—although this has always fallen below 1 percent.

*NHT* authors hold that strategic objectives guided Allied occupation planning to a large extent. Through policies of media censorship and mind control in history education, they say, the occupation defamed Japan so cleverly and effectively that postwar Japanese became steeped in national guilt and resolved never to wage war again—which removed permanently enfeebled the country. Textbooks accredited by the occupation forces—and largely carried over by the JTU-leftists after 1952—portrayed pre-1945 Japan as a force for unmitigated evil. This Tokyo Tribunal interpretation of the past, *NHT* authors assert, was not just ideologically biased; it was also bad history for being anachronistic. That is, it denounced Japan's acts of aggression based on latter-day moral values rather than judging those acts according to standards in place at the time when those acts were taken. Imperialist expansion and colonial rule were legal and morally acceptable, and indeed were seen as praiseworthy endeavors, until the post-1945 era. Japan was no more or less "guilty" on these counts at that time than Allied powers such as Britain, France, and the United States. Why, then, should Japan alone come under indictment in history textbooks? *NHT* authors concede that Japan must assume a fair share of moral condemnation for wartime atrocities. But, they protest, it is historically inaccurate to equate Japan with Nazi Germany, and thus unfair to demand similar degrees of penance and restitution.

The *NHT*-nationalist advocates portray themselves as empiricist followers of Ranke, who reject advocacy-driven leftist historical education in favor of telling "how it actually was at the time." Yet, as their Asian and left-wing Japanese adversaries stress, the *NHT* camp has its own political agenda: by arguing that Japan's past wars were not totally dishonorable, their stance makes war seem respectable and legitimate for Japan in the future.

### The Dispute Today

This controversy has lost much of its sizzle in recent years for two main reasons. First, the Japanese people have acquired rich, multiple sources of information about their past, so the lion's share of what most of them know about history derives from sources other than school textbooks, such

as the Internet, news media, and genres of popular culture such as *anime*. MoE-approved textbooks now do little to foster historical knowledge and to lead popular opinion—whether toward rearmament or toward anything else. Thus JTU-leftist arguments have mostly become irrelevant. Second, the *NHT*-nationalist camp has gained cogency from contemporary developments in East Asia, whatever one may think of its historical revisionist line, because nations other than Japan now pose far greater threats to world peace. Retrogression to ultra-nationalism and aggression is virtually impossible; thus, for many reasonable people, patriotic educational policies to wean Japanese citizens from unconditional pacifism seem increasingly sensible and even compelling.

*Bob Tadashi Wakabayashi*

**See also:** *Kokutai* and Ultra-nationalism; 1947 Constitution; Occupation of Japan; World War II; World War II, Japanese Atrocities; Yasukuni Shrine Controversy.

### Further Reading

Horio, Teruhisa. *Educational Thought and Ideology in Modern Japan*. Tokyo: University of Tokyo Press, 1988.

Ienaga, Saburô. *Japan's Past, Japan's Future*. Lanham, MD: Rowman and Littlefield, 2001.

Thurston, Donald. *Teachers and Politics in Japan*. Princeton: Princeton University Press, 1973.

# Hitotsubasi Keiki (Tokugawa Yoshinobu) (1827–1913)

Tokugawa Yoshinobu was born in Edo in 1827, the son of Tokugawa Nariaki, the *daimyō* of Mito. He lived in the capital until 1837, when he was sent to distant Mito to study at the Kokodan, or official clan school.

By 1847, Yoshinobu was being groomed for the political role he was to play in adulthood and returned to Edo as adopted heir of the Hitosubashi family, a collateral branch of the family. In 1858, the existing shōgun, Tokugawa Iesada, died in office, and Yoshinobu was considered his logical successor. However, a political row developed when senior councilor Ii Naosuke nominated his cousin, Tokugawa Yoshitomi, instead. Yoshitomi came to power as the youthful 14th shōgun Iemochi in Yoshinobu's place.

In 1860, antiforeign extremists assassinated Naosuke. Two years later, Yoshinobu was made guardian of Iemochi and commanded the guards outside his domain. In 1864, samurai extremists from Chōshū attempted to storm the palace gates, only to be defeated by Yoshinobu's quick actions. To prevent political order from unraveling further, he then prevailed upon young Iemochi to lead a military expedition against the insurgents. This campaign restored order to Chōshū without further fighting. However, in 1866, reformers under Takasugi Shinsaku had taken over the province, and a second major expedition was launched. This affair proved a bungling defeat for the Tokugawa shōgunate and nearly disastrous when Iemochi sickened and died while on campaign.

In 1867, Yoshinobu was finally installed as the 15th shōgun, and he made a determined effort to maintain the reins of power. However, the recent Tokugawa defeat only further emboldened the rebels.

Yoshinobu spent the first few months of his brief reign overhauling and modernizing the government, the bureaucracy, and the military. These changes did little to appease the rebel extremists, however, for their overwhelming concern was to disband the shōgunate completely and restore power to Emperor Meiji, who until this time had been only a figurehead ruler. Yoshinobu apparently toyed with the idea of resigning from office to continue on at the head of a body of leading samurai lords, but while visiting Kyoto for that purpose, fighting broke out between his men and Chōshū samurai. When the insurgents declared an "imperial restoration" and ordered Yoshinobu to surrender to the emperor, he refused. This act precipitated the short but bloody Boshin Civil War of 1868.

The shōgunate employed greater numbers of soldiers, but the men of Chōshū and Satsuma were better trained, led, and armed, and they defeated the government forces in several pitched battles around the imperial capital of Kyoto. Yoshinobu then withdrew his forces to Edo. As the imperialists gathered up additional strength before moving forward, Saigō Takamori, a leading Satsuma samurai, appeared in Edo and convinced Yoshinobu to submit to the emperor and avoid further bloodshed. The shōgun, sensing the political and military futility of his position, accordingly resigned on May 3, 1868, and went into house arrest in Mito, stripped of his titles. Loyalist rebels kept the fighting up for nearly a year before they were finally vanquished in northern Hokkaidō by imperial naval forces.

Yoshinobu was later officially pardoned, and he retired to Sumpu, the ancestral home of the Tokugawa clan. He lived the rest of his life in luxurious seclusion and received numerous awards and titles from the imperial government for his good behavior. Yoshinobu died at Tokyo in 1913, the last of the Tokugawa shōguns.

*Louis G. Perez*

**See also:** Boshin Civil War; Ii Naosuke; Meiji Emperor; Saigō Takamori; Tokugawa Nariaki.

**Further Reading**

Beasley, W. G. *The Meiji Restoration.* Stanford, CA: Stanford University Press, 1972.

Shiba Ryotaro. *The Last Shōgun: The Life of Tokugawa Yoshinobu.* Tokyo: Kodansha International, 1998.

Totman, Conrad. *The Collapse of the Tokugawa Bakufu, 1862–1868.* Honolulu: University of Hawaii Press, 1980.

# Hogen-Heiji-Gempei Wars (12th Century)

The rise of a feudal warrior (*bakufu*) government at Kamakura has its origins during a series of battles that blazed through the last half of the 12th century in and around the capital city Kyoto. At their common core were the political machinations of the retired emperor Go-Shirakawa. The result was to establish military control over the imperial house.

## The Hogen Rebellion (1156)

Chafing at the controls over the imperial house wielded by the Fujiwara family, Go-Shirakawa invented a series of political strategies to accrue actual power to himself and thereby slough off the regency imposed on the emperor by the Fujiwara. When his father Toba, the cloistered (retired) emperor, died in 1156, Go-Shirakawa managed to elbow aside another retired emperor Sutoku and have his own son Nijo installed as emperor. Go-Shirakawa hoped to control the child (and the imperial government itself) from his own cloister, just as the Fujiwara had long controlled infant emperors.

Sutoku had planned to install his own son in a similar manner, so he enlisted the support of Fujiwara no Yorinaga; Go-Shirakawa countered by putting Yorinaga's older brother Tadamichi forward as a candidate for the throne. Sutoku and Yorinaga summoned the support of Minamoto no Tameyoshi, head of the Minamoto clan, and Taira no Tadamasa. Go-Shirakawa and Tadamichi countered with Minamoto no Yoshitomo and Taira no Kiyomori, head of the Taira clan. At this juncture, the Fujiwara, Minamoto, and Taira clans were split, with factions of each family backing either side. The Minamoto and Taira clans were both offshoots (cadet) houses springing from the Yamato imperial clan itself. They had accrued considerable military power by coalescing tax-free estates (*shōen*).

Go-Shirakawa's forces won, thereby ending the so-called Hogen Disturbance. Nevertheless, the use of military forces as part of the process of choosing a new emperor set a very dangerous precedent. Before long, the victor warriors began to wield considerable power and influence over imperial politics.

## The Heiji Rebellion (1160)

Taira Kiyomori had shouldered aside his allies and had established real political power in the capital. He had banished or executed his chief enemies and was wielding considerable influence over the cloistered Go-Shirakawa. When Kiyomori learned that his former ally Minamoto Yoshitomo had joined with Fujiwara no Nobuyori in a plot, Kiyomori executed a brilliant strategy to catch them out. He left Kyoto in a feigned pilgrimage. When Yoshitomo and Nobuyori seized the opportunity to place the emperor Nijo under house arrest, Kiyomori sprang the trap. He lured the pair out of Kyoto and then surrounded them. Nobuyori fled, but Yoshitomo stood to fight. Yoshitomo was betrayed and killed by a "loyal" retainer. Kiyomori executed Yoshitomo's two eldest sons, but in an "act of Buddhist benevolence" spared the three younger sons Yoritomo, Noriyori, and Yoshitsune.

## The Gempei War (1180–1185)

Taira Kiyomori now consolidated his control over Kyoto and the surrounding provinces. Having executed his Minamoto and Fujiwara enemies, he seized their lands and distributed them within his family and allies. He installed himself as *Daijō Daijin* (prime minister), ruling with an iron fist over the Imperial government. He paid some public deference to the emperor and the cloistered Go-Shirakawa, but installed his own family as imperial ministers. Dressing in sumptuous silk, he strutted around the capital with considerable pomp and circumstance. His personal entourage outshone those of the imperial house. The popular adage at the time was "One is scarcely human if one is not Taira."

Go-Shirakawa seethed in anger, but he was powerless to do anything about it until finally in 1180 Kiyomori forced the abdication of Emperor Takakura. Kiyomori installed his own two-year-old grandson Antoku as the new emperor. Furious at being passed over, Go-Shirakawa's son, Prince Mochihito raised the standard for revolt. He was joined by Minamoto Yorimasa but Kiyomori cornered him and forced him to commit suicide.

Meanwhile, in far-away Kamakura, the young Minamoto Yoritomo declared himself the head of the Imperial Loyalists and began to form a coalition against the Taira.

Yoritomo had been in exile under the control of a Taira relative Hôjô Tokimasa. He married Tokimasa's daughter, Hôjô Masako, and seized upon the death of Yorimasa as an opportunity to become the head of the Minamoto clan. His father-in-law Tokimasa joined his coalition and before long, they moved toward Kyoto at the head of a coalition of former Taira allies.

Yoritomo several times had to struggle against his cousin Yoshinaka, but in 1181 they settled their differences. In that year Taira Kiyomori died and his son Munemori led the Taira coalition against the Minamoto. Yoritomo was joined by his half-brothers Noriyori and Yoshitsune, who led their own troops in support of Yoritomo. After four years of almost constant warfare, Yoritomo finally triumphed. In the ultimate deciding battle of *Dan-no-ura*, the young emperor Antoku and his grandmother Taira no Tokiko (Kiyomori's widow) were drowned in the naval battle.

Yoritomo finally triumphed, but he did not fully trust anyone and ultimately forced Yoshitsune to commit suicide in 1189. Noriyori was later (1193) killed as well. Instead of moving to Kyoto, Yoritomo chose to establish a new government in Kamakura. There, in 1192 he accepted the title of *seii taishōgun* ("barbarian-subduing generalissimo") from Go-Shirakawa (who died that year) over a new type of feudal government called *bakufu* ("tent government"). The *bakufu* ruled a coalition of *daimyō* (warlords) and maintained tight control over the imperial house that remained in Kyoto.

Ironically, Go-Shirakawa, who had begun the series of battles in an effort to expand his own power over the imperial house, ended up pretty much as he had started 36 years before, as a virtual prisoner. He merely exchanged masters, with the Fujiwara regents being replaced by Yoritomo and his successors. Unintentionally, Go-Shirakawa ushered in seven centuries of feudal warrior government.

In terms of Japanese history, the 12th-century feudal wars created the template for the study of the seven centuries of feudal warrior government. The so-called *gunki monogatari* ("Warrior Tales") became the foundation of such literature and have consistently colored how Japanese view their history. The exploits of the warriors became the trope of the *samurai* and *bushidō*.

*Louis G. Perez*

See also: Hôjô Masako; Kamakura *Bakufu*; Minamoto Yoritomo; Minamoto Yoshitsune; Warrior Tales.

## Further Reading

Brown, Delmer M., and Ichirō Ishida, eds. *Gukanshō: The Future and the Past*. Berkeley: University of California Press, 1979.

Mass, Jeffrey. *Yoritomo and the Founding of the First Bakufu: The Origins of Dual Government in Japan*. Stanford: Stanford University Press, 2000.

Varley, H. Paul. *Jinnō Shōtōki: A Chronicle of Gods and Sovereigns*. New York: Columbia University Press, 1980.

## Hôjô Masako (1157–1225)

Best known as the wife of Minamoto no Yoritomo (1147–1199), Masako was an active political figure who was instrumental in the creation of the Kamakura bakufu, Japan's first warrior government (1185–1333). Although never formally appointed regent, she was one of the most powerful individuals in that government for over two decades as she raised and supervised three young shōgun. She also was a key leader who rallied bakufu troops when an imperial army threatened to destroy Kamakura in the Jôkyû War of 1221.

Masako was the eldest daughter of Hôjô Tokimasa and his first wife Hôjô no Maki. She had two brothers, Munetoki and Yoshitoki, as well as several half-siblings. Based in rural Izu Province, the Hôjô was a minor branch of the powerful Taira warrior clan. Masako might have lived in obscurity if she had not met and married Yoritomo, heir to another powerful warrior clan, the Minamoto. Yoritomo had been a young boy when his father was executed in 1160 for attempting to oust the Taira. Yoritomo was sent into exile in Izu, to be watched by

Taira relatives like the Hôjô, but he became romantically involved with Masako around 1177. According to legend, Tokimasa initially opposed their marriage, but Masako ran away on a rainy night to be with Yoritomo rather than accept an arranged marriage to someone else. Tokimasa relented, and the two lived in the Hôjô compound for their first years of married life.

In 1180, Yoritomo, with the support of Masako, her family, and other eastern warriors, launched an armed uprising that became the Genpei War (1180–1185). Yoritomo's forces won the war, making him the most powerful warrior in the country and allowing him to create the Kamakura *bakufu*. According to *bakufu* records, Masako played an active role in supporting her husband during the war and was forced to flee enemy troops more than once. She was liked and respected by Yoritomo's retainers, who destroyed the house where his mistress was living on Masako's orders. She also was an important sponsor of Buddhist temples, was regarded as the first lady of Kamakura, and gave birth to four children: two girls (Ôhime and Sanman) and two boys (Yoriie and Sanetomo). Nevertheless, her most active leadership roles came after her husband's death in 1199.

With her father Tokimasa and brother Yoshitoki, Masako arranged for her son Yoriie to succeed his father and eventually become shōgun in 1202. Records suggest that he was an ineffective leader who mistreated his retainers and that only Masako could control him. When Yoriie became ill in 1203, Masako forced him to resign. Her father took power as the first shōgunal regent (*shikken*), and the title of shōgun was given to 11-year-old Sanetomo. Yoriie was exiled and assassinated the following year. Masako guided Sanetomo's administration and issued policies in his name. She and her brother forced their father from power in 1205 and suppressed uprisings by several eastern warrior families over the next two decades.

As Sanetomo did not father any children, Masako traveled to Kyoto in 1218 and negotiated for an imperial prince to become the next shōgun. Sanetomo's assassination in the following year gave the court an excuse to cancel the agreement. In 1221, retired emperor Go-Toba declared war on Kamakura (the Jôkyû War). Masako helped organize the defense: enemy agents were interrogated at her house, she was consulted on important decisions, and she delivered a stirring speech to the assembled vassals, reminding them of their obligations to her dead husband and inspiring them to fight for Kamakura. Her forces quickly defeated their opponents, and Masako again became guardian to a young boy: a three-year-old Fujiwara boy named Mitora, who would eventually become shōgun and set a pattern of adopted shōguns for the remainder of the Kamakura period.

Masako's prominence was widely recognized during the Kamakura period. The imperial court awarded her high rank, and her legal pronouncements were regarded as if they had come from a shōgun. Later historians, however, wrote of Masako as an evil, scheming woman who sacrificed her husband and children for politics. There is little evidence to support such a negative view, although it is difficult to reach firm conclusions about Masako's intentions because she left behind no diary. In any case, her important leadership role shows that women could be much more active in early warrior governance than they could in later times.

*Ethan Isaac Segal*

**See also:** Hogen-Heiji-Gempei Wars; Jôkyû War of 1221; Kamakura *Bakufu*; Minamoto Yoritomo.

## Further Readings

Collcutt, Martin. " 'Nun Shōgun': Politics and Religion in the Life of Hôjô Masako," in *Engendering Faith: Women and Buddhism in Premodern Japan*, edited by Barbara Ruch. Ann Arbor: Center for Japanese Studies, University of Michigan, 2002:165–188.

McCullough, William. "The *Azuma Kagami* Account of the Shôkyû War." *Monumenta Nipponica* 23, no. 1/2 (1968): 102–155.

## Hōjō Tokimune (1251–1284)

Hōjō Tokimune was born the eldest son of the regent (*shikken*) to the shōgun of the Kamakura *bakufu*. Two years after succeeding his father to the post at the age of 18, he was faced with the first of three incidents that threatened the *bakufu*. The Buddhist priest Nichiren had threatened the Hōjō clan by challenging the traditional Buddhist establishment and, therefore, the Hōjō rights to control the emperor through the office of shōgun. Tokimune sanctioned the rulings of lower officers by exiling Nichiren to Sado island in 1271.

A few years later, Tokimune had reasons for recalling Nichiren. Tokimune made peace with all religious leaders because he needed them to pray for national deliverance when the Mongols threatened to invade Japan.

When the Mongols made their first attempted invasion at Hakata Bay in northwest Kyushu, Tokimune called all of his feudal subordinates (*gokenin*) to rally to the defense of the country. He led a coalition of samurai armies to reinforce the defense in Kyushu. Before he could arrive, however, a typhoon sank most of the Mongol ships and turned the invasion into a splendid victory for Japan.

Tokimune then made the first of two fundamental mistakes. First, because the *bakufu* was really a coalition of *gokenin* military chieftans, the *bakufu* had neither a national treasury nor the wherewithal to adequately reward the valiant Kyushu defenders. Also, the traditional method of rewarding feudal vassals was to grant them the captured lands and possessions of the vanquished. Obviously, there were no such spoils of war from the Mongol defeat. Thus Tokimune chose to reward his own closest *gokenin*, who had traveled with him across the country. They were, after all, his closest territorial neighbors as well. Second, Tokimune also chose to reward the Buddhist and Shintō priests who had elicited nature to send the typhoon, which was designated as the "holy wind" (*kamikaze*).

The Kyushu *daimyō* justifiably felt ill used: not only were they not rewarded for their actions, but they were now charged by Tokimune to build and maintain an extensive stone wall to guard against future Mongol raids. Given that they had just suffered extensive losses in the attempted invasion, however, they could ill afford to do anything except complain.

Incredibly, seven years later, the almost exact scenario recurred with a second invasion in 1281. Again, Tokimune rewarded his allies and the priests but gave nothing to the Kyushu defenders. Many historians point to his actions as the root cause (in addition to the attempted Kemmu Restoration of the emperor Go-Daigo) for the eventual defeat of the *bakufu* 50 years later.

Tokimune did not live to see that event; he died in 1284. Before he died, he was heavily instrumental in establishing the official ties between the *bakufu* and the Zen monasteries that thronged to his capital. He had long been an adherent of Zen, but his personal Zen master Bukko took the opportunity to convince Tokimune to provide more assistance to the Zen temples throughout the country. Bukko was the Chinese Zen (Chan in China) master *Wuxue* who had come to Japan only the year before. Tokimune bestowed many favors and awards on him, and in return, Bukko led the campaign to recognize Tokimune as a Buddhist saint (*boddhisatva*) after his death

*Louis G. Perez*

**See also:** Go-Daigo; Mongol Invasions of Japan.

**Further Reading**

Conlan, Thomas. *In Little Need of Divine Intervention*. Ithaca, NY: Cornell University, 2001.

Sansom, George. *A History of Japan to 1334*. Standford, CA: Stanford University Press, 1958.

# Hong Kong, Battle of (December 8–25, 1941)

The colony of Hong Kong, consisting of 400 square miles of islands and an adjacent peninsula on the coast of Guangdong, South China, was both the headquarters of the Royal Navy's China Squadron and a significant entrepôt and commercial center. From the mid-1930s onward, the British Joint Chiefs of Staff believed that, in the event of attack by Japanese forces, Hong Kong would be indefensible.

During World War II, by June 1940, sizable Japanese forces blocked Hong Kong's access to the Chinese mainland. That August, Major General Sir John Dill, chief of the Imperial General Staff, recommended the withdrawal of the British garrison. Although Prime Minister Winston L. S. Churchill accepted this recommendation, it was not implemented. Some women and children were evacuated to Manila in the Philippines, and in October 1941, Britain accepted the Canadian government's ill-considered offer to send two Canadian battalions to reinforce the two Scottish and two Indian battalions already manning Hong Kong's defenses.

Even with this assistance, Hong Kong's defenses remained decidedly inadequate: 12,000 troops, augmented by the Hong Kong and Singapore Royal Artillery and the civilian Hong Kong Volunteer Defense Force, were too few to man the colony's main lengthy defense line (Gindrinker's Line), which ran 3 miles north of Kowloon in the New Territories. Air and naval forces comprised a pitiable 7 airplanes, 8 motor torpedo boats, and 4 small gunboats. It was generally known that many Japanese civilians in the colony were fifth columnists, agents simply awaiting the opportunity to facilitate a Japanese assault. The British government had no intention of sending any further assistance but merely expected its defenders to stave off the inevitable defeat as long as possible.

On December 8, 1941, as Japanese forces simultaneously attacked Pearl Harbor, a surprise raid on Kai Tak airfield by Taiwan-based Japanese bombers destroyed all 7 British airplanes. Twelve battalions of the 38th Division of the Japanese Twenty-Third Army, commanded by Lieutenant General Sano Tadayoshi, crossed the Shenzhen River separating the New Territories and mainland China. Churchill urged Hong Kong's defenders to resist to the end, but within 24 hours Japanese forces had breached Gindrinker's Line. British commander Major General Christopher M. Maltby ordered a retreat to Hong Kong island, and by December 12, Japanese troops held Kowloon.

Sano's artillery began heavy bombardments of British positions on Victoria, the central district, but Maltby refused a December 14 ultimatum to surrender and the following day repulsed a Japanese attempt to land troops on the island. A second attempt made three nights later succeeded, and Japanese forces swiftly advanced across the island to its southern coast, splitting British forces. Despite heavy losses, British troops fought fiercely, on December 20 compelling Sano to halt temporarily to regroup his forces. The advance soon resumed, however, and by December 24 Japanese units had destroyed the water mains, leaving their opponents as short of water as they were of ammunition.

On December 25, 1941, the British governor negotiated an unconditional surrender. Immediately afterward, the Japanese victors treated their defeated foes with great brutality, massacring many of the defending forces, Chinese and Western, including hospitalized wounded men. They raped and sometimes killed hospital nurses and other captured women. Surviving prisoners of war and Allied civilians were interned for the duration of the war, often in severe conditions, while the supposedly liberated Chinese population likewise experienced harsh and arbitrary rule and numerous atrocities.

Hong Kong remained under Japanese occupation until August 1945, when, despite the hopes of Chinese Nationalist leader Jiang Jieshi that it would revert to China, British forces reestablished control.

*Priscilla Roberts*

**See also:** Jiang Jieshi; Pearl Harbor, Attack on.

## Further Reading

Barham, Tony. *Not the Slightest Chance: The Defence of Hong Kong, 1941*. Hong Kong: University of Hong Kong Press, 2003.

Lindsay, Oliver. *The Lasting Honour: The Fall of Hong Kong, 1941*. London: Hamish Hamilton, 1978; 2d ed. London: Collins, 1997.

# I

## *Ichi-gō* Campaign (April–December 1944)

In spring 1944, World War II was going badly for the Japanese. With Lieutenant General Joseph W. Stilwell's forces progressing in northern Burma, the Japanese launched their last offensive in China. Known as the *ichi-gō* Campaign (Operation Number One), it was aimed primarily at the Nationalist forces; the Japanese strategic objectives were to destroy these forces, capture air bases in southeast China, consolidate control over eastern China, and secure control of the Beijing-Hankow-Canton railroad line. The Japanese also hoped to relieve some of the pressure on their forces in Burma and to establish a stronger base in China from which to resist any potential Allied invasion of the Japanese home islands.

The first phase began in March and lasted until July 1944, with the offensive being mounted on a broad front across central and south China. The Japanese aims were to press toward the Nationalist capital of Chongqing, open up direct communications with French Indochina, and capture airfields in southeast China being used by U.S. aircraft to attack Japanese ground forces and shipping. The early phase of the operation went well for the Japanese, with Nationalist forces quickly collapsing. This situation ended whatever hope remained among Western leaders that China might play a major role in the defeat of Japan.

In northern China during April and May, the Japanese cleared the Beijing-Hankow railway and took Henan Province, even though they had to move at night to avoid constant attacks from Major General Claire Chennault's 14th Air Force. Despite their air superiority, the Chinese Nationalist forces lost almost every time they met the Japanese. Some Chinese soldiers were even attacked by their own people, enraged by earlier mistreatment, and on occasion, starving peasants actually killed retreating Chinese troops and welcomed the Japanese.

Nationalist military failures exacerbated the already rocky relationship between Nationalist Chinese leader Jiang Jieshi and Stilwell, as well as that between Chennault and Stilwell. Stilwell was convinced that the key to restoring China lay in reopening a land supply route to Chongqing through Burma, whereas Chennault feared for the preservation of his airfields in eastern China. Jiang, realizing that the Americans would defeat the Japanese in due course, seemed more concerned with the threat posed to his regime by the Chinese Communists. In fall 1944, this rift led to Stilwell's dismissal.

Phase two of the *ichi-gō* Campaign began in July 1944 with a pincer movement by two Japanese armies, one from Wuhan and one from Canton, attempting to take Guilin and open a land route between central China and Southeast Asia. By November, all of Guangxi and eastern Hunan had been overrun, and the Japanese forces were threatening Guiyang, capital of Guizhou Province.

In the process, the Japanese army captured all but three of the U.S. airfields in south China. The Allies feared that if Guiyang fell, the Japanese might capture Kunming and Chongqing. The Japanese were not able to advance farther, however, and in December, they attacked Guiyang but were repulsed. The *ichi-gō* Campaign was over.

In early 1945, Japanese forces began limited offensives to consolidate the gains of 1944, but these failed to accomplish much, given that the threat of war with the Soviet Union forced military leaders to transfer several divisions to defend Manchuria and the Japanese mainland. Between May and July, the Nationalist Chinese used this situation to recover Guangxi and western Guangdong, but most Chinese lands captured by the Japanese during the *ichi-gō* Campaign remained in their hands until the end of the war. The *ichi-gō* offensive also greatly benefited Communist forces in China, who took advantage of the Nationalist defeats to occupy more territory and greatly expand their army.

*William Head*

**See also:** Burma Air Campaign; Jiang Jieshi (Ch'iang K'ai-shek); World War II, Continental Theater.

### Further Reading

Tuchman, Barbara. *Stilwell and the American Experience in China, 1911–1945*. New York: Macmillan, 1971.

Wilson, Dick. *When Tigers Fight: The Story of the Sino-Japanese War, 1937–1945*. New York: Viking, 1982.

## Ichikawa Fusae (1893–1981)

Ichikawa Fusae was born on May 15, 1893, in a small farming village in Aichi Prefecture. Her childhood was shaped by the regular physical abuse her mother endured at her father's hands and by his emphasis on educating all his children. That stress led her to graduate from a local primary school and then relocate to Tokyo to attend the Girls' Academy. Although she remained at the academy for only a few months because of homesickness, she later graduated from a teacher training school in Aichi. Ichikawa parlayed her education into two teaching positions before she left academia in 1917 to become the *Nagoya Newspaper*'s first female reporter. Her writings on women's issues and her subsequent work for women workers on behalf of the Yūaikai labor organization deepened her awareness of the discrimination women faced and propelled her to return to Tokyo and become an activist in the women's movement.

In 1919, Ichikawa responded to an appeal from Hiratsuka *Raichō* to found, with Hiratsuka and Oku Mumeo, the New Women's Association for the purpose of eliminating gender inequality. More specifically, the organization aimed to gain for women suffrage, revision of Article 5 of the Peace Police Law to allow women to join political parties and organize and attend political meetings, and passage of a law to prevent marriage by men infected with venereal disease. In support of these goals, Ichikawa and the association's women lobbied Diet members for support, submitted petitions to both houses of the national legislature, and wrote campaign letters for pro-suffrage candidates. The organization also held public lectures and classes and, beginning in October 1920, published a monthly periodical to advance its agenda and educate women in particular about politics. In 1922, these efforts won amendment to Article 5 to permit women to participate in political meetings, but the association disbanded later that year without achieving any other aims.

Lawmaker Ichikawa Fusae (left) hands a petition to Japanese Prime Minister Miki Takeo on December 28, 1974, in Tokyo, Japan. (Photo by Sankei Archivevia Getty Images)

In 1920, exhaustion and personal and ideological conflicts with Hiratsuka had driven Ichikawa to the United States. She officially resigned from the New Women's Association the following year and remained in the United States until 1924. While there she became acquainted with leading American suffragists Alice Paul and Carrie Chapman Catt. Their organizational activism and stress on political equality contributed to her decision to help establish the Women's Suffrage League less than a year after she returned to Japan. Under Ichikawa's leadership, this organization became the most vocal women's body demanding political equality in the prewar period, as members petitioned, lobbied, and educated for suffrage. The Mukden Incident of 1931 and the resulting rise of militarism and growing authoritarianism of the state, however, forced Ichikawa and fellow activists to take up other issues deemed more suitable for women, including the passage of legislation to protect mothers and children.

Ichikawa lamented the rise of fascism and criticized the military and state for pushing back the women's movement in the 1930s. As Japan moved toward total war, however, she came to see cooperation with the government as the best way for women to prove their worth and influence national policy. She joined a Home Ministry-sponsored movement in the mid-1930s to clean up elections and agitated for price controls and improved sanitation. After the outbreak of the Sino-Japanese War in 1937, she joined or assumed leadership positions in many state-supported organizations. Notable among those were the National Spiritual Mobilization Committee, the Women's Emergency Study Group, the Greater Japan Women's Association, and the Patriotic Press Association.

Immediately after Japan's surrender in 1945, Ichikawa resumed her calls for suffrage and equality as part of a study committee on postwar policies, and in November 1945 she joined with others to establish the New Japan Women's League. Her political activities were halted in March 1947, when American occupation forces purged her for her wartime collaboration. Freed to participate in politics again in October 1950, she returned to head the League, renamed the League of Women Voters of Japan later that year, before resigning to run for the House of Councillors as an independent in April 1953. She won her seat with the second highest number of votes received in the district of Tokyo. Ichikawa served until defeated in 1971, but was then reelected in 1974. In the Diet, she continued to agitate for greater rights for women, holding the Japan International Women's Year Conference in 1975 and pushing the government to ratify the UN's Convention on the Elimination of All Forms of Discrimination against Women in 1980. One of Japan's most important prewar feminists, she died on February 11, 1981, at the age of 87.

*Elizabeth Dorn Lublin*

**See also:** Hiratsuka *Raichō*; Kwantung Army Adventurism; Law on Assembly and Political Association of 1890; Occupation of Japan; Peace Preservation Law; Postwar Politics.

**Further Reading**

Molony, Barbara. "From 'Mothers of Humanity' to 'Assisting the Emperor': Gendered Belonging in the Wartime Rhetoric of Japanese Feminist Ichikawa Fusae." *Pacific Historical Review* 80, no. 1 (February 2011): 1–27.

Molony, Barbara. "Ichikawa Fusae and Japan's Pre-war Women's Suffrage Movement," *Japanese Women: Emerging from Subservience, 1868–1945*, edited by Hiroko Tomida and Gordon Daniels. Kent, UK: Global Oriental, 2005:57–92.

Molony, Kathleen. *One Woman Who Dared: Ichikawa Fusae and the Japanese Women's Suffrage Movement*. Unpublished doctoral dissertation, University of Michigan, 1980.

Vavich, Dee Ann. "The Japanese Woman's Movement: Ichikawa Fusae, A Pioneer in Woman's Suffrage." *Monumenta Nipponica* 22, nos. 3 and 4 (1967): 402–436.

## Ienaga Saburō (1913–2002)

Born sickly, Ienaga Saburō was talented in writing and was drawn to history. He passed his first intellectual milestone in middle school thanks to such books as G. H. Wells' *Outline of History* and Nishimura Shinji's *Age of Yamato*, which opened his eyes to the striking difference between the orthodox history, based on mythology, and objective history, based on scientific evidence.

After entering high school in 1931, Ienaga experienced an intellectual crisis. He found himself unable to accept the antiestablishment Marxist ideology and was on the brink of joining the widespread militarist trend following the Manchurian Incident. Soon thereafter, prompted by Tanabe Hajime's *Outline of Sciences*, he discovered the German Southwestern philosophy, which preached a clear break between *Sein* ("is") and *Sollen* ("ought") and helped him see through the logical structure of Japan's "national polity." According to Ienaga, this theory caused a "Copernican revolution" in his mind.

His lack of interest in history and the conservative atmosphere of the History Department made him bitter about his life in Tokyo University—at least until December 1935, when Ienaga took a field trip to Kyoto and Nara. The magnificent Buddhist art in these ancient capitals inspired him to work on the issue of "salvation" as his

Historian Ienaga Saburō speaks during a press conference in Tokyo on August 29, 1997. (AP Photo/Itsuo Inouye.)

thesis, starting his lifelong main field of research, intellectual history.

For a long time after the war, Ienaga could not recognize the epoch-making significance of Japan's new constitution, promulgated in 1946. It was not until 1952, with the reversal of the occupation policy—from demilitarization and democratization of Japan to rearming it and incorporating it into the anticommunist camp—well under way, that he realized that the hard-won peace and freedom were in danger of being lost again and decided that he must grip actively with problems of state and society Ienaga became a household name in Japan due to his lawsuit against the government for censoring his history textbooks for Japanese schools. In addition, he led a battle against moving Tokyo University of Education, where he was a professor since 1944, one hour east of Tokyo to become

Tsukuba University. The projected move was first introduced in 1963, as a way to increase the size of the campus, but Ienaga argued the real reason for it was to create an anti-democratic new university envisioned by the Ministry of Education and the financial circles. The administration threatened to fire Ienaga and two other faculty members for leading the opposition campaign. Despite the opposition of approximately 40 percent of the faculty and nearly all the students, the Diet forced through the Tsukuba University Law in 1973, incurring protests from 57 universities, 111 departments, and more than 8,000 individual scholars. Tokyo University of Education was closed in 1978, one year after Ienaga retired after teaching there for 33 years.

*Guohe Zheng*

**See also:** History Textbooks Controversy; Occupation of Japan.

**Further Reading**

Bellah, Robert N. "Ienaga Saburō and the Search for Meaning in Modern Japan," in *Changing Japanese Attitudes toward Modernization*, edited by Marius B. Jansen. Princeton, NJ: Princeton University Press, 1965:369–423.

Dore, R. P. "Notes and Comment: Textbook Censorship in Japan: The Ienaga Case." *Pacific Affairs* 43, no. 4 (Winter 1970–1971): 548–556.

Nozaki, Yoshiko. *Textbook Controversy and the Production of Public Truth: Japanese Education, Nationalism, and Saburo Ienaga's Court Challenges*. Ph.D. dissertation, University of Wisconsin, 2000.

## Ii Naosuke (1815–1860)

Ii Naosuke was born on November 29, 1815, in Hikone, Japan. He was the 14th son of Ii Naonaka, the *daimyō* of Hikone, Omi Province (present-day Shiga Prefecture).

Naosuke's ancestors had aided Tokugawa Ieyasu's campaign for power at the beginning of the Tokugawa shōgunate in the early 17th century.

Given his position in his family, little was demanded of Naosuke in his youth. He was allowed relatively free rein to pursue his interests, which included Zen Buddhism, swordplay, and the tea ceremony. However, at the age of 31, Naosuke was adopted by his elder brother, Ii Naoki, *daimyō* of Hikone. Naoki died heirless, and in 1850, Naosuke inherited the position of *daimyō*.

The Ii clan's traditional position as adviser to the Tokugawa shōguns meant that Naosuke was forced to look well beyond the bounds of his home domain. A pressing issue was how to respond to the demands of foreigners, such as U.S. Commodore Matthew Perry, for increased trade and interaction with Japan. Naosuke was initially in favor of strengthening Japan's defenses and maintaining the traditional Tokugawa policy of exclusion. However, in the mid-1850s, he underwent a change of opinion and began to favor opening Japan to the outside world.

An additional challenge was the fact that the 13th shōgun, Tokugawa Iesada, was ill and without an heir. The ailing shōgun appointed Naosuke to the office of Great Elder (*tairo*), a rarely filled position that was second in power and prestige only to the shōgun himself. Naosuke took forceful action to deal with the *bakufu*'s internal and external challenges. In July 1858, he approved the signing of the Harris Treaty, a commercial pact with the United States, without seeking imperial approval. He subsequently approved similar treaties with the Dutch, Russians, British, and French; opened the port of Yokohama to foreign trade; and sent an ambassador to the United States in 1859. He also announced that the issue of succession was an internal matter to be decided by the Tokugawa house, not by Japan's various domains, and arranged for Tokugawa Yoshitomi (renamed Iemochi) to succeed Tokugawa Iesada, who died later in 1858.

Both of those moves angered various powerful groups in Japan, including branches of the Tokugawa family and the leaders of reform-minded domains. Naosuke dealt with that opposition by initiating the "Great Persecution of the Ansei Period," forcing into retirement many reform-minded *daimyō* and jailing or punishing many others who criticized either the succession or the decision to sign treaties with the Western world.

The fact that Naosuke had unilaterally disregarded the wishes of the emperor (who had rejected a proposed treaty with the Americans in the spring of 1858) and the rulers of powerful domains increased opposition to the Tokugawa shōgunate in general and to Naosuke in particular. Many rallied around the cry "Revere the Emperor—Expel the Barbarians" (*sonno-jōi*). Samurai claiming loyalty to the emperor, many of whom hailed from the Satsuma, Mito, and Chōshū domains, embarked on a course of armed resistance and terrorism.

On the snowy winter morning of March 24, 1860, a band of Mito samurai attacked Naosuke as he left Edo Castle. Quickly overwhelming Naosuke's bodyguards, they killed Naosuke before he could even get out of his sedan chair. Attacks on other Tokugawa officials, as well as on foreigners in Japan, followed.

Largely discredited for decades, Naosuke's memory has been rehabilitated as growing numbers of Japanese have acknowledged the significance of his decisive leadership in an extremely difficult and important period of Japan's modern history.

*Kirk Larsen*

**See also:** Perry, Matthew; *Sonno-jōi;* Tokugawa *Bakufu* Political System; Tokugawa Ieyasu; Unequal Treaties.

### Further Reading

Duus, Peter, *Modern Japan*, Boston: Houghton Mifflin, 1998.

Lamberti, Matthew. (1972). "Tokugawa Nariaki and the Japanese Imperial Institution: 1853–1858." *Harvard Journal of Asiatic Studies* 32 (1972): 97–123.

## Ikeda Hayato (1899–1965)

Ikeda Hayato was a Japanese Liberal Democratic Party politician and Prime Minister of Japan (1960–1964). Born in Hiroshima Prefecture on December 3, 1899, he graduated from Kyoto Imperial University in 1925 with a degree in law. He joined the Finance Ministry and served as deputy finance minister during 1947–1948.

In the 1949 general election, Ikeda won election to the Diet from Hiroshima Prefecture as a Democratic Liberal. He was a protégé of Prime Minister Yoshida Shigeru. Ikeda served twice as Finance Minister (1949–1952, 1956–1957) and as Minister for International Trade and Industry (1952, 1959–1960). During the Allied occupation of Japan (1945–1952), he was responsible for implementing the Dodge Plan, an economic stabilization program. In 1951, Ikeda was a member of the Japanese delegation to the San Francisco Peace Conference, and from 1956 he formed his own faction within the ruling Liberal Democratic Party.

In July 1960, Ikeda assumed the premiership, taking over control from Kishi Nobusuke, who had split public opinion over revision of the United States–Japan Security Treaty. In contrast, Ikeda pursued a low-profile foreign policy, preferring to focus on domestic issues—above all, the economy.

Aiming to turn Japan into an economic great power, Ikeda launched a plan to double Japan's gross national product within a decade. This campaign enjoyed strong support from across the political spectrum. During his premiership, Japan joined the Organization for Economic Cooperation and Development (OECD) and secured full membership in the General Agreement on Tariffs and Trade (GATT) and the International Monetary Fund (IMF). Politically, Ikeda continued the policy of close cooperation with the United States. He saw Japan as constituting one of the so-called three pillars of the free world, alongside the United States and Western Europe. Ikeda also sought to improve relations with the People's Republic of China (PRC). Economic ties between Japan and PRC were strengthened during his time in office, but diplomatic relations were not established.

Poor health forced Ikeda to resign in October 1964. He died in Tokyo on August 13, 1965.

*Takemoto Tomoyuki and Christopher W. Braddick*

**See also:** Occupation of Japan; San Francisco Peace Treaty; Yoshida Shigeru.

### Further Reading

Braddick, C. W. *Japan and the Sino-Soviet Alliance, 1950–1964: In the Shadow of the Monolith*. New York: St. Antony's Series with Palgrave/Macmillan, 2004.

Edström, Bert. *Japan's Evolving Foreign Policy Doctrine: From Yoshida to Miyazawa*. Basingstoke, UK/New York: Palgrave, 1999.

## Ikkō *Ikki*

Ikkō refers to the Jōdo Shinshū or True Pure Land sect, founded by Shinran (1173–1263). *Ikki* means "alliance," usually of individual peasants or of villages to protest estate officials, military families to defend themselves against military governors, or even alliances of both to force the government to offer debt relief. Thus the word for alliance ("those of a single mind") came to mean "revolt" or "rebellion." In the Middle Ages, especially after 1333 and the beginning of a civil war of 60 years, as central authority broke down and local abuse increased, survival was possible only in groups. Even teamsters organized into such leagues, while merchants organized into guilds protect markets.

Ikkō *ikki* were alliances organized along sectarian lines: branch temples of Shinran's mausoleum, the Honganji ("original vow temple"), in Kyoto. Until the time of Shinran's descendant and eighth hereditary head of the lineage, Rennyo (1415–1499), the Honganji was still comparatively poor and weak compared with certain branch temple lines and the chief Tendai temple, Enryakuji on Mt. Hiei, which alternately claimed authority over Honganji and persecuted it. In 1465, Enryakuji burned down the Honganji, and Rennyo moved to Yoshizaki in Echizen. Rennyo worked intensively among the local elite: richer peasants, lower-ranking warriors, and the merchants and craftsmen; even mid-level warriors joined. The organizational strength lay in the fusion of the village government with the Shinshū congregation. The movement spread throughout central Japan and along the Japan Sea coast, from Kaga to Kii and Settsu to Owari. Shinshū fortifications dotted the area and adherents, known collectively as the Ikkō *ikki* ("the alliance of the completely dedicated," as adherents were known), emerged along with the various warlords of the area as a principal rival for political control during the period of fragmentation and unification after the civil war of 1466–1477, known as the Ōnin War.

The Honganji leadership faced different problems involving the group's adherents. If adherents refused to pay rent or taxes, the imperial court or military government (shōgun) would attempt to pressure Honganji to persuade adherents to pay or to control their rebelliousness. If military governors or, later, new warlords attempted to curtail temples' rights, including exemption from entry by officials, or impose taxes, Honganji would call on adherents to assemble in defense of its interests. In both cases, the leaders of Honganji used the promise to those who fought and died for Honganji of salvation through rebirth in the western Pure Land of Amida Buddha. Because Shinran had taught that rebirth occurred through Amida's grace alone (*tariki*) and that no one could be saved through one's own efforts (*jiriki*), the Honganji leadership was taking considerable liberties with the basic doctrine that formed the basis of Shinran's teachings as well as the basis of the organization as one with a distinct interpretation of the vows of Amida Buddha. Nevertheless, it is clear that, as dedicated as adherents were to the Honganji, they tended to fight with the Honganji only when their interests coincided with those of the Honganji.

Nevertheless, the congregations constituted a formidable military force. In 1488, the Honganji Ikkō *ikki* of Kaga rebelled and forced the military governor, Togashi Masachika, to commit suicide; the peasants and local military ruled the province through their parish organizations for 90 years until defeated by Oda Nobunaga (1534–1582). The Echizen congregations were not, however, able to prevent the Asakura from invading the province in 1506. In 1563, to make an arrest, a vassal of the Matsudaira, Sakai Masachika, invaded one of the three Honganji branch temples of Mikawa Province (either the Jōguji or the Honshōji), to which immunity from entry by officials had been granted by the father of Tokugawa Ieyasu; a Ikkō rebellion broke out the next year and nearly caused the future shōgun's death in the Battle of Azukizaka. The Ikkō adherents presented a serious obstacle to Oda Nobunaga from the time they blockaded Nobunaga in Kyoto when in 1568 he brought Ashikaga Yoshiaki (1537–1597) to assume the position of shōgun. It took more than 10 years for Nobunaga to resolve the issue with the Honganji adherents, who both supported and were supported by rivals of Nobunaga, such as the Mōri, the Uesugi, and the Takeda. For five years, Nobunaga laid siege to the Ikkō headquarters, the Ishiyama Honganji, located in what is now Ōsaka; only the intervention of the imperial court persuaded the 11th head of the Honganji Kennyo (1543–1592) to surrender. In 1602, Tokugawa Ieyasu finally broke the power of Honganji by dividing it in two.

*Sybil Thornton*

See also: Ashikaga *Bakufu*: Oda Nobunaga; Tokugawa Ieyasu.

**Further Reading**

Solomon, Michael. "The Dilemma of Religious Power: Honganji and Hosokawa Masamoto." *Monumenta Nipponica* 33, no. 1 (Spring 1978): 51–65.

Tsang, Carol Richmond. *War and Faith: Ikkō ikki in Late Muromachi Japan.* Cambridge, MA: Harvard University Press, 2007.

# Imjin War

Japanese military leader Toyotomi Hideyoshi launched a massive invasion of Korea in April 1592 that began the Imjin War. Although the Japanese invasion was ultimately thwarted by the exploits of Korean admiral Yi Sun Sin, the conflict had devastating long-term consequences for Korea.

Hideyoshi had unified all of Japan by 1590 and set his sights on conquering the Ming dynasty in China. After his demand for free passage through the Korean Peninsula was refused, Hideyoshi gathered a force estimated to number 150,000 and invaded the southern coast of Korea near Pusan on April 13, 1592. At first, the fighting was completely one-sided. The Japanese troops were experienced warriors armed with muskets they had obtained from Portugal, while the Korean land forces had little training and experience. Within three weeks, the Japanese forces had captured Seoul, and within three months, they had overrun most of the country.

Just as a complete Japanese victory appeared imminent, Admiral Yi entered the Imjin War and quickly turned the tide. Unlike the case with the Korean armies, Yi had revitalized the fleet under his command and was ready for combat. His secret weapon was the creation of "turtle ships," which were known in Korean as *kobukson*. Those warships had decks covered with a curved iron roof, like a turtle's back. Spikes protruded from the roof to prevent enemy soldiers from boarding, and the turtle ships were armed with cannons and other firearms that could fire in all directions.

Yi first used the turtle ships at Okpo, where he destroyed 26 Japanese ships without any losses. A series of victories quickly followed, culminating in the destruction of a Japanese fleet carrying reinforcements near Hansan Island on July 7, 1592. During the Battle of Hansan, Yi burned or sank more than 120 warships and destroyed most of a convoy carrying 100,000 Japanese soldiers. In Yi's final naval attack in 1592, he destroyed 133 Japanese vessels in Pusan harbor, again without suffering any losses. Yi's successes gave Korea complete control of the sea lanes around the peninsula, and the Korean navy was able to intercept most of the supplies and communications between Japan and Korea.

Bolstered by Yi's victories, large segments of the Korean populace, including Buddhist monks, rallied against the invaders, and guerrilla forces surfaced all over the country. The Korean guerrilla campaign took its toll on the Japanese troops, and the arrival of a Ming Chinese army forced the Japanese all the way back to the southern coast by May 1593. A stalemate developed, and negotiations dragged on for several more years. After peace talks broke down, the Japanese launched a second invasion in January 1597, but Korean and Chinese forces were able to hold off the Japanese troops and confine the fighting to the southern provinces. Following the death of Hideyoshi in September 1598, the Japanese forces were called back to Japan. While attacking the retreating Japanese forces in November, Yi was killed by a stray bullet while standing on the bow of his flagship.

The Japanese left widespread devastation in their wake. Numerous cities, towns, historic structures, and cultural treasures were destroyed; vast amounts of farmland lay in ruin; the economy was in shambles; and the Korean population was decimated, with tens of thousands killed and thousands more scholars and skilled workers taken captive to Japan. Korea never fully recovered from the Imjin War, and the country suffered severe famines into the next century.

*Louis G. Perez*

**See also:** Hansan Battle; Toyotomi Hideyoshi.

**Further Reading**

Lee, Ki-baik, *New History of Korea*. Seoul: Ilcho-gak, 1984.

Nahm, Andrew C., *Introduction to Korean History and Culture*. Seoul: Hollym International Corporation, 1993.

Sadler, A. L. "The Naval Campaign in the Korean War of Hideyoshi (1592–1598)." *Transactions* of *the Asiatic Society of Japan* 2, no. 14 (June 1937): 178–208.

# Inoue Kaoru (1836–1915)

Born into a low-ranking Chōshū samurai family, Inoue Kaoru rose to national prominence as part of the *sonno-jōi* ("Revere the Emperor—Expel the Barbarian") movement at the end of the Tokugawa era. Inoue studied Dutch and military arts in the domain school and was quickly recognized for his intelligence. In 1863, he joined with Takasugi Shinsaku to set fire to the British legation in Edo as a response to the earlier imperial edict to drive foreigners from Japan. Together with boyhood friend Itō Hirobumi (and with three others, they formed the Chōshū Five), Inoue went to Europe to study Western military science and returned just as Chōshū became involved in the bombardment of Western ships at Shimonoseki. Because of their Western knowledge, he and Itō rose quickly in han politics. Inoue was instrumental in the Chōshū alliance with Satsuma that brought down the Tokugawa.

In the early Meiji era, Inoue participated in a succession of important national reforms, including the Land Tax of 1873 and the abolition of the hans and establishment of the prefectural system (*haihan-chiken*). He was forced out of office because of his growing involvement with the Mitsui zaibatsu in 1873. Two years later, he returned to the government as a protégé of Kido Takayoshi. In 1885, Inoue became Japan's first Foreign Minister in the first Itō Hirobumi cabinet. As Foreign Minister, he came very close to revising the Unequal Treaties, engaging a series of conferences with all the signatories in Tokyo. The revision collapsed in 1887,

Inoue Kaoru (1836–1915) led early attempts to revise the Unequal Treaties. (J. Morris, *Makers of Japan*, 1906)

however, when it was disclosed that Inoue had agreed to a scheme whereby a separate judicial system would be temporarily employed for foreigner residents until Japan's law codes could be revised.

Inoue continued to serve in various ministries over the next 20 years and was generally recognized as part of the *genrō* oligarchy. He was often severely criticized because of his close relations with the Mitsui zaibatsu; some of his enemies called him "that Mitsui bank clerk." Although he never joined the political party movement, Inoue remained a close ally of Itō Hirobumi, who did.

*Larissa Castriotta Kennedy*

**See also:** Itō Hirobumi; Land Tax; Satchō Oligarchy; Shimonoseki, Bombardment of; *Sonno-jōi*; Unequal Treaties.

**Further Reading**

Craig, Albert M. *Chōshū in the Meiji Restoration*. Cambridge, MA: Harvard University Press, 1961.

Jansen, Marius B., and Gilbert Rozman, eds. *Japan in Transition: From Tokugawa to Meiji*. Princeton: Princeton University Press, 1986.

## International Military Tribunal for the Far East (1946–1949)

The International Military Tribunal for the Far East conducted trials of senior Japanese leaders after World War II. General of the U.S. Army Douglas MacArthur, heading the military occupation of Japan, established the International Military Tribunal for the Far East, popularly known as the Tokyo War Crimes Trials. The body held sessions in Tokyo from May 3, 1946, to November 12, 1948. Trials conducted by the tribunal were similar to those held at Nuremberg, Germany. The defendants were 28 senior Japanese military and civilian leaders, chosen from among 250 Japanese officials originally accused of war crimes. General Tōjō Hideki, who held various posts including Prime Minister and Chief of the General Staff, was the best-known defendant among the 18 military officers and 10 civilians charged. General MacArthur, with President Harry S Truman's support, exempted Emperor Hirohito from trial because of concerns over potential Japanese resistance to military occupation. More than 2,200 similar trials, including some held in Tokyo that preceded the tribunal, were conducted in areas formerly occupied by Japan, ranging from China to Pacific islands including Guam. The trials generated strong emotions, and they remain controversial to this day.

The Toyko tribunal consisted of 11 judges, one each from Australia, Canada, China, Great Britain, the Netherlands, New Zealand, the Soviet Union, the United States, France, India, and the Philippines. The Philippine justice was a survivor of the Bataan Death March. The tribunal's chief prosecutor, Joseph B. Keenan, was appointed by President Truman. Keenan's credentials included service as a former director of the U.S. Justice Department's Criminal Division as well as assistant to the U.S. Attorney General. His staff included 25 lawyers. The tribunal was not bound by the technical rules of evidence normally observed in a democracy and could admit any evidence that it chose, including purported admissions or statements of the accused.

The tribunal sought to establish clearly the principle that aggressive war was a crime and to prevent or deter future crimes against peace. Those who planned and initiated aggressive war in contravention of treaties, assurances, and international agreements were to be considered common felons. The tribunal also claimed jurisdiction over conventional war crimes and crimes against humanity, such as murder, mass murder, enslavement, deportation of civilian populations, and persecutions based on political or racial grounds in connection with other crimes under tribunal jurisdiction.

Some defendants were accused of being responsible for the actions of personnel under their command who had committed crimes against prisoners of war and civilian internees. These offenses included murder, beatings, torture, ill treatment, including inadequate provision of food and clothing and poor sanitation, rape of female nurses and other women, and the imposition of excessive and dangerous labor. Charges of murder were also leveled in cases involving the killing of military personnel who had surrendered, laid down arms, or no longer had means of defense, including survivors of ships sunk by naval action and crews of captured ships.

Seeking to conduct a fair trial, the tribunal gave each of those accused a copy of his or her indictment in Japanese, and trial proceedings were conducted in both English and Japanese. Defendants had a right to counsel, and the defense could question witnesses. Subject to court approval, the defense could also request the appearance of witnesses and the provision of documents. The mental and physical capacity of the accused to stand trial was also considered. After a conviction, the tribunal had the power to impose a death sentence or other punishment on a defendant.

Of the 28 original defendants, 25 were convicted. Seven (including Tōjō) were sentenced to death by hanging, 16 to life imprisonment, 1 to 20 years of incarceration, and another to 7 years in prison. The remaining 3 were not convicted, with 1 being declared mentally unstable and 2 dying before their trials ended.

As with the Nuremberg trials, the tribunal has been accused of promulgating "victors' justice," and some have called the proceedings racist. Nevertheless, fueled by horror at continuing military atrocities in places such as Bosnia and Cambodia, a legacy of the Tokyo and Nuremberg trials has been widespread international support for a permanent war crimes tribunal. The U.S. government, however, has resisted the formation of such a body, fearing that it could be politically influenced to harass American military forces operating overseas.

*Glenn E. Helm*

**See also:** MacArthur, Douglas; Shōwa Emperor (Hirohito); Tōjō Hideki; World War II, Japanese Atrocities.

## Further Reading

Kei, Ushimura. *Beyond the "Judgment of Civilization": The Intellectual Legacy of the Japanese War Crimes Trials, 1946–1949.* Translated by Steven J. Ericson. Tokyo: International House of Japan, 2003.

Maga, Timothy P. *Judgment at Tokyo: The Japanese War Crimes Trials.* Lexington: University Press of Kentucky, 2001.

Minear, Richard H. *Victors' Justice: The Tokyo War Crimes Trial.* Princeton, NJ: Princeton University Press, 1971.

Piccigallo, Philip R. *The Japanese on Trial: Allied War Crimes Operations in the East, 1945–1951.* Austin: University of Texas Press, 1979.

U.S. Department of State. *Trial of Japanese War Criminals: Documents 1. Opening Statement by Joseph B. Keenan, Chief of Counsel, 2. Charter of the International Military Tribunal for the Far East, 3. Indictment.* Washington, DC: U.S. Department of State, 1946.

## Ishiwara Kanji (1889–1949)

Ishiwara Kanji was a Japanese army general and head of the East Asian League. Born in Akita Prefecture, Japan, on January 18, 1889, he graduated from the Military Academy in 1909. Following routine service in Korea, Ishiwara entered the Army Staff College and graduated second in his class in November 1918. He spent the years from 1922 to 1924 in independent study in Germany, which exposed him to European military thought and gave him an opportunity to observe the results of World War I.

Ishiwara's experience in Europe, as well as his adherence to the Nichiren sect of Buddhism, led him to theorize that in the future, Japan would engage in an apocalyptic war with the United States. This struggle, which he dubbed "the Final War," was envisioned as a protracted total war in which airpower would play a decisive role. Ishiwara believed, however, that Japan could overcome its material inferiority by harnessing the economic resources of the Asian mainland, especially Manchuria and Mongolia. He published his theories in a book entitled *Thoughts on the Final Global War.*

In 1928, Ishiwara was posted to Manchuria, where he served as chief of operations for the Japanese Guandong (Kwantung) Army. Impelled by his sense of the urgency of preparing for the Final War, Ishiwara played a major role in planning and carrying out the Japanese army's seizure of Manchuria beginning in 1931. Shortly before the establishment of the puppet state of Manchukuo in 1932, he returned to Japan. Promoted to colonel, he headed the Operations Section of the army General Staff. After becoming a major general, he was put in charge of the General Staff's Operations Division. Nonetheless, Ishiwara's considerable earlier influence as a military theorist waned during the 1930s. Marginalized for his tacit support of a failed officers' rebellion in February 1936, as well as for his increasingly outspoken criticism of Japan's war with China (he was Chief of Staff of the Guandong Army in 1937 and 1938), he was promoted to lieutenant general but was forced into retirement in 1941.

Ishiwara headed the Toa Remmei (East Asian League), which opposed Premier Tōjō Hideki's policies during World War II. He briefly returned as an adviser to the "Surrender Cabinet" and urged that Japan conclude a peace agreement.

Following the war, Ishiwara was investigated by the Allied occupation authorities, who briefly considered trying him as a war criminal. Instead, he testified as a prosecution witness at the Tokyo War Crimes Trials in 1947. Ishiwara died in Akita Prefecture on August 15, 1949.

*John M. Jennings*

See also: February 26 Incident; International Military Tribunal for the Far East; Kwantung Army Adventurism; Manchukuo; Nichiren; Occupation of Japan; Tōjō Hideki.

## Further Reading

Barnhart, Michael A. *Japan Prepares for Total War: The Search for Economic Security, 1919–1941*. Ithaca, NY: Cornell University Press, 1987.

Peattie, Mark R. *Ishiwara Kanji and Japan's Confrontation with the West*. Princeton, NJ: Princeton University Press, 1975.

**Island Hopping.** *See* World War II, Pacific Theater.

## Isshi Incident

According to the *Nihon shōki* (720), on the 12th day of the sixth month of 645 C.E. (July 10, 645), at the formal reception of envoys from the three kingdoms of Korea, Soga no Iruka no Omi (Royal Chieftain) was attacked and wounded in the presence of the Great King Kōgyoku (594–661; reign 642–645) by her son, Prince Naka no Ōe (626–672; reign as Tenji 668–672) and Saeki no Komaro no Muraji (Chieftain). Naka no Ōe (whose father was Jōmei [reign 629–641]) claimed that the Soga were after the throne, and Iruka pleaded for an investigation; when Kōgyoku left the room to deliberate, Iruka was finished off by Komaro no Muraji and Katsuragi no Wakainukai no Amida no Muraji. The two other named conspirators were Nakatomi no Kamako (Kamatari; 614–669), Soga Kurayamada no Ishikawa no Maro, and Amanoinukai no Katsumaro, who passed a sword to Komaro no Muraji.

Naka no Ōe sent Iruka's body to his father Emishi and a general, Kose no Tokoda no Omi (died 658, the same general who had attacked Prince Yamashiro and forced him and his family to commit suicide), to attack him. Emishi's defenders, the Aya of Yamato Province, a Korean immigrant group, dispersed. The next day Emishi set fire to his residence and committed suicide with his family. On the 14th day (July 12), Kyōgoku abdicated in favor of her younger brother, Prince Karu (Kōtoku; 596–654; reign 645–654), and Naka no Ōe was created Prince Imperial. On the New Year, the first of a series of edicts were promulgated, which, over the next 60 to 70 years, would centralize the country and increase the power of the emperor on the model of Sui (581–618) and Tang (618–907) China.

The *Nihon shōki*, written by the victors and finished 75 years after the events, is not a completely reliable account: there is even doubt in some quarters that Kamatari had quite as big a role in the coup as portrayed. The text describes the rise and fall of the Soga clan against the background of the introduction of Buddhism, the increasing dependence on foreigners and foreign technology, problems in Korea, and the competition for the throne. The Soga were entrusted with Buddhist images and other items sent by the King Sǒngmyǒng (reign 523–54) of the Korean kingdom of Paekche in 552; they were chosen for this role apparently because they were not court ritualists and had risen on the basis of their control of specialists in imported agricultural and other technology—especially Koreans, some of whom were already practicing Buddhists. However, worship of a foreign religion was opposed by two of the chief officiants of court rituals: Mononobe no Moriya, supported by Nakatomi no Katsumi. It was bad enough when the Soga adopted Buddhism as a clan religion. When the dying Great King Yōmei (518–587; reign 585–587; grandson of Soga no Umako) accepted

Buddhism, however, Moriya and Katsumi abandoned the court and prepared to place their own candidate on the throne.

One month after Yōmei died, Moriya and Katsumi were defeated by Umako at the battle of Shigisan and Umako placed on the throne Sushun (grandson of his father Soga no Iname; reign 587–592), the youngest son of Kinmei (509–571; reign 539–571), but later had him assassinated. Suiko (554–628; reign 593–628; Y); reign 592–then ascended. As a daughter of Kinmei, full sister of Yōmei, widow of her half-brother Bidatsu, and mother-in-law of Prince Imperial Shōtoku (574–622; son of Yōmei and a daughter of Soga no Umako), she was the most influential woman in the imperial family and was able to keep the ambitions of the Soga in check. When Suiko died without appointing an heir, Soga no Emishi, Umako's son, backed Prince Tamura (Jomei, 593–641; reign 629–641) against Prince Yamashiro no Ōe, the son of Prince Imperial Shōtoku (574–622) and a daughter of Soga no Umako. After getting Tamura nominated, he killed Prince Yamashiro's backer Sakaibe no Marise, a son of Iname and his uncle.

Kōgyoku was less successful than Suiko in restraining the Soga, who seemed to rival the imperial family when they built palaces, constructed an armory, and surrounded themselves with bodyguards. In 643, Emishi's son Iruka ordered the assassination of Prince Yamashiro, who committed suicide with his family. This was the last straw for Naka no Ōe, Kamako, Ishikawa no Maro and the other nobles, who conspired to kill Iruka. By doing so, they broke the hold of the Soga clan on the imperial family and cleared the way for other families to ascend to the throne.

*Sybil Thornton*

**See also:** Early Mytho-histories: *Kojiki* and *Nihon shōki*.

## Further Reading

Asakawa Kan'ichi. *The Early Institutional Life of Japan: A Study in the Reform of 645 A.D.* New York: Paragon Book Reprint, 1963.

Brown, Delmer M., ed. *Cambridge History of Japan I: Ancient Japan.* Cambridge, UK: Cambridge University Press, 1993.

## Itagaki Taisuke (1837–1919)

Itagaki Taisuke was born on April 17, 1837, to one of the highest-ranking retainers to the lord of the Tosa clan in western Japan. At age 18, he was sent by his *daimyō* to Edo to study. Soon after his return to Tosa, Itagaki was exiled to a remote village for insulting Tosa officials. He spent his time studying and hunting before being called back to Tosa to take charge of a group of tax collectors. He was transferred to Edo in 1861 to supervise accounts and military affairs for the Tosa *daimyō*. By 1864, Itagaki had begun to openly identify with the lower samurai, against his own class, and to display anti-shōgun and anti-foreign sympathies.

By 1867, the leading clans of western Japan had agreed to work together to overthrow the shōgun. Itagaki secretly bought 300 U.S.-made rifles and armed his followers in Tosa. When the uprising began, he led the Tosa troops in the war against the forces loyal to the Tokugawa. Itagaki distinguished himself in defeating the Aizu clan in northern Japan in 1868. For his work, he was named *sanyo*, or cabinet consultant. In July 1870, he was raised to the rank of *sangi*, or councilor of state.

Many former samurai opposed the early Meiji reforms and began to rally around Saigō Takamori, a leader of the Satsuma clan and a close friend and ally of Itagaki. In 1873, the government debated whether

Japanese statesman Itagaki Taisuke (1837–1919). Itagaki played a role in the overthrow of the Tokugawa shōgunate and the development of the new government of the Meiji era. (J. Morris, *Makers of Japan*, 1906)

an expedition should be sent to Korea to punish it for hostile acts against Japanese citizens. When a majority of the government refused to declare war, Itagaki followed Saigō 's lead and resigned from the government. One reason Itagaki decided to resign was the way in which the Satsuma and the Chōshū clans had monopolized powerful positions in the government; they formed a powerful oligarchy that prevented leaders of other factions from participating in national decision making.

Itagaki met with other leaders who had left the government in protest, and they decided upon two goals. The first was to establish a large political association to arouse public emotions. The second was to submit a memorial to the government calling for the establishment of a representative national assembly. In 1874, Itagaki established the *Risshi-sha* (Institute of Aspiration) in Tosa. Itagaki became known as the "Rousseau of Japan," and Tosa became the "Mecca of Liberalism." Itagaki's followers took to calling themselves *Aikoku-koto* (The Public Party of Patriots). The memorial that Itagaki and his allies submitted to the government was rejected, but its publication in newspapers led to a national debate. The memorial borrowed heavily from Western liberal ideals, especially John Stuart Mill's *On Liberty* and Samuel Smiles's *Self-Help*. Itagaki's followers began to use the expression "popular rights" in their pronouncements.

The debates spawned by Itagaki's memorial led to growing discontent with the government. In January 1875, Itagaki met with government leaders at the Osaka Conference. Members of the Satsuma and Chōshū clans pledged themselves to the establishment of a constitutional monarchy and a representative legislature. In return, Itagaki agreed to return to the cabinet. The government hoped to defuse the growing crisis by reinstating the popular Itagaki, but in less than a year he resigned, charging that the legislative body represented the Satsuma and Chōshū leaders rather than the people.

In 1877, the Satsuma Rebellion broke out, led by Saigō. Itagaki refused to join the fighting but continued to press for more democratic government as a solution to the unrest in Japan. Saigō was defeated and committed suicide, ending the final armed challenge to Emperor Meiji's government. Itagaki and his followers, however, continued to call for reform, which caused the authorities to respond with repressive measures. Government leaders finally realized that reform was necessary, and on October 12, 1881, the emperor issued an edict announcing that a National Assembly (Diet) would be inaugurated 10 years hence in 1891.

In the same year, Itagaki founded the first real political party in Japan, the *Jiyuto* (Liberal Party). He traveled the country, speaking to large groups to familiarize them with the concepts of democratic government. During one speaking engagement, a would-be assassin stabbed Itagaki. According to legend, Itagaki responded by crying out, "Itagaki may die but liberty will live." Whether true or not, this slogan became a rallying cry for those working for popular rights.

Itagaki went to Europe in 1882 to study constitutional governments. During his absence, police repression nearly destroyed the Liberal Party. Upon his return, Itagaki revived the party in time for it to participate in the first session of the Diet in 1890. In the same year, a new constitution was instituted, based on the German model. Although Itagaki participated in several governments over the next decade, his great work was completed. He was more of an idealist than a pragmatic politician. When Itagaki died on July 11, 1919, he left a constitutional monarchy and representative legislature with true political parties for those who followed him.

*Louis G. Perez*

**See also:** Boshin Civil War; Jiyu Minken Undo; Saigō Takamori; Seinan (Satsuma) Rebellion; Tokugawa *Bakufu* Political System.

**Further Reading**

Fraser, Andrew. "The Osaka Conference of 1875." *Journal of Asian Studies* 26, no. 4 (August 1967): 589–610.

Giffard, Sydney. "The Development of Democracy in Japan." *Asian Affairs* 27, no. 3 (1996), 275–284.

# Itō Hirobumi

Itō Hirobumi was born on October 14, 1841, to poor farmers in Suo Province, in the Chōshū domain of Japan, and was given the name Hayashi Toshisuke. As a child, he was adopted by the Itō family, who were samurai of low rank. In his youth, he attended a private school headed by Yoshida Shōin. In 1859, Itō began to travel to Edo and Kyoto, where he met young samurai from other domains. Among them were advocates of the *sonno-jōi* movement. In December 1862, Itō participated in burning down the British legation in Edo.

In 1863, the leaders of the Chōshū domain conferred upon Itō the status of samurai and ordered him to go abroad to learn about the

One of the most prominent statesmen of modern Japan, Itō Hirobumi was involved in all levels of government from the beginning of the Meiji era in 1868 to his death at the hands of a Korean nationalist assassin in 1909. (J. Morris, *Makers of Japan*, 1906)

West. Itō and several other Chōshū samurai secretly stowed away on a ship bound for England. Itō stayed in London for six months, during which time he observed the technological superiority of this Western nation. He soon abandoned his anti-Western views and began to favor the opening of Japan.

When Itō learned that military forces in his native domain of Chōshū had fired upon Western ships in the Straits of Shimonoseki, he resolved to return to Japan to help settle the affair peacefully. Itō became a central figure in the formation of the alliance between the Satsuma and Chōshū domains.

With the formation of a new imperial government under Emperor Meiji in 1868, Itō became a councilor of state and was appointed a judge in the Bureau of Foreign Affairs. He also served simultaneously as governor of Hyogo Prefecture. In 1869, he became a minor official in the Ministries of Finance, Civil Affairs, and Industry.

As an official in the Ministry of Finance, Itō worked closely with Ōkuma Shigenobu. They advocated measures to open the nation to foreign trade, and helped to establish the first railroad system in Japan. In 1870, Itō traveled to the United States, where he studied the nation's currency system and fiscal affairs. Upon returning to Japan, he became director of the Tax Division and the National Mint. Itō also served as a high-level official in the Ministry of Public Works, where he was influential in the process of dissolving the old feudal domains and replacing them with the modern prefecture system.

In 1871, Itō accompanied Iwakura Tomomi and other leading statesmen to Europe and the United States, where they studied Western forms of government. The Iwakura Mission returned to Japan in 1873. Soon after, government leaders clashed over a proposal made by Saigō Takamori, who argued that Japan should invade Korea

for its refusal to recognize the legitimacy of the new Meiji government. Saigō resigned and returned to his native domain of Satsuma, where he subsequently led the unsuccessful Satsuma Rebellion against the Meiji regime.

In 1878, Itō became Minister of Home Affairs. He and Ōkuma subsequently became embroiled in a disagreement over the adoption of a constitutional form of government. Itō had Ōkuma ousted from office and assumed primary leadership in the Meiji government. Itō then traveled to Europe in 1882 to study constitutional systems. His meetings with Prussian legal experts Rudolf von Gneist and Lorenz von Stein led him to favor the German style of government, which was a constitutional system ruled by an absolute monarch. Upon returning home, Itō enlisted the assistance of two prominent statesmen, Itō Miyoji and Inoue Kowashi, to help draft a modern constitution.

During this period, Itō served as head of the Bureau for Organizational Studies, and he worked to revise the cabinet system. He also served as Minister of the Imperial Household, in which capacity he revised regulations pertaining to the imperial family. Itō was a central figure in drafting the Meiji Constitution. He was also influential in establishing the Imperial House Law, which established the Privy Council and assured the financial security of the imperial household.

Itō became Japan's first Prime Minister in 1885, and his first term lasted until 1888. He served simultaneously as the Minister of the Imperial Household and as President of the Privy Council.

With the promulgation of the new constitution on February 11, 1889, the nation's parliament, or Diet, was formed in 1890. In that year, Itō became president of the House of Peers in the newly formed legislature.

He became a personal counselor (*genrō*) to the emperor in the following year. From 1892 to 1896, he served as prime minister for a second time. In 1894, with the help of Foreign Minister Mutsu Munemitsu, Itō brought an end to the hated Unequal Treaties. Also in 1894, Japan entered into war against China over the suzerainty of Korea, soundly defeating the Chinese forces. Itō and Mutsu represented Japan in the talks that led to the Treaty of Shimonoseki (1895) and the subsequent Triple Intervention (1895).

Itō served as Prime Minister for a third time from 1898 to 1900. He met with strong opposition from the Kenseito (Constitutional Party) and, in response, formed his own political party, the Rikken Seiyūkai (Friends of Constitutional Government Party) in 1900. Tired of politics, Itō resigned as Prime Minister in 1901 and traveled to Russia in an attempt to strengthen trade relations between the two nations. He opposed factions that advocated close cooperation with the British and favored relations with Russia. His efforts failed, however; the Anglo-Japanese alliance was signed in 1902, and Japan went to war with Russia in 1904 over the issue of hegemony in eastern Asia, particularly Manchuria.

Following the conclusion of the Russo-Japanese War in 1905, Itō became the Japanese ambassador to Korea, and in 1906, he became Japan's first Resident General in Korea. During this time, Itō played a significant part in helping Japan usurp control over Korea's internal and foreign affairs and laid the foundation for the annexation of Korea. In 1909, when he became president of the Privy Council for the fourth time, Itō returned to Japan. Later that year, he left again for Korea, intending to mediate conflicts that had arisen over Japanese and Russian interests there. A Korean patriot named An Chung-kun assassinated him at a railway station in Harbin, China, on October 26, 1909, while Itō was en route to Korea.

*Louis G. Perez*

**See also:** *Genrō;* Iwakura Mission; Iwakura Tomomi; Meiji Constitution; Mutsu Munemitsu; Ōkuma Shigenobu; Russo-Japanese War; Saigō Takamori; Satchō Oligarchy; Seinan (Satsuma) Rebellion; Shimonoseki, Treaty of; Sino-Japanese War; *Sonno-jōi;* Triple Intervention; Unequal Treaties; Yoshida Shōin.

**Further Reading**

Akita, George. *Foundations of Constitutional Government in Modern Japan, 1868–1900.* Cambridge, MA: Harvard University Press, 1967.

Hamada, Kenji. *Prince Itō*. Tokyo: Sanseido, 1936

Oka, Yoshitake. *Five Political Leaders of Modern Japan: Itō Hirobumi, Ōkuma Shigenobu, Hara Takashi, Inukai Tsuyoshi, and Saionji Kimmochi.* Trans. Andrew Fraser and Patricia Murray. Tokyo: University of Tokyo Press, 1986.

# Itō Noe (1895–1923)

Itō Noe was born in 1895 in the village of Imajuku, Fukuoka Prefecture. Through the good offices of one of her uncle's neighbors in Tokyo, she was accepted into the private Ueno Girls' High School. A wedding to a young man from Imajuku was arranged for Itō. The formal engagement was announced in 1911, while Itō was still a student, though the wedding was scheduled for after her graduation in 1912. Itō returned to Imajuku but ran away after a few days to return to Tokyo; she had fallen in love with Jun Tsuji, her English teacher at school.

Jun introduced her to a newly published feminist magazine, *Seito* ("Bluestockings") the brainchild of feminist Hiratsuka *Raichō*. Hiratsuka was editor and introduced the first issue with her manifesto entitled *"Gen-shi josei wa taiyo de atta"* ("In the Beginning Woman Was the Sun"). This slogan was repeated on the cover of each subsequent issue and became a rallying cry for Japanese feminists of the time.

Itō first met with Hiratsuka in the spring of 1912 and submitted several of her poems. Hiratsuka decided to put the 17-year-old Itō to work for the magazine. In July 1912, Itō returned to Imajuku to dissolve her arranged marriage, and then returned to Tokyo with the support of Hiratsuka. She married Jun Tsuji and joined the staff of the magazine. Itō suggested that the magazine concentrate more on the problems confronting women and less on literary efforts. Beginning in January 1913, *Seito* published three consecutive issues that dealt only with the difficulties that Japanese society placed before women. The following month, the magazine sponsored its first public symposium. Many of the guest speakers were well-known critics, but the young Itō also addressed the symposium.

Criticism from governmental, educational, and journalistic sources followed swiftly. The February issue of *Seito* was banned from sale because of an article calling for liberation of all people and the common ownership of all property. Hiratsuka wished to escape the burden of editorship; thus, in January 1915, Itō became editor and publisher of *Seito*. She proclaimed that the magazine would not be limited by any philosophy or boundaries and that it would simply be for women. She organized debates to be published in *Seito* on such topics as chastity, abortion, and licensed prostitution. The debates continued until the last issue was published in February 1916.

Itō's philosophy continued to change and develop throughout this time. She began to question whether the equal rights sought by such feminists as Hiratsuka could bring true independence. She also met and fell in love with the anarchist Osugi Sakae. She divorced her husband to live with Osugi. He, in turn, divorced his wife, and the concurrent affair he was having with Kamichika Ichiko ended after she stabbed him. Itō and Osugi married, and she bore him five children, which Itō believed was the fulfillment of her role as a woman. "To marry and give birth is indeed the mission of the real woman. In fact, all women should fulfill this role," she wrote.

Itō spent the last seven years of her life helping Osugi in his anarchist activities. The two of them jointly produced a translation of the works of anarchists Emma Goldman and Peter Kropotkin into Japanese. Itō herself wrote 80 articles on feminism and anarchism, as well as several autobiographical novels. The couple was kept under police surveillance but continued to stay active in the anarchist movement. Itō claimed that "anarchists dealing only with abstract theory, no matter how dangerous they might appear, were left alone as long as they confined their interests to building personal philosophies." Although they kept a low profile, Itō feared that some untoward incident might cause the authorities to take more repressive measures against them. Unlike her earlier feminist writings, Itō's anarchist activities threatened the state itself.

A great disaster occurred on September 1, 1923, soon after the birth of Itō's seventh child. The Great Kanto Earthquake struck Tokyo, devastating the city and killing thousands. In the disorder that followed, Itō and Osugi were arrested. On September 16, the two anarchists were strangled in their cell by Captain Amakasu Masahiko of the Koji-machi Division of the Tokyo military police. Itō was only 28 years old, but she had lived according to her beliefs.

*Tim Watts*

**See also:** Great Kanto Earthquake; Hiratsuka *Raichō*; *Seito (Bluestockings)*.

### Further Reading

Duus, Peter. "Socialism, Liberalism, and Marxism, 1901–1931," in *Cambridge History of Japan, Vol. 6: The Twentieth Century*. New York: Cambridge University Press, 1988:606–653.

Miyamoto, Ken. "Itō Noe and the Bluestockings." *Japan Interpreter* 10, no. 2 (Autumn 1975): 190–203.

## Itō Yūko (1843–1913)

Itō Yūko was born in 1843 in Kagoshima, Japan, the son of a samurai warrior. As part of the garrison at Shimonoseki, Itō was highly impressed by this display of modern sea power when in September 1864 a combined British, French, Dutch, and U.S. squadron bombarded the Shimonoseki Straits, landing marines and demolishing the forts.

Itō soon entered the national naval school at Kobe. By 1869, he was chief officer of the warship *Fujisan*. As captain, he held a series of eight ship commands between 1871 and 1883, rising to rear admiral in 1886. In light of his exemplary service record, he served in the Naval Ministry during 1889–1890 and also functioned as president of the Naval Staff College.

In 1894, Itō was appointed commander of the Japanese fleet in anticipation of hostilities against China. He departed Sasebo Naval Base in July 1894. His adversary was the Chinese Peiyang Fleet, a motley array of two ironclad battleships, four light cruisers, and six torpedo boats. The Chinese forces were decidedly inferior to their adversaries in terms of drill and discipline. Nonetheless, they advanced to give battle on September 17, 1894, near the mouth of the Yalu River. In the ensuing five-hour action, Itō's warships sank five Chinese vessels, drowning nearly 1,000 sailors. Japanese losses totaled only 90 killed and 200 wounded.

Over the next several months, Japanese land forces attacked and slowly pushed the defenders out of their positions at Weihanwei. At that point, Itō, saddened by the fate of the Chinese commander who had once been his friend, wrote him a lengthy letter and entreated him to surrender rather than face disaster. "There need be no hostility between individuals," he declared. "The friendship between you and me is as warm as ever today." The Chinese commander responded by politely declaring the intention to fight to the last.

By February 4, 1895, the Japanese were in position to cut the harbor booms and remove the various mines and other obstacles guarding the entrance to Weihanwei Harbor. That evening, Itō sent in his torpedo boats despite freezing weather, and they sank the Chinese flagship, the *Ting Yuan*. The Japanese returned the following evening and sank an additional three vessels, whereupon the proud Chinese squadron ceased to exist. At that point, the Chinese offered to surrender Weihanwei to the Japanese on the condition that the prisoners be well treated. Itō agreed as promised but was shocked to learn that his old friend had committed suicide rather than be taken alive. As a final token of respect, Itō ordered a captured Chinese ship released and allowed to convey his friend's body back to China. As the ship departed, the entire Japanese squadron was held at attention and fired a parting salute.

Itō was honored upon his return home and promoted to full admiral in 1898. Between 1895 and 1913, he served as the senior member of the Navy General Staff and in 1907, was granted the title of viscount. He died in Tokyo in 1913, a major architect of Japanese naval power.

*John C. Fredriksen*

**See also:** Russo-Japanese War; Shimonoseki, Bombardment of; Sino-Japanese War.

**Further Reading**

Evans, David C., and Mark R. Peattie. *Kaigun: Strategy, Tactics, and Technology in the Imperial Japanese Navy, 1887–1941*. Washington, DC: Naval Institute Press, 1997.

Howarth, Stephen. *The Fighting Ships of the Rising Sun*. New York: Atheneum, *1983*.

## Iwakura Mission (1871–1873)

The Iwakura Mission was the first embassy of the newly formed Meiji government in 1868. It was the third overseas mission that the Japanese government sponsored in the 19th century, following the 1862 and 1865–1866 missions dispatched by the Edo regime.

Prince Iwakura Tomomi himself proposed an overseas mission in 1867. He argued that such a mission was necessary to affirm that (1) diplomatic policies rested in the realm of imperial authority, not with the Edo *bakufu*, and (2) to experience first-hand the Western culture and see what might be relevant to Japan. With the removal of the Edo *bakufu* in 1868, the aims of the mission were revised.

The new Meiji government gave its approval to the Iwakura Mission in October 1871, and the foreign legations were informed of this development in November 1871. The mission's aims were threefold: (1) to engage in preliminary talks on treaty revisions, (2)

to explore which aspects of Western cultures and systems would be applicable to Japan, and (3) to improve the image of Japan.

Iwakura was named ambassador. He had with him four vice-ambassadors: Ōkubo Toshimichi, Kido Takayoshi, Itō Hirobumi, and Yamaguchi Naoyoshi. The official historian and secretary to Iwakura was Kume Kunitake, who kept a detailed account that is vital in understanding the activities and decisions made by the embassy. On December 23, 1871, the Iwakura Mission departed Yokohama for the United States and Europe.

When the mission was finalized, it totaled 107 people (48 officials and 59 students, including five girls), who were divided into three groups. The political group would gather information on constitutions, laws, and regulations. The economic group would gather information on banking, taxation, currency, trade and industry, and railroad, telegraph, and postal services. The education group focused on curriculum and administration of all schools, including commercial and technical ones. All of these groups were to pay particular attention to all matters related to the military, including training, arsenals, and shipyards. To overcome the language barrier, the Meiji government called on some 60 students who were studying abroad to act as interpreters.

The mission reached San Francisco on January 15, 1872, and traveled to Washington, D.C., via train, arriving there on February 29. The journey would continue to Britain (August 17–December 16, 1872), France (December 16, 1872–February 17, 1873, Belgium (February 17–24, 1873), Germany (March 7–28, 1873), Russia (March 29–April 15, 1873), Germany (April 15–17, 1873), Sweden (April 23–30, 1873), Germany (May 1–8, 1873), Italy (May 9–June 2, 1873), and France (July 16–20, 1873). The mission returned to Japan on September 13, 1873.

The impact of the Iwakura Mission on Japan was profound, but mission was not without glitches. For example, at Washington, D.C., Secretary of State Hamilton Fish was open to negotiating a new treaty with Japan. The Japanese delegation realized that Iwakura did not have plenipotentiary powers, which resulted in Ōkubo and Itō hurrying back to Japan to obtain Letters of Credence. When they returned to Washington, D.C., they learned that the Japanese delegation had decided to hold treaty revision talks someplace in Europe after some preliminary unsatisfactory discussions with Fish. It was clear that the Japanese officials decided to focus more on the two other aims of the mission, but Iwakura made clear to U.S., British, and other governments that he was prepared to seek their views concerning treaty revision rather than conducting the actual negotiations.

The members of the Iwakura Mission were studious and keen observer of "things Western." A number of the delegates would fill important positions both in and out of the government. For example, Tanaka Fujimaro not only influenced the Japanese educational system, but was also among those leaders who called for the Meiji government to hire foreign experts (oyatoi) to assist Japanese in bringing about changes. Ōkubo saw the need to strengthen Japan; he was impressed by what he saw in Germany and with British industry. Kido found that parliamentary institution was a pillar of higher civilization. Members of the Iwakura Mission would be armed with knowledge of the West that would play an important role in the transformation of Japan.

*Roy S. Hanashiro*

**See also:** Itō Hirobumi; Iwakura Tomomi; Kido Takayoshi; Ōkubo Toshimichi; *Oyatoi.*

## Further Reading

Auslin, Michael. *Negotiating with Imperialism: The Unequal Treaties and the Culture of Japanese Diplomacy.* Cambridge, MA: Harvard University Press, 2004.

Beasley, William. *The Meiji Restoration.* Stanford: Stanford University Press, 1972.

Nish, Ian. *The Iwakura Mission in America and Europe.* Richmond: Japan Library, 1998.

Perez, Louis. *Japan Comes of Age: Mutsu Munemitsu and the Revision of the Unequal Treaties.* Madison: Fairleigh Dickinson University Press, 1999.

## Iwakura Tomomi (1825–1883)

Iwakura was born in Kyoto on October 26, 1825, to a family of lower nobility by the name of Horikawa. His childhood given name was Kanemaru, but he was later adopted by the more prestigious Iwakura family and given the name Tomomi. The court recognized his talents and in 1854, made him a chamberlain in the service of Emperor Komei. That year he joined a group of 88 court nobles in protesting the handling of treaty negotiations with the United States, which demanded that Japan open its ports to trade. Iwakura opposed such treaties with Western nations.

In 1860, Iwakura joined a political faction whose aim was to restore power to the emperor by arranging a marriage between the emperor's younger sister and the reigning shōgun. This act angered members of the growing anti-shōgun faction. As a result, in 1862, Iwakura was forced to resign his post, banned from the court, and exiled from Kyoto. He subsequently became a Buddhist monk and retired to a village north of Kyoto.

During the period of his confinement, Iwakura secretly corresponded with the

Iwakura Tomomi was an influential noble in the royal court of Japan during the important transition from the Tokugawa era to the Meiji period in the mid-19th century. He also led the Iwakura Mission (1871–1873) to study the Western nations. (J. Morris, *Makers of Japan*, 1906)

With his nomination to lead a diplomatic-study mission to Europe and the United States came the appointment as envoy extraordinary and minister plenipotentiary. In the latter months of 1871, Iwakura left for Europe accompanied by a number of government officials, including Itō Hirobumi and Ōkubo Toshimichi. The so-called Iwakura Mission returned to Japan in 1873. The goal of the mission to revise the Unequal Treaties with the United States failed, but members of the mission succeeded in gaining valuable information concerning governmental systems in the West.

Iwakura opposed the faction led by Saigō Takamori, whose ambition was to invade Korea because of that nation's refusal to recognize the sovereignty of the new Meiji government. Iwakura felt strongly that it was first necessary to build Japan's strength on the domestic front. He gained the support of the emperor and defeated the proinvasion faction led by Saigō, which resulted in his being attacked by a supporter of Saigō early in 1874.

Iwakura advocated a strong imperial institution and, as a consequence, ardently opposed the People's Rights Movement. He favored a system of government in which supreme power resided in the emperor alone. When in 1881 Ōkuma Shigenobu demanded the immediate drafting of a constitution and the formation of a national assembly, Iwakura allied himself with the more conservative faction led by Itō and had Ōkuma removed from his position as councilor of state. Iwakura sponsored Itō in traveling to Europe to study Western forms of constitutional government.

As head of the Peers' Club and director of the office in charge of the affairs of the court peerage, Iwakura acted as general supervisor of the nobility and served to protect the interests of the imperial family. He sought

faction of samurai advocating the overthrow of the Tokugawa government. When Emperor Komei died and was succeeded by Emperor Meiji in 1867, Iwakura received a pardon and was again allowed to reside in Kyoto. He soon joined Ōkubo Toshimichi and the Satsuma faction in plotting the restoration of power to the emperor. Iwakura was a leading figure at the court during the coup d'état that led to the Meiji Restoration in 1868.

Iwakura became a key figure in the new government. He was appointed to a number of important government posts and was integrally involved in the creation of the Charter Oath and the establishment of the prefectural system. Iwakura became Minister of Foreign Affairs in 1871, and later that year, he was appointed as Minister of the Right.

to expand the property holdings of the imperial house. With funds provided by family members of the nobility, he established the 15th National Bank and the Japan Railway Company. Iwakura also supported measures to ensure the livelihood of former samurai, whose social privileges had been rescinded under the reforms of the new Meiji government.

Throughout the early Meiji period, Iwakura had a strong influence on the emperor and made a name for himself as a shrewd political figure. He died on July 20, 1883, after a prolonged illness.

*Walter E. Grunden*

**See also:** Boshin Civil War; Charter Oath; Itō Hirobumi; Iwakura Mission; Jiyu Minken Undo; Meiji Emperor; Ōkubo Toshimichi; Ōkuma Shigenobu; Saigō Takamori.

**Further Reading**

Kido Takayoshi. *The Diary of Kido Takayoshi, Vol. 2.* Trans. by Sidney DeVere Brown, Tokyo: University of Tokyo Press, 1983–1986.

Morris, John. *Makers of Japan.* London: Methuen, 1906.

Shively, Donald H., ed. *Tradition and Modernization in Japanese Culture.* Princeton, NJ: Princeton University Press, 1971.

## Iwo Jima, Battle for (February 19–March 26, 1945)

By the end of 1944, American forces had secured control of the Mariana Islands to provide air bases for B-29 strategic bombers that could strike Japan. En route to Japan, these bombers flew over Iwo Jima (Sulphur Island). Located in the Japanese Bonin Islands, halfway between the Marianas and Japan, the pork-chop-shaped volcanic island of Iwo Jima is from 800 yards to 2.5 miles wide and 5 miles long, with a total area of some 8 square miles.

Iwo Jima housed a large radar facility that gave Tokyo advance notice of impending air attacks, as well as three airstrips for fighter aircraft used to harass the U.S. bombers. As a consequence, U.S. commanders formulated Operation Detachment to seize Iwo Jima.

Japanese leaders realized the strategic importance of Iwo Jima and began reinforcing it a year prior to the American invasion. Lieutenant General Kuribayashi Tadamichi, the island's commander, disregarded the traditional Japanese defensive doctrine of meeting the enemy at the shoreline and implemented a new strategy that relied on 1,500 interlocking strong points inland, designed for a battle of attrition. His force of 21,000 men dug out thousands of yards of tunnels in the soft volcanic rock to connect natural caves, underground bunkers, and man-made "spider-traps" from which concealed defenders could infiltrate and attack any enemy positions. These extensive subterranean complexes would also shield the defenders from extensive preliminary air and naval bombardment by U.S. forces. Japanese artillerymen also preregistered the beachheads to maximize the effectiveness of their own shelling. Kuribayashi ordered the defenders to die in place and to kill at least 10 Americans before dying themselves. He was, however, handicapped by a lack of freshwater. The absence of a natural harbor limited Japanese reinforcement of the island, and U.S. submarines also sank a number of Japanese supply ships, including one transport with a regiment of Japanese tanks.

Beginning in August 1944, U.S. Army aircraft in the Marianas subjected Iwo Jima to air strikes, and from December 8, the island came under daily attack. Three heavy cruisers bombarded Iwo Jima three times in December and twice in January. Then, for two weeks beginning in late January, Seventh Air Force bombed Iwo Jima day and night, and B-29s struck it twice. In all, U.S. forces dropped 6,800 tons of bombs and fired 22,000 rounds of 5-inch to 16-inch shells prior to the invasion, the heaviest bombardment of the Pacific war. Even so, the naval bombardment of the island, begun on February 16, 1945, lasted only three days—a far shorter period than V Marine Amphibious Corps commander Lieutenant General Holland M. ("Howlin' Mad") Smith had requested. Smith led a force of 80,000 men, supported by Admiral Raymond A. Spruance's 5th Fleet. Vice Admiral Richmond Kelly Turner had overall charge of the invasion.

On February 19, 1945, 30,000 U.S. Marines from the 3rd, 4th, and 5th Marine Divisions stormed ashore, only to encounter Iwo Jima's coarse, black volcanic sand. Heavy surf smashed the landing craft against the island's shelf, and the deep sand immobilized many vehicles on the beach. The resulting logjam of men and equipment on the beachhead provided prime targets for highly accurate Japanese artillery fire. With little or no cover, the Marines had no choice except to fight their way inland. One group wheeled south, toward the island's most prominent terrain feature, the 556-foot Mount Suribachi, while the majority of the Marines attacked northward toward the first airfield. On the fourth day after the initial landing, Marines reached the crest of Mount Suribachi, and although still under fire, they raised a small American flag. A few hours later, another group raised a second, larger flag as Associated Press reporter Joe Rosenthal impulsively snapped a photo. Rosenthal's picture of these five Marines and one navy corpsman planting the second flag became a Marine Corps icon and the symbol for American victory in the Pacific.

The photograph remains one of the most widely reproduced images of all time.

Marines assaulting the main line of resistance to the north waded through rain-soaked sand into a maze of Japanese pillboxes, bunkers, and caves. Assisted by flamethrowers, demolition charges, bazookas, tanks, and air support, they pushed their way through Kuribayashi's defenses for 36 days, sometimes advancing only a few feet per day. By March 26, 1945, nearly 70,000 Marines had conquered most of the island, at a cost of approximately 6,500 dead and 20,000 wounded. More than 95 percent of the Japanese defenders died during the same period, and pockets of Japanese resistance continued to emerge from concealed cave complexes throughout April and May, resulting in 1,600 additional Japanese deaths. Fewer than 300 Japanese were taken prisoner.

With the island firmly in U.S. possession, U.S. bombers pounded the Japanese homeland unabated. In the midst of the heaviest fighting on March 4, the first of 2,500 U.S. bombers made emergency landings on the island, and some 2,000 B-29s force-landed there from March to August. Given that these planes carried 10-man crews, this represented up to 20,000 airmen saved. The U.S. Army Air Forces moved to Iwo Jima and began to send long-range fighter escorts with the B-29s to Japan. From that point, the bombers mixed medium-level daytime raids with the low-level night attacks. Losses of Japanese planes mounted rapidly, while those of the B-29s continued to decline.

The struggle for Iwo Jima epitomized the courage and esprit of the Marine Corps during the war. Twenty-two Marines, four navy corpsmen, and one navy officer on Iwo Jima earned the Medal of Honor (almost half of them posthumously), accounting for one-third of all such medals won by Marines during the entire war. Fleet Admiral Chester Nimitz testified to the level of courage and bravery among the Americans fighting on Iwo Jima in stating, "Among the Americans who served on Iwo Jima, uncommon valor was a common virtue."

*Derek W. Frisby*

**See also:** World War II, Pacific Theater.

**Further Reading**

Alexander, Joseph. *Closing in: Marines in the Seizure of Iwo Jima*. Washington, DC: History and Museums Division, Headquarters, U.S. Marine Corps, 1994.

Bradley, James. *Flags of Our Fathers*. New York: Bantam Books, 2000.

Wright, Derrick. *The Battle for Iwo Jima, 1945*. Phoenix Mill, UK: Sutton Publishing, 1999.

# J

## Jiang Jieshi (Ch'iang K'ai-shek) (1887–1975)

Jiang Jieshi was born into a wealthy salt-merchant family in Fenghua County, Zhejiang Province, China. He was a serious student of Confucian classics and an admirer of Confucian scholar-generals Wang Yangming (1472–1529) and Zeng Guofan (1811–1872). In 1907, Jiang was admitted to the Baoding Military Academy in Tianjin. A year later, he entered Shinbu Military Academy (Zhenwu Xuexiao) in Japan. After graduating in November 1909, Jiang reported to the 19th Field Artillery Regiment of the Imperial Japanese Army at Takada, where he gained some real army experience. His division commander General Nagaoka later recalled that he was impressed by Jiang's loyalty and gratitude.

During his roughly three-year stay in Japan, Jiang was introduced to revolutionary ideas and became a member of the Alliance Society (Tongmeng Hui), an anti-Qing revolutionary organization founded by Dr. Sun Yat-sen in Japan in 1905. Upon hearing news of the Wuchang Uprising in 1911, Jiang rushed back to China to participate in the revolutionary movement, which succeeded in toppling the Manchu regime later that year. In January 1912, Sun founded the Republic of China (R.O.C.) as well as the Nationalist Party (Guomindang). However, he did not have strong military support for undertaking lasting political reform based on democratic and constitutional principles, and the country was soon controlled by warlords.

In 1924, Sun received financial support from Soviet Russia to establish the Whampoa Military Academy in Guangzhou and appointed Jiang to be its first commandant. The Academy gave Jiang a golden opportunity to train a dedicated group of military officers who were personally loyal to him and who later would play major roles in the battles against warlords and Japanese invaders. The sudden death of Sun in 1925 left a temporary political vacuum in the Guomindang and led to struggles among potential successors. In 1926, Jiang emerged as Sun's undisputed successor, took over Guomindang leadership, and launched the Northern Expedition (1926–1928) to reunify China by ending warlordism. A number of Whampoa graduates participated in this campaign. By the end of 1928, China was nominally reunified under the leadership of Jiang, who set up his government in Nanjing.

In 1931, Japan occupied Manchuria. Strong anti-Japanese sentiments soon spread across China. Even so, Jiang insisted on pursuing the unpopular policy of "pacifying the internal before resisting foreign aggression," meaning that he would deal with Japanese aggression only after eradicating the Chinese Communist Party (CCP). In December 1936, Jiang flew to Xi'an to direct anticommunist campaigns, but was arrested by two of his generals. They forced him to end the campaigns and accept a Guomindang-CCP alliance against Japanese invasion—an event known as the Xi'an Incident. When Jiang was released, he reluctantly kept his promise to forge a united front between the Guomindang and CCP. After the Xi'an Incident, Japan intensified its incursion of China. On July 7, 1937, Japan initiated the Marco Polo Bridge Incident and began an all-out effort to conquer China.

Anti-Japanese efforts under Jiang's leadership led China to a protracted war of resistance. Jiang adopted a strategy of "trading space for time." After his best troops sustained heavy losses in Shanghai and Nanjing in late 1937, Jiang moved his government to Chongqing, a city in China's interior province of Sichuan. The strategy slowed down the advances of Japanese troops and permitted Jiang to organize a number of successful counterattacks. By the end of 1938, however, Japanese troops had occupied the entire eastern seaboard, but victory over the entirety of China was nowhere near. Moreover, the United States decided to provide China with military assistance after its naval base in Pearl Harbor was attacked by Japanese fighter pilots in December 1937. With American involvement, China not only survived Japan's invasion but also became one of the "Big Four" Allied Powers.

After Japan's defeat in 1945, Jiang went on to fight a civil war with the Chinese Communists, whose victory forced Jiang to retreat his government and troops to Taiwan Island in 1949. He remained a leader of the ROC on Taiwan until his death in 1975.

*Yu Chang*

**See also:** Anti-Japanism in China; Atomic Bombs: Surrender of Japan; Manchukuo; Pearl Harbor, Attack on; Sun Yat-sen and the Japanese; Xi'an Incident.

**Further Reading**

Eastman, Lloyd E. *The Abortive Revolution: China under Nationalist Rule, 1927–1937.*

Cambridge, MA: Harvard University Press, 1972.

Eastman, Lloyd E. *Seeds of Destruction: Nationalist China in War and Revolution, 1937–1949.* Stanford, CA: Stanford University Press, 1984.

Taylor, Jay. *The Generalissimo: Chiang Kai-shek and the Struggle for Modern China.* Cambridge, MA: Harvard University Press, 2009.

# Jimmu Tennō (711 B.C.E.?–585 B.C.E.?)

According to Japan's oldest historical records, the *Kojiki* ("Record of Ancient Matters," 712) and the *Nihongi* ("Chronicles of Japan," 720), Jimmu Tennō (literally "Emperor of divine power") was the first emperor of Japan. His personal name is given as either Wakamikenu no Mikoto or Sano no Mikoto. Jimmu was the fourth son of Hiko Nagisatake Ugaya Fukiaezu no Mikoto, the great-grandson of the Shintō deity Amaterasu-Ōmikami and Tamayori-hime, the daughter of the sea deity Watatsumi. Even today, the Japanese Imperial line traces its descent and legitimization of power to Emperor Jimmu.

Although both the *Kojiki* and the *Nihongi* contain various narratives describing Emperor Jimmu's political and military achievements in conjunction with the origins of the Yamato kingdom (ancient Japan), he is considered to be more of a mythological figure than a historical one. One reason for this dispute is his age. Based on his dates, Emperor Jimmu would have been 126 years old when he died. Also, during his reign, which lasted from 660 B.C.E. to 585 B.C.E., he was known as Kamuyamato Iwarebiko; the title Jimmu Tennō was bestowed upon him posthumously in the eighth century. Historians believe that he might be a composite of

Emperor Sujin and Emperor Keitai, whose legends are almost identical. In fact, both Sujin and Jimmu have been called Hatsu Kuni Shirasu Sumera no Mikoto (literally "first sovereign of the country"). Thus Jimmu is sometimes identified with Sujin, who, according to tradition, built the first shrine dedicated to Amaterasu-Ōmikami.

Emperor Jimmu is most well known for his eastern campaign, which led to his ascension to the throne as recorded in the *Kojiki*. Jimmu, his brothers, and the local chieftain Sao Netsuhiko set out from Takachiho in southern Kyūshū (present-day Miyazaki Prefecture) eastward to conquer the eastern provinces and to exert their power of the entire country. Under the leadership of Jimmu's older brother, Itsuse no Mikoto, they reached Naniwa (close to present-day Ōsaka), where they were defeated by the local chieftain Nagasunehiko, and Itsuse no Mikoto was killed. Jimmu emerged as the new leader. When he realized that the party had been defeated because they battled eastward against the sun, he changed his direction and moved westward to Kumano. In a dream, the gods told Jimmu to follow the three-legged bird, Yatakarasu (literally "eight-span crow"), to Yamato to battle Nagasunehiko once more. This time, Jimmu emerged victoriously, received the gods' blessings, and built a palace at Kashihara (present-day Nara Prefecture), where he was crowned emperor. According to the *Kojiki*, Jimmu died at Kashihara and was buried at Unebi-yama, a mountain to the north of the city where his spirit can still be venerated today at a shrine called *Unebi-yama no ushitora no sumi no misasagi*.

*Monika Dix*

**See also:** Early Mytho-histories: *Kojiki* and *Nihon shōki*.

**Further Reading**

Brownlee, John. *Japanese Historians and the National Myths, 1600–1945: The Age of the Gods.* Vancouver: University of British Columbia Press, 1967.

Varley, H. Paul. *Japanese Culture: A Short History.* New York: Praeger Publishers, 1973.

Varley, H. Paul. *Jinnō Shōtōki: A Chronicle of Gods and Sovereigns.* New York: Columbia University Press, 1980.

# Jingū Kōgō

According to the *Kojiki* (712) and *Nihon shōki* (720), Jingū Kōgō was the consort of emperor Chūai, regent for 69 years, and mother of Ōjin (fourth to fifth centuries). Although Ōjin is documented in a number of Chinese and Korean histories, Jingū is not and has been removed from the list of rulers of Japan. Jingū is represented as going into a trance and giving an oracle directing an invasion of Silla. When her husband rejected the oracle, he suddenly died. Jingū is supposed to have used stones to delay the birth of her son, clad herself in armor, and led a successful invasion. On her return, she defeated other sons of her husband and secured the throne for her child. Later, she feted him on the occasion of his coming of age.

Although the existence of Jingū has been refuted, there are still things to be learned from the account of her life and reign. The first is the background of Japanese military action in Korea. The earliest records include a stele erected to the Koguryo King Kwang-gaet'o, on which mention is made of the Wa coming to Korea since 391, of making a treaty with Paekche in 1399, of having occupied Silla by 1400, of invading the area of the old Chinese commandery of Daifang and being repulsed in 1404, and of finally being wiped out in 1407. Relations with Paekche are indicated by the inscription, including the date of 369, on a seven-pronged sword held by the Isonokami Shrine indicates relations with Paekche, as do records in the *Book of Song* (*Song shu*; fifth to sixth centuries), which preserves instances of bestowing or recognizing titles of imperial commissar, general governor, and so forth over Korean countries on kings of Wa in 438, 451, and 477/78. The *Nihon shōki* records instances of war, receiving hostages, and accepting tribute from different countries in the Korean peninsula.

The nature of the relationship between Japan and Korea at this time is often hotly contested. What is not questioned is the function of including these records in the *Kojiki* and *Nihon* as convenient prefigurations of military actions taken by Japan in the seventh century, when the texts were first commissioned. The figure of Jingū leading the invasion of Korea provides a model for the Great King Saimei (reign 655–661), a woman, to go to the aid of Paekche, which had been occupied by Silla and Tang Chinese forces, as the head of a joint Paekche and Japanese army. She died at Asakura Palace (Hakata) in Kyushu before the expeditionary force departed, but any hope of reestablishing the kingdom was dashed by its defeat at the battle of Paekkang in 663.

In preliterate cultures, individual historical events cannot be remembered unless they are made to conform to traditional patterns. According to Akima Toshio, a collation of records of Jingū follows mythical structures: Jingū as the sea goddess with control of fish and water; Ōjin as the miraculous child born to her; the world under the sea as the land of the dead and the underworld as distant lands across the sea; the king's acquisition of wealth (Jingū finds a Nyoi pearl at Toyora) as *tama*, a jewel, or *tama*, spirit (as in *tama no fuyu*), through marriage with a shamaness able to transit between the underworld and the world of humans (Chūai rejects the gold and silver of Silla and dies; his son then is given them); the king as mediator between the two worlds with the help of the *wani*, the Wani clan that provides the consort (Ōjin marries a Wani woman) or even Wani, the legendary scholar sent from Paekche to Ōjin, who brought Confucianism and writing to Japan. The mythic structure of death and resurrection as travel to foreign lands and return in the Jingū's story was used in school books to encourage the population in the years up to the end of the war. Even the story of Ōjin is told in the pattern of "male initiation ritual myth": death and resurrection (return from the underworld as foreign country or sailing to Yamato on a funeral ship), purification (after his arrival in Yamato, Takeshiuchi no Sukene takes Ōjin to Ōmi and Wakasa to perform *misogi*), and marriage.

Other connections between Jingū and the seventh century are found in her name, Okinaga-tarashi-hime. She is made to descend from the Okinaga clan, as is Saimei's husband Jōmei (born 593; reign 629–641), whose posthumous name was Okinaga-tarashi-hi Hironuka and whose grandmother was a daughter of Okinaga no Made no Ō.

*Sybil Thornton*

**See also:** Early Mytho-histories: *Kojiki* and *Nihon shōki*.

## Further Reading

Akima Toshio. "The Myth of the Goddess of the Undersea World and the Tale of Empress Jingū's Subjugation of Silla." *Japanese Journal of Religious Studies* 20, no. 2/3 (June–September 1993): 95–185.

Como, Michael. *Shōtoku: Ethnicity, Ritual, and Violence in the Japanese Buddhist*

*Tradition* New York: Oxford University Press, 2008.

## Jiyu Minken Undo

The Movement for Popular Rights had its foundation in the political schism between the factions of the group that had overthrown the Tokugawa *bakufu*. The more conservative faction was the so-called Satchō (a conflation of the first syllables of Satsuma and Chōshū) oligarchy, which ultimately triumphed and became the leaders of the Meiji government for its first 30 years. The more liberal wing was composed primarily of the Tosa and Hizen side of the coalition.

The schism came about in 1873 primarily over the issue of whether to send a punitive expedition to Korea (*Seikanron*), although personality issues were involved as well. In January 1873, Etō Shimpei Itagaki Taisuke, Gotō Shojiro, and Soejima Taneomi had joined to sign a memorial to the emperor asking for a national assembly and a constitution. When the memorial was ignored, they resigned from the government. Saigō Takamori also resigned, but he did not join the liberals; instead, he went back to his home in Satsuma, where he founded a fencing school. Kido Takayoshi, Mutsu Munemitsu, and others resigned in 1874, mostly in protest to the Taiwan Expedition.

Etō was, like Saigō, a champion of the ex-samurai, who had been stripped of their special sociopolitical status through a series of reforms in 1871–1873. Within the year, Etō led a rebellion against the Meiji government centered in Saga. The rebellion was suppressed harshly by the newly formed commoner Imperial Army. Saigō refused to join Etō's uprising, as did the Tosa side of the liberals.

Itagaki formed a political coalition (it was not yet a real political party) that staged a series of public debates over the nature of government. He called this the *Jiyu Minken Undo*, which roughly translates into "People's Rights and Freedom Movement." The public debates were held all over the country, with sometimes thousands of people coming to hear the speakers. The public discussions often roamed far afield; a number of women speakers took the platform to call for women's rights, too.

The government had tried a number of methods to bring the dissidents back into the fold. After the failed Taiwan Expedition, Ōkubo Toshimichi, Itō Hirobumi, and Inoue Kaoru joined together to lure Kido, Gotō, Itagaki, Mutsu, and others to a conference held in Osaka in 1875. At that conference, the Satchō faction promised that a Senate (*Genrōin*) would be established, along with an Assembly of Prefectural Governors. A new Supreme Court was also promised.

When these promised institutions proved to be a chimera, Kido, Mutsu, Gotō, and Itagaki distanced themselves from the government and the *Jiyu Minken Undo* continued. The government passed a series of harsh Press Laws to stifle printed dissent. After Saigō's quixotic Satsuma Rebellion and the assassination of Ōkubo a year later, Itagaki and others formed the *Aikokusha* (Patriotic Society) and the *Domeikai* (Association for the Establishment of a National Assembly). In 1879, Iwakura Tomomi tried to bring the various political factions back together. He managed to get the emperor to call for written opinions on a proposed constitution.

Naturally, the imperial request fueled even more public debate. In 1880, the government passed even more stringent laws called, collectively, Laws of Public Meetings. The contretemps came to a head when Ōkuma Shigenobu was purged from the government in 1881 for having the temerity to submit an independent opinion on the constitution to the emperor instead of subsuming it together with the other government leaders, as was common practice. Itō flew into a rage and Ōkuma was purged. The government issued an imperial promise to grant a constitution a decade later. Not surprisingly, Ōkuma formed his own political party, the *Rikken Kaishinto* (Constitutional Reform Party).

This did not end the *Jiyu Minken Undo*, but the political parties could not cooperate enough to form a united front against the Satchō oligarchy. Unfortunately, the movement degenerated into violence. In the early 1880s, radical members of Itagaki's party, the *Jiyuto*, had made common cause with some of rural organizations that fostered a number of what have been called Agrarian Uprisings. By and large, these protests were spontaneous peasant-based spates of violence aimed at corrupt tax collectors and greedy moneylenders. The leadership of both parties began to distance themselves from the violence, particularly after Itagaki himself was the target of an attempted assassination in 1882. Itagaki, not surprisingly, withdrew from the movement for a time.

As the rural violence increased in 1883–1884, the government responded with harsher police suppression. The *Jiyuto* disbanded in October 1884, and Ōkuma *Kaishinto* soundly condemned the violence. The government seemed to have won as the nation turned its back on violence. The combination of Etō's Saga Rebellion, Seinan's Satsuma Rebellion, and the peasant riots seemed to have drained the will to protest from the people.

Itō seized control of the committee charged with the promulgation of the constitution. Those discussions took place in secret. Members of the *Jiyu Minken Undo* were effectively cut out of the process.

*Louis G. Perez*

**See also:** Inoue Kaoru; Itagaki Taisuke; Itō Hirobumi; Meiji-Era Peasant Uprisings; Mutsu Munemitsu; Ōkubo Toshimichi; Ōkuma Shigenobu; Saga Rebellion; Saigō Takamori; *Seikanron*; Seinan (Satsuma) Rebellion; Taiwan Expedition.

**Further Reading**

Akita, George. *Foundations of Constitutional Government in Modern Japan, 1868–1900.* Cambridge, MA: Harvard University Press, 1967.

Banno Junji. *The Establishment of the Japanese Constitutional System.* London: Routledge, 1992.

Bowen, Roger W. *Rebellion and Democracy in Meiji Japan.* Berkeley: University of California Press, 1980.

## Jôkyû War of 1221

Japan had a dual government during the Kamakura period (1185–1333): the warrior government (shōgunate or *bakufu*), based in Kamakura, supervised its retainers, while the imperial court in Kyoto administered the rest of the country. The two governments shared power, but their coexistence was an uneasy one. Tensions between them led to the Jôkyû War of 1221. In that year, retired emperor GoToba assembled military forces to destroy the warrior government, but a pre-emptive attack by Kamakura forces routed the imperial armies. As a result, the shōgunate gained power at Kyoto's expense and dominated the rest of the period.

There are various names given to these important events. Jôkyû (sometimes read Shôkyû) comes from the era name (1221 was the third year of the Jôkyû era). The conflict is sometimes referred to as an "incident," "disturbance," or "rebellion." Regardless of terminology, most scholars agree that the Jôkyû War was a major turning point in medieval Japanese history.

By the early 1200s, retired emperor GoToba was the most powerful figure in Kyoto. His chancellery was the final arbiter of important legal cases, and GoToba dominated the imperial family while his sons Tsuchimikado and Juntoku reigned as emperors. He and others at court viewed the Kamakura samurai as upstarts who overstepped the bounds of propriety by attempting to govern. Meanwhile, the Hôjô were trying to solidify their hold on Kamakura following Minamoto Yoritomo's death in 1199. In 1203, they created the office of shōgunal regent for themselves and replaced the second shōgun, Yoriie, with his younger brother, Sanetomo, who was more easily controlled. Sanetomo was also enamored with Kyoto culture, which may have helped smooth relations between the two capitals. But he did not father any children, leaving the *bakufu* without an heir.

In 1218, Sanetomo's mother (Yoritomo's widow) Hôjô Masako traveled to Kyoto seeking to adopt one of GoToba's sons as shōgunal heir. Although GoToba reluctantly agreed to the scheme, he backed out the next year when Sanetomo was assassinated. He probably sought to exacerbate the crisis in Kamakura leadership, seeing it as an opportunity to attack the *bakufu* while it was vulnerable. Unfortunately, surviving sources provide little information on GoToba's actions between 1219 and his declaration of war in 1221. One account of the war claims that GoToba was upset because Kamakura did not comply with his demand to remove two land stewards (*jitô*) from certain estates. Not only did Kamakura refuse the demand, but it also sent 1,000 troops to Kyoto and forced GoToba to designate a two-year-old Fujiwara boy as the next shōgun-to-be. Other sources, however, suggest that many warriors were unhappy with

Kamakura under the Hôjô, and GoToba went ahead with his plans to attack.

By the fifth month of 1221, the retired emperor had assembled 1,700 warriors in the capital. Most came from western and central Japan. Some fought because of ties to Kyoto; others because they disliked the Hôjô or felt that Kamakura had not adequately rewarded them. That same month, GoToba executed or arrested key warriors in Kyoto who were loyal to Kamakura and issued his war declaration, labeling the shōgunal regent, Hôjô Yoshitoki, as the enemy. Upon receiving the document, Kamakura leaders, including Yoshitoki and his sister Masako, debated their options. They considered taking defensive positions around Kamakura but instead chose to strike first. Vassals from 15 eastern provinces responded, and Yoshitoki and his son Yasutoki led them on a march for Kyoto. Most of the battles were fought in the Chûbu region during the first two weeks of the sixth month, with a final climactic battle at Uji River on the 14th day. Kamakura's forces proved victorious and entered Kyoto the next day.

GoToba tried unsuccessfully to raise additional troops from Mt. Hiei, but then surrendered, claiming that he had been misled by bad advisers. Kamakura, however, showed little mercy. Former emperors GoToba, Tsuchimikado, and Juntoku were exiled to Oki, Tosa, and Sado, respectively. Juntoku's young son, who had assumed the throne only months earlier, was forced to abdicate. Kamakura banned GoToba's direct descendants from the throne and chose one of his nephews to become the next emperor. Many ministers, advisers, and others who had fought for Kyoto were executed, while others lost their positions.

The changes were not limited to the capital, however. Kamakura reportedly confiscated more than 3,000 lands and/or titles that belonged to individuals who had sided with the court. These were given to warriors who had fought loyally for Kamakura. Until 1221, most Kamakura vassals were in eastern Japan. With the post-Jôkyû settlement, however, many lands in central and western Japan came under the control of eastern warriors. This change represented a major expansion of the shōgunate's power. To supervise those western vassals, Kamakura created a branch office in Kyoto, the Rokuhara tandai. The two samurai officials stationed there investigated and adjudicated disputes for western vassals and also spied on the imperial court to make sure that Kyoto would not rise up against Kamakura again.

*Ethan Isaac Segal*

**See also:** Hôjô Masako; Kamakura *Bakufu*; Minamoto Yoritomo.

## Further Reading

Mass, Jeffrey P. *The Development of Kamakura Rule, 1180–1225: A History with Documents*. Stanford, CA: Stanford University Press, 1979.

McCullough, William. "Shokyuki: An Account of the Shôkyû War of 1221." *Monumenta Nipponica* 19, no. 1/2 (1964): 163–215.

# K

## Kagoshima, Bombardment of

The Japanese term of Satsu-Ei Sensō, or Satsuma-Anglo War, is a much more appropriate name for the battle involving the bombardment of Kagoshima. The cause of the war was the Namamugi Incident (also known as the Kanagawa Incident) of September 14, 1862. British subjects Charles Richardson, Woodthorpe Clark, William Marshall, and Margaret Borradaile were traveling from the treaty port of Yokohama to the Kawasaki Daishi temple. As they passed through Namamugi village (in present-day Yokohama), they encountered a large entourage of the father of the Satsuma *daimyō*. Decorum called for individuals to dismount as the entourage passed. Richardson and others did not; this was taken as sign of disrespect and Satsuma samurai struck them down. Richardson was killed and the other two men were wounded, but Borradaile was unharmed.

The British government responded quickly. It demanded compensation, claiming that Anglo-Japanese Friendship Treaty granted Richardson and others extraterritoriality; it also stated that because Richardson and others were traveling on a road covered by the treaty, they were not obliged to follow Japanese custom. British Charge d'Affaires Edward St. John Neale demanded that the *bakufu* pay an indemnity of £100,000 (approximately $440,000 Mexican silver, or about one-third of the *bakufu*'s annual revenue), and make a formal apology. Neale also demanded trial and execution of the samurai involved, plus a compensation of £25,000 for the Richardson's family and the three other British subjects. Noncompliance would result in an attack on Edo. Neale stressed that the *bakufu* and Satsuma had to be dealt with separately. Ogasawara Nagamichi, representing the *bakufu*, negotiated with the British and offered an apology and agreed to pay the indemnity on July 2, 1863.

Satsuma officials, however, refused to comply with the British demands because those involved in the attack were loyal samurai, who reacted properly according to the rules of Japanese society. Therefore, the British claim of violating extraterritoriality simply did not apply, and the Satsuma officials saw no need to punish the two samurai or to pay compensation of £25,000.

The real reason for the Satsuma official position was that Satsuma strongly opposed the *bakufu*'s policy of forming treaties with Western nations and allowing foreigners to reside in Japan. Satsuma was a hotbed of the *jōi* ("Expel the Barbarian") movement. To punish the two samurai and to pay the compensation would indicate that Satsuma officials agreed with the British on the issue of extraterritoriality.

When the negotiation with Satsuma went nowhere, the British sent seven British vessels (HMS *Euryalus*, *Pearl*, *Perseus*, *Argus*, *Coquette*, *Racehorse*, and *Havoc*) under the command of Admiral Augustus Kuper. The ships arrived in Kagoshima on August 11, 1863, and anchored in deep waters away from the fortified beachfront of Kagoshima.

Forty samurai came aboard Neale's flagship MS *Euryalus*. They presented a letter to Neale claiming the samurai involved in Richardson's killing could not be located; stating that indemnity would be discussed after these samurai had been found; blaming the *bakufu* for not addressing the status of *daimyō* in the treaty; and indicating that Neale should continue the discussion with the *bakufu*. On August 14, Neale gave Satsuma officials 24 hours to bring the samurai involved in Richardson's murder to justice and pay the indemnity. Satsuma had no intention of doing so and let the 24-hour deadline lapse.

The stage for battle was set: British ships with 101 guns, including some revolving Armstrong model, versus Satsuma's 83 guns distributed among 10 batteries. The British first seized three Satsuma steam merchant vessels anchored in the bay. Because the total value of these vessels was $300,000 (Mexican silver), the British intended to use them hostage. The Satsuma responded by firing their cannons at the British. Quite surprised by the Satsuma's action, the British pillaged and burned the three Satsuma vessels, supposedly to free the British vessels that guarded these vessels. The British then launched an attack on Kagoshima. From a distance of about 400 yards from shore, the British fired at the city. Satsuma forces fired back. HMS *Racehorse* went aground and had to be towed by HMS *Coquette* and *Argus*. Captain Josling and Commander Wilmot of HMS *Euryalus* were both killed when a single cannon shot severed their heads. After three and half hours of fighting, 9 British were killed, 50 wounded, and several vessels damaged. The Satsuma lost five lives, along with the three steam vessels and five junks. Kagoshima was damaged considerably; approximately 500 houses were destroyed but no

British soldiers set foot on Kagoshima. On August 16, Kuper ordered the squadron to retreat to the entrance of the bay for repairs and then returned to Yokohama.

The Satsuma interpreted the British departure as their victory. After all, only five Satsuma lives were lost and the British were never able to land in Kagoshima. The Satsuma had repelled the British squadron. Rather than rejoicing, however, the Satsuma officials realized that they experienced firsthand the British firepower and began to reexamine their *jōi* position. Satsuma officials traveled to Edo and paid the compensation of £25,000. Although the samurai of the Namamugi Incident were never identified, the British agreed to work with the Satsuma and secured various items for them, including warships. The Satsuma-Anglo War marked the beginning of a close relationship between Satsuma and Britain and, at the same time, marked Satsuma's departure from *jōi* and embrace of *sonno* ("Revere the Emperor").

*Roy S. Hanashiro*

**See also:** Namamugi Incident.

**Further Reading**

Beasley, William. *The Meiji Restoration*. Stanford: Stanford University Press, 1972.

Fox, Grace. *Britain and Japan 1858–1883*. Oxford, UK: Oxford University Press, 1969.

Satow, Ernest. *A Diplomat in Japan*. Oxford, UK: Oxford University Press, 1968.

Totman, Conrad. *The Collapse of the Tokugawa Bakufu 1862–1868*. Honolulu: University of Hawaii Press, 1980.

## Kakitsu Disturbance

On the 24th day of the sixth month of the year corresponding to 1441, the sixth Ashikaga shōgun Yoshinori (born 1394; shōgun 1428)

was assassinated at a party in the house of a trusted vassal, Akamatsu Mitsusuke (born 1381), military governor of Harima, Mimasaka, and Bizen Provinces. The engagement was to celebrate the successful suppression of the most serious challenge to the shōgunate before the Ōnin War (1466–1477)—namely, the rebellion of Yūki Ujitomo (1398–1441), who had led a coalition of northern warlords in defense of two sons of the fourth Kamakura *kubō*, Mochiuji (1398–1439).

The enmity of Mitsusuke went back to 1427, when he inherited the headship of the family and the shōgun Ashikaga Yoshimochi (1386–1428) deprived him of Harima Province and bestowed it upon his favorite, Akamatsu Mochisada, a great-grandson of Akamatsu Norimura (Enshin; 1277–1350). Mitsusuke petitioned three times to be confirmed in his possessions and was refused; in a rage, he set fire to his mansion and retreated to Harima. Yoshimochi, equally enraged, took the two other provinces and sent an army after him including Mochisada's father Sadamura, who had received Mimasaka, and Akamatsu Mitsuhiro, who had received Bizen. Once Yoshimochi's homosexual relationship with Mochisada became known, Mochisada committed suicide and, in the end, with the support of other vassals of the shōgunate, Mitsusuke was reinstated.

In 1441, the same thing happened again. In 1437, it was rumored abroad that Yoshinori intended to deprive Mitsusuke of Harima and Mimasaka; in 1440, Yoshinori deprived Mitsusuke's brother Yoshimasa in Settsu Province of his fief and gave it to Akamatsu Sadamura, Mochisada's nephew. At this point, Mitsusuke planned Yoshinori's assassination with his brother Yoshimasa and son Noriyasu. During the party, some horses escaped the stables; amid the confusion, Yoshinori was caught, pushed to his knees, and beheaded by Azumi Yukihide.

Some of Yoshinori's attendants tried to fight back. Kyōgoku Takakazu died fighting; Ōuchi Mochiyo (born 1394) later died of his wounds. Sanjō Sanemasa (1409–1467; his sister Inshi was Yoshinori's second consort or Midaidokoro) drew the ceremonial sword given him by the shōgun but was cut down. Hatakeyama Mochinaga, Hosokawa Mochiyuki, Hosokawa Mochitsune, Isshiki Norichika, and Yamana Mochitoyo escaped. The conspirators took their time leaving the mansion, which they burned, and finally sauntered out with Yoshinori's head spitted on a sword. On the first day of the seventh month, Kikei Shinzui (1401–1469), a Zen monk, received the head of Yoshinori from Sakamoto Castle, where Mitsusuke had barricaded himself, and took it back to the capital to be buried in the Tōjiin, a subtemple of the Rinzai temple Tenryūji, on the sixth day.

The day after the assassination, officials of the shōgunate secured the succession to Yoshinori's son Yoshikatsu (1434–1443). Then, three armies led by Yamana Norikiyo, Akamatsu Sadamura, and Hosokawa Mochitsune began to converge on the borders of Harima Province, hovering there while waiting to attack. The first engagement was a failed attempt on the 25th day by Noriyasu to make a night attack on Sadamura. Mochitoyo finally left the capital on the 28th day. However, not until the first of the eighth month did Mochitoyo request official permission to take punitive action against Mitsusuke, which Emperor Hanazono (born 1419; reign 1428–1464) granted despite arguments that Mitsusuke had not acted against the emperor and the problem was a private matter. The main force finally invaded Harima on the 24th day and were fiercely resisted by Noriyasu. By the first day of the ninth month, Sakamoto Castle was no longer considered to be defensible and the Akamatsu removed to Kiyama Castle, although many members of Mitsusuke's forces deserted. The next day, the shōgunate army attacked, and Mitsusuke, his son, and another committed suicide.

The Kakitsu Disturbance was the culmination of Ashikaga tactics since Yoshimitsu (1358–1408; shōgun 1368–1394) for handling potential threats to their power in a situation in which the shōgun was only *primus inter pares*—one warlord among many, and not necessarily the strongest. Military governors (*shugo*) were rewarded with more provinces for service, but those who grew too powerful posed a threat to the shōgun. In such a case, the shōgun might take advantage of intrafamilial succession tensions, provoke resistance from one side, use the other side to take military action, and then split the family and its power. Yoshimitsu had used such tactics to break the Toki in 1389, the Yamana in 1392, and the Ōuchi in 1399. Before he was killed, Yoshinori had gone after several warlords. He had defeated his recalcitrant cousin in Kamakura Mochiuji in 1439 and in 1441 executed Mochiuji's sons Yasuō and Haruō, aged just 13 and 11.

*Sybil Thornton*

**See also**: Ashikaga Takauji; Ōnin War.

**Further Reading**

Carter, Steven D. *Regent Redux: A Life of the Statesman-Scholar Ichijō Kaneyoshi*. Ann Arbor, MI: Center for Japanese Studeis, the University of Michigan, 1996.

Varley, H. Paul. *The Ōnin War: History of its Origins and Background with a Selective Translation of the Chronicle of Ōnin*. New York: Columbia University Press, 1967.

## Kakure Kirishitan (750)

After Japan had closed it doors to the West in 1639, only a handful of Dutch traders were permitted to remain on the man-made island of Deshima in Nagasaki harbor. Christianity was strictly forbidden, with any remaining priests and Christians executed mercilessly. Approximately 150,000 Christians, mostly commoners, sustained the faith, with only rudimentary instruction. The practice they carried on underground was done so with a limited understanding of their newfound faith. Many of these Christians lost all contact with the missionaries and the institutional church, yet transmitted their Christian heritage through seven generations. They are known as *kakure* (hidden) *Kirishitan*.

When the United States forced Japan to open its door to trade in 1854, the ban against Christianity was still in force. European countries quickly followed the United States into Japan, and the Paris French Foreign Mission priests joined the diplomats and traders. These priests gained permission from the Vatican to have exclusive rights to proselytize Roman Catholicism in Japan at this time. The Japanese permitted them to build churches for the French in residence in Japan. In 1865, a group of *kakure Kirishitan* presented themselves to French priest Bernard Petitjean in his church in Nagasaki, opening a new world for the missionaries. Even so, persecutions of Christians continued, especially in the area of Urakami, Nagasaki; indeed, they did not end until 1873 when foreign diplomats protested and Japan brought down the signposts forbidding Christianity.

As the priests sought to find those who had hidden their faith over almost 250 years, they encountered many Japanese residents who did not welcome the missionaries. Catholicism was rigid in the 19th century, not open to the adaptation the Jesuits had allowed in the 16th and 17th centuries. Rather, the missionaries expected the newly discovered adherents to reform their mistaken beliefs and practices. This expectation, however, was not acceptable to Japanese who learned the faith from their parents and grandparents.

An estimated 30,000 of the *kakure Kirishitan* chose to practice the faith as taught to them by their ancestors. Many of the practices would be familiar to a Roman Catholic; what was missing was the meaning. The majority of the *kakure Kirishitan* resided in the Kurosaki area of Kyushu and offshore islands (Gōtō, Hirado, and Ikitsuki), while others lived on Honshu. Each group of *kakure Kirishitan* practiced its beliefs in isolation from the neighboring groups, so that the practices varied.

On the Gōtō Islands and in the Kurosaki area, the *higiricho* or *ocho* (calendar) was central to *kakure Kirishitan* practice, while in Hirado and Ikitsuki, it was the *nandogami* (closet gods). The calendar used by these Kirishitan was believed to have been transposed from the solar calendar of 1634, provided by the missionaries. As for the closet gods, that designation refers to objects considered sacred, such as hanging scrolls depicting images of Christ, or Mary; plaques representing the mysteries of the rosary; holy water, its container, and the stick to sprinkle it; *otempensia*, a bundle of hemp rope used by some Christians for self-discipline; and *omaburi*, small papers cut in the shape of a cross, used as charms for protection of home and field. In each of these articles, the connection to the original teachings of the missionaries is evident.

The officials of the *kakure Kirishitan* groups can be traced similarly to early belief. In no case did these officials see themselves as priests. Rather, they performed the works of the men (*dojuku*) trained by the priests to be assistants to them. For example, they could instruct, baptize, conduct religious prayer meetings, and assist the sick and dying to acknowledge sorrow for their faults before death.

Baptisms and funerals among *kakure Kirishitan* demonstrate a clear connection with Catholicism, but also with Shintō and Buddhist practices. Because beliefs had to be veiled under pain of death, it was natural to camouflage religious activities. How the meaning was carried over across the years is more difficult to determine. The *Tenchi hajimari no koto* ("The Beginnings of Heaven and Earth") provides a clue. This text contains recognizable elements of Christian teaching laced with Buddhist terms and concepts, as well as Japanese folk religion.

The encounter between the strictly orthodox 19th-century Catholic priests and the *kakure Kirishitan* was difficult. While these *kakure Kirishitan* are no longer in hiding, many still practice in secret. But their religious practices are on the wane. Because the offspring of these *kakure Kirishitan* often want to move to Tokyo or other larger cities, the faith is not being passed on to the next generations in great numbers. Many fear the *kakure Kirishitan* will disappear in the not too distant future.

*Ann M. Harrington*

**See also:** Dutch at Deshima.

**Further Reading**

Harrington, Ann M. *Japan's Hidden Christians*. Chicago: Loyola University Press, 1993.

Higashibaba, Ikuo. *Christianity in Early Modern Japan: Kirishitan Belief and Practice*. Boston: Brill, 2001.

Jennes, Joseph. *A History of the Catholic Church in Japan from its Beginnings to the Early Meiji Era, 1549–1871*. Revised ed. Tokyo: Oriens Institute for Religious Research, 1973.

Turnbull, Stephen. *The Kakure Kirishitan of Japan: A Study of Their Development,*

*Beliefs and Rituals to the Present Day.* Richmond, UK: Japan Library, 1998.

Whalen, Christal. *Beginning of Heaven and Earth: The Sacred Book of Japan's Hidden Christians.* Honolulu: University of Hawaii Press, 1996.

## Kamakura *Bakufu* (1185–1333)

When Minamoto Yoritomo finally triumphed in 1185 over the Taira coalition in the Gempei War, he established a military government at Kamakura. He accepted the title of *Sei-itai-shōgun* ("Barbarian-Subduing Generalissimo') in 1192, thereby establishing the dynasty (often called *shōgunate* by Western scholars) that would survive him for more than a century and would serve as the model for the subsequent two governments (Muromachi and Tokugawa) that would succeed after his fell.

The title *shōgun* had existed for more than two centuries but was mostly a sinecure for the imperial cadet houses. It was technically aimed at suppressing the warlike Ainu people in Japan's northern reaches. Yoritomo used it to derive imperial authority, but the power he wielded was based on his feudal relationships with other warlords. He demanded that his feudal vassals swear loyalty, but chiefly he required their military service. In exchange, Yoritomo left his subjects to themselves unless they disturbed the peace.

In many ways, the *bakufu* was a reflection of the decades of civil wars that brought Yoritomo to power. He chose to base it in Kamakura instead of Kyoto, as his predecessor Taira Kiyomori had done. Of course, the choice of location was obvious because Yoritomo's military power was in Kamakura along with his in-laws and allies the Hôjô. He also wished to keep his most trusted warrior vassals out of the sway of imperial intrigue and politics. The chief administrative organization he called the *mandokoro* (something like "chancellery"). Yoritomo appointed warlords to the ancient imperial office of *Shugo* ("military governor") and *jitō* ("land stewards") over the individual *shōen* ("manors"). Those offices existed in parallel with imperial governors, but Yoritomo's titles involved actual power, whereas the imperial ones were mainly sinecures for courtiers residing in Kyoto.

Because Yoritomo had spent his entire life at war, he trusted very few people and was almost paranoid about any possible rivals. He had eradicated the entire Taira family ("down to their dogs and chickens," one historian said) and had his own brothers and their heirs killed as well. He did not live long enough to firmly establish his own heirs. He died at age 52 in 1199. His young son Yoriie succeeded him; his father-in-law Hôjô Tokimasa became the regent (*Shikken*), but in reality, Yoritomo's widow, Hôjô Masako, became the power behind the throne. Yoriie was overthrown by relatives and was succeed by his brother Sanetomo. When the latter died in 1219, Masako engineered a series of shōgun and regents, but deposed them at will when either did not bow to her demands. Because Masako technically retired into a Buddhist convent at Yoritomo's death, she was often called *ama-shōgun*, or the "nun-general." Ultimately, she "adopted" an imperial prince to become shōgun. The system she established long survived her.

The *bakufu* was threatened by internal intrigue in Kamakura, but most seriously when in 1221 Emperor Go-Toba tried to regain power in what would be called the Jôkyû War. The rebellion was suppressed and the emperor was himself forced to abdicate to his young son. The *bakufu* struggled along, chiefly because every potential rebel was checked in his ambitions by the rest of the coalition.

The *bakufu* survived the two attempts at invasion of Japan by the Mongols in 1274 and 1281. Although those invasions are covered in another entry, but suffice it to say that the *bakufu* suffered collapse because of the very nature of the nature of government. Each warlord controlled his own manor and paid no tax or tribute to the *bakufu* except in the form of the rare military service when called upon to do so. There was no real national government; the *bakufu* functioned as a confederation. Consequently, there was no national treasury, and every feudal army answered only to its own warlord. When the shōgun failed to reward those warlords who had borne the brunt of fighting against the Mongols, the warlords began to search around for alternative coalitions.

Another emperor, Go-Daigo, raised the standard of imperial restoration in the early 1330s. After a protracted (and convoluted) civil war, Ashikaga Takauji, a relative of the Hôjô sent to quell the rebellion, turned on his colleagues and allied himself with Go-Daigo. The emperor was "restored" to power briefly, but was arrested by Ashikaga, who established a new *bakufu* in the Muromachi district of Kyoto. Go-Daigo escaped to Yoshino, where he established what has been called the Southern Court that existed until both sides of the imperial house reunited in Kyoto in 1392.

*Louis G. Perez*

**See also:** Ashikaga Takauj; Go-Daigo; Hogen-Heiji-Gempei Wars; Hôjô Masako; Jôkyû War; Minamoto Yoritomo; Mongol Invasions of Japan; Muromachi *Bakufu*; Southern Court (Yoshino); Tokugawa *Bakufu* Political System.

**Further Reading**

Mass, Jeffrey P. *The Kamakura Bakufu: A Study inn Documents*. Stanford: Stanford University Press, 1976.

Mass, Jeffrey P. *Warrior Government in Early Medieval Japan: A Study of the Kamakura Bakufu, Shugo and Jitō*. New Haven: Yale University Press, 1974.

## Kamikaze (*Tokkōtai*)

*Kamikaze* is the popular name given to World War II Japan's Special Attack Squads (*Tokubetsu kōgekitai*), commonly referred to by the abbreviation *tokkōtai*. This strategy was initiated during the final months of the Pacific War, when Japan's defeat seemed inevitable. In this strategy, Japanese fliers and sailors literally became human bombs, piloting planes and human torpedoes into enemy ships and other military targets. The name "kamikaze" literally means "god winds" and refers to the typhoons that, according to tradition, defeated the Mongol invasions of 1274 and 1281.

Accounts of Japanese suicide attacks date from the Russo-Japanese War, and the Japanese began to use the term *tokkōtai* shortly after the attack on Pearl Harbor, but in these cases the death of the soldiers, while likely, was not necessary for the success of the mission. The members of *tokkōtai* squads organized in the latter months of the Pacific War, however, were explicitly ordered to crash their crafts into enemy targets. Survival was not an option. Soon, Japanese war factories were producing planes and human torpedoes expressly designed to kill the operator.

Vice Admiral Ōnishi Takijiro devised the *tokkōtai* strategy, which he dubbed *shinpu*, the Chinese reading of the characters for kamikaze. The plan quickly won approval from the top command, although the psychological underpinning for a warrior's suicide can be traced to Japan's centuries-old *bushidō* tradition. Because the death of the soldiers was inevitable, the operation was made

A Japanese kamikaze pilot tries to crash his plane onto the deck of a U.S. Pacific Fleet warship on January 1, 1945. (Getty Images)

"voluntary" and was not an official navy or army operation. None of the military officers who approved the strategy ever participated in a kamikaze operation, although Ōnishi committed suicide the day after the emperor issued the imperial edict ending the war.

The first kamikaze mission occurred in the Philippines Battle of Leyte in October 25, 1944. Prior to the first mission's departure, Ōnishi met with the pilots, who drank ceremonial cups of sake before donning head bands with the rising sun. This ceremony became common practice for subsequent missions. Lt. Seki Yukio, a decorated flying ace who was persuaded to lead the first sortie, left a lock of hair for his mother. Leaving a memento for family also became part of the departure ritual because the pilots knew, if they were successful, there would be no physical remains to return to Japan.

Early in the strategy, the *tokkōtai* pilots flew "Zero" single-engine planes with a 557-lb bomb in the nose. The weight and placement of the bomb made the plane difficult to navigate and, once it began its final descent, impossible to pull out. Later, the kamikaze pilots flew gliders called *ōka* (cherry blossom planes), which were released from planes when within range of enemy targets. They had enough fuel to fly no more than 25 miles but carried more than a ton of explosives in the nose. Americans called the *ōka* "*baka*"—the Japanese word for "fool." Suicide boats were also used, but fortification of American-controlled ports soon made them ineffective. Human torpedoes (*ningen gyorai*) known as *kaiten* ("return to heaven") were also used. They would be lowered from ships when Allied vessels were in range. Originally, the torpedoes had a means for escape, but the mechanism was later removed.

The romantic interpretation of the *tokkōtai* described the pilots as young men whose zealous patriotism for the emperor and the nation was exploited by military leaders to volunteer for the missions. The majority of them were students from the navy flying school and university graduates. The government had reduced the length of college education, which increased the number of available pilots and sailors. Through the participants' final writings, however, it is revealed their volunteering was more often the result of intimidation and peer pressure, and the conditions of kamikaze bases were so harsh that the pilots were often demoralized. Trained and experienced pilots seldom volunteered to join the *tokkōtai* corps. Lt. Seki, for example, thought he could better serve the war effort as an instructor and reluctantly agreed to lead the first mission not out of loyalty to the nation or devotion to the emperor, but rather out of concern for his new bride's virtue should the home islands be invaded.

The success of the *tokkōtai* strategy is questionable. In total, 647 missions were launched between October 21, 1944, and the end of the war, which ended with the death of more than 2,000 suicide pilots and sailors. It is difficult, however, to determine how much damage the kamikaze actually inflicted on Allied ships and other targets and how much damage was done by conventional weapons. According to the United States, 43 ships were sunk by *tokkōtai* attacks and 288 damaged.

*R. W. Purdy*

**See also:** *Bushidō*; Mongol Invasions of Japan; World War II, Pacific Theater.

### Further Reading

Axell, Albert, and Kase, Hideaki. *Kamikaze: Japan's Suicide Gods*. London: Longman, Pearson Education, 2002.

Naito, Hatsuho. *Thunder Gods: The Kamikaze Pilots Tell Their Own Story*. Tokyo: Kodansha International, 1989.

Ohnuki-Tierny, Emiko. *Kamikaze, Cherry Blossoms, and Nationalism: The Militarization of Aesthetics in Japanese History*. Chicago: University of Chicago Press, 2002.

## Katsu Kaishū (1823–1899)

Born Katsu Yoshikuni in Edo on March 12, 1823, Katsu was son of a low-ranking Tokugawa retainer. He assumed the head of his family's household at the age of 15, when his father abdicated the position. His father's autobiography, *Musui's Story*, details the life of a petty samurai on the fringes of accepted society. Katsu himself found opportunities in Nagasaki, where he learned Dutch and studied Western military technology. He rose up as a naval officer for the Tokugawa. As foreign nations tried to open Japan to the west, the Tokugawa government appointed him as a translator.

In 1855, Katsu became the director of training at the Nagasaki Naval Center. He held that post until 1859, when he received a new commission. Katsu was assigned command of the *Kanrin-Maru*, a modern steam-powered Japanese warship, and escorted a Japanese delegation to San Francisco as they made their way to Washington, D.C., to formally ratify the Harris Treaty. The first of Japan's unequal treaties, the Harris Treaty opened Japan to the West after more than 200 years of self-imposed isolation. Katsu remained in San Francisco for two months, observing American life, culture, and technology. When he returned to Japan, he held high-level posts in the Tokugawa navy.

During Katsu's tenure as director of the Kobe Naval School in 1863 and 1864, the school attracted progressive thinkers and reformers. Katsu advocated reforming the Japanese navy, calling for a more modern, unified navy—one led by professionally trained men, not based on the hereditary domains and positions that had characterized the Tokugawa era. While open to foreign ideas, Katsu remained loyal to the Tokugawa government he served. After the shōgun's forces were defeated in 1866, the shōgun appointed him to negotiate with insurgent forces from the Chōshū domain. The Tokugawa remained in power, but the revolutionaries strengthened. As they were poised to invade in the spring of 1868, Katsu negotiated the surrender of the Tokugawa capital Edo. Arguing that cooperation was crucial to Japan remaining free from foreign colonization, Katsu facilitated a largely peaceful transition to the new Meiji government. He went into exile with the last Tokugawa shōgun.

Katsu was one of the few Tokugawa retainers who were later employed by the new Meiji government. In 1872, he became the Vice Minister of the Imperial Navy, and served as First Minister of the Navy from 1873 to 1878. He continued to serve the new government by advising on national policy, writing extensively about naval issues, and serving on the Privy Council until his death in 1899.

*Larissa Castriotta Kennedy*

**See also**: Boshin Civil War; Harris, Townsend; Unequal Treaties.

## Further Reading

Jansen, Marius B. *Sakamoto Ryōma and the Meiji Restoration.* New York: Columbia University Press, 1994.

Katsu, Kokichi. *Musui's Story: the Autobiography of a Tokugawa Samurai.* Tucson: University of Arizona Press, 1988.

## Kawakami Soroku (1848–1899)

Kawakami Soroku was born a samurai in Satsuma domain in 1848. Kawakami came of age as a traditional samurai. He learned to use the same weapons that had been used for centuries, along with new firearms. Kawakami distinguished himself during the Meiji Restoration by leading a punitive expedition to Hokkaidō. By the time of the Satsuma Rebellion in 1877, Kawakami was commander of the government's 13th Regiment. He remained loyal to the government and participated in the fighting against his clansmen. Kawakami had proven his ability and his loyalty, and he continued to rise in the Japanese Army.

In 1884, Gen. Ōyama Iwao, a senior member of the Army General Staff, departed Japan with a mission to study German military organizations. Kawakami was a strong supporter of the German model, and he was promoted to major general and made assistant chief of staff of the General Staff upon his return in 1885. In 1887, Kawakami went back to Germany to study for a year with Helmuth von Moltke, Sr., chief of the German General Staff. Once back in Japan, Kawakami was again made assistant chief of staff and was instrumental in implementing the German concepts and practices that he had observed.

Kawakami believed that only second-class Western nations were content merely to defend their frontiers. The goal of every truly great nation, he suggested, was "to radiate military power and in times of trouble call upon the soldierly strength of all citizens, thus taking insult from no quarter." The opportunity for intervention in Korea came in 1894.

Kawakami had advocated sending troops to Korea to provoke a fight with the Chinese after a local rebellion had led to both Japan and China sending troops. He had estimated how many troops it would take to provoke the Chinese and ensured that they were sent. By this time, Kawakami was the supreme force in the army. He had great charisma and was respected by soldiers and politicians alike, particularly Foreign Minister Mutsu Munemitsu. During the Korean crisis, the army began to influence the conduct of foreign affairs and brought about the Sino-Japanese War of 1894–1895. On July 23, 1894, Japanese troops attacked the Korean royal palace. On July 25, the Japanese Navy sank the *Kowshing*, a British vessel chartered to carry Chinese reinforcements; more than 1,000 Chinese soldiers drowned.

Kawakami served throughout the war as the senior staff officer at Imperial General Headquarters and directed the Japanese forces through the use of telegraphs. It was his plan that brought victory so quickly. Kawakami was rewarded for his part in the victory by promotion to general and by being named chief of the General Staff in 1898. He immediately began planning for a coming war with Russia but died in 1899 before it took place.

*Tim Watts*

**See also:** Mutsu Munemitsu; Ōyama Iwao; Sino-Japanese War.

**Further Reading**

Harries, Meirion, and Susie Harries. *Soldiers of the Sun: The Rise and Fall of the Imperial Japanese Army.* New York: Random House, 1991.

Lone, Stewart. *Japan's First Modern War: Army and Society in the Conflict with China, 1894–95.* London: Macmillan, 1994.

# *Kimigayo* (National Anthem)

On August 13, 1999, the Diet enacted a law officially recognizing what had until then served during the post-World War II era as Japan's de facto national anthem: *Kimigayo*. As the world's shortest national anthem, its lyrics are: "May your majesty's reign / last for a thousand—even eight thousand—generations, / until pebbles / become boulders / covered over with moss" (*Kimigayo wa / chiyo ni yachiyo ni / sazareishi no / iwao to narite / koke no musu made*).

With only a slight variation ("My lord . . . [*Waga kimi wa . . .*]" in the first line), this anonymous verse is found in the early 10th-century *Kokin wakashū* ("Collection of Ancient and Modern Poems"), where it heads the section "Felicitations." It first appeared in its present form in the early 11th-century collection *Wakan rōei shū* ("Collection of Japanese and Chinese Songs for Chanting"). While the latter version appears consistently to have been understood as addressed to the emperor, the referent of *kimi* in the *Kokinshū* verse is unclear. According to one theory, it is an allusive variation of a funeral elegy appearing in the *Man'yōshū*: "May this maiden's name / flow on through a thousand ages, / until the tips / of young pines at Himeshima / are covered with moss" (*Imo ga na wa / chiyo ni nagaremu / Himeshima no / komatsu ga ure ni / koke musu made ni*). It is further claimed that, in placing it in the "Felicitations" section, the compilers of the *Kokinshū* misunderstood its original elegiac intent.

Whatever its origins, since the 11th century this verse has been recited to wish longevity to the emperor and continued glory to his realm. While the word *kimi* had varied applications in the early 10th century, in later collections its usage in poetry narrowed specifically to reference the emperor, and commentaries through the Edo period consistently follow that interpretation. *Kimigayo* also appeared in Noh plays and other forms of theater, as well as in various genres of prose fiction.

In 1869, John William Fenton (1831–1890) arrived from Ireland to organize and train a naval band. Noting that Japan lacked a national anthem, he conferred with Ōyama Iwao (1842–1916), who, having agreed to select suitable lyrics, decided upon the current words of *Kimigayo*. Fenton composed a melody, and the new anthem was first performed before the emperor in 1870. The music was thought to be lacking the appropriate solemnity, however, and was not widely used.

In 1880, a new melody was composed by Hayashi Hiromori (1831–1896) and harmonized by Franz Eckert (1852–1916). This was adopted by the Imperial Household Agency and remained official through the end of the Pacific phase of World War II. It is the version in current use.

Although the Imperial Household Agency had already recognized this "military" version of *Kimigayo*, leaders at the Ministry of Education, acting independently, ordered its Department of Musical Research (*Ongaku torishirabe-gakari*, a forerunner of Tokyo University of the Arts) to compile a list of possible songs to serve as a national anthem. It appears that the intention was not to establish an "official"—or even a rival—version, but rather one that could be used in schools and for nonceremonial purposes. The submissions ranged from lyrics on the Three Sacred Treasures to a long poem praising Toyotomi Hideyoshi. Although the Ministry did not get around to reviewing the submissions until the following year (after which the plan was abandoned), the impetus to create a populist version of a national anthem was already evident in the inclusion in the Ministry's *Shōgaku shōkashū* ("Collection of Songs for Primary Schools") in 1882 of a third version version of *Kimigayo*. The first of its two verses was a variation of the traditional *Kokinshū* poem, while the second was by Minamoto no Yoritomo (1147–1199). The melody, reminiscent of a hymn, was attributed to a certain "Webb," but it remains

unclear who this person was. The use of *Kimigayo* and other patriotic songs in the *Shōgaku shōkashū* was an important part of the Ministry's policy of "imperialization" (*kōminka*) of the empire's non-Japanese populations.

Although *Kimigayo* lost its official status with Japan's defeat and the restructuring of the government under the Allied occupation, the 1880 version continued to be used unofficially, and was in fact sung at the ceremony inaugurating the new constitution on May 3, 1947. Beginning in the 1950s, the Ministry of Education periodically issued directives encouraging its use in schools, and in a 1977 publication referred to it as Japan's national anthem. In 1989, the government under the ruling Liberal Democratic Party began to require its use in school ceremonies, and even established punishments for noncompliance. These developments have not been uncontested; various groups consisting of both teachers and private citizens have opposed the anthem itself or its obligatory use. The objections have centered on its militaristic associations, or on what is seen as emperor worship in spite of the official explanation that the lyrics are meant simply as a benediction on the Japanese nation, with the emperor as its figurehead. Since the official recognition of *Kimigayo* in 1999, several hundred teachers and school employees have been punished for refusal to stand for the anthem.

*Roger K. Thomas*

**See also:** Minamoto Yoritomo; Toyotomi Hideyoshi.

## Further Reading

Chao, Hui-Hsuan. *Musical Taiwan under Japanese Colonial Rule*. Ph.D. dissertation, University of Michigan, 2009.

Fujita Yūji, ed. *"Kimigayo" no kigen: "Kimigayo" no honka wa banka datta*. Tokyo: Akashi Shoten, 2005.

Naitō Takatoshi. *Mittsu no Kimigayo: Nihonjin no oto to kokoro no shinsō*. Tokyo: Chūō Kōronsha, 1997.

Osa Shizue. *Kindai Nihon to kokugo nashonarizumu*. Tokyo: Yoshida Kōbunkan, 1998.

Xing Hang, ed. *Encyclopedia of National Anthems*. Lanham, MD: Scarecrow Press, 2003.

## Kim Ok-kyun (1851–1894)

Born into a poor family in Korea, Kim Ok-kyun was adopted at age 6 by a government official. He received an aristocratic education and served in several government offices after passing the national civil examination at 22. A disciple of Pak Kyusu (1807–1877), a politician and the earliest to advocate opening of the country, he discussed the West passionately with fellow disciples, along with ways to modernize Korea.

In July 1882, a mutiny took place in Seoul that not only left the Japanese legation destroyed and many pro-Japanese officials killed but almost took Queen Min's life. The aftermath of the mutiny deepened the split among Korean reformists. Moderate reformists wanted to keep the vassal-suzerain relationship with China and compromise with conservatives. Radical reformists, in contrast, sought to end the old relationship with China and start a fundamental reform. Kim Ok-kyun was the leader of the latter group, known as the Independent Party (*dongnipdang*). Upon hearing that Queen Min requested a crackdown on the mutineers by China, Kim Yun-sik and his fellow disciples were outraged and denounced the Queen as having "sold the country."

Kim Ok-kyun visited Japan both before and after the mutiny. What Japan had achieved since the Meiji Restoration deeply impressed him, convincing him that Korea should follow Japan's model in modernizing itself. On December 4, 1884, he launched the Gapsin Coup, which killed six key conservative officials and resulted in a pro-reform government. The new regime existed for only three days due to Chinese intervention, again at Queen Min's request. The failure of the coup has been attributed to its complete lack of mass participation, Kim's miscalculation of Japanese support, Chinese power in Korea, and Kim's lack of a strategy to deal with Queen Min. Becoming fugitives, Kim and eight other leaders of the coup took refuge in Japan.

Due to his reduced value to Japan's Korea agenda, Kim was received coldly during his 10 years of refugee life in Japan. He may have realized his mistake in relying too much on Japanese support for his reform, but it is less clear whether he realized that the support he did receive was lent ultimately to promote Japan's own interest, as shown, for example, in the writings of Fukuzawa Yukichi and Mutsu Munemitsu. On March 28, 1894, Kim Ok-kyun was assassinated in Shanghai by an assassin sent by Queen Min. When his body was sent back to Korea, it was dismembered and put on public display with the label "arch-traitor Kim Ok-kyun." Ten years after his death, a tomb was built for him in Aoyama Cemetery in Tokyo by his Japanese friends. The epitaph on the tombstone, by fellow reformist Pak Yong-hyo, well captures his life: "Born in an extraordinary time, with extraordinary talents, making no extraordinary achievements and meeting an extraordinary death."

*Guohe Zheng*

**See also:** Fukuzawa Yukichi; Korea Added to the Empire; Mutsu Munemitsu.

## Further Reading

Cook, Harold F. *Korea's 1884 Incident: Its Background and Kim Ok-kyun's Elusive Dream.* Seoul: Royal Asiatic Society, Korea Branch, 1972.

Duus, Peter. *The Abacus and the Sword: The Japanese Penetration of Korea, 1895–1910.* Berkeley: University of California Press, 1998.

Kim, Djun Kil. *The History of Korea.* Westport, CT: Greenwood Press, 2005.

Kleiner, Jergen. *Korea: A Century of Change.* River Edge, NJ: World Scientific Publishing Company, 2001.

Perez, Louis G. *Japan Comes of Age: Mutsu Munemitsu and the Revision of the Unequal Treaties.* London: Associated University Press, 1999.

## Kita Ikki (1883–1937)

Kita Ikki was born Kita Terujiro on Sado Island in Niigata Prefecture in 1883. He attended classes at Waseda University and was drawn to the study of evolutionary theory and social thought. In 1906, Kita self-published his first book, *Theory of the National Polity and Pure Socialism*, which was a critique of contemporary socialism and a rejection of the contemporary analysis of the *kokutai*, or national polity. The book was well received among Japanese intellectuals but was banned by the government.

Kita became part of the inner circle of the *Heiminsha*, a socialist organization, and forged close relationships with such radicals as Kōtoku Shūsui and Sakai Toshihiko. Kita also associated with Japanese nationals who supported socialist revolution in China. He became a member of the Chinese revolutionary group known as the *Tongmeng Hui* (United League), and made the acquaintance of the movement's leader, Song Jiaoren. Upon the outbreak of the 1911 Revolution in China, Kita traveled there hoping to participate. Following the assassination of Song in 1913, Kita was expelled from China for attempting to make public the facts surrounding his death.

When Kita returned to Japan, he began to write about his experiences in the revolution and published *Private History of the Chinese Revolution* in 1916. In the preface to the book, Kita outlined what he considered the fundamental principles of Asian nationalism and called upon Japanese citizens to support a revolution in China to expel the Western powers from Asia. Kita traveled to China again in 1916, but after experiencing first-hand the intense anti-Japanese sentiment expressed during the May Fourth movement of 1919, he became disillusioned with the movement and returned to Japan.

Later that year, Kita published *An Outline Plan for the Reconstruction of Japan*, in which he explained the steps he felt were necessary to build Asian nationalism and oust the nations of the West. His book advocated a coup d'état to overthrow the current Japanese government, suspension of the constitution, and three years of martial law under the army. It also argued for a major reorganization of Japanese society, stating that Japan should take a leading role in liberating China and India from the West. Kita's book became a primer for young, nationalistic army officers.

In 1920, Kita helped form the *Yûzonsha*, a right-wing political organization consisting of national socialist activists. He withdrew from the group in 1923 after a conflict with the organization's leaders over policy toward Russia. Nonetheless, Kita remained influential among a growing body of Japanese militarists, and he became a leading nationalist ideologue in the 1930s.

Kita's publications were seen by many as providing the ideological foundations for the attempted military coup d'état on February 26, 1936, in which a group of young army officers assassinated a number of prominent officials in an attempt to overthrow the government. Kita was accused of being an accessory to the coup and was arrested. After a trial by a military court in the following year, he was executed in 1937.

*Walter E. Grunden*

**See also:** February 26 Incident; Kōtoku Shūsui; May Fourth Movement; Young Officer Movement.

**Further Reading**

Shillony, Ben-Ami. *Revolt in Japan; The Young Officers and the February 26, 1936 Incident*. Princeton, NJ: Princeton University Press, 1973.

Wilson, George M. *Radical Nationalist in Japan: Kita Ikki, 1883–1937*. Cambridge, MA: Harvard University Press, 1969.

## Kitabatake Chikafusa (1293–1354)

Chikafusa was a member of the Murakami branch of the influential Minamoto family, or the Genji. He was an accomplished scholar and poet. In 1320, he was promoted to the office reserved for the highest-ranked courtier from the Minamoto family. A few years later he was appointed *dainagon* (great counselor) and entrusted by Emperor Go-Daigo with the task of tutoring one of his sons, Prince Tokiyoshi (1306–1330). However, when Tokiyoshi suddenly died in 1330, Chikafusa took the tonsure to show his loyalty and dedication to the prince. Even after relinquishing formal duties at the imperial court, Chikafusa remained an influential adviser.

Since the late 12th century, with the establishment of warrior government in Kamakura, imperial power had been significantly circumscribed by warrior families. In 1331, the Kamakura *bakufu*, then led by the Hōjō family, discovered a plot to overthrow it. As a result, Go-Daigo was exiled to Oki islands. Immediately, forces made up of warriors loyal to Go-Daigo came to the rescue. The *bakufu* dispatched local warrior leader Ashikaga Takauji (1305–1358) to suppress Go-Daigo's forces, but Takauji turned his back on the *bakufu* and supported the emperor. In 1333, the Kamakura *bakufu* was destroyed with the help of loyalist Nitta Yoshisada (1301–1338); Go-Daigo returned to Kyoto that year.

Between 1333 and 1336, Emperor Go-Daigo led an unsuccessful attempt to reassert imperial rule, which was called the Kemmu Restoration. The Restoration aimed to reduce the influences of local warrior families by giving power back to the court nobility. Go-Daigo's drastic measures to centralize power were quickly met with resistance from local warrior leaders. The Kemmu Restoration ended in failure when Ashikaga Takauji decided to assume de facto rule of Japan instead of continuing his support for Go-Daigo. To secure his rule, Takauji supported another imperial prince as a replacement for Go-Daigo.

In 1336, Chikafusa advised Go-Daigo to establish a separate imperial court at Yoshino, south of Kyoto. Hence, it was called the Southern Court. The emperor also took with him the Three Imperial Regalia, which were symbols of the legitimacy of imperial rule. Without the Regalia, the legitimacy of the emperor residing in the Northern Court was called into question, despite this ruler practically having the support of such powerful warrior leaders as Takauji and his allies. The resulting dynastic schism lasted until 1392. During this period, called the Southern and Northern Courts or the Nanbokuchō period, Chikafusa actively rallied support from local military leaders in various provinces. First, he traveled to the province of Ise and then to Hitachi, where he spoke out for the cause of Go-Daigo. It was during his sojourn in Hitachi that he wrote the *Jinnō shōtōki* ("Chronicle of the Direct Descent of Divine Sovereigns"), which justified the political legitimacy of the Southern Court by giving a historical account of imperial successions and rules from the Age of the Gods to the reign of Go-Daigo. This book described Japan as a divine land ruled by emperors in a single family line, an essential idea informing later development of emperorism, such as during the time of the Meiji Restoration in 1868.

In early 1344, after facing strong military suppression by the newly established Ashikaga *bakufu* (also known as the Muromachi *bakufu*) and realizing that most provincial barons had chosen to recognize the Northern Court, Chikafusa fled to Yoshino in great disappointment. However, he did not yet give up the idea of reclaiming Kyoto. When he was back in Yoshino in 1344, Chikafusa was immediately appointed to ministerial rank by Go-Daigo's son, Emperor Go-Murakami (1328–1368; reign 1339–1368). Under Chikafusa's leadership, the Southern Court recaptured Kyoto in 1352, but only for a few weeks. Without strong military support, the Southern Court was never able to challenge the Ashikaga *bakufu* and was reunited with the Northern Court in 1392.

*Yu Chang*

**See also:** Ashikaga Takauji; Boshin Civil War; Fujiwara Family; Kamakura *Bakufu*; Muromachi *Bakufu*; Nitta Yoshisada; Southern Court (Yoshino).

**Further Reading**

Goble, Andrew Edmund. *Kenmu: Go-Daigo's Revolution.* Cambridge, MA: Council on East Asian Studies, Harvard University, 1996.

Varley, H. Paul, trans. *A Chronicle of Gods and Sovereigns: Jinnō Shōtōki of Kitabatake Chikafusa.* New York: Columbia University Press, 1980.

## *Kokutai* and Ultra-nationalism

*Kokutai* is the most potent idea in the history of Japanese political thought. A key element of extremist or "ultra" nationalism, it did much to inspire the Japanese people in wars of aggression and in their creation of a Greater East Asian Co-prosperity Sphere. Western historians have rendered *kokutai* into English literally as "the national polity" or more abstractly as "the national essence." This ambiguity of translation reflects the fact that *kokutai* signified various things in different contexts, and these meanings changed greatly over time. Despite this diversity in meaning, the term always remained linked to a certain view of history—now disparagingly labelled *kôkoku shikan* or "the unfolding of imperial loyalism in Japan." This is somewhat comparable to Whig history, if defined as "the unfolding of liberalism in Britain," in that both interpretations are teleological in the sense of assuming that history is the realization of some hoped-for ideal over time.

### The Tokugawa Era (1600–1867)

Like much in the political vocabulary of premodern Japan, *kokutai* came from China. In traditional Chinese historical annals, this term usually meant "the ruling dynasty's honor or prestige" and was often used when a relatively weak ruling house like the Song (960–1279) faced the danger of invasion or suffered foreign occupation. Thus, in its Chinese inception, the word had undertones of defensive self-assertion, if not xenophobia, which Japanese scholars appropriated to foster ethnic nationalism in their own land. Nativists found in *kokutai* a convenient vehicle to propagate aspirations about "what is essential to make a land and people into a nation." This entailed instilling in all Japanese people devotion to the imperial court to override barriers to national unity posed by regional autonomy and hereditary class distinctions, as well as boosting military strength by enlisting support from commoners to augment the samurai class when Japan faced the threat of Western imperialism. Other nativists employed *kokutai* to support their contentions of timeless reverence by the Japanese people for a single imperial dynasty— claimed to be descended from the Sun Goddess—that "proved" moral superiority to China, where regicide and dynastic revolutions were the rule.

Nativism led to a form of loyalist thought that idealized Japanese history as a saga of imperial loyalism striving to assert itself against the forces of infidelity and ignorance. Loyalists asserted that the only proper form of government in Japan was for all land and people to come under direct imperial aegis, with no middlemen arbitrarily wielding the emperor's power and enjoying privileges relative to other subjects. Such a polity, the *kokutai*, existed in antiquity but lapsed after Fujiwara regents began to usurp imperial prerogatives in 858, and when warlords created a separate military regime in 1185—although neither group ever dared to overthrow the divine dynasty itself. There was one fleeting bright spot in these dark ages: the Kenmu Restoration achieved in 1333 on behalf of Emperor Go-Daigo by Kusunoki Masashige, who struggled against hopeless odds to sustain Go-Daigo's direct rule. In 1336, however, he succumbed to the forces of treachery

and obscurantism when Ashikaga warlords seized power. Thereafter, the *kokutai* fell to a nadir amid the anarchy of civil war and the chaos of political fragmentation until late-Tokugawa loyalists, inspired by the historical example of Kusunoki Masashige, abolished warlord hegemony in 1867 and achieved a second imperial restoration, this time under Emperor Meiji, with the aim of overcoming the 19th-century Western threat that Japan faced. Thus the emperor regained his proper position of de facto power, on top of his formal sovereign authority, in a centralized state. All land and all subjects once again came directly under his aegis—as in antiquity and during the short-lived Kenmu Restoration.

## Modern Times (1867–1945)

*Kokutai* lost much of its irrational mythical trappings under the impact of Enlightenment political and legal ideas derived from Western theories of the social contract that deemed the state and sovereign authority to be artificial creations designed by human societies in light of their needs. As a result, early in the Emperor Meiji's reign (1867– 1912), thinkers in Japan tended to downplay or ignore the mythical origins imputed to the imperial house by Tokugawa-era nativists. Instead, the early-Meiji thinkers often used *kokutai* to mean a nontangible "nationality" or "constitution," generically applicable to all nations, Japan included, in contrast to their concrete forms of government (e.g., republic or monarchy).

With the promulgation of the 1889 Meiji Constitution, the supreme law of the land, and the 1890 Imperial Rescript on Education, which inspired compulsory school curricula throughout Japan, *kokutai* reverted to its mythical roots peculiar to Japan. The constitution declared that the divine imperial dynasty should be "coeval with

Heaven and Earth"—that is, exist eternally—because the Sun Goddess had so decreed it. The emperor was declared "sacred and inviolable," and official commentaries on the constitution stressed that this factor made Japan's imperial dynasty decisively different from European monarchies despite similar wording in their constitutions. Thus "sacred and inviolable" entailed not just monarchic legal nonculpability, but also meant "above moral reproach and beyond rational questioning." The 1890 rescript, like all statements by the emperor, lacked any basis in positive law, but took on unassailable coercive power, so that conscientious objection, for example, became impossible after the emperor issued a rescript to declare war.

As a series of foreign and domestic crises beset Japan in the 1920s and 1930s, *kokutai* became *the* key element defining Japanese identity amidst the dizzying pace of modernization (which usually meant Westernization). Indeed, *kokutai* morphed into a rigid orthodox doctrine impervious to reason, similar to McCarthyism in Cold War America. One danger was that of revolution, perceived to stem from foreign ideas inimical to this *kokutai*. The 267-year-old Qing dynasty in China had fallen to revolutionaries in 1911. Among the great powers in Europe before 1914, only France had been a republic, but by 1919 only Britain remained a monarchy. Above all, the Soviet Union openly declared its intention to export the Bolshevik revolution. Hence it is no accident that the 1925 and 1928 Peace Preservation Laws banned attempts to alter the *kokutai* and the capitalist system on pain of torture and death.

The sense of crisis was exacerbated by wars, often of Japan's own making, such as the Manchuria Incident (1931–1933) and semicovert operations in China (1933–1937). War abroad exacerbated the sense of

danger from gullible Japanese at home betraying the *kokutai*, so liberalism and humanism joined Communism on Japan's prohibited list of dangerous ideas. The word "democracy" was banned because it literally translates as "an -ism under which the people are sovereign" (*minshushugi*)—which ipso facto was incompatible with the *kokutai* and imperial rule. In Japan's jingoist hothouse, politicians started a campaign to purge enemies of the Shōwa Emperor (Hirohito; reign 1926–1989) and to "clarify the *kokutai*." The Ministry of Education published its definitive teachers' guide for that purpose in 1937, the year that Japan invaded China to launch World War II in Asia.

After Japan expanded that war to include America and its Allies in 1941, *kokutai* assumed virulent aspects of ultra-nationalism. The military and government revived Kusunoki Masashige as a hero for all Japanese men, women, and children to emulate. No matter how hopeless the war might seem, they must fight and die for the emperor with no thought of surrender. After two atomic attacks in August 1945, some 3.1 million Japanese had died and Soviet forces had entered the northern part of Japan's colony, Korea. This Soviet influx helped in the eventual creation of a Communist regime, which remains there today. Only after Japan's leaders ensured that they had "preserved the *kokutai*"—that is, America agreed to not to harm the Shōwa Emperor—did they agree to surrender.

Japan's surrender ushered in a foreign army of occupation led by U.S. General Douglas MacArthur bent on pushing through democratic reforms, including a new "peace constitution," designed to dismantle the emperor's de facto powers, although his formal authority as a "symbol of the state and unity of the people" plus most of his ceremonial-religious acts of state were retained. Nevertheless, the consensus among postwar Japanese legal experts is that these democratic reforms put an end to the *kokutai*. To the utter chagrin of fringe right-wing extremists today, very few Japanese show any desire to re-embrace the irrational, emperor-centered ultra-nationalism of their wartime *kokutai*. Indeed, the term is now all but forgotten except when used as a homonym and portmanteau word, the "national athletic meets" (*kokumin taiiku taikai*) held annually.

*Bob Tadashi Wakabayashi*

**See also:** Ashikaga Takauji: Go-Daigo; Greater East Asia Co-prosperity Sphere; History Textbooks Controversy; Imperial Rescript on Education; Meiji Constitution; Mukden Incident: Lytton Report; Nativism, Rise of; ;1947 Constitution; Peace Preservation Law; Russian Invasion of Manchuria; Shōwa Emperor (Hirohito).

**Further Reading**

Hall, Robert King, ed. *Kokutai no hongi: Cardinal Principles of the National Entity of Japan*. Trans. John Owen Gauntlett. Cambridge, MA: Harvard University Press, 1949.

Minear, Richard H. *Japanese Tradition and Western Law*. Cambridge, MA: Harvard University Press, 1970.

Tsurumi, Shunsuke. *An Intellectual History of Wartime Japan, 1931–1945*. London: Routledge, 1986.

Wakabayashi, Bob Tadashi. *Japanese Loyalism Reconstrued*. Honolulu: University of Hawaii Press, 1996.

## Komura Jutarō (1855–1911)

Born to a samurai family from Kyushu, Komura Jutarō studied law in Tokyo on a domainal scholarship from 1871 to 1874. He continued his law studies at Harvard University as a government-sponsored overseas student and later entered the Foreign Ministry in 1884.

Toiling in the translation bureau for the better part of a decade, Komura was posted abroad by Foreign Minister Mutsu Munemitsu in 1893. Komura's distinguished performance abroad was rewarded with a series of increasingly important appointments. Following a stint in Beijing, which included serving as acting minister in the buildup to war with China, he became political affairs department chief and then Minister to Korea in 1895. While in Seoul, Komura penned the Komura-Weber memorandum with his Russian counterpart, Karl Weber, in which Japan and Russia agreed to jointly advise the Korean king and allowed both countries to station troops in important Korean cities.

Komura returned to Tokyo in 1896 to become Vice Minister, a stint that was followed by a series of postings as Minister, first to Washington (1898–1900), then to St. Petersburg, Russia (1900), and finally back to Beijing (1900–1901).General Katsura Tarō, whom Komura met in Manchuria during the Sino-Japanese War, chose Komura to be Foreign Minister in his cabinet in 1901. During that time, the Russian occupation of Manchuria and encroachment on Korea was the major issue confronting Komura in this role. Along with Katsura, Komura regarded Russia as a significant threat to Japan's position in Korea and strongly supported an alliance with Britain to counter that threat. The resulting Anglo-Japanese Alliance of 1902 allowed Komura to negotiate political and economic rights on the mainland from a position of power. When Russia failed to recognize Japanese rights throughout Korea, Komura was one of the more vocal proponents of war with Russia.

Komura traveled to the Portsmouth Peace Conference to personally negotiate the end of the war in 1905. The Japanese public roundly criticized Komura for failing to obtain an indemnity from Russia, despite the fact that he had negotiated Russia's cession to Japan of the Liaodong Peninsula and South Manchurian Railroad. In fact, Komura had pushed a hard line in negotiations over the indemnity to the point of nearly walking out, but the leadership in Tokyo instructed him to end the war even without reparations. Later in 1905, Komura secured Chinese recognition of the treaty terms concerning Manchuria in the Treaty of Peking.

The public outcry against the Portsmouth Peace Treaty forced the resignation of the Katsura cabinet in 1906. Komura became a member of the Privy Council but soon after accepted an ambassadorial appointment to London. In 1908, Katsura, forming his second cabinet, called Komura back to Tokyo to again serve as Foreign Minister. While in office, Komura sought to strengthen Japan's place on the continent and obtain recognition from the powers of that position. To this end, Komura orchestrated the Root-Takahira agreement (1908), in which the United States implicitly recognized Japanese control of Korea and southern Manchuria; reached an agreement with Russia (1910) over spheres of influence in Manchuria; and presided over the annexation of Korea (1910). Japan also regained tariff autonomy in 1911. When he died shortly after resigning office in 1911, Komura left a Japan that he had helped to transform in only a decade into a continental empire.

*Rustin Gates*

**See also:** Anglo-Japanese Alliance; Mutsu Munemitsu; Portsmouth Peace Treaty; Russo-Japanese War; South Manchurian Railroad.

**Further Reading**

Nish, Ian. *Japanese Foreign Policy, 1869–1942: Kasumigaseki to Miyakezaka.* London: Routledge & K. Paul, 1977.

Okamoto, Shumpei. "A Phase of Meiji Japan's Attitude toward China: The Case of Komura Jutarō." *Modern Asian Studies* 13, no. 3 (July 1979): 431–457.

# Konoe Fumimaro (1891–1946)

Born in Tokyo on October 12, 1891, Konoe Fumimaro was a member of one of the five highest-ranked aristocratic families in imperial Japan. His father, Prince Atsumaro, was a renowned Pan-Asian movement leader who founded Tōadōbun-shoin University in Shanghai.

A graduate of the Department of Law of Kyoto Imperial University, the young Konoe pursued a career in diplomacy and attended the Paris Peace Conference in 1919 as a junior member of the Japanese delegation. There, he observed the reality of international power politics, in which the

Outgoing Japanese Prime Minister Konoe Fumimaro (left), with his replacement, General Tōjō Hideki, following the transfer of power in 1941. (Bettmann/Corbis)

defeated became prey to the victors. Japan's failure to secure a statement on racial equality in the League of Nations Covenant disillusioned the young diplomat. Highly critical of the Anglo-American domination of the peace conference, Konoe published an article in 1920 attacking the hypocrisy of the postwar settlement.

Having served some years as a member of the House of Peers in the Japanese government, Konoe was appointed Prime Minister in 1937. His popularity was immense, and he enjoyed widespread support from both the military and the general public. Following the Marco Polo Bridge Incident of July 7, 1937, Konoe permitted the hard-liners in his cabinet to pursue an all-out war against China, thus making a fateful choice for Japan. In January 1938, he made the statement "*Shōkaiseki wo aiteni sezu*" ("We do not negotiate with Jiang Jieshi [Ch'iang K'ai-shek]"), which severely hampered peace negotiations with China. With the military stalemate in China, Konoe resigned in January 1939.

Konoe was once again called to the premiership in July 1940. In his second cabinet, a drastic political restructuring was carried out with the dissolution of existing political parties and establishment of the Taisei Yokusankai (Imperial Rule Assistance Association). Konoe became the first president of this organization, which was modeled on the one-party systems of Nazi Germany and the Soviet Union. While preparing for a total war at home, he agreed to the army's strategy of sending troops into northern French Indochina in September 1940. That same month, under the initiative of Foreign Minister Matsuoka Yōsuke, Japan concluded the Tripartite Pact with Germany and Italy. These actions further worsened already declining U.S.-Japanese relations. Faced with a diplomatic stalemate with the United States, Konoe resigned in July 1941 and was succeeded by General Tōjō Hideki.

After the tides of war turned, Konoe maneuvered carefully to rally anti-Tōjō elements in Japan to secure a negotiated peace with the Allies. In early 1945, he was designated as a special envoy to the Soviet Union to seek peace through a Soviet intermediary, which did not materialize. These actions did not, however, save Konoe from prosecution by the International War Crimes Tribunal in Tokyo after the war. Rather than face trial, he committed suicide before his arrest, on December 16, 1946, in Tokyo. His only son, Fumitaka, a junior army officer, was interned in Siberia and allegedly killed there by the Soviets.

*Tohmatsu Haruo*

**See also:** International Military Tribunal of the Far East; Jiang Jieshi (Ch'iang K'ai-shek); Matsuoka Yōsuke; Tōjō Hideki; Tripartite Pact; Versailles Treaty.

## Further Reading

Morley, James William, ed. *The China Quagmire: Japan's Expansion on the Asian Continent, 1933–1941*. New York: Columbia University Press, 1983.

Morley, James William, ed. *Deterrent Diplomacy: Japan, Germany, and the USSR, 1935–1940*. New York: Columbia University Press, 1976.

Morley, James William, ed. *The Fateful Choice: Japan's Advance into Southeast Asia, 1939–1941*. New York: Columbia University Press, 1980.

Morley, James William, ed. *The Final Confrontation: Japan's Negotiations with the United States, 1941*. New York: Columbia University Press, 1994.

Skillony, Ben-Ami. *Politics and Culture in Wartime Japan*. Oxford, UK: Clarendon Press, 1981.

## Korea Added to the Empire (1905–1910)

The Treaty of Portsmouth (September 5, 1905), which settled longstanding disputes between Russia and Japan in the latter's favor, included provisions that affected the sovereignty of a third country: Korea, then formally known as the Taehan Empire. Article II of the treaty acknowledged Japan's "paramount political, military and economical interests" in Korea, and stipulated that Russia "neither . . . obstruct nor interfere with measures for guidance, protection and control which the Imperial Government of Japan may find necessary to take in Korea." Japanese diplomats lost little time exercising their hard-won prerogative, persuading five of the Kwangmu Emperor Kojong's cabinet ministers to defy their sovereign's wishes and sign an agreement by which a Japanese Resident-General (tōkan) assumed responsibility for Taehan's external affairs and foreign trade, "until the moment arrives when it is recognized that Korea has attained national strength."

The signatures of these "five traitors" (Ulsa ojok) inspired a revival of the Korean martial tradition of "righteous armies" (uibyong), irregular peasant militias recruited by local gentry like those that had fought Japanese invaders in the 1590s. When the Residency-General disbanded the Taehan army in summer 1907, garrison troops in Seoul, Wonju, and elsewhere mutinied, opening fire on Japanese forces. Dispersing throughout the peninsula, they joined forces with the peasant militias in a guerrilla insurgency that resisted Japanese rule up until and well after the formal annexation of Korea in late August 1910.

Uibyong may never have posed a serious military threat to the Japanese presence, but proved to be enough of a nuisance to require a significant commitment of troops to the Korean peninsula. They attacked Japanese barracks and police stations, sabotaged telegraph facilities and railroads, and won a handful of skirmishes against the Japanese infantry and gendarmerie. Between 1907 and 1910, the colonial government reported 2,819 clashes between "brigands" and Japanese troops, with more than half of those (1,451) occurring in 1908 alone. The insurgents' most ambitious coordinated assault occurred in December 1907, when Yi Inyong and Ho Wi led some 10,000 guerrillas from Yangju to attack the Residency-General's headquarters; two Japanese infantry divisions—consisting of 20,000 soldiers—repelled the offensive a mere 12 kilometers from Seoul's East Gate. In its Report on the Suppression of Korean Insurgents (Chōsen bōto tōbatsu shi, 1913), the Japanese army claimed 19,461 rebels killed by the end of 1911.

The guerrillas were poorly equipped, using improvised, castoff, and outdated weapons such as muzzle-loading rifles. Enterprising arms dealers from Europe, China, and even Japan smuggled newer armaments to the rebels, but not in quantities sufficient to threaten the heavily armed Japanese forces. Although some historians insist that the insurgents were "supported by the populace," evidence also indicates that they alienated rural communities by extorting money, stealing food and supplies, and otherwise bullying the locals.

Royal ministers and officials known to be "friendly to Japan" (ch'inilp'a) became targets for patriotic assassins. In late 1907, 20 Korean members of a Japanese organization were murdered. On March 22, 1908, Durham White Stevens, an American diplomat appointed by the Japanese as adviser to Taehan's Foreign Office, was beaten up by four Korean immigrants in San Francisco, then shot the following day by two others. The most high-profile slaying was that of the first Resident-General, Itō Hirobumi, by An Chunggun on a train platform in Harbin, on October 26, 1908. Two months later, an attempt was made on the life of Premier Yi Wanyong, one of the "five Ulsa traitors." Condemning such violence, American philosopher George Trumbull Ladd excoriated Koreans as "a bloody race."

These terror tactics gave Japanese hardliners a pretext to advocate for outright annexation. Officials claimed that the violence had "induced certain classes of Koreans to tender to their Sovereign and the Resident-General a petition for Annexation." In late August 1910, the protectorate was abolished, the 518-year-old Yi dynasty dethroned, and Korea "brought under the direct administration of the Imperial Government."

The new post of Governor-General (sōtoku) was initially reserved for active-duty military officers. Although this legal requirement was rescinded in 1920, no civilian ever held the position. Considering the colony the most volatile in its formal empire, the Japanese government preferred to keep Korea in military hands.

The Korean insurrection elicited precious little sympathy abroad. Within that same decade, several major colonial powers had bloodied their own hands suppressing uprisings: the Americans in the Philippines; the British in South Africa; the Germans in Southwest Africa; and the Dutch in Bali. The Korean resistance and the Japanese counterinsurgency took place in a world in which colonial violence was unremarkable.

*E. Taylor Atkins*

**See also:** Itō Hirobumi; Portsmouth Treaty.

## Further Reading

Kang, Hildi. *Under the Black Umbrella: Voices from Colonial Korea, 1910–1945.* Ithaca: Cornell University Press, 2001.

McKenzie, F. A. *The Tragedy of Korea.* London: Hodder and Stoughton, 1908.

Yi Ki-baek. *A New History of Korea.* Trans. Edward W. Wagner. Cambridge, MA: Harvard University Press, 1984.

## Korean Question. *See Seikanron.*

## Korean War (1950–1952)

When North Korean forces invaded the southern portion of the peninsula on June 25, 1950, the status of Japan changed radically. Suddenly Japan became a staging area for American forces on their way to the new war. As such, it became the beneficiary of millions of dollars flooding into the Japanese economy. It quickly became apparent to both American and United Nations commanders that it would be infinitely cheaper and faster to obtain supplies for their forces in Japan rather than to ship them over from the United States or the rest of the world. Japanese industries leaped at the chance to produce whatever the U.S. and UN forces needed. By the end of 1950, nearly 75 percent of all the dry goods (e.g., uniforms, backpack, canteens, mess kits, tents) used by those troops were provided by Japan. More than $3.5 billion was sent to Japanese companies during the war, with these expenditures peaking at $809 million in 1953. Japanese manufacturing grew by 50 percent between March 1950 and 1951. The Japanese economy soared to prewar levels. Because most of Japan's industrial production was geared toward supplying the UN war effort, these payments amounted to 27 percent of Japan's total export trade. Japan's previous debts were quickly paid, and by January 1951 Japan began to enjoy a positive balance of payments.

In addition, Japan was almost magically transformed from a former enemy into what became known as "America's unsinkable aircraft carrier." The fall of China to the communists a year before had begun this transformation for Japan. This most recent incursion of the communists from North Korea, however, gave legitimacy to George Kennan's claims of the Domino Theory: that one Asian nation (and East Europe, in the case of the Soviet Union) would fall in turn to communism in a chain reaction. Certainly, after Mao Zedong sent 250,000 Chinese "volunteers" to Korea to respond to American incursions along the Yalu River in mid-October 1950, Japan became a staunch ally and the place to stop communism. American airbases in Japan became the home of virtually all of the air sorties during the war. American forces poured into Japan on their way to the peninsula. Millions of dollars were spent in Japan.

One negative result of the war was that 200,000 to 400,000 Koreans fled to Japan. Most of new immigrants were desperately poor. Their penury imposed a huge burden on their relatives who had remained in Japan after World War II. Another negative aspect was that Japan was forced into creating the Self-Defense Forces to protect Japan. Many Japanese protested that this represented a rehabilitation of Japan's hated military.

On balance, most scholars agree that the Korean War greatly benefited postwar Japan. Many argue that the very favorable nature of the San Francisco Peace Treaty of 1952, which formally ended World War II, can be attributed to Japan's role in the Korean War.

*Louis G. Perez*

**See also:** San Francisco Peace Treaty.

**Further Reading**

Forsberg, Aaron. *America and the Japanese Miracle*. Chapel Hill: University of North Carolina Press, 2000.

Vestal, James. *Planning for Change: Industrial Policy and Japanese Economic Development, 1945–1990*. Oxford, UK: Clarendon Press. 1993.

## Kōtoku Shūsui (1871–1911)

Kōtoku Shūsui was born Kōtoku Denjiro in Kochi on November 5, 1871. He moved to Tokyo in his mid-teens and began working as a journalist in 1893. From 1898 to 1903, Kōtoku was a columnist for the *Yorozu Choho* ("Everything Morning News"). He left the paper when it assumed a pro-war position during the Russo-Japanese War. Kōtoku founded the opposition *Heimin Shimbun* ("The Common People's Newspaper") with Sakai Toshihiko. It openly opposed the war and other government positions. The editors and journalists frequently ran into trouble with the government regarding their publication, and Kōtoku was jailed for five months in 1905.

Kōtoku began his political work as a socialist. In 1901, he and Sakai attempted to found the Japanese Social Democratic Party. They also translated and published Marx's *Communist Manifesto* in *Heimin Shimbun*. Kōtoku turned away from socialism, however, when, while in jail, he read Peter Kropotkin's *Fields, Factories and Workshops*, introducing Kōtoku to anarcho-communist ideas. In 1905, he traveled to the United States, where he could more freely criticize theeEmperor of Japan as a leading figure in Japan's capitalist economy. There Kōtoku became interested in syndicalism, an economic system proposed as an alternative to capitalism or socialism that focused on federations of workers to manage the economy, and anarcho-communism, which favored freedom from centralized government by having voluntary associations between workers. Kōtoku began a correspondence with Kropotkin, and by 1908 had translated his *Conquest of Bread* to Japanese.

At a June 1906 meeting to welcome him home, Kōtoku argued that a general strike—not pursuing parliamentary politics, the method favored by the Marxist political party—was the most effective way to achieve a revolution. His writings also reflected his changing outlook, arguing for direct action by the people, such as a general strike, rather than political solutions, such as universal suffrage. His new views precipitated a break between the anarcho-communists and the social democrats. Two new journals replaced the group's original publication in April 1907. The social democrats published the *Social News* and advocated for political solutions; the anarchists published the *Osaka Common People's Newspaper* and favored direct action by the people.

In the years that followed, crackdowns on labor unions and political organizations, as well as a repression of publications, contributed to a trend of using violence to achieve the goals of the anarchist movement. On May 20, 1910, the Japanese government arrested five anarchists in a plot to assassinate the emperor. They were accused of possessing bomb-making equipment in the High Treason Incident, as it was called. The initial arrests were followed by arrests of leftist political dissidents, including Kōtoku. His was also the highest-profile arrest. In spite of the fact that there was conclusive evidence against only five people, on January 18, 1911 a Japanese court convicted

25 men and one woman of planning the attack on the emperor. Even though Kōtoku had distanced himself from the group early on in the planning stages of the attack, and there was no evidence that he was involved in the plot, he was convicted of treason. Twenty-four of those convicted were sentenced to death; Kōtoku and 11 others were executed. Anarchists worldwide view him as martyr for their cause.

*Larissa Castriotta Kennedy*

**See also:** High Treason Incident; Russo-Japanese War.

**Further Reading**

Cronin, Joseph. *The Life of Seinosuke: Dr. Oishi and the High Treason Incident*. New York: White Tiger Press, 2007.

Notehelfer, Frederick George. *Kōtoku Shōsui: Portrait of a Japanese Radical*. Cambridge, UK: Cambridge University Press, 1971.

## Kusanagi-no-Tsurugi

Some Westerners point to the similarity of the tale of Excalibur in establishing the legitimacy of the imperial charisma. Neonationalists in Japan have created an aura around *Kusanagi*, which represents valor and purity. As a consequence, they become very angry when confronted with depictions of the sword in modern *manga* and *anime* illustrations in popular media.

Among Japan's many myths recorded in the *Kojiki* ("Record of Ancient Matters," 712) and the *Nihongi* ("Chronicles of Japan," 720), the one about *Kusanagi-no-Tsurugi* ("Grass-Cutting Sword") is one of the most well known because of its close ties to the Sun Goddess Amaterasu. Angered by the misdeeds of her brother, the god Susanoo, Amaterasu punished Susanoo by forcing him out of heaven and exiling him to

Izumo province in the worldly realm. In Izumo, Susanoo conquered the fearsome *Yamata-no-Orochi*, an eight-headed serpent that had been tormenting this province and its inhabitants for a long time. When Susanoo killed the beast, he found a sword in its tail which he called *Ama-no-Murakumo-no-Tsurugi* ("Sword of the Gathering Clouds of Heaven"). He presented this sword to Amaterasu as a peace offering to make up for his past misdeeds. This sword, along with the mirror and the jewel, constitute Amaterasu's Three Imperial Regalia, which are believed to be housed at Ise Shrine.

The sword's name change to *Kusanagi-no-Tsurugi* resulted from a later legend about the bravery of the distinguished warrior, Yamato Takeru, which can be traced back to the reign of the 12th Japanese sovereign, Emperor Keikō. One of the various treasures which Yamato Takeru received for protection from his aunt, a maiden at the Ise Shrine, was the *Ama-no-Murakumo-no-Tsurugi*. One time, Yamato Takeru was hiding from his enemy in a grassfield. When the enemy set fire to the grassland, Yamato Takeru drew his *Ama-no-Murakumo-no-Tsurugi* to cut through the burning grass and to escape from the fire. Miraculously, every time Yamato Takeru swung his sword in one direction, the wind also blew in the same direction, allowing him to direct the fire toward his enemy and to escape from the blaze. Following this incident, he renamed the sword *Kusanagi-no-Tsurugi*, meaning "Grass-Cutting Sword," in honor of its magic and protective power. According to legend, Yamato Takeru lost his life in a battle with a fierce monster because he did not carry his *Kusanagi-no-Tsurugi* sword with him at that time.

According to legend, the sword must be gathered together with the sacred curved jewel *(Yasakani no Magatama)* and sacred mirror *(Yata no Kagami)* to invest a new emperor at his ascension to the throne. It became part of the patriotic mythology surrounding State Shintō. Even scholarly discussion of anything relating to the emperor became taboo. The priests at Atsuta refuse to allow anyone to actually see the sword, even during the most recent investiture of the Heisei Emperor in 1989. At that ceremony it was reported to have been heavily wrapped in a special imperial cloth before it was whisked away by the priests.

*Monika Dix*

**See also:** Early Mytho-histories: *Kojiki* and *Nihon shōki*.

### Further Reading

Beasley, W. G. 1999. *The Japanese Experience: A Short History of Japan*. Berkeley: University of California Press.

Guirand, Felix. 1959. *New Larousse Encyclopedia of Mythology*. New York: Paul Hamlin.

## Kwantung Army Adventurism (1926–1936)

The Kwantung Army originated in the aftermath of the Russo-Japanese War, when the Portsmouth Treaty gave Japan control of Kwantung (Guandong) Province in south Manchuria as a leased territory. Formerly under Russian control, the territory included the Liaodong Peninsula, with its warm-water civilian port at Dalian and naval facilities and fortifications at Port Arthur. With the completion of the Chinese Eastern Railway by 1902, Russians had connected both of these Yellow Sea ports to the interior of the vast, resource-rich Manchurian region and ultimately to the Trans-Siberian Railway, which linked Russia's Pacific cold-water port, Vladivostok, to Europe. After 1905, Japanese also got control of the southern portion of the railway and a narrow strip of land around it through the interior of Manchuria. The military force that officially became the Kwantung Army in 1919 was charged with protecting Guandong and guarding the railway, which passed into the hands of the South Manchurian Railway Company (SMR), an enterprise jointly owned by the Japanese state and Japanese private capital.

Kwantung Army officers based in the leased territory and railway zone attempted to extend Japanese hegemony on the continent, using Manchuria as a buffer against Russian influence, and trying to maintain stability in the context of chaos following China's 1911 Revolution. In ways reminiscent of British relations with Princely States in India, Japanese cultivated relationships with warlords who became de facto rulers of Manchuria and northern China. Kwantung Army advisors especially assisted the warlord Zhang Zoulin (1875–1928), whose base was Fengtian, just outside of the leased territory. By 1918, Zhang gained control of the three provinces of Manchuria, an area larger than France and Germany combined. By the late 1910s and early 1920s, Zhang and his army were also receiving information, funds, weapons, training, and soldiers from the Kwantung Army. In 1926, Zhang wrested control of Republican China's last capital, Beijing, from other warlords, declaring himself Grand Marshal of the Republic of China. In an effort to unify China, Guomindang (Nationalist Party) forces under Jiang Jieshi marched north and attacked Zhang's troops south of Beijing in May 1928, leading to his army's retreat to that city. Japanese advisers then convinced Zhang to leave Beijing and return to Manchuria.

Despite the fact that some Japanese leaders thought they could work with Zhang, Kwantung Army officers were alarmed by the return of Zhang's army to Manchuria.

This concern, in part, led Colonel Kōmoto Daisaku to murder Zhang by blowing up his railcar as he traveled from Beijing back to Manchuria in June 1928. To deflect suspicion, Kōmoto used Russian bombs and planted the bodies of three Chinese vagrants, dressed like guerrillas, one of whom carried papers implicating Chinese in Zhang's assassination. Kōmoto lied to Japanese investigators about his illicit actions, but the truth leaked out. Kōmoto hoped that the disruption caused by Zhang's killing would be a pretext for Japanese imposition of order and a Japanese political takeover of Manchuria, but in 1928, Tokyo refused to respond as Kōmoto wished, with the cabinet even refusing the War Minister's request to send reinforcements to protect Japanese interests following Zhang's assassination.

In the period before the Mukden Incident of 1931, Chinese in Manchuria engaged in anti-Japanese actions, including boycotts of Japanese goods, discriminatory practices vis-à-vis Japanese nationals (including Koreans), harassment of Japanese businessmen and industrialists, disrespect of Japan's national symbols including its flag, taxes and tariffs designed to hamper Japanese economically, anti-Japanese public notices, rock-throwing at Japanese schoolchildren, Chinese military aircraft buzzing Japanese infrastructure, and construction of railways that competed with the SMR. At the same time, Manchuria, with its wide-open spaces compared to Japan, took on an aura of "paradise" from the Japanese perspective. Tensions preventing Japanese from enjoying "their" paradise came to the fore when Chinese forces under the command of Zhang Xueliang—Zhang Zoulin's son and successor, who allied himself with Jiang's republican government in Nanjing—summarily executed Nakamura Shintarō, a Kwantung Army Captain disguised as an agricultural expert, and three others working with him near the Inner Mongolian border. This incident occurred at nearly the same time as a dispute between Chinese and Korean farmers at Wanpaoshan, elsewhere in Manchuria, which was much sensationalized in press accounts. The stage was set for the Mukden Incident and Japanese attempts to impose order in Manchuria.

Lieutenant Colonel Ishiwara Kanji joined the Kwantung Army in 1928, and the following year Colonel Itagaki Seishirō was added to the army's staff. These middle-echelon officers had relationships with junior officers in Tokyo who pined for a Shōwa Restoration that would move Japan toward state socialism under the emperor. Reformist officers in both locales saw control of Manchuria as a panacea for all the ills of modern Japan. By early September 1931, Ishiwara and Itagaki had planned an incident that would drag the Japanese military and state into settlement of what they called the "Manchuria problem." They networked with Kwantung Army officers they could trust, like-minded officers in Tokyo, and leaders of Japan's army in Korea. Other officers, including the Kwantung Army's commander, were not privy to their conspiracy, but word of an imminent skullduggery leaked out. In mid-September, Foreign Minister Shidehara Kijūrō pressured War Minister Minami Jirō to intervene, which he did by dispatching Major General Tatekawa Yoshitsugu—a man known to be sympathetic to military solutions to Japan's problems; Tatekawa made it to Mukden by September 18. There, at a Japanese restaurant, he informed Ishiwara and Itagaki that Tokyo did not want such an event to occur. He then passed out from drinking too much or feigned doing so because he was actually in league with the conspirators.

That evening, Kwantung Army soldiers detonated a section of SMR-owned railway near Mukden so miniscule that a train was able to pass and reach its destination on schedule. Nonetheless, soon after the explosion, fighting erupted in and around Mukden. Japanese troops soon "found" documents incriminating Zhang Xueliang and three Chinese corpses in military attire near the explosion, all of which they used to blame the incident on Chinese. Unsurprised Kwantung Army officers who were not in on the conspiracy learned what had occurred, accepting the Mukden Incident as a *fait accompli*. They, along with reinforcements, proceeded to establish hegemony over the whole of Manchuria over the next five months, despite the wishes of Tokyo leaders, including the emperor himself. By February 1932, Japanese declared Manchukuo ("Land of the Manchu") with the last Qing emperor, Henry Pu-yi, as head of the new state. Puyi became puppet-emperor of the puppet-state two years later.

Following the creation of Manchukuo, the Kwantung Army ran the country's government, sharing a modicum of influence with the SMR. tension between the army and big business was ever-present, with mixed messages coming from Kwantung Army representatives who at times made anticapitalist proclamations. Japanese capital wanted to use Manchuria to dampen effects of the Great Depression, but the army was chiefly interested in using Manchurian resources in industrial development linked to war making. To the Kwantung Army—and to an extent to the SMR—Manchuria was also a place where experimentation would lead to a realization of utopian dreams that were harbingers of later Japanese discourses on "overcome modernity." By limiting private accumulation, the Kwantung Army sought to overcome problems wrought by capitalism without becoming communist. Its leaders also hoped that Manchukuo would become a stepping-stone toward a world of interracial harmony. Toward such ends, in July 1932, Ishiwara and others formed the Concordia Society (Kyōwakai), which was designed to ideologically defuse conflict in Manchuria, but also reflected sincere desires to use the puppet-state in the construction of a better world.

After the Mukden Incident, Japanese forces led by Major General Doihara Kenji of the army's Tokumukikan (Special Duties Organ) tried to wrest control of provinces of northern China from the Republic of China, making deals with warlords only loosely under Nanjing's control. By 1933, Kwantung Army troops had penetrated China both north and south of the Great Wall. Kwantung Army Lieutenant Colonel Tanaka Ryūichi later used illegally procured funds to finance a pro-Japanese, Inner-Mongolian independence movement under the would-be puppet-leader Prince Teh, who dreamed of a Greater Mongolia including the Soviet-backed Mongolian Peoples' Republic. In the winter of 1936, these Inner-Mongolian forces, with the assistance of Japanese advisers, battled Guomindang forces in Suiyuan Province, Inner Mongolia. This campaign commenced without the consent or even knowledge of either Tokyo or the Kwantung Army command. Following major setbacks to the Japanese-led forces in Suiyuan, the Kwantung Army sent a representative to Tokyo to ask for funds to carry on, but he was reprimanded by military leaders there, including Ishiwara Kanji, who recently had been transferred to the Army General Staff. The Suiyuan Incident—the last major military endeavor in Northeast Asia before the Marco Polo Bridge Incident in 1937—ended in an armistice between Prince Teh's forces and the Guomindang. In other words, Tanaka Ryūichi failed in his scheme to establish a second Manchukuo in Mongolia.

*Gerald Iguchi*

**See also:** Ishiwara Kanji; Jiang Jieshi (Ch'iang K'ai-shek); Manchukuo; Mukden Incident: Lytton Report; Pan-Asianism; Portsmouth Treaty; Pu-yi (Henry); Russo-Japanese War; Russo-Japanese War, Consequences; Shōwa Restoration; South Manchurian Railroad; Zhang Zuolin.

**Further Reading**

Barnhart, Michael A. *Japan Prepares for Total War: The Search for Economic Security, 1919–1941*. Ithaca: Cornell University Press, 1987.

Coox, Alvin D. *Nomonhan: Japan against Russia, 1939*. Stanford: Stanford University Press, 1985.

Drea, Edward J. *Japan's Imperial Army: Its Rise and Fall, 1853–1945*. Lawrence, KS: University of Kansas Press, 2009.

Duara, Prasenjit. *Sovereignty and Authenticity: Manchukuo and the East Asian Modern*. New York: Rowman and Littlefield, 2003.

Young, Louise. *Japan's Total Empire: Manchuria and the Culture of Wartime Imperialism*. Berkeley: University of California Press, 1999.

# L

## Language: Change in the Sixth to Eighth Centuries

Most archaeologists believe that the islands of Japan have had human occupation for at least some 30,000 years. No one knows when the first Japanese state appeared, but the Chinese chronicle *Records of Wei* speaks of a recognizable polity by the third or fourth century C.E. Little, too, is known of the earliest form of the Old Japanese language (*Jōko Nihongo*), as the Japanese had no indigenous writing system. Some inscriptions on wooden tablets, funerary items, and swords and art objects indicate that Chinese characters were used perhaps as early as the fourth century, but no real texts are found until much later. Some Japanese probably learned the Chinese language from immigrant Koreans in the fifth century.

In the fifth and six centuries, powerful families and hereditary clans (*uji*) formed the Yamato Court—named for the region of present-day Kyoto, Osaka, and Nara Prefecture—the first real government in Japanese history. They controlled the peasant population (*be*), who were grouped in caste-like fashion by occupation, residence, and family. By this time, contact between Japan and mainland Asia was growing, and many objects and ideas were borrowed from China. One powerful *uji* family, the Soga, gained predominance, and argued for the widespread acceptance of the newly imported religion of Buddhism. This was partly for political reasons; by advocating the adoption of Buddhism and its rituals,

the Soga clan hoped to consolidate its power. After defeating several families who opposed Buddhism, they prevailed under the reign of Empress Suiko (554–628) and her nephew and regent Prince Shōtoku (574–622)—Buddhism's first real patron in Japan. Shōtoku reformed the political system, initiated closer diplomatic relations with mainland Asia, and issued an imperial edit promoting Buddhism in 594. For the next several centuries, the politics and culture of Japan were shaped by Japanese views of the Sui and Tang Dynasties.

After its official acceptance, Buddhism spread rapidly, with several important monasteries and schools being established by the seventh century. For the next hundred years, Chinese and Korean monks an proselytizers often visited, bringing with them Chinese religious and philosophical books, and Chinese translations of original Buddhist Sanskrit texts. With Japanese having no writing system of its own, the Japanese elite enthusiastically took to the Chinese language and Chinese characters (*kanji*).

In reality, the two languages were quite mismatched, and the Chinese writing system was very difficult to apply to the Japanese language. The Chinese characters worked well for a language like Chinese that was uninflected for tense and most other features, had a word-order-based syntax, and had a monosyllabic vocabulary. In contrast, Japanese was polysyllabic, highly agglutinative, case-marked, with complex honorific and tense-based verbs. Also, the Chinese and Japanese phonological systems were quite different,

*Kanji* are Chinese characters used to write the Japanese language. They constitute one form of Japanese script, alongside *hiragana* and *katakana*. (Dreamstime.com)

with Chinese being tonal (where the pitch accent of a word could determine meaning).

While the first attempts to write Japanese in Chinese meet serious problems, the real reason prose was largely written in Chinese was due to the high prestige value it held throughout the Nara period (710–774). For several centuries the language of government, business, and official proclamations was done completely in Chinese. (Indeed, until the 19th century, most Japanese intellectuals had at least a reading knowledge of Chinese—a fact that has influenced much of the spoken and written Japanese language until the present). If nothing else, the vast literature of Chinese classics and religious texts were available to educated Japanese of the day.

However, not everything could be easily rendered in Chinese. There was also a vibrant vernacular indigenous Japanese literature found in poetry, verse, and song. There were

things like personal names, the names of historical and legendary emperors, and place names that also needed a way to be written down. The problem was how to do so. Chinese *kanji* were semantic ideograms, intending to mean some thing, rather than standing for sounds as in an alphabetic orthography. That is, the glyphs (at least initially) were intended to iconically represent their referent. For example, the *kanji* for "mountain," 山 (and pronounced *shān* in Chinese), was supposed to depict three peaks of a mountain range in the distance. Over time, the peaks were reduced to three vertical lines as the character became written often and quickly (much like reducing the picture of a person to a "stick figure" drawing). But while Japanese could simply use this character for their own word "mountain" (*yama*), they still needed ways to phonetically write things for which there were no Chinese characters (like a past-tense marker).

What was attempted was using some *kanji* for their semantic value and others for how they are pronounced. For example, probably everyone as seen a T-shirt with a saying like this on it, meaning "I love New York": I ♥ NY. Here, of course, we read the heart symbol for its semantic value, "love." However, suppose we replaced the "I" with a symbol for an eyeball, rendering the phrase on the T-shirt something like this: ☉ ♥ NY. Here the first symbol stands for its phonetic value, "eye," while the second symbol stands for its semantic value, "love." This is analogous to how early Japanese was written.

One advantage Chinese characters had was that because they represented one monosyllabic Chinese word, if the meaning of the character could be detached, the *kanji* could then be used to represent the sound of that syllable alone. Thus a kind of rebus-like system arose—in which certain Chinese characters (called *Man'yō-gana*, or *Man'yō* letters) were used for their phonetic value only—which allowed Japanese to write their native vocabulary. However, there were still many problems. First, if you saw the character for "mountain," for example, how would you know if you were supposed to read it for its semantic or phonetic value? There was no consensus on which *kanji* would be used as phonetic characters

for several centuries (until between 900 and 940, when a standardized set of syllabaries developed).

Another problem was there were a plethora of readings to choose from. Not only did every borrowed Chinese character potentially have an indigenous Japanese pronunciation (*kun-yomi*), but it could also use the Chinese pronunciation (*on-yomi*) that was brought with it when the *kanji* was imported. On top of that, Chinese characters were brought in at various times, and by people speaking differing Chinese "dialects" (actually often mutually unintelligible languages). Thus a *kanji* could have at least two readings—one Japanese-based and one Chinese-based. There were potentially numerous Chinese-based readings as well. This linguistic legacy has survived to the present, as seen in the following table showing four common characters—行, 子, 力, and 下—and their Japanese pronunciations, along with three of their possible Chinese pronunciations.

The turn of the sixth century saw the appearance of three of the most important books in Japanese history, both culturally and politically. (Many other works—such as the *Tennō-ki* ["Record of the Emperors," circa 620] solicited by Prince Shōtoku and other members of the Soga family in an attempt to justify their authority over the

| Kun-yomi | Three *On-yomi* readings | Kan-on | Go-on | Tō-on |
|---|---|---|---|---|
| 行 | *iku* | *kō* | *gyō* | *an* |
| 子 | *ko* | *shi* | *ji* | *su* |
| 力 | *chikara* | *riki* | *ryoku* | *roku* |
| 下 | *shita* | *ka* | *ge* | *a* |

Kun-yomi = Kun-yomi, or indigenous Japanese-reading of a character
On-yomi = On-yomi, or Sinified readings of a character
Kan-on = reading based on Han Dynasty (25 C.E.–220 C.E ) pronunciations
Go-on = reading based on Wu Dynasty (229 C.E.–280 C.E) pronunciations
Tō-on = reading based on Tang Dynasty (618 C.E.–907 C.E) pronunciations

aristocratic *uji* clans—have not survived.) They are the (1) the *Kojiki* (古書記, "Record of Ancient Matters"), probably compiled around 712; (2) the *Nihon-shōki* or *Nihon-gi* (日本書記 or 日本記, "Chronicle of Japan") complied in 720; and (3) the *Man'yō-shu* (万葉集, "The Collection of Ten Thousand Leaves) complied soon after 760. Interestingly, all three use different orthographic/linguistic experiments.

The 30 volumes of the *Nihon-shōki* are Japan's second oldest book. Instead of pure Chinese (*kambun*), the prose is written in *hentai kambun*, a Japanized version of Chinese using the *Man'yō-gana* script. Interspersed throughout are poems or songs (a single word covers both in Japanese) written in Old Japanese in *Man'yō-gana*. The *Man'yō-shu* is a book of more than 4,000 poems written in true indigenous vernacular Japanese, mostly between 645 and 759. It is written completely in *Man'yō-gana* script— in fact, the name comes from here—but not all scholars even today agree upon all the readings of all the characters, or the exact meaning of all the poems.

Besides being histories of the early days of Japan, the *Nihon-shōki* and the *Kojiki* are, in a sense, the scriptures of the indigenous Japanese religion, Shintō. They trace the unbroken imperial line from the Sun Goddess Amaterasu to the present, making the emperor the de facto head Shintō priest. These books have given a legitimacy to governmental authority for more than two millennia, and during periods of nationalism have been exalted as expressions of the Japanese spirit. While the prestige of Chinese literature occupied the minds of many of the elites, and even threatened the persistence of a vernacular Japanese literature, the *Man'yō-shu* showed a different side of the Japanese (Yamato) spirit. The *Man'yō-shu* has set the standard by which

all later Japanese poetry is judged, and is considered by many still to be the pre-eminent collection of Japanese verse.

*James Stanlaw*

**See also:** Early Mytho-histories: *Kojiki* and *Nihon shōki;* Jimmu Tennō; Language: Change in the 19th to 20th Centuries; Taika Reforms.

## Further Reading

Frellesvig, Bjarke. *A History of the Japanese Language*. Cambridge, UK: Cambridge University Press, 2010.

Habein, Yaeko Sato. *The History of the Japanese Written Language*. Tokyo: University of Tokyo Press, 1984.

Keene, Donald. *Seeds in the Heart: Japanese Literature from Earliest Times to the Late Sixteenth Century*. New York: Henry Holt, 1993.

Konishi, Jin'ichi. *A History of Japanese Literature. Vol. 1: The Archaic and Ancient Ages*. Princeton, NJ: Princeton University Press, 1984.

Martin, Samuel. *The Japanese Language through Time*. New Haven, CT: Yale University Press, 1987.

Miller, Roy Andrew. *Origins of the Japanese Language*. Seattle: University of Washington Press, 1980.

Shibatani, Masayoshi. *The Japanese Language*. Cambridge, UK: Cambridge University Press, 1990.

Seeley, Christopher. *A History of Writing in Japan*. Honolulu: University of Hawaii Press, 2000.

Takeuchi, Lone. *The Structure and History of Japanese: From Yamatokotoba to Nihongo*. New York: Longman, 1999.

## Language: Change in the 19th to 20th Centuries

The 19th century was a time of tremendous linguistic—as well as social and political—change in Japan. Previously, there was really no sense of a unified national Japanese language in the way we view things today. The Japanese language in the mid-19th century was hardly uniform, partly because the Tokugawa shōguns had done everything they could to keep cooperation among the various local warlords (*daimyō*) to a minimum. Contact and travel between the domains (han) was highly regulated. This contributed to the already substantial geographic dialect diversity in the country (often to the point of mutual unintelligibility). Nevertheless, concern about having a national language arose in earnest after contact with the West. In the mid-19th century, Japan was feeling tremendous pressure from the United States and Europe as they demanded increasingly unequal economic concessions.

Japanese leaders saw how the Western powers had decimated mainland Asia, and decided the best way to meet the threat was to Westernize their own country. Japan instantly modernized, going from an agrarian to an industrial economy within decades. Great social changes and upheavals occurred as the new Meiji government sought to develop a new consciousness among the people as it reevaluated all cultural and political institutions. Schooling, which had previously been reserved for the elite, became compulsory. This forced Japanese teachers and government officials to confront problems of language in ways they had not had to do previously. Simply put, the Japanese language as it stood in the 1860s posed many barriers to mass education, mass literacy, and ultimately a feeling of a pan-Japanese sense of identity.

A major concern of the Meiji leaders and intellectuals—as important as the political and economic problems facing them in the international arena—was what is often called *kokugo kokuji mondai*. This is usually translated as "Japanese language reforms" in English—that is, the problem (*mondai*) of instituting and promoting the national language (*kokugo*) and script (*kokuji*) in Japan. It was felt that until the notion of a "national language" (*kokugo*) became tied to the *kokutai*—the national polity—Japan could not advance economically or culturally. Language reform policy, then, became as much part of the political agenda as the educational agenda.

One of the first problems that needed addressing was to choose one of the many speech varieties available as the national language. Gradually, the speech patterns of the intellectuals of the new capital, Tokyo, became the standard almost by default. Nevertheless, the notion of an idealized *kokugo* demanded that all those who lived in the same political space believe they were speaking the same Japanese language. The actual variations of speech, as well as dialects, were by necessity ignored. *Kokugo-gaku*—literally, "the study of the national language"—was taken seriously by Japanese scholars. They turned to the ancient *Yamato kotoba* language of the ancient classics as the idealized ancestor of modern Japanese, free of Chinese influence, which was thought to reflect the true "Japanese spirit."

In fact, Japanese *was* highly influenced by Chinese in many inexorable ways. In terms of orthography, Japanese was written using Chinese characters. The Japanese borrowed the Chinese writing system when they imported Buddhism in the sixth century. Over the course of many centuries, a patchwork system was developed using Sino-Japanese characters for their semantic intent, and having an abbreviated set of approximately 100 *kanji* for use in two sets of syllabaries. These syllabaries allowed the Japanese to phonetically write things like adverbs and verb conjugations, for which

Chinese had no characters to offer. However, this writing system was not completely standardized, and one of the major things language reformers needed to do was script reform.

For one thing, there were thousands of *kanji* extant in Japanese and Chinese. Although certainly not all of them were needed for mass literacy, it was not clear which ones should be eliminated, or how. More importantly, a millennium ago when a *kanji* for a Japanese term was borrowed, usually the Chinese way of pronouncing that character was also taken in. This left a legacy where almost every *kanji* in Japanese had at least two readings: one based on the Japanese way of saying the referent and one (or more) based on Chinese. As a consequence, there was often some degree of uncertainty as to how a *kanji* should be read—even for one encountered before—as the reading could sometimes change depending on context.

Moreover, there was a vast discrepancy between the spoken and written forms of the Japanese language, regardless of the *kanji* used. The Japanese written language was highly Sinified in both vocabulary and literary style. In addition, when people in the 19th century wrote, they tried to approximate the classical Japanese forms (*wabun*) of a millennium ago rather than trying to depict how people were speaking. By the start of the Meiji period, the spoken and written languages were quite disparate, then, and for the most part only the well-educated segment of the population could read—or more importantly, actually interpret and understand—written Japanese beyond the basics with ease.

As a first attempt, language reformers established a Classical Standard (*bungo*) to be used only in writing, and a Colloquial Standard (*kōgo*) supposedly based on the spoken language. Given that even the new modernized Classical Standard of written

Japanese was still largely incomprehensible to those who knew only the spoken language, many attempts were made to more closely unify the spoken and written languages. Standardization came about through debates over how to reconcile these disparities. Many radical ideas were proposed by important figures, such as abolishing Japanese in favor of English, French, or Esperanto. Some advocated eliminating the use of *kanji* characters altogether while keeping the spoken language intact. In 1885, the Rōmaji Kai association was formed to promote the use of *rōmaji* ("Roman" letters, or the Latin alphabet) as a means of writing Japanese. Others wanted to use only one of the Japanese phonetic syllabary systems. In the end, the Ministry of Education decided to drastically reduce the number of *kanji*, and make the use of the phonetic syllabaries more consistent.

Kanda Takahira first used the term *genbun itchi*—the unification of the spoken and written language—in 1885. After much discussion, it was generally decided that a (rather idealized) version of the Tokyo dialect would become the Colloquial Standard and the basis of written Japanese. Futabatei Shimei wrote the first novel in the colloquial style in 1887, and by the turn of the century, most textbooks, novels, newspapers, and magazines had adopted some form of the Colloquial Standard.

Problems with the *kokugo* idea became more pronounced when Japan occupied other countries during the World War II. Schooling in *kokugo* (the "national language")—and not *nihongo* ("Japanese")—became the assimilation policy of choice in Japan's colonies throughout World War II. However, the language education policies in Korea, Manchukuo, and the so-called Greater East Asia Co-prosperity Sphere showed the poverty and internal contradictions of the *kokugo* idea, as Yeounsuk Lee clearly points out. In Japanese colonies, the promotion and dissemination of the Japanese language was always of primary importance for economic, military, and cultural reasons. It was thought that Japanese could act as a kind of goodwill lingua franca—*kyōeiken-go*, or Co-prosperity Language—uniting everyone under the greater Japanese empire. Once again, this policy brought up questions that had hardly been settled back in Japan: Which kind of Japanese was to be taught, which accent or dialect was to be used, how many *kanji* would students be exposed to, and which kind of word usage and style would be found in these overseas classroom? And here was a dilemma: If *kokogo* truly reflected the Japanese spirit, and was contained in the hearts of those of the "Japanese race," how could it be taught as an artificial or second language to foreigners? These problems were never solved.

After World War II, largely under suggestions proposed by reformers from the Supreme Commander of the Allied Powers (SCAP) during the American occupation, several changes were made to the Japanese language. The Colloquial Standard was abolished in official documents, and the written language became closer to the spoken vernacular. The number of *tōyō kanji*—those characters that were sanctioned for "daily use" in schools, books, and newspapers—were reduced to approximately 2,000. And while Japanese has enthusiastically borrowed English words ever since the country reopened its doors in the 19th century, the number of loanwords from English continued to grow exponentially in the 20th century. Many more of them were "made-in-Japan" terms for Japanese purposes, however, and were not necessarily transparent to native English speakers. These often reflected changing Japanese

cultural norms. For example, the use of the very productive English possessive pronoun *mai* ("my") seemed indicative of a new view that the values of group loyalty, which were thought to be the mainstay of Japanese society, were now being questioned. Terms such as *mai-hoomu* (owning "my home"), *mai-waifu* (adoring "my wife"), or *mai-peesu* (doing things at "my pace") suggest that personal interests and individual goals can compete with the traditional priority given to collective group responsibilities.

*James Stanlaw*

**See also:** Early Meiji (1868–1890) Political Reforms; Fukuzawa Yukichi; *Kokutai* and Ultra-nationalism; Language: Change in Sixth to Eighth Centuries; Nativism, Rise of.

## Further Reading

Burns, Susan. *Before the Nation: Kokugaku and the Imagining of Community in Early Modern Japan*. Durham, NC: Duke University Press Books, 2003.

Clark. Paul. *The Kokugo Revolution: Education, Identity, and Language Policy in Imperial Japan*. Berkeley: Institute of East Asian Studies, University of California, 2009.

Duke, Benjamin. *The History of Modern Japanese Education: Constructing the National School System, 1872–1890*. New Brunswick: Rutgers University Press, 2009.

Gluck, Carol. *Japan's Modern Myths: Ideology in the Late Meiji Period*. Princeton, NJ: Princeton University Press, 1987.

Gottlieb, Nanette. *Language and Society in Japan*. New York: Cambridge University Press, 2005.

Inoue, Miyako. *Vicarious Language: Gender and Linguistic Modernity in Japan*. Berkeley: University of California Press, 2006.

Lee, Yeounsuk. *The Ideology of Kokugo: Nationalizing Language in Modern Japan*. Honolulu: University of Hawaii Press, 2010.

Twine, Nanette. *Language and the Modern State: The Reformation of Written Japanese*. London: Routledge, 1991.

## Law on Assembly and Political Association of 1890

On July 25, 1890, shortly before the first session of the Imperial Diet, the Law on Assembly and Political Association (*Shukai oyobi Seishaho*) was issued by the Meiji government. It was one of a series of measures taken by Meiji oligarchs as a result of their concern about the rise of pro-democratic political parties and social groups centered on the Freedom and Popular Rights Movement. For the first time, the law explicitly prohibited women from engaging in any political activity, including holding or attending public meetings in which political discussion occurred, or from joining a political party.

Since the inception of the Freedom and Popular Rights Movement, which started in the mid-1870s and reached its peak around 1880, oligarchs had been hostile to this pro-democratic movement. Their desire to suppress pro-democratic momentum resulted in a series of regulations on public meetings and associations issued in the 1870s and the 1880s. One of the earlier countermeasures was the Assembly Ordinance (*Shukai Jorei*) of 1880, which required police permission for public assemblies and allowed discussion only of preapproved topics. Although the Assembly Ordinance prohibited police officers, teachers, and students from attending political meetings or joining political parties, it did not single out women as a category or prevent women from engaging in such activities. As a result, in the 1880s, women who were influenced by democratic ideals joined the Freedom and Popular Rights Movement and pressed for equal rights for women.

In October 1881, the government was pressured by pro-democratic forces within the government and society into issuing a rescript (*Kokkai Kaisetsu no Mikotonori*), promising the opening of the Meiji Parliament in 1890. On July 1, 1890, Japan's first national election was held, and liberal political parties secured the great majority of seats in the House of Representatives. Perceiving that it was just a matter of time before political parties would dominate the House, soon after the election, on July 25, the oligarchs passed the Law on Assembly and Political Association to impose even more stringent regulations on political parties and assemblies.

The law was largely based on the Assembly Ordinance and prescribed the same provisions, such as a mandatory police permit for any political meetings (clause 2) and a total ban on outdoor gatherings for political purposes (clause 6). Clause 28 stated that it was also prohibited for political parties to publicly advertise their public meetings or coordinate with other political parties. Unlike the previous measures, however, the law required police permits for outdoor meetings that were not political in nature (clause 7). In addition, Clause 8 stated that, while the Diet was in session, a public meeting or mass movement activity could not be held within approximately 12 kilometers from the Parliament. These provisions indicate that the government was concerned about the possibility that even public meetings of a non-political nature could be used for political purposes.

Another major provision that differentiated the law from the Assembly Ordinance is clause 4, which explicitly prohibited women, along with teachers and students, from participating in public assembly for political purposes. Clause 25 prevented women from joining political parties.

Likewise, clauses 5 and 26 prohibited foreigners from participating in political meetings as discussants and joining political parties, respectively. Clause 27 prohibited political parties from using emblems, flags, or banners. Many of these provisions were carried over in the Public Peace Police Law of 1900.

*Hiroyuki Yamamoto*

**See also:** Jiyu Minken Undo; Meiji Constitution.

### Further Reading

Garon, Sheldon. *Molding Japanese Minds: The State in Everyday Life*. Princeton: Princeton University Press, 1997.

Mackie, Vera. *Creating Socialist Women in Japan: Gender, Labour, and Activism, 1900–1937*. Cambridge, UK: Cambridge University Press, 1997.

Matsuo, Takayoshi. "The Development of Democracy in Japan—Taishō Democracy: Its Flowering and Breakdown." *Developing Economies* 4, no. 4 (December 1996): 612–637.

## League of Nations, Mandates

The League of Nations' Mandates System emerged in 1919 to cope with colonial and semicolonial territories held by German and Ottoman Empires at the time of World War I (1914–1918). Many of these territories had fallen directly under the control of Allied armies during the war. In calculating their disposition in the postwar era, Allied negotiators felt compelled to follow the general spirit of U.S. President Woodrow Wilson's claim that U.S. armies fought for "peace without victory" and not to endorse the territorial ambitions of European and Japanese colonial empires. In his famous Fourteen Points, Wilson declared that the "interests of [colonial] populations concerned must have

equal weight" with the imperial ambitions of the Allied states.

Established by the Treaty of Versailles, the Mandates System was formulated and overseen by the Permanent Mandates Commission, an agency of the League of Nations. The territories designated as mandates covered a wide variety of cultures and geographical zones, mostly in Africa and the Middle East. Although the collective goal of the Mandates System was to put occupied territories on a path to independence, the territories came under the direct supervision of established colonial powers.

Japan's participation in the Mandates System derived from the Japanese navy's occupation of German possessions in Micronesia in 1914. Japanese diplomats hoped to gain unambiguous political control over the territories at the Paris Peace Conference in 1919. Given Australian and American designs on the same territories, Japan's grudging acceptance of mandatory authority over these territories ultimately served Japan's strategic interests well.

The lands incorporated into the "South Seas Mandate" included islands and atolls spread across the Pacific island groups principally known as the Marshalls, Carolines, Marianas, and Palaus. The Mandates Commission deemed these territories to be of "low cultural, economic and political development" and, therefore, unprepared for full independence in a predatory world of large imperial states. Thus Japan received a "Class C" mandate for all German-controlled islands north of the equator and collectively ruled them under a single administrative body known as the Nan'yô (South Seas) Bureau. Under Class C status, Japan was permitted to subject the territories to direct rule of its domestic legal system and control was turned over to civilian authorities in 1922.

In accepting the mandate, mandatory powers agreed that "the well-being and development of such peoples form a sacred trust of civilisation" and that the powers labored on behalf of the League of Nations. Japan was obligated to report regularly to the Commission on progress in the islands.

Although Japan's reports projected rosy images of progress in the islands, the experience of Micronesia under Japanese mandate was little different from the experience of comparable Class C mandates under European control. While Class A mandates in the Middle East soon achieved some form of political independence, colonial powers were quick to integrate Class C mandates into established patterns of colonial control. For Micronesia, these patterns included immigration of Japanese nationals, often from economically depressed regions of the Japanese islands, notably Okinawa. Most of the population growth in Micronesia during the mandate period derived from this Japanese influx.

Whatever Japan's ambitions toward humane and progressively minded administration, it is hard to argue that the mandate was ruled in any way other than by and for Japanese interests. Japanese dominated economic activities on the islands. Japanese trading companies, often drawing on government support, took the lead in developing trade in tropical products, such as sugar cane, a commodity increasingly in demand in affluent Japan. Natural resources, notably phosphates, were exploited by Japanese mining companies for Japanese benefit. Japan sought to improve education on the islands, but schools were segregated, with schooling for Japanese residents being of longer duration than that of the local populace. In the face of these forces, indigenous populations declined in some areas.

The South Seas Mandate also fueled Japanese imagination about the nation and its place in Asia. The image of the South Seas as a tropical land populated by culturally distinctive "primitive" people attracted the interest of Japanese writers and social scientists. For military planners and free-wheeling expansionists, the South Seas fit into their vision of a "southward advance" of Japanese national power and cultural influence.

This position in "southern advance" ideology would ultimately have a profound effect on the course of the mandate. As part of the Washington Naval Treaty of 1922, Japan agreed not to build new naval and air stations on the islands. Despite Japanese and American recognition of the potential strategic value of a string of islands across the central Pacific, direct military preparations in the mandate did not begin until the late 1930s. These developments ensured that the mandate would become a central battleground in the Pacific Theater of World War II.

After the war, Japan's South Seas Mandate was replaced by United States' control of the area under the United Nations Trusteeship system. Most of the islands subsequently attained status as independent states.

*Michael A. Schneider*

**See also:** Versailles Treaty; World War II, Pacific Theater.

### Further Reading

Burkman, Thomas. *Japan and the League of Nations, Empire and World Order, 1914–1938*. Honolulu: University of Hawaii, 2008.

Peattie, Mark R. *The Nan'yō: The Rise and Fall of the Japanese in Micronesia, 1885–1945*. Honolulu: University of Hawaii Press, 1988.

Tadao, Yanaihara. *Pacific Islands under Japanese Mandate*. London: Oxford University Press, 1940.

## Leyte Gulf, Battle of (October 23–26, 1944)

The Battle of Leyte Gulf resulted from U.S. President Franklin D. Roosevelt's decision to follow the conquest of the Mariana Islands with the recapture of the Philippines. This idea was proposed by the commander of Southwest Pacific Forces, General Douglas MacArthur; the chief of naval operations, Ernest J. King, wanted to land on Formosa instead. The latter move made sound military sense, the former political sense.

On October 20, the U.S. 6th Army began an invasion of Leyte, with more than 132,000 men going ashore the first day. Warned by the preliminary bombardment, the Japanese put into effect their overly complicated contingency plan. The Naval General Staff in Tokyo had issued a directive for the Combined Fleet to seize the initiative "to crush the enemy fleet and attacking forces." The initial Japanese operation *Shō ichi-gō* (Operation Victory One) covered defense of the Philippine Archipelago, to which the Japanese decided to commit the entire Combined Fleet. The Combined Fleet commander, Admiral Toyoda Soemu, knew that should the Americans retake the Philippines, they would be in a position to cut Japan's access to oil from the Netherlands East Indies.

Prior to the battle, Japanese naval air strength had been severely reduced in the June 1944 Battle of the Philippine Sea ("the great Marianas turkey shoot"), and between October 12 and 14, U.S. carrier planes and army B-29 bombers struck Japanese airfields on Formosa, Okinawa, and the Philippines. These strikes denied the Japanese navy badly needed land-based air support and, by themselves, doomed the Japanese plan. The Japanese did add extra antiaircraft guns to their ships in an attempt to offset the lack of aircraft, but from an offensive standpoint they had to rely on naval gunnery and some 335 land-based planes in the Luzon area.

The Japanese plan was to destroy sufficient U.S. shipping to break up the Leyte amphibious landing. The Japanese attack included four prongs. A decoy force would draw U.S. naval covering forces north, while two elements struck from the west on either side of Leyte, to converge simultaneously on the landing area in Leyte Gulf and destroy Allied shipping there. At the same time, shore-based aircraft were to attack U.S. naval forces offshore.

On October 17, on receiving information that U.S. warships were off Suhuan Island, Toyoda alerted his forces. Logistical difficulties delayed the attack to October 25. Vice Admiral Ozawa Jisaburo's decoy Northern Force (3rd Fleet) consisted of the heavy carrier *Zuikaku*, three light carriers, two hybrid battleship-carriers, three cruisers, and eight destroyers. Ozawa had only 116 aircraft, flown by poorly trained pilots. His force sortied from Japan on October 20, and on the evening of October 22, it turned south toward Luzon. Japanese submarines off Formosa were ordered south toward the eastern approaches to the Philippine Archipelago, and shortly before October 23, what remained of the Japanese 2nd Air Fleet began to arrive on the island of Luzon.

The strongest element of the Japanese attack was the 1st Diversion Attack Force; on October 20, it refueled and split into two parts. The Center Force under Admiral Kurita Takeo included the giant battleships *Musashi* and *Yamato* with their 18.1-inch guns; Kurita also had three older battleships, 12 cruisers, and 15 destroyers. Center Force sailed northeastward, up the west coast

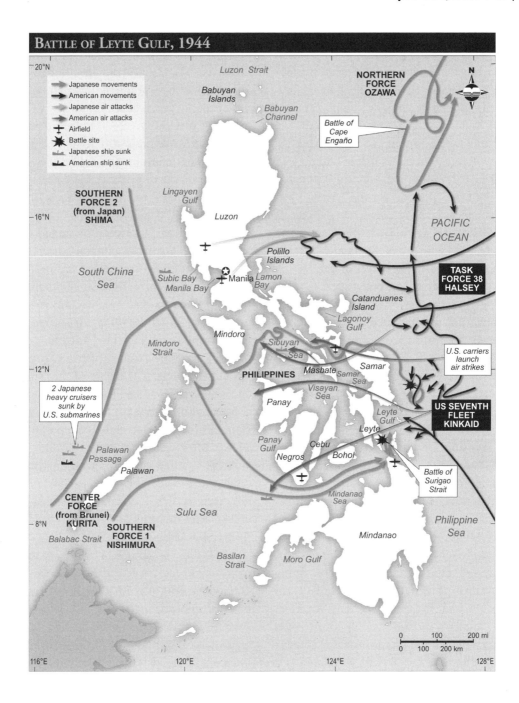

**BATTLE OF LEYTE GULF, 1944**

Japanese movements
American movements
Japanese air attacks
American air attacks
Airfield
Battle site
Japanese ship sunk
American ship sunk

20°N

Luzon Strait

NORTHERN FORCE OZAWA

N

Babuyan Islands

Babuyan Channel

Battle of Cape Engaño

SOUTHERN FORCE 2 (from Japan) SHIMA

Lingayen Gulf

16°N

Luzon

PACIFIC OCEAN

TASK FORCE 38 HALSEY

South China Sea

Subic Bay
Manila Bay

Manila

Lamon Bay

Polillo Islands

Catanduanes Island

Lagonoy Gulf

Mindoro

Mindoro Strait

Sibuyan Sea

Samar

U.S. carriers launch air strikes

12°N

2 Japanese heavy cruisers sunk by U.S. submarines

PHILIPPINES

Masbate

Samar Sea

Visayan Sea

Panay

Leyte Gulf

Leyte

US SEVENTH FLEET KINKAID

Palawan Passage

Panay Gulf

Cebu

Bohol

Negros

Palawan

Battle of Surigao Strait

CENTER FORCE (from Brunei) KURITA

Sulu Sea

Mindanao Sea

Philippine Sea

8°N

Balabac Strait

SOUTHERN FORCE 1 NISHIMURA

Basilan Strait

Moro Gulf

Mindanao

0     100     200 mi
0   100   200 km

116°E          120°E          124°E          128°E

of Palawan Island, and then turned eastward through the waters of the central Philippines to San Bernardino Strait. Meanwhile, the Southern Force (C Force) of two battleships, one heavy cruiser, and four destroyers, commanded by Vice Admiral Nishimura Shoji, struck eastward through the Sulu Sea in an effort to force its way through Surigao Strait between the islands of Mindanao and Leyte. The Southern Force was trailed by Vice Admiral Shima Kiyohide's 2nd Diversion Attack Force, which included two heavy cruisers, one light cruiser, and four destroyers. Shima's warships left the Pescadores on October 21, steamed south past western Luzon, and refueled in the Calamian Islands. Late in joining Nishimura's ships, Shima's force followed them into Surigao Strait.

Opposing the Japanese were two U.S. Navy fleets: Vice Admiral Thomas C. Kinkaid's 7th Fleet and Admiral William F. Halsey's 3rd Fleet, under the Pacific Fleet commander, Admiral Chester W. Nimitz, at Pearl Harbor. Leyte was the first landing to involve two entire U.S. fleets and also the first without a unified command, which would have unfortunate consequences.

The 7th Fleet was divided into three task groups. The first consisted of Rear Admiral Jesse B. Oldendorf's 6 old battleships, 16 escort carriers, 4 heavy cruisers, 4 light cruisers, 30 destroyers, and 10 destroyer escorts. The other two elements were amphibious task groups carrying out the actual invasion. The 7th Fleet had escorted the invasion force to Leyte and now provided broad protection for the entire landing area. As most of Halsey's amphibious assets had been loaned to Kinkaid, the 3rd Fleet consisted almost entirely of Vice Admiral Marc Mitscher's Task Force (TF) 38 of 14 fast carriers, with more than 1,000 aircraft, organized into four task groups containing 6 battleships, 8 heavy cruisers, 13 light cruisers, and 57 destroyers. The 3rd Fleet had the job of securing air superiority over the Philippines and protecting the landings.

The Battle of Leyte Gulf was actually a series of battles, the first of which was the October 23–24 Battle of the Sibuyan Sea. Early on October 23, the U.S. submarines *Darter* and *Dace* discovered Kurita's Center Force entering the Palawan Passage from the South China Sea, and they alerted Admiral Halsey, whose 3rd Fleet guarded San Bernardino Strait. The submarines sank two

Japanese heavy cruisers, the *Atago* (Kurita's flagship) and the *Maya*, and damaged a third. Kurita transferred his flag to the *Yamato*, and his force continued east into the Sibuyan Sea where, beginning in the morning of October 24, TF 38 launched five air strikes against it. The first wave of carrier planes concentrated on the *Musashi*, which absorbed 19 torpedoes and nearly as many bombs before sinking, taking down half of its 2,200-man crew. Several other Japanese ships were also damaged. On October 25, American pilots reported that Kurita had reversed course and was heading west; Halsey incorrectly assumed that this part of the battle was over. He did issue a preliminary order detailing a battle line of battleships known as TF 34, to be commanded by Vice Admiral Willis A. Lee. Admiral Kinkaid was aware of that signal and assumed TF 34 had been established.

Meanwhile, Japanese land-based planes from the 2nd Air Fleet attacked a portion of TF 38. Most were shot down, but they did sink the light carrier *Princeton* and badly damaged the cruiser *Birmingham*. Also, unknown to Halsey, Kurita's force changed course after nightfall and resumed heading for San Bernardino Strait.

Warned of the approach of the Japanese Combined Fleet, Admiral Kinkaid placed Oldendorf's six old 7th Fleet fire-support battleships (all but one a veteran of the Pearl Harbor attack), flanked by eight cruisers, across the mouth of Surigao Strait to intercept it. He also lined the strait with 39 patrol torpedo (PT) boats and 28 destroyers. In terms of naval warfare, the October 24–25 Battle of Surigao Strait was a classic case of "crossing the t." The PT boats discovered the Japanese moving in line-ahead formation, but Nishimura's force easily beat them back. Although the battleships often get the credit for the Surigao Strait victory, it was U.S. destroyers that inflicted most of the damage. Their converging torpedo attacks sank the battleship *Fuso* and three destroyers. The Japanese then ran into the line of Oldendorf's battleships, which sank all the Japanese warships save the destroyer *Shigure*. Nishimura went down with his flagship, the battleship *Yamashiro*.

Shima's force, bringing up the rear, then came under attack by the PT boats, which crippled a light cruiser. Shima's flagship collided with one of Nishimura's sinking vessels. Oldendorf's ships pursued the retreating Japanese. Another Japanese cruiser succumbed to attacks by land-based planes and those of Admiral Thomas L. Sprague's escort carriers. The rest of Shima's force escaped when Oldendorf, knowing his ships might be needed later, turned back. The battle was over by 4:30 a.m. on October 25.

Meanwhile, during the night of October 24–25, Kurita's force moved through San Bernardino Strait, issued from it unopposed, and turned south. In the most controversial aspect of the battle, Halsey left San Bernardino Strait unprotected near midnight to rush with all available units of the 3rd Fleet after Ozawa's decoy fleet, which had been sighted far to the north. Several of Halsey's subordinates registered reservations about his decision, but he would not be deterred. Compounding the error, Halsey failed to inform Admiral Kinkaid, who, in any case, assumed TF 34 was protecting the strait. Halsey's decision left the landing beaches guarded only by the 7th Fleet's Taffy 3 escort carrier group, commanded by Rear Admiral Clifton A. F. Sprague. It was one of three such support groups operating off Samar. Sprague had six small escort carriers, three destroyers, and four destroyer escorts.

Fighting off Samar erupted about 6:30 a.m. on October 24, as Taffy 3 found itself

opposing Kurita's four battleships (including the *Yamato*), six heavy cruisers, and 10 destroyers. The aircraft from all three of the Taffy groups now attacked the Japanese. Unfortunately, the planes carried fragmentation bombs for use against land targets; nevertheless, they put up a strong fight, harassing the powerful Japanese warships. Sprague's destroyers and destroyer escorts also joined the fight. Their crews courageously attacked the much more powerful Japanese warships, launching torpedoes and laying smoke to try to obscure the escort carriers. These combined attacks forced several Japanese cruisers to drop out of the battle.

Kurita now lost his nerve. By 9:10 a.m., his warships had sunk the *Gambier Bay*, the only U.S. carrier ever lost to gunfire, as well as the destroyers *Hoel* and *Johnston* and the destroyer escort *Samuel B. Roberts*. But Kurita believed he was under attack by aircraft from TF 38, and at 9:11 a.m., just at the point when he might have achieved a crushing victory, he ordered his forces to break off the attack, his decision strengthened by news that the southern attacking force had been destroyed. Kurita then exited through San Bernardino Strait. The four ships lost by Taffy 3 were the only U.S. warships sunk by Japanese surface ships in the entire battle.

At 9:40 p.m., Kurita's ships reentered San Bernardino Strait. As the Japanese withdrew, they came under attack by aircraft from Vice Admiral John S. McCain's task force from Halsey's fleet, losing a destroyer. Meanwhile, Sprague's escort carriers and Oldendorf's force returning from the Battle of Surigao Strait came under attack from land-based kamikaze aircraft, the first such attacks of the war. These attacks sank the escort carrier *St. Lô* and damaged several other ships.

At about 2:20 a.m. on October 25, Mitscher's search planes, from Halsey's force, located Ozawa's northern decoy force. In the Battle of Cape Engaño, Ozawa sent most of his planes ashore to operate from bases there; thus he had only antiaircraft fire with which to oppose the attack. While engaged against Ozawa, Halsey learned of the action off Samar when a signal came in from Kinkaid at 8:22 a.m., followed by an urgent request 8 minutes later for fast battleships. Finally, at 8:48 a.m., Halsey ordered McCain's TG 38.1 to make "best possible speed" to engage Kurita's Center Force. The task group was en route from the Ulithi to rejoin the other elements of TF 38. Because it had more carriers and planes than any of the three other task groups in Halsey's force, it made good sense to detach this unit.

At 10:55 a.m., Halsey ordered all six fast battleships and TG 38.2 to turn south and steam at flank speed, but they missed the battle. After the war, Kurita admitted his error in judgment; Halsey never did. In fact, Halsey said his decision to send the battleships south to Samar was "the greatest error I committed during the Battle of Leyte Gulf."

By nightfall, U.S. aircraft, a submarine, and surface ships had sunk all four Japanese carriers of Ozawa's force, as well as five other ships. This blow ended Japanese carrier aviation. The battle of annihilation that would have been possible with the fast battleships had eluded Halsey, yet, of Ozawa's force, only two battleships, two light cruisers, and a destroyer escaped.

Japanese losses in the Battle of Leyte Gulf came to 29 warships (4 carriers, 3 battleships, 6 heavy and 4 light cruisers, 11 destroyers, and 1 submarine) and more than 500 aircraft; in addition, some 10,500 seamen and aviators were killed. The U.S. Navy lost only 6 ships (1 light carrier, 2 escort carriers, 2 destroyers, and 1 destroyer escort) and more than 200 aircraft. About 2,800 Americans were killed, and another 1,000 were wounded. The Battle of Leyte Gulf ended the prospects for the Japanese fleet as an organized fighting force.

*Spencer C. Tucker*

**See also:** Macarthur, Douglas; World War II, Pacific Theater.

**Further Reading**

Cutler, Thomas J. *The Battle of Leyte Gulf, 23–26 October 1944*. New York: Harper Collins, 1994.

Field, James A., Jr. *The Japanese at Leyte Gulf: The Shō Operation*. Princeton, NJ: Princeton University Press, 1947.

Morison, Samuel Eliot. *History of United States Naval Operations in World War II. Vol. 12: Leyte*. Boston: Little, Brown, 1975.

## London Naval Conference

The London Naval Conferences of 1930 and 1935 were attended by the major naval powers of the world for the purpose of revisiting and adjusting the treaties signed at the Washington Naval Conference of 1921–1922. Although several important changes in international agreements took place in London, in the context of our present volume, the significance of these events lies in the fact that the 1930 conference threw into stark relief the dual power structure of the Japanese military. The controversy ignited by the 1930 conference marked the beginning of the end of the party governments in early Shōwa Japan. Nationalist activists would invoke the issues raised by the London Naval Treaty time and time again, as high-profile assassinations of politicians and the end of the party cabinet severely challenged the stability of the government in the years that followed.

The conference of 1930 sought to update the Washington System established by the Washington Conference Treaties of 1921 and 1922. Although the signers of the Washington Five Power Treaty agreed to limitations in the sizes of their respective navies, it soon became apparent that the treaty contained loopholes that could be exploited, most notably in the category of ships not restricted by the treaty. Under the London Naval Treaty, "auxiliary" crafts such as light cruisers and submarines, which had gone through major technological innovations since the Washington Treaties, were also included in the restrictions. Furthermore, the tonnage ratio was renegotiated, setting the ratio of heavy cruisers between the United States and Japan at 10:7, with the understanding that the ratio would than return to 5:3, the ratio set in Washington, by 1936 with the building of additional American ships.

Although the Minseitô administration led by Prime Minister Hamaguchi Osachi succeeded in securing the support of the Ministry of Navy in signing the treaty, the Navy General Staff, then headed by Katô Kanji, refused to grant its support. Many in the Japanese navy had hopes of raising the Japanese end of the ratio so that the country could achieve parity with the United States, arguing that this was crucial to Japan's national security and prestige. Facing a domestic fiscal crisis, the Hamaguchi administration was more interested in curbing military expenditures. Katô Kanji, who had battled with Katô Tomosaburô over this issue during the Washington Naval Treaty, was especially adamant about the need for better terms, and the split that had occurred between the "administrative" Ministry of Navy and the "fleet faction" of the Naval General Staff in Washington developed into a standoff.

Crucially, the minority party, the Seiyûkai, and various nationalist activists interpreted this split between the two navy factions as a constitutional issue that highlighted the Minseitô government's usurpation of Imperial authority. Under this interpretation, the Hamaguchi cabinet had no authority to sign the London Naval Treaty because the emperor's duty as supreme commander of determining the size and contents of the navy was delegated to the General Staff, which was independent of the Ministry of Navy and, therefore, of the cabinet. In other words, these parties argued that it was outside the jurisdiction of the Ministry of the Navy to authorize the Hamaguchi government's acceptance of the London Naval Treaty. Using this logic, enemies of the Minseitô government were able to argue that Hamaguchi had usurped the emperor's authority to manage the Imperial Navy out of his own political interests. What these arguments often failed to mention was the fact that the Privy Council had ratified the signing of London Naval Treaty, signifying the fact that it quite literally had the emperor's stamp of approval.

The political fallout from the signing of the London Naval Treaty was immense. Soon after, Prime Minister Hamaguchi was attacked by a nationalist activist; he died from his wounds five months later. Attacks upon party politicians and political liberalist would continue throughout the decade, marking a decisive end to the rule of party cabinets until after the war period. Furthermore, the much-publicized uproar against the 1930 signing of the London Naval Treaty signified the beginning of Japan's retreat from the Washington system. At the 1935 meeting of the London Naval Conference, the delegates from Japan were more forceful about the issue of naval parity, ultimately deciding to withdraw from the treaty system altogether.

*John D. Person*

**See also:** Party Cabinets; Rightwing Politics in Japan; Washington Naval Conference.

### Further Reading

Goldman, Emily O. *Sunken Treaties: Naval Arms Control between the Wars*. University Park: Pennsylvania University Press, 1994.

Iriye, Akira. *The Origins of the Second World War in Asia and the Pacific*. London: Longman, 1987.

Kobayashi, Tatsuo. "The London Naval Treaty, 1930," in *Japan Erupts: The London Naval Treaty and the Manchurian Incident, 1928–1932*, edited by James William Morley. New York: Columbia University Press, 1984:12–25.

O'Connor, Raymond G. *Perilous Equilibrium: The United States and the London Naval Conference of 1930*. Lawrence: University of Kansas Press, 1962.

## Loyalist Verse (*Shishi-gin*)

Strictly speaking, "loyalist verse" refers to various traditional genres of patriotic poetry written by loyalists of the Bakumatsu period, but it was also part of a broader current of ultra-nationalist writing that both preceded and survived the waning years of the shōgunate.

Traditional poetry in Japan could be most broadly categorized by language—Chinese and Japanese—both of which include many examples of loyalist verse. Chinese poems were written in lines of five or seven characters employing various schemes of rhyme, while the most common Japanese form, the *tanka*, consisted of only 31 syllables in lines of five and seven. Throughout most of Japan's literary history, the dominant mode in all forms had been one of lyricism—for the most part limited to topics of love, nature, and felicitation. Although verses praising the emperor are found in the earliest collections, poems charged with patriotic zeal had been unusual. Beginning with the late 18th century, not unlike many other cultural institutions, poetry was often appropriated to suit nationalist and even militarist ends. The "loyalists" (*shishi*) were united both by fervent devotion to the emperor and his rightful rule, and by contempt for anything that was seen as obstructing that right—most often the shōgunate. The rise of loyalist verse coincided with the availability through nativist scholarship of authoritative poetic models predating the dominance of lyricism, the growing perception of a foreign threat and the weakness of the shōgunate in responding to it, and calls from the court to "expel the barbarians." Within this environment, in the minds of the loyalists the emperor came to represent the Japanese spirit against foreign lands, especially the West.

Although it might be argued that many of the loyalists possessed more ardor than literary talent, they, along with most poets of a nativist stripe, were conscious of precedent and looked to ancient models for both diction and imagery. One frequently cited model was the third Kamakura shōgun, Minamoto no Sanetomo (1192–1219), who wrote such verses as the following: "Even were it a world / where mountains split asunder / and seas evaporate, / could my fealty to my sovereign / ever be divided?" (*Yama wa sake / umi wa asenamu / yo nari tomo / kimi ni futago-koro / waga arame yamo*).

Of the themes found in loyalist verse, the most common is apotheosis of the emperor and declarations of allegiance to him, as in this verse by Sakura Azumao (1811–1860): "Even in taking up / chopsticks to eat my meal, / at the thought / of his majesty's great blessings, / tears fill my eyes" (*Ii kuu to / hashi o toru ni mo / waga kimi no / ōmime-gumi / namida shi nagaru*). The famous

Chōshū loyalist Takasugi Shinsaku (1839–1867) expressed similar sentiments: "Of my mind, / completely given to my Lord, / I shall make a gem, / while my body, broken and crushed, / is but a piece of tile" (*Kimi no tame / tsukusu kokoro wa / tama to nashi / kudaku waga mi wa / kawara narikeri*).

Another common theme was defiance of foreign powers, as in these verses by Yoshida Shōin (1830–1959): "Though Yankee villains / in league with Europe / appear on our coasts, / if we are but prepared / what need have we to fear?" (*Abokuto ga / Yōra o yakushi / kitaru tomo / sonae no araba / nani ka osoren*); "By 'prepared' / I do not speak / of warships and cannons, / but of the Yamato spirit / unique to our blessed land" (*Sonae to wa / kan to hō to no / iinarazu / waga Shikishima no / yamatodamashii*).

Several events during the 1850s and 1860s solidified the identity of loyalists and gave impetus to their cause. The first major one was the Ansei Purge, conducted between 1858 and 1859, during which many loyalists were arrested. One who was executed, Rai Mikisaburō (1825–1859), remained defiant in one of his last verses: "My crime is this: / evidence / that my true feelings / for his majesty's reign / were not sufficiently deep" (*Waga tsumi wa / kimigayo omou / magkokoro no / fukakarazarishi / shirushi narikeri*). Another defining event was the Sakuradamon Incident of 1860, which resulted in the assassination of the Minister Ii Naosuke (1815–1860) by masterless samurai who saw him as having sold out to Western powers. One of the participants in the raid, Saitō Kenmotsu (1822–1860), evoked a historical incident to express his loyalist sentiments. In a poem in Chinese commemorating the unsuccessful attempt of a devoted retainer, Kojima Takanori, to rescue the exiled Emperor Godaigo (1288–1339; reign 1318–1339), he wrote: "Traversing myriad mountains and peaks shrouded in clouds, / Where will the imperial palanquin pass today? / With no gear but a straw raincoat I enter wild beasts' dens, / With but a single dagger I search out the abyss with its ferocious sea creatures. / But my patriotic fervor is greater than my lone strength, / And my undertaking to save the land proves fruitless. / Tears of vexation falling in streams become two columns of characters / Which I carve into a cherry trunk, an appeal to the heavens." There was also the Hamaguri Gate Rebellion (also known as the Kinmon Rebellion) of 1864, in which a body of anti-alien samurai—most from Chōshū—attempted unsuccessfully to take control of the imperial palace and force an edict of expulsion. One of the Chōshū samurai, Kusaka Genzui (1840–1864), expressed his zeal in the following Chinese verse: "Let the renown of our imperial land resound abroad; / For who could permit an alliance between court and traitor? / Our appeal to the former: give us the imperial sword / That we may cut down the shōgun to answer his majesty's virtue."

Although the popular image of the loyalist is that of a samurai—perhaps a *rōnin*—in reality those people who wrote patriotic verse and who came to be referred to as *shishi* reflected a diversity of backgrounds. Many noteworthy women poets emerged, among them the nun Nomura Bōtō (1806–1867), who was eventually imprisoned for her loyalist activities. She addressed this verse to young women: "If she but intently treads / a straightforward path, / then will even a delicate woman / be at all inferior / to a manly man?" (*Hitosuji no / michi o mamoraba / taoyame mo / masuraonoko ni / otori ya wa suru*). Like other women in the loyalist movement, Nomura sometimes played the role of peacemaker among factions of warriors: "These quarrels / among fellow warriors— / let us tone them down / and show the barbarians this: / the Yamato spirit" (*Mononofu no / tomoarasoi o / yawaragete / emishi ni miseyo / yamatodamashii*). One noteworthy loyalist from a peasant background was Matsuo Taseko (1811–1894), who described her audience at court in 1863 with the following lines: "Is this a spring night's dream? / Or is it reality?— / That on this day / such heavenly finery / should grace a low-born woman" (*Haru no yo no / yume ka utsutsu ka / shizu no me no / kumoi o kakeru / kyō no yosoi wa*). In addition, nativist poets from merchant-class backgrounds created verses that both inspired and were inspired by the loyalist cause. No doubt the best known of these is Tachibana Akemi (1812–1868), who was noted for such verses as the following: "It is a pleasure when, / in an age gone whoring / after things foreign, I see a man who has not / forgotten our divine land" (*Tanoshimi wa / emishi yorokobu / yo no naka ni / mi-kuni wasurenu / hito o miru toki*). Banbayashi Mitsuhira (1813–1864), the son of a Pure Land Buddhist priest, is also counted among the loyalists: "The barbarians / who, it is said, will arrive / in the spring— / would that I could show them / full cherry blossoms of his majesty's reign" (*Haru kakete / komu to iikemu / emishira ni / misebaya miyo no / hana no sakari o*).

The loyalists were a Bakumatsu phenomenon, but their legacy—including their poetry—continued through the Pacific phase of World War II. From *Junnan zenshū* ("Martyrdom: A Complete Collection") published in the second year of Meiji through the highly influential *Aikoku hyakunin isshu* ("One Hundred Patriotic Poets, One Verse Each") selected by Japan's literary luminaries and published in 1942, anthologies of patriotic verse were numerous, and the loyalists of the Bakumatsu always figured prominently among them.

*Roger K. Thomas*

**See also:** Go-Daigo; Ii Naosuke; Sakuradomon Incident; Yoshida Shōin.

**Further Reading**

Fujita Tokutarō. *Shishi shiikashū*. Tokyo: Shōgakkan, 1942.

Kuroiwa Ichirō. *Kinnō shishi shiikashū*. Tokyo: Shibundō, 1943.

Tanaka Takashi. *Ishin no uta: Bakumatsu sonnō shishi no zesshō*. Tokyo: Nihon Kyōbunsha, 1974.

Totman, Conrad D. *Early Modern Japan*. Berkeley: University of California, 1993.

Walthall, Anne. *The Weak Body of a Useless Woman: Matsuo Taseko and the Meiji Restoration*. Chicago: University of Chicago Press, 1998.

**Lytton Report.** *See* Mukden Incident: Lytton Report.

# MacArthur, Douglas (1880–1964)

Douglas MacArthur was born on January 26, 1880, at an army post near Little Rock, Arkansas; his father was General Arthur MacArthur, the U.S. Army's highest-ranking officer from 1906 to 1909. In 1903, the younger MacArthur graduated from West Point and then served as an engineering officer in the United States, the Philippines, and Panama. In 1913, he began a four-year stint at the War Department General Staff. After the United States declared war on Germany, MacArthur went to France to fight with the 42nd Division in the Champagne-Marne, St. Mihiel, and Meuse-Argonne operations. From 1919 to 1922, Brigadier General MacArthur was superintendent at West Point before serving two command tours in the Philippines. Promoted to general, he became U.S. Army Chief of Staff in 1930.

In 1935, MacArthur accepted a position as military adviser to the Philippine government, organizing Filipino defense forces over the next six years. In July 1941, the U.S. government recalled him to active duty and named him commander of U.S. Army Forces in East Asia. After Japan attacked Pearl Harbor, MacArthur commanded the defense of the Philippines, before fleeing to Australia in March 1942. He then supervised Allied military operations in the Southwest Pacific. Promoted in late 1944 to General of the Army, he became commander of U.S. Army Forces in the Pacific in April 1945 and then Supreme Commander for the Allied Powers (SCAP)

in August, in which position he accepted Japan's surrender and supervised the occupation of that country. Though at times autocratic, MacArthur efficiently enacted a series of political, economic, and social reforms that eliminated militarist, ultranationalist, and feudal habits before implementing the "reverse course" that transformed Japan into a Cold War security partner of the United States.

MacArthur, in his capacity as SCAP, presided nominally over the U.S. occupation of Korea. He rarely played a direct role in determining policy there, but was a consistent advocate of early U.S. military withdrawal. Never enthusiastic about the Harry S Truman administration's efforts to provide military and economic aid to South Korea, MacArthur outlined a strategy in 1949 excluding it from guarantees of U.S. protection. That same year, he lobbied vigorously for a U.S. defense commitment to Jiang Jieshi (Ch'iang K'ai-shek) after the Chinese Communists forced his flight to Taiwan. When North Korea attacked South Korea in June 1950, President Truman committed ground troops in response to MacArthur's recommendation. Named head of the United Nations Command, MacArthur pressed for the full use of U.S. military power in the conflict. After his Inchon landing succeeded in September 1950, he enthusiastically supported the administration's decision to destroy North Korea. By then, however, his relations with Truman were strained because of his pressure for stronger action to help the Chinese Nationalists topple the People's Republic of China (PRC).

During October 1950, as UN forces pushed northward, MacArthur downplayed the danger of Chinese intervention. At the Wake Island Conference, he assured Truman that the PRC's threat was a "bluff" and, even if carried out, would not impede achievement of U.S. war aims. After China's massive offensive in late November, MacArthur blamed the retreat and other battlefield problems on restrictions against attacking China, while rejecting the wisdom or feasibility of seeking an armistice. In March 1951, the front stabilized near the prewar border. Informed of Truman's impending ceasefire initiative, MacArthur torpedoed it when he issued a public demand that Chinese forces surrender or face attacks upon their homeland. Then came release of his letter to a congressman characterizing administration policy in Korea as appeasement. It was, however, Truman's plans to deploy atomic weapons for possible use in Korea that prompted his recall of MacArthur on April 11, 1951.

Politically ambitious, MacArthur had already increased Cold War tensions when he sought the Republican presidential nomination in 1948. After Truman fired him, he looked toward vindication and took his case directly to the U.S. public. Despite broad popular affection for the general as a war hero and frustration regarding Korea, neither average citizens nor most civilian and military officials favored a wider war. During the U.S. Senate's investigation of MacArthur's firing, the Joint Chiefs of Staff voiced opposition to his plan to escalate the war. In 1952, when the American people elected a general as president, it would not be MacArthur, but rather Dwight D. Eisenhower. MacArthur then dropped out of public life, making occasional public appearances. He died at Walter Reed Medical Center in Washington, D.C., on April 5, 1964.

*James I. Matray*

**See also:** Korean War; Occupation of Japan; Pearl Harbor, Attack on.

## Further Reading

Finkelstein, Norman. *The Emperor General: A Biography of Douglas MacArthur.* Bloomington, IN: AuthorHouse, 2001.

Perret, Geoffrey. *Old Soldiers Never Die: The Life of Douglas Macarthur.* Cincinnati, OH: Adams Media Corporation, 1997.

## Malaya Campaign (1941–1942)

Following World War I, the British government decided to develop Singapore into a large naval base, intended to defend against Japanese expansionism. Construction was slowed by the exigencies of the worldwide depression and was never completed. During the 1930s, the British built a series of airfields on the peninsula in the belief that Singapore and Malaya could best be defended from the air. Malaya's wartime population was approximately 5.5 million people, of whom only 2.3 million were indigenous Malay. The remainder were Chinese (2.4 million), Indians (750,000), and other nationalities, including British (100,000).

When the Japanese forces finally began their invasion of Malaya with landings along the northeastern coast on the night of December 7–8, 1941, the British were caught unprepared. With insufficient ships and aircraft to create a simultaneous presence in all theaters, Britain had been forced to establish priorities, and the theaters receiving most of the naval and air assets were the Atlantic and North Africa. Consequently, the defense of the peninsula was left to the army, which numbered some 88,600 Australian, British, Indian, and Malay troops. The principal ground units were the understrength 9th and 11th Indian Divisions and two brigades of the 8th Australian Division, as well as the 1st and

2nd Malaya Brigades at Singapore. The British had only 158 aircraft, mostly obsolete types, and no tanks. They also suffered a severe blow when Japanese aircraft sank their new battleship, the *Prince of Wales*, and battle cruiser, the *Repulse*, on December 10 when those warships attempted to oppose the Japanese landings.

The Japanese had devoted extensive planning to the Malayan operation, and the occupation of southern Indochina earlier in 1941 had formed part of their preparation. Malaya would provide them with tin and rubber resources, a strategic naval base at Singapore, and a jumping-off point for further expansion into the oil-rich Netherlands East Indies and the Indian Ocean.

The invading Japanese forces, commanded by General Yamashita Tomoyuki, went ashore beginning on the night of December 7–8. Some 60,000 men were gathered in three divisions, supported by Vice Admiral Ozawa Jisaburo's Malay Force, 158 naval aircraft, and 459 aircraft of the 3rd Air Division, as well as 80 tanks, 40 armored cars, and several artillery regiments. The Japanese quickly gained air superiority and began a rapid move southward. On December 15, in a desperate move, the British accepted an offer of cooperation from the Malayan Communist Party (MCP) and lifted the official proscription on both it and the Nationalist Party—the Guomindang (GMD; also known as Kuomintang [KMT]). Many members of these two parties were quickly trained in guerrilla warfare and sabotage at the 101st Special Training School, which had been hastily created at Singapore.

Kuala Lumpur fell on January 11. British, Australian, and Indian reinforcements, most of them poorly trained, were sent in through Singapore harbor to the retreating front but could do little to stem the Japanese advance. In a series of short battles in mid-January, the remaining British defenses in southern Malaya were broken, and on January 31, the defenders blew the causeway linking Singapore with the mainland.

Soon after the invasion had begun in December, General Sir Archibald Wavell, commander of Allied forces in the Far East, had visited Singapore and warned that the island's defenses had to be prepared should mainland units eventually be compelled to withdraw to it. Unfortunately, little serious effort was made to comply with this direction. On February 9, the Japanese landed on the island's northwest coast. Singapore was now crowded with refugees, its inhabitants demoralized, and its facilities stressed. On February 15, the British surrendered their remaining 70,000 troops. Most of the surviving graduates of the 101st Special Training School took to the jungles to carry on the fight, forming the Malayan People's Anti-Japanese Army (MPAJA) in March 1942.

Prime Minister Winston Churchill described the loss of Malaya as the greatest disaster in British military history. The loss clearly demonstrated that the British had grossly underestimated Japanese capabilities. Furthermore, their commanders had done a poor job in handling the ill-trained and inadequately equipped force they had sent to meet the invasion. The larger lesson of Malaya was that for commitments to be realistic, they had to be supported with sufficient resources.

The long-term repercussions were enormous and irreversible. Even though the British would return to Singapore and the Malay Peninsula at war's end, their stay would be temporary. European prestige and the omnipotent image of the white man in Southeast Asia were forever tarnished by the Malaya campaign, stoking the fires of nationalism and hastening decolonization.

*George M. Brooke III*

See also: Yamashita Tomoyuki.

**Further Reading**

Kirby, S. Woodburn. *Singapore: The Chain of Disaster*. London: Cassell, 1971.

Smyth, John. *Percival and the Tragedy of Singapore*. London: Macdonald, 1971.

## Manchukuo

Manchukuo was established in March 1932, following the Kwantung Army's seizure of Manchuria and eastern Inner Mongolia in the Mukden Incident. Because the Japanese army held the real power in the state, Manchukuo is commonly regarded as a "puppet state" in Western scholarship and as "false Manchukuo" in Chinese history.

Although Manchuria was the historical homeland of the Manchu people, whose Qing dynasty ruled over China from 1644 to 1912, by the early 1930s Han Chinese made up the majority of the population. Nonetheless, the Kwantung Army falsely claimed Manchukuo (literally, "Manchu state") was the result of a *native* Manchurian independence movement and declared Pu-yi, the former Qing emperor, to be head of state. In 1934, Pu-yi took the title of emperor as head of the renamed Great Manchu Empire (*Dai Manshu Teikoku*).

Despite this title, Pu-yi's decisions were subject to approval by the Japanese Kwantung Army, which retained control over the most important political body in Manchukuo, the General Affairs Board of the State Council. While Chinese held most government positions, they were supervised by higher-level Japanese officials, with the Japanese Director General of the Affairs Board on top. Nearly all Chinese in Manchukuo regarded the Japanese with contempt as an occupying force and often had to be persuaded or coerced into service. The landed elite tended to support the Manchukuo government, however, because it brought stability and implemented a crackdown on communist activities. The Japanese attempted to get the support of the different ethnic groups in Manchukuo through the creation of the Concordia Association. Although this authority was supposed to replace the Kwantung Army as the source of political power, the army increasingly used the Association to mobilize and keep tabs on the local population.

The main administrative goal of the Japanese was to develop the region into an industrial center for the greater empire. One way this was achieved was to integrate the Manchukuoan and Japanese economies into an autarkic bloc. Known as the "Yen bloc," the two economies maintained a unified currency system. Manchukuo, moreover, unified and reorganized its banking system to Japanese standards. Initially the government fueled industrial development, but over time it increasingly enlisted the capital and expertise of private enterprise in such efforts. Japanese *zaibatsu* and the government established joint ventures in nearly every industrial sector. Despite occasional "unease" within this partnership, the Japanese nonetheless achieved their goal, creating a large and modern industrial complex that tripled its production from 1933 to 1942.

In industrializing Manchukuo and integrating it with Japan's economy, the Japanese sought to create a "modern national defense state." Beginning in the mid-1930s, Japanese bureaucrats attempted to bring all Manchukuoan resources under state control and mobilize them in a more efficient and rational way. The foremost goal of this program was to provide the Japanese military with the resources and materiel necessary for waging protracted wars. With the outbreak of hostilities against China in 1937, Manchukuo became the supply base for the Japanese army's campaigns south of the Great Wall—a role it played until the end of World War II.

To facilitate Manchukuo's industrial development, Japanese officials attempted to modernize nearly all aspects of society. As the Japanese presence in Manchukuo grew, existing cities were expanded, utilizing the latest in urban planning and furnished with modern amenities. One of the most modern cities at the time, the new capital city of Xinjing (formerly Changchun) was the epitome of urban planning, including new buildings, wide streets, parks, and various public works. The newly expanded South Manchurian Railroad and its ultramodern train, the Asia Express, served to connect Manchukuo's planned cities. Middle-class Japanese professionals flocked to these cities to participate in Manchukuoan development and to live in an environment of modernity that surpassed even that in Japan. After 1932, the number of Japanese civilians rose by 800,000, and a total population of more than 1 million was attained by the 1940s.

Approximately 300,000 of these civilians settled in Manchukuo as part of a mass emigration program instituted by the Japanese government. Designed to both strengthen Japan's position in Manchukuo and relieve rural poverty in the Japanese countryside, the program ultimately failed to achieve its goal to send 5 million farmers to the plains of Manchuria over a 20-year period. Those settlers who did participate in the program were provided with land, often expropriated from Chinese farmers. They were also outfitted with farming tools, and managed by the government in an effort to maximize agricultural production. The emigration program included a strategic angle as well. Many of the immigrant farmers were settled along the Manchukuo-Soviet border and provided weapons to serve as a sort of

reserve force for the Kwantung Army. As the war worsened for the Japanese and the Kwantung Army's fighting capability diminished, the settlers on the border became the first line of defense against a Soviet invasion.

That invasion came on August 9, 1945, catching the Japanese by surprise. Some of the settlers fought alongside the overwhelmed Kwantung Army, others committed mass suicide, and still others desperately fled south away from the Russian advance. Very few escaped. Within eight days, the mechanized Russian army was in control of most of Manchukuo, having captured roughly 600,000 Japanese residents. Many of these Japanese were repatriated from 1946 to 1948, but a large number died in captivity or otherwise did not return to Japan. The state of Manchukuo was dissolved with the end of World War II.

*Rustin Gates*

**See also:** Kwantung Army Adventurism; Mukden Incident: Lytton Report; Russian Invasion of Manchuria; South Manchurian Railroad.

### Further Reading

Duara, Prasenjit. *Sovereignty and Authenticity: Manchukuo and the East Asian Modern.* New York: Rowman & Littlefield Publishers, 2003.

Yamamuro, Shin'ichi, and Joshua A Fogel. *Manchuria under Japanese Domination.* Philadelphia: University of Pennsylvania Press, 2006.

Young, Louise. *Japan's Total Empire: Manchuria and the Culture of Wartime Imperialism.* Berkeley, CA: University of California Press, 1998.

## Manila, Battle for (February 3–March 3, 1945)

Located on the big Philippine island of Luzon, Manila was one of the largest cities in Southeast Asia during the World War II era, with a population of more than 800,000 people. The Japanese commander in the Philippines, General Yamashita Tomoyuki, had 250,000 men on Luzon—a figure that had been grossly underestimated by General Douglas MacArthur's intelligence chief, Major General Charles A. Willoughby. Beginning on January 9, 1945, the 6th Army assaulted the western coast in the Lingayen Gulf. The Japanese made no effort to contest the landing, and that first day 68,000 men went ashore. They then drove southward toward Manila. The XIV Corps had the right flank, and I Corps on the left had the more difficult going.

Beginning on January 30, units of the 8th Army began landing north and south of Manila. XI Corps landed in the Subic Bay area, helping to seal off the Bataan Peninsula and preventing the Japanese from repeating the American defense of 1942. Meanwhile, on January 31, two regiments of the 11th Airborne Division went ashore at Nasugbu, about 45 miles southwest of Manila. On February 3, the division's remaining regiment was air-dropped on Tagaytay Ridge, 30 miles south of the city. The next day the 11th Airborne Division reached Paranaque, just south of Manila.

MacArthur urged a rapid advance. While the 37th Infantry Division pushed toward Manila from the north, the lighter and more mobile 1st Cavalry Division also drove on the city. MacArthur ordered the cavalry division to advance as fast as possible. Elements of the 1st Cavalry reached the northeastern outskirts of Manila on February 3, the first U.S. unit to do so. As darkness fell, one of its tanks smashed through the gates of Santo Tomas University, releasing 4,000 American prisoners held there.

Rear Admiral Iwabuchi Sanji now defied Yamashita's orders to withdraw from the city and used his 18,000 men (mostly naval personnel) to stage a fanatical, month-long, block-by-block and house-by-house defense of the city. As units of the 1st Cavalry and 37th Divisions closed on Manila, Iwabuchi's forces withdrew across the Pasig River, destroying its bridges and setting fire to the highly flammable residential areas. For the next several days, American forces battled these flames.

MacArthur had hoped that Manila would fall without significant damage to the city. On February 6, he announced in a communiqué that the complete destruction of the Japanese in Manila was "imminent." To save civilian lives, he ordered no air strikes. This order did not pertain to artillery fire, however, and its heavy use by both sides produced many civilian casualties. The doomed Japanese defenders also went on an orgy of murder and rape, killing thousands of innocent Filipinos.

By February 22, the 37th Division had driven the Japanese defenders into the old walled portion of the city (Intramuros) and the modern business district. In Intramuros, U.S. troops had to fight the Japanese, who were well dug in, one building at a time. Many buildings were simply turned into rubble by the unrestricted support fire, as breaching the buildings with infantry was virtually impossible.

By February 26, 1945, the remaining Japanese resistance was compressed into the three Philippine Commonwealth government buildings off the southeast corner of the walled city. The last organized Japanese resistance occurred in the Finance Building. Late on March 3, 1945, all organized resistance in the Manila area ended.

The Battle for Manila cost the Americans 1,010 personnel killed and 5,561 wounded. The Japanese lost perhaps 16,000 men in and around the city. In addition, more than

100,000 Filipino civilians were killed in the battle, and perhaps 70 percent of Manila was destroyed. The governmental center was damaged beyond repair, public transportation and electric power facilities were wrecked, and the water and sewer systems required extensive repair. Thirty-nine bridges, including the six major bridges over the Pasig River, were destroyed. Port facilities were so badly damaged that it was mid-April before any ships could unload at Manila Bay.

*Andrew J. Onello and Spencer C. Tucker*

**See also:** MacArthur, Douglas; Yamashita Tomoyuki.

**Further Reading**

James, D. Clayton. *The Years of MacArthur. Vol. 2: 1941–1945.* Boston: Houghton Mifflin, 1975.

Smith, Robert Ross. *The United States Army in World War II: The War in the Pacific— Triumph in the Philippines.* Washington, DC: U.S. Government Printing Office, 1963.

## *Maria Luz* Incident (1872)

On July 9, 1872, the *Maria Luz*, a Peruvian cargo ship bound from Macao to Peru, entered Yokohama harbor to refit after being damaged in a storm. While the ship was anchored there, a Chinese passenger leaped overboard and swam to the adjacent British ship HMS *Iron Duke*. The Chinese man claimed that he and 231 other Chinese laborers were being held in brutal captivity. The incident might have ended when the Chinese man was returned to the *Maria Luz* but another Chinese man escaped the next night.

The second escapee was turned over to acting British consul Robert Grant Watson, who took it upon his own authority to raid the ship with British marines. Watson then approached Japanese Foreign Minister Soejima Taneomi with evidence that the *Maria Luz* was packed with Chinese en route to be sold as slaves in Peruvian silver mines. Ricardo Herrera, the captain of the *María Luz*, appealed to Soejima with signed contracts indicating that the Chinese were not slaves, but were, in fact, indentured servants.

Virtually the entire foreign community counseled that because Japan had no jurisdiction in the matter, the *Maria Luz* should be allowed to sail on to Peru without further interference. Mutsu Munemitsu, the governor of the surrounding Kanagawa Prefecture, argued that although Japan had no treaty with Peru, the ship was immune from Japanese justice under the Most-Favored Nation and Extraterritorial clauses of the Unequal Treaties. He warned that Japan was in no military position to interfere should any foreign nation take up Peru's cause. When Justice Minister Etō Shimpei suggested that Mutsu should adjudicate the case, Mutsu resigned in protest. Mutsu's Vice governor Ōe Taku (a close friend and later co-conspirator in a case when both were convicted of treason in 1877) agreed to take the case. On August 30, Ōe ruled that the Chinese had been held against their will and freed them from their contracts.

The case became an international incident, as all foreign governments argued that Japan was clearly in the wrong. In June 1873, under considerable foreign pressure, the Japanese government requested that Tsar Alexander II of Russia arbitrate the issue as a neutral party. He agreed to hear the case and in 1875 ruled in Japan's favor.

The case became something of a diplomatic milepost. That same year it became the basis of new Japanese legislation, emancipating *burakumin* outcasts, prostitutes, and other forms of bonded labor. It was often cited as Japan's first salvo in the campaign to revise the hated Unequal Treaties. Ironically, 20 years later, Mutsu, now foreign minister himself, alluded to the case when he led the successful revision of the treaties in 1894.

*Louis G. Perez*

**See also:** Mutsu Munemitsu; Unequal Treaties.

**Further Reading**

Crawford, Suzanne Jones. "The *Maria Luz* Affair: A Study of Late Nineteenth Century Japanese Diplomatic Relations." *The Historian* 46, no. 4 (2007): 583–596.

Howell, David L. *Geographies of Identity in Nineteenth-Century Japan.* Berkeley: University of California Press, 2005.

Perez, Louis G. *Japan Comes of Age: Mutsu Munemitsu and the Revision of the Unequal Treaties.* Cranbury, NJ: Fairleigh Dickinson University Press, 1999.

## Maruyama Masao (1914–1996)

Maruyama Masao was born in Osaka in 1914, the second son of journalist and political commentator Maruyama Kanji. The young Maruyama was heavily influenced by his father's circle of intellectual friends, who were active participants of the liberal movement known as Taishō Democracy (1912–1926). In 1934, he entered the prestigious Tokyo Imperial University, where he met his mentor Professor Nambara Shigeru (1889–1974), who was a specialist in Western political thought at the Law Faculty. Maruyama was introduced to works by neo-Kantian philosophers and Marxist social theorists, which he read with great interest. In 1940, Maruyama was appointed assistant professor by his alma mater and began a teaching career that spanned more than three decades. In March 1945, he was drafted and was stationed in Hiroshima, where he experienced first hand the atomic bombing that took place on August 6, 1945. In September, Maruyama returned to Tokyo to resume his post. He retired in 1971 due to poor health and was appointed professor emeritus in 1974.

Maruyama's reputation as one of the most vocal critics of wartime ultra-nationalism and fascism was secured with the publication of "Chō-kokka shugi no ronri to shinri" ("The Theory and Psychology of Ultra-nationalism") in May 1946. The essay was widely seen as an intellectual attempt to free Japan from the curse of wartime imperialism that had paralyzed its people psychologically. In 1952, Maruyama published a ground-breaking study of the development of political thought preceding the rise of the modern Japanese state, entitled *Nihon seiji shisō shi kenkyū* ("Study of Japanese Political Thought"; translated as *Studies in the Intellectual History of Tokugawa Japan*). In this collection of essays, Maruyama traced the rise of the Nativist School of Thought in the 18th century as a reaction to Zhu Xi Neo-Confucian Orthodoxy and concluded that it was responsible for sowing the seeds of the emperor-centerd nationalistic ideology that had supported Japan's imperialistic expansion.

In 1964, Maruyama published *Gendai Nihon seiji no shisō to kōdō* (translated as *Thought and Behaviour in Modern Japanese Politics*), which sought to establish political science as an independent discipline of enquiry in Japan. In his retirement years, he worked on a commentary of Fukuzawa Yukichi's (1835–1901) *Bummeiron no gairyaku* ("An Outline of a Theory of Civilization," 1875), a seminal work informing Japan's modernization and nation-building process during the Meiji period (1868–1912).

In addition to publishing scholarly works critical of the prewar and wartime Japanese political system, Maruyama played an active role in promoting democratic ideals and encouraging the formation of civil society in the postwar years. He participated in a number of important and controversial public debates, including issues surrounding the San Francisco Peace Treaty (1951), the drafting of the postwar Constitution (1952), and the wartime responsibilities of the Shōwa Emperor and the Japanese Communist Party. In the 1960s and 1970s, when leftist students participated in the AMPO movement opposing the United States' continued military presence in Japan following the signing of the U.S.-Japan Mutual Peace Treaty, they criticized Maruyama for being a symbol of self-deceiving postwar democracy. At the height of the AMPO movement, Maruyama remained a faithful supporter of parliamentary politics, which he saw as essential for a democratic modern Japanese state.

*Yu Chang*

**See also:** AMPO: United States–Japan Security Treaty; Fukuzawa Yukichi; *Kokutai* and Ultra-nationalism; San Francisco Peace Treaty; Shōwa Emperor.

**Further Reading**

Barshay, Andrew E. "Imagining Democracy in Postwar Japan: Maruyama Masao as a Political Thinker." In *The Social Sciences in Modern Japan: The Marxian and Modernist Traditions*. Berkeley: University of California Press, 2004:197–239.

Bellah, Robert N. "Notes on Maruyama Masao." In *Imagining Japan: The Japanese Tradition and Its Modern Interpretation*. Berkeley: University of California Press, 2003:140–149.

Karube, Tadashi. *Maruyama Masao and the Fate of Liberalism in Modern Japan*, translated by David Noble. Tokyo: International House of Japan, 2008.

Kersten, Rikki. *Democracy in Postwar Japan: Maruyama Masao and the Search for Autonomy*. London/New York: Routledge, 1996.

Koschmann, J. Victor. "Maruyama Masao and the Incomplete Project of Modernity." In *Postmodernism and Japan*, edited by Masao Miyoshi and H. D. Harootunian. Durham: Duke University Press, 1989:123–142.

## Matsudaira Sadanobu

Matsudaira Sadanobu was born in 1758, under the name Katamaru. He was the third son of Tayasu Munetake, founder of one of the three junior houses of the Tokugawa family. He was also the grandson of Tokugawa Yoshimune, the eighth shōgun and author of the Kyoho Reforms. Sadanobu was in line for succession to the shōgunate.

In his youth, Sadanobu studied Confucianism, calligraphy, Japanese and Chinese poetry, painting, and the military arts. In 1774, he fell victim to a political scheme of the shōgun's councillor Tanuma Okitsugu, who ordered his adoption by Matsudaira Sadakuni, *daimyō* of Shirakawa. Sadanobu was removed from the line of succession to be shōgun, and a different house of the Tokugawa family provided the next shōgun. In 1783, however, Sadanobu succeeded his foster father as *daimyō* of Shirakawa and developed his own base of power. He worked to encourage education and military arts, and he promoted forestation and the improvement of agriculture. Sadanobu's measures soon showed results. The terrible Temmei famine of 1783–1787 killed millions throughout Japan; in Sadanobu's domain, however, not a single person died of starvation due to his frugal ways and the efficient transportation of food.

Sadanobu's achievements as *daimyō* did not go unnoticed. When Okitsugu fell from power in 1787, largely as a result of his corruption, Sadanobu was called upon to replace him as chief counselor to the shōgun.

The situation he faced was grim. Four years of bad harvests had been accompanied by riots in the cities and country, as well as earthquakes and volcanic eruptions. Political tension existed between the shōgun and the various *daimyō*s throughout Japan, due to Okitsugu's attempt to centralize power in the hands of the shōgun and his government. Sadanobu immediately instituted the Kansei Reforms. He began by purging the *bakufu* of Okitsugu's corrupt followers and promoting men of ability and moral standing. Sadanobu also encouraged simplicity and frugal ways in an attempt to limit consumption through sumptuary laws. Furthermore, he gave Edo greater economic independence from Osaka, and he built up Edo's cash and rice supplies against future emergencies. While devising a new purveyor system that gave the shōgunate more control over moneylenders, Sadanobu canceled the debts of the shōgunal retainers. He punished corrupt officials and merchants who did business with the government as well. Finally, Sadanobu reduced the *souko*, or conscript labor tax, which was imposed on farmers to maintain the main highways, and he undertook other measures designed to lighten the burden placed on the peasant class by the government.

Sadanobu's most controversial measure was the Prohibition on Unorthodox Learning (*Kansei Igaku no Kin*) of 1790, which limited the curriculum of the shōgunal academy to a narrow version of the Chu Hsi school of Neo-Confucianism. The strict religious orthodoxy did not apply to the people in general, but only persons who adhered to the official philosophy could hold governmental office. To enforce his ban, Sadanobu instituted a compulsory examination system,

the first of its kind in Japan. The prohibition also provided Japan with a consistent bureaucratic ideology that continued through the Meiji Restoration and beyond, and gave Japan's elite functionaries a tradition of public-spiritedness and dedicated service.

Two other issues absorbed much of Sadanobu's attention. In 1792, the Russian Adam Laxman tried to establish official trade relations with Japan. Sadanobu opted to continue the traditional Tokugawa policy of national seclusion. He avoided an open clash with Russia by promising token trade in Nagasaki. However, Sadanobu ordered the development of coastal defenses for Edo Bay as insurance. The second issue was the Title Incident of 1789, which arose Emperor Kokaku requested that a new title be issued to his father. The desired title, *daijo tenno*, was traditionally reserved for retired emperors. Despite growing pro-imperial sentiment among courtiers and samurai, Sadanobu refused the request. The discontent with Sadanobu's authoritarian handling of the affair, as well as resentment at his stringent sumptuary laws, contributed to his downfall. In 1793, the shōgun Tokugawa Ienari came of age and abruptly dismissed Sadanobu from his post.

In his retirement from the shōgunate, Sadanobu devoted his attention and time to his own domain of Shirakawa. He established an official school of Confucian studies known as the Rikkyokan. Sadanobu also distinguished himself as a poet, critic, and man of letters, as well as by taking an interest in archaeological matters. He died in 1829.

*Tim Watts*

**See also:** Tanuma Okitsugu.

## Further Reading

Hall, John Whitney. *Tanuma Okitsugo, 1719–1788: Forerunner of Modern Japan.*

Cambridge, MA: Harvard University Press, 1955.

Sansom, George Bailey. *A History of Japan*. 3 vols. Stanford, CA: Stanford University Press, 1958–1963.

## Matsukata Masayoshi (1835–1924)

Born in 1835 to a low-ranking samurai family in Kagoshima, Satsuma, Matsukata Masayoshi studied martial arts, calligraphy, and Confucian classics locally from age six and more formally in the Zoshikan domain school from age 13. From 1850, he served as a clerk in the domain treasury and participated in *daimyō* Shimazu Nariakira's efforts to modernize Satsuma's military defenses and develop the domain's economy to pay for it. He was later appointed to the domain's navy bureau in 1866 and was in the port city of Nagasaki to buy Western arms when the Tokugawa regime fell in 1868.

The new Meiji government appointed Matsukata governor of Hita in northern Kyushu in 1868; he served there until 1870, when he was transferred to Tokyo. Over the next few years, he headed government bureaus in charge of reforming Japan's land tax system and promoting industrialization. In 1878, Matsukata went to Europe as part of Japan's delegation to the third Paris World's Fair. There he met Leon Say, the French Finance Minister, whose free market approach to trade and finance Matsukata cited as a profound influence on his own economic thought.

Matsukata became Japan's Finance Minister in 1881 and quickly implemented the "Matsukata Deflation." To cover the costs of suppressing the Satsuma Rebellion in 1877, the government had issued nonconvertible paper currency. Matsukata moved to control inflation by reducing the amount of money in circulation and cutting government expenditures. He also reorganized the banking system around the central Bank of Japan, which was founded in 1882. Matsukata's tight money policies precipitated a severe depression and devastated farmers and small business owners, as Ministry of Agriculture and Commerce official Maeda Masana noted in the original draft of his 1884 economic development report. Although the social costs remained controversial, stability was restored to Japan's financial system by 1885.

Matsukata served as Prime Minister twice, in 1891–1892 and again in 1896–1898, but his authoritarian methods clashed with emerging political parties. Matsukata dissolved the Imperial Diet in 1891 when it moved to amend his cabinet's budget proposal. In the elections that followed, police suppressed political parties and government officials bribed voters. More successful as Finance Minister, Matsukata helped finance the First Sino-Japanese War of 1894–1895 with bonds and used the indemnity extracted from China to move Japan to the gold standard in 1898.

Matsukata retired from the cabinet in 1901 and traveled around the world in 1902, stopping in the United States, England, Belgium, France, Germany, Italy, Austria, and Russia before returning to Japan via the Trans-Siberian Railway. At Oxford University, he received an honorary doctorate of civil law. From 1903 to 1913, Matsukata served as president of the Japanese Red Cross. As a member of the Privy Council, he continued to advise the government, especially during the financing of the Russo-Japanese War in 1904. In 1917, Matsukata was appointed Lord Keeper of the Privy Seal. He retired from official posts in 1922 and died on July 2, 1924.

*John H. Sagers*

See also: Seinan (Satsuma) Rebellion; Sino-Japanese War.

## Further Reading

Bailey, Jackson H. "The Meiji Leadership: Matsukata Masayoshi." In *Japan Examined: Perspectives in Modern Japanese History*. Honolulu: University of Hawaii Press, 1983:114–143.

Reischauer, Haru Matsukata. *Samurai and Silk: A Japanese and American Heritage*. Cambridge, MA: Harvard University Press, 1986.

Sagers, John H. *Origins of Japanese Wealth and Power: Reconciling Confucianism and Capitalism, 1830–1885*. New York: Palgrave Macmillan, 2006.

## Matsuoka Yōsuke (1880–1946)

Born in the village of Morozumi in Yamaguchi Prefecture, Japan, on March 4, 1880, Matsuoka Yōsuke went to the United States at age 13, working his way through and graduating from the University of Oregon in 1900. After returning to Japan, he became a diplomat in 1904, and between 1904 and 1921, he developed close ties with the Japanese business community and military.

Matsuoka left the diplomatic service in 1921 to become a director of the South Manchurian Railroad and was its vice president from 1927 to 1929. The following year, he entered the Japanese Diet as a representative of the conservative Seiyūkai Party. In July 1932, he became Japan's representative to the League of Nations in Geneva, Switzerland, where he led the Japanese delegation in walking out following the league's acceptance of the Lytton Commission report on February 24, 1933. A staunch conservative, Matsuoka left the Seiyūkai Party in December 1933, advocating the abolition of political parties. In 1935, he rejoined the South Manchurian Railroad Company, serving as its president until 1939. He was also an adviser to the Japanese cabinet between 1937 and 1940.

From July 1940 to July 1941, Matsuoka served as the Japanese Foreign Minister, taking a strongly pro-Axis position. Outspoken and garrulous, he was known to his friends as "Mr. 50,000 Words." During his time as foreign minister, Japan joined Italy and Germany in the Tripartite Pact of September 1940. In March 1941, Matsuoka traveled to Berlin, where he held talks with Adolf Hitler and German Foreign Minister Joachim Ribbentrop. Hitler tried to turn the Tripartite Pact into an offensive alliance by convincing Matsuoka that Japan should join Germany in war against Britain, whereas Ribbentrop advocated a Japanese attack on Singapore. Matsuoka was noncommittal.

He then traveled on to Moscow to meet with Soviet leaders. There, on April 13, he signed a five-year nonaggression pact with the Soviet Union. Following the June 1941 German invasion of the Soviet Union, Matsuoka advocated that Japan join Germany in war against the Soviets, in violation of its neutrality pact with the USSR. He also urged an end to negotiations with the United States. In speeches in Japan, Matsuoka argued for Japanese control of the entire western Pacific.

Matsuoka alienated other members of Japan's cabinet not by his anti-American stance but by his ambition, his obnoxious behavior, and his flouting of the prime minister's position by holding unauthorized talks with the Germans. Indeed, Prime Minister Konoe Fumimaro and the entire cabinet resigned on July 16, 1941, so that the government could be reorganized without Matsuoka. The next day, Konoe again became prime minister—but with Vice Admiral Toyoda Teijiro as foreign minister.

Tuberculosis forced Matsuoka to retire from the political scene. At the end of the war, he flirted with the possibility of heading a military government, installed by a coup d'état and committed to a last-ditch resistance to any Allied invasion. He was arrested after the war and brought to trial before the International Military Tribunal for the Far East at Tokyo as a Class "A" war criminal. Matsuoka died in Tokyo on June 27, 1946, before a verdict could be rendered on his guilt or innocence.

*Spencer C. Tucker*

**See also:** International Military Tribunal for the Far East; Konoe Fumimaro; Manchukuo; Mukden Incident: Lytton Report; Russian Neutrality Pact; South Manchurian Railroad; Tripartite Pact.

**Further Reading**

Lu, David J. *Agony of Choice: Matsuoka Yōsuke and the Rise and Fall of the Japanese Empire, 1880–1946*. Lanham, MD: Lexington Books, 2002.

Lu, David J. *From the Marco Polo Bridge to Pearl Harbor: Japan's Entry into World War II*. Washington, DC: Foreign Affairs Press, 1961.

Teters, R. "Matsuoka Yōsuke: The Diplomat of Bluff and Gesture." In *Diplomats in Crisis: United States–Chinese–Japanese Relations, 1919–1941*, edited by R. D. Burns and E. N. Bennett, eds. Santa Barbara, CA: ABC-CLIO, 1974:275–296.

# May Fourth Movement (1919)

On May 4, 1919, more than 3,000 Chinese students assembled in central Beijing to denounce news emanating from the Paris Peace Conference. The conference negotiators, led by U.S. President Woodrow Wilson, had acquiesced to Japanese claims to former German-occupied territory in China's Shandong province. The decision unleashed the fury of nationalistic students, who had expected the territory to revert to Chinese control. Chinese officials, whom they viewed as complicit in Japanese actions, became targets of the students' ire. Brandishing flags and banners denouncing the officials as traitors to the nation, the students distributed a manifesto calling on the Chinese people to unite or face national annihilation. The protest eventually grew violent when one official was assaulted, another escaped the students' wrath only by means of a disguise, and two of their homes were destroyed. Over the next month, protests spread to other cities in China and eventually inspired strikes and anti-Japanese boycotts that convulsed Shanghai throughout June.

These events of May 4, 1919 gave political expression to vast undercurrents roiling Chinese intellectual and cultural life. For this reason, historians take the day's events as signaling a broader "May Fourth Movement," a crucial stage in rise of modern Chinese nationalism. May Fourth refers generally to an era that would have a profound impact on the subsequent history of East Asia. The generation that grew up under its shadow would carry the cultural, intellectual, and political controversies of the era with them into future battles. Most Chinese political leaders of the 20th century emerged from this May Fourth generation.

The May Fourth Movement united political issues with cultural criticism, giving the movement its distinctive character. For Chinese intellectuals, the betrayal at Paris by Western diplomats was symptomatic of China's feeble international status. China's weakness needed an explanation. Intellectuals blamed traditional Chinese culture and repudiated traditional values as the cause of endemic internal weakness. They decried China's moribund political culture and the old guard leadership that populated it. This iconoclasm, by extension, validated the regenerative force of youth. Student activism became a vital component in national politics. With the disillusion with Woodrow Wilson and the liberal West, Chinese thinkers turned to lessons from the Russian Revolution and Marxist-Leninism in seeking answers to China's malaise. In this sense, May Fourth nationalism was not simply a parochial nationalism, but instead saw the problems of the China in a global context and placed China in the flow of world history.

In foreign relations, May Fourth thinkers were staunchly anti-imperialist and identified Japan as the most immediate threat to Chinese national integrity. May Fourth nationalism was, therefore, sharply anti-Japanese. The organizers of the May 4 protests in Beijing had initially selected May 7 for the protests to commemorate Japan's ultimatum on that date in 1915 and China's humiliation over the Twenty-One Demands. Despite the staunch anti-Japanese sentiments, however, it is important to note that many May Fourth intellectuals and politicians had studied in Japan and were familiar with Japanese politics and society.

Japanese officials responded to the protests with predictable alarm. Most of them, however, refused to see the protests as a direct consequence of Japan's imperialistic policies. As evidence of how poorly Japanese officialdom grasped the significance of the movement, they quickly sought to place blame for it on foreign instigators, even accusing the American Minister in China of raising funds to support the protests. Other Japanese observers, however, appreciated that the May 4 protests, together with the March 1 protests against Japanese colonial rule in Korea, represented a fundamental challenge to the prevailing imperialist framework in East Asia. Yoshino Sakuzō, Tokyo Imperial University professor and political commentator, viewed the Chinese protests as part of the global thrust for popular representation. While the movement was undoubtedly anti-Japanese, Yoshino argued, the Chinese and Japanese people had shared interests in opposing militarism and autocratic bureaucracies in their respective governments.

In Paris, Chinese representatives refused to sign the Treaty of Versailles, much to the delight of Chinese nationalists. The dispute over the Shandong territory would be resolved at the Washington Naval Conference in 1922. The antagonism between Chinese nationalism and Japanese territorial ambitions expressed on May 4, 1919, however, would vex Sino-Japanese relations for decades, resulting in further strikes and protests against Japan and eventually in full-scale war in 1937.

*Michael A. Schneider*

**See also:** Twenty-One Demands; Versailles Treaty; Washington Naval Conference; World War I.

### Further Reading

Chow, Tse-Tsung. *The May Fourth Movement: Intellectual Revolution in Modern China.* Cambridge, MA: Harvard University Press, 1960.

Manela, Erez. *The Wilsonian Moment: Self-determination and the International Origins of Anticolonial Nationalism.* New York: Oxford University Press, 2007.

Schwarcz, Vera. *The Chinese Enlightenment: Intellectuals and the Legacy of the May Fourth Movement of 1919.* Berkeley: University of California Press, 1986.

## Meiji Constitution (1890)

After almost a decade of political wrangling, a constitution was promised to the Japanese nation in 1881. In the early 1870s, political leaders such as Ōkuma Shigenobu and

Itagaki Taisuke had led a public debate called the People's Freedom and Rights Movement (*Jiyu minken undo*). As part of this debate, there was widespread discussion of the nature of political sovereignty. Ōkuma and Itagaki had advocated for the creation of a constitution that would be a more liberal document based on British or French models. The more conservative elements of the government had triumphed, however, when Ōkuma was driven from the government in 1881. Itagaki and others had left the government in 1875.

Itō Hirobumi dominated the Constitutional Committee but was ably assisted by Inoue Kowashi, Itō Miyoji, Iwakura Tomomi, and Kaneko Kentaro They preferred a Prussian model and were helped in this regard by two German legal scholars, Rudolf von Gneist and Lorenz von Stein. A final draft of the constitution was submitted to Emperor Meiji in April 1888 and was promulgated to the nation without public debate on February 11, 1889. It came into effect on November 29, 1890.

In the Meiji Constitution, political sovereignty was fully vested in the emperor, who reserved all powers, granting limited political influence, if not power, to his subjects. Two houses of parliament (Diet) were created. Members of the House of Peers were to be appointed by the emperor, and members of the Lower House of Representatives were to be elected by a severely limited public electorate. The Lower House had very few powers except to pass the annual budget. Even then, the government, also appointed by the emperor, could function on the previous year's budget in the event of an impasse.

The emperor had direct command of the army and navy. He appointed ministers of those services, and they had direct access to the emperor himself without interference from the rest of the government, including the prime minister.

All civil and legal liberties (e.g., assembly, press, speech) were granted by the emperor, and could also be rescinded by the emperor at any time, for any reason. Only the emperor could amend the constitution, but either house had the right to submit petitions, which could be ignored by the emperor. No amendments were ever made to the constitution in the 57 years of its existence.

Two key elements did not appear in the constitution: the *genrō* and political parties. The *genrō* (senior statesmen) were members of the so-called Satchō Oligarchy (a conflation of the first syllables of the dominant regional Satsuma and Chōshū factions), who unofficially advised the emperor. Three were from Chōshū (Inoue Kaoru, Itō Hirobumi, and Yamagata Aritomo) and four were from Satsuma (Kuroda Kiyotaka, Matsukata Masayoshi, Ōyama Iwao, and Saigō Tsugumichi); they were later joined by Katsura Taro of Chōshū and the imperial courtier Saionji Kinmochi. The *genrō* took turns serving as the chief ministers during the entire 45 years of the Meiji era (only Ōyama did not serve as prime minister). They usually made all political decisions to be ratified by the emperor.

The framers of the constitution intended to preclude political parties in the Diet, but political expedience led to their formation and eventual takeover of the cabinet in 1918.

*Louis G. Perez*

**See also:** Inoue Kaoru; Itagaki Taisuke; Itō Hirobumi, Jiyu Minken Undo; Matsukata Masayoshi; Meiji Emperor; Ōkuma Shigenobu; Ōyama Iwao, Saigō Tsugumichi; Saionji Kinmochi; Yamagata Aritomo.

## Further Reading

Akita, George. *Foundations of Constitutional Government in Modern Japan, 1868–1900.* Cambridge, MA: Harvard University Press, 1967.

Beckmann, George M. *The Making of the Meiji Constitution: The Oligarchs and the Constitutional Development of Japan, 1868–1891*. Lawrence, KS: University of Kansas Press, 1969.

## Meiji Economic Reforms (1870–1880s)

The Meiji Restoration's leaders faced the immediate problem of how to revive the economy of the state captured in their successful coup d'état. Their plight in 1868 resembled that of rebels who commandeer a train, only to find it missing its locomotive engine. Although several Western governments and their arms traders had quietly aided the cause of the Restoration, the Western powers offered little to remedy the economic crisis. The samurai leaders, aware of what international indebtedness had wrought in China, did not rush to borrow from foreign banks. International lenders, seeing more risk than profit in financing young usurpers of uncertain staying power, matched their reluctance. Established avenues for raising funds easily at home also appeared limited. The former shōgunate's coffers were nearly empty and the domains debt-ridden. Many of Japan's once-thriving domestic markets in cotton and woven goods had collapsed owing to an influx of cheap machine-made imports from industrialized countries. Ignorance of international metallic exchange rates had resulted in outflow of gold, while inflation and economic uncertainty fed uprisings among city dwellers and farmers alike. Aside from immediate unrest generated by the domestic economic crisis, the new leaders of the imperial government also saw clearly that they must raise funds to defend Japan against presently quiescent but potentially aggressive Western states.

The first step in economic reform required neutralizing the opposition of the *daimyō* specifically, and the samurai generally, by reunifying the state around a restored imperial institution. The ruling clique accomplished this goal by initially assuring the continuance of at least half the *daimyō*'s revenue under the new order and the maintenance of stipends for members of the warrior class. In 1869, Chōshū, Satsuma, Tosa, and Hizen— the domains whose samurai led the Restoration—established the precedent of returning their lands to the emperor. Moved by persuasion and pressure, fellow *daimyō* lords followed suit, so that by 1871 Japan's 260 semi-autonomous domains had been completely replaced by 75 Tokyo-dependent prefectures. These new units constituted part of an increasingly integrated and unified system that enabled taxes, primarily from assessments on farm land, to flow to the center. Once the centralized administrative structure had been established, Japan's ministers determined how funds would be used for national ends (i.e., military strengthening and technological modernization) and how they would reallocated for local infrastructure building (e.g., constructing roads, railroads, and dams).

That the new central government had money to spend was thanks to land tax revenues that now flowed directly into the central treasury. The Tax Law of 1873 regularized taxes to make them universally assessed at 3 percent of the land's value and payable in cash. Whoever had been issued new land deeds would now be responsible for paying the tax, a shift from collective village-based tax responsibility that was commonplace during the Tokugawa period. The changes resulting from this policy became immediately apparent. The central government became better funded than the shōgunate had ever been, and the tax provided up to 70 percent of the state revenues for most of the Meiji period. The move also produced less immediately apparent outcomes. It provided land ownership to the farmers themselves while concentrating land in fewer hands. Tenancy rates increased, creating a surplus labor force of men and women who would soon flow to Japan's growing cities to work at state-subsidized textile mills, mines, steel plants, and shipyards. Other social-leveling reforms of the first Meiji decade intensified the secondary effects of the tax law. Decrees that freed commoners to pursue whatever calling they chose, voided old sumptuary laws, and mandated social equality (albeit qualified by official recognition of samurai bloodlines, creation of a new peerage, and special terminology for the former pariah class) also worked to invigorate the economy. The tax law was also the first part of the Meiji leaders "Rich Country, Strong Military" policy that planned for macro-economic growth through directed national investment made possible by forced contributions from the agrarian sector.

Although the agrarian tax reform helped fill government coffers from 1873, it proved insufficient to meet predictable and unpredictable expenses. Putting down the 1877 Seinan Rebellion (a civil war raised by samurai dissatisfied with the elimination of their stipends and near-total elimination of class privileges) added to government spending for modernization projects such as model factories and paying for Western technical expertise (rich salaries for "live machines"). The central government fed inflationary fires by repeatedly floating bonds and printing paper money to cover debts.

To control prices at home and restore foreign confidence in Japanese economic conditions, Finance Minister Matsukata Masayoshi implemented a retrenchment program that mandated severe cuts in government spending,

reductions in the currency supply, regressive taxes of commodities, and sale of government-subsidized factories and pilot projects at bargain basement prices. Historians are divided as to the necessity of such strong medicine, particularly given its impact on farmers, who saw agricultural commodity prices collapse and tenancy rates increase. Nevertheless, its effectiveness in stopping inflation, stabilizing prices, encouraging private-sector investment in the economy, and securing the confidence of foreign investors in Japan's economic prospects is beyond doubt. By the late 1880s, economic conditions were booming. Domestic investors demonstrated newfound confidence in creating a flood of joint stock companies. A new class of nationalistic entrepreneurs (*jitsugyōka*) worked closely with the central government to patriotically and profitably invest in Japan's industrial and financial future. The new confidence in the economy was also demonstrated by the Ministry of Finance through a greater willingness to seek foreign buyers of Japanese government bonds.

These rapid developments helped Japan achieve self-sustained growth and economic diversification during the 1890s. International trade relationships moved from exporting raw materials to providing finished goods, particularly textiles, to Asian markets. The development of heavy and chemical industries that enabled Japan to produce its own steel, locomotives, and battleships was also well under way by the first decades of the 20th century. The booming Meiji decades would be punctuated by years of busts brought on by Japanese military expansionism and exposure to downturns in international economic conditions. Nevertheless, thanks to specific centrally directed policies such as the Matsukata Deflation and the creation of hard and soft infrastructure, including transportation systems, a national bank, and educational institutions, the Japanese economy was rapidly transitioning from that of an isolated agrarian state to an internationally integrated industrial economy at the end of World War I.

*Michael Lewis*

See also: Matsukata Masayoshi; Meiji Land Tax.

### Further Reading

Crawcour, E. Sydney. "Economic Change in the Nineteenth Century." In *The Cambridge History of Japan: Volume 5, The Nineteenth Century*, edited by Marius B. Jansen. Cambridge, UK: Cambridge University Press, 1989: 569–617.

Jones, Mark, and Steven Erickson. "Social and Economic Change in Prewar Japan." In *A Companion to Japanese History*, edited by William M. Tsutsui. New York: Wiley-Blackwell, 2007: 172–188.

## Meiji Emperor (1852–1912)

Born Sachi No Miya on November 3, 1852, in Kyoto, as the son of Emperor Komei and Nakayama Yoshiko, Meiji was given the name Mutsuhito in his youth. As emperor, he assumed the name Meiji, meaning "enlightened rule." He became the crown prince in 1860 and ascended to the throne in 1867 at the age of 14. Because of his young age at the time of succession, the regent Nijo Nariyuki guided the early years of his rule. Meiji wed Ichijo Haruko, who became the Empress Shoken.

According to the Meiji Constitution (1890), the emperor was "sacred and inviolable." He held supreme authority over the state, and he controlled the military. In practice, Meiji wielded little actual power. The small, select circle of such elder statesmen (*genrō*) as Itō Hirobumi and Ōkubo Toshimichi advised the emperor in matters of state, and for the most part, the *genrō* ran the government. Emperor Meiji largely served to legitimate their actions with his public proclamations.

Emperor Meiji himself initially disliked European innovations, and he insisted on the preservation of traditional Japanese ceremonies and rites. For diplomatic purposes, however, he adopted Western-style ceremonial uniforms, particularly when dealing with the United States and the nations of Europe, and he eventually came to develop an appreciation of Western-style food, music, and sports. He studied the German language and European political theory, and he received numerous visitors of distinction from the West, including the Duke of Edinburgh in 1869 and former president of the United States Ulysses S. Grant in 1879.

Meiji served as supreme commander of the military forces during the Sino-Japanese War of 1894–1895 and the Russo-Japanese War of 1904–-1905 and took a deep interest in both wars. When the war with China broke out, Meiji traveled to the war headquarters in Hiroshima, where he attended military meetings throughout the day and night. He lived an austere lifestyle during that period, which led to exhaustion and possibly the illness that ultimately resulted in his death.

Meiji died on July 30, 1912, and a national shrine, Meiji Jingu, was erected in his honor in Tokyo. His passing symbolically marked the end of the era in which Japan was transformed from a semi-feudal agrarian society to an industrialized, modern nation-state.

*Walter E. Grunden*

See also: Charter Oath; Itō Hirobumi; Meiji Constitution; Ōkubo Toshimichi; Russo-Japanese War; Sino-Japanese War.

### Further Reading

Keene, Donald. *Emperor of Japan: Meiji and His World, 1852–1912*. New York: Columbia University Press, 2002.

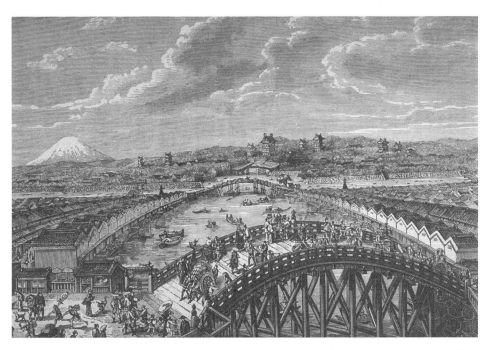

The population of Tokyo, Japan's largest city, reached more than 1 million in the late 19th century. The growth was due in part to the modernizing reforms of the Meiji Restoration. (Hulton Archive/Getty Images)

Large, Stephen S. *Emperors of the Rising Sun: Three Biographies*. New York: Kodansha International, 1997.

## Meiji-Era Peasant Uprisings

Prewar and early post-1945 studies of Meiji rural uprisings tended toward a simple two-sided view of exploited peasants reflexively responding to exploiters, usually wealthier fellow villagers or intruding tax officials. In recent decades, historians using micro-level village studies and analytical approaches particularly influenced by anthropology have found a greater diversity among participants than can be represented by the term "peasant." Their discovery of a wider range of motivations behind agrarian protests has also worked to replace a bifurcated analysis with one far more kaleidoscopic. In these newer studies, Meiji rural uprisings are often arrayed along several major intersecting axes depending on actors and actions. Among these, cultural, economic, and political uprisings are the most prominent and prevalent. Such a typology, however, by no means exhausts the hundreds of protests (and quasi-protests such as the millennial World Renewal or *Yonaoshi* pilgrimages) mounted during the Meiji decades. Even within broad categories, significant differences are evident.

Cultural protests during the first decade after the 1868 Restoration often sought to preserve pre-Meiji practices and social relationships. During the late 1860s and into the 1870s, rural residents demonstrated, petitioned, destroyed property, and physically attacked officials to protest the dissolution of *daimyō* domains, the emancipation of the pariah *burakumin*, the opening of Japan to Christian proselytizers, and mandatory smallpox vaccinations and cholera quarantines.

Some of these seemingly backward-looking protests made quite progressive demands. In the 1869 Bandori Riots in Tōyama, thousands of farmers carrying hempen banners and uniformly dressed in straw rain hats and capes (*bandori* or *mino*) made a customary call for the punishment of evil and corrupt officials as they clashed with government troops and attacked wealthier landowners and merchants to forestall Meiji reforms that the farmers claimed widened a growing gap dividing rich and poor. Their action, similar to earlier Tokugawa uprisings in tactics, was unprecedented in specifically seeking lower taxes *and* the inherently democratic right of villagers to select their own local headmen. The 1872 Wappa Uprising in Yamagata demonstrated an even more straightforwardly progressive protest in demanding revision of old methods of governance and taxation in favor of a new, more equitable system.

As the Bandori and Wappa protests make clear, economic grievances played an inextricable part in ostensibly culturally motivated rural uprisings. During the early 1870s, the Meiji central government repeatedly sent troops to newly created prefectures to put down popular protests over changes in the land tax system. Farmers in Fukuoka, Aichi, Gifu, Yamanashi, Fukushima, and Tōyama in parallel but independent protests sought to reverse regulations that required payment of uniform assessments in cash and legally concentrated more farmland in fewer hands. The economic hardship imposed on farmers by the 1872 Conscription Law, popularly derided as the "blood tax," also elicited opposition. The removal of young men—the most productive hands on family farms—added to new fiscal burdens arising from a flurry of centrally ordered but locally financed projects to build schools, roads, and levees. In Fukushima in 1882, the opposition to the newly installed governor's conscription of local labor to build a new prefectural road prompted actions ranging from demonstrations to recall the governor to an alleged plot to assassinate the state's local representatives.

Rural residents rose up with such great frequency because they likely found it ethically justified and practically effective. Protesters in the 1877 Tode Riots in Tōyama demonstrated motivations arising from *both* a still-valid popular understanding of the local moral economy and the cool calculation attributable to the rational peasant. The protests, locally described as yielding a "tax cut delivered at spear point," additionally achieved the rioters' essential demand that newly recognized holders of land deeds acknowledge the tenancy rights of landless farmers who had worked rice fields before and after the Meiji Restoration. This point, which was crucial to the economic viability of local tenants, was not mandated by the new centrally drafted national land tax law, but was nevertheless observed locally.

Within a decade of the 1868 Meiji Restoration, the political potential of rural protests became apparent to both former samurai opposed to rule by Tokyo's oligarchy and the leaders of the new Meiji government. Itagaki Taisuke, who originally intended only to organize exclusive self-help organizations for samurai who had been economically and socially dispossessed by Tokyo's reforms, soon sought to include disgruntled farmers in his movement for "freedom and popular rights." Prominent among his reasons was the flocking of farmers to political organizations critical of Tokyo's governance. From the mid-1870s into the 1880s, farmers by the hundreds of thousands signed petitions calling for lower taxes, a national assembly to represent their interests, and revision of unequal treaties with Western powers. Many of the petition signers later filled out the ranks of the Liberal Party formed in 1881 and pushed its program in the countryside thereafter. A more radical segment of the rural population joined former samurai in "violent incidents" (*gekika-jiken*) such as destroying government offices and plotting the assassination of Tokyo's local representatives. Although these actions were all successfully suppressed, uprisings such as the Fukushima Incident in 1882 and the Chichibu Incident in 1884 raised the possibility of a dangerous alliance of militant samurai leadership strengthened by massive rural support.

Even without the threat of rural rebellion of national proportions, the new imperial government found repeated troop mobilizations financially draining and politically distracting. In 1878, in a move in part undertaken to placate members of a new rural landlord class, local elites, and political figures capable of organizing regional support for and against central initiatives, Tokyo approved the opening of prefectural assemblies. Iwakura Tomomi, a court leader of the Restoration, later lamented the act and attempted to curtail the bodies as hotbeds of disloyal obstructionism. Although unsuccessful, his response typified the Meiji leaders' flexible views on controlling popular protest, urban as well as rural, through policies that alternated between "the candy and the whip."

The largest piece of candy came in 1881 as an imperial promise to open a national assembly and promulgate a written constitution within a decade. The final version of the Meiji Constitution was strong on imperial subjects' obligations and weak on citizens' rights. Nevertheless, by not

explicitly banning political parties or wider popular participation in politics, Asia's first written constitution provided space for parties gradually to grow and male suffrage to expand.

While promising a constitution, Tokyo authorities continued to wield the whip through centrally appointed governors empowered to prorogue local assemblies and reverse local legislation. The Home Ministry and other ministries also produced a steady stream of laws and ordinances that controlled freedom of speech, assembly, and political participation. The local and regional need for Ministry of Finance allocations to build dams, railroads, and ports also added to Tokyo's political leverage. The decline in rural protests led by local party bosses demonstrated the power of budgetary control to intimidate local politicos and dissipate ideological support for the Freedom and Popular Rights movement of the 1870s and 1880s.

Rural unrest did not end after promulgation of the Meiji Constitution and opening of Japan's National Assembly. Instances of Janus-faced rural uprisings, at times looking back to the pre-Meiji past for moral justification to deal with modern problems, can be seen in 20th-century disputes over tenants' rights, farmers' use of local rivers dammed for hydroelectric power generation, and the military's right to appropriate food resources during wartime. These protests, of course, differed from those of the *mino*-coated Bandori protestors seeking heavenly retribution. Later disputants less often resorted to direct action, but relied increasingly on organized tenant unions, law courts, and the modern media in seeking for redress for grievances. The industrialization of Japan's economy, a process that resulted in more Japanese working in factories than on farms in the 1930s, also saw unionization and strikes in the nation's burgeoning cities vie with rural protests as causes of concern for officials and social reformers.

*Michael Lewis*

**See also:** Itagaki Taisuke; Iwakura Tomomi; Jiyu Minken Undo; Meiji Constitutionn.

### Further Reading

Kelly, William W. *Deference and Defiance in Nineteenth-Century Japan.* Princeton: Princeton University Press, 1985.

Lewis, Michael. *Rioters and Citizens: Mass Protest in Imperial Japan.* Berkeley: University of California Press, 1990.

Vlastos, Stephen. "Opposition Movements in Early Meiji, 1868–1885." In *The Cambridge History of Japan, Volume 5: The Nineteenth Century*, edited by Marius B. Jansen. Cambridge, UK: Cambridge University Press, 1989:367–431.

## Meiji Ishin Shishi

When the shōgun's senior adviser Abe Masahiro solicited advice when crafting a response to American Commodore Matthew Perry's demands for a commercial treaty in 1853, he found little agreement among Japan's *daimyō*. Shimazu Nariakira of Satsuma favored stalling and building coastal defenses. Yamauchi Yōdō of Tosa wanted to keep foreigners out while studying military science. Tokugawa Nariaki of Mito advocated preparing for war rather than revealing weakness in the face of foreign threats. Fudai *daimyō* such as Hotta Masayoshi, Ii Naosuke, and Abe Masahiro himself, who were responsible of implementing policy, supported a compromise with Perry. Finally, the shōgunate negotiated the 1854 Kanagawa Treaty, which inflamed nationalist sentiments throughout Japan. Using the foreign crisis to their advantage,

court nobles began to exploit divisions within the shōgunate to reassert imperial authority.

With the foreign crisis and a growing rift between emperor and shōgun, ambitious young samurai saw an opportunity to expand their role in state affairs through radical action. Yoshida Shōin from Chōshū was a student of Western military science in Edo, where he studied with Sakuma Shozan. Captured in an attempt to stow away on one of Perry's ships, Yoshida was returned to Chōshū and, while under house arrest, operated a school promoting the idea of "revering the emperor and expelling the barbarians" (*sonno jōi*) through modernizing Japan's defenses.

Factionalism within the shōgunate was further aggravated when, during the negotiations leading to the 1858 Japan-U.S. Treaty of Amity and Commerce, the death of Shōgun Iesada precipitated a succession dispute. Tokugawa Nariaki of Mito supported his son Hitotsubashi Yoshinobu for the place atop the shōgunate, while Ii Naosuke pushed for Tokugawa Iemochi. When Iemochi became shōgun, Ii Naosuke became the most powerful leader in the shōgun's government and signed the American treaty in spite of widespread opposition. Afterward, Ii eliminated his opponents in the Ansei Purge of 1858–1859. *Daimyō* like Tokugawa Nariaki were placed under house arrest and lower-ranking critics like Yoshida Shōin were executed.

Ii Naosuke's dictatorial tactics and support for what many considered a humiliating treaty stirred the shishi to radical action. In March 1860, shishi from Mito and Satsuma attacked and killed Ii at the Sakurada Gate of Edo Castle. Henry Heusken, Townsend Harris's secretary, was killed in January 1861. Shishi attacked the British Legation at Tozenji in July 1861 killing two staff members and several Japanese guards. Charles Richardson was killed by Satsuma samurai at Namamugi in September 1862 when he rode his horse close to Shimazu Hisamitsu's procession. Troops in Chōshū fired on American, French, and Dutch ships in the Straits of Shimonoseki in the summer of 1863. In retaliation, British warships bombarded Kagoshima in Satsuma in August 1863 and French and American ships shelled Chōshū forts at Shimonoseki in 1864. The shōgunate also sent a punitive expedition against Chōshū that same year.

From 1864, the shishi adjusted their tactics as the futility of direct attacks became clear. Rather than continue campaigns of assassination, activists turned to political intrigue. Working with Ōkubo Toshimichi and Saigō Takamori from Satsuma and Kido Takayoshi of Chōshū, Sakamoto Ryōma helped overcome the long bitter rivalry between these major tozama domains to create an alliance in 1866 that eventually toppled the Tokugawa regime and proclaimed the restoration of the emperor Meiji in 1868. After the Meiji Ishin, many former shishi became key figures in the new government. Ōkubo Toshimichi, Kido Takayoshi, and Inoue Kaoru led the reforms that dismantled the feudal system. Itō Hirobumi drafted the Meiji Constitution, which invested all sovereignty in the emperor who was "sacred and inviolable." Yamagata Aritomo modernized Japan's military forces and was a key government leader into the 20th century.

Although the shishi had no clear revolutionary program and no organized political party, they contributed not only to the politics of the Meiji Ishin, but also to the evolution of Japanese nationalist ideology. Shishi understood Japan as a nation set apart from others, embraced the imperial institution as the ultimate focal point of Japanese loyalty, and in their zeal to prove their sincerity through radical action, helped bring more than two and a half centuries of Tokugawa rule to an end.

*John H. Sagers*

**See also:** Harris, Townsend; Heusken, Henry; Ii Naosuke; Inoue Kaoru; Itō Hirobumi; Namamugi Incident; Ōkubo Toshimichi; Saigō Takamori; Sakamoto Ryōma; Tokugawa Nariaki; Yamagata Aritomo; Yoshida Shōin.

**Further Reading**

Beasley, W. G. *The Meiji Restoration*. Stanford: Stanford University Press, 1972.

Craig, Albert M. *Chōshū and the Meiji Restoration*. Cambridge, MA: Harvard University Press, 1961.

Jansen, Marius. *Sakamoto Ryōma and the Meiji Restoration*. Princeton: Princeton University Press, 1961.

Koschmann, J. Victor. *The Mito Ideology: Discourse, Reform, and Insurrection in Late Tokugawa Japan, 1790–1864*. Berkeley: University of California Press, 1987.

## Meiji Land Tax (1873)

After five years of collecting land taxes using the systems used by individual *daimyō*, the Meiji government instituted a uniform national system. Various schemes had been proposed by Inoue Kaoru, Ōkuma Shigenobu, and Mutsu Munemitsu (all had served in the Tax Bureau in those first five years); the one instituted was a compendium of these approaches.

Previously, individual *daimyō* had collected a percentage of actual yield, paid as a portion of the crop itself. The new system was based on assessed evaluation of the land and was to be paid in cash. After an attempt to have farmers assess their own land, a nationwide land survey was conducted. The actual land was measured, old tax records scrupulously searched, and assessments were made using 5- to 10-year averages. Private land ownership was recognized for the first time in Japan with the issuing of land titles. Land bonds (*chiken*) were issued to the farmers assuring them that, although the land really belonged to the emperor, they had sole farming rights to it. They were required to sell their crops and pay the assessed tax in cash.

In many cases, the actual tax (3 percent) was lower than what farmers had been paying, particularly if they had been successful in hiding land or actual yield from the *daimyō*. In most cases, however, significant problems ensued.

The problems fell into five basic categories. First, the assessments were issued on assessed *potential* average yields of the land itself. Previously, peasants could make appeals to the *daimyō* if the crop had been damaged by natural phenomena (e.g., drought, hail, flood, locusts). Under the new system, tax collectors did not care if the farmers went into debt or even starved.

Second, farmers had no experience with actual grain markets. Farmers were trying to sell at harvest time; thus prices were lowest when supply was highest. Some farmers were lucky enough to enter into village cooperative schemes to store crops for later sale, or could sell grain futures contracts. Most poor farmers, however, were at the mercy of the market.

Third, unscrupulous moneylenders and corrupt tax collectors all too often took advantage of ignorant peasants. Land was sold to pay taxes, and farmers often ended up as tenant workers on land that they had previously farmed for generations.

Fourth, some land was not really conducive to regular taxation schemes. The swamps, foothills, and mountains had been used for centuries by hunters, gatherers, woodsmen, and fishers, and by peasants who could eke out additional subsistence in agricultural "downtimes." The farmers were now cut off from land where they used to harvest these "free" products.

Fifth, when the government instituted military conscription obligations, farmers lost their manpower in disproportionate numbers. Local epidemics also stripped manpower. If all the workers were ill at the same time, labor costs skyrocketed and farmers went into debt quickly.

Local peasant uprisings eventually forced the prefectural and national governments to make adjustments. The Meiji government lowered the tax rate to 2.5 percent in 1877 out of fear of further revolts.

On the whole, the new tax imposed a huge burden on the peasantry, but it was an obvious boon to the national government for a number of reasons. First, it gave the government a reliable budgetary tax revenue base. Bond revenue could be raised based on a predictable tax by which to pay off the bonds. Eventually, the government could tax grain wholesalers, sake dealers, and others who dealt in rice and other grain products. Second, the government was able to use the land registers for other purposes as well. They were reliable lists to be used for military conscription and even voting suffrage. The prefectural governments used the lists for a number of things, including education and law enforcement.

Social scientists have often cited the land tax reform as an introduction of capitalism and other social ills into Japan's rural areas. Socialists, communists, and anarchists often blame the tax system for imposing poverty and tenancy on the poor peasants. Also, because starving peasants were easy prey for demagogues, ultra-nationalist ideas grew disproportionately in the countryside.

*Louis G. Perez*

See also: Inoue Kaoru; Mutsu Munemitsu; Ōkuma Shigenobu.

## Further Reading

Nakamura, James I. "Meiji Land Reform, Redistribution of Income, and Saving from

Agriculture." *Economic Development and Cultural Change* 14, no. 4 (July 1966): 428–439.

Yamamura, Kozo. "The Meiji Land Tax Reform and Its Effects," in *Japan in Transition: from Tokugawa to Meiji*, edited by Marius B. Jansen and Gilbert Rozman. Princeton: Princeton University Press, 1986:382–399.

## Meiji Press Laws

Meiji-era press-control policies lay at the center of a constant struggle between control and freedom, with officials and writers alike advocating both healthy private debate and adequate national security, even as they argued over which was more important. The result was an era of lively interchange, when scores of press regulations made state power increasingly intrusive, yet left adequate (if decreasing) space for public discussion.

Japan's earliest modern press laws were prompted by the appearance of more than a dozen pamphlet-style "newspapers" in the spring of 1868, most of them critical of the regime that had just come to power. On June 18, the government issued its first press regulation, requiring official permission to publish. Two weeks later, it sent the young editor Fukuchi Gen'ichirō to jail and shut down his paper. Over the next seven years, officials issued successive press guidelines, providing for the registration of publications and detailing what could and could not be published (including "irresponsible criticism of the government"). Because the regulations provided few enforcement procedures, however, a vigorous, politically oriented press emerged in those years.

While authorities announced new press regulations repeatedly throughout the Meiji era, three ordinances—in 1875, 1897, and 1909—formed the essential structure that would dominate Japan's press until the end of World War II. Each of the laws restricted publications in its own way; yet, somewhat ironically, each gave sufficient space to assure that debate would be at least as lively as it was in the legally freer postwar era.

The 1875 *shimbunshi jōrei* (newspaper law), adopted in response to bitter editorial fights over issues such the creation of a legislature and Japan's relations with Korea, was the country's first comprehensive press ordinance. Going beyond the earlier decrees, it not only required prior approval for publishing, but also made editors responsible for a paper's content and insisted that significant news articles be signed. It proscribed a wide range of materials, including the publication of judicial proceedings, the criticism of laws, and the printing of anything that might provoke crime. And it provided for heavy punishment—fines of as much as 500 yen, jail terms as long as three years. Supplements a year later added provisions for the Home Ministry to suspend or ban papers. Moreover, an 1883 addition required papers to make a hefty security deposit, thus shutting down several radical, poorly financed journals.

While some papers toned down coverage as a result of this new law, public debate subsided very little. The editors of some journals risked heavy punishments by continuing to lambaste officials for a variety of "offenses," and the nation's leading editors staged an ingenious protest in which they drafted a set of "hypothetical" articles, asking which constituted a breach of the law. The government refused to respond to the editors, but by 1880 officials had fined hundreds of journalists and sent more than 150 to jail. Some papers skirted the law by hiring dummy "editors" to go to jail when the authorities struck.

Following the 1889 promulgation of the Meiji Constitution, which created a legislature and provided for freedom of the press "within the limits of law," journalists made constant demands for greater press freedom, and sympathetic legislators introduced repeated bills to end the Home Ministry's power to suspend or ban papers. The result was the passage of a new press law in 1897—after an intense outcry over the shutdown of one antigovernment journal—that changed the press-control system without altering it fundamentally. While the new law was praised for ending the administrative suspension of papers, it added new prohibitions, including forbidding the publication of anything that might besmirch the imperial household, and it gave the Home Ministry a new power—to stop the *distribution* of individual issues. The result was a wash. While bans and suspensions declined, the number of papers disrupted by a prohibition on distribution rose.

The final Meiji press law was passed in 1909. Throughout the early 1900s, the press had found endless ways to criticize the authorities: reporting on corruption, using codes to confuse censors, sponsoring citizen rallies to demand lower streetcar fares. Likewise, sympathetic politicians had continued their calls for more liberal laws. In the negotiations for a new bill, however, the conservatives proved more astute: the 1909 law maintained most of the old provisions and doubled the size of security deposits, thereby making it even more difficult for small, radical periodicals to stay in business. The established press, which had become increasingly commercialized, accepted the "revised" regulations with scarcely a complaint. Editors did not like the restrictions, but they were loath to write anything that might threaten their papers' profits. Only wartime defeat in 1945 would prompt genuine liberalization of Japan's press laws.

The sole time when these laws did not shape the government-press dance was when Japan went to war: against China in 1894 and Russia in 1904. Then, emergency orders and military rules took precedence. During the former conflict, for example, officials issued a series of battlefield rules that encompassed both pre-publication censorship and harsh penalties, with the result that more than 370 papers were suspended. The rules were even more far-reaching during the Russo-Japanese War, when both army and navy officials issued separate legal codes, prescribing who could cover the war and what reporters could wear, while requiring that articles be submitted to military censors and prohibiting the use of codes. Though reporters were patriotic to a fault, they used every imaginable ruse to get their stories around the authorities.

By the end of the Meiji era, the press-control system had produced three major results. First, it had made it clear that authorities and journalists stood in essential agreement on the government's fundamental right to maintain order and the press's right to engage in civil discourse. Second, the press-law enforcers had come to focus on two fronts: the political opinions of the far left and the more salacious (but not political) articles deemed likely to "injure public morals." Third, political comment, while still potent, had lost much of its fighting spirit—in part because of the laws and in part because of the press's rising profit orientation.

*James L. Huffman*

**See also:** High Treason Incident; Meiji Constitution; Otsu Incident; Peace Preservation Law; Russo-Japanese War; Sino-Japanese War; Triple Intervention.

**Further Reading**

Huffman, James L. *Creating a Public: People and Press in Meiji Japan.* Honolulu: University of Hawai'i Press, 1997.

Mitchell, Richard H. *Censorship in Imperial Japan*. Princeton, NJ: Princeton University Press, 1983.

Rubin, Jay. *Injurious to Public Morals: Writers and the Meiji State*. Seattle: University of Washington Press, 1984.

## Meiji Restoration. *See* Boshin Civil War.

## Midway, Battle of (June 3–6, 1942)

Beginning in January 1942, the Japanese military attempted to extend its defensive perimeter by seizing bases in Papua and New Guinea and in the Solomon Islands. By early March, these forces had taken the entire north coast of Papua and New Guinea and begun preparations for an amphibious invasion of Port Moresby. On May 7–8, these events resulted in the Battle of the Coral Sea, which ensued after the Japanese invasion force encountered an American carrier force. In the first naval battle in which neither fleet sighted the other, the aircraft carrier *Lexington* was sunk and the carrier *Yorktown* was heavily damaged. However, the Japanese had their light carrier *Shoho* sunk, and the loss of its air cover caused the invasion force to turn back. At the same time, the Americans damaged the carrier *Shokaku*. The Americans were able to repair the *Yorktown* in time for the next battle, whereas *Shokaku* could not be readied for that second and decisive fight. The second carrier, *Zuikaku*, also did not participate due to a shortage of aircraft. Thus, on balance, the Battle of the Coral Sea was a strategic U.S. victory.

A second battle soon developed after the Japanese turned their focus toward the strategic island of Midway. Despite the setback at Coral Sea, Japanese forces continued with their plans to seize Midway Island and bases in the Aleutians. Admiral Yamamoto Isoroku, Commander in Chief of the Combined Fleet, convinced the Imperial General Staff that the capture of Midway would allow Japan to pursue its Asian policies behind an impregnable eastern shield of defenses in the Central Pacific. The capture of Midway would serve as a dramatic response to the April 1942 U.S. raid on Tokyo. It would also deprive the United States of a forward base for submarines, and it would be a steppingstone to the capture of Hawaii. Perhaps most important, it would draw out the U.S. aircraft carriers, giving the Japanese the opportunity to destroy them.

Admiral Yamamoto sent out the bulk of the Japanese fleet. For this operation, he would use some 200 ships—almost the entire Japanese navy—including 8 carriers, 11 battleships, 22 cruisers, 65 destroyers, 21 submarines, and more than 600 aircraft. His plan called for diversionary attacks on the Aleutian Islands both to distract the Americans from Japanese landings on Midway and to allow the Japanese to crush the U.S. reaction force between their forces to the north and at Midway. The Aleutian operation would also secure the islands of Attu and Kiska, placing forces astride a possible U.S. invasion route to Japan.

Yamamoto correctly assumed that the U.S. Pacific Fleet commander, Admiral Chester W. Nimitz, would have to respond to a landing on Midway. When the Pacific Fleet arrived in the area, Japanese carrier and battleship task forces, waiting unseen to the west of the Midway strike force, would fall upon and destroy the unsuspecting Americans. Yamamoto believed that the *Yorktown* had been sunk in the Coral Sea fight and that the *Enterprise* and *Hornet* were not likely to be in the Midway area when the strike force attacked the island.

This miscalculation was one of several breakdowns in Japanese intelligence and communication that contributed to the eventual American victory.

For the Aleutian campaign, Yamamoto committed an invasion force of 2,400 men in three escorted transports, a support group of two heavy cruisers and two light carriers, and a covering force of four older battleships. The battle began in the Aleutians with air strikes on June 3, followed by landings three days later. The Aleutian phase of the operation went well for the Japanese. Carrier aircraft inflicted heavy damage on the U.S. base at Dutch Harbor, and the Japanese then made unopposed landings on Kiska and Attu. They maintained this toehold on continental U.S. territory until mid-1943.

Despite the Japanese success in the Aleutians, the action there proved to be superfluous to the coming battle at Midway. U.S. intelligence had broken the Japanese naval code, putting the basic outlines of the Midway plan into American hands and allowing the Americans to disregard the attacks on the Aleutians in favor of concentrating on Midway. The Pacific Fleet was ready with three fleet aircraft carriers, including the *Yorktown*. This ship had been hastily repaired at Pearl Harbor to allow operations in only 2 days (instead of an estimated 90 days) and was sent back to sea with an air group formed of planes from other carriers. *Yorktown* sailed just in advance of a picket line of Japanese submarines that Yamamoto hoped would intercept ships departing Pearl Harbor. The U.S. ships were concentrated in an ambush position some 350 miles northeast of Midway, awaiting the westward advance of Yamamoto's armada.

On June 3, American naval reconnaissance planes sighted, at a distance of 600 miles, the Japanese armada of some 185 ships

advancing on Midway. The battle began when Boeing B-17 Flying Fortress bombers from Midway Island struck without effect at the Japanese carrier strike force, about 220 miles southwest of the U.S. fleet. That same night, four Consolidated patrol bombers (PBYs) from Midway staged a torpedo attack and damaged an oiler, although the ship was able to regain its place in the formation.

Early on June 4, Nagumo sent 108 Japanese planes from the strike force to attack and bomb Midway, while the Japanese carriers again escaped damage from U.S. land-based planes. However, as the morning progressed, the Japanese carriers were soon overwhelmed by the logistics of almost simultaneously sending a second wave of bombers to finish off the Midway runways, zigzagging to avoid the bombs of attacking aircraft, and rearming to launch planes to sink the now sighted U.S. naval forces. American fighters and bombers, sent from Midway airfields, and aircraft from three U.S. carriers attacked the Japanese fleet. Three successive waves of U.S. torpedo-bombers were virtually wiped out during their attacks on the carriers; Japanese fighters and antiaircraft guns shot down 47 of 51 planes. The Japanese now believed that they had won the battle.

The Japanese First Air Fleet commander, Nagumo Chūichi, had ordered planes returning from strikes on Midway to rearm with torpedoes to strike the American ships. As this effort was in progress at about 10:30 a.m., 37 dive-bombers from the carrier *Enterprise* at last located the Japanese carriers in their most vulnerable state, while their decks were cluttered with armed aircraft, ordnance, and fuel. The Japanese fighters in the air were also down low, having dealt with the torpedo-bomber attacks. Within the span of a few minutes, three of the four Japanese carriers—the *Soryu, Kaga*, and *Akagi*—were in flames and sinking. Planes from the only intact Japanese carrier, the *Hiryu*, now struck back, heavily damaging the *Yorktown*. In late afternoon, the *Hiryu* also was hit and badly damaged. The Japanese crew abandoned the carrier the next day.

During the battle between the U.S. and Japanese naval forces, the two fleets neither saw each other nor exchanged gunfire; all contact was made by Japanese carrier-based planes and American land- and carrier-based aircraft. Yamamoto's first reaction on learning of the loss of three of his carriers was to bring up his battleships and recall the two light carriers from the Aleutians in hopes of fighting a more conventional sea battle. Ultimately, the loss of the *Hiryu* and Nagumo's gloomy reports led him to call off the attack on Midway. Yamamoto still hoped to trap the Americans by drawing them westward into his heavy ships, but the U.S. task force commander, Rear Admiral Raymond Spruance, refused to play his game and reported to Nimitz that he was unwilling to risk a night encounter with superior Japanese forces.

By the night of June 6, the Battle of Midway was over. It had been a costly defeat for Japan. In the battle itself, the Japanese had lost 4 aircraft carriers and 332 aircraft, most of which went down with the carriers. They also had a heavy cruiser sunk and another badly damaged. Three destroyers and a fleet oiler were damaged as well, and a battleship was slightly damaged. The Americans lost the aircraft carrier *Yorktown*, 1 destroyer, and 147 aircraft (38 of these being shore based).

The Japanese navy was still a formidable fighting force, but once it lost the four fleet carriers and their well-trained aircrews and maintenance personnel, the continued Japanese preponderance in battleships and cruisers counted for little. The subsequent Japanese defeat in the protracted fight for Guadalcanal was due principally to a lack of air assets. It can be reasonably stated that the Battle of Midway was indeed the turning point of the long struggle in the Pacific Theater.

*James H. Willbanks*

**See also:** Coral Sea, Battle of; Yamamoto Isoroku; World War II, Pacific Theater.

## Further Reading

Fuchida, Mitsuo, and Okumiya Masatake. *Midway: The Battle That Doomed Japan—The Japanese Navy's Story*. Annapolis, MD: Naval Institute Press, 1955.

Lord, Walter. *Incredible Victory*. New York: Harper and Row, 1967.

Morison, Samuel Eliot. *History of United States Naval Operations in World War II. Vol. 4: Coral Sea, Midway, and Submarine Actions, May 1942–August 1942*. Boston: Little, Brown, 1949.

Prange, Gordon W. *Miracle at Midway*. New York: McGraw-Hill, 1982.

## Minamoto Yoritomo (1147–1199)

Yoritomo was born in A.D. 1147. He was the son of Minamoto Yoshitomo and Fujiwara Suenori. His family, the Minamoto family, was a powerful military clan that descended from the imperial family. In 1158, at a very young age, Yoritomo received his first court title. A few years later, he was appointed as an administrator. Within a year of that promotion, however, the family participated in the rebellion called the Heiji Disturbance against the Taira family, the ruling military family of Japan. Yoritomo was sent into exile in Izu Province, and his father was killed, which led to the end of the rebellion.

During that time, Yoritomo married Hōjō Masako, who was a member of the Hōjō

Minamoto Yoritomo was the founder and first shōgun of the Kamakura shōgunate, which established the shōgunate system of government in Japan that lasted nearly seven centuries. (Corel)

clan and whose father was a Taira vassal. Yoritomo participated in another Minamoto-led rebellion against the Taira clan in 1180. The Japanese prince, Mochihito-o, had issued an imperial order asking the Minamoto clan to stop the Taira clan's incursions. That imperial edict gave Yoritomo and the rest of his family a justified reason to attack the Taira clan as well as others who were aligned against Yoritomo and his family. The rebellion even garnered support from disenfranchised Taira family members. During that conflict, Yoritomo set up his headquarters at Kamakura, which was not far from present-day Tokyo.

The civil war that resulted became known as the Gempei War. With the help of his cousin Minamoto Yoshinaka, Yoritomo managed to drive the Taira out of the capital of Kyoto. In 1183, the Minamoto clan was gaining ground in Japan. However, when Yoshinaka's troops caused unrest in Kyoto, Yoritomo and his half-brother Minamoto Yoshitsune, at the behest of Emperor Go-Shirakawa, took control of the capital from Yoshinaka. The battle against the Taira clan continued, and in 1184, the Minamoto clan, under the control of Yoshitsune and Minamoto Noriyori, won a decisive naval battle at Dannoura against the Taira clan. At that point, Yoritomo became the leader of the new warrior society that had developed over the course of the Gempei War.

After the war, Yoritomo decided to set up his independent military government at the city of Kamakura. Recognized by the imperial court in Kyoto, Yoritomo's government, with the aid of the samurai class of warriors, was responsible for maintaining law and order within Japan's provinces. There were now two structures with the power of rule in Japan: one staffed by courtiers and the other managed by warriors.

Because of his half-brother's success in Kyoto and at Dannoura, Yoritomo began to be jealous of Yoshitsune's control. Yoritomo levied imperial sanctions against his rival and hired police and stewards to hunt down his half-brother. Yoshitsune became a fugitive in his own country and eventually was sentenced to death. Those who had helped Yoritomo hunt Yoshitsune into submission later became department officials in Yoritomo's national governmental structure.

During the takeover, Yoritomo kept his government base at Kamakura, where his supporters and samurai were housed. In 1192, after Emperor Go-Shirakawa's death, Yoritomo claimed the title of supreme commander, or shōgun. That title gave him the power to act independently against any rebel he felt was a threat to his country and his control. It also marked the formal beginning of the Kamakura shōgunate.

During his remaining years, Yoritomo's policies helped ease relations between the various factions with the Japanese government as well as within society. Yoritomo died in 1199 from, according to some sources, a serious illness. His oldest son, Minamoto Yoriie, succeeded him as the second Kamakura shōgun.

*Kim Draggoo*

**See also:** Hogen-Heiji-Gempei Wars; Hôjô Masako; Kamakura *Bakufu*; Minamoto Yoshitsune.

### Further Reading

Hall, John Whitney, and Jeffrey P. Mass, eds., *Medieval Japan.* New Haven, CT: Yale University Press, 1974.

Perez, Louis G. *The History of Japan.* Westport, CT: Greenwood Press. 1998.

Yamamura, Kozo, ed. *The Cambridge History of Japan. Vol. 3: Medieval Japan.* Cambridge, UK: Cambridge University Press, 1990.

## Minamoto Yoshitsune (1159–1189)

Minamoto Yoshitsune, a warrior of the Tara and Kamakura eras, is one of Japan's most admired heroes. His meteoric rise to prominence in the Gempei War and his death at the hands of his half-brother, Minamoto Yoritomo, founder of the Kamakura *bakufu*, cast Yoshitsune as the quintessential "failed hero" and the term *hōgan biiki*, meaning "sympathy for the underdog" (literally "tears for the lieutenant"), was coined in his memory. The historical record on Yoshitsune is sparse, but his legacy has been embellished through Noh and Kabuki plays and other popular literary and artistic recreations. As one scholar noted, if Yoshitsune

had not existed, the Japanese would have invented him.

Yoshitsune was the ninth son of Minamoto Yoshitomo; his mother was Tokiwa Gozen, a beautiful, but minor lady-in-waiting. In 1160, Yoshitomo turned on his Taira allies and was killed in the Heiji War, which brought the Taira clan to prominence in Kyoto. While the Taira executed the adult Minamoto clan leaders, the male children, including Yoshitsune, were spared. As a youth, Yoshitsune was known as Ushiwakamaru and was sent to Kuruma Temple to study Buddhism. Ten years later, after learning his true Minamoto heritage, he ran away. For five years, he traveled throughout the country evading his sworn enemy, the Tairas, while honing his military skills. One of his most famous encounters was his defeat of the bandit monk, Benkei, who afterward became his trusted companion. Eventually, he was taken in by Fujiwara Hidehara in Mutsu Province (present-day Aomori).

Yoshitsune's first meeting with Yoritomo came in 1181, just after the outbreak of the Gempei War. The first command Yoritomo gave him was against their cousin, Minamoto Yoshinaka, whose antagonism of the court threatened Yoritomo's own military and political ambitions. After gaining a reputation through his defeat of Yoshinaka, Yoshitsune further distinguished himself in the Gempei War in the Battle of Ichinotani, where he routed the Taira by leading his forces down the steep Hiyodorigoe Cliff, and in the Taira's final defeat at the Battle of Dannoura.

Yoshitsune's reputation as a warrior won him the acclaim of the people and court, but drew the animosity of Yoritomo, who refused to grant him any titles. Defying Yoritomo's directive that the court bestow no honors without his approval, the former emperor Goshirokawa, perhaps hoping to exacerbate the tension between the two brothers, granted Yoshitsune the title lieutenant (*hōgan*) in the Bureau of Metropolitan Police, from which comes the expression "tears for the lieutenant." Although Yoshitsune claimed he was unable to decline the position, his acceptance further fueled Yoritomo's ire. It is not clear why Yoritomo became so hostile toward his younger brother. With the end of the Gempei War, Yoritomo may no longer have needed the bold and daring warrior. He may have also been jealous and saw Yoshitsune as a possible rival as he was establishing his own new powerbase. Also, because Yoshistune's mother was of minor court rank, Yoritomo never accepted his half-brother as an equal.

Tradition says that Yoshitsune was reluctant to recognize Yoritomo's hostility even after the first assassination attempts. Yoritomo pressured the court to declare his half-brother an outlaw, forcing Yoshitsune and a small cadre of his supporters, including Benkei and Yoshitsune's mistress Shizuka, to flee Kyoto and go into hiding. Yoshitsune finally took refuge again with Hidehara, but his protector was in his nineties and died a few months later. After Hidehara's death, Yoshitsune was vulnerable to assassination attempts and, according to legend, committed ritual suicide in 1189 at the age of 30 while Benkei held off the assailants.

*R. W. Purdy*

**See also:** *Hara-kiri* and *Seppuku*; *Heike monogatari*; Hogen-Heiji-Gempei Wars; Kamakura *Bakufu*; Minamoto Yoritomo.

#### Further Reading

McCullough, Helen Craig, trans. *Yoshitsune: A Fifteen-Century Japanese Chronicle*. Stanford: Stanford University Press, 1966.

Morris, Ivan. *The Nobility of Failure: Tragic Heroes in the History of Japan*. New York: Holt, Rinehart and Winston, 1975.

Varley, Paul. *Warriors of Japan as Portrayed in War Tales*. Honolulu: University of Hawai'i Press, 1994.

## Minobe Tatsukichi (1873–1948)

Born on May 7, 1873, in Takasago village near Kobe, Minobe Tatsukichi overcame financial challenges to graduate in political science from the Law Faculty of Tokyo Imperial University in 1897. In 1898, he married Kikuchi Tamiko, the daughter of University President Kikuchi Dairoku. After graduation, Minobe secured an assignment from the Ministry of Education to study comparative legislative systems in England, France, and Germany. While abroad between 1899 and 1902, he refined his organ theory of government, which suggested that the state was a corporate entity composed of various organs including the emperor. Based on his study abroad, the Imperial University bestowed upon Minobe the degree of doctor of law in 1903 (a practice common at the time). Minobe succeeded to his mentor's chair in administrative law and maintained a focus on constitutional law from a comparative perspective throughout his career.

Within the academic and legal order of the Meiji period, constitutional law was a preeminent field. Minobe studied the important question of the imperial institution and in 1912, published his thoughts on the organ theory of the state. This publication invited a fierce rivalry with Minobe's Tokyo Imperial University counterpart, Uesugi Shinkichi, who held the University's sole constitutional law chair and subscribed to his mentor Hozumi Yatsuka's assertion that the emperor was the embodiment of the state. Minobe lectured at other universities, including Chūō University, and served on a range of government committees. In 1920, Tokyo Imperial University established a second chair in constitutional law for Min-obe, reflecting the widespread influence of his thought. During a teaching career that lasted until 1934, Minobe's students included liberal activist Ishibashi Tanzan and the future Emperor Hirohito. Minobe was a prolific author, with works in four major genres including textbooks, scholarly articles and monographs, public commentary in major journals (such as *Chūō kōron* and *Kaizō*), and translations of foreign writing on law.

In 1932, Minobe joined the House of Peers by appointment, but his career in that body proved ill fated. In 1935, fellow House member Kikuchi Takeo denounced Minobe's constitutional theories, calling Minobe a traitor to the body politic. Minobe offered a rigorous defense of his academic writing and political record, yet in the face of pressure from Prime Minister Okada Keisuke he tendered his resignation, which his former student Emperor Hirohito accepted on September 1935. The Okada Cabinet criminalized his theories and writings, yet procurators refused to pursue criminal charges against Minobe even as ultra-nationalists demonstrated against him in the streets. Extremists turned to force of arms, making an assassination attempt on Minobe in February 1936 that left him injured. The uprising by young officers at the end of the month signaled the limits of Minobe's theories in the face of ascendant militarism and ultra-nationalism, which ultimately fueled war and destruction in East Asia.

After Japan's defeat, Minobe served on the Matsumoto Commission for the revision of the Meiji Constitution, on which he argued for preserving the document and the national polity (*kokutai*) that had once been his scourge. Following the imposition of the occupation-drafted constitution, Minobe complained that it was inappropriate to

Japan. An active constitutional scholar until the end, Minobe died on May 23, 1948.

*Darryl Flaherty*

**See also:** February 26 Incident; Shōwa Emperor.

**Further Reading**

Jansen, Marius B. *The Making of Modern Japan*. Cambridge, MA: Belknap Press, 2000.

Miller, Frank O. *Minobe Tatsukichi: Interpreter of Constitutionalism in Japan*. Berkeley, CA: University of California Press, 1965.

## Mishima Yukio (1925–1970)

Born Hiraoka Kimitake into a well-placed family in Tokyo on January 14, 1925, Mishima Yukio died by his own hand by ritual *hara kiri* or *seppuku* on November 25, 1970, in a theatrically attempted military coup at the Ichigaya headquarters of the Japanese Self-Defense Forces (S-DF) (*Jiei-tai*), an action that garnered world attention and raised concerns regarding an upsurge in Japanese militarism. At the time, he was arguably the most prominent Japanese novelist, playwright, essayist, and international personality.

Mishima had an overprotected, but emotionally chaotic, upbringing. Although a commoner, his grandmother strongly identified with her samurai background, and his grandfather was a former governor of Sakhalin, a Japanese colony. Mishima attended the prestigious Peer School, where his intelligence and abilities as a writer were recognized. As a student during World War II, his education was dominated by the indoctrination of nationalism.

In particular, Mishima was impressed by the *Hagakure* (The Book of the Samurai), compiled in the early 1700s and identified with the slogan "I have discovered that the Way of the Samurai is death." Another key influence would have been the 1937 *Kokutai no Hongi* (Cardinal Principles of the National Entity) which became almost a spiritual and nationalistic bible in the Japanese schools during the war, defending all aspects of traditional culture, especially Shintoism and the samurai ideal of *Bushidō*, and emphasizing one's duty and loyalty to the Emperor. Furthermore, his literary mentors during this time were absorbed by what was termed the Japanese Romantic School, which exalted traditionalism, the role of the emperor, and death as glorification of these ideals. These themes were evident in Mishima's earliest publications as a high school student, already under his pen name, and continued as themes throughout many of his literary works. He also revered the experience of personally meeting Emperor Hirohito, an honor bestowed upon him when he graduated first in his class from the Peers School.

In 1941, the National School Reform began placing increased emphasis on physical education in preparation for war service. Mishima, who was somewhat sickly as a youth, did not identify with this indoctrination, nor aspire to fight in the war having by his account an inferiority complex about his own physique and a distaste for sports, especially *kendo*. In fact, when he was formally called up for military service in February 1945, he was so physically weak, due both to chronic conditions and an acute lung inflammation, that he failed his physical exam and was sent home. His relationship to his own physique changed after he took up weight training in the mid-1950s, to remarkable effect. His body building led him back to *kendo* and to a course of physical conditioning, one of the forces that became increasingly synchronous for him with forging a samurai identity. Yet this emerging preoccupation with his physical presentation, romanticized in his extended autobiographical essay "Sun and Steel" (*Taiyo to Tetsu*, 1970), focused on the dialectic between the intellectual and physical self, and appears as much narcissistic as political.

Mishima's involvement in Japanese politics began to be more explicit in 1961. His short story "Patriotism" was set in the *Ni Ni Roku* (February 26 Incident) of 1936 that had attempted to overthrow the government and restore the emperor. In his fictionalized account, the chief character commits a highly romanticized *seppuku* upon the failure of the coup. With this publication, Mishima became publically identified with right-wing politics. His dissatisfaction with the direction of Japanese politics particularly with Article 9 of the Constitution of 1954 that defined the S-DF as a police force, rather than as an army, became increasingly central to his own identity. In April 1967, Mishima "enlisted" in the Self-Defense Forces (S-DF) (*Jieitai*), to which he had unusual access owing to his literary fame, and completed basic training—his first concrete step toward active association with the Japanese military. This was followed by increasing involvement with right-wing student groups, notably at Waseda University; he brought the first group of students to train with the S-DF in March 1968, and began seeking financial support from right-wing leaders to create a substantial student military group. Failing in this effort, he created the Tate no Kai (Shield Society, as in "shielding" the emperor) later that year. The left-wing student uprisings and protests of 1968–1969 further focused Mishima's resolve to use the Tate no Kai to take some type of action, initially through an act of *kirijini* (literally "going down fighting") in support of the emperor and against what he anticipated would be growing Communist-leaning actions As it became apparent that the uprisings were quieting down, this evolved into plans for the Ichigawa Incident and his plans for *seppuku*.

On the morning of November 25, 1970, Mishima, accompanied by four members of the Tate no Kai, entered the Ichigawa office of General Mashita, whom he knew and with whom he had made an appointment. Fighting off aides, seven of whom were injured, Mishima tied Mashita to his chair and demanded that the members of the 32nd Infantry be assembled outside. Wearing a kamikaze-style headband (white with a red sun), he addressed the 1,200 troops from a balcony. Police helicopters were already flying overhead, alerted to the incident by Mishima himself. When his speech was almost immediately drowned out by derisive cries from the soldiers, Mishima responded by yelling: "We are going to enter our protest against this constitution with our deaths. *Tennō Heika Banzai!* (Long live the Emperor!)" With that, Mishima turned back into the office. In front of the general, he committed *seppuku* by cutting his abdomen with a short sword; then Morita Masakatsu, his primary aide, acting as *kaishaku* (his second), cut off Mishima's head. Morita then committed *seppuku*, and one of the remaining three protestors cut off his head. At this point the remaining men were arrested.

The reaction to the incident was decidedly mixed. After initially calling him "insane," Prime Minister Satō said that Japanese "should respect Mishima's motives," and Defense Agency Director Nakasone called the suicide "a milestone in the evolution of Japanese thought." The Japanese press was flooded with articles about Mishima; his works, including his commentary on the *Hagakure*, were sold out at bookstores. Within a few weeks, six Tokyo department stores had run exhibitions of samurai swords. The Western press also gave the incident considerable coverage, although often with the culturally naïve perspective that Mishima was psychiatrically impaired or depressed. Those concerned with the political repercussions of Mishima's act quickly realized that no coordinated efforts were forthcoming from the right wing, and serious foreign analysis and concern ended with a sigh of relief.

In Japan sentiment soon shifted. General Mashita resigned to take responsibility for the incident. The Tate no Kai were ostracized and disbanded four months later. The three surviving participants were charged with illegal confinement, assault and battery, infliction of injuries, forcing others to exercise authority, and murder by request. It was the first time *kaishaku* had been tried under modern law. On April 27, 1972, the three dissidents were sentenced to four years' imprisonment at hard labor. Ironically, a few days prior to this event, on April 17, 1972, the Nobel laureate novelist Kawabata Yasunari, one of Mishima's mentors, committed suicide. Hardly an article about him was written without mention of Mishima, either to affirm or deny possible connection.

The motivation behind Mishima's suicide appears to have been extremely complex, consistent with the many aspects of his self-identity and social role. At least two overt political purposes were intended: reinstating the emperor as a symbolic god and spiritual head of Japanese culture, and protesting Article 9 of the Japanese Constitution. More personal reasons for his action included his long-standing fascination with death as the ultimate statement of purpose, a narcissistic fear of aging, and possibly a homosexual suicide pact with Morita, his "second." Evidence suggests that Mishima had been carefully planning the event for at least one year. He had turned in the final chapter of his final opus, a four-volume novel entitled *The Sea of Fertility*, shortly before the uprising. One explanation for the date, November 25, was that it was the original due date for the novel; another is that it coincided with the anniversary of the 1859 execution of Yoshida Shōin, a samurai-intellectual involved in the movement to overthrow the shōgunate and restore the emperor to central power. Yoshida's writings on *bushidō*, deeply influenced by Wang Yang-ming (*Yōmeigaku*) philosophy and the *Hagakure*, had appeared in the *Kokutai no Hongi*.

In the longer term, most Japanese had trouble accepting the exhibitionism apparent in the suicide. The individualist Mishima had overestimated the power of his personal appeal in Japan, and many of the people whom he was trying to reach responded with continued embarrassment both at his efforts to re-engage the samurai "spirit" and at the echoes of the militarism of the World War II era. His impressive body of work, while by no means obscure, arguably garners less attention and respect than it might otherwise, based on its promise and recognition during his lifetime, and Mishima remains known, perhaps as he desired, as much for the Ichigaya Incident as for his writing.

*Jean L. Kristeller*

**See also:** February 26 Incident; Self-Defense Forces (*Jieitai*), from the Bomb to Iraq; Yoshida Shōin.

**Further Reading**

Kristeller, Jean L. "Mishima's Suicide: A Psycho-cultural Analysis." *Psychologia* 16 (1973): 50–59.

Nathan, John. *Mishima: A Biography*. Boston: Little Brown and Company, 1974.

Stokes, Henry Scott. *The Life and Death of Yukio Mishima*. New York: Penguin Books, 1975.

# Mito School

The "Mito School" refers to a number of generations of Confucian scholars of the Tokugawa period (1603–1868) who were based in the Mito domain, in present-day Ibaraki Prefecture. Mito School scholars famously originated key ideas in modern Japanese national ideology, notably *kokutai* and *sonno-jōi*. These ideas influenced the Meiji Revolution, and continued to be used centrally in the ideology of the Japanese state until 1945.

Mito School scholars worked directly for the Lord of Mito Domain in the domainal academy. The traditional association of the Mito domain with scholarship began during the rule of domain lord Tokugawa Mitsukuni (1628–1701). Mitsukuni established a historical bureau in 1657, and began a project of compiling a complete history of Japan. This so-called *Dai Nihonshi* ("History of Great Japan") project continued into the 20th century, being taken over by national research institutes of the modern Japanese government.

Their intense work on historical interpretation and Confucian political thought led Mito School scholars to originate their own political ideas, particularly during the late 18th and early 19th centuries. The height of Mito School influence came during this later period, when Mito School scholars, among them Aizawa Seishisai, Fujita Yūkoku, and Fujita Tōko, developed a synthesis of nationalist and Confucian political thought that attracted a substantial following throughout Japan. The two most influential Mito works were Fujita Yūkoku's *Seimeiron* (1791) and Aizawa Seishisai's *Shinron*

(1825). In these works can be found the origins of the doctrine of *sonno-jōi* (Revere the Sovereign—Expel the Barbarians), which became the rallying cry of the Meiji Revolution. Aizawa, in particular, argued that the Tokugawa shōgunate should strengthen itself through using the charismatic power of the emperor to gain more direct power for the shōgunate so it could carry out a military buildup in preparation for Japan's inevitable confrontation with the expansionist West. Fujita and Aizawa's arguments emerged just as Western imperialism was growing as a major threat in East Asia. Within 15 years of *Shinron*'s appearance, the Western powers had defeated China in the Opium Wars. In this context, Mito School ideas were attractive for two reasons. On the one hand, they put forward a plan for transforming Japan into a military power capable of resisting the West; on the other hand, they followed Japanese Nativism in emphasizing the superiority of Japan over China. Given China's appearance of weakness in its confrontation with the West, the Mito School's emphasis of Japanese national identity and historic superiority, not only over the West, but also over China, was both novel and attractive.

Mito School political ideas, although emphasizing the potential power that could be wielded by giving the emperor a more central role in the polity, were developed to improve the political position of the shōgunate. It was envisaged that the emperor would enable the shōgunate to further centralize power, thereby increasing shōgunal power in relation to that of the *daimyō* and merchants. The Mito domain lord was a member of a secondary branch of the Tokugawa family and had a direct stake in the continuation of the shōgunate. The Mito School, therefore, was pro-shōgunate, with its "Revere the Emperor" ideology originally being designed to support the shōgunate and help the Tokugawa family. The anti-Western aspect of Mito School political ideas was also closely related to the political stance of the Mito domain lord. During most of the 19th century, the Mito domain lord was Tokugawa Nariaki, who led the hardline "Expel the Barbarians" faction in shōgunal politics. The increasing anti-Western line of Mito School writings during the mid-1800s, therefore, can also be seen partly as a kind of propaganda designed to support their lord's immediate political activities. It is one of the great ironies of Japanese history that the Mito School scholars who created the "Revere the Emperor—Expel the Barbarians" doctrine, which eventually became the rallying cry of anti-shōgunate rebels, were scholars working directly for a Tokugawa lord.

*Kiri Paramore*

**See also:** Aizawa Seishisai; *Kokutai* and Ultranationalism; *Sonno-jōi*; Tokugawa *Bakufu* Political System; Tokugawa Nariaki.

### Further Reading

Koschmann, Victor. *The Mito Ideology.* Berkeley: University of California Press, 1987.

Wakabayashi, Bob Tadashi. *Anti-foreignism and Western Learning in Early-Modern Japan: The New Theses of 1825.* Cambridge, MA: Harvard University Press, 1986.

## Mongol Invasions of Japan (1274, 1281)

In 1266, the Mongol emperor of China, Kublai Khan (1215–1294), sent a letter from "the Emperor of Great Mongolia" to the "King of Japan," delivered by a Korean envoy demanding that Japan submit to a tributary relationship or face invasion. Japan at the time was ruled by Hōjō Tokimune

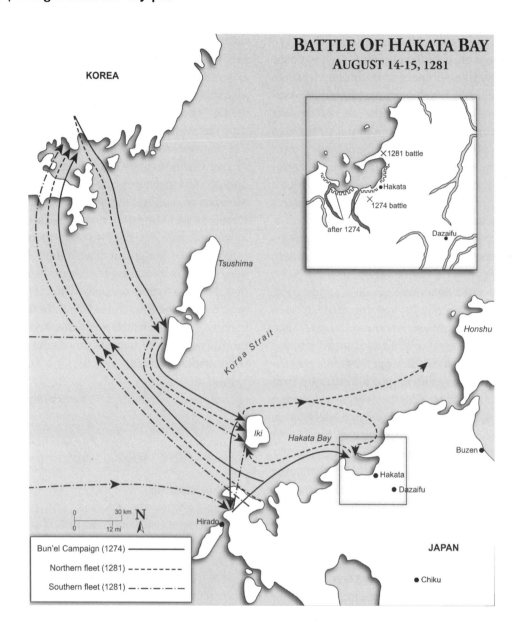

**BATTLE OF HAKATA BAY**
**AUGUST 14-15, 1281**

(1251–1284), regent for the Kamakura shō-gun. Although there was much debate about how to respond to the Mongol threat—news of what had happened to Korea was widely known in Japan—Tokimune decided to send back the envoys with no response. The Japanese emperor felt insulted by the letter, but could do little more than pray due to his marginalized position. Mongol envoys were dispatched four more times in as many years after that, but all were sent away.

In October 1274, Kublai sent an armada of 900 ships from the southern tip of Korea carrying more than 30,000 troops commanded by a Mongol general, with a Korean and a Chinese lieutenant. The soldiers were also a mixture of Mongols, Koreans, and Chinese. After quickly subduing the islands of Tsushima and Iki, the invaders landed in Hakata Bay. With superior weaponry, they easily gained upper hand in the battle on October 20. The Japanese abandoned Hakata and ran for their lives to Dazaifu. For reasons still unknown, the Mongol forces did not pursue the defeated Japanese but withdrew to their ships instead. That night, a typhoon suddenly blustered and destroyed the fleet. By one estimate, as many as 15,000 soldiers were drowned.

Despite the setback, Kublai renewed his demands in 1275. The envoy he dispatched, however, was ordered by Tokimune to be beheaded. Kublai's second envoy met the same fate in 1279. Anticipating another attack, the Kamakura *bakufu* reorganized the coastal defense, extending it to the western coast of Honshū. Moreover, it ordered preparation of small attack vessels and the construction of an earth-and-stone wall along Hakata Bay. The Imperial Court, meanwhile, ordered all temples and shrines to pray for Japan's victory.

In June 1281, two Mongol fleets, comprising a stunning total of 4,400 warships carrying 140,000 troops, set out for the second invasion of Japan. The Eastern Fleet from Korea arrived at Hakata on June 23 and landed troops at several places in northwest Kyūshū. But the Japanese, helped by the earth-and-stone walls, prevented them from gaining a foothold. Moreover, the smaller and easier-to-maneuver Japanese vessels harassed the invaders and set fire to their cumbersome ships. When the Southern Fleet from China arrived belatedly and the combined forces were preparing for a decisive attack on Hakata, another typhoon roared ashore on August 15 and 16. Of the 4,400 Mongol ships, only a few hundred survived. Most of the invaders drowned in the storm. The few thousand who survived were hunted and killed by the samurai.

The failure of the two invasions—known in Japan as the Battle of Bun'ei (*Bun'ei no eki*) and the Battle of Koan (*Kōan no eki*), respectively—has often been attributed to the lack of experience of Mongol cavalry in navy battles, the low morale of the Mongols' Korean and Chinese conscripts, and the determined resistance of the Japanese. Of course, the fortuitous typhoons were really the main reason for the Mongols' defeat. Kublai never gave up his ambitions toward Japan until his death in 1294. Most Japanese believed their victory was due to "the divine wind" (*kamikaze*), creating the myth that Japan was a country protected by gods—a myth to be invoked in World War II by Japanese suicide pilots. Nevertheless, fear of another invasion kept the Japanese on military alert for 20 more years.

Due to the Mongol invasions, the Kamakura shōgunate extended its control to the western provinces and concentrated power in the hands of the Hōjō family. This turn of events caused deep resentment among those vassals who were denied important posts. Moreover, widespread bitterness emerged among the warrior class, who expected rewards for their loyalty and sacrifice but got none because the shōgunate itself was exhausted by the war expenses and the victories over the Mongols yielded no booty or land. The Mongol invasions, therefore, contributed to the downfall of the Kamakura shōgunate, even though its power reached its peak during the crisis.

*Guohe Zheng*

**See also:** Hōjō Tokimune; Kamakura *Bakufu*; Kamikaze (*Tokkōtai*).

## Further Reading

Conlan, Thomas. *In Little Need of Divine Intervention*. Ithaca, NY: Cornell University, 2001.

Turnbull, Stephen R., and Hook, Richard. *The Mongol Invasions of Japan, 1274 and 1281.* Oxford, UK: Osprey Publishing, 2010.

## Mukden Incident: Lytton Report

In the Mukden Incident, Japanese soldiers based in northeastern China (then known as Manchuria) dynamited a section of a Japanese-owned railway and, after laying the blame on Chinese dissidents, used it as a pretext to launch a takeover of the entire region. The incident is usually dated as extending from the railway explosion of September 18, 1931, to the Tanggu Truce of May 31, 1933, which officially ended Sino-Japanese hostilities in the invasion of Manchuria. Some scholars mark its end with the Marco Polo Bridge Incident of July 1937 that began the Second Sino-Japanese War (1937–1945).

The origins of the Mukden Incident, also known as the Manchurian Incident and the September 18 Incident, stem from the acquisition of territorial and commercial interests in Manchuria following Japan's victory in the Russo-Japanese War in 1905. Japan's newly won spoils presented it with the "Manchurian problem" (*Manshū mondai*)—that is, the important tasks of securing, maintaining, and expanding Japanese interests in southern Manchuria. Initially, Japan focused on relations with Russia to solve the "problem," but Chinese nationalism supplanted the czar as the source of Japanese anxiety in the 1920s. By the early 1930s, the "problem" grew to encompass a whole host of Japanese concerns, including competing Chinese railways, an economic depression, and movements by Japanese residents in Manchuria.

The Japanese military and some prominent politicians had come to refer to Manchuria as Japan's "lifeline" (*seimeisen*) by the early 1930s. This rhetoric hardened Japan's resolve to protect its interests in the region in the face of rising Chinese nationalism and its demands of reclaiming sovereignty over all Chinese land. Many in the army believed Japan needed to be in control of Manchuria and its resources to properly wage a war against the Soviet Union, a conflict that was considered inevitable. Officers of the Japanese Kwantung Army, which was based in Manchuria and thus on the front line of a future war with the USSR, were perhaps the strongest supporters of this view.

Colonels Ishiwara Kanji and Itagaki Seishirō, both Kwantung Army staff officers, wrote operational plans for the military takeover of Manchuria in the summer of 1931. Believing they had the tacit approval of their superiors, Ishiwara and Itagaki enacted their plan on the night of September 18, 1931, by detonating a bomb on a section of the South Manchurian Railroad on the outskirts of the city of Mukden (Shenyang) and then ordering the capture of the city.

Due to the nonresistance policy of the acting ruler of Manchuria, Zhang Xueliang, the Kwantung Army was able to occupy the region quickly. By early 1932, Japan was in control of Manchuria, despite encountering some resistance in the north. The Japanese established the puppet state of Manchukuo in March 1932 and installed former Qing Dynasty Emperor Pu-yi as its head. Later, in January 1933, Japan invaded the neighboring province of Jehol (Rehe) and annexed it to Manchukuo.

During the Mukden Incident, the Chinese appealed to the League of Nations to intervene. With League sentiment running against Japan, Japanese delegates suggested a compromise that called for the League to dispatch a commission of inquiry to the region. The League Council unanimously agreed to the commission, mandating that it should prepare a report on the incident's origins and offer proposals for an equitable resolution.

Headed by Lord Lytton of Britain, the five-member commission arrived in Japan on February 29, 1932, to begin their six-month investigation, during which they visited with government officials in China and Japan and spent six weeks touring Manchuria. While in Manchuria, the commission received more than 1,000 letters from local Chinese citizens arguing that the Japanese were responsible for the Mukden Incident and the creation of Manchukuo. Lytton and his colleagues finished their fieldwork in the summer of 1932. Sensing that the commission's report would be critical of the establishment of Manchukuo, Japan opted to officially recognize the new state in September. The Japanese leadership hoped to mute questions of Manchukuo's legitimacy and force the commission to offer de facto recognition in its report.

The commission published its report in October 1932. Concerning the outbreak of the incident, the report stated, "The military operations of the Japanese troops . . . cannot be regarded as measures of legitimate self-defense." While initially seeming to refute Japanese claims, the report then noted, "In saying this, the Commission does not exclude the hypothesis that the officers on the spot may have thought they were acting in self-defense." This moderate assessment by the commission of the beginning of hostilities is characteristic of the report as a whole, which maintained a tone of impartiality throughout.

Even so, the report unequivocally stated that Japan had unlawfully violated Chinese sovereignty and international law with its military actions in Manchuria and its creation of Manchukuo, which would not have been possible without the assistance of the Japanese army and, therefore, was not the result of a native independence movement. To resolve the Sino-Japanese dispute, the commission proposed the creation of an autonomous government in Manchuria that would be formed through direct negotiations between Japan and China under the auspices of the League of Nations. While China would retain sovereignty over Manchuria, Japan, the report proposed, should be able to freely participate in the development of the economy.

Matsuoka Yōsuke was sent to Geneva, Switzerland, to argue Japan's position during the League's consideration of the Lytton Report in November 1932. His efforts at achieving conciliation were thwarted repeatedly by the cabinet in Tokyo, which refused to consider any League formula that denied the existence of Manchukuo. After months of debate, the League of Nations unanimously voted to endorse the report's proposal. Matsuoka and the rest of the Japanese delegation then walked out of the assembly hall. A month later, the Japanese government sent notice to the League of its intention to officially withdraw from that international body.

*Rustin Gates*

**See also:** Ishiwara Kanji; Kwantung Army Adventurism; Manchukuo; Matsuoka Yōsuke; Russo-Japanese War; South Manchurian Railroad.

## Further Reading

Nish, Ian. *Japan's Struggle with Internationalism*. London: Kegan Paul International, 1993.

Ogata, Sadako. *Defiance in Manchuria: The Making of Japanese Foreign Policy, 1931–1932*. Berkeley, CA: University of California Press, 1964.

Yoshihashi, Takehiko. *Conspiracy at Mukden: The Rise of the Japanese Military*. New Haven, CT: Yale University Press, 1963.

## Muromachi *Bakufu* (1338–1573)

The Muromachi *bakufu*, also known as the Ashikaga *bakufu* or shōgunate, was established by Ashikaga Takauji. The Muromachi period started in 1336, when Takauji took control of Kyoto, but the *bakufu* formally began when Takauji was proclaimed shōgun in 1338. The *bakufu* is named for the Muromachi district of Kyoto where the Ashikaga established their headquarters.

Ashikaga Takauji (1305–1358) became shōgun five years after overthrowing the Hōjō clan, who ruled as regents for the Kamakura *bakufu* (1185–1333). Takauji rebelled against the Hōjō to restore direct imperial rule to Emperor Go-Daigo. This resulted in the three-year period known as the Kemmu Restoration (1333–1336). However, Takauji soon broke with Go-Daigo and drove him from Kyoto, installing Emperor Kōmyō in his place. During the resulting long War between the Northern and Southern Courts (Nambokuchō) between 1336 and 1392, supporters of Go-Daigo and his line continued to resist the Ashikaga.

Takauji's government featured a mixture of feudal and bureaucratic authority. This dualism derived from the equal power initially held by Takauji's brother Tadayoshi, who took control of the bureaucracy inherited from the Kamakura *bakufu*. Takauji relied on his brother to run offices such as the Office of Land Titles and the Office of Adjudication, among others, while he managed military affairs through the Board of Retainers and the Office of Rewards. Tadayoshi's resolve to ensure effective bureaucratic governance conflicted with Takauji's prerogative as overlord to reward warriors for loyal service.

To prevail in the War between the Courts, Takauji needed to maintain the loyalty of warriors in the provinces. He achieved this goal through the appointments of provincial governorships (*shugo*) and by granting these governors powers to appropriate land from feudal estates (*shōen*) for their own purpose. This approach ran counter to Tadayoshi's efforts to appoint capable rulers as governors. Seizures of estate land by Takauji's warriors also clashed with Tadayoshi's efforts to maintain an effective adjudication process. Takauji eventually settled the conflict by forcing Tadayoshi from government in 1350.

Under the second shōgun, Takauji's son Yoshiakira (1330–1367), the governors became strengthened, particularly those Ashikaga cadet branches who ruled provinces in Central Japan. In 1362, the position of deputy shōgun (*kanrei*) was created. This position was rotated between the three most powerful cadet clans—the Hosokawa, Hatakeyama, and Shiba clans.

Ashikaga power reached its zenith under Yoshimitsu (1358–1408), the third Ashikaga shōgun. Under Yoshimitsu, the *kanrei* Hosokawa Yoriyuki (1329–1392) was instrumental in reining in the power of the governors in favor of the shōgun and providing stability, law, and order. Yoshimitsu's authority began to approach that of an autocratic monarch. He put an end to the War between the Courts, quelled two rebellions, and coerced the governors to reside in Kyoto. He also started a profitable trade with the Chinese Ming Empire. The Ming, in return, granted him the title "King of Japan." The Chinese trade enriched the *bakufu*, and more generally the Japanese economy; Chinese coinage was among the imports for which the Japanese had great need. Yoshimitsu was also a greater patron of the arts and of palaces and villas, and he encouraged such patronage among his vassals, leading scholars to call this era "Japan's Renaissance."

After Yoshimitsu's death, his son Yoshimochi and the deputy shōgun Shiba Yoshimasa rolled back some of Yoshimitsu's initiatives. They ended the China trade and returned a measure of power to the governors, reversing Yoshimitsu's centralization of power. Yoshimochi retired in favor of his son and successor Yoshikazu, who died after only two years as shōgun. Yoshimochi retook the shōgunal seat, and arranged for his brother Yoshinori to succeed him.

Yoshinori tried to reclaim the powers of his father Yoshimitsu, but this move proved unpopular among the retainer clans. He was eventually assassinated in 1441 by a vassal, Akamatsu Mitsusuke. Yoshinori was replaced by his eight-year-old son Yoshikatsu, who died within two years. His younger brother Yoshimasa was then named shōgun.

During this time, retainer clans such as the Hosokawa and Yamana dominated shōgunal politics. The Hosokawa clan controlled the deputy shōgun position during much of this era, while the Yamana were their biggest rivals. The infighting of these clans, fueled by the weakening personal power of the shōgun, erupted into the civil war known as the Ōnin War in 1467. This was the starting point for the Sengoku era. From this point forward, the Ashikaga shōguns were merely pawns for the Sengoku *daimyō* fighting for control of Kyoto. The Ashikaga shōgunate came to its formal end in 1573, when Oda Nobunaga exiled Ashikaga Yoshiaki from Kyoto.

*Philip Streich*

**See also:** Ashikaga Takauji; Civil Wars; Sengoku Era; Go-Daigo; Ōnin War.

**Further Reading**

Grossberg, Kenneth Alan. *Japan's Renaissance: The Politics of the Muromachi Bakufu*. Ithaca, NY: Cornall University Press, 2001.

Hall, John W., and Toyoda Takeshi, eds. *Japan in the Muromachi Age*. Berkeley, CA: University of California Press, 1977.

Sansom, George. *A History of Japan, 1334–1615*. Stanford: Stanford University Press, 1961.

## *Musha-e* (Warrior Prints)

In Japan, printing using carved wood blocks dates to the eighth century, while printed books illustrated with pictures printed in black ink date to medieval Japan. During the Edo period (1615–1868), woodblock prints illustrating the "floating world" of Yoshiwara, the pleasure center of Edo, became a popular art form among the merchant class living in the Tokugawa capital. Known as Ukiyo-e, or "pictures of the Floating World," the mass-produced prints, which emphasized fantasy and playfulness, featured prominent Kabuki actors in their famous roles, beautiful courtesans, scenes from classical literature, cultural heroes, and landscape scenes. Considered to be "low art" by the aristocracy, woodblock prints were an inexpensive alternative to hand-painted hanging and hand scrolls. The artist Hishikawa Moronobu (1625–1695) is credited with beginning the Ukiyo-e print tradition.

Creating a woodblock print was a team effort. The artist's original design was copied onto tracing paper, which was then placed face down and transferred onto a block of cherry wood. An engraver carved away the block, leaving relief lines that were inked by the printer. A separate block was carved for each color to be used in the print. The first prints were done in black ink on white paper; hand-applied red-orange was the first color introduced. Polychrome prints, called *nishihi-e*, were introduced in 1765. Mineral and vegetable dyes were initially used for color, and the introduction of aniline dyes in the 19th century broadened and brightened the color palette. Colors were layered individually by hand, beginning with the lightest. The paper provided the areas of white within the print, with black being the final color printed. The *kento*, or alignment mark, was used to ensure that the colors aligned correctly. Prints were issued in single sheets, as diptychs (two pages), and as triptychs (three pages).

Once the prints were completed, the publisher, which often commissioned the work, distributed them to an eager public. The publisher was also responsible for ensuring that the prints conformed to existing censorship rules. The Tokugawa *bakufu* strictly controlled the content and production of prints in an effort to protect public morality.

Over time, conventional iconography in the form of standardized subjects and figural poses evolved, although the personal styles of individual artists were easily discerned through drawing styles and color usage. Japan had a long history of rule by warriors, dating to the 12th century, making them popular artistic images. Early prints depicted Kabuki actors portraying popular samurai from literary and theatrical sources, as well as historical samurai. Characters from actor prints frequently were depicted with distorted facial features and exaggerated make-up, emphasizing either their ferocity or their comical nature. Popular artists who created actor prints included Katsukawa Shunko (1743–1812), Katsukawa Sunsho (1726–1792), Utagawa Toyokuni I (1769–1825) amd Utagawa Kunisada (1786–1865).

Warrior images in woodblock prints date to the 1660s. Popular samurai depictions included scenes from *gunki monogatari* (war tales), such as *Heike monogatari* ("Tale of Heike") and *Hogen monogatari* ("Tales of the Hogen Rebellion"), and individual figures such as the heroes of Suikoden and Miyamoto Musashi, the famous 17th-century rōnin swordsman. Many of these depictions featured action-packed battle scenes or moments of quiet contemplation as a samurai prepared for a coming battle.

*Musha-e* remained a minor woodblock print genre until the 19th century, when it increased in popularity after the Tempo Reforms of 1841–1843, which banned depictions of geisha and actors, who were seen as decadent and inappropriate, as well as richly embellished prints, which violated sumptuary laws. The artist Utagawa Kuniyoshi (1791–1861) is credited with establishing *musha-e* as an important genre. His brightly colored, boldly designed prints, resulting from the use of aniline dyes, feature fierce warriors in scenes of violent action. One of his most famous series of warrior prints is *Eight Hundred Heroes of a Japanese Water Margin, All Told*, which was based on a Chinese novel popularly adapted to include Japanese heroes in the 19th century.

The additional ban on illustrated commentary about present-day political events due to the fear of sedition led artists to disguise such commentary by recasting contemporary events in the past, using historical heroes in place of modern figures. The samurai occupied a privileged position in feudal society, celebrated for his nobility, courage, strength, and willingness to sacrifice himself for a noble cause, making him the perfect symbol for modern Japanese behavior as the country began to modernize in the second half of the 19th century. In addition to male samurai, the three women warriors—Empress Jingu, Tomoe Gozen, and Han Gaku—were popular characters in prints, emblems of wise and virtuous behavior who served as role models for contemporary women.

A stronger emphasis on native Japanese culture, in reaction to increasing Chinese and Western influences, also led to an increase in the popularity of warrior prints during the Meiji era (1868–1912). During this time of foreign wars, military conscription, and Japanese adoption of Western laws, clothing, and technology, the heroes of the past, with their ideals of loyalty, honor, and bravery, served as popular role models for a Japanese society trying to meld traditional culture and behavior with the demands of modernity as well as a reminder of Japan's past glories. The popularity of *musha-e* prints helped with this process.

*Deborah A. Deacon*

**See also:** Early Mytho-Histories: *Kojiki* and *Nihon shōki*; *Sensō-e* (War Prints).

## Further Reading

Keene, Donald, Anne Nishimura Morse, and Frederick Sharf. *Japan at the Dawn of the Modern Age: Woodblock Prints from the Meiji Era*. Boston: Museum of Fine Arts, Boston, 2001.

King, James, and Yuriko Iwakiri. *Japanese Warrior Prints 1646–1905*. Leiden/Boston: Hotei Publishing, 2007.

Kita, Sandy, Lawrence E. Marceau, Katherine L. Blood, and James Douglas Farquhar. *The Floating World of Ukiyo-e: Shadows, Dreams and Substance*. New York: Harry N. Abrams, 2001.

Meich, Julia. "Woodblock Prints and Photographs: Two Views of Nineteenth Century Japan. *Asian Arts* 3(Summer 1990): 36–63.

Smith, Lawrence. *The Japanese Print since 1900: Old Dreams and New Visions*. London: British Museum, 1983.

Yonemura, Ann. *Masterful Illusions: Japanese Prints in the Anne van Biema Collection*. Seattle/London: Arthur M. Sackler Gallery in association with the University of Washington Press, 2002.

# Mutsu Munemitsu (1844–1897)

Mutsu Munemitsu was born in 1844 to Date Munehiro, a high-level bureaucrat in the Tokugawa collateral Kii domain in Wakayama. As a young man, he took the name Mutsu to symbolize his break with his feudal past, joining Sakamoto Ryōma's revolutionary Kaientai in Nagasaki.

Despite taking no active role in the Meiji Restoration, Mutsu managed to join the new government as a protégé of Gōtō Shojiro and Kido Takayoshi. He held a number of minor posts, including the governorship of Kanagawa, before resigning during the *Maria Luz* Incident. Mutsu was head of the Land Tax Bureau during the period that the new tax was instituted. He traveled abroad a number of times before becoming tangentially involved in the Tosa Risshisha Incident while a member of the *Genrōin* during the Satsuma Rebellion. Convicted of treason with his friend Ōe Taku, he spent five years in prison from 1878 to 1883. While in prison, Mutsu learned English, translating Jeremy Bentham's *An Introduction to the Principles of Morals and Legislation* into Japanese.

Released from prison with the help of Itō Hirobumi and Inoue Kaoru, Mutsu went abroad to study with German legal scholars Rudolf von Gneist and Lorenz von Stein. He returned to Japan in late 1884, taking a minor position in the Ministry of Foreign Affairs. He was Foreign Minister Inoue's assistant in the treaty revision conferences in 1884–1885. In 1888, he was appointed minister to Washington, D.C., negotiating a treaty with Mexico that Foreign Minister Ōkuma Shigenobu hoped to use as leverage in breaking open the deadlocked Unequal Treaty negotiations.

Mutsu was elected to the Diet in 1890, but preferred to join Yamagata Aritomo's first

As foreign minister in 1894, Mutsu successfully negotiated a treaty with Great Britain, leading to the end of the Unequal Treaties. (John Clark Ridpath, *Ridpath's History of the World*, 1901)

cabinet as Minister of Agriculture and Commerce. With Gōtō Shojiro, he served as a conduit for bribes paid by the government to the Tosa Faction within the Diet to pass the first budget.

Mutsu resigned from the government as a protest against Matsukata Masayoshi's heavy-handed political election methods in the election of 1891. He became Foreign Minister in Ito's cabinet in 1892. Together with chief negotiator Aoki Shūzō (a protégé to Yamagata), he managed to negotiate a treaty with Great Britain only two weeks before the beginning of the First Sino-Japanese War. With Itō, he negotiated the Treaty of Shimonoseki but had to bow to foreign pressure in the Triple Intervention of 1895.

Mutsu resigned from the government due to poor health in 1896. Angry at being blamed for the Triple Intervention by the public, he wrote a defense of his handling of diplomacy, *Kenkenroku*. It circulated widely among his friends in manuscript form, but the book was not published until 1929 because Itō and others took issue with its "disturbing candor," chiefly because Mutsu frankly admitted that he and Itō had bullied China into war.

In 1897, Mutsu finally succumbed to tuberculosis while on convalescence in Hawaii. He is considered to be the Father of Japanese Diplomacy, and his statue dominates the entry to the present-day Foreign Ministry. Several of his protégés (Hoshi Toru, Komura Jutarō, Hara Takashi, Uchida Kōsai, and his son Mutsu Hirokichi) rose to political prominence chiefly through the Foreign Ministry after his death.

*Louis G. Perez*

**See also:** Hara Takashi; Inoue Kaoru; Itō Hirobumi; *Maria Luz* Incident; Matsukata Masayoshi; Ōkuma Shigenobu; Sakamoto Ryōma; Seinan (Satsuma) Rebellion; Sino-Japanese War; Triple Intervention; Unequal Treaties; Yamagata Aritomo.

**Further Reading**

Mutsu, Munemitsu. *Kenkenroku: A Diplomatic Record of the Sino-Japanese War, 1894–95*, translated by Gordon Berger. New York: Columbia University Press, 1995.

Perez, Louis G. *Japan Comes of Age: Mutsu Munemitsu and the Revision of the Unequal Treaties*. London: Fairleigh Dickinson University Press 1999.

Perez, Louis G. *Mutsu Munemitsu and Identity Formation of the Individual and the State in Modern Japan*. Lewiston, NY: Edwin Mellen Press, 2001.

# N

## Namamugi Incident

An incident of samurai assault on British nationals that occurred on September 14, 1862, the Namamugi Incident also became known in the West as the Richardson Affair or the Murder of Mr. Richardson. On that day, British subject Charles Lennox Richardson, in Japan en route home after 14 years as a successful merchant in Shanghai, went on a horseback ride along the East Sea Road with three of his compatriots, Yokohama residents Woodthorpe Charles Clark and William Marshall, and Mrs. Margaret Watson Borradaile, Marshall's cousin, who was visiting from Hong Kong. As they reached the central part of the village of Namamugi near Yokohama, the four encountered the armed retinue of Shimazu Hisamitsu, father of the *daimyō* of Satsuma and the de facto lord of that domain, heading southbound in the opposite direction. The assault took place when the Britons got too close to the 700-men retinue in a road around 5 to 8 meters in width. Richardson was cut many times in his left shoulder, abdomen, and ribs, and his head was virtually chopped off as the result of *todome*, the coup de grâce. His two male companions were seriously wounded. The doctor who examined Richardson's body and treated his wounded companions shortly after the incident was James Curtis Hepburn, an American better known for his romanization system to represent Japanese language.

Several different accounts of what caused the assault exist. One says that the Britons were trying to yield the road by turning their horses around when Satsuma retainers suddenly slashed them in a preemptive action to maintain the order of the procession, due to both the language barrier and the retainers' antiforeign zeal. Another says that the Britons, led by Richardson, arrogantly forced their way into the retinue and were attacked by Hisamitsu's retainers outraged at their flagrant violation of Japanese protocol to a lord. Still another story, which supports the preceding account, cites a more respectful Eugene Van Reed, an American, who dismounted, took off his hat, and bowed from roadside as the procession passed him along the same road a short while earlier. Whichever account is accurate, all agree that Hisamitsu's procession continued onward after the assault as if nothing had happened.

The incident reflects the widespread antiforeign sentiment that had emerged among many Japanese people since the country was forced open in 1854. After the incident the Satsuma samurai were cheered by many as heroes, and one prince even composed a poem to celebrate Hisamatsu as a righteous general who protected the emperor and the court from barbarians in "the battle of Namamugi."

Less frequently noted, however, is the role of the power dynamics between Satsuma and the Tokugawa shōgunate. Economically, the lord of Satsuma had been resentful about the shōgunate control of Satsuma's profitable foreign trade. Politically, Hisamitsu, trying to carry out the policy of the late Satsuma *daimyō* Shimazu Nariakira, had successfully lobbied the court earlier to send an imperial envoy to Edo to press the shōgunate for a political reform—the Bunkyū reform—to meet the challenge faced by Japan since the opening of the country. Hisamitsu was, in fact, on his way back from Edo after his mission was completed when the incident took place. As *tozama daimyō* had been denied a voice in Bukufu policymaking since the beginning of Tokugawa period, the shōgunate was understandably unhappy about the maneuver of Hisamitsu, who was not even a *daimyō*. Due to this power dynamic, the shōgunate informed foreign communities of the coming procession of the imperial envoy for the following day, but not the community of Hisamatsu—an omission that, in part, caused the incident.

Japan's foreign community in Yokohama was appalled by the incident and appealed to British government to take punitive action against Japan. Britain demanded an official apology and an indemnity of £100,000 from the *bakufu* and, from Satsuma, the execution of the perpetrators and an indemnity of £25,000. The *bakufu* complied with these demands, but Satsuma refused. Satsuma's refusal led to the British bombardment of Kagoshima, the domainal capital of Satsuma, known in history as the Bombardment of Kagoshima, or Anglo-Satsuma War.

*Guohe Zheng*

**See also:** Kagoshima, Bombardment of.

### Further Reading

Rennie, David. *The British Arms in North China and Japan*. London: Adamant Media Corporation, 2001.

Satow, Ernest. *A Diplomat in Ja.an*, Tokyo: Tuttle, 1921.

Takeda, Yasumi. *Namamugi ichijō* [The Namamugi Incident]. Tokyo: Chūō kōron sha, 1975.

# Nanjing Massacre

In July 1937, outright war began between Japan and China after the Marco Polo Bridge Incident. Chinese Nationalist forces under Guomintang President Jiang Jieshi (Ch'iang K'ai-shek) initially offered strong resistance to the Japanese invasion, holding out at Shanghai—the country's greatest port city and the site of a major international settlement—from August 13 to November 9, 1937.

The Nationalist troops then fell back, moving inland in the near rout to the Nationalist capital of Nanjing, a symbolic location home to more than 1 million Chinese. Jiang was not prepared to abandon it without a fight, but no defense or evacuation plans had been made. Another of Jiang's objectives in defending both Shanghai and Nanjing, home to numerous foreign embassies, was to attract worldwide attention and win foreign support for China's anti-Japanese war.

In early December, Japanese troops converged on Nanjing. After Chinese troops rejected Japanese demands to surrender, on December 9 the Japanese opened a massive assault. Three days later, the Chinese defenders fell back across the Yangtze River. The following day, the 6th, 9th, and 116th Divisions of the Japanese army entered the city as two Japanese navy flotillas arrived up the river. During the ensuing six weeks, the Japanese occupiers deliberately instituted a reign of terror, apparently designed to cow China's population into ready submission to Japanese invasion. Frustration over Jiang's refusal to surrender—Japanese leaders had expected him to capitulate before the end of 1937—might have been another factor contributing to the reign of terror.

Entering the city on December 13, Japanese forces fired on streets crowded with refugees, wounded soldiers, and civilians. They also fired on many thousands of refugees who were attempting to escape by swimming across the river. The occupying forces used machine guns, swords, bayonets, fire, live burial, and poison gas to massacre captured Chinese soldiers and any young men suspected of being such. Scattered atrocities and murders, often marked by great brutality, continued throughout the city for six weeks, as did heavy looting.

Counts of how many soldiers and civilians died in the Nanjing Massacre vary widely, ranging from 42,000 to 300,000. During this period, Japanese soldiers raped an estimated 20,000 women, most of whom were then killed.

The Nanjing Massacre shocked the West and generated extensive international sympathy for China, although this emotion did not necessarily translate into tangible support and assistance. It was an early example of the use of organized brutality to cow and terrorize civilian populations characteristic of many World War II military occupations. As the 21st century began, memories of the Nanjing Massacre remained bitter in China; a major museum commemorating the event exists in Nanjing. In contrast, Japanese officials sought for many decades to deny that the episode ever took place, or at least to minimize its scale, and it was omitted from official Japanese accounts of the war. In the late 1990s, however, several Japanese journalists and academics who investigated the subject mounted dedicated efforts to bring the event to the attention of the Japanese people.

*Priscilla Roberts*

**See also:** Jiang Jieshi (Ch'iang K'ai-shek); World War II, Japanese Atrocities.

**Further Reading**

Honda, Katsuichi. *The Nanjing Massacre: A Japanese Journalist Confronts Japan's National Shame*, edited by Frank Gibney. Armonk, NY: M. E. Sharpe, 1999.

Li, Fei Fei, Robert Sabella, and David Liu, eds. *Nanking: Memory and Healing*. Armonk, NY: M. E. Sharpe, 2002.

Wakabayashi, Bob Tadashi. *The Nanking Atrocity, 1937–1938: Complicating the Picture*. New York: Berghahn Books, 2007.

Yamamoto, Masahiro. *Nanking: Anatomy of an Atrocity*. Westport, CT: Praeger, 2000.

# Nara (Heijō-kyō) to Heian-kyō

In 784, Emperor Kammu (737–806; reign 781–806 ordered the erection of a new capital at Nagaoka and moved there that same year. In 793, repeated flooding caused by environmental degradation forced Kammu to move to a new capital, Heian-kyō (Kyoto).

Various reasons have been advanced for the move from Nara to Nagaoka, from Yamato to Yamashiro. It is clear, however, that a new capital was needed for what was a new lineage. With the death by smallpox of the childless Emperor Shōtoku (born 718; reign 765–770; reign as Kōken 749–758), the throne passed to her brother-in-law and Kammu's father Kōnin (709–782; reign 770–781), who was backed by a group of nobles led by Fujiwara Nagate (714–771; he gave one daughter to Kōnin) and Fujiwara Momokawa (732–779; he married one daughter to Kammu and one to Kammu's son Heizei). They had forged the letter in which Shōtoku supposedly nominated Kōnin as her heir. These nobles were determined to move the succession to the scholars and experienced bureaucrats descended from Tenji (born circa 625; reign 668–672), as opposed to the problematic line of Temmu (born circa 631; reign 672–686).

For example, Shōmu's daughter and Shōtoku's half-sister Princess Fuwa (died after 795) was involved in three failed major rebellions/intrigues: in 764 (rebellion of Fujiwara no Nakamaro, in which she lost her husband, a grandson of Temmu), in 769 (accused of using magic against Shōtoku), and even as late as 782 (she, her son, and a daughter were exiled for a plot against Kammu). Kōnin cut off the last of any connection with the Temmu line when he rid himself of his chief consort, Fuwa's sister Princess Inoue and her son by him, Prince Osabe. Inoue was accused of sorcery against her husband; mother and son were stripped of their titles, and Kammu was appointed crown prince. Two years later, Kōnin's sister died, and Inoue and Osabe were implicated in her death; they died in custody on the same day in 775, probably murdered, and probably at Momokawa's instigation. It is clear that Kammu considered his father to be the founder of a new lineage: in 785 he twice carried out Confucian legitimation rituals at Mt. Katano in which he recognized his father, rather than Amaterasu, as the founder of the lineage.

Lacking powerful connections within the imperial family itself, Kammu depended on Korean immigrant groups. Nagaoka was chosen because Yamashiro Province was the territory of various immigrant groups from Korea: the Hata, the Haji, and the Kudara no Konishiki family. These Korean lineages provided the financing, labor, and technical expertise for the building of Kammu's capitals, and received commensurate rewards. The Kudara no Konishiki were descended from a king of Paekche and, Kammu claimed, were relatives on his mother's side. In 783, he exempted the area from some taxes, the clan temple was endowed, and members of the family were awarded court ranks. A female member of the family was granted subsidies to build a residence. In 797, Kammu granted the entire clan

exemption from corvée duty. Kammu promoted Paekche descendants to high positions and appointed them to positions as officials and consorts in his household. Hata engineers built walls in Nagaoka and drained the area. The site of the palace was originally a residence of a chief of the Haji, workers in clay. They were his grandmother's family and had also married into the branches of the Fujiwara supporting Kammu.

Very importantly, the Hata provided Kammu with the technical expertise needed to deal with angry spirits of the dead created by the political upheavals of the past. Certainly, some of them had been created through his own connivance. For example, in 785, Kammu's crown prince, his full brother Sawara (750–785), was disposed of when he was implicated in the assassination in Nagaoka of Fujiwara no Tanetsugu (born 737); he died (of starvation, it is said) on the way to exile in Awaji. Kammu sought the protection of Hata shrines in Heian-kyō—Kamo, Fushimi Inari, and Matsuno'o—which were became some of the most important elements in the imperial cult.

The creation of this capital resulted gradually in changes. The concentration of the imperial family and nobility in the capital made it more difficult to raise a rebellion from a territorial base. The increasing control of the Fujiwara over the imperial "harem," the succession, and, thereby, over the bureaucracy decreased competitiveness. The gradual shift to private land assisted the development of dispersed power bases and a gradual lack of interest in the bureaucracy.

*Sybil Thornton*

**See also:** Fujiwara Family.

**Further Reading**

Shively, Donald H., and William H. McCullough, eds. *The Cambridge History of Japan II: Heian Japan.* Cambridge, UK: Cambridge University Press, 1999.

Van Geotham, Ellen. *Nagaoka: Japan's Forgotten Capital.* Leiden, Netherlands: Brill Academic Publishers, 2008.

# Nativism, Rise of

The cultural and intellectual movement known as Nativism arose in the latter half of the Tokugawa period (1600–1867) and had huge implications for modern nationalism and militarism in Japan until the end of World War II, which in East Asia is usually dated as lasting 1937 to 1945. Broadly speaking, Nativism took shape in two schools of thought: National Learning and Mito Learning. Both rejected the sinophilia then-dominant in East Asia as well as its political/diplomatic corollary, the Chinese world order—an interstate tribute system based on subservience to the emperor of China, reputed to be the fount of world civilization and morality. In the 1930s and 1940s, Japanese ultranationalists would apply this same Nativist formula to relativize Western culture, values, and institutions that also harbored pretensions of universal validity.

## National Learning

Adherents of the National Learning school derided what they deemed servility toward China by Tokugawa thinkers who embraced a sinocentric interpretation of progress in history—that is, the ancient Japanese had lived like beasts until they adopted writing, religion, government institutions, and moral culture from China, which ipso facto was the world's most advanced nation, with all other peoples being barbarians in need "sinification" or assimilation to Confucian ways. Following that sinocentric view, Japan was incapable of developing on its own; like all other barbarian societies, it could achieve civilization only to the extent that it became like China.

Scholars of National Learning turned that premise on its head. They retorted that ancient Japan *degenerated* after having imported Chinese moral and cultural ways, which corrupted the naturally pure and good Japanese. Their Nativist counter-interpretation held that the Chinese harped on Confucian virtues such as loyalty, yet in point of historical fact, committed regicide to overthrow 20-odd dynasties. In sum, Chinese people needed Confucian teachings because they were immoral by nature. By contrast, the Japanese had never formulated high-sounding moral tenets because they required none. They practiced virtue without being preached to, showing fidelity to one dynastic house, descended from the Sun Goddess, throughout history. This timeless reverence toward a single divine imperial dynasty supposedly proved that the Japanese were different from, and better than, the foreign peoples who repeatedly deposed their rulers. This precept became a core element in the concept of *kokutai*, or the unique state polity and national essence that made for Japanese moral preeminence in the world, which helped fuel foreign wars in the modern era.

Scholars of National Learning also contended that, whereas the Chinese emperor bestowed the right to rule on all other East Asian state leaders, the Japanese emperor invested Tokugawa shōguns with that right. This "imperial investiture," which lacked any grounding in fact, provided ideological confirmation of Japan's de facto detachment from the Chinese world order, with its shackles of political and military vassalage. Tokugawa Japan had unilaterally adopted a policy of national isolation; hence it was free to end that policy at any time. It could conclude treaties and wage wars with foreign powers as it saw fit under the modern Western nation-state system in light of its national interests. Thus, thinkers in this school held, Tokugawa Japan alone among East Asian nations enjoyed sovereign autonomy, which Meiji leaders would exploit to the hilt by encroaching on neighboring states that remained subject to Chinese diplomatic dictates. It is no accident that the otherwise pacifist Motoori Norinaga (1730–1801), a leading figure in this school, lauded exploits by Japanese forces under Toyotomi Hideyoshi (1537–1598), who invaded Korea twice in the 1590s.

Finally, one must note a revolutionary idea never explicitly evoked in National Learning—that is, by idealizing Japan's pristine society in high antiquity before the coming of Chinese ways, this school perforce also idealized the direct imperial government in ancient times that predated Nara, Fujiwara, and warrior forms of rule. Motoori remained a staunch Tokugawa supporter until his death in 1801, but unprecedented national crises, in tandem with Mito Learning, later thrust this implicit political ideal into the open during the Bakumatsu era (1853–1867).

## Mito Learning

The Mito Learning school emerged in the late 18th century and first half of the 19th century as a muscular Confucianism cum politicized *Bushidō*. As such, its adherents contended that teachings bequeathed by the sage-kings of ancient China more or less conformed with Japan's unique *kokutai*. Despite their disagreements, the Mito and National Learning schools shared attributes central to Nativism. Moreover, amid Western-induced Bakumatsu political and diplomatic crises, the stress that Mito Learning placed on Japanese martial prowess and loyalty led it first to justify Tokugawa rule and later to discredit it, which paved the way for restoring power to the reputedly divine imperial court in Kyoto.

In 1825, the *bakufu* issued a historic expulsion edict. It decreed that unauthorized Western ships, which were then beginning to frequent Japanese waters, be fired on and driven off without hesitation or warning—which clearly reflected the imperial will to maintain national isolation. Aizawa Seishisai (1782–1863), a leading Mito School thinker, wrote *New Theses* that same year in praise of the *bakufu*'s bold edict. He argued that, given this unprecedented Western threat, Japanese warriors must live up to their class ideology of *Bushidō*—the Way of the Samurai. For more than 200 years the samurai had enjoyed lucrative perquisites in society—such as guaranteed hereditary incomes—on the pretext of being ever-ready to die in loyal state service. Now, Aizawa in effect said, they would get their chance. His rousing message found widespread resonance among warriors, and *bakufu* political legitimacy came to rest on a capacity to "honor the emperor and expel the barbarians." Indeed, Tokugawa Nariaki (1800–1850), the *daimyō* of Mito domain and a relative of the ruling shōgunal house, observed that victory or defeat in civil wars had not mattered up to then because all combatants were Japanese, but if one inch of soil or one person in Japan should ever fall subject to a foreign state, damage to the *kokutai* would be unbearable.

After Britain's humiliating defeat of China in the first Opium War (1840–1842), *bakufu* leaders discreetly rescinded the 1825 expulsion edict. Nevertheless, in accordance with the Nativist "imperial investiture," court nobles instructed the *bakufu* to bolster national defenses in 1846, and this unprecedented rebuke went unpunished. In 1853–1854, a naval squadron led by U.S. Commodore Matthew Perry forced the *bakufu* to sign a treaty that ended national isolation by allowing a consul-general to reside in Japan, and Townsend Harris came to take up this post in 1856. He demanded and got a shōgunal audience at which he extorted a full-blown trade pact from *bakufu* leader Ii Naosuke—just as China was suffering defeat in the second Opium War in 1858. Ii signed the treaty, in a decision that countermanded the orders of the emperor in Kyoto, not the emperor in Beijing. This defiant act stirred up violent nationalistic opposition, first among samurai from Mito domain, who murdered Ii in 1860, and later throughout the nation as well. In 1863, two other Nativist hotbeds, the Chōshū and Satsuma domains, executed the expulsion edict that *bakufu* leaders had earlier rescinded, only to suffer a sound trouncing at the hands of modern Western armed forces. Random acts of violence against Westerners by individual samurai also met a similar fate. These abject failures persuaded younger samurai leaders to admit the impossibility of "honoring the emperor" and "expelling the barbarians," so they took the step of disestablishing their own class privileges and ending Tokugawa *bakufu* rule so as to restore the imperial court to power.

To sum up, by discrediting the Chinese world order and tribute system abroad, and by calling into question the bases of warrior supremacy at home, Nativism provided grounds for ethnic nationalism and imperial sovereignty to emerge in Japan by the mid-19th century. The key ideas in Nativism were as follows:

1. The Japanese are superior to all other peoples for having spontaneously revered a divine imperial dynasty throughout history.

2. Japan's emperor, not China's, invested Tokugawa shōguns with ruling authority but did so on condition that they uphold national isolation, which perforce meant preserving sovereignty and territorial integrity.

3. That point required shōguns to expel unauthorized foreigners who forced their way into Japan and the ruling warrior class to live up to its *Bushidō* ideology.

4. Failure on those counts would justify ending *bakufu* rule and the warrior class in the name of imperial loyalism, and creating a new polity and a commoner conscript army better suited to carrying out the preceding tasks.

*Bob Tadashi Wakabayashi*

**See also:** Ii Naosuke; *Kokutai* and Ultra-nationalism; Mito School; Perry, Matthew; *Sakoku*; Tokugawa *Bakufu* Political System; Toyotomi Hideyoshi.

**Further Reading**

Jansen, Marius. *China in the Tokugawa World.* Cambridge, MA: Harvard University Press, 1992.

Matsumoto, Shigeru. *Motoori Norinaga.* Cambridge, MA: Harvard University Press, 1970.

Nakai, Kate Wildman. "The Naturalization of Confucianism in Tokugawa Japan." *Harvard Journal of Asiatic Studies* 40, no. 1 (January 1980): 157–199.

Wakabayashi, Bob Tadashi. *Anti-foreignism and Western Learning in Early-Modern Japan.* Cambridge, MA: Harvard University Press, 1986.

# Navy, Modernized (1868–1894)

Much like the modern Japanese army, the Japanese navy in 1868 was hodgepodge of men, equipment, and facilities. Although it was initially subordinate to the army, the government gradually centralized the navy, updated its fleet, expanded shipbuilding facilities initiated by the Tokugawa shōgunate, sent foreign students abroad for training, and adopted and adapted the best practices of Western countries to form the most efficient navy in East Asia, which even rivaled some Western armadas.

During the early 17th century, the Tokugawa shōgunate banned the construction of ocean-going vessels and limited Japan's interaction with Western countries. By the 1850s, the growing European presence in the East Asian seas convinced the shōgunate to lift this ban. It called upon the large domains—in particular, Satsuma, Chōshū, Kaga, and Tosa—to develop and expand their costal defenses and naval technology. This was a decentralized effort; the shōgunate relied on the Dutch to build a naval training center in Nagasaki, sent students to Holland for further training, and later turned to the French for help. French representatives in Japan were enthusiastic partners of the shōgunate, despite wavering support back in France. The shōgunate, under the direction of Oguri Tadamasa and Kurimoto Joun, invited the French engineer Francois Verny, who had been building a shipyard in China, to build facilities in Japan. Verny chose Yokosuka as the location to build an iron foundry, arsenal, and dry dock; construction began in 1865. The French also opened a school in Yokosuka to train future Japanese navy men, which included classes in mathematics and French language. Satsuma, in contrast, purchased ships and arms from the British.

By the Meiji Restoration (1868), the domains mentioned previously possessed between 5 and 12 steamships. Most of the ships were obsolete by Western standards, having few armaments and little power, and, in many cases, represented nothing more than glorified transport barges. One American observer noted that Japan became the market for Western countries looking to sell their outdated ships. Naval considerations played little role in the fighting during the Restoration. One of the shōgunate's top naval men, Katsu Kaishū, who negotiated the capitulation of the Tokugawa forces, turned over some of the Tokugawa ships to the Satchō-led forces, while the rest were commandeered by the Enomoto Takeaki. Enomoto took the shōgunate's remaining fleet north to Hakodate, where he led a final battle against Satchō troops. He eventually surrendered, and returned the ships.

During the early Meiji period (1868–1912), concerns about a naval conflict with Western countries gave way to a focus on bolstering the Japanese army against invasion and possible domestic uprisings. Politics also favored the army's development over the navy—many early naval officials were former shōgunate officials, including those few who had any naval experience, such as Katsu Kaishū and Enomoto. Both men became navy ministers, but even they lacked significant knowledge of the sea. Still, the dearth of equipment and any significant naval tradition meant that the Meiji state could draw from a broad range of Western naval philosophies and new technologies. In 1870, the state officially adopted the British navy as its model, sending students to Great Britain for training, funding a British mission to Japan, and translating British naval texts. The British also helped the Japanese create a naval war college, and acquired the first ships specifically built for the Japanese market, which used the most recent technology.

The navy's importance grew during the 1880s. It received a larger share of the military budget and attracted greater attention from the Meiji oligarchs, especially after Satchō men began to dominate the top navy positions. Several statesman, such as Iwakura Tomomi, argued that a country's standing in the world was displayed by its navy's prowess—a position that represented a shift from older naval concerns over defense of the homeland to Japan as an imperial player. New French naval developments continued to influence the Japanese navy, especially a controversial organizational philosophy called the "Jeune Ecole." Rather than the relying on bulky fleet consisting of large warships, like the British model, this French school of thought emphasized small to medium-sized ships armed with light, fast-firing guns, especially torpedo ships. This model provided a solution to Japan's financial weaknesses; it could not afford a complete British-style fleet. Even so, Japan never completely abandoned its relationship with the British navy; in 1892, it purchased the *Yoshino*, the fastest cruiser in the world at the time.

Administratively, the Japanese navy finally became independent during the 1880s. Under the old British model, the top navy minister was beholden to a civilian bureaucracy; in contrast, the army followed the Prussian model and staffed its bureaucracy with royalty and others with direct links to the monarch. The state changed this model, creating a navy ministry that maintained equal footing with the army. This exacerbated competition between the army and navy for the public's attention and budget appropriations. One political strategy on the navy's part was to encourage a shared vision among citizens, businessmen, and politicians, to expand into the South Pacific (called "Nan'yō") which could become a place for migration, possible colonization, and adventure. The navy's attention southward rivaled the army's push toward the Asian continent, a source of tension that would never be resolved.

On the eve of Japan's first modern wars against China and Russia, the navy shifted from a haphazard mix of obsolete Western ships to one capable of defeating a navy as large as Russia's. Japan's initial naval weaknesses did not, however, put it too far behind the West; even during the 19th century, there was no consensus about how a navy should operate or how it should be equipped. Japan's naval modernization reflected the shifting trends in the West, allowing it to catch up quickly.

*Michael Wert*

**See also:** Imperial Rescript for Soldiers and Sailors; Iwakura Tomomi; Katsu Kaishū; Russo-Japanese War; World War I.

**Further Reading**

Evans, David C., and Mark R. Peattie. *Kaigun: Strategy, Tactics, and Technology in the Imperial Japanese Navy, 1887–1941.* Annapolis, MD: Naval Institute Press, 1997.

Peattie, Mark R. *Nan'yō: The Rise and Fall of the Japanese in Micronesia, 1885–1945.* Honolulu: Center for Pacific Islands Studies, University of Hawaii, 1988.

Schencking, J. Charles. *Making Waves: Politics, Propaganda, and the Emergence of the Imperial Japanese Navy, 1868–1922.* Stanford: Stanford University Press, 2005.

## New Guinea Campaign (March 8, 1942–September 13, 1945)

On January 23, 1942, Japanese forces under Major General Horii Tomitaro invaded New Britain, New Guinea, capturing Rabaul from its Australian garrison, known as Lark Force. Moving into mainland New Guinea on March 8, Japanese forces then occupied

Lae and Salamaua. The Australian defenders (code-named Kanga Force) retreated to the mountain town of Wau while the Japanese moved against the ports of Madang, Finschhafen, and Wewak. For the next 10 months, there was a stalemate as both sides poured resources into the Papuan Campaign.

When the Papuan Campaign ended on January 25, 1943, 1,000 Japanese survivors escaped into New Guinea. That month the Japanese dispatched to New Guinea Lieutenant General Adachi Hatazo's 18th Army. This group included the 6th Air Division. The Japanese 41st Division deployed to Wewak, the 20th Division deployed to Madang, and part of the 51st Division was dispatched to Lae/Salamaua.

To oppose the Japanese, General Douglas MacArthur had the U.S. 32nd and 41st Divisions and the Australian 6th and 7th Divisions and a militia brigade. The 32nd Division was not immediately available as a consequence of battle losses, and two of the brigades of the Australian 7th Division were temporarily deployed to Ceylon. The remaining brigade was sent to New Guinea to reinforce the militia brigade there. Australia was raising more militia, and its veteran 9th Division returned from Egypt in February. MacArthur also had the U.S. 5th Fleet as well as the Royal Australian Air Force and the small U.S. 7th Fleet comprising U.S., Australian, and Dutch warships.

To recover the initiative, Adachi ordered his 102nd Regiment to attack Wau on January 16. By January 28, the Japanese had driven Kanga Force to the edge of Wau Airfield, but the Australian 17th Brigade then flew in under Japanese fire to reinforce Wau. The fighting lasted until January 30, when the Japanese retreated to Salamaua. This defeat depleted the Japanese forces available to defend Lae/Salamaua. Thus, on

February 28, the bulk of the Japanese 51st Division boarded 8 merchantmen at Rabaul; escorted by 8 destroyers, this force sailed for Lae.

On March 1, Allied aircraft spotted this convoy in the Bismarck Sea. The Americans attacked with 181 aircraft. Employing skip-bombing techniques, during March 2–5 these planes destroyed all 8 Japanese transports and 4 destroyers, resulting in the loss of some 3,700 men. Only 850 Japanese soldiers ultimately reached Lae. In retaliation, the Japanese launched I Operation to destroy Allied air power in Papua and Guadalcanal. Between April 11 and April 14, Japanese aircraft struck Oro Bay, Milne Bay, and Port Moresby, destroying 2 Dutch merchantmen and 45 Allied planes. Japanese aircraft losses were even higher, however.

Both sides now slowly built up their forces. The Japanese used barges and submarines to reinforce Lae/Salamaua. The Americans flew troops into Wau. During April, the Australian 3rd Division assembled at Wau and began to push toward Salamaua. The Americans needed a coastal base for twin offensives against Lae and Salamaua, and in the 7th Fleet's first amphibious operation seized Nassau Bay on June 29, 1943. The Americans then moved up the coast toward Salamaua, linking up with the Australians on July 21. Distracted by this threat, the Japanese were surprised by a U.S. airborne drop on Nazab in the Markham Valley on September 1. Allied forces quickly constructed airfields to receive the 7th Division, which began an inland advance on Lae. The 9th Division then landed north of Lae on September 4. The encircled Japanese abandoned Salamaua on September 17 and Lae the next day and retreated into the interior.

Pursued by the 7th Division, the Japanese conducted a fighting withdrawal through the rugged terrain of the Markham and Ramu

Valleys. It took the Australians a month to overcome a key Japanese position at Sattleberg. To prevent these Japanese soldiers from reaching Finschhafen on the coast, the Australian 20th Brigade landed farther west at Scarlet Beach on September 22. Now isolated, the defenders of Finschhafen joined the Japanese exodus inland on October 2. The Japanese tried to retake Finschhafen by counterattacking Scarlett Beach on October 20, but their forces were defeated. The Allies had found a winning strategy. They used the Australians to engage the Japanese while American forces bypassed Japanese strongholds.

On December 23, 1943, U.S. Marines invaded New Britain Island. The Allies then constructed air bases there, enabling them to neutralize Japanese aircraft from Rabaul. On January 2, 1944, the U.S. 126th Regiment invaded Saidor and began a coastal drive on Madang. Meanwhile, the Australians pursued the Japanese overland toward Bogadjim, where a supply road led to Madang. Japanese defenses that were centered on Shaggy Ridge were taken on January 23.

On February 29, 1944, U.S. forces invaded the Admiralty Islands north of New Guinea, severing the Japanese 18th Army's lifeline to Rabaul. Then, on February 10, the Australians linked up with the Americans at Saidor. The Japanese High Command reacted to this event by withdrawing its defense line to Wewak, supported by a new base at Hollandia in Dutch New Guinea. The Japanese then sent their 6th Air Division from the Netherlands East Indies to defend these bases. Radio intercepts revealed these plans to MacArthur, who ordered an air offensive against Wewak and Hollandia. From March 30 to April 16, the 5th Air Force obliterated the 6th Air Division, destroying 390 planes and killing 2,000 Japanese pilots and air personnel.

After the fall of Bogadjim on April 17, 1944, the road to Madang was open to the Allies. Adachi evacuated his Madang headquarters, intending to fall back on Wewak and Hollandia. On April 24, the Australians entered Madang. Two days previously, U.S. forces had invaded Hollandia and Aitape. The Allied capture of Aitape 125 miles east of Hollandia blocked the escape of the 18th Army. Now desperate, Adachi used his dwindling resources to transport three regiments to Aitape. Their unexpected attack on July 11 drove the U.S. 32nd Division to the Driniumor River. Fighting continued until August 25, when the Japanese retired to Wewak.

During October 1944, the Australians replaced the Americans at Aitape. MacArthur's return to the Philippines was to be an American operation, with the Australians consigned to containing the bypassed Japanese. The Australian government, however, wanted Wewak retaken. This pointless offensive had little air or naval support, as that support had gone to the Philippines. On May 23, 1945, Wewak fell to the Australians, and Adachi retreated into the Prince Alexander Range for a last stand. The remnants of the 18th Army surrendered there on September 13, 1945.

*Jonathan "Jack" Ford*

**See also:** Coral Sea, Battle of; MacArthur, Douglas; World War II, Southwest Pacific Theater.

### Further Reading

Bergerud, Eric. *Touched with Fire: The Land War in the South Pacific*. New York: Penguin Books, 1996.

Miller, John Jr. *The United States Army in World War II: The War in the Pacific: Cartwheel: The Reduction of Rabaul*. Washington, DC: Center of Military History, U.S. Army, 1993.

# New Religions in Imperial and Postwar Japan

Amidst the socioeconomic, political, and cultural upheaval that characterized Japan between the mid-19th and mid-20th centuries, the nation's religious landscape changed dramatically. From the 1830s, the creation of several New Religions (*shinshūkyō*) gave the Japanese people new religious options. Their growth demonstrated that in the dawning modern era Japan's established religious institutions would have to compete for adherents. Indeed, in imperial (1868–1945) and early postwar (1945–present) Japan, millions of Japanese sought meaning in alternative belief systems beyond the officially approved religions of Buddhism, Shintō, and the recently revitalized Christianity.

Despite effective efforts by the imperial government to delimit, define, and enforce religious orthodoxy, New Religions materialized, and endured because of their capacity to attract religious seekers. They responded to the spiritual, social, and physical dilemmas created or exacerbated by Japan's modernization, gaining momentum in times of acute socioeconomic crisis and sociopolitical reconfiguration. Many Japanese were dissatisfied with the worldview and relevance of the established religions in these contexts. The appearance of charismatic founders with supernatural abilities and germane messages of hope and change was, therefore, often a welcome development.

During the 1830s and 1840s, two such figures founded Japan's two oldest New Religions in rural Honshū. From Imamura Shrine in Okayama, Shintō priest Kurozumi Munetada (1780–1850) preached faith in the Amaterasu, internal and social harmony, and human equality. Through intense sun worship the metaphysical sources of spiritual, physical, and emotional illness, and became a sage and healer for many shrine parishioners. In 1846, he and his followers founded the independent Kurozumi Kyōdan, a religious group that actively refuted rigid, encumbering class and gender divisions and religious hierarchies, distinguished itself from traditional Shintō, and attracted thousands of adherents. Eschewing these same social divisions and Shintō cosmology was the New Religion Tenrikyō (Teachings of Divine Wisdom), founded in 1838 by Nakayama Miki (1798–1887) near Nara. The religion's prophecies, benevolence- and reciprocity-centered worldview, safe childbirth rituals, and faith healing deviated greatly from Shintō, as did most elements of Kurozumi Kyōdan. However seeking shelter from persecution by competing priests and healers as well as by the government, both groups requested and sought and received recognition as Shintō sects, sheltered from persecution by competing priests and healers as well as by the government.

New Religions that lacked the protection of the established religions were most vulnerable to government oppression. Out of 1,000 New Religions in Imperial Japan, authorities targeted hundreds with increasingly harsh violence and destruction. The millenarian New Religion Oomotokyō, founded by impoverished Kyoto housewife Deguchi Nao (1836–1918) in 1892, provides a prime example. She and her son-in-law Deguchi Onisaburō (1871–1948) preached faith in and worship of Shintō deity Ushitora no Konjin, like the government-approved Konkōkyō sect from which Oomotokyō sprang. They also prophesied a Japanese military defeat and coming world renewal. After impressive growth of this sect during the 1910s, the police criminalized Oomotokyō for privileging Ushitora no Konjin over

Amaterasu and brutally besieged the organization in 1921 and 1935.

Although several approved Shintō sects had begun as New Religions, the Ministry of Education's religions bureau and the religions section of the Special Higher Police repeatedly targeted *shinshūkyō*. Alleging *lèse majesté*, fraud, and harmful, superstitions, and authorities acting under the Peace Preservation Law of 1900 (revised in 1925), authorities incarcerated leaders and believers, confiscated religious paraphernalia, and destroyed facilities. The lay Nichiren Buddhist New Religion Sōka Gakkai (Value-Creation Society), founded in 1930 by Tokyo educators Makiguchi Tsunesaburō (1871–1944) and Toda Josei (1900–1958), was an ideal target. Tsunesaburō, Toda, and others were arrested in 1943 for criticizing State Shintō ceremonies and war participation. Even the rapidly growing Shintō-derived New Religion Hitonomichi Kyōdan (The Way of Man) was forcefully disbanded in 1937, despite efforts to invoke the freedom of religion guaranteed in Article 28 of the Imperial Constitution.

With Japan's defeat in 1945 and the Allied occupation (1945–1952), New Religions reemerged with confidence. In the late 1940s, Miki Tokuchika (1900–1983) resurrected the Hitonomichi Kyōdan founded by his father, Miki Tokuharu (1871–1938). Working under the new name Perfect Liberty (PL) Kyodan, he advocated world peace. Unlike Konkōkyō and Kurozumikyō, the monotheistic nineteenth-century new religion Tenrikyō shed its pragmatic institutional and theological ties to Shintō and asserted its independence. Despite the death of founder Makiguchī Tsunesaburō in prison, Toda Josei revived and reshaped Sōka Gakkai after his release in 1945. The movement became Japan's largest New Religion, and its political reform agenda

was transformed into the groundbreaking Komeitō (Clean Government Party). From the ashes of the popular prewar Oomotokyō rose a modest reincarnation along with several thriving offshoots such as Sekai Kyūsei-kyō and Mahikari that work alongside other New Religions to offer meaning, moral guidance, and social support to millions of men and women in Japan and abroad.

*Garrett Washington*

**See also:** Occupation of Japan; Peace Preservation Law.

**Further Reading**

Clarke, Peter B. *Japanese New Religions: In Global Perspective*. Richmond, UK: Curzon, 2000.

Hardacre, Helen. *Kurozumikyō and the New Japanese Religions*. Princeton: Princeton University Press, 1986.

Ooms, Emily Groszos. *Women and Millenarian Protest in Meiji Japan: Deguchi Nao and Omotokyo*. Ithaca, NY: Cornell University Press, 1993.

# Newsreels

Newsreels—short news films about 10 minutes long—became popular in Japan during the 1930s as a result of the China War. At first they were produced and distributed by the three major newspapers and the Dōmei News Agency. Because of this association they were dubbed *me de miru shinbun* ("newspapers you watch"). In the late 1930s, after negotiations between the news companies and government representatives, the four operations were merged into *Nihon nyūsu eiga-sha* (Nippon newsreel company), which later was renamed *Nihon eiga-sha* (Nippon film company). From April 1940 until December 1945, this service was the sole producer of newsreels for Japanese theaters.

Besides producing the newsreel *Nihon nyūsu* for Japanese audiences, it also produced newsreels in English, French, Burmese, and Spanish for audiences throughout Japan's wartime empire.

The newsreel grew out of European film making. Although Thomas Edison and the Lumière brothers invented their movie cameras in the mid-1890s, the Lumière brothers' model was portable and could be taken to its subject. Soon European cameramen began to film "actualities," scenes of unmanipulated everyday life, and later "news films," film on a single newsworthy subject. In 1910, French film producer Charles Pathé released *The Pathé Journal*, a weekly film "magazine." The idea quickly spread across the English Channel and the Atlantic, with its popularity being greatly enhanced by its coverage of World War I.

The Lumières' *Cinématographe* and Edison's *Vitascope* were introduced to Japan within a year of their invention. The Boxer Rebellion of 1900 and the Russo-Japanese War of 1904–1905 were the subjects of Japan's earliest news films (*kirokueiga*, "documentary" or literally "record film"), but it was not until 1934 that the first newsreel, *[nyūsu eiga]* was produced by the Asahi Newspaper Company. Soon, *Asahi sekai nyūsu* was followed by the Mainichi Newspaper Company's *Daimai tonichi nyūsu* and the Yomiuri Newspaper Company's *Yomiuri nyūsu*. Within months of its creation in 1936, the Dōmei News Agency also launched its own newsreel operation with *Dōmei nyūsu*.

Just as images of World War I helped spur the popularity of newsreels in Europe and America, the China War did the same for Japan. The images of the war seized the public's attention and families hoped to enjoy a *sukuriin-gotaimen* ("meeting on the screen") with a father, brother, or son on the front.

Special newsreel theaters sprung up throughout the country, where for 10 *sen* one could see all four companies' newsreels plus short educational films and documentaries. Before the "China Incident" in 1937, there were no more than three newsreel theaters in Japan and all in Tokyo. By the end of that year, however, 23 newsreel theaters were operating in the cities of Kyoto, Osaka, and Kobe alone.

The demand for newsreels was further enhanced when the government issued in 1939 the new Film Law, which required theater operators to show newsreels or "culture films" with each screening of the feature movie. With the advent of both the war and the Film Law, the number of newsreel prints distributed in Japan more than doubled. Before the China War, the Asahi, Mainichi, and Yomiuri companies produced approximately 195 prints per week. Once the war started, the three companies, along with Dōmei's newly created operations, produced more than 510 prints per week. To keep up with the demand, the size of newsreel crews on the China front more than doubled by 1938 to 14 or 15 men. To fill the shortage of personnel, Dōmei and the newspaper companies drafted newsreel cameramen from their still photography departments. Cost overruns proved another worry for the operations, and by the end of the 1930s wartime rationing produced shortages of film stock.

For Japan's wartime government, there was also the issue of media control. This does not necessarily mean draconian control of the news media, but rather a way to limit the rivalry among the news companies. A single newsreel narrative was preferable to competing voices, even if their coverage of the war was positive. To the audience, however, the single most obvious reason for the merger was, as one writer put it as early as 1937, all the newsreels "simply show the same things." Some even thought it was unpatriotic for the news companies to profit from newsreels of the war.

In 1938, the Cabinet Information Department initiated discussion of a merger between the Dōmei and the *Asahi*, *Mainichi*, and *Yomiuri* newspapers. Dōmei president Furuno Inosuke was most enthused about the merger; *Yomiuri* president Shōriki Matsutarō opposed it. Furuno had been one of the foremost advocates of a national news organization and helped in the creation of both the Manchurian News Agency and Dōmei as national representative news agencies. Shōriki was a media mogul who saw the commercial value of news. Despite government support, Shōriki was able to delay the merger for nearly two years.

In April 1940, the four newsreel operations were merged as *Nihon nyūsu eigasha*. Furuno was named president, but in an apparent effort to appease Shōriki, the position was made nominal. After releasing some preliminary newsreels, the new company issued its first official *Nihon nyūsu* newsreel on June 11, 1940. Until the final months of the war, *Nihon nyūsu* was issued weekly. In March 1945, release dates became less regular. The newsreel continued to be released after Japan's surrender in August. During the Allied occupation, however, *Nihon nyūsu*'s nationalist production logo—a bird of prey perched on a globe with Japan and East Asia bathed in light and rays similar to Japan's wartime flag rotating around the globe—was replaced by "*Nihon nyūsu*" in block characters. The last *Nihon nyūsu* produced before Japan's surrender, number 254, was issued July 1, 1945; its final newsreel, number 264, was issued December 31, 1945. The next month the company was reorganized.

*R. W. Purdy*

**See also:** Boxer Rebellion; Dōmei News Agency; Russo-Japanese War.

**Further Reading**

High, Peter B. *The Imperial Screen: Japanese Film Culture in the Fifteen Years' War.* Madison: University of Wisconsin Press, 2003.

Nornes, Markus. *Japanese Documentary Film: The Meiji Era through Hiroshima.* Minneapolis: University of Minnesota Press, 2003.

Purdy, R. W. "*Hakkō Ichiu*™: Projecting "Greater East Asia." *Impressions: The Journal of the Japanese Art Society of America* 30 (2009): 106–113.

## Nichiren (1222–1282)

Nichiren was a Kamakura Period monk, at a time when an earlier aristocratic order, centered in the old capital at Kyoto had fallen, and an uncouth warrior government ruled from the archipelago's east. Previously, esoteric Buddhism prevailed, promising to make aristocrats into living Buddhas. With the relative chaos of Kamakura times, many questioned the efficacy of esotericism's time-consuming, expensive paths to salvation. New Buddhist thinkers spread the idea that the world had entered the third and most degenerate period of Buddhist history, *mappō*, the "end of the law."

Nichiren trained in the Tendai tradition, which focused on the *Lotus Sutra*'s teachings through an esoteric Buddhist lens. He developed an exclusive practice he believed appropriate in *mappō*, prescribing chanting the *daimoku* (*namu Myōhō Rengekyō*, "praise the *Lotus Sutra* of the wonderful law"). In locating all the power of Buddhism in this formula, Nichiren furthered Tendai tendencies to locate all the teachings of Buddhism in microcosm in the *sutra*, then to locate all of the teachings of the *Lotus* in its 16th chapter, where Śākyamuni reveals that he is a manifestation of an eternal metaphysical Buddha. The Buddha there reveals himself to be the immanent presence of utmost purity, erasing distinctions between immanence and transcendence, this-worldly defilement and otherworldly purity. Seeing no distinction between the *daimoku* and all the teachings of Buddhism, Nichiren believed chanting it awakened one, cultivating one's identification with the Buddha and precipitating visions of one's environment as a paradisiacal Pure Land.

Nichiren further eradicated dualism through what Jacqueline Stone calls "hierarchy inversions." For him, *mappō*—the worst time to be alive—was the best of times. Everything reversed according to his reading of the *Lotus Sutra*. The appropriate teaching for *mappō*, he argued, made marginal, inconsequential Japan the best place to be. It karmically linked the archipelago and the *Sutra*. Nichiren was aware of Buddhism's setbacks on mainland Asia, which he linked with *mappō*. He concluded that Japanese *Lotus* Buddhism would "return" to the continent, allegorizing this rebound by stating that just as earlier Buddhism he identified with the "moon tribe" (Indians) had traveled eastward, during *mappō* his more efficacious Buddhism from the eastern periphery of the cosmos would move westward like the all-powerful sun.

In modern times, novel interpretations of Nichiren's thinking conflated the salvation of Asia in the Buddhist sense that he proposed with a mission to save Asia and from Western imperialism. In 1901, Tanaka Chigaku (1861–1939) coined the term Nichirenism (*Nichiren-shugi*) to refer to modern, Nichiren-based teachings that he propounded. He called for "world unification," a desire for harmony juxtaposed with actual modern strife and dislocation from a non-Western perspective. Tanaka influenced army officer Ishiwara Kanji (1889–1949), who combined Nichirenism with his interpretation of world history. Ishiwara concluded that history's Final War, in which Japan had to acquire and use a weapon of unprecedented magnitude, would lead to a détente and everlasting peace in ongoing technological development. Ishiwara's desire to engineer this war led to the Mukden Incident, carried out by troops under his command, which initiated the 15 years of war in Asia and the Pacific that ended in 1945.

Other Nichiren-influenced figures played roles in the turbulent events of pre-defeat modern Japanese history. For example, Kita Ikki (1883–1937) influenced young army officers' eventual staging of a series of violent uprisings against what they saw as a corrupt political and economic order that prevented Japan from carrying out its soteriological mission. Their so-called Shōwa Restoration ended in their defeat and purge with the February 26 Incident in 1936. Inoue Nisshō (1887–1967) was a continental adventurer (*Tairiku Rōnin*) who studied Nichirenism with Tanaka after returning to Japan. In 1932, as a lay Nichiren "priest," he directed the Ketsumeidan (Blood Pledge Corps), a terrorist group he trained, to murder Finance Minister Inoue Junnosuke, industrialist Dan Takuma, and Prime Minister Inukai Tsuyoshi.

Scholars have dismissed intellectuals such as Tanaka, Ishiwara, Kita, and Inoue Nisshō as fascist reactionaries. Their actions, however, were inspired by a desire to transform the world into a better place, a Pure Land in reconfigured Nichiren Buddhist terms. Ishiwara imagined it as involving unending technological development that would improve human life immeasurably. In a sense, they were progressives. As with many supporters of militarism and imperialism in other modern nation-states such as the United States, Great Britain, or France, the stated goal of their utopian aggression can be understood in religious terms with religious aims, but also as reflecting desires for peace, harmony, and everlasting equity between nations across the globe.

*Gerald Iguchi*

**See also:** Continental Adventurers (*Tairiku Rōnin*); Ishiwara Kanji; Kamakura *Bakufu*; Kita Ikki; Kwantung Army Adventurism; Mongol Invasions of Japan; Pan-Asianism; Tanaka Chigaku; Young Officer Movement.

**Further Reading**

Peattie, Mark. *Ishiwara Kanji and Japan's Confrontation with the* West. Princeton: Princeton University Press, 1975.

Stone, Jacqueline, I. *Original Enlightenment and the Transformation of Medieval Japanese Buddhism*. Honolulu: University of Hawai'i Press, 1999.

Stone, Jacqueline, I. "Realizing This World as the Buddha Land," in *Readings of the Lotus Sutra*, edited by Stephen F. Teiser and Stone. New York: Columbia University Press, 2009.

Tanabe, George. "Tanaka Chigaku: The Lotus Sūtra and the Body Politic," in *The Lotus Sūtra and Japanese Culture*, edited by George and Willa Jane Tanabe. Honolulu: Hawai'i University Press, 1989.

Wilson, George. *Radical Nationalist in Japan: Kita Ikki, 1883–1937*. Cambridge, MA: Harvard University Press, 1969.

# Ninja

Perhaps nothing about the samurai tradition has captured Western fancy more than the idea of the *ninja*. Even long before the camp cartoon *Teenage Mutant Ninja Turtles* surfaced on American television in the mid-1980s, the world had seized upon the idea of the invisible assassin.

The historical *ninja* are almost impossible to pin down with any sense of documentary evidence, but given the fact that *ninja* were by definition secret, the idea of *ninja* historical documentation becomes an oxymoron. The very principle of *ninja* is couched in the name. The two kanji used can be pronounced alternately "*shinobi*" and taken to mean "to steal away," connoting subterfuge. Because the samurai ethic was based on honesty and openness, the idea of spying, sneaking into battle, and attempting to gain an unfair advantage was naturally anathema to the code of the warrior. Virtually all professional warriors eschew irregular guerrilla tactics, relegating such behavior to the cowardly mercenary. All armies welcome information gained by the spy, but can find few volunteers to fill this role among regular warriors.

Historical citations of secret spies and assassins abound from the virtual beginning of Warrior Tales, but they are the exception that proves the rule. Shōtoku Taishi allegedly used spies against his enemies in the sixth century, and various warriors employed espionage against the ultimate guerrilla enemies: the *emishi* (or Ainu). Fanciful stories abound about professional spies and assassins who trained in the hidden recesses of mountain valleys. Undoubtedly, many of the stories are clouded with reports of religious hermit *yamabushi* training in black magic to protect themselves from regular warriors.

The height of the *ninja* era is, however, the Sengoku era (1450–1570), when the country was embroiled in a century of almost continual civil warfare. The era is known as the Era of *Gekokujo* ("Subordinates conquering their lords"), when treachery was common. Legends grew about whole families of assassins being employed by rebel troops who turned against their feudal lords. Two such families allegedly trained in the hills of ancient Iga and Kōka in what is now Shiga Prefecture. A single day's walk from the ancient capital of Kyoto, yet far enough away to avoid the major warlord armies, these assassins supposedly sold their services to anyone who could pay.

Because they were not samurai, these ninja employed the "open hand" (karate) and jiujitsu ("yielding technique") martial arts and fashioned weapons from common agricultural tools. To counteract the extended castle siege warfare of the time, ninja reportedly specialized in climbing up "unscalable" castle walls, forging moats and rivers, and otherwise sneaking about unseen. Reputed to be virtually invisible due to their matte black costumes, they penetrated into closely defended redoubts. They probably dressed in ordinary clothing, blending in with the defenders. There is some evidence that they masqueraded as priests, blind masseurs, and as prostitutes and female entertainers. Indeed, there is ample evidence that many ninja were actually women; what better way to disguise an assassin or spy?

Stories abound about ninja being the critical difference in key battles such as Sekigahara, the 1614 siege of Osaka Castle, and the Shimabara Rebellion. If that is so, the Tokugawa bakufu understood how dangerous they might be. So Ieyasu himself is said to have taken steps to eradicate ninja after he established his government in the early 17th century.

Draconian methods of social control by the Tokugawa bakufu certainly would have made their continued existence difficult indeed. It was not until the Bakumatsu era in the mid-19th century, when many samurai became rōnin, that the legends of ninja began to surface again. Indeed, the bakufu created a semi-secret assassination corps of their own. The Shinsengumi ("Newly Selected Corps") was employed to ferret out and kill bakufu enemies in the 1860s.

Needless to say, the fame of the ninja probably superseded their numbers or their importance. Their notoriety has been hugely inflated by television, movies, and, of course, manga and anime. One simply has to type the five letters into any Internet search engine to witness their continued popularity.

*Louis G. Perez*

**See also:** Civil Wars, Sengoku Era; Rōnin; Shōtoku Taishi; Tokugawa Ieyasu.

**Further Reading**

Friday, Karl F. *The First Samurai: The Life and Legend of the Warrior Rebel, Taira Masakado*. Hoboken, NJ: Wiley, 2007

Turnbull, Stephen. *Ninja AD 1460–1650*. Oxford, UK: Osprey Publishing, 2003.

## Nishi Amane (1829–1897)

Nishi Amane was born into a samurai family in Tsuwano, in what is now Shimane Prefecture. In 1841, he began Confucian studies at his domain academy in Tsuwano. In 1853, Nishi was ordered to Edo after U.S. Admiral Matthew Perry's fleet had appeared there. On arrival in Edo, influenced by the events of time, Nishi began studying Dutch, then the main language of Western learning in Japan. In 1854, he renounced his obligation of service to his feudal lord and took up Western studies full time in Edo. Through these studies he came to know most of the experts on Western learning in Edo at the time, and also began to learn English. In 1858, when the shōgunate established its official academy of Western Learning (the *Bansho Shirabesho*), Nishi was appointed an assistant teacher, together with Tsuda Mamichi and Katō Hiroyuki.

In 1861, the shōgunate asked Nishi, together with Tsuda, to concentrate their studies on Western humanities and social science disciplines. The shōgunate also asked the U.S. government for help in placing Nishi and Tsuda at a university in the United States. U.S. authorities agreed, but the outbreak of the American Civil War precluded realization of this plan. Instead, the shōgunate dispatched Nishi and Tsuda to the Netherlands in 1863 to study law at Leiden University. This was the first time the Japanese government had sent any students to study formally at an overseas institution. Nishi and Tsuda were dispatched together with a party of shōgunal naval officers, who went to Rotterdam to study naval strategy and observe Dutch construction of a battleship for the shōgunate. In Leiden, Nishi and Tsuda studied law and politics with the liberal professor Simon Visseling, later Minister of Finance of the Netherlands. While in Leiden, they had the opportunity to observe the Netherlands during a period in which it was ruled by a reformist liberal government under Prime Minister Thorbecke. Nishi stayed two years in Leiden.

Nishi returned to Japan on the brink of the Meiji revolution. Nonetheless, in 1868, he managed to have his first major work published—*Bankoku kōhō*, a treatise explaining the principles of international law. Immediately after the Meiji Restoration, Nishi stayed with Tokugawa loyalists as they withdrew to their fiefs in present-day Shizuoka. Nishi was appointed the head of the post-Restoration Tokugawa Military Academy in their new base in Numazu, present-day Shizuoka Prefecture.

In 1870, when it became clear that no counter-revolution would materialize, Nishi joined other former Tokugawa loyalists in taking up offers of employment in the new Meiji government. He moved to Tokyo and became an official of the Ministry of the Army. In addition to his work drafting new military laws, he was active in Tokyo intellectual life as one of the founders of the Meiroku Group. During this period he authored a number of major works, including *Hyaku ichi shinron* and *Hyakugaku renkan*, which laid the basis of modern Japanese philosophical and social sciences. Through these works he famously "created" a number of key words in Sino-Japanese as translations for major Western academic words—notably the word *tetsugaku* (*zhixue* in Chinese) as a translation for philosophy. In the early 1880s, Nishi drafted a number of key documents for the emperor and military, including the Imperial Rescript for Soldiers and Sailors. In 1890, he was appointed a member of the House of Peers.

Nishi was a prime example of the *bunbu ryōdō* ethos of combining the scholarly and military arts. In the modern period, he managed to somehow combine two seemingly opposing roles in public life, one as a Westernizing liberal intellectual and the other as a military ideologue.

*Kiri Paramore*

**See also:** Imperial Rescript for Soldiers and Sailors; Perry, Matthew.

### Further Reading

Havens, Thomas. *Nishi Amane and Modern Japanese Thought*. Princeton, NJ: Princeton University Press, 1970.

Verwaijen, Frans Boudewijn. *Early Reception of Western Legal Thought in Japan, 1841–1868*. Ph.D. dissertation, Leiden University, 1996.

## Nitobe Inazō (1862–1933)

Nitobe Inazō was a scholar, diplomat, and educator. He was a devout Christian convert who lived in the West, married a Quaker woman, and was deeply influenced by Western thought. Nevertheless, he is perhaps best known for authoring one of the most influential books about Japan ever to be published in English, entitled *Bushidō*. In it, Nitobe explained that the "essence" of Japan was in large measure shaped by the "samurai warrior code of ethics" called *Bushidō* (the term literally means "way of the warrior"). While many Westerners take Nitobe's *Bushidō* to represent an old, authentic, and pure Japanese spirit, few know that his ideas were the product of both his Japanese roots and his Western learning.

*Bushidō* is a relatively recent idea, dating no earlier than the 19th century. Among the first significant contributions to the construction of this idea was Nitobe's *Bushidō*, first published in the United States in English (1899) and then in Japanese (1900). The book was highly influential in both countries. President Theodore Roosevelt enjoyed it so much he bought 60 copies to share with friends.

Samurai, or *bushi*, existed between the 9th and 19th centuries—warriors whose sole occupation was battle. The character "*bu*" in *bushi* consists of the elements for "halberd," a type of sword, and "stop"—thus it means "to stop a halberd" or "to make peace." The "*shi*" in *bushi* means "gentleman." While the social rank of *bushi* disappeared with the collapse of the Edo shōgunate and the Meiji Restoration in the latter half of the 19th century, the spirit of the *bushi* that existed in Japan for more 1,000 years continued to carry considerable influence.

Ironically, it was only *after* the samurai class ceased to exist that their legend truly began to grow. Various writers—Nitobe at the fore—created a powerful myth of this "warrior code," romanticizing the samurai's achievements. Writers painted an ideal picture of who the samurai had been, why they

were remarkable, and why they should be emulated. *Bushidō* came to represent a sort of "national ethic" for modern Japan and began to form the basis for much Japanese behavior we see today.

Various scholars have criticized Nitobe's *Bushidō* in recent years, in part because he ignored the viciousness and deception characteristic of all warrior classes. Some do not care for Nitobe's philosophizing about *Bushidō*, saying that he took his theory too far, perplexing many Japanese readers. Others say that his characterization of *Bushidō* stands in opposition to what others took to be Japan's "authentic *Bushidō*." Still others say that Nitobe unduly recast the "code" so that it could be better understood internationally.

Nitobe was not alone in constructing the *Bushidō* ideal, however. The appropriation of *Bushidō* by the Japanese military also played a significant role in constructing the *Bushidō* myth. The "Imperial Instructions to Soldiers and Sailors" (*Gunjin Chokuyu*), issued by the Emperor Meiji in 1882, was influential in spreading *Bushidō's* tenets, though it was not actually called *Bushidō* in the document itself. The *Gunjin Chokuyu* commanded Japanese soldiers to be loyal, brave, have faith, be simple, and be decorous—all characteristics said to have aptly described the samurai. In the age of national conscription, many young Japanese men were enamored by this idealized version of Japanese masculinity.

*Bushidō* is also supported by tenets borrowed from Zen Buddhism, giving it greater spiritual weight and influence over Japanese soldiers. Tapping into some of the most fundamental spiritual foundations supporting Japanese society, *Bushidō* incorporates Zen ideas of self-control, including *fudōchi* ("immovable wisdom"), *mushin* ("no mind"), and *muga* ("no self"). Like Zen monks, the samurai were supposed to seek and attain "enlightenment" (*satori*) to become role models and set a moral example. In the lead-up to World War II, these ideas were used to persuade Japanese soldiers to be stoic and brave and to put the nation before themselves. The *Bushidō* myth, which held that the samurai were role models because they were dutiful, were loyal, and set their master's well-being before their own, was thereby used to send Japanese soldiers into battle and, for some, to their deaths. Given that he saw himself as a bridge between Japan and the West, this was likely not Nitobe's intention.

*Aaron L. Miller*

See also: *Bushidō*; *Bushidō* in Japanese Sports; Imperial Rescript on Education; Zen Buddhism and Militarism.

### Further Reading

Nitobe, Inazō. *Bushidō: The Soul of Modern Japan*. New York: G. P. Putnam's Sons, 1905.

Suzuki, Daisetz Teitaro. *The Training of the Zen Buddhist Monks*. New York: University Press, 1965.

Yamada, Shōji. "The Myth of Zen in the Art of Archery." *Japanese Journal of Religious Studies* 28, nos. 1–2 (2001): 1–30.

## Nitta Yoshisada (1301–1338)

Nitta Yoshisada was one of the first warlords who responded to Emperor Go-Daigo's call to arms in the early stages of the Kemmu Restoration. Although his family had long been allied to the Minamoto house, he turned against the Kamakura *bakufu* and rallied to the "loyalist" forces surrounding the emperor. Nitta had long been a rival to Ashikaga Takauji, but chose to ally himself with him after Ashikaga had also turned against the *bakufu*.

Nitta led a force against Kamakura. When he was unable to approach the city from the landward side, he mounted a seaside attack. A myth sprang up surrounding that invasion in which he was reputed to have cast his golden sword into the waters to magically stem the approaching high tide. The defending Hōjō samurai, when faced with this surprise attack, refused to surrender. Nearly 900 of the defenders, including the last three *Shikken*, committed suicide rather than be taken prisoner.

Nitta was rewarded handsomely by Go-Daigo, becoming one of the imperial favorites. Indeed, historians suggest that it was Nitta's support that encouraged the emperor to defy Ashikaga, who had ambitions of his own. When Ashikaga turned against the emperor, Nitta rode against him while Go-Daigo fled Kyoto for Yoshino, where he established his "Southern Court" at Yoshino. Finally, in 1338, Nitta was surrounded and pinned under his fallen horse. Rather than be taken prisoner, Nitta tossed his famous sword into the air, magically decapitating himself. A number of his loyal samurai were awed by this new magic and chose to commit *junshi seppuku* ("suicide to accompany one's lord"), establishing a precedent for future stalwarts like Nogi Maresuke, who also committed *seppuku* after the death of the Meiji emperor in 1912.

Nitta became something of the paragon of imperial loyalty in later years. The adherents of *sonno-jōi* in the 1860s and the Young Officer *kōdōha* ("Imperial Way Faction") terrorists in the 1930s both invoked his memory.

*Louis G. Perez*

See also: Ashikaga Takauji; Go-Daigo; *Harakiri (Seppuku)*; Kamakura *Bakufu*; Nogi Maresuke; *Sonno-jōi*; Southern Court (Yoshino); Young Officer Movement.

## Further Reading

Goble, Andrew Edmund. *Kenmu: Go-Daigo's Revolution*. Cambridge, MA: Harvard University Press, 1996.

Sansom, George. *A History of Japan to 1334*. Stanford: Stanford University Press, 1958.

## Nogi Maresuke

Nogi Maresuke was born into a Chōshū samurai family in 1849. In 1868, Nogi fought for the imperial side in the Boshin Civil War. As a reward for his services, he was appointed a major in the 14th Infantry Regiment of the new Imperial Army. In that capacity, he participated in quelling antigovernment activity at Hagi in 1876. The following year, however, Saigō Takamori led the much larger Satsuma Rebellion against the Meiji government, and serious fighting erupted. In fierce combat, Nogi's regiment lost its regimental standard to the enemy, which remained a source of deep shame for the rest of his life. Intent on committing *sepuku* (ritual suicide) to atone for the disgrace, he was dissuaded by superiors to continue on in the service.

Nogi subsequently proved himself a talented officer and accepted a brigade command in 1878, rising to major general in 1885. He then conducted a military tour of Germany and returned with a new sense of military idealism based on the traditional samurai virtues of discipline and sacrifice.

Nogi commanded a brigade in the ground fighting in the Sino-Japanese War of 1894–1895 and conquered the Liaodong Peninsula and its major base of Port Arthur. He was subsequently promoted to lieutenant general and granted the title of baron. In 1895, Nogi was appointed governor of the newly acquired Taiwan. He remained there until 1898. Nogi played a prominent role in the Russo-Japanese War in 1904 by commanding the Japanese Third Army in the siege of Port Arthur. Initially, Nogi commanded a force of 80,000 men and 474 artillery pieces. Despite a two-to-one advantage in manpower on the side of Japan, the Russians' new technology of machine guns and barbed wire gave a tactical advantage to the defense. That advantage became readily apparent when the Japanese launched their first massed attack on August 7–8, 1904. Nogi captured the eastern hills of the outer defense, but at frightful cost. On August 19–24, Nogi again directed a frontal assault against the Chinese wall and 174 Meter Hill, which was repulsed with the loss of 15,000 men.

When heavy siege cannon failed to arrive in a timely fashion, the Japanese repeatedly attacked 203 Meter Hill on September 15–30 and were rebuffed again, suffering horrific casualties. That October, several large siege batteries were established that heavily pounded the Russians, but Japanese assault columns were nevertheless devastated by machine gun fire and repulsed. On November 26, Nogi launched another all-out assault against 203 Meter Hill and sustained 12,000 casualties, including the loss of both his sons. Undeterred by his losses, between November 27 and December 5, Nogi lost an additional 15,000 men but finally captured 203 Meter Hill. On January 2, 1905, the Russians finally surrendered Port Arthur to the victorious Japanese, who had sustained losses of 59,000 killed, wounded, and missing. Russian casualties amounted to approximately 31,000 men.

With Port Arthur secured, Nogi's Second Army marched north to join the main Japanese force under Marshal Ōyama Iwao at Mukden. In fierce fighting between February 21 and March 10, 1905, Nogi managed to force back the Russians and compelled them to withdraw. Hostilities concluded shortly after that, and despite his losses, Nogi returned home a war hero. He became a count in 1907 and was appointed director of the prestigious Peer's School (now Gakushuin University). There, he sought to imbue his students with an austere sense of national pride, discipline, and willingness to sacrifice.

Nogi demonstrated the sincerity with which he embraced the idea of sacrifice on September 13, 1912, when both he and his wife committed ritual suicide following the funeral of Emperor Meiji, whom he had served so loyally. Some viewed the act as a protest against the luxury and softness then prevailing in Japanese society. Nevertheless, despite his unimaginative qualities as a general, Nogi is viewed as a pristine patriot, the embodiment of loyalty and sacrifice. His house in Tokyo was designated as a national shrine and is visited by thousands of wellwishers every year.

*John C. Fredriksen*

**See also:** Boshin Civil War; Meiji Emperor; Ōyama Iwao; Russo-Japanese War; Saigō Takamori; Seinan (Satsuma) Rebellion; Sino-Japanese War.

**Further Reading**

Hargreaves, Reginald. *Red Sun Rising: The Siege of Port Arthur*. Philadelphia: Lippincott, 1962.

Sakurai, Tadayoshi. *Human Bullets: A Soldier's Story of Port Arthur*. Lincoln, NE: University of Nebraska Press, 1999.

Washburn, Stanley. *Nogi: A Man Against the Background of a Great War*. New York: H. Holt and Company, 1913.

# Nomonhan/Khalhin-Gol, Battle of (1939)

Small skirmishes between Manchurian and Mongolian border guards escalated in May 1939 into a clash between Japanese and Soviet forces, supporting their respective satellite states of Manchukuo and the Mongolian People's Republic, respectively. In late May, a Japanese reconnaissance unit of the 23rd Division that had crossed the Khalha River was encircled and annihilated by a Soviet mechanized battalion and Mongolian cavalry.

On reviewing the situation, the Japanese Kwantung Army leaders decided to repel the Soviets to settle the border dispute in Japan's favor. They ordered in Lieutenant General Komatsubara Michitarō's 23rd Division. In the process, Japan committed its infant tank corps of approximately 100 tanks and armored vehicles. In the resulting fighting, Japan lost more than 40 tanks within a week, and the rest were withdrawn. Thereafter, the only antitank weapons available to the Japanese infantry were 37-mm antitank guns and Molotov cocktail gasoline bombs.

Meanwhile, in June, General Georgii K. Zhukov was appointed commander in chief of the LVII Special Army Corps in the battle. He held the front line until the Japanese offensive lost its steam by mid-July. Both sides then began preparations for the next phase. As the Japanese contemplated a prolonged winter operation, the Soviets secretly assembled a massive force of two infantry divisions, tank and armored brigades, and more than 550 aircraft for a general offensive.

Zhukov mobilized several thousand trucks to maintain the 390-mile supply line between the railway terminal depot and the front line. The Soviets launched their counterattack on August 20, and within a week the entire Japanese front line had been cut off, encircled, and destroyed. The battle was virtually a fight between tanks and artillery on the Soviet side and small arms and bayonets on the part of the Japanese.

Although the Japanese achieved a minor tactical success in the final stage of the conflict (a night attack by Colonel Miyazaki Shigesaburo's regiment that pushed back a portion of the line), overall the battle was a shattering defeat for the Japanese Army. Its 23rd Division suffered a casualty rate of more than 70 percent. Total Japanese casualties came to 19,904 killed and wounded. Soviet and Mongolian casualties were even higher: 7,974 killed and missing and 15,925 wounded, for a total of 23,899. The Soviets lost some 350 aircraft and more than 300 tanks and armored vehicles during the fighting. The border dispute was settled in favor of the Soviets and Mongolians in an armistice arranged in Moscow in September 1939 between Soviet Commissar of Foreign Affairs Vyacheslav Molotov and Japanese Foreign Minister Tōgō Shigenori.

This battle demonstrated Japanese backwardness in artillery doctrine, armored warfare, and logistics. However, the Imperial Army, hampered by the continuing fighting in China, lacked the will, time, and resources to correct these defects before the start of the Pacific war in December 1941. In contrast, the fighting increased the Soviets' confidence in their integration of armor, artillery, and infantry, supported by in-depth logistical systems.

Politically, the Japanese army lost its confidence in a "northern advance" strategy into the Soviet Union and began seeking an alternative through expansion to the south, which inevitably led to increased friction with Britain and the United States. The Japanese military reversal at Nomonhan/Khalhin-Gol also induced Tokyo to sign a neutrality pact with the Soviet Union in April 1941. The Soviet Union, which concluded its own nonaggression pact with Germany on August 23, 1939, in the final stage of the Nomonhan battle, was now able to concentrate its attention on the partition of Poland between itself and Germany.

*Tohmatsu Haruo*

**See also:** Kwantung Army Adventurism; Manchukuo; Russian Neutrality Pact.

**Further Reading**

Coox, Alvin D. *Nomonhan: Japan against Russia, 1939.* Stanford, CA: Stanford University Press, 1988.

Drea, Edward. *In the Service of the Emperor.* Lincoln: University of Nebraska Press, 1998.

## Nozu Michitsura (1842–1907)

Born in Satsuma, Nozu Michitsura's family played an important role in organizing the anti-shōgunate forces during the Boshin Civil War of the 1860s. As a son of a newly ennobled family following the restoration of Emperor Meiji to the throne in 1868, Nozu had already risen to the rank of colonel in the Japanese Army when, in 1877, the young Meiji government was forced to quash the Satsuma Rebellion. Nozu commanded a brigade of the Japanese Army during that conflict. In the process, he earned a reputation as a loyal officer and able leader in the new national army.

Appointed to the rank of brigadier general in 1885, Nozu next saw combat during the Sino-Japanese War of 1894–1895. Initially under the command of Marshall Yamagata Aritomo, Nozu assumed full command of the First Army in November 1894 when Yamagata took ill. Nozu's forces were responsible for first securing the Japanese military base on the Korean Peninsula and then for driving the Chinese Army out of southern Manchuria.

A decade after the war with China, Nozu returned to the battlefield, now with the rank of full general, to command the Fourth Army during the Russo-Japanese War. The defeat of General Alexi Kuropatkin's Russian force on the battlefields of Manchuria proved that Japan was now a world power. Nozu's Fourth Army played a critical role during the conflict, driving the Russian Army northward out of the Liaodong Peninsula and toward the city of Mukden (Shenyang). The subsequent Battle of Mukden in early March 1905 proved disastrous for the Russian Army. Nozu's force of approximately 40,000 soldiers combined with a similar force from General Yasukata Oku's Second Army to drive out the Russians and occupy the strategic railway center, bringing Russia's territorial ambitions in Manchuria to an end. Nozu died a hero of the new Japanese Army in 1907.

*Robert Perrins*

**See also:** Boshin Civil War; Russo-Japanese War; Seinan (Satsuma) Rebellion; Sino-Japanese War; Yamagata Aritomo.

## Further Reading

Connaughton, R. M. *The War of the Rising Sun and Tumbling Bear: A Military History of the Russo-Japanese War, 1904–5*. New York: Routledge, 1988.

Kuropatkin, Alexei. *The Russian Army and the Japanese War*. New York: Kessinger Publications, 1909.

Munemitsu, Mutsu. *Kenkenroku: A Diplomatic Record of the Sino-Japanese War, 1894–1895*. Tokyo: University of Tokyo Press, 1982.

**Nun shōgun.** *See* Hôjô Masako.

## Occupation of Japan

On August 14, 1945, the Japanese government formally accepted the terms of the Potsdam Declaration for the surrender of Japan. The next day, Emperor Hirohito broadcast the news to the Japanese people. From then until April 28, 1952, when the San Francisco Peace Treaty went into effect, the country was under Allied control.

The occupation may be divided into two periods. The first began with the Japanese surrender in August 1945 and lasted until the Cold War spread into East Asia around 1948. It was characterized by faithful implementation of the Potsdam Declaration, which emphasized the complete democratization and demilitarization of Japan. The declaration called for the loss of territory, the elimination of militarism, the disbandment of the Japanese armed forces, the punishment of war criminals, and the creation of democracy. Japan was to be placed under military occupation until these goals were achieved. The second period, which lasted until the restoration of Japanese sovereignty in 1952, was marked by economic renovation and rearmament.

On August 30, General of the Army Douglas MacArthur arrived in Japan to assume his duties as supreme commander of the Allied occupation forces there, and the General Headquarters of the Supreme Commander Allied Powers (GHQSCAP) was soon established in Tokyo. The official Japanese surrender occurred onboard the U.S. battleship *Missouri* in Tokyo Bay on September 2, 1945. By the end of September, the U.S. military had occupied all of Japan.

The Far Eastern Commission, representing 11 nations, was vested with control over the occupation, and the U.S. government was supposed to implement its decisions. However, given developing sharp disagreements between the United States and the Soviet Union, Washington was determined to conduct the occupation with as little interference as possible by the Commission. Consequently, the Truman administration set out to establish the occupation regime and implement basic reform before the Far Eastern Commission officially began its work. The Commission was officially established in Washington, on February 26, 1946; by that time, most basic reforms in Japan were already in place. The Allied Council for Japan was an advisory body to the supreme Allied commander, established in Tokyo; the United States, Britain, China, and the Soviet Union were members. Because of the Soviet presence, MacArthur was determined to minimize the Council's involvement in the occupation.

The drastic reforms of Japan ordered by GHQSCAP were implemented by the cabinet of Prime Minister Shidehara Kijuro, established on October 9, 1945. When Shidehara visited MacArthur on October 11, the general informed him of the main points of reform he was to carry out. These measures included the emancipation of women, protection of workers, reform of the educational system, abolition of the feudal system, and democratization of the economy.

MacArthur strongly favored retaining the emperor, as he believed this would ease the occupation and reform process. Were the emperor system abolished, he feared Japanese anger might cause acts of terrorism against the numerous U.S. soldiers in Japan. MacArthur, however, viewed the emperor only as a figurehead, symbolizing the unity of the Japanese nation.

By the end of 1945, Japanese individuals charged with war crimes had been arrested and were detained in Sugamo Prison in Tokyo. The International Military Tribunal for the Far East opened at Ichigaya, Tokyo, on May 3, 1946. On November 12, 1948, 25 of 28 Japanese classified as Class A criminals were found guilty. Seven of these who received death sentences were executed on December 23, 1948.

GHQSCAP took particular interest in democratization and demilitarization provisions in the new constitution, promulgated on November 3, 1946. Article 9 renounced war as an instrument of state policy and denied the government the right to declare war. Japan was also completely disarmed, with no military establishment. The new constitution formally went into effect on May 3, 1947.

During 1946 and 1947, meanwhile, the Cold War began in Europe, precipitated by the Soviet occupation of Eastern Europe and disagreements over the future of Germany. In October 1949, the Communists won the Chinese Civil War. Most important for Japan, on June 25, 1950, the Democratic People's Republic of Korea (DPRK, North Korea) invaded the U.S.-supported Republic of Korea (ROK, South Korea). A major part of the U.S. occupation forces in Japan were immediately sent to Korea, leaving Japan suddenly vulnerable to attack. The Korean War thus brought the militarization of the U.S. strategic doctrine of containing communism and a decision to rearm Japan.

In these circumstances, by 1948, the Truman administration moved to review its policies toward Japan. Article 9 represented a real stumbling block to Japan's rearmament, but GHQSCAP found a loophole in the formation of the Japanese National Police Reserve Forces. On July 8, 1950, MacArthur sent Prime Minister Yoshida Shigeru a note requesting him to form such a force. The National Police Reserve Forces came into existence on August 10.

On September 8, 1951, Yoshida and a Japanese government delegation concluded the San Francisco Peace Treaty with 48 nations, not including the Soviet Union. Japan formally renounced all claims to territories formerly under its rule, including Korea, Taiwan, south Sakhalin Island, and the Kurile Islands. When the treaty went into effect on April 28, 1952, Japan recovered its full sovereignty, and the U.S. occupation formally came to an end. A U.S.-Japan security treaty was also signed on September 8, 1951. Under its provisions, the United States undertook to defend Japan, and Japan agreed to the stationing of U.S. forces on Japanese land.

*Saitō Naoki*

**See also:** International Military Tribunal for the Far East; Korean War; MacArthur, Douglas; 1947 Constitution; Potsdam Declaration; San Francisco Peace Treaty; Shidehara Kijuro; Shōwa Emperor; Yoshida Shigeru.

**Further Reading**

Dower, John W. *Embracing Defeat: Japan in the Wake of World War II*. New York: W. W. Norton/New Press, 1999.

Schaller, Michael. *The American Occupation of Japan: The Origins of the Cold War in Asia*. New York: Oxford University Press, 1985.

Schonberger, Howard B. *Aftermath of War: Americans and the Remaking of Japan, 1945–1952*. Kent, OH: Kent State University Press, 1989.

Ward, Robert E., and Yoshikazu Sakamoto, eds. *Democratizing Japan: The Allied Occupation.* Honolulu: University of Hawaii Press, 1987.

## Oda Nobunaga (1534–1582)

Born in June 1534 into a minor *daimyō* family in Owari Province around Nagoya, Oda Nobunaga waged war on his neighbors and drove his popular older brother from power. To prevent rival leader Imagawa Yoshimoto from establishing ties with the emperor and shōgun, Oda led an army of 2,000 men in a surprise attack on Imagawa and his army of 25,000 men at Okehazama in 1560, killing Imagawa and defeating his army. Oda also attacked the Saitō clan, destroying their hilltop castle of Inabayama in 1567.

Oda concluded a series of alliances with neighboring *daimyō* to protect his ranks. He then marched on Kyoto with 30,000 men and there restored Ashikaga Yoshiaki as shōgun on November 9, 1568.

Oda was ambivalent toward religion. Irreligious himself, he opposed the Buddhist warrior monks for political reasons. Although he appeared open to Christianity, this stance was a tactic to secure firearms brought to Japan by the Roman Catholic Portuguese.

Oda went to war with two rivals, the Asai and the Asakura, but the ensuing Battle of Anegawa on July 22, 1570, ended in a draw. Oda then sent his men to attack the Buddhist warrior monk stronghold on Mount Hiei near Kyoto. They killed the monks and destroyed their temples. When Oda distributed the land among his lieutenants, this action brought forth a powerful enemy in devout Buddhist *daimyō* Takeda Shingen, leader of the Takeda clan, who died shortly thereafter in 1573. Oda deposed Yoshiaki for plotting with his enemy, Shingen. The first Japanese military commander to employ large numbers of firearms (teppo), Oda used the massed firepower of some 3,000 musketeers to wipe out cavalry belonging to Shingen's son in the Battle of Nagashino in 1575. The Takeda commander Takeda Katsyori escaped, however. In a final battle against the Takedas, Oda defeated Takeda Katsyori in the Battle of Temmoku San in 1582.

Oda was at Nichiren Temple for a tea ceremony when he was attacked on June 21, 1582, by a vassal he had slighted, Akechi Mitsuhide. Unable to defend himself or escape, Oda committed suicide. The first of the great Japanese leaders who set out to unify the country, at the time of his death Oda controlled approximately one-third of Japan. Ruthless and ambitious, he was nonetheless a brilliant general who created the finest samurai army of Japanese history, winning many battles even though his forces were often outnumbered. A military innovator, he excelled at siege warfare and the use of advanced Western weaponry. Oda began the process of unifying Japan under a military government. His successors, Toyotomi Hideyoshi and Tokugawa Ieyasu, were both former hostages and vassals who employed many of his strategies and tactics.

*Spencer C. Tucker*

**See also:** Christian Era, Suppression; Firearms in Premodern Japan; Muromachi *Bakufu*; Tokugawa Ieyasu; Toyotomi Hideyoshi.

### Further Reading

Berry, Mary Elizabeth. *Hideyoshi.* Cambridge, MA: Harvard University Press, 1982.

Turnbull, Stephen. *Samurai: A Military History.* London: Osprey, 1977.

## Ōshio Yoshio (1659–1703) and the 47 Rōnin

In spring 1701, Asano Naganori, *daimyō* of Akō, was entrusted with the reception of an imperial envoy from Kyoto. The inexperienced country lord had been advised to seek guidance from Kira Yoshinaka, a senior *bakufu* protocol official. On April 21 of that year, Asano drew his sword in a corridor of the Edo castle and slashed Kira for some unknown reason, allegedly Kira's insult of Asano due to the latter's failure to provide the former with the expected bribe. The wounds were superficial, but Shōgun Tsunayoshi was so furious about this unseemly breach of decorum in the castle that he commanded Asano to commit *seppuku* on the same day. His lands were also confiscated and his retainers set adrift as rōnin, or masterless samurai. Twenty months later, on January 30, 1703, Ōshio Yoshio, the chief retainer of the domain, led 46 former samurai into Kira's mansion in Edo and killed him. Severing his head, they marched across the city carrying the trophy, offering it to Asano's grave in Sengakuji Temple. After six long weeks of debate, the *bakufu* finally issued a sentence of honorable death by *seppuku* to the 47 who had surrendered themselves. The order was carried out the same day, and the rōnin were buried in graves adjacent to that of their master.

The actions of the 47 rōnin have not been celebrated universally in Japan. In fact, heated debates on the incident occurred among Tokugawa Confucian scholars soon after the incident. Nevertheless, admirers of the 47 rōnin and their detractors alike failed to address the vital issue of why the actions of the 47 can be morally correct but legally wrong—an issue that betrays a fundamental contradiction of Japan's feudal society.

The incident acquired a literary life of its own. The word "Chūshingura" (literally "the treasury of loyal retainers.") did not appear until a puppet theater by that title was staged in 1748 in Osaka. While obviously based on the incident, the play altered it substantially, resulting in a piece that portrays the main characters as embodiment of absolute loyalty. For example, Yoichibei, a poor farmer, sells his daughter Okaru to the brothel so that his son-in-law Kampei can contribute funds to the revenge plot to restore his reputation as a loyal samurai after he failed to be with his lord when the slashing incident occurred. Similarly, Ōishi Yoshio, appearing as Yuranosuke in the play, devotes himself body and soul to the revenge mission, even pretending to be lost in dissipation in the pleasure quarters to put the enemy off guard. This piece, the most popular in the entire Japanese theatrical repertory, established Ōshio Yoshio and the 47 rōnin as paragon of loyalty in Japanese popular imagination. As pointed out by scholars such as historian Shigeno Yasutsugu, this piece, like its Kabuki adaptations, is full of fiction, as is true of other examples.

Meanwhile, the legend of the 47 rōnin continued to evolve, generating enormous amount of what a Japanese scholar calls "capacity," defined as "the ability of a single story to root itself in the national psyche in a way that encompasses so many issues for so many audiences in so many media." Indeed, the term "Chūshingura" has long been used to refer not only to the puppet theater from which the term originated and its countless adaptations, but also to the historical vendetta itself and all the retellings of it. On November 5, 1868, Meiji Emperor issued an imperial commendation of the Akō retainers; then, on February 7, 1873, to build a Western legal system, the Meiji government banned all types of vendetta, again creating a situation in which an action can be morally correct but legally wrong. As Japan embarked on the road to imperialism, Chūshingura was invoked repeatedly to promote loyalty of the Japanese to the emperor and the state, in the later days of World War II, in a "national revenge" against Britain and the United States.

In the postwar years, with censorship of ideas removed, the legend of Chūshingura began to show competing themes—so much so that it can be, and has been, used to justify almost any ideology or theory.

*Guohe Zheng*

**See also:** Tokugawa *Bakufu* Political System.

**Further Reading**

Brandon, James R., ed. *Chūshingura: Studies in Kabuki and the Puppet Theater.* Honolulu: University of Hawaii Press, 1982.

Keene, Donald, trans. *Chūshingura: The Treasury of Loyal Retainers.* New York: Columbia University, 1971.

Smith, Henry D. II. "The Capacity of Chūshingura." *Monumenta Nipponnica* 58, no. 1 (Spring 2003): 1–42.

Zheng, Guohe. "*Chūshingura* and Beyond: A Study of Japanese Ideal of Loyalty," in *Text and Presentation 2006*, edited by Stratos Constantinidis. Jefferson, NC: McFarland & Company, 2007:194–207.

## Okinawa, Invasion of (Operation Iceberg, March–June 1945)

Okinawa, the largest of the Ryukyu Islands and only 350 miles from the Japanese home island of Kyushu, had long been regarded as the last steppingstone to a direct Allied attack on Japan. The island is 60 miles long and at most 18 miles wide. Japanese leaders considered the defense of Okinawa to be their last chance to hold off an invasion of the homeland, and they were prepared for their forces to battle to the death. Allied strategists decided that a major amphibious operation, code-named Iceberg, would be mounted to take the island to secure harbor and airbase facilities for the projected attack on the Japanese home islands. Taking the island would also sever Japanese communications with south China.

Admiral Raymond Spruance, commander of 5th Fleet, had overall charge of the invasion operation. The covering force included 18 battleships and 40 carriers in Vice Admiral Marc A. Mitscher's Fast Carrier Force (TF-58) and the British component commanded by Vice Admiral H. B. Rawlings (TF-57, a battleship and four carriers, plus supporting ships, 22 in all). The lifting force of Vice Admiral Richmond K. Turner's Joint Expeditionary Force (TF-51) comprised some 1,300 ships. Operation Iceberg included the largest number of ships involved in a single operation during the entire Pacific war.

The land assault force consisted of U.S. Army Lieutenant General Simon Bolivar Buckner's 10th Army of some 180,000 men. The 10th Army included Major General Roy S. Geiger's III Marine Amphibious Corps (1st, 2nd, and 6th Divisions) and Army Major General John R. Hodge's XXIV Army Corps (7th, 27th, 77th, and 96th Divisions). The Japanese defenders were formed into the 32nd Army (Ryukus). It comprised four divisions (9th, 24th, and 62nd, plus the 28th on Sakishima) plus additional units. Lieutenant General Ushijima Mitsuru commanded approximately 130,000 men, including the 20,000-man Okinawan Home Guard. The Japanese constructed a formidable defensive system, particularly on the southern part of the island.

The invasion was originally scheduled for March 1, 1945, but delays in the Philippines campaign and at Iwo Jima caused Operation Iceberg to be delayed for several weeks. The operation began with the occupation of the Kerama Islets, 15 miles west of Okinawa, on March 16, 1945. Five days later, a landing was made on Keise-Jima, from which point artillery fire could be brought to bear on Okinawa itself. Then on April 1, Easter Sunday, the landing began with a feint toward the southeastern shore of the island. The real assault was made by 60,000 U.S. troops landing on the central stretch of Okinawa's west coast. They quickly seized two nearby airfields and advanced east to cut the island's narrow waist. The Marines and Army troops attained most of their initial objectives within four days.

Ushijima had concentrated the bulk of his defenders out of range of Allied naval guns off the beaches and behind the strong Shuri line at the southern end of the island. There, the Japanese planned to inflict as much damage as possible on the invaders, supported by the last units of the Imperial Fleet and kamikaze raids. U.S. forces encountered the Shuri line for the first time on April 4. They fought for eight days to take a ridge and clear the Japanese from numerous caves. Fighting was intense, as the Japanese defended every inch of ground. The 1st Marine Division finally took Shuri Castle on May 29. The Japanese then withdrew to the south to establish another defensive line at Yaeju Dake and Yazu Dake. Fierce fighting continued until most Japanese resistance had been eliminated by June 21. During the battle for Okinawa, both commanders died within five days of each other; General Buckner died of shrapnel wounds inflicted by Japanese artillery at a forward observation post on June 18, and General Ushijima committed suicide on June 23.

While the battle had raged ashore, fighting in the waters around the island was just as intense. Japanese kamikaze attacks reached their highest level of the war as the suicide pilots flung themselves against the Allied fleet. Several thousand pilots immolated themselves against U.S. and British ships, sinking 36 and damaging another 368. The largest kamikaze was the giant battleship

*Yamato*, dispatched to Okinawa with sufficient fuel for only a one-way trip. This ship was to inflict as much damage as possible before being destroyed; the Japanese hoped the *Yamato* might finish off the Allied fleet after the latter had been weakened by kamikaze attacks, then beach itself as a stationary battery. This mission came to naught on April 7 when the *Yamato* was attacked by U.S. carrier aircraft. Hit repeatedly by bombs and torpedoes, the battship sank long before reaching the invasion site.

Okinawa was officially declared secure on July 2. Both sides had suffered horrendous casualties. More than 107,000 Japanese and Okinawan military and civilian personnel died. On the U.S. side, the army lost 12,520 dead and 36,631 wounded. The Marines suffered 2,938 dead and 13,708 wounded. The navy lost 4,907 men killed and 4,874 wounded, primarily from kamikaze attacks. The navy was the only service in the battle in which the number of dead exceeded the number of wounded. This figure was greater than the navy's casualties in all U.S. wars to that date. The Battle of Okinawa was the costliest battle for the Americans of the Pacific war; it was cited to support the case for bringing the war to an end by means other than the invasion of Japan itself and certainly influenced the decision by the United States to use atomic bombs.

*James H. Willbanks*

**See also:** Iwo Jima, Battle for; Kamikaze (*Tokkōtai*).

## Further Reading

Appleman, Roy E., James M. Burns, Russell A. Gugeler, and John Stevens. *United States Army in World War II: The War in the Pacific. Okinawa: The Last Battle*. Washington, DC: U.S. Army, 1948.

Belote, James H., and William M. Belote. *Typhoon of Steel: The Battle for Okinawa*. New York: Harper and Row, 1970.

Gow, Ian. *Okinawa, 1945: Gateway to Japan.* Garden City, NY: Doubleday, 1985.

## Oku Yasukata (1846–1930)

Oku Yasukata was born the eldest son of Oku Riemon in Fukuoka Prefecture in 1846. He joined the new Imperial Army in 1871 and served as a junior officer in the Satsuma Rebellion of 1877. By 1894, Oku had risen to the rank of general in command of the Fifth Division in the first Sino-Japanese War. He was made a baron for his notable bravery and promoted to full general by 1902. In 1904, he held the office of Military Governor-General of the Tokyo region.

Oku commanded the Second Army in the Russo-Japanese War. Carried on 80 transport ships, his force began to land at Pitzuwo on May 5, 1904. To speed the landing, Oku's engineers constructed a landing jetty 1,000 feet long and 12 feet wide that ran directly from their junks and sampans.

Displaying the energy for which he became known, Oku advanced to Nanshan, where the peninsula narrowed to only 3,000 yards. The battle that followed was an omen of the combat that would occur in World War I. Trenches, barbed wire, machine guns, mines, and rapid-firing artillery all played prominent roles. Unable to go around the Russians, Oku sent his troops forward under heavy Russian fire. When this foray was initially repulsed, Oku displayed his determination. Despite heavy casualties, he ordered his soldiers to attack again and again. Aided by fire from Japanese Imperial Navy ships, Oku's troops eventually forced the Russians to retreat.

Oku and the Second Army then moved northward. Oku had captured railroad cars but no engines, so local Chinese workers were forced to pull the cars for miles over rivers and mountains to bring supplies to the Japanese soldiers. Oku defeated a Russian attempt to offer relief to the country's forces in Port Arthur in the Battle of Telissu on June 14. That battle set the pattern for the rest of the war: hard-fought battles, with heavy casualties on each side, and Japanese victory through outflanking attacks.

Displaying determination, energy, and daring, Oku contributed to victories in Tashihchiao, Liaoyang, and Mukden. Those defeats, along with the destruction of the Russian fleet at the Battle of Tsushima and a growing rebellion in western Russia, forced Tsar Nicholas II to sue for peace in 1905.

Oku was named a count in 1907 and was also promoted to field marshal, the highest rank in the army, in 1911. He served as chief of the General Staff from 1906 to 1912. He continued in the army until his death on July 19, 1930, having helped to establish a Japanese empire and demonstrating to his countrymen that Asians were not inferior to Europeans.

*Tim Watts*

**See also:** Russo-Japanese War; Seinan (Satsuma) Rebellion; Sino-Japanese War.

### Further Reading

Connaughton, R. M. *The War of the Rising Sun and Tumbling Bear: A Military History of the Russo-Japanese War, 1904–5.* New York: Routledge, 1988

Hargreaves, Reginald. *Red Sun Rising: The Siege of Port Arthur.* Philadelphia: Lippincott, 1962

Walder, David. *The Short Victorious War.* New York: Simon & Schuster, 1994.

## Ōkubo Toshimichi

Ōkubo Toshimichi was born on September 26, 1830, in the domain of Satsuma into a lower-class samurai family. In his youth, Ōkubo

Ōkubo Toshimichi was a 19th-century Japanese reformer who became involved in Meiji Restoration. (J. Morris, *Makers of Japan*, 1906)

became a close friend of Saigō Takamori, a more prominent samurai from the Satsuma domain. As a child, he concentrated on literary subjects, and in 1845, at the young age of 15, he became an aid to the archivist of the domain. In 1849, however, he was exiled with his family after his father became embroiled in a succession dispute concerning the lord of the domain.

Ōkubo was allowed to return in 1851, when Shimazu Nariakira became the new lord of Satsuma. Thereafter, he began to earn a reputation as a reformer in local government administration. He became a tax administrator in 1858. After Shimazu's death in 1858, Ōkubo became a staunch supporter of the pro-imperial anti-Tokugawa cause and helped to organize a group of radicals loyal to the emperor. Ōkubo advocated an attack on the government, but the leaders of the Satsuma

domain did not share his ambition. Nonetheless, his outspoken views gained him the ear of the new lord of the domain, and in 1862, Ōkubo was promoted from assistant superintendent of the treasury to personal attendant to the lord of the Satsuma domain.

For a while, Ōkubo became an advocate of the movement to promote cooperation between the imperial court and the Tokugawa government. Following a purge of anti-Tokugawa nobles, however he became convinced that the movement could not succeed. As a result, he joined the antigovernment faction led by Saigō.

A clash between Satsuma and British naval forces that resulted in the bombardment of Kagoshima in 1863 also forced Ōkubo to recognize the military superiority of the Western nations and the need to open Japan to the West. In 1866, Ōkubo assisted in the establishment of a naval training center in Satsuma, and the domain dispatched a few selected samurai to Great Britain to study.

Later in that year, Ōkubo and Saigō met with leading samurai from the Chōshū domain. Ōkubo played a key role in negotiating an alliance between the Satsuma and Chōshū domains, which subsequently joined forces to overthrow the Tokugawa government. In the following year, he gained the support of Iwakura Tomomi a court noble. In 1868, these radical antigovernment factions from Satsuma, Chōshū, and the imperial court combined to overthrow the Tokugawa regime.

As Ōkubo became a leading figure in the new Meiji government, he proposed changes in the court system and supported measures favoring the adoption of Western political and cultural customs. He became a Councilor of State in 1869; in 1871, he emerged as a key figure in the effort to replace feudal domains with a modern prefectural system. Ōkubo also implemented such significant social changes as prohibiting members of the former samurai from wearing swords and abolishing official discrimination against people of the outcast groups. Later in 1871, Ōkubo was appointed Minister of Finance and joined the diplomatic mission led by Iwakura.

Ōkubo returned to Japan in 1873 and was named the first director of the newly established Home Ministry. He then took a leading role in the effort to reform the land tax. In 1874, he was placed in charge of suppressing a samurai uprising in the Saga domain. Later, he opposed Saigō's plan to invade Korea, arguing that domestic development must have first priority.

Members of the *Jiyu Minken Undo* accused Ōkubo of being a despot and of ignoring their platform, but he was able to silence his critics by promising to gradually establish a constitutional form of government and to stop rioting among farmers by reducing land taxes. Under Ōkubo's political leadership, government forces suppressed the Satsuma Rebellion led by Saigō in 1877. Many former samurai of the Satsuma domain came to view Ōkubo as a traitor. On May 14, 1878, Ōkubo was assassinated by six disaffected samurai conspirators in the Akasaka district of Tokyo.

*Louis G. Perez*

**See also:** Boshin Civil War; Iwakura Mission; Iwakura Tomomi; Jiyu Minken Undo; Saigō Takamori; Seinan (Satsuma) Rebellion.

### Further Reading

Brown, Sidney D. "Ōkubo Toshimichi: His Political and Economic Policies in Early Meiji Japan." *Journal of Asian Studies* 21, no. 2 (1962): 137–265.

Iwata, Masakazu. *Ōkubo Toshimichi: The Bismarck of Japan*. Berkeley: University of California Press, 1965.

Murakami, Hyoe, and Thomas J. Harper, eds. *Great Historical Figures of Japan*. Tokyo: Japan Culture Institute, 1978.

# Ōkuma Shigenobu (1838–1922)

Ōkuma Shigenobu was born on March 11, 1838, in the Saga domain on the island of Kyushu. When he was 16, he joined the *sonno-jōi* ("Revere the Emperor—Expel the Barbarians") movement. As a consequence, he was expelled from the domain school in 1855. Later that year, he entered a *rangaku* school for "Dutch learning," and thereafter devoted himself to the study of Western subjects. After the bombardment of Shimonoseki by Western naval forces, Ōkuma began to advocate an alliance between the domains of Saga and Chōshū.

In 1866, without obtaining official permission to travel, Ōkuma left Saga for Kyoto in hopes of participating in a plot to

Count Ōkuma Shigenobu and Countess Ōkuma of Japan, circa 1906. Ōkuma was one of the most prominent statesmen of the late 19th and early 20th centuries in Japan, helping to shape the governments under Emperor Meiji after 1868 and Emperor Taishō after 1912. (J. Morris, *Makers of Japan*, 1906)

restore political power to the emperor. In 1868, he was made a domain representative and junior councilor in the new Meiji government in recognition of his early support of the restoration movement.

Ōkuma became an assistant in the Treasury Ministry in 1869 and soon rose to the position of Chief Assistant in the Treasury Ministry as well as in the Ministry of the Interior. He helped to establish the Ministry of Public Works. In 1873, he was promoted to Minister of the treasury, where he served until 1880. During that period, Ōkuma implemented significant reforms to modernize the nation's economic infrastructure, including establishing a national mint and unifying the currency system.

Following the Taiwan Expedition of 1874, Ōkuma was made chief of the bureau in charge of Taiwan affairs. In 1877, he took over the government bureau responsible for quelling the Satsuma Rebellion. During the suppression of those uprisings, Ōkuma came to depend on the Mitsubishi *zaibatsu* for the transportation of military supplies. Together with Iwasaki Yataro, the founder of Mitsubishi, Ōkuma assisted in the formation of the Mitsubishi Steamship Company, thereby cementing a close relationship with the Mitsubishi *zaibatsu* that would last for several years.

In 1878, Ōkuma was placed in charge of the bureau for land tax revision, where he attempted to enforce a series of unsuccessful programs geared toward financial retrenchment. Despite economic setbacks, his public popularity grew because he favored the immediate adoption of a British-style constitution and parliamentary government. Consequently, Ōkuma soon found himself the chief political rival and competitor of Itō Hirobumi, who championed the Prussian-style constitutional monarchy. In 1881, as the popular rights movement was gaining momentum,

Ōkuma publicly advocated the immediate establishment of a national assembly. That stand placed him in direct opposition to Itō, and as a result, he was forced out of office in 1881.

Following his resignation from government, Ōkuma established a political party called the Rikken Kaishinto (Constitutional Reform Party) in 1882. It adopted as its central platform the formation of a British-style parliament and political parties. Also in that year, Ōkuma founded the Tokyo Senmon Gakko, a higher school, which later became Waseda University. Ōkuma resigned as the leader of the Kaishinto Party in 1884.

In 1888, Itō sought to garner greater political and public support for his cabinet by offering Ōkuma a position as Foreign Minister. Ōkuma accepted this role and began a series of negotiations with the nations of the West to revise the unequal treaties. Opponents criticized Ōkuma for being too conciliatory to Western demands. In 1889, a member of a right-wing political organization attempted to assassinate him, and Ōkuma lost his right leg as a result of the attack. As a consequence, he retired from office.

Ōkuma soon experienced a political rebirth, when he was appointed privy councilor later that year. He served in that post from 1889 to 1891. In 1896, he formed yet another political party, the Shinpoto (Progressive Party). He served again as Foreign Minister from 1896 to 1897 and simultaneously as Minister of Agriculture and Commerce in 1897. He resigned both posts in 1898, when he came into conflict with Prime Minister Matsukata Masayoshi.

In 1898, Ōkuma merged the Shinpoto Party with the Jiyuto Party led by Itagaki Taisuke to form a new party called the Kenseito (Constitution Party). Together, they set out to form the first party cabinet with Ōkuma as Prime Minister. From

June 1898, Ōkuma served as Prime Minister and Foreign Minister. The success of the Kenseito Party was short -ived, however. The cabinet soon dissolved due to internal dissent, though Ōkuma remained as leader of the Kaishinto faction until his resignation in 1907.

Thereafter, Ōkuma served as chancellor of Waseda University until 1914, when he returned to the government and formed a second cabinet with the unanimous support of the ruling oligarchs. Ōkuma served as Prime Minister of Japan during World War I until conflict between Foreign Minister Kato Takaaki led to the resignation of the entire Ōkuma cabinet in October 1916. After that, Ōkuma withdrew from public life until his death on January 10, 1922.

*Walter E. Grunden*

**See also:** Itagaki Taisuke; Itō Hirobumi; Matsukata Masayoshi; Seinan (Satsuma) Rebellion; *Sonno-jōi;* Taiwan Expedition; Unequal Treaties.

## Further Reading

Ijichi, Junsei. *The Life of Marquis Shigenobu Ōkuma, a Maker of New Japan.* Tokyo: Hokuseido Press, 1940.

Lebra-Chapman, Joyce. *Ōkuma Shigenobu: Statesman of Meiji Japan.* Canberra: Australian National University Press, 1973.

## Ōnin War (1467–1477)

The Ōnin War was a conflict in Kyoto between powerful warlord houses over control of the Muromachi *bakufu.* The heads of the two warring sides were Hosokawa Katsumoto and his rival and father-in-law Yamana Sōzen. The Ōnin War marked the start of Japan's anarchic Sengoku era (1467–1600), also known as the Warring States Period, during which the *bakufu*'s ruling authority collapsed and Japan broke up into independent warlord-run domains.

The Ōnin War was the culmination of separate succession quarrels within the Hatakeyama clan, the Shiba clan, and the *bakufu* dynasty itself, the Ashikaga clan. The heads of the Hatakeyama and Shiba clans each served as governors *(shugo)* over multiple provinces, and together with the Hosokawa clan they rotated in the powerful position of deputy shōgun *(kanrei).* After the death of the third shōgun Ashikaga Yoshimitsu (1358–1408), the personal power of the shōgun declined sharply in favor of these deputy shōgunal clans and other powerful governor clans in Central Japan. At the mid-15th century, the two most powerful clans were the Hosokawa and Yamana clans.

Although the war's origins lie in the succession quarrels, it soon became a showdown between Hosokawa Katsumoto and Yamana Sōzen, long-time rivals within shōgunal politics. Prior to the Ōnin War, the two tried to reconcile differences when Katsumoto married Sōzen's daughter and adopted Sōzen's son as his heir. This effort ultimately failed when Katsumoto supported the restoration of the Akamatsu clan, whose leader had assassinated Shōgun Yoshinori in 1441. Yamana Sōzen had defeated the Akamatsu and had gained three of his six provinces from them. Hosokawa felt threatened by the Yamana gains, which placed Yamana on the western edge of Hosokawa territory. Akamatsu restoration would force Sōzen to return these territories. The situation worsened when Katsumoto's wife gave birth to a son, who replaced Sōzen's son as his heir. Whereas Sōzen and Katsumoto had previously taken the same opinion on the Hatakeyama and Shiba succession disputes, Sōzen now took the opposite side of

Katsumoto to prevent Katsumoto's influence in the *bakufu* from growing stronger.

These succession disputes still might not have led to war were it not for the shōgun's lack of leadership. The crisis within the shōgunal dynasty began when the eighth Ashikaga shōgun, Ashikaga Yoshimasa (1435–1490), tired of ruling and began planning his resignation. In 1464, Hosokawa Katsumoto brought Yoshimasa's brother Yoshimi into the *bakufu* to assist in administrative affairs. Yoshimi was thus in a position to succeed his brother. However, a year later, Yoshimasa's son Yoshihisa was born. This child then stood in the way of Yoshimi's ascendance to the shōgunal seat. Yamana Sōzen threw his support behind the infant to oppose Katsumoto and his favored candidate Yoshimi.

Meanwhile, the two sides in both the Hatakeyama and Shiba succession crises were already skirmishing in their provinces by the early 1460s. The inconsistent shōgun Yoshimasa alternated between supporting each side based on the advice of his competing advisers, Sōzen and Katsumoto. Sōzen and Katsumoto then began recommending to the shōgun that the other be formally censured by the shōgun. The Ōnin War started when the infighting of the Hatakeyama house spread to the capital. Yoshimasa ordered the Hosokawa and Yamana clans to stay out of the fighting, but this was ignored. Hosokawa Katsumoto, Yamana Sōzen, and the other two clans' disputants formed into two great sides, and small skirmishes quickly gave way to ever greater fighting involving tens of thousands of troops in the first half of 1467.

The details of the fighting itself are largely unremarkable. After the onset of fighting, the Ōnin War lacked the large-scale movements of troops that were characteristic of battles later in the Sengoku era.

Nevertheless, the vast number of troops situated in the crowded capital resulted in the destruction of much of the city. The initial fighting gave way to defensive standoffs that were occasionally interrupted by side skirmishes. Troops resorted to burning buildings as a favorite tactic, and looting was commonplace as a way to supply troops. Battles between allies of the two sides spread into western and central Honshu. The fighting raged on for more than 10 years and destroyed two-thirds of Kyoto. In 1473, the seventh year of fighting, both Hosokawa Katsumoto and Yamana Sōzen died, but the fighting continued.

The Ōnin War ended when the armies of both sides burned their strongholds and withdrew to their home provinces in 1477. After the war, the Hatakeyama and Shiba clans were weak enough from their succession disputes that the deputy shōgun post became essentially a Hosokawa position.

*Philip Streich*

**See also:** Civil Wars, Sengoku Era; Muromachi *Bakufu*.

### Further Reading

Berry, Mary Elizabeth. *The Culture of Civil War in Kyoto*. Berkeley: University of California Press, 1994.

Sansom, George. *A History of Japan, 1334–1615*. Stanford: Stanford University Press, 1961.

Varley, Paul. *The Ōnin War*. New York: Columbia University Press, 1967.

## Organ Theory of the State

Minobe Tatsukichi derived his theory of the emperor as an organ of the corporate state (*tennō kikansetsu*) from the line of thought of mentor Ichiki Kitokuro and the writings of German legal theorist Georg Jellinek.

A 1903 lecture offered early intimations of the theory, which was further articulated in 1912. Minobe refined his theory over the course of his career as a scholar of constitutional law at Tokyo Imperial University in competition with fellow constitutional scholar Uesugi Shinkichi. Minobe argued that the Meiji Constitution limited the emperor's power. By the 1920s, his theory had gained general acceptance, yet a competing vision of the emperor as the embodiment of the state (*kokutai*) cultivated by the military and ultranationalists overturned Minobe's approach in the mid-1930s.

The question of the emperor's proper place was prepositional. Was the emperor above, outside, or within the state as stipulated by the Meiji Constitution? Building on Jellinek's line of thought, Minobe answered this question by declaring that the emperor occupied a position above other state organs, yet within the bounds of the Constitution. The state was a corporate entity and served as the locus of sovereignty. Although by lineage the emperor had a right to rule, he also had a constitutional obligation to do so on behalf of the people through the corporate apparatus of the state. In support of his thesis that the Constitution limited the powers of the emperor, Minobe pointed to the emperor's act of granting the Constitution itself and the means by which he derived his legal authority. Where earlier analysts of the Constitution had focused on the first part of Article IV, which stated that "The emperor is the head of the empire, combining in himself the rights of sovereignty," Minobe focused on the second half, which stated that the emperor exercised these rights "according to the provisions of the present constitution." Minobe's reading pointed to new possibilities for the Diet and the people who enjoyed functions specified by the Meiji Constitution.

Constitutional drafter Itō Hirobumi laid out the opposing position to Minobe's organ theory in his *Commentaries*, a position sustained and promoted by law professor Hozumi Yatsuka and his successors. Imperial authority was absolute. Although the Constitution designated executive, legislative, and judicial branches, these entitities did not govern as organs of a corporate state. They, along with bodies such as the Privy Council, were agents of imperial will. The Japanese emperor occupied a unique position among world monarchs as the instantiation of a multimillennial body politic (*kokutai*) unfettered by any document. In other words, the emperor stood outside and above the Meiji Constitution.

Minobe was no populist. Along with Yoshino Sakuzō and others who sought greater opportunities for parliamentary politics, Minobe did not see sovereignty emanating from the people. Even so, the organ theory opened up possibilities for the legislative body in the corporate state. According to Minobe, the emperor was a constitutional monarch and Japan's political future was best served by vibrant parliamentarism. Minobe's views yielded fruit by the end of the 1910s, with the formation of Hara Takashi's political party cabinet in 1918. Minobe's appointment to a newly established chair of constitutional law at Tokyo Imperial University in 1920 signaled the arrival of his theory as orthodoxy. The organ theory enjoyed particularly strong support from party politicians and proponents of the new industrial economy. Yet even with the death of his constitutional law rival Uesugi in 1929, imperial absolutism under the rubric of the national polity claimed strong adherents, particularly within the military and in the House of Peers, a body that Minobe joined by imperial appointment in 1932.

During the mid-1930s, a coalition of ultranationalists and imperialists overturned Minobe's view of the relationship between the emperor and the state. In the wake of the Manchurian Incident (1931) and the ascent of the military in national politics, Peer Kikuchi Takeo accused Minobe of *lese majeste* and led the campaign to drive him from government. Minobe's speech in his own defense further inflamed critics. His opponents rejected his nuanced reading of the Constitution and drove Minobe to resign from the House of Peers in 1935. Minobe witnessed the suppression of his thought and the censure of his mentor and allies in succeeding years. In 1936, the Okada cabinet criminalized Minobe's theory on the structure of the state; in the following year, the government produced *The Fundamentals of the National Polity* (*Kokutai no hongi*), a text repudiating Minobe's theory and establishing a foundation for emperor worship and ultra-nationalism through World War II.

*Darryl Flaherty*

**See also:** Aizawa Seishisai; Hara Takashi; Itō Hirobumi; *Kokutai* and Ultra-nationalism; Minobe Tatsukichi; Party Cabinets.

### Further Reading

Ienaga, Saburō. *Minobe Tatsukichi no shisōshi teki kenkyū*. Tokyo; Iwanami shoten, 1964.

Miller, Frank O. *Minobe Tatsukichi: Interpreter of Constitutionalism in Japan*. Berkeley, CA: University of California Press, 1965.

## Orientalism

Edward Said's book *Orientalism* (1978) reinvented the term "Orientalism." Previously, Orientalism was a largely outdated word for a respectable scholarly field of interest—the study of "Eastern" societies, roughly defined as everywhere from the Muslim Middle East (including parts of Islamic North Africa that were and remain west of much of Europe) to the Far Eastern terminus of Eurasia in Japan. By 1978, "area studies" had largely replaced Orientalism as a focus of scholarly interest. Nonetheless, Said transformed Orientalism into a conceptual tool that he used to critically examine studies of "the East" going back to the Enlightenment, while also being useful as a critique of Orientalist traces in contemporary scholarship. Under the influence of thinkers including Michel Foucault and Nietzsche, Said examined Orientalism as a body of knowledge produced in the West, which did not necessarily have very much to do with actual places in Asia or Muslim Africa.

Nevertheless, Said suggested integral relationships between discourses on the Orient produced in the Occident and imperialism—namely, the depiction of Orientals as feminine compared to the masculine West; child-like compared to the adult West; static compared to the progressive West; despotic compared to the democratic West; and herd-like compared to Westerners' imagined autonomous individuality. Orientalism dovetailed with ideologies of imperialism as a humanitarian mission undertaken by people of European ancestry to assist helpless Orientals who were otherwise incapable of helping themselves. In scholarship since 1978, the concept of Orientalism has had fascinating ramifications in the context of studies of modern Japan.

Since the Meiji period, Japan been both Orientalized by the West and Orientalist vis-à-vis the rest of Asia. In fact, we can constructively reduce the basic problematic approach to Japanese modernity to this contradiction. It can be expressed by noting that Japan was one of the very few non-Western countries to never become a colony of the West in any formal sense, and Japan was the only non-Western country to itself practice fully modern imperialism by the late 19th century and up to 1945. Before post-World War II decolonization, Japan may have been the only country of the non-Western world to successfully industrialize and embrace the trappings of modern, liberal-capitalist society, complete with constitutional monarchy and a partially elected national parliament, with universal male suffrage after 1925. Nonetheless, history teaches us that imperialism and militarism are far from incompatible with liberalism and democratic political forms. Japan's becoming "modern" in every way was fully concomitant with overseas military aggression. Therefore, noting modern Japan's "successes" is not an entirely commendatory endeavor.

As scholars such as Stefan Tanaka have demonstrated, modern Japanese intellectuals learned the techniques of Orientalism rather quickly. Indeed, while contesting their place in a global hierarchy of nations and building an overseas empire, the Japanese began to use China to legitimize Japanese modernity and imperialism. They depicted what had formerly been the "Central Kingdom" as their own past, their own childhood, in ways that recall how Westerners such as Hegel represented the "East" (corresponding largely to today's Middle East) as the West's past and childhood.

Japanese leaders and intellectuals used evidence of Japanese "progress" and examples of Japanese culture in a doubled game at a series of World's Fairs (Chicago in 1893, St. Louis in 1904, and London in 1910). Specifically, they implicitly and explicitly claimed Japanese parity with the West and superiority vis-à-vis other non-Westerners because of industrialization, political developments, and

their own version of a civilizing mission in Taiwan, Korea, and parts of Manchuria. At the same time they suggested that as an Asian nation, Japanese maintained forms of spirituality associated with the Orient. Intellectuals such as Okakura Tenshin, Kita Ikki, Ishiwara Kanji, Ōkawa Shūmei, and D. T. Suzuki would ultimately claim or suggest that because Japan was both Asian and modern, it was able to synthesize the Occidental and Oriental. Japan could, therefore, lead the planet into a Japanese-led golden age.

On the one hand, such sentiments dovetailed with an ideology of Japanese-led pan-Asianism that served as an ideological basis for Japanese imperialism. This was especially so following Woodrow Wilson's rejection of the Japan-sponsored racial equality clause that was never inserted into the League of Nations Charter in 1919. After that, a marked Japanese tendency to ostensibly reject the West as a model intensified, which was the obverse of Japan supposedly leading Asian compatriots in a fight against Japanese imperialism. On the other hand, the ideologically double game of representing Japan as both Oriental and modern culminated in the early 1940s discourse attempting to characterize Japanese aggression abroad as "overcoming modernity."

Orientalism vis-à-vis Japan had many vicissitudes. As John Dower has shown, before Japan's 1945 defeat, Americans came to imagine the Japanese people in beastly or insect-like terms, underscoring the despotic, antidemocratic, and uncivilized pole of Orientalist representation. But as more recent research by Shibusawa Naoko has suggested, following defeat, Americans transformed Orientalist images of Japan into ones suggesting that Japanese were collectively cute children or exotically beautiful women. Shibusawa illustrates this process with reference to 1950s Hollywood films such as *Sayonara*

(1957, starring Marlon Brando), and *Geisha Boy* (1958, starring Jerry Lewis).

The postwar Orientalist image of Japanese that such popular cultural forms mirrored cohered with a Cold War imperative to rehabilitate Japan symbolically and materially, so as to make Japan into a U.S. client-state—something like a perpetual and Oriental adolescence compared with Americans as adult—as well as to transform Japan into a firm and loyal ally in the propaganda battles and real-world fight against communism. This also entailed using Japan as an exemplar for the rest of the usually decolonized and decolonizing non-white nation-states that, as contested regions between the Soviet Bloc and the "free world," collectively came to be called the Third World.

By the time Japan began emerging as an economic superpower in the 1970s and through the 1980s, many Japanese embraced what scholars know as *Nihonjinron* ("discourses on Japaneseness"), which we might view as insidiously ingenious strategies for engineering social discipline. Japanese were told that they were naturally or culturally harmonious and homogenous; that they had a tendency to almost magically get along with one another; and that they were inescapably inclined to not protest or ask superiors too many questions. Prime Minister Nakasone Yasuhiro infamously suggested that, compared with United States' multiculturalism, Japanese homogeneity explained and ensured Japan's ongoing "economic miracle." *Nihonjinron* took qualities previously and pejoratively associated with the Orient and transfigured them into virtues that—as a mark of implicit superiority—only Japanese were supposed to fully possess. In the sublimated warfare of global economic competition at the time, Japanese such as Nakasone were claiming that being herd-like—which is more or less the same thing as living in homogenous harmony with other Japanese— was Japan's not so secret weapon.

*Gerald Iguchi*

**See also:** Ishiwara Kanji; Kita Ikki; Occupation of Japan; Pan-Asianism; World War I, Consequences; World War II, Consequences; Zen Buddhism and Militarism.

## Further Reading

Dower, John. *War without Mercy: Race and Power in the Pacific War.* New York: Pantheon Books, 1986.

Ketelaar, James. *Of Heretics and Martyrs in Meiji Japan: Buddhism and Its Persecution.* Princeton: Princeton University Press, 1990.

Said, Edward. *Orientalism.* New York: Vintage Books, 1979.

Sharf, Robert. "The Zen of Japanese Nationalism." *History of Religions* 33, no. 1 (August 1993): 1–43.

Shibusawa Naoko. *America's Geisha Ally: Remaking the Japanese Enemy.* Cambridge, MA: Harvard University Press, 2006.

Tanaka, Stefan. *Japan's Orient: Rendering Pasts into History.* Berkeley: University of California Press, 1993.

Zachmann, Urs Matthias. "Blowing Up a Double Portrait in Black and White: The Concept of Asia in the Writings of Fukuzawa Yukichi and Okakura Tenshin." *Positions: East Asia Cultures Critique* 15, no. 2 (Fall 2007): 345–368.

## Osaka Castle, Battle of (1614–1615)

The Battle of Osaka Castle, fought by the forces of Tokugawa Ieyasu against supporters of Toyotomi Hideyori, marks the destruction of the Toyotomi house and the Tokugawa shōgunate's final consolidation of power. The battle was fought in two stages in the winter of 1614–1615 and again in the summer of 1615, and featured the last large-scale fighting by samurai armies in Japanese history.

The origins of the Osaka campaign lay in the continued presence of Hideyori, heir of Ieyasu's predecessor Hideyoshi, and the challenge he presented to the Tokugawa *bakufu*. When Hideyoshi died in 1598, Ieyasu and four other *daimyō* were tasked with ruling Japan in a collective regency for the five-year-old Hideyori until he came of age. Ieyasu, however, quickly supplanted the regency and defeated his challengers at the Battle of Sekigahara (1600). He established the Tokugawa shōgunate in 1603.

A decade later, the presence of the matured Hideyori at Osaka Castle grew to be a thorny issue for Ieyasu, who became determined to eliminate the one remaining challenge to the legitimacy of his clan's rule. In 1614, Ieyasu accused Hideyori of insulting the Tokugawa clan with an inscription at the Great Buddha that Hideyori was constructing. Ieyasu further accused Hideyori of recruiting *rōnin* and stashing stores of rice at Osaka Castle in preparation for war. As a result of the dispossession of the domains of the defeated *daimyō* at Sekigahara, many rōnin swarmed the countryside of western Japan, unable to find employment and banned by decree from becoming farmers. Hideyori became a rallying symbol for their opposition to the shōgunate. While it is debated whether Hideyori was truly preparing for war, with Ieyasu's accusations he nonetheless found himself in the position of needing to do so.

Several *daimyō* and thousands of rōnin pledged support to Hideyori and gathered at Osaka. Osaka Castle had been built on the ruins of the impregnable Ishiyama Honganji, whose militant Buddhist monks withstood Oda Nobunaga's sieges for 10 years. Its defenders improved the castle's defenses with greater walls and an additional outer moat. Hideyori amassed 90,000 defenders and enough armaments and rice to withstand a long siege.

Ieyasu gathered a force of 180,000 from his army and that of several *daimyō* and came to surround Osaka Castle by December 1614. He soon found that the castle was as impregnable as the Ishiyama Honganji had been against Nobunaga. After a month of ineffective tactics and skirmishes, Ieyasu became fearful that his own coalition of *daimyō* would break apart before Hideyori's surrender would come. While Ieyasu's *daimyō* allies had their own domains to manage and could not stay indefinitely, Hideyori's rōnin had nowhere to go and nothing to lose. Ieyasu turned to negotiation to draw Hideyori out.

A negotiated settlement was reached in late January 1615, and Ieyasu pretended to begin withdrawing his forces. Instead, he ordered his samurai to begin leveling the castle's defenses as quickly as possible. Within a month, they had filled in two moats over the protests of Hideyori's supporters.

In May, upon hearing that Hideyori was rebuilding his defenses and gathering more men, Ieyasu recommenced hostilities. This time, however, with their outer defenses decimated, Hideyori's army chose to venture out to fight the Tokugawa forces in the open. On June 3, 1615, the two sides met south of Osaka Castle. Despite a moment in the battle in which Hideyori's army appeared to have turned the tide, Ieyasu's two-to-one advantage in soldiers won out in the end. The Tokugawa forces penetrated the inner walls of the castle, and Hideyori retired into the castle's keep and committed suicide.

*Philip Streich*

See also: Sekigahara, Battle of; Tokugawa Ieyasu; Toyotomi Hideyoshi.

## Further Reading

Sansom, George. *A History of Japan, 1334–1615*. Stanford: Stanford University Press, 1961.

Totman, Conrad. *Tokugawa Ieyasu: Shōgun*. Union City: Heian International, 1983.

Turnbull, Stephen. *The Samurai: A Military History*. New York: Macmillan, 1977.

# Ōshio Heihachirō (1793–1837)

Ōshio Heihachirō was born in 1793 into a samurai family with the hereditary position of city police captain (*machi yoriki*) in the Osaka town-magistrate's office—a position that carried considerable authority but relatively low status. His discovery at age 15 that he had a heroic ancestor led to shame at "being a petty document writer in the company of jailers and municipal officials," motivating him to take up Neo-Confucian learning. At age 24, he chanced to read a book of moral maxims by the Chinese philosopher Lü Kun (1536–1618) that convinced him that his whole approach to learning— seeking moral principles externally—had been misguided. Finding that Lü had been deeply influenced by Wang Yangming (1472–1529), he began his lifelong study of the teachings of Wang and his followers.

Ōshio later won great fame through his resolute prosecution of three difficult legal cases. In 1830, disturbed over the attention these cases had brought him (and by his patron's retirement), he suddenly resigned his position, hoping to devote himself full-time to teaching Yōmeigaku (the Japanese pronunciation of Wang Yangming Study) at the private academy (the Senshindō) that he had set up in his residence. In 1833, he privately published his most famous philosophical work, *Senshindō sakki* ("Reading notes from the cave of mind cleansing"), which focuses on the intertwined spiritual practices of "returning to the Great Vacuity" (*ki Taikyo*) and "extending the inborn knowledge of the good" (to one's outward activities), while enjoining officials to devote themselves wholeheartedly to the welfare of the people.

In the same year, the country was struck by the severe (Tempo) famine. Although Ōshio repeatedly proffered policy advice to the new magistrate through his adopted son, his advice was angrily rejected. Burning with indignation, Ōshio distributed a fiery call-to-arms addressed to "the village headmen, elders, peasants, and tenant farmers in every village," calling for a righteous rebellion against the government he had once served. The mass support he expected did not materialize, and his band was soon defeated. Ōshio went into hiding; in 1837, when he was discovered, he committed suicide with his adopted son.

In a time when resentment against the Tokugawa government was growing in many quarters, Ōshio lived on in the popular mind as a rebel hero. His ideas, as well as his tactical errors, were carefully studied by those who led the anti-Tokugawa movement of the late 1850s and 1860s.

*Barry D. Steben*

**See also:** Matsudaira Sadanobu; Tanuma Okitsugu.

## Further Reading

Steben, Barry D. "Law Enforcement and Confucian Idealism in the Late Edo Period: Ōshio Chūsai and the Growth of His Great Aspiration." *Asian Cultural Studies* 22 (1996): 59–90.

Tetsuo Najita. "Ōshio Heihachirō (1793–1837)," in *Personality in Japanese History*, edited by Albert Craig and Donald Shively. Berkeley: University of California Press, 1970: 155–179.

## Ōtori Keisuke (1833–1911)

Born into a family of physicians in Akō han, Ōtori Keisuke entered into a Rangaku school for the study of Dutch. He later studied military science and English in Edo and was commissioned as an officer in the *bakufu* army in 1859. He trained with the French instructor Jules Benrose, who was a military adviser to the *bakufu*. Ōtori helped to train an 800-man (called Denshūtai) regiment using Western weapons and tactics. He quickly rose to a general's rank and would lead the unit in the Boshin War in early 1868. The Denshūtai won a small skirmish at Koyama only days before the *bakufu* surrendered Edo Castle, signaling an official end of the war.

Ōtori and a few hundred other troops refused to surrender, however, joining a group led by Enomoto Takeaki that escaped to the island of Hokkaidō. On Christmas Day 1868, the former *bakufu* troops there declared the Ezo Republic, electing Enomoto as president. Ōtori was elected Army Minister. The Republic was short-lived. In March, the castle at Hakodate was surrounded by the Meiji army, and Ōtori persuaded Enomoto and the others to surrender without further bloodshed.

Ōtori was convicted of treason and imprisoned until 1872. His reform work while in prison soon earned him an offer to join the Meiji government. He served in the Foreign Ministry, rising to be Ambassador to Korea at the time of the beginning of the first Sino-Japanese War. He was also actively engaged in education reform, at one time serving as the head of the Gakushuin Peers' School. He also helped to recover and write the history of the Ezo Republic and those who fought on the "wrong" side of the Boshin War.

*Larissa Castriotta Kennedy*

**See also:** Boshin Civil War, Consequences; Enomoto Takeaki; Sino-Japanese War, Causes.

### Further Reading

Hillsborough, Romulus. *Shinsengumi: The Shōgun's Last Samurai Corps.* New York: Tuttle Publishing, 2005.

Jansen, Marius B., and Gilbert Rozman, eds. *Japan in Transition: From Tokugawa to Meiji.* Princeton: Princeton University Press, 1986.

## Otsu Incident (1891)

On a visit to Japan on April 29, 1891, Russian Crown Prince Nicholas was attacked by Tsuda Sanzō, one of the policemen charged with his protection. Tsuda was prevented from killing the Tsarevich by Nicholas's cousin, Prince George of Greece and Denmark, who deflected the second sword slash with his own cane.

The Tsarevich was whisked away to the Imperial Palace in Kyoto, where he was treated by Japanese physicians. Tsuda was apprehended by two Japanese ricksha pullers. The following day, the Meiji Emperor, who had traveled by overnight train from Tokyo, visited the Tsarevich to apologize for Japan's "inhospitality."

The Tsarevich recovered and returned to Russia, leaving Japan in an uproar. The nation responded with more than 10,000 telegrams to the Tsarevich from private citizens expressing their shame, concern, and best wishes. One young woman, Hatakeyama Yuko, committed suicide by slitting her throat in front of the Kyoto Prefectural Office as a personal act of contrition.

The treatment of Nicholas's attacker became an international incident. Fearing a *causus belli*, the Meiji government moved to try Tsuda under Article 116 of the new Criminal Code, which called for the death penalty for attacks against Japan's royal family. When it became clear that Chief

Justice Kojima Iken would rule that the article would not apply, the government debated on what to do. Minister of Commerce Mutsu Munemitsu suggested that Japan could avoid the embarrassment by having Tsuda killed in prison while awaiting trial. Home Minister Saigō Tsugumichi and Foreign Minister Aoki Shūzō resigned to take responsibility for the lapse of security. Cooler heads prevailed, however, and Tsuda was sentenced to life imprisonment after a quick secret trial. Transferred to a bleak Hokkaidō prison, Tsuda died in September of that year.

Two years later, Foreign Minister Mutsu cited the incident as evidence that Japanese public opinion was rising to a fever pitch against foreigners because of the hated Unequal Treaties. Prime Minister Itō Hirobumi claimed that the trial of Tsuda proved that Japan's justice had progressed to such a level that foreigners could now trust Japanese justice and no longer needed the extraterritorial privileges embodied in the Unequal Treaties.

Some Japanese historians have pointed to the incident as a significant contributing factor leading to the Russo-Japanese War a decade later. By 1904, now Tsar Nicholas needed only to look into the mirror to see the nine-inch scar on his forehead as a reminder of Japanese perfidy and savagery.

*Louis G. Perez*

**See also:** Itō Hirobumi; Mutsu Munemitsu; Russo-Japanese War; Saigō Tsugumichi; Unequal Treaties.

**Further Reading**

Keane, Donald. *Emperor of Japan: Meiji and His World, 1852–1912.* New York: Columbia University Press, 2005.

Perez, Louis G. *Japan Comes of Age: Mutsu Munemitsu and the Revision of the Unequal. Treaties.* Cranbury, NJ: Fairleigh Dickinson University, 1999.

# Ōyama Iwao (1842–1916)

Ōyama Iwao was born on November 12, 1842, the son of a middle-ranked samurai in Satsuma. Ōyama joined his famous and popular cousin Saigō Takamori in the fight against the Tokugawa shōgunate as an officer of the imperial forces. In 1870, he was sent to study the French military system. It was here that Ōyama participated in the Franco-Prussian War as an observer. After his return to Japan in 1871, he became one of the central figures in Japan's new Imperial Army and—together with Yamagata Aritomo—the major architect of Japan's modern military system.

After a second period of study in France from 1874 to 1876, Ōyama was promoted to the rank of major general. During the Satsuma Rebellion of 1877–1878, he commanded a brigade of government forces on the side of the new central government. After the defeat of the rebellion and the creation of the Japanese General Staff in 1878, Ōyama became deputy chief of Japan's new supreme military institution and was promoted to the rank of lieutenant general. In 1882, he became Chief of General Staff, a position he was to hold until 1884, and again from 1899 to 1904. For more than 10 years—from 1880 to 1891 and again from 1892 to 1894—Ōyama served as an army minister in various Cabinets. Moreover, in his later years, he held important posts at the Japanese Imperial Court, serving as Supreme War Councillor to the emperor from 1898 to 1916 and Lord Keeper of the Privy Seal during 1914–1916.

During the Sino-Japanese War of 1894–1895, Ōyama left his ministerial post with the rank of general to take over the command of the Second Army, which succeeded in capturing the strategically important harbor town of Port Arthur in Southern Manchuria in a matter of hours. Only a few months later, Ōyama's army sailed across the Chihli Strait to the Chinese province of Shantung and captured the fortified city of Weihaiwei, thereby virtually blockading all maritime entrances to Tientsin and Beijing.

In 1898, Ōyama was promoted to field marshal, a rank to which only a few ascended in the whole history of the Japanese military. In 1899, he again became Chief of the General Staff. After five years, he left his post in Tokyo to became commander in chief of the Japanese forces in Manchuria during the Russo-Japanese War. The victories in Manchuria against the much stronger Russian forces, which culminated in the Battle of Liaoyang in August 1904 and the Battle of Mukden in March 1905, made Ōyama world famous. His military victories brought him promotion in the ranks of Japan's aristocracy. Ōyama was promoted to marquis in 1895, and in 1905 he reached the highest aristocratic rank of a prince.

After the victory over Russia, Ōyama retired from active service. He continued to hold his posts at the Imperial Court until he died in Tokyo on December 10, 1916.

*Sven Saaler*

**See also:** Russo-Japanese War; Saigō Takamori; Seinan (Satsuma) Rebellion; Sino-Japanese War: Yamagata Aritomo.

## Further Reading

Edgerton, Robert B. *Warriors of the Rising Sun: A History of the Japanese Military.* New York: Norton, 1997.

Jansen, Marius, ed. *The Emergence of Meiji Japan.* New York: Cambridge University Press, 1995.

## Oyatoi Gaikokujin

When the Tokugawa *bakufu* was replaced by the Meiji government in 1868, the Meiji leaders understood the dynamics of 19th-century world and saw that Japan was in a precarious situation. To survive the 19th-century world of Western imperialism, they perceived the need to strengthen Japan employing the concept of *fukoku kyō hei* ("rich nation, strong military"). An integral part of *fukoku kyō hei* was to institute reforms and changes along Western lines. Meiji leaders' approach was twofold: (1) to send students abroad and (2) to hire foreign experts to aid the Japanese in bring about reforms and changes. The hired foreigners were called officially *oyatoi gaikokujin*.

The *oyatoi* came from various nations and employed in many projects of the Meiji government. From educators to technocrats, they played a significant role in introducing such Western concepts as science, technology, education, and hygiene. Although the exact number of *oyatoi* during Meiji period is difficult to determine due to poor record keeping, a conservative figure is 2,050 individuals representing more than 25 countries. Britain provided the most (approximately half of all *oyatoi*), followed by France, the United States, and Germany. About two-thirds of the British *oyatoi* worked in the Public Works Ministry. This not only illustrates the close working relationship between Japan and Britain, but also demonstrates the Japanese recognition of British industrial might, and Japan's focus on building up its industrial and technological base.

The *oyatoi* received excellent salaries; for the British and Americans, it was at least double their salaries back home. The salaries of elite *oyatoi* exceeded all of Japanese officials' salaries, including those of generals/admirals and prime ministers. Thomas William Kinder, who was Director the Japanese Imperial Mint, received a salary of $1,045 (Mexican silver) per month, while the prime minister received ¥800 ($1 = ¥1). Three-fourths of the *oyatoi*'s salary were at the upper two levels of Japanese bureaucracy, meaning that there was a huge salary discrepancy between *oyatoi* and Japanese officials at all levels of bureaucracy.

In 1879, 66 percent of the Public Works Ministry's budget went to pay *oyatoi* and, throughout the Meiji period, this share never fell below 25 percent of the budget. Besides the salaries, the Meiji government usually paid for the *oyatoi*'s lodging, their passage to and from Japan, and their salary during the voyage. Kinder received a first-class cabin and salary of $522.50 to and from Japan and, at the Mint, his house was fully furnished and supplied with all necessary items.

Indeed, the *oyatoi* were expensive, but their overall contribution to Japan was profound. They did transmit Western knowledge to Japan, and some played a crucial role in shaping Meiji-era Japan. Hermann Roesler was employed in the Foreign Ministry and worked on commercial laws; this was an important task, because the treaty revision was approaching. Later, he served as an adviser to the Cabinet and worked closely with Itō Hirobumi on the Meiji Constitution. Richard Henry Brunton was hired to conduct coastal surveys and construct lighthouses. He and his staff of 25 men contributed to the safety of the shipping lanes in Japan. Kinder, as the director of the Mint, was involved in the construction of the Mint and was responsible for all aspects of coin production. He was crucial in the monetary reform of Japan.

The Meiji government would gradually decrease the number of *oyatoi*, and very few would be around by 1890. The Meiji government's decision was driven by several factors. Expense issue was a major concern, but the Meiji leaders saw that the transfer of Western knowledge to government officials and those in the private sector was occurring successfully. The *oyatoi* experience illustrated that they were "good teachers" and Japanese were "good learners." The *oyatoi* were involved in making Japan a "rich nation" with a "strong military." They were part of Japan's effort to repel Western imperialism. And, as Japan became a world power by the end of Meiji period, their footprints were clearly visible.

*Roy S. Hanashiro*

**See also:** Itō Hirobumi; Meiji Constitution.

## Further Reading

Beauchamp, Edward, and Akira Iriye, eds. *Foreign Employees in Nineteenth-Century Japan*. Boulder, CO: Westview Press, 1990.

Fox, Grace. *Great Britain and Japan, 1858–1883*. Oxford, UK: Clarendon Press, 1969.

Hanashiro, Roy. *Thomas William Kinder and the Japanese Imperial Mint, 1868–1875*. Leiden: Brill, 1999.

Jones, Hazel. *Live Machines, Hired Foreigners and Meiji Japan*. Vancouver: University of British Columbia Press, 1980.

# P

## Pacifism

Any examination of pacifism in the early 20th century must, of necessity, consider its historical moment of enunciation. From the 1874 Taiwan Expedition and the Boxer Rebellion (1899–1900), the First Sino-Japanese War (1894–1895), and the Russo-Japanese War (1904–1905), Japan moved inexorably toward militarism (1912–1945). This posturing was met with a variety of pacifist responses, the origins of which can be traced to a socialist bent in Imperial Japan that would culminate with development of those relatively short-lived political parties defining the early Shōwa period.

Were we to consider for a moment the seemingly tenuous link between the introduction of Western sports and the emergence of pacifism, the connection might initially seem anything but obvious. Hiraoka Hiroshi (1856–1934), an engineering student who had joined the Railway Bureau of the Ministry of Engineering at the urging of the politician Itō Hirobumi (1841–1909) upon completing technical studies in the United States, introduced the sport of baseball to his coworkers in 1878. With this development, the connection becomes somewhat more obvious: The popularity of baseball took off, owing in large part to an inherent expectation of a "level playing field." In fact, having often observed the Quaker-affiliated Philadelphia Phillies at play, Hiraoka became acutely aware that the intricacies of this sport and the ideology of Quaker-based Socialism shared "social pacifism" at their root. Taken together, then, they provided a teaching model for the newly acquired principles of organization, management, and business ethics.

Furthermore, Hiraoka's connection to Philadelphia and Minato ought not be underestimated, especially since the Evangelical Friends from Pennsylvania had in 1887 founded *Furendo Gakuen* in Minato, on the advice of two prominent figures in the development of a Japanese-styled pacifism: Uchimura Kanzô (1861–1930) and Nitobe Inazō (1862–1933).

At precisely the same time, Uchimura and his Japanese supporters could be found promoting their own pacifist agenda—one that in turn would serve as the precursor to the "Nonchurch Movement" (*Mukyōkai*) across northern Japan. Convinced that equality and egalitarianism above all else would determine how humans structure their lives, this group opted to practice an "authentic life," rooted concomitantly in faith and in social action. Uchimura's acquaintance with the Quaker faith and pacifism undoubtedly left a significant, lasting impression: returning to Japan in 1888, he immediately contacted Nitobe. Together they established the Friends School in Tokyo, the sole Friends' educational organization in Japan. Although the majority of its students shared no formal affiliation—nor were they expected to—all understood the principle of "Inner Light" and of pacifism at its central tenet.

Uchimura's other career as a journalist proved short-lived, in large part because of his pacifist views and his vocal opposition to the Russo-Japanese War. Even far more detrimental to his prospects, his lack of support for the war efforts necessarily called down the attentions of the Bureaus of Censorship and of the Army. Thereafter, he could do no more than sell his own highly personal monthly magazine, *Tokyo Zasshi* ("Tokyo Journal"); meager subscription fees notwithstanding, he supported himself by addressing Tokyo audiences on matters concerning a rise in militarism. Uchimura's words found an eager audience among the many curious, disenfranchised inhabitants in Tokyo; in the years that followed, this same audience would exercise considerable influence throughout postwar Japan.

Generally speaking, left-leaning parties, whether advocating socialism or socialist-pacifism, Marxism, or agrarianism, incurred the wrath of oligarchy or military alike. Most faced the inevitable—either being banned or forced underground. Left-socialist parties exerted little influence (and consequently no culpabilities) in governing the Japanese empire. "Popular" pacifism remained the single exception.

As the effects of increased industrialization and militarism spread across Japan, a much-stressed urban labor force pressed for a more equitable distribution of wealth, increased public services, and, at the very least, nationalization of certain means of production. Although representative of a greater demand, these calls for individual liberties soon fell before the needs of certain groups that gathered around common causes and that privileged matters of group over those of the individual. Put differently, concerns with constitutional development supplanted any vestige of individual social consciousness.

Similarly, the Society for the Study of Socialism (*Shakai Shugi Kenkyukai*), founded in October 1896, included among its diverse membership the likes of the eminent Meiji intellectual Abe Isō (1868–1912), the insurrectionary anarchist Kōtoku Shūsui (1871–1911), and the social actionist Katayama Sen (1859–1933). This collective reorganized in 1901 into Japan's first (notably short-lived) socialist party per se, the Socialist Democratic Party (*Shakai Min-shutō*). The government outlawed the group even as it came into being.

The socialist monthly magazine *Shinki-gen*, published in Japan between November 1905 and November 1906, fared little better. Its first issue (November 10) quickly set the tone for a wide-reaching socialist-pacifist movement, but just as quickly settled in as the central organ for "reformist-socialists," a group largely dominated by Christian social democrats. With Abe, Katayama, political dissident Ishikawa Sanshiro (1876–1956), and playwright Kinoshita Naoe (1869–1937) at its helm, *Shinkigen* eventually spoke for universal suffrage and social reform through parliamentary means. Not surprisingly, then, the first issue of the magazine began with a denial penned by Uchimura. "Although I am not a socialist," he stressed, "I cannot refrain from the greatest sympathy for … [such] gentlemanly work" (November 10, 1905). Thereafter, the magazine embraced an overtly humanistic worldview wherein its conception of socialism was both spiritually dominated and individually oriented. Thus, while their magazine frequently privileged Western religious motives (similar imagery provided a continuity to its cover), it nonetheless routinely criticized those Christian doctrines deemed particularly restrictive or repressive.

In February 1906, *Shinkigen* and the other materialist factions that had emerged from the *Heiminsha* movement found a certain unity under the umbrella of the Japan Socialist Party. Following in the footsteps of other similarly liberal groups, *Shinkigen* soon became the target of government repression: some 13 issues of the magazine saw light before it was banned. The Japan Socialist Party (*Nippon Shakaitō*) held on through February 1907, long enough to host its first congress. Immediately thereafter, it was banned.

Over the early decades of the 20th century, marked distinctions between pacifists and socialists went unnoticed, and any change in status translated into their indiscriminate ban. Unilateral movements grew increasingly tenuous and short-lived, as tensions grew rife and personalities and differences of approach came to a head. In spite of its anarchist underpinning, the Japan Socialist Party, originally a coalition representing the diversity of socialist beliefs, was subject to growing internal friction over time, delimiting its direction and possibility. Whereas extremist elements under Sakai Toshihiko (1871–1933) and Kōtoku favored direct action and violent overthrow, a far more measured pacifist agenda enjoyed the support of social moderate Katayama and reform-minded Tatsuji Tazoe (1875–1908). The latter favored a rational series of programs of social change. Grossly naïve, their coalition lacked stability, and the remains of the loosely connected group had collapsed within the year.

Thereafter, factions scattered as insignificant, brief political movements. Adherents found that their actions continued to attract police scrutiny and were summarily subjected to the increasingly restrictive Peace Preservation Laws. It was the execution of Kōtoku in the aftermath of the High Treason Incident in 1911, however, that landed the single most disruptive blow against early pacifism.

In 1920, historian Sakai and Meiji intellectual Yamakawa Hitoshi (1880–1958) attempted to resurrect various socialist splinter parties as the Japan Socialist League (*Nihon Shakai Shugi Dōmei*) by combining their social agendas with the activities of emerging labor unions and intellectual and anarchist groups. Although the organization swelled to some 3,000 members, irreconcilable differences in ideology underscored that nothing beyond empty propaganda might receive majority support. After the Japan Socialist League was suppressed in May 1921, no further attempts at finding unity in gross diversities were entertained thereafter.

Centrist socialism and its supporters, however, were slow to recognize the nature of such dissolutions. Opposing the anarchy of Sakai and Yamakawa, constitutional scholar Minobe Tatsukichi (1873–1948) and educator Yoshino Sakuzō (1878–1933) stressed that elements of Japan's traditional *kokutai* and the emperor system were compatible with democracy and socialism as a whole. A strident supporter of pacifism as part of the daily activities of the individual, Yoshino went on to found his own political party as an amalgam of Christian socialism, Confucian public morality, and syndicalism. Alongside the well-respected economist Fukuda Tokuzō (1874–1930), he dedicated his efforts toward the "propogat[ion of] ideals of democracy among the people." While such ideals enjoyed initial support and a certain guarded popularity among students and workers alike, only with the Allied occupation did these pacifist ideals gain wider berth among all of the peoples of Japan.

*James Wren*

**See also:** High Treason Incident; Itō Hirobumi; Kōtoku Shūsui; Minobe Tatsukichi; Nitobe Inazō; Russo-Japanese War; Sino-Japanese War; Taiwan Expedition; Uchimura Kanzô.

**Further Reading**

Howes, John F. *Japan's Modern Prophet: Uchimura Kanzo, 1861–1930*. Vancouver: University of British Columbia Press, 2006.

Marshall, Byron K. *Academic Freedom and the Japanese Imperial University, 1868–1939.* Berkeley: University of California Press, 1992.

Piovesana, Gino. *Recent Japanese Philosophical Thought, 1862–1994: A Survey.* London: Routledge, 1997.

Smith, Henry DeWitt. *Japan's First Student Radicals.* Cambridge, MA: Harvard University Press, 1972.

## Pal, Radhabinod (1886–1967)

Radhabinod Pal was born in the small village of Salimpur in the Kushtia district of Bangladesh. He studied math and constitutional law at Presidency College, Kolkata, and Law College of the University of Calcutta. A professor at the Law College from 1923 to 1926, Pal began to serve as a legal adviser to the Indian government in 1927. In 1941 he was appointed as a judge to the Calcutta High Court, and in 1944 the University of Calcutta appointed him Vice Chancellor. The Indian government sent Pal to Tokyo in 1946 as its representative on the bench at the Tokyo War Crimes Trials. In that role, Pal wrote one of three dissenting opinions issued by the tribunal. He finished out his career as part of the United Nations' International Law Commission, to which he was elected in 1952 and on which he served until 1966.

The International Military Tribunal for the Far East (commonly known as the Tokyo Trials) was established by Douglas MacArthur in January 1946 to carry out the intent of the Potsdam Declaration by punishing Japanese wartime leadership for crimes against peace and humanity. In addition, the tribunal charged high-level decision makers in the Japanese government with a new class of war crime: participation in a joint conspiracy to start and wage war.

In his dissent at the Tokyo Trials, Pal acknowledged and condemned the actions of the Japanese armed forces against civilian populations in its territories, and condemned Japanese treatment of prisoners of war (POWs). Nevertheless, he questioned the legitimacy of the Tokyo Trials. Because the 11 judges on the tribunal represented only the victors of World War II, he viewed the tribunal as a forum that gave victors the opportunity to retaliate against the Japanese. He argued that because the tribunal was motivated by a desire for vengeance or retribution, rather than impartial justice, the verdicts of the Tokyo Trials would not contribute to lasting peace. Pal believed that the exclusion of Western imperialism in East Asia, the use of the atom bomb, and strategic bombing of civilian targets from the list of charges proved that the tribunal was simply an opportunity for those who won the war to retaliate against the Japanese. Critics argue that Pal's dissent was politically motivated. They assert that having grown up under colonial British rule in India, Pal admired the Japanese government and military for standing up to Western imperialists.

On September 8, 1951, the Japanese government signed the San Francisco Peace treaty, in which Japan accepted the verdict of the tribunal. It was only after this event that Pal's dissent was made public. Some Japanese nationalists have taken passages from Pal's dissent out of context as evidence that Japanese atrocities during World War II never happened. In 1966, Emperor Hirohito awarded Pal the First Class Order of the Sacred Treasure for his role in the tribunal. After his death, a monument was dedicated in his honor at the Yasukuni Shrine outside Tokyo. Pal and his dissent remain controversial in India.

*Larissa Castriotta Kennedy*

**See also:** International Military Tribunal for the Far East; MacArthur, Douglas; Potsdam Declaration; Shōwa Emperor (Hirohito); Yasukuni Shrine Controversy.

## Further Reading

Brackman, Arnold C. *The Other Nuremberg: The Untold Story of the Tokyo War Crimes Trials*. New York: Morrow, 1987.

Minear, Richard H. *Victor's Justice: The Tokyo War Crimes Trial*. Princeton: Princeton University Press, 1971.

Pal, Radhabinod. *Crimes in International Relations*. Calcutta: University of Calutta, 1955.

Pal, Radhabinod. "In Defense of Japan's Case 1 and Case 2," in *Kenkyusha Modern English Readers 17*. Tokyo: Kenkyusha Syuppan Company, 1979.

Pal, Radhabinod. "Judgment," in *The Tokyo Judgment: The International Military Tribunal for the Far East, 29 April 1946–12 November 1948*, edited by B. V. A. Roling and C. F. Ruter. Amsterdam: University Press, 1977.

Ushimira, Kei. *Beyond the "Judgment of Civilization": The Intellectual Legacy of the Japanese War Crimes Trials, 1946–1949*, translated by Steven J. Ericson. Tokyo: International House of Japan, 2003.

## Pan-Asianism

Pan-Asianism is an ideology that espouses the principle of a fundamental unity among all Asians. It is difficult to provide generalizations about Pan-Asianist thought, however, because proponents of Pan-Asianism have emerged from a diverse range of personal backgrounds, intellectual commitments, and political ambitions. Building on the core assumption of Asian brotherhood, Pan-Asianists have generally argued that pan-Asian unity is the key to the eventual liberation of Asia from the political, economic, and cultural domination that Asia has faced since the 19th century. Theories of Pan-Asianism, therefore, received official sanction as the guiding ideology of Japan's military expansion during World War II in Asia (1937–1945). Nevertheless, it would be a mistake to view Pan-Asianism as nothing more than convenient ideological cover for Japanese militarism. Pan-Asianist ideas inspired writers in Japan and elsewhere in Asia for many decades before the war, serving as a running commentary on foreign relations and imperialism in Asia.

Pan-Asianist thinkers have shared common concerns, even though they could not draw from a coherent philosophical system. For most, Asian brotherhood was assumed to exist, but proponents struggled to define where that unity was actually rooted. For thinkers such as the Japanese art historian Okakura Tenshin and the Indian poet Rabinandrath Tagore, Asia was animated by an ideal, a spirit that could inspire its peoples to transcend their parochial divisions and the material facts of their colonial subjugation. Other thinkers pointed to shared cultural values, arising out of either the long reach of Chinese civilization or the social cross-pollination under Buddhism. Under the influence of Social Darwinist thought in the late 19th century, however, race became a common way to define Asian unity. These struggles to locate the exact source of Asian solidarity demonstrate the considerable degree to which Pan-Asianism has been defined reactively and negatively against European colonialism. Pan-Asianism emerged as a reaction against the military and cultural intrusion of "the West." Finally, Pan-Asianist thinkers invariably looked to Japan for leadership. If a rebirth and renovation of Asia could be achieved, Japan's modernization served as a model for other Asian societies and, for some, justification for Japan to take a leading role in bringing about that rebirth.

A common thread in Pan-Asianist thought in Japan, therefore, argued that Asia should be remade in Japan's image. Pan-Asianism, however, just as often included criticism of Japan's modernization and sought to remake Japanese society through the process of engineering an Asian renaissance. As a consequence, Japanese Pan-Asianists often found themselves regarded as marginal, even subversive, elements in their own society. This was certainly true of early Pan-Asian activists. In the Osaka Incident of 1885, Japanese authorities uncovered a conspiracy to foment revolutionary disturbances in Korea. The organizers, Ōi Kentarō and Fukuda Hideko, were liberally inspired democrats, seeking to overturn moribund autocratic governments in Asia as a means to counteract the failure of democracy in Japan. The Gen'yōsha, a right-leaning organization founded by Tōyama Mitsuru and others in 1881, engaged in antiliberal terrorist activities at home, but it would go on to support republican revolutionaries in China.

Japanese territorial expansion on the Asian continent in the late 19th century complicated the position of Pan-Asianists. Pan-Asian pioneer General Arao Sei (also Kiyoshi, 1859–1896) argued in 1895 that invading Korea and punishing China, as Japan had done during the Sino-Japanese War (1894–1985), appropriately expressed the nation's "long-term mission to raise up Asia." The official position of the Japanese government, however, was that Japan's military activities mirrored the behavior of other great powers, respected international law, and demonstrated that Japan's modernization had differentiated the country from other Asian societies. As prolific commentator Fukuzawa Yukichi put it, Japan was "leaving Asia" and thus joining the West.

No event did more to promote the vision of Japanese leadership in a pan-Asian renaissance than Japan's defeat of Russia in 1905. Japan's victory inspired pride among political activists throughout Asia, Africa, and the Middle East, and it turned Japan into a rendezvous point for Nationalists and Pan-Asianists. More fundamentally, in shaking the foundations of supposed "white" superiority, the war allowed proponents of pan-Asian unity, as well as those who feared it, to theorize more openly about an emerging global clash between "yellow" and "white" races.

The rise of internationalist thought after World War I ignited important changes in the main strands of Pan-Asianist thought. Where earlier Pan-Asianists might have been internationally minded, cosmopolitan, and even liberal democrats, Pan-Asianism in Japan became firmly planted as a right-wing, even radical, nationalist ideology, animated by virulent criticism of the West. This change grew in large measure from criticisms of the liberal internationalist order created by the Treaty of Versailles. Critics such as Prince Konoe Fumimaro and Ōkawa Shūmei saw the post-Versailles system as nothing more than a vehicle to enforce a new status quo dominated by the privileges of the "white states." The failure to include a "racial-equality proposal" in the Treaty and the subsequent 1924 ban on Japanese immigration to the United States further fueled such criticisms. Once again, Pan-Asianism played the role of oppositional ideology to the official Japanese policy of international cooperation. Right-leaning Pan-Asianist ideologues were further alarmed by the Leninist revolution in Russia and the nationalist movements it inspired among Asians against imperialism, including Japan's own imperialism in Asia.

By the 1930s, full-throated Pan-Asianist rhetoric had reached wider audiences. With their twin enemies of liberal internationalism and Marxist-Leninism, Pan-Asianists inspired Japanese military leaders to pursue aggressive tactics on the continent in the name of Asian unity. The key events of Japan's war in Asia—the Manchurian Incident of 1931, the construction of an East Asian economic regional bloc in northeast Asia, the invasion of China in 1937 and Prime Minister Konoe Fumimaro's declaration of a "new order in Asia," the puppet government of Wang Jingwei, and the declaration of the Greater East Asian Co-Prosperity Sphere—could all be seen as an official embrace of the Pan-Asianist ideology that had previously been viewed as subversive and marginal.

The official promotion of Pan-Asianist thought in wartime Japan, however, was a source of deep conflict. The radical and transformative character of Pan-Asianism did not sit well with conservative expansionists. The most ardent proponents of pan-Asian unity found Japan's military domination of Asia to be at odds with genuine unity among Asians. A truly radical Pan-Asianism would have to bring not only Western but also Japanese territorial aggression in East Asia to an end. In this vein, Ishiwara Kanji (1889–1949), architect of the Manchurian invasion in 1931, promoted a collective security organization called the East Asian League, which met with official disapproval. The pinnacle of official pan-Asian cooperation, the Greater East Asian Conference of 1943, faced difficulty in defining core values of Asian unity, resorting instead to internationalist-style slogans of mutual respect and cultural autonomy.

Discredited by Japan's defeat, Pan-Asianist ideas have struggled to regain credibility since the war, even when proposed by Asians other than Japanese. The economic growth of Asia, however, has brought about reconsideration of Pan-Asianism in the 21st century.

*Michael A. Schneider*

**See also:** Fukuzawa Yukichi; Gen'yōsha Nationalism; Greater East Asia Co-prosperity Sphere; Ishiwara Kanji; Konoe Fumimaro; Right-Wing Politics in Japan; Russo-Japanese War; Tōyama Mitsuru; Versailles Treaty.

**Further Reading**

Hotta, Eri. *Pan-Asianism and Japan's War 1931–1945*. New York: Palgrave Macmillan, 2007.

Iriye, Akira. *Power and Culture: The Japanese-American War, 1941–1945*. Cambridge, MA: Harvard University Press, 1981.

Jansen, Marius. *The Japanese and Sun Yat-sen.* Stanford: Stanford University Press, 1954.

Saaler, Sven, and J. Victor Koschmann. *Pan-Asianism in Modern Japanese History: Colonialism, Regionalism, and Borders.* New York: Routledge, 2007.

Saaler, Sven, and Christopher W. A. Szpilman, eds. *Pan-Asianism: A Documentary History.* 2 vols. Lantham, MD: Rowman & Littlefield Publishers, 2011.

## Party Cabinets (1918–1933)

The establishment of party cabinets in imperial Japan was a gradual process. It started in the Meiji era and peaked in 1924–1932, when the two main parties of the House of Representatives alternated in leading the government without interruption. This trend toward adoption of a parliamentary system of the British kind, however, lacked firm legal foundations because it depended entirely on constitutional practice. With the strengthening of both domestic and international conditions averse to liberal politics, from 1932 onward the parties had an increasingly marginal involvement in "national unity cabinets" dominated by the military and bureaucratic elites. In 1940, they finally dissolved into the Imperial Rule Assistance Association.

Under the Constitution of 1889, ministers of state exercised executive power as delegates of a sovereign monarch. In principle, they were autonomous from the bicameral Imperial Diet, as there were no specific provisions dealing with their appointment and removal. The authors of the fundamental law, representing the oligarchy who ruled the country at the time, had intended to protect the administration from the "tyranny of the majority" through this system. By custom, the emperor would appoint the premier upon advice of a few "elder statesmen," the *genrō*, who initially pursued the continuation of nonrepresentative government. However, as the annual budget and bills required approval of the elected Lower House, these "transcendent cabinets" (*chōzen naikaku*) soon had to acknowledge the parties as institutional partners. In 1898, the *genrō* consented to the formation of the Ōkuma-Itagaki cabinet, in which members of the majority party Kenseitō filled all key posts apart from those in the Army and Navy Ministries. Factionalism and hostility from both civil and military services caused the administration to fall apart within months, exposing party unpreparedness to take over the role of the oligarchs as a unifying force.

Two years later, the largest party agreed to reorganize as Rikken Seiyūkai under *genrō* Itō Hirobumi, who in 1903 passed the presidency on to his protégé Saionji Kinmochi. The Seiyūkai adopted a pragmatic policy of compromise with the established political elites, taking advantage of intermittent but growing participation in government to infiltrate the bureaucracy and strengthen its electoral base. The chief strategist was Hara Takashi, who became party president in 1914 and prime minister in 1918, in the wake of the "rice riots." Senior statesman Yamagata Aritomo, a fierce adversary of party expansion, recommended Hara for office as the only leader who could not only secure cooperation among state organs, but also be acceptable to public opinion in a time of worsening sociopolitical unrest. Though called the "commoner premier" because he was the first member of the Lower House to serve in this position, Hara pursued conservative policies on social issues and opposed immediate enactment of universal male suffrage. His cabinet sponsored instead a moderate enlargement of the franchise, along with administrative reforms that aimed at weakening what remained of the Meiji oligarchy. Concerned about the risk of Japan's diplomatic isolation after the country's interventions in China and Eastern Siberia, Hara responded with favor to the American initiative for an arms limitation conference in Washington, D.C.

The Seiyūkai main opponent in the Lower House, born as Rikken Dōshikai in 1913, grew to become the Kenseikai in 1916; it was similarly the outcome of an alliance between bureaucratic elements and an existing party. However, due to its later start and more liberal bent, the Kenseikai was less successful in building a network of elite supporters. The chances for a turnover in government increased after Hara's assassination in 1921, which left his party prey to factional strife. Following a short-lived attempt to keep the Seiyūkai in power, the emperor's advisers opted for "neutral cabinets" as a temporary settlement in view of the general election of 1924. Thanks to the Seiyūkai split, the Kenseikai emerged from the polls with a plurality, resulting in the appointment to premier of president Katō Takaaki. It was the first and only time that an election brought about a change in government in prewar Japan. In 1937 the Hayashi cabinet resigned after failing to win a majority, but this did not bring the parties back to power.

Saionji, the last surviving *genrō*, thereafter tried to smooth the transition to a parliamentary system by restricting the choice of the prime minister to the leader of either major party. This process was facilitated in 1927 by the merger of the Seiyūkai splinter group into the Kenseikai, which took the name of Rikken Minseitō. The Kenseikai-Minseitō carried out some political reforms, starting with universal male suffrage in 1925, and took a relatively liberal stance on the labor and tenancy questions. In foreign affairs, it promoted cooperative diplomacy with the Western powers and China. In contrast to the Seiyūkai's positive spending policy, the Minseitō pursued financial stability through deflation; these measures, however, amplified the impact of the Great Depression in Japan. At the same time, the Seiyūkai accentuated its conservative and nationalist tracts: at home, it engaged in suppression of the radical left; abroad, it opposed Chinese reunification under the Guomindang. It also attacked the Minseitō for pushing through the London Treaty despite opposition from the naval chief of staff.

Lacking constitutional guarantees and a mass base of support, the parties were unable to resist the political advance of the armed forces and "reformist bureaucrats" (*kakushin kanryō*) in the climate of national emergency of the 1930s. After the May 15 Incident of 1932, Saionji cautiously chose as premier the retired admiral Saitō Makoto, who formed a cabinet with the contribution of both Seiyūkai and Minseitō. This formula proved ineffective in forestalling the rise of the militarists and technocrats, who in the next few years achieved decisive control of the government.

*Andrea Revelant*

See also: Hara Takashi; Itagaki Taisuke; Itō Hirobumi; London Naval Conference; Ōkuma Shigenobu; Rice Riots; Saionji Kinmochi; Washington Naval Conference.

### Further Reading

Duus, Peter. *Party Rivalry and Political Change in Taishō Japan*. Cambridge, MA: Harvard University Press, 1968.

Mitani Taichiro. "The Establishment of Party Cabinets, 1898–1932," in *The Cambridge History of Japan*, Vol. 6, edited by Peter Duus. Cambridge, UK: Cambridge University Press, 1988:55–96.

Murai, Ryota. "Who Should Govern: The Political Reformation after the First World War in Japan." *Kobe University Law Review* 36, no. 1 (2002): 19–43.

## Peace Preservation Law (1925)

Japanese attempts to establish and enforce a law resembling the Peace Preservation Law (*Chian iji hô*) predate 1925. In 1900, the Peace Police Law was enacted for the purpose of suppressing labor movements. In February 1922, an early version of the Peace Preservation Law was introduced in the House of Peers, with the aim of combating communist organizing. This measure failed to pass due, in part, to its excessively vague wording. Yet, to bureaucrats in the Ministry of Justice, several of the high-profile incidents of the 1920s seemed to indicate the need for a law that criminalized socialist organizing. In 1921, Kondô Eizô was arrested for receiving funds from the Communist International for the purpose of building a Japanese Communist Party (JCP). In June 1923, members of the recently established JCP were arrested. Later that same year, Namba Daisuke, son of a member of the House of Representatives and a self-described socialist, was arrested for attempting to assassinate the Crown Prince, Hirohito. Communists and socialists were not the only cause for worry among law enforcement bureaucrats, however. The 1918 Rice Riots had signaled to lawmakers that mass movements could become a threat to the country's stability. Lastly, one of the main precursors to the Peace Preservation Law came in the form of an Imperial Rescript, which was announced to quell the frenzy in the wake of the Great Kanto Earthquake in 1923.

Although the first application of the law came shortly after its passage, when 38 students were arrested in Kyoto in 1925, the first large-scale application occurred on March 15, 1928, when approximately 1,600 members of proletarian parties were arrested. Arrests of suspected communists continued throughout the prewar period, and in some cases suspects were imprisoned indefinitely. The Special Higher Police (*Tokubetsu kôtô keisatsu*), which was in charge of ideological surveillance, was especially known for its brutality, and some suspects were even beaten to death. An especially famous case involved the proletarian writer Kobayashi Takiji (1903–1933), whose young career was cut short by the severe beating he received while in captivity.

Two major changes were eventually made to the Peace Preservation Law. In 1928, the punishment administered for breaking the law was made more severe, and was expanded to include the death penalty. Furthermore, the vague language of the first article was to some extent clarified, separating the language protecting the *kokutai* (the national polity) and the system of private property. The first article had initially outlawed actions and conspiracies aimed at "changing the *kokutai* or denying the private property system," which drew the ire of nationalist critics, who charged that it conflated the rule of the emperor with the system of capitalism. These changes accompanied a major strengthening of the police force,

including the expansion of the Special Higher Police. In the second major overhaul of the law in 1941, the seven articles were expanded to 65 articles, which spelled out in greater detail the punishable ideological and political offenses against the state covered by the law. Further, authorities were given the power to keep political criminals imprisoned longer than the term of their sentences as a preventive measure.

It is worth noting that despite the wide-ranging power of the Peace Preservation Law and its enormous influence in curbing leftist activism during the interwar period, there were also certain aspects of the law that made it inadequate for total ideological suppression. The most significant of these was the fact that its language was directed specifically at socialist and communists, when many of the direct threats against the state and private property rights, including assassinations of politicians, civil servants, and capitalists were in fact committed by ultra-nationalist activists. Although the Peace Preservation Law did nothing to prevent these acts, it was nevertheless one of the most powerful of the ideological policies enacted during the prewar era.

*John D. Person*

**See also:** Great Kanto Earthquake; Rice Riots; Right-Wing Politics in Japan.

**Further Reading**

Mitchell, Richard H. *Thought Control in Prewar Japan*. Ithaca: Cornell University Press, 1976.

Tipton, Elise. *The Japanese Police State: The Tokkô in Interwar Japan*. Honolulu: University of Hawaii Press, 1990.

# Pearl Harbor, Attack on (1941)

By early 1941, tensions between Japan and the United States had reached the breaking

Smoke rising from Hickam Field during the attack on Pearl Harbor on December 7, 1941. (National Archives)

point. Both sides visualized the same scenario for war in the Pacific. The Japanese would seize U.S. and European possessions in the Far East, forcing the U.S. Navy to fight its way across the Pacific to relieve them. Somewhere in the Far East, a great naval battle would occur to decide Pacific hegemony. In March 1940, commander of the Combined Fleet Admiral Yamamoto Isoroku scrapped the original plan—which called for using submarines and cruisers and destroyers with the Long Lance torpedo and savaging the U.S. battle fleet as it worked its way west—in favor of a preemptive strike against the U.S. fleet, which Roosevelt had shifted from San Diego to Pearl Harbor on the island of Oahu.

Yamamoto believed that such an attack, destroying the U.S. carriers and battleships, would buy time for Japan to build its defensive ring. Yamamoto also misread American psychology when he believed that such an attack might demoralize the American people and force Washington officials to negotiate a settlement that would give Japan hegemony in the western Pacific. With both sides edging toward war, U.S. Pacific Fleet commander Admiral Husband E. Kimmel and army Lieutenant General Walter C. Short made their dispositions for the defense of Oahu. Both men requested additional resources from Washington, but the United States was only then rearming, and little additional assistance was forthcoming.

The Japanese, meanwhile, trained extensively for the Pearl Harbor attack. They fitted their torpedoes with fins so that they could be dropped from aircraft into the shallow water of Pearl Harbor, and they also planned to use large armor-piercing shells to be dropped as bombs from high-flying aircraft. No deck armor would be able to withstand them.

Following the expiration of a self-imposed deadline for securing an agreement with the United States, Tokyo ordered the

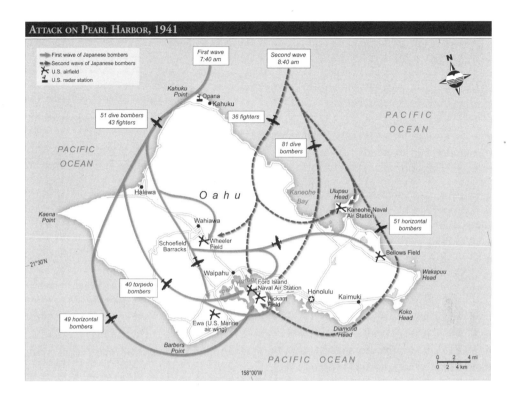

ATTACK ON PEARL HARBOR, 1941

attack to go forward. On November 16, 1941, Japanese submarines departed for Pearl Harbor, and 10 days later the First Air Fleet, commanded by Vice Admiral Nagumo Chaichi, sortied. This attack force was centered on six aircraft carriers: *Akagi, Hiryu, Kaga, Shokaku, Soryu,* and *Zuikaku.* They carried 423 aircraft, 360 of which were to participate in the attack. Accompanying the carriers were two battleships, three cruisers, nine destroyers, and two tankers.

Surprise was essential if the attack was to be successful. The Japanese maintained radio silence, and Washington knew only that the fleet had sailed. A "war warning" had been issued to military commanders in the Pacific, but few American leaders thought the Japanese would dare attack Pearl Harbor. Nagumo planned to approach from the northwest and move in as close as possible before

launching his aircraft, and then recover them farther out, forcing any U.S. air reaction force to fly two long legs.

Nagumo ordered the planes to launch beginning at 6:00 a.m. at a point approximately 275 miles from Pearl Harbor. Two events should have made a difference to the Americans but did not. First, before the launch, American picket ships off the harbor entrance detected one Japanese midget submarine. Second, they sank another. A total of five Japanese midget submarines were part of the operation. Carried to the area by mother submarines, they were to enter the harbor and then wait for the air attack. Probably only one succeeded.

At 7:50 a.m., the first wave of Japanese aircraft began the attack on the ships at Pearl Harbor and air stations at Ewa, Ford Island, Hickam, Kaneohe, and Wheeler. Most U.S. planes were destroyed on the ground. They were easy targets as Short, to avoid sabotage by the many Japanese residents on the island, had ordered the planes bunched together and ammunition stored separately. The attack achieved great success. Over some 140 minutes, the Japanese sank four of the eight U.S. battleships in the Pacific and badly damaged the rest. Seven smaller ships were also sunk, and four were badly damaged. A total of 188 U.S. aircraft were destroyed, and 63 were badly damaged. The attack also killed 2,280 people and wounded 1,109. The attack cost the Japanese only 29 aircraft and fewer than 100 air crew dead.

The chief drawbacks in the attack from the Japanese point of view were that the U.S. aircraft carriers were away from Pearl Harbor on maneuvers and could not be struck. In addition, the Japanese failed to hit the oil tank storage areas, without which the fleet could not remain at Pearl. Nor had they targeted the dockyard repair facilities. Nagumo had won a smashing victory but was unwilling to risk his ships. The task force recovered its aircraft and departed.

Yamamoto's preemptive strike was a brilliant tactical success. The Japanese could carry out their plans in the South Pacific without fear of significant U.S. naval intervention. However, the Pearl Harbor attack also solidly united American opinion behind a war that ultimately led to Japan's defeat.

*T. Jason Soderstrum*
*and Spencer C. Tucker*

**See also:** Yamamoto Isoroku.

### Further Reading

Clausen, Henry C. *Pearl Harbor: Final Judgment*. New York: Crown, 1992.

Prange, Gordon W., with Donald M. Goldstein and Katherine V. Dillon. *At Dawn We Slept: The Untold Story of Pearl Harbor*. New York: Harper and Row, 1975.

Russell, Henry Dozier. *Pearl Harbor Story*. Macon, GA: Mercer University Press, 2001.

Satterfield, Archie. *The Day the War Began*. New York: Praeger, 1992.

Toland, John. *Infamy: Pearl Harbor and Its Aftermath*. Garden City, NY: Doubleday, 1982.

Weintraub, Stanley. *Long Day's Journey into War: December 7, 1941*. New York: Dutton, 1991.

## Perry, Matthew (1794–1858)

Matthew Perry was born in South Kingston, Rhode Island, on April 10, 1794, and in 1809 he received his midshipman's warrant. He sailed for two years with his older brother, Lieutenant Oliver Hazard Perry, on board the schooner *Revenge* before transferring to the frigate *President*. In the War of 1812, he was wounded when a gun burst. Perry rose to lieutenant in February 1813. He served in the brief conflict with Algiers in 1815.

Over the next 30 years, Perry engaged in numerous sea and shore duties that established him as one of the foremost naval officers of his generation. He reached the level of master commandant in 1826, and from 1833 to 1837, he functioned as second-in-command of the New York Navy Yard.

Perry also helped lay the foundations of the U.S. Exploring Expedition. Rising to captain in 1837, he assumed command of the *Fulton*, the navy's first side-paddle steam warship, and also organized the first corps of naval engineers. Perry then conducted the navy's first gunnery school off Sandy Hook, New Jersey, during 1839–1840.

Promoted to commodore in June 1841, Perry was appointed chief of the New York Navy Yard. There he supervised the design and construction of two superb steam frigates, the *Missouri* and the *Mississippi*. By

1843, he was commanding the African squadron to suppress the slave trade. Two years later, he was detached to the newly established U.S. Naval Academy to help draw up its initial curriculum and serve on its board of examiners.

In the Mexican-American War (1846–1847), Perry was second-in-command of a blockading squadron under Commodore David Conner. He directed the *Mississippi* during operations against the ports of Frontera and Tabasco in October, and over the next two months participated in the captures of Tampico and Laguna. In March 1847, Perry succeeded Conner as squadron commander and then assisted the landing of General Winfield Scott's army at Veracruz. For the rest of the year, he led expeditions up the Tabasco River, capturing numerous forts and towns. Perry conducted blockade duty for the remainder of the war, before returning to the United States in 1848. He remained at New York until 1852, when he took on one of the most dramatic and significant diplomatic missions in American history.

Perry was assigned the task of "reopening" Japan to foreign trade by President Milliard Fillmore. He was given two steam frigates, *Mississippi* and *Susquehanna*, and two sloops of war, which he assembled in squadron strength at Naha, Okinawa, in May 1853. The Japanese would christen them the "black ships" on account of their drab color. Perry then sailed for Edo (Tokyo) Bay "to demand as a right, and not to solicit as a favor those acts of courtesy which are due from one civilized country to another."

Perry's squadron made its unannounced appearance in Japan on July 8, 1853. Perry, a man of great military bearing and dignity, politely but firmly refused to deal with local officials and demanded to negotiate with government representatives. The skittish bureaucrats were initially perplexed over which course of action to take, and at length two imperial dignitaries, Princes Idzu and Iwami, arrived. They received Perry ashore amid much pomp and ceremony, whereupon he delivered a letter from President Fillmore desiring trade and diplomatic relations. When the missive was politely accepted, Perry then announced he was leaving and would return in several months.

True to his word, Perry returned in February 1854 at the head of an even bigger squadron, and the *bakufu* signaled its willingness to negotiate. The commodore, polite and diplomatic as ever, took the precaution of showering his hosts with such marvels as a miniature steam train, a telegraph, and a printing press. Those gifts underscored the West's technological superiority and the benefits to be derived by trade. After much negotiation, the Treaty of Kanagawa was signed at Yokohama. The treaty provided for humane treatment of castaways, establishment of an American consul, and the opening of two ports to American goods. Perry then returned to the United States.

Soon after his return, Perry concluded his seafaring career and became a member of the navy's Efficiency Board. He also spent several years writing an extensive memoir on his experiences in Japan. He died in New York City on March 4, 1858, one of the most accomplished naval officers of American history.

*John C. Fredriksen*

**See also:** Tokugawa *Bakufu* Political System.

## Further Reading

Morison, Samuel E. *"Old Bruin": Commodore Matthew C. Perry, 1794–1858.* Boston/Toronto: Little, Brown, 1967.

Pineau, Roger, ed. *The Japan Expedition, 1852–1854: The Personal Journal of*

*Commodore Matthew C. Perry.* Washington, DC: Smithsonian Institution Press, 1968.

## Philippine Sea, Battle of (June 19–21, 1944)

Fought between the Japanese and U.S. navies and the largest aircraft carrier engagement in history, the Battle of the Philippine Sea virtually destroyed what remained of the Japanese naval aviation capability. In June 1944, U.S. forces launched Operation Forager to capture the Mariana Islands for use as bases for Boeing B-29 strategic bombing raids on Japan. On June 15, U.S. Marines invaded Saipan, northernmost of the principal Marianas. The Fifth Fleet was the main strike force. Task Force 58 provided support and protection; its assets included 7 fleet carriers, 8 light carriers, 7 battleships, 8 heavy cruisers, 13 light cruisers, 69 destroyers, and 956 aircraft.

Also on June 15, the Japanese First Mobile Fleet emerged from the Philippines through the San Bernardino Strait and headed northeast in Operation a-gō, which was intended to draw the U.S. fleet into a decisive battle that would reverse the course of the war in the Central Pacific. Assembled over the preceding month, First Mobile Fleet comprised 90 percent of Japan's surface naval strength: 5 fleet carriers, 4 light carriers, 5 battleships, 11 heavy cruisers, 2 light cruisers, 28 destroyers, and 473 aircraft. The Japanese believed their inferior aircraft numbers would be offset by the greater range of their planes and by the presence of 90 to 100 land-based aircraft on the islands of Guam, Yap, and Rota, with which they planned to attack the U.S. carriers to initiate the battle. As their own carriers came into range, their planes would launch a second strike, refuel and rearm on the islands, and then attack the Americans a third time while returning to the Japanese fleet.

The U.S. submarine *Flying Fish* reported the Japanese sortie from the Philippines. Leaving their older battleships and several cruisers and destroyers to protect the Saipan beachhead, the Americans joined Task Force 58 on June 18 to search for the Japanese. Misled by the commander of the Japanese land planes and unaware that most of them had been destroyed by attacks from the American undamaged carriers, the Japanese launched four attack waves on the morning of June 19, only to lose 346 planes in what the victors called the "Great Marianas Turkey Shoot." That same day, the U.S. submarine *Albacore* sank the *Taiho*, Japan's newest and largest carrier and the Japanese flagship; another U.S. submarine, the *Cavalla*, sank the Japanese fleet carrier *Shokaku*.

The Americans still did not know the precise location of the Japanese forces, and they did not move offensively toward the west for fear that the Japanese might flank them and get between the Saipan landing sites. Aerial night searches were deemed impractical because aircrews were exhausted and the moon was new. Although they dispatched extensive search missions through the morning and early afternoon of June 20, not until 4:00 p.m. were Japan's ships finally sighted, at the extreme range of the U.S. aircraft. Despite the realization that planes would return to their carriers in darkness and that many of them would probably exhaust their fuel beforehand, the Americans ordered a massive strike. The U.S. aircraft found the Japanese ships shortly before dark and sank another fleet carrier, the *Hiyo*, and 2 oilers; severely damaged 3 other carriers, a battleship, a heavy cruiser, and a destroyer; and eliminated all but 35 of the remaining Japanese aircraft.

The return flight of the U.S. aircraft became one of the most dramatic episodes of the Pacific war. Only 20 of the 216 aircraft sent out earlier had been lost in action, but 80 were lost in ditchings or crash landings. Ignoring the risk of Japanese submarines, the American carriers turned on all their lights to guide their fliers, and efficient search-and-rescue work recovered all but 49 airmen. The ships pursued the retreating Japanese from midnight until the early evening of June 21, but they were slowed by their destroyers' need to conserve fuel, whereas the Japanese accelerated the withdrawal begun after their losses on June 19.

Although it effectively destroyed Japanese naval air power, the Battle of the Philippine Sea quickly became controversial; the Americans were condemned for not steaming farther westward on the night of June 18–19. They also were criticized for not sending out night searches on June 19–20 that might have found the Japanese sooner and allowed the Americans more daylight for their air attack on the Japanese fleet, perhaps even creating conditions for a surface engagement. Such a scenario, however, might have resulted in much greater losses for the U.S. side with no more strategic benefits than were actually gained.

*John A. Hutcheson, Jr.*

**See also:** World War II, Pacific Theater; World War II, Southwest Pacific Theater.

### Further Reading

Spector, Ronald H. *Eagle against the Sun: The American War with Japan.* New York: Free Press, 1985.

Y'Blood, William T. *Red Sun Setting: The Battle of the Philippine Sea.* Annapolis, MD: Naval Institute Press, 1980.

## Port Arthur Siege (1904–1905)

For Japan, the necessary prerequisite to a land war in Manchuria was control of the seas. Aside from a few warships at Chemulpo (Inchon), Korea, the Russians had at Vladivostok 4 first-class cruisers and 17 torpedo boats. Their most powerful ships—7 battleships and 4 cruisers—were stationed at Port Arthur. Once the Japanese had decided to begin war against Russia, they cut the telegraph cable between Port Arthur and Korea early on February 7, 1904. Thus the Russians did not know of the earlier Japanese attack on Chemulpo, which had occurred without a formal declaration of war.

At 11:50 p.m. local time on February 8, Japanese Combined Fleet commander Admiral Tōgō Heihachirō launched an attack against Port Arthur, sending in his destroyers in a surprise torpedo attack. The Russian squadron had just returned to Port Arthur after a period at sea and was outside the harbor. The Russian battleships *Retvizan* and *Tsarevitch* and the cruiser *Pallada* were all hit and badly damaged. The *Pallada* ran aground near the harbor; both battleships attempted to make it to the dockyards but became grounded in the channel.

Near noon the next day, Tōgō brought up six battleships, five armored cruisers, and four protected cruisers to shell the Russian ships, shore batteries, and town from long range. The Russian ships, now anchored next to the forts, and the shore batteries replied. Only one Russian ship, the cruiser *Novik*, ventured out and fired a torpedo in the direction of the Japanese ships. Most of the Japanese vessels were hit by Russian shells, and Tōgō reluctantly ordered his ships to withdraw after about an hour.

Four Russian ships were damaged in the exchange, but all eventually returned to duty, as did the three ships badly damaged in the torpedo attack. The Japanese had suffered considerable damage to four battleships and a cruiser, among others. They sustained 132 casualties, whereas the Russians sustained

150 casualties. There were no pangs of conscience in Tokyo over the surprise attack, and only on February 10 did Japan formally declare war on Russia.

Frustrated at their inability to destroy the Russian naval forces at Port Arthur in the initial attack and to safeguard the lines of communication to Korea, Japanese leaders adopted attrition tactics at Port Arthur. On March 8, however, Russian Vice Admiral S. Ossipovitch Makarov took command there and initiated a series of sorties to harass the Japanese cruisers while avoiding contact with Tōgō's battleships. Both sides also laid mines, but Makarov was killed and the battleship *Petropav-lovsk* was lost when he ran it over a known Japanese minefield. In all, the Russians lost one battleship and the Japanese lost two battleships to mines off Port Arthur.

The Japanese forces put Port Arthur under siege from the land as well. Lieutenant General Baron Anatoli M. Stoessel commanded the Russian Port Arthur garrison of 40,000 men and more than 500 guns. During May 5–19, 1904, the Japanese Second Army, commanded by General Oku Yasukata, landed at Pitzuwu, 40 miles northeast of Port Arthur. The Japanese soldiers moved south but were halted at the Port Arthur outpost of Nanshan Hill. This key terrain feature guarded the entrance of the Liaodong Gulf and was held by 3,000 Russians.

On May 25, however, the Japanese flanked the Russian left guard by wading through the surf and in heavy fighting forced the garrison to withdraw. Japanese casualties totaled 4,500 of 30,000 men engaged, while the Russians lost 1,500 men. The capture of Nanshan Hill uncovered the port of Dairen, which became a Japanese base. Port Arthur was now cut off from the land side.

Japanese General Nogi Maresuke (who had captured Port Arthur from the Chinese in 1894) now concentrated his Third Army at Dalny. While the Second Army moved north to counter a Russian offensive, the Third Army took over the investment of Port Arthur. Three defensive lines—some of them incomplete—protected Port Arthur from the north. Stoessel, however, had insufficient food stocks for a protracted siege.

The Japanese steadily built their strength to more than 80,000 men and some 474 guns. On June 23, with his damaged ships repaired, Admiral Vilgelm Vitgeft, Makarov's successor, sortied. Tōgō, with only four battleships and a reduced cruiser force, prepared to meet the Russians, but Vitgeft returned to Port Arthur. His second attempt resulted in the August 10 Japanese victory in the Battle of the Yellow Sea in which Vitgeft was killed. Only one Russian cruiser was sunk in the battle; most of the ships made it back to Port Arthur.

The land fighting continued. On August 7–8, the Japanese forces attacked the hills constituting the Russians' outer defenses and were victorious in hard fighting. Three weeks later, during August 19–24, the Japanese struck again. Much of the fighting occurred at night, with Russian searchlights and flares illuminating the attackers and machine guns exacting a frightful toll. The Japanese lost 15,000 men; Russian losses were only 3,000 men.

Nogi now called for heavy siege guns and resorted to systematic siege operations, inching closer to the Russian positions. His third assault of September 15–30 was partially successful but failed to take its chief objective of 203 Meter Hill, the key point in the Russian defenses. In October 1904, the Japanese began shelling Port Arthur with 500-pound projectiles from 19 10.9-inch (28-centimeter) howitzers. From October 30 to November 1, the Japanese mounted their fourth assault, concentrating on 203 Meter

Hill, but were again defeated with heavy losses. A fifth attack on November 26 was also repulsed at a cost of 12,000 Japanese lives.

Finally, after an assault from November 27 to December 5 that claimed 11,000 Japanese soldiers, the attackers at last took 203 Meter Hill. It overlooked the harbor only 4,000 yards away, and its fall sealed the fate of the Russian fleet. The day after taking 203 Meter Hill, the Japanese opened fire on the Russian ships in the harbor. Japanese land assaults continued against the remaining Russian forts as well; the last fell on January 1, 1905. Stoessel surrendered his 10,000 starving men the next day. The Japanese captured considerable stocks of arms and foodstuffs, a shocking testimony to Stoessel's mismanagement. Japanese losses in the siege were 59,000 killed, wounded, or missing, and another 34,000 sick. The Russians suffered 31,000 casualties.

The Russian defeat at Port Arthur and in the battles at Mukden and Tsushima led to the Treaty of Portsmouth, which transferred control of Port Arthur to Japan.

*Spencer C. Tucker*

**See also:** Nogi Maresuke; Oku Yasukata; Sino-Japanese War; Tōgō Heihachirō.

### Further Reading

Walder, David. *The Short Victorious War: The Russo-Japanese Conflict, 1904–5*. New York: Harper and Row, 1973.

Warner, Denis, and Peggy Warner. *The Tide at Sunrise: A History of the Russo-Japanese War, 1904–1905*. New York: Charterhouse, 1974.

## Portsmouth Treaty

The Portsmouth Treaty was signed on September 5, 1905, near Portsmouth, New Hampshire, bringing a formal end to the Russo-Japanese War. The treaty was negotiated under the mediation of U.S. President Theodore Roosevelt, who won the 1906 Nobel Peace Prize for his efforts.

Although Tsar Nicholas of Russia and many of his officers in the military wanted to continue the Russo-Japanese War (1904–1905), the devastating naval defeat at Tsushima in late May 1905 persuaded the tsar of the necessity of bringing the war to a close. Additionally, the Revolution of 1905, which had started in January as a revolt against poor living and working conditions, threatened Russia's control over its military.

For its part, the Japanese side was also desirous of peace in 1905, despite not having suffered any defeats. The war effort was taking an enormous toll on both the army and the national economy. The costly victories at Port Arthur and Mukden led to a shortage of officers and capable fighting men in the army. Back home, the economy was being stretched thin by the loss of working men and the costs of the war. These costs amounted to seven times the total revenue of Japan in 1903, the year before the fighting started. Most of the war was financed through government bonds, with the leftover being covered by increased taxation, which simply exacerbated the hardships faced by the Japanese people.

The Japanese press and public, however, viewed the peace negotiations as premature. Due to strict government censorship, the press and public had no idea of the conditions of their military. Because the Japanese army and navy had not been defeated in any battle, the press and public had high expectations for further campaigns and victories. In peace negotiations, the general consensus was that Japan would win large concessions and an indemnity from Russia.

Before the war had even started, the Japanese government, uneasy with the risk involved in initiating a conflict with Russia, sent former Justice Minister and Roosevelt acquaintance Kaneko Kentarō to the United States to reestablish contact with the president and strengthen U.S.-Japan ties. The Japanese government asked Kaneko to approach Roosevelt in the spring of 1905 to ask his help in mediating a peace agreement.

Roosevelt agreed and confirmed the tsar's interest, and then formally offered his offices for mediation. Japan accepted his offer on June 10, and Russia accepted on June 12. The conference was scheduled for August in Portsmouth, chosen for its comfortable summer weather and privacy. The former Finance Minister Sergei Witte represented Russia, while the Foreign Minister Komura Jutarō headed the Japanese delegation. Witte formerly was one of the most powerful men in the Russian government, but he had been pushed out by the tsar over his moderate stance toward the Japanese. While still angry at his previous treatment, he nonetheless considered it his patriotic duty to answer his tsar's call for service. Russian Ambassador to Japan Roman Rosen, who had been asked to leave Tokyo after the outbreak of hostilities, accompanied him.

On the Japanese side, Komura was tasked with representing Japan because no one else was willing to risk his political future on the venture. Given the bellicosity and high expectations among the public regarding the negotiations, each possible candidate to serve as Japan's plenipotentiary realized that no matter what the outcome, he would be excoriated in the press.

The conference started on August 9, 1905. Komura presented his terms first: (1) Russia would acknowledge Japan's freedom of action in Korea; (2) both countries would withdraw troops from Manchuria; (3) Russia would cede the Liaotung Peninsula and the South Manchurian Railway to Japan; (4) Russia would cede Sakhalin, a long-disputed island north of Hokkaidō, to Japan; and (5) Russia would pay Japan a substantial indemnity payment to cover the costs of the war. The last two conditions were added by Komura, who felt that his initial instructions from Tokyo were too modest.

Ultimately, it was these two additions that proved to be the sticking points in coming to an agreement. From the start of the conference, the tsar's position had been that there would be no indemnity payment, nor would Russian land be surrendered. In the end, the Russians struck a compromise: in exchange for dropping the indemnity demand, Russia would cede the southern half of Sakhalin to Japan, in addition to accepting the first three terms. The treaty was signed on September 5, 1905. Even before the treaty was completed, news of the impending agreement incited antipeace riots in Tokyo.

*Philip Streich*

**See also:** Russo-Japanese War; Russo-Japanese War, Causes.

### Further Reading

Okamoto Shumpei. *The Japanese Oligarchy and the Russo-Japanese War*. New York: Columbia University Press, 1970.

Steinberg, John W., et al., eds. *World War Zero: The Russo-Japanese War*. Boston: Brill, 2007.

Westwood, J. N. *Russia against Japan, 1904–05*. Albany, NY: SUNY Press, 1986.

## Postwar Politics

The arrival of occupation forces at the end of August 1945 initiated the fundamental restructuring of the Japanese political system. While the specifics of that restructuring emerged over several years, the initial goals were disarmament and the introduction of peace and democracy as foundational values of the "new" Japan.

The first postwar Diet was elected in April 1946, with 80 percent of its members being elected to that body for the first time. Yoshida Shigeru became the first postwar prime minister, an office he held almost without interruption until 1954. One of the first tasks the Diet faced was adopting a new constitution. Drafted by occupation forces and selected Japanese political leaders, the Diet-amended Constitution took effect on May 3, 1947. Its signature features were the preservation of the emperor as a symbol of the nation, citizen sovereignty and rights, and the outlawing of war.

The effectiveness of efforts to democratize the economy and promote labor unions was so immediate that the progressive demands of civil society began to outpace the occupation's expectations. Growing militancy in the labor movement, coupled with the onset of the Cold War in Europe, led to a "reverse course" in occupation goals. Making Japan a reliable anti-communist ally of the United States became the new goal. A sweeping "red purge" aimed at industry and the state, the marketization of the economy, and the rehabilitation of former military leaders commenced.

Although it was not a belligerent in the Korean War, Japan reacted by establishing a national police force and a paramilitary, which became the Self-Defense Forces (*Jieitai*) in 1954. The United States and Japan signed a Mutual Security Treaty in 1951, and Japan regained its sovereignty the following year.

The formation of the Japan Socialist Party (JSP, *Nihon Shakaitō*) and Liberal Democratic Party (LDP, *Jiyū-Minshutō*) in 1955 marked the beginning of the so-called 1955 system, which remained the pattern for electoral competition until 1993. During that period, the LDP headed every government and the JSP was the main opposition party in a multiparty system.

LDP governments and the national bureaucracy, which remained intact through the occupation, succeeded in managing economic growth throughout the 1950s. Japan also normalized relations with the Soviet Union and joined the United Nations in 1956.

Throughout the 1950s, civil society groups organized around workers' rights, national education policy, and defense issues. Also, the irradiation of Japanese citizens on a fishing vessel near the Bikini Atoll in 1954 prompted the emergence of an anti-nuclear weapons movement.

As Japan and the United States prepared to renew their security treaty in 1959, many citizens who had gained political experience or come of age during the decade joined in a social movement (*Ampo*) against its renewal. Despite the mobilization of millions of opponents, Prime Minister Kishi Nobuske forced the Treaty of Mutual Cooperation and Security between the United States and Japan through the Diet in 1960 and then promptly resigned. The treaty assured a Cold War partnership between the two countries and a continued U.S. presence in Japan.

After the intense conflict of 1959–1960, the government turned toward managing the economy and raising living standards. Tension continued, however, over Japan's role in filling procurements for the U.S. war in Vietnam and the use of U.S. bases in the conflict. By the end of the decade, a radicalized student movement arose around these and other issues, but it collapsed due to infighting and loss of social support.

In the 1970s, the "Iron Triangle" of the LDP-led government, the bureaucracy, and large corporations was fully in place, but external conditions presented challenges. In particular, the oil- and Nixon-shocks caused economic hardships at home and concerns about Japan's defense posture. Despite these difficulties, the LDP continued to guard its rural electoral base through agricultural protectionism, received support from the business community thanks to infrastructure development, and benefited from malapportionment.

The 1970s also saw the rise of new citizens groups, including those concerned with environmental issues. Such worries began with the mercury poisoning case in Minamata in 1956, but activism increased as the environmental costs of Japan's rapid industrialization became widely apparent.

In the 1980s, confidence in the LDP weakened as a former prime minister and key faction leader Tanaka Kakuei was charged in a bribery scandal involving the Lockheed Corporation. Prime Minster Nakasone Yasuhiro, however, was able to weaken the opposition JSP by undercutting two of its constituent groups: the Japan Teachers' Union (*Nihon Kyōshokuin Kumiai*) and public railway workers.

Once an asset price "bubble" that had been rising for five years collapsed in 1991, a change in leadership seemed inevitable. When dozens of lawmakers defected from the party in 1993, the LDP temporarily lost power. Although it soon regained leadership of the government, it was dogged throughout the decade by persistently low economic growth, an AIDS-tainted blood scandal, and its handling of the 1994 Kobe earthquake (*Hanshin Awaji Daishinsai*).

The end of the Cold War led to the eclipse of the JSP as the main opposition party and its eventual breakup. Former members of the party, joining with LDP defectors and other opposition parties, formed the Democratic Party of Japan (*Minshutō*) in 1998.

In 1999, the LDP joined in a coalition with the New Kōmeitō (Clean Government) Party, and from 2001 to 2006 LDP Prime Minister Koizumi Junichirō headed the government. A charismatic leader, Koizumi pushed through privatization of the Japan Post Office. He also swung Japan closer to the United States after the terrorist attacks of September 11, 2001—sending the SDF to an active combat zone for the first time in its history. He raised the ire of China and South Korea, however, and stoked public debate with his visits to Yasukuni Shrine.

Following Koizumi, three more LDP prime ministers served in quick succession. The Democratic Party of Japan then formed its first government in 2009, after adding control of the House of Representatives to its capture of the House of Councillors in 2007.

The DPJ's first prime minister, Hatoyama Ichirō, resigned within a year of being elected largely due to his inability to clarify the government's position on U.S. base relocations. His successor, Kan Naoto, suffered a steady decline in public opinion ratings and, on March 11, 2011, faced the crisis of managing Japan's worst postwar disasters— a magnitude-9.0 earthquake off the eastern Tohoku coast, the devastating tsunami that followed, and the resultant breach of a nuclear power plant in Fukushima Prefecture.

*Benjamin A. Peters*

**See also:** AMPO: United States–Japan Security Treaty; Bikini Island Atomic Tests; Self-Defense Forces (*Jieitai*), from the Bomb to Iraq; Yasukuni Shrine Controversy; Yoshida Shigeru.

### Further Reading

Ikuo Kabashima and Gill Steel. *Changing Politics in Japan*. Ithaca, NY: Cornell University Press, 2010.

Neary, Ian. *The State and Politics in Japan*. Cambridge: Polity Press, 2002.

Rosenbluth, Frances McCall, and Michael F. Thies. *Japan Transformed: Political Change and Economic Restructuring*. Princeton, NJ: Princeton University Press, 2010.

# Pu-yi (Henry) (1906–1967)

Pu-yi was born in Beijing on February 7, 1906. His father was Zaifeng, the younger brother of the Guangxu emperor. Officially designated the adopted son of both the Guangxu emperor and the Tongzhi emperor, Pu-yi was chosen to serve as the 10th emperor of the Qing dynasty by the Empress Dowager Cixi prior to her death in November 1908. He became the Xuantong emperor and was formally enthroned early in 1909 before his third birthday.

On February 12, 1912, Pu-yi was obliged to abdicate because of arrangements made by his regents (principally his aunt Xiaoting, who was clearly the more capable of the two) and government official Yuan Shikai. Nevertheless, for more than a decade, loyal courtiers continued to visit the Forbidden City, where Pu-yi lived very much as he had before surrendering his imperial claim.

In June 1917, a fanatical Qing loyalist named Zhang Xun led 5,000 of his soldiers to Beijing from Anhui and reinstated Pu-yi as emperor. On July 1, he was enthroned as the Xuantong emperor for the second time. By July 12, the restoration had been squelched, and again Pu-yi was obliged to abdicate.

On November 5, 1924, Pu-yi was evicted from the Forbidden City by a powerful northern general named Feng Yuxiang and put under house arrest at Beifu, the palace of Pu-yi's father. Pu-yi left the palace and took refuge in the Japanese Embassy. The following year, he disguised himself as a student and slipped away to Tianjin, where he remained for the next six years under Japanese protection.

In 1931, Japanese troops took control of Manchuria. The following month, Pu-yi and a Chinese adviser were smuggled into South Manchuria by sea, and in March 1932, the state of Manchukuo ("land of the Manchus") was formally established by the Japanese. In 1934, when Manchukuo became "the Manchu imperial state," Pu-yi became the emperor. It was apparent from the outset, however, that regardless of the form taken by the government of Manchuria, it was a puppet regime fronting Japanese control.

Pu-yi's role in Manchukuo came to an abrupt halt with the Soviet Union's declaration of war on Japan in August 1945. When Japan surrendered, Pu-yi abdicated and was arrested by Soviet soldiers and was flown to the Soviet Union. He was imprisoned there for five years and then handed over to authorities in the People's Republic of China, who imprisoned him for nine more years. Finally, on September 25, 1959, Communist Party leader Mao Zedong granted Pu-yi amnesty, and before the end of the year, he returned to Beijing. In 1963, he was appointed to the National Political Library and Historical Materials Research Committee. He died of cancer at the age of 61 on October 17, 1967.

*Louis G. Perez*

**See also:** Manchukuo.

## Further Reading

Johnston, Reginald F. *Twilight in the Forbidden City.* London: Victor Gollancz Ltd., 1934.

Pu Yi, Henry. *The Last Manchu: The Autobiography of Henry Pu Yi, Last Emperor of China.* New York: Pocket Books, 1987.

# Q

## Qingdao, Siege of (August 23–November 7, 1914)

Between 1897 and 1913, Germans built from scratch a European-style fortress city on the tip of China's Shandong Peninsula. Located halfway between Tianjin and Shanghai, Qingdao commanded the entrance to Kaiochow Bay, the principal German navy base in the Pacific.

Qingdao contained extensive port facilities, including one of the largest dry docks in the world. The city was defended by a ring of small sea forts around the lower end of the peninsula, anchored by a major fort on the bay side and another on the Yellow Sea side. The main forts mounted 210-mm and 240-mm guns in revolving turrets.

Remembering all too well the Russian experience at Port Arthur during the 1904–1905 Russo-Japanese War, the Germans also constructed land defenses to thwart any ground attack from China. Qingdao's main defenses were set into two ranges of low hills that spanned the peninsula above the city. Four miles from the city, the inner defensive line was based on powerful Fort Bismarck in the center, supported by a fort at either end of the line. Fort Bismarck was equipped with 280-mm howitzers and 210-mm guns in reinforced concrete casemates, while the two flank forts had 105-mm and 120-mm guns in open batteries. Interspersed between the forts the Germans placed some 90 guns, ranging in size from 37 mm to 90 mm.

The far weaker outer line was 8 miles above the city, where the peninsula was 12 miles wide. Unfortunately for the Germans, the Qingdao garrison was never large enough for them to man both defensive lines adequately. The key terrain on the outer line, 1,200-foot-high Prinz Heinrich Hill on the southern flank, was never sufficiently fortified. Between the two lines of forts, the German intermediate defensive zone in the flat, marshy Haipo River valley contained five reinforced concrete redoubts, each with a garrison of about 200 troops.

Japan had signed an alliance with Great Britain in 1902, and the leaders in Tokyo saw in World War I an opportunity to eject Germany from east Asia. On August 15, 1914, using the justification of the Anglo-Japanese alliance, Japan issued an ultimatum to the Germans in Qingdao. They were given until August 23 to evacuate and abandon the colony without compensation. The German governor, navy Captain Alfred Meyer-Waldeck, rejected the ultimatum and prepared for a siege as the Germans began to evacuate nonessential civilians. Even before the Japanese ultimatum, on August 4 a German cruiser squadron under the command of Vice Admiral Maximilian von Spee departed Qingdao for the safety of open waters, not wishing to repeat the mistake the Russians had made 10 years earlier in allowing their ships to be bottled up at Port Arthur.

Even after calling in German reservists from all over Asia, Meyer-Waldeck still had only 4,600 troops in Quingdao. His sole remaining naval units were the obsolete Austrian cruiser *Kaiserin Elizabeth*, the torpedo boat *S-90*, and five small gunboats.

Japanese troops shell Qingdao (also known as Tsingtao) from the hill range overlooking the city, as burning oil tanks create clouds of smoke overhead, during World War I. (Reynolds and Taylor, *Collier's Photographic History of the European War*, 1916)

His air force consisted of one observation balloon and one Rumpler Taube monoplane, piloted by navy Lieutenant Günther Plueschow.

Believing themselves obligated to support the Japanese operation, the British sent the old pre-dreadnought *Triumph* and a token land force consisting of the 2nd Battalion, South Wales Borders from Tianjin, and a half battalion of the 36th Sikhs. British ground troops were under the command of Brigadier-General Nathaniel Barnardiston, who was outraged at being the first British commander to serve in the field under a non-European superior commander.

On September 2, the Japanese ground force, commanded by Lieutenant General Kamio Mitsuom, began coming ashore at Longkou Bay some 100 miles north of Qingdao. By the time the Japanese were ready to mount their main attack, they had more than 50,000 troops ashore, with another 10,000 still in reserve offshore. The 24th Heavy Artillery Brigade alone had in excess of 100 guns and howitzers larger than 120 mm. The German defenders were outnumbered at least 13 to 1.

On September 28, the Japanese attacked and captured Prinz Heinrich Hill, and the rest of the outer defensive line fell within hours. Continuing the fight from the intermediate defensive zone, the German artillery put up a stiff and effective resistance. On October 7, however, the sole German observation balloon broke loose of its mooring and drifted to sea. From that point onward, the German artillery was forced to fire blindly.

It took the Japanese most of October to move their heavy artillery forward for the attack on the intermediate defensive zone. In the meantime, most of the fighting took place at sea, with the German coastal batteries exchanging fire with the Japanese fleet, and the small handful of German fighting ships carrying out hit-and-run raids. On October 17, the torpedo boat *S-90* managed to sink the minelayer *Takashio*, with the loss of 250 Japanese sailors.

On October 31, the Japanese heavy artillery began firing on Qingdao itself. Their ground forces simultaneously began attacking the intermediate defensive zone using classic siege techniques. By November 1, Meyer-Waldeck knew that the end was near, and he ordered the systematic destruction of anything in Qingdao that might be useful to the Japanese. By November 5, Japanese artillery fire had neutralized almost all the German minefields and wire entanglements, and the German artillery was almost out of ammunition. Early on November 6, under orders from Meyer-Waldeck, Lieutenant Gunther Plüschow loaded Qingdao's war diaries and other secret papers into his monoplane and headed for neutral Chinese territory. Plüschow eventually made it back to Germany.

The last German position surrendered at 9:30 a.m. on November 7. The operation had cost the Japanese 1,445 killed and 4,200 wounded. The British lost 14 killed and 61 wounded. Despite the massive pounding they had taken from both sea- and land-based heavy artillery, the Germans suffered only 200 killed and 500 wounded.

Qingdao is significant as one of history's last large-scale actions involving coastal artillery. It also was one of the first major battles in which air, land, and sea power all combined to play key and mutually supporting roles. It was the only major World War I land battle in east Asia. Despite their relatively high casualty rate, the Japanese military demonstrated a mastery of joint operations far beyond the capability of most armies of 1914.

*David T. Zabecki*

**See also:** Anglo-Japanese Alliances; Port Arthur Siege; Russo-Japanese War.

## Further Reading

Burdick, Charles B. *The Japanese Siege of Tsingtao*. Hamden, CT: Archon, 1976.

Hoyt, Edwin P. *The Fall of Tsingtao*. London: A. Barker, 1975.

# R

## Red Army (Sekigun)

Most of the Sekigun or "Red Army Faction" members were highly educated students who had joined the Zengakuren student movements of the 1960s. These students participated in the more militant factions of the movement, where they were increasingly radicalized by the failures of the late 1960s. Frustrated by the inability of the movement to reach its goals as well as by declining student political movements, the Red Army Faction was formed.

The Sekigun comprised three separate and frequently overlapping groups. The first group, led by Takaya Shiomi, began as part of one of Zengakuren's more left-wing student organizations in 1968 and later became independent in 1969. The second group began as part of the original Sekigun under Takaya. This group was formed when it joined another left-wing group to become the Rengō Sekigun in 1971 under the leadership of Mori Tsuneo. The final group was formed in Lebanon in 1971 under Okudaira Takeshi and Shigenobu Fusako. It was originally part of the Rengō Sekigun, but later split with that group in 1972. This group is referred to as either the Arab Red Army (*Arabu Sekigun*) or the Japanese Red Army (*Nihon Sekigun*).

The Sekigun originally based themselves on Communist party structures, with their ideology focused on the concept of immediate and violent revolution. The members referred to themselves as "soldiers" and to their operations as "wars." They felt that the protests of the 1960s had been useless and that more militant and immediate action was needed to bring a more radical break with the status quo. They considered themselves revolutionaries, as opposed to terrorists. Their first operations focused on cities in Japan, but later operations were international in scope.

In September and October 1969, Sekigun first tried to get civilians in Tokyo, Osaka, and Kyoto to rise violently—group members described these actions as the Tokyo War, Osaka War, and Kyoto War, respectively. However, due to police intervention and raids, these uprisings were relatively benign. While a few Sekigun members attempted to throw Molotov cocktails at police stations, more than a hundred members were arrested before the conflict could escalate. In November 1969, police raided the group's military training exercise in Daibōsatsu. The remaining members of the Sekigun went underground.

In March 1970, a group of nine Sekigun members hijacked a Japan Airlines (JAL) airplane and flew it to Seoul, where they released the 129 passengers. They then flew on to North Korea, where the North Koreans reeducated them to become propagandists for the North Korean regime. Around the same time, Mori Tsuneo led Sekigun members in Japan to rob banks and incite violent popular uprising. In May 1972, another Sekigun group went to Lebanon to work with the Popular Front for the Liberation of Palestine to engage in further international terrorist operations. Their first action was an attack on Israel's Lod Airport (now Ben

Gurion International) in June 1972, which killed 26 people. In 1973, they hijacked a JAL flight in the Netherlands, later destroying the plane in Libya. In 1974, they attacked a Shell oil refinery to disrupt the oil supply from Singapore to other nations. Also in 1974, Red Army members took hostages at The Hague in an attempt to force the release of a jailed Red Army member. In 1975, they took hostages at the American and Swedish embassies in Malaysia to pressure the Japanese government to release five other Red Army members.

However, there was also internal strife in the group. In February 1972, Rengō Sekigun in Japan conducted a violent purge of its members. A total of 14 members were either beaten to death or tied up outside, where they froze to death. A nonmember was also killed during the purge. The five remaining members, led by Mori Tsuneo, then kidnapped a hostage and had a stand-off with police in an Asama Mountain Villa mountain lodge for 10 days. The hostage situation, called the Asama-Sansō Incident, was broadcast live and peaked at 89.7 percent viewership.

After this point, the Sekigun's terrorist acts were fewer and less influential. Many such acts—such as the crash of a Malaysian Airlines flight in 1977 and the arrest of a pipe bomb-carrying operative on the New Jersey Turnpike in 1988—appear to have been conducted by individual members. In 2000, Arab Red Army's leader, Shigenobu Fusako, was arrested in Osaka. She announced that the group had disbanded in 2001.

*Amanda Weiss*

**See also:** Zengakuren.

**Further Reading**

Farrell, William R. *Blood and Rage: The Story of the Japanese Red Army.* Lexington, KY: Lexington Books, 1990.

Steinhoof, Patricia G. "Hijackers, Bombers, and Bank Robbers: Managerial Style in the Japanese Red Army." *Journal of Asian Studies* 48, no. 4 (1989): 724–740.

Varon, Jeremy. *Bringing the War Home: The Weather Underground, the Red Army Faction, and Revolutionary Violence in the Sixties and Seventies.* Berkeley, CA: University of California Press, 2004.

## Rice Riots (1918)

The largest and last popular movement in Japan took place without any leadership or solid organization. The Rice Riots occurred from July to September 1918 and were a protest against economic hard times during World War I caused by inflation, especially a sharp rise in rice prices. Other factors contributing to the riot were the development of Taishō democracy, the influx of a large number of workers into urban areas that raised the level of rice consumption, the stagnation of rice production, and private hoarding of rice for profit during the Japanese intervention in Siberia.

In July 1918, a group of fishermen's wives in Tōyama devised a plan to halt rice shipments, a protest that quickly spread to other parts of Japan. Approximately 700,000 people—not only farmers and fishermen, but also day laborers, cartmen, roustabouts, factory workers, and the middle class—joined the movement. Because the police could not control the situation, the army dispatched more than 100,000 men to suppress riots in more than 100 locations, and 25,000 people were taken into custody.

The widespread rioting led to the resignation of Prime Minister Terauchi Masataki and his cabinet. Hara Takashi then became prime minister. His was the first cabinet based on a leading political party, the Seiyūkai. The Rice Riots spawned a number of specific protest movements that advocated labor and political reforms, including universal suffrage.

*Sugita Yoneyuki*

**See also:** Hara Takashi; Party Cabinets; Siberian Intervention; World War I.

### Further Reading

Dickinson, Frederick R. *War and National Reinvention: Japan in the Great War, 1914–1919.* Cambridge, MA: Harvard University Press, 1999.

Silberman, Bernard S., and H. D. Harootunian, eds. *Japan in Crisis: Essays on Taishō Democracy.* Ann Arbor, MI: Center for Japanese Studies, University of Michigan, 1999.

## Right-Wing Politics in Japan (1945–Present)

Japan has more than 800 right-wing groups (*uyoku*). They are recognizable in dark trucks playing a cacophony of martial music and militaristic propaganda.

Japan's surrender in 1945 and the demobilization of the Imperial Army led to a dispersal of ultra-nationalist elements by the Supreme Commander of the Allied Powers (SCAP). The revised education system prohibited teachings of militaristic and ultra-nationalistic ideologies. State Shintō was abolished, and the emperor's divinity was publicly renounced followed by a purge of right-wing elements from public office and the dissolution of ultra-nationalist organizations. Starting with the Great Japan Renovation Association (*Dai Nihon Isshin Kai*) in 1946, 233 right-wing organizations were dissolved by 1951. Some right-wing groups responded with violence and suicide. Led by Kageyama Shōhei, 14 members of the Great East Institute (*Daitō Juku*, established 1939) committed ritual suicide (*seppuku*).

Others, such as Tachibana Kōsaburō's Institute for Local Patriotism (*Aikyō Juku*), founded in 1931, dispersed into the countryside and built model agricultural villages.

Postwar right-wing organizations included the New and Powerful Masses Party (*Shinei Taishū Tō*), which was established in 1946 by Maki Kōnen (dissolved in 1947). However, the United States' "reverse course" policy (*gyaku koosu*), lifted the ban on many ultra-nationalists and led to the emergence of a right-wing movement. By 1951, evictions served against 210,000 previously purged militarists and ultranationalists were dropped. *Daitō Juku* was reestablished under the leadership of Kageyama Shōhei's son Masaharu, while Akao Bin's Great Japan Patriot's Party (*Dai Nihon Aikoku Tō*) was founded in 1951. These groups vehemently demanded a revision of the peace constitution and Japan's remilitarization. In 1960 a former member of *Aikoku Tō* assassinated the head of the Socialist Party, Asanuma Inejirō, when Ikeda's cabinet attempted to ease tensions after the fierce AMPO struggle.

In Japan's postwar political regime, the *uyoku* and Japan's mob-related organizations (*bōryoku dantai*) facilitated cozy relationships with the Liberal Democratic Party (LDP) under the leadership of Kishi Nobusuke (1896–1987), who became prime minister in 1957. As one of Japan's most influential postwar leaders, Kishi was the engineer of Japan's "1955 system." As a top bureaucrat in Manchuria and former Minister of Commerce and Industry, he was responsible for Japan's war industry and a close deputy to General Tōjō Hideki. Accused of being a Class A war criminal, Kishi was imprisoned with the controversial right-wing figures and political kingmakers Kodama Yoshio (1911–1984) and Sasakawa Ryōichi (1899–1995) in Tokyo Sugamo Prison until 1948. Kodama later served on the National Council of

Patriotic Societies (*Zen Nihon Aikokusha Dantai*), an umbrella organization of more than 800 right-wing groups—a connection that Kishi used to battle left-wing protests in the 1960 AMPO struggle. Emulating Italian fascists, Sasakawa founded the National Essence Mass Party (*Kokusui Taishū Tō*) in 1931. The organization was renamed as National League of Working People (*Zenkoku Kinrōsha Dōmei*) and dissolved following the purge of Sasakawa in 1946. Employing institutions such as the Kodama Agency (established in Shanghai in 1941), Kodama and Sasakawa accumulated considerable profits during the war through legal and illegal businesses, which they used to expand their political advantages after the war. Sasakawa secured exclusive rights for legal gambling in motorboat races and redistributed massive profits worth billions of yen to his Japan Shipbuilding Foundation, which later became known as the Nippon Foundation.

In response to the fledgling left-wing student movement during the 1960s and the student organization Zengakuren, the extremist right sought a "new nationalism" (*shin minzokushugi*) represented by student organizations such as Japan Student Union (*Nihon Gakusen Domei*) at Waseda University and the National Autonomous Student Council (*Zenkoku Gakusei Jichitai Renraku Kaigi*). These groups provided the basis for the emergence of a right-wing student movement and a "new right" (*shin uyoku*). Demanding the eradication of Zengakuren, the revision of Japan's peace constitution, and the return of the Soviet-occupied Northern Territories, these movements denounced the Japan-U.S. security treaty.

The famous writer Mishima Yukio and *Nichigakudō* member Morita Masakatsu founded the paramilitary Shield Society (*Tatenokai*) in 1967, which attempted a coup d'état. They entered the Japanese Self-Defense Forces' camp in Tokyo's Ichigaya district in 1970, where Mishima famously addressed the soldiers and claimed to restore the powers of the emperor. After these plans failed, Mishima and Morita committed *seppuku*. Right-wing groups such as the First Wednesday Association (*Issui Kai*), known for its construction of a lighthouse on the disputed Senkaku/Diaoyu islands, have since commemorated Mishima's failed attempt.

The recent past has seen a surge in political violence, ultranationalist influence, and a political shift to the right in Japan. Rightwing extremists have repressed public debate on delicate issues such as national identity, the imperial system, and war responsibility by intimidating and assaulting academics, journalists, and politicians. Accused of disrespect toward the emperor, the liberal-left *Asahi Shimbun* has repeatedly been the target of violence. The journalist Tomohiro Kojiro, a member of this group, was killed in 1987. In 2003 and 2006, Fuji Xerox's chief executive, Chairman Yotaro Kobayashi, and LDP politician Katō Kōichi suffered assaults after demanding the end of Prime Minister Koizumi Junichiro's visits to Yasukuni Shrine. The revelation of abductions of Japanese citizens by North Korea during the 1970s and 1980s in 2002 has subjected ethnic Koreans to *uyoku* intimidation. Deputy Foreign Minister Tanaka Hitoshi, leader of negotiations with North Korea, escaped a bomb assault in 2003.

Influential academics who contemplate female succession to the imperial line also fear the right-wing. Denying Japan's war atrocities and demanding a revision of history textbooks, the right-wing has engaged in a fierce struggle with Japan's Teachers Union (*Nikkyōso*). In 1999, the contested *kimigayo* (national anthem) and *hinomaru* (rising-sun flag) were officially recognized due to rightist political pressure. In 2006, Prime Minister Abe Shinzō amended the 1947 Fundamental Law of Education, promoting patriotism and tradition in schools. In the 1980s, LDP Prime Minister Nakasone Yasuhiro had argued for many of these policy changes. Territorial disputes with China, South Korea, and Russia have further revived Japan's right-wing movement. Today, *uyoku* members range from traditional rightists and Yakuza-linked groups to the "Net-Uyoku," who express their views on platforms such as "2-channel."

*Sebastian Maslow*

See also: AMPO: United States–Japan Security Treaty; Nativism, Rise of; Postwar Politics.

## Further Reading

Kaplan, David A., and Alec Dubro. *Yakuza: Japan's Criminal Underworld*. Berkeley: University of California Press. 2003.

Morris, Ivan I. *Nationalism and the Right Wing in Japan: Study of Postwar Trends*. London: Oxford University Press, 1960.

Samuels, Richard J. "Kishi and Corruption: An Anatomy of the 1955 System." *Japan Policy Research Institute Working Papers* 38 (December 2001).

## Rise of the Modern Army (1868–1894)

The modern Japanese army is an excellent lens for viewing a broad set of issues facing the young Meiji government. After the Tokugawa shōgunate collapsed, the oligarchs had to figure out how to fund the continuing development of the army inherited from the semi-autonomous domains and defeated shōgunate, how to deal with the samurai class, and how commoners could find a new role in defining Japan as a modern nation-state. Before 1868, no centralized national army existed in Japan. Reforms that began during the Bakumatsu period, however, carried over into the post-Restoration era.

Tokugawa shōgunal and domain armies consisted of samurai until the 19th century. By the mid-19th century, domains such as and even the shōgunate, formed militias that mixed the putatively unmartial commoners with low-ranking samurai. Much influence over the modern army came from the Chōshū domain, one of the two leading domains that defeated the shōgunate during the Meiji Restoration. Many Chōshū men dominated the government and army, and drew from earlier military innovations in those roles. For example, the Chōshū reformer Takasugi Shinsaku formed the *Kiheitai*, the "extraordinary units"—an allusion to Sun Tsu's *Art of War*. This mixed unit of samurai and commoners supported Chōshū's main army and engaged in guerrilla-style fighting tactics during the Boshin War. It represented the type of reforms implemented in the early Meiji army, outfitted soldiers with weapons purchased from abroad (the British), adopted foreign military tactics (from Dutch translations), and replaced traditional military training (swordsmanship) with bayonet drills. Yamagata Aritomo, Kido Kōin, and Ōmura Masajirō—all Meiji statesmen—were involved with the *Kiheitai*.

These developments occurred concurrently with similar army reform efforts undertaken by the shōgunate, which, like the navy, relied on French assistance. The French established infantry training facilities in Yokohama, sold weapons to the shōgunate, and helped reorganize the shōgunate's army. Moreover, the shōgunate encouraged its liege vassals to recruit able-bodied men from their fiefs to begin infantry drilling in Edo and Yokohama, and to create peasant militias throughout the Kanto plain surrounding Edo.

There was no initial consensus among the early Meiji leaders about how to centralize the army. Some, like Ōkubo Toshimichi, wanted to have an army dominated by the samurai; others, such as Ōmura Masajirō (often regarded as the father of the modern Japanese army), envisioned a national conscript army filled with commoners. Ōmura wanted to break the entrenched interests of the samurai nationally, and removing them from a privileged military position was the logical first step. Moreover, as the shōgunate discovered, samurai with old ideas about how to wage war dragged down military reform efforts. Even so, throughout the 1870s, early military academies in Yokohama and Osaka were dominated by ex-samurai, as were many of the officer and noncommissioned officer positions during the 1870s. The conscript army remained small throughout the 1870s, peaking at about 53,000 active soldiers in 1876, during an era of ex-samurai rebellions that culminated in the Seinan War in 1877.

Although the young Meiji army defeated the rebels, the fighting revealed significant weaknesses in the army's organization. Japan's army was administered according to the French model, which placed civilians in charge of the Army Ministry. After the first rebellion in 1874, the Japanese gradually shifted to a Prussian model, in which operational command was seated directly in the army's general staff. The French influence remained as a model for training and conscription, however. French-style firing ranges were established in Tokyo during the 1870s, and the French helped erect the Tōyama Army School. Even during the 1877 Satsuma Rebellion, the army used French military tactics of small-unit engagements. The initial conscription required all young men to serve three years of active duty and four years in the reserves, with exemptions for first sons, teachers, criminals, and those who could buy an exemption by paying a 270-yen fee. In fact, the conscription system is seen as one of the greatest legacies of military reform in the early Meiji period, as it broke the samurai dominance in the military and pushed forward the development of a truly national military. Nevertheless, due to poor wording in the 1872 decree for national conscription, anti-conscription riots spread throughout the countryside. The government explained that conscription amounted to a "blood tax," as the Westerners had referred to it, because men paid back their countries with their blood. Peasants understood the decree literally—they believed that mysterious figures dressed in white would come to take blood from young men.

After the French lost to the Prussians during the Franco-Prussian war (1870–1871), Japan gradually copied the Prussian army, especially the army's close relationship with the monarch and relative autonomy from civilian bureaucrats. The shift to a Prussian-German style of army expanded beyond bureaucratic considerations to the training and organization of troops. Major Klemens Wilhelm Jakob Meckel, famous for stating that Korea was "a dagger pointed at the heart of Japan," was the most influential of the new advisers. Under his three-year tenure, the Japanese army created a new training manual, abandoning the French one, and adopted Meckel's ideas on training. He emphasized a more holistic approach to training: inculcating fighting spirit in troops, teaching military history, and army communications. All of these measures represented a move away from the technique-centered French approach.

By the time Japan engaged in its first modern wars (the Sino-Japanese and Russo-Japanese Wars), the army was well on its way toward being one of the most modernized in the Asia. Based on reforms begun during the Bakumatsu period, the army reflected the government's modernization efforts more broadly, and was not simply confined to military considerations.

*Michael Wert*

**See also:** Imperial Rescript for Soldiers and Sailors; Ōkubo Toshimichi; Russo-Japanese War; Tokugawa Bakumatsu Military Reforms; World War II, Pacific Theater; Yamagata Aritomo.

### Further Reading

Harries, Meirion, and Susie Harries. *Soldiers of the Sun: The Rise and Fall of the Imperial Japanese Army.* New York: Random House, 1991.

Humphreys, Leonard. *The Way of the Heavenly Sword: the Japanese Army in the 1920s.* Stanford: Stanford University Press, 1995.

## Ritsu-ryō

*Ritsu-ryō* is the Tang and Sui Chinese legal system as applied in Japan until the Meiji Restoration (1868). *Ritsu* refers to the penal code, and *ryō* to the administrative code. Of the various codes produced by the Taika reforms (646–720), none survives—not even the last Yōrō code (completed and promulgated in 757). It has been reconstructed from a ninth-century commentary, the *Ryō no gige*.

The purposes of the reforms were to centralize power in the hands of the emperor, to effect direct extraction of men and materiel, and to delegate this function and its enforcement to a bureaucracy. All the people and all the land now belonged to the emperor. Peasants secured the right to farm the land through the payment of taxes in grain (about 3 percent), textiles (as well as salt and specialty items), corvée duty, and military service.

Taxation was based on the system of the Northern Wei dynasty (836–534/5), called the "equal field system." Every male of six received about 2,200 square meters, females two-thirds of that, and slaves one-third. Land was returned at death; registration and redistribution were carried out every six years. The land of temples, shrines, and private houses and gardens was not taxed. Various tax exemptions were granted for bringing waste land or abandoned fields under cultivation.

Officials responsible for taxation and administration were paid through grants of land. Thus local officials were paid from land assigned within the district and the province; bureaucrats in the capital were paid from estates near the capital. In both cases, positions were monopolized by certain families, so the land tended to be handed down as inherited patrimonies. Other abuses abounded. Corvée labor was expended on the development of the estates of local officials. Military service tended to be extended beyond the legal tour of duty and was spent on the estates of powerful nobles. The peasantry resisted these measures by absconding from service. Approximately one-third of able-bodied males still on the tax rolls were drafted until epidemics devastated the peasant population in the first third or so of the eighth century. The system was officially ended in 792, even though the country was still campaigning against the aborigines of the north.

During this era, the country of Japan was reorganized into provinces, districts, and townships. A network of official highways was established to facilitate the movement of taxes, mail, and officials. District officials were recruited from powerful families in the district. Provincial governors were appointed by the central bureaucracy, whose leaders were appointed by the emperor.

The central bureaucracy was divided into two divisions: the Department of Divinities and the Department of State. The Department of Divinities directed the worship of the *kami* of the realm. The Department of State controlled the eight ministries through a Council of State, composed of a Chancellor, three Ministers (Left, Right, and Center), and other officials and their assistants, for a total of something fewer than 30 officials. The Major Controller of the Left supervised the Ministries of Central Affairs, Civil Services, Ceremonies, and Taxation. The Major Controller of the Right supervised the Ministries of the Military, Justice, Treasury, and Imperial Household. All in all, some 5,000 to 10,000 people were employed by the government in Heian-kyō (Kyoto) alone—ministers, scribes, soldiers, and serving ladies.

No sooner had this system been set up than it began to fail. Foreign trade and embassies brought pestilence to the coast, and the highway system spread the diseases to the capital. Environmental degradation changed the climate, and the population decreased. There were not enough people to serve in the army and still farm the land. The army was privatized: instead of a conscript army, a militia led by mounted officers guarded the northern borders and policed the country. Land was privatized: land ownership was made legal in 743 and private estates were recognized in 749. The officials who had the power to grant tax exemptions used that power to develop portfolios of income from estates and to build up power blocks of clients with whom they shared the income of those estates. As more land was taken off the tax rolls, the income of the imperial treasury decreased, and concomitantly the number of positions in the

bureaucracy declined. Those lower-ranking aristocrats who could not find positions in the bureaucracy became the clients of the great and rich, who provided them with positions in the provinces, where they could create their own bases of wealth. Even the government was privatized, as it was conducted from the household offices of the Fujiwara family and extra offices created by the emperor.

*Sybil Thornton*

See also: Fujiwara Family.

## Further Reading

Batten, Bruce L. "Foreign Threat and Domestic Reform: The Emergence of the Ritsuryō State." *Monumenta Nipponica* 41, no. 2 (July 1, 1986): 199–219.

Miller, Richard J. *Japan's First Bureaucracy: A Study of Eighth-Century Government.* Cornell University East Asia Papers 19. Ithaca, NY: Cornell University Press, 1979.

## Russian Invasion of Manchuria (1945)

At the Yalta Conference in February 1945, Soviet leader Josef Stalin promised that the Soviet Union would enter the war against Japan "two to three months" after the conclusion of fighting in Europe. Against the Japanese, the Soviets amassed 1.5 million men, 28,000 guns and mortars, 5,500 tanks, and 4,370 aircraft; they faced the defending Japanese Kwantung Army, which (although it contained 1.2 million men, including forces in Korea, southern Sakhalin, and the Kuriles) was a shell of its former self. Many of its units had been transferred to Japan for the defense of the home islands. The Kwantung Army commander, General Yamada Otozō, called up 250,000 reservists for new units, pulled back his border forces, and planned a defense of central Manchuria, where the bulk of the population was located.

Japanese military intelligence, however, failed to perceive the extent of the Soviet buildup and believed the terrain in the Transbaikal, where the Soviets planned their main attack, would be impenetrable to armor. Fearing Japan's use of biological agents developed by Unit 731 at Harbin, the Soviets vaccinated their troops against plague and other diseases and issued masks to them. (In 1946, some Japanese involved in biological warfare were, in fact, tried by the Soviets for war crimes at Khabarovsk.)

The Soviets presented their declaration of war to Japanese Ambassador Satō Naotake in Moscow only minutes before they attacked. Soviet plans called for nearly simultaneous night attacks from the three fronts beginning after midnight on August 9, 1945, all to converge on the central plain of Manchuria. Vasilevsky later acknowledged that U.S.-supplied trucks and fuel landed at Vladivostok were vital in the Soviets' ability to launch this campaign as rapidly as they did.

The main attack was delivered by the Transbaikal Front of Marshal Rodion Malinovsky, operating from Mongolia. The Sixth Guards Tank Army, with 1,019 tanks and self-propelled guns, acted, in effect, as a forward detachment. The intent was to bypass Japanese strong points where possible to preempt the defenses of the Japanese Third Area Army. The Soviets raced for the 6,600-feet-high passes of the Greater Khingan Mountains and managed to cover 300 miles in only three days, encountering more problems from the terrain and fuel shortages than from the Japanese. The Japanese forces held onto Haliar until August 18. Changchun and Mukden (today's Shenyang) fell on August 21. Meanwhile,

air-landed troops entered Darien and Port Arthur on August 19, followed by forces sent via rail.

Driving from the Soviet Maritime Provinces, Marshal Kirill Meretskov's First Far Eastern Front had to overrun or bypass seven fortified districts held by the Japanese First Area Army. Attacking in a torrential thunderstorm, the Soviets skirted around most fortified areas, leaving their reduction to follow-on forces. Mutanchiang was held by Japanese forces until August 16. Soviet aircraft dominated the skies, with the few Japanese planes seeking refuge in Korea or Japan.

Although the Japanese Shōwa Emperor had signed the Imperial Rescript of Surrender on August 14 and the Kwantung Army's commander, General Yamada, had accepted it on August 18, the Soviets were determined to regain the territories lost in the 1904–1905 Russo-Japanese War. Thus Soviet forces continued combat operations in Korea until the armistice on September 2, by which time they had reached the 38th parallel, and in the Kuriles until September 5. The Soviets subsequently turned over a huge cache of Japanese weapons to the People's Liberation Army of Mao Zedong, including 3,700 guns, 600 tanks, and 861 aircraft.

During the campaign, the bulk of the Kwantung Army was not committed to battle, but the Soviets estimated 83,737 Japanese were killed, compared with Soviet casualties of more than 12,000 dead and nearly 25,000 wounded. More than 100,000 Japanese in Manchuria died after the ceasefire, and an estimated 594,000 Japanese prisoners were taken back to forced-labor camps in the Soviet Union. The last were not released until 1956, upon the normalization of relations between Japan and the Soviet Union.

*Claude R. Sasso*

See also: Atomic Bombs: Surrender of Japan; Kwantung Army Adventurism; Russo-Japanese War; Shōwa Emperor (Hirohito).

## Further Reading

Glantz, David B. *August Storm: The Soviet 1945 Strategic Offensive in Manchuria.* Leavenworth Paper no. 7. Fort Leavenworth, KS: Combat Studies Institute, U.S. Army Command and General Staff College, 1983.

Nimmo, William F. *Behind a Curtain of Silence: Japanese in Soviet Custody, 1945–1956.* Westport, CT: Greenwood Press, 1988.

Sasso, Claude R. *Soviet Night Operations in World War II.* Leavenworth Paper no. 6. Fort Leavenworth, KS: Combat Studies Institute, U.S. Army Command and General Staff College, 1982.

## Russian Neutrality Pact (1941)

When the Soviet Union and Germany concluded their nonaggression pact on August 23, 1939, the Japanese were caught by surprise. Later, when Japanese Foreign Minister Matsuoka Yōsuke visited Berlin in March 1941, Adolf Hitler ordered that he not be informed about Operation Barbarossa, Germany's plan to invade the Soviet Union.

On the way back to Tokyo, Matsuoka stopped in Moscow, where he concluded the Japanese-Soviet Neutrality Pact on April 13, 1941. This agreement guaranteed territorial inviolability as well as neutrality in case either power became involved in hostilities with a third nation. The agreement had far-reaching consequences, as it provided for Japanese neutrality when Germany invaded the Soviet Union in June 1941. The treaty was to be valid for five years, with an automatic extension for an additional five years unless one side declared otherwise.

Since 1939, Tokyo had sought an agreement with the Soviet Union to remove a threat from that direction as it attempted to conquer China. The Japanese first raised the idea of a nonaggression pact in May 1940, when the fall of France allowed Tokyo to contemplate a move against the European colonies in Southeast Asia, in which Soviet neutrality would be essential.

Negotiations between Japan and the USSR began in August 1940. During the ensuing talks, the Soviets pursued a cautious approach, suggesting a neutrality agreement instead of a nonaggression pact so as not to strain Russia's relationship with the Western powers, whereas the Japanese urged a more binding treaty modeled after the German-Soviet pact of 1939, with the undisguised goal of Japanese expansion southward. The Japanese memorandum resembled the content of the secret protocol of the German-Soviet pact, calling on the Soviet Union to recognize the traditional interests of Japan in Outer Mongolia and Manchuria, and to agree that French Indochina and the Netherlands East Indies lay within the Japanese sphere of influence. In return, Japan agreed to look favorably on a Soviet advance into Afghanistan and Iran.

The Japanese-Soviet Neutrality Pact of April 1941 greatly facilitated Japanese expansion in the southeastern Pacific and its attack on the United States. Josef Stalin's policy toward Japan in the summer and fall of 1941 resembled his attitude toward Germany before June 1941. He ordered his generals in the Soviet Far East to avoid any hostilities with Japan along their common border in Manchuria and Mongolia. Even if Japanese forces should attack, the Soviet Pacific Fleet was to withdraw northward.

Despite this treaty, Japan contemplated attacking the Soviet Union in the fall of 1941. Leaders of the Kwantung Army in Manchuria especially supported such a move, but Tokyo decided in favor of a move southward into the vacuum created by the temporary weakness of the European powers in Southeast Asia. Tokyo reached its decision on the basis of the outcome of earlier fighting with the Soviets, the difficult weather in Siberia, and the region's lack of oil and rubber, the two natural resources Japan needed most critically at that time.

The Neutrality Pact was of immense assistance to the Soviet Union in its war with Germany. Had Germany and Japan cooperated militarily against the Soviet Union, that country would probably have been defeated, and the Axis powers might have won World War II. Thanks to Japan's neutrality, the Soviet Far East provided the Soviet Western Front with 250,000 men between 1941 and 1944. The pact also allowed the Soviet Union to benefit from substantial and vital U.S. Lend-Lease aid. Simultaneously, Japan gained immensely from the pact. During its war with the United States, it received from the Soviet Union 40 million tons of coal, 140 million tons of wood, 50 million tons of iron, 10 million tons of fish, and substantial quantities of gold from Siberia and the Soviet Far East. Soviet trade helped make possible Japan's war with the United States.

The Soviet Union ultimately broke the nonaggression pact with Japan in 1945. At the February 1945 Yalta Conference, Stalin promised his Western allies that his country would enter the war against Japan "two or three months" after the end of the war in Europe, in return for territorial concessions in the Far East. Three months to the day, on August 8, 1945, the Soviet Union declared war on Japan.

*Eva-Maria Stolberg*

**See also:** Kwantung Army Adventurism; Manchukuo; Matsuoka Yōsuke; Russian Invasion of Manchuria.

## Further Reading

Haslam, Jonathan. *The Soviet Union and the Threat from the East, 1933–1941*. London: Macmillan, 1992.

Lensen, George A. *The Strange Neutrality: Soviet-Japanese Relations during the Second World War, 1941–1945*. Tallahassee, FL: Diplomatic Press, 1972.

## Russo-Japanese War (1904–1905)

The Russo-Japanese War began in the late evening of February 8, 1904, when a Japanese fleet under the command of Admiral Tōgō Heihachirō surprised and launched torpedoes at Russian warships anchored just outside the harbor at Port Arthur on the Liaotung Peninsula. The surprise attack was not an overwhelming success for the Japanese—only two battleships and one cruiser were damaged. Unfortunately for the Russians, those battleships were their two most modern.

War was formally declared by the Japanese only after the Port Arthur attack. Even so, the fact that Japan pulled off a surprise attack is a condemnation of Russian preparedness. On February 6, Japan informed the Russian government that it was cutting off diplomatic relations. Moreover, many observers and a few Russian officers had long thought war between the two countries to be inevitable. The Viceroy of the Far East, Admiral Yevgeny Alexeyev, however, had persuaded Tsar Nicholas that the Japanese would not start a war.

On the sea, there followed over the next three months a series of small-scale naval engagements, one of which resulted in the death of the Russian fleet commander, Admiral Stepan Makarov, on April 13, 1904. The Japanese made several attempts to physically block the harbor at Port Arthur with old

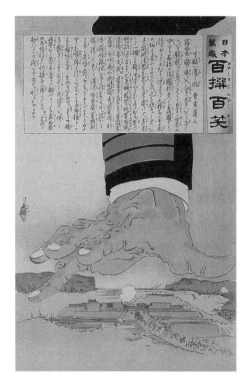

A Japanese poster depicts victory over the Russians. (Library of Congress)

ships. Admiral Tōgō, not able to fully block the harbor, settled for a naval blockade of Port Arthur.

By May 1904, the land war began to take shape. Three divisions of the Japanese army established themselves on the Manchurian side of Yalu River, ready to engage the Russians in the first major land battle of the war. These troops, under the command of General Kuroki Itei, had entered Korea in February and steadily made their way up to the Yalu. On the morning of May 1, these troops engaged and overwhelmed Russian defenses in the Battle of the Yalu. The Japanese army then moved southward and by the end of July 1904, the Japanese commander General Nogi Maresuke had a siege of Port Arthur in place.

At Port Arthur, the Russian fleet faced two unsavory options: they could remain inactive in the harbor and face the approaching Japanese army's artillery, or they could confront Tōgō's fleet and attempt to escape to Vladivostok. Reinforcements from the Russian Baltic fleet would take several months to arrive. On August 10, 1904, the Port Arthur fleet made an escape attempt, but no ships reached Vladivostok. A few damaged ships limped to third-party ports, where they were interned for the remainder of the war, while others returned to Port Arthur. The new Russian fleet commander, Makarov's successor Admiral Wilgelm Witgeft, was killed in action.

In late August 1904, the Battle of Liaoyang was fought north of the Liaotung Peninsula, with the Japanese suffering heavy casualties but nonetheless defeating a larger Russian force. This Russian defeat sealed Port Arthur's fate. In December 1904, the Japanese captured a strategic hill north of Port Arthur overlooking the harbor. From this vantage point, Japanese artillery accurately targeted ships in the harbor with devastating results. Four battleships and two cruisers were sunk over two days. On January 2, 1905, the Russian commander of Port Arthur, Anatoly Stoessel, surrendered. The Japanese suffered a staggering 60,000 casualties to the Russians' 30,000.

With the surrender of Port Arthur, the Japanese army turned its focus on the city of Mukden, home of Russia's Manchurian army. Due to the Japanese navy's domination at sea, the Japanese had been able to deploy troops unhindered. After the inconclusive Battle of Sandepu in late January 1905, the Japanese assaulted the entrenched Russian positions at Mukden starting on February 20. As in their previous land battles, the Japanese suffered heavy casualties, a result of their repeated frontal assaults against machine gun-protected trench defenses. Even so, they were able to compel Russian Commander-

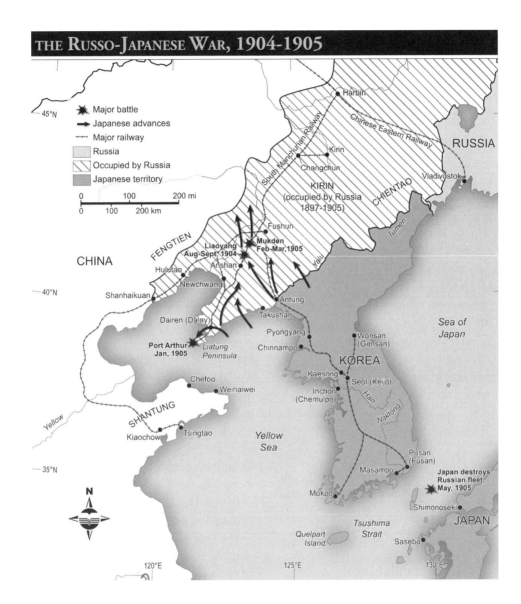

THE RUSSO-JAPANESE WAR, 1904-1905

in-Chief Alexsei Kurotpakin to order a withdrawal from Mukden on March 10.

Meanwhile, the Russian Baltic Fleet under Vice Admiral Zinovy Rozhestvensky was traveling halfway around the world to join the conflict. The magnitude of this undertaking in the age of coal power is astounding. The fleet required approximately 500,000 tons of coal to complete the trip, yet neutral ports were closed to

them by international law. The navy had to acquire a large fleet of colliers to supply at sea, an uneasy task itself. Also problematic was the weight of the ships' stores. One overladen ship grounded on a sandbank upon departure.

The Baltic Fleet set off mid-October 1904 and arrived in the Far East in May 1905. Rozhestvensky hoped to avoid contact and pass through the Tsushima Straits at night on the way to Vladivostok, but he was spotted and engaged by Tōgō's waiting fleet. Tōgō had been aware of the Baltic Fleet's voyage for months and had ample time to prepare for its arrival. The Battle of Tsushima of May 27–28 ended in catastrophe for Russia. The Baltic Fleet was destroyed, including eight battleships and more than 5,000 sailors, and Rozhestvensky was wounded and captured by the Japanese; Japan, for its part, lost a mere three torpedo boats.

While the Russian Baltic Fleet was still en route to the Yellow Sea, the Russians stalled entering peace negotiations. However, after the devastation at Tsushima, they quickly sued for peace. This was a boon for the Japanese, who were running dangerously low on men and munitions after the costly victory at Mukden and were sinking deeply into debt due to the war. Peace negotiations were undertaken with the mediation of U.S. President Theodore Roosevelt at Portsmouth, New Hampshire, in August–September 1905.

*Philip Streich*

**See also:** Nogi Maresuke; Portsmouth Treaty; Russo-Japanese War, Causes; Tōgō Heihachirō.

**Further Reading**

Steinberg, John W., et al., eds. *World War Zero: The Russo-Japanese War.* Boston: Brill, 2007.

Westwood, J. N. *Russia against Japan, 1904–05.* Albany, NY: SUNY Press, 1986.

## Russo-Japanese War, Causes

The causes of the Russo-Japanese War derive from the suspicion each country held of the other's expansionism in late 19th century, particularly after the Sino-Japanese War (1894–1895)

After the Sino-Japanese War, Japan won a favorable settlement from China, including the acquisition of the Liaotung Peninsula in southern Manchuria. This led Russia, which coveted Port Arthur, to intercede on China's behalf along with Germany and France in the "Triple Intervention"—a move that forced Japan to recede the peninsula back to China. The Japanese government acquiesced because it felt the country was too weak to withstand the European powers. Russia thus took by coercion what Japan had gained through war. In 1897, Russia signed a lease for Port Arthur.

Russia was simultaneously making inroads in Korea. The Russian ambassador was friendly with the Korean king, whose wife was murdered by Japanese agents in 1895; the king, in turn, granted concessions to Russia. This made Japan more nervous than Russian gains in Manchuria, so Japan broached the idea of a mutual exchange of spheres of influence with Russia: Japan would not interfere with Russian plans for Manchuria, and Russia would leave Korea to Japan. The Nishi-Rosen Agreement, which included those concepts, was signed in April 1898, but it fell short of the terms desired by Tokyo, as Russia wanted to keep its options open in Korea.

In the Boxer Rebellion in 1900, both Russia and Japan contributed large forces to the international coalition, but Russia quickly moved its forces from Beijing to Manchuria. After the withdrawal of international forces, Russia stayed on, leading other countries to believe that Russia sought a permanent occupation of Manchuria.

This ongoing presence gave momentum to the belief of some Japanese of the inevitability of war with Russia—an idea that first came into being when Russia announced its plans to build the Trans-Siberian Railroad in 1890. This feeling was held more by the younger generation of statesmen (i.e., Katsura Tarō, Komura Jutarō), however, while elder *genrō* statesmen such as Itō Hirobumi and Yamagata Aritomo advised caution. In

1901, Katsura became Prime Minister, replacing Itō in that role, and Komura became his Foreign Minister. To counter Russia's expansion, in 1902 the Katsura Cabinet signed the Anglo-Japanese Alliance. The treaty required that Great Britain aid Japan in the event that a third party came to Russia's assistance in a war with Japan.

In 1903, the Russians ignored a deadline that they had negotiated with China for a Manchurian withdrawal. The Japanese also feared that a Russian timber concession on the Korean side of the mouth of the Yalu River was being militarized with gun emplacements. Moreover, the Trans-Siberian Railroad was approaching completion. With these factors in mind, the Japanese pushed for new negotiations in July 1903.

Their opening position was stronger than the Manchuria-Korea exchange, Japan additionally wanted Russia to respect China's territorial integrity. Russia replied that Russian-Chinese relations were a bilateral Russian-Chinese matter, and furthermore that northern Korea should be kept neutral. Around this time, the Tsar appointed a hardliner, Admiral Yevgeny Alexeyev, as Viceroy of the Far East and commander of all matters military and diplomatic; he promptly sacked his finance minister Sergei Witte, who until then had been a voice of moderation. After receiving a Japanese reply to Russia's first counterproposal, Russian responses grew more intransigent. The Japanese felt that the Russians were delaying simply to buy time for a buildup of forces.

This, indeed, was Alexeyev's plan. He took advantage of the railway's partial completion in the fall to build up forces in Manchuria, even going as far as to occupy Mukden and expel the Chinese military. Meanwhile, naval forces were added at Port Arthur. Alexeyev took the further step of sending troops to the Manchurian-Korean border, though he believed that the Japanese would not start a war.

These moves and an uncompromising Russian counterproposal in December 1903 convinced Katsura, Komura, and the *genrō* that the Russians would never take the negotiations seriously. Sensing that their prospects simply worsened with time, on January 12, 1904, the Japanese government firmly decided for war, but put off the start until naval preparations were completed. Japan cut off relations with Russia on February 6, 1904, and launched a nighttime naval attack on Port Arthur on February 8.

*Philip Streich*

**See also:** Anglo-Japanese Alliance; Boxer Rebellion; Itō Hirobumi; Komura Jutarō; Portsmouth Treaty; Russo-Japanese War; Sino-Japanese War; Triple Intervention; Yamagata Aritomo.

### Further Reading

Malozemoff, Andrew. *Russian Far Eastern Policy, 1881–1904*. Berkeley, CA: University of California Press, 1958.

Nish, Ian. *The Origins of the Russo-Japanese War*. New York: Longman, 1985.

Okamoto Shumpei. *The Japanese Oligarchy and the Russo-Japanese War*. New York: Columbia University Press, 1970.

## Russo-Japanese War, Consequences

The effects of the Russo-Japanese War on Japan were decidedly mixed. On the one hand, the brilliant victory over a Western nation, coming on the heels of Japan's victory in the Sino-Japanese War, gave Japan international prestige as a modern military-industrial giant. On the other hand, it propelled Japan willy-nilly into the maelstrom of world politics. Some would argue that the war forced Japan into an eventual confrontation with the other budding world power, the United States. Some historians suggest that a sidelight to the negotiations to end the war led to the Taft-Katsura Agreement, whereby the United States agreed to accept Japan's predominance in Korea in exchange for an American presence in the Philippines. The treaty certainly convinced Japan of the need to extend the Anglo-Japanese Alliance, which, of course, dragged Japan into World War I.

Domestically, the war created unreasonable expectations on the part of Japan's population. The jingoistic Japanese press had led the people to believe that Japan could expect to win a huge war indemnity and considerable cession of land from the defeated Russians. The people had gorged on a steady stream of glorious Japanese military victories; it was reasonable to expect commensurate diplomatic gains as well. The peace treaty signed at Portsmouth, New Hampshire, gave Japan very little, however: the South Manchurian and Eastern Chinese Railways and the southern half of the bleak island of Sakhalin, but no indemnity to pay Japan's huge war expenses. Huge public riots in Tokyo's Hibiya Park on September 5, 1905, greeted Japan's returning diplomats. Thousands rioted and hundreds were injured (17 fatalities) as the crowd expressed its displeasure over the paltry settlement. Many historians suggest that the treaty and the riots led to the collapse of the Katsura Tarō cabinet on January 7, 1906.

Militarily, the war had a tremendous effect on Japan. Unfortunately, as had occurred the world over in the past, military leaders learn the wrong lessons from the war. The frontal infantry charges into machine guns should have taught the army that such human carnage (perhaps 50,000 deaths and four times

that number of wounded) must be avoided at all costs. Instead, military instructors everywhere taught young officers that such charges broke the will of the enemy and led to stunning victories. Some historians blame those lessons for the horrific trench warfare in World War I, for Japan's losses in the siege of Qingdao in 1915, and for the senseless slaughter in the island-hopping campaigns of the South Pacific in 1942–1945. The brilliant naval victory at Tsushima convinced Japanese naval leaders that a magnificent coup could turn the tide of war. Japan kept waiting for that heaven-sent conclusive victory in the naval battles on the Coral Sea, Midway, and in the Philippines 40 years later.

The economic costs of the war can never be known precisely. Japan had floated huge international loans, in expectations of a Russian indemnity that never came. Some economists argue that the war stimulated considerable domestic industrial growth and that the resulting international trade was also a considerable gain for Japan. Others, however, suggest that Japanese naval costs to protect that trade seriously damaged Japan's economy.

In terms of international relations, Japan's victory against Russia contributed to its plans for Korea and Manchuria, and ultimately led the country into the China Quagmire. One step dragged Japan into the next on the slippery slope toward disaster. At least two generations of Japanese paid heavily for Japan's heady victories in Northeast Asia. Japan had its own Manifest Destiny. Unfortunately, the human cost of the Greater East Asian Co-prosperity Sphere was the death of tens of millions of Japanese and East Asians.

Certainly for Russia, the war contributed significantly to the socioeconomic forces that brought down the tsarist regime in

1917. For the Koreans, it meant that the over-weaning Japanese presence on the peninsula blossomed into a full-fledged occupation. For Manchurians, it meant exchanging one imperialist overlord for another. For China, it meant yet another intruder trampling its citizens. Estimates of Chinese casualties in the Russo-Japanese War are as high as 20,000 deaths. China could expect many, many more deaths when Japan extended its presence in Manchuria to include all of China.

*Louis G. Perez*

**See also:** Greater East Asian Co-prosperity Sphere; Portsmouth Treaty; Sino-Japanese War.

## Further Reading

Nish, Ian Hill. *The Origins of the Russo-Japanese War*. London: Longman, 1985

Okamoto Shumpei. *The Japanese Oligarchy and the Russo-Japanese War*. New York: Columbia University Press, 1970.

Warner, Denis, and Peggy Warner. *The Tide at Sunrise: A History of the Russo-Japanese War 1904–1905*. London: TBS, 1975.

# S

## Saga Rebellion (1874)

In early 1874, Justice Minister Etō Shimpei resigned his position to protest the shabby way that ex-samurai were being treated by the Meiji government. Earlier in the decade, Etō had been an important member of the new government, helping to train the new national police force. Over time, however, he began to express concern about the plight of many ex-samurai, especially those in his home domain Hizen. A series of political and social reforms had stripped the samurai of their special social perquisites. They no longer had hereditary titles, employment, or stipends, and had even been forbidden to wear their distinctive hair styles or the two swords that characterized their social caste.

Etō and others—notably Saigō Takamori—had hoped to staff a punitive expedition to Korea with dispossessed samurai. When the government decided not to send an expedition, Etō and many others resigned from their government posts. Some within the government began to talk of sending a smaller expedition to Taiwan instead, but many others chose to rise in rebellion.

Clearly, Etō misread the situation. He led a force of ex-samurai in a raid against a government bank in Saga expecting other discontented groups to rise in sympathy. No help came. Instead, the newly trained imperial army was dispatched to put down the insurrection. Etō fled first to Satsuma and then to Tosa; in both places, he was denied assistance by his former allies. It is reported that Saigō later felt great regret for turning Etō aside, especially three years later when his own rebellion collapsed because his quixotic friends and allies refused him help as well.

Etō was captured in March, tried, convicted, and sentenced to death April 7, 1874. His friend Kido Takayoshi suggested clemency—perhaps Etō could lead a suicide mission at the head of the planned Taiwan Expedition? The government, especially Ōkubo Toshimichi, wanted to nip other rebellions in the bud, so Etō had to be made a public example. He was beheaded along with 11 other leaders, and their heads were displayed in public the day after conviction. It was the first public split of the forces that had allied to create the new Meiji state.

*Louis G. Perez*

**See also:** Ōkubo Toshimichi; Saigō Takamori; *Seikanron*; Taiwan Expedition.

### Further Reading

Harries, Meirion. *Soldiers of the Sun: The Rise and Fall of the Imperial Japanese Army.* New York: Random House, 1994.

McWilliams, Wayne C. "Etō Shimpei and the Saga Rebellion, Japan, 1874." *Proceedings of the International Symposium on Asian Studies* 2 (1979): 231–249.

## Saigō Takamori (1827–1877)

Saigō Takamori (given name, Takanaga) was born January 23, 1828, in Satsuma han (present-day Kagoshima Prefecture) on the southern island of Kyushu, far from the influence—and supervision—of the central

Tokugawa shōguns' government in Edo. Like many of the early Meiji revolutionaries, he was a low-ranking samurai, and served for 10 years as a minor han official. In 1854, Saigō went to Edo with Shimazu Nariakira, his Satsuma lord. When Ii Naosuke attempted to reestablish *bakufu* control over the pro-emperor han in the Ansei Purge, many *sonno-jōi* leaders' domains were punished or killed. Shimazu Nariakira died suddenly, so Saigō fled back to Satsuma. However, to placate the shōgunate, the Satsuma clan banished him to Amami Ōshima, a distant island in the Ryūkyū Archipelago.

In 1864, the new Satsuma lord Shimizu Hisamitsu rehabilitated Saigō, and sent him to command the Satsuma troops in Kyoto. The troops were ostensibly stationed there to help "guard" the emperor against all enemies, foreign and domestic. Chōshū extremists did, indeed, attack the Kimmon Gate of the Imperial Palace in their frustration to regain political influence in the court, and Saigō's troops (along with those from Aizu and Kuwana han) repelled them. Saigō was chosen to be one of the leaders of the shōgunate's military expedition to punish Chōshū han for the incident, but he secretly negotiated an agreement with Satsuma's Ōkubo Toshimichi and Chōshū's Kido Takayoshi—with Sakamoto Ryōma acting as middleman—which led to the Satsumu-Chōshū Alliance (*Satchō-Dōmei*) in 1866.

Under pressure owing to the growing military strength of the Satsuma and Chōshū domains, and with increasing imperial displeasure and collapsing popular support, the 15th shōgun, Tokugawa Yoshinobu, resigned in November 1867. In January 1868, Saigō's Satsuma and Chōshū forces pounded the shōgunate army south of Kyoto, emerging victorious after three days of heavy fighting. Even Saigō was surprised by the utter defeat of the Tokugawa military, which until this time had

the most numerous and best troops in Japan (including a French-trained infantry). The emperor formally retook power on January 3, during the so-called Meiji Restoration, as loyalist troops seized the Imperial Palace. Saigō, who wanted the Tokugawa further weakened, demanded that they forfeit their lands and money, and was not willing to make many concessions. In response, some Tokugawa vassals, unwilling to surrender, held out in various places in the north until June 1869, when the civil war finally ended.

Saigō became instrumental in the new Meiji government as local han were returned to imperial authority, the samurai class (and their income) abolished, and a conscript army established. In 1871, he served as the de facto head of the government when most other leaders went to the United States and Europe during the Iwakura Mission for 18 months. However, an international crisis developed when Korea would not recognize the legitimacy of the new Meiji emperor. Saigō offered to go to Korea to provoke an excuse for invasion by allowing himself to be assassinated. When the Iwakura Mission returned, its members quickly squelched this intemperate and impetuous plan, causing Saigō to resign and return home to Satsuma in October 1873.

While in Satsuma, Saigō established a number of private military academies for disaffected and idle ex-samurai and their followers. Some of them raided a government armory and naval yard, prompting a response from Tokyo, which eventually drew Saigō into the fray. Feeling compelled to side with the rebels, he reluctantly came out of retirement to lead a ragtag army of some 40,000 men against 300,000 well-trained and -equipped Meiji troops. Saigō died with his last 400 men at the Battle of Shiroyama, outside the city of Kagoshima, in a final hopeless charge on September 24, 1877.

Saigō died in a revolution against the very Meiji government he helped create. Yet, even during the Meiji period he was venerated—a bronze statue of him was erected in Ueno Park in Tokyo in 1898.

*James Stanlaw*

**See also:** Hitotsubashi Keiki; Ii Naosuke; Iwakura Mission; Meiji Emperor; Ōkubo Toshimichi; Sakamoto Ryōma; Seinan (Satsuma) Rebellion.

**Further Reading**

Keene, Donald. *Emperor of Japan: Meiji and His World, 1852–1912.* New York: Columbia University Press, 2002.

Ravina, Mark. *The Last Samurai: The Life and Battles of Saigō Takamori.* Hoboken, NJ: John Wiley & Sons, 2004.

Yates, Charles. *Saigō Takamori: The Man behind the Myth.* London: Routledge, 1995.

## Saigō Tsugumichi (1843–1901)

Saigō Tsugumichi was born on June 1, 1843, in Kagoshima, the capital of the feudal domain of Satsuma province. Saigō was always in the shadow of his older brother SaigōTakamori, probably the most famous hero of the Meiji Restoration.

Saigō fought on the side of the loyalist forces in the civil war against the Tokugawa. After the restoration, he was sent abroad in 1869 by the new government to study military organization in Russia, Germany, and France, along with Yamagata Aritomo. Soon, Saigō and Yamagata had become central figures in the young army of the new central government. In 1872, Saigō was granted the rank of a major general; he was later promoted to lieutenant general in 1874.

The Saigō brothers favored foreign expansion as a means to distract the samurai's attention from internal matters. Takamori favored Japanese expansion to Korea, while Saigō initiated preparations for an expedition to Taiwan to settle an old score. In 1871, inhabitants of the Ryukyu archipelago had been killed by natives of Taiwan. In 1873, China did acknowledge Japan's claim that the Ryukyuans were Japanese citizens but refused to pay an indemnity to Japan for the killings or start the punitive action against the murderers that Japan demanded. Consequently, the Japanese government ordered Saigō Tsugumichi to prepare for a military expedition in Nagasaki in February 1874.

In May 1874, Saigō led an army of 3,500 samurai, mostly from Satsuma, to Formosa and occupied the southern part of the island. Nonetheless, the Satsuma army suffered severe casualities due to tropical diseases such as malaria, rather than battlefield casualities. In October, China recognized Japanese sovereignty over Ryukyu and paid for the Taiwan expedition as well, so that the army could be withdrawn.

Only a few years later, Tsugumichi—as commander of the Imperial Guard troops—had to fight his own brother in the Satsuma Rebellion of 1877–1878. He proclaimed his loyalty to the emperor and refused to join his brother's rebellious forces. From then on, his career focused more on political matters than military ones. Saigō Tsugumichi was State Councilor from 1878 to 1885, Minister for Education in 1878, War Minister from 1878 to 1880, and Minister for Agriculture and Commerce from 1881 to 1884.

In his later years, Saigō also concentrated on gaining influence in the Japanese navy. Yamagata's Chōshū clan had attained complete dominance of the Japanese army, so Saigo's Satsuma clan decided to focus on gaining control of the navy. Saigō himself became admiral of the fleet in 1894 and served as the first Navy Minister for Japan from 1885 to 1890 and again from 1893 to

1898. In 1898, he was promoted to field marshal.

In 1892, together with Shinagawa Yajiro, Saigō co-founded the National Association, a pro-government group in the Lower House of the national legislature. For a short time, he was a member of the Privy Council as well. He also received noble titles for his services, becoming a viscount in 1884 and a marquis in 1895—the second highest rank of the Japanese aristocracy in Meiji Japan.

Saigō died on July 15, 1902, in Tokyo. In his last years, he was regarded as an elder statesman of Japan, but his influence never reached that of his powerful contemporaries Yamagata and Itō Hirobumi.

*Sven Saaler*

**See also:** Itō Hirobumi; Saigō Takamori; Seinan (Satsuma) Rebellion; Taiwan Expedition; Yamagata Aritomo.

### Further Reading

Hackett, Roger F. *Yamagata Aritomo in the Rise of Modern Japan, 1838–1922.* Cambridge, MA: Harvard University Press, 1971.

Iwao, Seiichi, ed. *Biographical Dictionary of Japanese History*, translated by Burton Watson. Tokyo: International Society for Educational Information, 1978.

## Saionji Kinmochi (1849–1940)

Saionji Kinmochi was born in Kyoto on December 7, 1849, the second son of Tokudaiji Kinito, a court noble. In 1852, he was adopted into the higher-ranking Saionji family. His elder brother, Tokudaiji Sanetsune, followed in the tradition of his father and became the Grand Chamberlain to Emperor Meiji. His younger brother, Tokudaiji Tomozumi, was adopted into the great merchant house of Sumitomo and became a prominent industrialist and business leader.

In 1867, at the age of 18, Saionji was appointed a junior councilor, and in 1868, he served as an imperial representative in battles against pro-Tokugawa factions in northern Japan. He was rewarded with an appointment as governor of Niigata Prefecture, but after serving in this post only a short time, he resigned in 1871 so that he could travel abroad to study.

Saionji traveled to France in 1871 and entered the Sorbonne, where he studied French language and law. He graduated in 1874 but remained in France until 1880. During this time, he studied under French legal scholar Emile Accollas, became an acquaintance of Georges Clemenceau, and met one of the most prominent intellectual

Saionji Kimmochi was a political leader in Japan whose career spanned the Meiji, Taishō, and Shōwa periods. Saionji had a moderating influence on Japanese politics as an elder statesman. (Library of Congress)

leaders of Japan during the Meiji Restoration, Nakae Chomin. After Saionji returned to Japan in 1880, he established a law school, the Meiji School of Law, the precursor of Meiji University. Also in that year, together with associates Nakae Chomin and Matsuda Masahisa, he founded the *Toyo Jiyu Shimbun* ("East Asian Free Press") newspaper. As president of the newspaper, Saionji strongly advocated popular rights and political freedoms.

In 1882, Saionji accompanied Itō Hirobumi to Europe to study constitutional systems. Upon his return to Japan in the following year, Saionji became a member of the House of Councilors. He was appointed envoy to Austria in 1885 and envoy to Germany in 1887. He served as Minister of Education in the second and third cabinets of Itō, vice president of the Upper House of the Diet, and adviser to the Privy Council. In 1900, Saionji served as acting prime minister, and he became president of the Privy Council. Also in that year, he became a founding member of the Rikken Seiyūkai (Friends of Constitutional Government Party) with Itō. He succeeded Itō as president of the party in 1903.

Saionji served as prime minister from 1906 to 1908, during which time he nationalized the railways. He became prime minister again in 1911, but his entire cabinet was forced to resign the following year after refusing to create two new divisions for the army. Upon his resignation, the newly enthroned Taishō Emperor elevated Saionji to the honorary status of *genrō*, or elder statesman. He became president of the Seiyūkai Party in 1913 but resigned the following year due to his inability to constrain the party's more vocal constitutional advocates. Saionji represented Japan at the Treaty of Versailles conference in 1919.

Saionji served as the chief political adviser to the Shōwa Emperor. As the last remaining *genrō*, from 1924, Saionji held considerable influence in determining who was to become prime minister. After the May 15, 1932, incident in which navy officers assassinated the prime minister, however, party cabinets were no longer formed, and the military began to dominate the government. Unable to constrain the increasing power of the military factions in government, Saionji resigned his position as elder statesman in 1937. He received a state funeral after his death on November 24, 1940.

*Walter E. Grunden*

**See also:** Itō Hirobumi; Iwakura Tomomi; Meiji Emperor; Shōwa Emperor (Hirohito); Taishō Emperor; Versailles Treaty.

### Further Reading

Connors, Lesley. *The Emperor's Adviser: Saionji Kinmochi and Pre-War Japanese Politics.* London: Croom Helm, 1987.

Harada Kumao. *Fragile Victory: Prince Saionji and the 1930 London Treaty Issue, from the Memoirs of Baron Harada Kumao.* Detroit: Wayne State University Press, 1968.

Oka, Yoshitake. *Five Political Leaders of Modern Japan: Itō Hirobumi, Ōkuma Shigenobu, Hara Takashi, Inukai Tsuyoshi, and Saionji Kimmochi*, translated by Andrew Fraser and Patricia Murray. Tokyo: University of Tokyo Press, 1986.

## Sakamoto Ryōma (1836–1867)

Sakamoto Ryōma—who also used the name Saidani Umetarō—was born into a country samurai family (*gōshi*) in 1835 in Tosa han (present day Kōchi Prefecture) in Shikoku Island, one of the backwater domains of the 19th-century Tokugawa shōgunate. He was the youngest of five children. The Sakamoto family bought their samurai title, having made their money running a sake brewery and pawn shop. Always rebellious and independent, Sakamoto left Tosa to study fencing in Edo; he was residing there when Commodore Matthew Perry's Black Ships came in 1853. After returning home, Sakamoto came under the influence of Takechi Zuisan, the anti-Tokugawa leader of the Tosa han and a *sonno-jōi* ("Revere the Emperor—Expel the Barbarians") loyalist.

Sakamoto became an activist and one of the self-styled "men of high purpose" (*shishi*). *Shishi* claimed that duty to a higher political calling was more important than traditional family responsibilities. Indeed, many of the *shishi* were only of modest rank, and many abandoned their obligations to their han domains to become a voluntary masterless samurai (*dappan rōshi*). They also believed in the divinity of the emperor, whom they insisted ruled the sacred and inviolable land of Japan as father-priest. The shōgunate was acceptable as long as the impure foreigners could be held at bay. When it became clear that this goal could not be met, the *shishi*'s actions became increasingly drastic.

Leaving Tosa again—this time illegally—Sakamoto went to Edo to become involved in national politics, taking up the itinerant life of a *dappan rōshi*. Believing that actions spoke louder than words, he soon became involved in a plot to assassinate Katsu Kaishū, the man designated to modernize the Tokugawa navy. When they met, Katsu convinced Sakamoto that modernizing Japan was the only way to counter the increasing Western threat. Sakamoto then became a staunch supporter of Katsu and recruited other followers to their cause. When Katsu lost favor with the shōgunate as the Tokugawa took an increasing hard line against dissidents in 1864, Sakamoto barely avoided assassination himself and fled to Satsuma han—which was becoming a center of anti-Tokugawa fervency—with the hotel maid who saved his life and who became his wife, Narasaki Ryō.

While in Satsuma, Sakamoto started a small private navy and cargo company carrying contraband to other rebellious domains, like Chōshū. In 1866, he negotiated an alliance between Satsuma and Chōshū—traditional rivals, and military powerhouses—in an effort to establish a united front against the Tokugawa government. He next persuaded his ancestral Tosa han to join them, and these domains, along with reformers in other places in the country, eventually reestablished imperial authority with surprising little violence. However, Sakamoto's plan was not simply to transfer power from the shōgun to the emperor. Instead, he pushed for a bicameral legislative body, valuing gold and silver on the international market, and allowing men of ability from *all* classes to be able to take part in government.

Sakamoto was assassinated on his birthday in 1867 at the age of 32, just two months before his longed-for Meiji Restoration took place. No one knows who actually killed him, even though Kondo Isami—the head of the *Shinsengumi*, one of the shōgunate's death squads—was executed for the crime when the *shishi* and reformers later took power. Thus began Sakamoto's elevation to status as a national hero.

Sakamoto continues to fascinate Japanese people of all political persuasions even today. NHK—Japan's public broadcasting network—aired a year-long historical television drama in 2010 based on his life ("*Ryō-maden*") starring popular singing star Masaharu Fukuyama. To celebrate the 60th anniversary of the Local Autonomy Law and the 175th anniversary of Sakamoto's birth, the Japanese mint released a limited edition ¥1,000 coin with his image. Daihatsu

Motors and Sapporo Beer also co-opted his image in their advertising campaigns. In a 2010 survey conducted by the Lifenet Insurance Company, more than 14 percent of respondents said that Sakamoto was "Japan's version of Barack Obama" because of his innovative leadership qualities, which changed the country.

*James Stanlaw*

**See also:** Katsu Kaishū Meiji Emperor; *Sonno-jōi.*

### Further Reading

Hillsborough, Romulus. *Ryōma: Life of a Renaissance Samurai.* San Francisco: Ridgeback Press, 1999.

Jansen, Marius. *The Making of Modern Japan.* Cambridge, MA: Harvard University Press, 2000.

Jansen, Marius. *Sakamoto Ryōma and the Meiji Restoration.* New York: Columbia University Press, 1995.

## Sakoku (1633–1854)

*Sakoku* literally means "closed country," referring to the foreign policy of the Tokugawa *bakufu.* The word *sakoku* was coined by Shizuki Tadao (1760–1806) in translating an essay appended to Englebert Kaempfer's *History of Japan* (1727). This essay, "Should Japan Remain Shut Up ... ," suggested that while free trade was generally better, for Japan it might be better to remain closed.

Before 1635, Japanese sailors roamed the seas of East and Southeast Asia. Large Japanese settlements existed in places such as Java and Thailand. Two significant changes in the 16th century served to catalyze the transformation of Japan into a closed country. One was the arrival of the first Europeans in 1543—three Portuguese mercenaries blown ashore on Tanegashima. The arquebuses they carried were copied within the decade and became a contributing factor to the second change—an extended period of civil war that was ended through armed conquest in 1591.

The Jesuit Francis Xavier came to Japan in 1549 to establish missions that, according to some estimates, made as many as 750,000 Japanese converts. Initially, there was no objection to Christianity. As Japan was forcibly unified first under Oda Nobunaga and then under Toyotomi Hideyoshi, however, Christianity served to highlight frictions between East and West that ultimately led to the policy of *sakoku.*

The first antiforeign laws were directed at priests. Toyotomi Hideyoshi passed the first anti-Christian legislation in 1587 for reasons that are still debated by scholars. This initial edict was not enforced, but in 1597 persecution began. That year the cargo of the silver-laden *San Filipe*, a Spanish ship that sank off the coast of Shikoku, was seized by the Japanese. According to tradition, the enraged captain told Hideyoshi that missionaries were just a vanguard for conquistadors. Hideyoshi responded by crucifying 26 Christians.

Hideyoshi died the following year, and Tokugawa Ieyasu, who seized power in 1600, did not officially initiate any anti-Christian activity. He passed the title of shōgun to his son Hidetada in 1605, but anti-Christian laws were issued in 1606, while Ieyasu was still actively involved in governmental affairs. In 1610, missions were banned. Christianity was again outlawed in 1622, leading to more executions and persecution. At that point, Christianity went underground but did not disappear. The Spanish, who had started trading with Japan in 1592, were expelled in 1624. The English had been unable to make their Japanese factory profitable and left of their own accord in 1623.

The third Tokugawa shōgun, Iemitsu, took office in 1623 and the *sakoku* edicts were issued under him. These edicts, issued from 1633 through 1641, broadly forbid Japanese citizens from going abroad, forbid any Japanese who were abroad from returning, and forbid Christianity. In 1636, Portuguese traders were required to move onto a small fan-shaped artificial island in Nagasaki harbor called Deshima. Only three years later, the Shimabara Rebellion led to their banishment. For a time, Dutch traders continued in Hirado, but in 1641 they were required to move to Deshima. This state of isolation and restricted trade is referred to as *sakoku*.

Although only one word, *sakoku*, is used to define this period, the way in which the "closed country" policy was enforced changed over time. For example, in 1806 policy stated that foreign ships in distress would be supplied with provisions before being sent on their way. Frictions led to a firmer stance in 1825; the *uchihari rei*, often translated as "no second thought," ordered that foreign ships be fired upon at sight.

Nevertheless, Japan was far from closed. Relations with Korea, which were damaged by attacks in 1592 and 1597, were reestablished in the early 17th century, resulting in infrequent embassies and limited trade through Tsushima. After the Qing dynasty took power in 1644, trade between China and Japan, which had been minimal due to a ban by the Ming government, increased dramatically. Chinese traders were required to stay in a walled compound in Nagasaki. There were also occasional exchanges with Siam and other Southeast Asian countries. Contact with Westerners was limited, but materials, objects, and even animals came to Japan from all over the world. Knowledge of geography, botany, medicine, and other sciences spread both through books and through contact with Westerners. Many modern scholars have demonstrated how porous the restrictions in Japan really were. Lacking a better word, many denote *sakoku* in quotes to convey the idea that Japan was closed in only certain ways.

Attempts were made to reopen trade with Japan throughout the *sakoku* period but only after Western activity in the Pacific increased dramatically in the mid-19th century did it become an important issue. In 1854, Commodore Matthew Perry negotiated the Treaty of Kanagawa using gunboat diplomacy, thereby "opening" Japan.

*Martha Chaiklin*

**See also:** Christian Era, Suppression; Dutch on Deshima; Oda Nobunaga; Tokugawa Ieyasu; Toyotomi Hideyoshi.

**Further Reading**

Chaiklin, Martha. *Cultural Commerce and Dutch Commercial Culture: The Influence of European Material Culture on Japan, 1700–1850*. Leiden: CNWS, 2003.

Chaiklin, Martha. "Exotic Bird Collecting in Early Modern Japan," in *JAPANimals*, edited by Greg Pflugfelder and Brett Walker. Ann Arbor: Center for Japanese Studies, University of Michigan Press, 2005.

Hellyer, Robert I. *Defining Engagement: Japan and Global Contexts, 1640–1868*. Cambridge, MA: Harvard University Asia Center, 2010.

Toby, Ronald P. *State and Diplomacy in Early Modern Japan: Asia in the Development of the Tokugawa Bakufu*. Stanford: Stanford University Press, 1991.

## Sakuradamon Incident (1860)

On March 24, 1860, 16 rōnin samurai from Mito han (along with one from Satsuma han) fell upon the Tokugawa *bakufu*

Tairō (Great Elder) Ii Naosuke as his palanquin was approaching the Sakuradamon (gate) of Edo Castle. Ii was fatally wounded, and his assassins then committed suicide. The assassins had come with a prepared written statement that read in part: "we have consecrated ourselves to be the instruments of Heaven to punish this wicked man, and we have taken on ourselves the duty of ending a serious evil, by killing this atrocious autocrat."

Ii had infuriated members of the *sonno-jōi* ("Revere the Emperor—Expel the Barbarians") faction by signing the Treaty of Amity and Commerce with the U.S. envoy Townsend Harris in 1858. Many self-designated patriots had warned Ii against allowing foreigners to enter Japan after Commodore Matthew Perry's visit to Japan a few years earlier. Ii ignored their threats and instead signed treaties with the Netherlands, Russia, Great Britain, and France. Ii also thwarted the attempt by the *daimyō* of Mito, Tokugawa Nariaki, to have his son Yoshinobu named heir to the ailing shōgun Iesada. Nariaki and his son were placed under house arrest, and a number of their supporters were been imprisoned. Ii executed a few opponents, notably the political firebrand Yoshida Shōin, for the temerity of criticizing his actions in what has been called the Ansei (after the era of that name) Purge.

Earlier, Ii had learned of several assassination plots being planned. In response, he reputedly said, "My own safety is nothing when I see the danger threatening the future of the country."

The *bakufu* responded to the assassination by initially refusing to even acknowledge that it had happened. It was announced that Ii had retired due to "ill health." Later in the year, the government softened Ii's harsh policies somewhat. The *bakufu* announced that it had agreed to Nariaki's suggested alliance of the Imperial House and the *bakufu* (*Kōbu Gattai*), forged by marrying the shōgun Iemochi to Imperial Princess Kazu-no-Miya. The compromise did not prove very effective, as the young Iemochi died a few years later and Yoshinobu became the final shōgun after all.

The political violence continued almost unabated as various factions within the movement slashed away at each other. Indeed, Ii's assassination opened the floodgates to an era of political violence that persisted for 70 years. More than a dozen assassinations occurred within the next decade alone. The victims included not only government leaders, but also foreigners (Henry Heusken, Townsend Harris's Dutch interpreter, in 1861; the young Englishman Charles Richardson in 1862; and assaults on the Russian Tsarevich in 1891 and Li Hung-chang in 1895) and the assassins themselves (Sakamoto Ryōma had planned to kill Katsu Kaishū, but was himself cut down in 1867).

The political renegades who styled themselves *rōnin* (literally "wave men"; "masterless samurai") and *shishi* ("men of spirit") were given license by an early Meiji commutation of their crimes led by Yamagata Aritomo. Decades later, the Young Officers who cut down a score of politicians and *Zaibatsu* leaders claimed to be spiritual descendents of the *sonno-jōi* assassins. Their heinous actions were condoned because of their alleged "purity of spirit" and "selfless patriotism." One historian has characterized the madness as "government by assassination."

Ironically, foreign patriots learned the same lessons and employed assassinations as well. In 1909, An Jung-geun, a Korean nationalist killed Itō Hirobumi. In 1932, a Korean patriot, Lee Bong-chang, tried to kill the Shōwa Emperor outside the same Sakuradamon gate by tossing a grenade under his carriage. Japan had sowed the wind and reaped the whirlwind.

*Louis G. Perez*

**See also:** Harris, Townsend; Heusken, Henry; Hitotsubashi Keiki; Ii Naosuke; Itō Hirobumi; Katsu Kaishū; Otsu Incident; Perry, Matthew; Sakamoto Ryōma; Shōwa Emperor (Hirohito); *Sonno-jōi*; Tokugawa Nariaki; Yamagata Aritomo; Yoshida Shōin.

## Further Reading

Beasley, W. G. "The Edo Experience and Japanese Nationalism." *Modern Asian Studies* 18, no. 4 (1984): 609–618.

Lamberti, Matthew. "Tokugawa Nariaki and The Japanese Imperial Institution: 1853–1858." *Harvard Journal of Asiatic Studies* 32 (1972): 97–123.

## San Francisco Peace Treaty (1951)

On March 17, 1947, General Douglas MacArthur publicly proposed an early peace treaty with Japan. However, differing attitudes among the European powers, the United States, the Soviet Union, and China over how best to approach such a treaty ultimately led to the postponement of any international conference on the subject.

Meanwhile, growing tensions between the Soviet Union and the United States enhanced Japan's political and strategic importance, leading the Americans to embark on a mission to reconstruct Japan both economically and politically. In light of growing tensions with the Soviet Union, together with the October 1949 communist victory in the Chinese civil war, U.S. policymakers, particularly those in the Pentagon, argued for the need to maintain U.S. military bases in Japan. Consequently, the United States became increasingly inclined to end its occupation of Japan.

The Americans made substantial moves toward securing a peace settlement after John Foster Dulles was appointed consultant to the State Department in April 1950. Dulles, with nonpartisan domestic support, initiated negotiations with other Allied countries beginning in September 1950. Meanwhile, the outbreak of the Korean War in June 1950 added urgency to these peace negotiations.

The terms for the peace treaty drafted by the United States in late 1950 were seen as lenient and were consequently opposed by the Soviet Union, Australia, New Zealand, and the Philippines. While no compromise could be reached with the Soviet Union, U.S. policymakers persuaded the other states to accept the treaty's nonpunitive principles. The final draft of the treaty was jointly prepared by the United States and Great Britain.

The peace conference opened on September 4, 1951 in San Francisco and was attended by 52 nations. The treaty itself was signed by representatives of 49 nations, including Japan, on September 8. Although their representatives were in attendance, the Soviet Union, Poland, and Czechoslovakia refused to sign the treaty.

The treaty stipulated Japan's abandonment of all territories acquired since 1895, including Korea, Taiwan, the Kurile Islands, and southern Sakhalin and its adjacent islands. American provisional control of the Ryukyu and Bonin islands was permitted, with an agreement to obtain ultimate authorization of the U.S. administration under a United Nations trusteeship. The document also established Japan's liability for payment of war reparations and drew attention to Japan's fragile economic situation. Later that same day, the United States and Japan also signed a security treaty (AMPO).

*Kuniyoshi Tomoki*

**See also:** AMPO: United States–Japan Security Treaty; Korean War; MacArthur, Douglas.

**Further Reading**

Dunn, Frederick S. *Peace-Making and the Settlement with Japan*. Princeton, NJ: Princeton University Press, 1963.

Yoshitsu, Michael M. *Japan and the San Francisco Peace Settlement*. New York: Columbia University Press, 1983.

## *Sankin kōtai* (Alternate Attendance)

The *sankin kōtai* was a political system established by the Tokugawa *bakufu* for exercising control over the 260-odd *daimyō* whose domains (han) were scattered in different provinces of Japan. This system grew out of previous practices in which feudal vassals were called upon to render services to their overlords, which were gradually formalized and made compulsory during the reign of the third Tokugawa shōgun, Iemitsu (1625–1651).

The *sankin kōtai* requirements were officially specified by the Laws of Military Households (*Buke Shohatto*) promulgated in 1635. Every summer during the course of the fourth lunar month, a group of *daimyō* would travel from their own domains to the shōgunal capital of Edo; simultaneously, their counterparts rotated (*kōtai*) back to their domains. During their stay in Edo, the *daimyō* attended (*sankin*) and rendered services to the Tokugawa shōgun.

In 1642, schedules and routes were further regularized for various groups of *daimyō* based on the locations of their domains and their other duties. For example, *fudai daimyō* (or hereditary vassals) whose domains were located in the nearby Kanto region were required to come to Edo more frequently. They attended the shōgun between the second and eighth lunar months of every year. *Daimyō* from distant provinces were allowed to fulfill their *sankin* duties every three years or even every six years. *Daimyō* who were responsible for coastal defense in Nagasaki in western Japan traveled to Edo in the 11th lunar month of the year and returned to their own domains in the second lunar month of the following year. Such arrangements were largely maintained through the better part of the Tokugawa era until 1862.

The *sankin kōtai* system was designed to achieve two main goals. First, by forcing *daimyō* to pay regular visits to Edo, the shōgun sought to exert political influence on these otherwise highly autonomous feudal lords. Throughout the Tokugawa era, power was shared between the *bakufu* and the han, leading to the so-called bakuhan system. Because the 260-odd *daimyō* had control over fourth-fifths of all the land in Japan, and many were not direct vassals or relatives of the Tokugawa family, the shōgun had to take extra precautions to prevent *daimyō* from rebelling against the *bakufu*. This was partly achieved by keeping all of the *daimyō*'s wives and children as semi-hostages in Edo and requiring all *daimyō* to reside in Edo for a period of time, usually one year for every other year, so that the *bakufu* could keep an eye on their activities. Moreover, the *daimyō* were required to demonstrate their loyalty and allegiance to the shōgun by participating in court ceremonies (such as exchanging customary gifts) and performing public duties such as building roads, repairing the shōgun's castle, and contributing men to guard the gates of shōgunal palaces.

Second, the system was meant to weaken the financial strength of potentially hostile *daimyō*. In addition to managing his own castle, a *daimyō* fulfilling *sankin kōtai* duties had to keep at least three more residential estates in Edo for his family and retainers. He also had to pay for the travel expenses of a retinue of several hundred retainers who accompanied him on regular journeys between his own domain and Edo, which was called a *daimyō* procession (*daimyō gyōretsu*).

The *sankin kōtai* system had major impacts for Japanese society in early modern times. Politically, it was a way for the *bakufu* to centralize its power and maintain political order in a largely feudal society. The system began as a device for maintaining and renewing political and personal ties between successive generations of Tokugawa shōguns and *daimyō*. Over time, it came to symbolize the political legitimacy and social prestige of both parties. Economically, the system represented a heavy financial drain on *daimyō*, but it contributed to the thriving commercial activities in the capital and the towns along the routes of *daimyō* processions. It indirectly benefited the rise of capitalism in Japan in early modern times. Socially, the system led to the gradual decline of the social influence of the samurai class, as many *daimyō* became indebted to moneylenders when they had to borrow money to pay for their *sankin*-related expenditures. As a result, the merchant class became socially and culturally more influential by the end of the 17th century.

*Yu Chang*

**See also:** Buke Shohatto; Tokugawa *Bakufu* Political System.

## Further Reading

Tsukahira, Toshio G. *Feudal Control in Tokugawa Japan: The Sankin Kōtai System.* Cambridge, MA: Harvard University Press, 1966.

Vaporis, Constantine Nomikos. *Tour of Duty: Samurai, Military Service in Edo and the Culture of Early Modern Japan.* Honolulu: University of Hawai'i Press, 2008.

# Sasakawa Ryōichi (1899–1995)

A wealthy rice market speculator, by the 1930s Sasakawa Ryōichi was deeply involved in fascist politics, founding the *Kokusui Taishūtō* (Ultranationalist Masses Party) in 1931. In 1932, he organized a paramilitary air corps, whose members wore black uniforms reminiscent of Italian fascists. After Japan's takeover of Manchuria, Sasakawa began to supply the Japanese military on the continent, also becoming involved in the lucrative, illicit opium trade that flourished there. Jailed in the mid-1930s for questionable activities, he was exonerated and released by 1939, after which he flew a Japanese-made bomber to Rome, where he met Italian leaders and posed in a kimono with his hero Mussolini.

In 1942, Sasakawa became a Diet member. He vigorously supported the ongoing war effort, and served as a shadowy nexus connecting organized crime and the ultra-right-wing on the one hand, and official government circles and the military on the other hand. Following Japan's defeat in World War II, occupation authorities arrested Sasakawa, charging him as a Class A war criminal. Seven wartime leaders were executed and 16 others received life sentences after trials conducted in Tokyo, but authorities released Sasakawa and accused war criminal and future Prime Minister Kishi Nobusuke without trial. Cold War imperatives stopped the Supreme Commander of the Allied Powers' (SCAP's) initial support for the Japanese left. In a "reverse course" policy, Americans began supporting the same individuals—or kinds of individuals—who had led Japan before its defeat in World War II.

While he was still being held for war crimes, seeing pictures of speedboat racing in *Life* magazine inspired Sasakawa to begin, when freed, to begin enriching himself again. This time, his focus was on organizing such boat races and, in turn, profiting from the gambling that accompanied them. In a *quid pro quo* move, Japan's Ministry of Transportation passed a Motorboat Racing Law in 1951, allowing Sasakawa to make immense profits from this gambling as long as he channeled some of those monies into the Japan Shipbuilding Industry Foundation. That foundation funded the renewal of Japan's key shipbuilding industry in the postwar period.

In 1962, the Japan Shipbuilding Industry Foundation was transformed into the Nippon Foundation. Using his newly renamed foundation, Sasakawa then created the United States–Japan Foundation, the Great Britain–Japan Foundation, the Scandinavia Sasakawa Foundation, and the Franco-Japan Foundation. Sasakawa attempted to use these organizations to fund universities and research around the world, including the University of Chicago, Massachusetts Institute of Technology, University of California at San Diego (UCSD), McGill University, and Australian National University. Scholars aware of these gifts' source vociferously refused them. At UCSD, for example, the late Masao Miyoshi and John Dower rhetorically asked the administration if it would accept money from Hitler when Sasakawa offered funds to the university.

In 1997, the Nippon Foundation spawned the Tokyo Foundation. Described as a think tank, this organization uses Sasakawa's wealth to develop what it calls "human resources" for the future. The Tokyo Foundation manages the Sasakawa Leaders Fellowship Fund (SYLFF) to support graduate studies and "education" in general. SYLF's Sasakawa-authored slogan is "the world is one family and all mankind are brothers and sisters." Karoline Postel-Vinay, Mark Selden, and others have suggested that the slogan is a transfigured reiteration of pre-1945 Japan's imperialist slogan, "*hakkō ichiu*" ("all the world under one roof"), and that as such it retroactively legitimizes pre-defeat Japan's militarism. As part of efforts to improve pre-defeat Japan's image, the Tokyo Foundation also funded promotion of Higashinakano Shūdō's *The Nanking Massacre: Facts versus Fiction* (2005).

Sasakawa's legacy seems mixed. After having a nefarious past and being accused of war crimes, he gave generous donations to organizations such as UNICEF and the World Health Organization. Such contradictions make sense if one understands how Japan's pre-defeat imperialist ideology resonated with anticommunist ideologies of liberal humanitarianism in the postwar era.

*Gerald Iguchi*

**See also:** International Military Tribunal for the Far East; Manchukuo; Right-Wing Politics in Japan.

**Further Reading**

Kirkup, James. "Obituary: Ryoichi Sasakawa." *The Independent*, July 20, 1995. Available at: http://www.independent.co.uk/news/people/obituary-ryoichi-sasakawa-1592324.html.

Postel-Vinay, Karoline, and Mark Selden. "History on Trial: French Nippon Foundation Sues Scholar for Libel to Protect the Honor of Sasakawa Ryōichi." *The Asia-Pacific Journal*, April 26, 2010. Available at: http://www.japanfocus.org/-Karoline-Postel_Vinay/3349.

Satō Seizaburō. *Sasakawa Ryoichi: A Life*, translated by Hara Fujiko. Norwalk, CT: Eastbridge, 2006.

## SatChō Oligarchy

Satchō is a conflation of the first syllables of the names of the two dominant regional Chōshū factions who unofficially advised the Meiji emperor after about 1880—Satsuma and Chōshū. Of the original seven men, three were from Chōshū (Inoue Kaoru, Itō Hirobumi, and Yamagata Aritomo) and four were from Satsuma (Kuroda Kiyotaka, Matsukata Masayoshi, Ōyama Iwao, and Saigō Tsugumichi). All were from lower-ranking samurai families, and all participated in the Boshin war that had ousted the Tokugawa *bakufu* and established the new Meiji government.

The fact that these men came to be special confidants of the Meiji emperor was an accident of nature more than indications of their exceptional acumen. They all seemed to work well together and were well received by the Meiji emperor. Otherwise, they were not particularly distinguished.

In fact, there were a dozen other early Meiji leaders who, simply because they did not survive the first two turbulent decades of the new era, did not become part of the oligarchy. Sakamoto Ryōma, for instance, was generally regarded as exceptionally charismatic and politically astute, but he was assassinated on the very eve of the Meiji Restoration in 1867. Ōmura Masujirō, from Chōshū, was an early proponent of universal military conscription, but was assassinated in 1869. Ōkubo Toshimichi and Saigō Takamori, both from Satsuma, died as a result of the aborted Satsuma Rebellion: Saigō killed himself, and Ōkubo was assassinated by other Satsuma men who blamed him for Saigō's death. Similarly, Etō Shimpei, from Hizen, was executed for his part of the Saga Rebellion. Kido Takayoshi of Chōshū died early (1877), as did Iwakura Tomomi (1883) and Sanjo Sanetomi (1891); the latter two were *kuge* (courtiers).

Many more men who could have been candidates for this oligarchy were weeded out for various reasons. Ōkuma Shigenobu, from Hizen, seemed destined to be part of

the oligarchy, but ran afoul of others, particularly Itō in 1881. Gōtō Shojiro and Itagaki Taisuke, both from Tosa, split from the government in 1873. Both later served in the government, but both were also involved in the Popular Rights Movement (*jiyu minken undo*) and later founded the Tosa wing of the Liberal Party (*Jiyutō*). Two other men became prominent but had earlier earned political stigmata that kept them out of the inner circle. Mutsu Munemitsu was from Kii, a Tokugawa-related domain, and was convicted of treason in 1878. Katsu Kaishū also was from a Tokugawa domain but later joined the Meiji government.

After the establishment of the Meiji Constitution in 1890, six members of the Satchō oligarchy took turns serving as the chief ministers during the entire 45 years of the Meiji era (only Ōyama did not serve as prime minister). They usually made all political decisions to be ratified by the emperor. They were able to make national laws by issuing imperial edicts; they kept rivals out of government, and channeled lucrative contracts to their business friends. After the sobriquet *genrō* ("senior statesmen") was coined by journalists to describe Itō's cabinet in 1892, the term became interchangeable with Satchō.

Because none of their political powers appeared in the constitution, when the *genrō* began to die out in the early 20th century, the government experienced a series of crises. After Kuroda (1900) and Saigō (1902) died, the remaining five *genrō* were joined by Katsura Taro of Chōshū and the imperial courtier Saionji Kinmochi.

*Louis G. Perez*

**See also:** Inoue Kaoru; Itagaki Taisuke; Itō Hirobumi; Iwakura Tomomi; Matsukata Masayoshi; Meiji Constitution; Meiji Emperor; Mutsu Munemitsu; Saga Rebellion; Saigō

Takamori; Saigō Tsugumichi; Saionji Kinmochi; Sakamoto Ryōma; Seinan (Satsuma) Rebellion; Yamagata Aritomo.

### Further Reading

Akita, George. *Foundations of Constitutional Government in Modern Japan, 1868–1900.* Cambridge, MA: Harvard University Press, 1967.

Pyle, Kenneth B. *New Generation in Meiji Japan: Problems of Cultural Identity, 1885–1895.* Stanford: Stanford University Press, 1969.

## Satō Eisaku (1901–1975)

Born on March 27, 1901, in Tabuse-chō in Yamaguchi Prefecture, Satō Eisaku graduated from the law school of Tokyo Imperial University in 1924. He then entered the Ministry of Railways, serving there until 1948. In 1947, he was appointed permanent Undersecretary of the Ministry of Railways but served in this post for just 13 months. In 1948, he became Chief Cabinet Secretary in the second Yoshida Shigeru government. Satō was chairman of the Policy Affairs Research Council of the Liberal Party in 1949 when he was elected to the Lower House of the Diet.

Satō held ministerial posts in the third and fourth Yoshida governments, including Minister of the Post Office (1951–1952) and Minister of Construction (1952–1953). In 1953, he became Director General of the Liberty Party (which merged with the Democratic Party in 1955 to become the Liberal Democratic Party), but he was forced to resign the position because of a ship-building company scandal during the fifth Yoshida cabinet in 1954. Satō subsequently became Minister of Finance during 1958–1960 under Prime Minister Kishi Nobusuke, Satō's elder brother by adoption.

In October 1964, Satō succeeded Ikeda Hayato as prime minister. During his seven years in office, Satō signed the 1965 Japan-Korea Treaty, which restored normal diplomatic relations between the two countries and enabled Japan to regain control of the Ogasawara Islands in 1968. Although U.S. troops and bases remained on Japanese soil, Satō managed to negotiate a reversion of Okinawa to Japanese sovereignty in 1972.

Satō was less successful in establishing closer ties to either the Soviet Union or the People's Republic of China (PRC). Public outrage over his agreement to allow U.S. troops to remain on Okinawa ultimately forced his resignation in November 1972. He was awarded the Nobel Peace Prize in 1974 for his antinuclear diplomacy, an award that caused considerable controversy. Satō died in Chiyodaku, Tokyo, on June 3, 1975.

*Kiichi Nenashi*

**See also:** Ikeda Hayato; Yoshida Shigeru.

### Further Reading

Lafeber, Walter. *The Clash: A History of U.S.-Japan Relations.* New York: Norton, 1997.

Reischauer, Edwin, O. *The Japanese Today: Change and Continuity.* Tokyo: Tuttle, 1988.

Schaller, Michael. *Altered States: The United States and Japan since the Occupation.* Oxford, UK: Oxford University Press, 1997.

**Satsuma Rebellion.** *See* Seinan (Satsuma) Rebellion.

**Seclusion.** *See Sakoku.*

## Seikanron

In 1873, a split over Korea policy separated the Meiji oligarchs into two camps. Following the Meiji Restoration, when the Japanese government claimed parity between its teen emperor and China's son of heaven, the Korean King Gojong balked. From 1869, the Korean government dismissed calls by Japanese envoys to open trade relations. With a caretaker government managing affairs in the absence of the Iwakura Mission abroad, Meiji militants called for punishment of Japan's neighbor—a demand that sparked the "Debate over Subduing Korea" (*Seikanron*). Calls for belligerence toward the peninsula transformed domestic politics while highlighting Japan's imperial ambitions.

In the wake of the Meiji Restoration, the question of what to do with unemployed samurai challenged the new Japanese government. While moderate oligarchs traveled abroad to consider measures for national strengthening, the remaining members of the government were active at home. Among them, Saigō Takamori fretted that fellow former samurai would sow strife in response to the policies adopted by the new regime, such as reversion of prefectures to the central state and reduced financial compensation for former samurai. In response, he and Itagaki Taisuke plotted to direct Japan's military strength outward as a means of defusing domestic tension.

Meiji-era hostility toward the Korean Kingdom in 1873 echoed earlier moments in Japan's history of political centralization. In the eighth century, rhetorical invasions of mythic dimension appeared in the *Record of Ancient Matters* (*Kojiki*) and *Chronicles of Japan* (*Nihon shōki*). These accompanied the emergence of the imperial court. During the 1590s, Toyotomi Hideyoshi's unification project included invasions of Korea. Compounding concerns about domestic politics, Saigō and others tallied up imagined insults to Japan's international dignity that included Korean recalcitrance and attacks on Ryukyuan sailors in Taiwan. Saigō and his supporters argued that the Meiji Empire should project military power across the Korea Strait.

A dual focus on domestic and international affairs characterized the debate over attacking Korea. Saigō's offer to serve as an envoy charged with provoking the Korean government appealed to supporters of an invasion. In addition to Saigō and Itagaki, Soejima Taneomi (acting Foreign Minister), Etō Shimpei (Minister of Justice), and Gōtō Shōjiro (Councilor) also supported measures against Korea. Their support foreshadowed subsequent thinking on the Korean peninsula: that Korea would fall to China or Russia; that military success in Korea would raise Japan's international profile; and that imperial adventures would answer popular enthusiasm for foreign domination.

Recent returnees from travels abroad and their allies opposed sending an expedition to Korea. Iwakura Tomomi, Kido Kōin, Ōkubo Toshimichi, and Itō Hirobumi all rejected Saigō's calls. Ōkubo articulated opposition to the plan, arguing both that Japan was ill equipped for a military adventure and that, regardless of its outcome, an attack would imperil tenuous relations with the treaty powers. In an audience before the Emperor Meiji, Iwakura successfully argued for an end to preparations for hostilities.

Proponents of hostilities resigned their government positions, taking their followers and allies with them. From Hizen to Satsuma, the Meiji government faced new and powerful military and then political opposition. Etō led an abortive uprising against the state in 1874. Saigō's Satsuma Rebellion threatened the Tokyo regime in 1877. Yet it was Itagaki's promotion of constitutional government through the movement for freedom and popular rights that had the greatest effect. In the wake of his resignation, Itagaki organized his followers into a national force that used public lectures, legal arguments, and political party-building to drive the Meiji government into promising to draft a constitution.

In the international arena, the debate marked a turning point in Japan's relationship with the treaty powers. With the encouragement of the U.S. government, Japan pressed its prerogatives against China and Korea. The 1871 murder of Ryukyuan sailors by Taiwanese aboriginals led foreign legal advisers such as Gustave Émile Boissonade to counsel the Meiji state to cement control over the archipelago and bolster its national sovereignty by pressing China. This logic led to the Taiwan Expedition of 1874 and then two years later, the Treaty of Kangwha, which forced international trade and treaty ports on Korea. It was in the context of the debate over subduing Korea that Meiji oligarchs first learned how international law could serve as a justification for asserting a place for the Empire of Japan in Asia.

*Darryl Flaherty*

**See also:** Boissonade de Fontarabie, Gustave Émile; Itagaki Taisuke; Iwakura Mission; Iwakura Tomomi; Jiyu Minken Undo; Korea Added to the Empire; Ōkubo Toshimichi; Taiwan Expedition.

## Further Reading

Dudden, Alexis. *Japan's Colonization of Korea: Discourse and Power.* Honolulu: University of Hawai'i Press, 2004.

Mayo, Marlene. "The Korean Crisis of 1873 and Early Meiji Foreign Policy." *Journal of Asian Studies* 31, no. 4 (August 1972): 793–819.

## Seinan (Satsuma) Rebellion (1877)

The Seinan War, which lasted from January 29 to September 24, 1877, in Japan, was the last armed challenge to the reforms of the Meiji government. Also known as the Satsuma Rebellion, its failure confirmed that the Meiji Restoration would go forward and that the samurai would no longer be a privileged class.

The samurai had been a hereditary warrior class of Japan since the 12th century. They were granted social and economic privileges in exchange for their military support. By the 19th century, however, the samurai were among those who had grievances against the Tokugawa shōgunate. The Satsuma samurai were especially notable among those who led the revolt that overthrew the shōgunate. Those men restored the emperor to power in Japan and initiated a series of reforms that launched the country on the road to modernity. By 1871, the samurai class was the only remaining vestige of feudalism in Japan, and the reformers began to change the samurai's status. They were given pensions that amounted to half of their former salaries, and were allowed to take up other professions. In 1873, the government offered the samurai the option of taking a lump sum instead of a pension. In 1876, the replacement of pensions by lump-sum payments was made mandatory.

While all the samurai were declining economically, the Satsuma samurai were especially angry at the government. In October 1873, their leader, Saigō Takamori, was politically discredited in a debate over war against Korea. He returned to Kagoshima, and thousands resigned their positions in the army and police to join him. Saigō provided for his supporters in the local government and built up a network of samurai who depended on him economically. He also established a network of military-oriented private schools and placed those facilities under the control of his samurai.

The central government in Tokyo grew more concerned about a possible revolt in

Kagoshima. To ward it off, Meiji leaders sent a naval unit to confiscate munitions that were held there. Young men in Kagoshima, however, attacked the naval yard and army munitions depot on January 29, 1877; they seized the supplies and fought against government troops. Saigō was surprised by his followers' actions, but he agreed to lead them to Tokyo to demand an explanation for the government's harassment. He soon was at the head of 40,000 men. The army was badly organized and poorly equipped and had no real plan except to march toward Tokyo.

On February 22, the army arrived at Kumamoto. Saigō decided to besiege the local garrison under General Tani Kanjo. Tani refused to surrender, and the siege dragged on for 50 days. Short of supplies and losing morale, Saigō 's army was forced to retreat when government reinforcements arrived. A total of 65,000 government troops were mobilized against the samurai and drove them back to Kagoshima. The new army consisted of former peasants and civilians, and they were able to defeat the hereditary warriors. By the time Saigō arrived back in Kagoshima, he had only about 400 men. In a final battle, Saigō ordered a desperate charge. When his forces were defeated, he committed suicide, which marked the end of the rebellion.

*Tim Watts*

**See also:** Saigō Takamori; Tokugawa *Bakufu* Political System.

**Further Reading**

Mounsey, Augustus Henry. *The Satsuma Rebellion*. Washington, DC: University Publications of America, 1979.

Ideishi Takehiko. *The True Story of the Siege of Kumamoto Castle*. New York: Vantage Press, 1976.

# *Seito (Bluestockings)* (1911–1916)

Established in 1911 as a literary magazine by Hiratsuka *Raichō*, Nakano Hatsuko, and Kiuchi Teiko, *Seito* rapidly became the primary outlet for feminism in Japan. Using an annuity intended to fund Hiratsuka's marriage, the magazine was named for the British feminist organization known as the Bluestockings. In her first editorial, Hiratsuka coined the famous phrase that became the metaphor for feminism in Japan: "In the beginning, Woman was truly the Sun, an authentic person. Now, Woman is the Moon, living off another, reflecting another's brilliance . . ."

Yosano Akiko's evocative poem "Mountain Moving Day," was published on the first page of that issue, which sold out its initial run of 1,000 copies. Thousands of women responded with subscription orders. For the next five years, most of the women who would become Japan's popular poets and writers contributed their literary work and their money to keep the journal afloat. In addition to the works of Okamoto Kanoko, Hayashi Fumiko, Yamakawa Kikue, Kamichika Ichiko, and Yamada Waka, the magazine also published translations of Western authors such as Anton Chekhov, Havelock Ellis, Emma Goldman, and Olive Schreiner. It published a translated version of Henrik Ibsen's *A Doll's House*.

As the journal became increasingly more devoted to politics and social reform, the Meiji government began to step in to suppress publication. A number of issues were banned by the government and on three occasions whole issues of the magazine were removed from bookstores after censors banned entire publishing runs as "injurious to public morals." The decidedly antiwar and socialist sentiments of its authors were not well received by an increasingly more militaristic government. The journal published discussions about controversial topics such as divorce, birth control, abortion, prostitution and other "women's problems." It continued to limp along for a number of years despite the heavy-handled government interference.

Tired of the constant struggle and in ill health, Hiratsuka turned over the editorship to the young firebrand Itō Noe in 1915. *Seito* continued to publish sporadically and clandestinely until 1916. By that time it had served as a springboard for many of its literary contributors and as cradle of "feminist consciousness" in Japan.

*Louis G. Perez*

**See also:** Hiratsuka *Raichō*; Itō Noe; Yosano Akiko.

### Further Reading

Bardsley, Jan. *The Bluestockings of Japan: New Woman Essays and Fiction from Seito, 1911–16.* Ann Arbor, MI: Center for Japanese Studies, 2007.

Lippit, Noriko Mizuta. "*Seito* and the Literary Roots of Japanese Feminism." *International Journal of Women's Studies* 2, no. 2 (March–April 1979): 232–245.

Sievers, Sharon L. *Flowers in Salt: The Beginnings of Feminist Consciousness in Modern Japan.* Stanford: Stanford University Press, 1983.

## Sekigahara, Battle of (1600)

The Battle of Sekigahara, the closing battle of the Sengoku era, saw Tokugawa Ieyasu (1542–1616) defeat a coalition led by Ishida Mitsunari. Three years later, Ieyasu formed the Tokugawa shōgunate.

In 1598, the ailing Toyotomi Hideyoshi (born 1536) called upon Japan's five most powerful *daimyō*—Ieyasu, Maeda Toshiie, Mōri Terumoto, Uesugi Kagekatsu, and Ukita Hideie—to serve as regents for his five-year-old heir, Hideyori. Of these

Himeji Castle passed into the control of Tokugawa Ieyasu after the Battle of Sekigahara in 1600. (Corel)

*daimyō*, Ieyasu was the most powerful, with an income twice that of Mōri and Uesugi. Hideyoshi also hailed five administrators (Ishida Mitsunari, Maeda Geni, Asano Nagamasa, Mashida Nagamori, and Natsuka Masaie) and tasked them with managing the state's day-to-day affairs.

After Hideyoshi's death in August 1598, Ieyasu began to push his advantage in influence over the other regents. His actions sparked rumors that he was maneuvering to fully take control for himself. The most likely source of these rumors was Mitsunari, the most ambitious of the administrators.

Mitsunari was a polarizing figure among the military elite. One of Hideyoshi's favored bureaucrats, he had served in Korea during the Imjin Invasion, from which he often sent back critical reports about Hideyoshi's commanders. After Hideyoshi's death, Mitsunari traveled back to Korea to arrange the withdrawal of the remaining troops. His management of this process further exacerbated the animosity for him among the generals. Mitsunari was known to oppose Ieyasu; he swayed the other regents to bring charges against Ieyasu, although these were dropped. Additionally, he was involved in several plots against Ieyasu, the exposure of which helped to drive more to Ieyasu's side in the developing dispute.

By the end of 1599, regency rule had disintegrated. Maeda Toshiie died, and Uesugi Kagekatsu became opposed to Ieyasu's dominating influence and returned to his northern domain. Ieyasu took sole control of decision making while maintaining a close watch over Mitsunari's political maneuvers. Virtually all of Japan's *daimyō* began to choose sides. Many western *daimyō* with strong loyalty to the Toyotomi house, such as Mōri Terumoto and Ukita Hideie, opposed Ieyasu. Meanwhile, many eastern *daimyō* and those with a strong distaste for Mitsunari threw their support behind Ieyasu.

In September 1600, Mitsunari publicly declared his opposition to Ieyasu. In Edo, Ieyasu gathered his forces and traveled west to face Mitsunari's army. The two forces met at the village of Sekigahara in Mino Province on the early morning of October 21. Ieyasu's eastern army numbered roughly 74,000 men. His troops were commanded by seasoned Tokugawa vassals such as Honda Tadakatsu and Ii Naomasa as well as Toyotomi generals such as Fukushima Masanori and Kuroda Nagamasa.

Though Mōri Terumoto was the western army's formal commander, he was kept back in Osaka and command was held by Mitsunari. The largest contingents at the fore of Mitsunari's army were those of Ukita Hideie and Konishi Yukinaga. On his right flank were the forces of Kobayakawa Hideaki and Wakisaka Yasuhara. The Mōri and Kikkawa clans stood ensconced behind nearby Mount Nangu, ready to attack the rear of the eastern army. The western army, with 80,000 men, outnumbered Ieyasu's eastern army.

The day was won for Ieyasu, however, as he had previously secured the defection of the Kobayakawa, Kikkawa, and Wakisaka forces. After the commencement of fighting, the Kikkawa clan refused to join in. His inaction forced the Mōri army behind him to stand their ground as well, ending the possibility of action upon the eastern army's rear. Meanwhile, Kobayakawa and Wakisaka turned and sent their forces onto the exposed right flank of Mitsunari's vanguard. This move sealed the fate of the western army. Not coincidentally, Kobayakawa had been a target of Mitsunari's critiques in Korea. After the Battle of Sekigahara, Mitsunari was publicly executed in Kyoto.

*Philip Streich*

**See also:** Civil Wars, Sengoku Era; Imjin War; Tokugawa Ieyasu; Toyotomi Hideyoshi.

**Further Reading**

Sansom, George. *A History of Japan, 1334–1615*. Stanford: Stanford University Press, 1961.

Totman, Conrad. *Tokugawa Ieyasu: Shōgun*. Union City: Heian International, 1983.

Turnbull, Stephen. *The Samurai: A Military History*. New York: Macmillan, 1977.

## Self-Defense Forces (*Jieitai*), from the Bomb to Iraq

Japan's postwar armed forces were founded on July 8, 1950, as the National Police Reserve (*Keisatsu Yobitai*) in the wake of the United States' involvement in the Korean War. They were renamed and inaugurated as the Self-Defense Forces (*Jieitai*) on July 1, 1954. Based on Article 9 of the Japanese Constitution, which disrupts the connection between soldiering and death presumably normalized elsewhere, the Self-Defense Forces operate under strict civilian control. The exact wording of Article 9 reads as follows:

Aspiring sincerely to an international peace based on justice and order, the Japanese people forever renounce war as a sovereign right of the nation and the threat of use of force as a means of settling international disputes. In order to accomplish the aim of the preceding paragraph, land, sea, and air forces, as well as other war potential, will never be maintained. The right of belligerency of the state will not be recognized.

The article forcefully disrupts the mutually reinforcing mechanisms of the potency of the state and the potency of its military men and women, creating a dramatically different framework for service members' negotiations of their militarized selves within a domestic, international, and historical setting.

Today Japan has a full-fledged military establishment, complete with three services (ground, maritime, and air), the latest military technology (tanks, ships, and planes, as well as a variety of state-of-the art weaponry, albeit no nuclear weaponry), and all of the organizational accompaniments common to armed forces (territorial divisions, brigades, and training methods). The army or Ground Self-Defense Force (GSDF) is the largest service branch and consists of approximately 148,000 troops, followed in size by the air force or Air Self-Defense Force (ASDF) with 46,000 troops, and the navy or Maritime Self-Defense Force (MSDF) with 44,000 service members. With 37.8 percent of the total military budget being devoted to it, the GSDF also claims the lion's share of Japan's military expenditures.

Since the 1950s, military-societal relations in Japan have undergone gradual but important shifts, typically in the aftermath of various engagements of the Self-Defense Forces. In 1960, when the Self-Defense Forces were on the brink of being mobilized to suppress domestic unrest, hundreds of thousands of ordinary citizens joined in protest against the renewal of the Treaty of Mutual Cooperation between Japan and the United States of America (*Nichibei Anzen Hosho Jôyaku*), which was to tie Japan permanently to U.S. security interests in the region. The protest became the largest mass demonstration in Japan's history. A year before the political unrest erupted, Sugita Ichiji, GSDF chief of staff, had sent his confidential Plan to Mobilize for the Maintenance of Order in 1960 to a number of high-ranking officers under his command. Many of these officers, he later recalled, did not want to even think about a possible mobilization of the Self-Defense Forces against the Japanese population and were hoping that the police would take care of suppressing the dissent. In such an inflammatory atmosphere, the strength of the antiwar and antimilitary sentiment of the public helped deter the Japan Defense Agency (JDA) from using force against the protesters.

The mass protest dissipated when Prime Minister Kishi Nobusuke—a former Minister of Commerce and Industry in Tōjō Hideki's government from 1941 to 1945, who had been jailed as a Class A war criminal until 1948—resigned owing to public furor over the treaty in July of that year. Subsequently, Ikeda Hayato took office and announced his income-doubling plan. The movement against the security treaty with the United States eventually splintered into local anti-U.S. military base movements. Grumbling about this issue remains audible in Okinawa, where protests are directed primarily against U.S. bases there.

The next watershed for military-societal relations in Japan came in the aftermath of the Persian Gulf War during the early 1990s, which had an impact on both the self-perception of service members and public opinion of the Self-Defense Forces. Japan contributed $12 billion to the Gulf War and in April 1991 sent mine sweepers to the Persian Gulf in the Self-Defense Forces' first international deployment ever, but the U.S. media fiercely criticized Japan for not putting its soldiers at risk. This criticism prompted the public relations apparatus within the JDA and on bases across Japan to engage in a more concerted effort of professional image-building and triggered a debate about Japan's responsibilities in the international arena and its contributions to international security (*kokusai kôken*).

Despite the doubts about the Self-Defense Forces' roles beyond Japan's borders, Japan's participation in international peacekeeping missions has been given post facto legitimacy, a strategy that might have boosted approval of the Self-Defense Forces as well. The first of such missions was to Cambodia in 1992, immediately after the law that regulates Japan's participation in peacekeeping missions (*Kokusai heiwa kyôryokuhô*) had passed the Diet on June 15, 1992, and had been implemented on August 10 of the same year. The Japanese contingent was accompanied by an impressive press corps that documented their every move. By then, the Japanese population's mainstream attitude toward the Self-Defense Forces had been transformed first from hostility to ignorance and then largely to apathy regarding the armed forces and security issues.

The majority of the Japanese population continues to oppose militarism at home and in wars abroad, but in the aftermath of the first peacekeeping missions they have also increasingly accepted a constrained international role for the Self-Defense Forces. The international criticism that Japan faced for its purely monetary contribution to the Gulf War coincided with increasing domestic support for Japan to play a larger political and possibly military role in the international arena. The Gulf War and the end of the Cold War also have cast doubt on the simple equation of overseas dispatches with any participation in an aggressive war.

A large-scale natural disaster marked another milestone on the Self-Defense Forces' march to public approval and a moment of intense media exposure. Initially, after the mobilization of the Self-Defense Forces to rescue survivors of the Kôbe-Awaji earthquake on January 17, 1995, the Self-Defense Forces came under intense scrutiny by national and international media for their lack of a prompt response and inadequate organizational skills. In the long run, however, the earthquake and its aftermath forced the modernization of disaster relief operation equipment and training, and later high-ranking commanders and soldiers alike viewed their involvement as highly rewarding and successful; various stories about the morale-boosting moments of saving someone's life circulated among the ranks for a long time. Subsequently, entire cohorts of newly recruited service members and cadets at the National Defense Academy (NDA) joined the Self-Defense Forces with the primary motivation of being dispatched to a disaster relief site, rescuing people who would be grateful to them, and possibly having all those deeds acknowledged in television reports. For practically all of those individuals—those who hope to participate in such a mission in the future, those who actually have participated in one, and even those who knew someone who has taken part in such a mission—rescuing people from the aftermath of a natural disaster had an enormous identity-building significance.

At the end of 1998, the press celebrated the 80-men unit from a GSDF base near Nagoya who had returned from Japan's first international disaster relief mission to Honduras in November and December 1998. The mission to Honduras and ongoing peacekeeping operations boosted service members' self-esteem and were highlighted by the military administration for two reasons: to communicate to politicians and to the national and international public that Japan's forces could perform well in an international arena and that they could be put to good use in terms of "contributing to the international community," and to gain visibility in a positive light

and in an ambiguously civilian/military context.

While the mission to Honduras contributed to a general sense in the Japanese population that the Self-Defense Forces could go abroad and carry out a peaceful operation, the North Korean "missile incident" in early 1999 raised new concerns about an impending military threat and contributed to debates about Japan's military capability and the functionality of the U.S.-Japan security alliance. Media addressed the failure of the Self-Defense Forces and the U.S. Forces Japan to prevent the incident; more generally, they questioned the actual military potency and functionality of the Self-Defense Forces in worst-case scenarios. The liberal press used the opportunity to problematize anew the constitutional legitimacy of the Self-Defense Forces. On the other side, the right exploited the opportunity to criticize the laws and regulations that, in their opinion, prevented the Self-Defense Forces from acting like what some commentators imagine as a "normal," "conventional," or "modern" military organization.

In 2006, Japanese newspapers reported all GSDF troops "safely home from their historic mission to Iraq," putting an end to two and one-half years of the first deployment of the Self-Defense Forces to a war zone since their foundation in 1954, albeit for a noncombat, humanitarian operation. The mission in Iraq increased Japan's international profile and strengthened ties with Japan's biggest ally, the United States. Subsequently, the JDA was transformed into the current Ministry of Defense in 2007, announcing on its homepage its existence "for further contribution to world peace." The Self-Defense Forces facility itself was moved from the shabby area of Roppongi to the fancy medieval castle meets 21st-century technology-style architecture in

Ichigaya. Suggesting that Japan had overcome the childlike state once attributed to it by General Douglas MacArthur, the international press claimed that the Iraq mission marked no less than Japan's transformation into a "grown-up nation" and a "normal state," and that its armed forces were on their way to becoming a "true military." Currently, the Self-Defense Forces are engaged in three United Nations peacekeeping operations (Golan Heights, Nepal, and Sudan) and three disaster relief operations (Haiti, Indonesia, and Pakistan).

Within Japan and the rest of Asia, the debate regarding the desirable condition of the armed forces and attempts at the renegotiation of the line that once used to be drawn very clearly between military and society continue.

*Sabine Frühstück*

**See also**: AMPO: United States–Japan Security Treaty; Ikeda Hayato; MacArthur, Douglas; Peace Preservation Law; Tōjō Hideki.

### Further Reading

Frühstück, Sabine. *Uneasy Warriors: Gender, Memory and Popular Culture*. Berkeley, CA: University of California Press, 2007.

Pekkanen, Saadia M., and Paul Kallender-Umezu. *In Defense of Japan: From the Market to the Military in Space Policy*. Stanford, CA: Stanford University Press, 2010.

Pyle, Kenneth. *Japan Rising: The Resurgence of Japanese Power and Purpose* (Century Foundation Books). New York: Public Affairs, 2008.

Samuels, Richard J. *Securing Japan: Tokyo's Grand Strategy and the Future of East Asia*. Ithaca, NY: Cornell University Press, 2007.

## Senninbari and "Comfort Bags"

Among the principal ways women provided relief, consolation, and encouragement to servicemen during Japan's 20th-century wars was the making and sending of comfort bags and thousand-stitch belts. The practice of providing comfort bags, usually referred to in Japanese as *imonbukuro*, first became popular in the United States during the American Civil War. In 1904, just after the outbreak of the Russo-Japanese War, the Japan Woman's Christian Temperance Union (WCTU) adopted it as a means to show patriotism, evangelize, and espouse reform principles.

The public, the government, and the military soon came to see the bags as an appropriate way for women to contribute to the war effort. That broader acceptance, prodded by WCTU activities intended to encourage widespread participation, turned the collection of comfort bags into a national project. Charged by the state with responsibility for all bags, the WCTU provided directions on how to sew bags, loaned out and sold empty ones to be filled, accepted empty bags and goods for insertion, and inspected all bags prior to shipment. The most common items included in the bags were needles, thread, buttons, socks, gloves, pencils, paper, and dried plums. WCTU members added to these temperance tracts, abstinence pledges, Bibles, and hymnal slips while removing perishable food, cigarettes, and salacious pictures. Free shipping from the War Department allowed for the sending of at least 60,000 bags during the Russo-Japanese War. Thereafter, urban and rural women's organizations periodically put together comfort bags for victims of natural disaster, with the largest number being sent after the 1923 Kanto earthquake. Nevertheless, comfort bags were predominantly a means of civic participation for women during wartime, and their provision to men in uniform once again became common after the Mukden Incident.

One additional item regularly included in comfort bags from the early 1930s through the end of the Pacific War was the thousand-stitch belt. The term *senninbari* literally means "stitches by a thousand people." Although it refers to a variety of cloth pieces women embellished and then gave to servicemen for good luck and protection, the overwhelming popularity of the belts made it synonymous with them.

Traditional Japanese belief posited that the source of a man's energy lay in his abdomen, and women's desire to keep that area safe provides one explanation for the preference for belts relative to items such as flags and headbands. The warmth a belt offered to men stationed in Manchuria, northern China, and Korea played a role as well. That comfort came partly from the fact that belts typically had at least two panels sewn together. They were most frequently made of white cotton and had cotton strings on each end for securing around a waist. Rectangular in shape, they ranged considerably in length and width, as each had to accommodate the girth of the intended wearer. While the adornments also varied, the majority of belts shared one or more characteristic feature. One was the addition of 1,000 stitches, each by a different woman, either knotted or continuous, and usually in red thread, the color of which represented good luck.

Both preprinted and handmade cloth was regularly marked with small circles in ink to identify where the stitches should go. The simplest pattern had the stitches in rows, while more decorative ones wrote out the characters for a prayer for continued success in battle, depicted a fierce tiger, or reproduced the Japanese flag. The tiger was a particularly symbolic motif and carried with it the hope that, like a tiger, the wearer of the belt would return safely after traveling thousands of miles.

Other typical features on belts included small pockets for holding written prayers and other kinds of amulets, and 5- and 10-yen coins sewn onto the exterior or between the panels. The holes in these coins made them easy to attach, but they were really sewn on because they represented a surpassing of four and nine. These numbers bear the same sounds in Japanese as the words for death and hardship, respectively, and the coins conveyed the wish that those off fighting would escape both. In addition to these features, many belts had at least one ink stamp from a temple or shrine, indicating that they had been officially blessed, and bore the name of the recipient, his unit, and the giving individual or organization.

The *Kokubo fujinkai* was the most prominent women's group engaged in the making and sending of belts. Indeed, this form of patriotic service was one of the defining activities of the society during the 1930s and early 1940s.

*Elizabeth Dorn Lublin*

**See also:** Mukden Incident: Lytton Incident; Russo-Japanese War; Women during World War II: *Kokubo Fujinkai and Aikoku Fujinkai*; World War II, Pacific Theater.

**Further Reading**

Bornter, Michael A. *Imperial Japanese Good Luck Flags and One-Thousand Stitch Belts*. Atglen, PA: Schiffer Publishing, 2008.

Lublin, Elizabeth Dorn. *Reforming Japan: The Woman's Christian Temperance Union in the Meiji Period*. Vancouver: University of British Columbia Press, 2010.

Smethurst, Richard J. *A Social Basis for Pre-war Japanese Militarism: The Army and the Rural Community*. Berkeley: University of California Press, 1974.

## Sensō-e (War Prints)

The Japanese tradition of depicting warriors in art dates to the Heian era (794–1185). As Japan modernized during the Meiji

Restoration, woodblock prints featuring historical samurai expressed the increasing sense of Japanese nationalism, imperialism, militarism, and cultural and racial identity. When Japan entered into international military conflicts, prints known as *sensō-e*, or war prints, were used to build international support as Japan promoted itself as a modern nation worthy of respect. With Japan's swift, decisive victory over China in the Sino-Japanese War (1894–1895), Japan was seen as the champion of progress in Asia and China as backward and antiquated. Woodblock print artists played a key role in creating these perceptions.

The woodblock print tradition reached its apex with the production of *sensō-e* during the Sino-Japanese War, when approximately 3,000 different prints were published. The inexpensive prints, which were produced quickly, proved popular both at home and abroad. Japan developed a new visual language in *sensō-e*, based on Western iconography, which made the prints more readily acceptable to a Western audience that viewed Asian art as inferior to Western art. The realistic depictions were seen by Japanese viewers as accurate representations of events at the front, despite the fact that very few artists had direct access to the action.

*Sensō-e* prints were a form of propaganda, emphasizing the heroism of individual Japanese military men in dramatic scenes that used standardized iconography such as a centrally placed gnarled pine tree, a fluttering "rising sun" flag, and a heroic figure in a Western-style uniform with raised sword leading his troops to victory against a distant enemy. Other common depictions included the compassionate warrior saving a small child from the chaos of war, small figures in large landscapes reflecting the loneliness of soldiers fighting far from home, and dramatic naval battles featuring fires, explosions, and ships sinking in heavy seas. Most of these prints were products of the artists' imagination rather than accurate depictions of actual events, with their colorful imagery supporting assertions of Japanese modernity and bolstering support for the war at home.

Most artists created colorful images of imagined battles and heroes from the comfort of Tokyo. Asai Chu (1856–1907), Koyama Shotaro (1857–1916), and Kuroda Seiki (1866–1924) were among the artists permitted to visit the front. Seiki, who was attached to the Second Army Division, published four volumes of pencil and ink sketches depicting the everyday lives of soldiers and Red Cross workers rather than action scenes. The best-known artists given access to the front were Kubota Beisen (1852–1906) and his sons Kensen (1875–1954) and Beisai (1874–1937). They produced images of the First Army Division's crossing of the Korean Peninsula for the newspaper *Kokumin Shinbun*. Their 10-volume *Illustrated Record of the Battles of the Sino-Japanese War* combined literati landscape painting traditions with Western figural techniques to create dramatic battle scenes. Among the more experienced artists who created prints in Tokyo were Kobayashi Kiyuchika (1847–1915) and Ogata Gekko (1859–1920).

The end of the Sino-Japanese War also signaled the end of the popularity of woodblock prints, although some prints were produced during the Russo-Japanese War (1904–1905). The majority of that war's imagery came in the form of the modern technology of lithographs and photographs, which were published in magazines and newspapers, providing nationalistic reporting and imagery to the general populace during the war. As with the Sino-Japanese War, access to the front was limited although the war was extensively covered by Western journalists, making it the most closely observed and recorded war to that time.

Although significantly fewer prints were produced during the Russo-Japanese War, they played an important role in popularizing it, serving as a form of propaganda that was both informative and celebratory. The prints contributed to a strong sense of national pride by depicting the Japanese military as chivalrous, disciplined, and modern, often braving treacherous conditions and succeeding despite incredible difficulties. They also created a psychological buffer for the Japanese people against the hardships of war. The war was dominated by sea battles, so prints of naval scenes were very popular, snapped up by a population hungry for information about Japanese successes. These prints, often modeled after Western images of Western wars, conveyed a sense of the dangers experienced by military men.

Watanabe Nobukazu (1874–1944), Mizuno Toshihata (1866–1908), and Migita Toshihide (1863–1925) were among the most well-known print artists of the time. As during the Sino-Japanese War, these artists created their works far from the front. The heroic figure leading his troops to victory, shown moving from right to left through the print to echo the Japanese movement through Asia, was a frequent theme in the *sensō-e* prints by Toshihata. Toshihide, who also produced prints during the Sino-Japanese War, was a successful figure painter who incorporated Western use of color, foreshortening, anatomical accuracy, and perspective into his works. His *sensō-e* prints frequently featured dignified lone figures fighting against impossible odds.

Although the Russo-Japanese War had ended by September 1905, worldwide interest in the Japanese success persisted until

the beginning of World War I. The proliferation of objects embellished with images of Japanese military heroes and successes contributed to a strong sense of national pride that continued unabated until World War II.

*Deborah A. Deacon*

**See also:** Boshin Civil War; *Musha-e* (Warrior Prints); Russo-Japanese War; Sino-Japanese War.

**Further Reading**

Chaikin, Nathan. *The Sino-Japanese War.* Privately published, 1983.

Clark, John. "Artists and the State: The Image of China," in *Society and the State in Interwar Japan*, edited by Elise K. Tipton. London: Routledge, 1997: 63–99.

Keene, Donald. "Prints of the Sino-Japanese War," in Shumpei Okamoto, *Impressions of the Front: Woodcuts of the Sino-Japanese War, 1894–5.* Philadelphia: Philadelphia Museum of Art, 1983:7–10.

Morse, Anne Nishimura. "Exploiting a New Visuality: The Origins of Russo-Japanese War Imagery," in Frederic A. Scharf, Anne Nishimura Morse and Sebastian Dobson, *A Much Recorded War: The Russo-Japanese War in History and Imagery.* Boston: Museum of Fine Arts Publications, 2005: 32–51.

Okamoto, Shumpei. *Impressions of the Front: Woodcuts of the Sino-Japanese War, 1894–5.* Philadelphia: Philadelphia Museum of Art, 1983.

*Seppuku.* See *Hara-kiri* and *Seppuku.*

# Shanghai, Battle of (August 13– November 9, 1937)

After the beginning of the second Sino-Japanese at Marco Polo Bridge on July 7, 1937, Japanese troops seized control of the Beijing-Tianjin area. On August 7, Jiang

Jieshi, the Guomindang (Nationalist) president of China, decided to retaliate by attacking Japanese forces stationed at the Japanese settlement in Shanghai in Jiangsu, China's leading port and major international commercial center. Japan and several prominent Western powers each administered part of an area of the city called the International Settlement, where their nationals enjoyed special extraterritorial privileges. To protect these rights, the Japanese government had installed its own garrison. Meanwhile, top Japanese naval officials urged forceful action in the Shanghai area, a hotbed of Chinese nationalist sentiment. At this sensitive time, several Japanese warships—together with naval vessels of other foreign nations—were also moored in Shanghai harbor. The situation in Shanghai grew increasingly explosive, and on August 9, Chinese soldiers killed two Japanese marines.

Jiang believed that the constricted conditions of street fighting in Shanghai would minimize Japanese superiority in logistics, tanks, and artillery and that the urban location would prove more advantageous to his own forces than the northern Chinese plains, the focus to date of Sino-Japanese military confrontation. By diverting Japanese attention to central China, he also hoped to allow beleaguered northern Chinese military units to regroup.

On August 11, Jiang ordered his troops to positions within the greater Shanghai area, carefully avoiding the foreign sections of the city. Japanese commanders rushed reinforcements to Shanghai, but when battle began on August 13, a mere 12,000 Japanese soldiers faced 80,000 Chinese. For a week, the battle hung in the balance, as Chinese units came close to driving their enemy into the Huangpu River.

From August 20, Japanese reinforcements arrived en masse by sea, landing on the banks of the Yangtze River and mounting what quickly became a siege of Shanghai. The Chinese government likewise poured men into Shanghai, where heavy fighting continued for almost three months, as both sides struggled for control of the city. Combat was brutal. On August 14, Chinese warplanes tried to bomb Japanese naval vessels in Shanghai harbor, but they merely succeeded in hitting civilian areas of the city. Japanese warships in the Yangtze and Huangpu Rivers responded with heavy point-blank fire against Nationalist positions, which continued throughout the battle. During the siege, a stray shell hit the U.S. cruiser *Augusta*, killing a crewman and wounding 18 others.

Hoping that the influential foreign residents of the city's International Settlement might conceivably serve as mediators and perhaps win overseas support for China, Jiang ordered Shanghai's defenders to hold out to the end, and for several weeks of bitter house-to-house fighting they did so. Between August and November 1937, 270,000 Chinese troops—constituting 60 percent of the city's Nationalist garrison and the core of Jiang's newly modernized Chinese army—were killed or wounded in the fighting, along with many thousands of civilians. Japanese casualties totaled some 40,000. Much of Shanghai was devastated, although both sides left the foreign settlements undisturbed.

At the beginning of November, a Japanese amphibious force landed at Hangzhou Bay 50 miles from Shanghai, threatening the city's rear. In what swiftly became a disorganized rout, Chinese forces evacuated Shanghai. Instead of retreating to newly built fortifications along the Shanghai-Nanjing railway line, they fell back farther to Nanjing, the Nationalist capital, which became the next Japanese target.

Jiang's decision to launch the Battle of Shanghai marked a deliberate extension to central China of Sino-Japanese conflict. It was a major strategic shift reflecting Jiang's new determination, after the Xi'an Incident and his rapprochement with the Communists, to move to outright opposition toward further Japanese incursions. It also constituted the real beginning of the Sino-Japanese War, which would last a further eight years.

*Priscilla Roberts*

**See also:** Jiang Jieshi (Ch'iang K'ai-shek); Xi'an Incident.

### Further Reading

Dorn, Frank. *The Sino-Japanese War, 1937–41: From Marco Polo Bridge to Pearl Harbor.* New York: Macmillan, 1974.

Wilson, Dick. *When Tigers Fight: The Story of the Sino-Japanese War, 1937–1945.* New York: Viking Press, 1982.

Yeh, Wen-hsin, ed. *Wartime Shanghai.* New York: Routledge, 1998.

## Shiba Ryōtarō and *Bushidō*

Shiba Ryōtarō (1923–1996) was a writer of historical fiction. Most of his prolific career was devoted to the portrayal of characters who are embodiment of *bushidō*.

In Shiba's view, a uniquely Japanese history started in the Kamakura period when the *bushi*, a class born of peasants, took control of the country. Until then, Japanese history was populated exclusively by the aristocracy of a centralized country, built on the Chinese model. Shiba summarizes *bushidō* in one motto—*nakoso oshikere* ("Cherish your name" or "Don't do anything shameful")—to be measured in terms of aesthetics (*bi*, how to act honorably), public-mindedness (*kō*, how to benefit society), and aspiration (*kokorozashi*, how to realize the two). As a novelist, Shiba presents his *bushidō* by portraying characters often

drawn from turbulent transitional times, such as the late 16th century, when violent rivalry among powerful warlords eventually led to a peaceful Japan, as seen in *The Tale of Stealing a Country* (*Kunitori monogatari*, 1965), *A New Tale of Toyotomi Hideyoshi* (*Shin taikōki*, 1968), and *The Battle of Sekigahara* (*Sekigahara*, 1966).

His best pieces, however, are set in the Bakumatsu and the Meiji periods when, in his view, *bushidō* was revealed at its best. Many of his protagonists are losers in the Meiji Restoration, such as Hijikata Toshizō in *Burn! Sword* (*Moe yo, ken*, 1964), the number 2 commander of the Shinsengumi that cracked down on the *sonno-jōi* radicals; Matsudaira Katamori in *The Protector of the Capital* (*Ōjō no goeisha*, 1968), who sacrificed his Aizu domain to keep the order of Kyoto, only to be labeled "a traitor to the emperor"; and Kawai Tsuginosuke in *The Pass* (*Tōge*, 1968), who led Nagaoka domain in a doomed resistance against Meiji government troops. These characters share the conviction that their actions are for the public good and they are willing to die holding to their beliefs rather than catering to the times. Characters from the winning side are either those who were later out of power but cherished their names, such as Saigō Takamori in *As If Soaring* (*Tobu ga gotoku*, 1975), portrayed sympathetically, or those who are successful but presented as plotters betraying *bushidō*, such as Iwakura Tomomi (1825–1883) and Ōkubo Toshimichi (1830–1878) in *The Water of Kamo River* (*Kamo no mizu*, 1968). This perspective sets Shiba decidedly apart from the orthodox history of the Meiji Restoration.

His most popular pieces are *Ryōma Goes* (*Ryōma ga yuku*, 1966) and *The Clouds above the Slope* (*Saka no ue no kumo*, 1972). The former tells of a runaway lower samurai from Tosa domain who single-handedly created the blueprint of a modern Japan state but excluded himself from any office in the new government; the latter describes the key role that two brothers from a small domain in Shikoku played in Japan's victory in the Russo-Japanese War (1904–1905).

Shiba was a tankman in World War II. This experience made him search Japanese history for an answer to the question of why his country should have plunged into "that stupid war." His works present the answer he discovered: the loss of Japan's proud *bushidō* ethics as seen, for example, in the pre-war Shōwa staff officers who led the country to disaster but took no responsibility for their actions. Many critics consider Shiba to be, in portraying *bushidō*, critical of the postwar loss of national identity among the Japanese, and his major contribution to be showing his compatriots what it means to be Japanese.

*Guohe Zheng*

**See also:** *Bushidō*; Iwakura Tomomi; Nitobe Inazō; Ōkubo Toshimichi; Saigō Takamori; Sakamoto Ryōma; Toyotomi Hideyoshi.

**Further Reading**

Chamberlain, Basil Hall. "The Invention of a New Religion." London: Watts & Co. 1912.

Gaskins, C., and V. Hawkins. *The Ways of the Samurai*. New York: Byron Preiss Visual Publications, 2003.

Morillo, Stephen. "Cultures of Death: Warrior Suicide in Medieval Europe and Japan." *Medieval History Journal* 4 (2001): 241.

Nitobe, Inazō. *Bushidō: Soul of Japan* (13th ed.). Rutland, VT: Charles E. Tuttle Company, 1969.

Shiba, Rotaro. *The Last Shōgun: The Life of Tokugawa Yoshinobu*, translated by Juliet Winters Carpenter. New York: Kodansha International, 1998.

Shiba, Rotaro. *Drunk as a Lord: Samurai Stories*, translated by Eileen Kato. New York: Kodansha International, 2001.

Yamamoto Tsunetomo. *The Art of the Samurai: Yamamoto Tsunetomo's Hagakure*, translated by Barry D. Steben. London: Duncan Baird Publishers, 2008.

## Shidehara Kijuro (1872–1951)

Shidehara Kijuro was born into a wealthy landlord family on August 11, 1872, in Osaka. He graduated from Tokyo University in 1895 with a degree in law. After passing the foreign service examination, he served in consulates in Korea, London, and Antwerp. In 1903, he married Iwasaki Masako, daughter of the head of Mitsubishi. In 1904, Shidehara entered the Foreign Ministry Office in Tokyo, where he served until 1911. In 1914, he was posted to Holland as Envoy Extraordinary and Minister Plenipotentiary. By 1915, Shidehara was appointed Vice Minister of Foreign Affairs, serving

Prime Minister Baron Shidehara Kijuro studies reports of election returns in an evening paper at his Tokyo home on April 10, 1946, as Japan holds its first postwar election. (AP Photo/Charles P. Gorry)

until 1919 in that office under five different ministers.

In 1919, Shidehara was appointed ambassador to the United States. He was one of Japan's delegates to the Washington Conference of 1921–1922. Although the main focus of the conference was naval disarmament, Shidehara arranged for the return of Shantung province to China and a reduction in Sino-Japanese tensions. He resigned in 1922 because of ill health but recovered enough to be appointed Foreign Minister in the Kato Takaaki cabinet in 1924. His diplomacy pursued friendly relations with Great Britain and the United States, while continuing a cooperative policy toward China.

Unlike other ministers, Shidehara avoided threats to use force in China but repeated a pledge to safeguard Japan's legitimate rights and interests. During the 1920s, he was under considerable pressure to approve military intervention in China. Although he refused, Japan's Kwantung Army in Manchuria sometimes acted on its own. At the Beijing Customs Conference during 1925–1926, Shidehara surprised foreign observers by immediately agreeing in principle to all of China's demands for tariff autonomy. He later pointed to this reasonable attitude with pride.

Shidehara served as Foreign Minister from 1924 to 1927 in two different cabinets. He fell from power in 1927 because he refused to allow Japanese gunboats to bombard Nanjing in retaliation for Chinese attacks on foreigners. When he returned as foreign minister in 1929, Shidehara continued to follow his hands-off policy toward China. In November 1930, Prime Minister Hamaguchi Osachi was seriously wounded by an assassin. Shidehara served as interim Prime Minister for four months. His failure to prevent the Kwantung Army from occupying all of Manchuria in September 1931 resulted in his removal from office. Between 1931 and 1945, Shidehara was in semi-retirement.

In October 1945, Shidehara became Japan's second postwar Prime Minister, replacing Higashikuni Naruhiko. He was selected because of his perceived pro-American attitude and because he had opposed the military intervention in China. He was ordered by the General Headquarters of the occupation forces to make reforms. Shidehara was most concerned with assuring that the emperor system survived in Japan. He encouraged Emperor Hirohito to publicly deny that he was divine. He also claimed to be the author of Article 9 of the 1947 Japanese constitution that outlawed war and vowed that Japan would never maintain armed forces. Evidence from others, including General Douglas MacArthur, supports Shidehara's claims.

Shidehara was the nominal head of the Nihon Shimpoto (Japanese Progressive Party). In Japan's first postwar election, in April 1946, he was defeated. He and his cabinet resigned in May. He was appointed state minister in the Yoshida Shigeru cabinet that succeeded his own. In the general election of 1947, Shidehara was elected to the Diet. After being reelected in 1949, he became speaker of the Lower House, holding that position until he died on March 10, 1951.

*Tim Watts*

**See also:** Kwantung Army Adventurism; MacArthur, Douglas; Washington Naval Conference; World War I; Yoshida Shigeru.

## Further Reading

Bamba, Nobuya. *Japanese Diplomacy in a Dilemma: New Light on Japan's China Policy, 1924–1929.* Vancouver: University of British Columbia Press, 1972.

Burns, Richard Dean, and Edward M. Bennett, eds. *Diplomats in Crisis: United States–Chinese–Japanese Relations, 1919–1941.* Santa Barbara, CA: ABC-CLIO, 1974.

Iriye, Akira. *After Imperialism: The Search for a New Order in the Far East, 1921–1931.* Chicago: Imprint Publications, 1990.

# Shimabara Rebellion (1637–1638)

Shimabara is a small peninsula in southwest Kyushu. In 1637–1638, peasant farmers in Shimabara and Amakusa, led by former samurai and accompanied by commoners, engaged in a revolt against local officials. Because both Shimabara and Amakusa had been led by samurai converts to Catholicism from the Arima and Konishi families, the area was home to a significant number of Christians. The incident, therefore, has often been viewed as a Christian rebellion. Most scholars today agree that the rebellion was not necessarily waged as a religious revolt. Rather, it broke out as a result of frustration with the economic oppression of the local overlords and the cruelty they meted out to the commoners.

Because these were remote areas of Japan, oppressed Christians from other areas sought refuge in Shimabara, adding more Christians to the already sizable numbers of believers. While they obviously worked to keep from being sought out based on their faith, their complaints were more basic. The Matsukura family took over Shimabara in 1614 and began the persecution of Christians. In addition, the *daimyō* took on massive work projects in the area to gain favor with the shōgun, for which he taxed the population beyond their ability to pay. Neighboring Amakusa suffered much the same fate, perpetuated by the anti-Christian *daimyō* Katakaka Terusawa.

The incident that sparked the overt rebellion came when an outraged father killed one of the *daimyō*'s henchmen who was torturing his daughter. The villagers rose up, and thus began a major assault on the shōgunal power in Japan by both Shimabara and Amakusa. A number of former samurai, many of whom were Christian, took on leadership positions and led the revolt. The local magistrates were unable to quell the rebels. The shōgun sent a commissioner to check out the problem, and the *bakufu*'s accompanying army was unsuccessful in quelling the rebellion.

Realizing profound shame in defeat, the shōgun then sent 120,000 men to defeat some 27,000 rebels, many of them women and children. When the rebels moved into the Hara Castle, surrounded on three sides by the sea, they held out there for 90 days. Eighty percent of the population in Shimabara and Asakusa took part in this standoff. Finally, the *bakufu* troops stormed the castle, killing all the survivors, including women and children. The shōgun's government lost 1,992 in death, and 10,656 wounded. The numbers of rebels killed is not clear but estimates range from 20,000 to 37,000, not counting women and children.

The length and the strength of the rebellion challenged the Tokugawa *bakufu* in a way it had not yet experienced. While Christianity was clearly an element of the rebellion, much more serious was the abusive nature of the *bakufu* leadership in both Amakusa and Shimabara. Also, slogans used by the rebels included Christian invocations, and their banners had recognizable Christian symbols. Yet underneath it all, the driving force was that the people were less and less able to survive crop failures beginning in the years after 1634, along with the increased taxation leveled by Matsukura. Those who failed to pay the additional taxes were subjected to torture and death; women, such as wives and daughters of rebels, faced humiliation and sale to brothels. It is clear that

Christianity was not the primary spark that started the rebellion, and this is the stance of most historians.

Yet, as a result of the Shimabara Rebellion, the last proscription against Christians was proclaimed by the government. These measures included the closing of Japan to all Westerners, with the exception of the Dutch, who were relegated to Deshima, a man-made isle off the shore of Nagasaki. Koreans and Chinese were allowed limited access. The ban against Christianity remained in effect officially until 1890, but in actual practice, until 1873.

*Ann M. Harrington*

**See also:** Dutch on Deshima; Tokugawa *Bakufu* Political System.

**Further Reading**

Boxer, C. R. *The Christian Century in Japan 1549–1650*. Berkeley, CA: University of California Press, 1951.

Elison, George. *Deus Destroyed: The Image of Christianity in Early Modern Japan*. Cambridge, MA: Harvard University Press, 1973.

Fujita, Neil S. *Japan's Encounter with Christianity: The Catholic Mission in Premodern Japan*. New York: Paulist Press, 1991.

Ward, Haruko Nawata. *Women Religious Leaders in Japan's Christian Century, 1549–1650*. Burlington, VT: Ashgate, 2009.

## Shimoda Treaty (1858)

After two years of desultory negotiations, United States Consul to Japan Townsend Harris finally managed to conclude a Treaty of Amity and Commerce between the two countries. Also often called the Harris Treaty, this diplomatic pact was the basis of the so-called Unequal Treaties (also called the Ansei Treaties, after the Japanese reign name). Commodore Matthew Perry had forced Japan to sign the first American treaty (Kanagawa) with Japan in 1854, and a prior Shimoda Treaty had been signed between Japan and Russia a year later.

Although isolated in a ruined rustic temple (Ryōsen-ji) in the remote Shimoda Peninsula, Harris had used the threat of impending European invasion to force the Tokugawa *bakufu* into signing the treaty. Under constant threat from antiforeign samurai (his Dutch interpreter Henry Heusken was later assassinated), Harris persevered for almost two years by reminding the Japanese what had happened to China a decade earlier during the so-called Opium Wars.

The main import of the treaty was that the additional Japanese ports of Edo (later changed to nearby Yokohama) and Osaka (later moved to Kobe) were opened to American trade and residence. The 1858 treaty contained the basic clauses that bound Japan into a hopelessly inferior position vis-à-vis to the 17 foreign nations that made up the basis of the so-called Unequal Treaties between 1858 and 1894. Modeled after the same group of treaties forced on China after 1842, the treaties contained six interlocking clauses that constrained the sovereignty of China and Japan (see the "Unequal Treaties" article for particulars): most-favored nation; extraterritoriality; no termination date or provision for revision; a scheduled (or conventional) import tariff restriction; unilateral; and treaty ports.

*Louis G. Perez*

**See also:** Heusken, Henry; Perry, Matthew; Tokugawa *Bakufu* Political System; Unequal Treaties.

**Further Reading**

Griffis, William Elliott. *Townsend Harris: First American Envoy in Japan*. Cambridge, MA: Cambridge University Press, 1895.

McMaster, John. "Alcock and Harris, Foreign Diplomacy in Bakumatsu Japan." *Monunmenta Nipponica* 22, nos. 3–4 (1967): 305–367.

## Shimonoseki, Bombardment of (1863–1864)

Shortly after the Tokugawa *bakufu* signed the initial "Unequal Treaties" with the United States and other Western nations, Chōshū han fired on Western ships as they sailed through the narrow straits at Shimonoseki. Chōshū had chosen to obey the Komei Emperor's order to "oust the barbarians," despite the fact that the *bakufu* and all other han ignored the order.

The Americans responded to this attack a few days later by shelling the coastal batteries on July 16, 1863, wounding three dozen Japanese and sinking two Chōshū ships. The French sent two ships a few weeks later and completely destroyed the small fishing village at the straits. The straits were then closed to Western ships through mid-1864 while the Americans, Dutch, and French sought reparations from the *bakufu*. The *bakufu* showed itself to be almost powerless against Chōshū, but was unwilling to pay reparations.

A new round of shelling started in July 1864. Finally, the Americans, British, Dutch, and French tired of the *bakufu* stalling and the Chōshū shelling, so they sent a combined fleet of a dozen ships to Shimonoseki in August. A coordinated attack hit the straits on September 5 and continued through the next two days when the Chōshū forces surrendered. Despite being outgunned, the Chōshū batteries and soldiers did significant damage on the allied forces, killing or wounding 72 men and damaging two of the British ships. Because the Americans were involved in their own civil war, and the French had most of their ships in Mexico supporting the ill-fated Maximillian Affair, neither sent significant forces to conduct the raid.

The *bakufu* negotiated the payment of a huge ($3 million) indemnity to be paid by Chōshū, which ultimately was reduced when the *bakufu* agreed to sign another round of "Unequal treaties" that included a uniform 5 percent scheduled tariff restriction and a promise to open an additional port (Hyogo) to Western commerce.

The debacle forced the *bakufu* to mount a punitive expedition against Chōshū, which ended in somewhat of a draw. Chōshū had shown itself as a primary "loyalist" (pro-emperor) anti-Western han, which brought it some fame and support from other han. It also allowed those Chōshū samurai who were more pro-Western to come to the fore in domain politics. As in the case of the Western bombardment of Satsuma forces at Kagoshima a year earlier, the Chōshū samurai were very impressed with the military power of the Western nations and soon came to realize that if Japan was to remain independent, it needed to modernize its military. Several Chōshū men (Kido Takayoshi, Inoue Kaoru, and Itō Hirobumi) who were later to lead the loyalist imperial forces against the *bakufu* had their first experiences in war at this time. They would later form a united front with men like themselves from Satsuma against the *bakufu*.

*Louis G. Perez*

**See also:** Inoue Kaoru; Itō Hirobumi; Kagoshima, Bombardment of; Unequal Treaties.

### Further Reading

Satow, Ernest Mason. *A Diplomat in Japan.* New York: Stone Bridge Press, 2006.

Tsuzuki Keiroku. *An Episode from the Life of Count Inouye.* Cornell, NY: Cornell University Press, 2009.

## Shimonoseki, Treaty of

The Treaty of Shimonoseki terminated the First Sino-Japanese War (1894–1895). Prime Minister Itō Hirobumi for Japan and Viceroy Li Hongzhang for China signed the treaty on April 17, 1895, in Shimonoseki, Japan, and the formal exchange of treaties occurred on May 8, 1895, in Yantai (Chefoo), China.

China sent a succession of three delegations to Japan to terminate the war—two before the destruction of the Chinese fleet, and one afterward. Within a week after the fall of Lüshun (Port Arthur), on November 26, 1894, China sent its first delegation (composed of Gustav Detring, the Tianjin commissioner of customs, and Alexander Michie, a British journalist) bearing a letter from Li Hongzhang to Itō Hirobumi. Because they lacked proper diplomatic accreditation from the Chinese government, Itō refused to receive them.

In the two months intervening between the first and second missions, the strategic city of Haicheng, the gateway to the Manchurian plain, fell on December 13 and became the most bitterly contested city of the war. China launched five unsuccessful counterattacks, which continued into March 1895.

Within a month of the first mission, China began organizing the second mission, hiring former U.S. Secretary of State John Watson Foster as a special adviser to two commissioners, Zhang Yinhuan, a mid-ranking diplomat, and Shao Youlian, the governor of Taiwan who became famous during the war for offering a reward for each severed Japanese head received. Upon their arrival in Hiroshima on January 31, 1895, again the Japanese noted the lack of proper negotiating credentials, calling off negotiations on February 2. Japan demanded China send a ranking diplomat with plenipotentiary powers. In the

intervening month and a half before the departure of the third mission, Japan took Weihaiwei on February 12, 1895, destroying China's only modern naval force, and occupied the key Manchuria port at Yingkou on March 6.

In the third mission, China sent its premier diplomat and longstanding quasi-foreign minister, Viceroy Li Hongzhang. On March 19, 1895, he arrived in the port of Shimonoseki. Negotiations were conducted in English, which Itō and Li's adopted son and nephew, Li Jingfang, spoke fluently. Japan rejected China's request for an immediate armistice, but took the Pescadores, islands off Taiwan, on March 26. After negotiations on March 24, before the police could intervene, a Japanese youth, Koyama Toyotaro, fired a single shot into Li Hongzhang's palanquin, seriously wounding him an inch below his eye. Foster called the wound "the most effective shedding of blood on the Chinese side during the entire war" because the Japanese felt compelled to offer a three-week armistice in Manchuria. The armistice did not apply to the Pescadores or Taiwan.

Negotiations resumed on April 1 between Li Jingfang and Foreign Minister Mutsu Munemitsu, when Mutsu presented a draft treaty reflecting the interests of key groups within the government: the navy wanted Taiwan, the army demanded the Liaodong Peninsula, and the Ministry of Finance emphasized a large indemnity. The draft treaty demanded the opening of numerous new treaty ports located deep inland in China, an indemnity of 300 million tael, and the restructuring of Japan's treaties with China on European lines to make them unequal treaties. To ensure Chinese fulfillment of the terms, Japanese terms included a temporary but highly symbolic occupation of Mukden (Liaoyang), the ancestral home of the Qing

Dynasty as well as the naval base at Weihai-wei. The terms appalled the Chinese, who began leaking information to the foreign press in the hopes of precipitating a third-party intervention.

When China demurred, Japan threatened to march on Beijing. On April 10, for the first time since the assassination attempt, Viceroy Li met with Count Itō and did his best to ameliorate the terms. In the end, Japan achieved its original war aim to expel China from Korea. In addition, the Liaodong Peninsula up to the Korean border, Taiwan, and the Pescadore Islands all became direct additions to the Japanese empire. China agreed to renegotiate its treaties with Japan on the basis of juridical inequality, putting Japan in conformity with the Western powers in exercising extraterritoriality in China.

Japan moderated only certain secondary aims during the negotiations. It reduced the indemnity from 300 to 200 million Kuping taels, which still covered the costs of the war and funded a major postwar rearmament program. It reduced its territorial demands by decreasing China's permanent cession of territory in Manchuria from a broader band of territory going deeper inland to the area from the Korean border westward to the port of Yingkou and including the strategic Liaodong Peninsula with its key ports of Lüshun and Dalian. Japan also reduced the number of new treaty ports with the elimination of the first three of the following seven: Beijing; Xiangtan, Hunan; Wuzhou, Guangxi; Shashi, Hubei; Chongqing, Sichuan; Suzhou, Jiangsu; and Hangzhou, Zhejiang. With the elimination of Wuzhou and Xiangtan, Japan also reduced its demands for the opening of rivers to international steam navigation with the elimination of the first two of the following four: the West River from Canton to Wuzhou, the Xiang River and Lake Dongting from the Yangtze River to Xiangtan, the upper Yangtze River from Yichang to Chongqing, and the Wusong River and canal from Shanghai to Suzhou and Hangzhou.

To ensure Chinese ratification of the treaty and subsequent payment of the indemnity, Japan no longer demanded to continue the occupation of Mukden, but remained in temporary possession of Weihaiwei and afterward acquired a lien on Chinese customs revenues until full payment of the indemnity. Japan also refused to cease offensive operations until China ratified the treaty. Although Japan promised to end its activities upon the exchange of ratifications, the country's offensive operations on Taiwan—now Japanese territory—continued through October 20, followed by a year-long insurgency. The plenipotentiaries signed the Treaty of Shimonoseki on April 17, 1895.

The terms outraged Chinese officials at home. Both the Guangxu Emperor and the Empress Dowager attempted to distance themselves from the treaty. Japan's threat to continue the war until the formal exchange of ratifications pressured the reluctant Guangxu Emperor to ratify the treaty or be deposed. Upon the third mission's return, the opposition to ratification became so intense that Li sent Foster in his stead to Beijing to persuade members of the Grand Council. Most had never been seen by a foreign envoy before.

Chinese and Japanese diplomats exchanged ratified treaties at Yantai on May 8. Li Jingfang assumed the onerous responsibility of formally handing over Taiwan to Japan. On July 21, 1896, the Sino-Japanese Treaty of Commerce and Navigation fulfilled Japan's demand to end the era of reciprocal treaty relations between the two countries. The war transformed Japan from the object of imperialism into one of the perpetrators.

The Chinese government at the time and future generations of Chinese historians blamed Li Hongzhang for the debacle. He lost both titles and power. In fact, the outcome of the war reflected, on the most superficial level, incompetent Chinese military strategy. More fundamentally, it reflected a failure to make broad internal reforms to update China's internal institutions in combination with the growing Han disenchantment with Manchu minority rule expressed in internal rebellions, which prevented the Manchus from overturning hallowed Han traditions to do so. Japan did not so much win the war as China lost it. No diplomat, regardless of stature, could have reversed the military debacle in the field.

Li's attempt to encourage a third-party intervention bore fruit in the Triple Intervention of Germany, Russia, and France that overturned Article 2 of the treaty ceding the Liaodong Peninsula to Japan. China agreed to increase the indemnity by 30 million Kuping taels in return for the territory.

*S. C. M. Paine*

**See also:** Itō Hirobumi; Mutsu Munemitsu; Sino-Japanese War; Triple Intervention.

### Further Reading

Foster, John Watson. *Diplomatic Memoirs*, vol. 2. Boston: Houghton Mifflin, 1909.

Lensen, George Alexander. *Balance of Intrigue: International Rivalry in Korea and Manchuria, 1884–1899*. 2 vols. Tallahassee: University Presses of Florida, 1982.

Kajima Morinosuke. *The Diplomacy of Japan 1894–1922*, vol. 1. Tokyo: Kajima Institute of International Peace, 1976.

Mutsu Munemitsu. *Kenkenryoku: A Diplomatic Record of the Sino-Japanese War, 1894–95*, translated by Gordon Mark Berger. Princeton: Princeton University Press, 1982.

Paine, S. C. M.. *The Sino-Japanese War of 1894–1895: Perceptions, Power, and Primacy*. Cambridge, UK: Cambridge University Press, 2003.

## Shōen and Rise of Bushi

*Shōen* refers to the privately held estates or manors of the late classical and medieval eras. The earliest *shōen* date back to the land law of 711, before the start of the Heian period, when aristocrats, the landed gentry, and temples were first permitted to cultivate unused land at their own expense. It was important that application to cultivate unused land be made to the government in Nara; the government had the right to confiscate land that was improperly developed. In 723, owners were granted the right to pass on the land to their descendants to the third generation, and in 743 this right to pass on land was expanded to perpetuity. After 743, the state also permitted landowners the right to buy and sell such private lands. This system represented a great change from the *ritsu-ryō* system, under which all land was the property of the state. Laborers on the early *shōen* were employed and paid; they were either farmers looking to augment their income or vagrants who abandoned their fields elsewhere. Although these economic developments seem antithetical to the *ritsu-ryō* system of state control, the government received revenue from and exercised a level of administrative control over the *shōen*.

Most of these early *shōen* disappeared, most likely as a result of increases in land taxes that made them less profitable. This earlier *shōen* system was gradually supplanted by a more independent form of *shōen* between the 10th and 12th centuries. These later *shōen* were distinguished by their exemption from taxes and eventually from administrative and penal law. This status was the result of the widespread creation of vertical alliances between rich landowners and powerful members of the imperial court. In this so-called System of Commendation, the *shōen* landholders transferred their property rights to a powerful figure in the imperial court. In return for a portion of the income from the *shōen*, this figure would then protect the rights of the *shōen* and gain its exemption from taxes and laws. The tax owed to the government essentially was transferred to the courtier. The landholder maintained true control over the *shōen*, however. In this way, the *shōen* and the individuals living on them became virtually independent of the state, and government tax officials were effectively barred from even entering these estates' grounds.

A sharp increase in the number of *shōen* occurred after the adoption of this system, accompanied by a corresponding diffusion of power from Kyoto to the many *shōen* spread across the country. This trend signaled the gradual breakdown of the *ritsuryō* state system. Much of this corruption could be blamed on the efforts of the powerful Fujiwara clan to enrich themselves at the expense of the state. The Fujiwara family came to dominate the imperial court and the throne itself as regents (*kampaku*), a position they first gained in 858. By the end of the ninth century, their rule of the state could be described as a dictatorship, with the *kampaku* issuing decrees as the emperor would. As the Fujiwara dominated the court, they were naturally best candidates for the commendation of *shōen* property rights. The nobility did not just serve as tools to protect the *shōen*; powerful courtiers often were able to amass their own *shōen* as well, sometimes through outright seizure of the *shōen* to which they formally held the rights.

Militarily, the weakness of the state was paralleled by the deterioration of the *ritsuryō* system's peasant conscript army. Service in the imperial conscript army was generally devastating for the peasant conscript and his family. Peasants had to furnish their own weapons and supplies. Families were neither supported nor compensated by the government for the loss of the head of the household and chief breadwinner. This inefficient system was abandoned near the end of the eighth century due to peace between Japan and the Korean kingdom of Silla on the Korean Peninsula (where Japanese troops had intervened in the sixth century) and the Chinese Tang empire.

There still existed fighting on the frontiers of northern Honshu against the indigenous peoples of Japan, called Ainu or *Emishi*. Large-scale wars between the Japanese and the indigenous peoples occurred in the 11th century (the Earlier Nine Years' War and the Later Three Years' War), and troops were garrisoned to protect against continuous smaller-scale raids against villages and government posts. Maintaining these armies was expensive for the imperial government, particularly as its revenue was being bled out by the spread of the tax-exempt *shōen* system.

The conscript army in the north was eventually replaced by mounted warriors skilled in archery who came from the landowning clans. These private warriors were more well versed in the skills of fighting through hunting and protecting and expanding their lands. Moreover, they were effective against the indigenous peoples, having adapted their tactics of fighting while on horseback from the indigenous fighters themselves. As these warriors (*samurai* or *bushi*) were more effective than the conscript army, over time the government and its local officials came to be totally dependent on these *bushi* supplied by the landed gentry.

As needed, local governors and deputies in the north were granted special titles and empowered to raise armies from the local *bushi* for policing and punitive missions against the indigenous peoples and rebel *bushi*. These appointments and the resulting armed forces became regularized in some locales and even morphed into hereditary offices. It was such local officials who created the first retainer bands in the 10th century. A governor's retainers could be used as administrators and tax collectors in addition to their policing, security, and military functions. This practice was eventually copied by the more powerful landowners, who needed greater bands of men on a permanent basis to protect and manage the large expanses of *shōen* under their control. As these warriors continued in the service of the family of a landowner after his death, a system of permanent vassalage to the landowner's clan was instituted. Thus, as *shōen* spread across the country and the state simultaneously withdrew from providing for security, *shōen* landowners and local officials (who also owned *shōen*) came to accumulate bands of *bushi* retainers to protect and manage their territories and provide peace and order in the surrounding area.

Over time, these developments led to the rise of the warrior class. The provincial landowners and their *bushi*, with an emerging monopoly on the means of coercion, rose quickly in prominence in contrast to the nobility, the religious orders, and the peasants (though it must be noted that Buddhist sects maintained their own monk warriors (called *sōhei*). The Fujiwara clan, which dominated the imperial court, also owned great *shōen* and counted military leaders among their number, but they are not typically described as a warrior clan. They were more successful in manipulating court politics to achieve their goals. The two clans that overtook the Fujiwara and came to dominate late Heian Japan—the

Taira and Minamoto clans—came from the nascent warrior class. Both clans were descended from the imperial family, but grew powerful as land barons in the provinces separated from the imperial family.

The rebellions of two *bushi* from the Taira clan mark key points in the accession of the bushi. In the 10th century, the Taira family dominated the Kantō area. In 939, Taira no Masakado rebelled against the government, took control of several provinces in the Kantō area, and proclaimed a new independent government. The Fujiwara sent commanders from their clan, who had to ally with local warriors, including several of Masakado's Taira cousins, to put down the rebellion. A similar rebellion in the east by Taira no Tadatsune also drew the court to contract with local Taira rivals to fight as the government's representatives. They were unsuccessful, however, so the government turned to a Minamoto leader, Yorinobu, to put down the rebellion in 1031. Tadatsune held an obligation to Yorinobu from two decades ago and surrendered without a fight. The Minamoto clan began to gain influence from this point on, even drawing the allegiance of fighters from their future rivals, the Taira clan. The Taira and Minamoto would later fight for hegemony over Japan in the Gempei War (1180–1185), from which would emerge the first military dictatorship, the Kamakura shōgunate of the Minamoto clan (1192–1333).

While the idealized behavior of the *bushi* as described later in the code of conduct known as *bushidō* would not be developed until the medieval age, the rise of the *bushi* contains instances of such behavior, such as Tadatsune's surrender to Yorinobu.

*Philip Streich*

See also: Ainu, Military Resistance to, *Bushidō*; Fujiwara Family; Hogen-Heiji-Gempei Wars; *Ritsu-ryō*. Taira Masakado

## Further Reading

Farris, William Wayne. *Heavenly Warriors: The Evolution of Japan's Military, 500–1300*. Cambridge, MA: Harvard East Asian Monographs, 1992.

Friday, Karl. *Hired Swords: The Rise of Private Warrior Power in Early Japan*. Stanford, CA: Stanford University Press, 1992.

Morris, Dana. "Land and Society," in *The Cambridge History of Japan: Vol. 2, Heian Japan*, edited by D. Shively and W. McCullough. New York: Cambridge University Press, 1999:183–235.

Takeuchi Rizō. "The Rise of the Warriors," in *The Cambridge History of Japan: Vol. 2, Heian Japan*, edited by D. Shively and W. McCullough. New York: Cambridge University Press, 1999:644–709.

## Shōtoku Taishi (573–621 C.E.)

Shōtoku Taishi (literally "Prince Shōtoku") was an imperial prince and regent of Japan who lived during the Asuka period, which dates from the late sixth to the early seventh century. His given name was Umayado no ōji (literally "Prince of the stable door") because he was born next to a horse stable. He was the middle son of Emperor Yōmei (reign 585-587) and Princess Hashihoto no Anahobe.

Shōtoku's father, Emperor Yōmei, aided his son's political advancement, but it was predominantly Shōtoku's aunt, Empress Suiko (reign 592–628), who exerted the greatest influence on his career. Empress Suiko's official rule lasted until 628, but in 593 she appointed Shōtoku as regent, thereby making him head of state.

Shōtoku's family belonged to the Soga, a powerful clan during the Asuka period whose members promoted Buddhism, with the goal of making it a state religion. As a member of this clan, Shōtoku was educated in Chinese language, literature, culture, and religion, including Buddhism, Daoism, and Confucianism. This influence of Chinese culture had a lasting effect on Shōtoku's reign, especially in terms of government and religion.

Born at a time when ancient Japan was made up of warring clans, Shōtoku aimed at unifying the country under a centralized government. In 604, he announced a system of 12 new ranks among members of the court, with each rank being associated with a particular government office. This system was based on talent, loyalty, and service. In this way, Shōtoku combined Chinese bureaucracy with Japanese clan leadership. This measure was followed by Shōtoku's Seventeen-Article Constitution, which was promulgated in the same year. The unique aspect of this constitution was that it did not focus on laws and rules, but rather on Confucian virtues of moral human conduct to achieve good government. For example, the constitution instructed officials how to be righteous, distribute rewards and punishment, and respect superiors. In this way, it emphasized that harmony should be valued and disputes should be avoided, which was Shōtoku's successful attempt at developing a unified country.

In addition to politics, religion underwent a make-over under Shōtoku's reign, especially regarding the introduction and popularization of Buddhism. Shōtoku was a devout Buddhist who built 46 Buddhist temples in the vicinity of the capital of Nara. The most famous of these temples include Shitennōji in present-day Ōsaka and Hōryūji in Ikaruga, Nara Prefecture. Today Hōryūji is the oldest wooden building in the world and a world heritage site. Shōtoku built his temples with two aims in mind: to introduce Buddhism as a state religion to the Japanese, and to improve Japanese society as a whole through Buddhism. Therefore, temples were not solely places of worship, but also places that fostered the education and welfare of the people.

As part of Shōtoku's effort to promote a greater understanding of Buddhism among the Japanese (Japan's indigenous belief is Shintō), Chinese monks visited Japan and Japanese priests and students went to China to study. Shōtoku himself followed the Buddhist teachings and copied sutras. After his death in 621, he was deified as a Buddhist saint. Many images depict Shōtoku as a young boy with his hair tied up and his hands in prayer, indicating his understanding, popularization, and devotion to Buddhism.

*Monika Dix*

**See also:** Seventeen-Article Constitution.

**Further Reading**

Como, Michael A. *Shōtoku: Ethnicity, Ritual and Violence in the Japanese Buddhist Tradition*. New York: Oxford University Press, 2008.

Beasley, W. G. *The Japanese Experience: A Short History of Japan*. Berkeley: University of California Press, 1999.

Varley, H. Paul. *Japanese Culture: A Short History*. New York: Praeger Publishers, 1973.

# Shōwa Emperor (Hirohito) (1901–1989)

In Japan, Emperor Hirohito is commonly referred to as Emperor Shōwa. Born at the Aoyama Palace in Tokyo on April 29, 1901, as the oldest son of Emperor Taishō, he was named Hirohito by his grandfather the Emperor Meiji. His imperial title was Michinomiya. Hirohito was heir to the chronically ill and frail Emperor Taishō.

During a six-month period in 1921, Hirohito traveled in Europe, and his visit to Great Britain and his meeting with King George V profoundly shaped his view of constitutional monarchy.

On December 25, 1926, Hirohito ascended to the throne on the death of his father, ushering in the Shōwa period in Japanese history. His reign spanned more than six decades. The new emperor's close advisers included political moderates who desired close relations with Britain and the United States. They also hoped that Hirohito might reverse the decline in popular reverence for the imperial throne that had occurred in the Taishō period.

In his early years as emperor, Hirohito and his imperial entourage found Prime Minister Tanaka Giichi's hard-line China policy at best problematic. This was one reason why Hirohito harshly reprimanded the military officer-turned-politician over his response to the June 1928 assassination of Zhang Zuolin in Manchuria. When Tanaka's successor Hamaguchi Osachi was placed in a politically untenable position over the 1930 London Naval Disarmament Treaty, Hirohito did voice unequivocal support for cooperation with Britain and the United States and threw his support behind the beleaguered prime minister. Although these actions no doubt illustrated Hirohito's desire for peace, they inexorably enmeshed him in the rough-and-tumble political process and made his entourage vulnerable to attack by hard-liners.

These experiences in the early years of his reign and his observations of European governments led Hirohito to conclude that he must defer to cabinet decisions. On the basis of this particular understanding of his constitutional function, Hirohito chose, despite personal reservations, to accept policies presented to him by the cabinet at key historical junctures, such as the outbreak of the military conflict with China in 1937 and the attack on Pearl Harbor.

Hirohito rendered an independent political judgment only twice: (1) when the cabinet was unable to act effectively on the attempted coup by army junior officers on February 26, 1936, and (2) when Japan accepted the Potsdam Declaration, when he called on the Japanese people to surrender at the end of World War II. Such studied self-restraint did not make him a hapless stooge. As head of state under the Meiji constitutional system, Hirohito often expressed his concerns and opinions to those who made policy recommendations to him, but he usually upheld the cabinet's decision.

After the war, some Western historians alleged that Hirohito had been sympathetic to Japanese expansionist policies, but the available documentation largely contradicts this view. During the war, Hirohito's role as commander in chief became more pronounced, but his reprimands and exhortations to the military during the conflict should be understood in their proper historical context. As a wartime head of state, he acted to try to win the war. Although threatened with military revolt, Hirohito decided to accept the Potsdam Declaration, risking a possible coup d'état when he made the decision to surrender.

In the new postwar Japanese constitution, the emperor became the symbol of the nation. In keeping with the new constitutional principle of popular sovereignty, the emperor carried out certain ceremonial duties with the advice and approval of the cabinet. In 1971, Hirohito traveled to Europe, and in 1975 he went to the United States. Hirohito died in Tokyo on January 7, 1989.

*Kurosawa Fumitaka*

**See also:** February 26 Incident; London Naval Conference; Meiji Emperor; Pearl Harbor, Attack on; Potsdam Declaration; Taishō Emperor; Tanaka Giichi; Zhang Zuolin.

## Further Reading

Bix, Herbert P. *Hirohito and the Making of Modern Japan*. London: Duckworth, 2001.

Kawahara, Toshiaki. *Hirohito and His Times: A Japanese Perspective*. New York: Kodansha, 1990.

Large, Stephen S. *Emperor Hirohito and Shōwa Japan: A Political Biography*. London/New York: Routledge, 1992.

Wetzler, Peter. *Hirohito and War: Imperial Tradition and Military Decision Making in Prewar Japan*. Honolulu: University of Hawaii Press, 1998.

## Shōwa Restoration

A vaguely defined political slogan, the "Shōwa Restoration" was the professed goal of the Young Officer Movement's rebellion in the February 26 Incident of 1936. The central tenet of the ideology undergirding calls for a Shōwa Restoration was the belief that the Meiji Restoration of 1868, in which the Meiji Emperor was "restored" to his rightful place as sovereign over the Japanese people, had yet to be completed or had been derailed. In either case, it was the emperor's advisers—or so the belief went—who were responsible for the need for imperial restoration due to their usurpation of the throne's power. Restoration proponents believed that these advisers forced the emperor to consent to policies that were enacted merely to benefit their own interests, not those of the Japanese people.

This belief in the necessity for continuing the Meiji Restoration had been voiced as early as the 1870s, most notably around the time of the Satsuma Rebellion, and continued sporadically into the Taishō period. Radical rightists in the late 1920s began employing the term "Shōwa Restoration" in their rhetoric against Japan's adoption of Western capitalism and liberalism and in their argument for unifying the nation under the Shōwa Emperor.

The Young Officer Movement was the strongest advocate, in both rhetoric and actions, of a Shōwa Restoration. Beginning in the Military Academy in Tokyo in the 1920s, the Young Officer Movement sought the political and social reconstruction of Japan. Ideologically, proponents of this view were most influenced by ultranationalist philosopher Kita Ikki and his *Basic Plan for National Reorganization*. Included in Kita's *Plan* were curbs on personal and corporate wealth and a limited nationalization of property. According to the Young Officers, the emperor, following a coup in which he would reclaim his place as the "people's emperor," would lead the reform efforts. In their scheme, the Young Officers sought to create a Japan with less social inequality by ridding it of the powerful "privileged classes," including such groups as party politicians, industrialists, and senior military officers. In carrying out this plan, the Young Officers believed that they would be the successors of the low-ranking samurai of the Bakumatsu era. Just as the patriotic lower samurai of the 1860s toppled the Tokugawa shōgunate, so the Young Officers would purge the corrupt advisers surrounding the throne in the 1930s. While Kita influenced the Young Officers, it would be a mistake to say that he offered them a Shōwa Restoration plan of action that they followed in February 1936.

In the early morning of February 26, 1936, members of the Young Officer Movement attempted to enact a Shōwa Restoration by leading their army units in a takeover of central Tokyo. They hoped that the emperor would endorse their rebellion and that army reformers, spurred into action, would carry out the restoration. After occupying important government buildings and sending assassination squads to the residences of prominent members of the government, the leaders of the movement presented their "Manifesto to the Uprising" to army leaders. In this prepared statement, the Young Officers called on the war minister to carry out a Shōwa Restoration, but they failed to offer concrete steps as to how this goal was to be achieved, other than by removing the "evil advisers" of the emperor.

Civilian sympathizers met during the rebellion to enlist public support by publishing the *Shōwa Restoration Bulletin*. The publication relayed news of the uprising in the capital and requested people to call on the emperor to proclaim a Shōwa Restoration. This civilian effort failed, however, in part because the bulletins were mailed and reached recipients after the rebellion had ended.

For his part, the emperor did not support either the rebels or their call for his restoration. The emperor branded the Young Officers "mutineers" and ordered the rebellion to be put down. The dream of a Shōwa Restoration was quashed by the Shōwa Emperor himself.

*Rustin Gates*

**See also:** February 26 Incident; Kita Ikki; Shōwa Emperor (Hirohito); Young Officer Movement.

**Further Reading**

Najita, Tetsuo. *Japan: The Intellectual Foundations of Modern Japanese Politics.* Chicago: University of Chicago Press, 1980.

Shillony, Ben-Ami. *Revolt in Japan: The Young Officers and the February 26, 1936 Incident.* Princeton, NJ: Princeton University Press, 1973.

## Siberian Intervention

Following the Russian Revolution of 1917, Russia entered a period of civil war that lasted until the founding of the Soviet Union in 1922. The main forces invoved in this unrest were the Red Army of the Bolshevik revolutionaries, who were pitted against the counter-revolutionaries or "White Russians," ranging from moderate socialists (Mensheviki) to conservatives advocating the restoration of the tsarist regime. In these conflicts, counter-revolutionary forces were supported by foreign troops. In northern Russia and on the Crimean front, French and British troops intervened on the side of counter-revolutionary forces. In the Far East, a multinational force was dispatched to the city of Vladivostok. The bulk of these troops consisted of units of the Japanese Imperial Army; the commander of the international force was a Japanese general.

The notion of military intervention during the Russian civil war had first been put forth by the French Marshal Ferdinand Foch. He had suggested occupying sections of the Trans-Siberian Railroad to prevent the Bolsheviks from reaching Vladivostok, where large amounts of ammunition were stored during World War I. Moreover, a body of Czech nationals and former prisoners of war from the army of the Austro-Hungarian Empire had organized themselves into the Czech Legion, a formidable military force that had become a major factor in the civil war in Siberia. Foch argued that these troops had to be guaranteed passage out of Siberia before being redeployed on the battlefields of Western Europe.

As a result of the military situation in Russia, it was clear that Japan and the United States would share most of the burden of any military intervention. In August 1918, the two governments signed an agreement stipulating that both states would send a military force of 7,000 men to Vladivostok, but would refrain from larger military adventures and from attempts to colonize the region. While the United States restricted the zone of military engagement largely to the city of Vladivostok and its surroundings, the Japanese Army, without approval from the government in Tokyo, increased its forces in Eastern Siberia by the end of 1918 to 72,000 men and enlarged the area of engagement along the Trans-Siberian Railroad as far to the west as the Transbaikal region and the Baikal Sea. For decades, the Japanese army had been a strong advocate of expansion to the north, and its actions were now supported by a group of pro-interventionists in the Foreign Ministry, as well as in the business sector and the media.

A leading force in shaping Japanese public opinion were the "Nine Doctors," a group of nine academics under the leadership of Professor Tomizu Hirondo from Tokyo Imperial University. Tomizu had been given the nickname "Professor Baikal," since, as early as 1905, following the Russo-Japanese War, he had asserted that Russia would have to cede all of its Far Eastern possessions as far to the west as Lake Baikal. In 1918, Tomizu and other academics published a book titled *Arguing in Favor of Intervention* (*Shuppei-ron*), about the need for Japan to occupy these territories. Apart from creating a safety zone between Japan and Russia, Tomizu suggested the Japanese occupation would counter the danger of possible attacks on Japan by German Zeppelins and U-boats using Vladivostok as a military base.

Thus, in late 1918, Japanese troops occupied large regions of Eastern Siberia and the Russian Far East. They remained in place until late 1922, and in the north of Sakhalin until 1925. This was Japan's largest military commitment between the Russo-Japanese War and World War II. Japan not only occupied Russia's Far Eastern and Eastern Siberian territories, but also attempted to turn these territories into a part of Japan's informal empire as a buffer state. However, anti-Bolshevik governments supported by Japan—such as those of Admiral Aleksandr Kolchak (1874–1920) and Ataman Grigory Semyonov (sometimes spelled Semenov; 1890–1946), collapsed one by one under the attacks of Bolshevik partisan forces. The American Expeditionary Force under the command of Major General William Graves retreated in 1920 in response to the deteriorating situation. In late 1920, a short-lived Far Eastern Republic was founded—under Bolshevik auspices—and its merging with Russia marked the foundation of the Soviet Union in 1922.

For Japan, the Siberian Intervention was a disaster. Indeed, it has been dubbed "Japan's Vietnam" by Japanese historians such as Wada Haruki, due to the character of the military engagement, which was largely a war of Japanese regular troops against partisan forces. This resistance against Japanese intrusion also has to be seen in the larger context of resistance against Japanese colonialist-imperialist expansion in East Asia, with almost simultaneous insurgencies against Japanese colonial rule in Korea and Japanese expansion into China. The intervention caused strong anti-Japanese feelings in the Soviet Union and became a burden for Japanese-Soviet relations in the years to come.

*Sven Saaler*

**See also:** Russo-Japanese War.

### Further Reading

Graves, William S. *America's Siberian Adventure*. Cape & Smith, 1931. Available at: http://www.marxists.org/archive/graves/1931/siberian-adventure/index.htm.

Ôtani Masao. *Shuppei-ron* [On Intervention]. Tokyo: Minyûsha, 1918.

White, John Albert. *The Siberian Intervention*. Princeton, NJ: Princeton University Press, 1950.

## Siemens-Vickers Scandal (1914)

In January 1914, Karl Richter, a German expatriate working for the German construction company Siemens in Tokyo, sold some stolen documents to the international news service Reuters. The internal company documents indicated that Siemens had been paying bribes to Japanese Navy authorities in return for a virtual monopoly over naval construction contracts. After Reuters published the documents, a number of Japanese newspapers started their own investigations, which turned up the names of several Japanese naval personnel who had accepted bribes. Additionally, it was discovered that the British company Vickers had paid naval authorities for the contract to build the Japanese cruiser *Kongō*.

The ensuing scandal gripped the imagination of Japan for more than a month, resulting in huge public demonstrations in Tokyo in early February. Both houses of the Japanese Diet then refused to pass the 1914 Navy budget pending further investigation. The scandal hit the government of Prime Minister Admiral Yamamoto Gonnohyōe, who was also concurrently Navy Minister. He was forced to resign in disgrace a month later.

In May, a naval court-martial reduced the Russo-Japanese War hero Yamamoto in rank (as well as his predecessor Admiral Saitō Makoto) and sentenced several naval procurement department bureaucrats to prison. Ironically, when World War I broke out in August 1914, Vickers was quietly allowed to finish the *Kongō* and the imprisoned naval authorities were quietly pardoned.

The scandal seriously damaged the heretofore pristine reputation of Japan's military. The "selfless and patriotic" military had already been besmirched as part of the Taishō political crisis two years before. Two decades later the so-called Young Officer Movement (especially the Imperial Way faction) would cite this scandal as part of its argument that the elder leadership of the army and navy had been corrupted by the *Zaibatsu* economic cliques.

*Louis G. Perez*

**See also:** Russo-Japanese War; Yamamoto Gonnohyōe; Young Officer Movement.

**Further Reading**

Haley, John Owen. *The Spirit of Japanese Law.* Athens, GA: University of Georgia Press, 1998.

Hoare, J. E. *Britain and Japan: Biographical Portraits, Vol. III.* London: Routledge Curzon, 1999.

# Singapore, Battle for (February 8–15, 1942)

Throughout the 1930s, British governments neglected Pacific defenses, as budgetary constraints forced retrenchment. Moreover, from 1939 onward, fighting in Europe and North Africa was Britain's priority, diverting additional men and resources from the Far East, where Singapore was complacently considered impregnable.

The Japanese plan for attacking the British colony called for an approach to Singapore from the north by land. The British had designed Singapore's defenses primarily to meet a seaborne attack. Although some of the big guns were capable of firing against land targets, they lacked the high-explosive shells for use against attacking troops.

The drive on Singapore began with the Japanese invasion of northern Malaya on December 8, 1941. By January 15, 1942, the British III Corps of the 8th and 11th Indian Divisions had been forced back to the defensive line in Johore, which was held by the 8th Australian Division. By the end of January, the Japanese had driven British forces back across the Straits of Johore into a defensive position on Singapore Island.

The Straits of Johore protected the northern and western shores of Singapore Island. The straits varied in width from 600 to 2,000 yards and were crossed only by a 70-foot-wide causeway that the British cut but could not destroy. Singapore island was largely covered by jungle growth and plantations that sharply limited observation and fields of fire. Save for several towns, the population was concentrated on the southeast coast in Singapore Town, a city of 1 million. The key location around Bukit Timah village in the center of the island contained a large depot of military stores and the three reservoirs for the island's water supply.

Lieutenant General Arthur E. Percival commanded 85,000 defending troops. Japanese commander Lieutenant General Yamashita Tomoyuki had only 30,000 men of the 25th Army. Although the attackers were short of ammunition and other supplies, their aircraft dominated the skies. Percival deployed the bulk of his troops too far forward, defending 30 miles of front to make his stand on the island's beaches. Most of the men were poorly trained, and all were exhausted and dispirited after weeks of battle and defeat. Moreover, they had been outfought by a battle-hardened enemy skilled in infiltration and tactics suitable for the jungle terrain. The defending force of Indians (now consolidated into the 11th Division) and the 8th Australian Division had been reinforced on January 29 by the 11th British Division and, a few days earlier, by the partially trained 44th Indian Brigade. The only other troops were fortress troops, with two Malayan brigades and volunteers. All but one of the island airfields were within reach of Japanese artillery fire, and the few remaining fighter aircraft were thus redeployed to Sumatra, from which they could provide only limited air support. Yamashita planned to throw the British off balance by feinting east of the causeway and making his major attack to the west of it.

On the morning of February 8, the Japanese attacked. Two divisions crossed in landing craft against the Australian 22nd Brigade west of the Kranji River. Although the Australians sank many landing craft, they were too thin on the ground to hold the line. By the next morning, the Japanese had taken Ama Keng and were attacking Tengah Airfield. The defenders then withdrew to establish a line on the narrow neck of land between the Kranji and Jurong Rivers. Meanwhile, on the evening of February 9, the Japanese successfully attacked the 27th Australian Brigade, creating a gap between the brigade and the Kranji-Jurong line. The Japanese soon bypassed that line, which was never properly prepared or occupied by the defenders. A British counterattack attempting to restore the position failed.

By February 11, the Japanese had seized and repaired the causeway, allowing them to send additional resources, including tanks, onto the island and advance toward Nee Soon village. On February 12, Percival ordered a withdrawal to a perimeter marked by Bukit Timah road, MacRitchie and Pierce reservoirs, and Paya Lebar-Kallang. Heavy fighting began south of Bukit Timah road on February 13, where for 48 hours the Australians held off the attackers, and along Pasir Pajang ridge, where Malayan forces stubbornly repulsed the Japanese. On February 14, however, the defenders were forced back to what proved to be their final line.

London had ordered Percival to continue the fight and not surrender. However, conditions in the city were shocking, with dead and dying in the streets and loss of the water supply imminent. Reserves of food and ammunition for the troops had been seriously depleted by loss of the depots. Meanwhile, the British evacuated certain key personnel by sea who were essential to the later war effort, and demolitions destroyed heavy guns, aviation fuel, bombs, and other equipment. Many of Percival's troops simply deserted, including the engineers who were to destroy the naval dockyard.

When it was clear that nothing was to be gained by further resistance, on February 14 Prime Minister Winston Churchill authorized Percival to surrender. Percival also had the welfare of civilians to consider when on February 15 he surrendered his 70,000 troops unconditionally to Yamashita. The Japanese had taken Malaya and Singapore in only 70 days. The loss of Singapore was the greatest defeat of British forces since the 1781 Battle of Yorktown, and it had immense repercussions for British prestige in Asia.

*Philip L. Bolté*

**See also:** Malaya Campaign; World War II, Continental Theater.

## Further Reading

Allen, Lous. *Singapore, 1941–1942*. Newark: University of Delaware Press, 1977.

Brooke, Geoffrey. *Singapore's Dunkirk*. London: Cooper, 1989.

Warren, Alan. *Singapore, 1942: Britain's Greatest Defeat*. New York: Hambledon, 2002.

## Sino-Japanese War (1894–1895)

The First Sino-Japanese War began with a Japanese naval attack on Chinese troop transports on July 25, 1894, and ended with the signing of the Treaty of Shimonoseki on April 17, 1895, and the formal exchange of treaties on May 8, 1895, at Yantai. It resulted in the reversal of the traditional East Asian balance of power, with the transformation of Japan into an internationally recognized power at China's expense.

The original battle for dominance in Korea escalated to effectively eliminate Chinese sea power for the next century, create the beginnings of a Japanese empire with the Chinese cession of Taiwan and the Pescadores, and undermine Koreans' sovereignty over their peninsula. The war marked the beginning of a Russo-Japanese competition for empire on the Asia mainland that lasted until the end of World War II.

Japan had responded to the Industrial Revolution by both modernizing its technological capabilities and Westernizing its civil and military institutions, whereas China had focused narrowly on acquiring modern armaments. Japanese leaders believed their national security depended on containing Russian expansion in Asia and creating a Japanese empire on a par with those of the great Western powers. Russia's announcement in 1891 of its plan to build a trans-Siberian railway threatened these ambitions. Changes in the regional balance of power and Russo-Japanese rivalries were the underlying causes of the war. Escalating instability in Korea, including the massive Tonghak peasant rebellion and infighting within the royal house of the Yi dynasty, represented the proximate cause. When the king of Korea requested Chinese military aid, Japan sent troops, too.

Chinese soldiers raise their hands in surrender to armed Japanese soldiers in September 1938. (Hulton-Deutsch Collection/Corbis)

Japan completed the domestic phase of its modernization program with the conclusion of treaty revision with Britain on July 16, 1894, on the basis of juridical equality. Nine days later, Japan fired the opening shots of the First Sino-Japanese War, beginning the foreign policy phase of the conflict. This war would be the first of three that sought to contain Russia and stake out the Japanese empire—the other two wars were the Russo-Japanese War and the Second Sino-Japanese War.

China and Japan both possessed state-of-the-art navies, which experts considered roughly comparable. Although Japan had faster ships, China's two largest battleships had gun ranges and armor that should have made them unsinkable by Japan's navy. China, however, lacked a modern army under unified command. Unlike Japan, China's army had no hospital, commissariat, or engineering divisions. Also, many of its soldiers lacked rifles, whereas Japanese soldiers had a standard kit and thorough training.

Although China tried to avoid war, on July 25, 1894, Japan attacked three Chinese naval ships off Seoul near Feng Island and later that day sank *Kowshing*, a British-owned but Chinese-leased troop transport. Japanese soldiers then fought Chinese forces south of Seoul, winning at Sŏnghwan on July 29. Both countries formally declared war on 1 August.

China lost the war by ceding the initiative to Japan and failing to coordinate its land and naval forces. Two pairs of key battles determined the outcome, followed by a coda in Taiwan and a Triple Intervention that determined the postwar territorial settlement. Fighting concentrated in four theaters: Korea, Manchuria, Shandong, and Taiwan.

It took a month and a half for both sides to build up their forces. Then, in a three-day period in mid-September 1894, in the first pair of key battles, Japan defeated China decisively on land and sea, accomplishing its original objective of ejecting China from Korea. On September 16, Japan overran China's prepared positions at P'yŏngyang after China failed to contest Japan's dangerous river crossing or attack its vulnerable supply lines. Chinese forces then fled all the way to Manchuria, ceding Korea to Japan.

On September 17, the Japanese navy sought out the Chinese fleet, sinking four Chinese vessels near the mouth of the Yalu River without losing any ships. Again Chinese forces ceded the initiative and never again crossed the Weihaiwei-Yalu line, allowing Japan to deploy and supply its troops at will. Had China targeted troop transports or supply ships, Japan would have been hard-pressed to continue fighting.

Hostilities then concentrated in Manchuria. On the Manchuria bank of the Yalu, during the Battle of Juliancheng, China again failed to contest the Japanese river crossing. On October 26, the city fell and Japanese forces pursued inland. On December 13, the strategic city of Haicheng fell but Chinese kept trying to retake it until March 2, 1895. Haicheng was the most bitterly contested city in the war because it linked the mountainous terrain in Korea with the Manchurian plain and ancestral lands of the Qing dynasty.

The second pair of key battles took place over the winter of 1894–1895 at Lüshun and Weihaiwei. China failed to contest the landing of Japanese troops on the Laiodong Peninsula, the location of China's main naval base at Lüshun (Port Arthur), which had the only facilities to repair capital ships. Japan took the narrow neck of the peninsula in the Battles of Jinzhou and Dalian on November 5–6 and 7–9, respectively. On November 21–22, Lüshun fell and a Japanese massacre of Chinese civilians ensued. In every other battle, Japanese forces meticulously followed the laws of war.

Meanwhile, Japan took China's second naval base at Weihaiwei during the the Shandong campaign by blockading the Chinese fleet in port, taking the city by land, and destroying the fleet trapped in port. On February 12, 1895, Weihaiwei fell, ending Chinese naval power for more than a century.

On February 20, Japan ordered its navy to take the Pescadore Islands off Taiwan; it occupied them on March 20. In the hard-fought Taiwan campaign, Japan took Taipei on June 6, Taizhong on August 26, and Tainan on October 21. On November 20, Japan declared victory, although guerrilla fighting persisted for a year.

China sued for peace after the fall of Lüshun as a delaying tactic while trying—unsuccessfully—to organize a European intervention. The inadequate negotiating credentials of China's emissaries made clear its purpose was delay not negotiations. In the time that Japan rejected China's first two diplomatic missions, Weiheiwei fell, costing China its navy. China's longstanding, quasi-foreign minister, Li Hongzhang, lead the properly accredited third mission. On March 19, he arrived in Japan; on April 17, he concluded the Treaty of Shimonoseki terminating the war. The Taiwan campaign coincided with these negotiations.

Although China ceded to Japan Taiwan, the Pescadores, and the Liaodong Peninsula, on April 23 Russia, Germany, and France organized the Triple Intervention, forcing Japan's return of Liaodong Peninsula in exchange for a larger indemnity from China. The intervening powers, particularly Russia, did not want Japanese troops in proximity to Beijing. The indemnity exceeded Japan's war costs and funded a massive postwar arms spending binge that prepared Japan to fight the Russo-Japanese War a decade later.

Russia feared a rising power on its vulnerable Siberian frontier and responded with an unprecedented postwar eastward focus of its foreign policy and infrastructure investments. Between 1896 and 1898, Russia acquired railway concessions in Manchuria larger than any other foreign concession in China. In 1898, Russia completed the humiliation of Japan by claiming the Liaodong Peninsula for itself. Japan would finally gain the peninsula in the Russo-Japanese War.

The Western powers interpreted China's uninterrupted losses in the battlefield as proof of its inability to reform and responded by creating alternative administrative structures to oversee their economic interests. The so-called Scramble for Concessions included Japanese domination of the Fujian province across from Taiwan, Russian domination of Manchuria, French domination of China's three southernmost provinces, German domination of Shandong, and British domination of the Yangtze River valley.

The war and the Scramble for Concessions had a far more profound impact on China than did the Opium Wars. The latter had involved small coastal forces, whereas Japanese troops had marched deep inland into the core lands of the ruling Manchus. Moreover, Japan's rejection of Sinification for Westernization and its uninterrupted military victories undermined the legitimacy not only of Manchu minority rule but also of the Confucian order itself, whose legitimacy was based on a superiority that China could no longer claim. The war ended China's Self-Strengthening Movement in failure and precipitated the equally unsuccessful Hundred Days' Reforms in 1898.

Japan became a recognized international power, as indicated by the Anglo-Japanese alliance of 1902, when Britain, the dominant superpower, negotiated its only long-term alliance between the Napoleonic Wars and World War I. Japan was the only non-Western rising power until China emerged to fill that role a century later. Victory in war legitimated the highly controversial Meiji reforms in an outpouring of nationalism.

Popular beliefs giving the military exclusive credit for Japan's success blinded the Japanese to the diplomatic prerequisites for successful war termination and began the fatal tilt in the distribution in political power at home from civil to military leaders. The Japanese also failed to recognize China's own contributions to its defeat. Had China practiced a sound military strategy of attacking Japan's vulnerable sea lines of communication and drawn Japanese troops inland, Japan could not have won the war at an acceptable cost. The outcome of the Russo-Japanese War a decade later reinforced these misconstrued lessons, when Japan fought another highly dysfunctional state.

*S. C. M. Paine*

**See also:** Russo-Japanese War; Shimonoseki, Treaty of; Triple Intervention; World War II.

### Further Reading

Eastlake, Warrington, and Yamada Yoshi-aki. *Heroic Japan: A History of the War between China and Japan.* 1897. Reprint, Washington, DC: University Publications of America, 1979.

Elleman, Bruce A. *Modern Chinese Warfare, 1795–1989.* London: Routledge, 2001.

Lone, Stewart. *Japan's First Modern War: Army and Society in the Conflict with China, 1894–95.* London: St. Martin's Press, 1994.

Oh, Bonnie Bongwan. *The Backgrouwnd of Chinese Policy Formation in the Sino-Japanese War of 1894–1895.* Ph.D. dissertation, University of Chicago, 1974.

Paine, S. C. M. *The Sino-Japanese War of 1894–1895: Perceptions, Power, and Primacy.* Cambridge, UK: Cambridge University Press, 2003.

## Sino-Japanese War (1937). *See* World War II, Continental Theater.

## Sino-Japanese War, Causes

At the time of the Sino-Japanese War of 1894–1895, the government of Japan claimed that the causes for its first "modern" war were primarily self-defense. It is clear from the personal and diplomatic correspondence of the country's leaders, however, that they were more interested in acquiring Korean and Chinese territory than in any other more altruistic motives. Japan had learned from Great Britain, Germany, France, Russia, and the other imperialist nations of the world that if Japan was to take its rightful place among the leaders in East Asia, it must acquire territory. Colonies would provide raw materials for Japan's industries as well as ready and secure markets for its manufactured goods.

Japan had already acquired the Ryukyu archipelago at the expense of China in the 1870s, but now it turned its attentions to Taiwan, Korea, and Manchuria. Those territories were possessions or client states of China. Japan had fished in these troubled waters for at least two decades. In 1873, it had only narrowly averted a punitive raid to Korea; a year later, it had dispatched another raid to punish the natives of Taiwan. In 1882, a Korean military mutiny had forced Japan to send warships to protect its citizens. Two years later, an attempted coup was mounted by a group of pro-Japanese Korean reformers. A group of Japanese sympathizers had provided aid and shelter for Koreans wishing to follow Japan's Meiji Restoration model for modernization. This bloody civil war was finally suppressed by resident Chinese troops, but not before a number of Japanese were killed or seriously wounded. That uprising had been settled diplomatically by the Tientsin Treaty (1885), which required both nations to notify the other when one intended to send troops to Korea.

In 1894, Kim Ok-kyun, a Korean reformer who had been a longtime resident of Japan, was murdered by Chinese agents in Shanghai. Kim's butchered body was paraded around China. Japan demanded an investigation and an apology because Kim had allegedly been killed in the Japanese settlement (he had been killed in a Japanese restaurant). The issue continued to fester.

A seemingly heaven-sent opportunity presented itself in 1894 when China notified Japan that it had been asked by Korea to send troops to help put down the native Tonghak Rebellion. It had been common practice for the Koreans to ask for Chinese help because they considered Korea to be part of China's Tributary System. Now Japan willfully misinterpreted the Treaty of Tientsin (it required only notification) by announcing that it, too, would send troops to protect Japanese citizens in Korea.

Prime Minister Itō Hirobumi and Foreign Minister Mutsu Munemitsu agreed that this was an excellent opportunity to take advantage of a political vacuum in the northeast. Most of Japan's political leadership agreed with them. Yamagata Aritomo had long advocated extending what he called the "Line of Sovereignty" (Japan's physical borders) outward to a "Line of Advantage" that included the mineral-rich Manchuria as well as Korea, which Otto von Bismarck allegedly had called "a dagger pointing at the heart of Japan." Another army leader,

Kawakami Soroku, had joined the Itō-Mutsu cabal, giving his whole-hearted support for a war with China. In a series of cabinet meetings Itō and Mutsu argued for "positive measures" in Korea. What they meant was eventual war. In his controversial memoirs (*Kenkenroku*) of the war, Mutsu stated:

> In the event a Sino-Japanese conflict occurred, we were determined to have the Chinese be the aggressors, while we ourselves assumed the position of the aggrieved party.

When Japan dispatched 2,800 troops to Korea, the Chinese, of course, resisted. They requested that the matter be referred to a third-party international referee. While Britain and Russia considered this request, the Japanese army precipitated hostilities in early June when it attacked the Korean royal palace, captured the king, and installed a pro-Japanese government in Seoul. This new Korean government demanded that China recall its troops.

In the meantime, Mutsu had asked his ambassador Ōtori Keisuke to avoid outright war while delicate negotiations to end the Unequal Treaties dragged to a conclusion in London. He feared that Great Britain might extort more concessions, or might even join the Russians in mediation. On the evening that he received telegraph notification that the treaty had been concluded on July 16, he cabled Ambassador Ōtori in Seoul that he could now take "whatever measures" were needed to begin the war. Ōtori and the army officers in Seoul decided on a naval confrontation to be followed quickly by army action.

On July 25, 1894, Japan stopped the British-owned but Chinese-leased ship *Kowshing* off Seoul near Feng Island.

When warned that the Japanese were about to board the ship to search for "war contraband," the British crew abandoned it, only moments before the Japanese fired on the ship and sunk it and the thousand Chinese troops aboard. A few days later, Japan attacked Chinese troops south of Seoul. Both countries formally declared war on August 1.

*Louis G. Perez*

**See also:** Itō Hirobumi; Kawakami Soroku; Mutsu Munemitsu; Russo-Japanese War; Taiwan Expedition; Unequal Treaties; Yamagata Aritomo.

### Further Reading

Lone, Stewart. *Japan's First Modern War: Army and Society in the Conflict with China, 1894–1895*. New York: St. Martin's Press, 1994.

Mutsu Munemitsu, *Kenkenroku: A Diplomatic Record of the Sino-Japanese War, 1894–95*, translated by Gordon Berger. Tokyo: University of Tokyo Press, 1982.

Paine, S. C. M. *The Sino-Japanese War of 1894–1895: Perceptions, Power, and Primacy*. Cambridge, UK: Cambridge University Press, 2003.

## Sino-Japanese War, Consequences

At the end of the Sino-Japanese War of 1894–1895, Japan occupied considerable Chinese territory, and for all intents and purposes it had won every battle of the war. The Chinese were summoned to Shimonoseki to negotiate a humiliating treaty to end the ignominious war. All things considered, the results could have been even worse for China. After some silly posturing by China, its chief delegate Li Hongzhang was shot in the face by a Japanese zealot. The Japanese were embarrassed, of course, particularly since only a few years earlier a Japanese policeman had attacked Russia's visiting Tsarevitch in the Otsu Incident. Japan appeared to be unable to channel the patriotism of its citizens. It was now pressured by other nations to show some leniency to Li and China.

The resulting Treaty of Shimonoseki initially granted Japan the island of Taiwan and a leasehold on the Liaoning Peninsula, the entry point into Manchuria. Japan also was assured the "full and complete independence and autonomy" of Korea, which really meant that China officially renounced its ancient tributary role as a protector of the peninsula. Lastly, Japan was given a huge indemnity (equal to 7.45 million kilograms of silver) sufficient to cancel its considerable debts incurred to pay for the war. If Japan wished to exult in its victory and spoils of war, the celebration was very short-lived.

Almost immediately after the treaty was signed, Russia, Germany, and France announced that it was not in the "best interests of the world" to allow Japan to take Liaoning. The three argued that this would set off a ruinous scramble among the European powers to counter Japan's acquisition. Japan was "counseled" to exact a larger indemnity (an additional 1.12 million kilograms of silver) from China in lieu of Liaoning. This so-called Triple Intervention caught Japan by surprise. There was very little chance of Japan enforcing the Treaty of Shimonoseki in the face of the thinly veiled threat of a joint intervention by the three powers. Itō Hirobumi and Mutsu Munemitsu, the chief negotiators for Japan, managed to pacify their more bellicose peers, some of whom advocated war against one or more of these European bullies. Japan swallowed this bitter pill, though virtually every Japanese resident understood that this would mean war against at least Russia in the future. For his part, Mutsu began to quietly sound out the British as possible allies in the inevitable war to recover Liaoning. Seven years later, those tentative inqueries bore fruit in the Anglo-Japanese Alliance of 1902.

Generally speaking, the consequences of its first "modern" war were decidedly mixed for Japan. To be sure, the war signaled that Japan was now to be considered among the international powers, not only in East Asia, but in the world as well. The victories against China had surprised most of the world powers, except for the British naval tutors of Japan's new navy and the German advisers who had helped Japan's army to modernize. It is generally acknowledged that Japan's new status forced the rest of the world to change how they treated Japan. The hated Unequal Treaties were very quickly revised. Great Britain had been the first to break the deadlock only two weeks before the war had started, and Germany was next to follow suit within a few months after the war. The rest of the Western powers quickly fell into line. By 1899, all 17 nations who were parties to the Unequal Treaties had done so.

The acquisition of Taiwan was also a mixed blessing. The initial costs of trying to administer the island were prohibitive. It was not until Gōtō Shinpei was appointed governor a few years later that the island began to show a profit for Japan.

Within a few years, it became clear that war with Russia was probably inevitable. Not only did the scars of the Triple Intervention still ache, but Russia had added insult to injury by coercing the Chinese to grant it a 99-year leasehold over Manchuria. The Russians began to build the Eastern Chinese and South Manchuria Railways with which to drain the mineral wealth of Manchuria down to a new warm-water port at the tip of the peninsula at Dalian that the Russians began to call Port Arthur. Also, the Russians refused to withdraw their troops from Korea—troops that were originally sent to help put down the Chinese Boxer Rebellion in 1900. Those actions probably forced Japan and Great Britain into each other's arms in the Anglo-Japanese Alliance of 1902.

One might argue that the Russo-Japanese War was caused by the Sino-Japanese War. One might also argue that Japan's seizure of Korea in 1910 was a direct result of the war begun in Korea a decade earlier. Its territorial and colonial ambitions dragged Japan into a series of wars and negotiations. The costs for Japan can scarcely be overestimated. When it won in China in 1895, it became a world power that had to defend every inch of newly acquired Chinese, Manchurian, and Korean territory. The spoils of war proved to be very expensively won for Japan.

Of course, to lay all of the ills of Japanese military expansionism at the door of the Sino-Japanese War would be ludicrous. Japan had many opportunities to avert this disaster in the intervening years. Absent World War I and the Great Depression, the country might well have heeded calmer voices and cooler heads might have prevailed. Suffice it to say, Japan's thrust into northeast Asia in 1894 made the Pandora's Box of evils more difficult to avoid.

*Louis G. Perez*

**See also:** Anglo-Japanese Alliance; Colonization of Taiwan; Gōtō Shinpei; Itō Hirobumi; Mutsu Munemitsu; Otsu Incident; Russo-Japanese War; Shimonoseki, Treaty of; Triple Intervention; World War I.

### Further Reading

Lone, Stewart. *Japan's First Modern War: Army and Society in the Conflict with China, 1894–95*. London: St. Martin's Press, 1994.

Paine, S. C. M. *The Sino-Japanese War of 1894–1895: Perceptions, Power, and Primacy.* Cambridge, UK: Cambridge University Press, 2003.

## *Sōhei* ("Monk Warriors")

Given the pacifist and renunciation aspects of Buddhism, the idea of "monk warriors" should certainly classify as an oxymoron. Yet like medieval European Christianity (e.g., the Crusades), armed religious men across Asia rose to defend the faith. As in Europe, the *sōhei* were primarily lay organizations, and often degenerated into little better than mercenary bands who fought on the side of whomever could pay best. The *sōhei* were ordinarily housed in Buddhist temple grounds and formed a religious brotherhood through several generations. They commonly intermarried within the brotherhood, employing a communalist approach to their lives. Orphans and widows were absorbed into the fraternity with barely a ripple in the body politic. Most practiced a communal ownership of all possessions.

The first recorded instances of *sōhei* were involved in inter-temple rivalries in and around Kyoto and Nara in the mid-10th century. The adherents and acolytes of the four largest temples in the country (Enryaku-ji, Kōfuku-ji, Mii-dera, and Tōdai-ji) occasionally swarmed out of their temple compounds not only to engage one another in brief brawls, but also to intimidate government officials who displeased their ecclesiastical leaders.

As the country succumbed to one imbroglio after another in the subsequent centuries, the *sōhei* were employed extensively because their forces were constantly primed for battle. Indeed, some historians argue that the *sōhei* were the first full-time professional warriors. Until the samurai were sequestered in castles in the 14th century, however, they were part-time warriors at best. They often were *shōen* administrators, cultivators, or artisans who sprang to their lord's colors only in times of emergencies.

The height of *sōhei* influence was the Sengoku era (1470–1600), when the entire country was at almost constant civil war. The *sōhei* of Enryaku-ji on Mount Hiei overlooking Kyoto were almost constantly embroiled in one skirmish or another. Oda Nobunaga found them to be so nettlesome that he surrounded the mountain and destroyed the entire temple complex and all its residents.

Another brand of Buddhist *sōhei*, the *ikkō-ikki* of the *Jōdo Shinshū* Buddhist sect, carved out a huge territory around ancient Kaga province. These worthies were a mix of peasants, monks, woodsmen, and fishers who were especially fierce warriors because they shared a belief in a Pure Land Buddhism, which promised them instant salvation in holy war.

Toyotomi Hideyoshi, and Tokugawa Ieyasu after him, fought the *ikkō-ikki* in a series of battles until Ieyasu finally eradicated them in the early 17th century. Indeed, one of the most effective methods that Ieyasu employed to pacify the country after a century of civil war was to dispossess the major temples of their extensive lands and *sōhei*.

*Louis G. Perez*

**See also:** Oda Nobunaga; Tokugawa Ieyasu; Toyotomi Hideyoshi.

### Further Reading

Adolphson, Mikael S. *The Teeth and Claws of the Buddha: Monastic Warriors and Sōhei in Japanese History.* Honolulu: University of Hawai'i Press, 2007.

Turnbull, Stephen. *Japanese Warrior Monks AD 949–1603.* Oxford, UK: Osprey Publishing, 2003.

## Sonno-jōi

The combination of the separate doctrines of *sonno* (revere the sovereign) and *jōi* (expel the barbarians) as markers of an exclusivist Japanese ideology is usually traced to Aizawa Seishisai's political treatise *New Theses* (*Shinron*) of 1825. *Sonno* and *jōi* as separate political ideas have a much longer history, however—one that originates in Chinese Confucian political thought. The rise of Confucianism as the primary vocabulary of political discourse in Japan during the Tokugawa period led to the doctrine of *sonno* becoming an important term in political thought from the 17th century onward. The interpretation of *sonno* became a political issue in Tokugawa Japan, because due to the particular nature of the political settlement under the shoguante, it was debatable who the "sovereign" referred to in the doctrine actually was. Japan was, in effect, ruled by the shōgun, who controlled not only the local feudal lords, but also the imperial family. Yet the shōgunate also officially justified its power by claiming that the shōgun ruled on behalf of the emperor. In the 17th and early 18th centuries, Japanese Confucian scholars such as Yamaga Sokō and Arai Hakuseki argued that because the shōgun was carrying out the practical duties of a sovereign, he should be regarded as the sovereign under the *sonno* doctrine. This interpretation defined the sovereign in practical terms. The person who was carrying out the tasks of the sovereign—that is, bringing peace to the realm—deserved to be revered. This notion, by association, justified governance in terms of its social utility: ensuring peace and welfare.

Other scholars in the 18th century, notably the nativist Motoori Norinaga, regarded the emperor in Kyoto as the sovereign. They contrasted the position of the "unbroken" Japanese imperial line to the constant changes of dynastic lineage in China. Their view that the emperor rather than the shōgun was sovereign of Japan thereby rested on a definition of "sovereign" that justified the legitimacy of that position in terms of its history in leading a distinct ethnic group or nation, rather than in terms of its capacity to bring order or peace. This later interpretation led to governance being justified in terms of ethnocentrism, rather than social utility or effectiveness. According to major scholars of Japanese history such as Maruyama Masao, this perspective had consequences for the development of Japanese politics during the modern period.

Aizawa Seishisai's *New Theses*, written while Aizawa was serving the Mito lord Tokuagawa Nariaki, sought to employ the charismatic or religious power of the emperor to strengthen the shōgunate. Therefore, while Aizawa's political ideology was primarily Confucian, he adopted major elements of Motoori Norinaga's Japanese nativism—notably, many of his ideas about the status of the emperor. Aizawa's *sonno-jōi* doctrine argued that the Japanese people's loyalty to the emperor could drive out the Western threat, but it envisaged that outcome happening under the leadership of the Tokugawa shōguns. In the 1850s, however, the Tokugawa shōgunate's inability to militarily defeat Western maritime incursions into Japan weakened its claims to power. By not being able to "expel the barbarians," the shōgunate failed to carry out its traditional military defensive role, and by not defending the national integrity of Japan, it also failed to play a national leadership role. Enemies of the shōgunate were, therefore, able to use the *sonno-jōi* doctrine to attack the shōgunate.

Internal political rifts within the shōgunate, culminating in the arrest of Tokugawa Nariaki and the suppression of other Mito domain samurai, also meant that many Mito domain-inspired *sonno-jōi* followers lost trust in the shōgunate. Thus, by 1860, *sonno-jōi* had become the label for a broad social movement that opposed the shōgunate's handling of the issue of Western incursion, and was prepared to advocate overthrow of the shōgunate. This movement is mainly associated with samurai who were influenced by the ideas of the likes of Aizawa. However, the *sonno-jōi* movement also received major support from merchants and villagers under the influence of the nativist *sonno-jōi* ideas of Motoori Norinaga and Hirata Atsutane.

After the Meiji Restoration, although Japan opened to the West, the *sonno-jōi* doctrine continued to play a major role in national ideology. The doctrine of *sonno* (revere the sovereign) was converted to *chūkun* (loyalty to the emperor), and *jōi* (expel the barbarians) to *aikoku* (love for the country). This *chūkun-aikoku* doctrine played a similar role to *sonno-jōi* as a rallying cry for later Japanese wars, particularly against China in the late 19th and early 20th centuries. Postwar Japanese thinkers, notably Maruyama Masao, argued that *sonno-jōi*'s original ethnocentric characteristics had been passed on to the modern Japanese state, and had provided part of the background to the development of fascist militarism in the 1930s.

*Kiri Paramore*

**See also:** Aizawa Seishisai; Maruyama Masao; Tokugawa *Bakufu* Political System; Tokugawa Nariaki.

### Further Reading

Maruyama Masao. *Studies in the Intellectual History of Tokugawa Japan*. Tokyo: University of Tokyo Press, 1974.

Tadashi Wakabayashi, Bob. *Anti-foreignism and Western Learning in Early-Modern Japan: The* New Theses *of 1825*. Cambridge, MA: Harvard University Press, 1986.

## South Manchurian Railway

The South Manchurian Railway was something of a war prize. It had its origins as the Russian-owned China Far East Railway but became Japanese property as part of the Treaty of Portsmouth settlement ending the Russo-Japanese War in 1905. When title was turned over to Japan, a semi-private company (commonly called *Mantetsu*, the shortened form of its title) was formed to administer its considerable holdings.

Gōtō Shimpei, the former governor-general of Taiwan, was appointed the first president of the company in late 1906. He served for 30 months, instituting many improvements to create what he called the "most modern railway in Asia." *Mantetsu* was converted from the Russian gauge to the standard world gauge (4 feet, 8.5 inches), employing American-made rail and rolling stock. This complicated the transfer of goods from the northern spur of the China Far East Railway, which remained in Russian hands, because the two systems did not mesh. Of course, it also ensured that the Russians could not use their own railstock if they ever decided to invade Manchuria.

Like the American Union and Southern Pacific Railways, *Mantetsu* controlled much more than the railway itself. It developed coal mines, electric generators, sawmills, pulp plants, and chemical plants, and maintained shipping ports along the Liaoning Peninsula. It also built hotels and warehouses and established an ambitious land office to accommodate the thousands of Japanese who emigrated to the area in the next three decades. It actively encouraged the development of soybean and wheat fields, and it built mills and processing plants to process those and other agricultural products. By the late 1920s, more than half of the world's supply of soybeans came from *Mantetsu*.

In many ways, the South Manchurian Railway became a paragon for Japan's colonization efforts abroad. The government appointed very able men in its administration, including several with experience in the foreign ministry (notably Uchida Yasuya and Matsuoka Yōsuke). In the 1920s, the railway had been touted as a model of government and commercial cooperation. *Mantetsu* was noted for its very liberal social policies, particularly for its treatment of female employees. It employed urban planners and other social reformers, creating model communities with spacious homes, public parks, schools, libraries, utilities, sewers, and waste processing plants.

In the late 1920s and beyond, the company fell in with bad elements. Because it was protected by the Japanese Imperial Army (also called the Kwantung Army), *Mantetsu* became embroiled in world politics. Until 1926, it had a complicated relationship with the Manchu warlord Zhang Zuolin. Zhang used his troops to augment the Kwantung Army; in return, he received subsidies from *Mantetsu* that he used to build up his considerable private army. When Zhang began to make overtures to Jiang Jieshi and the Guomintang, officers in the Kwantung Army began to plot against him. Finally, when it became obvious that Zhang had thrown his lot in with Jiang, the Kwantung Army assassinated him in 1928.

After the Manchuria Incident, also engineered by the rogue Kwantung Army in 1931, *Mantetsu* fell under the sway of the army. It maintained close relations with the army and became a huge economic enterprise.

Indeed, nearly one-fourth of all the tax revenue from Japan's commercial sector came from *Mantetsu* alone. The fact that the company was only semi-privately owned made it a model for the army's idealized plan for the Shōwa Restoration. The idea was that once the national government was "cleansed" of its pernicious *Zaibatsu*-controlled politicians, the rest of Japan's economy would be rebuilt using *Mantetsu* as its model.

The army had used the railway's extensive expertise in the development of the puppet state of Manchukuo. Even worse, after World War II accelerated, *Mantetsu* employed Koreans, Chinese, and Manchurians as forced labor. Because it was so intertwined with the Kwantung Army, the company participated in the atrocious behavior demonstrated by Japan's army. During the war, thousands of Asians died in its employ. Asian slaves and allied prisoners of war labored in horrific conditions in its mines, forests, chemical plants, and other war industries.

At the end of the war, Russia invaded Manchuria and seized most of *Mantetsu*'s properties. The Russians pulled up the very railway roadbed, rails, and rolling stock, carrying them away to Russia, returning some of it only after the Chinese communists triumphed after 1949. Of course, *Mantetsu* itself came to an end, being abolished by the Allied occupation authorities in 1945.

*Louis G. Perez*

**See also:** Gotō Shinpei; Jiang Jieshi (Ch'iang K'ai-shek); Kwantung Army Adventurism; Mukden Incident: Lytton Report; Matsuoka Yōsuke; Portsmouth Treaty; Russo-Japanese War; Uchida Yasuya (Kōsai); Zhang Zuolin.

**Further Reading**

Itō Takeo. *Life along the South Manchurian Railway: Memoirs of Itō Takeo*, translated by Joshua Fogel. Armonk, NY: M. E. Sharpe, 1988.

Young, Louise. *Japan's Total Empire: Manchuria and the Culture of Wartime Imperialism.* Berkeley: University of California Press, 1999.

## Southern Court (Yoshino)

Japan's imperial house was briefly bifurcated in 1336 when Emperor Go-Daigo was ordered deposed by Ashikaga Takauji in favor of his cousin. Go-Daigo had attempted to wrest power from the Kamakura *bakufu* in the so-called Kemmu Restoration. Ashikaga had briefly backed the emperor, but then placed him under house arrest. Go-Daigo escaped to Yoshino in the mountains south of Kyoto, where he established what has been called the Southern Court.

Until 1392, the rival courts vied for recognition. As long as the Ashikaga (also called Muromachi after the section of Kyoto where it was based) *bakufu* resided in the capital, however, the "Northern Court" was treated as the only legitimate house. In 1392, a deal was struck whereby the two houses were to alternate in power, and the Yoshino branch returned to Kyoto.

Obviously, a historical controversy arose about which house should be considered legitimate. The issue was finally settled at the end of the Meiji era in 1911, when it was declared that the line had continued "unbroken" through Go-Daigo's Southern Court issue.

*Louis G. Perez*

**See also:** Ashikaga Takauji; Go-Daigo.

### Further Reading

Ponsonby-Fane, Richard Arthur Brabazon. *The Imperial House of Japan.* Kyoto: Ponsonby Memorial Society, 1959.

Thomas, Julia Adeney. *Reconfiguring Modernity: Concepts of Nature in Japanese Political Ideology.* Berkeley: University of California Press. 2001.

## State Shintō

The term "State Shintō" (*kokka shintō*) does not have a single definition. Shintō scholars argue that the term should be used only after the establishment of the Shrine Office (Jinja Kyoku) inside the Home Ministry in 1900, which took on the task of regulating the shrines and priests. Others dispute that the term applies to the patronized state religion from 1868 to 1945, which also served as background for the state rites and as a legitimate symbol of the country. Hozumi Yatsuka was probably the most important Meiji theorist who first joined the fundamental Shintō doctrines to the family concept of the state and molded them into a comprehensive theory of monarchical absolutism. He stated that the foundation of the Japanese nation's unique *kokutai* and national morality was an ancestor religion. Some scholars actually place State Shintō within the *kokutai*, "national body" ideology.

Shintō, which means "way of the gods," is an ethnic religion that does not follow any doctrines and is said to contain the essence of Japanese ethnic identity. Furthermore, it derives from Kannagara, which is an ancient expression implying the sanctity of the reign of the emperor. It reasserts the belief that Japan is a "sacred nation" and can be interpreted as "the way of the emperor" as well as "the way of the people." Reverence and worship of the imperial ancestors who claimed direct descent from Amaterasu Ōmikami, the Sun Goddess enshrined in the Grand Shrines of Ise, is a pervasive element of imperial Shintō. Historical evidence indicates that Jimmu Tennō, the first emperor of Japan, established the nation (according to Kannagara) by receiving the divine message of the ancestral gods as he undertook his great mission.

Until the shrine mergers of 1905–1929, Shintō was a highly localized religion, with each village having its own place of reverence (*sanpai*) where local heroes were enshrined. Shintō deifies emperors and heroes along with mythological deities. Just as the various gods (*kami*) ensured the abundance of crops and well-being of the people, so the emperor as kami watched over the nation and was responsible for its integrity. There was no set of doctrines to follow, which had the result that the rites of individual shrines were subject to great variations.

The sacerdotal corps were enlisted from the local male population, and the teachings were esoterically handed down from one generation to the next. However, with the emergence of state patronage, not only the organizational structure but also the ideological direction of Shintō came to be crystallized. Although shrines were closely connected to the ancient Japanese state by "worship of the gods and government as one" (*saisei itchi*), their symbiosis was strengthened during the State Shintō period. This entailed the shrines becoming sanctifiers of government directives and policies.

With the opening of Japan in the second half of the 19th century and after the first euphoria of embracing everything Western—despite the numerous rebellions that tried to hinder this process—the majority of leading intellectuals in the country settled for "Eastern ethics as base, Western techniques as means" (*tōyō dōtoku, seiyō gei*), which meant that they feverishly started to construct ideologies for "Japanism." Shintō, as the spiritual root and life blood to the nation's historical legitimacy and continuity, was an integral part of this process. The old values of reverence, filial piety, duty, national devotion,

obedience, and deep respect for hierarchy came to acquire new meaning, and the emperor, the nation, and Shintō came to be regarded as one in accordance with these ideas.

As discussed earlier, Hozumi's *kokutai*, which can be translated as "national polity," "national essence," "body politic," and "state structure," refers to the Japanese nation and national spirit itself—a category defined by blood and ethnicity (*minzoku no dantai*) and referenced as "ethnic nation-state" (*kokuminzoku*), similar to the German *Volksstaat*. As the nation was equated with the emperor, paying respects to his portrait on a regular basis in the shrines connected all Japanese subjects to every other Japanese subject in the country. This spiritual unity was rather unique among the fascist-militarist countries prior to World War II. Also, the Japanese emperor was not revered or worshipped because of his individual accomplishments or personal merits, but rather because he was regarded as the spiritual head and origin of the country, embodying the very essence of Japanese-ness by connecting his subjects to a transcendental creation that had its mythological beginnings in ancient times.

Kakehi, another radical Shintō ultra-nationalist state theorist, asserted that "the imperial state is a corporation (*dantai*), and intrinsic being of one heart and body." In other words, one's own life has never been one's own; it comes from the emperor. Kakehi referred to the state as "universal great life" (*fuhenteki daiseimei*), a term composed of the elements for "emperor and his subjects."

According to the official government stance of the time, Chapter 3, Article 28, of the Meiji Constitution (1889) dealing with freedom of religious belief was not to be applied to Shintō observances. Indeed, adherence to such practices was made obligatory for every Japanese subject, regardless of individual religious beliefs (although at the time of the Meiji Constitution, it was forbidden to adhere to any other religion—the ban on Christianity was still in force for Japanese citizens) even after it was lifted for foreign nationals. Given that the shrines were to be treated as ethical institutions promoting patriotism, people were required to show proof of their transcendent patriotic commitments to the all-inclusive national ethic (*kokumin dōtoku*). As the nation was considered one with the emperor, and the emperor, in turn, was regarded as a direct descendant from Amaterasu, this perspective takes only a short leap from ethics to supra-religious practices and then back again. The debate on whether practicing obeisance at Shintō shrines is considered religious or not remained in full swing for decades and lasted for the entire duration of State Shintō. The 1932 Yasukuni Incident, during which students of the Jesuit-founded Sophia University refused to pay their respects at the shrine, merely rekindled the argument. With regard to the history of Shintō, it was separated from Buddhism in 1868—a division that did not occur peacefully—and state patronage of the latter gave way to support of the former.

The Great Promulgation Campaign (Taikyū Senpo Undō, 1870–1884) saw state sponsorship of Shintō at its peak and prompted state officials to propagate the doctrine, entrusting Shintō priests to ensure its proper dissemination. For the first time in Japanese religious history, shrine affiliations became obligatory, both nonreligious and egalitarian at the same time, serving census functions through the registration system. The emphasis here focuses on the nonreligious and egalitarian aspects of such practice: prior to State Shintō, associations

with a shrine did not have the clearly pyramid-like structure pointing toward the Grand Shrines of Ise, the emperor, and Amaterasu herself. Instead, adherents were content with the kami that were enshrined in the local village shrine.

State support of Shintō eventually declined, but even the years 1880–1905 saw many important shrine constructions. The Yasukuni Shrine in Tokyo rose to prominent status at this time and necessitated the formation of the first National Association of Shrine Priests in 1900.

With Japanese victories in both the Sino-Japanese and Russo-Japanese wars, the annexation of Korea (1910), and the colonization of Manchuria (1931), feelings of patriotism were greatly enhanced and fanned by enthusiastic shrine priests. In addition to mandatory shrine reverence, education was the most powerful channel of national indoctrination. The state overtly subsidized the training of shrine priests, and their influence in the education system gained even more meaningful momentum when graduates of Shintō schools (Kokugakuin University) automatically qualified to teach in public schools. Priests made sure that the portrait of the emperor was properly venerated and that the Imperial Rescript on Education (1890) was enforced at grassroots levels. Schoolchildren were taken on frequent visits to the Grand Shrines of Ise, while adults organized their reverence by village work groups.

The peak in the influence of State Shintō occurred between 1930 and 1945, when the country was gearing up for total war and has already had its feet on the Korean Peninsula. Several factions also sprang up that were independent of the 13 officially recognized Shintō sects. These sectarian versions were purged during 1935–1937; in particular, the ones that did not vehemently support the state's ideology were annihilated completely. Thus, only those versions of Shintō were tolerated that served the nation's nationalist and Pan-Asianist aspirations.

*Judith Erika Magyar*

**See also:** Imperial Rescript on Education; Jimmu Tennō; *Kokutai* and Ultra-nationalism; Meiji Constitution; Pan-Asianism; Russo-Japanese War; Sino-Japanese War; State Shintō, Exporting to the Colonies.

### Further Reading

Hardacre, Helen. *Shintō and the State, 1968–1988*. Princeton, N.J.: Princeton University Press, 1991.

Lebra, Joyce C. *Japan's Greater East Asia Co-prosperity Sphere in World War II: Selected Readings and Documents*. Oxford, UK: Oxford University Press, 1975.

Skya, Walter A. *Japan's Holy War*. London: Duke University Press, 2009.

Tanaka, Stefan. *Japan's Orient*. Los Angeles: University of California Press, 1993.

## State Shintō, Exporting to the Colonies

After winning both the Sino-Japanese and Russo-Japanese wars, annexing Korea (1910), and colonizing Manchuria (1931), feelings of patriotism in Japan were greatly enhanced by the evolution of the Pan-Asianist ideology, which regarded all of Asia as an integral whole. Furthermore, the establishment of the Greater East Asia Co-prosperity Sphere in 1940 propagated the idea that Japan was to be the leader in East Asia, with other nations contributing to the development and well-being of the Sphere according to their own individual capacities. Japanese ideologists saw nothing strange in the fact that they regarded Japan as the sole leader of the pact: according to their value system, other East Asian nations were not deemed as capable as the Yamato nation. Racial supremacy was recognizable in almost every aspect of Japanese conduct during the occupation of East Asia, and the introduction of Shintō was no exception

As it is unique to Japan, the only time Shintō sought foreign converts was during the colonial years of imperialism. State Shintō (*kokka shintō*) encompassed several means of control through shrine attendance both in Japan and in the colonies, albeit to varying degrees. In the occupied countries, many of the shrines were erected to satisy the desires of Japanese immigrants who wished to continue their practices from the homeland.

Colonial subjects in East Asia were to pay their respects to Japanese deities as a means of showing submission to imperial authority. They did not do so by their own free will but were either gently or more forcefully coerced. For example, the last Manchu emperor was made to worship Amaterasu as a way of showing his good intentions toward Japan. The majority of colonial shrines were dedicated to Amaterasu and to other Japanese deities. Often, the very founders of the actual colony were enshrined to be worshipped as the kami identified with particular places, sometimes originating from the place of worship. The shrines in the colonies were under direct supervision of the Japanese military.

In Korea, in an effort to secure total support for the war, the government initiated the "Movement for the General Mobilization of the National Spirit." This network of administrative units served not only as a controlling mechanism over the population, but also as a rapid means of communication and information flow. To attain spiritual unity, all people were coerced into attending Shintō shrine events regularly and praying for the victory of the Japanese forces.

Because food rationing was administered through these patriotic groups, the system worked with remarkable efficiency.

Despite the fact that colonial subjects and Japanese immigrants were supposed to be equal, the shrines of colonials were to be inferior in Shintō. When Koreans asked that their Korean founders be enshrined in the Korean Shrine, their hopes were dashed. The Japanese argument suggested that there was no reason why Korens could not worship the imperial deities; moreover, the privilege of being enshrined was permitted only for "real" Japanese.

In addition to mandatory shrine reverence, education was the most powerful channel of national indoctrination. Japanese education for the indigenous populations placed special emphasis on elementary schooling. In Taiwan, the Japanese-language elementary schools were attended by 65 percent of the Taiwanese children; the picture was similar in Korea. On the peninsula, more than half of school-age children attended elementary school by 1940.

In 1940, there were 137 shrines in Manchuria, 368 in Korea, and 18 in Taiwan, one of which was for a Chinese deity. After the annexation of Korea, the journal of the Shintō priesthood asked its readers to travel as missionaries to the "forsaken land" that had been under the spell of Buddhism and Confucianism for so long. In an answer to this call, as many as 61 Shintō priests migrated to Korea by 1935 and 66 priests moved to Taiwan by 1941.

Shrines were erected mostly in Taiwan, Korea, and Manchuria. In the strongly Catholic Philippines and Muslim Indonesia, however, the occupying forces adopted a more tolerant spirit toward the population. As long as there were no significant skirmishes with authorities, religious practices were not curtailed substantially in these regions.

*Judith Erika Magyar*

**See also:** Colonization of Taiwan; Greater East Asia Co-prosperity Sphere; *Hakkō Ichiu*; Korea Added to the Empire; Manchukuo; Pan-Asianism, Russo-Japanese War; Sino-Japanese War; State Shintō.

**Further Reading**

Hardacre, Helen. *Shintō and the State, 196–1988*. Princeton, NJ: Princeton University Press, 1991.

Lebra, Joyce C. *Japan's Greater East Asia Co-prosperity Sphere in World War II: Selected Readings and Documents*. Oxford, UK: Oxford University Press, 1975.

**Student Movement.** *See* Zengakuren.

## Sun Yat-sen (1866–1925) and the Japanese

Sun Yat-sen, known as Son Bun (Ch. Sun Wen) in Japan and as Sun Zhongshan or "father of the Republic" (guofu) in China, is the best-known Chinese historical figure in Japan, alongside Mao Zedong. His memory is kept alive in Japan not only in scholarly circles, but also among the wider public. Since 1984, the Japanese port city of Kobe has hosted a Sun Yat-sen memorial hall. In 1998, the Japanese daily *Asahi* included a ·phrase by Sun as the only Chinese in its list of representative quotes for understanding the 20th century; "will you become the running dog of Western rule of might or the stronghold of Eastern rule of right." Sun ended his famous speech on Greater Asianism (Dai Ajiashugi), delivered in Kobe in November 1924, with this sentence. This speech has since been regarded as his admonitory legacy to Japan.

Chinese nationalist leader Sun Yat-sen in 1923. Sun founded his Nationalist Party (Guomindang) while living as an exile in Japan. (UPI/Bettmann/Corbis)

Although he died in 1925, Sun's legacy played a prominent role during the most aggressive and hostile period in Sino-Japanese history—the "Fifteen Years War" (1931–1945) or, as the war is known in China, the "Anti-Japanese War of Resistance." Sun was appropriated not only by the Japanese military and the foreign ministry, which even published his collected writings in seven volumes (1939–1940), but also by the pro-Japanese Chinese collaborationist regime of Wang Jingwei (1883–1944). Wang made every effort to present himself as Sun's legitimate successor and to keep the memory of Sun's pro-Japanese and Pan-Asianist spirit alive. While some scholars regard Sun's pan-Asianism as a proof of his unfailing admiration of Japan, others interpret his last message to Japan as an open critique of the country's betrayal of Asia and China.

Until Sun's last visit to Japan in 1924, the country had alternately functioned as a model, a refuge, a place of political and economic support, and a source of disappointment to him. While Japan remained Sun's partner of first choice until his death, he became increasingly disappointed with the prevalence of Japanese imperialist policy toward China. By the early 1920s, he had become estranged from the Japanese, whom he had always considered as siblings to the Chinese. During his lifetime, Sun established close links with Japanese thinkers, politicians, and activists through his frequent visits to Japan.

Born in 1866 in southeastern China near Guangzhou in today's Guangdong Province,

Sun left China when he was 14 years old to study medicine in Hawaii and then moved to Hong Kong. In 1895, after China's defeat in the First Sino-Japanese War, he led his first insurrection against the Qing (Manchu) dynasty. When it failed, Sun was banned from Hong Kong and went into exile in Japan for the first time. During his second stay in Japan, in 1898, Sun took on a Japanese name (Nakayama Shō) and befriended the Japanese Sinophile writer Miyazaki Tōten (1870–1922). Tōten became, in his own words, "a faithful follower of Sun's heroic plans" and Sun's main contact in Japan. He also introduced Sun to influential Asianist activists and Japanese politicians, including future Prime Minister Inukai Tsuyoshi (1855–1932) and Tôyama Mitsuru (1855–1944), founder of the Pan-Asianist Gen'yōsha society. In Tōten and other Japanese Asianists, Sun thought he had found comrades for his project of the "revival of Asia" and the liberation and modernization of China along the Japanese model. Famously, Sun referred to the Meiji Restoration as "the first step of the Chinese Revolution."

In August 1905, Sun brought several anti-Qing forces together and founded the Revolutionary Alliance (Tongmenghui) in Tokyo. The party journal, *Minbao* ("People's Daily"), was printed in Tōten's house, and counted "an alliance of the two peoples of China and Japan" as one of its six key principles. The Japanese government, however, was neither supportive of Sun's activities nor receptive to outspokenly Pan-Asianist undertakings. Under pressure from the Japanese government, Sun eventually left Japan for the United States.

While the Chinese Revolution of 1911 led to the overthrow of the Qing and the establishment of the Chinese Republic in 1912, Sun failed to unify the country against the separatist warlords and General Yuan Shikai's military rule. After Yuan undermined the power of the Chinese National Assembly in 1913, Sun was forced into exile again and came to Japan, for the first time upon official invitation by the Japanese government. During his stay, Sun first publicly elaborated the idea of close Sino-Japanese cooperation as the core of a wider pan-Asian alliance under the banner of Greater Asianism. This theme became a key topic in Sun's approach to Japan, although Pan-Asianist inclinations were largely met with skepticism in Japan until the early 1930s.

Also in Japan, in 1914 Sun married his second wife Song Qingling (1893–1931), of the famous Song clan. Upon his return to China in 1916 and in the following decade until his death, Sun attempted to extend his political power base from Guangzhou, where in 1919 he reorganized the National Party (Guomindang). Despite successfully recruiting military and political allies, such as Jiàng Jieshi (1887–1975) and the newly founded Communist Party, he failed to form a national government. In 1924, he accepted an invitation by northern militarists to a conference about national reconstruction. On his way there, Sun fell ill; he died in Beijing of liver cancer on March 12, 1925.

Sun's main politico-intellectual legacy is the Three Principles of the People (*Sanmin zhuyi*) which have loosely been translated as nationalism (*minzu zhuyi*), democracy (*minquan zhuyi*), and socialism (*minsheng zhuyi*). In Japan, however, Sun is best known for his Pan-Asianism. In his last public speech made in Japan only months before his death, he praised the Japanese for their achievements and their successful resistance against Western aggression. Sun also called for pan-Asian solidarity and cooperation centering on Sino-Japanese friendship. At the end of his speech, however, he warned Japan not to abandon its true characteristics of the Kingly Way (*ōdō*) as an Oriental nation and presented the Japanese with the choice of joining either the West or the East. *Ōdō* was later used by Japanese propaganda as the principle of peaceful and harmonious coexistence of different races and nationalities in Japanese-occupied Manchuria (Manchukuo). Although the historicity of this final passage of his speech is disputed, his speech is frequently reduced to that part. This theme of Japan either joining Asia or the West, most famously addressed in Fukuzawa Yukichi's "Datsu A Ron" ("On Leaving Asia," 1885), has remained a central concern in public political discourse in contemporary Japan. While historically Sun was viewed in Japan mainly as an Utopian idealist who lacked a sense of realism and the power to implement his policies effectively, today he is often portrayed as a pioneer of Sino-Japanese friendship and as someone who, had he lived, could have helped prevent the antagonism between China and Japan from developing in a full-scale war in the 1930s and 1940s.

*Torsten Weber*

**See also:** Fukuzawa Yukichi; Jiang Jieshi (Ch'iang K'ai-shek); Manchukuo; Pan-Asianism.

## Further Reading

Bergère, Marie-Claire. *Sun Yat-sen*, translated by Janet Lloyd. Stanford, CA: Stanford University Press, 1998.

Etō, Shinkichi, and Harold Z. Schiffrin, eds. *China's Republican Revolution*. Tokyo: University of Tokyo Press, 1994.

Jansen, Marius B. *The Japanese and Sun Yat-sen*. Cambridge, MA: Harvard University Press, 1954.

Schiffrin, Harold Z. *Sun Yat-sen, Reluctant Revolutionary*. Boston: Little Brown, 1980.

# T

## Taiheiki

The *Taiheiki*, or *Chronicle of Great Peace*, belongs to the war tale genre (*gunki monogatari*). It is a fictional history of the 14th-century War of the Northern and Southern Courts. The narrative depicts Emperor Go-Daigo's conquest of the Kamakura shōgunate, continues with Go-Daigo's transformation into a despot and Ashikaga Takauji's establishment of the Muromachi shōgunate; and concludes with the rise of Hosokawa Yoriyuki and Ashikaga Yoshimitsu in 1367, ostensibly putting and end to the turmoil caused by prominent warriors whose internecine rivalries had theretofore threatened the new shōgunate's stability.

The *Taiheiki* is often didactic, leaning heavily on quotes from Chinese canonical texts and legends. In particular Confucian, classics, the notions of virtuous government and the mandate of heaven are invoked throughout the tale, and the absence, of those qualities in a regime or individual is a clear sign of impending doom. Also evident is an attempt at formulating an ethic for the warrior class. These themes are not unique to the *Taiheiki* and appear elsewhere, most notably in the *Heike monogatari*; however, in contrast to the latter's focused Buddhist treatment of the Genpei wars, the diffuse way in which themes interact reveals the complexity of thought in medieval Japan, making the *Taiheiki* a distinctive addition to the canon.

Evidence suggesting that it is not the product of a single author further complicates the issue. Its creation was likely a group effort headed by one or more individuals associated with Hossōji temple, and led by a priest name Echin. Barring the discovery of further information, the mystery of authorship is likely to remain unsolved.

The *Taiheiki* played an important role in the formation of samurai culture identity and ideology since its creation. Many warriors considered the *Taiheiki* a legitimate history of Japan and wanted the text amended to include the names of their ancestors. In the Sengoku era (1477–1600), warriors admired many of the characters: *daimyō* and strategists considered the text to be a primer on military tactics and ethics.. Episodes about Kusunoki Masashige, Go-Daigo's general par excellence, were particularly adored in this and later eras: the tale of his suicide at the Battle of Minatogawa remains one of the most iconic in war tales.

Samurai and commoner alike in the Tokugawa period (1600–1868) found similar themes to admire, despite the vastly changed social landscape. They enjoyed the *Taiheiki* both as a written work and in interpretive discussions called *Taiheiki-koshaku* or roadside narratives called Taiheiki-yomi. One of the leading early Tokugawa period ideologues, Hayashi Razan, encountered the text in his youth through such lectures. By the late 17th century the *Taiheiki* was the subject of several commentaries and it became a favorite among artists and entertainers: the *bunraku* play *Chūshingura*, about the famed Forty-Seven Rōnin, would be set against the background of the *Taiheiki* to avoid censorship.

Toward the end of the 19th century, the tale was particularly beloved by samurai seeking to topple the Tokugawa shōgunate, as its narrative provided numerous examples of selfless loyalty to the emperor. The Taiheiki was a source of inspiration for "men of high purpose" (*shishi*), and also had a role in the formation of the slogan "Revere the Emperor—Expel the Barbarian" (*sonno-jōi*). The pre-World War II Japanese government tapped into the work's ideological potential to inculcate loyalty in its soldiers and citizens: reading about loyalty and self-sacrifice as embodied by characters like Kusunoki and Nitta Yoshisada were textbook staples, indispensable for training soldiers, such as the *kamikaze*, who would be willing to sacrifice themselves for emperor and nation.

*Jeremy Sather*

See also: Ashikaga Takauji; *Bushidō*; Early Mytho-histories: *Kojiki* and *Nihon shōki*; Go-Daigo; Kamakura *Bakufu*; Kitabatake Chikafusa; Muromachi *Bakufu*; Nitta Yoshisada; *Sonno-jōi*; Southern Court (Yoshino).

## Further Reading

Conlan, Thomas. *State of War: The Violent Order of Fourteenth Century Japan*. Ann Arbor: Center for Japanese Studies, University of Michigan, 2002.

Friday, Karl. *Samurai, Warfare, and the State in Early Medieval Japan*. New York: Routledge, 2004.

Goble, Andrew E. *Kemmu: Godaigo's Revolution*. Cambridge, MA: Harvard University Press, 1996.

McCullough, Helen Craig. *Taiheiki: A Chronicle of Medieval Japan*. New York: Columbia University Press, 1959.

Sato, Hiroaki. *Legends of the Samurai*. Woodstock: Overlook Press, 1995.

Varley, Paul. *Warriors of Japan as Portrayed in the War Tales*. Honolulu: Hawaii University Press, 1994.

# Taika Reforms

The Taika reforms brought Chinese customs to Japan in the seventh century A.D. The Taika, or "great change," reforms had their roots in the mid-sixth century, when officials of the ruling Yamato clan in Japan, in an attempt to strengthen the power of their state, began sending emissaries to the Chinese court to learn from the example of the Tang dynasty. One of the earliest changes to come from China was the Buddhist religion, first introduced to Japan in 552. After 600, Japan adopted new court ranks based on the Chinese system. Most significantly, Japan adopted a document outlining the rights of its central government, which used ideals of Confucianism and Buddhism and borrowed heavily from Chinese government protocol. The Taika reforms, introduced by Naka-no Oe (Tenji Emperor) following a coup in 645, built on this foundation of Chinese government ideals to make the broadest changes yet in the Japanese system.

The Taika reforms established a provincial administration system; a new system of taxation, such public works as roads and post stations; and a census—all based on similar institutions in the Chinese Tang government. In imitation of the Chinese system, private land ownership was abolished and replaced by lifetime grants of land from the emperor. The traditional Japanese system of occupational communities protected by elite patrons, the *be*, was also abolished to bring Japanese craftsmen more in line with their Chinese counterparts. The reforms were far-reaching, although their implementation was often slow. For example, the first Japanese census was not compiled for more than three decades, until 670.

The Taika reforms also had unintended effects on Japanese society. Provincial administrators developed a feudal system to rival the power of the central government, and the Buddhism imported from China gave the priesthood authority that rivaled that of the Yamatos. Ultimately, the reforms that were designed to strengthen the Yamatos' power in Japan weakened it, contributing to the rise of samurai and feudalism.

*Jessica Sedgewick*

See also: Buddhism Copes with Imperialism.

**Further Reading**

Asakawa, Kan'ichi. *The Early Institutional Life of Japan: A Study in the Reform of 645.* New York: A. D. Paragon Book Reprint, 1963.

Batten, Bruce. "Foreign Threat and Domestic Reform: The Emergence of the Ritsuryo State." *Monumenta Nipponica* 41, no. 2 (Summer 1986): 199–219.

## Taira-no-Masakado (died 940)

Because he led the first recorded rebellion against the Heian-era government, Taira-no-Masakado has taken on the aura of the "first bushi." Born the son of Taira no Yoshimochi, an important land owner in the Kanto region, he briefly served the imperial regent Fujiwara no Tadahira in the capital. In 939, however, Masakado rebelled against the government and briefly installed himself as the Shinnō ("new emperor"), conquering two provinces in the Kanto. He was quickly declared a rebel, and a bounty was placed on his head. Before the imperial troops sent from Heian-kyō could reach the far-off Kanto, however, his cousin Taira no Sadamori caught and killed Masakado at the Battle of Kojima in 940.

Masakado's head was severed, preserved in salt, paraded through the provinces, and finally hung from a tree in the capital as a warning to all others who might rebel. In death, Masakado has taken on a curious notoriety. A written account, the *Shōmonki*, surfaced in the early 940s and various legends sprang up about him. His head was reputed to have unearthed itself and flown magically back to the Kanto. Rumors of his new tomb multiplied, and several temples claimed to be his final resting place. The one most commonly associated with him is in the Ōtemachi section of Tokyo.

The brief rebellion, *Jōhei Tengyo no ran*, is often called Japan's "first feudal battle." Several superstitions and myths surround Masakado's legend. He is generally considered to be a protecting kami who watches over Tokyo. His image has appeared in several *manga* and *anime*, and is a popular character in various role-playing video games.

*Louis G. Perez*

See also: Fujiwara Family.

**Furthur Reading**

Friday, Karl. *The First Samurai: The Life and Legend of the Warrior Rebel Taira Masakado.* Hoboken, NJ: John Wiley & Sons, 2008.

***Tairiku.*** *See* Continental Adventurers (*Tairiku Rōnin*).

## Taishō Emperor (1879–1926)

The third son of Emperor Meiji, Taishō was born to an imperial concubine named Yanagihara Naruko on August 31, 1879. Yoshihito was the personal name given to the future emperor and the name by which he was known during his life. Soon after his birth, Taishō contracted what was diagnosed to be meningitis. Although he recovered, the experience left him in poor health for his entire life. As was traditional at the time, responsibility for the future emperor's upbringing was given at first to Count Nakayama Tadayasu, Meiji's maternal grandfather. Taishō's education contained little formal schooling and instead concentrated on physical fitness. When he was older, he received more intellectual training.

In 1887, the future emperor was designated crown prince. Unlike those heirs who preceded him, he was the first to be educated publicly. He attended the Peers' School, now known as Gakushuin University. Taishō studied Western subjects as well as the traditional Japanese and Chinese classics. After eight years of formal schooling, he was assigned tutors and lecturers. Because those in charge of the future emperor recognized the importance of the West to Japan's future, his teachers included Frenchmen, Englishmen, and Americans. Other aspects of the imperial family's life changed as well. After 1905, the emperor's children were allowed to reside with him, contrary to past custom. Monogamy for the royal family was also established in 1924, and the imperial concubinage by which Taishō was born was abolished.

Taishō's health remained a concern to Japanese leaders for his entire life. When Meiji died in 1912, his son had to be certified as fit to reign. His health quickly declined after his coronation that year. By 1919, he was unable to perform basic ceremonies of state, including convocations of the Imperial Diet. He spent more and more time at imperial villas away from the Imperial Palace in Tokyo. In 1921, Taishō's eldest son, Crown Prince Hirohito, was made regent for the emperor.

During Taishō's reign, Japan began the process of coming to grips with the problems of modern democracy. Political parties became more important, and the power of the elected Imperial Diet increased. The influence of nonelected government organs, like the *genrō* ("elder statesmen"), declined. For many liberals, the Taishō era was an interlude of democracy between the authoritarianism of the Meiji era and the militarism of the 1930s. It was also during Taishō's reign that for the first time in modern Japanese history, a popular demonstration brought down the government in the so-called Taishō Political Crisis of 1912.

Taishō died on December 25, 1926. He was succeeded by his son, the Shōwa Emperor (Hirohito).

*Tim Watts*

**See also:** Meiji Emperor; Shōwa Emperor (Hirohito).

**Further Reading**

Bix, Herbert P. *Hirohito and the Making of Modern Japan*. New York: Harper Collins, 2000.

Large, Stephen S. *Emperors of the Rising Sun: Three Biographies*. New York: Kodansha International, 1997.

Seagrave, Sterling, and Peggy Seagrave. *The Yamato Dynasty: The Secret History of Japan's Imperial Family*. New York: Broadway Books, 1999.

## Taiwan Expedition (1874)

In 1871, Paiwan aborigines murdered 54 Ryukyuan sailors off the southern tip of the island of Taiwan (then called Formosa). In 1874, the Japanese government demanded that China punish the aborigines and pay reparations to Japan. The Chinese government refused, citing two reasons: (1) China did not claim sovereignty over the aborigines and (2) Japan had no territorial sovereignty over the Ryukyu Islands.

In reality, both claims were technically accurate. For centuries the Qing dynasty had claimed Taiwan to be part of its territory but had never exercised any governmental authority over the island. Also, the Satsuma *daimyō* had exercised some loose authority over the Ryukyus for two centuries, but the Tokugawa *bakufu* did not actually recognize the island chain as part of Japan.

The issue was a Japanese red herring. The new Meiji government hoped to use the Taiwan Incident as a way to defuse ex-samurai discontent. A year earlier, Saigō Takamori had tried to get the government to attack Korea in response to another alleged slur on Japanese pride. He hoped to lead an expedition manned by thousands of ex-samurai who were at loose ends after being disenfranchised by the Meiji government. Stripped of their rights to wear two swords, their distinctive topknot hair styles, and their lifetime stipends, the ex-samurai were spoiling for a fight. The earlier Saga Rebellion had served as a warning that these men were an explosive force. Saigō was denied his Korean Expedition because the government feared a war with China that might give Western nations the excuse to intervene in Japanese affairs.

Taiwan looked like a safer, though no less quixotic, adventure. Saigō demurred, but his younger brother Tsugumichi was dispatched with some 3,600 soldiers. The expedition stumbled about, mostly because the Taiwanese did not wish to fight Japan or anyone else. A minor success in a desultory skirmish at Stone Gate was declared a major Japanese victory on May 22, 1874. Nevertheless, it soon became clear that the real Japanese enemy was indigenous diseases. It was later reported that the official 531 Japanese war casualties were actually deaths from the various fevers for which the Japanese had no natural immunities.

In any case, the Taiwan Expedition was officially declared a glorious victory and Tsugumichi returned to Japan as something of a hero. The expedition did not dissipate the ex-samurai's discontent, as evidenced by the Satsuma Rebellion led by Tsugumichi's elder brother a few years later. Ironically, the Qing government could do little better than the Japanese in conquering Taiwan. A year later, it dispatched some 300 Chinese soldiers to that island; nearly two-thirds of them were killed or wounded in a Paiwan aborigine ambush.

Japan and China submitted the Taiwan Question to British arbitration a few years later. The issue was settled when the British confirmed Japanese sovereignty over the disputed Ryukyu Islands in 1879.

Nevertheless, the Taiwan Expedition was celebrated as Japan's first battle in its war of imperial expansion. The government erected monuments to Japan's victory on Taiwan 20 years later when the island became part of the empire as part of the peace settlement after the First Sino-Japanese War of 1894–1895. The souls of Japan's war dead became enshrined as part of Japan's Glorious War Dead at the Yasukuni Shrine.

*Louis G. Perez*

**See also:** Saga Rebellion; Saigō Takamori; Saigō Tsugumichi; Sino-Japanese War; Yasukuni Shrine.

**Further Reading**

Eskildsen, Robert. "Of Civilization and Savages: The Mimetic Imperialism of Japan's 1874 Expedition to Taiwan." *American Historical Review* 107, no. 2 (2002): 388–418.

Leung, Edwin Pak-Wah. "The Quasi-War in East Asia: Japan's Expedition to Taiwan and the Ryūkyū Controversy." *Modern Asian Studies* 17, no. 2 (1983): 122–134.

Nishida Masaru. "Japan, the Ryukyus and the Taiwan Expedition of 1874: Toward Reconciliation after 130 years." *Japan Focus* (November 21, 2005): 436–439.

# Takahashi Korekiyo (1854–1936)

At five a.m. on February 26, 1936, soldiers broke down the doors to the Tokyo home of Finance Minister Takahashi Korekiyo. Two of their officers went to the room where Takahashi slept and brutally murdered him with both a pistol and a sword. Why did these young terrorists kill Takahashi on that cold February morning? They did so, as one of them later testified during his court martial, because Takahashi advocated an economic, foreign, and military policy for Japan that was radically different from the one proposed by the Japanese military.

Although Takahashi is best known for his economic ideas about how to grow the Japanese economy by raising the standard of living for all of the Japanese people ("rich country, prosperous people," as he wrote in an 1885 memorandum, rather than "rich country, strong army,"), he developed in the first decades of the 20th century a comprehensive view of how Japan, a second-level power, should operate in the world of the great powers, which emphasized "going along" with the United States and Great Britain, rather than "going alone." Takahashi realized that Japan, with an economy the size of Italy's and with a heavy reliance on the Anglo-Americans and their empires for capital, markets, raw materials, and technology, could not afford an autonomous foreign policy and an autarkic economy. Not only would Japan lose if it went to war with the British and Americans, but even its military, without access to American and British capital and American petroleum and scrap iron, would make itself weaker in the process.

Takahashi began developing his ideas about economic development, which focused on increasing exports and domestic demand, and the concomitant idea that defense spending was "unproductive" and should be held to a level commensurate with the size of Japan's economy, as early as the 1880s. During that era, under the guidance of Maeda Masana in the Agriculture and Commerce Ministry, Takahashi was involved in researching and writing a grassroots, bottom-up proposal for industrial growth—one that would emphasize agriculture and raw silk, not heavy industry from the West, which the military favored. In the years during and after the end of World War I, Takahashi developed these ideas into a comprehensive view of economic, foreign, and military policy that he explained in a series of memoranda and published articles in the early 1920s. He advocated the following principles:

1. Civilians should lead and the military follow in making Japan's foreign policy.
2. Japan should carry out a peaceful foreign policy.
3. Japan should avoid yen diplomacy and military intervention in its China policy.
4. The Japanese army's and navy's general staffs should be abolished and civilians appointed as army and navy ministers to unify foreign and defense policy under the civilian control of the prime and foreign ministers.
5. Military spending should be reduced sharply. While Prime Minister in 1921–1922, the Takahashi cabinet negotiated the Washington Naval Disarmament Treaty that limited the tonnage of Japan's capital ships to three-fifths of that of the United States and Great Britain. In 1923, Takahashi advocated cutting the army's budget by 50 percent.

6. Japan should cooperate with the United States and Great Britain because Japan did not have either the economic power or the capital, natural resources, or technology to compete with them. Takahashi, as nationalistic a Japanese subject as anyone, resented American attitudes toward Japanese immigrants, but he also understood the realities of power: even with the 5-5-3 ratio in place, Japan paid four times more per capita for its battleships that the United States did. It could not afford to compete with the Anglo-American powers.

7. Diplomatic cooperation with the powers did not mean that Japan could not compete with them in expanding its export trade. Takahashi, ever the nationalist, was committed to growing Japan's economy, not to some abstract idea of worldwide economic development.

8. Government should be decentralized, and in some cases even privatized. In this vein, Takahashi advocated that the Ministry of Education be abolished and control over primary education be turned over to local government. He also suggested that control over the land tax be given to localities to pay for the costs of the education system; that prefectural governors be elected, not appointed; that universal suffrage be established.; and that all of the national universities be privatized, so all universities could compete on an even playing field.

9. In a remarkable memorandum in 1920 to Prime Minister Hara Takashi, and then in a magazine article published in January 1923, Takahashi wrote that the Allied powers in World War I—"countries committed to justice and humanity"—had won the war over German and Austrian militarists who believed that they could achieve their ends only through force. Thus Japan should "put new wine in new wine skins," by rejecting the German model and replacing it with a system that was concerned with "the richness of people's lives."

When Takahashi stepped down from the Finance Ministry in 1927, he thought that, at age 73, his public life was over. Nevertheless, in December 1931, in the midst of a worldwide economic crisis, he became Finance Minister once again, and served in that post for all but a few months of the remaining years of his life. As Finance Minister during the World Depression, Takahashi introduced countercyclical exchange rate, monetary, and fiscal policies—he left the gold standard to devalue the yen, encouraged lower interest rates, and increased government spending to stimulate economic recovery. Japan returned to full employment by 1935–1936, half a decade earlier than most of the world's developed nations.

As government spending increased, so did the Japanese military's demands for more funds. Takahashi did not want to give the army and navy more money, but understood that politically he had no choice. The cabinet, not the Finance Ministry, created the annual budget, and the army and navy ministers could bring down the government if their demands were not met. Thus, during his four years as Finance Minister (1931–1936), Takahashi fought a constant battle with successive army and navy ministers to hold down military spending. During this half-decade, he went on record in opposition to the dispatch of military forces to Shanghai in February 1932; to the use of Japanese capital in the development of Manchuria because the monies could better be used to buy raw materials from the Americans, British, and their colonies; to the concept of the "crisis of 1936," which generals such as Araki Sadao talked about; and to the integration of the Manchurian and Japanese monetary systems, because to Takahashi, Manchuria, even after the establishment of Manchukuo, was still part of China. As he said in November 1935, during the debate over the 1936 budget:

> If the military pushes for larger budgets unreasonably, I think they will lose the trust of the people … Our country is poor in natural resources and I doubt that we can compete in an autarkic economic environment. We must think about our position in the world and form a budget in keeping with our people's wealth.

In other words, Takahashi understood that Japan, which had been anointed a world power after World War I, was not a power in the same way that the United States and Great Britain were. Cooperation with the two great powers, no matter how they might aggravate Japan with anti-immigration and tariff laws, was in Japan's best interest. Japan was not rich and strong enough to "go alone."

The murderous events of February 26, 1936, marked a turning point in Japanese history. Those who advocated a policy of cooperation rather than confrontation with the world's powers were either killed or silenced by fear of being killed. As one Diet member told Takahashi, when asked why he did not join in the fight against militarism, "pistols are scary." Oddly, the army's leaders used the suppression of a coup d'état attempt by their own lower-ranking officers to increase the military's grip on the helm of the Japanese state. Men like Takahashi

Korekiyo, who advocated, and while in office carried out, a policy of cooperation with other world powers and limitations on military spending were gradually replaced by army officers and their civilian "new bureaucrat" compatriots, and Japan moved from cooperation to autonomy in foreign policy, autarky in the economy, war, and defeat.

*Richard J. Smethurst*

**See also:** Araki Sadao; February 26 Incident; Hara Takashi; Tanaka Giichi; World War I.

## Further Reading

Byas, Hugh. *Government by Assassination.* New York: Alfred A. Knopf, 1942.

Singleton, John, ed. *Learning in Likely Places: Varieties of Apprenticeship in Japan.* Cambridge, UK: Cambridge University Press, 1998.

Smethurst, Richard J. *From Foot Soldier to Finance Minister: Takahashi Korekiyo, Japan's Keynes.* Cambridge, MA: Harvard University Press, 2007.

Storry, Richard. *The Double Patriots: A Study of Japanese Nationalism.* New York: Houghton Mifflin, 1957.

Wilson, George M., ed. *Crisis Politics in Japan.* Tokyo: Sophia, 1970.

## Takeda Shingen (1521–1573)

The subject of several historical and fictional works in Japanese scholarship, literature, and cinema, Takeda Shingen remains one the most well-known warlords of the Sengoku era. A general of great repute, he is best known for his fierce rivalry with Uesugi Kenshin (1530–1578), with whom he fought five times at Kawanakajima in Shinano Province between 1553 and 1564. Shingen and Uesugi both allied off and on with a third rival in the Kanto region, the Go-Hōjō clan.

Takeda Shingen was born in Kai Province on December 1, 1521, to clan leader Takeda Nobutora (1493–1574). Following historical custom, Shingen was known by various names over his lifetime: Katsuchiyo during his childhood, and Harunobu after his coming of age. In 1559, he took the name Shingen, by which he is commonly known, after taking the monk's habit. Due to his father Nobuntora's general unpopularity among clan elders, Shingen overthrew his father and took control of the clan in 1541.

Shingen devoted much of his life to gaining control of Shinano Province to his north. Shinano was a large province that was held by several weaker warlord houses. It was through his campaigning in the northern part of Shinano that Shingen began his rivalry with Uesugi Kenshin of Echigo Province. Several Shinano lords who had combined their forces to withstand Shingen fled to Echigo Province, where they begged Kenshin to challenge Shingen. Kenshin agreed, resulting in the First Battle of Kawanakajima in 1553. This and each successive battle at Kawanakajima (1553, 1555, 1557, 1561, and 1564) resulted in a draw. However, Shingen was eventually able to conquer most of Shinano Province.

In the mid-1560s, Shingen began to enter into alliance negotiations with a rising power to his southwest, Oda Nobunaga. His expansionist tendencies, however, would soon bring him into conflict with Nobunaga and his close ally, Tokugawa Ieyasu. In 1567, Shingen invaded Suruga Province, directly to his south and the last remaining province of the once powerful Imagawa clan. The Imagawa were in the midst of a long decline that began after Imagawa Yoshimoto was defeated in 1560 by Nobunaga at Okehazama. At the same time, Ieyasu was invading the Imagawa domain from the west. Their mutual expansion into the same territory led to border clashes and an end to the prospective alliance with Nobunaga. Furthermore, Ieyasu formed an alliance with Kenshin in 1570, leading to an encirclement of Shingen.

Aware of his precarious position, Shingen started preparations to oppose Nobunaga. After fighting had broken out between the Asakura/Azai coalition and Nobunaga in May 1570, Shingen began secretly corresponding with the warlords opposing Nobunaga, as well as with Shōgun Yoshiaki, who was planning to rebel against Nobunaga. But Shingen could not move against Nobunaga until his rear was secured from attack by Kenshin. This impediment was resolved in the winter of 1571–1572, when the Go-Hōjō clan broke their alliance with Kenshin and allied with Shingen.

On November 8, 1572, after months of preparation, Shingen launched his campaign to challenge Ieyasu and Nobunaga. The campaign was initially very successful. In coordination with the other warlords fighting Nobunaga, Shingen called for an encirclement of Nobunaga while he pushed through Ieyasu's forces. Although Asakura and Azai decided to return home for the winter, Shingen nonetheless continued his westward push. Shōgun Yoshiaki publicly rebelled against Nobunaga and raised a small force in Kyoto. Then fate struck: Shingen suddenly took ill, left his campaign, and died in May 1573. His death temporarily ended the Takeda threat to Nobunaga. His successor Katusyori consolidated power over the Takeda clan leadership and took the army back into the field, but he was defeated in 1575 at the Battle of Nagashino.

*Philip Streich*

**See also:** Civil Wars, Sengoku Era; Oda Nobunaga; Tokugawa Ieyasu.

### Further Reading

Lamers, Jeroen. *Japonius Tyrannus: The Japanese Warlord Oda Nobunaga Reconsidered*. Leiden: Hotei Publishing, 2000.

Sansom, George. *A History of Japan, 1334–1615*. Stanford: Stanford University Press, 1961.

## Tanaka Chigaku (1861–1939)

Born Tada Tomonosuke, Tanaka Chigaku was placed in the care of the Nichiren priest Kawase Nichiren when his father died. He broke with the sect in 1879 to join the lay Buddhist organization Nichiren-kai. He changed his name (Chigaku means "wisdom and learning") to signal his break with the parent organization.

Tanaka created a religious syncretism of Nichiren Buddhism and Nativist Shintō that preached that Japan was destined to rule the world by reason of its virtuous purity. He popularized the phrase *hakkō ichiu*, which can be translated "the whole world under one roof." According to Tanaka, Jimmu, the human descendent of the Shintō Sun Goddess Amaterasu-omi-kami, used the phrase when he ascended the throne to become Japan's first emperor in 660 B.C.E. The phrase, quoted in the *Nihon shōki*, is literally "eight cords: one roof"—to Tanaka, it meant that Japan was divinely destined to rule the entire world.

A charismatic preacher and lecturer, Tanaka soon gathered a loose organization of adherents around him, which evolved into the Kokuchukai (National Pillar Society) in 1914. An adept poet and dramatist, he had a gift for turning a phrase. Notably, he linked the Nichiren prayer "Hail the Lotus Sutra" (*Namu myoho rengekyo*) with his own "Imperial Japan Forever" (*Nippon teikoku ban-banzai*).

Tanaka traveled around Japan preaching his militant Buddhism (surely an oxymoron). He taught that Nichiren had been a 13th-century avatar of Japanism. He began to apply his teachings to Japan's expansionism during the First Sino-Japanese War, when he hailed the war as Japan's first step in realizing *hakkō ichiu*. He praised Japan's defeat of Russia in 1904–1905 as the beginning of an anti-Christian crusade. In addition, Tanaka advocated that Japan continue to expand onto the Asian continent after its acquisition of Korea. He preached that it was Japan's sacred mission to "save Asia" from the twin evils of Christianity and communism.

Among Tanaka's later adherents was an army officer, Ishiwara Kanji, who incorporated Tanaka's teaching into his own Plan for Manchuria. Out of that came the Kwantung Army's Manchurian Incident in 1931 as well as the formation of Japan's puppet state Manchukuo a year later.

After the establishment of Manchukuo, Tanaka stepped up his travels to lecture to Japanese emigrants and soldiers in Korea and Manchuria. Only his advancing age and illness slowed him down. He was widely published, and his popularity persisted even after his death in 1939. His phrase *hakkō ichiu* was immortalized in 1940 when it was carved into the stele that commemorated the 2,500th-anniversary celebration of the founding of Japan.

*Louis G. Perez*

**See also:** *Hakkō Ichiu;* Ishiwara Kanji; Manchukuo; Mukden Incident: Lytton Report; Russo-Japanese War; Sino-Japanese War.

### Further Reading

Edwards, Walter. "Forging Tradition for a Holy War: The *Hakkō Ichiu* Tower in Miyazaki and Japanese Wartime Ideology."

*Journal of Japanese Studies* 29, no. 2 (2003): 289–324.

Lee, Edwin. "Nichiren and Nationalism: The Religious Patriotism of Tanaka Chigaku." *Monumenta Nipponica* 30, no. 1 (1975): 19–35.

## Tanaka Giichi (1864–1929)

Born on June 22, 1864, in the Chōshū Hagi domain of Japan, Tanaka Giichi graduated from the Japanese Military Academy and served in the 1904–1905 Russo-Japanese War as the chief of operations. After the war, Tanaka held several key positions within the Ministry of War and on the Army General Staff. He pressed for an expansionist foreign policy on the Asian mainland while he overhauled military training and effected greater coordination between military and civilian education.

Tanaka was appointed Army Minister in the Hara Takashi cabinet in 1918 and cooperated with Hara in withdrawing Japanese troops from Siberia. Tanaka understood the nature of modern warfare as total war and sought to incorporate the lessons of World War I into army preparedness and training reform. His service in the Hara cabinet and his strategic vision shaped Tanaka as a politician. Awarded the title of baron in 1920, he served as Army Minister again in the second cabinet of Yamamoto Gonnohyōe in 1923. Then, in April 1925, he assumed the presidency of the Rikken Seiyūkai Party on the recommendation of Takahashi Korekiyo and left the army.

Tanaka was elected to the House of Peers the following year. In April 1927, he became Prime Minister and Foreign Minister simultaneously. He convened the Eastern Council two months later to refashion Japan's China policy, a move widely perceived as reflecting his hard-line position on Chinese affairs.

The so-called Tanaka Memorial, cited by a Chinese journal in December 1927 as evidence of Japan's expansionist intent, allegedly evolved from this conference and was presented to Emperor Hirohito. In all likelihood, this document, containing many stylistic and factual errors, was fabricated. Tanaka was reprimanded by the emperor for his handling of the bombing death of Zhang Zuolin in July 1929, and his cabinet collapsed as a result. Tanaka died in Tokyo on September 29, 1929.

*Kurosawa Fumitaka*

**See also:** Hara Takashi; Russo-Japanese War; Shōwa Emperor (Hirohito); Siberian Intervention; World War I; Yamamoto Gonnohyōe; Zhang Zuolin.

### Further Reading

Bamba, Nobuya. *Japanese Diplomacy in a Dilemma: New Light on Japan's China Policy, 1924–1929.* Vancouver, Canada: University of British Columbia Press, 1972.

Morton, William F. *Tanaka Giichi and Japan's China Policy.* New York: St. Martin's Press, 1980.

Nish, Ian. *Japanese Foreign Policy in the Interwar Period.* Westport, CT: Praeger, 2002.

## Tanaka Memorial

The Tanaka Memorial was alleged to be a secret report of a 1927 meeting held by then Prime Minister Tanaka Giichi and the leaders of Japan's Army, Navy, Finance and Foreign Ministries. The memorial outlined a four-step plan to conquer the world.

The authenticity of the document is still questioned among historians. Mention of the memorial was first made in a Chinese Nationalist (Guomintang) Party organ, *China Critic*, in 1929. In the article, the author claimed to have read a copy of the memorial in which Tanaka had stated that Japan planned to seize Manchuria, defeat China, establish forward naval bases in the Pacific, and then ultimately conquer the United States and the world. An English translation of the article appeared in the house organ of the American Communist Party in 1931, but most international experts dismissed the report as a thinly disguised plot by Guomintang propagandists. Herbert Armstrong published an article on the memorial in the American *Plain Truth* magazine in 1934. Coming on the heels of Japan's actions in Manchuria in 1931 and the establishment of the puppet regime of Manchukuo a year later, the memorial took on some credence. American propagandists, including Frank Capra in his wartime movie series *Why We Fight*, gave the memorial more publicity.

Most scholars consider the memorial to be a hoax, pointing to the fact that no authentic Japanese-language copy was ever discovered. Indeed, no copy was introduced into evidence at the International Military Tribunal for the Far East, which investigated war crimes committed during World War II. Most historians consider it to be a rather heavy-handed (though admittedly remarkably effective) piece of wartime propaganda.

*Louis G. Perez*

**See also:** International Military Tribunal for the Far East; Manchukuo; Mukden Incident: Lytton Reprt; Tanaka Giichi.

### Further Reading

Coble, Parks M. *Facing Japan: Chinese Politics and Japanese Imperialism, 1931–1937*. Cambridge, MA: Harvard University Press, 1991.

Stephan, John T. "The Tanaka Memorial (1927): Authentic or Spurious?" *Modern Asian Studies* 7, no. 4 (1973): 733–745.

## Tanuma Okitsugu (1719–1788)

Tanuma Okitsugu was born in 1719 in Kii han. When his *daimyō*, Tokugawa

Yoshimune, was summoned to Edo to become the eighth shōgun, Okitsugu and his father accompanied him. Okitsugu became a page (*kosho*) to Yoshimune's son, Ieshige. In 1745, Tokugawa Ieshige succeeded his father to become the ninth shōgun. Okitsugu remained in his service as Ieshige's personal attendant. Okitsugu's rose to the rank of chamberlain (*sobashu*) in 1751.

In 1760, Ieshige relinquished his position in favor of his son Tokugawa Ieharu, who continued to rely on Okitsugu. In 1767, he was promoted to Grand Chamberlain (*sobayonin*). In 1772, Okitsugu was named a Councilor of State, as well as Grand Chamberlain. Okitsugu was the only man to ever hold both offices simultaneously.

His first son, Okitomo, also entered the shōgunate service; he became a junior councilor in 1783. Other men related by marriage to Okitsugu or his followers held most of the key positions of government, especially in the finance commissioner's office (*kanjo bugyo*).

Part of Okitsugu's rise to power was based on his skill in learning the weaknesses of superiors and colleagues and taking advantage of them. He appreciated money and openly approved of bribery. He was alleged to have said, "Gold and silver are treasures more precious than life. A man whose wish is to serve is so strong that he offers bribes for an appointment shows thereby that his intentions are loyal." Office seekers realized the higher the desired office, the larger the bribe would need to be.

The "Okitsugu period" (1767–1786) was characterized by many problems and disasters, both human and natural, and Okitsugu was blamed for exercising undue influence over the weak shōguns. A number of peasant uprisings and mob violence occurred in the cities. Famine was common, agricultural revenues fell off, and the people faced a heavy tax burden. Even natural disasters were blamed on Okitsugu, including the eruption of Mount Asama in 1783 and epidemic diseases in the 1780s. Nevertheless, Okitsugu did seek to ease the nation's troubles.

His policies were designed to centralize power under the shōgun at the expense of the *daimyō*, who exercised nearly total control over their fiefs. His fiscal policies were designed to increase tax income and create new sources of revenue for the shōgun. Some policies were traditional, such as reclamation of arable land through draining of swamps and riparian works designed to increase irrigation facilities. Okitsugu created monopolies on copper, iron, vegetable oil, silk, lime, and ginseng in exchange for payments by merchants.

Foreign trade in certain products increased; copper, shellfish, and dried seafood were exported from Nagasaki in exchange for gold and silver. Okitsugu dispatched a mission to negotiate trade terms with the Russians, and he organized a new guild of merchants intended to support foreign trade, granting them special privileges and taxing them heavily. Okitsugu ordered silver coins be minted, to supplement the gold currency already in use. Other schemes to reform Japan's economy, however, such as setting up a shōgunate revolving-loan fund for the *daimyō*, were largely unsuccessful.

Okitsugu's enemies continually pointed to his corruption and blamed him for many of the nation's problems. Thus, when shōgun Tokugawa Icharu died in 1786, Okitsugu quickly fell from power. He and his son were removed from their positions and stripped of many of their holdings. Okitsugu died in 1788.

*Tim Watts*

See also: Tokugawa *Bakufu* Political System.

**Further Reading**

Hall, John Whitney. *Tanuma Okitsugo, 1719–1788: Forerunner of Modern Japan.* Cambridge, MA: Harvard University Press, 1955.

Screech, Timon. *Secret Memoirs of the Shōguns: Isaac Titsingh and Japan, 1779–1822.* London: Routledge Curzon, 2006.

## Tarawa, Battle of (November 20–24, 1943)

In December 1941, a Japanese task force seized Tarawa—part of the Gilbert Islands, which stretch some 500 miles along the equator. Tarawa is a hook-shaped atoll with a lagoon formed by a coral reef just beneath the ocean surface. The barb in the hook is formed by 2-mile-long, triangular-shaped Betio Island, less than 300 acres of coral sand and coconut palms rising no more than 15 feet above sea level.

The Japanese constructed an airfield there, and by November 1943, they had turned Betio into a fortress. Rear Admiral Shibasaki Keiji commanded 5,000 naval infantry troops who manned reinforced concrete blockhouses, coconut-log bunkers, and gun pits, all connected by a network of tunnels and trenches. Heavy guns in hardened revetments commanded virtually every approach to the island, prompting Shibasaki to remark that Betio could not be taken by a million men in a hundred years.

The Central Pacific commander, U.S. Admiral Chester W. Nimitz, decided to seize the Gilbert Islands in a joint assault by the army and the Marines as the first test of offensive amphibious operations. V Amphibious Corps was responsible for the landing, code-named Operation Galvanic.

The 2nd Marine Division would seize Tarawa, while the army's 27th Infantry Division landed at Makin.

V Corps staffers decided the portion of Betio that faced the lagoon was the least heavily defended terrain, and they designated landing areas there as Red Beaches 1, 2, and 3. A disadvantage to those sites was the precise navigation required for the landing craft to pass into the lagoon and then maintain formation as they approached the beaches. Amphibious doctrine called for landings at high tide so the landing craft could clear defensive obstacles. Unfortunately, the planners did not have reliable tide charts, and when November 20, 1943, was designated as D-Day, the tides would not be favorable to the Marines. By then, U.S. aircraft had flown hundreds of sorties against Betio, saturating the island with bombs as ships of the Fifth Fleet pounded the island's defenses one last time. Faulty U.S. reconnaissance reports indicated that nothing was left alive on Betio.

At 9:00 a.m., almost two hours after the last bombardment began, three reinforced battalions of the 2nd Marine Regiment attacked Red Beaches 1, 2, and 3. Japanese heavy guns opened up, unleashing a deadly hail of fire into the tightly packed amphibious tractors (amphtracs) as they neared the reef, paused briefly to climb over it, and then landed on the beaches. However, the shallow-draft Higgins boats that followed could not get over the reef. A nightmare for the Marines began when they were forced to debark into the water about 600 yards from the shore. Withering Japanese machine-gun fire met the Marines, who were unable to return fire as they slowly waded toward shore laden with equipment. A small seawall afforded little cover from Japanese small-arms fire as navy corpsmen set up aid stations.

By afternoon, the Marines had penetrated no more than a few hundred feet in many places. Their leaders requested that reserves be committed in a message that emphasized the precariousness of the situation, stating, "Issue in doubt." Of the 5,000 Marines who landed that day, almost 1,500 became casualties. During the night, the Japanese threatened with counterattacks, snipers, and infiltrators. Many Marines had drained their canteens and emptied their cartridge belts. The wounded suffered and could only wait for evacuation in the morning.

The morning saw little improvement. Stiff resistance compelled the attackers to destroy each Japanese strong point at a heavy price, as U.S. Navy destroyers provided fire support at dangerously close ranges. The day of November 21 ended with more of Betio in Marine hands, but the island was not yet secure. At midmorning on November 22, the Marines began their final assault on the Japanese command post, where they poured gasoline down air vents and then ignited it, killing those inside, including Shibasaki. Many Japanese committed suicide as the Marines cleared the western portion of the island and pushed the remaining defenders into a narrow tail of land in the east.

The final Japanese act entailed a series of nighttime banzai attacks, in which mobs of enemy soldiers charged Marine positions with drawn swords and bayonets. They were cut down by artillery and machine-gun fire from the exhausted Marines. Commanders declared the battle over on the morning of November 23, after 76 hours of horrendous fighting.

The Japanese had 4,690 men killed; only 17 prisoners were taken, along with 129 Korean laborers. The desperate Japanese defense of the island cost the Marines and the navy 1,027 dead, 88 missing, and 2,292 wounded. The casualties shocked an American public that viewed the fight on Tarawa as evidence that there would be no cheap victories as the battles were carried to the Japanese homeland. The Battle of Tarawa brought many changes in fighting tactics, including improved naval fire support and significant increases in firepower ashore, to include more automatic weapons, tanks, explosive charges, and flamethrowers.

*Steven J. Rauch*

See also: World War II, Pacific Theater.

### Further Reading

Alexander, Joseph H. *Utmost Savagery: The Three Days of Tarawa.* Annapolis, MD: Naval Institute Press, 1995.

Russ, Martin. *Line of Departure: Tarawa.* New York: Doubleday, 1975.

## *Tenko* (Political Conversion)

The term *tenko* ("changing directions") was first used in the public statement issued by Sano Manabu and Nabeyama Sadachika on June 8, 1933, announcing their joint repudiation of their former Marxist political loyalties. The two members of the Japan Communist Party (JCP) had been imprisoned for treason since mid-1929. In their statement, they explained that they had been "reborn" into the national essence (*kokutai*) and now swore loyalty to the emperor.

Within the year, more than 500 former members of various leftist political parties joined the two and issued their own public *tenko* statements. By 1940 virtually every member of the JCP had renounced their former Marxist ideologies, and by 1942 almost all former leftist parties had been dissolved and their members had joined the new ultra-nationalist Imperial Rule Assistance Association (*taisei yokusansai*).

A number of former leftists wrote that they had been heavily influenced by the new political ideologies expressed by Sano and Nabeyama, but also by Josef Stalin's actions in the late 1920s. Several cited Stalin's sacrifice of the Chinese Communist Party in Jiang Jieshi's "White Terror" and Extermination Campaigns of 1926–1936 and, of course, Stalin's alliance with Jiang again in 1936 in the so-called Second United Front aimed at Japan. They claimed that it had been Stalin who had repudiated the essential socialist ideologies in favor of Russian national interests. A number of *tenko* claimed that their own conversions were merely minor shifts from proletarian internationalism to petty bourgeois nationalism. In other words, they maintained their beliefs in the long-term benefits of socialism, but were now just making minor adjustments in their short-term strategies.

In addition to the political "conversions," a number of authors underwent a *tenko* and began to write in favor the emperor-centered nationalism (*tennō taisei*). The best-known former leftist writers who underwent *tenko* included Shimaki Kensaku, whose "Quest for Life" (*Seikatsu no tankyu*) was basically apolitical, and Hino Ashihei, whose "Wheat and Soldiers" (*Mugi to heitai*) confessed his involvement in the 1937 China Incident and praised the heroism of Japanese soldiers.

Similarly, the *tenko* term has also been applied to many Japanese who underwent a wartime religious conversion from other religions to State Shintō. Notable members of this group include Akamatsu Katsumaro and Kurata Hyakuzo, who had been adherents of Pure Land Buddhism and now joined the *tennō taisei* loyalists after a public *tenko*. Also, one of Japan's "New Religions," *Omotokyo*, began to support the state in the mid-1930s after experiencing a decade of religious persecution.

*Louis G. Perez*

See also: Jiang Jieshi (Ch'iang K'ai-shek).

## Further Reading

Hoston, Germaine. "A Marxism and National Socialism in Taishō Japan: The Thought of Takabatake Motoyuki." *Journal of Asian Studies* 44, no. 1 (November 1984): 43–64.

Hoston, Germaine. "Tenkō: Marxism and the National Question in Prewar Japan." *Polity*16, no. 1 (Autumn 1983): 96–118.

Steinhoff, Patricia G. *Tenko: Ideology and Societal Integration in Prewar Japan.* New York: Garland, 1991.

**Teppo.** *See* Firearms in Premodern Japan.

## Tōgō Heihachirō (1848–1934)

Born at Kajiya, Satsuma, on January 27, 1848, Tōgō Heihachirō joined the Satsuma domain navy in 1866 and was a gunnery officer in the 1868 Boshin War. He entered the new Imperial Navy as a cadet in 1871, then apprenticed with the Royal Navy and studied mathematics at Cambridge University during 1871–1878.

After being promoted to lieutenant commander in 1879, Tōgō received his first ship command. Promoted to captain in 1888, he took command of the cruiser *Naniwa* and sailed it to Hawaii in 1893 during unrest surrounding the coup against Queen Liliuoikalani. On July 26, 1894, in the *Naniwa*, he began the 1894–1895 Sino-Japanese War off Korea, sinking by torpedo the British transport *Kowshing*, which was carrying Chinese troops. Tōgō then participated in the Battle of the Yalu River on September 17, 1894, and commanded naval forces that seized Taiwan. Promoted to rear admiral in 1895, he headed the Naval Technical Council and the Higher Naval College during 1895–1896. He commanded the Japanese squadron in the suppression of the 1900–1901 Boxer Rebellion in China. In October 1903, he took command of the Standing and Combined Squadrons, virtually the entire Japanese fleet.

Flying his flag in the battleship *Mikasa*, Tōgō began the 1904–1905 Russo-Japanese War with a surprise attack on the Russian Far Eastern Fleet at Port Arthur on February 7, 1904, and then carried out a blockade there. Promoted to full admiral in June, he won the Battle of the Yellow Sea on August 10, repulsing an attempt by the Lüshunkou Squadron to reach Vladivostok. He then annihilated Russia's Baltic Fleet, which had steamed halfway around the world, in the Battle of Tsushima Straits on May 27–28, 1905, the only decisive fleet action in the history of the steel battleship. This defeat brought Russia to the negotiating table and made Tōgō a national hero.

Tōgō was chief of the Naval General Staff during 1905–1909 and was made a count in 1907. Although virtually retired, he was

Tōgō Heihachirō was honored as a war hero in Japan, after leading the decisive naval victory against Russia at Tsushima in 1905. (J. Morris, *Makers of Japan*, 1906)

promoted to admiral of the fleet in 1913 and then oversaw the studies of Crown Prince Hirohito. Tōgō formally retired in 1921, although he continued to have considerable influence on naval policies. He supported the Big Navy advocates, opposing the 1930 London Navy Treaty and thereby helping to widen the split in the navy between the treaty faction and the fleet faction. Tōgō died in Tokyo on May 30, 1934, the day after he was named a marquis.

*Spencer C. Tucker*

See also: Boshin Civil War; Boxer Rebellion; London Naval Conference; Russo-Japanese War; Shōwa Emperor (Hirohito); Sino-Japanese War.

### Further Reading

Kirby, E. Stuart. "Heihachirō Tōgō: Japan's Nelson," in *The Great Admirals: Command at Sea, 1587–1945*, edited by Jack Sweetman. Annapolis, MD: Naval Institute Press, 1997:326–348.

Ogasawara, Nagayo. *Life of Admiral Tōgō*, translated by I. Jukichi and I. Tozo. Tokyo: Seito Shorin Press, 1934.

## Tōjō Hideki (1884–1948)

Tōjō Hideki was born in Tokyo, Japan, on December 30, 1884, into an old samurai family. His father, an accomplished army general, enrolled his son in the Military Academy and the Army Staff College, from which he graduated with honors in 1914. He was a military attaché in Switzerland and Germany and taught at the Army Staff College before accepting a position within the Army Ministry. By 1929, Tōjō had also become commander of the prestigious First Infantry Regiment.

Tōjō rose to major general in 1933. In 1935, he was transferred to the Kwantung Army in Manchuria as head of military police. He distinguished himself by arresting major conspirators of the February 26, 1936, coup attempt and was rewarded with a staff post within the Kwantung Army.

When the Sino-Japanese War of 1937–1945 erupted in July 1937, Tōjō personally led two infantry brigades in a lightning conquest of Inner Mongolia, his only experience with combat in the field. When presiding General Ishiwara Kanji began pressing for containment of hostilities with China, Tōjō, who supported total war, worked to arrange his ouster. By then, he was the most influential officer in the Kwantung Army.

In May 1938, Tōjō returned to Tokyo as Army Vice Minister under Prime Minister Konoe Fumimaro. He handled his duties with such adroitness that he earned the nickname "the Razor." Tōjō opposed the efforts of Army Chief of Staff Tada Shun, who sought peace negotiations with the Chinese, and continually pushed for expanded war on the Chinese mainland, and possibly with the Soviet Union. He became a vocal proponent of the Tripartite Pact with Germany and Italy, and supported Japan's occupation of Indochina following the 1940 defeat of France.

At home, Tōjō sought to instill greater domestic harmony by absorbing all parties into the Imperial Rule Assistance Association, thereby muting all criticism of foreign policy. Though ostensibly pushing the nation toward conflict, Tōjō's popularity was too great to ignore, and Premier Konoe had little recourse but to retain him in his third cabinet of July 1941.

When Konoe steadfastly opposed a war against the Western powers as unwinnable, Tōjō deftly maneuvered the resignation of his cabinet. Tōjō was then appointed Prime Minister in October 1941 while also holding the post of Army Minister. He authorized continued negotiations with the United

States for a possible end to its trade embargo with Japan while simultaneously preparing the nation for war. "If Japan's hundred millions merge and go forward," he declared, "wars can be won with ease." When it became apparent that U.S. President Franklin D. Roosevelt would not rescind his demand for a Japanese evacuation of China, Tōjō authorized the navy to attack U.S. military installations in Pearl Harbor, the Philippines, and elsewhere in December 1941.

The initial phase of World War II in the Pacific was characterized by a lightning series of Japanese victories over British and U.S. forces. These successes boosted Tōjō's prestige at home and led to greater acceptance of his views on the legitimacy of force. By June 1942, however, the U.S. victory at the Battle of Midway had stopped Japanese expansion in its tracks and commenced a long string of heavy defeats. By 1943, Tōjō had assumed the additional post of Military Procurement Minister, and the following year, he became Chief of the General Staff. When the fall of Saipan in July 1944 placed Japan in the range of U.S. bombers, however, Prince Konoe arranged for Tōjō's dismissal as Prime Minister.

When Allied authorities came to his residence with an arrest warrant, Tōjō tried and failed to kill himself. Upon recovering, he was put on trial by an international war tribunal for crimes against humanity and was sentenced to death. He accepted all responsibility for the outbreak of hostilities to absolve the emperor of any blame. He was subsequently hanged on December 23, 1948.

*John C. Fredriksen*

**See also:** February 26 Incident; International Military Tribunal for the Far East; Ishiwara Kanji; Konoe Fumimaro; Kwantung Army Adventurism; Shōwa Emperor (Hirohito); Tripartite Pact; World War II, Pacific Theater.

## Further Reading

Browne, Courtney. *Tōjō: The Last Banzai.* New York: Holt, Rinehart and Winston, 1967.

Butow, Robert J. C. *Tōjō and the Coming of the War.* Stanford, CA: Stanford University Press, 1969.

Coox, Alvin D. *Tōjō.* New York: Ballantine Books, 1975.

Hoyt, Edwin Palmer. *Warlord: Tōjō against the World.* Lanham, MD: Scarborough House, 1993.

## Tokugawa *Bakufu* Political System

The Tokugawa *bakufu* political system represented a mixture of pre-Tokugawa shōgunal institutions and innovations implemented by the early Tokugawa shōgun. Hereditary *daimyō* continued to rule over semi-autonomous domains, relying on their own lands for resources, and supported by samurai loyal only to them. The shōgunate established a general set of rules for maintaining tenuous control over the *daimyō*, but relied upon *daimyō* cooperation to maintain domestic stability and even international relations—for example, by asking *daimyō* to engage with the Ryukyu Kingdom, Korea, and the Ezo lands to the north. The Tokugawa shōgunate devoted its attention to a centered, but not centralized, rule over Japan. Much of its administration was focused in Edo and, to a lesser extent, the surrounding Kanto region, with offices in key cities such as Osaka, Kyoto, and Nagasaki. In many ways, however, the Tokugawa shōgunate mirrored the domains. For example, it depended on its own lands—nearly one-fourth of all land in Japan—for economic resources. Likewise, it created similar recruitment and promotion structures for its own samurai.

Of the nearly 22,500 Tokugawa samurai, nearly 17,000 worked within the shōgunate's bureaucracy. Many of these samurai received little compensation and were generally underemployed; some even struck out on their own as rōnin, finding various odd jobs where they could. Managing these lower-ranked samurai, often called "housemen" (*gokenin*), was a constant struggle for the shōgunate. The regime wanted housemen to use their time constructively—for example, by maintaining preparation for possible military activity. Some acted as intendents who managed the Tokugawa lands located throughout the Kanto plain that surrounded Edo. Others worked as minor functionaries in the various magistrate offices. The rest of the Tokugawa liege vassals, known as the "bannermen" (*hatamoto*), ranged in rank and income from 500 to 9,500 *koku*, a rank just below *daimyō*. Although many were indistinguishable from housemen, bannermen could theoretically claim special privileges—for example, having an audience with the shōgun. Bannermen staffed the mid-level bureaucratic positions: the Edo city magistrate, commissioners of finance and foreign relations, and inspectors. Each position brought with it financial benefits on top of their hereditary stipends. More importantly, these roles gave ambitious vassals a chance to affect Tokugawa policy. A small percentage of bannermen also managed fiefs, similar to *daimyō* domains, from which they could draw material and human resources.

Above the liege vassal samurai were the vassal *daimyō* (*fudai*), whose putatively close connection to the Tokugawa progenitor, Ieyasu, made them trustworthy for protecting the Tokugawa realm. This group also staffed the higher posts, such as the Keeper of Osaka Castle, the Kyoto Deputy, Master of Court Ceremony, and the Magistrate of Temples and Shrines. More importantly, they filled the highest positions, acting as the junior and senior councilors who set Tokugawa policy. Although the title "Great Councilor" (*tairō*) existed, it was largely titular, except when it was occupied by Ii Naosuke. None of the previously described positions were permanent, and mechanisms were in place to break political impasses, such as the ability to create ad hoc committees, create new magistrate offices, or assign trusted men to concurrent positions. Some office-holding *daimyō* were essentially glorified bannermen: they might have small fiefs, but lacked the castle stronghold that defined the classic image of a *daimyō*. Instead, they spent most of their time in Edo focused on their shōgunate duties.

Many of the roughly 23 Tokugawa-relative *daimyō* (*shimpan*) were, like the outer *daimyō* (*tozama*), shut out from formal shōgunate positions. Nevertheless, the "Three Houses" (*sanke*) were important because they provided a pool of heirs should the shōgun fail to produce one. Moreover, the smallest of the three, the Mito domain, maintained a hereditary role, by custom, as adviser to the shōgun. Although close to the Tokugawa legacy, the proximity of these domains did not lead to simple acquiescence to the shōgunate. In Mito's case, the early 19th-century *daimyō*, Tokugawa Nariaki, criticized the Tokugawa shōgunate for not "expelling the barbarians" from Japan.

Several informal channels existed within the shōgunate that allowed outsiders to gain at least a minority voice. *Daimyō*, regardless of their status, as well as noble families in Kyoto could influence the shōgun and shōgunal politics through their "women of the great interior" (*Ōoku*)—hundreds of women who served the shōgun and managed his domestic needs. Thus they played an important function in the political cliques that tied together key liege vassals, noble families, and *daimyō*. Moreover, wealthy merchants and other commoners who lent money to the shōgunate submitted memorials regarding, for example, how to reform shōgunal finances. Gradually the shōgunate allowed input from outer *daimyō* and court nobles, thus weakening its position as the ruling institution in Japan.

*Michael Wert*

**See also:** Buke Shohatto; Civil Wars, Sengoku Era; Ii Naosuke; Muromachi *Bakufu*; Tokugawa Ieyasu; Tokugawa Nariaki.

### Further Reading

Bolitho, Harold. *Treasures among Men: The Fudai Daimyo in Tokugawa Japan*. New Haven: Yale University Press, 1974.

Totman, Conrad D. *Early Modern Japan*. Berkeley: University of California Press, 1993.

Totman, Conrad D. *Politics in the Tokugawa Bakufu, 1600–1843*. Cambridge, MA: Harvard University Press, 1967.

## Tokugawa Bakumatsu Military Reforms

By the 19th century, leaders within the shōgunate, and *daimyō* throughout Japan, bemoaned the backward state conditions of their military organization and technology, and complained about the deteriorating state of the samurai class as a reliable pool of skilled warrior-bureaucrats capable of maintaining stability in Japan. The shōgunate's solution was to streamline its military organization, eliminate inefficiency, provide new sources of military technology from Western countries, and reinvigorate samurai physical and moral training. The first reforms were brief, occurring in 1854, the year that treaties were signed with the United States. They consisted of cost cutting, expanding coastal defenses, and encouraging military drills and frugality among the samurai. Domains carried out these reforms as they saw fit—for example, increasing the number of schools available for samurai learning and martial arts. The reform did little to change the Tokugawa military, however, as other domestic concerns attracted the shōgunate's attention—major reform would have to wait until the 1860s.

The most expansive institutional military changes occurred as one part of a broad effort called the "Bunkyū Reforms" of 1862. These reforms included a shifting of the political relationship between the shōgunate and the court, whereby the shōgunate recognized itself as subordinate to the emperor, and institutional reforms such as the weakening of the alternate attendance system (*sankin kōtai*). On the military front, the shōgunate increased purchases of Western weaponry, like the newly invented Minie rifle, which possessed greater range and accuracy than previously available rifles. The shōgunate encouraged domains to buy warships, and even sent men abroad for training. It also established firing ranges. Other reforms included a complete reorganization of the military structure, using a Dutch model of "tactics of three combat arms," which employed light infantry armed with Minie rifles, artillery units, and heavy and light cavalry. Taking advantage of its close relationship to France, the shōgunate invited several military advising missions to Japan. From the mid-1860s and throughout the early Meiji period, French drill and military science continued to influence the modern Japanese military. This included a French-led construction of an arsenal, dockyard, and iron works at Yokosuka, with plans to build a shipyard that would buttress the shōgunate's navy.

However, traditional weaponry, such as units of pike-wielding samurai, remained.

The shōgunate also redefined its retainers' roles. On the one hand, it no longer required the lowest-ranking men to support the army with their labor, but instead asked them to pay a tax on their stipend—an attempt to accrue more funds for reforms. On the other hand, fief-holding bannermen were asked to send men from their fiefs to Edo and elsewhere for training.

Reforms did not happen at once, but were implemented in piecemeal fashion throughout the 1860s. Many of the reforms changed over time—for example, even units consisting of fief-holding bannermen were eventually disbanded and their military duties converted into tax obligations. Large domains also carried out similar reforms, especially the Satsuma domain, which relied on the British for new weapons and warships. Moreover, the shōgunate and domains included more commoners in their militaries. Shōgunate offices throughout the Kanto regions, such as the Iwahana intendent station in Kōzuke Province, ordered local peasant elites to form militias. These militias, and their counterparts in domains such as Chōshū, were burdensome for peasant populaces who had to provide their manpower and funding. At the same time, the peasant militias allowed young peasants from elite families to build upon their swordsmanship training, presenting them with an opportunity to act out fantasies of being a warrior. In at least one domain, a popular fencing instructor who was a commoner was hired to teach his "realistic" style to the domain's samurai, as part of the daimyō's effort to remilitarize them.

For the shōgunate, the military reforms were too little, too late. It lacked the funds to buy the full range of weapons and training it needed. Moreover, many high-ranking samurai resisted the reforms. For example, they did not want to pay the new obligatory taxes or train with Western rifles, an activity more suitable to low-ranking men or commoners. Nevertheless, many of these reforms influenced the military development during the Meiji period, especially the use of commoners in the army instead of samurai. In addition, the Meiji government continued to support the French-constructed Yokosuka naval base, and used French models for infantry.

*Michael Wert*

**See also:** Bakumatsu Fencing Schools and Nationalism; Navy, Modernized; Rise of the Modern Army; *Sankin kōtai* (Alternate Attendance); Tokugawa *Bakufu* Political System; Tokugawa Economic Reforms.

**Further Reading**

Medzini, Meron. *French Policy in Japan during the Closing Years of the Tokugawa Regime.* Cambridge, MA: Harvard University Press, 1971.

Rogers, John M. *The Development of the Military Profession in Tokugawa Japan.* Ph.D. dissertation, Harvard University, 1998.

Totman, Conrad D. *The Collapse of the Tokugawa Bakufu, 1862–1868.* Honolulu: University Press of Hawaii, 1980.

## Tokugawa Ieyasu (1543–1616)

Tokugawa Ieyasu was born Matsudaira Takechiyo on January 31, 1543, near Nagoya; he was the son of the *daimyō* Matsudaira Hirotada. Seeking to expand his lands from the mountains onto the plains of Mikawa, Hirotada made an alliance with the neighboring Imagawa clan and sent his six-year-old son to live with the Imagawa as a hostage. There, Ieyasu learned military and administrative skills and even led forces on behalf of the Imagawa. During his dozen years with the Imagawa, Ieyasu learned of his father's murder in 1549 and the gradual dissolution of his family's holdings.

In 1560, Oda Nobunaga defeated the Imagawa in battle. Ieyasu returned to his family's domains and reasserted control. He changed his name to Tokugawa Ieyasu and allied himself with Nobunaga. Ieyasu profited greatly from his alliance with Nobunaga and expanded his rule to five provinces. He paid a price, however, by having to prove his loyalty by first killing his wife and then ordering the suicide of his son.

When a subordinate assassinated Nobunaga in 1582, one of his generals, Toyotomi Hideyoshi, succeeded him and continued the task of unification. Hideyoshi clashed with Ieyasu in 1584, but a peace was soon made, and Ieyasu married Hideyoshi's sister.

In 1589, Ieyasu joined Hideyoshi in a campaign against Hōjō, a powerful *daimyō* with lands on the plains in the eastern provinces of the Kanto. Hideyoshi then ordered Ieyasu to move his domain to the Hōjō lands, perhaps hoping to isolate his greatest rival. However, that region was agriculturally rich, and Ieyasu instead grew stronger, consolidating his base and building an imposing headquarters at Edo. He also avoided participation in Hideyoshi's ruinous Korean campaigns. When Hideyoshi died in 1598, his son and heir, Toyotomi Hideyori, was only five years old. Although Hideyoshi had made all the *daimyō* pledge their loyalty to his son, the barons soon set about scheming to gain power. Ieyasu, who was officially the regent, emerged as the leader of one of two factions. In 1600, his forces crushed his opponents in the Battle of Sekigahara.

Ieyasu then became the undisputed lord of Japan. He dispossessed the *daimyō* who had opposed him of their lands, and either distributed those lands to loyal *daimyō* or reserved them for the Tokugawa clan. The emperor, powerless but prestigious, named Ieyasu shōgun in 1603.

Ieyasu was not an absolutist ruler; he settled for obedience from the *daimyō* and granted them considerable autonomy within their domains. He did require that all *daimyō* spend part of each year (*sankin kōtai*) at his court in Edo and leave their wives and children as hostages when they were not there. That system allowed Ieyasu to watch for and punish any signs of disloyalty. He also kept the *daimyō* busy expanding the castle at Edo and overseeing and paying for the work of thousands of artisans and laborers. By the time of his death, the castle was the largest in the world, a maze of moats, stone walls, and wooden parapets, stocked with enough supplies to withstand a prolonged siege.

Hideyoshi had sought to ban Spanish and Portuguese Catholic missionaries after a half-century of proselytizing in Japan. In about 1600, Dutch and English traders arrived in the country; unlike the Iberians, they were willing to trade without bothering about proselytizing the Japanese. Ieyasu was anxious to learn from the foreigners and benefit from their trade goods, particularly firearms; he even made the stranded English sailor William Adams an official adviser. By 1612, Ieyasu became convinced that Japanese Christians represented a threat to his power. He therefore banned missionary work, sought to eradicate Christianity, and even executed some recalcitrant Japanese converts. His successor, Tokugawa Hidetada, would continue such persecution with notorious ferocity. As for foreign trade, Ieyasu allowed it to continue only at the port of Nagasaki.

In 1614, Ieyasu decided to destroy the supporters of Hideyoshi's son Hideyori, the only potential rival to the Tokugawa. After contriving to increase tensions by accusing Hideyori of planning rebellion, Ieyasu led an army to Osaka in 1614 and laid siege to its castle. Early in 1615, Ieyasu offered a peace in return for the destruction of the castle's outer defenses. When that was done, Ieyasu resumed his attack and took the castle. Hideyori and his family committed suicide.

Ieyasu, through war, adept alliances, skilled administration, and outright treachery, had completed the unification of Japan begun by Nobunaga and Hideyoshi and ended its long era of political chaos. By carefully planning for his succession, he ensured that the Tokugawa shōgunate would survive his death. After the destruction of Osaka, Ieyasu returned to Sumpu, became ill, and died on June 1, 1616.

*Ryan Reed*

See also: Oda Nobunaga; *Sakoku*; *Sankin kōtai* (Alternate Attendance); Sekigahara, Battle of; Toyotomi Hideyoshi.

**Further Reading**

Sadler, Arthur L. *The Maker of Modern Japan: The Life of Tokugawa Ieyasu*. London: George Allen & Unwin, 1937.

Totman, Conrad D. *Politics in the Tokugawa Bakufu, 1600–1843*. Cambridge, MA: Harvard University Press, 1967.

## Tokugawa Loyalism: Boshin War

The number of supporters of the Tokugawa shōgunate dwindled after its second punitive mission against the Chōshū domain failed in 1866. Few vassal *daimyō* (*fudai*) answered the shōgunate's call to arms, and among those who did, their large armies fought without enthusiasm. Some fought only because they happened to be near Chōshū, such as the Kokura domain, which was invaded by Chōshū samurai. In 1867, the last shōgun, Yoshinobu, led a coalition army to Kyoto to "free" the emperor from the grasp of enemy influences, but was stopped in the villages of Toba-Fushimi, where the shōgunate lost again, despite outnumbering its opposition. Preempting those who desired to eliminate him as an enemy of the court, Yoshinobu returned his title of shōgun to the emperor, resigning from his position as head of the shōgunate.

Following the loss at Toba-Fushimi, many vassal *daimyō* hedged their bets and declared loyalty to the court. Most of them did not participate in the fighting, some refused to resist the court, and others claimed that because the shōgun had resigned, there was nothing left to defend. From the winter of 1868 to the summer of the following year, a mixed group of *daimyō*, samurai, and commoners fought against the advancing Satsuma- and Chōshū-led armies, many, but not all, in the name of Tokugawa loyalism. In general, resistance occurred in three interconnected regions: Edo and the surrounding countryside, the domains of the Northeast, and a final battle in the north at Hakodate.

The most fervent Tokugawa loyalists could be found among the Tokugawa liege vassal samurai, whose fate was tied to the shōgunate. Oguri Tadamasa, who had served the shōgunate as a finance commissioner and foreign affairs magistrate, was the most vocal among those who wanted to fight against Satsuma and Chōshū. After his view failed to convince the shōgun to fight, the shōgun fired him. He retired to his fief and was later executed, the only shōgunate vassal to suffer this fate. Other colleagues formed units of low-ranking samurai and commoners, like their emperor-zealot counterparts, the *shishi*, to maintain stability in Edo. The largest of these, the Shōgitai, eventually received authority to protect Yoshinobu. The group quickly amassed 3,000 to 4,000 members who engaged in guerrilla warfare against the invading army. They were finally defeated by government troops during the battle of Ueno in the summer of 1868.

Many loyalists fled to the northwest, where they joined 26 domains to fight against the Meiji government's troops, in what is called the Boshin War. Although some were vassal *daimyō* of the Tokugawa family, little evidence suggests that they fought out of a sense of loyalty to the Tokugawa family. In fact, they imitated the imperial loyalist domains by propping up their own imperial family member, Prince Rinnōji, and created a royalty-centered government like the new Meiji one. Even so, much of the fighting occurred in the Aizu domain, one of the three *daimyō* families closely related to the Tokugawa. The Aizu-led coalition lost in the fall of 1868.

Former shōgunate samurai and survivors of the fighting in Aizu led a final rebellion against the emperor's armies under the leadership of Enomoto Takeaki, head of the shōgunate's navy. Rather than turn over the shōgunate's eight warships, as negotiator Katsu Kaishū had promised, Enomoto sailed them from Edo to the north in the summer of 1868. Disaffected samurai, *daimyō*, and even a few French military advisers who worked for the shōgunate joined him in Hakodate, Hokkaidō. Enomoto attempted to establish a rival government, the republic of Ezo. This group held the first elections on the Japanese islands, but failed to convince a Tokugawa family member to come lead their newly formed nation. Thousands of troops clashed with the government's army, losing to them in the summer of 1869. Enomoto was later pardoned and became Minister of the Navy.

The Boshin War and Tokugawa loyalism was short-lived, having been destroyed by the fall of 1869. Many former Tokugawa samurai, like Enomoto and Katsu Kaishū, found employment with the Meiji government, especially in vital fields such as foreign affairs, finance, and the navy. The bloodiest fighting in Aizu scarred local history there, much as warfare affected the American South after the Civil War. Even in Aizu today, when people there refer to "the war," it signifies not World War II, but the Boshin War.

*Michael Wert*

**See also:** Aizu Samurai Spirit; Boshin Civil War; Hitotsubashi Keiki (Tokugawa Yoshinobu); Katsu Kaishū; Meiji Ishin Shishi; Mito School; Tokugawa Bakumatsu Military Reforms.

**Further Reading**

Hillsborough, Romulus. *Shinsengumi: The Shōgun's Last Samurai Corps.* North Clarendon, VT: Tuttle Publishing, 2005.

Medzini, Meron. *French Policy in Japan during the Closing Years of the Tokugawa Regime.* Cambridge, MA: Harvard University Press, 1971.

Najita, Tetsuo, and J. V. Koschmann. *Conflict in Modern Japanese History: The Neglected Tradition.* Princeton, NJ: Princeton University Press, 1982.

Shiba, Gorō, Mahito Ishimitsu, and Teruko Craig. 1999. *Remembering Aizu: The Testament of Shiba Gorō.* Honolulu: University of Hawai'i Press.

Totman, Conrad D. *The Collapse of the Tokugawa Bakufu, 1862–1868.* Honolulu: University Press of Hawaii, 1980.

## Tokugawa Nariaki (1800–1860)

Born in Mito-han in 1800, Tokugawa Nariaki studied with the Mito scholars Aizawa Seishisai and Fujita Tōko, both of whom were key advisers. His political outlook followed their ideas of *sonno-jōi* and *koku-tai*, holding that the shōgunate should utilize the charismatic power of the emperor to militarily mobilize the entire nation, including the peasantry, against the Western threat. His early adoption of these doctrines led to radical political, social and economic reform in the Mito domain.

From 1833 through to 1844, Nariaki rationalized the taxation system, hired experts in Western learning to advise him on coastal defense and battleship construction, trained troops in Western military tactics, established a state school system, combined Confucian and Shintō religious institutions, and taxed Buddhist temples and rich samurai to fund increased military spending. These reforms challenged powerful groups within Mito and beyond. Actions such as his confiscation of temple bells for reuse in arms manufacture became hugely controversial. In 1844, the extent of political conflict in Mito led the shōgunate to censure Nariaki. He was stripped of his position as domain lord and put under house arrest in Edo, with his 13-year-old son assuming the office of domain lord. Nariaki's detention ended within months, and by 1849 he was again politically active in Mito.

Nariaki's focus switched, however, to national shōgunate politics. He continually lobbied for increased coastal defense across Japan. Admiral Matthew Perry's arrival in 1853 vindicated Nariaki's position and propelled him into a more powerful position in the shōgunate. He was immediately given shōgunal responsibility for implementing a defensive buildup along Japan's coasts. Conflicts between himself and the shōgunate leadership, however, led to his resignation from this post in 1855.

From this point, Nariaki sought to directly take control of the shōgunate by aligning with other Tokugawa nobles to have one of his sons become the next shōgun. When this attempt failed in 1858, Nariaki instead secured an imperial command from the emperor in Kyoto, handing responsibility for the defense of Japan directly to the Mito domain. This direct challenge to the power of the shōgunate resulted in a brutal shōgunal crackdown on Nariaki and his Mito domain samurai supporters in Edo. Mito samurai and their supporters who had not been captured launched acts of urban insurgency in Edo, including the assassination of shōgunal Senior Councilor Ii Naosuke in front of the Sakurada gate of Edo Castle in March 1860.

Five months later, Nariaki died in Mito. The suppression of the *sonno-jōi* faction of the Tokugawa house, personified by Nariaki, ironically drove many young samurai who had supported them into the hands of the anti-shōgunate militia and domains, which later carried out the Meiji Restoration, thereby ending the Tokugawa house's rule of Japan.

*Kiri Paramore*

**See also:** Aizawa Seishisai; Ii Naosuke; Perry, Matthew; Sakuradamon Incident; *Sonno-jōi*.

**Further Reading**

Paramore, Kiri. *Ideology and Christianity in Japan*. New York: Routledge, 2009.

Tadashi Wakabayashi, Bob. *Anti-foreignism and Western Learning in Early-Modern Japan: The New Theses of 1825*. Cambridge, MA: Harvard University Press, 1986.

**Tokugawa Yoshinobu.** *See* Hitotsubashi Keiki.

# Tokyo, Bombing of (March 9–10, 1945)

By February 1945, the U.S. 20th Air Force's strategic bombing campaign against Japan was in trouble. The new commander of its combat operations from the Marianas, Major General Curtis LeMay, knew he had been given the assignment in January to get results. He had reorganized the staff, instituted new training, and designed new maintenance programs, but the achievements of his high-altitude precision-bombing attacks remained disappointing. Besides technological problems with the hastily fielded B-29 Superfortress, the biggest difficulty he faced was the weather. Overcast skies and jet stream winds at normal bombing altitudes obscured targets and negated flight patterns.

Other theater commanders were trying to gain control of the expensive B-29s, and LeMay knew he could be relieved (just as his predecessor had been) if he did not produce significant success. He had gained some experience with fire raids in China and had conducted some experiments over Japan. Although unsure how higher headquarters would react to a departure from precision bombing, LeMay and his staff decided to destroy key targets by burning down the cities around them. This result would be achieved with low-level, mass night raids. These tactics would avoid high winds, reduce the strain on the B-29s' problematic engines, allow aircraft to carry more bombs, and exploit weaknesses in the Japanese air defenses.

The first raid employing these new tactics, Operation Meetinghouse, was conducted against Tokyo beginning on the night of March 9. The selected zone of attack covered six important industrial targets and numerous smaller factories, railroad yards, home industries, and cable plants, but it also included one of the most densely populated areas of the world: Asakusa, with a population of more than 135,000 people per square mile. For the first time, XXI Bomber Command had more than 300 bombers on a mission—

325, to be exact—and they put more than 1,600 tons of incendiary bombs on the target.

Before the firestorm ignited by Operation Meetinghouse had burned itself out, between 90,000 and 100,000 people had been massacred. Another million were rendered homeless. Sixteen square miles were incinerated, and the glow of the flames was visible 150 miles away. Victims died horribly as intense fires consumed the oxygen, boiled water in canals, and sent liquid glass rolling down streets. The B-29 crews fought superheated updrafts that destroyed at least 10 aircraft. They also wore oxygen masks to avoid vomiting from the stench of burning flesh. A total of 14 Superfortresses were lost on the mission.

The attack on Tokyo was judged a great success. It resuscitated the flagging strategic bombing campaign against Japan and restored the hopes of Army Air Forces leaders that the B-29s could prove the worth of independent airpower by defeating an enemy nation without the need for an invasion. Operation Meetinghouse set the standard for the incendiary raids that dominated 20th Air Force operations for the remainder of the war.

*Conrad C. Crane*

**See also:** World War II, Pacific Theater.

**Further Reading**

Cortesi, Lawrence. *Target: Tokyo*. New York: Kensington Publishing, 1983.

Edoin, Hoito. *The Night Tokyo Burned*. New York: St. Martin's Press, 1987.

Werrell, Kenneth P. *Blankets of Fire: U.S. Bombers over Japan during World War II*. Washington, DC: Smithsonian Institution Press, 1996.

## Tokyo Rose (1916–2006)

Toguri D'Aquino achieved notoriety as one of several women who broadcast from Tokyo between 1943 and 1945. "Tokyo

Mrs. Iva (Tokyo Rose) Toguri D'Aquino, imprisoned for her alleged anti-American activities during World War II, was released from a federal women's reformatory in 1956. (Library of Congress)

Rose" was a moniker created by her listeners, as there is no trace of the name in broadcast records. Born in Los Angeles on July 4, 1916, she graduated from the University of California in Los Angeles with a B.S. degree in zoology in January 1940 and pursued graduate work there until June, when she began working with her father's business. In July 1941, she sailed for Japan without a U.S. passport, planning to visit a sick aunt and to begin the study of medicine. By September 1941, D'Aquino had decided to return permanently to the United States and applied for a passport, but that application was still in State Department hands when the war began.

By mid-1942, D'Aquino had worked as a typist for a news agency in Tokyo and then for Radio Tokyo. In November 1943, she began to host Zero Hour on Radio Tokyo, part of the Japanese psychological warfare designed to lower U.S. military morale. The 75-minute program was broadcast early each evening. Toguri was variously introduced as Orphan Ann, Orphan Annie, "Your favorite enemy Ann," or "Your favorite playmate and enemy, Ann." The program was popular because it featured recorded big-band music.

Only in early 1944 did D'Aquino become aware that U.S. troops had given her—and other Japanese women broadcasting over Radio Tokyo—the "Tokyo Rose" title. She was the only American citizen given that nickname; the others were all Japanese. In April 1945, she married Felipe D'Aquino, a Portuguese citizen of Japanese-Portuguese ancestry.

Following her postwar admissions to the press about her wartime role as well as inflammatory stories by columnist Walter Winchell, among others, D'Aquino was arrested by the U.S. Army in September 1948 and taken to the United States to stand trial for treason. Federal Bureau of Investigation (FBI) inquiries into her activities took several years (the nearly 750-page FBI report is available on the Internet). Her treason trial began in San Francisco on July 5, 1949, and ended on September 29, when the jury delivered a guilty verdict. On October 6, 1949, she was sentenced to 10 years of imprisonment, fined $10,000, and stripped of her American citizenship. She became only the seventh person to be convicted of treason in U.S. history.

On January 28, 1956, D'Aquino was released after serving six years and two months of her sentence. She fought several efforts at deportation and went to work in the Chicago area. In November 1976, she filed a third petition seeking a presidential pardon (she had applied unsuccessfully in 1954 and 1968). She received a full pardon on January 19, 1977, from President Gerald Ford. She died in Chicago on September 26, 2006.

*Christopher H. Sterling*

**See also:** World War II.

**Further Reading**

Duus, Masayo. *Tokyo Rose: Orphan of the Pacific.* Tokyo: Kodansha International, 1979.

Howe, Russell Warren. *The Hunt for "Tokyo Rose."* Lanham, MD: Madison Books, 1990.

## Tôyama Mitsuru (1855–1944)

Born in Fukuoka in 1855, Tôyama Mitsuru was a central figure of the political right in late 19th- and early 20th-century Japan. He is particularly well known as one of the co-founders of the right-wing political society Gen'yôsha ("Dark Ocean Society," 1881) and its de facto leader. The Gen'yôsha was founded and had its headquarters in Fukuoka, a town in western Japan. While most of the early members of the Gen'yôsha had participated in the antigovernmental Movement for Freedom and Civil Rights, the association became increasingly more statist in later years—a situation that led, for example, to the close cooperation of some Gen'yôsha members with the Japanese Imperial Army as spies on the Asian continent or as interpreters. Due to this close relationship with the army, Tôyama has also been called "the army's chief contact man in civilian life."

Although Tôyama is usually characterized as a right-wing activist and politician, his activities also included support for the leaders of various national independence and modernization movements throughout Asia, including Kim Ok-kyun from Korea, Rash Behari Bose from India, Sun Yat-sen from China, and Emilio Aguinaldo from the Philippines.

Throughout his life, Tôyama created a network of contacts involving such leaders and pan-Asian activists. He considered this network essential to equip Asia for successful resistance against Western imperialism. It was, first of all, this anti-Westernism underlying Tôyama's activities (but also his shying away from publicity) that led to his portrayal in the Western media as a dark, conspiratorial figure. Publications of Tôyama's associates, in contrast, describe him as "the silent and unseen hero of Japan" and "the man behind the political scene." Western media were less fond of Tôyama's activities. On October 6, 1944, *The New York Times* published an obituary under the heading "Tōyama of Japan, Terrorist Leader," describing Tôyama as "One of World's Most Evil Men," and the "unofficial emperor" of Japan. The newspaper directly compared Tôyama to Hitler.

The comparison with Hitler is also found in a less polemical publication—an academic article on the Gen'yōsha published by Japanologist Herbert Norman in the same year. The charge of terrorism stemmed from the Gen'yōsha's reputation of not eschewing violence and blackmail to achieve its objectives, particularly in its early years. Japanese and foreign accounts often agreed that Tôyama and his Gen'yōsha were, indeed, to be ranked among the "masters of political bullies and cutthroats in Japan." This assessment, of course, is not completely without reason. In 1889, for example, Tôyama supported an assassination attempt on Foreign Minister Ōkuma Shigenobu. Although in later years Tôyama and his compatriots became closer to government circles, Tôyama was never directly involved in politics and never assumed public office or held ministerial positions.

Contrary to popular wisdom, the Gen'yōsha was little concerned with foreign policy issues, instead advocating emperor worship and domestic patriotism as its main objectives. Foreign policy issues were rather the domain of the numerous offshoots of the Gen'yōsha, such as the notorious Kokuryûkai ("Black Dragon Society," founded 1901) and the Anti-Russia Society (Tairo Dôshikai, founded 1903). However, Tôyama was also highly active in these associations, supported their advocacy of foreign expansion, and was a firm supporter of Japanese expansion into Manchuria as well as a strong advocate of Japan's wars—against Russia in 1904, against China from 1931/1937, and against the Western powers in 1941.

*Sven Saaler*

**See also**: Gen'yōsha Nationalism; Kim Ok-kyun; Ōkuma Shigenobu; Sun Yat-sen and the Japanese.

## Further Reading

Norman, E. H. "The Gen'yōsha: A Study in the Origins of Japanese Imperialism." *Pacific Affairs* 17, no. 3 (1944): 261–284.

Saaler, Sven. "Taishō-ki ni okeru Seiji Kessha. Kokuryūkai no Katsudō to Jinmyaku [Political Societies in the Taishō Era: The Activities and the Social Network of the Kokuryūkai]," in *Demokurashii to Chūkan Dantai: Senkanki Nihon no Shakai Shūdan to Nettwaku* [Democracy and Intermediary Organizations: Social Organizations and Networks in Interwar Japan], edited by Inoki Takenori. NTT Shuppan, 2008: 81–108.

## Toyotomi Hideyoshi (1536–1598)

Born in modest circumstances around 1536 near Nagoya, home of the Oda clan, Toyotomi Hideyoshi's childhood name was Hiyoshimaru. As a youth, he joined the Imagawa clan under the name Kinoshita Tokichiro Hashiba. He had joined the Oda clan as a servant, but by dint of his ability he soon rose to become an important general under Oda Nobunaga, eventually taking the name of Toyotomi Hideyoshi.

Hideyoshi fought in the Battle of Okehazanna in June 1560 and planned the successful attack on Saitō Castle in 1567. He fought in many other battles, and was rewarded for his services with territory in Omi Province. In the Battle of Nagashimo in June 1575, Hideyoshi commanded the left under Oda Nobunaga.

Hideyoshi was besieging the Mori clan at Takamatsu Castle when he learned of the assassination of Oda Nobunaga and his son by Oda Nobunga's vassal Akechi Mitsuhide on June 21, 1582. Hideyoshi then rushed

Toyotomi Hideyoshi was instrumental in the 16th-century unification of Japan after a century of civil war. (Library of Congress)

south and defeated Akechi in the Battle of Yamazaki on July 4, establishing his own de facto control over the Oda clan. He still had to contend with, battle against, and for the most part defeat rivals for Oda Nobunaga's holdings during 1583–1584, among whom the most formidable was Shibata Katsuie. Hideyoshi defeated Shibata in the Battle of Shizugatake in Omi on April 20–21, 1583, after which Shibata committed suicide.

Given the name of Toyotomi by the emperor in 1584, Hideyoshi was now de facto ruler of Japan. Because of his peasant origins, he was unable to secure from the emperor the title of shōgun, which would have given him de jure power. Toyotomi requested the last shōgun to adopt him but was refused, whereupon he assumed the title of *kampaku* (regent). Toyotomi then set about consolidating his control. He campaigned against the Ikkō Buddhist sects during 1584–1585, and then launched campaigns on the islands of Shikoku in 1585 and Kyushu during 1586–1587. Following the latter campaign, which yielded an indecisive result, Toyotomi issued the Sword-Hunt Edict in 1588, which limited the wearing of swords to samurai and hereditary *daimyō*. By forbidding ordinary people the right to bear arms, the transition of the samurai into a professional military class was completed. This remained the case for the next three centuries. Toyotomi expelled Christian missionaries from Japan in 1587 and effectively abolished slavery by halting the sale of slaves in 1590. He also campaigned against the Hōjō clan of central Honshu, the last remaining threat to his authority, and was victorious over them in the siege of Odawara in 1590. Toyotomi set up a political structure centered on a council of the leading *daimyō*, while the regent held real authority.

Fearing a possible revolt by the samurai because of inactivity and wishing to distract them from domestic affairs, Toyotomi mounted a major invasion of Korea during 1592–1593. Although the Japanese experienced early success and occupied most of the Korean Peninsula, further advance was halted by Chinese intervention. When peace negotiations faltered, Toyotomi invaded Korea for a second time during 1597–1598 but was largely unsuccessful. His later years were marked by periods of insanity. Toyotomi died suddenly on September 18, 1598. His political successor Tokugawa Ieyasu benefited much from Hideyoshi's organizational genius.

*Spencer C. Tucker*

**See also:** Imjin War; Oda Nobunaga; Tokugawa Ieyasu.

## Further Reading

Berry, Mary Elizabeth. *Hideyoshi*. Cambridge, MA: Harvard University Press, 1982.

Dening, Walter. *The Life of Toyotomi Hideyoshi*. 3rd ed. London: Kegan Paul, Trench, Trubner, 1930.

## Tripartite Pact

The Tripartite Pact was signed between Italy, Germany, and Japan in Berlin on September 27, 1940. Creating an alliance informally known as the "Rome-Berlin-Tokyo Axis," it provided for cooperation between the signatories to establish and maintain a "new order" in East Asia and Europe, with the Italians and Germans responsible for its creation in Europe and the Japanese in Asia. The treaty was to run for 10 years and be renewed as expiration approached. Article 3 provided for mutual support if any of the signatories were attacked by a third party not currently at war with the signatories.

The treaty contained a provision that it would not affect current agreements with the USSR, which applied to the German-Soviet Non-Aggression Pact of August 23, 1939. A secret supplemental protocol, not published at the time, was agreed to on December 27, 1940. It clarified that in case of an attack the signatories would convene a committee charged with verifying the attack and then activating Article 3. The Germans and Italians also reiterated their commitment to assist Japan should it be attacked by the United States. The parties also promised to share newly developed military technology, which in reality rarely happened, although Germany did share some jet aircraft technology.

In the end, the Tripartite Pact proved to be an empty alliance, as all of the signatories were the aggressors during World War II and, therefore, were never able to call upon their allies under Article 3. The Axis alliance did not function as a true alliance except between the Germans and Italians, who in fact cooperated to a large degree both in Europe in general (albeit with the Germans essentially making all major decisions) and in the attack on the Soviet Union in June 1941. Japan was left to deal with its problems in the Pacific by itself.

*Lee Baker, Jr.*

**See also:** World War II, Pacific Theater.

## Further Reading

Bernd, Martin. *Japan and Germany in the Modern World*. Providence, RI: Berghahn Books, 1995.

Meskill, Johanna. *Hitler and Japan: The Hollow Alliance*. New York: Atherton Press, 1966.

## Triple Intervention

Russia, Germany, and France intervened, in the so-called Triple Intervention, in the settlement of the First Sino-Japanese War (1894–1895) to force Japan to relinquish the Liaodong Peninsula to China. Control of the peninsula would have put Japanese military forces within easy reach of Beijing and in a position to blockade the Gulf of Bohai.

During the war, the Japanese Foreign Ministry made every effort to forestall foreign intervention. It declared Shanghai, the center of British investments, outside the sphere of hostilities. The Japanese government also protected Chinese in Japan from violence. A lawyer was assigned to each Japanese army corps and fleet to prevent any breaches in international law. Meanwhile, China's long-standing quasi-foreign minister, Viceroy Li

Hongzhang, made every effort to encourage foreign intervention to counterbalance Japan.

On April 23, 1895, six days after the signing of the Treaty of Shimonoseki, the ministers of Russia, Germany, and France called on the Japanese Foreign Ministry in Tokyo. They strongly recommended that Japan return the Liaodong Peninsula to China, with the unstated implication that their combined naval forces would ensure that Japan did so. If they had intervened militarily, the Treaty of Shimonoseki would have become a dead letter, and Japan would no longer have been negotiating with China, a defeated power, but with three European great powers. As a result, Japan rapidly agreed to return the disputed territory in return for an increase in China's war indemnity.

There is disagreement over whether Germany or Russia masterminded the intervention. France became involved only through its alliance with Russia. After the French loss of the Franco-Prussian War in 1871, French foreign policy focused on defense against Germany and the restoration of lost territories. In 1894, the Franco-Russian alliance became the bedrock of French security, which meant that France felt compelled to support Russia in Asia. Tsar Nicholas II of Russia had ambitions for empire and commerce in Asia as evidenced by his decision, announced in 1891, to build the very expensive Trans-Siberian Railroad to promote expansion eastward. German interests also stemmed from a desire for empire in Asia as well as the even more important goal of constraining its two main rivals in Europe, Russia and Britain. Kaiser Wilhelm II of Germany tried to stir Russian fears of a "yellow peril" to deflect Russian attention from Europe to Asia, which Russia did until its defeat in the Russo-Japanese War made clear where its real national interests lay.

As a preliminary to negotiations following the Triple Intervention, on May 10, 1895, the Meiji Emperor issued an imperial rescript returning the territory. Despite heavy government newspaper censorship, 40 Japanese subjects reportedly committed *seppuku* (ritual disembowelment) to express their outrage. The Japanese public believed their country had won the Liaodong Peninsula in a just war to protect vital Japanese national security interests on the Asian mainland.

Li Hongzhang, the negotiator of the Treaty of Shimonoseki, also negotiated the Liaodong Convention, returning the peninsula to China in exchange for an addition of 30 million Kuping taels to the war indemnity. Baron Hayashi Tadasu and Li Hongzhang signed the Liaodong Convention on November 8, 1895, in Beijing, and Japan completed the evacuation on December 25, 1895, removing the dockyard equipment to the Japanese naval base at Sasebo.

During the negotiations, Russia pressured Li to remove a clause promising not to cede the peninsula to any other power. Hayashi conceded this point, much to his later regret. On March 27, 1898, Russia claimed the Liaodong Peninsula for itself as part of a vast Russian railway concession through the heart of Manchuria. Thus Li Hongzhang's attempt to use Russia to neutralize Japan ultimately failed. China simply lost the disputed territory to Russia instead of Japan.

Hayashi believed that Li had ceded the Liaodong Peninsula in the Treaty of Shimonoseki, while realizing that the other powers would not tolerate it. He wrote that Li "was only too delighted to let Japan have the sensation of owning the place as a preliminary to the chagrin of losing it." Throughout the war, the Russians had repeatedly made clear to all that they would not tolerate a Japanese occupation of the peninsula. The

Japanese Foreign Ministry proved unable to convince the Imperial Japanese Army of the futility of including this territorial demand. Nevertheless, the diplomats reaped the blame for this army blunder. Foreign Minister Mutsu Munemitsu expressed a common lesson drawn by the Japanese: "diplomacy shorn of military support will not succeed, however legitimate its aims might be." The public supported a massive postwar rearmament program that positioned Japan to defeat Russia the following decade.

The Japanese public honored their military officers for winning the war and excoriated their diplomats for allegedly losing the peace. This widely accepted interpretation of events set in motion the gradual shift in power within Japan from civil to military institutions. The Russo-Japanese War soon accelerated the shift.

*S. C. M. Paine*

**See also:** Hayashi Tadasu; Meiji Emperor; Mutsu Munemitsu; Shimonoseki, Treaty of; Sino-Japanese War.

### Further Reading

Hayashi Tadasu. *The Secret Memoirs of Count Tadasu Hayashi*, edited by A. M. Pooley. New York: G. P. Putnam's Sons, 1915.

Iklé, Frank W. "The Triple Intervention: Japan's Lessons in Diplomacy and Imperialism." *Monumenta Nipponica* 22, nos. 1–2 (1967): 122–130.

Kajima Morinosuke. *The Diplomacy of Japan 1894–1922*, vol. 1. Tokyo: Kajima Institute of International Peace, 1976.

Lensen, George Alexander. *Balance of Intrigue: International Rivalry in Korea and Manchuria, 1884–1899*. 2 vols. Tallahassee: University Presses of Florida, 1982.

Mutsu Munemitsu. *Kenkenryoku: A Diplomatic Record of the Sino-Japanese War, 1894–95*, translated by Gordon Mark Berger. Princeton: Princeton University Press, 1982.

Paine, S. C. M. *The Sino-Japanese War of 1894–1895: Perceptions, Power, and Primacy*. Cambridge, UK: Cambridge University Press, 2003.

## Tsushima, Battle of (1905)

In the summer of 1904, the Russian government decided to make one last effort to win its war with Japan and sent the Baltic Fleet on a voyage around the world to the Far East. If the Russians could gain control of the sea, they could cut off Japanese forces in Manchuria and bombard Japanese coastal cities, forcing Japan to retreat from the war. On October 15, Rear Admiral Zinovi Petrovitch Rozhdestvenski's 36 warships set out on this long journey. The most powerful units were the four new 13,500 ton Borodino-class battleships: the *Borodino, Alexander III, Orel,* and *Kniaz Suvarov* (flagship).

The voyage went badly from the start. On October 21 off the Dogger Bank in the North Sea, jittery Russian crews opened fire on their own cruiser, the *Aurora,* and the British Hull fishing fleet, mistaking them for Japanese torpedo boats and sinking several trawlers. This incident almost brought war with Britain.

After the fleet rounded Portugal, some ships proceeded eastward through the Mediterranean Sea and the Suez Canal, while the main detachment continued south around Africa. The British, being a Japanese ally, refused to supply coal, and the Russians were forced to secure it from German colliers. The lack of coaling stations led Rozhdestvenski to order the ships to take on whatever fuel they could, placing it in every possible space and precluding training and gunnery practice.

# BATTLE OF TSUSHIMA, OCTOBER 27, 1905

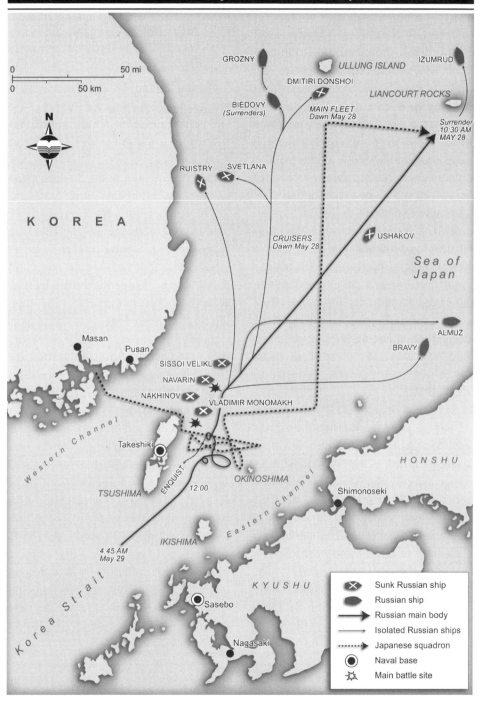

0 — 50 mi
0 — 50 km

N

GROZNY

ULLUNG ISLAND

IZUMRUD

DMITIRI DONSHOI

LIANCOURT ROCKS

BIEDOVY
(Surrenders)

MAIN FLEET
Dawn May 28

Surrender
10:30 AM
MAY 28

RUISTRY

SVETLANA

K O R E A

CRUISERS
Dawn May 28

USHAKOV

Sea of
Japan

Masan

Pusan

ALMUZ

SISSOI VELIKL

BRAVY

NAVARIN

NAKHINOV

VLADIMIR MONOMAKH

Takeshiki

HONSHU

ENQUIST    12:00

OKINOSHIMA

TSUSHIMA

Shimonoseki

Eastern Channel

Western Channel

4:45 AM
May 29

IKISHIMA

K Y U S H U

| | Sunk Russian ship |
| | Russian ship |
| ➤ | Russian main body |
| → | Isolated Russian ships |
| ·····➤ | Japanese squadron |
| ◉ | Naval base |
| ✸ | Main battle site |

Sasebo

Nagasaki

Korea Strait

Reunited at Madagascar, on March 16 the fleet started across the Indian Ocean, refueling five times at sea; this was an unprecedented feat. Rozhdestvenski hoped to get to Vladivostok without battle, but the fleet made one last stop to take on supplies and coal at Cam Ranh Bay in French Indochina.

Rozhdestvenski sent most of his auxiliary vessels to anchor at the mouth of the Yangtze River, and he timed his advance through the Tsushima Straits to be at night. He also sent two cruisers toward the east coast of Japan in an attempt to persuade the Japanese that the entire fleet would follow.

At sea for eight months, the Russians would meet Fleet Admiral Tōgō Heihachirō's modern, efficient, battle-tested Japanese fleet in its home waters. Tōgō gambled that Rozhdestvenski would choose the most direct route to Vladivostok, by means of the Tsushima Straits, and planned a trap there. The Japanese also had cut off Vladivostok by sowing 715 mines at the entrance to Peter the Great Bay.

On the night of May 26–27, Japanese picket ships sighted the Russian fleet in the straits. Tōgō's ships immediately left their bases, dumping coal as they went to increase their speed. Tōgō relied on radio messages to keep informed of the location of the Russians. (Tsushima was the first naval battle in which the radio was used.) The total Russian fleet consisted of 8 battleships, 8 cruisers, 9 destroyers, and several smaller vessels. The firepower was slightly to the Russian advantage, but this was offset by the fact that the Japanese crews were far superior to the Russians in gunnery.

Tōgō had 4 battleships, 8 cruisers, 21 destroyers, and 60 torpedo boats. Many factors favored Tōgō. His ships had been recently overhauled and repaired. The Japanese ships were, on the average, 50 percent faster than the Russian vessels, even the newest of which were fouled from the long voyage. Tōgō's men were fresh, eager, and battle-tested and were sailing in their own waters and led by highly skilled officers.

On the afternoon of May 27, trailed by Japanese cruisers, the Russians sailed past Tsushima Island. When the Russian ships came out of some fog at 1:19 p.m., Tōgō in the battleship *Mikasa* to the northeast at last sighted his prey. The Russian ships were steaming in two columns. Rozhdestvenski had his flag in the *Suvarov*, the lead ship in the starboard column.

The Russians assumed that Tōgō would turn south and bridge the gap, allowing his battleships to fire on the weaker Russian divisions. This approach would have left the Russian ships headed toward Vladivostok, with the Japanese moving in the opposite direction. Instead, Tōgō made a daring move, ordering his cruisers to make a 270-degree turn to the northeast to cut the Russians off from Vladivostok. This brought the Japanese ships onto a course parallel to that of the Russians; with their superior speed they would turn east and cross the Russian "T."

This maneuver carried grave risks, because during the long turn Tōgō exposed his whole line of ships to the full broadsides fire of the Russian fleet. Seconds after the *Mikasa* began its turn, the *Suvarov* opened fire at a range of about 6,400 yards. As the fleets formed into two converging lines, each blasted away at the other. Rozhdestvenski altered course slightly to port, reducing the range, but the Russian fire rapidly deteriorated as the range closed. The Russians scored few direct hits.

Russian fire damaged three Japanese ships, hit many others, and forced a cruiser out of the battle line. But soon the *Suvarov* was on fire, and another battleship, the *Oslyabya*, was holed in its side. The Japanese concentrated their fire on these two crippled battleships, and their superior gunnery gradually held sway.

By nightfall, the Japanese victory was nearly complete. Wounded in the battle, Rozhdestvenski yielded command to Rear Admiral Nicholas Nebogatov. That night Tōgō sent his destroyers and torpedo boats to finish off those Russian vessels that were not already sunk or that had escaped.

Of 12 Russian ships in the battle line, 8 were sunk, including 3 of the new battleships; the other 4 were captured. Of the cruisers, 4 were sunk, 1 was scuttled, and 3 limped into Manila and were interned; only 1 made it to Vladivostok. Of the destroyers, 4 were sunk, 1 was captured, 1 was interned at Shanghai, and 2 reached Vladivostok. Three special service ships were sunk, 1 was interned at Shanghai, and 1 escaped to Madagascar. Tōgō lost only 3 torpedo boats. Although other ships suffered damage, all remained serviceable. The Russians lost 4,830 men killed or drowned and almost 7,000 were taken prisoner. Japanese personnel losses were 110 killed and 590 wounded.

In just one day, Russia ceased to be a major Pacific power. Fifty years would pass before it regained status at sea. The battle confirmed Japan's position as the premier military power of the Far East and led the Japanese to believe that wars could be turned by one big battle. Ironically, the Battle of Tsushima was also the only major decisive fleet action in the history of the steel battleship. Only the gun had counted—but in the future, underwater or aerial weapons would often exercise the dominant influence at sea.

Tōgō's victory at Tsushima forced the Russian decision to sue for peace. Although Russia might have raised new armies to continue the war, popular discontent and revolutionary outbreaks threatened the government's very survival.

*Spencer C. Tucker*

**See also:** Tōgō Heihachirō.

**Further Reading**

Busch, Noel F. *The Emperor's Sword: Japan versus Russia in the Battle of Tsushima.* New York: Funk and Wagnalls, 1969.

Hough, Richard. *The Fleet That Had to Die.* New York: Viking, 1958.

Westwood, J. N. *Witnesses of Tsushima.* Tokyo: Sophia University, 1970.

## Twenty-One Demands (1915)

After Japan's successful invasion of German possessions in the Shandong Peninsula in 1914, Japan's Foreign Minister Katō Takaaki moved to gain formal recognition of Japanese claim to this territory. In January 1915, Japan's minister in Beijing presented a list of 21 points of negotiation to the Yuan Shikai government. This list of proposals subsequently gained notoriety as "the Twenty-One Demands."

Japan's proposals contained widely divergent aims and reflected a number of areas of concern over its position in China relative to the other powers active in China: Great Britain, France, Germany, Russia, and the United States. With Germany removed by military force, the proposals aimed to ensure Chinese recognition of Japan's new gains in Shandong. They attempted to shore up Japan's position in Manchuria by extending the leasehold on colonial possessions in the Liaodong Peninsula (the Kwantung Leased Territory) and on the south China coast, adjacent to Japan's colony Taiwan. Other proposals aimed to supplant the position of Japan's ally Britain in the Yangtze River valley and block further European expansion in China. In these proposals, Japan hoped to secure mining rights and railroad concessions, and expand the influence of Japanese advisers in regions of special interest.

Many of the proposals were ambiguously worded, none more so than the notorious subset of the proposals known as "Group 5." This set of the proposals sought a comprehensive shift in Japan's position in China, giving Japan greater influence over the central government of the country, but also giving Japanese rights to own land, engage in religious activities, and administer police activities throughout China. From the perspective of the imperialist age in which they emerged, these proposals might not have appeared either outlandish or inconsistent with privileges that other imperialist powers already enjoyed. Japan's bare-knuckled diplomatic techniques also differed little from the behavior of other powers in China.

There is no doubt, however, that Japan's imperialist gambit was ill timed. With European states distracted by war, Japan sought to shift the balance of power when other states felt insecure. Japan's own behavior—insisting that negotiations remain secret and hiding the contents of "Group 5" from British and American diplomats—betrayed the government's discomfort with its timing. China's negotiators decided they had no alternative but to expose the full contents of the demands to the international community. As an indication of the consequences of such diplomatic fumbling, U.S. Minister to China Paul S. Reinsch, who had previously been tolerant of Japan's imperialist ambitions, was transformed into a harsh critic.

Under this scrutiny, Japan withdrew most of the proposals from Group 5 but issued an ultimatum threatening military action if China did not accede to the remaining demands. In the face of the ultimatum, Chinese negotiators relented and final agreements over the limited set of demands were signed on May 25, 1915.

The ultimate impact of the episode was symbolic beyond what Japan's policymakers had intended. For Chinese nationalists and Japan's critics, the Twenty-One Demands became emblematic of the naked aggressiveness of Japanese designs on China. The negotiations displayed the weakness of the nominal Chinese government and its inability to act independently of the competing imperial interests of the great powers. The experience of the Twenty-One Demands would color Chinese perceptions of Japanese behavior for decades.

For many Japanese observers and later historians, the Twenty-One Demands demonstrated weaknesses in Japan's diplomatic strategy. For them, Japan's foreign policy remained reactive and opportunistic, without clear guiding principles or a sense of national purpose behind it. In Japanese politics, the episode served as further evidence of the loss of the Meiji era (1868–1912) consensus over national goals. This lack of consensus would afflict Japan's foreign relations in the era between the wars.

*Michael A. Schneider*

**See also:** Party Cabinets; Versailles Treaty; World War I.

### Further Reading

Dickinson, Frederick R. *War and National Reinvention: Japan in the Great War, 1914–1919.* Cambridge, MA: Harvard University Asia Center, 1999.

Iriye, Akira, ed. *The Chinese and the Japanese: Essays in Political and Cultural Interactions.* Princeton: Princeton University Press, 1980.

La Fargue, Thomas Edward. *China and the World War.* Stanford: Stanford University Press, 1937.

# Uchida Yasuya (Kōsai) (1865–1936)

A five-time Foreign Minister, Uchida Yasuya was a key foreign policymaker in interwar Japan. Born in Kumamoto on September 29, 1865, he entered the Foreign Ministry in 1887 upon graduation from Tokyo University and was dispatched as special assistant to Japanese Ambassador to the United States Mutsu Munemitsu. Uchida assisted Mutsu in drafting a treaty with Mexico that became Japan's first "equal" treaty.

Uchida's first ambassadorial appointment was to Qing China in 1901. From Beijing, he became alarmed at Russian encroachment in northern Korea. In cables to Tokyo, Uchida openly advocated removing the Russian threat by force. Following the Russo-Japanese War in 1905, Uchida joined Foreign Minister Komura Jutarō in negotiating Chinese acceptance of the terms of the Portsmouth Peace Treaty.

After serving in Austria (1907–1909), Uchida returned to Washington, D.C., as ambassador. While in this role in 1911, Uchida was appointed Foreign Minister in the second Saionji Kinmochi cabinet. The major foreign policy issue confronting Uchida in his first term as Foreign Minister was the overthrow of the Qing dynasty in China in the Nationalist revolution. Initially, Uchida backed the falling Qing regime, but he soon shifted his approach by linking Japanese policy to that of its ally, Great Britain. Both approaches had the goal of securing Japanese treaty rights in China in the face of an uncertain political atmosphere on the mainland. In failing to support the Chinese revolutionaries, Uchida angered Pan-Asianists in Japan, including some Parliamentarians, who had been advocating independence for China for decades. Accordingly, many were happy to see Uchida resign when the Saionji cabinet fell in the Taishō Political Crisis of 1912.

Uchida's next major assignment was as Ambassador to Russia in 1917. Arriving in the Russian capital mere weeks before the Russian Revolution, Uchida had a front row seat to the communist takeover that allowed him to grasp the lasting changes that Lenin and his counterparts were effecting. As a result, he advocated early Japanese recognition of the Soviet Union and opposed the Siberian Expedition because he felt it would irreparably harm Soviet-Japanese relations.

Uchida guided Japan's post-World War I foreign policy during his second stint as foreign minister from 1918 to 1923 in the successive cabinets of Hara Takashi, Takahashi Korekiyo, and Yamamoto Gonnohyōe. Under Uchida's watch, Japan participated in the Paris Peace Conference, helped to found the League of Nations, and agreed with the Western powers to a set of multilateral treaties known collectively as the Washington Treaties, which established a new cooperative framework for international relations in East Asia and the Pacific. In all of these efforts, Uchida pursued a policy of cooperation with the Western powers and instituted the policy of "coexistence and co-prosperity" with China that sought to maintain Japanese interests on the mainland while not intervening in Chinese politics. This policy was limited to China south of the Great Wall; Uchida continued to defend and extend Japanese interests in Manchuria throughout the period.

Later, in 1928, Uchida sparked controversy when he, as Japanese representative, signed "in the names of the people" the No War Pact. Conservative politicians in the Privy Council, of which Uchida was a member, claimed Uchida had violated the sovereignty of the emperor and demanded an amendment to the Pact. Uchida's firm stance in opposition politically damaged Prime Minister Tanaka Giichi, who had originally appointed Uchida representative signing ceremony in Paris.

Roughly a month before the Mukden Incident in 1931, Uchida was made President of the South Manchurian Railroad. After some hesitation, he threw his support behind the Kwantung Army's seizure of Manchuria and creation of Manchukuo. In meetings with Japanese leaders as well as the Lytton Commission, Uchida argued that Manchukuo would finally solve Japan's "Manchurian problem" (*manshū mondai*). The strongest expression of this argument came in August 1932 when Uchida, newly installed as Foreign Minister in the Saitō Makoto cabinet, announced to the Diet that he was so committed to Japan's official recognition of Manchukuo that he "would not give up one inch even if the country is turned into scorched earth." Uchida continued his bluster by refusing to compromise on the issue of Manchukuo during negotiations over the Lytton Report. His intransigence, in part, led to Japan's withdrawal from the League of Nations in 1933. Uchida resigned as minister

due to health reasons soon after and later died of pneumonia in 1936.

*Rustin Gates*

**See also:** Hara Takashi; Manchukuo; Mukden Incident: Lytton Report; Mutsu Munemitsu; Russo-Japanese War; Siberian Expedition; South Manchurian Railway; Washington Naval Conference.

## Further Reading

Gates, Rustin. *Defending the Empire: Uchida Yasuya and Japanese Foreign Policy, 1865–1936*. Unpublished doctoral dissertation, Harvard University, 2007.

Gates, Rustin. "Pan-Asianism in Prewar Japanese Foreign Affairs: The Curious Case of Uchida Yasuya." *Journal of Japanese Studies* 37, no. 1 (Winter 2011): 1–27.

Gates, Rustin. "Solving the 'Manchurian Problem': Uchida Yasuya and Japanese Foreign Affairs before the Second World War." *Diplomacy & Statecraft* 23, no. 1 (March 2012): 23–43.

## Uchimura Kanzô (1861–1930)

Though the son of a samurai retainer, Uchimura Kanzô was educated in Western learning and became proficient in English. A member of the "Sapporo Band" of Protestant converts from the graduates of the Sapporo Agricultural College, he was baptized by a Methodist missionary and helped start a church in Hokkaidō. After spending several years in the United States and studying at Andover College, he returned to Japan in 1888. Though critical of missionaries and aspects of Western religion, Uchimura never rejected his newfound faith. His work, *How I Became a Christian* (1895), originally written in English, gives his account of his early years and is still widely read today. Uchimura eventually formulated the idea of *mukyôkai* ("non-church") Christianity as a Japanese form of Christianity without denominations or ecclesiastical structure. Uchimura also considered the Japanese samurai ethic to be a virtuous tradition onto which Christianity could be grafted, thereby creating a new "sanctified *bushidō*" ethic for Japan. Although he acknowledged universal aspects of Christianity, he argued that he was a true patriot who held fast to both of the "two J's"—Jesus and Japan—and believed that Japan had a special destiny in the historical development of Christianity.

In 1891, while teaching in the prestigious First Higher School in Tokyo, Uchimura hesitated, on Christian principle, to bow before the Imperial Rescript on Education during a school ceremony. This act elicited a barrage of anti-Christian sentiments throughout Japan, and resulted in his dismissal from the school. Although it was interpreted by many contemporaries as disrespect toward the emperor, Uchimura's refusal has also been viewed as an example of individualistic opposition to the deification of the emperor that accompanied Japan's growing imperialism. Uchimura initially supported the Sino-Japanese War in 1894, but regretted this decision after the war and criticized Japan's treatment of Korea. As an editor of the popular periodical *Yorozu Chôhô*, he became a well-known columnist and writer. In 1903, prior to the outbreak of the Russo-Japanese War, Uchimura became an avowed pacifist; he remained so throughout the rest of his life.

Uchimura was a popular public speaker, and he addressed large audiences, particularly after World War I. One of the enduring legacies of Uchimura was his *deshi* (students). In his weekly meetings, he attracted prominent men, including the future Tokyo University professor Yanaihara Tadao, who challenged Japanese expansionism during the 1930s, and Tanaka Kôtarô, Chief Justice of the Japanese Supreme Court after the war. Whether viewed as an indigenizing Christian leader, a scathing political critic, or a revered teacher, Uchimura functioned as a kind of prophet—one motivated by an individual faith and courage who had a great impact on both his own time and beyond. The words inscribed on his tombstone, "I for Japan, Japan for the World, the World for Christ, and All for God," reveal the breadth of his hopeful religious vision for Japan and the world.

*James M. Hommes*

**See also:** *Bushidō*; Christian Era, Suppression; Nitobe Inazō; Pacifism.

**Further Reading**

Howes, John F. *Japan's Modern Prophet: Uchimura Kanzo 1861–1930*. Vancouver/Toronto: UBC Press, 2005.

Moore, Roy A., ed. *Culture and Religion in Japanese-American Relations: Essays on Uchimura Kanzo, 1861–1930*. Ann Arbor, MI: University of Michigan Press, 1981.

Willcock, Hiroko. *The Japanese Political Thought of Uchimura Kanzo (1861–1930): Synthesizing Bushidō, Christianity, Nationalism, and Liberalism*. Lewiston: Edwin Mellen Press, 2008.

**Ultra-nationalism.** *See Kokutai* and Ultra-nationalism.

## Unequal Treaties

In the 19th century, Japan was saddled with a series of foreign treaties that locked it into international inferiority for half a century. Starting with the 1858 Shimoda Treaty (also called the Harris Treaty) with the United States, 17 western nations forced Japan to sign the humiliating treaties under thinly veiled threats of imperialist intervention.

The treaties included six salient clauses. First, a Scheduled (or Conventional) Tariff limited Japan's power to impose import duties to a mere 5 percent of imported value. Given that most international tariffs ranged between 10 and 20 percent at the time, Japan was denied valuable revenue. Even worse, Japan was unable to raise protective tariffs to nurture its native products. Many foreign powers plied a ruinous Coasting Trade, whereby foreign trading ships would take on Japanese-made products in one Japanese port and declare that the goods were now their own and, therefore, limited to the 5 percent scheduled tariff. Thus it became cheaper to ship Japanese-made goods from one Japanese port to another on foreign ships than on Japanese ships.

Second, none of the treaties contained provisions for revision or termination dates. That omission made them, in effect, eternal. Third, the treaties applied only to foreigners in Japan and not to Japanese abroad, making the treaties unilateral. Fourth, a number of Japanese ports were open to foreign ships in addition to the historical port of Nagasaki. These so-called Treaty Ports were open to alien residence and trade. Eventually other ports (notably Yokohama and Kobe) became self-governing settlements where foreigners were allowed to practice their own religions (Christianity remained technically illegal in Japan until the mid-1870s).

By far the most despised clauses were the last two. The fifth is commonly called Extraterritoriality. Under this provision, foreigners were granted immunity from Japanese justice. Foreigners could be arrested by Japanese authorities if they broke laws, but then had to be turned over to their Resident Consuls for what became known as Consular Jurisdiction. Japanese could bring lawsuits against foreigners, but the foreign consuls administered alien justice in the language of the foreigner. Generally speaking, the overwhelming majority of Consular Jurisdictional cases were administered fairly because the Westerners wanted to appear "civilized." Nevertheless, the appearance of favoritism was impossible to avoid—separate is perceived as inherently unequal.

The final insult added to injury has been called a "most vile bit of diplomacy." That was the Most Favored Nation clause. Unlike the 21st-century meaning of the term, which implies granting one's international friends the best benefits so as to curry good relations, this clause was mean-spirited. To preclude Japan from using the natural self-interest of Western nations against each other, the clause automatically granted the same concessions made to one nation, to all nations. Because the clause also worked "in reverse," however, Japan was locked into circular logic: every nation had to agree to every change conjointly. The result was "All for one; one for all; and none for Japan."

From very early on, the Japanese hated the treaties. Not only did they rob Japan of tariff revenue, but they also deprived it of national sovereignty. Extraterritoriality implied that Japanese law was inferior. The treaties were humiliating.

Japan tried to revise the treaties as quickly as possible. One of the chief purposes of the Iwakura Mission of 1872–1873 was to discover what must be done to get rid of the Unequal Treaties. American Secretary of State Hamilton Fish had instructed that if Japan wished to revise them, then Japan must first reform its legal and political systems to allay any Western fears of Japanese justice. German Chancellor Otto von Bismarck had also told Japanese leaders that if they wished to revise the treaties, Japan must learn Germany's lesson: might makes right. Become powerful, he suggested, and the Western nations would accept Japan as an equal.

As Japan went about those social, political, economic, and military reforms, a series of Japanese foreign ministers tried various revision schemes. Inoue Kaoru first tried separate negotiations with the Western powers. Once he decided that the Most Favored Nation made piecemeal revision impossible, he called all the nations to Tokyo to negotiate jointly at two sessions in 1882–1883 and again 1884–1886. The major sticking point was, of course, extraterritoriality. Few nations wanted to be accused by their citizens of having abandoned them to what was generally accepted "uncivilized savage justice." Inoue very nearly engineered a compromise by which special international "Mixed Courts" with a majority of foreign justices would preside over any Westerner as a defendant. An uproar ensued among the Japanese public, who correctly saw the compromise as a abrogation of judicial sovereignty.

Ōkuma Shigenobu, who succeeded Inoue, tried a number of tactics to revise the treaties. One was to negotiate a completely equal treaty with Mexico in 1888 in hopes of using it to shame the Western nations into similar revisions. His chief negotiator with the Mexican government was Minister to Washington Mutsu Munemitsu, who warned him that the Western nations had simply to invoke the Most Favored Nation clause to take advantage of all concessions made to Mexico without having to surrender anything in return. That was precisely what happened, so Ōkuma had to shelve the Mexican Treaty. Ōkuma also tried to break the deadlock by negotiating secretly with the top Western nations. He reached a compromise that would have created a temporary Mixed Court for a few years until extraterritoriality could be phased out gradually. In addition, he promised that the Western nations would receive regular updates as Japan revised its legal codes. When the story leaked into the press, another public uproar ensued. This time it also included an assassination attempt on Ōkuma, who lost a leg in an explosion.

Four years later, Mutsu became foreign minister. Mutsu adduced the Ōkuma attack as well as one on Tsarevich Nicholas in the Otsu Incident of 1891 to warn the Western nations that Japanese public opinion was at such a fever pitch that further violence against foreign residents in Japan was a risk if the treaties were not promptly revised. He also threatened to unilaterally renounce the treaties. Finally, Mutsu managed to get the British to negotiate in secret, reasoning that Britain was the real deadlock. He finally managed to sign an "equal" treaty with Britain in July 1894. Actually, there was a five-year phasing-out period of extraterritoriality. Perhaps the public would have risen again in outcry against this plan, but at that precise moment the Sino-Japanese War broke out and public attention shifted to more patriotic matters. Cynical historians suggest that Mutsu probably engineered the treaty and war within a week of each other. Mutsu's plan worked, and the other nations quickly fell in line behind Britain's example, especially when Japan sounded defeated China in the 1894–1895 war.

Most historians agree that the need for treaty revision had been the impetus for the wrenching social, political, legal, economic and military reforms that were accomplished in its name.

*Louis G. Perez*

**See also:** Inoue Kaoru; Iwakura Mission; Mutsu Munemitsu; Ōkuma Shigenobu; Otsu Incident; Shimoda Treaty; Sino-Japanese War.

## Further Reading

Auslin, Michael R. *Negotiating with Imperialism: The Unequal Treaties and the Culture of Japanese Diplomacy.* Cambridge, MA: Harvard University Press, 2004.

Perez, Louis. *Japan Comes of Age: Mutsu Munemitsu and the Revision of the Unequal Treaties.* Madison, NJ: Fairleigh Dickinson University Press, 1999.

# Unit 731

Unit 731 was the Japanese army's secret biological warfare unit. Established under the command of Lieutenant Colonel Ishii Shiro in Harbin, Manchuria, in August 1936, Unit 731 was officially known as the Epidemic Prevention and Water Purification Bureau. Some 3,000 personnel worked to produce bacteria for anthrax, bubonic plague, cholera, dysentery, tetanus, typhoid, typhus, and other infectious diseases.

To develop methods to disperse biological agents and enhance their effectiveness, Unit 731 infected prisoners of war. At least 3,000 of these individuals died in the experiments. Unit personnel referred to the prisoners—mostly Chinese, Koreans, and Soviets—as *maruta* (logs) because the Japanese informed the local Chinese that the Unit 731 facility was a lumber mill. U.S., British, and Australian prisoners were also used as human guinea pigs.

Unit 731's activities were outrageous crimes against humanity. After infecting a prisoner with the virus, researchers might then cut open his body, sometimes while he was still alive, to determine the effects of the disease. No anesthetics were employed, as these medications might affect the results. Medical researchers also confined infected prisoners with healthy ones to determine how rapidly diseases spread. In addition,

Unit 731's doctors conducted experiments on compression and decompression and the effects of extreme cold on the body, subjecting limbs to ice water and then amputating them to determine the effects. The Japanese army also repeatedly conducted field tests using biological warfare against Chinese villages.

In a more widespread use of biological warfare, Japanese aircraft spread plague-infected fleas over Ningbo in Zhejiang Province in eastern China in October 1940, causing 99 deaths. The Chinese government correctly concluded that an epidemic of plague in these areas was caused by Japanese biological weapons, and it publicized its findings. Japanese troops also dropped cholera and typhoid cultures into wells and ponds. In 1942, germ-warfare units deployed dysentery, cholera, and typhoid in Zhejiang Province.

At the end of the Pacific phase of World War II, Ishii and other researchers escaped to Japan. They left behind their laboratory equipment, as well as plague-infected mice that produced outbreaks of the disease in the Haerbin area between 1946 and 1948. The U.S. government feared that the Japanese might employ biological warfare against North America via balloon bombs from Japan, but such a plan was never carried out.

After the Japanese surrender, the United States did not bring Ishii and his colleagues before the International Military Tribunal for the Far East for their crimes. Instead, they were granted immunity in exchange for providing information on the experiments to U.S. authorities, which Washington officials considered invaluable in the United States' own biological warfare program. The Soviet government did prosecute 12 members of the unit at Khabarovsk in December 1949, all of whom admitted their crimes. They were convicted and received sentences of from 2 to 25 years in a labor camp.

*Kotani Ken*

**See also:** International Military Tribunal for the Far East.

**Further Reading**

Harris, Sheldon. *Factories of Death*. London: Routledge, 1994.

Williams, Peter, and David Wallace. *Unit 731*. New York: Free Press, 1989.

**U.S.-Japan Security Treaty.** *See* AMPO: United States–Japan Security Treaty.

# V

## Versailles Treaty (1919)

The Treaty of Versailles (signed June 1919) was the most important of the series of international treaties that emerged from the Paris Peace Conference (1919–1920) to bring a formal end to World War I. Not merely content to map out solutions to issues raised by the defeat of the German and Austrian-Hungarian Empires, the treaties' authors established a framework for international relations in the postwar world, most notably in the form of the League of Nations. Thus the Treaty of Versailles had a practical impact on international politics, but it also became a symbol of an approach to peace-making and international co-operation during subsequent decades.

Japan had specific and general aims in the negotiations over the treaty. The country sought formal recognition of its territorial gains acquired during the war, foremost among them former German possessions in China's Shandong Peninsula. More broadly, Japan sought affirmation of its new great power status and intended to enjoy the prestige accorded full members of the international community. Japanese Prime Minister Hara Takashi recognized that U.S. President Woodrow Wilson would have a decisive influence over treaty negotiations and determined that affirming Japan's great power status depended in large part on Japan adopting a co-operative posture toward the United States and other Allied powers. The official head of the delegation, Marquis Saionji Kinmochi, and the lead negotiator, Baron Makino

Nobuaki, were widely viewed as pro-British and pro-American in their worldviews.

Acceptance of Japanese territorial claims in Shandong was achieved, albeit with controversy. Wilson had advocated for peace without territorial aggrandizement and, as a victor on the Allied side, China's delegation hoped that occupied German possessions in the Shandong Peninsula would revert to Chinese control. Both hopes would be frustrated by the Shandong controversy. The Japanese delegation pushed hard for recognition of its claim to these territories, having already enlisted British and French support for its claim in secret negotiations during the war. Fearing a Japanese refusal to join the proposed League of Nations, Wilson acceded to the Japanese territorial claim. The Chinese delegation refused to sign the final treaty, and public protests erupted in China on May 4, 1919, against Japan's successful imperialist maneuvering.

As a major signatory power to the Treaty of Versailles, Japan gained recognition of its status as a major world power. Japan would receive control over German possessions in the south Pacific as well under the system of colonial mandates set out in the treaty. Japan's acceptance of the treaty signaled the nation's assent, at least in general terms, to the Wilsonian ideals contained within it. For this reason, the Treaty of Versailles and the League of Nations were part of a complex political calculus within Japan among outright supporters of Wilson's ideas, those who recognized the importance of the treaty and the postwar international system, and those who found Wilson's ideas repugnant and antithetical to the security needs of the Japanese state. The treaty's impact on Japanese public opinion and society, therefore, was complicated and uneven. Japanese commentators who praised Wilson's democratic values, for example, castigated him for his reckless idealism when his principles of "national self-determination" invited anti-Japanese protests in Korea and China.

No issue embodied these conflicting currents of public opinion more deeply than the "racial equality proposal." This proposal began as an effort by Japanese diplomats to ensure that Japanese nationals would not suffer legal discrimination as immigrants outside Japan, especially in the United States. What began as a limited Japanese attempt to protect its nationals, however, was transformed in the course of international public discussion into a general call for a clear statement of racial equality in the final draft of the Treaty of Versailles. Japan, in effect, became the advocate for a universal principle it did not adopt even within its own empire. Japanese and Chinese delegations put aside their disputes over Shandong to find common cause in advocacy for a racial equality clause.

In the face of Australian opposition and Wilson's decision that such a sweeping proposal required unanimous support, the racial equality clause was omitted from the final draft of the Treaty. Wilson's critics in Japan lashed out at his apparent hypocrisy: voicing universal principles of equality and democracy while leaving the discriminatory policies of the great powers unchecked. Future Prime Minister Prince Konoe Fumimaro argued that the Treaty of Versailles amounted to no more than the endorsement of a global status quo dominated by the Western powers. This argument served as a rallying cry among Pan-Asianist writers, who viewed Wilson's principles as poisonous to Asian societies. They called on other Asian peoples to unite and resist the racial discrimination of the "white" powers perpetuated in the post-Versailles world.

Despite these negative public perceptions of the Treaty of Versailles, Japan had benefited from the treaty. It had achieved its wartime diplomatic goals, significantly enhancing its strategic position in the Pacific Ocean while assuring its position as a major power in international politics. American-educated author and colonial studies scholar Nitobe Inazō was elevated to a position of Undersecretary of the League of Nations, the most prominent international position for a Japanese official to date. Although Japanese diplomats would operate within the Treaty of Versailles framework for the next decade, Japan would eventually break from it decisively in the Mukden Incident of 1931.

*Michael A. Schneider*

**See also:** American Anti-alien Movement; League of Nations, Mandates; Konoe Fumimaro; May Fourth Movement; Mukden Incident: Lytton Report; Pan-Asianism; Washington Naval Conference; World War I.

**Further Reading**

Burkman, Thomas. *Japan and the League of Nations, Empire and World Order, 1914–1938.* Honolulu: University of Hawaii, 2008.

Dickinson, Frederick R. *War and National Reinvention: Japan in the Great War, 1914–1919.* Cambridge, MA: Harvard University Asia Center, 1999.

Macmillan, Margaret Olwen. *Paris 1919: Six Months That Changed the World.* New York: Random House, 2002.

Manela, Erez. *The Wilsonian Moment: Self-determination and the International*

*Origins of Anticolonial Nationalism.* New York: Oxford University Press, 2007.

Shimazu, Naoko. *Japan, Race, and Equality: The Racial Equality Proposal of 1919.* London: Routledge, 1998.

## Violence in Wartime Cinema

Paradoxically, depiction of sheer bodily violence in Japanese cinema during one of the most violent times in its history could be considered minimal, especially when compared with films made in either earlier or later times. The main reason for that distinction lies in new regulations during the 1930s and 1940s that restricted the cinematic portrayal of certain phenomena, violence among them. However, it would be a mistake to think that violence simply disappeared from the screen during these days. In fact, violence remained prevalent within Japanese films; it just took on different shapes, styles, and effects. First and foremost, on the psychological level, things were never more violent, and the impact that these films had on their audience may have had a gruesome effect that exceeded the ramifications of all types of violence depicted in Japanese cinema before and after.

With the exception of very few "auteuristic" films by directors such as Ozu Yasujirō, Naruse Mikio, Shimizu Hiroshi, and perhaps even Kinoshita Keisuke, whose works tended to be polemic, versatile, and consistent with their own style, rather than any governmental code, the blunt majority of films during the World War II era seem to have dealt with one idea more than anything else—namely, the notion of self-sacrifice. War films from the late 1930s and into the 1940s depicted men who were eager to die for the nation or for the sake of serving the emperor. These men often spent their last breath on whispering "*tennō heika banzai*" (long live the emperor) with an unmistakable expression of accomplishment on their faces.

In the war films that first appeared in the latter half of the 1930s, wounded soldiers are very often depicted as insisting upon returning to the battlefield, no matter how severe their situation is. This phenomenon can be seen clearly in films such as *Gonin no Sekkōhei* (*Five Scouts*, Tasaka, 1938) and *Shanhai Rikusentai* (*Shanghai Report*, Kumagai, 1939), as well as in what can be called "training movies," in which young men are portrayed enduring extreme hardship while training to become soldiers. These films, which were often commissioned by the navy or other official governmental bureaus, stressed a need to overcome one's given weaknesses or other, mainly physical, limitations to achieve the ultimate goal of the nation and the emperor. While the training experiences themselves are to be overcome in Yamamoto Kajiro's *Hawai Mare Oki Kaisen* (*The War at Sea from Hawaii to Malay*, 1942) and *Kato Hayabusa Sento-Tai* (*Colonel Tateo Katō's Flying Squadron*, 1944), in Watanabe Kunio's *Kessen no Ozora-e* (*To the Sky of Decisive Battle*, 1943) a young boy is an embarrassment to his family because of his physically weak and sometimes even ill nature. It is only after he recovers from his sickness and is accepted by a military training institution that he is able to regain affection from them.

*Heitai-San* (*Soldier*, Bang, 1944) is yet another very typical training story, albeit one that takes place in the occupied Korean peninsula. While the screenplay was written by a Japanese writer, and while the movie is spoken solely in the Japanese language, the majority of the people involved in its production—including the main cast and the director himself—are Korean. This is another manifestation of the psychological violence with which the Japanese propaganda machine worked to win the hearts and minds of the people in its expanding colonies, enforcing Japanese ideals, and casting off local cultural way of life. In many of these films, a local woman is portrayed resisting the growing Japanese influence, which is symbolized in an all-good Japanese man. The woman then falls in love with the man and finally comes to the conclusion that the Japanese are liberating the colonial population and seek only the well-being of the locals. Infamous for her acting in the role of such a woman is the Japanese actress Ōtaka Yoshiko, who was born in occupied Manchuria and is also known by the name Shirley Yamaguchi and chiefly by the Chinese name Lee Koran. In one of her films, *Soshū no Yoru* (*Suchow Night*, Nomura, 1942), she portrayed exactly such a role of a rebellious Chinese woman, who during the course of the film is pacified and even turns supportive of the Japanese, after falling for a Japanese physician. This film and several others with similar plots were given different endings according to the places they were scheduled to be screened, so as to maximize their manipulative, and therefore violent, effect on their viewers in Japan and in its occupied territories.

*Rea Amit*

**See also:** Newsreels.

**Further Reading**

Abe Nornes, Mark, and Yukio Fukushima. *Japan/America Film Wars: World War II Propaganda and Its Cultural Contexts*. Chur, Switzerland/Langhorne, PA: Harwood Academic Publishers, 1994.

Anderson, Joseph L., and Donald Richie. *The Japanese Film: Art and Industry*. Princeton, NJ: Princeton University Press, 1982: 126–158.

Baskett, Michael. *The Attractive Empire: Transnational Film Culture in Imperial Japan*. Honolulu: University of Hawai'i Press, 2008.

Gerow, Aaron. "Narrating the Nation-ality of a Cinema: The Case of Japanese Prewar Film," in *The Culture of Japanese Fascism*, edited by Alan Tansman. Durham, NC: Duke University Press, 2009.

High, Peter B. *The Imperial Screen: Japanese Film Culture in the Fifteen Years' War, 1931–1945*. Madison: University of Wisconsin Press, 2003.

# W

**War Crimes Tribunal.** *See* International Military Tribunal for the Far East.

**Warrior Monks.** *See Sōhei.*

## Warrior Tales

*Gunki monogatari* ("war tales") and *rekishi monogatari* ("historical tales") are two genres of writing that emerged during the late Heian period and flourished throughout the medieval age and mark a new development in the recording of history. They share a common focus on historical events and actors, and they are generally written either in *kanbun* (a hybrid form of Chinese) or Japanese (*wabun*). This language choice contrasts with that of the official histories, which are more commonly recorded in Chinese. *Gunki* and *rekishi monogatari* are in the main organized into long, narrative chapters, a style standing in stark contrast to the dated, chronological form usually associated with official histories that preceded them. For the most part, authorship of *gunki* and *rekishi monogatari* is impossible to discern, and often works of these genres are thought to represent edited compilations rather than works produced by a single author.

The *gunki monogatari* genre took shape at a time when *rekishi monogatari* had already emerged, and *gunki monogatari* share many of that more general category's characteristics. The rubric of *rekishi monogatari* refers to a hybrid narrative form addressing history broadly speaking; *rekishi monogatari* tend to contextualize their subjects in terms of large historical significance. They developed as a response to the traditional variety of historiographic writing associated with the *Rikkokushi* ("Six National Histories"), works written in Chinese and, on the whole, not interested in warrior affairs.

The most memorable early *rekishi monogatari*, *Eiga monogatari* ("A Tale of Flowering Fortunes") and *Ōkagami* ("The Great Mirror") describe the life and times of the great Fujiwara regent Michinaga. Unlike earlier official histories, these works adopt a far more personal tone: both are long, narrative accounts rather than records of daily entries, and both position themselves to tell the kind of stories that official histories as a rule eschewed. *Eiga monogatari*, attributed with a fair degree of certainty to a lady in service to Michinaga's wife, Rinshi, describes life "behind the screens" in Michinaga's household. The narratorial voice is far closer to that of the fictional *Genji monogatari* than to that of a traditional history.

*Ōkagami* is perhaps even more important as an antecedent for *gunki monogatari*. There, we find multiple narrators—the two main ones are men of implausibly advanced age—in conversation with one another recounting stories about Michinaga and his kin. The work is notable for reproducing the "storytelling in a round" format more familiar in fictional works. *Ōkagami* was the first of a series of *kagami mono* ("mirror pieces") utilizing aged narrators to talk about present times and the past. In its characterization of history as something that is remembered and spoken in the colloquial language of the people, rather than neutrally rendered in Chinese and organized under dated entries, it represents a new mode of historical writing and questions more traditional forms.

The move toward narrative history, the privileging of voice, and the introduction of characters beyond the central courtier government found in early *rekishi monogatari* represent a sea change in how, for whom, and by whom history was being recorded. Because they were not in Chinese, they were comprehensible to wider audiences. Perhaps even more importantly, their format suggested that it was not simply the daily activities of the court, but rather the private lives of men and women, that represented what was most important, or at least most telling, about the past and present.

The *gunki monogatari* are more specific in focus, than *rekishi monogatari*, but similarly vary in form, style, and content. Extant *gunki monogatari* range in length from 30 or so to more than 500 pages in modern printed editions, and their literary quality varies dramatically. Needless to say, their historical reliability is extremely questionable, and the appearance of monsters, deities, and other supernatural figures is not uncommon to the genre.

The best known of the *gunki monogatari*, *Heike monogatari* and *Taiheiki*, describe the events of the realm at war—the former, the Genpei War of 1180–1185, and the latter, the battles of the Northern and Southern Courts Period. The cast of characters in each is large, and there is no sole protagonist. By contrast, *gunki monogatari* like *Soga monogatari* ("The Tale of the Revenge of the Soga Brothers") and *Gikeiki* ("The Story of Yoshitsune") describe the lives of individual warriors, following them from birth to death. In the case of *Gikeiki*, the actual battlefield heroics of the protagonist, Yoshitsune, are elided completely.

Most *gunki monogatari* are marked by a strong narratorial voice and a mixed style: some passages replicate the voice of a storyteller, some quote older Japanese or Chinese texts, some include apparently verbatim citation of a contemporary document. Most have connections to oral storytelling or other performance traditions. Many comprise a number of variant texts, ranging from narratives written in *kanbun* or Chinese to more widely circulating versions in Japanese. Works such as *Heike monogatari* and *Soga monogatari* are framed as Buddhist or Confucian parables; other texts, such as *Gikeiki* or *Taiheiki*, have less clearly defined agendas. The best-known *gunki monogatari* interpret the past and give birth to the future. Both *Heike monogatari* and *Taiheiki* weave myths from the *Nihon shōki* ("Record of Japan," 720 C.E.) into their narrative as they strive to explain the rise of the warriors and the chaotic times they describe, while at the same time creating a cast of memorable characters and situations that would be recreated, reinterpreted, and expanded in medieval narrative and drama.

*Gunki monogatari* arose as a genre in the late Heian period with tales of military conquests in the provinces, including the defeat of Taira Masakado (recorded in *Shōmonki* ["The Story of Masakado"]), and remained popular throughout the medieval period. In the Tokugawa period, many were published in book form; *Taiheiki*, in particular, was extremely popular reading material for the burgeoning urbanites of Edo and Osaka.

*Gunki monogatari* episodes became the basis for other works especially Noh or *kōwakamai* plays. Popularity of such episodes led to widespread knowledge of the major events and characters of the civil conflicts occurring during the medieval period. The common knowledge of the contents of *gunki monogatari* contributed to early manifestations of shared cultural identity, primarily as that associated with the samurai class. During Japan's period of imperial expansion in the early 20th century, many tales and heroes from the *gunki monogatari* would be mobilized to encourage military and domestic patriotism. Characters such as Minamoto Yoshitsune and Kusunoki Masashige, with their already long and illustrious literary and cultural pedigrees, became icons to be revered and imitated; the trope of the indefatigable underdog as hero was a particularly powerful image as Japan went to war against larger and more militarily established nations.

The degree to which *gunki monogatari* were histories for their contemporary audiences, should not be underestimated; they are inheritors of the *rekishi monogatari* tradition of asserting new ways of engaging the past and explaining the present during the turbulent age of the Genpei War, in the Mongol Invasions, through the War of the Northern and Southern Courts, and into the Sengoku ("Warring States") period. Their popular appeal certainly stems from their engaging narratives of personal valor and suffering, but their complex relationship to earlier historical genres and their focus on actual events suggest their important role as popular history throughout the medieval period. Moreover, their embeddedness in Japanese culture has allowed them to remain accessible as sources of historical memory in recent times.

*Elizabeth A. Oyler*

**See also:** *Heike monogatari*; Kamakura *Bakufu*; *Taiheiki*.

## Further Reading

Bialock, David T. *Eccentric Spaces, Hidden Histories: Narrative, Ritual, and Royal Authority from* The Chronicles of Japan *to* The Tale of the Heike. Stanford, CA: Stanford University Press, 2007.

Cogan, Thomas J. *The Tale of the Soga Brothers*. Tokyo: University of Tokyo Press, 1987.

McCullough, Helen C. *Ōkagami: The Great Mirror*. Princeton, NJ: Princeton University Press, 1980.

McCullough, Helen C. *The Tale of the Heike*. Stanford, CA: Stanford University Press, 1988.

McCullough, Helen C. *Yoshitsune: A Fifteenth-Century Japanese Chronicle*. Stanford, CA: Stanford University Press, 1966.

McCullough, Helen C., and William H. McCullough. *A Tale of Flowering Fortunes: Annals of Aristocratic Life in the Heian Period*. Stanford, CA: Stanford University Press, 1980.

Oyler, Elizabeth A. *Swords, Oaths, and Prophetic Visions: Authoring Warrior Rule in Medieval Japan*. Honolulu: University of Hawaii Press, 2006.

Varley, Paul. *Warriors of Japan as Portrayed in the War Tales*. Honolulu: University of Hawaii Press, 1994.

# Washington Naval Conference (1921–1922)

The Washington Naval Conference was a diplomatic event initiated by the United States significant for the series of treaties that would serve as important guidelines in setting the territorial and military agendas of the Pacific powers. After clashing with the United States over the territorial gains Japan had made in World War I, Japanese observers were suspicious of the United States' motives in East Asia. At the same time, the postwar recession made it difficult to sustain an arms race with the

United States. With Japan's treaty with Britain also under threat, Prime Minister Hara Takashi sought to strengthen diplomatic ties with the United States to boost economic exchange between the two emerging powers and improve its image on the international stage. Although Hara was assassinated days before the opening of the conference, his basic stance toward international cooperation and economic competition was maintained by the delegation representing Japan, led by Baron Shidehara Kijûrô and Navy Minister Katô Tomosaburô, who went on to adopt the measures of the resultant treaty as Prime Minister in 1922.

The Four-Power Treaty, signed by the United States, Britain, France, and Japan, served as a pact of nonaggression between these four Pacific powers. The United States was interested in breaking the Anglo-Japanese Alliance, which had soured to some extent its relationships with the two other powers, and which threatened the stability of U.S. interests in the Pacific owing to the possibility of having to face two formidable navies at once. At the same time, Japan wanted assurance that the United States and British would not, in turn, form an alliance against Japan once the Anglo-Japanese pact was abolished. By guaranteeing the mutual respect of their rivals' territories and stating that no single power would be attacked by an alliance of the others, the four powers formed a framework that would allow them to avoid any major confrontation with their rival navies.

If the Four-Power Treaty spelled out the political understanding of the Pacific policy of the powers, the Five-Power Treaty mapped out its technical aspects. The latter treaty was an agreement formed by the four aforementioned powers with the addition of Italy, which was interested in establishing

naval parity with France. The most significant aspect of the Five-Power Treaty was the establishment of basic ratios that set the maximum allowable size of each of the participating navies. This was a very controversial issue in Japan, as the country agreed to limit the size of its navy to 60 percent of the size of the U.S. and British navies. In the context of establishing parity in the Pacific, however, even this limitation of arms on the part of Japan put the country at an advantage, considering its proximity to the area in question. as well as the fact that its forces were concentrated in the Pacific. Nevertheless, the basic fact that the Imperial Navy was restricted from maintaining overall parity with its rivals was demeaning to some in the navy, and the issue would later be revisited at the London Naval Conference in 1930.

Finally, the Nine-Power Treaty outlined the agreed-upon direction of the powers' policy regarding China, though in practice it was perhaps not as successful as the two other treaties. Signed by the United States, Belgium, Britain, France, Italy, Japan, the Netherlands, Portugal, and China, the treaty in theory sought to pave the way toward an independent, modern China, while maintaining the interests of each of the parties in the rich resources and markets of the territory. Yet, the signers failed to develop concrete interpretations of the vaguely termed language of the treaty, and as China became more unified through the 1920s, the treaty quickly became ineffective.

The results of the Washington Naval Conference—or the "Washington System," as it became known—were largely modified by the London Naval Treaty of 1930, which was then abandoned by both France and Japan in 1935 and 1936, respectively. Nevertheless, the Washington System is significant in that it represented the first large-scale attempt to put limitations on arms building among the Great Powers, and in this sense it is often viewed as a success.

*John D. Person*

**See also:** Anglo-Japanese Alliance; Hara Takashi; London Naval Conference; Navy, Modernized; Shidehara Kijuro.

**Further Reading**

Asada, Sadao. "Japan's Special Interests and the Washington Conference, 1921–1922." *American Historical Review* 67 (October 1961): 62–70.

Goldman, Emily O. *Sunken Treaties: Naval Arms Control between the Wars.* University Park: Pennsylvania University Press, 1994.

Iriye, Akira. *The Origins of the Second World War in Asia and the Pacific.* London: Longman, 1987.

LaFeber, Walter. *The Clash: A History of U.S.-Japan Relations.* New York & London: W. W. Norton & Company, 1997.

Nish, Ian. *Japanese Foreign Policy in the Interwar Period.* Westport, CT: Praeger, 2002.

# Western Medicine in Imperial Japan

In the Meiji period, the Japanese government, as part of its overall drive to modernize, embarked on a comprehensive program to acquire Western medicine. The growth of medicine was predicated on the transfer of knowledge, and the establishment of public and private institutions dedicated to medical education, research, public health, and health care. The most significant organizations involved in this effort were Tokyo University, the Japanese Red Cross Society, the Institute of Infectious Diseases, the Army Medical Bureau's School of Medicine, and the Sanitary Bureau, as well as hundreds of local medical schools and hospitals. Tokyo University, founded in 1877 from a number of existing educational institutions including Igakko, a medical school, quickly became a conduit for Western medical knowledge. In the early 1870s, numerous German physicians served as medical instructors at Igakko and later Tokyo University. The first were Benjamin Mueller, who taught internal medicine, and Theodore Hoffman, a specialist in surgery. In 1874, Albert Wernich replaced Mueller; Wernich was, in turn, replaced by Erwin Baelz in 1876. Baelz taught internal medicine and stayed at Tokyo University until 1901. These instructors, as well as other German physicians, trained Japan's first generation of Western medical practitioners and instructors.

The Japanese government also sent hundreds of its brightest young students to Europe (primarily Germany) to study medicine. Beginning in the 1870s, Germany was the destination of more than 90 percent of all Japanese students engaged in medical studies overseas, because Germany was the world leader in medicine at the time, having established the first advanced training programs in this field in its university system. By the first decade of the 20th century, as many as 150 Japanese medical students per year were studying in Germany. Japanese overseas students engaged in advanced studies in all medical fields, including, but not limited to, pathology, bacteriology, internal medicine, anatomy, and physiology. These German-educated specialists then returned to Japan to research and teach in Japanese universities, hospitals, and research centers.

Perhaps the most successful Japanese student to study in Germany was Kitasato Shibasaburo, a bacteriologist who worked in Robert Koch's laboratory at the University of Berlin from 1886 to 1891. Koch's work provided the foundation for germ theory, the concept that disease is caused by a specific microbial pathogen. He demonstrated this fact with his isolation of the anthrax bacillus (1877), the tubercle bacillus (1882), and the *Vibrio cholerae* bacterium (1883). In 1893, two years after returning from his studies in Germany, Kitasato became the director of the newly founded Institute of Infectious Diseases in Japan, an organization patterned after the Koch's research center. The institute was the single most significant medical research organization in Japan at the time and very quickly registered two important discoveries. In 1894, Kitasato isolated the causative agent for the plague during an outbreak in Hong Kong. Three years later, in 1897, Shiga Kiyoshi, a researcher at the institute, isolated the pathogen for dysentery.

In 1874, Japan's Ministry of Education announced the Regulations on Medical Practice (*Isei*), which established standards for the education and practice of medicine. In 1875, the Home Ministry took over the responsibility for public health and medical matters. A year later, it imposed strict guidelines for the licensing of all physicians, including national examinations in physics, chemistry, anatomy, physiology, pathology, pharmacology, and internal medicine. The new licensing standards were designed to curtail the practices of those individuals who only wanted to train in Chinese medicine. By 1880, 1,396 physicians had passed the national examination and nearly every prefecture in Japan had established a publicly funded medical school that also included a hospital. The Home Ministry registered 626 public and private hospitals by 1882.

The outbreak of war in 1914 separated Japan from the source of its medical knowledge, Germany. The Japanese medical community had no choice but to become more

self-reliant. By this time, Japan had constructed a viable medical infrastructure more than capable of producing its own physicians, hospitals, and research.

*Roberto Padilla II*

**See also:** *Bunmei kaika.*

### Further Reading

Bartholomew, James. *The Formation of Science in Japan: Building a Research Tradition.* New Haven: Yale University Press, 1989.

Jannetta, Ann. *The Vaccinators: Smallpox, Medical Knowledge, and the "Opening" of Japan.* Stanford: Stanford University Press, 2007.

Johnston, William. *The Modern Epidemic: A History of Tuberculosis in Japan.* Cambridge, MA: Harvard University Press, 1995.

Nakamura, Ellen Gardner. *Practical Pursuits: Takano Choei, Takahashi Keisaku, and Western Medicine in Nineteenth-Century Japan.* Cambridge, MA: Harvard University Press, 2005.

Oberlander, Christian. "The Rise of Western 'Scientific Medicine' in Japan: Bacteriology and Beriberi," in *Building a Modern Japan: Science, Technology, and Medicine in the Meiji Era and Beyond*, edited by Morris Low. New York: Palgrave Macmillan, 2005:13–36.

## Women during World War II: Kokubo Fujinkai and Aikoku Fujinkai

The *Aikoku fujinkai* (Patriotic Women's Association) and the *Kokubo fujinkai* (National Defense Women's Association) stand out as the two most prominent organizations to mobilize and direct women's support of Japan's military establishment and community in the 20th century. The older of the two, the *Aikoku fujinkai* was established in 1901 by Okumura Ioko, the well-to-do daughter of a temple priest with kinship ties to the imperial family, for the purpose of providing comfort and aid to the families of wounded and killed servicemen, along with the injured themselves.

Backing from the Home Ministry and Okumura's skill at recruiting officers from among the political, social, and economic elite and the imperial household gave the *Aikoku fujinkai* an air of prestige. Its high dues strengthened that aura by restricting membership to the middle and upper classes. While the association had only 14,000 members in late 1902, the Russo-Japanese War and surging patriotic sentiment resulted in significant growth, and by late 1905 its roster had increased to include 465,000 names.

During that war, members sent off and welcomed back servicemen with ceremonial messages. They also provided those in arms with a variety of material goods (typically in comfort bags), paid house and hospital calls on the bereaved and wounded, and attended funerals. Such functions remained central to the *Aikoku fujinkai*'s aim after the war, though the organization did also give pensions to war widows and orphans, job training to wives, school supplies to children, and free lodging to families of hospitalized soldiers and sailors, with the necessary money coming from dues and fund-raising campaigns.

In 1917, partly to compete with the many new women's organizations in existence, the *Aikoku fujinkai* revised its mission statement to commit members to the provision of relief more generally. Activities initiated over the next two decades sought to mold good military wives and healthy future recruits. These efforts included giving free medical check-ups and haircuts to youth, along with eye exams to adults; running

children's libraries and organizing children's afterschool activities; and opening maternity hospitals and providing midwives for at-home births. *Aikoku fujinkai* members also offered child care; operated vocational schools for girls, women, and the blind; distributed food, money, and other essentials in response to natural disasters, bad crops, and epidemics; carried out campaigns to encourage thrift; and instructed the public about civic duty and "proper" behavior through entertainment and publications. Such outreach contributed to steady organizational growth in terms of numbers of members and branches, and, by the early 1930s, the association enjoyed a membership of approximately 1.5 million affiliated with branches, primarily urban, throughout the Japanese empire.

In the wake of the 1931 Mukden Incident and resulting increases in troop mobilization at home and deployment overseas, the *Aikoku fujinkai* experienced another surge in members. The 1930s also saw the organization face significant competition for the first time from another women's group. That challenge came from the *Kokubo fujinkai*, which had itself emerged in response to the Mukden Incident. More specifically, in 1932, Yasuda Sei and Mitani Eiko, a pair of Osaka housewives, saw that thousands of men were being shipped out to China and Manchuria without families nearby to see them off. Yasuda and Mitani gathered several dozen women from their neighborhood association and together began comforting those soon to depart from the Osaka port or train station with hot tea, small gifts, prayers, and shouts of "banzai." Before long, the group expanded its support services to include welcoming back returning servicemen, helping those wounded in the line of duty, and returning the remains of deceased servicemen to family. Such grassroots support for the military almost immediately drew the attention of the Army Ministry, which had no real influence over the *Aikoku fujinkai* and was eager to find a means to mobilize women in line with its own agenda. The opportunity to affiliate came in the summer of 1932 when Yasuda and Mitani traveled to Tokyo and met with army officials about opening a branch in the capital and establishing a national organization. The former task was accomplished within months, and, by 1934, the *Kokubo fujinkai* had evolved into a nationwide association with 1 million members. By 1936, that figure exceeded 3.6 million, far surpassing the *Aikoku fujinkai*'s roughly 2.3 million members.

The *Kokubo fujinkai*'s phenomenal growth in its early years owed much to army involvement, as military commanders founded branches and local reserve organizations prodded women to join. Attempts to organize within workplaces and affiliate with village women's groups—in short, to take advantage of existing concentrations of women—contributed to the organization's growth as well. Even more important were the facts that, unlike the *Aikoku fujinkai*, the *Kokubo fujinkai* required minimal dues and membership was open to all women, regardless of socioeconomic standing or occupation. This characteristic was epitomized by the white apron members wore whenever engaged in association business. Such apparel erased class differences at the same time that it advertised the organization's work. It also legitimized women's public outreach by linking them with the domestic sphere and asserting that members were involved in activities suitable to their roles as wives and mothers.

This notion, made even more explicit with the *Kokubo fujinkai's* motto "National defense begins in the kitchen," was one that the Army promoted as it sought to use the *society* to spread the official ideology of the "good wife and wise mother." Some women undoubtedly joined in support of that stance. Many more signed up because of the public nature of the association's activities and the opportunities those activities provided for members to escape the drudgery of household duties and socialize with others under the guise of patriotic service.

As the *Kokubo fujinkai* grew, its core activities remained fundamentally the same as those first undertaken in Osaka. Wearing the ubiquitous white apron, often with a sash bearing the name of the organization in big, bold print, members continued to see off and welcome back servicemen at train stations and ports with refreshments and words of encouragement. They also helped return remains and gave solace to the bereaved. In addition, many attended reservists' musters and reviews and provided ceremonial rice boiled with red beans to those in uniform. They assisted the families of men killed in action by preparing and serving food at funerals, and sent those stationed in barracks and on the battlefield comfort bags filled with letters, photos, and useful sundries. Increasingly these bags contained *senninbari* or "thousand-stitch belts," which members had made as amulets. Additional activities, which likely had more of a social than a service component for many, included visits to temples, shrines, and model kitchens, along with classes in cooking, cloth dyeing, and recycling.

The scale of these activities and the similar ones of the *Aikoku fujinkai* exploded following the Marco Polo Bridge Incident and the initiation of full-scale hostilities between Japan and China in 1937. The same was true of their memberships, as the *Kokubo fujinkai*'s roster grew to 8.85 million names by

June 1941 and the *Aikoku fujinkai*'s membership expanded to 7.5 million by December of that same year. With the *Kokubo fujinkai*, membership essentially became compulsory for adult married women as the army tightened its control, particularly at the local level. One consequence of that measure and intensified state efforts at mobilization of resources before and after the Pearl Harbor attack was the addition of new activities for *Kokubo fujinkai* women. As men grew scarcer at home, directives called on members to fight fires, serve as marshals during fire raids, provide morale-boosting entertainment, contribute labor on farms, help with land reclamation and road repairs, and attend lectures on topics ranging from public hygiene to the progress of the war. Women in both organizations were also compelled to buy government bonds, donate metal for munitions, and otherwise economize to deal with scarcities of daily goods.

Compulsion took a different form in February 1942, when the government forced the *Kokubo fujinkai* and the *Aikoku fujinkai* to merge with other national women's groups into the *Dai Nippon fujinkai* (Greater Japan Women's Association). The nearly 20 million women who automatically became members of this new organization were enjoined to boost the morale of servicemen, conserve resources, increase production, and otherwise support the military with the end goal being to lead Japan to victory. Women continued to do essentially the same things they had done previously, with two notable exceptions. The declining fortunes of the military after the Battle of Midway led the government to impose a moratorium on public send-offs to keep troop deployments secret, thereby eliminating this activity from women's repertoire. Women also began training with bamboo spears for the anticipated landing of American troops.

Persistent rivalries and flaws in the program of total state control ultimately undermined the *Dai Nippon fujinkai* and led to its dissolution in the summer of 1945. Women's efforts to provide solace and assistance to the military community nonetheless continued on a voluntary basis and as part of work, neighborhood, and village groups for World War II's remaining few weeks.

*Elizabeth Dorn Lublin*

**See also:** Pearl Harbor, Attack on; Russo-Japanese War; Senninbari and "Comfort Bags"; World War II, Pacific Theater.

**Further Reading**

Morita, Keiko. "Activities of the Japanese Patriotic Ladies' Association (*Aikoku Fujinkai*)," in *Women, Activism, and Social Change*, edited by Maja Mikula. New York: Routledge, 2005: 49–70.

Wilson, Sandra. "Family or State? Nation, War, and Gender in Japan, 1937–45." *Critical Asian Studies* 38, no. 2 (2006): 209–238.

Wilson, Sandra. "Mobilizing Women in Interwar Japan: The National Defense Women's Association and the Manchurian Crisis." *Gender and History* 7, no. 2 (August 1995): 295–314.

# World War I

Military operations in East Asia during World War I were limited, bearing no resemblance to the catastrophic war that shook Europe. On the diplomatic front, however, Japanese politicians were ambitious, eager to promote Japan's imperial interests in region. Despite this relative calm, Japanese leaders would see East Asia transformed by the war. None would have predicted that the war's impact on Japanese politics,

American troops march past Japanese marines in Siberia during World War I. (National Archives)

society, and its foreign relations would be so far-reaching in ways they neither anticipated nor desired.

Japanese greeted the outbreak of war in Europe in August 1914 as an opportunity. Citing provisions of the Anglo-Japanese Alliance, Japan declared itself on the side of the Allied Powers and demanded German surrender of possessions in China's Shandong Peninsula. Faced with the German refusal, Japan acted swiftly, landing a military force in Shandong in September 1914. The campaign to capture the key city Qingdao, along with its military installations in Jiazhou Bay, took two months and cost Japan approximately 400 lives. In October, the Japanese navy faced no resistance when it occupied German-controlled islands in the Pacific north of the equator—that is, the island groups known as the Marshalls, Marianas, Carolines, and Palaus.

Japanese diplomats moved aggressively to translate these military successes into a broad refashioning of the imperial balance of power in China. The so-called Twenty-One Demands of January 1915 aimed to expand Japanese influence throughout the country. When the Yuan Shikai government in Beijing balked at what it perceived as excessive demands and bullying tactics, Japanese leaders responded with a threat of force. Japan and China ultimately agreed to a reduced set of the demands. The benefits to Japan from the episode were mostly offset by the enmity it excited among the Chinese population and the suspicions it invited in the eyes of Japan's preoccupied allies. The United States and Japan would attempt to smooth over these frictions with the Lansing-Ishii Agreement of 1917, without clear success.

As the war dragged on in Europe, Japanese businesses capitalized on opportunities to assist Allied war procurement and, in some cases, replace European firms in Asian markets. The resulting economic boom in Japan produced many newly moneyed entrepreneurs, filled government tax coffers, and significantly strengthened Japan's international balance of payments.

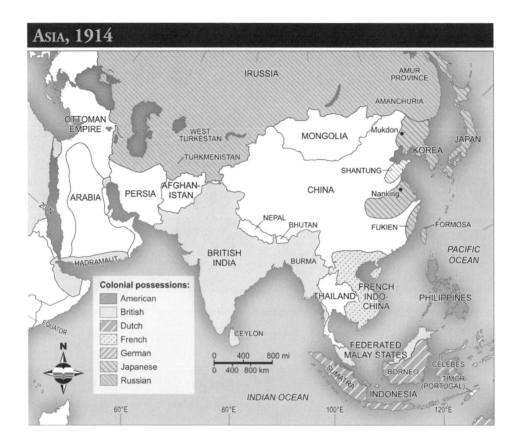

ASIA, 1914

Colonial possessions:
- American
- British
- Dutch
- French
- German
- Japanese
- Russian

From this position of strength, Japanese politicians continued to meddle in Chinese affairs, opposing Yuan Shikai's attempts to install himself as a new Chinese emperor and eventually seeking to depose him.

After Yuan's death in mid-1916, Japan attempted to use its rising financial clout to bolster its position in Beijing. Under the direction of Prime Minister Terauchi Masatake, businessman Nishihara Kamezō negotiated loans with Yuan's successor Duan Qirui. He also urged Duan to bring China into the war on the Allied side, indirectly setting the stage for conflict with Japan over the occupied German possessions. Duan, however, squandered the funds on unsuccessful military adventures, which only exacerbated China's political fragmentation. Japan did not garner significant

political benefit and the loans were never repaid. Once they were exposed, however, the Nishihara Loans fueled anger over Japan's unilateral policies in China.

Events during the final year of World War I collided with a stunning ferocity. The Russian Revolution of 1917 threw Japanese military planning for the region into turmoil. Japan would ultimately join in the U.S.-led expedition to Siberia to support the faltering anti-Bolshevik forces. The wartime boom had created new wealth and supported rising expectations across economic classes and political allegiances. It also ignited inflation. Prices of consumer goods, especially rice, rose out of control, exacerbated by government procurement for the Siberian Expedition, with speculators eventually driving prices even higher. The result was mass upheaval. Popular protests broke out first in rural Tōyama Prefecture but eventually spread throughout the country. The Rice Riots pulled down the Terauchi government, forcing Japanese leaders to endorse Hara Takashi as Japan's first commoner prime minister.

In some ways, World War I benefited Japan. The Japanese empire grew significantly as a result of the war. Japan's rising political and economic status was recognized through its full participation in the postwar peace settlement under the Treaty of Versailles.

The war, however, also upset traditional patterns of political power within the country and throughout the region. New groups and new ideologies would play a larger role in managing the nation, including calls for expanded democratic politics. Events such as the May Fourth Movement (1919) in China demonstrated that Japan's wartime policies had invited direct opposition to its imperial ambitions. By the war's end, Japan found itself confronted with a new international political environment, an unresolved intervention in Siberia, an East Asia inflamed by anti-Japanese nationalist movements, and a domestic populace seething with anticipation about an uncertain future.

*Michael A. Schneider*

**See also:** Anglo-Japanese Alliance; Hara Takashi; May Fourth Movement; Rice Riots; Siberian Expedition; Twenty-One Demands; Versailles Treaty.

### Further Reading

Burkman, Thomas. *Japan and the League of Nations, Empire and World Order, 1914–1938.* Honolulu: University of Hawaii, 2008.

Dickinson, Frederick R. *War and National Reinvention: Japan in the Great War, 1914–1919.* Cambridge, MA: Harvard University Asia Center, 1999.

Dunscomb, Paul E. *Japan's Siberian Intervention, 1918–1922: "A Great Disobedience against the People."* Lantham, MD: Lexington Books, 2011.

Lewis, Michael. *Rioters and Citizens: Mass Protest in Imperial Japan.* Berkeley: University of California Press, 1990.

## World War I, Causes

Clearly, World War I was unlike any other military action in Japan's history, because Japan had no choice in whether to join the fray. The country was obligated by the terms of the Anglo-Japanese Alliance to come to the aid of Great Britain. The first Anglo-Japanese Alliance (1902–1910) redounded to Japan's benefit because Great Britain's neutrality in the Russo-Japanese War (1904–1905) deterred France and Germany from aiding their erstwhile ally Russia. There would be no repeat of the Triple Intervention (1895) when French and German threats helped to wrest the Liaoning Peninsula away from Japan after it had won it in the first Sino-Japanese War (1894–1895).

While Japan had negotiated the end of the Russo-Japanese War at Portsmouth, New Hampshire, in 1905, Japan's chief negotiator Komura Jutarō had met with British diplomats to extend the Anglo-Japanese Alliance to include mutual protection throughout all of East Asia. Thus, after the alliance was renewed in 1911, Japan was obligated to come to Britain's aid in the event the British empire went to war with two or more enemies. Japan dutifully did so on August 23, 1914.

Britain's enemies (Germany, Austro-Hungary, and the Ottoman Empire) had no troops in East Asia except for Germany's leasehold at Qingdao in China's Shandong Peninsula. Japan was reticent to attack Germany because of its long-time affinity with the German military tutors who helped prepare Japan's army for its previous wars. Nevertheless, Japan laid siege at Qingdao and achieved a costly victory there in September 1914.

*Louis G. Perez*

**See also:** Anglo-Japanese Alliance; Qingdao, Siege of; Russo-Japanese War; Sino-Japanese War; Triple Intervention.

**Further Reading**

Dickinson, Frederick. *War and National Reinvention: Japan in the Great War, 1914–1919*. Cambridge, MA: Harvard University Press, 1999.

## World War I, Consequences

Allied with Britain, France, Russia, and eventually the United States, Japan formally went to war with Germany, Austria-Hungary, and Ottoman Turkey in World War I. In 1914, Japanese army units invaded Shandong province from the north, overrunning the German garrison at Qingdao with ease. Next, the Japanese navy appropriated the German-held Palau, Caroline, Marshall, and Mariana archipelagos. In general, Japan took advantage of the West's preoccupation with the war in Europe to dominate Asia economically and move toward heavier forms of industrialization.

In an effort to preserve such gains, Japanese officials presented the Twenty-One Demands to China's Yuan Shikai regime in 1915, demanding continued or expanded territorial rights in South Manchuria, Shandong, and Inner Mongolia. They also insisted upon Chinese joint ownership of key iron works and mandated that China purchase weapons from Japan. Furthermore, the Twenty-One Demands required the Chinese government to accept Japanese "advisers" at various levels and insisted that Chinese open no new ports to nation-states other than Japan.

Following the beginning of the 1917 Bolshevik Revolution, troops of various capitalist countries invaded Russia, with most leaving by 1920. Japanese troops remained in Siberia until 1922, however. There, in addition to making attempts to contain communism, Japanese maintained control of the East Siberian Railway and access to other assets and resources of Asian Russia.

In 1919, a Japanese delegation to the Paris Peace Conference at Versailles aimed to keep possessions taken from Germany. Japan's Western allies had already convinced Japanese to largely drop the Twenty-One Demands. China, however, had supported the victorious side in the war and expected the return of Shandong to China; its leaders were deeply disappointed that Japanese forces remained in control there until 1922, In that year, the Washington Naval Conference, which limited the number of Japanese warships vis-à-vis the navies of the United States, Britain, France, and Italy, also successfully pressured Japan to relinquish claims to Shandong and to withdraw from Siberia. Japan continued to possess the formerly German Pacific islands as the Japanese South Seas (Nan'yō). These territories officially remained League of Nations mandates, but became fully incorporated into Japan's empire.

The Japanese delegates at Versailles pushed for inclusion of a "racial equality" clause in the League of Nations charter, something staunchly opposed by British and Australian representatives. The Chinese delegation—opposed to Japan in every other way—also supported the clause. On April 11, at a meeting chaired by U.S. President Woodrow Wilson, 11 out of 17 delegates voted to include the clause, but Wilson refused to acquiesce. Japanese leaders were unlikely to extend equality to their colonized subjects, but passing the clause would have signaled full Western acceptance of Japan in the club of modern, imperialist nation-states. Limitations on the Japanese navy negotiated in 1922 and restrictions on Japanese immigration into Anglo-Saxon countries in the interwar period, combined with Japan's diplomatic failure at Versailles, collectively pushing Japanese to superficially reject what increasingly appeared to be slavish imitation of the West. The power of Pan-Asianist discourse as an ideological basis for Japanese imperialism grew concomitantly.

Ironically, in 1919, Chinese and Koreans began to challenge the authority of Japanese leadership and question the legitimacy of Japanese colonialism as never before. China reacted to the Shandong problem and other indignities with the May Fourth Movement, which included anti-Japanese demonstrations and boycotts of Japanese commodities. Influenced by Wilson's "self-determination" rhetoric, Koreans began to protest Japanese oppression and call for independence with the March First Movement. Despite Japanese moves to soften colonial rule in Korea, and despite a general Japanese turn to "the East" during the interwar period, little could offset post-1918 anti-Japanese sentiment in Asia.

*Gerald Iguchi*

**See also:** Anglo-Japanese Alliance; Anti-Japanism in China; May Fourth Movement; Pan-Asianism; Right-Wing Politics in Japan; Siberian Expedition; Twenty-One Demands; Versailles Treaty; Washington Naval Conference; World War I; World War I, Causes.

### Further Reading

Aydin, Cemil. *The Politics of Anti-Westernism in Asia: Visions of World Order in Pan-Islamic and Pan-Asian Thought.* New York: Columbia University Press, 1993.

Burdick, Charles B. *The Japanese Siege of Tsingtao: World War I in Asia.* Hamden, CT: Archon Books, 1976.

Gordon, Paul Lauren. "Human Rights in History: Diplomacy and Racial Equality at the Paris Peace Conference." *Diplomatic History* 2, no. 3 (Summer 1978): 257–278.

Humphreys, Leonard A. *The Way of the Heavenly Sword: The Japanese Army in the 1920s.* Stanford: Stanford University Press, 1996.

Peattie, Mark R. *Nan'yō: The Rise and Fall of the Japanese in Micronesia, 1885–1945.* Honolulu: University of Hawaii Press, 1992.

## World War II

Most Japanese call World War II the Greater East Asia War (*Dai Tō-A Sensō*), but others refer to it as the Pacific War because fighting was not restricted to East Asia at all. One of the most difficult tasks in recounting the history of the war is that of periodization. Everyone knows when the war ended (August 15, 1945), but there is much contention about when it began. For Americans, of course, the war began early on Sunday morning, December 7, 1941, when Japan attacked Pearl Harbor. For the Japanese, however, their country had really been at war for considerably longer.

Most Japanese historians mark the beginning of Japanese engagement in the war as the night of July 7, 1937, when Chinese and Japanese forces exchanged gunfire at the Marco Polo Bridge just outside Beijing. Most Chinese prefer that the beginning actually be noted as September 18, 1931, when Japan's Kwantung Army faked an attack on the South Manchurian Railway in an effort to overrun Manchuria. Still others, particularly those of the Marxian persuasion, claim that Japan's assault on Chinese sovereignty can be traced to June 4, 1928, when the same Kwantung Army assassinated the Manchu warlord Zhang Zuolin.

Most historians generally consider that the underlying the causes for the war were Japan's overweening imperialist ambitions in Asia. Japanese apologists compare Japan's ambitions to those of the American Manifest Destiny. That is to say, Japan had as much right to dominate Northeast Asia as the United States had to conquer most of North America and to dominate South America as well. Japanese territorial ambitions can be traced back to the first Sino-Japanese War (1894–1895), when Japan announced its intentions to control its periphery. Having added the Ryukyu Islands to its possessions in the 1870s, Japan now acquired Taiwan and the nearby Penghu Islands as part of the Treaty of Shimonoseki (1895). It also acquired the Liaotung Peninsula and guaranteed the political independence of Korea. Liaotung was wrested away from Japan in the so-called Triple Intervention of the same year. A decade later, Japan won Liaotung again (as well as the Kurile Island and the southern half of the island of Sakhalin) after the Russo-Japanese War (1904–1905).

Korea was annexed in 1910, and Japan continued to force its neighbors to recognize its predominance in Northeast Asia for two decades after. Liaotung was returned to Chinese sovereignty after the Washington Naval Conference of 1922, but only after Japan briefly tried to extend its power over the Chinese Shandong Peninsula (captured from Germany in World War I).

A new generation of Japanese saw China's descent into warlordism as an opportunity to seize Manchuria and even Mongolia and northern China in the late 1920s and early 1930s. Whether Japan was serious about creating Pan-Asianism in this period is debatable, but soon after the seizure of

Manchuria and the establishment of the puppet regime in Manchukuo, many Japanese began to bandy about the term "Greater East Asia Co-prosperity Sphere." Japan hoped to create an Asian sphere of nations "liberated" from Western colonialism. It envisioned that it would economically and even politically dominate that coalition much as England led the British Commonwealth.

At the beginning of the war with China in 1937, Japan seemed destined to once again trounce China as it had four decades earlier. It quickly seized Beijing and Tianjin. Japan's government tried time and again to limit the escalation of the war in the initial stages. It hoped to convince China to agree to an armistice that left Japan in control of most of northern China. The recent Second United Front (December 1936) had forged an uneasy alliance between the Nationalist (Guomindang) forces led by Jiang Jieshi and the Chinese Communist Party only recently seized by Mao Zedong. The alliance seemed determined to resist Japanese expansion.

After the initial Japanese victories, the Chinese made the Japanese pay dearly for these victories. Chinese resistance stiffened in the Battle of Shanghai, and Japan found it necessary to send more troops and ships to the area at the end of November 1937. At this point Japan began to bomb civilian areas of the city from the sea and air. It also began to show evidence of the atrocities that would plague the war. Captured soldiers were summarily shot; civilians were tortured and killed.

The Chinese government declared its capital Nanjing to be an "Open City" and fled west along the Yangtze River. Under international rules of war, the Open City designation meant that the military forces were leaving and declared that the city would be undefended. The Japanese responded to the few guerrilla snipers around the city by roaring into Nanjing with full military might. Even worse, for the next two weeks the army seemed to have gone crazy. Noncombatants were massacred, women were raped and then killed, and whole areas of the city were put to the torch. Western (primarily business-men and missionaries) witnesses reported the atrocities to the press, but the Japanese government denied all charges.

If the Japanese military intended to use this terror against civilians strategically, it was badly mistaken. The guerrillas who con-tinued to fight the Japanese used the atroc-ities as a recruiting device to bring peasants into their ragtag armies. Indeed, during the rest of the war, the guerrillas were able to use Japanese atrocities to convince the Chinese population that surrender was hope-less. If Japan continued to brutalize captives, better to "die on one's feet than to live on one's knees."

By mid-1938, the war had settled into what even the Japanese call "the China Quagmire." The Japanese ruled most of coastal China and made forays into the hin-terlands. The Guomindang refused to sur-render from their wartime capital of Chongqing in far-off Sichuan. The Commu-nists conducted a very effective guerrilla campaign mostly in northern and western China, striking against the Japanese forces when they least expected. The guerrillas occasionally even won conventional victo-ries at Changsha and Guangxi in 1939, but mostly they would hit and run. The Japanese could never really find the guerrillas and resorted to more atrocities against civilians who seemed to be harboring the guerrillas. Coupled with Japan's air attacks against Chinese cities, the civilian casualties mounted into the millions.

Because the United States, Russia, and Great Britain had from the beginning of the war sent aid to the Chinese, the Japanese fooled themselves into thinking that if that meager aid was cut off, the Chinese would surrender. The Japanese conducted costly air raids against the so-called Burma Road supply lines over the Himalayan foothills. Despite cutting off most British and American aid, the Chinese refused to surrender.

For their part, the Americans thought that they could force Japan to stop its aggression and began to deny Japan the iron and oil that the country needed to continue the war. That step, in turn, convinced Japan that to obtain these essential raw materials, it needed to expand into Southeast Asia. In a circle of world madness, the United States demanded that Japan evacuate China. Japan decided that its only recourse was war with the United States.

It is clear that most of Japan's leadership knew that it could not hope to defeat the dis-tant United States in total war. At best, its military leaders argued, Japan could force the "soft" Americans to realize that war in Asia was not in its long-term best interests. In a similar madness, the United States believed that Japan could be intimidated into giving up its territorial acquisitions of the previous half-century—which was as likely as if, in the middle of the Spanish-American War, the United States would have been forced into giving up all its acquisitions since 1840. Thus Japan moved into French Indochina, the United States blockaded all industrial products in response, and Japan decided to attack the Americans and British. Both sides were self-righteously convinced that they had been forced into war by the irrational actions of the other.

*Louis G. Perez*

**See also:** Jiang Jieshi (Ch'iang K'ai-shek); Kwantung Army Adventurism; Manchukuo;

Pearl Harbor, Attack on; Russo-Japanese War; Shimonoseki, Treaty of; Sino-Japanese War; Triple Intervention; Washington Naval Conference; World War II, Pacific Theater; Zhang Zuolin.

### Further Reading

Butow, Robert. *Tōjō and the Coming of the War.* Princeton: Princeton University Press, 1965.

Spector, Ronald H. *Eagle against the Sun: The American War with Japan.* New York: Vintage Books, 1984.

## World War II, Consequences

In assessing the consequences of World War II, first and foremost one must consider that millions of people were killed during the war. Even if one accepts only the most conservative estimates, perhaps 30 million people died in the Asian part of the fighting (a similar number in the rest of the world). Estimates suggest that only 20 to 25 percent of the dead can be categorized as regular combatants; the rest were civilians. The Japanese conducted an atrocious war in every sense of the word. Japanese Imperial Army troops behaved horribly. They massacred civilians, bombed cities, blew up dams and levees, burned crops in the field, and employed biological warfare wherever they went. Rape, torture, and murder were common. Little wonder that Asians still consider the Japanese to have been subhuman and brutal.

Scholars all over the world have struggled to explain why the Japanese behaved as they did. Some blame brutal military training. Such "transfer of aggression," in which brutalized troops take out frustrations on the weak, only partially explains the bestial behavior, however. Other academics claim that the irrational Japanese racist "land of the gods" nationalism demonized all non-Japanese; it was, therefore, permissible to torture, maim, and kill with complete amorality. Yet others point at the ideas of *bushidō* that dehumanized Japanese troops. If surrender is cowardly, then captured enemies deserved to be treated with contempt and brutality. Whatever caused this behavior, Japan's military forces devastated and destroyed everyone and everything they encountered.

Second, Japan destabilized political systems throughout Asia. Many Japanese were probably sincere in their goals of "liberating" Asians from their old Western imperialist masters; many more used the ideas of Pan-Asianism as a shield and cover for their own imperialist ambitions. The results were mixed. Virtually all Asians who cooperated or collaborated with Japan refused to return to their own colonial roles after the war. Several nationalist movements had their beginnings during this era, or were highly encouraged by the Japanese war. The Indian National Army under Subhas Chandra Bose fought valiantly alongside the Japanese against British forces in Burma. Although Bose died in an airplane accident, many of the officers and men in his army returned to India to become leaders in that country's independence movement. Similarly, the foundations of the Burmese National Army can be traced to the experience of native troops against Britain. Likewise, many among the leadership of the postwar South Korean army served in the Japanese Imperial Army.

Other Asians got their first taste of military service in the various armies fighting against the Japanese. Certainly at the head of this group are the guerrilla leaders of the Chinese Communist Party. Many Chinese residents of Taiwan blame the Japanese for the fact that a communist government sits

World War II, Consequences | 481

in Beijing instead of a "rightful" Guomintang one. The communists were able to pose as saviors of China and to discredit Jiang's nationalist forces as cowardly for having sat out the war in remote Chongqing. Kim Il-sung and others in the leadership of North Korea fought along with the Chinese Communists. Ho Chi-minh and other Vietnamese also fought against the Japanese, as did Indonesians, Filipinos, and Chinese Muslims. Later, many native Asians were able to parlay their anti-Japanese credentials into important positions in postwar Asian movements and governments.

Moreover, the war helped to destroy the old European colonial systems and usher in American and Russian ones. Like the empires of Japan, Germany, and Italy, the Dutch Empire did not survive the war; the French and British systems made brief postwar comebacks, but crumbled in the 1950s and 1960s. The nascent American and Russian systems emerged from their ashes, with the Cold War and the paranoia of the Domino Theory replacing the horrors of World War II.

Third, World War II destroyed the Japanese imperial political system. Some scholars consider the "Ultra-nationalist" period (1933–1945) to have been an aberration. They point to the development of party cabinets, universal male suffrage, and the high level of literacy in the 1920s as the natural and normal political evolution that was "hijacked" by militarists. Be that as it may, World War II destroyed the emperor-centered State Shintō system. The loss of the war and the revelation of Japanese war atrocities completely destroyed whatever credibility the old system still enjoyed. An entire generation of postwar Japanese subjects remember the privation, shame, and humiliation of the postwar era. Japanese

postwar cinema has done an excellent job of reminding everyone of the horrors of war. Little wonder that most Japanese dismiss the arguments of the Neo-Conservatives who advocate a return to the old ideas. Without question, many of the most vocal advocates of pacifism and against nuclear warfare can be found in Japan. Obviously the pro-American political system in Japan is a direct result of the war and subsequent Allied occupation.

Similarly, Japanese society was changed by the war. Most of the so-called nobility was swept away, as were those who considered themselves inheritors of the samurai tradition. The new generation of postwar Japanese found their heroes among entrepreneurs, inventors, and "salary-men." Certainly Japanese education changed radically. Neo-Confucian values became passé and even evil—to be replaced with the virtues of science and humanism. Without doubt, the role and status of women in Japanese society changed because of the war and later occupation. Indeed, many scholars argue that the liberal nature of the postwar Constitution would not have been possible without World War II and the Allied occupation.

*Louis G. Perez*

**See also:** Jiang Jieshi (Ch'iang K'ai-shek); 1947 Constitution; World War II, Japanese Atrocities.

## Further Reading

Dower, John. *Embracing Defeat: Japan in the Wake of World War II.* New York: W. W. Norton, 1999.

Gordon, Andrew, ed. *Postwar Japan as History.* Berkeley: University of California Press, 1993.

Hane, Mikiso. *Eastern Phoenix: Japan Since 1945.* Boulder, CO: Westview Press, 1996.

# World War II, Continental Theater

When Americans talk about World War II against Japan, they really mean the Pacific Theater. Almost all American involvement against the Japanese occurred in the South Pacific. In reality, the war on the Asian continent involved more men and war materiel; it was twice as long; and it resulted in perhaps 10 times the number of casualties suffered in the Pacific Theater.

Japanese fighting in World War II began in July 1937 with the Marco Polo Bridge Incident. At the beginning of the war, Japan seemed destined to once again trounce China as it had four decades earlier. Japanese forces quickly seized Beijing and Tianjin and moved down the coast. Japan's government tried time and again to limit the escalation of the war in the initial stages. It hoped to convince China to agree to an armistice that left Japan in control of most of northern China. The recent Second United Front (December 1936) had forged an uneasy alliance between the Nationalist (Guomindang) forces led by Jiang Jieshi and the Chinese Communist Party only recently seized by Mao Zedong, however, and this alliance seemed determined to resist Japanese expansion.

After the initial Japanese victories, the Chinese made the Japanese pay dearly for

**JAPANESE EXPANSION IN CHINA**

July 1937-July 1938

July 1938-July 1939

July 1939-December 1941

its early successes. Chinese resistance stiffened in the Battle of Shanghai, to the point that Japan found it necessary to send more troops and ships to the area at the end of November 1937. At this stage of the war, the Japanese government lost control of its own forces. The military leadership seized the reins of the war and began to ignore orders from Tokyo. They began to bomb civilian areas of Shanghai from both the sea and the air. They also began to turn a blind eye to atrocities that would persist throughout the war. Captured soldiers were summarily shot; civilians were tortured and killed.

The Chinese government declared its capital Nanjing to be an "Open City" and fled west along the Yangtze. Under international rules of war, the Open City designation meant that military forces were leaving and that the city would be undefended. The Japanese forces responded to the few guerrilla snipers around the city by roaring into Nanjing with full military might. Even worse, for the next two weeks the army seemed to have gone crazy. Noncombatants were massacred, women were raped, and whole areas of the city were put to the torch. Western (primarily businessmen and missionaries) witnesses reported the atrocities to the press, but the Japanese government denied all charges and forced Westerners to leave.

If the Japanese military intended to use this terror against civilians strategically, it was badly mistaken. The guerrillas who continued to fight the Japanese used the atrocities as a recruiting device to bring peasants into their ragtag armies. Indeed, during the rest of the war, the guerrillas were able to use Japanese atrocities to convince the Chinese population that surrender was hopeless. If Japan continued to brutalize captives, better to "die on one's feet than to live on one's knees."

By mid-1938, the war had settled into what even the Japanese call "the China Quagmire." The Japanese ruled most of coastal China and made forays into the hinterlands. The Guomindang refused to surrender from their wartime capital of Chongqing in far-off Sichuan. The Communists conducted a very effective guerrilla campaign mostly in northern and western China, striking against the Japanese soldiers when they least expected. The guerrillas occasionally even won conventional victories at Changsha and Guangxi in 1939, but mostly they would hit and run. The Japanese could never really find the guerrillas and resorted to more atrocities against civilians who seemed to be harboring the guerrillas. Coupled with Japan's air attacks against Chinese cities, the civilian casualties mounted into the millions.

By 1940, the Japanese army was scattered all over China and was having great difficulties coordinating and supplying its forces. Each time the army conquered an area, another battle flared up miles away, and then another and another. One Japanese general later confessed, "It was like trying to put out a prairie fire by stamping on it." The communist-led guerrillas employed classic hit-and-run tactics. The Japanese responded with scorched-earth tactics that drove even more displaced peasants into the guerrilla ranks.

In 1940, Japan missed an excellent chance to split the Chinese ranks. The Japanese had been trying to cultivate allies among China's Muslim minorities and regional warlords, but with no real success. The Japanese were heavy-handed in their treatment of Chinese and loathe to allow them any real power or control over their native regions. Now, however, a national figure emerged. Wang Jingwei, a handsome and charismatic colleague of Sun Yat-sen in the pre-revolutionary period, presented himself as an alternative to Jiang Jieshi. Educated in Japan, Wang had been a rival to Jiang when Sun died in 1925. When Jiang had prevailed, Wang had continued working in the political back-channels of China. In 1940, he was designated as President of the Executive Yuan and Chairman of the Government of National Salvation. Had the Japanese army accorded him any real power, perhaps more Chinese would have flocked to his puppet regime. As it was, the Japanese generals treated him with contempt. A ragtag army of deserters, cutthroats, rapists, and thieves was formed in support of Wang, but they specialized in rape, graft, corruption, and cowardice. The Chinese peasantry hated them even more than they did the haughty Japanese.

The pattern of establishing puppet regimes varied little throughout the areas that the Japanese military had conquered. Along with Wang's regime, Japan installed the former emperor of China "Henry" Pu-yi, as emperor of Manchukuo; Ba Maw, as head of the State of Burma; Subhas Chandra Bose, as head of state of the Provisional Government of Free India; José P. Laurel, as President of the Second Philippine Republic; as well as "liberated" governments in Thailand (Siam) and Cambodia. All of these entities were part of the Greater East Asia Co-prosperity Sphere (*Dai-tō-a Kyōeiken*), which Japan styled after the British Commonwealth. All were given lip service as "independent allied nations," but accorded little more than hollow promises. The local Japanese military commanders gave them no power and usually treated their leaders with thinly veiled contempt. With the exception of Burma, all of the nations repudiated the Japanese-led alliance after the war.

In 1940, China's communist-led guerrillas began a wide-scale campaign against the Japanese in the north. They cut Japanese supply lines, blew up rail lines, and destroyed a Japanese-controlled coal mine. The Japanese response was a full-scale scorched-earth campaign, killing perhaps millions of defenseless peasants. The campaign was called the "Three-All Campaign" ("loot all, burn all, kill all") by the Chinese. Along with committing rape, murder, and arson, Japanese troops blew up the dams and levees on the rivers, causing devastation in a area of north China about the size of France. About this same time, some Japanese army units (notably the notorious Unit 731) began to conduct "scientific" experiments on captured enemy soldiers and civilians. The army also dropped biological pathogens on Chinese cities.

Russia, as part of China's Second United Front, had provided China with aid since 1937. Russian "volunteers" served with Chinese military units, in some cases flying Russian planes in aid of the war. With the signing of the Japanese-Soviet Neutrality Pact of 1941, however, Russian aid stopped. The United States and Great Britain provided aid as well, mostly over the so-called Burma Road, a thin cordon over the Himalayan foothills. Japan reasoned that if it could cut off that aid, China would surely buckle. Thus Japan began to bomb the Burma Road. In 1941, the United States quietly formed the American Volunteer Group (AVG), or Flying Tigers, to replace the withdrawn Soviet volunteers and aircraft. This quixotic ragtag group began to fly supplies over the Himalayas ("over the hump," they called it).

When Japan attacked Pearl Harbor, the United States and Great Britain became China's allies in the war. In many ways, the entry of the Western allies changed the nature of the war in China. Jiang Jieshi seemed to be content to send surrogates occasionally against the Japanese, preferring to marshal his men and materiel for the future battle against his erstwhile communist allies after the war. He preferred "trading space for time." Some of his troops were sent to help the British-led fight against the Japanese in Burma in 1944. For their part, the communists continued to use guerrilla warfare to build up support among the Chinese peasantry.

The Japanese government began to siphon men and materiel away from the Asian continent to fight against the Americans in the South Pacific, though more than 2 million men remained in China and Manchuria. When the war came to an abrupt halt in August 1945, hundreds of thousands of Japanese civilians in China were abandoned by their military. Nearly a half million captives were captured by invading Soviet forces in Manchuria. In some cases, they were forced by the Russian army into slave labor. Ironically, tens of thousands died from the same horrific conditions that the Japanese had imposed on captive Manchurians, Chinese, and Koreans in the preceding decade.

War casualties are highly debated and politicized. The most reliable numbers are only estimates. China lost more than 9 million civilians and perhaps another 3 million combatants in World War II. Japan had perhaps 1.75 million people killed during the war, probably two-thirds of whom were lost in the Continental Theater.

*Louis G. Perez*

**See also:** Jiang Jieshi (Ch'iang K'ai-shek); Pearl Harbor, Attack on; Russian Invasion of Manchuria; Russian Neutrality Pact; Unit 731; World War II, Pacific Theater.

### Further Reading

Hsiung, James C., and Steven I. Levine, eds. *China's Bitter Victory: The War with Japan, 1937–1945* Armonk: M. E. Sharpe, 1992.

Myers, Ramon Hawley, and Mark R. Peattie. *The Japanese Colonial Empire, 1895–1945*. Princeton: Princeton University Press, 1984.

Wilson, Dick. *When Tigers Fight: The Story of the Sino-Japanese War, 1937–1945*. New York: Viking Press, 1982.

# World War II, Japanese Atrocities

Moral definitions of "atrocious" conduct are slippery to start with, and change over time. Moreover, "atrocities" are not always the same as "war crimes," which often go unpunished for political reasons. To torpedo a merchant ship without first evacuating its crew was an atrocity in World War I and was made a war crime in 1922—yet this was a routine practice devoid of moral stigma by the 1940s. The saturation fire-bombing of cities to massacre civilians was illegal during World War II, but the United States never faced criminal charges for it. Most people today consider the use of nuclear weapons in war to be criminally atrocious, yet it remains perfectly legal. With these vexing issues in mind, this article examines four atrocities that Japan committed from 1931 to 1945: drug trafficking, chemical/biological warfare, the "Rape of Nanjing," and prisoner of war (POW) abuse. (Comfort women receive treatment elsewhere in this volume.)

### Drug Trafficking

Japanese carpetbaggers smuggled drugs into China under extraterritoriality, with support from consular authorities and the army, starting in the 1910s. Aided by Chinese puppet regimes, traffickers spread south of the Great Wall in the 1930s, and firms such as Mitsui and Mitsubishi joined in with Foreign Ministry collusion. Thereafter, Japanese field armies and civil bureaucrats ran drug operations through puppet states that ordered widespread cultivation of opium, bought up crops, processed poppies into opium paste, refined this material into hard drugs, and exported the finished products to South East Asia and other parts of China. The army used this illicit income to purchase war materiel and to fund machinations such as the Shanghai Incident of 1932, in which Chinese thugs were paid to kill Japanese priests. That pretext justified Tokyo's dispatch of three army divisions, ostensibly to protect its nationals in China, but actually to divert attention from the takeover of Manchukuo—a puppet state that earned 12 percent of its revenue from drugs.

Chinese domestic law, plus four international treaties ratified by Japan, outlawed trafficking. Nevertheless, Chinese warlords, crime syndicates, and even the central Guomindang government all relied on opium for revenue, so Japan felt no qualms about following suit. It also expanded drug trafficking operations to include narcotics such as heroin, morphine, and cocaine. Even so, Japan escaped sentencing on drug-related charges at the Tokyo war crimes trials in 1946–1948.

### Chemical/Biological Warfare

Toxic gases caused approximately 1 million casualties in World War I, of which some 90,000 (9 percent) were fatal. Japan did not ratify the 1925 Geneva Convention that banned the use of poison gas in war, and apart from Italy in Ethiopia, it was the sole World War II belligerent to employ this weapon in combat. Although initially disdaining this tactic, Japanese commanders began using nonlethal tear gas in 1937 to incapacitate Chinese troops from afar before killing them by bullet or bayonet at close quarters. Reliance on lethally toxic agents like lewisite became common by 1938. Japan used gas 2,091 times in China to cause about 90,000 casualties, of which some 10,000 (11 percent) were fatal, but it did not use gas against the United States for fear of retaliation in kind.

Japan was exceptional in waging germ warfare as well. Unit 731 and three other secret units scattered pathogen-infested vermin and fleas on Chinese towns from 1938 to 1945. These units also experimented on humans through injections of, or exposure to, germ strains in an effort to measure their potencies, in the process killing some 3,000 persons, code-named "logs." At the war's end, the army ordered that biological arms factories and laboratories be razed and that poison-gas canisters be buried, but approximately 400,000 of them still remain and continue to produce casualties today. High-ranking commanders, including Emperor Hirohito, approved the deployment and use of chemical and biological weapons against China, but U.S. prosecutors at the Tokyo trials granted immunity from prosecution and other lucrative perquisites to persons suspected of these two war crimes in return for access to research findings.

### "Rape of Nanjing"

Also known as the "Nanjing Massacre," this event comprised large-scale barbarous acts of murder, plunder, arson, and rape—which violated the laws of war and international treaties ratified by Japan—during a six-week seizure of Nanjing city and its environs in December 1937–January 1938. This horrific event did take place, but there is room for honest debate about its scale, its degree of illegality at the time, and the nature of Japanese turpitude. Implying similarities to the Nazi Holocaust, Chinese maximalists insist on victim tolls of 300,000 to 340,000 massacred and tens of thousands raped.

By contrast, verdicts at the Tokyo war crimes trials estimated 100,000 to 200,000 persons massacred and 20,000 raped. Although the rapes are impossible to quantify, recent research shows that massacres of civilians and of POWs in detention number roughly 46,000 inside the city of Nanjing and more than 100,000 if its environs are included. The variation in numbers stems from difficulties in sorting civilians murdered in cold blood from belligerents killed in accordance with the laws of war in 1937. Japanese troops hunted down those whom they considered "defeated stragglers" or what we now call "unlawful combatants"—that is, troops who did not lay down arms in surrender. Many of these men discarded uniforms, concealed their weapons, and blended into civilian crowds to be indistinguishable from noncombatants.

Japanese troops presumed that these former soldiers were guerrillas waiting for a chance to strike back, and so considered them legitimate targets on mop-up operations. That was the case even in Nanjing's designated refugee safety zone, because large-scale caches of weapons were found in this area, which the Chinese had agreed to demilitarize. By contrast, Chinese and Western observers did not know about the arms caches and viewed these "defeated stragglers" as "ex-soldiers" fleeing for their lives with no desire to resist and, therefore, no different from helpless refugees. This judgment call was hard to make in 1937; it is virtually impossible to sort out today.

The judicial bench at Tokyo ordered two Japanese individuals—one general and one diplomat—to be executed for the "Rape of Nanjing." They were found guilty of "crimes against peace," or conspiring to wage aggressive war—not "crimes against humanity" like genocide, as with Nazi convicts at Nuremberg. Defense counsels at Tokyo argued that "conspiring to wage aggressive war" was legal in 1937 but prosecutors and justices—all from the victorious Allies—made this a "crime" retroactively in 1946 to win convictions. The bench also conceded that this pair was guilty only of "omission," or not effectively using their authority to halt illegal acts by troops on the ground, which in effect meant they committed criminal negligence. They were not guilty of "commission," or directly ordering illegal acts. Nonetheless, Japan had to accept the verdicts and punishments to obtain a peace treaty.

## POW Abuse

Roughly 27 percent of U.S. and British POWs (35,756 of 132,134), as well as 35.9 percent of Australian POWs (8,033 of 22,376), died in Japanese detention from 1941 to 1945. Indeed, more Australians were killed in captivity than in combat. Allied POWs died from forms of abuse outlawed by a 1929 Geneva Convention that stipulated humane treatment in food, clothing, housing, medical care, and working conditions. Japan refused to ratify this Convention, but later pledged to "apply it *mutatis mutandis* [with needed changes]." The Allies took this term to denote compliance with the Convention "as if formally ratified," but Tokyo had meant "in light of Japanese law and socioeconomic conditions," which implied that foreign POWs would not automatically be entitled to better treatment and higher living standards than Japanese nationals, for that is what the Convention enjoined. As a result, sick and wounded Allied POWs at Bataan, for example, were made to trek 106 kilometers without food, water, and medical care in intense heat while enduring beatings and what their captors excused as "mercy killings." In addition, large numbers of POWs were dragooned to Japan and forced into slave labor under pathological conditions.

If viewed "in light of Japanese law and socioeconomic conditions," such forms of maltreatment were clearly illegal but not necessarily atrocious or abusive. In fact, roughly 60 percent of Japanese military deaths in the war (1.4 million of a total 2.3 million such deaths) resulted from starvation and disease—not combat. In the 1940s, surrender was forbidden to troops under any circumstances, so Japanese soldiers often died after combat had ended and their continued role as belligerents was meaningless, especially on islands "hopped over" by U.S. forces. These Japanese "defeated stragglers" died from a form of abuse designed by their commanders to prevent them from becoming POWs. Some 5,700 Japanese stood trial for Class B and C war crimes, mainly involving POW abuse, and approximately 930 were executed. Here again, Japan's acceptance of guilt and punishment was required to obtain a peace treaty.

## Some Causes

Japan's conduct exceeded the bounds of civilized behavior in the mid-20th century if measured against Western standards. In addition to their massive murder, rape, pillage, and enslavement of Asians, Japanese troops humiliated, abused, and killed Caucasian POWs. Although wanton cruelty existed aplenty, it was not the *main* cause of atrocities in 1931–1945, so simplistic demonizing of Japan is unwarranted. Instead, economic weakness and a drastically changed attitude toward Western cultural/moral norms in this wartime era offer more a compelling explanation.

Humane treatment was a frill that Japan could ill afford for its own nationals, much less for its enemies. It had won sharp, short, 19th-century-style wars against Qing China, Tsarist Russia, and Wilhelmian Germany. In contrast, as with the frog in Aesop's fable versus the cow, Japan in 1931–1945 was too poor to wage total war on four fronts with several enemies more populous, rich, mechanized, and scientifically advanced than itself. Atrocities seemed like a cheap panacea. Scant mechanization in agriculture and industry kept Japanese production levels down and left comparatively little surplus manpower for military conscription—hence the reliance on slave labor. Narcotics raised money—not readily forthcoming from state coffers—to finance puppet regimes, to pacify occupied areas, and to buy materiel needed for aggression. Without resorting to dirty tactics and illegal weapons, Japan could not defeat China while preparing to invade the USSR and actually attacking the United States and Britain. Penury also explains Japan's penchant for surprise attacks before declaring war, which was legally and morally acceptable in 1894 and 1904, but not in 1941. To survive at Nanjing as elsewhere, Japanese troops had to forage (i.e., plunder)—a method of provisioning that recalls medieval Mongol hordes, not modern armies. From the armed robbery of food and fuel, which was deemed permissible, it was a short step to torching dwellings as well as to killing the men and raping the women who resisted.

Japan won accolades for its humane treatment of European POWs in 1904 and 1914—if not Asian POWs in 1894. In that earlier era, however, surrender was allowed to Japanese troops as part of "civilization and enlightenment" modeled on Western cultural norms. By contrast, in the 1940s, capture was forbidden, so troops felt justified in giving enemies no quarter, following what they misperceived as "traditional Japanese" values, such as fighting to the last man. The high command held that obeying the Geneva Convention's provisions on POWs would be a one-sided burden; even worse, Japanese troops might desert to the foe, hoping to obtain the humane treatment they were normally denied. Ultimately, this indigence precluded Japan's adherence to international law so the Japanese government bore culpability for starting and prolonging a war in which its forces could not but violate legal norms recently enacted by a world seeking to make warfare less savage.

*Bob Tadashi Wakabayashi*

**See also:** Atomic Bombs: Surrender of Japan; Comfort Women; World War II, Pacific Theater.

## Further Reading

Harris, Sheldon H. *Factories of Death: Japanese Biological Warfare, 1932–1945, and the American Cover-up.* New York/London: Routledge, 2002.

Norman, Michael, and Norman, Elizabeth. *Tears in the Darkness: The Story of the Bataan Death March and Its Aftermath.* New York: Farrar, Straus and Giroux, 2009.

Tanaka, Yuki. *Hidden Horrors: Japanese War Crimes in World War II.* Boulder, CO: Westview Press, 1996.

Wakabayashi, Bob Tadashi ed. *The Nanking Atrocity, 1937–38: Complicating the Picture.* New York/London: Berghahn Books, 2007.

## World War II, Pacific Theater

### 1941–1942

On December 7, 1941, Japanese carrier-based planes attacked the U.S. Pacific Fleet, which was at anchor in Pearl Harbor on a sleepy Sunday morning. The Japanese had caught the Americans in Hawaii by surprise, and their ambassador arrived late with what was essentially a Japanese declaration of war. The Japanese mauled the American surface fleet, but the American carriers were away on maneuvers. Despite initial heavy damage, only two battleships were total losses—the *Oklahoma* and the *Arizona*.

Japan had awoken the sleeping American giant.

This was a grim time for the United States, with only a temporary victory on December 8, at Wake, when its Marine defenders held off an initial Japanese attack. While the United States recovered from the shock of the sneak attack, the Japanese took Wake, Guam, and the Dutch East Indies, and the invasion of the Philippines began on December 22. Japanese forces also attacked down the Malay Peninsula and forced the surrender of the vital British fortified port of Singapore on February 15, 1942. President Franklin Roosevelt and his senior advisers decided to launch a raid on the Japanese home islands. They named this raid after its colorful leader James Doolittle. His B-25s flew off of the navy's carrier *Hornet* on April 18, and dropped modest bomb loads on Japan. Most of his men landed in China, but the Japanese captured eight others, three of whom they executed. To counter the negative impact the Doolittle raid had on Japanese morale, Admiral Yamamoto Isoroku would later push up an already planned attack on Midway Island. Part of this attack consisted of a supporting attack on the Aleutians.

Due to the success of the Japanese on the Philippines, President Roosevelt ordered General Douglas MacArthur to leave his soldiers in the Philippines and command the Pacific forces from Australia. MacArthur's forces in the Philippines surrendered on April 9. During the infamous Bataan Death March, the Japanese killed roughly 10,000 American and Filipino prisoners of war, while the remainder faced slow starvation and brutal treatment in squalid prison camps. Meanwhile, the Japanese continued their expansion in the central, southern, and southwest Pacific islands.

The Japanese expansion included an attempt to seize New Guinea. If the Japanese

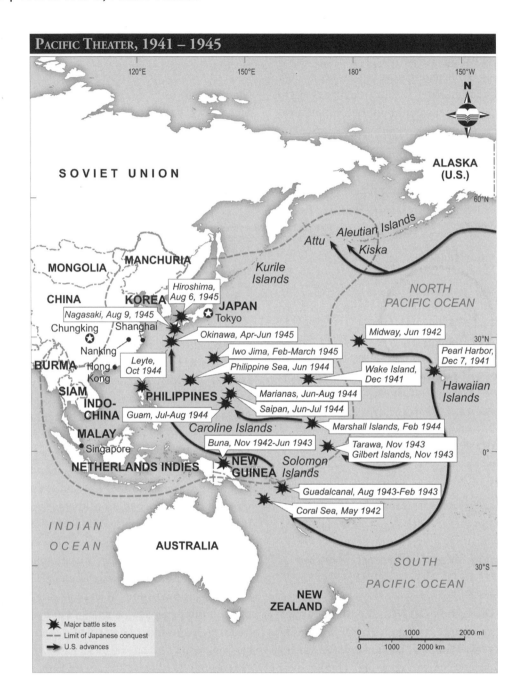

## PACIFIC THEATER, 1941 – 1945

SOVIET UNION

ALASKA (U.S.)

MONGOLIA   MANCHURIA

CHINA   KOREA

Nagasaki, Aug 9, 1945

Chungking   Shanghai

Nanking

BURMA   Hong Kong

SIAM   INDO-CHINA

MALAY

Singapore

NETHERLANDS INDIES

Hiroshima, Aug 6, 1945

JAPAN
Tokyo

Okinawa, Apr-Jun 1945

Iwo Jima, Feb-March 1945

Philippine Sea, Jun 1944

Leyte, Oct 1944

PHILIPPINES

Marianas, Jun-Aug 1944

Saipan, Jun-Jul 1944

Guam, Jul-Aug 1944

Caroline Islands

Buna, Nov 1942-Jun 1943

NEW GUINEA   Solomon Islands

Kurile Islands

Attu   Aleutian Islands
Kiska

NORTH PACIFIC OCEAN

Midway, Jun 1942

Pearl Harbor, Dec 7, 1941

Wake Island, Dec 1941

Hawaiian Islands

Marshall Islands, Feb 1944

Tarawa, Nov 1943
Gilbert Islands, Nov 1943

Guadalcanal, Aug 1943-Feb 1943

Coral Sea, May 1942

INDIAN OCEAN

AUSTRALIA

SOUTH PACIFIC OCEAN

NEW ZEALAND

Major battle sites
Limit of Japanese conquest
U.S. advances

0   1000   2000 mi
0   1000   2000 km

took the island, it was a natural springboard to cut off and conquer Australia. The Japanese sent a naval force with landing troops to take Port Moresby and, thereby, all of New Guinea. The U.S. Navy interceded, which resulted in the Battle of the Coral Sea on May 8. This battle was a key engagement for several reasons. It was the first naval battle where the two surface fleets were never in visual range; instead, U.S. and Japanese airplanes fought. The Japanese sunk the USS *Lexington* and damaged the

*Yorktown* but abandoned their amphibious assault on Port Moresby. Instead, Japan attempted to take Port Moresby via the Kokoda Trail over the rugged, mountainous spine of New Guinea. However, Australian soldiers, steep mountains, and dense jungle slowed and then halted the advancing Japanese troops.

As the Japanese prepared to attack Midway, the change in schedule had several effects. First, not all of the Japanese carriers were able to participate in the attack. Second, the Japanese had to use a great deal of radio traffic to coordinate the attack, which facilitated U.S. code-breaking efforts. This code-breaking intelligence—known as Magic—allowed the United States to know that the Japanese were going to attack Midway; thus Admiral Chester Nimitz laid what he hoped was a trap with the *Hornet*, *Yorktown*, and *Enterprise*. Luck was with Nimitz and his forces on June 4 and 5—U.S. aircraft sunk four Japanese carriers and killed many of Japan's experienced aircrews. Despite the loss of the *Yorktown*, America had won the initiative in the Pacific.

While the Japanese, Australians, and Americans fought on New Guinea, American Marines landed on the island of Guadalcanal in the Solomon Islands on August 7. The fighting for Guadalcanal raged for months. American air power could assist the troops only during daylight hours, which allowed the Marines to take and hold an air strip that they would later rename Henderson Field. At night, when the U.S. carriers withdrew, the Japanese surface fleet, with its outstanding night fighting capability, brought supplies, reinforcements, and naval gunfire. This see-saw dynamic continued until the United States could bring in additional air power due to the victory at Midway. As additional air and sea forces arrived, American Marines and soldiers secured Guadalcanal in November.

## 1943–1944

On January 2, 1943, MacArthur's Australian and American forces took Buna on the east coast of New Guinea. The next American endeavor was MacArthur's Operation Cartwheel, which began on June 29. Forces under Halsey's command sought to attack through the Solomon Islands to Bougainville, while MacArthur's forces planned to attack along the north shore of New Guinea and then to the western end of New Britain. These were the first campaigns using the "island hopping" tactics of taking only those areas necessary to stage the next "hop" and avoiding enemy strength. Island hopping also involved amphibious assaults, naval gunfire support, joint air support, and, on certain occasions, paratroopers and land assaults. By December 1943, Operation Cartwheel had isolated the key Japanese base of Rabaul, and MacArthur decided to let Rabaul "wither on the vine" rather than risk immense casualties taking a neutralized base.

While Operation Cartwheel was under way, the Joint Chiefs of Staff approved the U.S. Navy's separate drive through the Central Pacific, which Admiral Chester Nimitz commanded. Thus Nimitz's and MacArthur's drives became known as a twin axis or twin drive strategy. Nimitz's first target was the coral atoll of Tarawa in the Gilbert Islands. Tarawa was a bloody learning experience for the United States and amphibious warfare. The Japanese were well entrenched and the United States did not have a sufficient or effective naval bombardment. The Japanese also demonstrated their will to fight and die for their country on November 20—only 17 of 5,000 Japanese defenders survived.

For their part, the Marines suffered 1,000 dead and 2,000 wounded. Meanwhile, the army took the island of Makin to complete U.S. control of the Gilbert Islands.

The next step in the Central Pacific drive was the Marshall Islands. The navy had debated how to take control of the Marshalls, but Nimitz decided on taking Kwajalein to avoid strong Japanese positions in the eastern Marshalls. After studying Tarawa carefully, Marines and soldiers fought for Kwajalein from January 31 to February 4, 1944, experiencing a fraction of the casualties of Tarawa. The success of Kwajalein led to Nimitz pushing up the timetable. Thus U.S. forces attacked Eniwetok on February 18, rather than in May. After a carrier air raid neutralized the nearby Japanese base of Truk, Marines and soldiers defeated the Japanese garrison on Eniwetok on February 21.

While American industry steadily increased the size of the U.S. sea, air, and land capabilities, U.S. forces wore down the smaller Japanese forces. Additionally, U.S. submarines and air power began decimating the Japanese merchant marine, which limited the amounts of raw materials reaching the Japanese factories in the home islands. This American *guerre de course* set the stage for MacArthur's seizure of Biak and Nimitz's attack on the Mariana Islands.

Nimitz targeted Saipan, Tinian, and Guam, and the landings brought out the Japanese fleet for what the Japanese hoped would be a decisive, tide-turning victory. The Japanese got their decisive naval battle, but it did not turn the tide of the war. The Americans had roughly 500 fighters and 400 bombers compared to 200 fighters and 200 bombers for the Japanese. The Americans now had superior aircraft and the U.S. pilots had gained experience as well. The resultant aerial Battle of the Philippine Sea is also known as the Marianas Turkey Shoot, as they Japanese lost roughly 300 planes compared to 30 American planes lost. Meanwhile, MacArthur's forces successfully seized Biak and its airfield on June 7; thus U.S. aircraft could now reach the Philippines. Nimitz's forces also secured Saipan, Tinian, and Guam through heavy fighting from June 15 to late August. Like Biak, these islands were home to key airbases; control of Saipan and Tinian allowed the United States to begin attacking the Japanese home islands with the B-29 strategic bomber.

The United States was poised to begin cracking the inner circle of Japanese defenses in mid- to late 1944. In September of that year, MacArthur took the island of Morotai to prepare to invade the Philippines. Another supporting attack for the Philippine operation called for the seizure of Peleliu in the Palau Islands by Nimitz's forces beginning on September 15 and ending in late November. Peleliu proved to be a bloody assault on heavily fortified ridges, in which the Marines suffered their highest casualty rate of the war: 40 percent. The heavy casualties on Peleliu were even more unfortunate as the island proved to be of little use to support the invasion of the Philippines.

While the Marines fought for the bloody ridgelines of Peleliu, MacArthur planned the recapture of the Philippines. He would first take Leyte Island to prepare for subsequent operations to retake the main island of Luzon. The American assault on Leyte began on October 20, 1944, but the Japanese did not let this foray go unchallenged. The Japanese Navy launched its final effort, which resulted in the Battle of Leyte Gulf from October 24 to October 26. Like many previous Japanese naval operations, it was very complex. The battle involved forces converging on Leyte Gulf while a diversionary carrier force acted as bait to draw away the U.S. carriers from the invasion site. Despite losses, the Japanese carrier ruse drew away the aggressive Admiral William "Bull" Halsey, thus leaving the invasion force with little air support. Meanwhile, Japanese surface vessels attempted to reach the invasion site through Surigao Strait, but were caught in narrow waters by a prepared U.S. force that included some of the repaired battleships damaged in Pearl Harbor; these U.S. forces devastated this group of Japanese vessels. Farther north, another group of Japanese vessels moved through the San Bernadino Strait with only a few U.S. escort carriers barring their path. News of the defeat at Surigao Strait and Halsey's attempt to return, as well as a fear of the unknown, made the Japanese commander to withdraw. With the invasion site secure, the Marines and soldiers fought a successful, grinding battle to liberate Leyte.

## 1945

In early 1945, MacArthur was ready to take the island of Luzon and the Philippine capital of Manila. General Yamashita Tomoyuki decided to cede the cities and defend the mountainous areas of northern Luzon, which he held until the Japanese surrender in World War II. Some of Yamashita's subordinates disobeyed him and fought for every inch of Manila, which is sometimes referred to as the Stalingrad of the Pacific due to the ferocious house-to-house fighting. Additionally, the Japanese attacked the supporting U.S. vessels with suicide attacks—the kamikaze.

While the fighting raged in the Philippines, the U.S. strategic bombing campaign had picked up intensity. At the same time, the U.S. submarine efforts had all but wiped out the Japanese merchant marine, which never adopted the convoy system that served the Allies so well in the Battle of the Atlantic. Thus Japanese industry was essentially crippled. The long B-29 flight from the Marianas to Japan showed the need for an emergency landing strip. An early warning radar on Iwo Jima in the Volcano Islands and the need for a landing strip made Iwo Jima the next U.S. target. U.S. Marines landed on Iwo Jima on February 19, 1945, resulting in one of the bloodiest battles in Marine Corps history—6,821 Marines died and few of the 21,000 Japanese troops defending the island survived.

One of the final steps before the invasion of the Japanese home islands was to secure a base of operations in the Ryukyu Islands. The United States chose Okinawa to seize for a base of operations, and made an amphibious assault on April 1, 1945. The vicious land combat combined with massive, incessant kamikaze attacks made the battle for Okinawa costly for both sides. Japan lost roughly 70,000 soldiers and 80,000 civilians; the United States suffered more than 65,000 casualties on land, at sea, and in the air.

The Japanese kamikaze tactics, tenacious defense, and other political factors led President Harry Truman to decide to use atomic bombs on Japan. On August 6, 1945, the United States dropped an atomic bomb on Hiroshima. The Soviets attacked Japanese forces in Manchuria on August 8, and the United States dropped another atomic bomb on Nagasaki on August 9. The Shōwa Emperor surrendered on August 15, 1945. The official surrender occurred on the decks of the U.S. battleship *Missouri* on September 2, 1945.

*Captain Jonathan P. Klug*

**See also:** Atomic Bombs: Surrender of Japan; Kamikaze (*Tokkōtai*); MacArthur, Douglas; Pearl Harbor, Attack on; Russian Invasion of Manchuria; Shōwa Emperor (Hirohito); Yamamoto Isoroku.

## Further Reading

Costello, John. *The Pacific War 1941–1945: The First Comprehensive One-Volume Account of the Causes and Conduct of World War II in the Pacific.* New York: Atlantic Communications, 1981.

Murray, Williamson, and Allan R. Millet. *A War to Be Won: Fighting the Second World War.* Cambridge, MA: Belknap Press of Harvard University Press, 2000.

Spector, Ronald H. *Eagle against the Sun: The American War with Japan.* New York: Vintage Books, 1984.

Stokesbury, James L. *A Short History of World War II.* New York: William Morrow and Company, 1980.

## World War II, Southwest Pacific Theater

The Southwest Pacific Theater of World War II comprised the geographical area known to the Japanese as the Southern Resource Area as well as the Southeast Area; to the Allies, it was known as the Southwest Pacific Area (SWPA). Major land areas in this theater were the Philippine Islands, the Netherlands East Indies, New Guinea, Australia, the Bismarck Archipelago, and the Solomon Islands. In August 1942, the boundary was redrawn to exclude Guadalcanal and certain others of the Solomon Islands.

Japan entered the SWPA in a quest for oil. Oil powered Japan's economy and its armed forces, and the U.S. embargo of oil had helped trigger the Japanese decision to go to war against the United States. Dependent on foreign oil imports and rapidly using up its stocks, Japan needed to secure oil, the absence of which would paralyze Japanese industry within a year and immobilize the fleet within two years. Oil resources in the Netherlands East Indies, Japanese leaders believed, would make Japan self-sufficient in that vital commodity.

The Japanese Southern Army headquarters in Saigon, French Indochina, supervised army operations from the Philippines southward. Navy leaders, meanwhile, decided that U.S. airfields and fleet bases could not be tolerated on the flank of this advance. Japanese Lieutenant General Homma Masaharu's 14th Army with two divisions invaded the Philippines beginning on December 8, 1941. U.S. resistance in the Philippines officially ended on May 7, 1942. Meanwhile, Lieutenant General Imamura Hitoshi's 16th Army invaded the Netherlands East Indies with three divisions beginning on December 20. Dutch resistance there ceased on March 8.

The Japanese had only a marginal shipping capacity during the war. By May 1942, the Japanese were securing oil from their conquests in the Pacific, but the fleet was using just 42 percent of its merchant tanker capacity. Iron, manganese, chrome, and copper awaited exploitation in the Philippines. In addition, the Japanese desperately needed bauxite from the Netherlands East Indies for aircraft aluminum. Nickel was available from the Celebes. Local Japanese commanders were inefficient at developing these resources, and what materials the Japanese did extract from Borneo, Java, and Sumatra encountered shipping bottlenecks.

As the Japanese pushed southward, their navy engaged in several actions. The Battle of the Java Sea largely destroyed the American-British-Dutch-Australian (ABDA) fleet. The United States won a small victory against Japanese transports in the Battle of Makassar Strait. There was also a fight at Badung Strait, and the Allied cruisers *Houston* and *Perth* were destroyed in the Battle of Sunda Strait. The short-lived ABDA

Command collapsed in early March 1942, and the Japanese breached the Malay Barrier.

The startling successes of their initial campaigns encouraged the Japanese navy leadership to propose that five divisions invade Australia. Shipping and logistics, however, posed insurmountable problems: Japan, already short of shipping capacity, had lost 700,000 tons of shipping—nearly 12 percent of its total capacity—as a result of being sunk or severely damaged in the first four months of war. The Japanese army had never considered operating in the SWPA and had not planned how to campaign over such a large area and with such extended lines of communications. Japanese army planners estimated that to capture Australia would require 12 divisions and 1.5 million tons of shipping. The Japanese did not have the military assets and resources for such an operation. Australia was simply one continent too far.

Rather than invade Australia, Imperial General Headquarters in Tokyo ordered six of the divisions that had participated in the southern operations back to the Japanese home islands, China, and Manchuria. Planners redirected their logistical effort to the northwest and west when they should have been building bases—especially air bases—and establishing and supplying garrisons in the south.

On March 30, 1942, the U.S. Joint Chiefs of Staff established the Southwest Pacific Area. General Douglas MacArthur received command. The SWPA succeeded the ABDA area formed on January 15 as well as the Australia–New Zealand Area (ANZAC) established at the end of January. The first priority was to strengthen lines of communications to Australia and to build up logistics and air power. The air war here would be primarily land based.

Japan landed troops on New Guinea in February and March 1942. Its military leaders sought Port Moresby on the south coast as an air base, as part of Japan's campaign to cut the lines of communications to Australia and to deny the port as a base for Allied counterattacks. In the May 1942 Battle of the Coral Sea, the U.S. Navy deflected the Japanese seaborne invasion attempt. The Japanese then attempted to seize Port Moresby by land, crossing over the Owen Stanley Mountains. Australian forces fought a delaying action south toward Port Moresby that weakened the Japanese and ultimately halted this thrust. The Australians then drove the Japanese back to New Guinea's north coast. A Japanese landing at Milne Bay failed, boosting Allied morale.

On July 2, 1942, the U.S. Joint Chiefs of Staff ordered MacArthur to begin an offensive to clear the Japanese from New Guinea. This effort was limited by the availability of forces and because the Americans' army and navy were both constrained by the priority given to Europe. The long fight for Buna concluded in late January 1943. The Australians and Americans executed shore-to-shore and ship-to-shore operations up New Guinea's coast. Rabaul on New Britain was initially a target, but the Americans chose to bypass that major Japanese bastion, instead simply cutting it off from outside resupply.

Although progress was slow, the Allies kept the initiative, imposed a tremendous drain on Japanese resources, and prevented the Japanese from consolidating their conquests. Weather, disease, and inhospitable terrain inflicted heavy losses on all combatants in this theater, but especially on the Japanese. Particularly devastating to the Japanese was the loss of so many of their air assets, and the destruction of Japanese transports in the Battle of the Bismarck Sea gave Japan a stark warning of the precariousness of its position.

The Americans launched almost every operation so as to extend their air umbrella and logistics closer to the Philippines. The strategy of island hopping, which made use of growing U.S. Navy strength in the theater, allowed U.S. forces to advance, yet bypass strong Japanese ground forces. Allied shipping constraints and a shortage of service troops proved greater impediments to the advance than shortfalls in combat troops.

The SWPA was the location of one of two major U.S. offensives (comprising mainly land-based air and ground forces) aimed at Japan. The second location was the Central Pacific, in which the U.S. offensives largely relied on carrier air and sea power. The Japanese had insufficient assets to counter both offensives and were often off balance as they tried to maneuver against the two. The Japanese were simultaneously heavily committed in Burma and China and had to maintain major forces in Manchuria as a check on potential action by the Soviet Union.

The American SWPA and Central Pacific offensives indirectly supported each other early in the campaigns, and then directly supported each other as they converged at the Luzon-Formosa-China coast area. The speed, flexibility, and mass of the two Allied thrusts neutralized the defender's traditional advantage of interior lines of communications. Coordination between the U.S. Army and Navy regarding current and future operations was critically important.

The Japanese regarded campaigns in New Guinea as a means to delay their enemies, reduce enemies' resources, and gain time to reorganize for a counteroffensive. Rather than weakening the Allies, however, the campaigns in this area became a drain on Japanese manpower, ships, and aircraft. Allied air power cleared Japanese from the air and sea. Nowhere did the Japanese stop the advance, nor could they sustain the attrition that went with it.

The vast majority of Japanese troop and logistics shipping occurred in SWPA waters. Oil moved north through these waters, and U.S. submarines attacked the vital Malaya/Netherlands East Indies–Japan line of communications. Japan lost half its cargo-carrying capacity in 1944 to air and submarine attacks. Critical oil and raw materials required for war production in the home islands were sent to the ocean bottom.

The Battle of the Philippine Sea in June 1944 largely destroyed what remained of Japanese naval aviation. Japanese navy leaders then developed plans for a decisive battle, depending on the avenue of the U.S. advance. When the Americans invaded the Philippines in October, the Japanese immediately initiated their plan, which resulted in the Battle of Leyte Gulf—the greatest naval battle, in terms of ships and numbers of men engaged, in history. In the ensuing battle, the U.S. Navy all but destroyed the Japanese Navy as an organized fighting force.

The inability of Japan to transport men and supplies to Leyte and the country's similar difficulties in supplying and reinforcing Luzon hastened Japan's defeat in the Philippines. The U.S. conquest of the Philippines enabled U.S. air power there to sever the seaborne supply lines between the Japanese home islands and its Southern Resource Area. U.S. Navy forces swept into the South China Sea in January 1945 and cut Japanese lines of communications with Indochina. The American conquest of the Philippines, the ability of carrier task forces to go wherever they pleased, and the strangulation wrought by the submarine fleet completely isolated the Southern Resource Area.

Large Japanese ground forces remained in Indochina and in the Netherlands East

Indies, but they could play no role in defense of the home islands, nor could raw materials reach the home islands. This fact made MacArthur's use of Australian forces in Borneo in mid-1945 all the more questionable; it was a campaign with little strategic value.

The last operations in the SWPA were American preparations for the invasion of Japan. The Philippines provided staging areas for 18 U.S. Army divisions, large numbers of aircraft, logistics organizations, and hundreds of ships. With Japan's surrender in August, operations in the SWPA came to an end. The conclusion of hostilities did not bring peace, however, as wars in which indigenous peoples sought independence from their colonial occupiers soon began.

*John W. Whitman*

**See also:** Coral Sea, Battle of; Leyte Gulf, Battle of; MacArthur, Douglas; Philippine Sea, Battle of.

## Further Reading

Bergerud, Eric. *Fire in the Sky. The Air War in the South Pacific*. Boulder, CO: Westview Press, 2000.

Morton, Louis. *United States Army in World War II: The War in the Pacific. Strategy and Command: The First Two Years*. Washington, DC: U.S. Army Center of Military History, 1989.

## Xi'an Incident (1936)

In 1931, Japan's imperialistic designs on China became overt after the Kwantung Army occupied and set up the puppet state Manchukuo in northeastern China. Manchuria had previously been ruled by the warlord-turned-Guomindang general, the Young Marshal Zhang Xueliang. At the time, Jiang Jieshi adopted the policy of "pacifying the internal before resisting foreign aggression" and ordered Zhang not to put up any resistance against Japanese encroachment. Zhang and Yang Hucheng, another warlord-turned-Guomindang general, were ordered to engage in campaigns against the Chinese Communists, who were driven out of their base in Jiangxi Province by late 1934. Approximately 100,000 Communists undertook the Long March, desperately trying to avoid annihilation. By late 1935, a fraction of them arrived in the remote area of Yan'an in Shaanxi Province and managed to survive Guomindang's pursuits and attacks.

By December 1936, Zhang and Yang had stationed their troops in Xi'an City of Shaanxi Province and were prepared for final extermination of the beleaguered Communist Red Army in Yan'an. However, both men were sympathetic toward the Communists. With their firm anti-Japanese stance, the Communists had gained popularity among the Chinese public and even some of the soldiers who fought against them. Moreover, both Zhang and Yang saw Japan as a greater threat to China than the Communists.

In October and December 1936, Jiang twice flew to Xi'an to boost the morale of his anti-Communist troops. On both occasions, Zhang and Yang made desperate attempts to convince Jiang to end his anti-Communist campaigns and focus on fighting the Japanese. When all of their attempts proved futile, they decided to force Jiang to accept their view by kidnapping him and his entourage in the morning of December 12, 1936.

The news of Jiang's capture shocked the world, with his fate having profound repercussions for the various parties involved in the region, including the Guomindang, the Chinese Communist Party (CCP), Japan, and the Soviet Union. Guomindang leaders in Nanjing decided to deploy troops to suppress Zhang's forces in the name of rescuing Jiang, but Jiang's wife Song Meiling (1898–2003) was highly suspicious of the effectiveness of such a hasty military action. She also understood well that some Guomindang leaders, especially those with close connections with Japan, had much to gain from Jiang's death. Therefore, she asked for a delay of troop deployment and flew to Xi'an with her brother Song Ziwen (T. V. Soong; 1894–1971) to negotiate directly with Zhang and Yang for the release of her husband.

Upon hearing the news of Jiang's capture, some CCP leaders naturally wanted him executed. However, they soon realized the important role played by Jiang in unifying China and resisting Japanese invasion. Mao Zedong, the CCP leader, sent his representatives to participate in the negotiation of Jiang's release. Soviet leader Joseph Stalin also strongly opposed the execution of Jiang, as he feared that a divided Guomindang after Jiang's death would provide ample opportunities for the Japanese to take advantage of a chaotic China and threaten Soviet interests in it.

In Xi'an, Song Meiling was able to convince her husband to end his anti-Communist campaigns, at least for the time being, and not to kill Zhang and Yang for their rebellious act. As a result, on December 25, 1936, Zhang and Yang released Jiang and his entourage. Both men also accompanied Jiang back to Nanjing, where they were immediately placed under house arrest. Following the Xi'an Incident, the resultant Guomindang-CCP coalition was perceived by Japan as a sign that armed conflict between the two nations was inevitable. Starting from July 1937, China embarked on an eight-year journey to resist Japanese invasion. In retrospect, the Xi'an Incident was a turning point in China's war of resistance against Japan, as Jiang was forced to confront squarely the Japanese invaders sooner than he had expected.

In 1949, while Jiang was losing the civil war with the CCP, Jiang had Yang executed. Zhang fared better. After 1949, he remained under house arrest in Taiwan and was only released in 1991 after both Jiang and his son had died.

*Yu Chang*

**See also:** Jiang Jieshi (Ch'iang K'ai-shek); Manchukuo.

**Further Reading**

Taylor, Jay. *The Generalissimo: Chiang Kai-shek and the Struggle for Modern China*. Cambridge, MA: Harvard University Press, 2009.

Wong, Young-tsu. "The Xi'an Incident and the Coming of the War of Resistance," in *China in the Anti-Japanese War, 1937–1945: Politics, Culture, and Society*, edited by David P. Barrett and Larry N. Shyu. New York: Peter Lang, 2001:15–50.

Wu Tien-Wei. *The Sian Incident: A Pivotal Point in Modern Chinese History*. Ann Arbor: University of Michigan Press, 1976.

# Y

## Yalu River, Battle of (1894)

The opening naval battle of the Sino-Japanese War, fought on September 17, 1894, was in many ways a metaphor for China's 19th-century military failures. Although the Chinese Beiyang fleet was superior in the number of ships and guns, it fared poorly and lost what should have been an easy victory due to incompetence and corruption.

Many of the shells fired by the Chinese were filled with cement or sand instead of high explosives by corrupt military suppliers. One gun had been sold on the black market and another had not been seated because the space was used by the sailors to store pickles. The Chinese ships were actually sailed by Westerners because the Chinese officers were by and large inexperienced in actual warfare. The Chinese naval high command was attended by Western advisers (a German army major, an American ensign, and a British sub-lieutenant) because the leaders were political sinecures.

The Japanese ships, although inferior in number, tonnage, and guns, acquitted themselves splendidly. Admiral Itō Sukeyuki maneuvered his fleet brilliantly, flanking the Chinese fleet and placing the smaller Chinese ships between himself and the larger array, making it impossible for the Chinese to fire without hitting their own ships. In fact, the Chinese flagship destroyed its own mast in one salvo during the confusion.

The Japanese severely damaged a dozen Chinese ships, sinking five with an estimated 850 Chinese killed, with about the same number wounded. Four Japanese ships were damaged, but none sunk. Perhaps 180 Japanese sailors dead and another 200 wounded made Japan the clear victors of the day. Yet at the time, the foreign observers initially considered the battle as a Chinese victory since the original objective of the battle was to cover a landing of Chinese soldiers, a task that was accomplished.

Within a day, however, even the Chinese admitted that the battle had been a humiliating defeat for China. The Beiyang fleet did not play a significant role in the rest of the short war. Many foreigners consider the battle as an apt exemplar of a disastrous war that China should have won.

*Larissa Castriotta Kennedy*

**See also:** Sino-Japanese War.

### Further Reading

Paine, S. C. M. *The Sino-Japanese War of 1894–1895: Perceptions, Power, and Primacy.* London: Cambridge University Press, 2002.

Wright, Richard N. J. *The Chinese Steam Navy 1862–1945.* London: Chatham Publishing, 2000.

## Yalu River, Battle of (1904)

The Battle of Yalu River in 1904 was an early engagement of the Russo-Japanese War. At the end of April 1904, Russian forces under General Vera Zasulich met Japanese forces under the command of

# BATTLE OF THE YALU (YELLOW SEA) SEPTEMBER 17, 1894

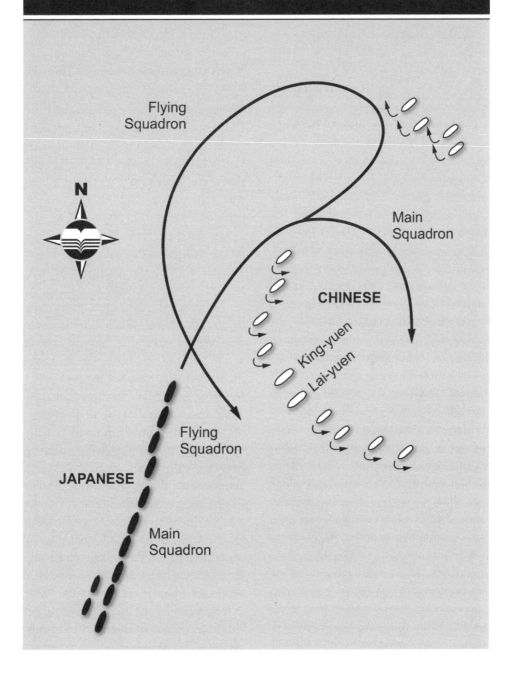

General Kuroki Tamemoto at the point where the Yalu River meets the Ai River. The Japanese forces consisted of the three divisions of the First Army: 2,000 cavalry, 28,000 infantry, and 128 field guns, including some brand new Krupp 4.7-inch howitzers. The Russian forces were the Eastern Detachment and had 5,000 cavalry, 15,000 infantry, and only 60 guns.

Strategically, the Battle of Yalu River showed the use of subterfuge, a relatively new concept in this context. Between April 25 and 27, Japanese engineers built a bridge intended as a diversion. The Russians fired on it, showing the Japanese where the Russian guns were. Tactically, the battle was dominated by new technologies. The Japanese Krupp howitzers could fire from farther away than the Russian artillery. Thus the safe distance for the Russians guns was greater than their effective range. Both sides in this conflict were equipped with breech-loading rifles, but only the Japanese grasped what this meant on a tactical level. The Japanese troops attacked in a long line, allowing them to cover a large field of fire. The Russians mocked this strategy and attacked using tactics best suited for single-shot muzzle-loading weapons.

The battle itself was surprisingly one sided. The Japanese attacked in the morning on May 1, and by 5:30 p.m., the Russian forces were retreating in disarray. The majority of the Russians escaped, and casualties were relatively minor: 1,300 Russians dead and 600 captured; 160 Japanese dead and 820 wounded. Symbolically, however, the Japanese had shown that an Asian army could win against a European power. As with much of the Russo-Japanese War, this symbolic victory was more significant than the military victory.

*ABC-CLIO*

**See also:** Russo-Japanese War.

**Further Reading**

Jukes, Geoffrey. *The Russo-Japanese War, 1904–5.* Oxford, UK: Osprey, 2002.

Nish, Ian. *The Origins of the Russo-Japanese War.* London: Longman, 1985.

## Yamagata Aritomo (1838–1922)

Yamagata Aritomo was born on June 14, 1838, into a low-ranking samurai family in Hagi, a castle town in Chōshū domain. His father had literary and scholarly interests that were shared by Yamagata. Yamagata was schooled by his father and through private instruction in classical Chinese and Japanese literature. He also learned to fence, to fight with a spear, and to defend himself through the martial techniques of *jujitsu*. Yamagata's father died in 1860.

Yamagata participated in Chōshū domain's loyalist movement, which played a considerable role in restoring the emperor to power in 1868. To maintain Chōshū power, Yamagata proposed an expansion of the domain's army and navy. In addition, he placed considerable emphasis on sending able Japanese men abroad "to become intimately acquainted with world conditions and to acquire practical knowledge about warships, artillery, military systems and administration." In 1869, Yamagata selected himself as fit for such a mission, traveling to Paris, London, Belgium, Holland, Prussia, Russia, and the United States to study institutions and most especially the military systems of each country. He most admired the militaristic style of the Prussians.

One year later, Yamagata returned to Tokyo and reported directly to the imperial palace of Emperor Meiji. Given the position of Assistant Vice Minister of Military Affairs, he took major steps toward organizing a

Yamagata Aritomo was the prime minister of Japan from 1889 to 1890 and again from 1898 to 1900. He is also known as the architect of the modern Japanese Army. (Library of Congress)

modern national army. The first step called for standardization of military systems. Second was the organization of an imperial body-guard to constitute the first important military unit under the direct command of the emperor. Yamagata also believed it was important to abolish the domains to concentrate all power in the emperor. The adoption of a system of conscription took five years.

Yamagata's progress through the military ranks was rapid. He was War Minister from 1873 to 1878 and led the government forces that quelled the 1877 Satsuma Rebellion led by Saigō Takamori. The following year, Yamagata adopted the Prussian-style general-staff system that separated military command from administrative functions.

As first Chief of Staff of the Army from 1878 to 1882 and again from 1884 to 1885, Yamagata solidified the independence of the military directly under the emperor and fostered the loyalty of servicemen to the throne by promoting the Imperial Rescript to Soldiers and Sailors in 1882.

Next, Yamagata moved into the political arena—a shift that did not undermine his influence in the military. Toward the end of the century, his stellar rise in the civilian bureaucracy paralleled his ascent in the military. He served as Home Minister from 1883 to 1889, during which time he reorganized the ministry, the police, and local government systems. In late 1888, Yamagata took his second trip abroad to study local governments, always keeping one eye on foreign military systems. As Minister of State, he enjoyed the status that permitted him to travel among the upper circles of governments. For three decades prior to his death in 1922, he was part of a small group of elite statesmen (*genrō*) who were close advisers to the emperor on critical domestic and foreign policy issues.

For a time, Yamagata alternated with Itō Hirobumi as Prime Minister from 1889 to 1890 and again from 1898 to 1900. He held the post of Justice Minister from 1892 to 1893, and subsequently became President of the Privy Council. He strengthened the Privy Council's power by requiring the emperor's cabinet to obtain Privy Council approval of 10 categories of ordinances, including any change in civil-service rules.

In 1910, Yamagata became one of the founders of the Imperial Military Reservist Association. He wanted to mobilize reserves in time of war and achieve the greater ideal that "all citizens are soldiers" by spreading patriotic military values to the public.

Until 1918, Yamagata was perhaps the most conservative bulwark against party politics. In that year, he finally gave his support to the naming of Hara Takashi as Japan's first party politician Prime Minister.

Among Yamagata's enjoyments in later life were his poetry, landscape architecture, and the rituals of a tea master. Yamagata died on February 1, 1922.

*Walter E. Grunden*

**See also:** Hara Takashi; Itō Hirobumi; Meiji Emperor; Rescript to Soldiers and Sailors; Saigō Takamori; Seinan (Satsuma) Rebellion.

### Further Reading

Hackett, Roger F. *Yamagata Aritomo in the Rise of Modern Japan, 1838–1922.* Cambridge, MA: Harvard University Press, 1971.

Hunter, Janet, ed. *Concise Dictionary of Modern Japanese History.* Berkeley: University of California Press, 1984.

## Yamamoto Gonnohyōe (1852–1933)

Yamamoto Gonnohyōe was born on November 26, 1852, in Kagoshima, the capital of Satsuma, As a young man, Yamamoto fought in the Boshin Civil War. Afterward, he entered the Japanese Navy Academy, from which he graduated in 1874.

During the Sino-Japanese War of 1894–1895, Yamamoto acted as a staff officer in the Imperial Headquarters in Shimonoseki. In the following years, he rose quickly in the hierarchy of the navy. From 1898, he served as Navy Minister for almost eight years in various cabinets, making the navy a political tool of the Satsuma clan in Japanese politics.

In 1904, Yamamoto achieved the rank of admiral. He became one of the major opponents of the Chōshū clan, led by Yamagata Aritomo, in Japanese politics. The two men frequently clashed. While Yamagata pursued a continental defense strategy directed against Russian expansionism in East Asia,

Yamamoto advocated a maritime defense strategy and demanded the expansion of the navy. Because Japan was an archipelago, Yamamoto argued, naval expansion had to be given top priority as the country's foremost defense. Yamamoto was even ready to give up Japan's colonies on the Asian Continent to allow the expansion of the navy. Yamagata considered colonies essential in the framework of Japan's national defense and in the struggle with the imperialist powers of the West.

Yamamoto soon became politically active as well. He pursued a policy of allying the Satsuma clan to the new political factions to challenge the supremacy of the predominant Chōshū clan. This policy proved remarkably successful when in 1913, Yamamoto was named Prime Minister and formed a coalition cabinet with the strongest party in the Diet—the Seiyūkai. To secure the party's support, however, Yamamoto had to include three Seiyūkai members in his cabinet, and three of his other cabinet members had to join the party, which left only four cabinet posts for Yamamoto's free disposal. The cabinet did succeed in passing reforms, which aimed at reducing the privileged position of the military in Japanese politics, thereby reducing the political influence of the army and of the Chōshū clan, which controlled the army. However, Yamamoto's cabinet had to resign in April 1914 due to a corruption scandal in the navy, known as the Siemens-Vickers scandal. Although Yamamoto was not directly involved in the imbroglio, he was still considered the ultimate authority of the navy and, therefore, responsible for its conduct.

In the following years, Yamamoto acted behind the political scenes, being awarded with the aristocratic rank of baron in 1902 and the rank of count in 1907. In 1923, he was again asked to form a cabinet. After the devastating Great Kanto Earthquake of September 1, 1923, reduced Japan to a state of emergency, the country needed a powerful authority to organize its recovery. Yamamoto formed his second cabinet, which was proclaimed a "Cabinet of National Union." He became not only Prime Minister, but Foreign Minister as well. The cabinet's main task was to restore law and order and start rebuilding the devastated area around the capital. Yamamoto's second cabinet resigned in December 1923, amid more political squabbling.

Yamamoto died on December 8, 1933, in Tokyo. He never achieved the status of elder statesman—the ultimate title of the Japanese political elite during this period—though few could doubt his lasting influence.

*Sven Saaler*

**See also:** Boshin Civil War; Great Kanto Earthquake; Satchō Oligarchy; Siemens-Vickers Scandal; Sino-Japanese War; Yamagata Aritomo.

### Further Reading

Najita, Tetsuo. *Hara Kei in the Politics of Compromise, 1905–1915*. Cambridge, MA: Harvard University Press, 1967.

Schencking, J. Charles. *Making Waves: Politics, Propaganda, and the Emergence of the Imperial Japanese Navy, 1868–1922*. Stanford: Stanford University Press, 2005.

## Yamamoto Isoroku (1884–1943)

Born in Nagaoka on April 4, 1884, Yamamoto Isoroku was the biological son of the former samurai Takano Sadayoshi and the adoptive son of Yamamoto Tatewaki. Educated at the Naval Academy (1901–1904), he fought in the 1904–1905 Russo-Japanese War and took part in the great Japanese naval victory in the Battle of Tsushima. Yamamoto attended the Naval Staff College in 1915 and 1916.

Initially trained in gunnery, Yamamoto became a leading advocate of naval air power during the 1920s and 1930s. Between 1919 and 1921, he studied English at Harvard University. Promoted to captain in 1923, he served as naval attaché in Washington, D.C., from 1926 to 1928. That experience persuaded him of the United States' unlimited economic potential and the relatively low quality of the U.S. Navy.

On returning to Japan, Yamamoto became chief of the navy's technical service in 1930 and was promoted to rear admiral the next year. He pushed for the development of modern aircraft for the navy. In 1933, he took command of the 1st Naval Air Division. Yamamoto headed the Japanese delegation to the 1935–1936 London Naval Conference, where he presented Tokyo's position that it would no longer abide by the 5-5-3 naval ratio with the United States and Britain. He returned home a hero. Appointed Vice Minister of the Navy in 1936, Yamamoto opposed his government's decision to proceed with construction of the giant Yamato-class battleships, believing they were a waste of precious resources. Unable to overcome the reliance on traditional battleships, Yamamoto nonetheless pushed ahead the construction of aircraft carriers, long-range bombers and flying boats, and the new Zero fighter.

Appointed commander in chief of the Combined Fleet in August 1939 and promoted to full admiral in November 1940, Yamamoto opposed the Tripartite Pact and the movement toward war with the United States. Although he allegedly remarked privately that Japanese forces would "run wild" for six months to a year, he had "utterly no confidence" after that. Nonetheless, he rejected the Japanese Navy's original plan to lie in wait for the U.S. Pacific Fleet in the Far East, after the American ships had been savaged by submarine and torpedo attacks.

Instead, Yamamoto devised a preemptive strike against the Pacific Fleet anchorage at Pearl Harbor in the Hawaiian Islands. He hoped that by crippling U.S. naval power at the war's outset, Japan might use the breathing spell that would ensue to conquer the Southern Resource Area and erect an impregnable defensive barrier.

Yamamoto did what he could to prepare his fleet for war, purging ineffective officers and insisting on realistic, rigorous—even dangerous—training, both day and night, so that when war came, the fleet was the best trained in the world, certainly at night fighting. However, he ignored technological advances, such as radar, which Japanese ships did not receive until 1943.

The success of the Pearl Harbor attack on December 7, 1941, enhanced Yamamoto's prestige, which he used to persuade the Naval General Staff to accept his overly complex Midway plan in April 1942. Designed to draw out the remnants of the U.S. Fleet, specifically the carriers absent from Pearl Harbor on December 7, Yamamoto's Midway campaign ended in disaster on June 4–6 with the Combined Fleet's loss of four fleet carriers, a blow from which the Japanese Navy never recovered.

Although the tide of the Pacific war clearly shifted in favor of the Allies after Midway, U.S. leaders remained wary of Yamamoto's leadership. Accordingly, when U.S. intelligence learned that Yamamoto intended a one-day inspection trip to the northern Solomons in April 1943, with the approval of President Franklin D. Roosevelt, aircraft intercept his plane. On April 18, P-38 fighters shot down Yamamoto's aircraft near Buin in southern Bougainville Island, killing the admiral. His remains were recovered and returned to Tokyo, where he was honored with a state funeral.

*Bruce J. DeHart*
*and Spencer C. Tucker*

**See also:** London Naval Conference; Pearl Harbor, Attack on; Russo-Japanese War.

## Further Reading

Agawa Hiroyuki. *The Reluctant Admiral: Yamamoto and the Imperial Navy.* Tokyo: Kondansha International, 1979.

Hoyt, Edwin P. *Yamamoto: The Man Who Planned Pearl Harbor.* New York: McGraw-Hill, 1990.

Potter, John D. *Yamamoto: The Man Who Menaced America.* New York: Viking, 1965.

Wible, J. T. *The Yamamoto Mission: Sunday, April 18, 1943.* Fredericksburg, TX: Admiral Nimitz Foundation, 1988.

# Yamashita Tomoyuki (1885–1946)

Yamashita Tomoyuki was born in Osugi Nara on November 8, 1885. He graduated from the Military Academy in 1908 and the War College in 1916. Trained as an infantry officer, he served on the General Staff in 1918 and then was resident officer in Germany, from 1919 to 1921. Promoted to major in 1922 and to lieutenant colonel in 1923, he served concurrently as military attaché to Austria and Hungary (1927–1929). Promoted to colonel in 1929, Yamashita then commanded a regiment before serving in the Army Ministry (1932–1936). He next commanded a brigade in the Korea Army (1936–1937) and was promoted to lieutenant general in 1937. Yamashita was chief of staff of the North China Area Army between 1937 and 1939 in World War II before commanding the 4th Division (1939–1940).

Recalled to Tokyo in July 1940, Yamashita became inspector general of army aviation. In November of that year, Minister of War General Tōjō Hideki, who saw Yamashita as a rival, sent him on a six-month military mission to Germany and Italy. On his return to Japan in June 1941, Yamashita warned against going to war with Great Britain and the United States until Japanese forces could be modernized—unwelcome advice that produced his exile to command the Guandong (Kwantung) Army in Manchukuo.

In November 1941, just weeks before the Pacific war, Yamashita received command of the 25th Army. In a campaign lasting 70 days (from December 7, 1941, to February 15, 1942) and while outnumbered by the British, Yamashita conquered Malaya and Singapore and earned the nickname "Tiger of Malaya."

Shortly thereafter, Prime Minister Tōjō engineered Yamashita's transfer back to Manchuria. After languishing there for two years, Yamashita received command of the 14th Area Army. From October 20, 1944, to September 2, 1945, he directed an effective defense of the Philippines. Surrendering to U.S. forces at the end of the war, he was arrested and tried as a war criminal for failing to control the Naval Defense Force, which committed atrocities in Manila in February 1945. Yamashita had ordered that Manila not be held and certainly had not ordered the atrocities committed there, but the court ruled him responsible for the actions of his subordinates. Sentenced to death, he was hanged on February 23, 1946.

*Bruce J. DeHart*

**See also:** Tōjō Hideki.

**Further Reading**

Hoyt, Edwin P. *Three Military Leaders: Heihachirō Tōgō, Isoroku Yamamoto, Tomoyuki Yamashita*. New York: Kodansha International, 1993.

Lael, Richard. *The Yamashita Precedent*. Wilmington, DE: Scholarly Resources, 1982.

Potter, John D. *The Life and Death of a Japanese General*. New York: New American Library, 1962.

Taylor, Lawrence. *A Trial of Generals: Homma, Yamashita, MacArthur*. South Bend, IN: Icarus Press, 1981.

## Yasukuni Shrine Controversy

Built in 1869 and named "the Shintō shrine for national pacification" in 1879, Yasukuni now houses close to 2.5 million persons who died for the emperor in domestic and foreign conflicts since 1853. Japanese servicemen were taught that they would be enshrined as "heroic spirits" at Yasukuni after dying in combat— the highest form of consecration for an imperial subject. Until August 1945, bereaved families who lost kin in action were honored by being invited to biannual memorial services where the emperor enshrined each new cohort of war dead. Parents of those who died enjoyed respect, social status, and war pensions. Worship at Yasukuni was obligatory for all imperial subjects regardless of their religious creed and unlike other Shintō shrines, Yasukuni fell under Army and Navy Ministry administration with its operating expenses supplied by the imperial government. The Allied occupation (1945–1952), however, stripped Yasukuni of state support in an effort to democratize Japan under the tenets such as "freedom of belief" and "the separation of church and state" as stipulated in the "McArthur peace constitution."

Thus, in the postwar era, Yasukuni became a corporate religious body no different from Buddhist temples, Christian churches, and ordinary Shintō shrines. Between 1969 and 1973, five bills to revive its public support came before the Diet, which rejected all five, so Yasukuni's yearly budget of roughly 2 billion yen ($24.3 million) comes from

Japanese officers visit the Yasukuni Shrine, a war memorial in Tokyo, Japan. (Library of Congress)

nongovernment sources, mainly private donations. Some 6 million persons visit the shrine annually, including the Dalai Lama in 1980. Still, Yasukuni remains fraught with highly controversial issues related to modern Japan's history and the commemoration of its war dead.

## Detractors

Detractors hold that the essence of Yasukuni lies in, ultra-nationalis, militarism, imperialism, and emperor-biased discrimination. Traditional religious beliefs before 1853, by contrast, were liberally inclusive. Japan's "true" tradition called for consoling the fallen spirits of friend and foe alike, be they foreign invaders or rebels to the throne. Moreover, civilian victims, numbering almost 873,000 in World War II, also died for the emperor and thus should be viewed as equally worthy of enshrinement, but are debarred it.

Consecration at Yasukuni, then, is a privilege reserved for military personnel—a policy that, not coincidentally, also applies to state pensions and benefits, which are denied to bereaved civilian families. Approximately 2 million of Yasukuni's 2.5 million "heroic spirits" were enshrined after the Allied Occupation in an effort to revive emperor-state values, and the government was illegally complicit by providing names of war dead to be enshrined. Postwar Yasukuni priests enshrined these 2 million war dead, normally without consent from bereaved families and sometimes against their express wishes, which violates freedom of belief.

The enshrined include more than 50,000 former colonial subjects (Koreans and Taiwanese), whom the postwar government stripped of Japanese citizenship, which deprived them of pensions and other benefits enjoyed by bereaved military families. Fully

99.2 percent of Yasukuni's "heroic spirits" died waging wars of aggression, and its on-site historical museum denigrates the suffering of foreign victims by glorifying Japanese imperialism. In 1969, priests decided to consecrate 14 Class A war criminals as "martyrs," and implemented that decision in 1978. These men were convicted in the Tokyo war crimes trials and subsequently executed, or else died either during those proceedings or they died while in prison after sentencing.

These facts, detractors assert, place Yasukuni Shrine beyond the pale of reputability, which makes visits by the emperor, prime ministers, and other public officials abhorrent, to say nothing of unconstitutional for violating freedom of belief and the separation of church and state. This is unacceptable for postwar Japan, which rejoined the comity of nations after vowing to honor the tenets of pacifism and democracy and after accepting the guilty verdicts at the Tokyo war crimes trials as legally binding and morally valid.

Detractors set the rank-and-file, drafted to die for their country in a war of aggression, apart from the Class A war criminals who ordered them to perpetrate that aggression. Thus very few detractors insist that bereaved families have no right to console the spirits of loved ones by visiting Yasukuni, and fewer still argue that that the shrine should be dismantled. Instead, they hold that, for Japanese citizens and public officials to honor the war dead properly and avoid legitimate foreign criticism, the following criteria must be met: (1) leaders must make further, more sincere, statements of apology for war crimes as well as pay more official compensation; in addition, (2) Yasukuni priests must de-enshrine the souls of Class A war criminals and expurgate exhibits at the historical museum (which the shrine refuses to do) or (3) Japan must build an alternative commemorative institution untainted by its sordid history.

## Defenders

Defenders of the Yasukuni Shrine retort that virtually all states—some with more sordid histories—have religious or semi-religious sites such as public cemeteries and monuments where state officials, free from foreign censure and interference, honor those who died for their country. This was true at Yasukuni in earlier postwar days; emperors and prime ministers regularly paid their respects until the 1980s, when Asian governments began unjustifiably to criticize the practice.

Given its postwar makeover as a nonofficial entity, Yasukuni presents nothing to warrant rebuke. Unlike in the pre-1945 era, no one "worships" there in a militaristic sense, and anyone who dislikes the shrine for any reason is free to stay away. Emperors and prime ministers visit the Grand Shrine at Ise periodically, and Tokyo City officials hold Buddhist memorial services for war victims annually. Why do detractors attack only visits to Yasukuni as unconstitutional? Democracy cuts both ways, so detractors must honor the constitutional rights and freedoms accorded to Yasukuni. Under the separation of church and state, the government cannot forbid anyone—when acting as a private individual—from exercising his/her rights to freedom of belief by visiting a particular church, synagogue, mosque, or other religious site. Of course, defenders would like leaders to visit Yasukuni in an official rather than a private capacity.

Also, unless a religious body is judged in court to have violated some law, no one can interfere in its doctrinal matters by, for example, forcing it to de-enshrine spirits. In 1965, Yasukuni went so far as to build a sub-shrine on its premises expressly to honor souls previously excluded—foreign nationals who died fighting against Japan as well as Japanese such as Saigō Takamori, who died rebelling against the emperor.

Finally, Yasukuni houses the souls of more than 8,000 Class B and C war criminals. Will detractors next demand that these men, along with the Class A criminals, also be deleted as bad apples?

For defenders of the Yasukuni Shrine, this controversy turns on the moral injustice and illegality of the Tokyo war crimes trials plus unfair parallels drawn to Nazi Germany. Morally speaking, the detractors' logic on Class A war criminals forces one to vilify Socrates forever as an irredeemably evil pariah just because some law court convicted and executed him. Defenders protest that Japanese sentiment calls for absolution of a person's crimes after death or after that individual has paid his or her debt to society; even former enemies concurred with that point, they say. During the 1950s, Japan requested pardons for all war criminals still in prison, and the Allied powers agreed. As a result, some of the released Class A convicts assumed cabinet posts and represented Japan at respected international bodies such as the United Nations General Assembly.

Legally speaking, the Nuremberg comparison is invalid. No suspects at Tokyo were found guilty of heinous "crimes against humanity" such as the Holocaust. Instead, they were convicted of conventional war crimes and "crimes against peace"— plotting and waging of aggressive war— which was not actually illegal in the 1930s and 1940s. Instead, it was trumped up as a crime so as to extract punitive verdicts later on, although the victors were also guilty. Moreover, defenders assert, imperial Japan had arguably legitimate grounds to wage war—an argument made at the Yasukuni historical museum. Detractors are free to dispute that argument by citing Japanese atrocities, but must respect the shrine's right to present another viewpoint on the issue under constitutional guarantees of free inquiry and expression.

Ultimately, shrine defenders contend, the detractors' demands violate the constitution and democratic principles. What is more, some 6 million Japanese freely visit Yasukuni each year from a genuinely felt need and desire to do so; nothing suggests that an alternative commemoration site would have such a broad appeal, so there is no cogent reason to build one. Yasukuni Shrine does not symbolize or support anything so egregiously evil or offensive—such as apartheid, ethnic cleansing, jihad, or fatwa—that foreign criticism and interference are warranted. The Yasukuni view of history is disputable, but does not lie outside the confines of acceptable debate.

*Bob Tadashi Wakabayashi*

**See also:** Comfort Women; International Military Tribunal for Far East; Nativism, Rise of; 1947 Constitution; Saigō Takamori; World War II, Japanese Atrocities.

### Further Reading

Breen, John ed. *Yasukuni, the War Dead, and the Struggle for Japan's Past*. New York: Columbia University Press, 2008.

Hardacre, Helen. *Shintô and the State, 1868–1988*. Princeton: Princeton University Press, 1989.

Seraphim, Franziska. *War Memory and Social Politics in Japan, 1945–2005*. Cambridge, MA: Harvard University Press, 2006.

## Yosano Akiko (1878–1942)

Yosano Akiko was born on December 7, 1878, in Sakai, a commercially important seaport near Osaka. Her father owned a

Yosano Akiko, perhaps the best-known antiwar poet, was also a frequent contributor to the feminist journal *Seito* (*Bluestockings*). (National Diet Library, Japan.)

prosperous confectionary store and was so despairing over the birth of another daughter instead of a first son that he sent the infant Akiko to live with an aunt. She returned around age two following the birth of her brother, Chuzaburo, but did not thereafter develop strong ties with her parents. Akiko resented the better treatment that her younger siblings received, the expectation that she would become a self-abnegating wife and mother herself, and her parents' persistence in locking her in her room at night to safeguard her chastity. She found an outlet in reading, however, and spent hours devouring the Japanese literary classics in her father's extensive library.

After graduating from a girls' middle school, Akiko began working in the sweet shop, reading in her spare time and eventually writing poetry. Her efforts to publish some of her poems in *Venus* (*Myojo*) led to her acquaintance with Yosano Tekkan, then a leading figure in the world of poetry thanks to his publication of the magazine and position as founder of the New Poetry Society. Their relationship soon turned romantic, and in 1901, she fled Sakai for Tokyo to become his wife over the strenuous opposition of her parents.

That same year, Akiko published her first collection of 31-syllable poems (*tanka*). Titled *Tangled Hair* (*Midaregami*), this volume attracted considerable attention, complimentary and critical, because of her frankness in describing her sensual feelings and love for Tekkan. It also helped to establish her reputation as one of the most influential poets of the time. That standing was solidified in September 1904 when she published in *Venus* a 40-line poem called "Brother, Do Not Give Your Life" ("Kimi shinitamo koto nakare"). She had originally penned this poem for Chuzaburo after he had been deployed to Port Arthur to fight in the Russo-Japanese War. Fearful that he would sacrifice his life in a suicide mission, she questioned whether their parents had intended for him to die young, prodded him to think about whether the fate of Port Arthur really mattered to his life as heir to the confectionary store, implored him to consider the feelings of their mother and his wife, and questioned the emperor for sending others in his stead to kill and die. This critique of war as causing senseless suffering and death was one of only a small number of published pieces that challenged the very popular Russo-Japanese War, and it gave rise to intense hostility, to the point that Akiko's house was stoned and she was labeled a traitor to Japan.

The notoriety stemming from Akiko's first collection and this antiwar poem generated a flood of requests for public and private talks and for manuscripts. Akiko responded by becoming a regular lecturer, including for the Accomplished Women's Literary Society, and by writing prolifically. She continued to produce poems, and the publication of a number in Hiratsuka *Raichō's* feminist literary journal *Blue Stockings* (*Seito*) contributed to its early success. She also increasingly wrote literary criticism and commentaries on issues ranging from politics to education to women's issues. Her opinions on the latter led to her involvement in a public debate with Hiratsuka and others in 1918 over state protection for mothers. The primary breadwinner for her family, which came to include 11 children, Akiko argued from experience and with force about the importance of women's economic independence and equality of opportunity.

After a 1928 trip to Manchuria and Mongolia with Tekkan, Akiko began to write in support of Japan's overseas military expansion. Departing from her earlier opposition to war and militarism, the latter expressed most notably in a 1918 essay, she composed poems and commentaries that called on women to demonstrate their loyalty and asserted that the military's actions in China were only intended to bring the Chinese peace and prosperity. She also praised Japanese soldiers who had died in battle and, in one verse penned soon after the attack on Pearl Harbor, exhorted her fourth son, Augyusuto, then a lieutenant in the navy, to fight bravely. Such compositions have done little to diminish her reputation as the author of Japan's most famous antiwar poem, "Brother, Do Not Give Your Life." Also known as one of the country's most important feminist writers whose works fill 20 volumes, Akiko died on May 29, 1942, due to uremia and complications from a brain hemorrhage.

*Elizabeth Dorn Lublin*

**See also:** Hiratsuka *Raichō*; Pacifism; Pearl Harbor, Attack on; Russo-Japanese War; *Seito* (*Bluestockings*).

## Further Reading

Rabson, Steve. "Yosano Akiko on War: To Give One's Life or Not—A Question of Which War." *Journal of the Association of Teachers of Japanese* 25, no. 1 (April 1991): 45–74. Special issue on Yosano edited by Laurel Rodd Rasplica.

Rodd, Laurel Rasplica. "Yosano Akiko and the Taishō Debate over the 'New Woman,' " in *Recreating Japanese Women, 1600–1945*, edited by Gail Lee Bernstein. Berkeley: University of California Press, 1991: 175–198.

Yosano Akiko. *Travels in Manchuria and Mongolia: A Feminist Poet from Japan Encounters Prewar China*, translated by Joshua A. Fogel. New York: Columbia University Press, 2001.

## Yoshida Shigeru (1878–1967)

Born in Yokosuka, Kanagawa Prefecture, Japan, on September 22, 1878, Yoshida Shigeru graduated from Tokyo Imperial University in 1906. He entered the Ministry of Foreign Affairs and served as Deputy Foreign Minister in 1928 and then Ambassador to Italy and Great Britain during 1936–1938. During World War II, he tried to bring the war to an end with an early Japanese surrender but was arrested by the military police.

During the U.S. occupation after the war, Yoshida headed the Japan Liberal Party and served as Prime Minister during May 1946–May 1947 and again during October 1948–December 1954. While he was in office, the Cold War heated up, altering U.S. policy toward Japan. President Harry S Truman's administration recognized Japan's geopolitical importance in East Asia and changed its policies to revitalize Japan's economy, retain the use of Japanese military bases, and rearm Japan. Demand for Japanese rearmament became far stronger after the outbreak of the Korean War in June 1950.

In January 1951, Yoshida held a series of talks with U.S. diplomat John Foster Dulles, assigned to negotiate a peace treaty with Japan. Dulles wanted Japan to conclude a peace treaty as a U.S. ally and to maintain adequate armed forces. Yoshida agreed to an alliance with the United States but resisted Dulles's request for rearmament. Yoshida ultimately compromised with Dulles and secretly promised to create Japanese security forces. On September 8, 1951, Yoshida signed the San Francisco Peace Treaty. That same day, he also signed the United States–Japan Security Treaty.

In October 1952, Yoshida created the National Security Forces, which succeeded the National Police Reserve established in 1950. With continuous pressure from Washington officials to strengthen Japan's defense forces, he transformed the National Security Forces into the Self-Defense Forces in June 1954. A few months before this transition, the U.S.-Japan Mutual Defense Assistance Agreement was signed, strengthening military and economic ties between the two nations. By that time the Japanese economy was flourishing, as the Korean War had pumped billions of dollars into Japanese factories.

Yoshida's diplomacy put top priority on Japanese economic development, followed by retaining defense forces at the minimum level possible. Yoshida remained a strong supporter of the Guomindang (GMD, Nationalist) government on Taiwan. In domestic matters, he increased centralization of government.

The year 1954 saw the biggest challenge to his diplomacy. The *Lucky Dragon* incident in March caused massive protests against U.S. testing of nuclear weapons. The *Lucky Dragon* was a Japanese fishing vessel that became caught in radioactive fallout after an American nuclear test in the Pacific Ocean.

Yoshida's political power and popularity decreased during this tumultuous year, and his premiership came to end in December 1954. He died on October 20, 1967, in Oiso, Kanagawa Prefecture, Japan.

*Iikura Akira*

**See also:** Korean War; Occupation of Japan; San Francisco Peace Treaty; Self-Defense Forces (*Jieitai*), from the Bomb to Iraq.

**Further Reading**

Dower, John W. *Empire and Aftermath: Yoshida Shigeru and the Japanese Experience, 1878–1954*. Cambridge, MA: Harvard University Press, 1979.

Finn, Richard B. *Winners in Peace: MacArthur, Yoshida, and Postwar Japan*. Berkeley: University of California Press, 1992.

Schaller, Michael. *Altered States: The United States and Japan since the Occupation*. Oxford, UK: Oxford University Press, 1997.

# Yoshida Shōin (1831–1859)

Yoshida Shōin was born in Chōshū, in 1831, the son of a low-ranking samurai. At an early age, he was adopted by his uncle Yoshida Taisuke, an influential teacher of the Yamaga school of military science. The highly intelligent Shōin matured into an adept student of warfare and its instruction. He was precocious enough at the age of 9 to lecture on military science before the lord of his domain. By the time he was 17, he was regarded as a master of the Yamaga school teachings. By 1848, he was employed as an instructor and a leading authority on military strategy, ethics, and Chinese classics.

In 1850, Shōin was allowed to tour western Kyushu, and the following year, he accompanied the *daimyō* to Edo (present-day Tokyo). Shōin became influenced by new avenues of thought, especially the school of Sakuma Shozan, who advocated Western learning and military science. In 1851, he slipped away and made an unauthorized visit to schools in northeastern Honshu for additional enlightenment. After returning, Shōin was arrested for traveling without permission, stripped of his samurai status, and imprisoned. Apparently, his local lord had second thoughts about restricting this talented, head-strong subject, and permission to travel freely was eventually granted.

After a decade of traveling, learning, and lecturing, Shōin was back in Edo when Commodore Matthew Perry's squadron made its appearance at Shimoda in 1853. Shōin was acutely aware that Western military technology was vastly superior to the antiquated samurai methods of the Middle Ages, and he wished to learn more. He hastened to Nagasaki after hearing that a Russian ship had landed there, but arrived after it had departed. He then returned to Edo. When Perry returned in 1854, Shōin brazenly stowed aboard his flagship, intending to visit America and learn the secrets of modern technology. However, he was caught and promptly arrested. For violating the shōgunate's strict injunctions against foreign contact, Shōin was placed in confinement.

Shōin was released from prison after a year in jail but remained under house arrest. He then spent the next 10 years devoting himself to writing and teaching. Shōin opened a small school of military thought, the Shokka Sonjuku, which became closely associated with the *sonno-jōi*, a movement demanding an end to the Tokugawa shōgunate, imperial restoration, and expulsion of all foreigners from Japan. First, however, he felt that young men should be sent abroad to Europe and America to learn Western technology and enhance national defense. Shōin's teachings made indelible impressions on his many students, two of whom, Takasugi Shinsaku and Yamagata Aritomo, played major roles in overthrowing the Tokugawa government in 1868.

Together with several of his students, Shōin planned the assassination of Manabe Akikatsu, a high-ranking Tokugawa official. When word of the plot leaked out to local Chōshū officials, they promptly arrested Shōin and several of his followers out of fear of being implicated themselves. He was then taken to Edo, tried for treason, and found guilty. The severe penalty of death was levied at the insistence of *bakufu* minister Ii Naosuke, who wished to set an example for any other contemplated acts of rebellion. Thus Shōin was executed in 1859 at the age of 29. His martyrdom served as a rallying point for anti-Tokugawa forces, including many of Shōin's former students. In 1868, they succeeded in orchestrating the Meiji Restoration.

*John C. Fredriksen*

**See also:** Boshin Civil War; Ii Naosuke; Perry, Matthew; *Sonno-jōi;* Yamagata Aritomo.

### Further Reading

Huber, Thomas M. *The Revolutionary Origins of Modern Japan.* Stanford, CA: Stanford University Press, 1981.

Van Straelen, H. J. J. M. *Yoshida Shōin, Forerunner of the Meiji Restoration.* Leiden: Brill, 1952.

**Yoshino Court.** *See* Southern Court.

# Young Officer Movement

The Young Officer Movement originated among army cadets at the Military Academy in Tokyo during the mid-1920s. Senior officers who were part of what became known as the *kōdōha* (Imperial Way Faction) nurtured the movement's formation. One such officer was General Mazaki Jinzaburō, who took charge of the curriculum at the academy in 1923, and was the academy's head from 1925 to1927. Mazaki appealed to young men because when other military leaders were focusing on the mechanization and rationalization of the army, he stressed patriotic Japanese spirit. Another *kōdōha* officer, General Araki Sadao, served as Inspector General of Military Education between 1929 and 1931. He then became War Minister between 1931 and 1934. Araki is the source of the term *kōdōha* because he often used the Japanese prefix "*kō*" (imperial), referring to the Japanese army as "*kōgun*" (imperial army), Japan as "*kōkoku*" (imperial country), and his way of doing everything as "*kōdō*" (the imperial way). He also discoursed on Japan's divine mission, referring to Japan's unique capacity to overcome the evils of Western imperialism and capitalism while resisting the internationalism of communism. Symbolizing the value of Japan's singularity, Araki changed army regulations and allowed officers to carry Japanese-style swords—forged at the nationalist Yasukuni Shrine—replacing the European-style swords that became regulation equipment during the Meiji period.

Ideologically, several sources nurtured the Young Officers. When Mazaki ran the Military Academy, he encouraged cadets to attend lectures at the Institute for Social Research, which Ōkawa Shūmei and others founded in 1923. There they were lectured on Japan's uniqueness and soteriological mission. The cadet Nishida Mitsugu became enamored with Ōkawa's thinking, and soon he and a group of his compatriots were attending meetings of the Yūzonsha (Survivors Society), which Ōkawa founded in 1919 with Kita Ikki. Kita Ikki was a *tairiku rōnin* (continental adventurer) who, working with the Kokuryūkai (Black Dragon or Amur River Society), helped facilitate the Chinese Revolution of 1911. In 1919, Kita wrote *Nihon kaizō hōan takō* ("Outline Plan for the Reorganization of Japan"), a reformist pamphlet arguing that Japan be organized along socialist lines, meaning limiting private and corporate accumulation of capital. Kita propounded a military revolution, if necessary, that would make a "people's emperor" of Japan's monarch. Characterizing Japan as the world's proletariat, Britain as the world's primary capitalist, and Russia as the planet's biggest landlord, Kita believed that revolutionary Japan's reformation would lead to liberation of the world. Soon after its publication, the state banned Kita's work. Censored versions were published, but complete handwritten versions circulated among Young Officers, becoming their "bible."

Modern incarnations of Nichiren Buddhism—also known as Nichirenism—constituted another ideological foundation of the Young Officer Movement. Kita Ikki converted to such thinking around 1916, and he exposed the Young Officers to it. Inoue Nisshō, a lay Buddhist leader of the Ketsumeidan (Blood Pledge Corps), was also a Nichirenist who had connections with Nichirenist leader Tanaka Chigaku. Nisshō especially influenced Young Officers of the navy. While training at the Naval Air School in Tsuchiura, Ibaragi Prefecture, these officers visited Inoue's nearby unconventional temple, which also served as a school for the civilian terrorists who joined his group. In the modern period, some Japanese appropriated the 13th-century monk Nichiren's teaching that the *Lotus Sutra* ordained that the Japanese Buddhism he espoused would travel westward to reinvigorate the Buddhism of continental Asia during the degenerate age of *mappō* (the end of the Buddhist dharma). Nichirenist thought reinterpreted this to mean that the *Lotus Sutra* taught that the modern Japanese political body (*kokutai*), as an expression of the compassionate teachings of Buddhism, had to expand its influence across Asia, saving the continent from various evils.

Nichirenist and reformist thought of a wide variety combined in the thinking of the Young Officers, who deduced a need to reorganize Japan by removing what separated the emperor from his people, meaning eradicating the privileged classes constituted by industrialists and politicians. Their notion of a Japanese mission also resonated with the Pan-Asianism embraced many Japanese before 1945. According to Japanese Pan-Asianism, Japan needed to unify Asia and lead a fight against the West, with which the Young Officers associated all of modernity's shortcomings. As they understood it, however, the West's contamination of Japan necessitated a national purge before Japan could save the world. The long decade after World War I filled the Young Officers with a particular sense of urgency. Anglo-Saxon powers denied passage of the racial equality clause that the Japanese delegation to Versailles in 1919 wished to insert in the League of Nations charter, seeming to make it clear that those powers would never accept the Japanese as equals. The Japanese public disparaged the army and the government cut military expenditures. Military men deemed treaties signed in Washington in 1922 and

London in 1930, which limited the size of the Japanese navy, humiliating. The Great Depression particularly affected Japan's rural population, from which the majority of military conscripts originated. In reaction to such developments, Young Officers involved themselves in several violent incidents during the 1930s.

In October 1930, Lieutenant Colonel Hashimoto Kingoro formed the Sakurakai (Cherry Blossom Society). Members held ranks no higher than lieutenant colonel. Following Kita's blueprint, the group advocated the violence of radical reform, yet it also gained tacit support from senior army officers, including War Minister and General Ugaki Kazushige, who called them a "study group." The Sakurakai planned a coup later known as the March 1931 Incident. The conspiracy involved mass demonstrations over labor legislation, with rioters then storming the Diet building. While supposedly protecting the Diet, the army planned to surround the building and demand the resignation of the cabinet. Ōkawa and other civilians attempted to sow disorder outside the Diet, but failed. Ugaki then withdrew his support. Next came the October Incident of 1931, which was also abortive. The Sakurakai planned a coup that would involve aerial bombardment of the cabinet while in session, and assassination of other members of the privileged classes whom they thought came between the emperor and his people. Civilians Nisshō, Ōkawa, and Nishida (a civilian by then) were also involved. The putschists wanted to make Araki Prime Minister, but when War Minister Minami Jirō and Araki learned of the conspiracy, they squelched it, managing to dissolve the Sakurakai. They prosecuted no one, however, allowing conspirators to proceed with their careers with a figurative slap on the wrist.

New Prime Minister Inukai Tsuyoshi made Araki War Minister in 1931, satisfying the army Young Officers, but junior naval officers proceeded with attempts at reform through violence. Fujii Hitoshi was one such officer. He worked with Nisshō, planning attacks on politicians. After Fujii was killed in action in Shanghai in 1932, a plot involving naval officers (including their new leader Koga Kiyoshi), army cadets, Inoue, and agrarian reform activist Tachibana Kōsaburō occurred and became known as the May 15 Incident. On that day, naval officers and army cadets went to the residence of Inukai, shooting and killing him. Another group of naval officers threw bombs at the home of Lord Keeper of the Privy Seal Count Makino Nobuaki, causing no harm. Tachibana and other civilians attempted to disable Tokyo's power generators with explosives, but this effort also failed. Tachibana associates also shot and wounded Nishida in retaliation for his failure to support army involvement in the day's events. Involvement of the civilians associated with Ōkawa led to his trial and sentencing to five years' imprisonment, of which he served only two years. Nisshō was likewise tried and imprisoned for the May 15 Incident as well as for his role in the Ketsumeidan Incident earlier in the year, during which civilian terrorists killed former Finance Minster Inoue Junnosuke and Mitsui Enterprises director Dan Takuma. Nisshō received a life sentence, but was released in 1940.

The February 1936 Incident was the end of the Young Officer Movement. The members of this movement led their troops in a mutinous takeover of central Tokyo, killing an Inspector General of Military Education, an Imperial Grand Chamberlain, the Finance Minister, and the Lord Keeper of the Privy Seal. They expected the emperor to embrace their attempts to remove the corrupt and greedy individuals surrounding him, but the emperor rejected their efforts, ordering them to return to their barracks. Afterward, the military tried and executed the remnants of the Young Officer Movement, along with Kita and Nishida.

We can trace the chain of events that led to the 1936 mutiny to the Young Officers' affection for Mazaki. In 1933, opponents of the *Kōdōha* who were known as the *tōseiha* (control faction) began their own takeover of the military. By 1935, they had removed Mazaki from the influential position of Inspector General of Military Education. In retaliation, Lieutenant Colonel Aizawa calmly called upon the *tōseiha*'s Major General Nagata Tetsuzan, head of the Military Affairs Bureau, and killed him with a sword. In the context of a public trial in which Aizawa was gaining public sympathy, army leaders decided to transfer the First Division of Tokyo, home of the majority of the Young Officers, to Manchuria. This pushed the Young Officers into their last desperate attempt to facilitate the radical reform they envisioned.

*Gerald Iguchi*

**See also**: Araki Sadao; February 26 Incident; Hashimoto Kingoro; Kita Ikki; *Kokutai* and Ultra-nationalism; Nichiren; Pan-Asianism; Shōwa Restoration; Tanaka Chigaku.

## Further Reading

Large, Stephen S. "Nationalist Extremism in Early Shōwa Japan: Inoue Nissho and the 'Blood-Pledge Corps Incident', 1932." *Modern Asian Studies* vol. 35 no. 3 (July 2001): 533–564.

Shillony, Ben-Ami. *Revolt in Japan: The Young Officers and the February 26, 1936 Incident*. Princeton, NJ: Princeton University Press, 1973.

Storry, Richard. *The Double Patriots: A Study of Japanese Nationalism.* Westport, CT: Greenwood Press, 1973.

Victoria, Brian Daizen. "The Ethical Implications of Zen-Related Terrorism in 1930s Japan." Available at: www.acmuller.nvet-zen-sem-2004-victoria.html.html.

Wilson, George. *Radical Nationalist in Japan: Kita Ikki and 1883–1947.* Cambridge, MA: Harvard University Press, 1969.

# Z

## Zaibatsu

Originally the term *Zaibatsu* (literally "financial clique") was used to indicate family-owned businesses like Mitsui, Mitsubishi, Sumitomo, and Yasuda that used business acumen to build large financial conglomerates tied to national contracts. Those companies had existed in the Tokugawa period and had been chosen for lucrative programs in the Meiji Reform period. In many cases, *Zaibatsu* leaders were given favorable terms based on friendship and marriage relationships. For instance, Nakamigawa Hikojiro, vice-president of a Mitsui-owned bank, was a nephew of Fukuzawa Yukichi and a protégé of Inoue Kaoru. The head of the Furukawa *Zaibatsu* had adopted Mutsu Munemitsu's eldest son. Obviously, contracts to supply the government's burgeoning army, naval, communication, and construction enterprises had been very lucrative.

In the so-called Matsukata Deflation of 1881, Japan's pilot industries (e.g., naval construction, silk-reeling, chemicals, metallurgy) had been sold off to *Zaibatsu* friends in an attempt to balance the national budget. Of course, those companies had profited enormously from those transactions. After the Russo-Japanese War, a new, "second tier" of *Zaibatsu* emerged, including Okura, Furukawa, and Nakajima.

The meaning of the term *Zaibatsu* began to change somewhat when those businesses began to wield enormous political power by virtue of their close ties to the political parties in the early 1920s. The Rikken Seiyūkai political party was tied by marriage and patronage to the Mitsui group, which also had very strong connections with the army. Similarly, the Rikken Minseito was connected to the Mitsubishi group and the navy.

A major political scandal erupted in 1914 when it was revealed that naval ministry leaders had been taking bribes from the German industrial giant Siemens and the British naval construction company Vickers in exchange for major contracts. The public outrage caused the fall of the Yamamoto Gonnohyōe cabinet.

Naturally, the lesser political parties (particularly the leftist ones) complained bitterly about "sweetheart deals," "no-bid contracts," and union-busting practices employed by the major *Zaibatsu*. Campaign contributions sealed the closed system for the *Zaibatsu* and their major political parties. With the advent of the worldwide economic depression in the early 1920s, the conservative parties began to complain as well. The more radical elements within the military, particularly the Imperial Way Faction in the army, railed at the "unholy alliance" of corrupt politicians, *Zaibatsu* leaders, and the top elements within the bureaucracy.

When Manchukuo was created as a puppet state by the Imperial Army, the major *Zaibatsu* were cut out of the financial picture as contracts were granted to a new group (*shinko zaibatsu*) of companies that included Nissan. Of course, after the war with China erupted in 1937 and commenced with the Allies after 1942, all of the *Zaibatsu* were needed to feed the enormous military machine needed for World War II.

The interior of the Mitsubishi plant, Kobe, Japan, circa 1925. Mitsubishi was founded as a shipping company in 1870, but by the early 20th century it had become a major industrial conglomerate (*Zaibatsu*). (Library of Congress)

During the first phase of the American occupation (1945–1949), the *Zaibatsu* were targeted for complete dissolution. The reasoning was that the "military-industrial complex" (President Dwight Eisenhower's phrase) precluded open, honest economic competition and stifled political democracy. The largest combines were broken up into their constituencies. Many of the smaller companies could not compete, and bankruptcy became all too common in the late 1940s. With the fall of China to the Communists in 1949 and the beginning of the Korean War in 1950, the second phase (the "reverse course") of the Allied occupation demanded a "reintegration" of Japan's industry to help fight the Communists.

Japan's response was the *keiretsu* system. The word *keiretsu* means "series" or "subsidiary," and refers to a more horizontal integration. Undert this system, vertical control by family ownership, holding companies, and interlocking directorships were no longer allowed. Of course, ownership of key blocks of controlling shares remains common, as does the practice of subsidiaries absorbing "excess" employees shed by their "parent" company in economic downturns.

*Louis G. Perez*

**See also:** Inoue Kaoru; Korean War; Manchukuo; Matsukata Masayoshi; Mutsu Munemitsu; Russo-Japanese War; Siemens-Vickers Scandal; Yamamoto Gonnohyōe.

## Further Reading

Hirschmeier, Johannes, and Yui Tsunehiko. *The Development of Japanese Business, 1600–1973*. London: George Allen & Unwin, 1975.

Marshall, Byron K. *Capitalism and Nationalism in Prewar Japan: The Ideology of the Business Elite, 1868–1941*. Stanford: Stanford University Press, 1967.

## Zen Buddhism and Militarism

The links between militarism and Zen Buddhism in modern times have been well documented. The Zen Buddhist organizations of both the Sôtô and the Rinzai sects lent moral and practical support to the Japanese military and its policies from the late 19th century to the end of World War II in 1945. After the war, it took decades before either sect would attempt to atone for its role in the Japanese war efforts. Despite popular images suggesting that Zen and the martial arts were closely linked historically, the origins of this association are themselves modern and based on the need of all Buddhists to prove their patriotism following the rise of the new Meiji government in 1868. Since then, the idea that Zen Buddhism and samurai warrior ideals were historically intertwined has risen to the level of common sense—yet it is a classic example of the modern invention of tradition.

This is not to say there was no historical link between Zen Buddhism and the warrior class, but most samurai in medieval Japan were adherents of Pure Land Buddhism rather than of Zen Buddhism. The links that did exist were primarily institutional, although a small number of samurai were themselves Zen practitioners, just as some other samurai were practitioners of the Tendai, Shingon, Nichiren and other sects. In medieval Japan, the Kamakura *bakufu* and its successor, the

Muromachi *bakufu*, both patronized Rinzai schools of Zen Buddhism. Under both regimes, the Rinzai monasteries were organized into a Five Mountain (*Gozan*) system. Based on this system, the monasteries served the *bakufu* in various roles, including conducting rites and rituals and composing letters and documents in classical Chinese (the equivalent of medieval European Latin) for use in foreign relations. One regent to the Kamakura *bakufu*, Hôjô Tokiyori (1227–1263), was indeed a genuine practitioner who received transmission from a Chinese monk. For most samurai leaders, however, Zen Buddhism played an important role culturally, administratively, and in foreign affairs; few were themselves Zen practitioners. During the Edo period, Zen Buddhist temples flourished as an administrative structure useful to the government on the village level, but samurai were no more attracted to Zen practice than before.

With the fall of the Edo *bakufu* in 1868, a powerfully nationalistic ideology came to the fore, with adherents who pushed for the rejection of foreign influences, including Buddhism. Under the slogan of *haibutsu kishaku* ("abolish Buddhism and destroy Shakyamuni"), tens of thousands of Buddhist temples were destroyed between 1868 and 1874, monks were forced to enter lay life, the financial foundations of temples were undercut, and some even believed that organized Buddhism in Japan might collapse completely. In response to this crisis, Buddhist leaders strove to show that they were as nationalistic and patriotic as any other Japanese subjects.

From this time forward, ideologically Japanese Buddhist leaders, including Zen leaders, emphasized the notion of *on* or "debt of gratitude" to the *tennō* (sovereign) and to the state. Traditionally, Buddhists applied this concept broadly to parents, ruler, all sentient beings, and the Three Treasures of the Buddha, Dharma, and Sangha. From the late 19th century, however, Buddhist leaders asserted that the debt of gratitude to the *tennō* was equal to the debt owed to the historical Buddha.

The link between Japanese militarism and Zen Buddhism began a new, active stage from the time of the Russo-Japanese War in 1904–1905. Shaku Sôen, a highly respected Zen priest, served on the front as a military chaplain in this war. After the war ended, increasingly large numbers of Japanese Army officers started to sit *zazen*, the Zen meditation previously practiced mostly by monks and a small number of lay students. Growing numbers of influential Zen teachers openly supported Japan's imperialistic ventures abroad and the rise of martial values at home. Priests and lay writers alike began to emphasize a link between bushidō ("The Way of the Warrior") and the stoic virtues of Zen practice. Most works on this subject tended to cast this link in an ahistorical context, overlooking the fact that *bushidō* itself was an 18th-century concept, created during the great peace of the Edo period during which the samurai spent more time theorizing about the martial arts and less time practicing them than during previous centuries.

This is not to say that all Zen priests accepted this new ideology. There were notable exceptions, such as Uchiyama Gudô (1874–1911), a Sôtô priest who became an anarcho-socialist and was executed because of suspected links with a plot to assassinate the Japanese sovereign. Nevertheless, Zen priests who opposed Japanese militarist expansion and later the war efforts were a very small minority.

During the 1930s, the ideology of imperial-state Zen (*kôkoku Zen*) emerged. It envisioned Zen practice as a way of realizing the "fundamental spirit of the unity of sovereign and subjects." The Zen project of letting go of the ego was transformed into a means of serving the sovereign on the battlefield. The degree to which Japanese militarism and Zen became intertwined was perhaps best expressed by the teacher Harada Daiun (1870–1961), when he wrote in 1939:

> [If ordered to] march: tramp, tramp, or shoot: bang, bang. This is the manifestation of the highest Wisdom [of Enlightenment]. The unity of Zen and war of which I speak extends to the farthest reaches of the holy war.

After 1945, the Zen sects quickly developed the same amnesia with regard to decades of enthusiasm for Japanese militarism that most members of the society experienced. It was not until the American Sôtô Zen priest Brian Daizen Victoria started a concerted examination of the role of Zen organizations played in support of Japanese militarism and the publication of his *Zen at War* that Japanese Zen leaders publicly recognized and atoned for their predecessors' roles in supporting militarism and war. Ironically, the mythos of a link between Zen and the martial arts also became one of the attractions that drew many Europeans and Americans to Zen from the 1950s, and not a few became dedicated and sincere Zen practitioners.

*William Johnston*

**See also**: Kamakura *Bakufu*; Muromachi *Bakufu*; Russo-Japanese War.

### Further Reading

Ketelaar, James. *Of Heretics and Martyrs in Meiji Japan: Buddhism and Its Persecution*. Princeton: Princeton University Press, 1990.

Victoria, Brian Daizen. *Zen at War*, 2nd ed. Lanham, MD: Rowman and Littlefield, 2006.

Victoria, Brian Daizen. *Zen War Stories*. London: Routledge Curzon, 2003.

## Zen Buddhism in Japanese Sports

The samurai "warrior code of ethics," called *bushidō*, is supported by ideas borrowed from Zen Buddhism, and both Zen and *bushidō* occupy important positions in Japanese sports. The samurai sought to become role models and "set a moral example and to do so they borrowed Zen ideas of self-control, such as *fudōchi* ("immovable wisdom"), *mushin* ("no mind"), and *muga* ("no self") and strived to reach "enlightenment" (satori) through Zen practice. This transfer of idea (from Zen to *bushidō*) gave *bushidō* greater spiritual weight and influence over Japanese soldiers and, later, athletes. Throughout the 20th century, *bushidō* became both an ethic of self-restraint and the masculine ideal. Because of an intimate link seen between mind and body in both Zen meditation (and Zen "ascetic practice") and in sports, Zen Buddhism came to carry considerable influence in modern Japanese sports.

Buddhism came to Japan from China in 552. By then it was already more than 1,000 years old. The teachings of Gautama, the historic Buddha, noted that the world was a place of suffering caused by man's desires and acquisitiveness, and suggested that a man could be released from this suffering if he could achieve enlightenment. Doing so required following an "eightfold path" of right views, right intentions, right speech, right livelihood, right effort, right mindfulness, and right concentration. Following this path could be difficult if one was plagued by bad karma from a previous life.

Although many sects exist in Japanese Buddhism, Zen has had the most influence on the samurai and on Japanese sports because of the attention paid to mental training and preparation. The "mindlessness" advised by Zen meditation is considered an essential means toward achieving enlightenment—and for some athletes, the calm needed to perform under pressure. Japanese divers, for example, cite samurai Miyamoto Musashi's concept of *munenmusō* ("free from all ideas and thoughts") as the state of "consciousness" that they take down to the depths of the ocean.

The connection between Zen and sports is perhaps most evident in Japanese baseball. The samurai's sword is often referred to as his "soul and many Japanese talk about their baseball bats as if they were sacred in the same way. Baseball great Oh Sadaharu, for example, recommends the virtues of a Zen approach to hitting. The Zen monk Takuan (1573–1645), who was said to have influenced many samurai, including Munenori (1571–1646), once wrote a book entitled *Fudōchi Shinmyōroku* ("Divine Record of Immovable Wisdom"), a remarkably similar title to that of superstar baseball player Hideki Matsui's 2007 autobiography, *Fudōshin* ("An Immovable Mind"). Both books emphasize the importance of an unwavering mental attitude and a sense of calm, poise, and stability. This suggests that the bridge between Takuan and Matsui, Zen and baseball, and the four centuries that stand between them, is *bushidō*.

The emphasis on "ascetic practice" (*shūgyō*), a Zen practice, is the spiritual justification lurking behind much of Japanese sports training. The idea of *shūgyō* originated among Zen Buddhist monks, and has come to be one of the primary means through which many Japanese coaches build the character of their charges. *Shūgyō* has many meanings: (1) following the Buddhist commandments and finding enlightenment through specific religious actions, practicing Buddhist teachings, and concentrating one's efforts on the Buddhist path; (2) taking religious action that aims to make union with the existence of gods and to purify the spirit through repression of the bodily desires; or (3) the pilgrimage that scholars and artists take to perfect their trade. Oki, a kendo coach, writes:

> When I think of *shūgyō*, I think of the image of a master swordsman, climbing a mountain, sipping a valley river's water, receiving instruction from a teacher, and swinging a wooden sword against an imaginary opponent. (Oki 2001:146)

In the martial arts, such imaginary training was for the purpose of learning *kata*—"form." Because there were no "practice games," apprentices had to train themselves by *imagining* battle. These ideas have also found relevance in modern Japanese sports. The "monastic tradition" (*shūdō*) has been integral in helping invent tradition in modern Japanese sports. One example of *shūgyō* in Japanese sports is the ritual of shaving one's head to symbolize membership on a team. This practice is rather common in high school baseball and boys' basketball. The ritual derives its legitimacy from Buddhism. Buddhist monks (*obōsan*) shave their heads in an undertaking called *teihatsu* to remind themselves of their many duties. Thus *shūgyō* is related to the body, and as with the shaving of one's head, the body is altered to indicate that someone is undertaking special, serious training toward a specific goal (e.g., victory in a battle, sports match, or enlightenment.

*Aaron L. Miller*

**See also:** *Bushidō*; *Bushidō* in Japanese Sports; Nitobe Inazō; Zen Buddhism and Militarism.

## Further Reading

Oki, Masahiro. *Katsu tame no kantokujutsu*: *Dakara taibatsu wa hitsuyō da* [Coaching Techniques for Winning: That Is Why Corporal Punishment is Necessary]. Tokyo: Bungeisha, 2001.

Sogawa, Tsuneo. "What Should Be Taught through Budō?," in *Budo Perspectives*, edited by A. Bennett. Auckland, New Zealand: Kendo World Publications, 2005:185–202.

Sugimoto, Atsuo. *Supotsu bunka no henyō* [Transformations in Sports Culture]. Kyoto: Sekaishisōsha, 1995.

Suzuki, Daisetz Teitaro. *The Training of the Zen Buddhist Monks*. New York: University Press, 1965.

## Zengakuren

Zengakuren was an expansive student governing body representing numerous student groups from around Japan. At present, Zengakuren might best be defined as an amorphous political identity currently used as a foundational myth for many dissident groups. Its full title is *Zen Nihon Gakusei Jichi-kai Sorengo*, or All-Japan Federation of Student Self-Government Associations. While the Zengakuren still exists, its primary period of political activity and social influence was from the postwar period to the 1970s.

During the Allied occupation era, the Supreme Commander for Allied Powers (SCAP) sponsored the formation of student groups to encourage democracy in schools around Japan. In September 1948, incensed over administrative disagreements, rising tuition, and the privatization of education, more than 100 of these groups united to form the Zengakuren. Zengakuren's basic tenets focused on the promotion of the ideals of freedom, democracy, and antifascism. However, alarmed by the socialist leanings of many student members and Zengakuren's close ties to the Japanese Communist Party (JCP), SCAP frequently limited or outright banned the early political protests of these groups.

In its early stages, Zengakuren had strong ties to the JCP. However, the group was so all-encompassing that its ideologies, motives, and political movements were not always uniform. Even from the early 1950s, Zengakuren began to fracture into smaller groups. By the late 1950s, part of the expansive organization's diverse membership was strongly opposed to the JCP. During this period, the Zengakuren fragmented into several splinter groups.

In 1958, one of the most famous of these groups—the Bund group—was formed by people who had either quit or been expelled from the JCP for their radical behavior. Bund called itself the Communist League, but it was not officially affiliated with the JCP. The Bund group itself later fractured into numerous factions, including the radical Red Army Faction.

The 1960s were Zengakuren's most active and influential years. Japan's postwar move toward economic prosperity also brought with it issues related to the U.S.-Japan alliance, bureaucracy, and individual identity. Most of the struggles of this period focused on opposing AMPO, Okinawa military bases, and the construction of Narita Airport.

All throughout 1960, students attempted to circumvent the ratification of the US-Japan Security Treaty (AMPO) by surrounding the Diet and even attacking the U.S. Press Secretary's car. Frequently, attendance at their protests numbered in the hundreds of thousands and inspired great popular support in the wider society. However, despite these efforts, the AMPO treaty was passed at night by the Diet without any opposition parties present. Prime Minister Kishi later signed the AMPO treaty into law on January 19, 1960, to the disappointment and frustration of the student protestors.

The events of 1960 merely foreshadowed the tenor of the following decade. The failure of the 1960 anti-AMPO movement led to a great sense of disillusionment in the democratic process. After this failed movement, the student groups and the JCP split into factions once again. Despite great popular dissatisfaction, popular movements had proved ineffective.

Mid-1960s protests focused on opposing Narita Airport, the Japan-Korea Treaty (normalization of Japanese and South Korean relations), and the Vietnam War. In 1967, students protested Prime Minister Satō's visit to the Vietnam War region by attempting to block his plane's departure at Haneda airport.

Another struggle began as a specific set of grievances arose among the medical faculty on the Tokyo University campus in January 1968, with the protest later spreading nationwide. At Tokyo University, students formed a struggle committee, occupied the main administration building, and barricaded several departments. In November of that year, students also held Professor Hayashi Kentarō hostage for eight days. The protests soon spread throughout schools in Japan and continued unabated throughout 1969.

In 1970, the students again reunited to combat AMPO, the inclusion of bases at Okinawa in the return of Okinawa to Japan, and the creation of Narita airport. In that same year, Mishima Yukio, one of the ideological heroes of the radical student movement, committed suicide to protest postwar Japan's lack of traditional values. The loss of Mishima, the failure of these movements, and Zengakuren's perceived association with violence resulted in a decline in public support and a rising sense of disenchantment with protests and democratic movements. The Zengakuren eventually faded from public consciousness. As a group, Zengakuren members are still active, but their power has declined drastically since the final Narita airport movement in the 1970s. At present, there are five distinct groups that claim to be inheritors of the 1950's–1960's Zengakuren legacy.

*Amanda Weiss*

**See also:** AMPO: United States–Japan Security Treaty; Anti-Narita Airport Movement; Red Army (Sekigun).

## Further Reading

Apter, David E., and Sawa, Nagayo. *Against the State: Politics and Social Protest in Japan*. Cambridge, MA: Harvard University Press, 1984.

Dowsey, Stuart. *Zengakuren: Japan's Revolutionary Students*. Berkeley, CA: Ishi Press, 1970.

Kersten, Rikki. "The Intellectual Culture of Postwar Japan and the 1968–1969 University of Tokyo Struggles: Repositioning the Self in Postwar Thought." *Social Science Japan Journal* 12, no. 2 (2009): 227–245.

## Zhang Zuolin (1873–1928)

Zhang Zuolin was born in 1873 in Liaoning Province. The fourth child of a peasant family, he had no formal education and limited prospects. His father died when Zhang was nine years old. His mother later remarried the village veterinarian.

Zhang turned to the military at the age of 20 and enlisted in the Yijun, a unit commanded by Song Qing. He fought against the Japanese in the Sino-Japanese War of 1894–1895. His troops fought on the side of the Japanese in the Russo-Japanese War and harassed Russian forces in Manchuria. After the war, his unit was officially organized into a regiment, and Zhang swiftly moved up the ranks of the armed forces in Manchuria.

During the Chinese Revolution of 1911, Zhang used his troops to guard Mukden (Shenyang) and put down a local revolt. In the ensuing years, he expanded his power to include all of Manchuria and parts of Inner Mongolia—that is, virtually all the provinces northeast of the Great Wall of China. From 1919 onward, he ruled Manchuria as a nearly autonomous state. For example, ignoring the nominal authorities in Beijing, Zhang signed a separate Mukden-Soviet treaty with the Soviets in 1924. He proved adept at playing various warlords, the Soviets, and the Japanese off one another. Zhang was even able to place one of his followers, Liang Shiyi, in the position of premier in Beijing for a brief time in 1921. A coalition of opposing warlords finally ousted Liang and forced Zhang to cede control of the north China plain to others.

In 1924, Zhang forged a new alliance with the warlord Feng Yuxiang and moved his forces south; he took control of the area around Beijing and moved even farther southward into the Yangtze River region. In 1926, he joined his erstwhile enemy Wu Peifu in an alliance and adopted a virulent anti-Soviet stance. Zhang covered his Beijing headquarters with the slogan "Absolutely destroy Communism" and launched an anticommunist purge in 1927. He sent his troops to raid the Soviet embassy in Beijing and captured many Chinese Communists who were hiding there. Among them was the cofounder of the Chinese Communist Party, Li Dazhao, whom Zhang executed along with 19 others.

Zhang had originally planned to move his forces south to counter the 1926 Northern Expedition of Jiang Jieshi and the Chinese Nationalist Party. Inexplicably, however, he changed his mind and waited for the Nationalists to move north from their newly acquired territory in the Yangtze River basin. The Nationalists began to move on Beijing in 1928. Despite being delayed by a ferocious clash with Japanese forces in Shandong, the ultimate triumph of the Nationalists appeared inevitable. Japanese officials offered Zhang cooperation and protection if he would retreat with his forces to Manchuria.

Zhang agreed to do so but was assassinated when a bomb planted by officers of the Japanese Kwantung Army destroyed his private railway car in June 1928. After a struggle for succession, Zhang's son, Zhang Xueliang (the "Young Marshal"), inherited control of the forces of his father. Several of Zhang's other sons served in the military of either the Nationalists or the Communists.

*Kirk Larsen*

**See also:** Jiang Jieshi (Ch'iang K'ai-shek); Kwantung Army Adventurism; Russo-Japanese War; Sino-Japanese War.

**Further Reading**

McCormack, Gavan. *Chang Tso-Lin in Northeast China, 1911–1928: China, Japan, and the Manchurian Idea*. Stanford, CA: Stanford University Press, 1977.

Spence, Jonathan D. *The Search for Modern China*. New York: Norton, 1990.

# Primary Documents

## Seventeen-Article Constitution, 604

*This document is reputed to have been written by Shōtoku Taishi, regent for the Empress Suiko in 604. Rather than a proper constitution, it was a Buddhist-inspired exhortation to the people of Japan.*

**I.** Harmony is to be valued, and an avoidance of wanton opposition to be honored. All men are influenced by class-feelings, and there are few who are intelligent. Hence there are some who disobey their lords and fathers, or who maintain feuds with the neighboring villages. But when those above are harmonious and those below are friendly, and there is concord in the discussion of business, right views of things spontaneously gain acceptance. Then what is there which cannot be accomplished!

**II.** Sincerely reverence the three treasures. The three treasures, Buddha, the Law and the Priesthood, are the final refuge of the four generated beings, and are the supreme objects of faith in all countries. What man in what age can fail to reverence this law? Few men are utterly bad. They may be taught to follow it. But if they do not betake them to the three treasures, how shall their crookedness be made straight?

**III.** When you receive the Imperial commands, fail not to obey them scrupulously. The lord is Heaven, the vassal is Earth. Heaven overspreads, and Earth bears up. When this is so, the four seasons follow their due course, and the powers of Nature obtain their efficacy. If the Earth attempted to overspread, Heaven would simply fall in ruin. Therefore when the lord speaks, the vassal listens; when the superior acts, the inferior complies. Consequently when you receive the Imperial commands, fail not to carry them out scrupulously. Let there be a want of care in this matter and ruin is the natural consequence.

**IV.** The Ministers and functionaries should make decorous behavior their leading principle, for the leading principle of the government of the people consists in decorous behavior. If the superiors do not behave with decorum, the inferiors are disorderly: if inferiors are wanting in proper behavior, there must necessarily be offences. Therefore it is that when lord and vassal behave with propriety, the distinctions of rank are not confused: when the people behave with propriety, the Government of the Commonwealth proceeds of itself.

**V.** Ceasing from gluttony and abandoning covetous desires, deal impartially with the suits which are submitted to you. Of complaints brought by the people there are a thousand in one day. If in one day there are so many, how many will there be in a series of years? If the man who is to decide suits at law makes gain his ordinary motive, and hears causes with a view to receiving bribes, then will the suits of the rich man be like a stone flung into water while the complaints of the poor will resemble water cast upon a stone. Under these circumstances the poor man will not know where to take their complaints. Here too there is a deficiency in the duty of the Minister.

**VI.** Chastise that which is evil and encourage that which is good. This was the excellent rule of antiquity. Conceal not, therefore, the good qualities of others, and fail not to correct that which is wrong when you see it. Flatterers and deceivers are a sharp weapon for the overthrow of the State, and a pointed sword for the destruction of the people. Sycophants are also fond, when they meet, of dilating to their superiors on the errors of their inferiors; to their inferiors, they censure the faults of their superiors. Men of this kind are all wanting in fidelity to their lord and in benevolence towards the people. From such an origin great civil disturbances arise.

**VII.** Let every man have his own charge and let not the spheres of duty be confused. When wise men are entrusted with office, the sound of praise arises. If unprincipled men hold office, disasters and tumults are multiplied. In this world, few are born with knowledge: wisdom is the product of earnest meditation. In all things, whether great or small, find the right man, and they will surely be well managed. On all occasions, be they urgent or the reverse, meet but with a wise man, and they will of themselves be amenable. In this way will the State be lasting and the Temples of the Earth and of Grain will be free from danger. Therefore, did the wise sovereigns of antiquity seek the man to fill the office, and not the office for the sake of the man.

**VIII.** Let the Ministers and functionaries attend the Court early in the morning and retire late. The business of the state does not admit of remissness and the whole day is hardly enough for its accomplishment. If, therefore, the attendance at Court is late, emergencies cannot be met. If officials retire soon, the work cannot be completed.

**IX.** Good faith is the foundation of right. In everything let there be good faith, for in it there surely consists the good and the bad, success and failure. If the lord and the vassal observe good faith one with another, what is there which cannot be accomplished? If the

lord and the vassal do not observe good faith towards one another, everything without exception ends in failure.

**X.** Let us cease from wrath and refrain from angry looks. Nor let us be resentful when others differ from us. For all men have hearts, and each heart has its own leanings. Their right is our wrong, and our right is their wrong. We are not unquestionably sages, nor are they unquestionably fools. Both of us are simply ordinary men. How can any one lay down a rule by which to distinguish right from wrong? For we are all, one with another, wise and foolish, like a ring which has no end. Therefore, although others give way to anger, let us on the contrary dread our own faults, and though we alone may be in the right, let us follow the multitude and act like them.

**XI.** Give clear appreciation to merit and demerit and deal out to each its sure reward or punishment. In these days, reward does not attend upon merit nor punishment upon crime. All you high functionaries who have charge of public affairs, let it be your task to make clear rewards and punishments.

**XII.** Let not the provincial authorities or the Kuni no Miyakko levy exactions on the people. In a country there are not two lords; the people cannot have two masters. The sovereign is the master of the people of the whole country. The officials to whom he gives charge are all his vassals. How can they, as well as the Government, presume to levy taxes on the people?

**XIII.** Let all persons entrusted with office attend equally to their functions. Owing to their illness or to their being sent on missions, their work may sometimes be neglected. But whenever they become able to attend to business, let them be as accommodating as if they had cognizance of it from before, and not hinder public affairs on the score of their not having had to do with them.

**XIV.** All you ministers and functionaries! Be not envious. For if we envy others, they in turn will envy us. The evils of envy know no limit. If others excel us in intelligence, it gives us no pleasure; if they surpass us in ability, we are envious. Therefore, it is not until after a lapse of five hundred years that we at last meet with a wise man, and even in a thousand years we hardly obtain one sage. But if we do not find wise men and sages, how shall the country be governed?

**XV.** To turn away from that which is private, and to set our faces towards that which is public—this is the path of a Minister. Now if a man is influenced by private motives, he will surely feel resentments, and if he is influenced by resentful feelings, he will surely fail to act harmoniously with others. If he fails to act harmoniously with others, he will surely sacrifice the public interests to his private feelings. When resentment arises, it interferes with order, and is subversive of law. Therefore, in the first clause it was said that superiors and inferiors should agree together. The purpose of that first clause is the same as this.

**XVI.** Let the people be employed (in forced labor) at seasonable times. This is an ancient and excellent rule. Let them be employed, therefore, in the winter months, when they are at leisure. But from Spring to Autumn, when they are engaged in agriculture or with the mulberry trees, the people should not be so employed. For if they do not attend to agriculture, what will they have to eat? If they do not attend to the mulberry trees, what will they do for clothing?

**XVII.** Decisions on important matters should not be made by one person alone. They should be discussed with many. But small matters are of less consequence. It is unnecessary to consult a number of people. It is only in the case of the discussion of weighty affairs, when there is a suspicion that they may miscarry, that one should arrange matters in concert with others, so as to arrive at the right conclusion.

*Source:* Brinkley, Frank, and Dairoku Kikuchi. *A History of the Japanese People from the Earliest Times to the End of the Meiji Era.* New York: Encyclopedia Britannica Company, 1915: 140–141.

## Charter Oath, 1868

The Charter Oath, also called the Five Article Oath, was written by a group of politically minded men—notably Yuri Kimimasa and Kido Takayoshi. It was read by courtier Sanjo Sanetomi at the enthronement of the Meiji Emperor on 7 April 1868.

By this oath, we set up as our aim the establishment of the national wealth on a broad basis and the framing of a constitution and laws.

Deliberative assemblies shall be widely established and all matters decided by open discussion.

All classes, high and low, shall be united in vigorously carrying out the administration of affairs of state.

The common people, no less than the civil and military officials, shall all be allowed to pursue their own calling so that there may be no discontent.

Evil customs of the past shall be broken off and everything based upon the just laws of Nature.

Knowledge shall be sought throughout the world so as to strengthen the foundation of imperial rule.

*Source:* Reprinted in McLaren, W. W. *Japanese Government Documents.* Bethesda, MD: University Publications of America, 1979.

## Imperial Rescript for Soldiers and Sailors, 1882

*The government of Japan issued the following code of conduct for military men under the seal of the Meiji Emperor on January 4, 1882. The first draft was written by Nishi Amane, then an Army Ministry bureaucrat. It was extensively edited by Inoue Kowashi, the author of the Meiji Constitution and Imperial Rescript on Education eight years later.*

*Every military man was obliged to memorize the entire rescript and repeat it verbatim when called upon to do so.*

... Soldiers and Sailors, We are your supreme Commander-in-Chief. Our relations with your will be most intimate when We rely upon you as Our limbs and you look up to Us as your head. Whether We are able to guard the Empire, and so prove Ourself worthy of Heaven's blessings and repay the benevolence of Our Ancestors, depends upon the faithful discharge of your duties as soldiers and sailors. If the majesty and power of Our Empire be impaired, do you share with Us the sorrow; if the glory of Our arms shine resplendent, We will share with you the honor. If you all do your duty, and being one with Us in spirit do your utmost for the protection of the state, Our people will long enjoy the blessings of peace, and the might and dignity of Our Empire will shine in the world. As We thus expect much of you, Soldiers and Sailors, We give you the following precepts:

1. The soldier and sailor should consider loyalty their essential duty. Who that is born in this land can be wanting in the spirit of grateful service to it? No soldier or sailor, especially, can be considered efficient unless this spirit be strong within him. A soldier or a sailor in whom this spirit is not strong, however skilled in art or proficient in science, is a mere puppet; and a body of soldiers or sailors wanting in loyalty, however well ordered and disciplined it may be, is in an emergency no better than a rabble. Remember that, as the protection of the state and the maintenance of its power depend upon the strength of its arms, the growth or decline of this strength must affect the nation's destiny for good or for evil; therefore neither be led astray by current opinions nor meddle in politics, but with single heart fulfill your essential duty of loyalty, and bear in mind that duty is weightier than a mountain, while death is lighter than a feather. Never by failing in moral principle fall into disgrace and bring dishonor upon your name.

[The second article concerns the respect due to superiors and considerations to be shown inferiors.]

3. The soldier and the sailor should esteem valor.... To be incited by mere impetuosity to violent action cannot be called true valor. The soldier and the sailor should have sound discrimination of right and wrong, cultivate self-possession, and form their plans with deliberation. Never to despise an inferior enemy or fear a superior, but to do one's duty as soldier or sailor—this is true valor. Those who thus appreciate true valor should in their daily intercourse set gentleness first and aim to win the love and esteem of others. If you affect valor and act with violence, the world will in the end detest you and look upon you as wild beasts. Of this you should take heed.

4. The soldier and the sailor should highly value faithfulness and righteousness.... Faithfulness implies the keeping of one's word, and righteousness the fulfillment of one's duty. If then you wish to be faithful and righteous in anything, you must carefully consider at the outset whether you can accomplish it or not. If you thoughtlessly agree to do something that is vague in its nature and bind yourself to unwise obligations, and then try to prove yourself faithful and righteous, your may find yourself in great straits from which there is no escape.... Ever since ancient times there have been repeated instances of great men and heroes who, overwhelmed by misfortune, have perished and left a tarnished name to posterity, simply because in their effort to be faithful in small matters they failed to discern right and wrong with reference to fundamental principles, or because, losing sight of the true path of public duty, they kept faith in private relations. You should, then, take serious warning by these examples.

5. The soldier and sailor should make simplicity their aim. If you do not make simplicity your aim, you will become effeminate and frivolous and acquire fondness for luxurious and extravagant ways; you will finally grow selfish and sordid and sink to the last degree of baseness, so that neither loyalty nor valor will avail to save you from the contempt of the world.

These five articles should not be disregarded even for a moment by soldiers and sailors. Now for putting them into practice, the all important thing is sincerity. These five articles are the soul of Our soldiers and sailors, and sincerity is the soul of these articles. If the heart be not sincere, words and deeds, however good, are all mere outward show and can avail nothing. If only the heart be sincere, anything can be accomplished. Moreover these five articles are the "Grand Way" of Heaven and earth and the universal law of humanity, easy to observe and to practice. If you, Soldiers and Sailors, in obedience to Our instruction, will observe and practice these principles and fulfil your duty of grateful service to the country, it will be a source of joy, not to Ourself alone, but to all the people of Japan.

*Source:* Kyokai, Nihon Gaiji. *The Japan Year Book*, Vol. 1. Foreign Affairs Association, 1933:225–227. Translation from *The Imperial Precepts to the Soldiers and Sailors: The "Boshin" Imperial Rescript*. Also cited in Tsunoda, et al. *Sources of Japanese Tradition II*. New York: Columbia University Press, 1958: 198–200.

## Imperial Rescript on Education, 1890

In an attempt to reinstitute Neo-Confucian principles into Japanese society, the Japanese government issued the following document over the seal of the Meiji Emperor on October 30, 1890. It was chiefly written by Inoue Kowashi, one of the principal architects of the Meiji Constitution. This is the official English translation issued the same day.

Know ye, Our subjects:

Our Imperial Ancestors have founded Our Empire on a basis broad and everlasting and have deeply and firmly implanted virtue; Our subjects ever united in loyalty and filial piety have from generation to generation illustrated the beauty thereof. This is the glory of the fundamental character of Our Empire, and herein also lies the source of Our education.

Ye, Our subjects, be filial to your parents, affectionate to your brothers and sisters; as husbands and wives be harmonious, as friends true; bear yourselves in modesty and moderation; extend your benevolence to all; pursue learning and cultivate arts, and thereby develop intellectual faculties and perfect moral powers; furthermore advance public good and promote common interests; always respect the Constitution and observe the laws; should emergency arise, offer yourselves courageously to the State; and thus guard and maintain the prosperity of Our Imperial Throne coeval with heaven and earth.

So shall ye not only be Our good and faithful subjects, but render illustrious the best traditions of your forefathers. The Way here set forth is indeed the teaching bequeathed by Our Imperial Ancestors, to be observed alike by Their Descendants and the subjects, infallible for all ages and true in all places. It is Our wish to lay it to heart in all reverence, in common with you, Our subjects, that we may thus attain to the same virtue.

The 30th day of the 10th month of the 23rd year of Meiji (October 30, 1890)

*Source:* Monroe, Paul. *A Cyclopedia of Education*, Vol. 3. New York: Macmillan, 1918: 521.

## Korean-Japanese Treaty (1894)

*The Monroe Doctrine of 1823, while asserting U.S. hegemony over the Americas, had conversely stated the country's noninterference in the Far East. Therefore, the United States played no role in this treaty signed by representatives from Korea and Japan on July 25, 1894. The treaty called for Korea to assist Japanese forces in expelling Chinese forces from the country. The stated goal was an independent Korea. The Japanese had been gaining power in Asia for years and were just preparing to launch a concerted effort to increase their territorial holdings and influence within the region, particularly as the previous dominant power, China, seemed to be crumbling. Long considered an extension of China, Korea fell under increasing Japanese control during this period. Much had changed by 1904, when Japan went to war against Russia, which was challenging its influence in Korea. The Spanish-American War, and the United States' acquisition of the Philippines, had given Americans the opportunity to wield influence over Asian affairs. The United States brokered the Japanese-Russian peace treaty and made a side deal with Japan pledging noninterference with Korea in return for Japan's noninterference in the Philippines. Japan formally annexed Korea in 1910.*

The Korean Government hereby commissions the envoy extraordinary and minister plenipotentiary of Japan, who resides at Seoul, Korea, to expel the Chinese forces from the Korean Kingdom on behalf of the Korean Government.

Both Governments having agreed mutually to aid each other and help in attacking the Chinese and in defending themselves. And in order to insure the success of this joint action of both countries, the undersigned commissioners of each country are given full power to ratify the treaty, as follows:

### Article I

This treaty is an agreement to expel the Chinese forces from the Korean Kingdom, and to strongly establish the independence of Korea, as well as to fulfill the privileges and immunities which are enjoyed by both countries.

### Article II

As Japan has undertaken to attack the Chinese, Korea shall have to exert the utmost efforts in all possible ways to facilitate the movements of the Japanese troops to and fro and in preparing provisions for these troops.

### Article III

This treaty shall be abolished on the date of making a treaty of amity with China.

Wherefore the commissioners of both countries have hereunto set their seals and signatures this 26th day of the seventh moon of the five hundred and third year of Ta Chosen (Korea) and the 29th day of August of the twenty-seventh year of Meiji (August 25, 1894).

Kim Yun-Sik, (Korean) Minister for Foreign Affairs

K. OTori, Envoy Extraordinary and Minister Plenipotentiary of Japan to Korea

*Source:* United States Department of State. *Papers Relating to the Foreign Relations of the United States.* Washington, DC: Government Printing Office, 1985: 93–94.

## Japanese Treaty of Korean Annexation (1910)

*When the United States acquired the Philippines as the spoils of victory in the Spanish-American War, it began to consider commercial opportunities in Asia. First, the United States and Great Britain cooperated in promoting the so-called Open Door policy to establish equal access to trade with China. The various powers that wielded influence in China grew concerned about aggressive Russian behavior in China. This led to the Russo-Japanese War (1904–1905), which U.S. President Theodore Roosevelt helped to end. Roosevelt won the Nobel Peace Prize for his role. At the same time, the United States and Japan signed a secret accord in which the United States promised to give Japan a free hand in Korea in return for Japan's promise to do the same regarding the United States and the Philippines. By this one-sided treaty, Japan forcibly annexed Korea, which had long been dominated by China, on August 22, 1910. The change in Korea's status indicated the dramatic shift in power that occurred in Asia in the late 19th and early 20th centuries, as China suffered increasingly from internal dissension and foreign encroachment, while Japan emerged as a formidable military and industrial power. Korea remained tied to the Japanese empire until Japan's defeat in World War II.*

His Majesty the Emperor of Japan and his Majesty the Emperor of Korea having in view the special and close relations between their respective countries, desiring to promote the common weal of the two nations and to assure permanent peace in the Extreme East, and being convinced that these objects can be best attained in the annexation of Korea to the Empire of Japan, have resolved to conclude a treaty of such annexation and have, for that purpose, appointed as their plenipotentiaries—, that is to say, his Majesty the Emperor of Japan Viscount Masakata Terauchi, his Resident-General, and his Majesty the Emperor of Korea Ye Wan Yeng, his Minister-President of State, who upon mutual conference and deliberation have agreed to the following articles:—

### Article I
His Majesty the Emperor of Korea makes complete and permanent cession to his Majesty the Emperor of Japan of all rights of sovereignty over the whole or Korea.

### Article II
His Majesty the Emperor of Japan accepts the cession mentioned in the preceding article and consents to the complete annexation of Korea to the Empire of Japan.

### Article III
His Majesty the Emperor of Japan will accord to their Majesties the Emperor and ex-Emperor and his Imperial Highness the Crown Prince of Korea and their consorts and helm such titles, dignities, and honors as are appropriate to their respective ranks, and sufficient annual grants will be made for the maintenance of such titles, dignities and honors.

### Article IV
His Majesty the Emperor of Japan will also accord appropriate honor and treatment to the members of the Imperial House of Korea and their heirs other than those mentioned in the preceding article, and funds necessary for the maintenance of such honor and treatment will be granted.

### Article V
His Majesty the Emperor of Japan will confer peerages and monetary grants upon those Koreans who, on account of meritorious services, are regarded as deserving such special recognition.

### Article VI
In consequence of the aforesaid annexation the Government of Japan assumes the entire government and administration of Korea and undertake to afford full protection for the persons and property of the Koreans obeying the laws there in force and to promote the welfare of all such Koreans.

### Article VII
The Government of Japan will, so far as circumstances permit, employ in the public services of Japan in Korea those Koreans who accept the new regime loyally and in good faith and who are duly qualified for such services.

### Article VIII
This treaty, having been approved by his Majesty the Emperor of Japan and his Majesty the Emperor of Korea, shall take effect from the date of its promulgation.

**Imperial Japanese Rescript Attached to the Proclamation and Treaty of Annexation**
We, attaching highest importance to the maintenance of permanent peace in the Orient and the consolidation of lasting security to our Empire, and finding in Korea constant and fruitful sources of complication, caused our government to conclude in 1905 an agreement with the Korean Government by which Korea was placed under the protection of Japan in the hope that all disturbing elements might thereby be removed and peace assure forever. For the four years and over which have since elapsed, our government have exerted themselves with unwearied attitude to promote reforms in the administration of Korea, and their efforts have, in a degree, been attended with success, but at the same time, the existing regime of government in that country has shown itself hardly effective to preserve peace and stability, and in addition the spirit of suspicion and misgiving dominates the whole peninsula.

In order to maintain public order and security, and to advance the happiness and well-being of the people, it has become manifest that fundamental changes in the present system of government are inevitable.

We, in concert with his Majesty the Emperor of Korea, having in view this condition of affairs, and being equally persuaded of the necessity of annexing the whole of Korea to the Empire of Japan in response to the actual requirement of the situation, have now arrived at the arrangement for such permanent annexation. His majesty the Emperor of Korea and the members of his Imperial House will, notwithstanding the annexation, be accorded due and appropriate treatment. All Koreans, being under our sway, will enjoy growing prosperity and welfare, and with assured repose and security will come a marked expansion in industry and trade. We confidently believe that the new order of things now inaugurated will serve as a fresh guarantee of enduring peace in the Orient. We order the establishment of a Governor-General of Korea. The Governor-General will under our direction exercise the command of the army and the navy and have general control over all administrative functions in Korea. We call upon all our officials and authorities to fulfil their respective duties in appreciation of our will, and to conduct the various branches of administration in consonance with the requirements of the occasion, so that our subjects may long enjoy the blessings of peace and tranquility.

### Announcement of the Japanese Foreign Office, August 29, 1910

1. Korea shall hereafter be named "Chosen."
2. The Government-General shall be established in Chosen.
3. The Residency-General and its accessory offices will be in existence for the present, and the Resident-General will exercise the functions of the Governor-General.
4. The issue of special passports for the people of Chosen is abolished, and hereafter the Chosens will be treated on an equal footing as the Japanese in the matter.

At the same time as the promulgation of the Annexation Treaty, which took place today, an Imperial Rescript was issued granting amnesty to a number of prisoners, both of grave and minor offences, on account of extenuating circumstances, and also granting diminution or exemption of the taxes non-paid in past years and taxes to be collected during this year.

*Source: American Journal of International Law, Supplement, Vol. 6. New York: American Society of International Law, 1912.*

# League of Nations: Report on Japanese Invasion of Manchuria, 1933

*In 1932, Japan launched an attack against the Chinese state of Manchuria, quickly defeating Chinese resistance and establishing a brutal occupational rule over the region. Alarmed by Japan's openly aggressive actions and seemingly ever-increasing territorial ambitions in Asia, the League of Nations formed a committee to investigate the Manchurian invasion that same year. On February 24, 1933, the committee submitted this report, an excerpt of which appears below. Many historians consider the Japanese invasion of Manchuria as the opening phase of World War II.*

### Part Two: Chief Characteristics of the Dispute

Since September 18, 1931, the activities of the Japanese military authorities, in civil as well as in military matters, have been marked by essentially political considerations. The progressive military occupation of the Three Eastern Provinces removed in succession all the important towns in Manchuria from the control of the Chinese authorities, and, following each occupation, the civil administration was reorganised. A group of Japanese civil and military officials conceived, organised, and carried through the Manchurian independence movement as a solution to the situation in Manchuria as it existed after the events of September 18th, and, with this object, made use of the names and actions of certain Chinese individuals and took advantage of certain minorities and native communities that had grievances against the Chinese administration. This movement, which rapidly received assistance and direction from the Japanese General Staff, could only be carried through owing to the presence of the Japanese troops. It cannot be considered as a spontaneous and genuine independence movement.

The main political and administrative power in the "Government" of "Manchukuo," the result of the movement described in the previous paragraph, rests in the hands of Japanese officials and advisers, who are in a position actually to direct and control the administration; in general, the Chinese in Manchuria, who, as already mentioned form the vast majority of the population, do not support this "Government" and regard it as an instrument of the Japanese. It should also be noted that, after the Commission of Enquiry completed its report and before the report was considered by the Council and the Assembly, "Manchukuo" was recognised by Japan. It has not been recognised by any other State, the Members of the League in particular being of opinion that such recognition was incompatible with the spirit of the resolution of March 11th, 1932.

The situation which led up to the events of September 18th, 1931, presents certain special features. It was subsequently aggravated by the development of the Japanese military operations, the creation of the "Manchukuo Government" and the recognition of that "Government" by Japan. Undoubtedly the present case is not that of a country which has declared war on another country without previously exhausting the opportunities for conciliation provided in the Covenant of the League of Nations; neither is it a simple case

of the violation of the frontier of one country by the armed forces of a neighbouring country, because in Manchuria, as shown by the circumstances noted above, there are many features without an exact parallel in other parts of the world. It is, however, indisputable that, without any declaration of war, a large part of Chinese territory has been forcibly seized and occupied by Japanese troops and that, in consequence of this operation, it has been separated from and declared independent of the rest of China. . . .

*Source:* League of Nations. *Report on Japanese Invasion of Manchuria*, released February 24, 1933.

# Potsdam Declaration, July 26, 1945

*After Germany surrendered to the Allied Powers, U.S. President Harry S Truman, Soviet Union President Josef Stalin, and British Prime Minister Clement Atlee (having replaced Winston Churchill midway through the conference after elections in Great Britain) met in Potsdam and issued the following proclamation to the Japanese government (the proclamation was also made in the name of Chinese President Jiang Jieshi, who did not attend the conference). The last nine words were a veiled inference to atomic weapons.*

(1) We, the President of the United States, the President of the National Government of the Republic of China, and the Prime Minister of Great Britain, representing the hundreds of millions of our countrymen, have conferred and agree that Japan shall be given an opportunity to end this war.

(2) The prodigious land, sea and air forces of the United States, the British Empire and of China, many times reinforced by their armies and air fleets from the west, are poised to strike the final blows upon Japan. This military power is sustained and inspired by the determination of all the Allied Nations to

prosecute the war against Japan until she ceases to resist.

(3) The result of the futile and senseless German resistance to the might of the aroused free peoples of the world stands forth in awful clarity as an example to the people of Japan. The might that now converges on Japan is immeasurably greater than that which, when applied to the resisting Nazis, necessarily laid waste to the lands, the industry and the method of life of the whole German people. The full application of our military power, backed by our resolve, will mean the inevitable and complete destruction of the Japanese armed forces and just as inevitably the utter devastation of the Japanese homeland.

(4) The time has come for Japan to decide whether she will continue to be controlled by those self-willed militaristic advisers whose unintelligent calculations have brought the Empire of Japan to the threshold of annihilation, or whether she will follow the path of reason.

(5) Following are our terms. We will not deviate from them. There are no alternatives. We shall brook no delay.

(6) There must be eliminated for all time the authority and influence of those who have deceived and misled the people of Japan into embarking on world conquest, for we insist that a new order of peace, security and justice will be impossible until irresponsible militarism is driven from the world.

(7) Until such a new order is established and until there is convincing proof that Japan's war-making power is destroyed, points in Japanese territory to be designated by the Allies shall be occupied to secure the achievement of the basic objectives we are here setting forth.

(8) The terms of the Cairo Declaration shall be carried out and Japanese sovereignty shall be limited to the islands of Honshu, Hokkaido, Kyushu, Shikoku and such minor islands as we determine.

(9) The Japanese military forces, after being completely disarmed, shall be permitted to return to their homes with the opportunity to lead peaceful and productive lives.

(10) We do not intend that the Japanese shall be enslaved as a race or destroyed as a nation, but stern justice shall be meted out to all war criminals, including those who have visited cruelties upon our prisoners. The Japanese Government shall remove all obstacles to the revival and strengthening of democratic tendencies among the Japanese people. Freedom of speech, of religion, and of thought, as well as respect for the fundamental human rights shall be established.

(11) Japan shall be permitted to maintain such industries as will sustain her economy and permit the exaction of just reparations in kind, but not those which would enable her to re-arm for war. To this end, access to, as distinguished from control of, raw materials shall be permitted. Eventual Japanese participation in world trade relations shall be permitted.

(12) The occupying forces of the Allies shall be withdrawn from Japan as soon as these objectives have been accomplished and there has been established in accordance with the freely expressed will of the Japanese people a peacefully inclined and responsible government.

(13) We call upon the government of Japan to proclaim now the unconditional surrender of all Japanese armed forces, and to provide proper and adequate assurances of their good faith in such action. The alternative for Japan is prompt and utter destruction.

*Source:* U.S. Department of State. *A Decade of American Foreign Policy: Basic Documents, 1941–49*. Washington, DC: Government Printing Office, 1950.

# The Constitution of Japan, 1947

After a desultory postwar attempt by the Japanese government to revise the Meiji Constitution, Douglas MacArthur, Supreme Commander of Allied Powers (SCAP), appointed an ad hoc committee of American occupation staffers to "suggest revisions."

The resulting document was written principally by American attorneys Milo Rowell and Courtney Whitney. The articles about equality between men and women are reported to be written by female staffer Beate Sirota. The "example" was presented to the Japanese on February 13, 1946. Japanese legal scholars tinkered with it somewhat but changed very little from the original draft. It was enacted on May 3, 1947, and has never been amended.

The preamble suggests why it still is called "The Peace Constitution":

We, the Japanese people, acting through our duly elected representatives in the National Diet, determined that we shall secure for ourselves and our posterity the fruits of peaceful cooperation with all nations and the blessings of liberty throughout this land, and resolved that never again shall we be visited with the horrors of war through the action of government, do proclaim that sovereign power resides with the people and do firmly establish this Constitution. Government is a sacred trust of the people, the authority for which is derived from the people, the powers of which are exercised by the representatives of the people, and the benefits of which are enjoyed by the people. This is a universal principle of mankind upon which this Constitution is founded. We reject and revoke all constitutions, laws ordinances, and rescripts in conflict herewith. We, the Japanese people, desire peace for all time and are deeply conscious of the high ideals controlling human relationship and we have determined to preserve our security and existence, trusting in the justice and faith of the peace-loving peoples of the world. We desire to occupy an honored place in an international society striving for the preservation of peace, and the banishment of tyranny and slavery, oppression and intolerance for all time from the earth. We recognize that all peoples of the world have the right to live in peace, free from fear and want. We believe that no nation is responsible to itself alone, but that laws of political morality are universal; and that obedience to such laws is incumbent upon all nations who would sustain their own sovereignty and justify their sovereign relationship with other nations. We, the Japanese people, pledge our national honor to accomplish these high ideals and purposes with all our resources.

The first eight articles describe the role of the emperor. The most revolutionary are Articles 1 and r:

### Article 1
The Emperor shall be the symbol of the State and the unity of the people, deriving his position from the will of the people with whom resides sovereign power.

### Article 4
The Emperor shall perform only such acts in matters of state as are provided for in this Constitution and he shall not have powers related to government. 2) The Emperor may delegate the performance of his acts in matters of state as may be provided for by law.

The most controversial article was the so-called Peace Article:

### Article 9
Aspiring sincerely to an international peace based on justice and order, the Japanese people forever renounce war as a sovereign right of the nation and the threat or use of force as means of settling international disputes. 2) In order to accomplish the aim of the preceding paragraph, land, sea, and air forces, as well as other war potential, will never be maintained. The right of belligerency of the state will not be recognized.

The sections dealing with women are Articles 14, 24, and 26:

### Article 14
All of the people are equal under the law and there shall be no discrimination in political, economic or social relations because of race, creed, sex, social status or family origin.

### Article 24
1) Marriage shall be based only on the mutual consent of both sexes and it shall be maintained

through mutual cooperation with the equal rights of husband and wife as a basis. 2) With regard to choice of spouse, property rights, inheritance, choice of domicile, divorce and other matters pertaining to marriage and the family, laws shall be enacted from the standpoint of individual dignity and the essential equality of the sexes.

**Article 26**
1) All people shall have the right to receive an equal education correspondent to their ability, as provided for by law. 2) All people shall be obligated to have all boys and girls under their protection receive ordinary education as provided for by law. Such compulsory education shall be free.

*Source:* Nihonkoku Kenpō (Constitution of Japan), Ch.1, Art. 1 and 4; Ch.2, Art. 9; Ch.3, Art. 14, 24, and 26. Available at: http://www.solon.org/Constitutions/Japan/English/english-Constitution.html. Accessed June 30, 2012.

# United States–Japan Security Treaty, 1951

*The United States–Japan Security Treaty was signed at the height of the Cold War (and six years after the end of World War II) on September 8, 1951, and went into effect on April 28, 1952. The treaty was designed to provide Japan with a strong basis for economic and social recovery after World War II. By signing the treaty, the United States committed itself to defending Japan; in return, Japan provided bases for U.S. forces. With the United States' assurance of Japan's security—along with generous financial aid—Japan was able to achieve a successful economic recovery.*

SECURITY TREATY BETWEEN THE UNITED STATES OF AMERICA AND JAPAN

Japan has this day signed a Treaty of Peace with the Allied Powers. On the coming into force of that Treaty, Japan will not have the effective means to exercise its inherent right of self-defense because it has been disarmed.

There is danger to Japan in this situation because irresponsible militarism has not yet been driven from the world. Therefore Japan desires a Security Treaty with the United States of America to come into force simultaneously with the Treaty of Peace between the United States of America and Japan.

The Treaty of Peace recognizes that Japan as a Sovereign nation has the right to enter into collective security arrangements, and further, the Charter of the United Nations recognizes that all nations possess an inherent right of individual and collective self-defense.

In exercise of these rights, Japan desires, as a provisional arrangement for its defense, that the United States of America should maintain armed forces of its own in and about Japan so as to deter armed attack upon Japan.

The United States of America, in the interest of peace and security, is presently willing to maintain certain of its armed forces in and about Japan, in the expectation, however, that Japan will itself increasingly assume responsibility for its own defense against direct and indirect aggression, always avoiding any armament which could be an offensive threat or serve other than to promote peace and security in accordance with the purposes and principles of the United Nations Charter.

Accordingly, the two countries have agreed as follows:

ARTICLE I
Japan grants, and the United States of America accepts, the right, upon the coming into force of the Treaty of Peace and of this Treaty, to dispose United States land, air and sea forces in and about Japan. Such forces may be utilized to contribute to the maintenance of international peace and security in the Far East and to the security of Japan against armed attack from without, including assistance given at the express request of the Japanese Government to put down large-scale internal riots and disturbances in Japan, caused through instigation or intervention by an outside power or powers.

## ARTICLE II

During the exercise of the right referred to in Article I, Japan will not grant, without the prior consent of the United States of America, any bases or any rights, powers or authority whatsoever, in or relating to bases or the right of garrison or of maneuver, or transit of ground, air or naval forces to any third power.

## ARTICLE III

The conditions which shall govern the disposition of armed forces of the United States of America in and about Japan shall be determined by administrative agreements between the two Governments.

## ARTICLE IV

This Treaty shall expire whenever in the opinion of the Governments of the United States of America and Japan there shall have come into force such United Nations arrangements or such alternative individual or collective security dispositions as will satisfactorily provide for the maintenance by the United Nations or otherwise of international peace and security in the Japan Area.

Signed September 8, 1951. Entered into effect April 28, 1952.

*Source:* United States Department of State. *American Foreign Policy 1950–1955: Basic Documents Volumes I and II*. Department of State Publication 6446, General Foreign Policy Series 117. Washington, DC: United States Government Printing Office, 1957.

# Chronology

| | | | |
|---|---|---|---|
| **1500–250** **B.C.E** | Jōmon era of hunters and gatherers | **806** | Introduction of Shingon Buddhism |
| **250 B.C.E–** **A.D. 250** | Yayoi era; iron and wet-rice introduced | **939** | Revolt of Taira Masakado |
| **140–160** | Himiko and Iyo shaman-emperors | **1002–1019** | Murasaki Shikibu writes *Tale of Genji* |
| **2nd century C.E.** | Jingū Kogo | **1086–1129** | *Insei* (Cloister) government established by Emperor Shirakawa |
| **250–550** | Kofun or Tomb period; horse-mounted warrior culture | **1159–1160** | Heiji War |
| **552** | Introduction of Buddhism to Japan | **1175** | *Jōdo* Pure Land Buddhism founded by Hōnen |
| **604** | Seventeen-Article Constitution of Shōtoku Taishi | **1192** | Founding of Kamkura *bakufu* by Minamoto Yoritomo |
| **645** | Taika Confucian Reforms; the Isshi Incident | **1224** | True Pure Land sect founded by Shinran |
| **702** | Taihō Code promulgated | **1253** | Nichiren sect founded |
| **710** | First imperial capital in Nara | **1274 and** **1281** | Attempted Mongol invasions |
| **712** | *Kojiki* issued | **1333–1334** | Kemmu Restoration under Emperor Go-Daigo |
| **714** | *Nihongi* issued | **1333** | Founding of Ashikaga *bakufu* |
| **794** | Transfer of capital to Heian-kyō (Kyoto) | **1336–1392** | Southern Imperial Court in Yoshino |
| **805** | Introduction of Tendai Buddhism | **1441** | Kaikitsu War |
| | | **1467–1477** | Sacking of Kyoto (Ōnin War) |

| 1543 | Portuguese arrive in Japan at Tanegashima |
|---|---|
| 1549 | Francis Xavier in Japan |
| 1582 | Suicide of Oda Nobunaga |
| 1587 | Sword hunt and military unification by Toyotomi Hideyoshi |
| 1587 | Anti-Christian edict by Hideyoshi |
| 1592–1598 | Korean (Imjin) invasion |
| 1597 | Twenty-six Christians crucified at Nagasaki |
| 1598 | Death of Hideyoshi |
| 1600 | Battle of Sekigahara |
| 1603 | Tokugawa Ieyasu becomes shōgun; foundation of Tokugawa *bakufu* |
| 1614 | Battle of Ōsaka Castle; Toyotomi Hideyori dies |
| 1622 | Beginning of anti-Christian persecutions |
| 1637–1638 | Shimabara Rebellion; *Sakoku* instituted |
| 1641 | Dutch moved to Deshima Island |
| 1769–1786 | Tanuma Okitsugu runs *bakufu* |
| 1787–1793 | Matsudaira Sadanobu runs *bakufu* |
| 1812 | Golovnin Incident |
| 1825 | An edict to drive off foreign vessels is issued |
| 1833–1836 | The Tempō famine |
| 1837 | Ōshio Heihachirō leads an insurrection |

| 1841 | Rōjū Mizuno Tadakuni initiates the Tempō Reforms |
|---|---|
| 1849 | The woodblock artist Hokusai dies |
| 1853 | Commodore Matthew Perry arrives |
| 1854 | The Treaty of Kanagawa is signed with the United States |
| 1858 | Ii Naosuke is appointed great councilor (tairō); a commercial treaty with the United States is concluded; the woodblock artist Hiroshige dies |
| 1860 | Ii Naosuke assassination at Sakuradamon |
| 1861 | Henry Heusken assassinated |
| 1862 | Namagugi Incident, in which Charles Richardson is assassinated |
| 1866 | Tokugawa Yoshinobu (Keiki) established as last shōgun |
| 1867 | Shōgun Keiki restores political power to the imperial court |

## Meiji Period (1868–1912)

| 1868 | A new government is established; Tokyo (formerly Edo) becomes the capital; Charter Oath issued |
|---|---|
| 1869 | Four major *daimyō* relinquish control over their han to the imperial government |
| 1871 | The han are replaced by prefectures; the postal system is introduced; Tokugawa class distinctions are eliminated; |

the Iwakura Mission is dispatched to the West

**1872** The Tokyo-Yokohama Railroad is opened; the freedom to buy and sell land is granted; compulsory elementary education is instituted; *Maria Luz* Incident

**1873** The Gregorian calendar is adopted (December 3, 1872, of the old lunar calendar is converted to January 1, 1873); universal military conscription and a new land tax are instituted; Seikanron controversy

**1874** A request for the establishment of a national assembly is submitted by Itagaki and others

**1874** Saga Rebellion; Taiwan Expedition

**1876** The wearing of swords by former samurai is banned

**1877** Saigō Takamori leads the Satsuma Rebellion

**1879** The Ryukyu Islands become Okinawa Prefecture

**1881** A national assembly is promised by the government

**1884** The peerage is created; the Chichibu Uprising occurs

**1885** The cabinet system is adopted; Itō Hirobumi becomes the first prime minister

**1887** Electric lighting is introduced

**1888** The Privy Council is established

**1889** The Meiji Constitution is promulgated

**1890** The first Diet convenes; the Imperial Rescript on Education is issued

**1891** Otsu Incident, in which the Tsarevitch is attacked

**1894** Kim Ok-kyun assassinated

**1894** A treaty revision is agreed upon between Japan and England

**1894** First Peace Preservation Law

**1894–1895** The Sino-Japanese War

**1895** Triple Intervention by Russia, Germany, and France

**1898** The Ōkuma-Itagaki cabinet is formed

**1900** Public Order and Police Law; Boxer Rebellion in China

**1902** The Anglo-Japanese Alliance is concluded

**1904–1905** The Russo-Japanese War is concluded by the Treaty of Portsmouth

**1910** Korea is annexed; Kōtoku Shūsui and others are executed

**1912** Emperor Meiji dies

## Taishō Period (1912–1926)

**1914** Japan enters World War I; Siege of Qingdao

**1914** Siemens-Vickers Scandal

| | |
|---|---|
| **1915** | The Twenty-One Demands are presented to China |
| **1918** | The Hara cabinet is formed. |
| **1918–1922** | Siberian Intervention |
| **1919** | Treaty of Versailles; May Fourth Movement in China |
| **1921** | The Washington Conference on naval arms limitations convenes |
| **1923** | The Great Kanto Earthquake; Itō Noe assassinated |
| **1925** | Universal manhood suffrage is enacted; radio broadcasting commences |
| **1925** | Second Peace Preservation Law |
| **1926** | Emperor Taishō dies |

## Shōwa Period (1926–1989)

| | |
|---|---|
| **1930** | London Naval Conference |
| **1931** | The Manchurian Incident |
| **1932** | Prime Minister Inukai is assassinated; party government ends |
| **1933** | Lytton Report; Japan withdraws from the League of Nations |
| **1935** | Minobe Tatsukichi's organ theory of the state is condemned |
| **1936** | Prominent leaders are assassinated by radical militarists; the Anti-Comintern Pact with Germany is concluded; Xi'an Incident |
| **1937** | War with China breaks out; Battle of Shanghai; Nanjing Massacre |
| **1939** | Battle of Nomonhan |
| **1940** | Japanese troops move into French Indochina; a tripartite alliance with Germany and Italy is concluded |
| **1941** | Japan attacks Pearl Harbor, beginning the Pacific war; Corregidor Battle; Battle of Malaya |
| **1942** | The Battle of Midway (June); Bataan Death March; Guadalcanal Battle |
| **1943** | Battle for Tarawa |
| **1944** | The tide of war shifts; Saipan falls; Prime Minister Tōjō resigns; U.S. bombers carry out massive air raids on Japanese cities; Battle of Leyte Gulf |
| **1945** | U.S. troops land in the Philippines and Okinawa; atomic bombs are dropped on Hiroshima and Nagasaki; Russia enters the war; Japan surrenders; Allied occupation under General Douglas MacArthur begins |
| **1946** | A new constitution is promulgated |
| **1948** | General Tōjō and others are executed |
| **1951** | The peace treaty is signed in San Francisco |
| **1951** | A United States–Japanese Mutual Security Agreement is signed |
| **1952** | The Allied occupation ends |
| **1954** | Bikini Atoll Incident |

| | |
|---|---|
| **1955** | The Liberal Democratic Party (LDP) is formed |
| **1956** | Japan is admitted to the United Nations |
| **1960** | A new United States–Japan Mutual Security Agreement is concluded |
| **1964** | Japan hosts the Olympic Games in Tokyo |
| **1965** | Ienaga Saburō, a prominent historian, files the first of his three lawsuits against the Ministry of Education, charging that the process of textbook approval is unconstitutional |
| **1970** | Mishima Yukio commits suicide |
| **1971** | The United States agrees to relinquish control of Okinawa by 1972 |
| **1972** | Prime Minister Tanaka visits China and normalizes relations |
| **1973** | Arab oil embargo and energy crisis |
| **1975** | Emperor Hirohito visits the United States |
| **1975** | Prime Minister Miki Takeo visits the Yasukuni Shrine as a "private individual" on the 30th anniversary of the end of World War II |
| **1978** | Fourteen Class A war criminals (convicted by the International Military Tribunal for the Far East), including Tōjō Hideki, are quietly |

| | |
|---|---|
| | enshrined as "Martyrs of Shōwa" at Yasukuni Shrine |
| **1979** | Prime Minister Ohira Masayoshi visits the Yasukuni Shrine |
| **1980** | Japan produces more automobiles than the United States |
| **1980–1982** | Prime Minister Suzuki Zentaro visits the Yasukuni Shrine |
| **1982** | Honda opens its first car plant in the United States |
| **1983** | Prime Minister Nakasone Yasuhiro visits the Yasukuni Shrine |
| **1983** | President Ronald Reagan visits Japan |
| **1984** | Matsui Yayori publishes a short article in *Asahi Shinbun* on the subject of "comfort women," the first time any major newspaper addresses the issue |
| **1985** | Prime Minister Nakasone Yasuhiro visits the Yasukuni Shrine |
| **1986** | The Equal Employment Opportunity Law comes into effect to protect women's rights |
| **1987** | Privatization of national railways begins |
| **1987** | An Okinawan supermarket owner burns the Japanese flag in protest of Japan's treatment of Okinawa |
| **1988** | Recruit Scandal: Prime Minister Takeshita resigns after |

accepting bribes from the Recruit Company

**1988** Supreme Court rules that Nakaya Yasuko cannot prevent the government from enshrining the soul of her deceased husband (killed while serving in the Self-Defense Forces) at Yasukuni Shrine

**1989** Emperor Hirohito dies; Crown Prince Akihito is enthroned as Heisei Emperor

## The Heisei Era (1989– )

**1990** Nagasaki mayor Motoshima Hitoshi survives an assassination attempt after suggesting that Hirohito assume blame for World War II atrocities committed in his name

**1991** Japan pledges billions of dollars to support the Gulf War but refuses to send troops, citing Article 9 of the Peace Constitution

**1991** In a Diet session, the Japanese government denies the involvement of the wartime state and its military in the matter of "comfort women."

**1991** Mount Unzendake in southern Japan erupts, leaving 43 people dead and nearly 2,300 homeless

**1992** Historian Yoshimi Yoshiaki publishes documentary evidence proving the Japanese government was actively involved in the wartime "comfort women" program

**1992** Mohri Minoru is the first Japanese astronaut in space

**1992** Kanemaru Shin is forced to resign his Diet seat for taking bribes from the Sagawa Kyubin Company

**1992** Itami Jūzō, a film director, is attacked and seriously injured by Japanese mobsters upset over his unflattering portrayal of yakuza in a film

**1992** Prime Minister Miyazawa Kiichi officially apologizes to South Korea over the "comfort women" issue

**1992** Prime Minister Miyazawa Kiichi visits the Yasukuni Shrine

**1993** The LDP loses its majority in the Diet lower house for the first time since 1955

**1993** As millions of Japanese watch on television, Crown Prince Naruhito marries commoner Owada Masako in an elaborate Shintō religious ceremony

**1993** American Chad Haaheo Rowan becomes the first non-Japanese Sumo Grand Champion (Yokozuna), under the name Akebono

**1993** An Earthquake measuring magnitude 7.8 strikes northern Japan, killing 196 people

**1994** The LDP returns to power

**1994** Ōe Kenzaburo, Japanese novelist, wins the Nobel Prize for literature

| | |
|---|---|
| **1994** | Japan fires a rocket to the moon |
| **1995** | The Japanese government creates the Asian Women's Fund to receive private contributions to aid "comfort women" |
| **1995** | The Aum Shinrikyo religious cult, under the leadership of Asahara Shōkō, releases deadly sarin gas in the Tokyo subway, killing seven people and injuring hundreds more |
| **1995** | The Kansai Earthquake strikes in Kobe, causing $100 billion in property losses and killing more than 5,000 people |
| **1995** | On the anniversary of the end of World War II, Prime Minister Murayama makes the first official apology to other Asian countries for Japan's wartime atrocities |
| **1995** | U.S. President Bill Clinton formally apologizes to Japan for the rape of a young girl by three U.S. Marines in Okinawa |
| **1996** | Tupac Amaru guerillas capture the Japanese ambassador in Peru |
| **1996** | Prime Minister Hashimoto Ryūtarō visits the Yasukuni Shrine |
| **1997** | The consumption tax is raised from 3 percent to 5 percent over loud public outcry |
| **1997** | Japan signs an international agreement promising to remove remnants of chemical warfare agents left in China after World War II |
| **1997** | In response to historian Ienaga Saburō's third lawsuit alleging government interference in textbook content, Supreme Court finds partially for Ienaga |
| **1998** | The Winter Olympic Games are held in and around Nagano |
| **1998** | Prime Minister Obuchi issues an apology to the people of South Korea for 35 years of brutal colonial rule |
| **1999** | *Kimigayo* is reinstated as the national anthem; "Rising Sun" is reinstated as the official national flag. |
| **1999** | The Health Ministry approves Viagra (after six months of consideration) but still holds back approval for the birth control pill (which was in consideration for nine years) |
| **1999** | The Tokaimura nuclear power plant accident exposes at least 7- people to various levels of radiation and ends up taking the lives of 2 people |
| **2000** | Empress Dowager Nagako (Hirohito's widow) dies |
| **2000** | Ota Fusae is elected governor of Osaka, becoming the first woman governor in Japan |
| **2000** | A new 2,000-yen bill is released into circulation by the Bank of Japan—the first |

release of a new banknote since 1958

**2001** The U.S. submarine *Greeneville* sinks the Japanese fishing vessel *Ehime Maru* near Honolulu, Hawaii; nine people on the *Ehime Maru* die as the trawler sinks

**2001** Prime Minister Mori and Russian President Putin sign an accord for return of two Kurile Islands, Etorofu and Kunashiri, to Japan

**2001** First case of mad cow disease in Japan

**2001** The United States turns over to Japanese authorities an American serviceman accused of rape

**2001** Prime Minister Koizumi makes a surprise visit to Yasukuni Shrine

**2001** Prime Minister Koizumi visits China and South Korea in an attempt to smooth relations between those countries

**2001** Japan dispatches two destroyers and a supply ship to the Indian Ocean to support U.S. forces fighting in Afghanistan; it is the first time for Japan has sent military ships outside of its own waters since the end of World War II

**2001** Crown Princess Masako gives birth to a daughter, and lineage controversy ensues

**2002** Japan and Korea cohost the 2002 Soccer World Cup

**2002** North Korean leader Kim Jung Il allows five Japanese who had been kidnapped 20 years earlier to return to Japan

**2002** A Tokyo court acknowledges for the first time Japan's use of biological weapons before and during World War II

**2002–2006** Prime Minister Koizumi visits Yasukuni Shrine

**2002** Koizumi is the first prime minister to visit North Korea

**2004** Japan dispatches Army Self Defense Forces to Samawah, in southern Iraq—the first time troops have been deployed to an active war zone since World War II

**2004** The death sentence for Aum Shinrikyo leader Asahara is confirmed

**2004** Nonradioactive steam leaks from Mihama nuclear power plant, killing four workers and severely burning seven others

**2004** Japan applies for a permanent seat on the United Nations Security Council, but is rejected

**2005** Anti-Japanese protest in Beijing

**2005** Princess Sayako (age 36), the emperor's only daughter, quits the monarchy and marries Yoshiki Kuroda, a 40-year-old commoner

**2005** Bills finally pass both houses of the Diet to privatize the postal system

**2005** More than 100 people are killed when a commuter train crashes near Amagasaki

**2006** North Korea test-fires missiles over the Sea of Japan

**2006** Japan agrees to pay $6 billion of the $10 billion cost for transferring 8,000 U.S. Marines from Okinawa to Guam

**2006** Crown Prince's younger brother, Akishino, and his wife have a baby boy, the first male heir to the imperial throne born since the mid-1960s; he is named Hisahito and is now third in line to the throne

**2007** Japan recalls ships that supported fighting in Afghanistan

**2007** Radiation leaks, burst pipes, and fires at Kashiwazaki nuclear power plant follow a 6.8 magnitude earthquake near Niigata

**2007** Nagasaki mayor Ito Itcho is assassinated by yakuza

**2007** The Japanese whaling fleet sets sail on a six-month mission described as scientific research

**2007** The Asian Women's Fund (founded in 1995) dissolves; it had provided 285 women in the Philippines, South Korea, and Taiwan with 2 million yen ($17,800) each in compensation, helped set up nursing homes for Indonesian former sex slaves, and offered medical assistance to some 80 Dutch former sex slaves

**2008** A U.S. Marine accused of raping a young girl in Okinawa surrenders to Japanese jurisdiction (the case is later dropped)

**2008** A defamation lawsuit filed against novelist Ōe Kenzaburo over statements that military officers ordered civilians to commit mass suicide in Okinawa during World War II is rejected in Osaka district court

**2008** The District Court of Nagoya rules that Japan's 2004 dispatch of air force troops to Iraq breached the country's pacifist constitution

**2008** Former Agricultural Minister Shimamura Yoshinobu joins 159 other lawmakers to pray at the Yasukuni Shrine; Prime Minister Fukuda Yasuo does not attend

**2008** Tokyo prosecutors arrest Tamio Araki, former president of Pacific Consultants International, and three other company executives for allegedly misusing 120 million yen of government funds meant for the disposal of about 400,000 chemical weapons that Japanese troops left behind in China at the end of the war

**2008** A poll by *Yomiuri* newspaper finds that 43.1 percent of the Japanese population supports keeping the 1947 pacifist constitution as is, against 42.5 percent who back revisions

**2009** DPJ leader Hatoyama Yukio is elected prime minister as the head of a coalition with the Social Democratic Party and People's New Party.

**2010** Prime Minister Hatoyama says Japan may rethink U.S. military bases after a city on Okinawa elects a mayor opposed to hosting a major air base

**2010** Japan's economy grows by less than first estimated in the final quarter of 2009; on an annualized basis, economic growth is 3.8 percent, down from the initial estimate of 4.6 percent

**2010** Prime Minister Hatoyama Yukio apologizes for not keeping an election promise to move the United States' Futenma military base—unpopular with many locals—from Okinawa

**2010** Prime Minister Hatoyama quits; Finance Minister Kan Naoto takes over after a vote in the party's parliamentary caucus

**2010** The ruling coalition loses majority in elections of the upper house of the Diet

**2011** On March 11, a magnitude 9.0 earthquake and tsunami hit Japan; approximately 20,000 people are killed; the Fukushima Dai-ichi nuclear reactor crisis begins

**2011** Japan wins the Women's World Cup in Soccer

**2011** Prime Minister Kan Naoto is replaced by Noda Yoshihiko

# Glossary

***Aikoku fujinkai* (Patriotic Women's Association):** Group formed by Okumura Ioko in 1901. Merged with *Kokubo fujinkai* into *Dai Nippon fujinka* in 1942.

***Aikoku-koto* (Public Party of Patriots):** Group founded by Itagaki Taisuke in 1874.

**Ainu:** Premodern non-Japanese peoples. See also *Emishi* and *Ezo*.

**Ainu Culture Revitalization Law (*Ainu bunka shinkō hō*):** Law established in 1997 to improve the status of the Ainu.

**Alternate attendance:** See *Sankin kōtai*.

**AMPO:** 1960 "Treaty of Mutual Cooperation and Security"; commonly known by the Japanese abbreviation *Nippon-koku to Amerika-gasshūkoku to no Aida no Sōgo Kyōryoku oyobi Anzen Hoshō Jōyaku.*

**Amur River Society (Black Dragon Society):** See *Kokuryūkai*.

**Ansei Purge:** Ii Naosuke's punishment of anti-*bakufu* men (1858–1859) when *daimyō* such as Tokugawa Nariaki were placed under house arrest and lower-ranking critics such as Yoshida Shōin were executed.

***Ashigaru*:** Foot soldiers, often musketeers during the Sengoku era.

**Baien Incident:** Unsuccessful suicide pact of Morita Sohei and Hiratsuka *Raichō* in 1908.

***Bakufu*:** Literally "tent government"; military rule of the country by a hereditary *shōgun*, as opposed to rule by the imperial court and the emperor.

***Bandori*:** Rural straw rain capes. See also *Mino*.

***Banzai* ("1,000 Years"):** Traditionally the salute to the emperor repeated three times; akin to "Long Live the Emperor." Because of wartime newsreels, for American audiences "*Banzai*" became emblematic of Japan like "Heil Hitler" was for Germany.

**Battle of Bun'ei (*Bun'ei no eki*):** 1274 Mongol Invasion. See also Battle of Koan.

**Battle of Koan (*Kōan no eki*):** 1281 Mongol Invasion. See also Battle of Bun'ei.

**Battle of Midway:** June-4–5, 1942.

**Battle of the Coral Sea:** May 8, 1942.

***Biwa hōshi* ('biwa priests"):** Minstrels who accompanied their singing of War Tales with the *biwa*, or Japanese lute.

**Black Dragon Society (Amur River Society):** See *Kokuryūkai*.

**Black ships (*kurofune*):** Commodore Matthew Perry's ships, which sailed into Tokyo Bay in 1853.

**Blood Pledge Corps:** See *Ketsumeidan*.

**Blood tax:** Universal military conscription.

**Bluestockings:** See *Seito*.

**Boddhisatva:** Buddhist saint.

*Bōryoku dantai*: Postwar organizations allied with the yakuza mob.

**Boxer Rebellion:** "Righteous and Harmonious Fists"; common title given to the peasant uprising in that occurred in northeast China in 1898–1900.

**"Brother, Do Not Give Your Life":** See "Kimi shinitamo koto nakare."

**Buke Shohatto ("Laws of Military Households"):** Tokugawa *bakufu* law promulgated in 1635.

*Burakumin*: Hereditary pariah class.

*Bushidō* ("the Way of the Warrior"); sociopolitical ethos of the samurai.

**Castle towns:** See *Jokamachi*.

**Charter Oath (*Gokajō no seimon*):** Statement of political principles promulgated in March 1868 by the new Meiji government..

**Cherry Blossom Society:** See Sakurakai.

*Chian iji hô*: See Peace Preservation Law of 1925.

**Chrysanthemum Throne:** Euphemism for Japan's imperial institution.

**China Quagmire:** Inability to find an early peaceful settlement to Japan's invasion of China after 1937.

*Ch'inilp'a* ("friendly-to-Japan"): Korean collaborators targeted by Korean nationalists.

*Chise* (in the Ainu language): Thatch houses.

*Chōzen naikaku* ("transcendent cabinets"): Meiji *genrō*'s preference for cabinets formed without political party members.

**Chūshingura ("the treasury of loyal retainers."):** Bunraku puppet theater play (1748) about the Akō Incident of the 47 Rōnin.

**Closed country:** See *Sakoku*.

**Colonization Commission (*kaitakushi*):** Meiji government commission established in 1869 to colonize Hokkaidō.

*Companhia*: Confraternities of Japanese Christian believers in the 16th to 17th centuries.

**Constitution Party:** See Kenseito.

**Constitutional Reform Party:** See Rikken Kaishinto.

**Control Way Faction:** See Tōsei-ha.

*Dai Manshu Teikoku* ("Great Manchu Empire): Designated name of Manchukuo after 1934.

*Daimoku* (*namu Myōhō Rengekyō*; "praise the *Lotus Sutra* of the wonderful law"): Nichiren's chanted formula for salvation.

*Daimyō* ("Great Name"): Territorial warlord during Sengoku and Edo eras.

*Daimyō gyōretsu*: *Daimyō* procession on *Sankin kōtai*.

*Dai Nippon fujinkai* (Greater Japan Women's Association): Group formed in February 1942 when *Kokubo fujinkai* and *Aikoku fujinkai* merged.

*Dai-toa-kyoeiken*: See Greater East Asia Co-prosperity Sphere.

*Dai Tō-A Sensō* ("Greater East Asia War"): Common Japanese name for World War II.

*Dappan rōshi* ("masterless samurai"): See *Rōnin*.

*Datsu A Ron* ("On Leaving Asia"): Fukuzawa Yukichi's modernization argument, 1885.

*Dekasegi*: Late 19th-century émigrés; migrating workers to North America and Hawai'i.

**Dōbunkai ("Common Culture Association"):** Pan-Asianist organization founded in 1898, which became the Tōa (East Asia) Dōbunkai.

**Dodge Plan:** An economic stabilization program developed by Joseph Morrell Dodge in Allied-occupied Japan in 1948.

*Dōjō:* Fencing academies.

*Dojuku* **("fellow lodgers"):** Japanese lay Christian preachers in the 16th to 17th centuries.

*Domeikai:* Association for the Establishment of a National Assembly founded by Itagaki Taisuke and others in the 1870s.

**Dutch Studies:** See Rangaku.

**"Eastern ethics as base, Western techniques as means":** See *tōyō dōtoku, seiyō gei.*

*Emishi:* Premodern non-Japanese peoples. See also Ainu and *Ezo.*

**Emperor-centered nationalism (*tennō taisei*):** Name given to the ultra-nationalist form of government of Japan from the mid-1930s to 1945.

**Extraterritoriality:** A clause in the Unequal Treaties that reserved all judicial jurisdiction over foreigners who lived in Japan to their national courts.

*Ezo:* Premodern non-Japanese peoples. See also Ainu and *Emishi.*

**"Flying over the hump":** Allied supply of China flying over the Himalayas, 1942–1944.

*Fudai daimyō:* Trusted vassals who had served Tokugawa Ieyasu prior to the Battle of Sekigahara (1600). Compare to *Tozama* and *Shimpan.*

*Fuhenteki daiseimei* **("universal great life"):** State Shintō principle that one's life is not one's own; it is granted by the emperor.

*Fukoku-Kyōhei* **("Rich Country, Strong Military"):** Slogan of early Meiji political reformers.

*Fumi-e* **("Treading on pictures"):** Tokugawa anti-Christian device, forcing everyone to step on icons to prove themselves not Christian.

**Gakushuin:** The Peers' School.

*Gekika-jiken* **("violent incidents"):** Generic name for peasant uprisings in the Meiji era.

*Gekokujō* **("those below topple those above"):** Treachery; overthrowing one's feudal lord.

*Genbun itchi* **("unity of spoken and written language"):** Program to clarify Japanese language in 1885.

*Genrō* **("Senior Statesmen"):** Seven members of the so-called Satchō Oligarchy.

**Gen'yōsha ("Dark Ocean Society"):** Ultra-nationalist organization founded by Toyama Mitsuru in 1881.

*Gokajō no seimon:* See Charter Oath.

*Gokenin* **("housemen"):** Lower-ranked samurai who served *daimyō* as do-all retainers. Compare with *Hatamoto.*

*Goningumi* **("Five villages"):** Groups of five or more villages responsible for reporting "hidden" Christians during the Tokugawa era.

*Gōshi:* Country samurai family.

*Go-sanke* **("Three Houses"):** Close relatives of Tokugawa, important because they provided a pool of heirs should the shōgun fail to produce one. Includes *Mito, Owari,* and *Kii.*

*Gozan* **("Five Mountains"):** *Rinzai Zen* Buddhist monasteries system.

**Greater East Asia Co-prosperity Sphere (*dai-toa-kyoeiken*):** Asian collaborators, 1940–1945.

**Greater East Asia War (*Dai Tō-A Sensō*):** World War II.

**Great Learning for Women:** See *Onna daigaku.*

**Great Manchu Empire (*Dai Manshu Tei-koku*):** Designated name of Manchukuo after 1934.

**Great Treason Incident:** See High Treason Incident.

***Gunki monogatari* ("War Tales"):** Medieval literary genre including *Heike monogatari* et al.

**Guomindang:** Nationalist Party of China, founded by Sun Yat-sen and dominated by Jiang Jieshi after 1925.

***Gyaku koosu* ("reverse course"):** American change in Japanese occupation policy after 1947, favoring conservative political factions over former leftist allies.

***Haibutsu kishaku* ("abolish Buddhism and destroy Shakyamuni"):** Anti-Buddhist movement in early Meiji.

***Hakkō Ichiu* ("eight cords, one roof"):** Ultra-nationalist slogan popularized by Tanaka Chigaku.

***Hanshin Awaji Daishinsai*:** 1995 Kobe earthquake.

***Hara-kiri*:** Ritual suicide, also known as *seppuku*. See also *Junshi*.

***Hatamoto* ("bannermen"):** Middle-ranking liege vassals who served *daimyō*. Compare with *gokenin*.

**High Treason Incident:** Plot to assassinate the Emperor in 1910. Led to execution of many leftists in 1911.

**Historical tales:** See *Rekishi monogatari*.

***Hōgan biiki* ("tears for the lieutenant"):** Sympathy for the underdog.

***Hon'in* ("senior retired emperor"):** A retired emperor in the *insei* (cloister) government.

**Igakko:** A medical school founded in 1877 from a number of existing educational institutions; it later became part of Tokyo University.

***Ikkō* ("single purpose"):** Self-governing villages, all members of the Jōdo Shinshu sect of Buddhism.

**Imperial Rule Assistance Association (Taisei Yokusankai):** Dissolution of all political parties in 1940 to be replaced with a single pro-government party.

**Imperial Way Faction:** See *Kōdōha*.

**Income Doubling Plan:** Economic reform launched by Ikeda Hayato in 1960.

***Insei* ("cloister government"):** An alternative source of political power used by retired emperors to rule over successor emperors (sons or grandsons} in the late 11th century.

**"In the Beginning Woman was the Sun" ("*Genshi josei wa taiyo de atta*"):** Opening line of Hiratsuka *Raichō* poem; it became the slogan of the *Seito* (*Bluestockings*) journal.

**Iron Triangle:** The postwar Liberal Democrat Party (LDP)-led government, the bureaucracy, and large corporations.

***Iwor*:** Ainu well-defined territory.

**Japan Socialist League (*Nihon Shakai Shugi Dōmei*):** Group briefly established in 1920 from remnants of other disbanded socialist parties.

**Japan Socialist Party (*Nippon Shakaitō*):** Political party that existed briefly in 1907 but was quickly banned.

**Japan Teachers' Union (JTU; *Nihon Kyōshokuin Kumiai*):** Post-war union for teachers.

**Japón:** Area around Coria del Río in southern Spain populated.by Japanese descendants of émigrés who settled there in the 17th century.

***Jinja Kyoku* ("Shrine Office"):** Home Ministry office for State Shintō, established in 1900.

***Jinnō shōtōki* ("Chronicle of the Direct Descent of Divine Sovereigns"):** Document written by Kitabatake Chikafusa about 1336.

*Jiriki kyūsai* ("self-redress"): Revenge.

*Jitsugyōka*: Nationalistic entrepreneurs in early (1870–1880) Meiji Japan; investors in national economic programs.

*Jiujitsu* ("**yielding technique**"): A martial art.

*Jiyuto* (**Liberal Party**): Japan's first real political party, founded by Itagaki Taisuke in 1881.

*Jitsugaku* ("**practical knowledge**"): Name commonly given to Western or Dutch (Rangaku) studies during final years of the Tokugawa *bakufu*.

*Jiyu Minken Undo*: The "People's Rights and Freedom Movement" in the 1870s.

*Jokamachi* ("**Castle towns**"): The sprawling cities that sprang up around medieval castles.

*Jōko Nihongo* ("**Old Japanese language**"): The Japanese language as it existed before the influence of Chinese in the seventh century.

*Junshi*: Suicide of a vassal, following the suicide of one's lord. See also *Hara-kiri* and *Seppuku*.

*Kagamimono* ("**mirror works**"): Tradition of writing in the 11th century.

*Kaishaku*: An attendant or "second" who would behead the victim committing suicide after the initial cut had been made.

*Kaisho* (**Dutch: "Geldkamer"**): Tokugawa official in charge of setting prices for silk brought to Nagasaki by Dutch; an office established in 1698.

*Kaitakushi*: See Colonization Commission.

*Kaiten* ("**Return to Heaven**"): Kamikaze. See also *Ningen gyorai* and *Ōka*.

*Kakure kirishitan* ("**hidden Christians**"): Illegal Christian adherents during the Tokugawa era.

*Kakushin kanryō* ("**reformist bureaucrats**"): The conservative bureaucracy of the 1930s.

*Kami*: Ancestral spirits in Shintō, all descending from Sun Goddess Amaterasu.

**Kamikaze ("Divine Winds"):** Suicide air pilots in World War II; also known as *Tokkōtai* ("Special Attack Squads" [*Tokubetsu kōgekitai*]). See also *Kaiten* and *Ōka* (cherry blossom planes).

*Kampaku*: See Regent. See also *Sessho*.

*Kanbun*: A hybrid form of written Chinese that was popular among the warrior class during the medieval period.

**Kanji:** The Sino-Japanese written characters.

*Kannagara* ("**natural religion**"): Ancient expression implying the sanctity of the reign of the emperor in Shintō.

*Kanrei*: The office of deputy shōgun, established during the Muromachi *bakufu* (1362).

**Karate ("open hand"):** A martial art.

**Karayuki-san ("someone who goes to China"):** Euphemism for Japanese prostitutes abroad (especially in Shanghai).

*Kataribonkei*: Recited-text lineage of Warrior Tales. See also *Yomihonkei*.

*Keiretsu* ("**System**"): Economic integrated conglomerations that replaced *Zaibatsu* in Japan in the post-World War II era.

*Kenseito* (**Constitution Party**): A coalition party jointly founded by Itagaki Taisuke and Ōkuma Shigenobu in 1898.

*Ketsumeidan* ("**Blood Pledge Corps**"): 1932 assassination plot.

*"Kimi shinitamo koto nakare"* ("**Brother, Do Not Give Your Life**"): Yosano Akiko's antiwar poem of 1904.

*Kirishitan Shumon aratame-yaku*: Christian Suppression Office, which was established in 1640.

*Kirokueiga* ("record film"): Newsreel documentary.

*Kōbugattai*: Movement to unite the Tokugawa *bakufu* and the imperial court by marrying Shōgun Iemochi to Imperial Princess Kazu-no-Miya.

*Kobukson* ("turtle ships"): Ships used by the Koreans in the Imjin War of 1592 to defeat the Japanese.

*Kōdōha* ("Imperial Way Faction"): Young Officer radicals in the Japanese army in the late 1920s through mid-1930s, who became allied with General Araki Sadao.

**Kokka shintō:** State Shintō.

*Kôkoku Zen* ("imperial-state Zen"): An attempt to create state-controlled Zen Buddhism during the 1930s.

*Koku*: Unit of dry volume measurement, about 5 bushels of rice.

*Kokubo fujinkai* (**National Defense Women's Association:** A group founded in 1932 by Yasuda Sei and Mitani Eiko; it merged with *Aikoku fujinkai* into *Dai Nippon fujinka* in 1942.

*Kokuchukai* ("National Pillar Society"): Organization founded by Tanaka Chigaku in 1914.

*Kokudaka*: Assessed Tokugawa-era tax, based on usual annual yield and collected in kind.

*Kokugo kokuji mondai* (**"Japanese language reforms"**): Program to create a national language in the early Meiji era.

*Kokumin* ("citizen"): Name used to indicate people loyal to the nation. Also can be read as "the people."

*Kokumin dōtoku* ("all-inclusive national ethic"): State Shintō principle that everything is dependent on the emperor.

*Kokuminzoku* ("ethnic nation-state"): State Shintō principle similar to the German *Volksstaat*.

*Kokuryūkai* ("Black Dragon Society; Amur River Society"): A Pan-Asianist organization founded in 1901.

*Kokutai*: National essence or national polity under State Shintō.

*Kome-hyappyo* ("100 bags of rice"): Kobayashi Torasaburo, suggested that 100 donated bales of rice be sold to build a school for the future education of the Nagaoka people in 1869.

*Kotan*: Ainu independent villages.

**Kōtoku Incident:** See High Treason Incident.

*Kun-yomi*: Indigenous Japanese-reading of a kanji character. See also *On-yomi*

*Kurofune*: See Black ships.

**Law on Assembly and Political Association** (*Shukai oyobi Seishaho*): Law promulgated in 1890 to enumerate what constituted a legal political assembly.

**Laws of Military Households (Buke Shohatto):** Set of laws promulgated in 1635 to establish a moral code for samurai.

*Machi yoriki*: Tokugawa-era municipal police captain.

*Manshū mondai* ("Manchurian problem"): Euphemism for the incursion into Manchuria by the Kwantung Army in 1931.

*Mantetsu*: Shortened form of South Manchurian Railway.

*Manyōgana*: Seventh-century system of writing so named because the poetic anthology *Manyō'shū* used the style.

*Mappō* ("the end of the Buddhist dharma"): Prophesized degenerate age, predicted to occur 2,000 years after the death of Buddha.

**"Masterless samurai":** See *Dappan rōshi* and Rōnin.

*Me de miru shinbun* ("newspapers you watch"): Newsreels.

**Meiji land tax:** A tax on landowners promulgated in 1871 and put into effect in 1873.

*Mino*: Rural straw rain hats. See also *Bandori*.

*Minshushugi* ("**people are sovereign**"): Usually translated as "democracy."

*Minzoku no dantai* ("**blood and ethnicity**"): Nationalistic principle of State Shintō.

*Mukyōkai* ("**Nonchurch Movement**"): Early Meiji nonsectarian Christian organization.

*Nakoso oshikere* ("**Cherish your name**" or "**Don't do anything shameful**"): Honor aspect of *bushidō* creed.

*Namu Myōhō Rengekyō* ("**praise the *Lotus Sutra* of the wonderful law**"): Nichiren's *daimoku* chanted formula for salvation.

*Nandogami* ("**closet gods**"): The hidden icons of *kakure Kirishitan*.

**Nan'yō ("South Seas"):** Former German Pacific islands (primarily Marshalls, Carolines, Marianas, and Palaus) given to the Japanese in 1919 as part of the League of Nations mandates under the Treaty of Versailles.

"**Nationalistic entrepreneurs**": See *Jitsugyōka*.

*Nemawashi* ("**Preparing the roots**"): Traditional consensus-building and compromise.

"**Newspapers you watch**" (*me de miru shinbun*): Newsreels.

**New Woman's Association:** See *Shin Fujin Kyokai*.

*Nihonjinron* ("**discourses on Japaneseness**"): Postwar argument that Japan is unique and should not be compared to other cultures.

*Nihon Kyōshokuin Kumiai*: Japan Teachers' Union (JTU).

*Nihon-machi* ("**Japan-towns**"): Cities throughout Asia where Japanese merchants lived after about the 14th century.

*Nihon nyūsu eiga-sha*: Japan Newsreel Company.

*Nihon Sekigun* ("**Japanese Red Army**"): Usually shortened to *Sekigun*; the leftist antigovernment union of terrorists.

*Nihon Shakai Shugi Dōmei* (**Japan Socialist League**): A group briefly established in 1920 from the remnants of other disbanded socialist parties.

*Nikkyōso* (*Nihon Kyōshokuin Kumiai*): Japan's Teachers Union.

*Ningen gyorai* ("**Human torpedoes**"): Kamikaze. See also *Kaiten* and *Ōka*.

**Ninja:** Semi-mythical medieval "invisible" assassins. The two kanji can also be read *shinobi*.

*Nippon Shakaitō* (**Japan Socialist Party**): Group that existed briefly in 1907 but was quickly banned.

*Nippon teikoku ban-banzai* ("**Imperial Japan Forever**"): Slogan invented by Tanaka Chigaku.

**Nishihara Loans:** Loans made by Japan to the Chinese warlord Duan Qirui in 1916 to try to force China to accede to the Twenty-One Demands.

**Nonchurch Movement** (*Mukyōkai*): Early Meiji nonsectarian Christian organization.

*Ōka* ("**cherry blossom planes**"): Kamikaze planes.

*Omaburi* ("**Protectors**"): Small papers cut in the shape of a cross, used as charms for protection of home and field by *kakure Kirishitan*.

*On* ("**debt of gratitude**"): Confucian social obligation and duty during the premodern period.

*Onna daigaku* ("**The Great Learning for Women**"): A didactic text for samurai women written by Kaibara Ekken in 1672.

*On-yomi*: Sinified readings of a kanji character. See also *Kun-yomi*.

*Ōoku* ("women of the great interior"): Influential women within the Tokugawa *bakufu* castle in Edo.

**Organ Theory**: Minobe Tatsukichi's theory that the emperor was an organ of the corporate state (*tennō kikansetsu*).

*Otempensia*: A bundle of hemp rope used by some *kakure Kirishitan* for self-discipline.

**Peace Preservation Law (*Chian iji hô*)**: Law promulgated in 1925 intended to reign-in political dissidents.

**People's Rights and Freedom Movement:** See *Jiyu Minken Undo*.

**"Picture brides"**: A scheme used to bring women to overseas Japanese communities in the 19th century.

**Progressive Party:** See Shinpoto.

**Rangaku ("Dutch Studies")**: Generic name given to all Western sciences during the Tokugawa era.

**"Reformist bureaucrats" (*kakushin kanryō*)**: The conservative bureaucracy of the 1930s.

**Regent (*sessho*)**: Office held by the Fujiwara family in the Heian era to control a child (or female) emperor; it was first held by Fujiwara Yoshifusa in 858. See also *Kampaku*.

*Rekishi monogatari* ("historical tales"): Medieval literary genre.

**"Revere the Emperor—Eliminate the Evils"**: See *Sonno-tōkan*.

**"Revere the Emperor—Expel the Barbarians"**: See *Sonno-jōi*.

**"Reverse course" (*Gyaku koosu*)**: American change in Japanese occupation policy after 1947.

**"Revolutionary Alliance":** See Tongmenghui.

**"Rich Country, Strong Military"**: See *Fukoku-kyohei*

**Rikken Kaishinto (Constitutional Reform Party)**: A political party founded by Ōkuma Shigenobu in 1882.

**Rikkenseiyūkai (Friends of Constitutional Government)**: A political party founded by Itō Hirobumi in 1890; also called Seiyūkai.

*Rikkokushi* ("Six National Histories"): History document written in the medieval period.

*Ritsu-ryō* ("Criminal and Administration Codes")**: Reforms instituted in seventh-century Japan emulating the Confucian political system of Tang China.

**Rock Springs Massacre of 1885:** An event in which Wyoming miners rampaged through a settlement of Chinese workers as part of a labor dispute with the Union Pacific Railway.

*Rōnin* ("wave men"): "Masterless" samurai cast adrift from their *daimyō*, especially in the Tokugawa Bakumatsu era.

**Root-Takahira Agreement (1908)**: Agreement in which the United States implicitly recognized Japanese control of Korea.

*Ryūha*: Traditional swordsmanship styles.

*Saisei itchi* ("worship of the gods and government as one")**: The underlying principle of State Shintō.

*Sakoku* ("closed country")**: The Tokugawa national policy of isolating Japan after about 1640.

**Sakurakai (Cherry Blossom Society)**: An ultra-nationalist radical organization founded by Hashimoto Kingoro and Isamu Cho in 1930.

*Sankin kōtai* ("alternate attendance")**: System of political control enforced by the Tokugawa government.

*Sanmin zhuyi*: See Three Principles of the People.

*Sanyo* (**cabinet consultant**): An official in the early Meiji government.

**Satsuma- Chōshū Alliance (***Satchō-Dōmei***)**: A political/government alliance formed in 1866.

**Seikanron:** The controversy over whether to invade Korea in 1873.

*Seimeisen* (**"life line"**): Manchuria as Japan's chief industrial partner after about 1935.

*Seii taishōgun* (**"Barbarian-Subduing Generalissimo"**): Military deputy office that came to be the hereditary head of the feudal-era *bakufu*. Commonly shortened to *shōgun*.

**Seito (***Bluestockings***)**: A feminist journal founded by Hiratsuka *Raichō* in 1912.

**Seitosha (Bluestockings Association):** A feminist organization founded by Hiratsuka *Raichō* in 1911.

**Seiyūkai:** See Rikkenseiyūkai.

**"Senior Statesmen":** See *Genrō*.

**Senkaku islands:** Disputed islands (versus China) located between Taiwan and Okinawa in the East China Sea. The Chinese call them Diaoyu.

*Seppuku*: Ritual suicide. See also *Hara-kiri* and *Junshi*.

*Sessho*: See Regent.

*Shakai Minshutō* (**Socialist Democratic Party**): A political party founded in 1901 after the Society for the Study of Socialism (*Shakai Shugi Kenkyukai*) was disbanded.

*Shakai Shugi Kenkyukai* (**Society for the Study of Socialism**): A political party founded in 1896. It was later reestablished in 1901 as the Socialist Democratic Party (*Shakai Minshutō*).

*Shidai Zaibatsu* (**"Big Four"**): Financial clique involving Mitsubishi, Mitsui, Sumitomo and Yasuda.

*Shimpan* (**"family"**) *daimyō*: Branch houses of Tokugawa Ieyasu. Compare to *Fudai* and *Tozama*.

*Shin Fujin Kyokai* (**New Woman's Association**): A women's group founded by Hiratsuka *Raichō* with feminists Ichikawa Fusae and Oku Mumeo in 1920.

*Shinkigen*: A socialist monthly magazine briefly published in 1905–1906.

*Shinko Zaibatsu* (**"new group"**): Financial cliques that surfaced after the establishment of Manchukuo in 1932.

*Shinobi*: Alternate reading of kanji commonly read as *ninja*.

**Shinpoto (Progressive Party):** A political party founded by Ōkuma Shigenobu in 1896.

*Shinsengumi* (**"Newly Selected Corps"**): A special assassination corps employed by the Tokugawa *bakufu* at the end of their era of rule.

*Shinshūkyō* (**"New Religions"**): The creation of several religious movements from the 1830s.

*Shishi* (**"men of purpose"**): Bakumatsu terrorists who attacked Tokugawa loyalists, claiming to be divinely inspired on behalf of the emperor.

*Shōen*: Tax-free estates granted to local leaders in return for land reclamation, military, or religious purposes.

**Shōgun:** Literally, "a commander of a force"; a military rank and historical title for a hereditary military ruler of Japan.

**Shōgunate:** Name commonly given to the (*bakufu*) government of the shōgun.

**Shukai oyobi Seishaho:** Law on Assembly and Political Association passed in 1890.

**"Six National Histories":** See *Rikkokushi*.

**Socialist Democratic Party (*Shakai Minshutō*):** A political party founded in 1901 after the Society for the Study of Socialism (*Shakai Shugi Kenkyukai*) had been disbanded.

**Society for the Study of Socialism (*Shakai Shugi Kenkyukai*):** A political party founded in 1896. It was later reestablished in 1901 as the Socialist Democratic Party (*Shakai Minshutō*).

**Sōhei:** Buddhist warrior monks.

**Sonno-jōi ("Revere the Emperor—Expel the Barbarians"):** Slogan of the royalists during the Bakumatsu era.

**Sonno-tōkan ("Revere the Emperor—Eliminate the Evils"):** Slogan used by 1930s Young Officer radicals in the army to advocate the Shōwa Restoration.

**Sōtoku:** Japanese Governor-General of Korea, after the 1910 annexation.

**Southern Court:** An imperial split that started when the emperor Go-Daigo fled to Yoshino in 1336. The "Southern Court" was reconciled with the "Northern Court" in Kyoto in 1392.

**"Special Higher Police":** See *Tokubetsu kôtô keisatsu*.

State Shintō (*kokka shintō*) established as a political ethos in 19th century. Incorporated Shintō national symbols to legitimize Meiji government.

**Sukuriin-gotaimen ("meeting on the screen"):** Instances when a family at a movie theater glimpsed a father, brother, or son at the war front in a newsreel during World War II.

**Tairo ("Great Elder"):** Chief counselor of the Tokugawa *bakufu*. The role was most famously held by Ii Naosuke.

**Tanka:** Traditional poetry form consisting of only 31 syllables in lines of five and seven syllables.

**Tenko ("changing directions"):** Political conversion by leftists in the 1930s and 1940s.

**Tennō kikansetsu:** See Organ Theory.

**Tennō taisei:** See Emperor-centered nationalism.

**Teppo:** Arquebus gun introduced into Japan in the mid-16th century.

**Three-All Campaign ("loot all, burn all, kill all"):** Japan's scorched-earth campaign in northern China in 1941.

**Three Principles of the People (*Sanmin zhuyi*):** Concepts expressed by Sun Yat-sen to create nationalist-socialist government. See Tongmenghui.

**Tōa Dōbunkai ("East Asia Common Culture Association"):** See *Dōbunkai*.

**Todome:** Chopping off of the head; the *coup de grâce* in sword warfare.

**Tōkan:** The Japanese Resident-General in Korea during 1905–1910.

**Tokkōtai:** Special Attack Squads (*Tokubetsu kōgekita*); also known as Kamikaze.

**Tokubetsu kôtô keisatsu ("Special Higher Police"):** A police squad empowered by the Peace Preservation Law of 1925.

**Tonghak ("Eastern School"):** Korean peasant rebellion, 1893–1894.

**Tongmenghui ("Revolutionary Alliance"):** Chinese political party founded in August 1905 by Sun Yat-sen in Tokyo.

**Toriasukainin:** Private immigration agents in Yokohama and Kobe after 1885.

**Tōsei-ha ("Control Way Faction"):** Group of less radical older officers in the Japanese Army in 1920s and 1930 who became allied with Tōjō Hideki.

**Tōyō dōtoku, seiyō gei ("Eastern ethics as base, Western techniques as means"):** Syncretist idea of Meiji modernizers.

*Tōyō kanj* ("**daily use characters**"): Some 2,000 Sino-Japanese written characters sanctioned by the government for common use in postwar books, newspapers, and other popular printed materials.

*Tozama* ("**outsider**") *daimyō*: Former enemies of Tokugawa Ieyasu prior to the Battle of Sekigahara. Compare to *Fudai* and *Shimpan*.

"**Transcendent cabinets**" (*chōzen naikaku*): Meiji *genrō*'s preference for cabinets formed without political party members.

**Turtle ships**: See *Kobukson*.

*Uibyong*: Irregular anti-Japanese peasant militias in Korea.

*Uji*: The premodern hereditary clans in Japan.

*Uyoku*: Postwar political right-wing groups.

"**Violent incidents**" (*gekika-jiken*): Generic name for peasant uprisings.

*Wakō* ("**Japanese pirates**"): Name given to multi-ethnic pirates between Japan and China beginning in the 13th century.

"**Warrior Monks**": See *Sohei*.

"**War tales**": See *Gunki monogatari*.

*Yomihonkei*: Recited-text lineage of Warrior Tales. See also *Kataribonkei*.

*Yonaoshi*: Meiji-era quasi-protests such as the millennial World Renewal or pilgrimages.

*Yumiya no narai* ("**learning the bow and arrow**"): The samurai martial arts.

*Zaibatsu* ("**financial clique**"): Economic-industrial conglomerates (e.g., Mitsui, Miysubishi) that existed from the 1880s to 1945.

*Zazen*: Zen meditation.

*Zen-Nihon Gakusei Jichikai Sōrengō* ("**All-Japan Federation of Student Self-Government Associations**"): Proper name of the student postwar organization Zengakuren.

# Bibliography

Abe Nornes, Mark, and Fukushima, Yukio. *Japan/America Film Wars: World War II Propaganda and Its Cultural Contexts*. Chur, Switzerland/Langhorne, PA: Harwood Academic Publishers, 1994.

Adachi, Ken. *The Enemy That Never Was: A History of the Japanese Canadians*. Toronto: McClelland and Stewart, 1976.

Adachi Nobuko, ed. *Japanese and Nikkei at Home and Abroad: Negotiating Identities in a Global World*. NY: Cambria Press, 2010.

Adachi Nobuko, ed. *Japanese Diasporas: Unsung Past, Conflicting Presents, and Uncertain Futures*. London/New York: Routledge, 2006.

Adachi Nobuko. Racial Journeys: The Japanese-Peruvians in Peru, the United States, and Japan. *Japan Focus* (refereed electronic journal). Available at: http://japanfocus.org/. Accessed September 7, 2007.

Adolphson, Mikael S. *The Teeth and Claws of the Buddha: Monastic Warriors and Sōhei in Japanese History*. Honolulu: University of Hawai'i Press, 2007.

Agawa Hiroyuki. *The Reluctant Admiral: Yamamoto and the Imperial Navy*. Tokyo: Kondansha International, 1979.

Akima Toshio. "The Myth of the Goddess of the Undersea World and the Tale of Empress Jingū's Subjugation of Silla." *Japanese Journal of Religious Studies* 20, nos. 2/3 (June–September 1993): 95–185.

Akita, George. *Foundations of Constitutional Government in Modern Japan, 1868–1900*. Cambridge, MA: Harvard University Press, 1967.

Alexander, Joseph H. *Utmost Savagery: The Three Days of Tarawa*. Annapolis, MD: Naval Institute Press, 1995.

Alexander, Joseph. *Closing In: Marines in the Seizure of Iwo Jima*. Washington, DC: History and Museums Division, Headquarters, U.S. Marine Corps, 1994.

Allen, J. Michael. "The Price of Identity: The 1923 Kanto Earthquake and Its Aftermath." *Korean Studies* 129 (1996): 64–93.

Allen, Louis. *Singapore, 1941–1942*. Newark: University of Delaware Press, 1977.

Ames, Roger. "*Bushidō*: Mode or Ethic?," in Nancy Hume, ed., *Japanese Aesthetics and Japanese Culture: A Reader*. Albany, NY: State University of New York Press, 1995: 223–240.

Anderson, Joseph L., and Donald Richie. *The Japanese Film: Art and Industry*. Princeton, NJ: Princeton University Press, 1982: 126–158.

Appleman, Roy E., James M. Burns, Russell A. Gugeler, and John Stevens. *United States Army in World War II: The War in the Pacific. Okinawa: The Last Battle*. Washington, DC: U.S. Army, 1948.

Apter, David, and Nagayo Sawa. *Against the State: Politics and Social Protest in Japan*. Cambridge, MA: Harvard University Press, 1984.

Asakawa Kan'ichi. *The Early Institutional Life of Japan: A Study in the Reform of 645 A.D.* New York: Paragon Book Reprint Corp., 1963.

Aston, W. G. *Nihongi: Chronicles of Japan from the Earliest Times to A.D. 697. C.E.* New York: Tuttle, 1972.

Auslin, Michael R., *Negotiating with Imperialism: The Unequal Treaties and the Culture of Japanese Diplomacy.* Cambridge, MA: Harvard University Press, 2004.

Aydin, Cemil, *The Politics of Anti-Westernism in Asia: Visions of World Order in Pan-Islamic and Pan-Asian Thought.* New York: Columbia University Press, 1993.

Azuma, Eiichiro. "Wakamatsu Colony," in Brian Niiya, ed. *Encyclopedia of Japanese American History: An A-to-Z Reference from 1868 to the Present.* New York: Checkmark Books, 2000: 406.

Azuma, Eiichiro. *Between Two Empires: Race History and Transnationalism in Japanese America.* NY: Oxford University Press, 2005.

Bailey, Jackson H. "The Meiji Leadership: Matsukata Masayoshi," in *Japan Examined: Perspectives in Modern Japanese History.* Honolulu: University of Hawaii Press, 1983.

Ball, Howard. *Justice Downwind: America's Atomic Testing Program in the 1950s.* New York: Oxford University Press, 1986.

Bamba, Nobuya. *Japanese Diplomacy in a Dilemma; New Light on Japan's China Policy, 1924–1929.* Vancouver: University of British Columbia Press, 1972.

Banno Junji. *The Establishment of the Japanese Constitutional System.* London: Routledge, 1992.

Barham, Tony. *Not the Slightest Chance: The Defence of Hong Kong, 1941.* Hong Kong: University of Hong Kong Press, 2003.

Barnhart, Michael A. *Japan Prepares for Total War: The Search for Economic Security, 1919–1941.* Ithaca, NY: Cornell University Press, 1987.

Barrow, Clayton J., ed. *America Spreads Her Sails: U.S. Sea Power in the 19th Century.* Annapolis, MD: Naval Institute Press, 1973.

Barshay, Andrew E. "Imagining Democracy in Postwar Japan: Maruyama Masao as a Political Thinker," in Andrew Barshay, ed. *The Social Sciences in Modern Japan: The Marxian and Modernist Traditions.* Berkeley: University of California Press, 2004: 197–239.

Bartholomew, James. *The Formation of Science in Japan: Building a Research Tradition.* New Haven: Yale University Press, 1989.

Baskett, Michael, *The Attractive Empire: Transnational Film Culture in Imperial Japan.* Honolulu: University of Hawai'i Press, 2008.

Batten, Bruce. "Foreign Threat and Domestic Reform: The Emergence of the *Ritsuryō* State." *Monumenta Nipponica* 41, no. 2 (Summer 1986): 199–219.

Beasley, W. G. *The Japanese Experience: A Short History of Japan.* Berkeley: University of California Press, 1999.

Beasley, W. G. *The Meiji Restoration.* Stanford, CA: Stanford University Press, 1972.

Beauchamp, Edward, and Akira Iriye, eds. *Foreign Employees in Nineteenth-Century Japan.* Boulder, CO: Westview Press, 1990.

Beckmann, George M. *The Making of the Meiji Constitution: The Oligarchs and the Constitutional Development of Japan, 1868–1891.* Lawrence, KS: University of Kansas Press, 1969.

Bellah, Robert N. "Ienaga Saburō and the Search for Meaning in Modern Japan," in Marius B. Jansen, ed. *Changing Japanese Attitudes toward Modernization.* Princeton, NJ: Princeton University Press, 1965: 369–423.

Bellah, Robert N. "Notes on Maruyama Masao," in Robert Bellah, ed. *Imagining Japan: The Japanese Tradition and Its Modern Interpretation.* Berkeley: University of California Press, 2003: 369–423.

Belote, James H., and William M. Belote. *Typhoon of Steel: The Battle for Okinawa.* New York: Harper and Row, 1970.

Bendersky, J. W. *The Jewish Threat: Anti-Semitic Politics of the U.S. Army.* New York: Basic Books, 2000.

Bergerud, Eric. *Fire in the Sky: The Air War in the South Pacific*. Boulder, CO: Westview Press, 2000.

Bergerud, Eric. *Touched with Fire: The Land War in the South Pacific*. New York: Penguin Books, 1996.

Bernd, Martin. *Japan and Germany in the Modern World*. Providence, RI: Berghahn Books, 1995.

Berry, Mary Elizabeth. *Hideyoshi*. Cambridge, MA: Harvard University Press, 1982.

Bialock, David T. *Eccentric Spaces, Hidden Histories: Narrative, Ritual, and Royal Authority from The Chronicle of Japan to The Tale of the Heike*. Stanford, CA: Stanford University Press, 2006.

Bix, Herbert P. *Hirohito and the Making of Modern Japan*. New York: Harper Collins, 2000.

Black, John R. *Young Japan: Yokohama and Yedo 1858–79*. Oxford, UK: Oxford University Press, 1969.

Blacker, Carmen. *The Japanese Enlightenment: A Study of the Writings of Fukuzawa Yukichi*. Cambridge, UK: Cambridge University Press, 1964.

Blackwood, Thomas. "Bushidō Baseball? Three 'Fathers' and the Invention of a Tradition." *Social Science Japan Journal* 11, no 2 (2008): 223–240.

Blair, Alexander. "Justice Undone: The Trial of General Araki Sadao." *International Journal of Interdisciplinary Social Sciences* 5, no. 4 (Fall 2001): 107–120.

Blum, Ron. *The Siege of Port Arthur: The Russo-Japanese War through the Stereoscope*. New York: Harcourt-Brace, 1987.

Blusse, Leonard, Willem Remmelink, and Ivo Smits, eds. *Bridging the Divide: 400 Years of the Netherlands and Japan*. Leiden: Hotei Publishing, 2000.

Bornter, Michael A. *Imperial Japanese Good Luck Flags and One-Thousand Stitch Belts*. Atglen, PA: Schiffer, 2008.

Bowen, Roger W. *Rebellion and Democracy in Meiji Japan*. Berkeley: University of California Press, 1980.

Boyd, Carl. *The Extraordinary Envoy: General Hiroshi Æshima and Diplomacy in the Third Reich, 1934–1939*. Washington, DC: University Press of America, 1980.

Braddick, C. W. *Japan and the Sino-Soviet Alliance, 1950–1964: In the Shadow of the Monolith*. New York: St. Antony's Series with Palgrave/Macmillan, 2004.

Bradford, James C., ed., *Captains of the Old Steam Navy: Makers of the American Naval Tradition*. Annapolis, MD: Naval Institute Press, 1986.

Bradley, James. *Flags of Our Fathers*. New York: Bantam Books, 2000.

British Documents on Foreign Affairs. *Reports and Papers from the Foreign Office Confidential Print, Part One, Series E: Asia, vol. 8*. Frederick, MD: University Publications of America, 1989.

Brooke, Geoffrey. *Singapore's Dunkirk*. London: Cooper, 1989.

Brown, Delmer M., ed. *Cambridge History of Japan I: Ancient Japan*. Cambridge, UK: Cambridge University Press, 1993.

Brown, Delmer M., and Ichirō Ishida, eds. *Gukanshō: The Future and the Past*. Berkeley: University of California Press, 1979.

Brown, Sidney D. "Ōkubo Toshimichi: His Political and Economic Policies in Early Meiji Japan." *Journal of Asian Studies* 21, no 2 (February 1962): 137–265.

Browne, Courtney. *Tōjō: The Last Banzai*. New York: Holt, Rinehart and Winston, 1967.

Brownlee, John. *Japanese Historians and the National Myths, 1600–1945: The Age of the Gods*. Vancouver: University of British Columbia Press, 1967.

Brownlee, John S. *Political Thought in Japanese Historical Writing, from Kojiki (712) to Tokushi Yoron (1712)*. Waterloo, ON: Wilfrid Laurier University Press, 1991.

Buckley, Roger. *US-Japan Alliance Diplomacy, 1945–1990*. New York: Cambridge University Press, 1992.

Burdick, Charles B. *The Japanese Siege of Tsingtao: World War I in Asia*. Hamden, CT: Archon Books, 1976.

Burkman, Thomas. *Japan and the League of Nations, Empire and World Order,*

*1914–1938*. Honolulu: University of Hawaii, 2008.

Burns, Richard Dean, and Edward M. Bennett, eds. *Diplomats in Crisis: United States–Chinese–Japanese Relations, 1919–1941.* Santa Barbara, CA: ABC-CLIO, 1974.

Busch, Noel F. *The Emperor's Sword: Japan vs. Russia in the Battle of Tsushima.* New York: Funk and Wagnalls, 1969.

Butow, Robert J. C. *Japan's Decision to Surrender.* Stanford, CA: Stanford University Press, 1954.

Butow, Robert. *Tōjō and the Coming of the War.* Princeton: Princeton University Press, 1965.

Byas, Hugh. *Government by Assassination.* New York: Alfred A. Knopf, 1942.

Byrd, Martha. *Chennault: Giving Wings to the Tiger.* Tuscaloosa: University of Alabama Press, 1987.

Carter, Steven D. *Regent Redux: A Life of the Statesman-Scholar Ichijō Kaneyoshi.* Ann Arbor, MI: University of Michigan Press, 1996.

Chaiklin, Martha *Cultural Commerce and Dutch Commercial Culture: The Influence of European Material Culture on Japan, 1700–1850.* Leiden: CNWS, 2003.

Chao, Hui-Hsuan. *Musical Taiwan under Japanese Colonial Rule.* Ph.D. dissertation, University of Michigan, 2009.

Chen, Edward I. "Gōtō Shimpei, Japan's Colonial Administrator in Taiwan: A Critical Reexamination." *American Asian Review* 13, no. 1 (1995): 29–59.

Ch'i Hsi-sheng. "The Military Dimension, 1942–1945," in James C. Hsiung and Steven I. Levine, eds. *China's Bitter Victory: The War with Japan, 1937–1945.* Armonk, NY: M. E. Sharpe, 1992: 157–184.

Ch'i Hsi-sheng. *Nationalist China at War: Military Defeats and Political Collapse, 1937–45.* Ann Arbor: University of Michigan Press, 1982.

Chow, Tse-Tsung. *The May Fourth Movement: Intellectual Revolution in Modern China.* Cambridge, MA: Harvard University Press, 1960.

Clarke, Peter B. *Japanese New Religions: In Global Perspective.* Richmond, UK: Curzon, 2000.

Clausen, Henry C. *Pearl Harbor: Final Judgment.* New York: Crown, 1992.

Cleary, Thomas, trans. *The Code of the Samurai: A Modern Translation of the Bushidō Shoshinshū of Taira Shigesuke* [Daidōji Yūzan]. Rutland, VT: Tuttle, 1999.

Coble, Parks M. *Facing Japan: Chinese Politics and Japanese Imperialism, 1931–1937.* Cambridge, MA: Harvard University Press, 1991.

Cogan, Thomas J. *The Tale of the Soga Brothers.* Tokyo: University of Tokyo Press, 1987.

Como, Michael. *Shōtoku: Ethnicity, Ritual, and Violence in the Japanese Buddhist Tradition* New York: Oxford University Press, 2008.

Conlan, Thomas. *In Little Need of Divine Intervention.* Ithaca, NY: Cornell University Press, 2001.

Connaughton, R. M. *The War of the Rising Sun and Tumbling Bear: A Military History of the Russo-Japanese War, 1904–5.* New York: Routledge, 1988.

Connors, Lesley. *The Emperor's Adviser: Saionji Kinmochi and Pre-War Japanese Politics.* London: Croom Helm, 1987.

Cook, Harold F. *Korea's 1884 Incident: Its Background and Kim Ok-kyun's Elusive Dream.* Seoul: Royal Asiatic Society, Korea Branch, 1972.

Cooper, Kent. *Barriers Down.* New York: Farrar and Rinehart, 1942.

Coox, Alvin D. *Nomonhan: Japan against Russia, 1939.* Stanford, CA: Stanford University Press, 1988.

Coox, Alvin D. *Tōjō.* New York: Ballantine Books, 1975.

Cortesi, Lawrence. *Target: Tokyo.* New York: Kensington, 1983.

Costello, John. *The Pacific War 1941–1945: The first Comprehensive One-Volume Account of the Causes and Conduct of World War II in the Pacific.* New York: Atlantic Communications, 1981.

Craig, Albert M. *Chōshū and the Meiji Restoration.* Cambridge, MA: Harvard University Press, 1961.

Craig, Albert M. *Civilization and Enlightenment: The Early Thought of Fukuzawa Yukichi.* Cambridge, MA: Harvard University Press, 2009.

Craig, William. *The Fall of Japan.* New York: Dial Press, 1967.

Crawcour, E. Sydney. "Economic Change in the Nineteenth Century," in Marius B. Jansen, ed. *The Cambridge History of Japan: Volume 5, The Nineteenth Century.* Cambridge, UK: Cambridge University Press, 1989, 423–487.

Crawford, Danny J. *The 2nd Marine Division and Its Regiments.* Washington, DC: History and Museums Division, Headquarters, U.S. Marine Corps, 2001.

Crawford, Miki Ward, Katie Kaori Hayashi, and Shizuko Suenaga. *Japanese War Brides in America: An Oral History.* Santa Barbara: ABC-CLIO, 2010.

Crawford, Suzanne Jones. "The *Maria Luz* Affair: A Study of Late Nineteenth Century Japanese Diplomatic Relations." *The Historian* 46, no. 4 (August 2007): 583–596.

Cronin, Joseph. *The Life of Seinosuke: Dr. Oishi and the High Treason Incident.* Kyoto: White Tiger Press, 2007.

Crowley, James. *Japan's Quest for Autonomy: National Security and Foreign Policy, 1930–1938.* Princeton, NJ: Princeton University Press, 1966.

Cutler, Thomas J. *The Battle of Leyte Gulf, 23–26 October 1944.* New York: Harper Collins, 1994.

Daniels, Roger. *The Politics of Prejudice: The Anti-Japanese Movement in California and the Struggle for Japanese Exclusion.* Berkeley: University of California Press, 1962.

de Bary, William Theodore, et al., eds. *Sources of Japanese Tradition,* vol. 2. 2nd ed. New York: Columbia University Press, 2005.

Dening, Walter. *The Life of Toyotomi Hideyoshi.* 3rd ed. London: Kegan Paul, Trench, Trubner, 1930.

Dickinson, Frederick R. *War and National Reinvention: Japan in the Great War, 1914–1919.* Cambridge, MA: Harvard University Asia Center, 1999.

Doolittle, James H. *I Could Never Be So Lucky Again.* New York: Bantam Books, 1991.

Dore, R. P. "Notes and Comment: Textbook Censorship in Japan: The Ienaga Case." *Pacific Affairs* 43, no. 4 (Winter 1970–1971): 548–556.

Dorn, Frank. *The Sino-Japanese War, 1937–41: From Marco Polo Bridge to Pearl Harbor.* New York: Macmillan, 1974.

Dower, John W. *Embracing Defeat: Japan in the Wake of World War II.* New York: W. W. Norton/New Press, 1999.

Dower, John W. *Empire and Aftermath: Yoshida Shigeru and the Japanese Experience, 1878–1954.* Cambridge, MA: Harvard University Press, 1979.

Dower, John. *Peace and Democracy in Two Systems: External Policy and Internal Conflict.* Berkeley: University of California Press, 1993.

Dower, John. *War without Mercy: Race and Power in the Pacific War.* New York: Pantheon Books, 1986.

Dowsey, Stuart. *Zengakuren: Japan's Revolutionary Students.* Berkeley, CA: Ishi Press, 1970.

Drea, Edward J. *In the Service of the Emperor: Essays on the Imperial Japanese Army.* Lincoln: University of Nebraska Press, 1998.

Drea, Edward J. *Japan's Imperial Army: Its Rise and Fall, 1853–1945.* Lawrence, KS: University of Kansas Press, 2009.

Duara, Prasenjit. *Sovereignty and Authenticity: Manchukuo and the East Asian Modern.* New York: Rowman and Littlefield, 2003.

Dubreuil, Chisato O., and William W. Fitzhugh, eds. *Ainu: Spirit of a Northern People.* Washington, DC: Arctic Studies Center, National Museum of Natural History, Smithsonian Institution, in association with University of Washington Press, 1999.

Dudden, Alexis. *Japan's Colonization of Korea: Discourse and Power.* Honolulu: University of Hawai'i Press, 2004.

Dunn, Frederick S. *Peace-Making and the Settlement with Japan.* Princeton, NJ: Princeton University Press, 1963.

Dunscomb, Paul E. *Japan's Siberian Intervention, 1918–1922: "A Great Disobedience against the People."* Lantham, MD: Lexington Books, 2011.

Duus, Masayo. *Tokyo Rose: Orphan of the Pacific.* Tokyo: Kodansha International, 1979.

Duus, Peter. *The Abacus and the Sword: The Japanese Penetration of Korea, 1895–1910.* Berkeley: University of California Press, 1998.

Duus, Peter. *Modern Japan,* Boston: Houghton Mifflin, 1998.

Duus, Peter. "Socialism, Liberalism, and Marxism, 1901–1931," in *Cambridge History of Japan, Volume 6: The Twentieth Century.* New York: Cambridge University Press, 1988: 622–675.

Eastlake, Warrington, and Yamada Yoshi-aki. *Heroic Japan: A History of the War between China and Japan.* 1897. Reprint, Washington, DC: University Publications of America, 1979.

Edgerton, Robert B. *Warriors of the Rising Sun: A History of the Japanese Military.* New York: Norton, 1997.

Edoin, Hoito. *The Night Tokyo Burned.* New York: St. Martin's Press, 1987.

Edström, Bert. *Japan's Evolving Foreign Policy Doctrine: From Yoshida to Miyazawa.* Basingstoke, UK/New York: Palgrave, 1999.

Elleman, Bruce A. *Modern Chinese Warfare, 1795–1989.* London: Routledge, 2001.

Esenbel, Selçuk. "Japan's Global Claim to Asia and the World of Islam: Transnational Nationalism and World Power, 1900–1945." *American Historical Review* 109, no. 4 (October 2004): 1140–1170.

Evans, David C., and Mark R. Peattie. *Kaigun: Strategy, Tactics, and Technology in the Imperial Japanese Navy, 1887–1941.* Annapolis, MD: Naval Institute Press, 1997.

Falk, Stanley Lawrence. *Bataan: The March of Death.* New York: Norton, 1962.

Farrell, William R. *Blood and Rage: The Story of the Japanese Red Army.* Lexington, KY: Lexington Books, 1990.

Farris, William Wayne. *Heavenly Warriors: The Evolution of Japan's Military, 500–1300.* Cambridge, MA: Harvard East Asian Monographs, 1992.

Farris, William Wayne. "Sacred Texts and Buried Treasures: Issues in the Historical Archaeology of Ancient Japan." *Monumenta Nipponica* 54, no. 1 (1998): 123–126.

Field, James A., Jr. *The Japanese at Leyte Gulf: The Shō Operation.* Princeton, NJ: Princeton University Press, 1947.

Finkelstein, Norman. *The Emperor General: A Biography of Douglas MacArthur.* Bloomington, IN: Author House, 2001.

Finn, Richard B. *Winners in Peace: MacArthur, Yoshida, and Postwar Japan.* Berkeley: University of California Press, 1992.

Ford, Daniel. *Flying Tigers: Claire Chennault and the American Volunteer Group.* Washington, DC: Smithsonian Institution Press, 1995.

Fox, Grace. *Great Britain and Japan, 1858–1883.* Oxford, UK: Clarendon Press, 1969.

Frank, Richard B. *Downfall: The End of the Imperial Japanese Empire.* New York: Random House, 1999.

Frank, Richard B. *Guadalcanal: The Definitive Account of the Landmark Battle.* New York: Random House, 1990.

Fraser, Andrew. "The Osaka Conference of 1875." *Journal of Asian Studies* 26, no. 4 (August 1967): 589–610.

Friday, Karl F. *The First Samurai: The Life and Legend of the Warrior Rebel, Taira Masakado.* Hoboken, NJ: Wiley, 2007.

Friday, Karl. *Hired Swords: The Rise of Private Warrior Power in Early Japan.* Stanford, CA: Stanford University Press, 1992.

Friday, Karl F. *Samurai, Warfare and the State in Early Medieval Japan.* London: Routledge, 2003.

Frühstück, Sabine. *Uneasy Warriors: Gender, Memory and Popular Culture in the Japanese Army.* Berkeley: University of California Press, 2007.

FRUS, United States Department of State. *Papers Relating to the Foreign Relations of the United States, Japan: 1931–1941,* vol. I. Washington, DC: U.S. Government Printing Office, 1931–1941: 224–229. Available at: http://digital.library.wisc.edu/1711.dl/FRUS.FRUS193141v01.

Fuchida Mitsuo and Okumiya Masatake. *Midway: The Battle That Doomed Japan: The Japanese Navy's Story.* Annapolis, MD: Naval Institute Press, 1955.

Fujita, Neil S. *Japan's Encounter with Christianity: The Catholic Mission in Pre-modern Japan.* New York: Paulist Press, 1991

Fujita, Shozo. "The Spirit of the Meiji Revolution." *Japan Interpreter* 6, no. 1 (Spring 1970): 78–88.

Fujita Tokutarō. *Shishi shiikashū.* Tokyo: Shōgakkan, 1942.

Fujita Yūji, ed. *"Kimigayo" no kigen: "Kimigayo" no honka wa banka datta.* Tokyo: Akashi Shoten, 2005.

Fukuzawa, Yukichi. *The Autobiography of Yukichi Fukuzawa.* New York: Columbia University Press, 1966.

Gailey, Harry. *The Liberation of Guam: 21 July–10 August, 1944.* Novato, CA: Presidio Press, 1988.

Garon, Sheldon. *Molding Japanese Minds: The State in Everyday Life.* Princeton: Princeton University Press, 1997.

Gaskins, C., and V. Hawkins. *The Ways of the Samurai.* New York: Byron Preiss Visual Publications, 2003.

Geotham, Ellen Van. *Nagaoka: Japan's Forgotten Capital.* Leiden, Netherlands: Brill Academic Publishers, 2008.

Gerow, Aaron. "Narrating the Nationality of a Cinema: The Case of Japanese Prewar Film," in Alan Tansman, ed. *The Culture of Japanese Fascism.* Durham, NC: Duke University Press, 2009 134–55.

Giffard, Sydney. "The Development of Democracy in Japan." *Asian Affairs* 27, no. 3 (1996): 275–284.

Glantz, David B. *August Storm: The Soviet 1945 Strategic Offensive in Manchuria.* Leavenworth Paper no. 7. Fort Leavenworth, KS: Combat Studies Institute, U.S. Army Command and General Staff College, 1983.

Glines, Carroll V. *The Doolittle Raid: America's Daring First Strike against Japan.* New York: Orion, 1988.

Goble, Andrew Edmund. *Kenmu: Go-Daigo's Revolution.* Cambridge, MA: Harvard University Press, 1996.

Golovnin, Vasili, M. *Narrative of My Captivity in Japan during the Years 1811, 1812 and 1813.* 2 vols. Richmond, UK: Japan Library, 2000.

Gong, Gerrit, and Teo, Victor, eds. *Reconceptualising the Divide: Identity, Memory, and Nationalism in Sino-Japanese Relations.* Newcastle, UK: Cambridge Scholars, 2010.

Gordon, Andrew, ed. *Postwar Japan as History.* Berkeley: University of California Press, 1993.

Gordon, Beate Sirota. *The Only Woman in the Room.* Tokyo: Kodansha International, 1997.

Gordon, Paul Lauren. "Human Rights in History: Diplomacy and Racial Equality at the Paris Peace Conference." *Diplomatic History* 2, no. 3 (1998) 257–278.

Gow, Ian. *Okinawa, 1945: Gateway to Japan.* Garden City, NY: Doubleday, 1985.

Graves, William S. *America's Siberian Adventure.* NY: Cape & Smith, 1931. Available at: http://www.marxists.org/archive/graves/1931/siberian-adventure/index.htm.

Greenlaw, Olga. *The Lady and the Tigers: Remembering the Flying Tigers of World War II,* edited by Daniel Ford. San Jose, CA: Writers Club Press, 2002.

Griffis, William Elliott. *Townsend Harris: First American Envoy in Japan.* Cambridge, UK: Cambridge University Press, 1895.

Grossberg, Kenneth Alan. *Japan's Renaissance: The Politics of the Muromachi Bakufu.* Ithaca, NY: Cornell University Press, 2001.

Guirand, Felix. *New Larousse Encyclopedia of Mythology*. New York: Paul Hamlin. 1959.

Hackett, Roger F. *Yamagata Aritomo in the Rise of Modern Japan, 1838–1922*. Cambridge, MA: Harvard University Press, 1971.

Haley, John Owen. *The Spirit of Japanese Law*. Athens, GA: University of Georgia Press, 1998.

Hall, John W. *Government and Local Power in Japan, 500–1700: A Study Based on Hizen Province*. Princeton: Princeton University Press, 1966; Ann Arbor, MI: University of Michigan Press, 1999.

Hall, John Whitney, *Tanuma Okitsugu, 1719–1788: Forerunner of Modern Japan*. Cambridge, MA: Harvard University Press, 1955.

Hall, John Whitney, and Jeffrey P. Mass, eds. *Medieval Japan: Essays in Institutional History*. New Haven: Yale University Press, 1974.

Hall, John W., and Toyoda Takeshi, eds. *Japan in the Muromachi Age*. Berkeley, CA: University of California Press, 1977.

Hall, Robert King, ed. *Kokutai no hongi: Cardinal Principles of the National Entity of Japan*, translated by John Owen Gauntlett. Cambridge, MA: Harvard University Press, 1949.

Hamada, Kenji. *Prince Itō*. Tokyo: Sanseido, 1936.

Hamel, Eric M. *Guadalcanal: Decision at Sea: The Naval Battle of Guadalcanal, November 13–15, 1942*. New York: Crown, 1988.

Hammer, Joshua. *Yokohama Burning: The Deadly 1923 Earthquake and Fire That Helped Forge the Path to World War II*. New York: Simon & Schuster, 2006.

Hanashiro, Roy. *Thomas William Kinder and the Japanese Imperial Mint, 1868–1875*. Leiden: Brill Academic Publications, 1999.

Hane, Mikiso. *Eastern Phoenix: Japan Since 1945*. Boulder: Westview Press, 1996.

Harada Kumao. *Fragile Victory: Prince Saionji and the 1930 London Treaty Issue, from the Memoirs of Baron Harada Kumao*. Detroit: Wayne State University Press, 1968.

Hardacre, Helen. *Kurozumikyō and the New Japanese Religions*. Princeton: Princeton University Press, 1986.

Hardacre, Helen. *Shintō and the State, 1968–1988*. New Jersey: Princeton University Press, 1991.

Hargreaves, Reginald. *Red Sun Rising: The Siege of Port Arthur*. Philadelphia: Lippincott, 1962.

Harries, Meirion. *Soldiers of the Sun: The Rise and Fall of the Imperial Japanese Army*. New York: Random House, 1994.

Harries, Meirion, and Susie Harries. *Soldiers of the Sun: The Rise and Fall of the Imperial Japanese Army*. New York: Random House, 1991.

Harrington, Ann M. *Japan's Hidden Christians*. Chicago: Loyola University Press, 1993.

Harrington, Peter. *China, 1900: The Eyewitnesses Speak; The Boxer Rebellion as Described by Participants in Letters, Diaries and Photographs*. London: Greenhill Books, 2000.

Harris, Sheldon H. *Factories of Death: Japanese Biological Warfare, 1932–1945, and the American Cover-up*. New York/London: Routledge, 2002.

Harris, Townsend. *The Complete Journal of Townsend Harris*, 2nd ed., edited by Mario E. Cosenza. Tokyo/Rutland, VT: Charles E. Tuttle, 1958.

Haslam, Jonathan. *The Soviet Union and the Threat from the East, 1933–1941*. London: Macmillan, 1992.

Havens, Thomas. *Fire across the Sea: The Vietnam War and Japan 1965–1975*. Princeton, NJ: Princeton University Press, 2006.

Havens, Thomas. *Nishi Amane and Modern Japanese Thought*. Princeton, NJ: Princeton University Press, 1970.

Hayashi, Saburo. *Kogun: The Japanese Army in the Pacific War*. Westport, CT: Greenwood Press, 1959.

Heazle, Michael, and Knight, Nick, eds. *China-Japan Relations in the Twenty-*

*First Century: Creating a Future Past?* Cheltenham, UK/Northampton, MA: Edward Elgar, 2007.

Hesselink, Reinier H. "The Assassination of Henry Heusken." *Monumenta Nipponica* 49, no. 3 (Autumn 1994): 331–351.

Heusken, Henry. *Japan Journal, 1855–1861*, translated by Jeannette C. van der Corput and Robert A. Wilson. New Brunswick, NJ: Rutgers University Press, 1964.

Higashibaba, Ikuo. *Christianity in Early Modern Japan: Kirishitan Belief and Practice.* Boston: Brill, 2001.

High, Peter B. *The Imperial Screen: Japanese Film Culture in the Fifteen Years' War, 1931–1945.* Madison: University of Wisconsin Press, 2003.

Hillsborough, Romulus. *Shinsengumi: The Shōgun's Last Samurai Corps.* New York: Tuttle, 2005.

Hirschmeier, Johannes, and Yui Tsunehiko. *The Development of Japanese Business, 1600–1973.* London: George Allen & Unwin, 1975.

Hoare, J. E. *Britain and Japan: Biographical Portraits, Vol. III.* London: Routledge Curzon, 1999.

Honda, Katsuichi. *The Nanjing Massacre: A Japanese Journalist Confronts Japan's National Shame*, edited by Frank Gibney. Armonk, NY: M. E. Sharpe, 1999.

Horio, Teruhisa. *Educational Thought and Ideology in Modern Japan.* Tokyo: University of Tokyo Press, 1988.

Hotta, Eri. *Pan-Asianism and Japan's War 1931–1945.* New York: Palgrave Macmillan, 2007.

Hough, Richard. *The Fleet That Had to Die.* New York: Viking, 1958.

Howarth, Stephen. *The Fighting Ships of the Rising Sun.* New York: Atheneum, 1983.

Howe, Russell Warren. *The Hunt for "Tokyo Rose."* Lanham, MD: Madison Books, 1990.

Howell, David L. *Geographies of Identity in Nineteenth-Century Japan.* Berkeley, CA: University of California Press, 2005.

Howes, John F. *Japan's Modern Prophet: Uchimura Kanzo, 1861–1930.* Vancouver: University of British Columbia Press, 2006.

Hoyt, Edwin P. *The Fall of Tsingtao.* London: A. Barker, 1975.

Hoyt, Edwin P. *Three Military Leaders: Heihachirō Tōgō, Isoroku Yamamoto, Tomoyuki Yamashita.* New York Kodansha International, 1993.

Hoyt, Edwin P. *Yamamoto: The Man Who Planned Pearl Harbor.* New York: McGraw-Hill, 1990.

Hoyt, Edwin Palmer. *Warlord: Tōjō against the World.* Lanham, MD: Scarborough House, 1993.

Hsiung, James C., and Steven I. Levine, eds. *China's Bitter Victory: The War with Japan, 1937–1945* Armonk: M. E. Sharpe, 1992.

Huber, Thomas M. *The Revolutionary Origins of Modern Japan.* Stanford, CA: Stanford University Press, 1981.

Humphreys, Leonard A. *The Way of the Heavenly Sword: The Japanese Army in the 1920s.* Stanford, CA: Stanford University Press, 1996.

Hunt, Michael H. *The Making of a Special Relationship: The United States and China to 1914.* New York: Columbia University Press, 1983.

Hunter, Janet, ed. *Concise Dictionary of Modern Japanese History.* Berkeley: University of California Press, 1984.

Hurst, G. Cameron. *Armed Martial Arts of Japan: Swordsmanship and Archery.* New Haven: Yale University Press, 1998.

Hurst, G. Cameron III. *Insei: Abdicated Sovereigns in the Politics of Late Heian Japan.* New York: Columbia University Press, 1976.

Hyoe Murakami and Thomas J. Harper, eds., *Great Historical Figures of Japan.* Tokyo: Japan Culture Institute, 1978.

Ideishi Takehiko. *The True Story of the Siege of Kumamoto Castle.* New York: Vantage Press, 1976.

Ienaga, Saburō. *Minobe Tatsukichi no shisōshi teki kenkyū.* Tokyo: Iwanami shoten, 1964.

Ienaga, Saburô. *Japan's Past, Japan's Future.* Lanham, MD: Rowman and Littlefield, 2001.

Ijichi, Junsei. *The Life of Marquis Shigenobu Ōkuma, a Maker of New Japan*. Tokyo: Hokuseido Press, 1940.

Ikeda, Masako Kobayashi. *French Legal Advisor in Meiji Japan (1873–1895): Gustave Émile Boissonade de Fontarabie*. Ph.D. thesis, University of Hawaii, 1997.

Inoue, Mitsusada. *Introduction to Japanese History before Meiji*. Tokyo: Kokusai Bunka Shinkokai (Japan Cultural Society), 1962.

Irish, Ann B. *Hokkaido: A History of Ethnic Transition and Development on Japan's Northern Island*. Jefferson, NC: McFarland & Company, 2009.

Iriye, Akira. *After Imperialism: The Search for a New Order in the Far East, 1921–1931*. Chicago: Imprint Publications, 1990.

Iriye, Akira, ed. *The Chinese and the Japanese: Essays in Political and Cultural Interactions*. Princeton: Princeton University Press, 1980.

Iriye, Akira. *Power and Culture: The Japanese-American War, 1941–1945*. Cambridge, MA: Harvard University Press, 1981.

Ishimitsu, Mahito. *Remembering Aizu: The Testament of Shiba Gorō*, edited and translated by Teruko Craig. Honolulu: University of Hawai'i Press, 1999.

Iwao, Seiichi, ed. *Biographical Dictionary of Japanese History*, translated by Burton Watson. Tokyo: International Society for Educational Information, 1978.

Iwata, Masakazu. *Ōkubo Toshimichi: The Bismarck of Japan*. Berkeley: University of California Press, 1965.

Jaffe, Richard ed. "Religion and the Japanese Empire." *Japanese Journal of Religious Studies* 37, no. 1 (2010): 1–7.

James, D. Clayton. *The Years of MacArthur. Vol. 2, 1941–1945*. Boston: Houghton Mifflin, 1975.

Jannetta, Ann. *The Vaccinators: Smallpox, Medical Knowledge, and the "Opening" of Japan*. Stanford: Stanford University Press, 2007.

Jansen, Marius, ed. *The Emergence of Meiji Japan*. New York: Cambridge University Press, 1995.

Jansen, Marius, *The Japanese and Sun Yat-sen*. Stanford: Stanford University Press, 1954.

Jansen, Marius B. *The Making of Modern Japan*. Cambridge, MA: Belknap Press, 2000.

Jansen, Marius B. "The Meiji Restoration," in Marius B. Jansen, ed. *The Cambridge History of Japan: Vol. 5, The Nineteenth Century*. Cambridge, UK: Cambridge University Press, 1989.

Jansen, Marius B. *Sakamoto Ryōma and the Meiji Restoration*. New York: Columbia University Press, 1994.

Jennes, Joseph. *A History of the Catholic Church in Japan from Its Beginnings to the Early Meiji Era, 1549–1871*. Revised ed. Tokyo: Oriens Institute for Religious Research, 1973.

Johnston, Reginald F. *Twilight in the Forbidden City*. London: Victor Gollancz, 1934.

Johnston, William. *The Modern Epidemic: A History of Tuberculosis in Japan*. Cambridge, MA: Harvard University Press, 1995.

Jones, Hazel. *Live Machines, Hired Foreigners and Meiji Japan*. Vancouver, BC: University of British Columbia, 1980.

Jones, Mark, and Erickson, Steven. "Social and Economic Change in Prewar Japan," in William M. Tsutsui, ed. *A Companion to Japanese History*. New York: Wiley-Blackwell, 2007: 112–145.

Ka, Chih-ming. *Japanese Colonialism in Taiwan: Land Tenure, Development and Dependency, 1895–1945*. Boulder, CO: Westview Press, 1995.

Kabashima Ikuo and Gill Steel. *Changing Politics in Japan*. Ithaca, NY: Cornell University Press, 2010.

Kang, Hildi. *Under the Black Umbrella: Voices from Colonial Korea, 1910–1945*. Ithaca, NY: Cornell University Press, 2001.

Kaplan, David A., and Alec Dubro. *Yakuza: Japan's Criminal Underworld*. Berkeley: University of California Press. 2003.

Karube, Tadashi. *Maruyama Masao and the Fate of Liberalism in Modern Japan*, translated by David Noble. Tokyo: International House of Japan, 2008.

Katsu, Kokichi. *Musui's Story: the Autobiography of a Tokugawa Samurai*. Tucson: University of Arizona Press, 1988.

Kawahara, Toshiaki. *Hirohito and His Times: A Japanese Perspective*. New York: Kodansha, 1990.

Keene, Donald. *Emperor of Japan: Meiji and His World, 1852–1912*. New York: Columbia University Press, 2002.

Kei, Ushimura. *Beyond the "Judgment of Civilization": The Intellectual Legacy of the Japanese War Crimes Trials, 1946–1949*, translated by Steven J. Ericson. Tokyo: International House of Japan, 2003.

Kelly, William W. *Deference and Defiance in Nineteenth-Century Japan*. Princeton: Princeton University Press, 1985.

Kelly, William. "The Spirit and Spectacle of School Baseball: Mass Media, Statemaking and 'Edu-tainment' in Japan, 1905–1935." *Senri Ethnological Studies* 52 (2000): 218–235.

Kersten, Rikki. *Democracy in Postwar Japan: Maruyama Masao and the Search for Autonomy*. London/New York: Routledge, 1996.

Kersten, Rikki. "The Intellectual Culture of Postwar Japan and the 1968–1969 University of Tokyo Struggles: Repositioning the Self in Postwar Thought." *Social Science Japan Journal* 12, no. 2 (2009): 227–245.

Ketelaar, James. *Of Heretics and Martyrs in Meiji Japan: Buddhism and Its Persecution*. Princeton: Princeton University Press, 1990.

Kidder, Jonathan Edward. *Himiko and Japan's Elusive Chiefdom of Yamatai*. Honolulu: University of Hawai'i Press, 2007.

Kido Takayoshi. *The Diary of Kido Takayoshi*, vol. 2, translated by Sidney DeVere Brown. Tokyo: University of Tokyo Press, 1983–1986.

Kim, Djun Kil. *The History of Korea*. Westport, CT: Greenwood Press, 2005.

Kimura, Hiroshi. *Kurillian Knot: A History of Japanese-Russian Border Negotiation*.

Stanford, CA: University of Stanford Press, 2008.

Kinmonth, Earl H. "Fukuzawa Reconsidered: Gakumon No Susume and Its Audience." *Journal of Asian Studies* 37, no. 4 (August 1978): 677–696.

Kirby, E. Stuart. "Heihachirō Tōgō: Japan's Nelson," in Jack Sweetman, ed. *The Great Admirals: Command at Sea, 1587–1945*. Annapolis, MD: Naval Institute Press, 1997: 326–348.

Kirby, S. Woodburn. *Singapore: The Chain of Disaster*. London: Cassell, 1971.

Kirkup, James. "Obituary: Ryoichi Sasakawa." *The Independent*, July 20, 1995, 23A.

Kitaoka, Shin'ichi. "The Army as a Bureaucracy: Japanese Militarism Revisited." *Journal of Military History* 57, no. 5 (October 1993): 67–86.

Kiyoko, Takeda. "Ichikawa Fusae: Pioneer for Women's Rights in Japan." *Japan Quarterly* 31, no. 4 (1984): 410–415.

Kleiner, Jergen. *Korea: A Century of Change*. River Edge, NJ: World Scientific Publishing, 2001.

Koginos, Manny T. *The Panay Incident: Prelude to War*. Lafayette, IN: Purdue University Studies, 1967.

Koschmann, J. Victor. "Maruyama Masao and the Incomplete Project of Modernity," in Masao Miyoshi and H. D. Harootunian, eds. *Postmodernism and Japan*. Durham: Duke University Press, 1989: SSS55–SSS69.

Koschmann, J. Victor. *The Mito Ideology: Discourse, Reform, and Insurrection in Late Tokugawa Japan, 1790–1864*. Berkeley: University of California Press, 1987.

Kristeller, Jean L. "Mishima's Suicide: A Psycho-cultural Analysis." *Psychologia* 16 (1973): 50–59.

Kuroiwa Ichirō. *Kinnō shishi shiikashū*. Tokyo: Shibundō, 1943.

Kuropatkin, Alexei. *The Russian Army and the Japanese War*, translated by Alexander Bertram Lindsay. New York: E. P. Dutton, 1909.

Lael, Richard. *The Yamashita Precedent.* Wilmington, DE: Scholarly Resources, 1982.

La Fargue, Thomas Edward. *China and the World War.* Stanford: Stanford University Press, 1937.

Lafeber, Walter. *The Clash: A History of U.S.-Japan Relations.* New York: Norton, 1997.

Lamberti, Matthew. "Tokugawa Nariaki and the Japanese Imperial Institution: 1853–1858." *Harvard Journal of Asiatic Studies* 32 (1972): 97–123.

Lamers, Jeroen. *Japonius Tyrannus: The Japanese Warlord Oda Nobunaga Reconsidered.* Leiden: Hotei Publishing, 2000.

Large, Stephen S. *Emperor Hirohito and Shōwa Japan: A Political Biography.* London/New York: Routledge, 1992.

Large, Stephen S. *Emperors of the Rising Sun: Three Biographies.* New York: Kodansha International, 1997.

Lebra, Joyce C. *Japan's Greater East Asia Co-prosperity Sphere in World War II: Selected Readings and Documents.* Oxford, UK: Oxford University Press, 1975.

Lebra-Chapman, Joyce. *Ōkuma Shigenobu: Statesman of Meiji Japan.* Canberra: Australian National University Press, 1973.

Lee, Ki-baik. *New History of Korea.* Seoul: Ilcho-gak Company, 1984; Leiden: Brill, 1999.

Lensen, George. *The Russian Push toward Japan.* Princeton, NJ: Princeton University Press, 1958.

Lensen, George A. *The Strange Neutrality: Soviet-Japanese Relations during the Second World War, 1941–1945.* Tallahassee, FL: Diplomatic Press, 1972.

Leung, Edwin Pak-Wah. "The Quasi-War in East Asia: Japan's Expedition to Taiwan and the Ryūkyū Controversy." *Modern Asian Studies* 17, no. 2 (1983): 432–455.

Lewis, Michael. *Becoming Apart: Local Politics and National Power in Toyama, 1868–1945.* Cambridge, MA: Harvard University Press, 2000.

Lewis, Michael. *Rioters and Citizens: Mass Protest in Imperial Japan.* Berkeley: University of California Press, 1990.

Li, Fei Fei, Robert Sabella, and David Liu, eds. *Nanking: Memory and Healing.* Armonk, NY: M. E. Sharpe, 2002.

Lindsay, Oliver. *The Lasting Honour: The Fall of Hong Kong, 1941.* London: Hamish Hamilton, 1978; 2d ed. London: Collins, 1997.

Lone, Stewart. *Japan's First Modern War: Army and Society in the Conflict with China, 1894–95.* London: St. Martin's Press, 1994.

Lord, Walter. *Incredible Victory.* New York: Harper and Row, 1967.

Lu, David J. *Agony of Choice: Matsuoka Yōsuke and the Rise and Fall of the Japanese Empire, 1880–1946.* Lanham, MD: Lexington Books, 2002.

Lu, David J. *From the Marco Polo Bridge to Pearl Harbor: Japan's Entry into World War II.* Washington, DC: Foreign Affairs Press, 1961.

Lublin, Elizabeth Dorn. *Reforming Japan: The Woman's Christian Temperance Union in the Meiji Period.* Vancouver: University of British Columbia Press, 2010.

Lundstrom, John B. *The First Team and the Guadalcanal Campaign.* Annapolis, MD: Naval Institute Press, 1994.

Mackie, Vera. *Creating Socialist Women in Japan: Gender, Labour, and Activism, 1900–1937.* Cambridge, UK: Cambridge University Press, 1997.

Macmillan, Margaret Olwen. *Paris 1919: Six Months That Changed the World.* New York: Random House, 2002.

Maga, Timothy P. *Judgment at Tokyo: The Japanese War Crimes Trials.* Lexington: University Press of Kentucky, 2001.

Maja Mikula, ed. *Women, Activism, and Social Change.* New York: Routledge, 2005: 49–70.

Mallonée, Richard. *Battle for Bataan: An Eyewitness Account.* New York: I Books, 2003.

Malozemoff, Andrew. *Russian Far Eastern Policy, 1881–1904.* Berkeley, CA: University of California Press, 1958.

Manela, Erez. *The Wilsonian Moment: Self-determination and the International*

*Origins of Anticolonial Nationalism.* New York: Oxford University Press, 2007.

Marshall, Byron K. *Academic Freedom and the Japanese Imperial University, 1868–1939.* Berkeley: University of California Press, 1992.

Marshall, Byron K. *Capitalism and Nationalism in Prewar Japan: The Ideology of the Business Elite, 1868–1941.* Stanford: Stanford University Press, 1967.

Maruyama Masao. *Studies in the Intellectual History of Tokugawa Japan.* Tokyo: University of Tokyo Press, 1974.

Mass, Jeffrey P. *The Development of Kamakura Rule, 1180–1225: A History with Documents.* Stanford, CA: Stanford University Press, 1979.

Mass, Jeffrey. *Yoritomo and the Founding of the First Bakufu: The Origins of Dual Government in Japan.* Stanford: Stanford University Press, 2000.

Masterson, Daniel M., with Sayaka Funada-Classen. *The Japanese in Latin America.* Urbana/Chicago: University of Illinois Press, 2004.

Matsuo, Takayoshi. "The Development of Democracy in Japan: Taishō Democracy: Its Flowering and Breakdown." *Developing Economies* 4, no. 4 (December 1996): 612–637.

Mayo, Marlene. "The Korean Crisis of 1873 and Early Meiji Foreign Policy." *Journal of Asian Studies* 31, no. 4 (August 1972): 793–819.

McCormack, Gavan. *Chang Tso-Lin in Northeast China, 1911–1928: China, Japan, and the Manchurian Idea.* Stanford, CA: Stanford University Press, 1977.

McCullough, Helen C. *Ōkagami: The Great Mirror.* Princeton, NJ: Princeton University Press, 1980.

McCullough, Helen C. *The Tale of the Heike.* Stanford, CA: Stanford University Press, 1988.

McCullough, Helen C. *Yoshitsune: A Fifteenth-Century Japanese Chronicle.* Stanford, CA: Stanford University Press, 1966.

McCullough, Helen C., and William H. McCullough. *A Tale of Flowering Fortunes: Annals of Japanese Aristocratic Life in the Heian Period*, Stanford, CA: Stanford University Press, 1980.

McCullough, William. "Shokyuki: An Account of the Shôkyû War of 1221." *Monumenta Nipponica* 19, nos. 1/2 (1964): 163–215.

McKenzie, F. A. *The Tragedy of Korea.* London: Hodder and Stoughton, 1908.

McMaster, John. "Alcock and Harris: Foreign Diplomacy in Bakumatsu Japan." *Monumenta Nipponica* 22, nos. 3–4 (1967): 305–367.

McWilliams, Wayne C. "Etō Shimpei and the Saga Rebellion, Japan, 1874." *Proceedings of the International Symposium on Asian Studies* 2 (1979): 231–249.

Medzini, Meron. *French Policy in Japan during the Closing Years of the Tokugawa Regime.* Cambridge, MA: Harvard University Press, 1971.

Meskill, Johanna. *Hitler and Japan: The Hollow Alliance.* New York: Atherton Press, 1966.

Miller, Frank O. *Minobe Tatsukichi: Interpreter of Constitutionalism in Japan.* Berkeley, CA: University of California Press, 1965.

Miller, John, Jr. *The United States Army in World War II: The War in the Pacific: Cartwheel: The Reduction of Rabaul.* Washington, DC: Center of Military History, U.S. Army, 1993.

Miller, Richard J. *Japan's First Bureaucracy: A Study of Eighth-Century Government.* Cornell University East Asia papers 19. Ithaca, NY: Cornell University Press, 1979.

Minear, Richard H. *Japanese Tradition and Western Law.* Cambridge, MA: Harvard University Press, 1970.

Minear, Richard H. *Victors' Justice: The Tokyo War Crimes Trial.* Princeton, NJ: Princeton University Press, 1971.

Miwa, Kimitada. *Japanese Policies and Concepts for a Regional Order in Asia, 1938–1940.* Tokyo: Sophia University, 1983.

Miyajima, Toshimitsu. *Land of Elms: The History, Culture, and Present Day Situation of the Ainu People.* Etobicoke, ON: United Church Publishing House, 1998.

Miyamoto, Ken. "Itō Noe and the Bluestockings." *Japan Interpreter* 10, no. 2 (Autumn 1975): 190–203.

Moore, Roy A., ed. *Culture and Religion in Japanese-American Relations: Essays on Uchimura Kanzo, 1861–1930.* Ann Arbor, MI: University of Michigan Press, 1981.

Morillo, Stephen. "Cultures of Death: Warrior Suicide in Medieval Europe and Japan." *Medieval History Journal* 4 (2001): 241.

Morinaga, Maki I. *Secrecy in Japanese Arts: "Secret Transmission" as a Mode of Knowledge.* New York: Palgrave Macmillan, 2005.

Morison, Samuel Eliot. *History of United States Naval Operations in World War II. Vol. 4, Coral Sea, Midway, and Submarine Actions, May 1942–August 1942.* Boston: Little, Brown, 1949.

Morison, Samuel Eliot. *History of United States Naval Operations in World War II. Vol. 5, The Struggle for Guadalcanal, August 1942–February 1943.* Boston: Little, Brown, 1948.

Morison, Samuel E. *History of United States Naval Operations in World War II. Vol. 7, Aleutians, Gilberts and Marshalls, June 1942–April 1944.* Boston: Little, Brown, 1951.

Morison, Samuel Eliot. *History of United States Naval Operations in World War II. Vol. 8, New Guinea and the Marianas, March 1944–August 1944.* Boston: Little, Brown, 1953.

Morison, Samuel Eliot. *History of United States Naval Operations in World War II. Vol. 12, Leyte.* Boston: Little, Brown, 1975.

Morison, Samuel E. *"Old Bruin": Commodore Matthew C. Perry, 1794–1858.* Boston/Toronto: Little, Brown, 1967.

Morita, Keiko. "Activities of the Japanese Patriotic Ladies' Association (Aikoku Fujinkai)," in Women, Activism, and Social Change, edited by Maja Mikula. New York: Routledge, 2005: 49–70.

Morley, James William. *The China Quagmire: Japan's Expansion on the Asian Continent, 1933–1941.* New York: Columbia University Press, 1983.

Morley, James William, ed. *Deterrent Diplomacy: Japan, Germany, and the USSR, 1935–1940.* New York: Columbia University Press, 1976.

Morley, James William. *The Fateful Choice: Japan's Advance into Southeast Asia, 1939–1941.* New York: Columbia University Press, 1980.

Morley, James William. *The Final Confrontation: Japan's Negotiations with the United States, 1941.* New York: Columbia University Press, 1994.

Morris, Dana. "Land and Society," in D. Shively and W. McCullough, eds. *The Cambridge History of Japan: Vol. 2, Heian Japan.* New York: Cambridge University Press, 1999:183–235.

Morris, Ivan I. *Nationalism and the Right Wing in Japan: Study of Postwar Trends.* London: Oxford University Press, 1960.

Morris, Ivan. *The Nobility of Failure: Tragic Heroes in the History of Japan.* New York: Holt, Rinehart and Winston, 1975.

Morris, John. *Makers of Japan.* London: Methuen, 1906.

Morton, Louis. *United States Army in World War II: The War in the Pacific. Fall of the Philippines.* Washington, DC: Office of the Chief of Military History, Department of the Army, 1953.

Morton, Louis. *United States Army in World War II: The War in the Pacific. Strategy and Command: The First Two Years.* Washington, DC: U.S. Army Center of Military History, 1989.

Morton, William F. *Tanaka Giichi and Japan's China Policy.* New York: St. Martin's Press, 1980.

Mounsey, Augustus Henry. *The Satsuma Rebellion.* Washington, DC: University Publications of America, 1979.

Mueller, Joseph N. *Guadalcanal 1942: The Marines Strike Back.* London: Osprey, 1992.

Murray, Williamson, and Millet, Allan R. *A War to Be Won: Fighting the Second World War*. Cambridge, MA: Belknap Press of Harvard University Press, 2000.

Mutsu, Munemitsu. *Kenkenroku: A Diplomatic Record of the Sino-Japanese War, 1894–95*, translated by Gordon Berger. New York: Columbia University Press, 1995.

Myers, Ramon Hawley, Mark R. Peattie, and Ching-chih Chen. *The Japanese Colonial Empire, 1895–1945*. Princeton, NJ: Princeton University Press, 1984.

Nahm, Andrew C. *Introduction to Korean History and Culture*. Seoul: Hollym International Corporation, 1993.

Naitō Takatoshi. *Mittsu no Kimigayo: Nihonjin no oto to kokoro no shinsō*. Tokyo: Chūō Kōronsha, 1997.

Najita, Tetsuo. *Hara Kei in the Politics of Compromise, 1905–1915*. Cambridge, MA: Harvard University Press, 1967.

Najita, Tetsuo. "Ōshio Heihachirō (1793–1837)," in Albert Craig and Donal Shively, eds. *Personality in Japanese History*. Berkeley: University of California Press, 1970: 155–179.

Nakamura, Ellen Gardner. *Practical Pursuits: Takano Choei, Takahashi Keisaku, and Western Medicine in Nineteenth-Century Japan*. Cambridge, MA: Harvard University Press, 2005.

Nakamura, James I. "Meiji Land Reform, Redistribution of Income, and Saving from Agriculture." *Economic Development and Cultural Change* 14. no. 4 (July 1966): 428–439.

Nathan, John. *Mishima: A Biography*. Boston: Little, Brown, 1974.

Neary, Ian. *The State and Politics in Japan*. Cambridge: Polity Press, 2002.

Nimmo, William F. *Behind a Curtain of Silence: Japanese in Soviet Custody, 1945–1956*. Westport, CT: Greenwood Press, 1988.

Nish, Ian H. *Alliance in Decline: A Study in Anglo-Japanese Relations, 1908–23*. London: Athlone Press, 1972.

Nish, Ian H. *The Anglo-Japanese Alliance: The Diplomacy of Two Island Empires 1894–1907*. London: Athlone Press, 1966.

Nish, Ian. *Japanese Foreign Policy in the Interwar Period*. Westport, CT: Praeger, 2002.

Nish, Ian. *The Origins of the Russo-Japanese War*. New York: Longman, 1985.

Nishida Masaru. "Japan, the Ryukyus and the Taiwan Expedition of 1874: Toward Reconciliation after 130 years." *Japan Focus* 21 (November 2005): 436–439.

Nitobe, Inazō. *Bushidō: Soul of Japan*. 13th ed. Rutland, VT: Charles E. Tuttle, 1969.

Norman, E. Herbert. "The Gen'yōsha: A Study in the Origins of Japanese Imperialism." *Pacific Affairs* 17, no. 3 (September 1944): 261–284.

Norman, Michael, and Elizabeth Norman. *Tears in the Darkness: The Story of the Bataan Death March and Its Aftermath*. New York: Farrar, Straus and Giroux, 2009.

Notehelfer, F. G. *Kōtoku Shūsui: Portrait of a Japanese Radical*. Cambridge, UK: Cambridge University Press, 1971.

Nozaki, Yoshiko. *Textbook Controversy and the Production of Public Truth: Japanese Education, Nationalism, and Saburo Ienaga's Court Challenges*. Ph.D. dissertation, University of Wisconsin, 2000.

O'Brien, Phillips Payson, ed. *The Anglo-Japanese Alliance, 1902–1922*. London: Routledge Curzon, 2004.

Oberlander, Christian. "The Rise of Western 'Scientific Medicine' in Japan: Bacteriology and Beriberi," in Morris Low, ed. *Building a Modern Japan: Science, Technology, and Medicine in the Meiji Era and Beyond*. New York: Palgrave Macmillan, 2005: 13–36.

Ogasawara, Nagayo. *Life of Admiral Tōgō*, translated by I. Jukichi and I. Tozo. Tokyo: Seito Shorin Press, 1934.

Oh, Bonnie Bongwan. *The Backgrouwnd of Chinese Policy Formation in the Sino-Japanese War of 1894–1895*. Ph.D. dissertation, University of Chicago, 1974.

Oka, Yoshitake. *Five Political Leaders of Modern Japan: Itô Hirobumi, Ôkuma*

*Shigenobu, Hara Takashi, Inukai Tsuyoshi, and Saionji Kinmochi*, translated by Andrew Fraser and Patricia Murray. Tokyo: University of Tokyo Press, 1986.

Okamoto Shumpei. *The Japanese Oligarchy and the Russo-Japanese War*. New York: Columbia University Press, 1970.

Oki, Masahiro. *Katsu tame no kantokujutsu: Dakara taibatsu ha hitsuyō da* [Coaching Techniques for Winning: That Is Why Corporal Punishment Is Necessary]. Tokyo: Bungeisha, 2001.

Okihiro, Gary Y. *Cane Fires: The Anti-Japanese Movement in Hawaii 1865–1945*. Philadelphia: Temple University Press, 1991.

Ōkubo Yasuo. *Nihon kindaihō no chichi: Bowasonaado*. Tokyo: Iwanami, 1977.

Olsen, Edward A. *U.S.-Japan Strategic Reciprocity: A Neo-Internationalist View*. Stanford, CA: Hoover Institution Press, 1985.

Olson, L. A. *Hara Kei: A Political Biography*. Unpublished doctoral dissertation, Harvard University, 1954.

Ooms, Emily Groszos. *Women and Millenarian Protest in Meiji Japan: Deguchi Nao and Omotokyo*. Ithaca, NY: Cornell University Press, 1993.

Osa Shizue. *Kindai Nihon to kokugo nashonarizumu*. Tokyo: Yoshida Kōbunkan, 1998.

Ōtani Masao: *Shuppei-ron* [On Intervention]. Tokyo: Minyûsha, 1918.

Oyler, Elizabeth A. *Swords, Oaths, and Prophetic Visions: Authoring Warrior Rule in Medieval Japan*. Honolulu: University of Hawaii Press, 2006.

Paine, S. C. M. *The Sino-Japanese War of 1894–1895: Perceptions, Power, and Primacy*. Cambridge, UK: Cambridge University Press, 2003.

Paramore, Kiri. *Ideology and Christianity in Japan*. New York: Routledge, 2009.

Park, Yune-hee, *Admiral Yi Sun-Sin and His Turtleboat Armada: A Comprehensive Account of the Resistance of Korea to the 16th Century Japanese Invasion*, Seoul: Hanjin, 1973.

Peattie, Mark R. *Ishiwara Kanji and Japan's Confrontation with the West*. Princeton, NJ: Princeton University Press, 1975.

Peattie, Mark R. *The Nan'yō: The Rise and Fall of the Japanese in Micronesia, 1885–1945*. Honolulu: University of Hawaii Press, 1988.

Pekkanen, Saadia M., and Paul Kallender-Umezu. *In Defense of Japan: From the Market to the Military in Space Policy*. Stanford: Stanford University Press, 2010.

Perez, Louis G. *The History of Japan*. Westport, CT: Greenwood Press, 1998.

Perez, Louis G. *Japan Comes of Age: Mutsu Munemitsu and the Revision of the Unequal Treaties*. London: Associated University Press, 1999.

Perez, Louis G. *Mutsu Munemitsu and Identity Formation of the Individual and the State in Modern Japan*. Lewiston, NY: Edwin Mellen Press, 2001.

Perret, Geoffrey. *Old Soldiers Never Die: The Life of Douglas Macarthur*. Cincinnati, OH: Adams Media Corporation, 1997.

Perrin, Noel. *Giving Up the Gun: Japan's Reversion to the Sword, 1543–1879*. Boulder: Shambhala, 1979.

Piccigallo, Philip R. *The Japanese on Trial: Allied War Crimes Operations in the East, 1945–1951*. Austin: University of Texas Press, 1979.

Pineau, Roger, ed. *The Japan Expedition, 1852–1854: The Personal Journal of Commodore Matthew C. Perry*. Washington, DC: Smithsonian Institution Press, 1968.

Piovesana, Gino. *Recent Japanese Philosophical Thought, 1862–1994: A Survey*. London: Routledge, 1997.

Ponsonby-Fane, Richard Arthur Brabazon. *The Imperial House of Japan*. Kyoto: Ponsonby Memorial Society, 1959.

Postel-Vinay, Karoline, and Mark Selden. "History on Trial: French Nippon Foundation Sues Scholar for Libel to Protect the Honor of Sasakawa Ryōichi." *Asia-Pacific Journal* 17-4-10 (April 26, 2010): 56–78).

Potter, John D. *The Life and Death of a Japanese General*. New York: New American Library, 1962.

Potter, John D. *Yamamoto: The Man Who Menaced America*. New York: Viking, 1965.

Prange, Gordon W. *Miracle at Midway*. New York: McGraw-Hill, 1982.

Prange, Gordon W., with Donald M. Goldstein and Katherine V. Dillon. *At Dawn We Slept: The Untold Story of Pearl Harbor*. New York: Harper and Row, 1975.

Preston, Diana. *The Boxer Rebellion: The Dramatic Story of China's War on Foreigners That Shook the World in the Summer of 1900*. New York: Walker, 2000.

Pu Yi, Henry. *The Last Manchu: The Autobiography of Henry Pu Yi, Last Emperor of China*. New York: Pocket Books, 1987.

Purdy, R. W. "Fanning the Flames or Holding the Blaze at Bay? Furuno Inosuke and Japan's Wartime Press," in Louis G. Perez, ed. *Mutsu Munemitsu and Identity Formation of the Individual and the State in Japan*. Lewiston, NY: Edwin Mellen Press, 2001: 266–286.

Purdy, R. W. "Nationalism and News: 'Information Imperialism' and Japan, 1910–1936." *Journal of American–East Asian Relations* (Fall 1992): 295–323.

Pyle, Kenneth. *Japan Rising: The Resurgence of Japanese Power and Purpose*. New York: Public Affairs, 2007.

Ravina, Mark. *The Last Samurai: The Life and Battles of Saigō Takamori*. Hoboken, NJ: Wiley, 2004.

Reischauer, Edwin, O. *The Japanese Today: Change and Continuity*. Tokyo: Tuttle, 1988.

Reischauer, Haru Matsukata. *Samurai and Silk: A Japanese and American Heritage*. Cambridge, MA: Harvard University Press, 1986.

Robinson, Greg. *A Tragedy of Democracy: Japanese Confinement in North America*. New York: Columbia University Press, 2009.

Rogers, John M. "Arts of War in Times of Peace: Swordsmanship in *Honchō Bugei Shōden*, Chapter 5." *Monumenta Nipponica* 45, no. 4 (Winter 1990): 413–447.

Rogers, John M. *The Development of the Military Profession in Tokugawa Japan*. Ph.D. thesis, Harvard University, 1998.

Romanus, Charles F., and Riley Sunderland. *United States Army in World War II: China-Burma-India Theater: Stilwell's Command Problems*. Washington, DC: Office of the Chief of Military History, Department of the Army, 1956.

Rose, Caroline. *Sino-Japanese Relations: Facing the Past, Looking to the Future?* London/New York: Routledge Curzon, 2005.

Rosenbluth, Frances McCall, and Michael F. Thies. *Japan Transformed: Political Change and Economic Restructuring*. Princeton, NJ: Princeton University Press, 2010.

Rubin, Jay. *Injurious to Public Morals: Writers and the Meiji State*. Seattle: University of Washington Press, 1984.

Russ, Martin. *Line of Departure: Tarawa*. New York: Doubleday, 1975.

Russell, Henry Dozier. *Pearl Harbor Story*. Macon, GA: Mercer University Press, 2001.

Saaler, Sven. "Taishō-ki ni okeru Seiji Kessha: Kokuryūkai no Katsudō to Jinmyaku [Political Societies in the Taishō Era: The Activities and the Social Network of the Kokuryūkai]," in Inoki Takenori, ed. *Demokurashii to Chūkan Dantai: Senkanki Nihon no Shakai Shūdan to Nettwaku* [Democracy and Intermediary Organizations: Social Organizations and Networks in Interwar Japan]. Tokyo: NTT Shuppan, 2008: 81–108.

Saaler, Sven, and J. Victor Koschmann. *Pan-Asianism in Modern Japanese History: Colonialism, Regionalism, and Borders*. New York: Routledge, 2007.

Saaler, Sven, and Christopher W. A. Szpilman. "Introduction: The Emergence of Pan-Asianism as an Ideal of Asian Identity and Solidarity, 1850–2008," in Sven Saaler and Christopher W. A. Szpilman, eds. *Pan-Asianism. A Documentary History. Vol. 1: 1859–1920.* Lanham, MD: Rowman & Littlefield, 2011: 1–41.

Saaler, Sven, and Christopher W. A. Szpilman, eds. *Pan-Asianism: A Documentary History.* 2 vols. Lantham, MD: Rowman & Littlefield, 2011.

Sadler, A. L. "The Naval Campaign in the Korean War of Hideyoshi (1592–1598)." *Transactions of the Asiatic Society of Japan, Series 2*, 14 (June 1937): 178–208.

Sadler, Arthur L. *The Maker of Modern Japan: The Life of Tokugawa Ieyasu.* London: George Allen & Unwin, 1937.

Sagers, John H. *Origins of Japanese Wealth and Power: Reconciling Confucianism and Capitalism, 1830–1885.* New York: Palgrave Macmillan, 2006.

Said, Edward. *Orientalism.* New York: Vintage Books, 1979.

Sakaki, Atsuko. *Obsessions with the Sino-Japanese Polarity in Japanese Literature.* Honolulu: University of Hawaii Press, 2006.

Sakurai, Tadayoshi. *Human Bullets: A Soldier's Story of Port Arthur.* New York: Kegan Paul, 2005.

Samuels, Richard J. *Kishi and Corruption: An Anatomy of the 1955 System.* Japan Policy Research Institute Working Papers, no. 38 (December 2001).

Samuels, Richard J. *Securing Japan: Tokyo's Grand Strategy and the Future of East Asia.* Ithaca: Cornell University Press, 2007.

Sansom, George. *A History of Japan to 1334.* Stanford: Stanford University Press, 1958.

Sasso, Claude R. *Soviet Night Operations in World War II.* Leavenworth Paper no. 6. Fort Leavenworth, KS: Combat Studies Institute, U.S. Army Command and General Staff College, 1982.

Satō Seizaburō. *Sasakawa Ryoichi: A Life*, translated by Hara Fujiko. Norwalk, CT: Eastbridge, 2006.

Satterfield, Archie. *The Day the War Began.* New York: Praeger, 1992.

Schaller, Michael. *Altered States: The United States and Japan since the Occupation.* Oxford, UK: Oxford University Press, 1997.

Schaller, Michael. *The American Occupation of Japan: The Origins of the Cold War in Asia.* New York: Oxford University Press, 1985.

Schencking, J. Charles. *Making Waves: Politics, Propaganda, and the Emergence of the Imperial Japanese Navy, 1868–1922.* Stanford: Stanford University Press, 2005.

Schonberger, Howard B. *Aftermath of War: Americans and the Remaking of Japan, 1945–1952.* Kent, OH: Kent State University Press, 1989.

Schroeder, Paul W. *The Axis Alliance and Japanese-American Relations, 1941.* Ithaca, NY: Cornell University Press, 1958.

Schultz, Duane. *The Doolittle Raid.* New York: St. Martin's Press, 1988.

Schwarcz, Vera. *The Chinese Enlightenment: Intellectuals and the Legacy of the May Fourth Movement of 1919.* Berkeley: University of California Press, 1986.

Screech, Timon. *Secret Memoirs of the Shōguns: Isaac Titsingh and Japan, 1779–1822.* London: Routledge Curzon, 2006.

Seagrave, Sterling, and Peggy Seagrave. *The Yamato Dynasty: The Secret History of Japan's Imperial Family.* New York: Broadway Books, 1999.

Sharf, Robert. "The Zen of Japanese Nationalism." *History of Religions* 33, no. 1 (August 1993): 1–43.

Shiba, Ryotaro. *Drunk as a Lord: Samurai Stories*, translated by Eileen Kato. New York: Kodansha International, 2001.

Shiba, Ryotaro. *The Last Shōgun: The Life of Tokugawa Yoshinobu.* Tokyo: Kodansha International, 1998.

Shibusawa Naoko. *America's Geisha Ally: Remaking the Japanese Enemy.* Cambridge, MA: Harvard University Press, 2006.

Shillony, Ben-Ami. *The Emperors of Modern Japan.* Leiden: Brill, 2008.

Shillony, Ben-Ami. *Politics and Culture in Wartime Japan*. Oxford, UK: Clarendon Press, 1981.

Shillony, Ben-Ami. *Revolt in Japan: the Young Officers and the February 26, 1936 Incident*. Princeton, NJ: Princeton University Press, 1973.

Shimazu, Naoko. *Japan, Race, and Equality: The Racial Equality Proposal of 1919*. London: Routledge, 1998.

Shimbori Michiya. "Zengakuren: A Japanese Case Study of a Student Political Movement." *Sociology of Education* 37, no. 3 (Spring 1964): 229–253.

Shinoda, Minoru. *The Founding of the Kamakura Shōgunate 1180–1185, with Selected Translations from the Azuma Kagami*. New York: Columbia University Press, 1960.

Shively, Donald H., ed. *Tradition and Modernization in Japanese Culture*. Princeton, NJ: Princeton University Press, 1971.

Shively, Donald H., and William H. McCullough, ed. *The Cambridge History of Japan II: Heian Japan*. Cambridge, UK: Cambridge University Press, 1999.

Siddle, Richard. *Race, Resistance, and the Ainu of Japan*. New York: Routledge, 1996.

Silberman, Bernard S., and H. D. Harootunian, eds. *Japan in Crisis: Essays on Taishō Democracy*. Ann Arbor, MI: Center for Japanese Studies, University of Michigan, 1999.

Siniawer, Eiko Maruko. *Ruffians, Yakuza, Nationalists: The Violent Politics of Modern Japan, 1860–1960*. Ithaca: Cornell University Press, 2008.

Sjöberg, Katarina. *The Return of the Ainu: Cultural Mobilization and the Practice of Ethnicity in Japan*. Langhorne, PA: Harwood Academic Publishers, 1993.

Skya, Walter A. *Japan's Holy War*. London: Duke University Press, 2009.

Smethurst, Richard J. *A Social Basis for Prewar Japanese Militarism: The Army and the Rural Community*. Berkeley: University of California Press, 1974.

Smith, Henry DeWitt. *Japan's First Student Radicals*. Cambridge, MA: Harvard University Press, 1972.

Smith, Robert Ross. *The United States Army in World War II: The War in the Pacific—Triumph in the Philippines*. Washington, DC: U.S. Government Printing Office, 1963.

Smyth, John. *Percival and the Tragedy of Singapore*. London: Macdonald, 1971.

Sogawa, Tsuneo. "What Should Be Taught Through Budō?," in A. Bennett, ed. *Budo Perspectives*. Auckland, New Zealand: Kendo World Publications, 2005: 14–22.

Solomon, Michael. "The Dilemma of Religious Power: Honganji and Hosokawa Masamoto," *Monumenta Nipponica* 33, no. 1 (Spring 1978): 51–65.

Spector, Ronald H. *Eagle against the Sun: The American War with Japan*. New York: Free Press, 1985.

Spence, Jonathan D. *The Search for Modern China*. New York: Norton, 1990.

Steben, Barry D. "Law Enforcement and Confucian Idealism in the Late Edo Period: Ōshio Chūsai and the Growth of His Great Aspiration." *Asian Cultural Studies* 22 (1996): 59–90.

Steinberg, John W., et al., eds. *World War Zero: The Russo-Japanese War*. Boston: Brill, 2007.

Steinhoof, Patricia G. "Hijackers, Bombers, and Bank Robbers: Managerial Style in the Japanese Red Army." *Journal of Asian Studies* 48, no. 4 (1989): 724–740.

Stephan, John T. "The Tanaka Memorial (1927): Authentic or Spurious?" *Modern Asian Studies* 7, no. 4 (1973): 733–745.

Stokes, Henry Scott. *The Life and Death of Yukio Mishima*. New York: Penguin Books, 1975.

Stokesbury, James L. *A Short History of World War II*. New York: William Morrow and Company, 1980.

Stone, Jacqueline I. *Original Enlightenment and the Transformation of Medieval Japanese Buddhism*. Honolulu: University of Hawai'i Press, 1999.

Stone, Jacqueline I. "Realizing This World as the Buddha Land," in Stephen F. Teiser and Jacqueline I. Stone, eds. *Readings of the Lotus Sutra*. New York: Columbia University Press, 2009: 112–133.

Sugimoto, Atsuo. *Supotsu bunka no henyō* [Transformations in Sports Culture]. Kyoto: Sekaishisōsha, 1995.

Sun, Laichen. "Military Technology Transfers from Ming China and the Emergence of Northern Mainland Southeast Asia (c. 1360–1527)." *Journal of Southeast Asian Studies* 34 no. 3 (2002): 495–517.

Sunada Ichiro. "The Thought and Behavior of Zengakuren: Trends in the Japanese Student Movement." *Asian Survey* 9, no. 6 (June 1969): 457–474.

Suzuki, Daisetz Teitaro. *The Training of the Zen Buddhist Monks*. New York: University Press, 1965.

Takekoshi Yosaburo. *Japanese Rule in Formosa*. Taipei: Longman's Green and Company, 1997.

Takeuchi Rizō. "The Rise of the Warriors," in D. Shively and W. McCullough, eds. *The Cambridge History of Japan: Vol. 2, Heian Japan*. New York: Cambridge University Press, 1999: 644–709.

Tanabe, George. "Tanaka Chigaku: The Lotus Sūtra and the Body Politic," in George Tanabe and Willa Jane Tanabe, eds. *The Lotus Sūtra and Japanese Culture*. Honolulu: Hawai'i University Press, 1989.

Tanaka, Stefan. *Japan's Orient: Rendering Pasts into History*. Berkeley: University of California Press, 1993.

Tanaka Takashi. *Ishin no uta: Bakumatsu sonnō shishi no zesshō*. Tokyo: Nihon Kyōbunsha, 1974.

Tanaka Yuki. *Hidden Horrors: Japanese War Crimes in World War II*. Boulder, CO: Westview Press, 1996.

Tanaka, Yuki. *Japan's Comfort Women: Sexual Slavery and Prostitution during World War II and the US Occupation*. London: Routledge, 2002.

Tanaka Yuki. "Oda Makoto, Beheiren and 14 August 1945: Humanitarian Wrath against Indiscriminate Bombing." *Japan Focus: The Asia-Pacific Journal* (September 28, 2007): 22–43.

Taylor, Lawrence. *A Trial of Generals: Homma, Yamashita, MacArthur*. South Bend, IN: Icarus Press, 1981.

Teters, R. "Matsuoka Yōsuke: The Diplomat of Bluff and Gesture," in R. D. Burns and E. N. Bennett, eds. *Diplomats in Crisis: United States–Chinese–Japanese Relations, 1919–1941*. Santa Barbara, CA: ABC-CLIO, 1974: 275–296.

Thomas, Julia Adeney. *Reconfiguring Modernity: Concepts of Nature in Japanese Political Ideology*. Berkeley: University of California Press, 2001.

Thurston, Donald. *Teachers and Politics in Japan*. Princeton: Princeton University Press, 1973.

Titus, David A. *Palace and Politics in Prewar Japan*. New York: Columbia University Press, 1974.

*Tokushi yoron (1712)*. Waterloo, ON: Wilfrid Laurier University Press, 1991.

Toland, John. *Infamy: Pearl Harbor and Its Aftermath*. Garden City, NY: Doubleday, 1982.

Toland, John. *Rising Sun: The Decline and Fall of the Japanese Empire, 1936–1945*. New York: Random House, 1970.

Totman, Conrad D. *The Collapse of the Tokugawa Bakufu, 1862–1868*. Honolulu: University Press of Hawaii, 1980.

Totman, Conrad D. *Early Modern Japan*. Berkeley: University of California, 1993.

Tregaskis, Richard. *Guadalcanal Diary*. New York: Random House, 1943.

Tsang, Carol Richmond. *War and Faith: Ikkō ikki in Late Muromachi Japan*. Cambridge, MA: Harvard University Press, 2007.

Tsunoda Ryusaku et al., eds. *Sources of Japanese Tradition*, Vols. 1 & 2. New York: Columbia University Press, 1958.

Tsurumi, Shunsuke. *An Intellectual History of Wartime Japan, 1931–1945*. London: Routledge, 1986.

Tuchman, Barbara. *Stilwell and the American Experience in China, 1911–1945*. New York: Macmillan, 1971.

Turnbull, Stephen. *Japanese Warrior Monks AD 949–1603*. Oxford, UK: Osprey, 2003.

Turnbull, Stephen. *The Kakure Kirishitan of Japan: A Study of Their Development, Beliefs and Rituals to the Present Day.* Richmond, UK: Japan Library, 1998.

Turnbull, Stephen. *Ninja AD 1460–1650.* Oxford, UK: Osprey, 2003.

Turnbull, Stephen. *Samurai: A Military History.* London: Osprey, 1977.

Turnbull, Stephen R., and Hook, Richard. *The Mongol Invasions of Japan, 1274 and 1281.* Oxford, UK: Osprey, 2010.

Uchida, Yoshiko. *Samurai of Gold Hill.* Berkeley: Creative Arts Book Company, 1985.

Udagawa Takehisa. *Teppō denrai: heiki ga kataru kinsei no tanjō* [The Arrival of the Musket: The Birth of the Early Modern as Told by Military Weapons]. Tokyo: Chuo Koronsha, 1990.

U.S Department of State. *Trial of Japanese War Criminals: Documents 1. Opening Statement by Joseph B. Keenan, Chief of Counsel, 2. Charter of the International Military Tribunal for the Far East, 3. Indictment.* Washington, DC: U.S. Department of State, 1946.

Van Straelen, H. J. J. M. *Yoshida Shōin: Forerunner of the Meiji Restoration.* Leiden: Brill, 1952.

Varley, H. Paul. *Japanese Culture: A Short History.* New York: Praeger, 1973.

Varley, H. Paul. *Jinnō Shōtōki: A Chronicle of Gods and Sovereigns.* New York: Columbia University Press, 1980.

Varley, H. Paul. *The Ōnin War: History of Its Origins and Background with a Selective Translation of the Chronicle of Ōnin.* New York: Columbia University Press, 1967.

Varley, Paul. *Warriors of Japan as Portrayed in the War Tales.* Honolulu: University of Hawaii Press, 1994.

Varon, Jeremy. *Bringing the War Home: The Weather Underground, the Red Army Faction, and Revolutionary Violence in the Sixties and Seventies.* Berkeley, CA: University of California Press, 2004.

Verwaijen, Frans Boudewijn. *Early Reception of Western Legal Thought in Japan, 1841–1868.* Ph.D. dissertation, Leiden University, 1996.

Victoria, Brian. *Zen at War.* 2nd ed. London: Rowman & Littlefield, 2006.

Victoria, Brian Daizen. *Zen War Stories.* London: Routledge Curzon, 2003.

Vining, Elizabeth Gray. *Windows for the Crown Prince: An American Woman's Four Years as Private Tutor to the Crown Prince of Japan.* New York: Harper Collins, 1952.

Vlastos, Stephen. "Opposition Movements in Early Meiji, 1868–1885," in Marius B. Jansen, ed. *The Cambridge History of Japan: Vol. 5: The Nineteenth Century.* Cambridge, UK: Cambridge University Press, 1989.

Wakabayashi, Bob Tadashi. *Anti-foreignism and Western Learning in Early-Modern Japan:* The New Theses *of 1825.* Cambridge, MA: Harvard University Press, 1986.

Wakabayashi, Bob Tadashii. "Comfort Women: Beyond Litigious Feminism." *Monumenta Nipponica* 52, no. 2 (Spring 2003): 157–178.

Wakabayashi, Bob Tadashi. *Japanese Loyalism Reconstrued.* Honolulu: University of Hawaii Press, 1996.

Wakabayashi, Bob Tadashi, ed. *The Nanking Atrocity, 1937–38: Complicating the Picture.* New York/London: Berghahn Books, 2007.

Walder, David. *The Short Victorious War: The Russo-Japanese Conflict, 1904–5.* New York: Harper and Row, 1973.

Walker, Brett L. *The Conquest of Ainu Lands: Ecology and Culture in Japanese Expansion, 1590–1800.* Berkeley: University of California Press, 2001.

Ward, Haruko Nawata. *Women Religious Leaders in Japan's Christian Century, 1549–1650.* Burlington, VT: Ashgate, 2009.

Ward, Robert E., and Yoshikazu Sakamoto, eds. *Democratizing Japan: The Allied Occupation.* Honolulu: University of Hawaii Press, 1987.

Warner, Denis, and Peggy Warner. *The Tide at Sunrise: A History of the Russo-Japanese*

*War, 1904–1905.* New York: Charterhouse, 1974.

Warner, Denis Ashton, and Peggy Warner. *The Tide at Sunrise: A History of the Russo-Japanese War, 1904–1905.* Portland, OR: Frank Cass, 2002.

Warren, Alan. *Singapore, 1942: Britain's Greatest Defeat.* New York: Hambledon, 2002.

Washburn, Stanley. *Nogi: A Man Against the Background of a Great War.* New York: H. Holt, 1913.

Weinstein, Martin E. *Japan's Postwar Defense Policy, 1947–1968.* New York: Columbia University Press, 1971.

Weintraub, Stanley. *Long Day's Journey into War: December 7, 1941.* New York: Dutton, 1991.

Weisgall, Jonathan M. *Operation Crossroads: The Atomic Tests at Bikini Atoll.* Annapolis, MD: Naval Institute Press, 1994.

Werrell, Kenneth P. *Blankets of Fire: U.S. Bombers over Japan during World War II.* Washington, DC: Smithsonian Institution Press, 1996.

Westwood, J. N. *Russia against Japan, 1904–05.* Albany, NY: SUNY Press, 1986.

Westwood, J. N. *Witnesses of Tsushima.* Tokyo: Sophia University, 1970.

Wetzler, Peter. *Hirohito and War: Imperial Tradition and Military Decision Making in Prewar Japan.* Honolulu: University of Hawaii Press, 1998.

Whalen, Christal. *Beginning of Heaven and Earth: The Sacred Book of Japan's Hidden Christians.* Honolulu: University of Hawaii Press, 1996.

White, John Albert. *The Siberian Intervention.* Princeton, NJ: Princeton University Press, 1950.

Whiting, Robert. *You've Gotta Have Wa.* New York: Vintage, 1990.

Whitman, John W. *Bataan: Our Last Ditch—The Bataan Campaign, 1942.* New York: Hippocrene Books, 1990.

Wible, J. T. *The Yamamoto Mission: Sunday, April 18, 1943.* Fredericksburg, TX: Admiral Nimitz Foundation, 1988.

Willcock, Hiroko. *The Japanese Political Thought of Uchimura Kanzo (1861–1930): Synthesizing Bushidō, Christianity, Nationalism, and Liberalism.* Lewiston: Edwin Mellen Press, 2008.

Williams, Peter, and David Wallace. *Unit 731.* New York: Free Press, 1989.

Wilson, Dick. *When Tigers Fight: The Story of the Sino-Japanese War, 1937–1945.* New York: Viking Press, 1982.

Wilson, George M. *Radical Nationalist in Japan: Kita Ikki, 1883–1937.* Cambridge, MA: Harvard University Press, 1969.

Wilson, Sandra. "Family or State? Nation, War, and Gender in Japan, 1937–45." *Critical Asian Studies* 38, no. 2 (2006): 209–238.

Wilson, Sandra. "Mobilizing Women in Interwar Japan: The National Defense Women's Association and the Manchurian Crisis." *Gender and History* 7, no. 2 (August 1995): 295–314.

Wright, Derrick. *The Battle for Iwo Jima, 1945.* Phoenix Mill, UK: Sutton, 1999.

Wright, Richard N. J. *The Chinese Steam Navy 1862–1945.* London: Chatham, 2000.

Xing Hang, ed. *Encyclopedia of National Anthems.* Lanham, MD: Scarecrow Press, 2003.

Yamada, Shōji. "The Myth of Zen in the Art of Archery." *Japanese Journal of Religious Studies* 28, nos. 1–2 (2001): 1–30.

Yamamoto, Masahiro. *Nanking: Anatomy of an Atrocity.* Westport, CT: Praeger, 2000.

Yamamoto Tsunetomo. *The Art of the Samurai: Yamamoto Tsunetomo's Hagakure,* translated by Barry D. Steben. London: Duncan Baird Publishers, 2008.

Yamamoto Tsunetomo. *Hagakure: Book of the Samurai,* translated by William Scott Wilson. Tokyo: Kōdansha International, 2002.

Yamamura, Kozo, ed. *The Cambridge History of Japan. Vol. 3: Medieval Japan.* Cambridge, UK: Cambridge University Press, 1990.

Yamamura, Kozo. "The Meiji Land Tax Reform and Its Effects," in Marius B. Jansen and Gilbert Rozman, eds. *Japan in*

*Transition: from Tokugawa to Meiji.* Princeton: Princeton University Press, 1986: 382–399.

Yamazaki, Tomoko. *Sandakan Brothel No. 8: An Episode in the History of Lower-Class Japanese Women*, translated by Kren Colligan-Taylor. London/New York: M. E. Sharpe, 1999.

Yates, Charles L. *Saigō Takamori: The Man behind the Myth*. London: Kegan Paul International, 1995.

Y'Blood, William T. *Red Sun Setting: The Battle of the Philippine Sea*. Annapolis, MD: Naval Institute Press, 1980.

Yeh, Wen-hsin, ed. *Wartime Shanghai*. New York: Routledge, 1998.

Yi Ki-baek. *A New History of Korea*, translated by Edward W. Wagner. Cambridge, MA: Harvard University Press, 1984.

Yoshitsu, Michael M. *Japan and the San Francisco Peace Settlement*. New York: Columbia University Press, 1983.

Young, Arthur Morgan. *Japan in Recent Times, 1912–1926*. Westport, CT: Greenwood, 1973.

Young, Donald J. *The Battle of Bataan: A History of the 90-Day Siege and Eventual Surrender of 75,000 Filipino and United States Troops to the Japanese in World War II*. Jefferson, NC: McFarland, 1992.

Young, Louise. *Japan's Total Empire: Manchuria and the Culture of Wartime Imperialism*. Berkeley: University of California Press, 1999.

Zachmann, Urs Matthias. "Blowing Up a Double Portrait in Black and White: The Concept of Asia in the Writings of Fukuzawa Yukichi and Okakura Tenshin." *Positions: East Asia Cultures Critique* 15, no. 2 (Fall 2007): 345–368.

Zheng, Guohe. *From Patriotism to Imperialism*. Ph.D. dissertation, The Ohio State University, 1997.

Zheng, Yongnian. *Discovering Chinese Nationalism in China: Modernization and International Relations*. Cambridge, UK/New York: Cambridge University Press, 1999.

# Editor and Contributors

**Volume Editor**

Louis G. Perez
Professor of Japanese History
Illinois State University
Normal, Illinois

**Contributors**

Nobuko Adachi
Associate Professor of Anthropology
Illinois State University
Normal, Illinois

Rea Amit
Ph.D. candidate
Tokyo Geijutsu Daigaku
Tokyo, Japan

E. Taylor Atkins
Professor of History and Director of Under-
graduate Studies
Northern Illinois University
DeKalb, Illinois

Lee Baker, Jr.
University of Cincinnati

Tim Barnard
University of Memphis

Christopher W. Braddick
Professor of International Political History
Musashi University

Martha Chaiklin
Assistant Professor of History
University of Pittsburgh
Pittsburgh, Pennsylvania

Yu Chang
Independent scholar
Hong Kong

Deborah A. Deacon
Dean of Graduate Studies
Harrison Middleton University
Tempe, Arizona

Bruce J. DeHart
History Department
University of North Carolina at Pembroke

Monika Dix
Assistant Professor of Japanese Language,
Literature, and Culture
Saginaw Valley State University
University Center, Michigan

Kim Draggoo
Independent scholar

Darryl Flaherty
Assistant Professor of History
University of Delaware
Newark, Delaware

Paul E. Fontenoy
Curator of Maritime Research
North Carolina Maritime Museum

John C. Fredriksen
Independent scholar

Sabine Frühstück
Professor of Modern Japanese Cultural
Studies
Department of East Asian Languages and
Cultural Studies
University of California
Santa Barbara, California

Rustin Gates
Assistant Professor of History
Bradley University
Peoria, Illinois

Walter E. Grunden
Associate Professor
Bowling Green State University

Roy S. Hanashiro
Professor of History
University of Michigan
Flint, Michigan

Ann M. Harrington
Professor Emeritus of History
Loyola University
Chicago, Illinois

William Head
U.S. Air Force Historian
Maxwell Air Force Base

Glenn E. Helm
Director, Navy Department Library
Washington Navy Yard

Jim M. Hommes
Ph.D. candidate in History

University of Pittsburgh
Pittsburgh, Pennsylvania

Roger Horky
Texas A&M University

Captain C. J. Horn
United States Military Academy
Department of History
West Point, New York

James L. Huffman
Professor Emeritus of History
Wittenberg University
Springfield, Ohio

Gerald S. Iguchi
Assistant Professor of History
University of Wisconsin
La Crosse, Wisconsin

Akira Iikura
Associate Professor
Josai International University

Lance Janda
Associate Professor
Cameron University

John M. Jennings
Department of History
U.S. Air Force Academy

William Johnston
Professor of History
Wesleyan University
Middletown, Connecticut

Larissa Castriotta Kennedy
Instructor in History
Illinois State University
Normal, Illinois

Captain Jonathan P. Klug
U.S. Air Force Academy

Kotani Ken
National Institute for Defense Studies
Tokyo, Japan

Jean L. Kristeller
Professor of Psychology
Co-Director, Center for the Study of Health,
Religion and Spirituality
Indiana State University
Terre Haute, Indiana

Kuniyoshi Tomoki
George Washington University

Kurosawa Fumitaka
History Department
Tokyo Women's Christian University

Kirk Larsen
Associate Professor
Brigham Young University

Joel Legassie
Ph.D. candidate in History
University of Victoria
Victoria, British Columbia, Canada

Michael Lewis
Professor of History
University of Sydney
Sydney, Australia

Elizabeth Dorn Lublin
Associate Professor of History
Wayne State University
Detroit, Michigan

Judith Erika Magyar
Ph.D. candidate in Political Science
Waseda University
Tokyo, Japan

Sebastian Maslow
Doctoral student, Graduate School of Law

Tohoku University
Japan

James I. Matray
Professor and Chair of History
Department of History
California State University, Chico

Aaron L. Miller
Assistant Professor and Hakubi Scholar
Kyoto University, Japan

Saitō Naoki
Independent scholar

Kiichi Nenashi
Professor
Kwansei Gakuinn University

Elizabeth A. Oyler
Director, East Asian Studies
Assistant Professor of Japanese
University of Illinois
Urbana, Illinois

Roberto Padilla II
Assistant Professor of History
University of Toledo
Toledo, Ohio

S. C. M. Paine
Professor of Strategy and Policy
U.S. Naval War College
Newport, Rhode Island

Kiri Paramore
Assistant Professor of Asian Studies
Universiteit Leiden
Leiden, Netherlands

John D. Person
Ph.D. candidate
Department of East Asian Languages and
Civilizations

University of Chicago
Chicago, Illinois

Benjamin A. Peters
Miyazaki International College
Miyazaki, Japan

R. W. Purdy
Associate Professor of History
John Carroll University
University Heights, Ohio

Ryan Reed
Independent scholar

Andrea Revelant
Assistant Professor
Department of Asian and North African
Studies
Ca' Foscari University of Venice
Dorsoduro, Venezia

Sven Saaler
Associate Professor of Modern Japanese
History
Sophia University
Tokyo, Japan

John H. Sagers
Associate Professor of History
Linfield College
McMinnville, Oregon

Claude R. Sasso
William Jewell College

Jeremy Sather
Ph.D. candidate in Japanese Literature
University of Pennsylvania

Michael A. Schneider
Chairman and Professor of History
Knox College
Galesburg, Illinois

Jessica Sedgewick
Independent scholar

Ethan Isaac Segal
Associate Professor of History
Michigan State University
East Lansing, Michigan

Richard J. Smethurst
Professor of History
University of Pittsburgh
Pittsburgh, Pennsylvania

T. Jason Soderstrum
Iowa State University

James Stanlaw
Professor of Anthropology
Illinois State University
Normal, Illinois

Barry D. Steben
National University of Singapore

Philip Streich
Haverford College
Haverford, Pennsylvania

Christopher H. Sterling
George Washington University

Eva-Maria Stolberg
Institute of Russian History

Sugita Yoneyuki
Osaka University of Foreign Studies

Yasuhiro Takeda
Professor of International Relations
Japanese National Defense Academy

Kunihiko Terasawa
Ph.D. candidate in Religion, Temple
University

Adjunct Professor of Religion
St. Joseph University
Philadelphia, Pennsylvania

Roger K. Thomas
Professor of Japanese
Illinois State University
Normal, Illinois

Sybil Thornton
Associate Professor of History
Arizona State University
Tempe, Arizona

Tohmatsu Haruo
Associate Professor
Tamagawa University, Japan

Takemoto Tomoyuki
Lecturer
Hanazono University

Spencer C. Tucker
Senior Fellow
Military History, ABC-CLIO, Inc.

Bob Tadashi Wakabayashi
Professor Emeritus of History
York University
Toronto, Ontario, Canada

Garrett Washington
Mellon Postdoctoral Fellow in Japanese
History
Visiting Assistant Professor in History
Oberlin College
Oberlin, Ohio

Tim J. Watts
Content Development Librarian
Kansas State University

Torsten Weber
Research Associate
School of Humanities and Social Sciences
Jacobs University
Bremen, Germany

Amanda Weiss
Ph.D. candidate
Graduate School of Interdisciplinary Information Studies
University of Tokyo
Tokyo, Japan

Michael Wert
Assistant Professor of History
Marquette University.
Milwaukee, Wisconsin

James Wren
Professor Emeritus of East Asian Language
and Literature
San Jose State University
San Jose, California

Hiroyuki Yamamoto
Terasaki Postdoctoral Fellow Comparative
Politics
University of California
Los Angeles, California

Guohe Zheng
Professor of Japanese
Ball State University
Muncie, Indiana

# Index

Note: page numbers in **bold** font indicate main entries.

# About the Editor

**Louis G. Perez** is Professor of Japanese History at Illinois State University in Normal, Illinois. He is the author of *Modern Japan: A Historical Survey*; *The History of Japan*; *Daily Life in Early Modern Japan*; *Mutsu Munemitsu and Identity Formation of the State and Individual in Modern Japan: Essays in Honor of Ian Mutsu*; *Japan Comes of Age: Mutsu Munemitsu and the Revision of the Unequal Treaties*; and *The Dalai Lama*. Perez is a U.S. Army veteran of the Vietnam War. His father was also an Army veteran of World War II, serving in the "island-hopping" campaigns of the South Pacific.